Audubon Wildlife Report 1985

Audubon Wildlife Report 1985

The National Audubon Society, founded in 1905, is dedicated to conserving plants and animals and their habitats, to promoting wise use of land, water, and energy, and to protecting life from the many global environmental problems that now threaten it. With more than half a million members, 500 chapters, 10 regional offices, and a staff of nearly 300, the Audubon Society is a powerful force for conservation research, education, and action.

Audubon Wildlife Report 1985

Amos S. Eno, Project Director
Roger L. Di Silvestro, Editor

The National Audubon Society
New York, New York

Acknowledgments

Thanks for help in the preparation of the Audubon Wildlife Report 1985 are owed to the following National Audubon Society staff: Jim Leape, who prepared the Legal Development sections of most of the agency and program reports and whose advice on other sections and chapters was invaluable; Mary McCarthy, whose generosity with her talent on a computer keyboard resulted in the graphs used in this book; Claire Rusowicz, who helped with extensive proofreading of the material at many stages of its development; Mercedes Lee, who helped track down photos and wrote the biographical notes that accompany the Species Accounts section; Ruth Norris, who helped with promotion of the publication as well as with proofreading; and Chris Wille, whose editorial guidance and diverse publications experience provided indispensible expertise every step of the way.

Design by Robbin Gourley
Printed by Dartmouth Printing Company
Published by National Audubon Society
950 Third Avenue, New York, New York 10022

ISBN 0-930698-21-5 (1985 Volume)
     0-930698-20-7 (Volume Set)

Printed on recycled paper

The Audubon Wildlife Report 1985

DEDICATION

FOR CLEO LAYTON, whose 50 years of dedicated service at the Department of the Interior is a record unlikely ever to be equaled. To all who knew and worked with him, Cleo's dedication, knowledge, humor, and industry were a source of inspiration and strength.

Few individuals in federal service have contributed so much to the perpetuation of America's park and wildlife resources.

PREFACE

T HIS PROJECT ORIGINATED as the brainchild of Ken Berlin, whose fertile imagination and perspicacity have fostered many worthy projects on behalf of wildlife protection.

Nat Reed became both midwife and wet nurse to the project as it emerged from inception to creation. His sure and steady support has resulted in the publication of this first annual AUDUBON WILDLIFE REPORT.

This report would not have been possible without the timely and generous support of:

Etaienne Boegner; Hugh H. Chatham Co.; Hugh H. Chatham, Sr.; the Clark Foundation; the James R. Dougherty, Jr. Foundation; Sophie Englehard; Amos Eno; the Jamee & Marshall Field Foundation; the Forbes Foundation; the Four Arts Society; Henry J. Heinz, II; Essie Johnson; W. Alton Jones; Robert H. Kanzler; Bill Lane, of *Sunset* magazine; Dan W. Lufkin; Mote Marine Lab., Inc.; Louis Marx, Jr.; the Packard Foundation; Mrs. Sumner Pingree; Nathaniel P. Reed; Alita Davis Reed; Adrian Weaver Reed; J. Verner Reed; Andrew G. C. Sage II; Benno C. Schmidt; Peter Sharp; Mr. and Mrs. Peter J. Solomon; the Weyerhaeuser Foundation; and Robert Winthrop.
Amos S. Eno

FOREWORD

FOR ABOUT A century, the development of wildlife management has been recorded in widely scattered literature. It may be found in the proceedings of seminars and conferences, in hearings and laws, and in the cryptic security of scholarly journals. Few libraries have an abundance of information on the conservation movement, and often what is available is outdated. The most elementary needs of students, as well as the requirements of professionals at all levels, have been poorly served.

Clearly, a single source that amasses the history, legislation, current issues, and statistics important to conservationists would be a time-saver for nearly anyone with serious concerns in the wildlife field. This report fulfills that need. It and successive annual volumes will include the many diverse elements that contribute to the formulation of American wildlife policy. They will feature essential history, descriptions of agencies and missions, objective exploration of issues and legal aspects, and important biological findings. They should be a reliable aid to those who labor in the various branches of federal and state governments, in legislative chambers, in resource agency field units, in editorial precincts, and in the national and local offices of citizen organizations.

Aside from such uses, the continuing series will have a special place in Audubon's environmental education program. School libraries can make available at modest cost a ready reference for students. The indexed, easily readable accounts will fill out key events and benchmarks of the past and impart a state-of-the-art knowledge of today's doings. By design, they will become a growing source for the planning of workshops, field activities, term papers, and speaking assignments. Also, students will acquire a source for elementary reference and documentation practices.

What Americans call progress tends to follow a recognizable pattern: Whenever a significant public need arises, some remarkable individual emerges from the nation's woodwork to answer it.

This could describe the origin of the AUDUBON WILDLIFE REPORT. In recent years, a progressively insistent idea has spurred Amos S. Eno, the report's originator, to tackle this monumental task. With the 1985 volume, he presents the first installment of a work of ambitious proportions. Its launching brings together in fortunate combination a viable public service, a capable sponsoring organization, and the confidence of farsighted supporters.

Amos S. Eno has unusual credentials for coordinating this project. He worked in the Department of the Interior during the early 1970s, a period of constructive innovation. He understands the technical foundations of wildlife management. He knows about public pressures, congressional foibles, and state relationships. For more than a dozen years he has studied the legislative process. Now his efforts have yielded this fine report.

In this first of the series, the surefooted treatment of subjects as diverse as wildlife in the national parks, federal aid programs, and inland fisheries bespeaks a reassuring sophistication. However, the wide-ranging coverage shows that the AUDUBON WILDLIFE REPORT cannot be a one person job. Thus Part III, which contains accounts on the status of individual, often endangered, species, includes the contributions of eminent authorities: Ogden on condors, Rose on manatees, and Servheen on grizzlies.

These condensed histories and thumbnail studies will be the basis for future additions and updating. As they accumulate, adapting to changing needs, the reports will take on unique encyclopedic value.

The wildlife report suggests that our confrontation with basic environmental problems and wildlife management challenges is being systematized. The complexity of natural systems and the confusing variety of human influences make this analytical approach increasingly necessary. The 1985 Audubon report lays down an important foundation. Lines of communication are established, and the collection of information is under way. Everything augurs well for this useful public service. It will be an expanding record of what has been and what is now.

Durward L. Allen
Purdue University
April 1985

INTRODUCTION

by Amos S. Eno

T HE CONSERVATION MOVEMENT in America emerged late in the 19th century in response to the wholesale depletion of fish and wildlife resources across the continent. The decimation of vast herds of plains buffaloes by hide hunters, of herons, egrets, and terns by plume hunters, and the decline of native fisheries inspired a general concern for the protection of these resources. In subsequent years public and private agencies responsible for the conservation of fish and wildlife emerged, often by fits and starts, in response to many discrete natural resource crises.

Today the responsibility for management of our wildlife, including fish and other living resources, is vested in a multitude of public and private agencies. Federal jurisdiction, limited to a relatively small number of species, is shared by five principal agencies, the U.S. Fish and Wildlife Service, National Marine Fisheries Service, U.S. Forest Service, Bureau of Land Management, and National Park Service. In addition, many other departments, bureaus, and commissions fulfill lesser roles.

The individual states, responsible for the management of all resident fish and wildlife, vary widely in their respective management policies and institutions. Additionally, a welter of private conservation groups manages wildlife habitat and maintains an abiding interest in monitoring federal and state wildlife programs.

Often it is hard even for wildlife professionals to make sense of the diverse panoply of agencies, laws, and interested parties. This muddle is further complicated by the controversy that frequently surrounds wildlife management. Those familiar with environmental issues in general and wildlife conservation in particular know that these subjects are fertile breeding grounds for divergent philosophies and opinions.

No one disputes, however, that the protection and management of wildlife is a public charge. But wildlife presents unique problems for public administration. For unlike the land and water upon which wildlife depends, most species are mobile. In many cases this mobility is spectacular, as in the bipolar migrations of the arctic tern or the circumpolar wanderings of the albatross. This mobility presents unique difficulties for those charged with wildlife management, because all wildlife species exhibit a

XV

whimsical disregard for international, state, and local boundaries. Even plants present analogous problems when their populations are fragmented in patches across national and state borders.

In response, numerous international treaties and federal/state compacts, and innumerable cooperative management arrangements, have resulted. This in turn compounds the complexities of species management, invites general public confusion, and geometrically complicates public and private responses to species suffering severe population declines and extinctions.

Public interest in the plight of our wildlife resources has contributed substantially to the resuscitation of the wildlife-oriented publishing industry. Seemingly every wildlife agency and every interested organization publishes a journal, report, or text describing its mission or point of view. However, a principal shortcoming in this new conservation literature is the lack of a comprehensive document that details the scope of the principal public agencies responsible for wildlife: their histories and evolution, their present jurisdictions, a description of their multifaceted programs, and the status of their charges. This report attempts to fill that void by placing in one volume a wealth of current information on the laws, policies, regulations, and science used by the public agencies responsible for administering our wildlife resources. Of necessity this report is a bit of a catchall, but it will grow amoeba-like each year to incorporate an ever-broadening array of programs relating to wildlife.

The impetus for initiating the annual AUDUBON WILDLIFE REPORT was a desire to provide lawmakers, decision-makers in federal and state government, wildlife professionals, and conservationists with a tool that will make their work easier and more efficient. We recognize that it is virtually impossible to be impartial in such an undertaking, but we have attempted to make this report as evenhanded as possible. For the first time, we are providing in a single volume an examination of the legislative history that underlies today's principal wildlife conservation programs, descriptions of the federal agencies that are mandated by Congress to implement wildlife law, an in-depth discussion of current wildlife trends, issues, and problems, and an appendix of species information, agency budgets, contacts, and information sources.

The report is divided into four parts. Part One provides an overview of the U.S. Fish and Wildlife Service. It explains how FWS is run, who runs it, how it is funded, and what it does to meet its legal obligations to wildlife.

Part Two is a comprehensive review of the major federal wildlife programs and the agencies that implement them. Each chapter is broken into eight subsections:*

  I. Introduction — a brief statement describing the agency or program.
 II. History and Legislative Authority — an examination of the federal laws that underpin the agency or program.
III. Organization and Operations — an outline of agency roles and responsibilities, including organizational structure, administration, budgeting, and research.
 IV. Current Program Trends — an examination of significant management activities and trends.
  V. Current Issues — discussion of the specific problems and concerns that conservationists confronted in 1983 and 1984.

---

*The chapters on wetlands and on the Bureau of Land Management are subdivided by program. The chapter on the U.S. Fish and Wildlife Service did not follow this outline completely because to have done so would have caused repetition with subsequent chapters on FWS agencies and programs.

VI. Legislation — bills enacted during the 98th Congress (1983-1984) and how they affect wildlife programs.
VII. Legal Developments — a discussion of significant court cases decided in recent years.
VIII. Status of the Resource — an assessment of the resources managed by the agency or program.

The third part focuses on selected wildlife species that illustrate the full range of wildlife conservation management and research issues. Acknowledged experts prepared the 12 chapters in this section. Each chapter is divided as follows:*

I. Species Description and Natural History — what the species looks like, where and how it lives.
II. Significance of the Species — a discussion of its biological importance and its value to man.
III. Historical Perspective — an examination of the developments that led to the species' current status.
IV. Current Trends — a discussion of the problems and successes presently affecting the species.
V. Management — a description of what wildlife professionals are doing to protect and preserve the species.
VI. Prognosis — a prediction about what could happen to the species within the near future.
VII. Recommendations — a discussion of what should be done to ensure the species' survival.

Part Four is an extensive appendix that lists information contacts within the agencies and provides budget information and other data.

Future volumes will follow the same format, but the agency featured in Part One will change yearly. Next year, the U.S. Forest Service will be highlighted in Part One, the species section will be nearly doubled, and the report will cover selected state as well as federal programs. The number of federal agencies covered also will be expanded.

As with any new publication, some shortcomings and oversights will appear. Any suggestions or comments for making future editions more useful should be sent to:

Amos S. Eno   Roger Di Silvestro
Wildlife Report Project Director   Wildlife Report Editor
National Audubon Society   National Audubon Society
645 Pennsylvania Avenue S.E.   950 Third Avenue
Washington, DC 20003   New York, New York 10022

*The chapter on Hawaiian birds does not follow the outline, however, because it covers several species and so did not fit this format.

PART I.
Featured Agency

A wood duck chick views the world from an artificial nest box. Fish and Wildlife Service programs have helped many once beleaguered species, such as the wood duck.

The U.S. Fish and Wildlife Service

by William J. Chandler
W.J. Chandler Associates

INTRODUCTION

THE FISH AND Wildlife Service (FWS) is the federal government's lead agency for conserving and managing the nation's fish and wildlife resources. Its activities range from managing 89.9 million acres within the National Wildlife Refuge System, to conserving plant and animal species threatened with extinction, to advising other federal agencies on how to manage wildlife on their lands, to regulating the import and export of wildlife species, and enforcing all federal wildlife laws.

FWS operates on a budget of nearly $600 million and employs some 6,000 people in offices scattered throughout the states and territories. These offices include:

- A national headquarters staff in Washington, D.C.;
- Seven regional offices responsible for all FWS activities within their geographic area;
- Four hundred twenty-four national wildlife refuges;
- Seventy-three fish hatcheries;
- Thirty-two fishery assistance offices and seven fishery resources coordinators;
- Fifty-nine Ecological Services Field Offices;
- Nine research centers and laboratories;
- Thirty-eight Cooperative Research Units.

An understanding of the constitutional basis of federal wildlife authority is a necessary backdrop to any description of FWS activities. This authority is discussed below.

FWS traces its roots to the establishment of a U.S. Commission on Fish and Fisheries in 1871 and the commencement of research on economic ornithology by the Division of Entomology, Department of Agriculture, in 1885. A brief history of the evolution of these fish and wildlife bureaucracies is given below.

All FWS activities are organized into eight programs. Program policies are established by FWS headquarters staff and implemented by FWS regional and field offices. Detailed descriptions of FWS efforts to conserve and manage various groups of species and lands are provided in other chapters in this book.

LEGISLATIVE AUTHORITY

Both the federal government and the states have authority under the Constitution for conserving and managing wildlife, but nowhere is this authority specifically defined. The 10th Amendment to the Constitution reserves to the states all powers not delegated to the federal government nor expressly prohibited the states. These state powers, generally referred to as the police powers, enable a state to undertake a variety of actions on behalf of its citizens, including the management of wildlife.

The Constitution also assigns certain powers to the federal government, such as the power to regulate interstate commerce. These are paramount to state powers. Congress uses these federal authorities as it deems necessary to accomplish innumerable and diverse objectives. To the extent that Congress uses its federal powers to conserve wildlife, such action may pre-empt state authority.

The federal courts play a key role in this process by interpreting the often general language of the Constitution so as to more clearly delineate state and federal powers. In the case of wildlife, a subject not mentioned in the Constitution, the Supreme Court is the ultimate arbiter of federal and state wildlife authority.

The historical development of federal wildlife law is extensively treated in Michael J. Bean's *The Evolution of National Wildlife Law.*[1] A short overview of the constitutional basis for federal wildlife authority is given here.

Initially, the Supreme Court dealt with wildlife cases that focused mainly on the authority of states to regulate the taking of fish, game, and shellfish. In a series of cases in the 19th century, the court determined that the states did have the authority to control and regulate wildlife and went so far as to declare in *Geer v. Connecticut*[2] in 1896 that there was a "common property in game" that the state had the authority to regulate "as a trust for the benefit of the people." In essence, this case "articulated a general theory of state 'ownership' of wildlife,"[3] which the states later relied upon to challenge the validity of federal wildlife-regulation efforts. The state ownership doctrine was used only once by the court. In *The Abby Dodge,*[4] a 1912 decision, the court barred federal regulation of the harvest of sponges in Florida's territorial waters on the ground that the regulation of such harvest was exclusively within the power of the state. Since then, the ownership doctrine "has received no authoritative judicial support" and "has been given a quiet interment."[5]

In 1900, the federal government became directly involved in wildlife regulation when Congress passed the Lacey Act.[6] This statute authorized the secretary of Agriculture to conserve and restore bird species and to regulate the import of foreign wildlife. It also prohibited interstate commerce in wildlife killed in violation of state law. The Lacey Act represented the first clear assertion of federal authority over wildlife — a matter previously the exclusive domain of the states — and was a harbinger of things to come.

When Congress passed other wildlife laws, the Supreme Court inevitably found its attention focused on cases of state-federal conflict over authority to regulate wildlife. In resolving these cases over the years, the court moved away from its state-ownership doctrine and found ample reasons to uphold federal laws on the basis of the federal government's treaty-making, federal-property, and interstate-commerce powers.

In 1920, the court in *Missouri v. Holland*[7] upheld federal regulation of migratory birds on the ground that the law in question, the Migratory Bird Treaty Act of 1918, implemented a migratory-bird-protection treaty between the United States and Canada and was thus a valid exercise of the federal government's treaty power. The case opened the door to the making of other treaties with foreign nations for the conservation and management of fish or wildlife of common interest. The major types of treaties concluded to date include those protecting migratory birds and various fisheries and regulating commerce in endangered plant and animal species.

The Constitution gives Congress the power to "make all needful Rules and Regulations respecting the Territory or other Property belonging to the United States."[8] In a 1976 decision, *Kleppe v. New Mexico*,[9] the Supreme Court declared that the government's power to regulate the use of federally owned lands "necessarily includes the power to regulate and protect the wildlife living there." The decision contravenes the long-standing assertion by states that they have the exclusive authority to regulate wildlife on federal lands.

Congress also has the constitutional power to regulate interstate commerce. The Supreme Court has interpreted broadly this power to permit federal regulation of a host of commerce-related activities, including the taking of fish and wildlife. In *Douglas v. Seacoast Products, Inc.*,[10] the court held that Congress has the power to regulate the taking of fish in state waters in cases where there is some related effect on interstate commerce. It also held, in *Andrus v. Allard*,[11] that the Migratory Bird Treaty Act was a valid exercise of the interstate-commerce power. More recently, in *Palila v. Hawaii Department of Land and Natural Resources*,[12] a federal district court held that "a national program to protect and improve the natural habitats of endangered species preserves the possibilities of interstate commerce in these species and of interstate movement of persons, such as amateur students of nature or professional scientists who come to a state to observe and study these species."

Bean concludes that "it is clear that the Constitution, in its treaty, property and commerce clauses, contains ample support for the development of a comprehensive body of federal wildlife law and that, to the extent such law conflicts with state law, . . . [federal law] takes precedence."[13] However, such a conclusion

> does not automatically divest the states of any role in the regulation of wildlife or imply any preference for a particular allocation of responsibilities between the states and the federal government. . . . In designing such a system, for reasons of policy, pragmatism, and political comity, it is clear that the states will continue to play an important role either as a result of federal forebearance or through the creation of opportunities to share in the implementation of federal wildlife programs.[14]

For their part, the states continue to view their role in wildlife management as primary on the basis of state ownership of fish and resident wildlife. In 1970, the International Association of Fish and Wildlife Agencies issued the following policy statement:

> The Association hereby declares that the title, ownership and jurisdiction of fish and resident wildlife indisputably rests with the individual states of the United States;
> - that such title, ownership and jurisdiction shall be independent of the jurisdiction or ownership of land;
> - that the states shall have the exclusive right to manage, regulate and control fish and resident wildlife;
> - and that this dictum of states' rights is absolutely essential for the protection and preservation of the American heritage of fish and wildlife.[15]

The Department of the Interior has attempted to clarify the role and responsibilities of the states and the federal government in wildlife management in a 1983 policy statement, "Department of the Interior Fish and Wildlife Policy: State-Federal Relationships."[16] According to the Department of the Interior, the states have the "basic role" of managing fish and resident wildlife, "especially where states have primary authority." Congress has "reaffirmed the basic responsibility and authority of the states to manage fish and resident wildlife on Federal lands," and the states retain "concurrent" jurisdiction with the federal government over wildlife such as migratory birds and endangered species for which the secretary of the Interior has been given specific management responsibilities.*

History of the U.S. Fish and Wildlife Service

FWS history reaches back to the second half of the 19th century, a time when two concerns about wildlife arose. One was a recognition that the nation's bountiful fish and wildlife populations were not inexhaustible, a fact brought home by the precipitous decline of various species locally, regionally, and nationally. The other was a perception that wildlife species, especially birds, could have both positive and negative effects on agriculture and that these relationships should be studied and publicized. A corollary idea was that beneficial species should be protected while harmful species should be controlled or exterminated.

Each of these concerns helped precipitate congressional action to involve the federal government in wildlife management. As a result, the predecessor organizations of today's FWS were born. In 1871, Congress created a Commission on Fish and Fisheries to investigate the decline of "food fishes." In 1885, it appropriated funds to the Department of Agriculture for the study of economic ornithology. A year later, it established a Division of Economic Ornithology and Mammalogy within the department to study the food habitats, distribution, and migrations of birds and mammals and their relation to agriculture, horticulture, and forestry. Thereafter, each of these bureaucracies followed independent courses of development until their successor organizations — the Bureau of Fisheries in the Department of Commerce and the Bureau of Biological Survey in the Department of Agriculture — were merged in 1940 into the Fish and Wildlife Service within the Department of the Interior.

This section provides a brief overview of the development of the two bureaucracies that grew into FWS. More detailed discussions of the principal statutes that guide FWS today are found in the chapters on migratory birds, inland fish, endangered species, refuges, wetlands, marine mammals, federal aid, and animal damage control.

U.S. Fish Commission

In 1871, Congress created the post of commissioner of Fish and Fisheries and named Spencer Fullerton Baird of the Smithsonian Institution as the first commissioner. Initially, the purpose of the fish commission was to investigate the population status of "food fishes of the coast and the lakes of the United States" to determine if declines had occurred and, if so, the causes for those declines. The commission also was directed to make recommendations regarding "protective, prohibitory, or precautionary measures" necessary to protect fisheries.

Based on these investigations, Congress soon expanded the commission's activities to include the propagation and distribution of fish and fish eggs throughout the nation. The first federal fish hatchery was created in 1872. Thereafter, numerous

---

*It must be emphasized that this is a policy statement, based on the department's interpretation of federal and state statutory authority, not a legal opinion.

hatcheries were created around the country. The states followed suit, creating their own fish commissions, and joined the federal government in introducing non-native species into United States waters and transplanting native trout from one state to another.

By 1889 the commission had been given two additional duties, the development of commercial fishing and the collection of statistics on fishery production. The appropriations bill for the commission that year provided funds to increase the supply of food fishes, lobsters, and shellfish by artificial propagation and stocking or other means; to investigate the causes "of the decrease of food fishes in the lakes, rivers, and coast waters of the United States, and for the study of the waters of the interior in the interest of fish culture;" to study fishing methods and the relationships between fish species in various fisheries; to explore ocean fishing grounds for the purpose of developing commercial fishing; and to collect and compile statistics on all fisheries in the United States.

In 1903, the fish commission was transferred to the newly created Department of Commerce and renamed the Bureau of Fisheries. Its location within Commerce was indicative of the bureau's principal mission: the promotion of commercial fishing. The bureau's functions remained much the same as those of its predecessor: the collection and analysis of scientific information and statistics on fish and fishery production, the improvement of fish-culture techniques, and the propagation of fish for use in the restoration of depleted fisheries of commercial significance.

Commencing in the 1920s, Congress recognized the need to protect inland fish and their habitats from the adverse impacts of federal dams and to mitigate fishery losses caused by water-resource-development projects. The Federal Power Act of 1920 authorized the secretary of Commerce to recommend construction of fish passageways at dams licensed by the commission. A 1935 amendment mandated the construction of such recommended facilities. Another measure, the Fish and Wildlife Coordination Act of 1934, required all federal dam-building agencies to consult with the Bureau of Fisheries prior to construction and to include fish lifts and ladders if they were deemed necessary and economically practicable.

Congress also began passing laws to undertake the restoration of specific fisheries. The purpose of the Mitchell Act of 1938 was to help rectify the damage done by federal dams to the salmon and steelhead fishery of the Columbia River Basin. The act authorized fish surveys, construction of fish passageways and other facilities, habitat protection and restoration measures, and the propagation of salmon at hatcheries for restocking the river.

In 1939, the Bureau of Fisheries was transferred to the Department of the Interior as part of a move by President Roosevelt to put all wildlife matters in one department. In 1940, the Fisheries Bureau, along with the Bureau of Biological Survey, which had been transferred from Agriculture to Interior, was merged into the new Fish and Wildlife Service.

After World War II, a rising demand for recreational fishing opportunities led FWS to become more involved in fish propagation and conservation for sport uses. Congress addressed the recreational fishing issue in 1950 by passing the Dingell-Johnson Act, which authorized a federal grant-in-aid program to help states conserve sport fish and to provide sport fishing recreation opportunities. The program was funded by an excise tax on fishing tackle.

The increased attention given by FWS to the conservation and use of inland fish for sport uses was not welcomed by commercial fishing interests, which regarded such efforts as a distraction from the previous emphasis on commercial fisheries. In addition, the conservation of certain fisheries for sport use often meant tighter harvest restrictions for commercial users of the same resource.

The conflict between sport and commercial fishing came to a head in 1956, when commercial-fishing interests promoted the creation of a separate U.S. Fish Commission that would be more attendant to their wishes. The move failed, but compromise legislation split FWS into two separate bureaus: the Bureau of Sport Fish and Wildlife and the Bureau of Commercial Fisheries.

Congress continued through the 1950s and 1960s its practice of passing legislation to help restore specific inland fisheries or fish species. These measures included the Great Lakes Fishery Act of 1956, fishery-mitigation measures for the Colorado River Storage Project (also in 1956), and the Anadromous Fish Conservation Act of 1965, which authorized a federal grant-in-aid program to states to conserve and restore anadromous fish species in all areas of the United States.

Another significant milestone was the creation of a program to better conserve and utilize sport-fish resources on federal lands. The Sikes Act of 1960 and later amendments authorized FWS, in cooperation with the states, to assist federal land-managing agencies to develop fishery-resource-management plans for their lands. The National Wildlife Refuge Administration Act of 1966 authorized the use of national wildlife refuges for fishing as long as the refuge is compatible with the major purposes for which it was established.

In 1970, another government reorganization effort, designed to put all ocean resources into one agency, led to the abolishment of the Bureau of Commercial Fisheries and the transfer of FWS marine fishery activities — both commercial and sport — back to the Department of Commerce. These activities were assumed by the National Marine Fisheries Service (NMFS), a new bureau under the National Oceanic and Atmospheric Administration. The reorganization left jurisdiction over inland fish with the Bureau of Sport Fisheries and Wildlife, which was renamed the U.S. Fish and Wildlife Service in 1974. Jurisdiction over anadromous species in inland waters, however, was divided between NMFS and FWS.

Although statutes passed since 1970 have given FWS added responsibilities for certain fishery resources of national significance, the activities conducted today by the FWS Fishery Resources Program are pretty much the same as those of 1970. They include the propagation and culture of fish for stocking purposes; the restoration of depleted, nationally significant fishery resources through restocking, habitat rehabilitation, and protection; the provision of technical assistance to federal land-managing agencies and Indian tribes; the promotion of fishery use on appropriate wildlife refuges; the enforcement of federal fish laws; and the conduct of research.

The Division of Economic Ornithology

Like the fish commission, the Division of Economic Ornithology and Mammalogy was created primarily as a research body.[17] But rather than study declining populations of wildlife, the division's initial charge was to investigate the food habits, distribution, and migrations of North American birds and mammals in relation to agriculture, horticulture, and forestry and to promote economic ornithology and mammalogy, the study of both wildlife benefits and damages to agriculture and other interests.* This thrust grew out of a recognition in scientific circles that birds help protect agricultural crops from insects and that such bird-plant relationships should be

---

*Congress made an appropriation to the Department of Agriculture's Entomological Division in 1885 to commence the study of economic ornithology. In 1886, the Division of Economic Ornithology and Mammalogy was created by Congress to expand the research effort.

further elucidated and made known to farmers. A corollary recognition was that introductions of non-native birds, a practice then growing in frequency, could harm native birds or crops.[18]

The history of the division and its successor agency has been extensively treated in *The Bureau of Biological Survey*,[19] by Jenks Cameron, a source used for much of this section. Cameron identifies four areas of sequential emphasis by the bureau during the period 1885 to 1929: first economic ornithology, then studies of the geographic distribution of species, next a brief return to economic ornithology, and finally a direct effort to protect game and other desirable species of birds and animals and the repression of undesirable species.

In the early years, 1885 to 1905, the division conducted studies on the food habitats of birds and on birds and mammals that were economically beneficial. By 1890, however, the division was placing increasing emphasis on studies of the distribution of plants and mammals, an emphasis that continued to grow throughout the decade and into the early part of the 20th century. A number of field biological surveys were conducted during this period, particularly in the West, and the division mapped the "life zones" of various species. In 1896, the division was renamed the Division of Biological Survey to reflect its new emphasis.

Meanwhile, other forces were at work that eventually would redirect the division's priorities. The expansion of agriculture and ranching in the United States led to increased human conflicts with wildlife and to demands that the federal government do something to help protect crops and livestock from wildlife depredations. As a result, in 1905 the division created a new section concerned solely with studying the relations of mammals to agriculture. At about the same time, growing public pressure to have the federal government take action to help protect game birds being decimated by market hunters and plume birds killed for the millinery trade led to passage of the Lacey Act of 1900, which involved the division in supporting the enforcement of state game laws and in the conservation, propagation, and stocking of wild game and other birds.

By the time the division was enlarged to bureau status in 1905, its biological survey function was on the wane and its involvement with wildlife that had tangible economic or other benefits or that threatened human economic activity was on the rise. The bureau refocused its efforts on economic ornithology and became more deeply involved in the control of harmful mammals. In 1907, the bureau issued its first publication on how to destroy wolves and coyotes. The bureau continued its study of and advisory role on predator control until 1915, when Congress appropriated funds to the bureau for the direct control of predators and other animals that resided on federal lands. This work later was expanded to cover private lands as well.

The Lacey Act enlarged the powers of the Biological Survey by authorizing it to pursue the preservation, distribution, introduction, and restoration of game and other wild birds. The act also prohibited the import of any wild bird or animal without a federal permit and forbade interstate commerce in animals and birds killed in violation of state laws, a provision that dealt a severe blow to market hunting. Its passage marked the onset of national regulatory efforts to protect, conserve, and manage wildlife.[20]

In 1903, another highly significant event occurred that presaged a total transformation in the division's priorities: the creation by President Theodore Roosevelt of the first national wildlife refuge on Pelican Island, Florida. Management responsibility for this and other bird and big-game refuges set aside on public-domain lands by Roosevelt was given to the survey. Refuge management eventually grew to be the largest single activity conducted today by FWS. Following Roosevelt's lead, Congress also started creating refuges, principally for big-game species, on a limited basis. This modest effort changed when concern over declining migratory waterfowl populations reached a peak in the 1920s. In 1929, Congress passed the Migratory Bird Conservation Act, authorizing the purchase of private lands for migratory-bird refuges. This act, in essence, created a national refuge system. Later legislation expanded the list of species that could be protected by refuges to include all forms of wildlife and endangered animal and plant species.

In 1913, the Bureau of Biological Survey became directly involved in regulating the hunting of wildlife when Congress passed the Migratory Bird Act. This law declared all migratory birds to be under the protection of federal law and prohibited the hunting of all species except as allowed by the secretary of Agriculture. To head off state challenges to the law's constitutionality, the federal government signed a migratory bird protection treaty with Canada, which accomplished the same purpose as the 1913 law. The implementing legislation for the treaty, the Migratory Bird Treaty Act of 1918, was upheld by the Supreme Court in 1920.

In the 1930s, Congress launched three additional federal wildlife initiatives. The Pittman-Robertson Act authorized a grant-in-aid program to assist states in the restoration of game populations. The Fish and Wildlife Coordination Act was passed to authorize the bureau to consult with federal dam building agencies so as to provide fish and wildlife benefits whenever possible in connection with reservoir projects. And the Duck Stamp Act required waterfowl hunters to buy duck stamps; receipts were used for the acquisition and management of migratory-bird refuges.

The Fish and Wildlife Service Since 1940

The Bureau of Biological Survey was transferred to the Department of the Interior in 1939 and merged in 1940 with the Bureau of Fisheries into the new Fish and Wildlife Service. At this point, many of the principal wildlife activities of today's FWS already were established. These included the protection, conservation, and management of migratory birds; the control of predators and other wildlife; law enforcement; the management of wildlife refuges; the administration of a federal grant-in-aid program for state wildlife restoration efforts; consultation with federal dam-building agencies to mitigate project impacts on wildlife; and research.

Since 1940, several new statutes have added to the agency's wildlife responsibilities. Amendments to the Fish and Wildlife Coordination Act and several other statutes have enabled the service to expand its preconstruction consultation activities with federal development agencies to cover a wide variety of development projects. The Sikes Act of 1960, as amended, authorized FWS to work cooperatively with the states in the preparation of wildlife-management plans for federally owned lands managed by the Forest Service, the Bureau of Land Management, the Department of Defense, and the Department of Energy. Such work is conducted as part of the FWS technical-assistance program.

Several other statutes have broadened FWS emphasis on game species to include all forms of wildlife. The Endangered Species Act of 1973 involved FWS in the identification and protection of plant and animal species endangered with extinction and the regulation of trade in such species. This effort is now one of the major FWS resource-management programs. The Marine Mammal Protection Act of 1972 gave FWS exclusive management authority over five species of marine mammals found in United States waters. Finally, the Fish and Wildlife Conservation Act of 1980 (the Nongame Act) authorized a federal grant-in-aid program to the states for the conservation of nongame species of wildlife. However, this act has yet to be funded by Congress.

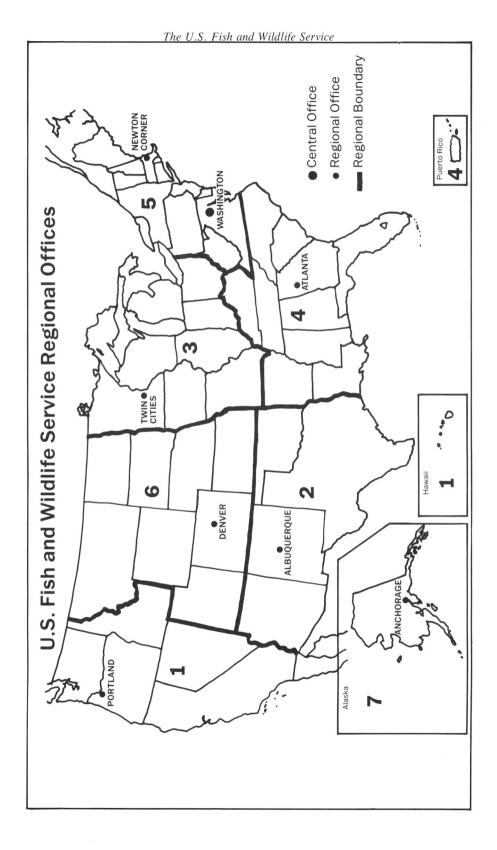

U.S. Fish and Wildlife Service Regional Offices

ORGANIZATION AND OPERATIONS

Roles and Responsibilities

The broad mission of FWS is to "provide the federal leadership to conserve, protect and enhance fish and wildlife and their habitats for the continuing benefit of people."[21] In pursuit of this mission, FWS uses a Program Management System to plan, budget, and evaluate its many activities. The system links and coordinates the eight FWS programs:

- Habitat Resources
- Wildlife Resources
- Fishery Resources
- Endangered Species
- Federal Aid
- Executive Direction
- Administration and Related Support Services
- Cooperative Research Units

A program focuses either on a specific natural resource, a special skill or function, or a cluster of activities useful for management purposes. Each program is divided into a number of "subactivities" that reflect the major functions conducted by FWS personnel under the program. These subactivities are used for budgeting purposes, and each is a line item in the FWS annual budget justification document.

Each FWS program is managed by an FWS executive, referred to as the "program manager," stationed in the Washington office. The program manager is responsible for setting program goals, objectives, and policies, allocating budget and staff to FWS regional and field offices to implement the program, and monitoring and evaluating results. Program managers report directly to the FWS director but do not directly supervise the field personnel who implement the program.

Programs are implemented by seven regional offices and the Office of Research and Development, which supervise field units (refuges, hatcheries, laboratories, etc.) located in their geographic or functional areas. Regional directors report directly to the FWS director. They are responsible for ensuring that national program objectives are transformed into appropriate objectives within their area of responsibility and accomplished on time and within budget ceilings.

The national program offices and regional and field offices are linked together by the three main components of the Program Management System: planning, budgeting, and evaluation. These activities are conducted in such a way that information flows back and forth between the program managers and regional and field offices. Hence the management system is described as one that is "top down, bottom up." Decisions regarding national objectives and budget are made by the director based on advice from program managers and regional directors. Four meetings of the Directorate, the FWS policy-making body, composed of key FWS officials, are held each year to address major problems and issues.*

Planning

FWS prepares a variety of national, regional, and field station plans to guide its work. These plans are hierarchical in that field plans must be consistent with regional plans and regional plans consistent with national plans.

---

*The FWS Directorate is composed of the director, deputy director, staff assistant to the deputy director, the chiefs of the offices of legislative services and equal opportunity, the assistant directors for planning and budget, public affairs, and administration, all regional directors, and the program managers.

U.S. Fish and Wildlife Service

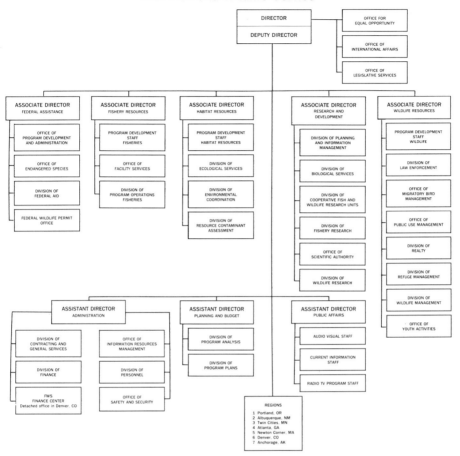

National Plans. Several different types of national plans are prepared by the Washington office to provide overall policy guidance to regional and field offices. They include:

- The Service Management Plan, which provides overall direction for FWS for a five- to ten-year period.
- Program management documents, which outline more specific program objectives for a five-year period.
- Special national plans that address a unique problem, such as the National Waterfowl Management Plan, the National Disease Contingency Plan, and the National Pollution Response Plan.
- National Objectives for Species of Special Emphasis, a handbook of national population and distribution goals for 54 animal species that FWS has identified as being of high biological, legal, or public interest. National Species of Special Emphasis objectives serve as one important guide for resource-management activities undertaken by regional offices.

Regional Plans. Each regional office prepares a Regional Resource Plan that contains objectives and strategies for meeting population and distribution goals for all NSSEs within the region as well as for some other species of regional interest known as "regional species of special emphasis." Regional plans have a five-year planning horizon and are updated periodically. The regional resource plan serves as one of the key resource planning guides for all field units. FWS regions prepare internal "operational plans" that specify how regional-plan objectives will be attained, by whom, and at what cost. These operational plans form one basis of the region's annual budget proposal.

In addition, regional offices coordinate the preparation of endangered species recovery plans. Each plan is assigned to a lead region for preparation. Completed recovery plans then must be approved by the Office of Endangered Species in Washington and by the FWS director.

Field Plans. Field plans are prepared to guide the operational activities of field stations such as wildlife refuges, hatcheries, and laboratories, or of field personnel engaged in the control or management of wildlife or fish populations not located on refuges. Such plans include:

- Refuge master plans
- Alaska refuge comprehensive conservation plans
- Refuge management plans
- Law enforcement strategy plans
- Hatchery management plans
- Research and development plans (for research facilities)
- Animal damage control plans
- Fish and wildlife management plans (for populations on non-service lands)

Field plans are prepared for a two-year period and must be approved by the regional director.

Budgeting

The FWS budget process begins with a Directorate policy conference in November. The purpose of the conference is to identify national budget issues for inclusion in the fiscal-year budget beginning two years hence. After receiving advice from his management team, the director issues a Director's Policy Memorandum identifying the general issues and priorities that he wishes to emphasize in the budget. In concert with the director's memorandum, each program manager then issues a Program Manager Strategy Statement that further elaborates the director's priorities for each program.

Using these guidelines and their regional resource operational plans, the regional directors prepare regional budget proposals. After these proposals are submitted and reviewed, the program managers prepare a Program Manager Strategy Paper that consolidates regional budget proposals into a national program proposal.

At a national budget meeting held the following April, the Directorate establishes service-wide budget priorities and makes a recommendation for the FWS budget. The director then makes a final decision on the budget proposal and forwards it to the assistant secretary for Fish and Wildlife and Parks. Next the budget is sent to the secretary of the Interior for review, adjustment, and approval, then on to the president's Office of Management and Budget, where it is again reviewed and adjusted. A final FWS budget is submitted to Congress in late January or early February as part of the president's annual budget request.

In Congress, three committees in each house have responsibilities related to the FWS budget. The authorizing committees with jurisdiction over fish and wildlife — the Merchant Marine and Fisheries Committee in the House and the Environment and Public Works Committee in the Senate — may hold hearings on the proposed budget and make recommendations to the budget committees regarding funding levels. The budget committees set overall spending limits for all federal agencies. Guided by these limits, the appropriations committees determine the final size and content of the budget. After holding hearings, each House and Senate appropriations subcommittee on Interior makes recommendations for FWS spending levels in their respective versions of the annual Interior appropriations bill. Each bill then must be approved by the full appropriations committees and voted on by all members of each legislative body. House and Senate differences are resolved by a conference committee, and the final appropriations bill is approved and sent to the president for signature.

Once FWS knows what its appropriation will be, it schedules its work for the new fiscal year. Each program manager issues a Program Advice that allocates money and work-force levels called "full-time equivalent positions," to each region to achieve the tasks specified in the budget and plans. Regional directors in turn prepare annual work-plan advices, which provide funds, personnel allotments, and work guidance to their field units. Each field unit then prepares its own annual work plan.

Evaluation

FWS annually evaluates its programs to determine if they attain policy and program objectives identified in service plans and work schedules. The evaluations provide feedback for establishing or modifying program objectives. A mid-year and end-of-year evaluation conference is held by the Directorate to report on progress and to identify problems and ways to solve them.

Program Descriptions

Each FWS program is responsible for the implementation of a variety of activities authorized by federal wildlife and other laws and for achieving objectives designated in a variety of FWS plans. A brief overview of each program is given here; more in-depth discussions of key resource-management programs are provided in following chapters. In addition, FWS law-enforcement, international, and wildlife-permit activities are discussed.

Habitat Resources

While the other three resource programs focus on wildlife species, the Habitat Resources Program focuses on wildlife habitat and particularly on the impacts of human activities — including federally permitted, licensed, or constructed projects — on that habitat. The program places heavy emphasis on protection of wetlands, one of the most important and most threatened habitat types.

The FY 1985 budget for habitat resources was $49.2 million,* about eight percent of the total FWS budget. The program had 911 full-time equivalents (FTEs), about 14 percent of the FWS total. Just under a third of the program's budget is allocated to research and slightly more than a third to reviewing federal projects, permits, and licenses. The principal activities conducted by the habitat-resources program include:

- Reviewing and making recommendations for preventing or reducing the adverse impacts of federal water resource development projects on fish and wildlife. In 1985, FWS expects to review approximately 1,500 federal projects, more than half of them sponsored by the Corps of Engineers.
- Reviewing and making recommendations on applications for federal permits and licenses, primarily Section 404 and Section 10 permits issued by the Corps

*This amount includes $4.6 million for the Cooperative Research Units Program discussed later in this section.

of Engineers, and permits and licenses for hydroelectric facilities issued by the Federal Energy Regulatory Commission. In 1985, FWS expects to review 16,000 Corps permit applications plus 5,000 notices of planned dredge and fill activities that may require individual permits. It also expects to carry out 2,295 consultations related to Federal Energy Regulatory Commission permits and licenses.

- Insuring FWS compliance with the National Environmental Policy Act (NEPA) by preparing guidance for use by FWS personnel on NEPA requirements, reviewing various FWS actions to determine adherence to NEPA, and coordinating with other elements within FWS in the preparation and review of other agencies' environmental impact documents.
- Monitoring pesticides and toxic chemicals to develop and provide information on the build up of persistent chemicals and pollutants in fish and wildlife populations; providing emergency response action in the case of major spills; and collecting samples, conducting field assessments, and providing technical expertise and assistance on matters of fish and wildlife contamination.
- Conducting the National Wetlands Inventory, including preparation of a wetlands map that shows the characteristics and extent of the nation's wetlands and deep-water habitats — and the issuance of periodic reports on wetlands status and trends.
- Conducting a variety of research studies regarding human impacts on fish and wildlife habitat, with a primary focus on environmental contaminants and a lesser emphasis on the impacts of energy and mineral development and land and river modification.

Many of the activities in the Habitat Resources Program, including federal project investigations, review of permits and licenses, and most reviews of other agencies' environmental impact statements, are carried out by staff in 59 FWS Ecological Services field offices.

Wildlife Resources

The Wildlife Resources Program is the largest and most diverse of the four FWS resource-management programs. Its activities range from managing the National Wildlife Refuge System, to coordinating the use of aircraft in FWS operations, to conducting specific management actions for the benefit of marine mammals such as the polar bear. The FY 1985 Wildlife Resources Program budget of $146.5 million constitutes about 25 percent of the FWS budget. The program has 2,840 FTEs, 43 percent of the FWS total.

The Wildlife Resources Program has lead responsibility for all service activities relating to mammals, birds, reptiles, amphibians, crustaceans, and terrestrial mollusks except species listed under the Endangered Species Act, which are the responsibility of the Endangered Species Program. Principal activities include:

- management of 89.9 million acres of land in the National Wildlife Refuge System, including 424 refuges, 149 waterfowl production areas, and 58 wildlife management areas;
- enforcement of federal wildlife laws through its Division of Law Enforcement;
- management of 816 migratory bird species and three species of marine mammals,* and the provision of technical assistance on wildlife management to

*Polar bear, walrus, and northern sea otter. The southern sea otter and the West Indian manatee are the responsibility of the Endangered Species Program.

Indian tribes, federal, state and local agencies, private industry, and foreign governments;

- control of damage caused by certain species of migratory birds and mammals through the provision of technical and operational assistance to federal, state, local, and private agencies and organizations;
- conduct of wildlife research, especially relating to migratory birds, marine mammals, and animal damage control.

Several offices of the Wildlife Resources Program provide services for the rest of FWS. These include the Division of Realty, which acquires lands and waters and other real property in support of all FWS programs; the Division of Law Enforcement; the Office of Public Use Management, which develops guidelines for the public use of refuges and for public participation in all FWS programs; and the Office of Youth Activities, which coordinates all federally funded youth-employment programs, such as the Youth Conservation Corps, on FWS lands.

The Fishery Resources Program has responsibility for all FWS activities relating to the conservation and management of fish. Program jurisdiction includes all freshwater species of the inland waters and species of anadromous fish when they reside in inland waters. Most program efforts, however, are focused on about 40 species or species groups that are caught for market or sport. The FY 1985 budget for the Fishery Resources Program, $46.1 million, constitutes 7.8 percent of the FWS budget. The program has 887 FTEs, about 13 percent of the total. The principal activities conducted by the program include:

- operation and maintenance of 73 federal fish hatcheries that propagate about 300 million fish annually for stocking and for mitigating fishery losses caused by federal water projects;
- implementation of the Lower Snake River Compensation Plan, a program to mitigate damage caused to anadromous and other fish resources by the construction of four federal dams in the state of Washington;
- promotion of fishing on the 125 units of the National Wildlife Refuge System that have significant fisheries;
- enforcement of federal fish protection laws with primary concentration on illegal commercial fishing for anadromous species and Great Lakes fish;
- provision of technical and operational assistance to other federal agencies, states, and Indian tribes for the management of selected anadromous, Great Lakes, and inland fisheries or fish species;
- conduct of scientific research on fish habitat and ecology, resource use, and fish propagation;
- coordination of grants to states under the Anadromous Fish Conservation Act for the conduct of various research, conservation, restoration, and management projects.

In addition, the associate director for Fisheries supervises the Office of Facility Services, which coordinates a service-wide maintenance, construction, and rehabilitation program for all physical facilities at refuges, fish hatcheries, research laboratories, and other FWS facilities. FWS ranks construction priorities on a service-wide basis and seeks appropriations for the most significant items in its annual budget request.

Endangered Species

The Endangered Species Program is responsible for identifying, listing, protecting, and managing all species of animals and plants that are threatened or endangered with extinction. Although both foreign and United States species are listed under the

15

Endangered Species Act, FWS necessarily focuses its management efforts on 331 listed species that occur in the United States.

The Endangered Species Program budget for FY 1985, $27 million, constitutes 4.6 percent of the FWS budget. The program has 405 FTEs, six percent of the FWS total. The principal activities conducted by the Endangered Species Program include:

- listing species determined to be threatened or endangered based on FWS status surveys;
- enforcing, through the Division of Law Enforcement, laws that protect endangered species from harm and from illegal trade;
- consulting with and providing advice to other federal agencies to ensure that their development activities and other actions do not jeopardize listed species or their critical habitat;
- preparing and implementing recovery plans for listed United States species;
- conducting research to develop tools and techniques for more effectively managing listed species;
- coordinating a state grant-in-aid program for the cooperative management of endangered species.

Federal Aid

The Federal Aid Program is responsible for coordinating two grant-in-aid programs to states for fish and wildlife restoration, conservation, and management. The Federal Aid in Fish Restoration Act, also known as the Dingell-Johnson Act (D-J), authorizes matching grants to states for up to 75 percent of the cost of projects undertaken to enhance sport fish resources and fishing opportunities. The Federal Aid

Fish and Wildlife Service Budget
Fiscal Year 1985

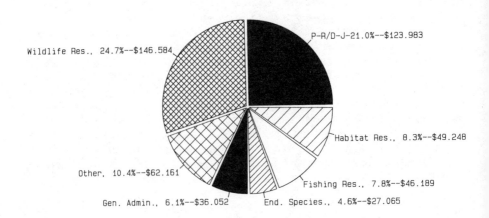

P-R/D-J—21.0%—$123.983

Wildlife Res., 24.7%—$146.584

Habitat Res., 8.3%—$49.248

Other, 10.4%—$62.161

Fishing Res., 7.8%—$46.189

Gen. Admin., 6.1%—$36.052

End. Species., 4.6%—$27.065

FWS BUDGET, FY 1985
TOTAL = $ 592, 142, 000

in Wildlife Restoration Act, also known as the Pittman-Robertson Act (P-R), authorizes matching grants to the states for up to 75 percent of the cost of projects designed to restore, conserve, manage, and enhance species of birds and mammals and to educate hunters in the skills, knowledge, and attitudes necessary to be safe and responsible.

These programs are funded by federal excise taxes on fishing tackle (D-J) and on firearms, ammunition, and archery equipment (P-R). Tax receipts are allocated for state use on an annual basis. In FY 1985, the total federal aid program budget of $123.9 million represents the second largest program budget of the eight FWS programs and constitutes 21 percent of the total FWS budget. Of this amount, $38 million is for D-J program expenditures and $85.9 million for P-R projects. These programs have 90 FTEs, one percent of the total.

The Division of Federal Aid in Washington coordinates both the P-R and D-J programs on behalf of the associate director for Federal Assistance. The division's responsibilities include ensuring that state projects are "substantial in character and design," monitoring the projects as they progress and seeing that the projects comply with other federal laws, such as the National Environmental Policy Act and the Endangered Species Act.

States are given wide latitude in their selection of projects to be funded. The principal types of projects excluded from funding include public relations, law enforcement, and commercial activities. The D-J program funds about 400 projects each year, the P-R program nearly 600. Typical D-J projects include research on fishery problems, surveys and inventories of fish species, creation and improvement of waters suitable for fish, and providing access to fishing areas. Projects conducted under the P-R program include researching wildlife problems, species surveys and inventories, acquisition and improvement of wildlife habitat, providing facilities and access to wildlife areas, and providing training in hunter safety.

Executive Direction and Administration

The Executive Direction Program is responsible for overall FWS management. The program is headed by the deputy director of FWS, who supervises all associate directors, regional directors, and various other Washington offices that conduct activities with a national scope. Most goals of the program have to do with internal management: correcting problems, improving efficiency, facilitating communication, and developing and maintaining a professional staff.

The direction program coordinates FWS cooperation with other federal agencies, the states, nonprofit conservation organizations and international agencies. The program also is responsible for FWS public relations efforts, which include enhancing public understanding of fish and wildlife resources, developing public support for FWS objectives, and involving the public in FWS decisions affecting fish and wildlife.

The Administration and Related Support Services Program is responsible for providing high-quality administrative support to all FWS management and operational levels. It is the FWS business-management arm. Support services is supervised by the assistant director - Administration. Services personnel are located in the Washington office, seven regional offices, and the Denver Finance Center.

The program is concerned with four administrative functions: personnel management and organization; contracting and general services; financial management; and safety and security. Its principal goals are to insure that all FWS administrative business is conducted in compliance with all laws and regulations and that all appropriated monies are accounted for.

Together the Executive Direction and support services programs have an FY

Fish and Wildlife Service FTES
Fiscal Year 1985

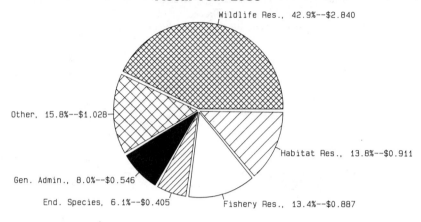

FWS FTES, FY 1985
TOTAL = $ 6,617,000

1985 budget of $36 million, about 6.1 percent of the total FWS budget. There are 546 FTEs allotted to the two programs, about eight percent of total staff positions.

Cooperative Research Units

The Cooperative Research Units Program is responsible for coordinating a fish and wildlife research and training program at certain state land grant colleges and universities. This research effort, cooperatively sponsored and funded by the federal government, the states, participating universities, and the Wildlife Management Institute, commenced in 1935 and was given statutory authority by the Cooperative Unit Act of 1960.

The cooperative unit program is supervised by the associate director for Research and Development. In FY 1985, the budget for the program is $4.6 million,* about the same amount it has received since FY 1980. These funds are used principally to pay for salaries of the FWS co-op unit leader and his or her assistant. A small amount also provides base funding for the unit. Nearly all funds to pay for specific research projects come from contracts and grants provided by FWS, the states, and other federal agencies. The program has 57 FTEs.

In FY 1984, FWS operated 25 cooperative fishery research units, 20 wildlife units, and four combined fish and wildlife units at 31 universities in 29 states. FWS has initiated a move to combine separate fishery units and wildlife units that currently exist

---

*Funding for the cooperative units is included in the Habitat Resources activity in the FWS budget.

at the same university in order to improve administrative efficiency and reduce program costs. Fifteen of the 24 affected universities now have combined units.

According to FWS, about 90 percent of all research conducted by the units is oriented toward solving fish and wildlife management problems. The other 10 percent is basic research. Fish and wildlife agencies in nine states rely exclusively on their cooperative units to satisfy agency research needs. In many other states, the units conduct a substantial portion of the state-agency research. At any given moment, the units are involved in more than 600 research projects.

FWS Projects Conducted in FY 1983 and FY 1984

| | Number of Projects | | |
| | | | (% of all |
	1983	1984	Projects)*
Animal Damage Control	19	12	(1.7%)
Biological Services	104	87	(12.4%)
Endangered Species	43	60	(8.5%)
Environmental Contamination Evaluation	43	50	(7.1%)
Fishery Resources	254	220	(31.4%)
Interpretation and Recreation	4	3	(0.4%)
Ecological Services	46	46	(6.5%)
Mammals and Non-Migratory Birds	154	122	(17.4%)
Migratory Birds	99	100	(14.2%)
TOTAL	766	700	

*Percent does not add up to 100% due to rounding.
Source: U.S. Fish and Wildlife Service

In addition to their research contributions, the units also help train a cadre of fish and wildlife management professionals employed by federal and state fish and wildlife agencies, universities, and the private sector. Of the 150 unit graduates in FY 1983, more than 70 percent found employment in fish and wildlife biology.

International Activities

FWS is involved in a variety of efforts to provide advice and technical assistance to foreign nations and to otherwise promote international conservation efforts. These are carried out pursuant to a number of different laws, treaties, and other authorities and are the responsibility of several different programs within FWS.

The major authorities for FWS international efforts are the following:

- The Western Hemisphere Convention (Convention on Nature Protection and Wildlife Preservation in the Western Hemisphere[22]), signed in 1940 and implemented in the United States by the Endangered Species Act of 1973.* The convention's main concerns are habitat conservation and the protection of species in trade.
- The Convention on International Trade in Endangered Species of Wild Fauna and Flora (CITES),[23] a multinational agreement ratified by 85 countries to regulate international trade in certain critical species listed in its appendices.
- Section 8 of the Endangered Species Act of 1973, which allows excess foreign currencies held by the United States to be spent on conservation of foreign

*The first appropriation to carry out convention-related activities, $150,000, was made in FY 1983.

19

species listed as threatened or endangered species by the United States, encourages conservation agreements with foreign countries and provides federal personnel and financial assistance for training foreign conservation personnel.

Within FWS, the Office of International Affairs is most directly involved in international conservation. International Affairs has lead responsibility for the Western Hemisphere Convention, which accounts for a major portion of the office's activities. Office priorities include the training of Latin American wildlife personnel; studies, mapping, and project planning for migratory-bird conservation in Latin America; information exchanges including translation into Spanish of scientific and wildlife management manuals; and a variety of bilateral projects with certain Latin American countries. The office also is responsible for overseeing the use of excess foreign currencies to conserve listed endangered species abroad. When available, such currencies generally are used to provide training and support to local government or to nongovernmental organization conservation efforts. Excess-currency projects presently operate only in India and Pakistan.

In addition, the office coordinates or carries out more than a dozen conservation activities in collaboration with the Soviet Union under the bilateral US-USSR Environmental Agreement.[24] These activities primarily support travel of United States or Soviet scientists to conduct research and monitoring. Finally, environmental education in developing countries is an increasingly important part of the office's activities.

The Office of Endangered Species has an important role in implementing the international aspects of the Endangered Species Act. In particular, the Office of Endangered Species makes a substantial effort to compile data and information on imperiled species worldwide, collaborates with the International Union for Conservation of Nature and Natural Resources Conservation Monitoring Centre in exchanging data on the status of foreign species, and prepares listing proposals for all foreign species listed under the Endangered Species Act. However, the office's most important contribution to international wildlife conservation has been identified simply as the close interaction and exchange of data between United States and foreign biologists, which can strongly influence foreign conservation programs.

Two other offices have important international responsibilities related to the implementation of CITES. The Office of Scientific Authority, a unit within the FWS Research and Development arm, serves as the United States "scientific authority" for CITES-related actions. Its major responsibilities are to review work on listings of species to be covered by the convention, to advise on the issuance of permits for the export of listed species, and generally to collect, analyze, and disseminate data and information on critical species of flora and fauna. The actual issuance of permits under CITES is carried out by the Federal Wildlife Permit Office, a unit supervised by the associate director - Federal Assistance. The permit office is the United States management authority for convention activities.

Other offices with more limited international responsibilities include the Office of Migratory Bird Management, which is involved in international conservation efforts pursuant to United States migratory-bird treaties with four other nations; the FWS research divisions, which provide technical assistance to foreign countries, disseminate wildlife research literature, and conduct some research on species that reside in other countries; and the Division of Law Enforcement, which enforces wildlife protection and trade laws.

The Division of Law Enforcement

Although it is supervised by the Wildlife Resources Program, the Division of Law Enforcement is responsible for enforcing all fish and wildlife statutes administered by FWS, including laws that pertain to fish and endangered species — resources that are the management responsibility of other FWS programs. Both the Fishery Resources and Endangered Species Programs include enforcement line items within their budgets to pay for work done by the Division of Law Enforcement, and program staff provide advice and guidance to the division concerning law-enforcement measures needed to protect fish and endangered species from illegal takings and other harm.

FWS employs 156 special agents nationwide to investigate wildlife crimes and enforce federal laws. The division staff in Washington develops regulations and program guidelines for all FWS law-enforcement operations and coordinates investigations that transcend regional boundaries. The division also has a Special Operations Branch through which it carries out major nationwide undercover operations.

In the field, all operations except those of the Special Operations Branch are organized into seven districts,* each under the supervision of a special agent in charge. The special agent in charge supervises a number of special agents who enforce a broad range of laws, including the Migratory Bird Treaty Act, the Endangered Species Act, the Lacey Act, the Marine Mammal Protection Act, the Duck Stamp Act, and the Airborne Hunting Act. Overall, FWS focuses its limited resources on large-scale and commercially motivated violations and more specifically on illegal wildlife imports, illegal trade in domestic wildlife, interstate commerce in illegally taken fish, violations of migratory bird hunting laws, and illegal big-game hunting.

In 1982, the declared value of wildlife imports and exports in the United States was $799 million. The importation of certain wildlife is prohibited by the Endangered Species Act, which establishes felony penalties for knowing violations of CITES, the principal organ regulating international commerce in wildlife. In addition, the Lacey Act imposes penalties for importation of wildlife taken or exported in violation of the laws of a foreign country. To enforce these laws, the Division of Law Enforcement has 56 wildlife inspectors who work with customs agents to monitor wildlife imports and exports.** Since FWS inspectors are able to inspect only 20 to 25 percent of incoming wildlife shipments, and species or species parts that are illegally imported often are difficult to identify, FWS directs undercover investigations to monitor international trade in wildlife and apprehend violators of United States laws.

Domestic wildlife trade is regulated by the Endangered Species Act, the Migratory Bird Treaty Act, and the Bald Eagle Protection Act, which prohibit, with few exceptions, the taking, possession, or sale of species they protect. In addition, the Lacey Act prohibits interstate commerce in any wildlife and fish taken in violation of state or Indian tribal laws. To prosecute fish and wildlife violations, FWS conducts investigations of taxidermists and other wildlife dealers and purchases illegally obtained wildlife in undercover "sting" operations. In 1984, for example, "Operation Falcon" obtained 400 birds of prey illegally taken for use in falconry.

Other high priorities include halting the violation of migratory-bird-hunting restrictions. FWS has addressed this recently by focusing on large, commercial violators, such as hunting clubs and outfitters that bait their fields or use electronically recorded calls to lure waterfowl. To stem the taking of big game out of season and in non-hunting areas, FWS agents have conducted undercover investigations in cooperation with state officials.

---

*A district covers the same geographic area as a region.

**All wildlife imports and exports are required to be shipped through a designated port of entry: New York, Miami, New Orleans, Chicago, Dallas, Fort Worth, Los Angeles, San Francisco, Seattle, and Honolulu.

Wildlife Permits

FWS has primary responsibility for issuing permits for the export, import, and certain uses of plant and animal species protected or regulated by federal or international law.* Most FWS permits are processed by the Wildlife Permit Office, which issues permits for different purposes under several laws as follows:

- permits required under the Endangered Species Act;
- permits for species under FWS jurisdiction pursuant to the Marine Mammal Protection Act (permits for other species are issued by National Marine Fisheries Service);
- export or import permits required for plant and animal species listed by CITES;
- and, import permits for wild animals regulated under the Lacey Act because they are considered "injurious" to the environment, to people, or to plants and animals.

FWS regional special agents-in-charge process permits required under the Migratory Bird Treaty Act and the Bald Eagle Protection Act. In the case of bald eagles, an endangered species, or migratory birds listed under CITES, applicants must apply to both the Wildlife Permit Office and the appropriate special agent-in-charge. The FWS Office of Migratory Bird Management, Bird Banding Laboratory, handles all bird-banding permits.

CURRENT PROGRAM TRENDS

In FY 1985, the total FWS budget appropriation, prior to any later recissions or supplemental funds, was $592.1 million — about nine percent of the Interior Department's budget. The FWS personnel limit was 6,617 FTEs.

FWS allocates funds and personnel slots to implement its programs through various budget appropriation accounts. An appropriation may be further subdivided into activity accounts.

While FWS is constrained by federal laws as to what it can spend its funds doing, the agency has relatively wide latitude to choose which of many authorized activities merit focus. Thus the annual FWS budget provides a good idea of what wildlife issues and problems FWS considers most important. Wildlife Resources constitutes the largest part of the budget, 24.7 percent, followed by Federal Aid, 21 percent. Habitat Resources, 8.3 percent, and Fishery Resources, 7.8 percent, are about a third the size of the Wildlife Resources account. Endangered Species constitutes 4.6 percent of the budget, yet is responsible for directly managing many more species than any other program.**

The cost of land acquired by FWS is funded from two accounts: Land Acquisition, which provides $63.2 million from the Land and Water Conservation Fund for purchases of refuges and endangered species habitat, and the Migratory Bird Conser-

---

*Under the Animal Welfare Act, the U.S. Department of Agriculture issues permits for wildlife exhibited in circuses, roadside zoos, or similar commercial activities, insuring that facilities are adequate and animals are treated humanely. U.S. Department of Agriculture also is responsible for enforcing all regulations governing the export or import of plants.
**In actual practice, the Wildlife Resource Program focuses its efforts on 48 species of game birds, seven nongame birds, three marine mammals, and a few damage-causing mammals and birds. The Fishery Resources Program focuses on about 40 species of sport fish. The Endangered Species Program is responsible for managing 331 United States species; recovery plans have been prepared for 196 of these.

vation Account, which includes direct appropriations ($21.3 million) made under the Wetlands Loan Act and duck stamp receipts ($16.4 million), all of which are placed in the migratory-bird-conservation fund to be used to purchase migratory-bird habitat. Altogether, $100.9 million was budgeted in FY 1985 — 17.1 percent of the total budget — for the cost of administering land acquisition and the cost of the land itself.

FWS Activity Accounts for FY 1985

Appropriation Account/Activity Account	FY 1985 Budget (in millions)
• Resource Management	$305.138
—Habitat Resources	(49.248)
—Wildlife Resources	(146.584)
—Fishery Resources	(46.189)
—Endangered Species	(27.065)
—General Administration	(36.052)
• Construction and Anadromous Fish	24.298
• Land Acquisition (under the Land and Water Conservation Fund)	63.218
• Migratory Bird Conservation Account	37.642
• National Wildlife Refuge Fund	12.685
• Miscellaneous Permanent Appropriations	
—Federal Aid/Fish	38.086
—Federal Aid/Wildlife	85.872
—Proceeds from Sales	.200
• Contributed funds	3.838
• Operation and Maintenance of Quarters	20.915
TOTAL	$592.142*

*Total includes an additional $250,000 for payment of rewards authorized by federal wildlife laws.
Source: FWS, Budget Justification FY 1985

Certain FWS management functions cut across several of the eight FWS programs and are thus funded under several budget accounts. The largest such function is "operation and maintenance" (O&M) of refuges and fish hatcheries. FY 1985 funding for servicewide O&M functions was $128.3 million (2,547 FTEs) and constituted 21.6 percent of the total budget. A second crosscutting function, Research and Development, received $43 million (892 FTEs) in FY 1985, 7.2 percent of the budget. Included in this total are funds for the operation and maintenance of research facilities. A third crosscutting function is Law Enforcement, which received funds from three different FWS programs: wildlife resources, fishery resources, and endangered species. The total law enforcement budget in FY 1985 was $19.5 million (389 FTEs), about 3.3 percent of the budget.

REFERENCES

1. Michael J. Bean, *The Evolution of National Wildlife Law* (New York: Praeger Publishers, 1983).
2. 161 U.S. 519 (1896).
3. Op. cit., Michael J. Bean, *The Evolution of National Wildlife Law*, p. 16.

4. 223 U.S. 166 (1912).
5. Op. cit., Michael J. Bean, *The Evolution of National Wildlife Law*, p. 28.
6. Act of May 25, 1900, Ch. 553, 31 Stat. 187 (currently codified at 16 U.S.C.A. 701, 337-3378 and 18 U.S.C.A. 42).
7. 252 U.S. 416 (1920).
8. U.S. Constitution, Article IV, Sect. 3.
9. 426 U.S. 529 (1976).
10. 431 U.S. 265 (1977).
11. 444 U.S. 51 (1979).
12. 471 F. Supp. 985 (D. Ha. 1979), aff'd on other grounds, 639 F.2d 495 (9th Cir. 1981).
13. Op. cit., Michael J. Bean, *The Evolution of National Wildlife Law*, p. 28.
14. Ibid.
15. International Association of Fish and Wildlife Agencies, Proceedings: 60th Annual Convention, September 16-18, 1970 (Washington, D.C.: IAFWA, 1970), p. 126.
16. 48 Fed. Reg. 11642-11645 (1983).
17. Act of June 30, 1886, 24 Stat. 100.
18. Jenks Cameron, *The Bureau of Biological Survey* (Baltimore: The Johns Hopkins Press, 1919), pp. 1-21.
19. Op. cit., Jenks Cameron, *The Bureau of Biological Survey*.
20. Id., p. 82.
21. U.S. Department of the Interior, Fish and Wildlife Service, Service Management Plan (Washington, D.C.: Fish and Wildlife Service, September 1982).
22. Convention on Nature Protection and Wildlife Preservation in the Western Hemisphere (1940), T.S. No. 981, U.N.T.S. No. 193.
23. Convention on International Trade in Endangered Species of Wild Fauna and Flora, March 3, 1973, 27 U.S.T. 1087, T.I.A.S. No. 8249.
24. Agreement on Cooperation in the Field of Environmental Protection, May 23, 1972, 23 U.S.T. 845, T.I.A.S. 7345.

PART II.
Federal Agencies and Programs

LEN RUE JR.

The federal migratory bird management program is responsible for some 800 species, but focuses primarily on waterfowl such as these snow geese.

Migratory Bird Protection and Management

by *William J. Chandler*
W.J. Chandler Associates

INTRODUCTION

THE FEDERAL GOVERNMENT has treaty and legislative authority to protect, manage, and conserve 816 species of native migratory birds that are identified in four bird-protection treaties between the United States and the foreign nations with which it shares these migrants. Authority over migratory birds was assumed by the federal government in 1916 when it became clear that the states were not adequately protecting waterfowl or other bird species. The states, however, retain authority over nonmigratory birds, principally members of the order Galliformes (pheasants, quail, grouse) and introduced, nonnative species such as the European starling.

Migratory bird conservation is the responsibility of the U.S. Fish and Wildlife Service (FWS), an agency of the Department of the Interior. FWS classifies migratory birds into two categories, game and nongame. Game includes 162 species that legally may be hunted. Game species are further subdivided into waterfowl and shore and upland game birds. Nongame (unhunted) birds include 654 species, some 80 percent of all migratory species under federal authority. Since 103 of the game species no longer are hunted, the effective number of nongame species is 757, 93 percent of all federally protected species.

By necessity, the management of wide-ranging birds is accomplished through a partnership between FWS and its counterpart agencies at the state level. State fish and wildlife agencies have established four flyway councils (Atlantic, Mississippi, Central, and Pacific) to provide advice and cooperative assistance to the federal government in the management of waterfowl species that pass through or occupy their territories. The states also conduct research and banding programs, acquire and manage habitat, manage a few federally acquired waterfowl refuges, and assist in the enforcement of federal hunting regulations and bird protection laws.

Several private, nonprofit organizations conduct programs that complement FWS migratory bird activities. Ducks Unlimited leases and manages habitat for migratory waterfowl, primarily in Canada. The Nature Conservancy acquires significant wetlands within the United States in order to protect them from development, and either resells the lands to federal or state conservation agencies or retains them as nature reserves. The National Audubon Society acquires and manages bird refuges and conducts bird research projects.

Certain game birds have received intensive study and management over the years. This is because more information is needed about game species to ensure that they are not overhunted and because federal wildlife laws tend to emphasize game species. Nongame species have received considerably less attention from FWS. Although these birds have been protected from hunting since 1916, relatively little has been done by the federal government to gather a comprehensive body of information on their status and habitat needs. In 1965, FWS took a step toward remedying this situation by establishing a breeding bird survey that monitors yearly population trends for about 500 nongame species, but adequate information is obtained for only half of these.

Today, FWS migratory bird management remains focused on game management. Important game species include 44 species of ducks, geese, and swans, and six species of doves, coots, woodcocks, sandhill cranes, rails, and gallinules. While FWS does conduct a few activities to benefit the hundreds of nongame species, the budget for these activities is only a tiny fraction of that devoted to game birds.

HISTORY AND LEGISLATIVE AUTHORITY

Most of the major federal statutes dealing with migratory birds were passed between 1900 and 1934, a time when the public recognized that America's wildlife resources would not withstand unregulated hunting and unlimited habitat destruction. Although most of these early laws have been amended, their principal emphasis remains much the same as when enacted. Migratory bird laws address five principal subjects: the regulation of hunting and other takings or uses of birds, the acquisition of land for the protection of significant habitat in federally owned refuges, the financing of refuge purchases with a federal stamp fee for waterfowl hunters, the prevention or mitigation of adverse impacts on migratory bird habitat caused by water resource projects, and the control of bird species that cause crop damage or other problems for man.

Origin of Federal Control

Congress first asserted federal authority to conserve and manage migratory birds by passing the Migratory Bird Act of 1913.[1] This measure aimed to protect all birds from hunting, especially during the nesting season, in order to save them from extinction. It placed all migratory game and insectivorous birds under federal protection and prohibited their hunting or taking except when permitted by federal regulations issued by the secretary of Agriculture. (The Bureau of Biological Survey, an FWS predecessor, was then a unit of the Department of Agriculture.)

The 1913 act was promptly challenged in federal court as a violation of the states' constitutional power to manage wildlife, and lower courts found the law unconstitutional. While the case was on appeal to the Supreme Court, Senate proponents of federal authority over migratory birds passed legislation authorizing the president to negotiate a migratory bird protection treaty with Great Britain on behalf of Canada. The Senate's strategy was based on the presumption was that the federal government's treaty making power would withstand any constitutional challenge by the states.[2]

A Convention for the Protection of Migratory Birds[3] was signed August 16, 1916, by the United States and Great Britain and was soon ratified by the Senate. A major reason for the treaty, according to its text, was to protect birds from "indiscriminate slaughter" by sport, market, and subsistence hunters. The treaty identified three categories of birds: game, insectivorous, and other nongame. It established open and closed seasons for game birds, prohibited the hunting of insectivorous birds, and prohibited the hunting or taking of other nongame birds except for certain species hunted by Native Americans for subsistence. The treaty also promulgated a 10-year hunting moratorium for certain game-bird species and established a procedure for providing special protection for the wood duck and eider. It banned the shipment or export of all migratory birds or their eggs during the closed season and authorized the issuance of permits for the killing of any birds that "may become seriously injurious to the agricultural or other interests in any particular community."

In 1918, Congress passed the Migratory Bird Treaty Act,[4] providing statutory authority for implementing the convention in the United States. The act gave the secretary of Agriculture responsibility for overseeing United States compliance with the treaty. It directed the secretary to issue regulations governing the hunting or other taking, sale, possession, and shipment of migratory bird species covered by the convention and required that the regulations be compatible with treaty terms. Otherwise, the statute generally prohibited the hunting or taking of all bird species not excepted by the regulations. The law also made it illegal to ship birds, dead or alive, across state lines if such action is contrary to the laws of the state of origin; made violation of the law a misdemeanor, punishable by a $500 fine or six months in jail or both; gave states discretionary authority to provide further protection to migratory birds so long as such actions are not inconsistent with the treaty; allowed continued use of migratory birds for scientific or propagation purposes until the secretary issued specific regulations governing such activities; and repealed the Migratory Bird Act of 1913.

The 1918 law was challenged in court by the state of Missouri, which argued that the states owned all wildlife within their borders and therefore had legal jurisdiction over it (*Missouri v. Holland*[5]). In 1920, the Supreme Court upheld the supremacy of the federal treaty-making power as a source of authority for the federal regulation of migratory birds and extinguished forever state claims to exclusive jurisdiction over wildlife.[6]

With its right to manage migratory birds firmly established, the federal government later signed migratory bird protection treaties with Mexico[7] (1936), Japan[8] (1972), and the Soviet Union[9] (1976), each of which was implemented by technical amendments to the 1918 treaty act. While all subsequent treaties were patterned after the convention with Great Britain, they contained certain unique provisions appropriate to their respective goals. Together, the four treaties give the federal government the authority to protect and manage a total of 816 species of birds.

Migratory Bird Refuges

Although it regulated hunting, the 1918 act soon was deemed insufficient to conserve migratory birds because it made no provision for habitat protection. Duck and geese populations continued to decline because interior wetlands required by them were drained, a prolonged drought dried up ponds and wetlands used by prairie-nesting ducks, and hunting pressure continued. A lengthy public debate over how to properly conserve waterfowl populations eventually led to passage of the Migratory Bird Conservation Act of 1929.[10] The major purpose of the measure was creation of a national system of publicly financed bird refuges to help the United States more effectively meet its obligations under the treaty with Canada.

The 1929 statute authorized federal acquisition of land by purchase or donation and protection of land through rental agreements in order to preserve both waterfowl and other migratory birds. All federally protected refuges were to be "inviolate sanctuaries," which meant they were closed year-round to migratory bird hunting. The law established a Migratory Bird Conservation Commission, composed of executive, congressional, and state officials, to approve all land acquisitions under the act and required that any purchase of land be approved by the legislature of the state where acquisition occurs. Absent from the law were two proposals that had provoked considerable controversy and delayed its passage: use of the refuges as "public shooting grounds" where migratory bird hunting would be allowed, and a federal stamp-fee requirement for hunters.

Although the 1929 law called for the purchase of bird refuges, few appropriations for this were made during the Great Depression. The Migratory Bird Hunting Stamp Act of 1934,[11] also known as the Duck Stamp Act, provided a means for financing these acquisitions. The act required all migratory waterfowl hunters aged 16 or older to purchase a one-dollar, federal migratory bird hunting stamp, in essence an annual federal stamp fee. All stamp-sale revenue was placed in a special migratory bird conservation fund from which monies could be withdrawn at any time. Originally, 90 percent of the funds were allocated to the identification, acquisition, maintenance, and development of "inviolate migratory bird sanctuaries" in accordance with the goals of the Migratory Bird Treaty Act; for the maintenance and development of other refuges already administered by the federal government and frequented by migratory game birds; and for research on migratory waterfowl. The remainder was made available for covering administrative expenses, including enforcement, associated with any migratory bird treaty, the 1918 treaty act, the 1929 law, and the Duck Stamp Act.

Later amendments to the Duck Stamp Act increased the price of the stamp and changed the uses of the migratory bird conservation fund. The stamp was raised to two dollars commencing in 1949, three dollars in 1959, five dollars in 1972, and $7.50 in 1979. The 1949 amendments[12] also authorized the secretary of the Interior to set aside "wildlife management areas" on up to 25 percent of any land acquired with duck-stamp revenue and to allow hunting of resident and migratory game birds there. Thus the requirement of the 1929 Migratory Bird Conservation Act that refuges be "inviolate sanctuaries" was modified.

In 1951, Congress increased the amount of the fund allocated for administration and enforcement of migratory bird statutes from 10 to 15 percent, lowering the sum for acquisition and maintenance of refuges to 85 percent. In 1958, the allocation formula again was revised, effective July 1, 1960, to require exclusive use of fund revenues, less the cost of administering the Stamp Act, for land acquisition. This change was made because of concerns that wetlands drainage was outpacing the purchasing program and that as a result significant migratory waterfowl habitat was being lost. In addition, the 1958 amendments[13] authorized the purchase of fee title or perpetual conservation easements of small prairie wetlands, also known as prairie potholes, used by nesting ducks. These wetlands, scattered throughout nine states, are designated "waterfowl production areas" and constitute an important part of the national wildlife refuge system.

The 1958 Duck Stamp Act amendments also gave the secretary authority to administer as a "wildlife management area" up to 40 percent of any area set aside for migratory birds under any law. On these areas, migratory game birds or other resident wildlife species could be hunted pursuant to federal regulations. The hunting of resident species was expanded further in 1966 when Congress passed the National Wildlife Refuge System Administration Act,[14] authorizing the secretary to permit hunting of any resident wildlife species on any lands within the national wildlife refuge system if the secretary determined that hunting was compatible with the major purposes for which the areas were established.

In response to increased drainage of prairie wetlands, Congress accelerated the acquisition of migratory bird habitat by passing the Wetlands Loan Act of 1961.[15] This statute provided for the direct appropriation of up to $105 million to the migratory bird conservation fund for the purchase of refuges and for purchase and easement of waterfowl production areas. The $105 million was considered an advance appropriation that eventually was to be repaid by use of 75 percent of the annual duck-stamp revenues once the loan authority expired. Congress in 1976 increased the loan authority to $200 million and has extended the loan authority through FY 1986. Some $175 million had been appropriated by FY 1985.

Mitigation of the Effects of Water Projects

In addition to establishing refuges, Congress recognized the need to protect significant migratory bird habitat by preventing or mitigating the adverse impacts of federal development projects. The Fish and Wildlife Coordination Act of 1934[16] permitted development of migratory bird resting and nesting areas on waters newly impounded by federal agencies provided that such use was not inconsistent with the primary purpose of the waters or the constitutional rights of the states. It also authorized the Bureau of Biological Survey to consult with federal water resource agencies about obtaining wildlife uses of existing impoundments. The act called for the survey to cooperate with and assist federal, state, and other agencies in increasing the supply of game species, combating wildlife disease, and developing a nationwide wildlife conservation program. It also authorized studies on the effects of pollutants on wildlife and surveys of wildlife on public lands in order to develop a program for maintaining adequate wildlife populations.

The Fish and Wildlife Coordination Act was revised substantially in both 1946 and 1956. The 1946 amendments[17] authorized the secretary of the Interior to cooperate with federal, state, and private agencies in the development and protection of all wildlife species and their habitat, in controlling wildlife disease, in minimizing damages caused by "overabundant" species, and in providing public hunting areas. It also mandated that water-project agencies consult with the FWS and state wildlife agencies before construction, in order to prevent loss of and damage to wildlife resources and their habitats. Recommendations for preventing adverse impacts on wildlife had to be included in the project report, and the cost of any recommended wildlife-protection measure adopted by the water resource agency was to be made part of the total project cost. Federal water project agencies were required to make adequate provision for development of impoundments and associated land areas for wildlife, provided that such use was consistent with the primary purposes of the project. Water project wildlife areas that provide significant benefits to the national migratory bird management program are administered by the secretary of the Interior. All other areas are managed by state wildlife agencies.

The Coordination Act was revised again in 1958[18] in an attempt to give wildlife equal importance in water resource planning and construction. Whereas the 1946 law did not specifically require water resource agencies to include wildlife mitigation measures in project design, the 1958 statute required the project plan to include "such justifiable means and measures for wildlife purposes as the . . . agency finds should be adopted to obtain maximum overall project benefits." Furthermore, the 1958 law specifically authorized federal water resource agencies to alter incomplete projects to incorporate wildlife-protection measures and to acquire lands to protect wildlife habitat. Left unchanged was the earlier requirement that all wildlife measures be consistent with the primary purposes of the water project.

Responsibility for the management of wildlife areas associated with water projects remained with the secretary of the Interior, but he was given the discretion to delegate it to other agencies through cooperative agreements. The 1958 law also gave the secretary the option of transferring lands valuable to the national migratory bird program to state wildlife agencies if he and the state jointly determined that state management would be in the public interest. However, only a few migratory bird areas eventually were transferred to the states under this authority. Finally, the 1958 amendments for the first time attempted to deal with habitat destruction caused by drainage, impoundment, or other projects built under the Watershed Protection and Flood Prevention Act of 1954,[19] administered by the Department of Agriculture. The secretary of the Interior was authorized to recommend wildlife-protection measures for such projects, but acceptance of these recommendations occurred only if the local organization of private landowners sponsoring the project and the secretary of Agriculture approved.

Under the Coordination Act, 34 waterfowl refuges comprising 1,003,969 acres in 20 states have been established in conjunction with federal water projects.[20] The most recent refuges established under Coordination Act authority are Felsenthal, Arkansas, (64,510 acres) and Big Stone, Minnesota, (10,794 acres), both authorized in 1975. Few refuges are being created now in connection with water projects because fewer reservoirs are being built, and those that are being built do not have significant migratory bird benefits.

The Coordination Act was supplemented in 1965 by another measure, the Water Project Recreation Act,[21] which provides uniform policies for the provision of both recreation and fish and wildlife benefits in multipurpose water resource projects. The Recreation Act requires that recreation and fish and wildlife benefits be provided at any project where it is reasonable to do so.

Prohibition of Federal Assistance for Wetlands Drainage

In 1962, Congress employed a new tactic to discourage the drainage of wetlands. An amendment to the Soil Conservation and Domestic Allotment Act[22] prohibited federal assistance to farmers for the drainage of wetlands in North Dakota, South Dakota, and Minnesota, the principal prairie duck breeding areas of the United States. The provision, also referred to as the drainage referral amendment or the Reuss amendment, required the secretary of Agriculture to withhold technical and financial assistance for drainage projects if the secretary of the Interior "has made a finding that wildlife preservation will be materially harmed on that farm by such drainage and that preservation of such land in its undrained status will materially contribute to wildlife preservation." This finding must be filed with the secretary of Agriculture within 90 days of the application for drainage assistance. Within a year after he files his finding, the secretary of the Interior or the state must offer to lease or purchase the wetland; otherwise the prohibition against federal assistance expires. If an offer is tendered but refused by the landowner, the prohibition remains in effect for a five-year period commencing on the date the secretary's finding is filed.

The drainage referral amendment was useful in preventing the drainage of some wetlands in the 1960s, but FWS does not have readily available statistics on how many drainage projects were blocked, how many purchase offers were tendered, or how many acres ultimately were purchased. Eventually, the Department of Agriculture moved away from providing assistance for drainage projects that destroyed migratory bird habitat. In 1970, the Department of Agriculture was directed by the Water Bank Act[23] to promote wetlands conservation. Under this law, the department signs 10-year conservation agreements with farmers who agree to maintain wetlands and water bodies on their property. In exchange, the farmer receives an annual payment from the federal government. In 1975, the Soil Conservation Service adopted a wetlands protection policy that prohibited technical assistance to farmers for draining certain types of wetlands. The policy was strengthened in 1977 and still is in force.[24]

Prevention of Damage Caused by Birds

Congress has dealt in several statutes with the problem of crop depredations caused by migratory birds. The 1916 treaty with Canada permitted the killing of any birds that may seriously injure agricultural or other interests. Amendments to the Coordination Act in 1946 authorized the secretary of the Interior to cooperate with other federal, state, and private agencies in minimizing damage caused by "overabundant" species.

In 1948, the Lea Act[25] was passed to deal exclusively with depredations in California caused by wintering ducks and geese that ate unharvested crops. The law authorized the rental or purchase of up to 20,000 acres to provide feeding areas for waterfowl in an effort to keep them off private agricultural lands until crops were harvested. Hunting also was permitted on any of these lands at the option and under the management of the state of California.

The Waterfowl Depredations Control Act of 1956[26] authorized the secretary of the Interior to requisition surplus grains held by the Commodity Credit Corporation for use in luring waterfowl flocks away from agricultural crops in areas where depredations are a problem. The Surplus Grain for Wildlife Act of 1961[27] authorized the secretary to use surplus grains for feeding migratory birds and resident game species threatened with starvation due to adverse winter weather conditions.

In summary, existing treaties and legislation enable FWS to regulate the hunting or other taking, possession, sale, shipment, and trade of 816 migratory bird species. FWS is authorized to purchase land and conservation easements to protect migratory bird habitat and to fund these purchases with receipts from the sale of federal duck stamps to hunters and with direct appropriations from Congress that eventually must be repaid from future duck-stamp revenues. FWS consults with federal water resource agencies and with the Department of Agriculture in an attempt to minimize the adverse impacts of large and small water projects on wetlands. The federal government has exclusive authority to manage migratory birds on federal refuge system lands. The secretary of the Interior may permit the hunting of migratory birds on up to 40 percent of a migratory bird refuge. Hunting is permitted on all portions of waterfowl production areas. Various statutes authorize FWS to control migratory birds that threaten agricultural crops or human health; this includes the killing of these birds when necessary.

ORGANIZATION AND OPERATIONS

Responsibilities and Roles

FWS has sole authority for coordinating and supervising all federal migratory bird management activities. Its principal functions include conducting population surveys and research, development of annual hunting regulations, acquisition and management of migratory bird refuges, control of bird depredations on private lands, review of federal water resource projects to prevent or mitigate their damage to migratory bird habitat, provision of grants to states for wildlife restoration projects, and enforcement of all federal migratory bird statutes regulating the taking of, and commerce in, federally protected species.

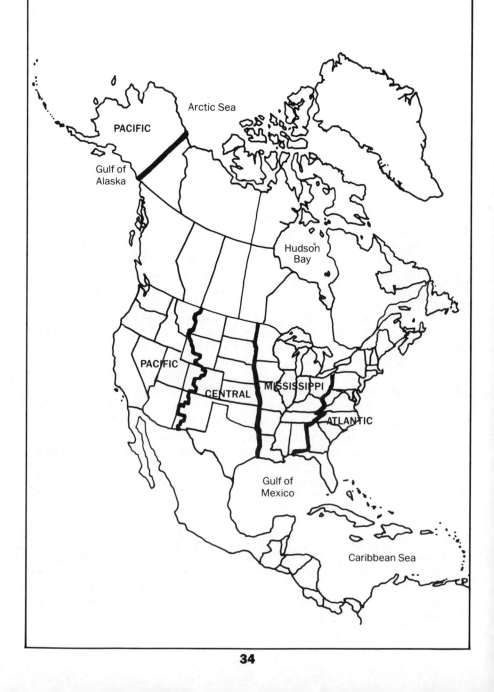

Administrative Waterfowl Flyways of the United States

FWS encourages state cooperation in all aspects of federal wildlife programs, and the states play an active role in migratory bird management through four flyway councils. The states work closely with FWS in developing annual hunting regulations for waterfowl and migratory shore and upland game birds and play a major role in enforcing federal laws, since they collectively are able to field a much larger number of law enforcement officers than is the federal government. States also acquire and manage waterfowl refuges, conduct research and population surveys, and control bird depredations on private lands under cooperative agreements with FWS.

Congressional Committees

Four Congressional committees have primary jurisdiction over migratory bird matters. The Senate Committee on Environment and Public Works and the House Committee on Merchant Marine and Fisheries have exclusive jurisdiction over migratory birds. These two committees authorize all new migratory bird laws and have the power to oversee and recommend amendments to all existing laws. The appropriations committees of the House and Senate actually determine how much money is spent on FWS programs annually. The subcommittee on Interior and Related Agencies of each appropriations committee reviews in detail the annual FWS budget request and allocates funds among various fish and wildlife programs.

Agency Structure and Function

FWS separates its activities into eight programs, each supervised by a national program manager. Planning, budgeting, and evaluation are carried out within this program structure. The Wildlife Resources Program, directed by the associate director for Wildlife Resources, has responsibility for migratory birds as well as other wildlife species of federal interest that are not listed as threatened or endangered under the Endangered Species Act. (All listed species are the responsibility of the Federal Assistance Program and the Office of Endangered Species.)

The associate director for Wildlife Resources is responsible for setting national program goals, providing policy guidance to regional and field offices, preparing the annual budget, and evaluating performance for all wildlife resources activities. The associate director is assisted by two deputy associate directors who in turn supervise various offices and divisions of the Wildlife Resources Program. Migratory bird responsibilities are spread throughout these units. In addition, some migratory bird activities are conducted through other programs by FWS offices that are not supervised by the associate director for Wildlife Resources.

The Office of Migratory Bird Management, contrary to its name, does not coordinate all migratory bird activities. The office's principal functions are to conduct national population and hunting-harvest surveys, coordinate the national bird-banding program for game and nongame birds, monitor raptor migration, assist in the preparation and implementation of migratory bird management plans including the National Waterfowl Management Plan and the United States portion of the North American Waterfowl Management Plan, develop federal hunting regulations for migratory game birds on an annual basis, and provide liaison with state migratory bird programs. Other key offices with migratory bird responsibilities are the Division of Refuge Management, which provides guidance for managing the national refuge system; the Division of Realty, responsible for acquiring all lands for refuges; the Division of Law Enforcement, which enforces migratory bird statutes as well as other wildlife laws; and the Division of Wildlife Management, which controls problems or depredations caused by waterfowl, blackbirds, and other birds.

OFFICES RESPONSIBLE FOR MIGRATORY BIRD ACTIVITIES OF THE U.S. FISH AND WILDLIFE SERVICE

Activity	Office and Supervisor
1. Annual population and harvest surveys	Office of Migratory Bird Management, Associate Director — Wildlife Resources
2. Bird banding program	Office of Migratory Bird Management, Associate Director — Wildlife Resources
3. Breeding bird survey	Division of Wildlife Research, Assistant Director — Research and Development
4. Basic and applied research	Division of Wildlife Research and Division of Cooperative Fish and Wildlife Research Units, Assistant Director — Research and Development
5. Annual hunting regulations	Office of Migratory Bird Management, Associate Director — Wildlife Resources
6. Land acquisition	Division of Realty, Associate Director — Wildlife Resources
7. Management of migratory bird refuges	Division of Refuge Management, Associate Director — Wildlife Resources
8. Enforcement of migratory bird laws	Division of Law Enforcement. Associate Director — Wildlife Resources
9. Control of bird depredations	Division of Wildlife Management, Associate Director — Wildlife Resources
10. Review of federal actions and permits impacting migratory birds	Division of Ecological Services, Associate Director — Habitat Resources
11. Provisions of grants to states for migratory bird projects	Division of Federal Aid, Associate Director — Federal Assistance

Source: U.S. Fish and Wildlife Service, 1984.

Three national-level offices that are not supervised by the associate director for Wildlife Resources have significant migratory bird responsibilities. The Division of Wildlife Research conducts an annual breeding-bird survey to monitor population trends of about 500 nongame species. This division also conducts or coordinates basic and applied research on migratory birds. The Office of Ecological Services, Habitat Resources Program, reviews all federal actions and federal permits for water and other development projects to identify impacts on migratory birds and other species and makes recommendations for preventing or mitigating damage to wildlife. The Division of Federal Aid supervises the distribution of federal grants to states under the Pittman-Robertson Act[28] for the acquisition, restoration, and development of lands that benefit migratory birds and other wildlife.

The actual implementation of wildlife resources program activities is carried out by personnel in FWS regional and field offices. Each regional director is assisted by an assistant regional director for Wildlife Resources and by a special agent-in-charge who runs law enforcement activities. At the field level, migratory bird activities are conducted by refuge managers and other field personnel.

Planning

Objectives for migratory bird operations are identified in a series of interrelated plans prepared by FWS at the national, regional, and field levels. National plans include the Service Management Plan,[29] which provides broad guidance and long-term

National Organization
Wildlife Resources Program
Fish and Wildlife Service

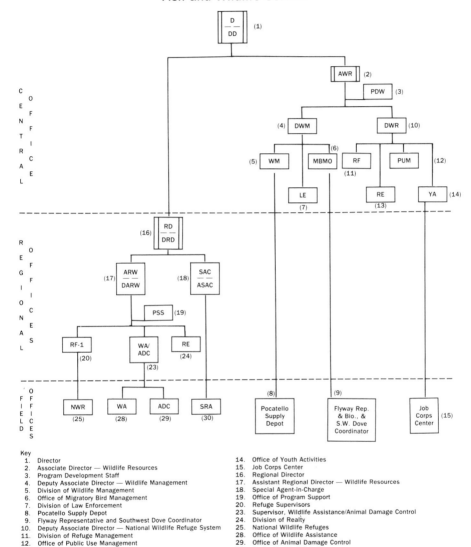

Key
1. Director
2. Associate Director — Wildlife Resources
3. Program Development Staff
4. Deputy Associate Director — Wildlife Management
5. Division of Wildlife Management
6. Office of Migratory Bird Management
7. Division of Law Enforcement
8. Pocatello Supply Depot
9. Flyway Representative and Southwest Dove Coordinator
10. Deputy Associate Director — National Wildlife Refuge System
11. Division of Refuge Management
12. Office of Public Use Management
13. Division of Realty

14. Office of Youth Activities
15. Job Corps Center
16. Regional Director
17. Assistant Regional Director — Wildlife Resources
18. Special Agent-in-Charge
19. Office of Program Support
20. Refuge Supervisors
23. Supervisor, Wildlife Assistance/Animal Damage Control
24. Division of Realty
25. National Wildlife Refuges
28. Office of Wildlife Assistance
29. Office of Animal Damage Control
30. Senior Resident Agents

Source: Fish and Wildlife Service, July 1983

policy direction for all FWS programs; the Program Management Document: Migratory Birds,[30] which provides a five-year statement of resource goals, objectives, problems, strategies, and policies; and special plans, which address specific resources or problems from a national perspective.

Examples of special plans relevant to migratory birds include the National Waterfowl Management Plan[31] and the Migratory Bird Disease Contingency Plan.[32] The waterfowl plan defines general objectives for the cooperative management of waterfowl by FWS and the states and provides a basis for the more detailed flyway plans that state flyway councils prepare for individual waterfowl populations. The disease-contingency plan provides guidance for dealing with disease outbreaks that from time to time occur in waterfowl populations.

In addition, FWS prepares national species of special emphasis plans for waterfowl populations that have been designated national species of special emphasis (NSSE). An NSSE plan provides a comprehensive statement of FWS population and management goals for an individual species. Initial objectives for NSSE plans are contained in *National Objectives for National Species of Special Emphasis*.[33] NSSE plans currently are under preparation for 54 species, but none have been approved formally.

Planning objectives and strategies identified in national plans are broken down into more specific objectives, strategies, and activities at the regional and field levels. Each of the seven FWS regional offices prepares a regional resource plan to guide the operations of field units and personnel that it supervises. A Regional plan covers five years and focuses FWS efforts on the management of NSSEs and other species considered significant within the region but not nationally. The plan takes into account endangered species recovery plans to ensure that management activities for migratory birds and other wildlife do not adversely affect endangered species that occupy the same habitat.

Field plans provide operational guidance to FWS personnel who operate refuges and research laboratories or who conduct resource management programs at the regional or subregional level. Field plans that must incorporate national and regional migratory bird objectives include refuge master plans, the long-range management documents for national wildlife refuges (referred to, for Alaska refuges, as comprehensive conservation plans); refuge management plans, prepared for specific refuge management activities such as waterfowl production; research and development plans, which guide the work of each research facility; animal damage control plans, formulated for each state where waterfowl and other species cause economic loss or human health or safety problems; fish and wildlife management plans, which establish recommended goals and actions for species on federal lands in cases where a federal agency has requested FWS assistance; the Bristol Bay Cooperative Management plan, an economic development and natural resources management plan for the Bristol Bay region prepared by several cooperating federal, state, and local agencies; and law enforcement strategy plans, developed to protect waterfowl and other fish or wildlife that are illegally hunted or taken from the wild.

Budgeting

Funds for migratory bird activities are allocated through the FWS budget process. The various national, regional, and field plans prepared by FWS provide the basis for budget formulation and justification. Each region develops a budget proposal that proposes expenditures for various FWS resource management programs. Regional budget proposals are evaluated and merged by the FWS national office directorate, comprised of the director, the associate directors, and the regional directors. The proposed budget is then reviewed by the Interior Department and the Office of Management and Budget, either of which may make revisions.

Next the budget is submitted to Congress as part of the president's annual budget. Hearings are held by both the authorizing committees, which make recommendations on the proposal to the House and Senate budget committees, and by the appropriations subcommittees on Interior and related agencies. Additions and deletions to the budget are made by the Interior appropriations subcommittees, and a final budget is approved sometime between June and November for the federal fiscal year, which begins October 1.

Appropriated funds then are allocated by FWS to its various programs, and its annual work plans are adjusted and made final. Periodic evaluations are made by FWS to determine if its annual work objectives have been met.

Migratory bird activities are conducted under various FWS programs. Since program budgets are subdivided into functional categories, such as research, law enforcement, and refuge management, which cover a variety of wildlife species, it is impossible to break out the precise amount allocated to migratory birds.

This was not always the case. From FY 1974 to FY 1983, FWS arranged its budget in a combination of functional and resource categories. During that period the Wildlife Resources budget was subdivided into four categories: migratory birds, mammals and nonmigratory birds, animal damage control, and interpretation and recreation. Migratory birds was further subdivided into four functional categories: refuges, law enforcement, research, and management.

In FY 1984, FWS revised its budget format to emphasize functional activities within major resource programs. Under this arrangement, it is no longer possible to determine easily how much money is allocated to a specific class of wildlife such as migratory birds. For the transitional year, however, FWS included a breakdown showing how the new budget would have been displayed under the old format.

According to figures supplied by FWS, migratory birds received $56.7 million in appropriations in FY 1980, or about 56 percent of the total Wildlife Resources budget. By FY 1983 this figure had grown to $65.1 million, still 56 percent of the wildlife

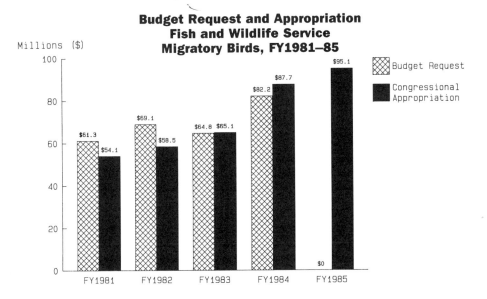

**Budget Request and Appropriation
Fish and Wildlife Service
Migratory Birds, FY1981–85**

resources account. In FY 1984, the year FWS revised its budget format, FWS stated that $82.2 million or 65 percent of the $126.1 million requested for the Wildlife Resources Program was for migratory birds. Congress ultimately approved $135 million in FY 1984 for Wildlife Resources. Assuming that roughly 65 percent or $87.7 million went to migratory birds, spending jumped 35 percent over the FY 1983 level.

In FY 1985, $146.5 million was appropriated to Wildlife Resources in the regular appropriations bill for the Department of the Interior. Assuming that approximately 65 percent of this amount also is for migratory bird-related activities, the "migratory bird appropriation" is about $95.1 million, an eight-percent increase over 1984. In sum, the FWS budget allocation for migratory bird management increased approximately 46 percent from FY 1983 to FY 1985. This shift was a direct reflection of an FWS decision to spend more money on waterfowl management.

Statistics for the number of employees engaged primarily in migratory bird management activities are not available.

Research

The role of FWS research is to support the needs of the various resource programs. With regard to migratory birds, the Wildlife Resources Program establishes research needs and objectives that then are carried out by the Division of Wildlife Research with funds provided from the wildlife resources budget. Actual supervision of research, however, is the responsibility of the assistant director for research and development, who oversees all FWS research activities and personnel. A substantial amount of the wildlife resources research budget — about 75 percent — is spent on migratory birds. The principal areas of research are:

1. Waterfowl population status: Studies on population status, including the development of census and survey techniques, investigation of factors affecting the productivity and mortality of birds, and the effects of environmental factors and hunting regulations on waterfowl populations.

2. Waterfowl ecology, habitat requirements, and habitat manipulation: General research aimed at increasing the productivity of waterfowl on both national wildlife refuges and elsewhere.

3. Waterfowl health: Research on the causes, diagnosis, control, and prevention of migratory bird diseases such as avian cholera and duck plague, and on lead poisoning. Research results are transferred to refuge personnel in order to train them in reducing the likelihood of disease outbreaks.

4. Nongame migratory birds: The primary research emphasis is on monitoring nongame bird populations to identify species with declining populations. Study areas include improvement of survey methods and identification of significant habitats.

5. Bird damage control: Studies to define and develop standard methods for measuring bird-caused damage, to develop chemical and non-chemical wildlife control methods, and to assess the ecological effects of these methods on the controlled species and the general environment.

Migratory bird research is conducted at four facilities. The Patuxent Wildlife Research Center, in Laurel, Maryland, specializes in migratory bird population survey and status assessment work; the Northern Prairie Wildlife Research Center, in Jamestown, North Dakota, addresses waterfowl habitat and management requirements; the National Wildlife Health Laboratory, in Madison, Wisconsin, specializes in disease prevention and control; and the Denver Wildlife Research Center, in Colorado, conducts research on Alaska-nesting geese, seabirds, and riparian ecology, and maintains the North American bird collection in cooperation with the Smithsonian.

The annual FWS budget justification document identifies principal research emphases of the wildlife resources program for the current and upcoming fiscal years. In the "wildlife research" category for FY 1984:

> wildlife research will continue to be focused on studies to improve black duck winter surveys, to assess impacts of land management on waterfowl production, to determine habitat requirements of wintering waterfowl, and to develop improved monitoring methods for population trends of nongame birds. In addition, we will continue efforts to diagnose and control wildlife disease, provide ecosystem analyses on selected . . . refuges and evaluate factors influencing population dynamics of waterfowl, especially the mallard. . . .[34]

For FY 1985, FWS has budgeted additional funds for determining the causes of the decline of the black duck population and to develop better information on population status and trends of geese that nest in Alaska.

In the "animal damage control research" category, FWS focuses on identifying and assessing damage caused by birds, developing methods to control damage, and assessing the environmental impacts of control methods both on the target species and on other species and the environment. The research emphasis for FY 1984 and 1985 is blackbird damage to corn, rice, and sunflower crops and reduction of health hazards and economic losses resulting from blackbird and starling winter roosts.

In addition, considerable research on migratory birds is conducted by "cooperative units" located at various state universities. Such research frequently is executed in cooperation with the state fish and wildlife agency and FWS.

CURRENT PROGRAM TRENDS

Under the leadership of Director Robert Jantzen, a Reagan appointee, FWS is reviewing its approach to migratory bird management and changing its priorities, a process that is likely to continue for several years. A major factor compelling this review is a drive to decrease federal spending and reduce the national deficit.

Reform is taking two major directions. First, the FWS NSSE planning process, initiated in 1981, has taken hold, and 45 migratory bird species have been designated as priorities for intensified management because of their high biological, legal, or public interest. Second, Jantzen has made improvement of waterfowl management a top priority. As a consequence, traditional FWS emphasis on ducks and geese has been reinforced and augmented while management actions on behalf of migratory shore and upland game birds and nongame species have been de-emphasized. This emphasis is reflected in the migratory birds identified as national species of special emphasis: 34 are waterfowl species or populations, four are upland game species, and seven are nongame species.

New Waterfowl Priorities

Five years ago, the approach to migratory bird management could be characterized as "keeping score," one official said. Waterfowl populations were monitored from year to year and hunting regulations adjusted when populations showed increases or decreases from the previous years. Now, FWS is trying to take a more positive, aggressive approach to protecting and enhancing the resource over the long term. As a result, certain waterfowl activities are being enhanced and new directions are being charted.

Thirty-four duck and goose species or populations have been identified as NSSEs. Of these, six duck species and three goose populations have been selected for further intensive management. These are the pintail, black duck, canvasback, red-head, mallard, and wood duck, and the Pacific Flyway populations of the white-fronted goose, the cackling goose (a race of the Canada goose), and the brant. Population objectives for each now are being explored in consultation with state wildlife agencies, as are habitat needs and other management requirements. It is expected that more funds will be devoted to the management of these nine NSSEs than is now the case.

All nine waterfowl species face habitat loss and degradation problems that must be eliminated or mitigated. An FWS waterfowl habitat strategy team tentatively identified 11 key habitat areas used by these species that must be protected through purchases, conservation easements, voluntary landowner agreements, or other measures. The acquisition of significant, privately owned tracts in these areas would cost an estimated $600 million over 10 years. Even if this money is obtained and spent, the strategy team concluded that waterfowl species will continue to be threatened until the nation "mandates a halt to further net loss in quality or quantity of wetlands."[35]

Waterfowl Conservation Measures on Private Farmland

FWS is increasing its efforts to work cooperatively with the Department of Agriculture to preserve and enhance waterfowl habitat on private lands. Many farm programs funded by the Department of Agriculture have adverse consequences for wetlands used by waterfowl, especially in the prairies of North and South Dakota. Wetlands are drained to bring more land into subsidized crop production, set-aside lands do not have adequate requirements for cover that would benefit waterfowl, eroding soils are filling up FWS-protected wetlands, and farmers are removing nesting cover from the uplands that surround wetland breeding areas. To address these problems, FWS has created a staff position in the Division of Wildlife Management whose occupant works with the Department of Agriculture and others to promote wildlife conservation requirements in federal agricultural programs.

Increased Waterfowl Production on FWS Lands

Research sponsored by FWS has shown that under certain conditions predation — by, for example, skunks, racoons, foxes, and even ground squirrels — wreaks havoc on nesting waterfowl, often destroying up to 90 percent of the eggs. Predator damage increases significantly when agricultural practices destroy waterfowl nesting cover. FWS is testing an array of predator control methods to help nesting ducks achieve higher reproductive success on federal wildlife refuges and waterfowl production areas. Such methods include the construction of nesting islands, use of electric fences, planting of suitable nesting vegetation, and selective use of predator poisons.

Wetlands Acquisition

Even though FWS has been acquiring lands for migratory birds since the 1930s, it has not been able to acquire sufficient acreage to protect waterfowl populations adequately. The amount of federal acquisition needed is directly related to the amount of privately owned wetlands that are destroyed by agriculture and development activities. The greater the destruction of privately owned wetlands, the more important it becomes for FWS to own and manage refuges that protect waterfowl breeding stocks.

Traditionally, Congress has eschewed regulatory methods to prevent the destruction of waterfowl habitat, leaving land acquisition as the only alternative. But despite previous attempts by Congress to accelerate wetlands acquisition, FWS has not received sufficient appropriations to meet its acquisition goals.

In the 1950s, FWS and state fish and wildlife agencies jointly determined that

12.5 million acres of waterfowl habitat in the conterminous United States should be protected in federal and state refuges in order to maintain species populations at then-existing levels. FWS took responsibility for eight million acres, 3.5 million of which already were owned, and the states for 4.5 million acres, of which two million were owned.

In 1976, FWS revised its acquisition strategy to target 33 types of wetlands that should be protected to save significant migratory bird habitat. The total acreage goal was 3,825,000, of which 1,878,000 already had been acquired during the period FY 1962-76. That left 1,947,000 to be acquired either in fee or by easement from FY 1977 to FY 1986. FWS will not meet this goal. At the end of FY 1984, it had acquired only 59 percent of the 3,825,000-acre objective.

Canadian Waterfowl Program

Even if FWS were to be successful beyond its wildest expectations in conserving waterfowl habitat in the United States, the fact remains that the majority of ducks and geese that winter in the United States breed in Canada. For example, approximately 80 percent of all prairie ducks nest in Canada, mostly on privately owned lands. Thus the number of wintering waterfowl in the United States is highly dependent on habitat-protection efforts in Canada. The same economic pressures and incentives leading to the draining of small wetlands in North and South Dakota also are at work in Canada. Waterfowl are viewed by some Canadian farmers as pests since they can consume significant amounts of unharvested grain. Wetlands may be viewed as obstacles to farm machinery and plowed under. Growth of Canadian agriculture inevitably puts pressure on wetlands that can be converted to cropland.

In 1983, the Canadian Wildlife Service released its Waterfowl Management Plan for Canada,[36] the first step in a process designed to develop a national strategy for waterfowl conservation. The plan provides the framework for the development of provincial action plans to conserve waterfowl during the period 1983-88. The provincial plans will be followed by a national operational plan to guide the Canadian Wildlife Service's efforts.

Whether this process will proceed according to schedule is in doubt. In 1984, Canada announced budget cutbacks that would reduce the Canadian Wildlife Service staff from 370 to 286, a 23-percent reduction. The service's capital and operating budgets would be reduced by $3.8 million, a 17-percent decrease, and its habitat-acquisition program terminated.[37]

Stabilized Hunting Regulations Study

This year marks the end of a five-year study conducted by FWS in cooperation with the states and the Canadian Wildlife Service to determine the effects of stabilized hunting regulations on duck populations and harvests. Usually, open seasons, daily bag limits, and other hunting regulations are adjusted routinely in accordance with annual population fluctuations on the theory that such adjustments have a significant impact on the survival rate of duck populations from year to year. However, some studies have suggested that hunting at current levels does not significantly effect mallard populations. This might be true for other species, too. If so, it may not be necessary to adjust hunting regulations on a yearly basis if other factors such as environmental conditions and habitat availability are the major determinants of population size. The present study will help FWS to evaluate the significance of non-hunting mortality on duck populations, the relationship between hunting mortality and other causes of death, and the role of recruitment in affecting population size. In sum, the stabilized hunting regulations study is a means to help increase FWS knowledge

43

about waterfowl management in order to develop more cost-effective management strategies. Results of the study are expected to be available beginning in 1986.

Migratory Shore and Upland Game Species

Migratory shore and upland game birds have never received the same level of attention that FWS devotes to waterfowl. The perception has been that birds in this category are not as greatly threatened by hunting pressure or habitat loss as are waterfowl.

Historically, FWS has paid the most attention to three bird species — woodcock, mourning dove, and sandhill crane — that are sought by hunters. FWS conducts annual population-trend surveys for each. The states conduct their own population and hunter-harvest surveys for other species, such as the band-tailed pigeon and white-winged dove. As it does for waterfowl, FWS, with the advice of the states, sets annual seasons and regulations for migratory shore and upland game birds that are hunted.

Four species have been designated NSSEs: woodcock, mourning dove, white-winged dove, and six distinct populations of sandhill crane, only two of which are hunted. The woodcock is of special concern since the population-trend survey shows a gradual but continuing decline in the eastern population.

In the mid-1960s, FWS initiated a modest accelerated research program for shore and upland game birds to collect basic data on their population sizes, biology, and habitat needs. Commencing in FY 1968, $250,000 was budgeted annually: $175,000 for state research grants and $75,000 for FWS research and program coordination. The program was terminated in FY 1982 as part of an FWS budget-reduction effort because it was not viewed as a pressing need. Presently, very little research is being done on any migratory shore and upland game species despite information about significant gaps in these species.

Nongame Migratory Bird Management

FWS is responsible for managing 654 nongame migratory species. Another 103 birds legally are considered game, but since currently they are not hunted, they are in essence nongame. In the late 1970s and early 1980s, FWS was expanding its nongame activities and identified several objectives it intended to pursue to improve its understanding and management of nongame. One major objective was the identification of nongame species in danger of decline and the causes of their predicament. Another was the preparation of a national nongame management plan patterned after the national plan for waterfowl. Neither of these objectives has been fully attained.

In July 1982, the Office of Migratory Bird Management released a report, "Nongame Migratory Bird Species with Unstable or Decreasing Population Trends in the United States."[38] The report presents a list of 28 birds "with some evidence of unstable or declining populations in significant portions of their range during the past 10-15 years." The list includes nine wading birds, five raptors, three marine birds, four shore birds, and seven passerines.

The list is only a preliminary step in assessing the true status of these birds. FWS used a wide variety of available data in compiling the list, not all of which is considered definitive. Furthermore, little information on the causes of population declines was obtained. The study recommended a number of additional measures to refine the list, including the incorporation of new data sources, periodic updating of the list, development of practical survey programs for species not adequately monitored by the breeding bird survey, and special investigations of species such as the common loon, roseate tern, and loggerhead shrike. No action, however, has been taken to implement most of these recommendations.

FWS has identified five of the 28 declining species as NSSEs — interior least tern, roseate tern, piping plover, spotted owl, and trumpeter swan — species that require increased research and management attention. In addition, two raptors not on the declining list — the western population of the golden eagle and the osprey — are on the NSSE list. Nongame species also may be designated as "regional species of special emphasis" by FWS regional offices, a designation that may provide some increased management attention.

A draft "Nongame Migratory Bird Management Plan for the United States"[39] was completed in 1983 and cited as an FWS accomplishment in its FY 1985 budget request to Congress. The draft plan identifies general goals, objectives, policies, and strategies for the conservation and management of nongame migratory birds to achieve compliance with the objectives of migratory bird treaties and legislation. The plan represents the first synthesis of what FWS does or intends to do for nongame birds. Since its submittal, FWS has taken no action to seek public comment on the draft plan, to revise it, or, ultimately, to implement it.

In sum, FWS has no special program or comprehensive plan to guide its efforts in complying with treaty and legislative requirements that call for the protection and conservation of nongame migratory birds as well as game species. The modest nongame research undertaken in the 1970s has been reduced drastically. While FWS recognizes the need for better monitoring and research on nongame populations and the need for national coordination of nongame migratory bird efforts, it has been unwilling to reallocate some of its resources from either waterfowl or other resource management activities to nongame activities. Instead, FWS appears to await the creation of a new source of federal funding specifically designated for nongame species that would allow the states to conduct nongame migratory bird projects with federal grant assistance as authorized by the Fish and Wildlife Conservation Act of 1980.[40] FWS will submit a report to Congress in 1985 that assesses potential new sources of funding to finance nongame activities authorized by the act.

Meanwhile, 36 states since 1977 have established nongame programs financed by special funds. These programs cover the full spectrum of nongame wildlife, including migratory birds. States may conduct conservation activities for bird species under federal authority as long as such activities are consistent with federal laws and regulations. FWS currently does not coordinate these individual state activities.

CURRENT ISSUES

Disputes over the management of migratory birds are not uncommon among federal and state wildlife agencies, sport hunting organizations, and wildlife conservation groups. At times, FWS is able to settle these disputes itself, but frequently Congress or the courts resolve disagreements. Three current migratory bird issues include a long-lived dispute over how to prevent toxic lead poisoning in waterfowl, the decline of goose populations in the Pacific Flyway, and the effects of tropical deforestation on nongame birds.

Toxic Poisoning from Lead Shot

For almost 10 years, the issue of how to prevent the poisoning of waterfowl by spent lead shot had kept FWS, state wildlife agencies, and conservation and hunter organizations at loggerheads. As yet, no completely satisfactory resolution appears to be in sight.

It has been known for decades that migratory waterfowl are being poisoned by spent lead shot ingested while feeding. More recently, it has been recognized that other migratory species have been poisoned as well, either from direct ingestion or, as is the case for scavenging birds such as the bald eagle, from eating the flesh of other birds that contains lead shot. FWS estimates that two to three million waterfowl die annually from toxic lead poisoning.

In 1976, FWS banned the use of lead shot for waterfowl hunting in certain areas with high accumulations of spent shot. Problem areas were jointly identified by FWS and state wildlife agencies, and hunters were required to use steel shot, the only effective, non-toxic replacement for lead.

The FWS "hotspot" approach to the lead shot problem was considered too weak by some who thought a nationwide ban on lead shot was in order. However, the local bans precipitated vehement opposition from some hunters who believed that steel shot cripples more birds than does lead because of its ballistic characteristics and that consequently waterfowl populations would benefit little from a change to steel shot. Opposition also was expressed because of the alleged damage to gun barrels and the greater cost of steel-shot shells. Some state wildlife agencies agreed with these hunters, especially the agencies in Maryland, Louisiana, and California.

Eventually, hunter and state wildlife agency opposition led to an amendment, added by Senator Ted Stevens (R-Alaska) to the FY 1979 Interior Appropriations Bill, which requires FWS to obtain state approval before designating steel-shot zones on any lands within a state, including federal refuge lands. This language also was added to the appropriations bill each year through FY 1983 and incorporated by Interior into its own budget request for FY 1984 and 1985.

In 1983, FWS modified its policy to require steel shot for waterfowl hunting on federal refuges only if a lead-poisoning problem has been documented by verified deaths or if high levels of lead are found in soft-tissue samples in conjunction with gross lesions and clinical signs of lead poisoning. In cases where a state agency has documented evidence of lead poisoning on land near or adjoining a federal refuge, the state may request FWS to include the refuge in a lead-free zone established by the state. FWS will respond favorably to such requests.

FWS continues to identify steel-shot zones for designation with state concurrence. Five additional steel-shot zones were proposed for designation for the 1984-85 hunting season, all on national wildlife refuges: Stillwater, Nevada; Missisquoi, Vermont; Benton Lake, Montana; and Tule Lake and Lower Klamath, California. If adopted, a total of 65 national wildlife refuges, along with many waterfowl production areas, would be classified as steel-shot areas.

More recently, FWS has been prompted to take action to protect birds that die from indirect ingestion of lead shot, such as the bald eagle. In 1984, the National Wildlife Federation petitioned FWS to designate six counties as nonlead areas for the 1984-85 hunting season and another 89 counties for the 1985-86 season on the basis that 109 bald eagles, an endangered species, have been lead poisoned to some degree since 1966 in these counties. FWS is studying the request and plans to make its own proposal in 1985.

Since the lead-shot controversy erupted in 1976, the need to switch to steel shot has begun to gain greater acceptance. Individual states and flyway councils are moving toward the position that steel shot should be used in all waterfowl hunting, not just in certain designated problem areas. For instance, Nebraska and Iowa will require statewide use of steel shot for waterfowl hunting in 1985. Nevertheless, some states remain adamantly opposed to a nationwide ban on lead-shot use. FWS intends to propose new guidelines in 1985 for designating steel-shot zones, but remains wedded to the position that a national ban is unnecessary.

The Effects of Tropical Deforestation on United States Birds

An issue of growing interest to conservation organizations in the United States is the effect of tropical deforestation on 332 Nearctic species, birds that breed in the United States in the summer and winter in the tropics. A few studies have shown that populations of certain Nearctic migrants have disappeared from parts of their North American range. The reason for their disappearance has not been adequately explained. One theory holds that the decline of certain species in the United States is a result of forest fragmentation. A conflicting theory states that land-use changes — especially deforestation — in the tropics of Mexico and of Central and South America are the major cause of decline.

Although FWS has devoted some resources to document the problem, the level of commitment is inadequate. In cooperation with the World Wildlife Fund, FWS in 1983 published a report, "Nearctic Avian Migrants in the Neotropics,"[41] about these species and their apparent decline. It also initiated in 1983 a modest, three-year research and training program to gather field data on forest fragmentation in the neotropics in cooperation with Latin American biologists. The study will be completed in 1986 or 1987 but is not expected to produce a definitive answer on the cause of species disappearance or decline.

Until such evidence is obtained, FWS cannot fully meet its treaty and legislative responsibilities to protect and conserve all species of migratory birds. Obtaining adequate scientific evidence will require a much larger commitment of research dollars than is currently being expended.

The Management of Geese That Nest in Alaska

A steady decline in the populations of four species of geese — black brant, greater white-fronted goose, emperor goose, and cackling Canada goose — that breed in Alaska's Yukon-Kuskokwim (Y-K) Delta and winter in the Pacific Flyway has created a major controversy among sport hunters, Alaskan Native Americans, and government agencies over what has caused the trend and what action should be taken to reverse it. Sport hunting groups cast the blame on Native American residents of the Y-K Delta, whose spring/summer goose harvests are in violation of the 1916 bird-protection treaty between the United States and Canada, and on FWS, which has refused to enforce the treaty's prohibition against subsistence hunting. A suit has been filed by these groups to prevent the service from allowing any harvest of the four species during the closed season.

Although FWS officials agree that subsistence harvests are a major cause of goose population declines, they contend that the type of enforcement called for by sporthunters is impossible, unnecessary, and counterproductive to the survival of the geese. Enforcement of hunting season regulations and bag limits would be extremely difficult, according to FWS, which has only six law-enforcement officers in the entire state. The delta alone covers 70,000 square miles. Past attempts to arrest and fine Native Americans for hunting violations have had little success and have resulted in a deterioration of relations between Native Americans and government agencies. Another reason FWS has not enforced the treaty is because it recognizes the traditional, cultural, and subsistence importance of the spring/summer goose harvest to Native Americans. Sport hunting groups take special exception to this argument, claiming that subsistence hunting is an anachronism since Alaskan natives use modern weapons and airplanes and their communities are rapidly expanding and modernizing.

Cooperation between government agencies and the Native American community is essential for several reasons. Better quality research is needed in the Y-K Delta to determine the precise effect of subsistence hunting on goose populations and to design an overall goose-management plan for the Pacific Flyway. Research in the past has been insufficient. Without the cooperation of Native Americans, the precise nature and dimensions of the problem will remain unknown.

Another factor compelling cooperation is the millions of acres of Native American inholdings within the national wildlife refuge and park systems, a consequence of the Alaskan Natives Claims Settlement Act of 1971 and the Alaskan National Interest Lands Conservation Act of 1980. These inholdings contain some of the most significant goose habitat in Alaska and represent a crucial bargaining chip for Alaskan natives since they could develop them.

FWS is pursuing two avenues to better manage Y-K geese. For the short term, FWS in 1984 signed a cooperative agreement with Y-K Native Americans, sport hunting groups, and state fish and wildlife agencies. Known as the Hooper Bay agreement, it requires Native Americans to stop hunting cackling Canada geese and to restrict their harvest of white-fronted geese and brant to periods before egg-laying and after fall flight. Another agreement, the Yukon-Kuskokwim Goose Management Plan, calls for a cooperative monitoring and law enforcement program in the Native American communities, along with other improvements. The plan should be made final in 1985.

For the long term, FWS wants the Senate to ratify a Protocol on Subsistence Hunting of Migratory Birds, an amendment to the 1916 migratory bird treaty with Canada which would legalize subsistence hunting and give the secretary of the Interior the authority to regulate Native American hunting activity. In short, the protocol would provide a legal basis for FWS cooperative agreements. Canada signed the protocol in 1979, but United States ratification of the protocol has been stalled because some sport hunting groups and environmental organizations object to the vague wording of the document. FWS has acknowledged these complaints and is working with the Canadian Wildlife Service to resolve the problem.

Meanwhile, FWS has budgeted $205,000 for research on Alaska-nesting geese in FY 1985. These funds will be used to research the ecology, productivity, and habitat requirements of goose populations and to evaluate the importance of natural mortality, fall hunting, and spring/summer subsistence hunting on population levels.

LEGISLATION

The 98th Congress (1983-84) considered several proposals to protect wetlands that provide migratory bird habitat. These included provisions to provide more money for wetlands acquisition by federal and state agencies, to extend the Wetlands Loan Act and abolish the requirement for repayment of previous loans, to accelerate the inventory of wetlands, to prohibit certain types of federal financial assistance for activities that destroy wetlands, to provide tax incentives to private landowners who conserve wetlands, and to revise the mitigation requirements of the Fish and Wildlife Coordination Act. Ultimately, only an extension of the Wetlands Loan Act was enacted.

Emergency Wetlands
The issue that received the most attention was how to accelerate wetlands protection, a subject that periodically has received congressional attention since the Migratory Bird Conservation Act of 1929 first authorized the purchase of wetlands as refuges for migratory birds. A comprehensive wetlands conservation measure, the Protect Our Wetlands and Duck Resources Act (S. 978, H.R. 2268), was submitted by the Reagan

administration in early 1983. This legislation was treated by House and Senate authorizing committees as one of many recommendations for drafting their own bills.

Eventually, the House passed H.R. 3082, the Emergency Wetlands Resources
Act, the purpose of which was to intensify protection of the nation's wetlands through
a variety of means. The bill would have:

1. increased the amount of money placed in the migratory bird conservation fund
    for refuge purchases by authorizing admission fees to certain wildlife refuges
    and increasing the price of a duck stamp from the current $7.50 to $15.00 by
    1989;
2. established a new Wetlands Conservation Fund of $75 million annually to
    provide up to $50 million per year for grants for state wetlands conservation
    projects, including acquisition, establishment of new or enhancement of exist-
    ing wetlands, and preservation of existing wetlands; and to provide an addi-
    tional $25 million to FWS for the acquisition of priority wetlands identified by
    a national wetlands priority conservation plan to be prepared by the Interior
    Department;
3. accelerated the National Wetlands Inventory Project, the purpose of which is
    to classify and map all coastal and inland wetlands of the United States, by
    authorizing additional sums to complete work in the conterminous states by
    FY 1989;
4. required a periodic report on the status of wetlands in the conterminous United
    States;
5. mandated a comprehensive report to Congress on the causes of wetlands
    destruction and loss to include an analysis of federal laws and programs that
    induce wetlands destruction and a discussion of the costs borne by the federal
    government as a result of wetlands destruction;
6. repealed the provision of the Wetlands Loan Act that calls for repayment of all
    appropriations made under the act, about $175 million through FY 1985; and
7. sanctioned construction of a jetty project at Oregon Inlet, North Carolina, that
    requires the taking of land from a national park and refuge.

The Senate measure, S. 1329, also known as the Emergency Wetlands Resources
Act, was reported by two committees — Energy and Natural Resources and Environment and Public Works — but never went to the floor. The Senate bill was similar in
most ways to the House bill with two exceptions. It credited approximately $10 million
annually in import duties on fire arms to the migratory bird conservation fund and
extended the Wetlands Loan Act through FY 1993. In addition, the Energy Committee
voted to delete the authority for user fees at wildlife refuges, something the Environment and Public Works Committee already had approved. This intercommittee disagreement was never settled because the bill never reached the floor.

Both the House and Senate are expected to reconsider the emergency wetlands
measures in the 99th Congress. The bills are expected to be reintroduced in substantially the same form as the versions that expired.

Wetlands Loan Act Reauthorization

Since no action was taken on comprehensive wetlands legislation, Congress had
to deal with the expiring Wetlands Loan Act on a separate basis. In 1983, a one-year
extension was passed, and in 1984 the program was extended through FY 1986. No
changes were made in the act's requirement that loaned funds be repaid out of duck-
stamp revenues.

Other Legislation

Other legislation affecting wetlands did not proceed very far. The House passed a bill, H.R. 5755, that amended the Fish and Wildlife Coordination Act, but the Senate took no action on the measure. The House bill authorized wildlife mitigation actions for development projects on "offsite lands," that is on lands not in the immediate vicinity of a project that causes damage to wildlife. The bill also required federal construction agencies to fund FWS studies so that FWS can make recommendations for protecting wildlife, including migratory birds, affected by water resource projects. It is likely that a bill similar to H.R. 5755 will be reconsidered in 1985.

Congress also held hearings on two different measures, S. 1675 and H.R. 5900, to provide tax incentives for private landowners who sell or donate their land for conservation purposes or who undertake conservation measures on their land. Certain provisions of the House measure dealt specifically with wetlands. H.R. 5900 authorized the secretary of the Interior, upon application of a property owner, to designate a privately owned wetland as a "wetland enhancement area" if the secretary determines that the land requires improvement or protection to preserve or enhance its wetland characteristics. Landowners would be eligible to receive a 15-percent tax credit for the cost of implementing conservation measures approved by the secretary on their land.

The idea of amending the tax code to promote land-conservation activities by private citizens has been talked about for several years. As yet, no such measures have been approved by the tax committees of either house.

LEGAL DEVELOPMENTS

In the past few years, the courts have repeatedly affirmed the broad authority of FWS to manage migratory birds. In a series of criminal prosecutions under the Migratory Bird Treaty Act, the courts upheld convictions for offenses ranging from hunting waterfowl over baited fields (*United States v. Brandt*[42]) to abrogation of conservation easements held by FWS (*United States v. Seest*[43]).

In civil litigation, the courts have upheld FWS migratory bird management decisions. The courts approved an FWS decision to allow continued hunting of black ducks, despite recent population declines (*Humane Society of the United States v. Watt*[44]), and rebuffed Nevada's challenge to FWS authority to protect migratory birds on the Ruby Lake National Wildlife Refuge (*Nevada v. United States*[45]). The Supreme Court also rejected an attempt by North Dakota to limit the FWS authority to acquire interests in land under the Migratory Bird Hunting Stamp Act of 1934 and the Wetlands Loan Act of 1961. The prairie potholes of North Dakota are some of the richest waterfowl breeding areas in the United States. In 1961, FWS began acquiring easements to protect these wetlands, using duck-stamp funds. These areas, known as waterfowl production areas, became part of the National Wildlife Refuge system. The Wetlands Loan Act requires the governor's approval for the acquisition of lands or interests in lands and water, and for 16 years a succession of North Dakota governors had approved the easement purchase program. In 1977, however, the state enacted statutes attempting to limit the acquisition program. The United States filed suit, arguing that the North Dakota statutes were an unconstitutional infringement on federal authority. The Supreme Court agreed, holding that a state's consent, once given, to allow easement purchases, could not be conditioned or withdrawn (*North Dakota v. United States*[46]).

RESOURCE STATUS

FWS does not have a centralized, comprehensive system for monitoring the 816 migratory birds under its authority, but it does attempt to monitor population trends of several hundred species. Certain species of ducks and all goose populations are monitored intensively through a variety of survey methods and census techniques. Three upland game species — woodcock, mourning dove, and sandhill crane — also are surveyed annually. Population-trend information for all other birds is collected yearly by the national breeding bird survey. Coordinated by FWS but conducted principally by volunteers, the breeding bird survey provides population and distribution information on about 500 bird species. Hindered by limitations and biases, however, the survey yields adequate data for only half of these. FWS also coordinates counts of migrating raptors at six different locations around the country.

Ducks

FWS, in cooperation with the Canadian Wildlife Service and the states, uses aerial surveys and other methods to develop annual breeding-population estimates for 14 species of ducks that can be surveyed on selected breeding grounds in Alaska, Canada, and the United States: mallard, gadwall, wigeon, green-winged teal, blue-winged teal, northern shoveler, pintail, redhead, canvasback, scaup (greater and lesser are counted as one), bufflehead, common goldeneye, ruddy, and ring-necked duck. Survey findings are published annually in a report, "Status of Waterfowl and Fall Flight Forecast."[47] Since these surveys do not cover all breeding areas for each species, the population estimates do not represent the total breeding population of each species. Nonetheless, when aggregated these estimates do represent a substantial portion of all breeding ducks for the 14 species. The 1984 breeding-duck population of 38 million represents a one-percent decline from the 1983 total of 38.6 million, but is six percent below the 1955-83 average of 40.5 million.

Total Estimated Duck Breeding Populations in North America, 1955-84, in Areas with Comparable Annual FWS Surveys*

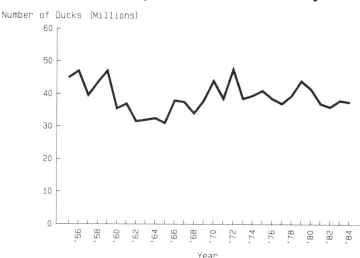

SOURCE: Fish and Wildlife Service, "1984 Status of Waterfowl and Fall Flight Forecast"

* (Excluding scoters, eiders, mergansers, and old squaws)

FWS also prepares annual estimates of the total number of the 14 species that breed just in the 50 areas that FWS itself surveys by air. This total is referred to as the "duck breeding population of North America," a slight misnomer since it covers only breeding populations in the United States Great Plains and Canada.

The annual total of the North American breeding-duck population has varied from a low of 30 million in 1965 to a high of 48 million in 1956. A major factor causing population fluctuations is climate. During periods of drought, some wetlands dry up, leaving less breeding habitat for prairie-nesting ducks. Drought conditions have persisted since 1980 in various parts of the prairie. When more precipitation occurs, population levels are expected to increase. No discernible decline in the total duck population has occurred over time. But since each species has its own unique biological requirements, behavior patterns, and habitat needs, it is important to examine the population trend for individual species making up the aggregate population.

FWS makes population estimates for 10 of the 14 species surveyed on their breeding grounds. In 1984 the estimated breeding population of five species declined from its average size of the previous 29 years (1955-83): mallard, by 30 percent; green-winged teal, by 16 percent; blue-winged teal, by 22 percent; pintail, by 38 percent; and canvasback, by one percent. The other five species showed increases: gadwall, by 21 percent; wigeon, by 26 percent; northern shoveler, by 13 percent; redhead, by 19 percent; scaup, by 21 percent.

No breeding-population surveys or population estimates are made for 23 other duck species for several reasons, principally because FWS does not consider them to be in jeopardy. FWS obtains information on hunting mortality for these nonsurveyed ducks through its annual harvest survey, which covers all waterfowl. Generally, the 23

DUCK BREEDING POPULATION ESTIMATES FOR 14 SPECIES IN COMPARABLE ANNUAL SURVEY AREAS, 1983–1984 (EXCLUDES SCOTERS, EIDERS, OLDSQUAWS, AND MERGANSERS) (ESTIMATES IN THOUSANDS)

Survey Area	1983	1984	Percent Change
Alaska-Old Crow	4,494	5,109	+14
N. Alberta-Northwest Territories	9,744	10,661	+9
N. Saskatchewan-N. Manitoba-W. Ontario	4,325	3,364	−22
S. Alberta	3,169	2,860	−10
S. Saskatchewan	7,539	5,355	−29
S. Manitoba	1,428	838	−41
Montana	823	750	−9
Wyoming	306*	585	+91
Colorado	70**	110	+57
North Dakota	2,999	3,974	+33
South Dakota	2,537	3,301	+30
Nebraska	142	154	+8
Minnesota	568	621	+9
California	219	123	−44
Wisconsin	235	249	+6
Total	38,598	38,054	−1

*No survey in 1983, figure represents long-term average.
**No survey in 1983, figure represents 1982 results, as habitat conditions were judged similar in both years.
Source: Fish and Wildlife Service, "1984 Status of Waterfowl and Fall Flight Forecast."

species are not hunted heavily, nor is FWS aware of other threats to their existence.

FWS has designated seven duck species as NSSEs: mallard, pintail, canvasback, redhead, wood duck, black duck, and ring-necked duck. NSSE plans for each are in various stages of completion. An NSSE plan sets population-size objectives, establishes habitat conservation goals, and identifies other significant research and management needs. It must be emphasized that these plans are in the formative stage, may change with time and experience, and should not be regarded as final. The status reports that follow for each species are based principally on information taken from FWS draft NSSE plans, from "1984 Status of Waterfowl and Fall Flight Forecast," and from information provided by FWS personnel. Generally, range and biological information was obtained from *A Guide to Field Identification: Birds of North America*.[48]

Mallard

The mallard is the most abundant and widely distributed game duck in North America and a favorite of hunters. A surface feeder, it is commonly found in ponds and freshwater marshes. The mallard's principal breeding grounds stretch from the northern prairies all the way to Alaska.

The estimated breeding population in surveyed areas averaged 8.4 million during the period 1955-83. In 1984 the population numbered 5.9 million. According to FWS, this decline is attributable to habitat loss, the single most important factor determining abundance, and to recent droughts. Although mallard numbers fluctuate normally in response to precipitation cycles, the population did not respond as greatly to favorable water conditions in the mid-1970s as it did in earlier periods. According to FWS, this probably was due to the long-term effects of habitat destruction.

The vast majority of mallards are produced in the prairie and parkland wetlands of the United States and Canada, habitat that is decreasing because of destruction by

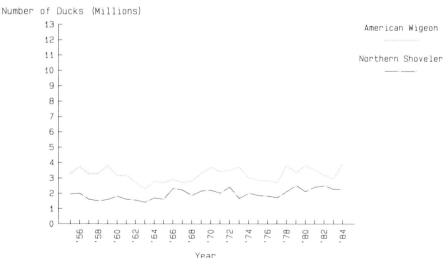

American Wigeon and Shoveler Breeding Population Estimates, 1955-84, in Areas With Comparable Animal Surveys

Number of Ducks (Millions)

American Wigeon

Northern Shoveler

Year

SOURCE: Fish and Wildlife Service, "1984 Status of Waterfowl on Fall Flight Forecast"

Mallard, Pintail and Green-Winged Teal
Breeding Population Estimates, 1955-84, in Areas
With Comparable Annual Surveys

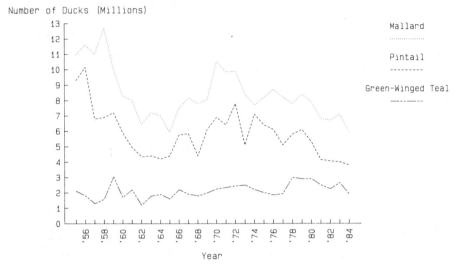

SOURCE: Fish and Wildlife Service, "1984 Status
of Waterfowl on Fall Flight Forecast"

farmers and ranchers. For instance, in the Couteau du Missouri counties of North Dakota, half the grasslands used for livestock was converted to croplands between 1965 and 1975. The lack of adequate nesting cover leads to increased vulnerability to predation. The mallard's nesting success is about half of what it was in the 1930s.

Migration habitat currently is considered adequate to support a fall flight of 19.2 million birds. Mallards readily accept and use new, man-made reservoirs, which compensate to some degree for the destruction of natural water bodies used during migration.

The mallard winters on ponds, lakes, marshes, and brackish coastal waters throughout the United States. Several key wintering habitats, such as the flooded bottomland hardwoods of the Mississippi River Delta and grasslands in California's central valley, are being converted to croplands, and portions of mallard populations are being dispersed to other areas. An opportunist, the mallard is expanding its range by adapting to man-created habitats such as farm drainage ditches and reservoirs.

The mallard breeding-population objective established by FWS is 10.8 million birds, a goal set in 1974. This would produce an estimated fall flight of 19.2 million and allow hunters to kill 6.5 million, a number roughly the same as the estimated average annual retrieved take during 1974-81.

FWS predicts that the mallard population will continue to decline until prairie wetland destruction is stopped. In addition, the success of breeding pairs must be increased significantly by the maintenance of adequate cover on private farmland near wetlands and by predator control actions.

Northern Pintail

The pintail is another widely distributed North American duck avidly sought by hunters. It breeds principally in Canada and Alaska, and winters along the Pacific,

Scaup, Blue-Winged Teal and Gadwall
Breeding Population Estimates, 1955-84, in Areas
With Comparable Annual Surveys

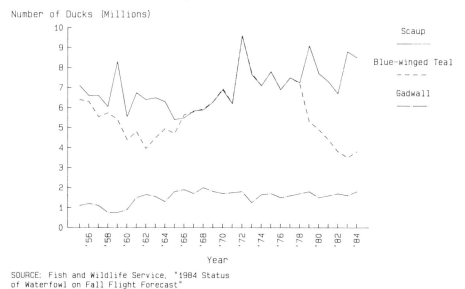

SOURCE: Fish and Wildlife Service, "1984 Status
of Waterfowl on Fall Flight Forecast"

Atlantic, and Gulf coasts and in Mexico. The pintail feeds on aquatic vegetation, seeds, and snails.

The estimated pintail breeding population in surveyed areas fluctuated greatly from 1962 to 1981, ranging from 4.1 to 7.8 million, with an average of 6.9 million. A drought in the prairie breeding areas from 1981 to 1983 has led to a short-term decline and a new low of 3.6 million birds in 1984. This decline is expected to reverse itself with an increase in precipitation and the improvement of prairie habitats.

Pintail production is greatest in the northwest quadrant of North America. Alaska is the most important United States breeding area, followed by the Dakotas and Montana. Breeding habitat in Alaska is relatively secure since most of the significant nesting areas are within national wildlife refuges. Breeding habitat in the Canadian and United States prairies is declining as wetlands and upland cover are converted to agriculture.

Pintails migrate through all four flyways, with heaviest concentrations in the Pacific, followed in order by the Central, Mississippi, and Atlantic. The destruction of migration habitat is a gradual, ongoing process, but habitat is considered adequate at present. Key areas of concern during the next 10 years are the Klamath Basin in California; the Great Salt Lake, Utah; and the playa lakes in the Texas panhandle.

Pintails winter throughout the southern half of the United States, in Pacific coast states, and in Mexico. Ninety percent of the birds in the United States winter in just three states: California, 58 percent; Texas, 18 percent; and Louisiana, 15 percent. FWS considers winter habitat the most important of all habitat needs. Key wetlands need to be conserved in all three states. In addition, the maintenance of certain agricultural lands in rice, soybeans, and small grains is vital to pintail winter food needs.

The total breeding population objective for the pintail is 6.9 million. About 80 percent, or 5.5 million, are assumed to breed in surveyed areas. The fall flight objective is 15.1 million and the hunter harvest objective, 1.1 million.

Canvasback

The canvasback is a prized game duck whose population constitutes approximately two to four percent of all North American ducks. The canvasback is a diver that feeds on both vegetation and animal matter. Its breeding range extends from the Dakotas to Alaska, and it winters principally along the Atlantic and Pacific coasts.

The 1984 breeding population estimate in surveyed areas was 569,000, up from 528,000 in 1983. The population fluctuated widely in the 1970s, with a low of 423,000 in 1978 and a high of 706,000 in 1975. No long-term downward trend can be discerned from breeding estimates, but the species must be watched carefully because of its low numbers and the potential difficulty in reversing a precipitous decline once it starts.

The canvasback uses four main breeding habitats: the prairies and parklands of the United States Great Plains and Canada, the deltas of major rivers in northern Canada, Yukon Flats and other inland marshes of Alaska, and the boreal forest marshes and lakes in Canada. Approximate percentages of the breeding population are: Canadian parklands, 34 percent; Saskatchewan Delta, five percent; Athabaska Delta, three percent; MacKenzie Delta, one percent; Old Crow Flats, one percent; Alaska, 12 percent; northern boreal forest, 24 percent; prairie potholes of the United States and Canada, 17 percent; and intermontane regions of the United States and Canada, three percent.

The most serious threat to breeding habitat is the drainage and degradation of parkland and prairie wetlands in Canada and the United States. Destruction of nesting cover adjacent to wetlands suppresses the reproductive success of canvasbacks by increasing their susceptibility to predation.

Canvasbacks follow several migration routes to their wintering areas along the Atlantic, Gulf, and Pacific coasts. Birds migrating through the Midwest to the Atlantic and Gulf coasts once staged on midwestern lakes, but many of these have become so polluted or altered by development that migrating flocks are now concentrating in the upper Mississippi River. Such concentration — up to 200,000 birds — is considered a problem because it places a substantial portion of the population at risk from a disease outbreak or from a contaminating oil or chemical spill. Birds wintering along the Pacific coast face similar development pressures along their migration routes.

About half of all canvasbacks counted in winter surveys from 1960 to 1971 were on the Atlantic coast, one fourth along the Gulf coast, and one fourth along the Pacific coast. In the East, Chesapeake Bay used to be the most important wintering area, but pollution has eliminated most of the vegetation preferred by the duck. Pollution and other problems such as human disturbance and habitat loss also afflict canvasback populations on San Francisco Bay and Mobile Bay.

FWS has set the breeding-population goal for the canvasback at 625,000, which would require a nine-percent increase from the 1984 population estimate of 569,000. If achieved, this population would produce a fall flight of 1,070,800 canvasbacks and support a hunter take of 267,000.

Achievement of these goals is dependent upon several required actions: causes for the current high mortality rates for juvenile canvasbacks must be identified and resolved; predators of nesting birds and young must be controlled; better statistics must be gathered on hunting mortality and age-sex ratios; hunters must be educated to identify and kill male canvasbacks only; illegal hunting must be controlled; and present canvasback habitat must be maintained or enhanced. A drop of the breeding

Redhead and Canvasback Breeding Population Estimates, 1955-84, in Areas With Comparable Annual Surveys

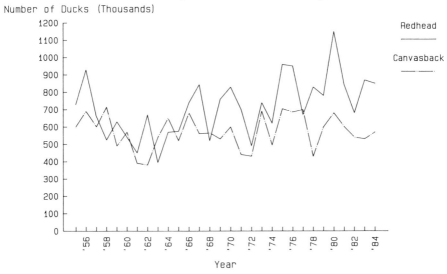

Number of Ducks (Thousands)

Redhead

Canvasback

Year

SOURCE: Fish and Wildlife Service, "1984 Status of Waterfowl on Fall Flight Forecast"

population to 400,000 would cause FWS to consider restricting the hunting of the species.

Redhead

The redhead is a prairie-breeding duck that commonly winters in protected coastal bays and estuaries. It feeds by diving underwater and eating vegetation and animal foods.

The redhead breeding-population estimate in surveyed areas for 1984 was 849,000. The population has fluctuated widely since 1969, with a low of 489,000 in 1972 and a high of 1,146,000 (1980). According to FWS, no discernible population trend, either up or down, has occurred in the past 15 years. However, redhead juveniles are suffering a high mortality level that is not attributable to legal hunting.

The most extensive North American breeding habitat of the redhead is the prairies and parklands of the Dakotas, Minnesota, and western Canada. A second important area is the intermontane region of Oregon, Washington, Nevada, California, Utah, Idaho, Montana, Colorado, and British Columbia. Redheads also breed in the northern boreal forest of Canada.

Redheads are highly dependent on small seasonal and semipermanent wetlands in the prairies and parklands. The continued drainage of these areas poses a significant long-term threat to the breeding population. In the Great Basin, heavy irrigation demands often leave redhead breeding marshes without sufficient water. In addition, intensive farming and grazing have damaged or destroyed emergent vegetation around marsh edges, reducing the quantity and quality of nesting cover.

The large majority of redheads migrate either through the Great Plains to wintering areas along the Gulf coast, or through staging areas in the Midwest to the Chesapeake Bay and the Florida coast. Migrating redheads are broadly dispersed and use a

57

variety of aquatic habitats for staging and migration. Consequently, loss of migration habitats is not currently as critical a problem for redheads as it is for other species such as the canvasback.

An estimated 80 percent of redheads winter along the Gulf coast from Florida to the Yucatan peninsula. This habitat is threatened by dredge and fill activities, pollution from herbicides, and potentially catastrophic oil spills. In the East, redhead habitat in Chesapeake Bay is threatened by declining water quality that has destroyed the redhead's preferred foods. FWS does not know precisely how this affects redhead winter survival.

The FWS breeding-population objective for the redhead is 875,000, three percent above the 1984 estimate in surveyed areas. Redheads have exceeded that objective in three of the last 15 years: 974,000 in 1974, 946,000 in 1975, and 1,146,000 in 1980. A breeding population of 875,000 could produce a fall flight of 1.5 million, from which hunters would be allowed to take 376,000. The harvest objective has not been attained for 15 years.

Attainment of these management objectives depends on several factors: causes of the high juvenile mortality must be identified and reduced; predators of nesting redheads must be controlled, especially on refuges; reliability of hunter-take estimates must be increased; the redhead's age-sex ratio must be improved; present breeding, migration, and wintering habitats must be maintained in their current condition or improved; and enforcement of hunting regulations must be maintained at the current level.

Wood Duck

The wood duck is a common duck found in open woodlands around lakes, swamps, rivers, and streams. It is found in all states east of the 100th meridian and in southern Canada, the Pacific coast states, and some Rocky Mountain states.

The wood duck has made a dramatic comeback since the 1930s, when populations were low. Restricted hunting combined with an increase in suitable woodland-pond habitats have enabled the duck to expand into areas where it previously was absent.

FWS studies show that the estimated annual wood duck harvest by hunters has averaged about a million birds from 1971 to 1980, up from 640,000 the previous decade. The breeding population estimate, extrapolated exclusively from harvest data, was around 3.2 million in 1982, double the 1970 estimate.

Wood ducks nest in tree cavities or man-made nesting boxes near ponds, streams, and tree-filled marshes. Juveniles are reared on these water bodies, where they forage for insects and are protected from predators. Wintering habitat consists of wooded streams, flooded bottomland hardwood forests, and other similar areas in the southeastern United States and the Central Valley of California.

All forms of habitat for wood ducks — breeding, rearing, migration, and wintering — are considered adequate at present. A need exists, however, to protect key areas from future loss via conservation easements or other means. FWS has identified seven core wood duck breeding and wintering habitat areas. For instance, FWS estimates that 300,000 acres of interior wetlands and river bottomlands in the lower Mississippi drainage area should be protected from drainage. About 4.5 million wetland acres already have been drained there in the last 20 years.

The FWS breeding population objective for the wood duck is to maintain the estimated 3.2 million birds. This would produce a fall flight of about 6.8 million and a hunter take of 1.3 million, which was the estimated harvest in 1981.

BREEDING POPULATION ESTIMATES FOR
10 SPECIES OF DUCKS, 1955–84
(IN THOUSANDS)

Year	Mallard	Gadwall	American wigeon	Green-winged teal	Blue-winged teal	Northern shoveler	Pintail	Redhead	Canvas-back	Scaup*
1955	10,345	1,106	3,333	2,076	6,436	1,965	9,251	733	595	7,100
1956	11,711	1,202	3,712	1,898	6,267	2,084	10,124	928	692	6,595
1957	10,946	1,102	3,208	1,293	5,449	1,744	6,856	684	600	6,535
1958	12,904	687	3,372	1,618	5,799	1,515	6,889	524	713	6,040
1959	10,292	683	3,779	3,153	5,300	1,649	7,228	641	481	8,220
1960	8,206	873	3,165	1,630	4,303	1,859	5,769	542	575	5,566
1961	8,290	1,422	3,219	2,216	4,833	1,625	4,860	437	396	6,764
1962	6,144	1,610	2,721	1,119	3,890	1,633	4,299	664	385	6,398
1963	7,360	1,578	2,209	1,754	4,587	1,435	4,361	396	523	6,564
1964	6,974	1,223	2,630	2,051	4,943	1,685	4,111	560	658	6,326
1965	5,948	1,692	2,695	1,526	4,628	1,607	4,301	568	505	5,383
1966	7,401	1,976	2,901	2,219	5,616	2,272	5,777	747	683	5,421
1967	8,205	1,638	2,637	1,944	4,715	2,244	5,870	846	556	5,877
1968	7,586	2,098	2,783	1,805	3,697	1,811	4,225	502	557	5,971
1969	8,065	1,837	3,192	1,991	4,514	2,150	6,390	749	530	6,338
1970	10,379	1,698	3,752	2,259	5,633	2,269	7,004	834	601	6,930
1971	9,843	1,733	3,425	2,352	5,426	2,052	6,291	693	441	6,149
1972	9,867	1,776	3,428	2,407	5,673	2,505	7,875	489	429	9,527
1973	8,781	1,198	3,665	2,444	4,866	1,657	5,114	754	696	7,535
1974	7,392	1,562	3,003	2,221	5,437	2,060	7,165	613	493	7,045
1975	8,109	1,672	2,862	2,038	6,441	1,994	6,387	974	706	7,846
1976	8,637	1,478	2,699	1,844	5,023	1,818	6,045	946	686	6,973
1977	8,226	1,546	2,678	1,952	4,626	1,616	4,971	688	702	7,490
1978	7,695	1,593	3,808	2,978	4,497	2,162	5,664	833	423	7,125
1979	8,444	1,889	3,388	2,920	5,278	2,555	6,070	774	606	9,135
1980	8,003	1,459	3,857	2,925	4,903	2,050	5,420	1,146	688	7,690
1981	6,757	1,479	3,555	2,515	4,076	2,403	4,227	825	594	7,253
1982	6,684	1,690	3,159	2,247	3,879	2,540	4,112	674	543	6,549
1983	7,107	1,536	2,923	2,574	3,381	2,237	4,086	866	528	8,788
1984	5,974	1,799	3,979	1,804	3,870	2,223	3,664	849	569	8,402
1955-83 Ave.	8,493	1,484	3,164	2,137	4,970	1,972	5,888	712	572	6,936
Percent Change in 1984 from:										
1983	−16	+17	+36	−30	+14	−1	−10	−2	+8	−4
1955-83 Ave.	−30	+21	+26	−16	−22	+13	−38	+19	−1	+21

*Includes greater and lesser scaup.
Source: Fish and Wildlife Service. "1984 Status of Waterfowl and Fall Flight Forecast."

Ring-Necked Duck

The ring-necked duck is considered a minor game species nationally, but is avidly hunted in Minnesota, Wisconsin, Michigan, and in some southeastern states. The ring-neck breeds in sedge marshes and on bog lakes, as well as on woodland ponds and small lakes. Its principal breeding habitat is in the boreal forests and prairies of Canada and in midwestern states around the Great Lakes. The species winters in southern coastal marshes, along the Pacific Coast, and in Mexico.

FWS lacks adequate data on the breeding-population size. Based on what data there is, the population seems to fluctuate between 200,000 and 800,000 annually, with an average of 450,000 to 500,000.

The breeding population is in a suspected decline based on midwinter survey counts, especially in the Atlantic Flyway, and on hunter-take estimates that in 1983 showed a high United States kill of 519,000 from an estimated fall flight population of a million. Also, hunting mortality estimates show a national decline of 25 percent from 1980 to 1981, and a parallel decline in numbers harvested in Minnesota. Declining harvests are another indication that the population itself may be declining. In addition, ring-necked ducks appear to be highly vulnerable to poisoning from ingesting spent lead shot.

Ring-neck breeding pairs are dispersed widely among small ponds, lakes, and bogs. This dispersion makes it difficult to obtain good breeding population estimates and to establish secure breeding refuges. The status of breeding habitat overall is not well known, but some localized threats have been identified. These include destruction of bog habitat by peat mining, lakeshore development, and acid rain impacts on one of the duck's preferred foods, aquatic invertebrates. Favored migration habitat includes wild rice beds in Minnesota, which are attracting ring-necked ducks in increasing numbers. Most of these privately owned areas are not protected by conservation easements, and FWS-owned refuges with wild rice beds are scarce.

The southeastern states provide key wintering habitat for the ring-necked duck. About 30 percent of the entire population winters in the coastal regions of Florida, Louisiana, and Texas. Wetlands destruction is the principal threat to wintering ducks.

The FWS breeding-population objective for the ring-neck is 500,000. This would produce a fall flight of about a million birds and a harvest objective of 400,000.

Black Duck

The black duck is a surface-feeder whose range covers the eastern half of North America. It breeds principally in Canada and winters on shallow ponds and coastal waters of the eastern United States. The black duck feeds primarily on aquatic insects and vegetation.

No reliable aerial survey can be made of the black duck breeding population because the ducks nest in low densities throughout the boreal forests of eastern

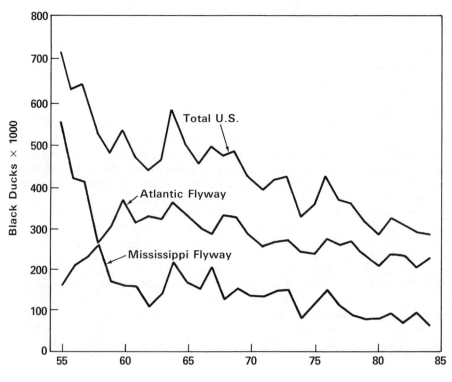

Black Duck Count — Mid-Winter Survey, 1955-84

Canada. Instead, breeding population estimates are extrapolated from an annual mid-winter waterfowl survey and other data.

The winter population count in surveyed areas has declined steadily and substantially since 1955, averaging a 2.7-percent drop yearly between 1955 and 1983 and 1.6 percent between 1963 and 1983. The rate of decline in the Mississippi Flyway is 3.4 percent, and in the Atlantic Flyway 2.3 percent. In 1984, the black duck winter population in the Mississippi Flyway was estimated to be 61,300, down 35 percent from the 1974-83 mean. In the Atlantic Flyway, the winter count was 226,600, down six percent from the 1974-83 mean. Reasons for the decline are poorly understood, but include habitat destruction, hybridization with mallards, and hunting. The Humane Society of the United States has charged that the allowed hunter kill has been too high in view of the long-term population decline. Prompted by a Humane Society suit to prohibit black duck hunting, FWS in 1983 promulgated regulations designed to reduce the hunter kill by 25 percent.

The majority of black ducks breed in Canada, but their southern breeding range extends into the upper Midwest, New England, and along the east coast south to Virginia and North Carolina. FWS believes that urbanization and agriculture have destroyed black duck breeding habitat in the southern part of the range, but the extent of this destruction is undocumented. Other adverse impacts may include pesticides used in forestry and acid rain. Migration habitat presently is considered adequate, with no substantial threats known.

Destruction of wintering habitat has occurred along the east coast and losses continue. For example, 98,000 acres of wetlands were destroyed from 1954 to 1968 in 13 states from Maine to South Carolina. Habitat loss is occurring on both a small and large scale. While the large losses, such as the conversions of lowland forests in the Atlantic coastal plain to agriculture, are more recognizable, the cumulative effect of small land-use changes by individual landowners could be substantial. FWS Region 5 has identified 458,000 acres of black duck habitat that is currently in private ownership.

The FWS breeding population objective for the black duck is 1.6 million. Achievement of this objective would produce an estimated fall flight of three million ducks and a hunter take of 710,000 annually. Between 1962 to 1982, hunting mortality averaged 675,000, of which 52 percent occurred in the United States, the rest in Canada.

To make progress toward these objectives, FWS has initiated a series of actions, principally designed to gather more information on the duck's status. The FY 1985 budget for FWS Wildlife Resources Program includes $243,000 to better manage black duck populations, to improve winter counts in the Atlantic Flyway, to explore methods for reliably surveying the breeding population, and to conduct an information program informing hunters of the black duck's decline. Another $250,000 is allocated to research to improve population-survey methods for black ducks wintering on interior wetlands of the Mississippi Flyway, to develop more reliable measures of the total black duck population, to identify causes of black duck mortality, and to determine whether hunter-take levels have been a factor in the duck's decline.

Geese

The six species of native North American geese are Canada, greater white-fronted, snow, Ross', emperor, and brant. All breed principally in Alaska and Canada. The emperor goose winters mainly along the Alaska coast. The other five species migrate south to the United States and Mexico. Twenty-seven distinct populations of

ESTIMATED POPULATIONS OF GEESE (IN THOUSANDS) IN SELECTED AREAS DERIVED FROM FALL, WINTER, AND SPRING SURVEYS IN COMPARABLE ANNUAL SURVEY AREAS

| | Flyway | | | | | | | | | | | |
| | Pacific Jan. | | | Central Dec. | | Mississippi Dec. | | Atlantic Jan. | | Midcontinent | | |
Species	1982	1983	1984	1982	1983	1982	1983	1983	1984	1982	1983	1984
Canada geese	283	293	223	640	661	771	729	889	822			
White-fronted geese	117[1]	92[1]	113[2]							300[2]	263[2]	77[7]
Snow geese	661[3]	445[3]	526[3]	1000	966	832	589	185[4]	180[4]	1756[5]	1494[5]	
Brant	121[6]	109[6]	133[6]					124	127			

[1]November 1981, '82 and '83 survey
[2]March survey
[3]Includes Ross' geese
[4]Greater snow geese from St. Lawrence River May photo surveys
[5]December survey
[6]Includes Mexico
[7]Incomplete March Survey
Source: Fish and Wildlife Service, "1984 Status of Waterfowl and Fall Flight Forecast."

various goose species have been identified. FWS manages them as individual units. All of these populations have been designated NSSEs.

Generally, most populations of geese are in good shape. FWS, in cooperation with the states and Canada, conducts spring, fall, and winter surveys to estimate the size of goose populations in selected areas and to monitor population trends from year to year. FWS uses these estimates along with climate, weather, and reproduction information to forecast changes in the size of the fall flight of each goose population.

The estimated hunting mortality of all geese killed in the United States during the 1983-84 hunting season was 2.04 million. This represented a 21-percent increase above the 1.69 million harvest level of 1982-83.

It is beyond the scope of this report to discuss the status of each of the 27 distinct goose populations. Instead, trends and problems will be identified by administrative flyway.

Atlantic. No major population declines have occurred in any goose population that winters along the east coast, but distribution problems exist. The Canada goose is deserting its more southern winter range and spending more time farther north. This distribution change means less hunting opportunities in North Carolina and other southern states. The Atlantic Flyway Council is conducting a three-year study to determine the causes of the distribution changes.

The Atlantic brant population declined precipitously in the mid-1970s because of poor nesting and wintering conditions. The majority of this flock winters in New Jersey, where biologists fear that its coastal habitat is being lost and degraded by development. Hunting of brant has been allowed since 1982, but would be prohibited if the population dropped below 100,000. An estimated 127,000 wintering birds were reported in 1984.

Mississippi. Goose populations in the Mississippi Flyway are considered to be in satisfactory to excellent shape. None are suffering severe population declines or habitat problems. Valley populations have increased significantly since their low numbers in the 1940s. However, hunt allocation of Mississippi Valley Canada geese is disputed among the flyway states.

Central. No goose populations in the Central Flyway are in decline or have serious habitat problems. One flock, the Great Plains population of giant Canada geese, is under intensive management to restore it to its former size and range in 10 midwestern states. The initial population objective of 15,000 breeding pairs already has been met, and efforts are being made to increase that number to 25,000 by the year 2000.

Concern exists that the midcontinent population of snow geese is damaging its own breeding habitat in the Arctic because of its large flock size. Annual grasses in that area have not seeded for nearly a decade. This situation could conceivably lead to a sudden drop in population numbers in the future, but recent data show that the flock is spreading out to other nesting areas. The Canadian Wildlife Service has initiated research to determine the magnitude of the problem.

Pacific. In contrast to the goose populations of other flyways, some Pacific Flyway populations have suffered serious declines or are threatened with decline. These include the cackling and dusky races of the Canada goose and the Pacific populations of the greater white-fronted goose, the Pacific brant, and the emperor goose, which breeds and winters principally in Alaska. Two other populations, the Aleutian Canada goose and the tule race of the greater white-fronted, have experienced increases, but remain small in total number.

A major threat to Pacific goose populations is the destruction of California wintering habitat. For instance, 93 percent of the Central Valley wetlands have been destroyed since 1900, and the attrition continues. Approximately 120,000 acres of private agricultural lands currently are managed for waterfowl by private sporting clubs but are susceptible to conversion to other incompatible uses.

Another problem is overhunting of Pacific goose populations by Alaskan Native Americans and sportsmen. The amount of subsistence hunting of goose species that nest in Alaska is not well documented, but is believed to be high. A more extensive treatment of the problems afflicting geese that breed in the Alaskan Arctic and winter in the Pacific Flyway may be found in the chapter on arctic geese.

The Pacific brant population has decreased because of the movement of wintering birds south into Mexico. The causes for this shift are not well documented or understood.

Swans

Only two species of swans are native to North America. One, the tundra swan (formerly called the whistling swan) is hunted; the other, the trumpeter swan, is not. The mute swan, introduced from Europe, is commonly seen in parks and is not hunted.

The tundra swan breeds in Alaska and the Canadian Arctic and winters in large flocks in fresh or brackish shallow water, principally in three Pacific and three Atlantic coastal states. If adequate natural foods are not available, it will eat agricultural crops and forage for shellfish.

FWS monitors the overall swan population through surveys of the eastern and western wintering populations. The size of both the eastern and western flocks has grown substantially since FWS began making yearly surveys. The estimated eastern wintering population has increased at a two-percent annual rate since 1928 and now numbers between 70,000 and 90,000. In 1984, the flock numbered 81,000 compared with 86,500 in 1983. This amount of change from year to year may be the result of distribution shifts at the time of the survey.

The western population has increased from 15,000 to 20,000 in the late 1940s to an annual average of 59,000 from 1973 to 1982. The 1984 flock estimate was 62,000, compared with 67,000 the preceding year.

The breeding habitat of the tundra swan in Alaska and Arctic Canada is considered secure, as is its migration habitat. In the winter, swans congregate principally in a few locations along the Pacific and Atlantic coasts. The average distribution of the eastern flock from 1970 to 1979 was: Maryland 51 percent, Virginia 8 percent, and North Carolina 39 percent. For the western population, the figures are: California 84 percent, Oregon 10 percent, Washington two percent, Nevada two percent, Utah two percent.

The major winter habitat problem is the disappearance of aquatic vegetation from Chesapeake Bay. As a result, swans are feeding more in winter wheat fields and commercial shellfish beds. Although such depredations now are considered minimal, they could pose a real problem were the eastern population allowed to grow.

One habitat-related problem that may be affecting the swan is toxic poisoning from lead shot ingested during winter feeding. The swan is known to be susceptible to lead poisoning because it is a bottom-feeder, but FWS has no comprehensive data to indicate the severity of the problem.

To ensure that eastern flock depredation problems do not get out of hand, FWS wants to stabilize the population within a range of 60,000 to 80,000 birds. Recreational hunting is the chief way to keep the population at that level. Although swans have not been hunted on the east coast for decades, hunters are interested in establishing an annual swan hunt. Maryland has proposed such a hunt several times, but negative public reaction has killed the proposal. North Carolina, however, permitted swan hunting in 1984.

The minimum winter population objective for the western population is 38,000. A drop below this number would lead to the closure of the annual hunt. Since the western population has averaged 59,000 between 1973 and 1982, a large increase in hunting would have to occur before the population dropped to the minimum. From 1970 to 1981, the three states that allow tundra swan hunting — Utah, Montana, and Nevada — issued 3,500 hunting permits, but the kill average was 1,504 per year, both for bagged and unretrieved birds. Like the eastern population, the western flock is causing some depredation problems. Interest has increased among California and Oregon hunters for an annual swan hunt in those states.

Migratory Shore and Upland Game Birds

In addition to waterfowl, federal law permits the hunting of sandhill cranes, four species of rails (king, clapper, Virginia, and sora), purple and common gallinules, coots, woodcocks, snipe, and six species of pigeons and doves (white-crowned pigeon, band-tailed pigeon, scaly-naped pigeon, mourning dove, zenaida dove, and white-winged dove). FWS sets annual hunting regulations for each species.

FWS, in cooperation with states and Canada, conducts rangewide population surveys and develops population estimates for sandhill cranes, woodcocks, and mourning doves — all heavily hunted species. Other upland game species are either unmonitored because they are widely distributed and lightly hunted, as are snipe, or are monitored by state fish and wildlife agencies if hunted intensively at the local level, as are white-winged doves. It is beyond the scope of this report to provide status information on all upland game birds. Detailed discussions of significant species may be found in *Management of Migratory Shore and Upland Game Birds in North America*.[49] FWS has designated four upland game species as NSSEs: the mourning dove, woodcock, sandhill crane, and white-winged dove. The status of the three NSSE species monitored by FWS are covered here.

Mourning Dove

The mourning dove is common in suburbs and farmlands in all states except Alaska. Generally, the dove nests in trees and feeds on grains and seeds. It has the longest nesting season of any game bird in the United States and has expanded its range northward during the past several decades. Mourning doves were hunted in 37 states, including Hawaii, in 1984.

The fall dove population is estimated to be between 350 and 600 million birds. FWS annually monitors mourning dove population trends by means of a call-count survey that records the number of doves heard calling along randomly selected road routes throughout the country. Results are reported in "Mourning Dove Breeding Population Status."[50] Using survey data, FWS develops for each state a "breeding density index" that is used to detect yearly changes in dove populations. FWS has established three mourning dove management units to reflect independent population segments: eastern, central, and western. The breeding density index fluctuates annually both within states and within the three management units. FWS uses statistical methods to determine whether or not these changes represent significant increases or declines.

Despite the appearance of rather large changes in the breeding density index, these fluctuations are not statistically significant when compared with data from previous years. The mourning dove population has remained stable over the long term throughout the past decades.

Man's alteration of the landscape has been highly favorable to the mourning dove. Favored nesting habitats include immature forest stands and the edges of forests that border open agricultural lands. Although a great deal of suitable habitat is available, some is being destroyed by agricultural practices, reclamation projects, and housing developments. In spite of these losses, habitat is still generally favorable for doves in most of the nation.

FWS has prepared a draft management plan for the dove. The basic objective of the plan is "to perpetuate and enhance mourning dove populations that will sustain an annual harvest by hunting and provide traditional opportunities for enjoyment of the resource by nonhunters." Specifically, the plan calls for maintaining the most recent three-year average breeding density index in each management unit at levels within 20 percent of the 1973 to 1982 long-term average (i.e. eastern, 17.2; central, 25.4; western, 11.7). All these goals are being met now. In addition, the plan calls for implementation of a nationwide harvest survey to provide additional information with which to make management decisions. The plan also outlines research to develop a better understanding of the bird's habitat requirements and of the forces that may be adversely affecting breeding and wintering habitat.

Woodcock

The woodcock is a popular game bird throughout eastern North America. It inhabits moist woodlands, swamps, thickets, and abandoned farm lands. Woodcock breeding range covers most of the eastern states, including Texas and the southeast portion of Canada. Birds at the northern end of the range migrate south during winter.

FWS annually monitors the woodcock breeding population by means of an annual singing ground survey in which the average number of males heard calling is counted along randomly selected routes. The resulting number provides an index to measure increases or decreases in the overall population. A second source of data is an annual hunter survey that provides wing samples from harvested woodcocks. The wings are analyzed for age and sex data and information on hunter success. Woodcock population trends are reported in the FWS annual publication, "Status of American Woodcock."[51]

Two woodcock populations are recognized by FWS. The eastern population is comprised of birds in all coastal states from Florida to Maine, West Virginia, Pennsylvania, Canada's Atlantic coastal provinces, and Quebec. The central region includes Ontario, midwestern and Gulf coast states and those in between.

Eastern woodcocks have declined at a mean annual rate of 2.8 percent between 1966 and 1984. Between 1983 and 1984, the breeding population index of singing males dropped 11.5 percent, from 1.92 to 1.70 males heard per route.

The central population shows an overall increase of 1.3 percent annually during the same period. Between 1983 and 1984, the population index increased slightly from 3.03 to 3.04, the first positive move in the index since 1978.

Over the next few years, the total woodcock population is expected to remain stable or decrease. A principal factor believed to be responsible for this trend is the loss of favorable breeding habitat. The woodcock prefers early successional stages of forests, but many of these are being replaced with climax vegetation unfavorable to the woodcock. Increased development of woodcock habitat is also thought to be a factor causing decline. Continued loss of southeastern bottomland forests to agriculture may become a serious problem for the central population.

FWS would like to maintain the breeding index at 2.25 males per route in the eastern region and 3.5 in the central, but since it controls so little of the woodcock's habitat, reaching this goal will be difficult. The estimated hunter harvest is about two million birds annually. However, a survey of hunter success indicates a downward trend that follows the population decline. FWS is considering more restrictive hunting regulations for the woodcock for the 1985-86 season.

Sandhill Crane

The sandhill crane is a wading bird that is fairly common in prairies and fields, where it often is seen in large flocks. Its breeding areas include Alaska and arctic Canada, the Rocky Mountain states, and the lake states of the Midwest, Oregon, and California.

FWS monitors crane populations principally through winter and staging area surveys and has good data for the six recognized populations, except the eastern one. Population size estimates for surveyed areas are as follows:

Eastern	20,000
Midcontinent	540,000
Rocky Mountain	16,000
Lower Colorado River Valley	1,700
Central Valley	3,200
Pacific Flyway	25,000
Total	605,900

The eastern population, not presently hunted, is expected to increase in size. The midcontinent population, which is hunted, is increasing by as much as six percent per year. Midcontinent-population mortality from hunting averaged 10,600 in Central

Flyway states between 1977 and 1981, and FWS believes that the annual hunter take has stabilized. FWS wants to maintain the midcontinent population between 486,000 and 594,000 cranes.

The Rocky Mountain population is greatly reduced from its historic levels, but has staged a comeback from about 250 birds in the mid-1940s to as many as 15,000 by 1971. FWS intends to recolonize Utah and Colorado with more birds. Highly limited hunting of this population occurs in Arizona and Wyoming.

The lower Colorado population is being managed in order to increase its size from 1,700 to about 2,600 by the year 2000. Principal use of this flock is for viewing. No hunting is permitted. FWS intends to increase the Central Valley population to an upper limit of 4,000. No hunting of this flock is allowed.

The Pacific population is being managed in order to maintain the 20,000 to 25,000 wintering cranes in California. Pacific cranes are hunted only in Alaska, where the 10-year harvest average was 229.

Nongame Migratory Birds

Since 1965, FWS has conducted a breeding-bird survey designed to detect trends in population for about 500 species. The survey does not provide a total count of bird populations or even of the breeding population for each species. Rather, the survey samples the number of different birds heard or observed along 1,850 randomly selected road routes throughout the United States during one morning each year. The number of birds per species heard per route is the yearly index that is used to determine population trends. By analyzing survey data over a number of years it is possible to determine significant increases or decreases in some species. The breeding-bird survey also provides a fairly precise measure of birds that are expanding their range.

Although the survey collects information on about 500 species, adequate population data is obtained for only 250. The survey inadequately samples certain habitats, such as marshes and other areas with no vehicular access, and collects insufficient information on rare birds and certain species whose habits make them hard to find on a regular basis.

Based on an analysis of breeding-bird survey data and other information, FWS prepared a 1982 report that identified 28 species with unstable or decreasing population trends during the last 10 to 15 years: nine wading birds, five raptors, three marine birds, four shore birds, and seven passerines. Eighteen of the species are associated with coastal and wetland habitats, three are open woodland and forest species, six inhabit fields or grasslands, and three occupy mixed habitats.

FWS has no plans to conduct follow-up investigations to more accurately assess the biological status of the 28 declining species, nor to update the list as a routine activity. However, five of the 28 have been selected as NSSEs — least tern, roseate tern, piping plover, spotted owl, and trumpeter swan — which eventually should mean increased attention from FWS. Two other nongame birds designated as NSSEs are the osprey and the western population of the golden eagle.

FWS conducts counts of migratory raptors at six different locations. These surveys, in effect since 1977, are done in collaboration with private conservation organizations. About 250,000 raptors are monitored.

Most monitored raptor populations are stable or increasing. The red-shouldered hawk has shown declining numbers at several locations, but no long-term decline can be confirmed until several more years' data are accumulated. Significantly, raptors affected by pesticides in the 1960s and 1970s no longer show declines. These include the bald eagle, peregrine falcon, merlin, and Cooper's hawk.

A five-year study to develop a technique for monitoring breeding populations of

NONGAME MIGRATORY BIRD SPECIES WITH
UNSTABLE OR DECREASING POPULATION TRENDS
IN THE UNITED STATES

Species	FWS Regions Where Status is of Concern	Significant or Negative BBS Trend	BBS or Other Data Indicating Decline	No BBS Data Available	Apparent Population Decline	Small Population Size	Restricted Habitat
					Primary Reason for Listing		
Common Loon	5		x		x		
Reddish Egret	2, 4		x			x	x
Least Bittern	1, 3, 4, 5, 6			x	x		x
American Bittern	3, 5	x			x		x
Wood Stork	4		x		x		x
White-faced Ibis	1, 6			x		x	x
Trumpeter Swan	1, 6		x			x	
Red-shouldered Hawk	3, 5			x	x		x
Ferruginous Hawk	1, 2			x	x	x	
Northern Harrier	1, 2, 3, 5, 6	x			x		x
Black Rail	1, 2, 4, 6			x	x		x
Piping Plover	3, 5, 6			x	x		x
Snowy Plover	1, 2, 4, 6			x	x		x
Long-billed Curlew	1, 6			x			x
Upland Sandpiper	3, 5		x		x		x
Gull-billed Tern	4, 5			x	x	x	x
Roseate Tern	4, 5		x		x	x	x
Least Tern	2, 3, 6			x	x		x
Black Tern	3, 6	x			x		x
Barn Owl	4, 5			x	x		x
Spotted Owl	1, 2			x		x	x
Loggerhead Shrike	3, 5		x		x		
Bell's Vireo	1, 6		x		x		x
Golden-cheeked Warbler	2			x			x
Baird's Sparrow	6		x		x		
Henslow's Sparrow	3, 5		x		x		
Seaside Sparrow	4			x			x
Bachman's Sparrow	3, 4		x		x		

BBS = Breeding Bird Survey
Source: Fish and Wildlife Service, 1982.

woodland-nesting raptors recently was completed by the University of Maryland under contract to FWS. Field studies to validate the recommended survey method are under way in several states.

REFERENCES

1. Act of March 4, 1913, Ch. 145, 37 Stat. 828.
2. James B. Trefethen, *An American Crusade for Wildlife* (New York: Winchester Press and the Boone and Crockett Club, 1975), pp. 153-154.
3. Convention for the Protection of Migratory Birds, August 16, 1916, United States - Great Britain (on behalf of Canada), 39 Stat. 1702, T.S. No. 628.

4. Ch. 128, 40 Stat. 755.
5. 252 U.S. 416 (1920).
6. Michael J. Bean, *The Evolution of National Wildlife Law* (New York: Praeger Publishers, 1983), pp. 20-21.
7. Convention for the Protection of Migratory Birds and Game Mammals, February 7, 1936, United States-Mexico, 50 Stat. 1311, T.S. No. 912.
8. Convention for the Protection of Migratory Birds and Birds in Danger of Extinction, and Their Environment, March 4, 1972, United States-Japan, 25 U.S.T. 3329.
9. Convention Concerning the Conservation of Migratory Birds and Their Environments, November 19, 1976, United States-U.S.S.R., 29 U.S.T. 4647.
10. Act of February 18, 1929, Pub. L. No. 770, Chap. 257, 45 Stat. 1222.
11. Act of March 16, 1934, Pub. L. No. 124, Chap. 71, 48 Stat. 451.
12. Act of August 12, 1949, 63 Stat. 599.
13. Pub. L. 85-585, 72 Stat. 486.
14. Pub. L. 89-669, 80 Stat. 926.
15. Pub. L. 87-383, 75 Stat. 813.
16. Act of March 10, 1934, Pub. L. No. 121, Chap. 55, 48 Stat. 401.
17. Act of August 14, 1946, Pub. L. No. 732, Chapt 965, 60 Stat. 1080.
18. Pub. L. 85-624, 72 Stat. 563.
19. Act of August 4, 1954, Chap. 656, 68 Stat. 666.
20. U.S. Department of the Interior, Annual Report of Lands Under Control of the U.S. Fish and Wildlife Service as of September 30, 1984 (Washington, D.C.: Division of Realty, Fish and Wildlife Service, 1984), pp. 22-23.
21. Pub. L. 89-72, 79 Stat. 213.
22. Pub. L. 87-732, 76 Stat. 696.
23. Pub. L. 91-559, 84 Stat. 1468.
24. U.S. Department of Agriculture, Soil Conversation Service, General Manual 190, Section 410.26, March 1984.
25. Act of May 18, 1948, Pub. L. 534, Chap. 303, 62 Stat. 238.
26. Act of July 3, 1956, Pub. L. 654, Chap. 512, 70 Stat. 492.
27. Pub. L. 87-152, 75 Stat. 389.
28. Act of September 2, 1937, Chap. 89, 50 Stat. 917.
29. U.S. Department of the Interior, Fish and Wildlife Service, Service Management Plan (Washington, D.C.: Fish and Wildlife Service, September 1982).
30. U.S. Department of the Interior, Fish and Wildlife Service, Program Management Document: Migratory Birds (Washington, D.C.: Fish and Wildlife Service, March 18, 1982). Note: This plan will be replaced by a program management document for the entire wildlife resources program in 1985.
31. U.S. Department of the Interior, Fish and Wildlife Service, A National Waterfowl Management Plan for the United States (Washington, D.C.: Fish and Wildlife Service, March 1982).
32. U.S. Department of the Interior, Fish and Wildlife Service, "Migratory Bird Disease Contingency Plan" (unpublished draft, Fish and Wildlife Service, April, 1982).
33. U.S. Department of the Interior, Fish and Wildlife Service, *National Objectives for National Species of Special Emphasis* (Washington, D.C.: Fish and Wildlife Service, 1983).
34. U.S. Department of the Interior, Fish and Wildlife Service, Budget Justifications, F Y 1985 (Washington, D.C.: Fish and Wildlife Service, 1984), p. 137.

35. U.S. Department of the Interior, Fish and Wildlife Service, "Waterfowl Habitat Strategy Report," (unpublished memorandum, Fish and Wildlife Service, January 30, 1984), p. 2.
36. Canadian Wildlife Service, "Waterfowl Management Plan for Canada, an Overview," *Environment Canada* (March, 1983).
37. *Outdoor News Bulletin*, November 30, 1984, p. 1.
38. U.S. Department of the Interior, Fish and Wildlife Service, "Nongame Migratory Bird Species with Unstable or Decreasing Population Trends in the United States" (unpublished report, Office of Migratory Bird Management, July 1982).
39. U.S. Department of the Interior, Fish and Wildlife Service, "Nongame Migratory Bird Management Plan for the United States" (unpublished draft report, Office of Migratory Bird Management, 1983).
40. Pub. L. 96-366, 94 Stat. 1322.
41. U.S. Department of the Interior, Fish and Wildlife Service, *Nearctic Avian Migrants in the Neotropics* (Washington, D.C.: U.S. Department of the Interior, July 1983).
42. 717 F.2d 955 (6th Cir. 1983).
43. 631 F.2d 107 (8th Cir. 1980).
44. 551 F. Supp. 1210 (D.D.C. 1982), aff'd. 713 F.2d 865 (D.C. Cir. 1983).
45. 731 F.2d 633 (9th Cir. 1984).
46. 460 U.S. 300 (1983).
47. U.S. Department of the Interior, Fish and Wildlife Service, and Canadian Wildlife Service, "1984 Status of Waterfowl and Fall Flight Forecast" (Washington, D.C.: U.S. Department of the Interior, 1984).
48. Chandler S. Robbins, Bertel Bruun and Herbert S. Zion, *A Guide to Field Identification, Birds of North America* (New York: Golden Press, 1983).
49. G. C. Sanderson, editor, *Management of Migratory Shore and Upland Game Birds in North America* (Washington, D.C.: International Association of Fish and Wildlife Agencies, 1977).
50. U.S. Department of the Interior, Fish and Wildlife Service, "Mourning Dove Breeding Population Status" (Washington, D.C.: U.S. Department of the Interior, June 1984).
51. U.S. Department of the Interior, Fish and Wildlife Service, "Status of American Woodcock" (Washington, D.C.: U.S. Department of the Interior, June 1984).

The brown pelican is among the 828 species protected by the federal Endangered Species Act, the first law designed to stem human-caused extinctions.

The Endangered Species Program

by Dennis Drabelle
Special to National Audubon Society

INTRODUCTION

SINCE 1966, THE federal government has recognized formally that preserving wildlife in danger of extinction is a national concern. Although the federal endangered species program is ever evolving, one feature has remained constant: the collection of information to identify species in jeopardy, determine their behavioral characteristics, and locate the habitat essential to their survival. This emphasis on gathering scientific information has been embodied in the list of endangered and threatened wildlife and plants, in the documentation that supports the listing of species, and in the preparation and implementation of recovery plans for listed species.

Extinctions occur naturally, but usually are slow in rate and number. Extinctions caused by man, however, constitute a quantum leap in the subtraction of species. During the last 350 years, more than 100 avian species have died out at an increasingly accelerated rate: In the first 200 years, 25 bird species became extinct; in the last 150 years, 78 disappeared.[1]

Harvard biologist Edward O. Wilson estimates that worldwide the current annual extinction rate is 1,000 species yearly, expected to rise past 10,000 a year by 1990.* "During the next thirty years fully one million species could be erased,"[2] he wrote. This could result in as much as a 10 percent loss in the variety of living things.

In establishing the endangered species program, Congress appears to have had human-caused extinctions uppermost in mind. The first clause of the Endangered Species Act of 1973[3] declares, "various species of fish, wildlife, and plants in the United States have been rendered extinct as a consequence of economic growth and development untempered by adequate concern and conservation." However, the act also protects foreign species and species whose existence is jeopardized by nonhuman causes. As of December 31, 1984, the federal list of endangered and threatened wildlife and plants contained 828 species, including 331 found in the United States. In addition, several thousand species of vertebrates, invertebrates, and plants have been identified as candidates for listing.

---

*One major reason for the acceleration is the rapid loss of tropical rainforest habitat to development in Third-World countries.

HISTORICAL PERSPECTIVE AND LEGISLATIVE AUTHORITY

Although the first legislation to deal specifically with endangered species was not enacted until l966, federal efforts to conserve jeopardized species began much earlier. In l900, Congress passed the Lacey Act,[4] which made it a federal crime to transport across state lines wildlife killed in violation of state laws. Congress did this partly to prevent the imminent extinction of birds slaughtered to provide showy plumes for millinery. In l903, when President Theodore Roosevelt established Pelican Island in Florida as the first national wildlife refuge, he was acting to protect the brown pelican. Over the years numerous other refuges have been established to reverse the decline of a particular species, among them Red Rock Lakes National Wildlife Refuge in Montana for the trumpeter swan, Key Deer National Wildlife Refuge in Florida, and Attwater Prairie Chicken National Wildlife Refuge in Texas.

Sometimes the protection of habitat can by itself forestall the extinction of a jeopardized species. In other cases more drastic measures are required. The whooping crane was one such species, and the elaborate campaign to preserve it marked a turning point in federal protection of vanishing species.

The federal effort to save the crane began in l945 with the establishment of the Cooperative Whooping Crane Project by the U.S. Fish and Wildlife Service (FWS) and the National Audubon Society. Yet by the mid-l950s the species seemed to be in an irreversible decline, numbering only some 40 individuals. The bird's plight sparked heated debate in the Department of the Interior. Some biologists thought that nature should be allowed to take its course. Others advocated the extreme measure of capturing every remaining member of the species and establishing a captive-breeding program.

Dr. Ray C. Erickson[5], who worked for both the Refuge and Wildlife Research divisions of FWS, urged a middle course: a test program of captive breeding with a surrogate species, the closely-related and more plentiful sandhill crane. If that project succeeded, its techniques could be applied to the whooper.

Twice rejected, Erickson's proposal won approval when he recast it as a New Frontier initiative in the early days of the Kennedy administration. After polishing the techniques of captive breeding, rearing, and release with sandhill cranes at the FWS Patuxent Wildlife Research Center in Laurel, Maryland, Erickson and his colleagues applied them to some of the remaining whooping cranes.

The results more than 20 years later are impressive: a main flock of about 90 birds that migrates between Wood Buffalo National Park in Alberta, Canada, and Aransas National Wildlife Refuge in Texas; a second, newly-established flock that migrates between Grays Lake, Idaho, and Bosque del Apache, New Mexico, national wildlife refuges; and about 35 captive cranes at Patuxent.

At about the same time that Erickson's proposal was being implemented, FWS established an in-house Endangered Species Committee to compile with plant experts at the Smithsonian Institution a list of wild species thought to be in jeopardy. This work, the forerunner of the present endangered species list, was the first federal effort to address the problem of declining species in a systematic way.

In l966, Congress passed the Endangered Species Preservation Act,[6] which directed all heads of federal agencies to protect native forms of wildlife that were threatened with extinction. It also authorized the expenditure of funds to acquire habitat for threatened wildlife and made identification of jeopardized species an official responsibility of the secretary of the Interior. But this law lacked enforcement authority and made the naive assumption that existing authorities were adequate to protect declining species. That same year the Interior Department published the "red book," the first effort to identify species whose existence was in jeopardy.

In 1969, Congress replaced the 1966 act with the Endangered Species Conservation Act.[7] The new law increased the authorization of funds for habitat acquisition and introduced two major innovations. One was a provision that made it a crime to import or export any member of an endangered species, whether it was endangered domestically or worldwide. The second was a provision that expanded the secretary's responsibility from identifying only native jeopardized species to establishing and maintaining a global list of such species. In addition, the 1969 act directed the secretaries of Interior and State to convene an international ministerial meeting for the purpose of producing a treaty for "the conservation of endangered species."

The meeting was held in 1973 and resulted in the Convention on International Trade in Endangered Species of Wild Fauna and Flora (CITES).[8] The treaty, binding only on participating nations,* attempts to regulate trade in wildlife products by classifying species chosen by CITES members into three categories, each of which constitutes an appendix to the treaty. The extent to which signatory nations agree to regulate trade in a species depends upon the appendix in which it is listed.

Although the 1969 Endangered Species Act was revolutionary in the annals of conservation law, it nevertheless had serious shortcomings. Only species perilously close to extinction were listed, putting the act's protective measures into effect largely after the fact. Also, the act failed to provide protection for jeopardized populations of otherwise stable species. It included no prohibition on the taking of listed species, and obligations to avoid adverse impacts by federal projects were limited to a few designated agencies. Finally, the act was limited to protecting only vertebrates, mollusks, and crustaceans, although extinction threatened all categories of wildlife.

Congress attempted to remedy these shortcomings by passing the Endangered Species Act of 1973.[9] It required all federal agencies to conserve endangered wildlife, opened protection to all plants and animals, and created two categories of protected species — endangered, which covers those in danger of extinction throughout all or a significant part of their ranges, and threatened, those likely to become endangered within the foreseeable future throughout all or a significant portion of their ranges. The 1973 act also made it a crime for anyone to violate regulations issued by the Interior secretary for protection of threatened species. In addition, the act provided for the listing of critical habitats, which are areas essential to the survival of listed species. This was a major new form of protection.

The 1973 act and subsequent amendments formalized the listing process, which remains the prerequisite for protection and recovery of jeopardized species. Species listing or a change in listed status begins either on the initiative of the agency having jurisdiction to protect the species — FWS for terrestrial species, the National Marine Fisheries Service (NMFS) in the Department of Commerce for most marine species — or with the filing of a petition by a private party. The appropriate secretary — Interior for terrestrial species, Commerce for marine** — must respond to petition requests within 90 days and must determine whether to propose the species for listing within the following nine months. If the secretary decides that a species should be proposed for listing, he publishes a notice to that effect in the *Federal Register* as well as in local newspapers in areas that the proposal might affect and notifies affected state and local governments and relevant scientific bodies.

---

*As of May 24, 1984, the signatory nations numbered 86.

**For the sake of convenience, discussions of the listing and protection of species in this chapter will for the most part be limited to FWS and the secretary of the Interior.

Once a species has been proposed for listing, a final decision is required within a year although the secretary can extend this deadline up to six months under certain circumstances. During that time, FWS gathers data on the species and attempts to define its critical habitat, which usually is identified in the proposed listing material. Under the 1982 amendments,[10] however, designating critical habitat is not a prerequisite to listing. The secretary may even decide not to designate critical habitat if to do so would provide a roadmap for lawless hunters and collectors. For various reasons — primarily because about two-thirds of all listed species were listed before critical habitat determinations became a statutory requirement — critical habitat has been designated for only 64 listed species, a small fraction of the total.

Section 4(b)(7) of the act allows the secretary to shortcut timetables and procedural requirements for listing when he perceives an "emergency posing a significant risk to the well-being of any species." Emergency listings are valid for 240 days, after which they expire. The Interior secretary's responsibilities also include reviewing the endangered and threatened species list every five years to determine whether any species should be removed and whether the status of any species should be changed.

The act treated plants somewhat differently from animals: it required the secretary of the Smithsonian Institution to prepare a report on endangered and threatened plant species, complete with recommendations on how to conserve them. The report identified more than 3,000 plant species as candidates for listing. Subsequently, the secretary of the Interior issued a notice of review covering plants included in the Smithsonian report and drawing upon other information. The notice is an FWS attempt to determine the probable status of various plant taxa.[11] FWS in 1982 followed up the comprehensive notice of review for plants with a second that covers vertebrates and a third, in 1984, that covers invertebrates. Using these notices, federal and state agencies can begin to consider the conservation of declining species well in advance of their formal listing.

Species listed as endangered can be relisted as threatened when sufficient progress has been made toward their recovery. Fully recovered species can be delisted. Similarly, threatened species can be relisted as endangered or delisted if circumstances warrant. This gives the revised act the flexibility to protect species before they are all but extinct and to protect jeopardized populations of a species even though the species as a whole may be in satisfactory shape.

The second significant provision of the 1973 act is the consultation requirement established by Section 7. Section 7 requires federal agencies to consult the secretary of the Interior to insure that agency actions and use of agency funds do not jeopardize listed species or their critical habitat. The consultations may be informal in the earlier stages. Some are no more than oral opinions made by FWS biologists that no jeopardy to a listed species or its critical habitat would result from proposed agency actions. If an agency wants a formal no jeopardy opinion, the appropriate FWS regional director is authorized to issue one. If, on the other hand, it appears that a proposed action will result in jeopardy, the consultation would culminate in a written opinion by the secretary "detailing how the agency action affects the species or its critical habitat."

The purpose of Section 7 is to require federal agencies to plan their projects so that they will not harm listed species. When first enacted, however, the section spawned several controversial lawsuits brought by private parties who sought to stop the construction of federal projects already under way and on which millions of dollars already had been spent.

A 1978 amendment to the act tempered the stringency of Section 7. Under the amended section, the head of the federal agency whose project is affected, the governor of an affected state, or a permit or license applicant can petition a special Endangered Species Committee for an exemption from act prohibitions. The committee, composed of the heads of six federal agencies plus an ad hoc member from any state affected by the project, reviews the petition and may grant an exemption if a number of conditions are met. Among these are a determination that no reasonable and prudent alternatives to the agency action exist and establishment by the committee of mitigation and enhancement measures — such as species propagation and transplantation, and habitat acquisition and improvement — designed to help minimize the adverse effects of the action. Only two cases have been brought to the committee during the six years of the committee's existence. Both petitions involved cases specifically addressed by the 1978 amendment.

Critical habitat, as used in Section 7, is a central feature of the act's enforcement mechanism. Although some species have been hunted to extinction, most man-made extinctions are caused primarily by habitat destruction. Section 7 emphasizes the importance of protecting habitat vital to a species' survival and requires federal agencies to plan their projects with consideration for the critical habitats of listed species.

Once a species has been listed, FWS is supposed to prepare a species recovery plan. This is a technical document that spells out the means by which FWS proposes to restore the species to numbers that permit its delisting. Although the plans are required by the act, their format and timing are left to the secretary's discretion. Recovery plans, often prepared by independent experts under federal contract, summarize species data and outline species management programs. Because FWS has no authority to implement recovery plans outside the United States, they are prepared only for domestic listed species.

Section 10 authorizes the secretary to permit activities otherwise prohibited by the act. These include activities performed for scientific purposes or to enhance the propagation or survival of a species, or takings that are incidental and unavoidable to the carrying out of an otherwise lawful activity.

Section 8 of the act directs the secretary to encourage the conservation of fish, wildlife, and plants in other countries. This provision has led to a modest program whereby FWS provides advice and technical assistance to such countries as India and Pakistan to conserve species such as the Indian rhinoceros, Asiatic lion, black buck, and Asian elephant. In addition, FWS is authorized to use foreign currency accruing to the United States in those countries to assist in the development and management of endangered species programs. Under this authority FWS has, for example, assisted Egypt in inventorying its endangered species and India in gauging the adequacy of its wintering habitat for the endangered Siberian crane.

The act was amended again in 1982, after the Reagan administration considerably slowed the listing process by requiring FWS to consider the economic impacts of listing. Congress, in the new amendments, made it clear that listing decisions were to be based solely on biological considerations and that economic impacts were to be considered only in the designation of critical habitat. However, the 1982 amendments also made it possible for federal agencies to take actions that might incidently kill listed species provided that the killing does not threaten the existence of the species. This provision was designed to keep the act from stopping federal projects that might wipe out local populations of listed animals and plants.

The amendments also permitted the Interior and Commerce secretaries to give private developers permits for killing listed species provided that the killing is "incidental to, and not the purpose of, the carrying out of an otherwise lawful activity."

ORGANIZATION AND OPERATIONS

Roles and Responsibilities

FWS is responsible for listing and protecting terrestrial wildlife and plants. With the exception of the polar bear, sea otter, marine otter, walrus, manatee, and dugong — marine mammals protected by FWS — NMFS is responsible for listing and protecting marine species, including fish and the remaining marine mammals — whales and other cetaceans, seals, and sea lions.* However, NMFS is responsible for sea turtles only when the turtles are in the water. FWS is responsible when the turtles are on land.

In addition to requiring all federal agencies to ensure that their actions do not jeopardize the continued existence of any listed species or result in the adverse modification of critical habitat, the act directs federal agencies to carry out programs for the conservation of listed species. In practice, this responsibility devolves primarily upon three agencies in addition to FWS and NMFS: the National Park Service and Bureau of Land Management (BLM) in the Department of the Interior and the U.S. Forest Service in the Department of Agriculture. These agencies carry out their responsibilities under the act primarily by participating in efforts to recover listed species found on their lands. For example, most grizzly bears in the lower 48 states are found on National Park Service or Forest Service lands, so the National Park Service and Forest Service play principal rolls in implementing the recovery plan for this threatened species.

The listing of species sometimes creates conflicts with other activities, such as logging, road construction, grazing, mining, and oil and gas exploration. Accordingly, multiple-use agencies, such as BLM and the Forest Service, devote attention to unlisted dwindling species in order to lessen the likelihood that they will need to be listed. For example, the Forest Service has designated the spotted owl, which some have suggested should be listed, as a sensitive species. The agency's two Pacific coast regions have been cooperating in the development of a management plan for this species. In its draft form the plan, designed to maintain viable populations of the species and prevent the necessity of listing it, includes the establishment of spotted owl management areas where logging and other destructive activities would be prohibited.

Many states have their own endangered species programs which conserve species that — regardless of their national status — are in danger of extinction within the state. In addition, Section 6 of the act directs the secretary to carry out the national endangered species program by cooperating "to the maximum extent practicable with the States." In practice, this cooperation mostly has taken the form of joint research projects and cooperative agreements whereby a state assumes the primary responsibility for one or more endangered species within its borders.

If the secretary determines that a state's proposed program for conserving endangered species meets certain criteria under the act, he signs an agreement with the state. The agreement makes the state eligible for federal grants that may defray as much as three-fourths of the cost of approved programs. Using funds obtained in this way, Missouri has purchased caves as habitat for endangered bat species; Florida has posted signs and otherwise warned boaters in manatee habitat that the species is endangered and vulnerable to injury by boat propellers; and New York, New Jersey, and Pennsylvania have pooled resources to restore bald eagle populations in their states. As of the end of FY 1984, 39 states and two territories had entered into cooperative agreements.

---

*As of October 1984, NMFS had listed only seven species. Several others under its jurisdiction, however, were listed by the 1973 Act.

For the remaining states and territories, the reasons for not entering into such agreements vary. Some states do not have adequate programs. Others, mindful of the fluctuations in federal funding, are not interested in tying their programs to the federal purse.

Congressional Committees

The Endangered Species Act must be reauthorized periodically by Congress, usually every three years. The next reauthorization is due in 1985. The congressional committees responsible for reauthorization, which includes establishment of appropriations ceilings, as well as for oversight and other substantive matters concerning the Endangered Species Program, are the House Committee on Merchant Marine and Fisheries and the Senate Committee on Environment and Public Works. The appropriations committees of the House and Senate — particularly the subcommittees on Interior and related agencies — annually determine how much money, within the established ceilings, will be spent on endangered species.

Agency Structure and Function

The Endangered Species Program is one of eight programs administered by FWS. It is supervised by the associate director for Federal Assistance, who also administers the Federal Aid Program and the wildlife permitting activity. The Office of Endangered Species in Washington is responsible for the overall management of the Endangered Species Program, including review and evaluation of field-station and regional-office activities and policy development. The office is divided into two branches. The Branch of Management Operations oversees Section 7 consultations, Section 6 state grants, and recovery plan implementation. The Branch of Biological Support manages the listing process.

FWS regional offices implement most endangered species program activities. Though some activities, such as listing proposals and recovery plans, may originate at the field-station level, the appropriate regional office is responsible for reviewing and forwarding them to Washington. The Endangered Species Office, subject to review by the associate director for Federal Assistance and the FWS director, is responsible for reviewing and approving all listing proposals, grant proposals, and recovery plans.

The primary responsibility for Section 7 consultations lies with the regional directors. The Endangered Species Office receives copies of consultation documents and keeps them in a central file for review during program evaluation.

Enforcement of the criminal provisions of the act is the responsibility of the Division of Law Enforcement in the Wildlife Resources Program. Administration of the permitting system for activities otherwise prohibited by the act is the responsibility of the Wildlife Permit Office.

Planning

As with other FWS programs, the Service Management Plan[12] provides long-term policy guidance for the Endangered Species Program. The five-year Program Management Document[13] for the Endangered Species Program provides a five-year statement of resource goals, objectives, problems, strategies, and policies. The Program Advice serves as a one-year plan and allocates personnel and funds. Operational planning is carried out largely through the preparation of notices of possible candidates for the list, the listing process itself, and the preparation of recovery plans.

A crucial document in operational planning is the Endangered and Threatened Species Listing and Recovery Priority Guidelines[14] adopted by FWS in 1983. The guidelines assign priorities for listing on the basis of three criteria: the magnitude of threats to the continued existence of a species, the immediacy of the threats, and the taxonomic position of the species. Under the last criterion a monotypic genus — that is, a plant or animal species that is the only representative of its genus — has priority over a species in a genus with more than one species, and a species has priority over a subspecies.

Four criteria govern recovery priorities: the degree of threat to the species (a more general assessment than that required for the two separate threat criteria, magnitude and immediacy, that apply to listing); the species' potential to benefit from a recovery plan; the species' taxonomic position; and the degree of conflict between the species and development projects or other forms of economic activity.

Budgeting

The Endangered Species Program budget is a line item in the FWS budget. It consists of separate subactivities for listing, consultation, recovery, research and development, grants to the states, and law enforcement. In order to fund and staff law enforcement for the program, the Office of Endangered Species annually allocates monies and full-time employees from its own budget to the Division of Law Enforcement.

FY 1985 ENDANGERED SPECIES BUDGET

	Appropriation	Full-time Employees
Listing	$2,967,000	57
Protection	7,363,000	150
Consultation	2,593,000	76
Recovery	5,985,000	57
Research	4,237,000	65
Grants	3,920,000	—
Total	$27,065,000	405

Source: FWS, Office of Endangered Species.

Research

Federal endangered species research, directed by the FWS Patuxent Research Center, is of two types: ecological studies and captive propagation. Ecological studies are devoted to collecting "information on the distribution, behavioral, ecological, physiological, genetic, and pathological characteristics of the species under study to identify and evaluate limiting factors and find means of correcting them."[15] A notable example is the just completed, six-year survey of Hawaiian forest birds, about 20 of which are endemic to the state and nearly extinct.

Captive breeding compensates for the slow breeding of some species and the reduced gene pools of others. The goal may be to replenish existing populations by releasing individuals from the captive stock or, as in the case of the whooping crane, to create a second wild population. At present the Patuxent Center has captive propagation programs under way for five endangered species: the whooping crane, Mississippi sandhill crane, masked bobwhite quail, bald eagle, and Puerto Rican parrot. It also is breeding Andean condors as a surrogate for the California condor. The California condor, an endangered species that numbers fewer than 20 individuals in the wild, is the subject of captive propagation efforts at a field station in California.

FWS has conducted captive propagation research on the Hawaiian goose, the peregrine falcon, and the black-footed ferret. Although a great deal was learned about the ferret, the efforts to breed it in captivity were not successful. As a follow-up to the Hawaiian-forest survey, FWS is likely to undertake captive breeding of some Hawaiian endemic avian species.[16]

CURRENT PROGRAM TRENDS

Listing

The prerequisite to protecting an endangered or threatened species is listing, a complex, lengthy process that must comply with the rule-making requirements of the Administrative Procedure Act.

During its early years, the Reagan administration viewed the Endangered Species Program as an obstacle to economic progress. The response of Interior Secretary James Watt and his assistants was twofold: to complicate and slow the listing process and to cut funding for all aspects of the Endangered Species Program except consultation.

The administration slowed the pace of listing by invoking Section 4(b)(2) of the Endangered Species Act. This section directs the Interior secretary to consider the economic impact of designating any area critical habitat and permits him to "exclude any area from critical habitat if he determines that the benefits of such exclusion outweigh the benefits of specifying such areas as part of the critical habitat. . . ." Although this directive appeared to be limited to critical habitat determinations, the administration interpreted it in conjunction with President Reagan's Executive Order 12291, which called for a documented determination of the economic impacts of all federal agency rule-makings, so that listing was considered to be a rule-making action covered by the economic-impacts requirement. FWS was required to assemble voluminous data on the economic impacts of each proposed listing and, by implication, to decline to list species where the economic effects of doing so would be grave.

The result was that the highly complex listing process was further complicated and the length of time required to list a species increased by a full year. The number of species listed annually plummeted. According to Lynn Greenwalt, FWS director under presidents Nixon, Ford, and Carter, "During calendar years 1976 through 1980, the service listed almost 350 species as endangered or threatened. However, during the [Reagan] administration's tenure from 1981 to 1983, a total of only 18 species, including two emergency cases under threat of suit by the National Audubon Society, were processed."[17] Moreover, the new requirement proved unnecessary: in no case did FWS determine that merely listing a species would have significant economic impacts.

In 1982, Congress clarified its intent by stating unequivocally that listing decisions are to be made solely on the basis of biological data.* That clarification — along with a congressional directive for FWS to prepare annual progress reports on efforts to reduce the backlog of species proposed for listing — broke up the listing logjam. Whereas in 1981 only four species were listed and in 1982 only 10, the number rose to 23 in 1983, and 47 in 1984.

Subsequent to the congressional clarification, FWS formally gave notice, on October 25, 1983, that it would no longer prepare environmental assessments pursuant to the National Environmental Policy Act of 1969 for listing actions. This decision, based upon relevant case law and the advice of the Council on Environmental Quality, reflects the rationale that merely listing a species as endangered or threatened inherently has no adverse environmental impacts.

---

*This leaves the economic-impact requirement still applicable to critical habitat determinations.

NUMBERS OF SPECIES LISTED PER CALENDAR YEAR

	1973*	1974	1975	1976	1977	1978	1979	1980	1981	1982	1983
Mammals	158	3	2	85	1	1	28	1	0	0	0
Birds	170	0	3	36	3	0	1	0	0	0	0
Fishes	39	0	3	2	5	2	1	4	0	1	3
Reptiles	28	0	1	27	4	7	2	8	0	1	17
Amphibians	6	0	0	7	2	0	0	1	0	0	0
Insects	0	0	0	8	0	0	0	5	0	0	0
Snails	1	0	0	0	0	7	0	0	1	0	0
Clams	0	0	0	24	1	0	0	0	0	0	0
Crustaceans	0	0	0	0	0	1	0	0	0	2	1
Plants	0	0	0	0	4	18	36	2	3	6	2
Total	402	3	9	189	20	36	68	21	4	10	23

*Species listed previous to the 1973 Act.
Source: FWS, Office of Endangered Species.

Consultation

On several occasions during the early years of the Endangered Species Act, the prohibitions of Section 7 interfered with the ongoing activities of federal agencies, especially dam-building by the Army Corps of Engineers, the Tennessee Valley Authority, and the Bureau of Reclamation. Recently, however, the consultation process established by that section has been working as originally contemplated: to help avoid conflicts. Agencies have been consulting with FWS during the planning stages of their projects, and conflicts with endangered species or their critical habitats have been averted before substantial commitments to the projects were made. The list itself,

SECTION 7 CONSULTATIONS BY FWS, FY 1979–81

FY	Informal Consultations	Formal Consultations/No Jeopardy/Jeopardy		
1979	1,585	980	858	87
1980	2,374	729	647	68
1981	3,535	483	422	30
Totals:	7,494 (1)	2,192 (2)	1,927 (3)	185 (4)

1. Informal consultation does not result in a biological opinion. When agencies notify FWS early in their planning process, often formal consultation is avoided, as indicated by the yearly (average 30 percent) increase in the number of informal consultations with the corresponding yearly (average 30 percent) decrease in the number of formal consultations and jeopardy opinions.

2. Ninety formal consultations were canceled or withdrawn with no endangered species problems nor impacts to the projects. Thirty-eight consultations are continuing as of January 1982.

3. Of the 1,927 no jeopardy biological opinions, 493 (26 percent) also included activities that "would promote the conservation of listed species."

4. Of the 185 jeopardy biological opinions (eight percent of formal consultations), 54 (29 percent) also included specific project activities that "are not likely to jeopardize" listed species. The purpose of the act is to inform the public and project sponsors that a problem exists. Alternatives, suggested through consultation, offer project sponsors a means of proceeding with the project while avoiding further impacts to the species or habitat.

Source: U.S. Fish and Wildlife Service, Office of Endangered Species.

the determination of critical habitats for listed species, and the comprehensive notices of potential candidates for listing have served as planning guidance for federal agencies. To further improve their planning, agencies such as the U.S. Forest Service have been developing in-house biological expertise to solve some problems without FWS advice. The most recent FWS comprehensive review of Section 7 consultations, covering 1979 to 1981, showed trends toward more informal consultations and fewer jeopardy findings.

Recovery

Fifty-five new recovery plans were approved in 1984. About 60 percent of the listed United States species now are covered by recovery plans. If this yearly rate continues, within a few years plans will have been approved for all but the most recently listed species. However, implementation of recovery activities often is slow, and only 10 percent of the listed species are known to be stable or increasing, while the status of most is unknown.

RECOVERY PLANS* BY CALENDAR YEAR

1977	4	1981	5
1978	7	1982	29
1979	13	1983	33
1980	11	1984	55

Total 152

*Several recovery plans cover more than one species.
Source: FWS, Office of Endangered Species.

Plants

Historically, plants have taken second place to animals in listing priorities. This has been a function of limited time, funds, and personnel; agency prejudices; and the greater visibility and appeal of animals. The 1983 FWS guidelines for listing priorities, however, do not differentiate between plants and animals, and recently FWS has been attempting to reduce the large backlog of plants to be listed. Though FWS does not have an overall count of the number of botanists it employs, the agency has been hiring more of them in recent years.

By the end of 1983, 71 plant species had been listed. By the end of 1984, the number was 86. Thirty-two plant species have approved recovery plans.*

CURRENT ISSUES

Funding and Personnel

A review of basic statistics for the Endangered Species Program shows the magnitude of identified work that remains to be accomplished. More than 3,800 species of plants and animals have been identified as candidates for listing, and Defenders of Wildlife has calculated that at present listing rates, 166 years will be required to list current candidates.[18] Other aspects of the program also are lagging. By the end of 1984, critical habitat had been determined for only 64 of the 331 listed United States species, and only 157 recovery plans had been approved.

In the early years of the Reagan administration, the budget process was used as a

---

*As of October 1, 1984, the 32 plant plans constitute 17 percent of the 183 plans in effect.

method of undermining the program, which was viewed as an obstacle to economic progress. In FY 1982, for example, the administration's budget requests for all categories of the endangered species program except Section 7 consultations represented an overall 35 percent decrease in the amounts requested by the Carter administration for that year. Congress, however, appropriated substantially greater amounts than were requested. Even with the congressional increases, the total appropriation was 22 percent below that for the previous fiscal year.

FY 1982 PRESIDENT'S BUDGET REQUESTS FOR ENDANGERED SPECIES (FWS AND STATE GRANTS) AND FINAL APPROPRIATIONS ($000)

	Budget Requests				Congressional Action		
						Increase	% Change
				%	Final	over Reagan	From
Activity	Carter	Reagan	Difference	Change	Appropriation	Request	Reagan
Section 15 (FWS):							
Listing	$ 3.443	$ 1.957	−$1.486	−43	$ 1.987	+$30	+2
Law Enforcement	5.761	4.618	−1.143	−20	5.672	+1.054	+23
Consultation	2.380	2.413	+33	+1	2.459	+46	+2
Recovery (including							
Research &							
Development)	7.494	6.067	−1.427	−19	7.651	+1.584	+26
Section 6 (Grants)	3.920	0	−3.920	−100	0	0	—
Total	$22.998	$15.055	−$7.943	−35	$17.769	+$2.714	+18

Source: Defender's Report (see Reference 19. p. 5.)

Similarly reduced requests and similar congressional reactions characterized the endangered species budget in fiscal years 1983 and 1984. For fiscal year 1985, funding for the program increased markedly.

ENDANGERED SPECIES PROGRAM FUNDING

Fiscal Year	Administration's Request (in thousands)	Appropriation
1983	$16,550	$18,459
1984	17,361	19,947
1985	25,242	27,065

Progress in carrying out the endangered species program also is a function of the number of personnel tied to the program. The number of full-time equivalent employees has increased from 224 in FY 1981 to 405 by early FY 1985. This apparent growth is due more to changes in how FWS defines and allocates employee positions than it is to additions in the work force.

In its early years the Reagan administration proposed a severe cutback in the use of moneys from the Land and Water Conservation Fund to acquire habitat to be added to the National Wildlife Refuge System for listed species. This was part of an across-the-board strategy of reducing use of the fund for federal land acquisition. As noted by Defenders of Wildlife, "Overall, Land and Water Conservation Fund requests have fallen from an average $560 million during FY 1978 to FY 1981 to an average $85 million during FY 1982 to FY 1985."[20]

Despite all the controversy that has centered on its funding, the endangered species program, responsible for 331 United States species and nearly 200 recovery plans, receives only 4.6 percent of the total FWS budget. In contrast, the Wildlife Resources Program, responsible for managing 48 game bird species, seven nongame bird species, three marine mammal species, and a few damage-causing birds and mammals, receives 24.7 percent of the FWS budget. The Fisheries Program, which manages only 40 sport-fish species, receives 7.8 percent of the total FWS budget.

LAND AND WATER CONSERVATION FUND DISBURSEMENT FOR ENDANGERED AND THREATENED SPECIES

Fiscal Year	Administration Request (in thousands)	Congressional Appropriation (in thousands)
1981	$ 8,320	$ 7,658
		−9,291*
1982	-0-	1,900
1983	998	9,800
1984	-0-	27,400
1985	14,500	31,600

*This figure represents a rescission of funding. The Interior Department not only returned the amount appropriated in FY 1981 to the Treasury, but also $1,633,500 in unspent funds left over from the previous fiscal year.

Source: FWS, Office of Endangered Species.

Reintroductions

FWS sometimes reintroduces a species to former range where it has been extirpated or introduces one to new areas. Reintroductions have aroused some opposition. State officials in New Mexico, for example, expressed misgivings about the reintroduction of the whooping crane at Bosque del Apache National Wildlife Refuge because it might have an adverse effect on the hunting of other refuge birds. A reintroduction proposal in the draft recovery plan for the southern sea otter in California has triggered opposition from commercial fishermen concerned that establishment of additional populations of this threatened subspecies will accelerate the decline of the marketable shellfish on which the otter feeds. Oil and gas developers are concerned that the otter will interfere with their projects in coastal waters.*

To allay these kinds of concerns, Congress in the 1982 amendments to the Endangered Species Act made special provision for experimental (reintroduced or newly established) populations of listed species. Under Section 10(j), experimental populations are divided into those that are "essential to the continued existence of a species" and those that are nonessential. Reintroduced essential populations are to be treated as threatened species under the act even if the species as a whole is listed as endangered. A nonessential population is to be treated as if it were a species proposed to be listed, which means that critical habitat is not designated for the population. These changes were designed to give FWS flexibility in the management of experimental populations. Since Section 10(j) went into effect, one experimental-population action has been made final: a second population of the endangered Delmarva fox squirrel was established. A second proposal, for establishing experimental populations of the Colorado squawfish and the wound fin, currently is under consideration.

*At present, an environmental impact statement for the proposed reintroduction of the otter is being prepared, and the decision as to whether to carry it out will be made in 1985.

Status of Endangered Species Recovery Plans
October 1, 1984

The following Recovery Plans have been approved:

Alabama Cavefish 9/17/82
Alala (Hawaiian Crow) 10/28/82
Aleutian Canada Goose 3/7/79
American Crocodile 2/13/79
Antioch Dunes (2 P, 1A) 3/21/80
Appalachian Monkeyface Pearly Mussel
7/9/84
Arizona Trout 8/20/79
Attwater's Prairie Chicken 12/16/83
Bald Eagle (Chesapeake Population) 5/19/82
Bald Eagle (Northern States) 7/29/83
Bald Eagle (Southeastern States) 8/3/84
Bald Eagle (Southwest Population) 9/8/82
Bayou Darter 9/8/83
Big Bend Gambusia 9/19/84
Birdwing Pearly Mussel 7/9/84
Black-footed Ferret 6/25/78
Blue Pike 6/29/76
Blunt-nosed Leopard Lizard 4/18/80
Bonytail Chub 5/16/84
Bunched Arrowhead (P) 9/8/82
California Brown Pelican 2/3/83
California Condor 4/9/75
California Least Tern 4/2/80
Cape Sable Seaside Sparrow 4/6/83
Channel Islands Species (4P, 3A) 1/26/84
Chapman's Rhododendron (P) 9/8/83
Chittenango Ovate Amber Snail 3/24/83
Clay Phacelia (P) 4/12/82
Clear Creek Gambusia 1/14/82
Colorado Squawfish 3/16/78
Columbian White-tailed Deer 10/21/76
Comanche Springs Pupfish 9/2/81
Cui-ui 1/23/78
Culebra Island Giant Anole 1/28/83
Cumberland Bean Pearly Mussel 8/22/84
Cumberland Monkeyface Pearly mussel 7/9/84
Davis' Green Pitaya (P) 9/20/84
Delmarva Peninsula Fox Squirrel 11/6/79
Desert Slender Salamander 8/12/82
Devils Hole Pupfish 7/15/80
Dromedary Pearly Mussel 7/9/84
Dusky Seaside Sparrow 4/26/79
Eastern Brown Pelican 7/19/79
Eastern Cougar 8/2/82
Eastern Indigo Snake 4/22/82
Eastern Timber Wolf 6/5/78
Eureka Valley Dunes (2 P) 12/13/82
Everglade Kite 3/11/83

Fine-rayed Pigtoe Pearly Mussel 9/19/84
Flat-spired Three-toothed Snail 5/9/83
Florida Panther 12/16/81
Furbish Lousewort (P) 6/30/83
Gila Trout 1/12/79
Gila & Yaqui Topminnow (2 species) 3/15/84
Golden Coqui 4/19/84
Gray Bat 7/8/82
Greenback Cutthroat Trout 11/11/77
Green-blossom Pearly Mussel 7/9/84
Green Pitcher Plant (P) 5/11/83
Grizzly Bear 1/29/82
Gypsum Wild Buckwheat (P) 3/30/84
Hairy Rattleweed (Wild Indigo) 3/19/84
Harper's Beauty (P) 9/13/83
Hawaiian Forest Birds (4 species) 2/3/83
Hawaiian Hawk 5/9/84
Hawaiian Monk Seal (NMFS) 4/1/83
Hawaiian Sea Birds (2 species) 4/25/83
Hawaiian Vetch (*Vicia menziesii*) (P) 5/18/84
Hawaiian Waterbirds (3 species) 6/19/78
Higgins' Eye Mussel 7/29/83
Houston Toad 9/17/84
Humpback Chub 8/22/79
Indiana Bat 6/1/76
Iowa Pleistocene Snail 3/22/84
Kauai Forest Birds (6 species) 7/29/83
Kendall Warm Springs Dace 7/12/82
Kern Primrose Sphinx Moth 2/8/84
Key Deer 6/10/80
Kirtland's Warbler 10/22/76
Laysan Duck 12/17/82
Leopard Darter 9/20/84
Leatherback Sea Turtle (Sandy Point) 10/23/81
Light-footed Clapper Rail 7/3/79
Maryland Darter 2/2/82
Masked Bobwhite 2/15/78
Maui-Molakai Forest Birds (7 species) 5/30/84
McDonald's Rock-cress (P) 2/28/84
Mesa Verde Cactus (P) 3/30/84
Mexican Wolf 8/9/82
Mississippi Sandhill Crane 10/24/79
Moapa Dace 2/14/83
Mohave Tui Chub 9/12/84
Mona Boa 4/19/84
Mona Ground Iguana 4/19/84
Morro Bay Kangaroo Rat 8/18/82
Mountain Golden Heather (P) 9/14/83
Navasota Ladies'-tresses (P) 9/21/84

Nellie Cory Cactus (P) 9/20/84
Nene 2/14/83
Noonday Snail 9/7/84
Northern Monkshood (P) 9/23/83
Northern Rocky Mountain Wolf 5/28/80
Okaloosa Darter 10/23/81
Orange-footed Pearly Mussel 8/30/84
Oregon Silverspot Butterfly 9/22/82
Owens River Pupfish 9/17/84
Ozark Big-eared and Virginia Big-eared Bat
  (2 species) 5/8/84
Painted Snake Coiled Forest Snail 10/14/82
Pale Lilliput Pearly Mussel 8/22/84
Palila 1/23/78
Pahrump Killifish 3/17/80
Palos Verdes Blue Butterfly 1/19/84
Pecos Gambusia 5/9/83
Pebles Navajo Cactus (P) 3/30/84
Peregrine Falcon (Alaska) 10/4/82
Peregrine Falcon (Eastern) 8/20/79
Peregrine Falcon (Pacific) 10/12/82
Peregrine Falcon (Rocky Mountain/South-
  west) 8/3/77
Persistent Trillium (P) 3/27/84
Plymouth Red-bellied Turtle 3/26/81
Puerto Rican Parrot 11/30/82
Puerto Rican Plain Pigeon 10/14/82
Puerto Rican Whip-poor-will 4/19/84
Raven's Manzanita (P) 7/10/84
Red-cockaded Woodpecker 8/24/79
Red Hills Salamander 11/23/83
Red Wolf 7/12/82
Robbins' Cinquefoil (P) 7/22/83
Rough Pigtoe Pearly Mussel 8/6/84

San Diego Mesa Mint (P) 7/10/84
San Joaquin Kit Fox 1/31/83
Santa Cruz Long-toed Salamander 9/28/77
Schaus Swallowtail Butterfly 11/17/82
Shiny Pigtoe Pearly Mussel 7/9/84
Slackwater Darter 3/8/84
Slender Chub 7/29/83
Snail Darter 5/5/83
Socorro Isopod 2/17/82
Sonoran Pronghorn 12/30/82
Southern Sea Otter 2/3/82
Spotfin Chub 11/21/83
St. Croix Ground Lizard 3/29/84
Stock Island Tree Snail 3/8/83
Tennessee Purple Coneflower (P) 2/14/82
Truckee Barberry (P) 6/20/84
Unarmored Threespine Stickleback 12/27/77
Valley Elderberry Longhorn Beetle 8/1/84
Virginia Fringed Mountain Snail 5/9/83
Virginia Round-leaf Birch (P) 3/3/82
Warm Springs Pupfish 11/10/76
Watercress Darter 6/25/80
West Indian Manatee 4/15/80
White Wartyback Pearly Mussel 9/19/84
Whooping Crane 1/23/83
Woundfin 7/9/79
Yellowfin Madtom 6/23/83
Yellow-shouldered Blackbird 5/25/83
Yuma Clapper Rail 2/4/83
Total:
      Plans   158
      Species   183
A = Animal species
P = Plant

LEGISLATION

No legislative changes were made in the program during the 98th Congress. The 1985 reauthorization is not expected to result in many drastic changes, but one major controversy could surface: an attempt by western water users to amend the act so that it does not limit their use of water under state water laws.

This concern was sparked most recently by the federal court decision in *Riverside Irrigation District v. Andrews*, discussed below. The possible legislative consequences of this decision, which dealt with both the Endangered Species Act and the 404 permit program of the Clean Water Act, are discussed in the chapter on wetlands.

LEGAL DEVELOPMENTS

The Endangered Species Act has spawned extensive litigation. In recent years, this litigation has focused on the responsibilities imposed upon federal agencies by Section 7 and the scope and effect of the prohibitions imposed on private citizens by Section 9.

Four recent cases demonstrate the broad authority and responsibility imposed upon federal agencies by Section 7. *Carson-Truckee Water Conservancy District v. Clark*[20] reviewed the Interior Department's decision to operate the Stampede Dam in California so as to provide stream flows adequate to conserve two listed fish species, the cui-ui and the Lahontan cutthroat trout. This meant selling no water from the dam and reservoir project. Water users in Nevada sought to compel sale of water from the reservoir on the grounds that some water could be sold without jeopardizing the continued existence of the fish. The Ninth Circuit, however, affirmed the secretary's decision to give first priority to conservation of the fish, holding that, under Section 7, he must not only avoid "jeopardizing" protected species, but also act to promote their recovery.

In *Riverside Irrigation District v. Andrews*,[21] Under Section 7(a)(2), a Colorado district court reviewed the decision of the Corps of Engineers to deny permission under the Clean Water Act for a dam on a tributary of the South Platte River. The Corps had found that the dam would adversely affect whooping crane habitat 250 miles downstream. The dam builders argued that the Clean Water Act did not authorize the Corps to take any action that would affect water rights under state law. The court ruled, however, that such authority existed in Section 7 of the Endangered Species Act.

In *Roosevelt Campobello International Park Commission v. the Environmental Protection Agency (EPA)*,[22] the First Circuit reviewed EPA's issuance of a Clean Water Act permit for construction of an oil refinery and deep-water port at Eastport, Maine. Both FWS and NMFS had issued biological opinions finding that oilspills from the project were likely to jeopardize the continued existence of bald eagles and right and humpback whales. EPA rejected these determinations, however, finding that the risk of oilspills was "minute." The First Circuit disagreed. Citing the requirement, added in 1979, that agencies use "the best scientific and commmercial data available" in determining whether their actions are likely to jeopardize a protected species, the court held that EPA could not issue the permit until it had obtained "real time simulations" of tanker traffic to and from the refinery, because such studies "would contribute a more precise appreciation of risks."

When reviewing the act's proscriptions on taking and sale of protected species (Section 9), the courts reached mixed results. In *Sierra Club v. Clark*,[23] a Minnesota federal court reviewed the secretary's approval of regulations allowing a sport trapping season for gray wolves. The court held that such takings could be permitted only "in the extraordinary case where population pressures . . . cannot otherwise be relieved." The court also overturned regulations relaxing the restrictions on government take of wolves in areas with predation problems. On appeal, the Eighth Circuit affirmed the district court's ban on sport trapping but remanded the case for further consideration of the reasonableness of the predator control program.[24]

In *U.S. v. Dion*,[25] the Eighth Circuit reviewed the prosecution of several Indians for taking and sale of bald eagles. The defendants argued that their tribe's treaties with the United States conferred upon them the right to take and sell bald eagles. FWS responded that any such treaty right had been abrogated by the Endangered Species Act. Sitting *en banc*, the Eighth Circuit held that the Indians' treaties allowed continuation of their traditional activities, including the take but not sale of bald eagles. Finding no express congressional intent to abrogate these treaty rights in the language or history of the Endangered Species Act, the court held that the Indians could not be prosecuted for exercise of those rights. The case was therefore remanded to a panel of the court for determinations whether the alleged activities were so protected.

In a pair of cases,[26] *H.J. Justin & Sons. v. Deukmejian* and *Man Hing Ivory and Imports v. Deukmejian*, the Ninth Circuit has reviewed California's efforts to supplement the federal prohibitions contained in Section 9. The court held that the state can regulate or ban trade in species not listed under the federal statute. But the state cannot forbid trade in listed species (in this case, the African elephant), if that trade has been authorized by federal regulations.

Finally, the courts have reviewed the new "incidental take" provisions (Section 10(a)), added to the act in 1982. In *Friends of Endangered Species v. Jantzen*,[27] a California district court considered the San Bruno Mountain project, the first development project approved under those provisions. After lengthy negotiations, the project developers had agreed to a "conservation plan" for the endangered mission blue butterfly whose critical habitat included the project site. Opponents challenged the methodology used by FWS in approving the plan and the adequacy of review under the National Environmental Policy Act. The court, however, affirmed the FWS finding that, although the project would cause some incidental take of the endangered butterfly, it nonetheless would yield a net benefit to the species by placing 74 percent of its habitat under public control. The court upheld the Interior Department's approval of the project.

RESOURCE STATUS

The period during which the Endangered Species Program has been in existence — less than 20 years since inception of the list and less than a dozen since the 1973 act provided the program with its basic authorities — is too short for a large number of recoveries to have been achieved. Until the program builds a more substantial track record, the act's effectiveness is difficult to assess.

FWS has a rudimentary system for measuring the results of its recovery efforts. Each recovery plan lists steps to be implemented during the next three to five years. These steps are given one of three priorities. The highest priority is assigned to actions that must be taken to prevent extinction of the species. Second priority actions are those that maintain the current status of the species. Last are the actions that would assure progress toward complete recovery. Theoretically, priority one actions are taken first, but in actual practice priority items two and three often are executed before priority one steps.

Twice yearly, FWS solicits from its regional offices reports that give the highlights achieved in implementing recovery plans. These approved data, however, are not aggregated into a single assessment for species such as the bald eagle, for which recovery efforts are under way in more than one region. Nor does FWS prepare a summary assessment of whether each listed species has declined or improved in status since the previous report.

FWS is in the process of developing an automated data-processing system to track the implementation of recovery plans, but no firm date is set for its completion. The system would help ensure that each step in a given plan is carried out on schedule. For the near term, implementation of this system is probably the single most important action FWS could take to provide for meaningful assessment of the endangered species resource.

FWS is developing one additional automated data base, the Endangered Species Information System, which it hopes to have ready for use in FWS regional offices in FY 1986 and later for other federal agencies. The purpose of the system is to provide a broad range of biological, locational, status, and other information on species listed as threatened or endangered. The system will have detailed narratives and key-word files for information searches. It also will be cross referenced with certain other existing data bases.

REFERENCES

1. Greta Nilsson, *The Endangered Species Handbook* (Washington, D.C.: The Animal Welfare Institute, 1983), pp. 2-3.
2. Edward O. Wilson, *Biophilia* (Cambridge: Harvard University Press, 1984), p. 122.
3. 87 Stat. 884 (codified at 16 U.S.C.A. 1531-1543).
4. 31 Stat. 187, 32 Stat. 285 (codified at 16 U.S.C.A. 701,702).
5. Much of the information about the inception of the captive propagation effort for the whooping crane derives from a telephone conversation with Dr. Erickson in January 1985.
6. 80 Stat. 926 (repealed 1973).
7. 83 Stat. 275.
8. March 3, 1973, 27 U.S.T. 1087, T.I.A.S. No. 8249, Art. II §1.
9. 87 Stat. 884 (codified at 16 U.S.C.A. 1531-1543).
10. 96 Stat. 1411 (codified at 16 U.S.C.A. 1533(b)(6)(c)(ii).
11. U.S. Department of the Interior, "Endangered and Threatened Wildlife and Plants: Review of Plant Taxa for Listing as Endangered or Threatened Species," *Federal Register*, vol. 45, No. 242, Monday, December 15, 1980, pp. 82480-82569.
12. U.S. Fish and Wildlife Service, Service Management Plan (revised), September 1982.
13. U.S. Fish and Wildlife Service, Endangered Species Program Management Document, April 1983.
14. *Federal Register*, September 21, 1983, pp. 43098-43105.
15. U.S. Fish and Wildlife Service, Endangered Species Technical Bulletin, vol. 2, no. 11, February, 1977, p. 6.
16. For more details on endangered species research techniques, see Nathaniel P. Reed and Dennis Drabelle, *The United States Fish and Wildlife Service* (Boulder: Westview Press, 1984), pp. 110-19.
17. Testimony of Lynn A. Greenwalt before the Subcommittee on Interior and Related Agencies of the Committee on Appropriations, U.S. House of Representatives, May 5, 1983, p. 22.
18. Defenders of Wildlife, "Saving Endangered Species: A Report and Plan for Action," May 1984, p. 15.
19. Ibid., p. 11.
20. *Carson-Truckee Water Conservancy District v. Clark*, 741 F.2d 257 (9th Cir. 1984), *cert den* U.S.L.W., 105 S. Ct. 1842 (1985).
21. *Riverside Irrigation District v. Andrews*, 568 F. Supp. (D.Col. 1983), *aff'd* 758 F.2d 508 (10th Cir. 1985).
22. *Roosevelt Campobello International Park Commission v. U.S. Environmental Protection Agency*, 684 F.2d 1043 (1st Cir. 1982)
23. *Sierra Club v. Clark*, 577 F. Supp. 783 (D. Minn. 1984).
24. *Sierra Club v. Clark*, 755 F.2d 608 (8th Cir. 1985).
25. *U.S. v. Dion*, 752 F.2d 1261 (8th Cir. 1985). The Ninth Circuit has held otherwise. *U.S. v. Fryberg*, 622 F.2d 1010 (9th Cir. 1980).
26. *H.J. Justin & Sons v. Deukmejian*, 702 F.2d 758 (9th Cir. 1983); *Man Hing Ivory and Imports v. Deukmejian*, 702 F.2d 760 (9th Cir. 1983).
27. *Friends of Endangered Species v. Jantzen*, 20 E.R.C. 1645, 1811 (N.D. Cal. 1984).

The federal fisheries program protects and manages the many species important both to commercial and weekend fishermen.

Inland Fisheries Management

by *William J. Chandler*
W.J. Chandler Associates

INTRODUCTION

INLAND FISH* ARE managed cooperatively by the federal government and
the states, although primary responsibility for the conservation and management of
fish in state territorial waters rests with the states. Federal involvement in both inland
and ocean fisheries management began in 1871.

Federal fishery policy has evolved into two distinct bodies of authority: one for
inland fishery resources, implemented principally by the U.S. Fish and Wildlife
Service (FWS), Department of the Interior; and one for ocean fisheries, implemented
by the National Marine Fisheries Service (NMFS), a unit of the National Oceanic and
Atmospheric Administration, Department of Commerce.

The principal exception to this division of authority is jurisdiction over anadromous fish, migratory species such as salmon and shad which spend part of their lives in
freshwater and part in estuary and ocean waters. Over the years both FWS and NMFS
have been given various responsibilities — some exclusive, some overlapping, and
some joint — for anadromous species. However, in no instance has the federal
government pre-empted state authority to regulate the harvest of anadromous species
in state internal waters.** In addition, because some anadromous fish spawn in United
States waters but are harvested in ocean waters by both United States and foreign
fishermen, the federal government has found it necessary to conclude several international treaties to conserve these stocks. Thus, the management of anadromous species
is a highly complex, cooperative venture involving federal agencies, states, foreign

---

*"Inland fish" generally is used to mean all fish species found in the internal fresh waters of the
United States, including those in lakes, rivers, streams, ponds, and estuaries. Ocean fish
includes marine species harvested in coastal, ocean, and high-seas fisheries. For management
purposes, anadromous fish may be considered as either inland or ocean species.

**In contrast, the management of migratory birds was pre-empted by the federal government in
1916 because of the inability of the states to collectively manage species that crossed state and
international borders. In certain limited situations, the federal government may pre-empt state
authority to regulate the harvest of certain anadromous fish species, but the exercise of such
authority is the exception, not the rule.

nations, and American Indian tribes that have treaty rights to harvest anadromous fish in certain fisheries.

In addition, federal land-managing agencies also play a significant role in the management of fish within their waters. Generally, such management is conducted in accordance with state laws and regulations, because the states have legal responsibility and authority for managing fish on all federal lands except national wildlife refuges. Federal agencies, however, are responsible for managing the habitat their lands provide.

About 750 species of fish, including anadromous species, are found in the inland waters of the United States. FWS management activities focus on about 40 species or groups of species, principally those with commercial, sport, or Indian ceremonial value, and on another 51 species that have been listed under the Endangered Species Act as threatened or endangered with extinction.* This chapter covers fishery resources of sport or commercial value that are managed to some degree by the FWS Fishery Resources Program. The role of NMFS in the management of anadromous species also will be discussed.

Through its Fishery Resources Program, FWS propagates fish for stocking, conducts research, provides technical assistance to federal and state agencies and Indian tribes, administers a program of federal grants to the states for anadromous species conservation, mitigates fishery losses caused by federal water resource projects, and enforces federal fish conservation laws. Approximately half of the Fishery Resources Program for FY 1985 is allocated to fish propagation at federal hatcheries and another 25 percent to research.

HISTORY AND LEGISLATIVE AUTHORITY

Federal involvement in the management of inland fish has evolved piecemeal over the past 115 years. The scores of appropriation acts and other laws that have been passed can be grouped into six categories:

1. Legislation that established a U.S. Fish and Fisheries Commission in 1871 and subsequent appropriations acts that expanded its activities to include, among other things, the propagation of fish at federal hatcheries.
2. Laws that guided the fishery bureaucracy through several organizational transformations.
3. Laws that deal with avoiding or mitigating the adverse affects of water resource projects on fish.
4. Statutes aimed at conserving and managing important fisheries or fish species or at mitigating specific fishery losses.
5. Laws that authorize nationwide fish conservation and management activities, including activities on federal lands.
6. Various statutes authorizing fish surveys, investigations, and general research.

The U.S. Fish Commission
Federal involvement in fishery resource management began in 1871 with the creation of a U.S. Commissioner of Fish and Fisheries.[1] The first commissioner, Spencer Fullerton Baird of the Smithsonian Institution, was charged with investigating

---

*The number of listed species is current to February 1, 1985. All endangered species, including fish, are the responsibility of the FWS Endangered Species Program.

the decline of food fishes of the coasts and lakes, ascertaining the causes of decline, and making recommendations regarding the protection of fish stocks.

The first federal fish hatchery was established in 1872 along the McCloud River at Baird, California, for the purpose of propagating salmon.[2] Thereafter, Congress established numerous federal hatcheries around the country to help stem the decline of local fisheries.* Today, fish propagation remains one of the principal activities of the FWS Fishery Resources Program.

After establishment of the federal fish commission, numerous states created their own commissions. Together, the federal government and the states launched far-reaching propagation and transplantation campaigns that included augmentation of salmon stocks in the Pacific Northwest, introduction into United States waters of non-native species such as the European carp and brown trout, and translocation within the United States of native species such as the rainbow trout and salmon. The federal commission also encouraged state fish commissions to introduce black bass into ponds, streams, and lakes throughout the country.[3]

Evolution of the Fish Bureaucracy

In 1903, the fish commission was transferred into a newly established Department of Commerce and Labor and was renamed the Bureau of Fisheries.[4] Like its predecessor, the bureau's function was to conduct surveys and research, collect statistical information on fisheries, develop fish-culture methods, and propagate fish for stocking purposes. In 1939, the bureau was transferred to the Department of the Interior, where it was merged in 1940 with the Bureau of Biological Survey, another transferred agency, into the new Fish and Wildlife Service.

The merger of the fisheries bureau into an agency whose primary mission was conservation was unsatisfactory to commercial fishermen, who eventually lobbied to establish a fish bureaucracy more attuned to their concerns. Legislation was introduced in the House in 1956 to remove all fisheries activities from Interior and place them in a separate U.S. Fisheries Commission. The bill was strongly opposed by conservation organizations that wanted fisheries management to remain with FWS because of the agency's emphasis on resource conservation. A compromise was made that split FWS into two agencies: the Bureau of Sport Fisheries and Wildlife and the Bureau of Commercial Fisheries, both of which reported to a single commissioner of fish and wildlife.[5]

Yet another reorganization took place in 1970 when President Nixon created the National Oceanic and Atmospheric Administration (NOAA) within the Department of Commerce to manage all activities relating to the conservation and development of ocean resources. Most functions of the FWS Bureau of Commercial Fisheries, including activities related to certain marine mammals and fish, regulation and development of the commercial fishing industry, and the promotion of marine sport fishing, were transferred to NOAA's National Marine Fisheries Service (NMFS). The Bureau of Sport Fisheries and Wildlife retained authorities related to inland fisheries, both commercial and sport.[6] The bureau was renamed the U.S. Fish and Wildlife Service in 1974.[7]

One anomaly of the 1970 reorganization is that anadromous fish species, which utilize marine, estuarine, and freshwater environments, were not assigned to either agency exclusively but rather to both. Discussions were held at the time about placing

*Private individuals and states also established hatcheries, commencing in the 1860s.

anadromous responsibilities with just one agency, but no agreement could be reached between Commerce and Interior (see the Current Trends section for a more detailed discussion of anadromous jurisdiction).

Avoiding and Mitigating the Impacts of Dams on Fish

Commencing around the turn of the century, the federal government began sponsoring the construction of dams throughout the West, first for irrigation purposes under the Reclamation Act of 1902[8] and later for power, flood control, water supply, and recreational use. These dams often caused precipitous declines of various fish stocks, especially anadromous stocks, which migrate far inland to spawn.

As the adverse impacts of dams on fisheries became widely recognized, Congress attempted to do something about the problem. The Federal Water Power Act of 1920[9] established a Federal Power Commission, known today as the Federal Energy Regulatory Commission, and authorized it to issue licenses to private parties for the construction, operation, and maintenance of dams, water conduits, reservoirs, and other irrigation and power developments. The law directed the commission to issue licenses for projects on certain federal lands only after a finding that a license would not be incompatible with the purposes for which the lands were set aside or acquired. Any license issued must stipulate the conditions required by the federal land-managing agency to protect adequately its land.

In addition, the law authorized the secretary of Commerce to recommend the inclusion of fishways in navigation facilities constructed as part of a dam or water diversion project. Later, this authority was transferred to the Interior secretary. Acceptance of the secretary's recommendations by the navigation authority, originally discretionary, was made mandatory by the Public Utility Act of 1935,[10] which amended the Power Act.

Congress addressed the adverse impacts of dam projects on fish more comprehensively in the Fish and Wildlife Coordination Act of 1934.[11] The act required federal dam-building or licensing agencies to consult with the Bureau of Fisheries before issuing a license or commencing construction and to include fish lifts and ladders as part of the project if they were deemed necessary and "economically practicable." The act also authorized a variety of other measures for the benefit of fish. These included directing the secretary of Commerce to assist federal, state, and other agencies in rearing, stocking, and increasing the supply of fish and in combating fish diseases; in undertaking research on the effects of water pollution on fish and shellfish; in using federal water impoundments for fish-culture stations where such use is not inconsistent with the primary use of the project; and in surveying fish resources on all federal lands.

Amendments to the Fish and Wildlife Coordination Act in 1946 and 1958 strengthened federal requirements for fish mitigation. As amended, the act requires water resource agencies to give "equal consideration" to fish and wildlife conservation in project development; to consult with FWS, NMFS, and the states on all projects for the control or modification of streams or water bodies in order to determine how to prevent loss of or damage to fish and wildlife resources; and to give "full consideration" to the recommendations of the secretaries of the Interior and Commerce. In addition, the law requires water resource agencies to include "justifiable" wildlife and fish protection measures in their projects; to assess wildlife losses and benefits associated with all new projects recommended for construction; and to provide for the conservation, maintenance, and management of wildlife resources in project lands and waters. The act also authorized the secretary of the Interior to recommend wildlife conservation measures for small water projects constructed under the Watershed Protection and Flood Prevention Act, but incorporation of these measures is left to the discretion of the secretary of Agriculture and the local private organization sponsoring the project.

Another mitigation measure, the Estuary Protection Act of 1968,[12] requires the Interior secretary to make recommendation on how water development plans and projects submitted to Congress by other federal agencies can be designed to protect estuarine resources. This provision is supposed to provide a coordinating mechanism to assist in the preservation of rapidly diminishing estuary areas, habitat for many saltwater and anadromous fish species. However, since the law does not give the secretary any more authority than he has under the Coordination Act, its effects have been minimal.

More recently, Congress passed the Public Utility Regulatory Policies Act, amending the Federal Power Act and establishing a program to expedite the licensing by the Federal Energy Regulatory Commission of small hydroelectric power projects in connection with existing dams. The act authorizes the commission to grant license exemptions to hydro projects of five megawatts or less and to man-made conduits used for the generation of 15 megawatts or less. However, the act requires the commission to consult with FWS and the state fish and wildlife agency in accordance with the Fish and Wildlife Coordination Act and to include as part of the license exemption "such terms and conditions as the Fish and Wildlife Service and the State agency each determine are appropriate to prevent loss of, or damage to, such resources and to otherwise carry out the purposes of" the Fish and Wildlife Coordination Act.[13]

The Conservation and Management of Significant Fisheries

Columbia River Basin. Congress has passed a number of measures to stem the decline of significant fisheries and fish species around the nation and to mitigate losses caused by federal dams. The first area to be addressed was the salmon and steelhead fishery in the Columbia River Basin. The Mitchell Act of 1938 authorized the secretary of Commerce to establish salmon hatcheries in Washington, Oregon, and Idaho and directed him to conduct whatever investigations were necessary to facilitate conservation of the basin fishery, to improve feeding and spawning habitat, to facilitate fish migration over obstructions, and "to perform all other activities necessary for the conservation of fish in the Columbia River Basin in accordance with law."[14] The act was amended in 1946 to permit transfer of federal funds to the states for their cooperative assistance in fish conservation activities.

Under authority of the Mitchell Act, the secretary of Commerce, in cooperation with FWS, other federal agencies, the states, and Indian tribes with treaty fishing rights in the basin, conducts the Columbia River Fisheries Development Program.* The main purpose of the program is to increase the abundance of the basin's steelhead trout and five species of salmon, principally through the artificial propagation and release of fish from 22 hatcheries and three rearing ponds. Since 1949, some $147 million has been spent on the program.**

Lower Snake River Compensation Plan. In addition to the general, basinwide conservation program authorized by the Mitchell Act, Congress has passed specific legislation dealing with the Lower Snake River, a major tributary to the Columbia. Between 1960 and 1975, the federal government constructed four power dams on the

---

*Authority for administering the Mitchell Act was given to the secretary of the Interior as a result of the 1939 transfer of the Bureau of Fisheries to Interior, but was returned to Commerce when NMFS was created in 1970.
**Through FY 1984. Most of the work accomplished has been for the benefit of coho and chinook salmon.

Lower Snake. Completion of the first structure in 1962 was followed a few years later by a marked decline in the populations of salmon and steelhead trout even though fish ladders had been installed in the dams.* By 1977, dam-related fishery losses were calculated at $35 million annually.

Congress passed legislation to mitigate fish and wildlife losses in 1976. Section 102 of the Water Resources Development Act of 1976[15] authorized the Lower Snake River Fish and Wildlife Compensation Plan. The major elements of the plan include construction by the U.S. Army Corps of Engineers, and operation by the secretary of the Interior, of 22 fishery installations, including 11 hatcheries, and the acquisition and development of lands for habitat development and public access to the fishery. Most of the completed fishery installations are operated and maintained by the states under cooperative agreement with FWS. Completion of all facilities is scheduled for 1988.

Other Pacific Salmon Conservation Measures. Congress has passed two other pieces of legislation applicable to anadromous fish conservation in the Pacific Northwest. The Salmon and Steelhead Conservation and Enhancement Act of 1980[16] was enacted to deal with several federal court decisions in the 1970s that determined that treaties signed in the 1850s entitled certain American Indian tribes to half of the allowable catch of salmon and steelhead trout in the Washington and Oregon portions of the Columbia River Basin and in certain marine and inland fisheries of western Washington. These rulings threatened the economic viability of the commercial salmon fishing industry and threw state programs and procedures for harvest allocation and fishery management into turmoil.

The Salmon and Steelhead Conservation Act established a compensation scheme for commercial fishermen who could no longer maintain their businesses and sought to enhance planning and coordination among salmon and steelhead managers in order to help prevent a further decline of the fishery and to increase fish stocks so that as many fishermen as possible could use the resource. It established the Washington State and Columbia River conservation areas for fishery management purposes; created the Salmon and Steelhead Advisory Commission under authority of the secretary of Commerce and made NMFS a voting member, FWS a nonvoting member; and authorized the commission to prepare a report with recommendations for the "development of a management structure (including effective procedures, mechanisms, and institutional arrangements) for the effective coordination of research, enhancement, management and enforcement policies for the salmon and steelhead resources of the Columbia River and Washington conservation areas, and for the resolution of disputes between management entities. . . ." The statute requires the secretary of Commerce, in consultation with the secretary of the Interior, to approve the report. Once the report is approved, the act authorizes the secretary of the Interior to provide financial assistance to the states and the Indian tribal governments for the preparation of fish enhancement plans and projects if they agree to abide by the report and coordinate fish management efforts. The statute also requires the secretary of the Interior, in consultation with Commerce, to monitor and evaluate all enhancement projects. All state and Indian plans must meet certain standards prescribed by the secretary of the Interior before he approves them. Appropriations of up to $70 million for salmon projects and $14 million for steelhead projects are authorized for the period 1982 to 1992. Federal assistance for project implementation is limited to 50 percent of the total cost.

The report establishing the management structure for the Columbia River Basin

---

*It was later determined that a substantial loss of juvenile fish occurs when they pass through dam turbines during downstream migration.

fishery has been prepared by the advisory commission and is expected to be approved by the secretary of Commerce in 1985. As yet, no enhancement grants have been made.

The other Pacific salmon conservation measure is the Pacific Northwest Electric Power Planning and Conservation Act of 1980.[17] This law is intended to encourage the conservation and efficient use of electric power and the development of natural resources in areas served by the Federal Columbia River Power System, which is administered by the Bonneville Power Authority. Among other provisions, the act requires the development of regional plans and programs for "protecting, mitigating, and enhancing fish and wildlife resources" in the Columbia River and its tributaries in the states of Washington, Oregon, Idaho, and Montana.

The law establishes a Pacific Northwest Electric Power and Conservation Planning Council consisting of representatives of the four states and requires it to prepare and maintain a fish and wildlife program to deal with the adverse affects of hydroelectric dams.* The council must consult with NMFS, FWS, state fish and wildlife agencies, Indian tribes, and others in preparing the program. Once the program is completed, the act requires the Bonneville Power Authority to use its legal and financial authorities to protect, mitigate, and enhance fish and wildlife adversely affected by any Columbia River System hydroelectric facility in a manner consistent with the wildlife program. The act requires other federal water resource agencies — the Corps of Engineers, Bureau of Reclamation, Federal Energy Regulatory Commission — to exercise their water resource management responsibilities in a manner "consistent with the purposes of this Act and other applicable laws, to adequately protect, mitigate, and enhance fish and wildlife . . . in a manner that provides equitable treatment for such fish and wildlife."

The council's wildlife program, first issued in 1982, contains 220 measures designed to benefit fish and wildlife.[18] Administration of about 100 of these is assigned to the Bonneville Power Authority for funding. The remainder are assigned to other federal, state, and Indian agencies and entities. The power authority from FY 1981 to FY 1984 spent $35.5 million on fish and wildlife projects required by the act.

The Great Lakes and Upper Colorado River Fisheries. Congress confronted two other significant fishery problems in the 1950s: the decline of important fish species in the Great Lakes and fish losses caused by a series of dams constructed in the Upper Colorado River Basin. The five Great Lakes once supported a substantial commercial fishery. Important species included lake trout, sauger, walleye, and yellow perch. All of these species suffered substantial declines in numbers because of overexploitation, pollution, predation by the sea lamprey, and other factors. In 1954, the United States signed a treaty with Canada, the "Convention on Great Lakes Fisheries,"[19] which established a Great Lakes Fishery Commission in order to control sea lamprey depredations and to coordinate and conduct research designed to maintain sustained production of significant commercial and sport species.** The treaty was implemented by the Great Lakes Fisheries Act of 1956,[20] which authorizes the secretary of the Interior to undertake a sea lamprey control program and other actions on behalf of the United States commissioners. The sea lamprey was brought under control by 1962, but fish-stock restoration is far from complete.

In 1956, Congress authorized construction of the Colorado River Storage Pro-

---

*The wildlife program does not address activities such as irrigation, logging, and other practices that have degraded fish habitat.
**The commission has no power to establish any catch quotas.

ject,[21] a series of dams and related facilities designed to harness the waters of the Upper Colorado for irrigation, flood control, power generation, and water supply. The act directs the secretary of the Interior to "investigate, plan, construct, operate and maintain" public recreation facilities to conserve wildlife and other values. It also requires the secretary to construct and maintain facilities to mitigate losses of fish and wildlife and to improve the fishery through propagation and release of fish. Two fish and wildlife hatcheries were established in connection with the project in order to propagate kokanee salmon and rainbow, cutthroat, and brook trout for release in reservoirs and tailwaters.

Anadromous Fish Conservation. The Mitchell Act established a conservation program for anadromous fish, but it applied only to stocks in the Columbia River Basin. Since anadromous stocks were declining in other regions as well, Congress passed comprehensive legislation to deal with the problem. The Anadromous Fish Conservation Act of 1965[22] established a federal-state cooperative grant program for conserving and restoring outside the Columbia River Basin anadromous species* that had been depleted by federal, state, and private water resource projects or for which the United States has international treaty obligations. Both the secretaries of the Interior and Commerce are authorized to sign cooperative agreements with the states and to share the implementation cost of conservation projects. In addition, each agency is authorized to conduct research, biological surveys, and engineering investigations; clear streams; construct and operate devices to protect fish habitat and migration; and construct and operate hatcheries to conserve anadromous species.**

Congress authorized $211 million for state grants through FY 1984, of which $88.9 million was appropriated, about half through NMFS and half through FWS. States use their grant funds for construction, research, fish propagation, facility operation and maintenance, coordination, and planning. The principal species benefiting from state programs are coho and chinook salmon, steelhead trout, Atlantic salmon, striped bass, river herring, and shad.

Atlantic Salmon Restoration. One Atlantic coast anadromous species that has received special attention from FWS is the Atlantic salmon, which was nearly extirpated from the rivers of New England by dams, pollution, and habitat destruction. In 1947, Maine launched a salmon restoration effort, and other New England states eventually followed suit. FWS joined this effort in 1967 and now is the lead federal agency in the restoration program.

Atlantic salmon restoration is threatened by commercial take of salmon in ocean waters off the coasts of North America and Greenland, a fishery that intercepts salmon stocks that spawn in United States waters. To lessen this threat, the United States concluded a "Convention for the Conservation of Salmon in the North Atlantic Ocean"[23] with Canada and several European nations that fish for salmon. The treaty establishes a North Atlantic Salmon Conservation Organization to regulate the taking of salmon in ocean waters and to promote the conservation and enhancement of all salmon stocks that use the North Atlantic. The treaty also establishes a North American Commission comprised of certain New England states and Canadian provinces to improve cooperation in the management of Atlantic salmon stocks that spawn in one country but are harvested by the other.

The Atlantic Salmon Convention Act of 1982,[24] which implements the treaty,

---

*The act applies to all anadromous species and to other fish species in the Great Lakes and Lake Champlain that ascend streams to spawn.
**Administration of the Anadromous Fish Conservation Act was jointly assigned to Commerce and Interior under the reorganization plan of 1970.

gives the secretary of Commerce, in cooperation with the Interior secretary, the lead role in supplying information on salmon originating in United States waters and in executing other technical and regulatory functions required by the convention. Any United States objection to or approval of salmon conservation measures required by the organization must have the concurrence of both secretaries.

More recently, Congress has approved an interstate compact between four New England states for restoring salmon to their rivers. The compact is discussed in the section on legislation.

North Atlantic Striped Bass. Another species that has drawn special federal attention is the striped bass. The North Atlantic race of this prized commercial and sport fish, found in coastal and estuarine waters from New England to North Carolina, declined precipitously during the 1970s. In response, Congress amended the Anadromous Fish Conservation Act in 1979 to authorize a joint NMFS-FWS study of the problem.[25] Although no definitive reasons for the decline have been identified, the NMFS-FWS report issued in FY 1984 recommended harvest restrictions to help restore the population. Congress passed legislation to reduce harvests the same year (see legislation section of this chapter and the separate chapter on striped bass).

Nationwide Fish Conservation Programs

Grants to States for Sport Fish Restoration. As recreational fishing grew after World War II, the federal government launched a major grant program to assist states in providing more public sport-fishing opportunities. The Federal Aid in Sport Fish Restoration Act of 1950, commonly referred to as the Dingell-Johnson Act,[26] authorized a permanent program of federal financial assistance to the states for the restoration and management of fish that have "material value in connection with sport or recreation in the marine and/or fresh waters of the United States." Under the act, receipts collected from a 10-percent excise tax on fishing tackle and other gear are allocated yearly to the states and territories for the management of sport-fish resources. States are reimbursed for up to 75 percent of the cost of implementing projects that meet broad federal statutory guidelines and requirements.

States have wide latitude in their selection of projects. Nearly 400 projects are funded each year for such activities as research on fishery problems, surveys and inventories, acquisition of fish habitat, creation and improvement of water bodies, and provision of public access and facilities related to fishing. The Dingell-Johnson program is administered by the FWS Federal Aid Program (see the federal aid chapter for further details).

Fishery Management on Federal Lands and Wildlife Refuges. During the 1960s, Congress passed several pieces of legislation to guide fish conservation efforts on federally managed lands and on national wildlife refuges. Under terms of the Sikes Act of 1960,[27] FWS, in cooperation with the Defense Department and state fish and wildlife agencies, was authorized to develop plans for fish and wildlife resources conservation on military reservations. The plans are implemented by Defense Department personnel. A 1974 amendment substantially broadened the act's coverage. It directed the secretaries of Interior, Agriculture, and Energy to cooperate with state fish and wildlife agencies in the development of comprehensive plans for the conservation and rehabilitation of fish and wildlife on lands under their jurisdiction. The Sikes Act provides the basis for FWS assistance to other federal land managing-agencies in conducting fisheries management. Formerly, FWS paid the costs of such assistance, but today most costs are reimbursed by the benefiting federal agency.

Congress has promulgated several laws pertaining to fishing and fish management on units of the National Wildlife Refuge System.* The Fish and Wildlife Act of 1956[28] established a general national policy of "maintaining and increasing the public opportunities for recreational use of our fish and wildlife resources, and stimulating the development of a strong, prosperous, and thriving fishery and fish processing industry." It authorized the secretary of the Interior to conduct investigations on the abundance, availability, and biological requirements of fish resources, to collect statistics on sport fishing, to conduct educational and extension services relative to sport fishing, and to "take such steps as may be required for the development, advancement, management, conservation, and protection of fisheries resources. . . ."

The Refuge Recreation Act of 1962[29] more directly addressed the use of refuges for fishing. It authorizes the secretary to administer refuges, hatcheries, and other Interior-administered fish and wildlife conservation areas for public recreational purposes when recreation is an appropriate "incidental or secondary use." The statute also permits the acquisition of land for recreational development and authorizes the secretary to establish use fees and issue use permits to recreationists.

The recreational use of refuges was further amplified by the National Wildlife Refuge Administration Act of 1966.[30] The law authorizes the Interior secretary to permit the use of refuges for any purpose, including fishing, if he determines that such use is "compatible with the major purposes for which such areas were established." Refuge regulations for both hunting and fishing must be consistent with state fish and wildlife laws to the extent practicable.

Management of fish and wildlife resources on federal lands and refuges in Alaska is governed by the special requirements of the Alaska National Interest Lands Conservation Act of 1980.[31] In recognition of the established subsistence uses of fish and wildlife by native and non-native rural Alaskans, the act requires that federal lands, including wildlife refuges, be managed to enable rural residents to engage in subsistence activities, consistent with "sound management principles" and the "conservation of healthy populations of fish and wildlife." The law establishes six regional advisory councils to advise the secretary of the Interior in the development and implementation of a strategy for the management of fish and wildlife within each region that accommodates subsistence use. It also authorizes the secretary to conduct research on fish and wildlife resources and on subsistence uses of federal land and to prepare a periodic report on the status of fish and wildlife resources on public lands that are subject to subsistence uses.

Fish Research

Finally, many federal statutes have authorized general- and special-purpose research on fisheries and fish. Today, FWS carries out its basic research and development activities under six principal statutes. The Fish and Wildlife Coordination Act authorizes assistance to federal, state, and other agencies in development, protection, rearing, and stocking of fish. The Fish and Wildlife Act of 1956 directs the Interior secretary to provide continuing research, extension, and information services and to take necessary steps to develop, manage, protect, and conserve fishery resources.

Four other statutes authorize more focused research activities. The Great Lakes Fisheries Act authorizes research on the Great Lakes fishery resources. The Fish-Rice Rotation Farming Program of 1958[32] authorizes the secretary of the Interior to estab-

---

*Only a few refuges so far have been established for the primary purpose of conserving fish. These include Togiak, Bechorof, and Alaska Peninsula in Alaska; San Bernadino, Arizona; and Ash Meadows, Nevada. However, a number of refuges established for other purposes possess substantial fish resources.

lish experimental stations to develop methods for the commercial production of fish on flooded rice acreage in rotation with rice-field crops. The National Aquaculture Act of 1980[33] called for the preparation of a national aquaculture plan for promoting the commercial culture of fish, shellfish, and plants in controlled aquatic environments. Preparation of the plan was assigned to the secretaries of Agriculture, Commerce, and Interior. Although no appropriations have ever been made to carry out the law, a national plan[34] was prepared and issued in 1983. The act also authorizes other research and development activities associated with aquaculture, including experimental projects. Finally, the Alaska National Interest Lands Conservation Act authorizes a variety of fisheries research on national wildlife refuges in Alaska.

ORGANIZATION AND OPERATIONS

FWS, through its Fishery Resources Program, is responsible for most federal inland fish management activities. The specific responsibilities of the Fishery Resources Program are as follows:

1. Restore Depleted Fisheries Resources of National Significance. The focus is on economically significant, depleted fish stocks subject to interjurisdictional management, including Pacific salmon and steelhead trout, Atlantic salmon, anadromous striped bass, fish of the Great Lakes, and other anadromous species of the Atlantic and Gulf coasts.

2. Mitigate Fishery Resources Damaged by Federal Water Resource Projects. Anadromous species and other fish have been affected severely by water-development projects, especially federal dams on western rivers. FWS determines mitigation requirements for water resource projects, implements the mitigation plan, and operates mitigation-related facilities such as hatcheries.

3. Assist with the Management of Fisheries on Federal Lands. FWS directly manages fisheries on national wildlife refuge lands and provides technical assistance to other federal agencies for the management of fish on their lands. In addition, FWS serves as a technical adviser to Indian tribes on fish and wildlife management.

4. Maintain a Leadership Role for Scientific Management of National Fishery Resources. FWS directs its research and development toward activities and problems beyond the capabilities of the states to address. Such activities include maintaining brood stocks of certain fish species, fish disease prevention, registering drugs and chemicals used in fish management, and providing technical training to fishery personnel of other federal and state agencies.

Jurisdiction Over Anadromous Species

Both FWS and NMFS have responsibilities for the management of anadromous species when the fish are in inland waters. This division of management began in 1970 when NMFS was established within the Department of Commerce to take responsibility for marine fishery resources and Bureau of Commercial Fisheries functions were transferred from Interior to Commerce. NMFS and FWS each wanted jurisdiction over anadromous fish in inland waters. Ultimately, a compromise was reached.

NMFS was given authority over anadromous fish in marine waters and exclusive authority to administer the Columbia River Fisheries Development Program authorized by the Mitchell Act. NMFS also was authorized to administer the Commercial Fisheries Research and Development Act,[35] under which federal grants are provided to the states for research on and development of commercial fishery resources, including anadromous fish. NMFS and FWS were given joint authority to administer the

Anadromous Fish Conservation Act, another federal grant-in-aid program designed to conserve, enhance, and develop anadromous fish stocks. In addition, both agencies retained authority under the Fish and Wildlife Coordination Act to review federal water resource projects that affect fisheries resources and to make recommendations to mitigate the projects' adverse effects.

In 1976, Congress passed the Magnuson Fishery Conservation and Management Act,[36] establishing a fishery conservation zone that extends 200 miles offshore and within which the federal government has exclusive authority to manage ocean-fishery resources, including anadromous species. NMFS administers the act and, by its approval of catch levels set by regional fishery management councils, plays a pivotal role in the conservation of anadromous fish species.

State and Private Roles

The states are recognized as having primary authority to manage fish within their territorial waters. This includes the key power to regulate the commercial or sport taking of fish. In addition, the states conduct a variety of fisheries activities, including surveys and assessments, research, propagation and stocking, and habitat conservation and restoration.

Several private organizations conduct fish enhancement or conservation projects that complement state and federal fish management activities. The Nature Conservancy acquires lands and waters that provide habitat for fish and wildlife species, and manages these areas as nature preserves. The Sport Fishing Institute funds fisheries research and training programs and disseminates information on trends in fisheries research and management. The Izaak Walton League conducts a Save Our Streams program in which its chapters "adopt" streams and work to ensure that water quality is preserved. Trout Unlimited provides volunteers and funds to enhance stream habitats for salmonid fish.

U.S. Fish and Wildlife Service
Fishery Resources

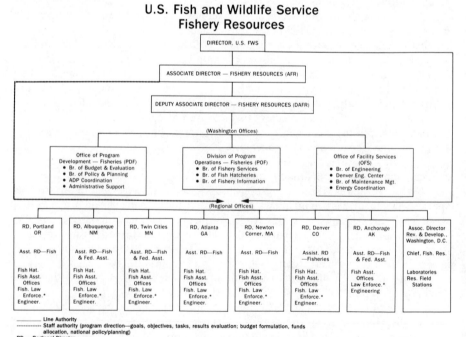

Congressional Committees

Five congressional committees have jurisdiction over federal freshwater fisheries programs. In the Senate, the Subcommittee on Environmental Pollution of the Committee on Environment and Public Works authorizes legislation dealing with FWS fish and wildlife programs of FWS; the National Ocean Policy Study, a special subunit of the Senate Committee on Commerce, Science, and Transportation, has jurisdiction over legislation dealing with activities conducted by NMFS. Appropriations for FWS fisheries programs are made by the Senate Appropriations Subcommittee on Interior and Related Agencies, those for NMFS by the Subcommittee on State, Commerce, Justice and the Judiciary.

In the House, the Subcommittee on Fisheries and Wildlife Conservation and the Environment of the Merchant Marine and Fisheries Committee is responsible for legislation administered by both FWS and NMFS. Appropriations for FWS fisheries activities are made by the House Appropriations Subcommittee on Interior and Related Agencies, those for NMFS programs by the Subcommittee on Commerce, Justice, State and the Judiciary.

The Fishery Resources Program

Within FWS, the Fishery Resources Program, headed by an associate director for Fishery Resources, has management responsibility for all freshwater fish species except those listed as endangered or threatened under the Endangered Species Act.* The associate director sets national program goals, prepares the program budget, provides policy guidance to FWS regional and field offices, and evaluates overall program performance.** At the national level, the associate director is assisted by a deputy associate director, and by a Division of Program Development and a Division of Program Operations.

Significant fishery management activities also are conducted by other FWS programs or offices that are not supervised directly by the fishery program manager. The Habitat Resources Program in the Office of Ecological Services reviews the impacts of federal water resource projects on fisheries and, with the assistance of fishery program personnel, determines fish mitigation requirements during the planning phase of water development projects. The Federal Aid Program administers annual grants to the states for sport-fish conservation and restoration projects under the Dingell-Johnson Act. The Cooperative Research Units Program, administered by the Division of Cooperative Fish and Wildlife Research Units, supervises a cooperative federal, state, and university research program on fish and wildlife resources. The Wildlife Resources Program's Division of Law Enforcement enforces federal laws regulating the taking and trade of fish, and the Division of Refuge Management, in consultation with the Fishery Resources staff, supervises the management of fishery resources on national wildlife refuges.

The actual implementation of fishery program activities is carried out by FWS personnel in regional and field offices. Each regional office has an assistant regional director of Fishery Resources who manages fisheries activities within a multistate region.** The assistant regional director is assisted by a deputy and several divisional

---

*Listed species are the responsibility of the Endangered Species Program and will not be dealt with in this chapter.
**The associate director for Fishery Resources also supervises the Office of Facility Services, which coordinates the construction and maintenance of all FWS facilities.
**In some regions, the assistant director manages both the fishery and federal aid programs.

supervisors who oversee FWS field personnel within geographically distinct areas. At the field level, FWS maintains 34 fishery assistance offices, 73 fish hatcheries, and seven fishery resource coordinators.*

Planning

Fishery program activities are guided by objectives identified in a series of interrelated plans prepared by FWS national, regional, and field offices. Plans with a national scope include the Service Management Plan, [37] which provides overall, servicewide goals and long-term policy guidance; the Program Management Document-Fishery Resources, [38] which identifies program objectives and strategies for a five-year period; the annual Fishery Resources Program Advice, [39] which allocates funds and personnel to the regions for the accomplishment of specified tasks; the Fishery Resources Program's Statement of Responsibilities and Role;[40] and program element plans,** which implement FWS responsibilities identified in the program statement.

FWS also prepares nationwide objectives for national species of special emphasis (NSSEs), defined as species or groups of species that have high biological, legal, and public interest. Eleven fish or fish groups have been selected as NSSEs, and initial population and distribution objectives for them are contained in National Objectives for National Species of Special Emphasis.[41]

Fishery management objectives and strategies identified in national plans are transformed into appropriate regional and field objectives and strategies in various operational plans prepared at those levels. Each regional office prepares a regional resource plan, a five-year plan that focuses the region's management efforts on NSSEs and certain other species considered to be of regional, but not national, significance. Regional Resource Plans contain individual resource plans for fish species of concern to the region.

At the field level, FWS prepares fishery management plans for individual fishery resources or species (including fishery plans for national wildlife refuges), mitigation plans, hatchery development plans, and special plans pertaining to the management of interjurisdictional fisheries.

Research

Most fish research is conducted by the Division of Fishery Research under the supervision of the associate director for Research and Development. The division's role is to provide support to the Fishery Resources Program, which supplies the division with operating funds and with guidance on how funds should be spent. Research constitutes 24 percent of the Fishery Program budget in FY 1985.

There are three principal areas of fishery research:

1. Habitat. Habitat research on species of interest, including studies of the ecological relationships among fish species and the probable effects of changes in water quality or habitat modification.

2. Resource Use. Investigation directed at assessing and allocating fish resources. Research projects include predicting the response of fish communities to the harvest of certain species, developing methods to identify fish stocks both temporally and spatially, determining the impact of artificially propagated fish on natural stocks, and solving fishery problems identified by resource managers.

---

*The coordinators represent FWS on fishery matters for the Columbia, Merrimack, Snake, Susquehanna, Connecticut, and Delaware rivers and the Chesapeake Bay.
**Program element plans, of which there are 21, currently are under preparation.

3. Fish Husbandry. Research to support the propagation and culture of fish in hatcheries, especially those operated by FWS. Activities include investigations of fish production techniques, health, genetics, carrying capacity of hatcheries, and performance of stocked fish relative to naturally reproduced populations.

Fishery research is conducted at one national research center with five satellite laboratories, four other major laboratories, and 28 field stations. The National Fisheries Center in Leetown, West Virginia, administers the five satellite labs and a training academy for fishery personnel. The National Fishery Research Laboratory at La-Crosse, Wisconsin, specializes in the study and registration of drugs and chemicals used in fishery research and management, including those used to control the sea lamprey, and on the ecology of fish in the upper Mississippi River Basin. The Great Lakes Fishery Laboratory conducts studies in all five Great Lakes. The Seattle National Fishery Research Laboratory investigates factors that limit fish populations in freshwater and estuary environments, factors affecting fish health, and methods for more efficient use of hatchery-reared anadromous fish in supplementing natural stocks. The Gainesville National Fishery Research Laboratory conducts surveys of exotic fish introduced to United States waters and investigates the potential impacts of these species on native fish and wildlife.*

Budget and Staff

The various national, regional, and field plans prepared for fishery activities provide one basis for formulating and justifying the Fishery Program's annual budget request. Each region submits a budget request to the national office to cover its projected needs for the fiscal year two years hence. Regional requests are evaluated and reshaped by the FWS national office directorate, comprised of the director, associate directors, and regional directors. The proposed FWS budget then is reviewed by the Interior Department and the president's Office of Management and Budget before it is submitted to Congress as part of the president's annual budget. Hearings are held by the authorizing committees of both houses, which make recommendations to the House and Senate budget committees, and by the appropriations subcommittees on Interior and related agencies. Additions and deletions to the FWS budget are made by the appropriations subcommittees, and a final budget is approved by Congress sometime between June and November for the federal fiscal year beginning October 1.

Appropriated funds then are allocated by FWS to its various programs, and its annual work plans are adjusted and made final. Periodic evaluations are made by FWS to determine if its annual work objectives have been met by its employees.

The FY 1985 Fishery Resources Program budget of $46.1 million constitutes about 7.8 percent of total FWS expenditures. The $46.1 million was distributed as follows:

Activity	Amount in Millions	Percent of Total
Hatchery operation	$24.6	53.3
Lower Snake mitigation	$ 4.5	10.0
Refuge fishery operations	$ 2.1	4.5
Population management (technical assistance)	$ 1.7	3.7
Law enforcement	$ 2.1	4.5
Research	$11.1	24.0
Total	$46.1	100.0

*According to FWS, 40 species of foreign fish have established reproducing populations in United States waters. An additional 58 species have been identified in United States waters, but are not yet known to be established.

The Fishery Resources Program also administers activities funded under the Construction and Anadromous Fish Account of the FWS budget. For FY 1985, $24.2 million was appropriated to this account: $4 million for grants to states under the Anadromous Fish Conservation Act and $20.2 million for the servicewide construction program.

Budget trends over the period are difficult to determine because FWS changed its budget format in FY 1984. The two activities that can be compared — hatcheries and research — have grown slightly since 1981. Hatcheries received 55.4 percent of the FY 1981 budget versus 53.3 percent in FY 1985, research received 28.8 percent in FY 1981 versus 24 percent in FY 1985. Staff size, measured in full-time equivalent positions, has dropped slightly from 1,037 in FY 1981 to 1,011 in 1985.

PROGRAM TRENDS

Under the Reagan administration, a redefinition of the Fishery Resources Program begun by FWS in the 1970s has reached fruition. New program policies have led to the transfer of some federal fish hatcheries to other entities, a new emphasis on evaluating the effectiveness of fisheries mitigation for federal water projects, and a concerted effort to maximize the use of fish resources on national wildlife refuges. In addition, FWS has identified 11 species of fish or groups of fish as NSSEs. FWS already has reshaped its budget to reflect its redefined role and has prepared regional resource plans for the NSSEs to guide the management efforts of field personnel.

Redefinition of Fishery Program

Re-examination of the responsibilities, roles, and objectives of the fishery program commenced in the 1970s, when concerns were raised about the FWS policy of stocking hatchery-reared fish free of charge for privately owned farm ponds and state-owned or state-managed waters. Concern also was raised about the desirability of maintaining federal hatcheries that benefit primarily state fishing programs. In addition, Congress raised questions about the FWS practice of providing technical assistance on fisheries to other federal land-managing agencies and the Bureau of Indian Affairs without reimbursement. FWS gradually in the late 1970s terminated its practice of stocking farm ponds nationwide except in eight Southeastern states, and closed or transferred several hatcheries that benefited primarily state fishery programs.* In addition, congressional appropriations committees in FY 1981 required FWS to seek reimbursement for costs of technical services provided to other federal agencies.

When the Reagan administration took office in 1981, the redefinition of the fisheries program was intensified and development of a Responsibilities and Role Statement was begun.** In essence, FWS now concentrates its efforts on species and fisheries for which it has a clear legislative responsibility and toward nationally significant, interjurisdictional fishery resources that have been depleted.

Since FWS does not have exclusive authority to regulate any inland fish species or fishery, it works cooperatively with the states in the conduct of its activities. The Fishery Resources Program is viewed as a catalyst that ensures that fishery resource

---

*Today, FWS expends about $600,000 annually to raise warm-water fish species for release in farm ponds in Kentucky, Tennessee, Mississippi, Georgia, Florida, North Carolina, Louisiana and Arkansas. FWS intends to terminate this activity by 1990.

**The statement was issued March 20, 1985.

Anadromous Fish Conservation Act Program

Legislative authorizations and congressional appropriations to the U.S. Fish and Wildlife Service and the National Marine Fisheries Service under the Anadromous Fish Conservation Act.

STATE GRANTS (Section 4 — Authorization expires 9/30/85)

Fiscal Year(s)	Amounts Authorized	Appropriated to FWS	Appropriated to NMFS	Total Appropriated
1966–70	$25,000,000	$8,215,000	$8,110,000	$16,325,000
1971	6,000,000	2,321,000	2,000,000	4,321,000
1972	7,500,000	2,332,000	2,000,000	4,332,000
1973	8,500,000	2,333,000	2,500,000	4,833,000
1974	10,000,000	1,833,000	2,000,000	3,833,000
1975	20,000,000	2,633,000	1,790,000	4,423,000
1976	20,000,000	4,388,000	2,500,000	6,888,000
1977	20,000,000	3,513,000	2,000,000	5,513,000
1978	20,000,000	3,513,000	2,000,000	5,513,000
1979	20,000,000	3,611,000	2,000,000	5,611,000
1980	11,000,000	3,712,000	2,000,000	5,712,000
1981	13,000,000	2,700,000	4,000,000	6,700,000
1982	15,000,000	0	3,000,000	3,000,000
1983	7,500,000	3,000,000*	2,750,000*	5,750,000
1984	7,500,000	3,400,000*	2,800,000*	6,200,000
1985	7,500,000	3,430,000	3,000,000	6,430,000
Subtotal	$218,500,000	$50,934,000	$44,450,000	$95,384,000

*Some of this money was used to fund striped bass research and consequently was not disbursed to the states.

problems and opportunities are identified in a timely fashion and that helps state, Indian and other federal agencies to correct fisheries problems. Only if a clear need for federal action exists will FWS undertake additional fishery management activities.

Fish Hatchery Terminations

With the new emphasis on nationally significant species and fisheries, FWS initiated efforts in FY 1983 to close or transfer hatcheries that used less than half their fish production for federal activities such as mitigation and fishery restoration. FWS recommended a total of 31 hatchery closures or transfers. Ultimately Congress approved 19 terminations during FY 1983 to 1985. The operation of 18 terminated hatcheries has been assumed by state, local, or Indian tribal governments. One has been turned over to a university. The fish production from terminated hatcheries that was used to meet federal management responsibilities and goals will be reassigned to some of the remaining 73 FWS hatcheries.

Evaluation of Mitigation Activities

A long-standing activity of the Fishery Resources Program has been to mitigate the damage federal water resource projects have caused to fishery resources, especially anadromous species. In the past, FWS mitigation efforts have focused primarily on providing hatchery-reared fish to compensate for the loss of naturally reproducing stocks. Under the new fisheries policy, FWS responsibility has been expanded to include evaluation of mitigation measures implemented by water resource agencies and their effectiveness in achieving fishery enhancement goals. To the greatest extent possible, FWS will seek to have project beneficiaries or the development agency pay for all mitigation work.

U.S. Fish a
FY 1981–FY 1985 Budget Appropriations/

Fiscal Year	President's Budget/ Appropriation	Fishery Resources Total	Hatchery O&M	LSRCP[1]
FY 1985	President's Budget	$44,148	$22,799	$4,591
	Appropriation	46,189	24,582	4,499
FY 1984	President's Budget	34,025	20,302	—
	Appropriation	42,007	23,222	3,737
FY 1983	President's Budget	32,852	20,121	—
	Appropriation	48,339	24,724	—
FY 1982	President's Budget[3] (Carter)	46,442	24,243	—
	Amended Reagan (March)	37,628	22,494	—
	Amended Reagan (Sept.)	31,828	19,882	—
	Appropriation[3]	37,262	22,983	—
FY 1981	President's Budget	34,951	19,822	—
	Appropriation	41,004	22,513	—
	(Adj. Approp.)[3]	(36,374)	(20,152)	

[1]Prior to FY 1984, funds for the Lower Snake River Compensation Plan were included within Hatchery Operations and Maintenance.

[2]Under the Service's current budget structure established in FY 1984, the Fishery Resources Activity is divided into six Subactivities including: Hatchery Operations and Maintenance; Lower Snake River Compensation Plan (LSRCP); Refuge Operations and Maintenance; Fishery Law Enforcement; Population Management; and Fishery Research and Development. Prior to FY

Increased Fishing on Refuges

Another major initiative of the Reagan administration is to increase public use of national wildlife refuges, including their use for fishing, as long as such use is compatible with refuge purposes. According to FWS, fishery resources on refuges have not been managed optimally in the past. A concerted effort began in FY 1984 to improve this situation. FWS now is rating refuge recreational fishing potential and developing fishery management plans for refuges that have significant fish resources or that have problems associated with fishery resources. Through December 1984, 58 fishery management plans had been completed, and 14 were in draft form. Another 53 are needed. Thus a total of 125 units, or about 30 percent of all refuges, eventually will have fishery management plans. Fishing may be allowed on a refuge irrespective of whether a fish management plan exists. During FY 1984, fishing was permitted on 188 refuges.

Regional Resource Planning

Concurrent with its effort to redefine the fishery program, FWS in 1981 instituted a new planning process for the management of fish and wildlife species that are of national biological, legal, or public interest. By the end of FY 1984, 54 species or species groups had been identified as NSSEs. These included nine fish of commercial or sport value — coho, chinook, sockeye, and Atlantic salmon; steelhead, cutthroat, and lake trout; striped bass; and a group of three Great Lakes perch — one endangered species, the cui-ui, and one pest species, the sea lamprey.

For the most part, the NSSE identification process simply re-identified fish

dlife Service
ǝnt's Budget for Fishery Resources ($000)

Refuge O&M	Population Manage- ment	Law Enforcement	Research & Development	YCC	Jobs Bill
$2,217	$1,758	$2,187	$10,596		
2,173	1,723	2,143	11,069		
2,162	1,663	227	9,671		
2,181	1,733	329	10,805		
Fishery Assistance[2]					
	2,975	225	9,531		
	3,216	227	11,184	1,155	7,833
	9,970	232	11,997		
	3,753	227	11,154		
	2,274	223	9,449		
	3,550	225	10,504		
	4,609	141	10,379		
	6,481	157	11,853		
	(5,591)	(142)	(10,489)		

1984, funds for Population Management and Refuge O&M were included in the Fishery Assistance Subactivity.

[3]Through the FY 1982 budget request, General Administrative Services was included in the various programs under the Resource Management Appropriation (approximately 10.5%). In the FY 1982 appropriation bill, Congress removed this funding from the programs and established a separate account. The FY 1982 appropriation reflects this action. An adjusted appropriation line is shown in FY 1981 reflecting the removal of the General Administrative Services.

species that already were the focus of FWS management efforts. In addition to the 11 NSSEs, FWS regional offices also have identified certain other species of interest in their regions. These regional species of special emphasis (RSSEs) also receive management attention.

REGIONAL SPECIES OF SPECIAL EMPHASIS: FISH

Region 1
   Lahontan Cutthroat Trout

Region 2
   Rainbow Trout
   Humpback Chub
   Woundfin
   Gila Topminnow
Region 3
   None

Region 4
   Brook Trout
   Rainbow Trout
   Brown Trout
Region 5
   American Shad

Region 6
   Paddlefish
   Rainbow Trout
Region 7
   None

The regional resource plan contains specific management objectives to be achieved for each nationally and regionally significant species. Operational plans then are prepared to achieve those objectives. The plan is revised at least every two years.

CURRENT ISSUES

Inland fishery management has been rife with conflict since the mid-1930s, as commercial and sport fishermen have fought over harvest allocations in different fisheries around the country and against dams, pollution, and other human activities that destroy or degrade fish habitat. Recent controversies include disputes over the management of the striped bass, whose Atlantic population has collapsed over the past 10 years, and over the implementation of an Atlantic salmon restoration project in New England. In addition, two relatively new threats to fish resources currently are under debate: the construction of numerous small hydroelectric dams around the country and acid precipitation. With the exception of the striped bass, which is covered in a separate chapter, these controversies are discussed in the following sections.

Atlantic Salmon Restoration

A long-standing state and federal effort to restore naturally spawning populations of Atlantic salmon to the rivers of New England is threatened with failure by construction of new hydroelectric dams on restoration rivers, increasing water acidity, and excessive harvest of the stocks in ocean fisheries. Unless all of these threats are alleviated, the restoration program, on which $76 million already has been spent, could be doomed.

The sea dwelling race of Atlantic salmon was virtually extirpated from New England by 1900. The only exceptions were salmon that spawned in a few rivers in Maine. Causes for the decline include numerous dams, water pollution, habitat alteration, and overfishing. It is estimated that some 300,000 adult salmon annually entered 28 major rivers to spawn in pre-Colonial times, with the Connecticut, Merrimack, Androscoggin, Kennebec, and Penobscot receiving most of these fish. Today, approximately 7,000 adult salmon — 1,000 of them naturally reproduced and 6,000 hatchery produced — are estimated to use 16 rivers.

Seven rivers in Maine — the Dennys, East Machias, Machias, Pleasant, Ducktrap, Narragaugus, and Sheepscot Rivers — have relatively stable salmon populations. The Kennebec River has only a remnant population. The remaining New England rivers where the species presently occurs — St. Croix, Union, Saco, Merrimack, Pawtucket, Connecticut, Penobscot, and Androscoggin — have runs generated almost entirely from hatchery fish.

In 1947, the state of Maine launched a program to increase the numbers of salmon returning to state waters. Since then, the effort has grown into a New England-wide effort involving three federal agencies, nine state agencies, private conservation organizations, and the salmon-producing and salmon-harvesting nations of the North Atlantic. Coordination of the restoration effort is performed by FWS. The goal of the program is to restore self-sustaining populations of salmon in 18 rivers, especially the Merrimack, Connecticut, and Penobscot Rivers, in order to support a recreational fishery. The restoration objective of 54,000 returning adults by the year 2000 would support an annual sport harvest of some 12,000 salmon and provide an estimated 140,000 angler-days of recreation each year.

The principal threat to the restoration effort is the construction of hydroelectric dams at old and new dam sites on rivers targeted for restoration. The impetus for most of these projects is federal statutes that provides various incentives for construction by private parties of small hydroelectric facilities. (See discussion below of the small-hydro issue.)

Dams pose two threats to Atlantic salmon. First, an estimated five to 20 percent of the fish encountering just one dam while migrating upstream to spawn will not cross the barrier even if it has the most sophisticated fish passageways. The more dams encountered, the fewer the number of fish ultimately reaching their spawning grounds upstream. Second, a significant percentage of juvenile fish returning to the ocean are killed when they pass through hydroelectric turbines.

Continued federal licensing of small hydro dams could virtually end the Atlantic salmon restoration effort, according to FWS. A potential test case is brewing over a proposed hydroelectric facility at Sewell's Falls on the Merrimack River near Concord, New Hampshire. The Merrimack is one of the principal restoration rivers. The Federal Energy Regulatory Commission is likely to issue a decision on licensing this 19-foot, 4.95 megawatt structure sometime in 1985. Conservation organizations, the state of Massachusetts, NMFS, and FWS oppose the licensing of the dam. Power from the dam is not needed, they say, but because public utilities are required by federal law to buy small-hydro-produced electricity at favorable prices an artificial incentive spurs the building of the dam.

Hydroelectric proponents argue that the Atlantic salmon restoration effort should be re-evaluated for its cost-effectiveness because the $76 million already expended has shown little tangible results. Restoration advocates counter that the payoff will not be seen until near the end of the program, when the program will amply justify itself. Many observers believe that a decision by the energy regulatory commission to issue the license would set a precedent for the issuance of many other licenses on other restoration rivers. Conservation organizations are likely to sue to block the construction if the license is granted.

Another problem hampering the restoration effort is the high take of United States-spawned salmon stocks in ocean fisheries. Salmon spawned in Canadian and United States waters migrate to ocean waters off Greenland, where an estimated 50 to 60 percent of all adult salmon that otherwise would return to United States waters to spawn are caught by European fishermen.

The United States signed an international treaty in 1982 that established the North Atlantic Salmon Conservation Organization for the purpose of regulating the harvest of salmon and implementing other conservation measures. In 1984, the West Greenland Commission, a subunit of the salmon conservation organization, reduced the total allowable harvest of Atlantic salmon off West Greenland from 1,190 to 870 metric tons, a decrease of about 240,000 fish. This action was compelled by a sharp decline in the salmon harvest, which dropped from 1,100 tons in 1981 to about 300 tons in 1982 and 1983. This was the first reduction in the salmon harvest quota since the 1,190-ton limit was set in 1972, but is still three times the level of the 1982 and 1983 catches, making it arguably a weak protective measure.

Finally, a new, less obvious threat now jeopardizes the salmon-restoration effort: acid precipitation. Many scientists suspect that increasing acid levels in New England streams and rivers are having a significant effect on the hatching of salmon eggs and the growth of juvenile fish. Although these effects have not been well-documented, FWS recently dropped a proposal to use several tributaries of Miller's River, itself a tributary to the Connecticut, as nursery habitat for juvenile salmon because the waters had become too acidic (see the discussion on acid precipitation in this section).

Impacts of Small-Hydro Development on Fisheries

Federal laws promoting the construction of new small hydroelectric facilities and the rehabilitation of existing dams have provoked an avalanche of controversy over the environmental effects of this program, especially its impacts on anadromous fish stocks that already have been severely depleted in numbers and distribution. The Fish and Wildlife Coordination Act requires that federal water resource agencies give fish and wildlife resources equal consideration with other project objectives. However, critics charge that the Federal Energy Regulatory Commission, administrator of the small hydro-program, has ignored environmental and other concerns and is seeking to license as many dams as possible. This approach, say commission critics, also ignores the agency's responsibility under the Federal Power Act to ensure that all licensed projects "will be best adapted to a comprehensive plan for improving or developing a waterway or waterways for the use or benefit of interstate or foreign commerce, for the improvement and utilization of water-power development, *and for other beneficial uses, including recreational purposes . . .*"[48] (emphasis added).

The small-hydro program was authorized by the Public Utilities Regulatory Policies Act of 1978,[49] a measure passed to promote various forms of renewable energy such as geothermal and solar power. Among other things, the law authorizes the Federal Energy Regulatory Commission to develop a process for licensing small-hydroelectric projects of 15 megawatts or less at existing dams not producing electricity. The act also contains provisions that promote the sale of electricity produced by small-hydro facilities and authorizes the commission to waive licensing requirements for power projects that produce less than five megawatts, as long as the exempted projects maintain environmental review procedures and meet terms and conditions recommended by FWS and the state fish and wildlife agency. In addition, changes in tax laws have encouraged private investment in small-hydro projects.

All this has led to a tremendous upsurge in project license requests. According to Representative James Weaver (D-Oregon), in 1983 the Federal Energy Regulatory Commission received more than 1,000 preliminary permit applications for small-hydro projects, compared with an average of 20 applications per year in the 1960s and 1970s.[50]

Any dam, depending upon its design and location, could pose a substantial threat to existing fisheries or to attempts to restore depleted fish stocks. The Federal Energy Regulatory Commission's implementation of the small hydro-program has drawn intense criticism precisely on this score because many of the license requests have been for projects in the Pacific Northwest and New England, both areas of significant or potentially significant anadromous fisheries.

In the Pacific Northwest, the Federal Energy Regulatory Commission has licensed or exempted from licensing 138 projects since the end of 1980; as of March 1984, the Bonneville Power Administration estimated that 553 small-hydro projects had been approved or were in some stage of the licensing procedure. Many of these projects are located on the same river or stream.[51] In New England, projects are proposed for several restoration rivers, including the Androscoggin and Penobscot in addition to the Merrimack (described above).

The Federal Energy Regulatory Commission is required by a number of different federal statutes to give adequate consideration to all river uses, including the protection of fishery resources, in deciding whether or not a proposed project is in the public interest. However, critics charge that the commission has pursued a one-dimensional mission of power promotion and that environmental considerations have been disregarded almost completely. Criticism has been heaped on the agency by members of Congress, state natural resource agencies, and conservation organizations, many of whom leveled their charges at a hearing before the House Subcommittee on Energy Conservation in late 1984. Among other things, the commission was accused of failing to consider the cumulative effects of multiple small-hydro proposals on single rivers and river basins; ignoring state water resource and energy development plans; granting so many preliminary license permits that federal, state, and local natural resource agencies cannot review them adequately; failing to comply with provisions of the

Northwest Power Act that require the commission to protect and enhance fishery resources affected by dams; not enforcing promised modifications in licensed facilities that would mitigate damages to fish or other resources; excluding NMFS as a participant in the licensing process; misinterpreting its authority under the Public Utility Regulatory Policies Act by licensing the construction of small-hydro projects at new sites rather than just at existing dams; and licensing dams that are not needed because of a failure to adequately consider the public need for power generated by small-hydro facilities.

Legislators from the Pacific Northwest and New England introduced bills last year that would correct some of the alleged abuses. These include proposals to permit states to zone certain rivers for hydroelectric development and others for protection, and to require the Federal Energy Regulatory Commission to abide by this zoning; to require commission licensing actions to be consistent with state, local, or regional water resource plans (the commission now has the authority to override these plans); to require the commission to consider the cumulative effects of its hydropower licensing program; and to delegate the small-hydro licensing program to the states. Legislation promoting some kind of comprehensive river planning is expected to receive serious consideration in the 99th Congress by the House Energy and Power Committee because of the interest of its Chairman, Representative John Dingell (D-Michigan), in the issue.

Meanwhile, the commission's management of the small-hydro program was found wanting in three 1984 federal court decisions. The courts held that the commission must comply with license provisions proposed by the Department of the Interior to protect lands under the department's jurisdiction; that the commission has no authority to exempt dam projects under five megawatts from licensing if they are constructed at new dam sites; and that the commission cannot issue or renew power licenses for large or small facilities while deferring implementation of fish protection measures nor ignore the substantive obligations of the Northwest Power Act, which requires the commission to give equitable treatment to fish and wildlife, or of the Fish and Wildlife Coordination Act, which requires equal consideration of fish in water resource development projects (see the Legal Developments section of this chapter for further details).

Effects of Acid Precipitation on Fish

The widespread environmental damage caused by acid precipitation has been publicized greatly during the past several years. A variety of fish species and fisheries in both the United States and Canada have been affected severely by increasing levels of acidity in streams, rivers, and lakes. Yet despite the mounting evidence of massive damage to fish and other resources, the federal government has refused to take decisive action to control sources of air pollution — coal-burning power plants, industrial coal and oil burners, and automobiles — that produce sulfur dioxide particulates which combine with atmospheric moisture to form acid precipitation.

The acidity or alkalinity of liquids is measured by a pH test. Values may range from 0, highly acidic, to 14, highly alkaline, with 7.0 being neutral. Each decline in pH between 7.0 and 0 indicates a large jump in acidity, since pH is computed on a logarithmic scale. Thus a pH of five is 10 times as acidic as six, and a pH of four is 100 times as acidic as six.

Normal precipitation has a pH level that typically ranges from 5.6 to 8.0. A pH level below 5.6 qualifies the precipitation as abnormally acidic. No fish species are known to successfully reproduce in water with a pH below five.

Although acid precipitation affects nearly every aspect of the environment, fish are among the more seriously affected. As the pH level of water drops toward the more acidic range, the normal ionic salt balance within a fish is disturbed, and the fish begins to lose body salts to the surrounding water. If salt losses exceed intake, fish go into shock, lose equilibrium, and eventually die. Large-scale fish kills frequently result from pulses of acidity produced when snow melts in the spring and releases large quantities of acid into rivers and streams.

Increased acidity also releases dissolved metals from soils. For fish, the most serious toxic metal is aluminum. Generally, aluminum levels above two parts per million in water are fatal to species such as brook trout, and levels as low as 0.2 parts per million usually are fatal to its fry.

The loss of entire fish populations in abnormally acidic streams or lakes usually occurs because of successive failures in the reproductive cycle. Acidic waters inhibit the development of fish reproductive organs and facilitate the development of a mucous that suffocates eggs and fry. Since such reproductive failure often is very hard to detect, this effect of acid precipitation may not manifest itself until an entire water body is depopulated. Research has shown that such popular game fish as smallmouth bass, brown trout, Atlantic salmon, walleye, striped bass, and northern pike are among the first species to be affected adversely by acid rain.

Today, the pH of precipitation over much of the eastern United States is abnormally acidic, measuring below 4.4, and values as low as 2.1. have been recorded. Furthermore, acid precipitation is not limited to the Northeast. Washington state receives precipitation with an annual average pH of 4.9, and the area around Pasadena, California, averages 3.9.

The ecological response of an area to acid rain depends on the natural buffering ability of the land. Among the areas with the least amount of natural buffering ability are the Appalachian Mountains, Wisconsin, Minnesota, northern Michigan, parts of the Sierra and Rocky Mountains, and much of eastern Canada.

The most extensive studies in the United States on the effects of acid precipitation on fish have been done in the Adirondack Mountains of New York state, where rainfall currently averages below pH 4.2. A study completed in the late 1970s by Dr. Carl Scofield of Cornell University showed that of the 217 high-elevation ponds and lakes tested in the Adirondacks, 51 percent had pH values less than five, and 90 percent of these were devoid of all fish life. Comparable data from 1929 to 1937 indicates that at that time only four percent of these lakes were below pH five and devoid of fish.[52]

FWS currently is conducting liming experiments — the application of lime or soda ash to lakes and the placement of limestone gravel in spawning streams used by brook trout — to determine their effectiveness in lowering acid levels. Similar studies are being conducted independently by several states. Although liming can have immediate positive effects, it is merely a temporary solution usually practiced only in lakes with a slow water turnover rate.

Conservation groups and some members of Congress have been promoting legislation to combat the acid precipitation problem ever since the Clean Air Act came up for reauthorization in 1981, but the effort has stalled repeatedly. The general approach of the legislation has been to reduce sulfur emissions from midwestern power plants, believed to be the source of most acid precipitation in the Northeast. Opposition to acid precipitation legislation has come from Midwestern utilities and members of Congress who claim that the cost of reducing emissions would soar; from eastern states with high-sulfur coal who fear that switching to western low-sulfur coal would cost them jobs and hurt state economy; and from the Reagan administration, which has insisted that more study is needed before requiring expensive controls.

Two important acid precipitation bills were introduced in the 98th Congress,

S. 768 and H.R. 3400, but neither passed. S. 768, sponsored by Senator Robert Stafford (R-Vermont), was reported by the Senate Environment Committee and would have required that sulfur dioxide emissions be reduced by 10 million tons from 1980 levels within a 10-year period. H.R. 3400, introduced by Representatives Henry Waxman (D-California) and Gerry Sikorski (D-Minnesota), called for an eight-million-ton reduction within 10 years, but included provisions intended to address the concerns of control opponents. It would have required the top 50 sulfur polluters to reduce emissions by installing pollution-control equipment rather than switching to low-sulfur coal, thus protecting the interests of high-sulfur-coal-producing states, and would have financed 90 percent of the capital costs by charging a nationwide tax on non-nuclear electricity production, thus spreading the costs. However, the bill died in the House Health and Environment Subcommittee of the Energy and Commerce Committee by a 10 to nine vote, stalling further action on the Clean Air Act in the 98th Congress.

Meanwhile, several acid-rain-related lawsuits have been filed. The most prominent suit has been brought by the states of New York, Pennsylvania, and Maine against the Environmental Protection Agency (EPA). These states petitioned EPA for relief under Section 126 of the Clean Air Act, which allows any state to petition the EPA administrator to request a finding that a major source of air pollution outside the state is emitting pollutants that prevent the petitioning state from achieving compliance with clean-air standards. After EPA failed to act on the petition, the states sued in 1984 to force EPA to answer it. In October 1984, a district court judge ruled that EPA did have to respond, and in January 1985, EPA formally denied the petition. The three states, joined by New Hampshire, Vermont, Massachusetts, Connecticut, and New Jersey, have since appealed the denial.

LEGISLATION

The 98th Congress (1983-84) passed a number of bills dealing with inland fishery resources and considered still others that are expected to be reintroduced in the 99th session. Measures enacted include:

Yakima River Salmon Restoration

Congress passed three separate measures[53] to speed the restoration of severely depleted salmon stocks on the Yakima River Basin in the state of Washington. Historically, salmon entering the river to spawn were estimated to number 500,000 to 600,000. Today's run is estimated at 2,000. Collectively, the measures authorize the secretary of the Interior to construct and operate fish-passage facilities at dams in the basin; provide $4.8 million in appropriations to expedite the construction of such facilities at two Bureau of Reclamation dams; and authorize the Yakima Indian tribe, the state of Washington, and other entities to receive credit toward any future financial obligations they may owe for water facilities constructed under the proposed Yakima Enhancement Project, provided that they advance money to build fish facilities associated with the project. The wildlife program of the Northwest Power Planning Council has recommended a number of fish enhancement measures for the Yakima. The $4.18 million appropriation would go toward funding some of these measures.

Trinity River Restoration

Public Law 98-541[54] was passed to restore depleted anadromous stocks on the Trinity River in California. Two dams constructed in the river in the 1950s and 1960s as part of the Central Valley Project diverted some 80 percent of the river flow to agricultural use. Lack of flow, combined with erosion from timbering in the watershed, led to sediment buildup in the river, which destroyed spawning beds and habitat. It is estimated that chinook salmon populations have dropped 80 percent and steelhead populations 60 percent from pre-dam levels.

In 1976, Congress directed the Trinity River Task Force to prepare a comprehensive management program to correct fish and wildlife problems in the basin. The new law gives the secretary of the Interior the authority to implement a fish restoration program in cooperation with state, Indian, and local agencies. The goal of the program is to restore fish and wildlife populations to the levels that existed prior to dam construction. The measure authorizes appropriations of $33 million over a 10-year period to implement the program and up to $2.4 million yearly for operation and maintenance of fish passageways and other facilities. The $33 million for capital costs must be shared by state and local governments (15 percent) and public utilities, water districts, and other direct purchasers of water and power from the Trinity dams (50 percent).

Interstate Compact to Conserve Atlantic Salmon

Public Law 98-138[55] gives congressional consent to an interstate compact signed by Connecticut, Massachusetts, New Hampshire and Vermont for the restoration of Atlantic salmon in the Connecticut River watershed to numbers as near as possible to their historical abundance. Under the compact, the states will establish a Connecticut River Atlantic Salmon Commission, composed of two representatives of each state and the regional directors of FWS and NMFS. The commission's duties include the making of recommendations for stocking programs, management procedures, and research projects; the encouragement of state acquisition of river bed and river bank lands; and, most significant, the regulation of the taking of Atlantic salmon on the main stem of the Connecticut River.* In addition, the commission has the authority to issue a Connecticut River Basin salmon license and to use license receipts to finance restoration work by its member states.

Striped Bass Moratorium

The continued decline of the striped bass population in the mid-Atlantic states prompted congressional consideration of a federally imposed moratorium on bass take along the Atlantic coast in view of inadequate state conservation and management practices. Ultimately, Congress passed the Atlantic Striped Bass Conservation Act,[56] a measure sponsored by Representative Gerry Studds (D-Massachusetts). The act mandates a reduction in the striped bass catch from Maine to North Carolina by requiring each affected state to establish catch limits by July 1, 1985, with take recommendations made in the Interstate Fisheries Management Plan for Striped Bass[57] prepared by the Atlantic States Marine Fisheries Commission.** Should any state fail to comply, the secretary of Commerce is authorized to declare a moratorium on the catching of striped bass in that state's coastal waters. The moratorium would end when the commission notifies the secretary that the state has taken appropriate remedial action.

---

*The commission does not have authority to regulate harvests on tributary streams, a power the states retained for themselves.
**The plan would achieve an estimated 55-percent reduction in the striped bass take. Interior and Commerce are to review the commission's catch plan and make recommendations on its effectiveness to both the commission and Congress. In addition, the act extends authority for the Emergency Striped Bass Study through FY 1986.

commission's catch plan and make recommendations on its effectiveness to both the commission and Congress. In addition, the act extends authority for the Emergency Striped Bass Study through FY 1986.

Aquaculture Act Reauthorization

No funds have ever been appropriated to implement the Aquaculture Act of 1980, although a National Aquaculture Development Plan[58] was prepared in 1983. The Reagan administration consistently has opposed implementation of the act on the grounds that it duplicates existing authorities. Congress, on the other hand, has reauthorized the program yearly, despite lack of funding.

In addition to reauthorizing the program through FY 1985[59], Congress also considered a measure, H.R. 2676, that would have given the secretary of Agriculture the lead role in aquaculture development. Among other provisions, the bill would have:

- established the secretary of Agriculture as permanent chairman of the Joint Subcommittee on Aquaculture;
- created an Office of Aquaculture Coordination and Development within Agriculture;
- authorized the secretary of the Interior to study exotic species introduced by aquaculture;
- created a National Aquaculture Board to assess aquaculture studies and activities; and
- maintained the departments of the Interior and Commerce in cooperative roles in aquaculture development.

H.R. 2676 was reported by the House Merchant Marine and Agriculture committees, and a similar measure, S. 1101, was reported by the Senate Commerce and Agriculture committees. However, neither measure was voted on by the House or Senate. The Aquaculture Act must be reauthorized for FY 1986. A measure similar to H.R. 2676 is expected to be reintroduced in 1985.

National Hatchery System

Late in the 98th Congress, the House Subcommittee on Fisheries and Wildlife Conservation held a hearing on H.R. 6213, a proposal introduced by Subcommittee Chairman John Breaux (D-Louisiana), that would establish a National Fish Hatchery System. Such a system is necessary, said Breaux, because the Reagan administration's initiative to close or transfer a number of federal hatcheries precipitated unresolved concerns about hatchery funding and operations. At the hearing, Breaux said the controversy is fueled partially by the lack of a consistent policy to guide hatchery operations and that H.R. 6213 would bring stability and order to the hatchery program.

As proposed, H.R. 6213 would establish a national hatchery system to be administered by FWS to include all FWS hatcheries and other federally supported hatcheries. The system is supposed to produce fish for mitigating the impacts of federal water projects, restore significant species in interjurisdictional waters, stock waters under federal and state fishery jurisdiction, initiate reasearch and development, and implement endangered species recovery. The bill also requires restoration plans for all species produced by the hatcheries, reimbursement of fish-production costs by the agency for which the fish are produced, and phase-out of fish production that benefits private users. Breaux intends to reintroduce a hatchery bill in 1985.

Anadromous Fish Grants

Section 4 of the Anadromous Fish Conservation Act authorizes a federal grant-in-aid program for the states. Administered jointly by NMFS and FWS the grant program aid program for the states. Administered jointly by NMFS and FWS the grant program is up for reauthorization in 1985. The Reagan administration repeatedly has attempted to end the program, but Congress has continued to appropriate funds for it, including $6.4 million each for FY 1984 and FY 1985.

LEGAL DEVELOPMENTS

Over the past decade, the courts have delineated the appropriate allocation of fishing rights between Indians and non-Indians and among states along the same water body. The courts also have clarified the responsibilities of federal agencies, especially the Federal Energy Regulatory Commission, to give adequate consideration to the protection of fish resources affected by their projects.

The most important cases concerning Indian treaty fishing rights were decided in the 1970s and early 1980s. These cases have arisen in several states.* However, the issue has been most exhaustively litigated in the state of Washington.** These cases are well summarized in Michael Bean's *The Evolution of National Wildlife Law*[60].

The courts have held that the allowable harvest of anadromous fish must be allocated fairly not only between Indians and other fishermen, but also among upstream and downstream states. When Idaho sued Oregon and Washington for a larger share of the allowable anadromous-fish harvest on the Columbia-Snake River system, the Supreme Court held in *Idaho v. Oregon*[61] that such relief could be provided under the common-law doctrine of equitable apportionment — a doctrine originally developed for allocation of water rights. The court denied relief to Idaho, however, because the state had failed to prove that it was suffering substantial injury.

In more recent cases, the courts have demanded that federal agencies more carefully consider the effects of their actions on fish resources. In a challenge to the Westway Highway project in New York City, the district court found in *Action v. West Side Highway Project*[62] that the Corps of Engineers had failed to consider the possibly significant effects of the project on striped bass spawning in the Hudson and enjoined construction pending completion of a supplementary environmental impact statement to study those effects. In a series of challenges to Federal Energy Regulatory Commis-

---

*See *Eastern Band of Cherokee Indians v. North Carolina Wildlife Resources Commission*, 588 F.2d 75 (4th Cir. 1978) (state cannot regulate fishing by non-Indians on Indian reservations); *United States v. Michigan*, 653 F.2d 277 (6th Cir. 1981) (state may not regulate Indian gill-net fishing in Lake Michigan unless absence of regulation will cause irreparable harm to fish resource) (see also *United States v. Michigan*, 520 F. Supp. 207 (D. Mich. 1981) (same case on remand); *White Earth Band of Chippewa Indians v. Alexander*, 518 F. Supp. 527 (D. Minn. 1981) (state may enforce fish and game laws against non-Indians on the Indian reservation).
**See *Puyallup Tribe v. Dep't of Game*, 414 U.S. 44 (1973) (state regulation banning net fishing of steelhead trout but allowing sport fishing unlawfully discriminated against Indians); *Puyallup Tribe v. Dep't of Game*, 433 U.S. 165 (1977) (Indians' take of fish on their reservation may not exceed their allocated share of entire fish catch); *United States v. Washington*, 384 F.2d 312 (W.D. Wash. 1974), aff'd, 520 F.2d 676 (9th Cn. 1975), cert. den., 423 United States 1086 (1976) (states may regulate Indian fishing only to extent essential for conservation of fish resources and must assure Indians a 50 percent share of harvestable fish); *Washington v. Washington State Commercial Passenger Fishing Vessel Ass'n*, 443 United States 658 (1979) (largely affirming district court's allocation in *United States v. Washington, supra*, but requiring that fish Indians take on their reservation be counted toward their total share); *United States v. Washington*, 694 F.2d 1374 (9th Cir. 1983) (Indian share of fish take includes fish produced in state fish hatcheries).

sion licensing decisions, the courts have found even more substantial obligations in the Federal Power Act. Reviewing a hydroelectric project licensed by the commission, the Supreme Court in *Escondido vs. La Jolla*[63] firmly rejected the commission's assertion of absolute authority over such projects. The court held that, under Section 4(e) of the Power Act, if a power project is located on federal lands or Indian reservations, the agency responsible for those lands may impose upon the project any conditions necessary to protect the lands. This decision suggests that the courts will find similar authority in Section 18 of the act, which provides that the Federal Energy Regulatory Commission "*shall require* the construction, maintenance, and operation by a licensee at its own expense of *such fishways as may be prescribed by the Secretary of the Interior* or the Secretary of Commerce as appropriate"[64] (emphasis added).

These restrictions on the commission's authority take on new significance in light of a recent Ninth Circuit decision in *Confederated Tribes v. Federal Energy Regulatory Commission.*[65] Reviewing the commission's decision to relicense the Rock Island Dam in Washington, the court held that a relicensing decision is subject to the same legal restrictions as the original licensing decision. The court specifically held that the commission could not issue a new license while deferring consideration and implementation of fishery protection measures. The decision also suggests that relicensing may provide the Interior Department an opportunity to demand that adequate fishery protection measures be imposed.

Finally, in recent years FWS, in concert with NMFS, has undertaken an aggressive program to enforce federal and state laws that regulate commercial taking of fish. In particular, in several undercover sting operations FWS has used the Lacey Act to prosecute dealers selling catfish illegally taken in the Midwest, walleye and lake trout illegally taken from the Great Lakes, and striped bass illegally taken from the depleted Chesapeake Bay bass population.

RESOURCE STATUS

FWS, through its Fishery Resources Program, collects a variety of data on the biological status of about 40 species of inland fish that are of sport or commercial value. This information is scattered among FWS regional and field offices and research stations. No national aggregation of status data exists, and no effort routinely and regularly has been made to update and assess the information collected in the field. Little if any data is collected by FWS on the other 700 or so species of freshwater fish except by the Office of Endangered Species, which monitors species threatened or endangered with extinction.*

This section discusses the status of the 11 fish species or fish groups identified by FWS as national species of special emphasis.**

Columbia Basin Salmon and Steelhead

FWS has identified three anadromous fish of the Columbia River Basin as NSSEs: coho salmon (*Oncorhynchus kisutch*), chinook salmon (*Oncorhynchus*

---

*The Atlas of North American Freshwater Fishes[66] summarizes distributional and other biological information on fresh-water species. It was financed by FWS, the Sport Fishing Institute, and the North Carolina State Museum.

**All information in this section has been obtained from FWS or NMFS unless otherwise indicated. For data on Pacific salmon and steelhead, see especially 1984 Ocean Salmon Fisheries Review[67] by the Pacific Fishery Management Council.

tshawytscha), and steelhead trout (*Salmo gairdneri*). Coho and chinook salmon are harvested commercially and also are prized game fish. The steelhead trout, formerly the subject of commercial harvest, is now taken primarily for sport.

Salmon and steelhead in the Columbia River Basin have declined dramatically since the beginning of the 20th century. It is estimated that anadromous fish runs in the Columbia River itself have dropped 70 percent from historic levels.[68] The principal cause for this decline is the construction of numerous federal irrigation and power dams that have blocked the migration of fish and altered their habitat. Other causes contributing to the decline include land-use practices that have degraded spawning habitat and water quality and the excessive take of fish.

Coho, chinook, and steelhead populations divide into numerous subgroups that return to spawn in the same river or stream segment where they were born. Population estimates developed for the subgroup are expressed in terms of the number of adult fish passing a particular river point during upstream migration. The number of a given species returning yearly to the mouth of the Columbia to spawn is called the inriver run size.*

Coho Salmon. Coho salmon stocks have declined since 1970, when the number of adults returning to the Columbia River reached their highest peak —approximately 872,000 — since construction of the McNary Dam in 1953. The worst year was 1977, when inriver run size dropped to an estimated 87,000. The decline was precipitated by excessive take and habitat destruction. More recently, El Nino, a warm ocean current that reduces salmon food sources, has moved northward and helped cause stock declines.

Chinook Salmon. Chinook salmon in the Columbia River Basin are divided into spring, summer, and fall races. Spring chinook are divided further into stocks destined for areas above and below Bonneville Dam, the Columbia River dam closest to the Pacific Ocean. Spring chinook destined for areas above Bonneville have declined significantly since the early 1970s. In 1972, the inriver run size was estimated at 269,500. By 1984, it had dropped to an estimated 47,400. Several factors are responsible for the dwindling stocks including loss of habitat to numerous dams above Bonneville and a high mortality rate of smolts when they pass through dam turbines during downstream migration. Spring chinook runs destined for areas below Bonneville seem to be maintaining their size. Inriver run size in 1971 was an estimated 98,900. In 1984 it was 113,100.

Summer chinook stocks, all destined for areas above Bonneville Dam, are in the worst condition. Inriver run size in 1971 was an estimated 71,900, but for the last few years estimates have averaged only 20,000. Again, loss of habitat and dam-related mortality has had a major impact. Also significant are farming and timbering land-use practices that damage the tributaries where summer chinook spawn.

Fall chinook stocks are divided between those destined for areas above and below the pool located behind the Bonneville Dam. Those destined for areas above the pool have shown a remarkable recovery during the last two years, mainly as a result of harvest restrictions and improved passage over dams. Inriver run size averaged approximately 100,000 during the 1970s, but dropped to a low of 66,300 in 1981, only to rebound in 1984 to 130,600. Fall chinook below Bonneville have declined, as a result of El Niño, from an inriver run size of about 160,000 during the 1970s to a low of 87,600 in 1983.

Steelhead Trout. Upper river steelhead trout stocks did poorly in the 1970s,

---

*The inriver run size is an estimate developed from inriver catch data and counts of fish made at various river impediments such as dams or waterfalls.

STATE RECOMMENDED GOALS FOR COLUMBIA RIVER BASIN ANADROMOUS FISH			
	Pre-McNary Goals* (Base run size)	*Current Run Levels (5-yr. ave. 1975-79)*	*Fishery Reduction Since McNary Dam*
Spring chinook	300,000	101,000	− 199,000 (66%)
Summer chinook	200,000	41,000	− 159,000 (79%)
Fall Chinook	400,000	294,000	− 106,000 (26%)
Sockeye	200,000	55,000	− 145,000 (72%)
Coho	164,000	45,600	− 118,400 (72%)
Summer steelhead	400,000	124,000	− 276,000 (69%)

*These goals were represented as the run sizes of the various stocks which could have been maintained prior to the construction of McNary Dam in 1953. In the case of coho, the goal was based on the size of the run in 1967.
Source: "1984 Columbia River Basin Fish and Wildlife Program."

reaching an inriver run size low of 85,000 in 1975. Recently, however, stocks have improved to an estimated inriver run of 360,000 for 1984. The turnaround is the result of several management actions: improved fish passage around dams, increased and improved hatchery production, state designation of the steelhead as a sport species only, and voluntary restraints on harvests by Native Americans. No specific population data is available for lower-river steelhead trout.

Overall Basin Objectives. State fish and wildlife agencies have recommended management goals for desired levels of anadromous fish entering the Columbia River. FWS conforms its hatchery propagation and habitat-improvement activities to help support these goals, but attaining them may be difficult considering the high demand for these species and the pressure on the states and NMFS to keep ocean-harvest levels high. Also, certain stocks, such as summer chinook, may never recover unless habitat loss is stopped and degraded areas are restored.

Great Lakes Fish

The Great Lakes provide a significant fishery for commercial and sport fishermen of the United States and Canada. The depletion of certain species because of inadequately regulated take, habitat degradation, predation by the sea lamprey,* and the recognition that coordinated efforts were required to maintain fishery productivity, led to a 1954 treaty between the United States and Canada to establish the Great Lakes Fishery Commission. The commission's purposes include research, eradication of the sea lamprey, and the recommendation of fishery rehabilitation measures for adoption by the Great Lakes states and provinces. Its powers do not include setting catch levels for Great Lakes fish stocks. FWS has responsibility for providing the United States commissioners with technical advice and support and for conducting research, lamprey control, and other activities undertaken by the United States.

FWS focuses most of its activities on lake trout (*Salvelinus namaycush*), walleye (*Stizostedion vitreum vitreum*), and yellow perch (*Perca flavescens*) — all commercial

---

*The sea lamprey is believed to have entered Lake Ontario via the St. Lawrence River. It was discovered in Lake Erie in 1921 and by 1946 was found in lakes Michigan, Huron, and Superior.

and sport species — and on the sea lamprey. All of these species are found in each of the Great Lakes. Sea lamprey and lake trout prefer colder, deeper water and are in greater abundance in lakes Huron, Superior, and Michigan, while yellow perch and walleye prefer warmer, shallower water and are concentrated in lakes Erie and Ontario and in the bays and shorelines of lakes Michigan and Huron.

Walleye and Yellow Perch. The walleye has made a strong recovery after declining precipitously in the late 1960s. No specific population data on the species is available prior to 1976, but the Canadian commercial take in Lake Erie, by far the largest walleye catch, reached a peak of 9.3 million pounds in 1956 and dropped to only 333,000 pounds in 1968. Estimates for western Lake Erie, beginning in 1976, show a general increase in walleye stocks, from a low of 12.6 million fish in 1977 to a high of 43.7 million in 1983. Recent Canadian commercial harvests also have improved, averaging one to two million pounds yearly from 1979 to 1982.

Walleye stocks in Erie declined rapidly in the 1960s because of excessive take, pollution, and spawning-habitat degradation. They recovered slightly in the early 1970s because mercury contamination closed the walleye commercial fishery in the western basin of Lake Erie. It remains closed in Michigan and Ohio, but since the Canadians fully reopened their side in 1976 pollution cleanup and strict catch limits in Lake Erie have enabled walleye stocks to return to their former abundance. Concern now exists that walleye stocks may have exceeded sustainable levels and are beginning to deplete their food sources.*

Yellow perch stocks have declined steadily since the early 1970s. Specific population data are unavailable, but in Lake Erie, which has the largest concentration of yellow perch, United States and Canadian commercial catches peaked from 1957 to 1970, averaging some 20 million pounds annually, then dropped in the 1970s to between 10 and 15 million pounds and reached a low in 1983 of six million pounds. As with the walleye, pollution, excessive take, and habitat modification primarily are responsible for the yellow perch decline. Although stocks are depressed, the yellow perch is not considered threatened with extirpation from Lake Erie. No significant harvest restrictions have been established, though recommendations now are being formulated through the Great Lakes Fishery Commission.

A new threat to both yellow perch and walleye is the recent expansion of white perch (*Morone americana*), a nonindigenous commercial and sport species believed to have entered the Great Lakes through the St. Lawrence Seaway from its habitat in the Northeast. Found almost exclusively in Lake Ontario in the past, the white perch is beginning to populate the other lakes, particularly Lake Erie.** Fishery-management agencies are concerned that white perch may compete with walleye and yellow perch for the same food sources and may eat walleye eggs. More research is needed, however, and no action to reduce white perch stocks has been taken.

The harvest of both walleye and yellow perch is regulated by the Province of Ontario and the various Great Lakes states, which have primary management responsibility for both species. FWS provides advice to the states on harvest quotas through the Great Lakes Fishery Commission, undertakes research, and provides technical assistance. FWS goals for the two species are identical: to rehabilitate stocks in lakes Michigan, Huron, Erie, and Ontario and maintain present stocks in Lake Superior; and

---

*A decline from 44 million to 31 million between 1983 and 1984 indicates declining food availability.
**Samples taken to measure trends in abundance of newly hatched white perch showed a jump from two fish per hour of sampling in 1980 to 7,000 per hour in 1984.

to increase populations so that by 1990, the overall harvest of both walleye and yellow perch is 20 percent above 1983 levels.

Lake Trout and Sea Lamprey. Once the premier species of the Great Lakes, the lake trout has declined steadily over the past 50 years. Specific population data or estimates are not available, but commercial harvest in the three upper Great Lakes dropped by more than 90 percent, from a range of 40 to 65 million pounds between 1920 and 1929, to a range of one to five million pounds between 1970 and 1979. Recent assessments indicate that some growth of naturally reproducing stocks has occurred in lakes Superior, Michigan, and Huron.

The slight recovery is primarily the result of a successful program to control the sea lamprey. Starting in 1961, sea lamprey spawning runs on tributary streams and rivers were treated chemically. Success was evident the following year in Lake Superior, where surveys showed an 84 percent reduction in adults. Today, chemical treatment, combined with 24 tributary barrier dams that block access to spawning areas, have reduced sea lamprey populations by more than 90 percent in Lake Superior. Similar reductions have been achieved in lakes Michigan and Huron. Lakes Ontario and Erie are just beginning to undergo treatment.

With the success of the sea lamprey program, the main impediment to lake trout recovery is excessive take. Despite the stocking of 83.5 million hatchery-produced lake trout in the three upper Great Lakes between 1965 and 1980, natural reproduction has been minimal because few fish are allowed to reach optimum spawning age. According to fishery scientists, total annual mortality in the lake trout population should not exceed 40 to 45 percent in order to restore naturally reproducing populations, but current mortality rates often exceed 70 to 80 percent.

FWS has been the lead agency for carrying out sea lamprey control in United States waters.* Also, the region's five FWS hatcheries produce 95 percent of the lake trout provided by the United States. Canada's current hatchery production of lake trout is minimal.

The FWS goal of cutting the sea lamprey populations to 10 percent or less of pretreatment levels in all the Great Lakes has been achieved in all but a few areas where chemical and mechanical controls are not economically feasible. For lake trout, the FWS objective is to develop naturally reproducing stocks in each lake by the year 2010 and to restore stocks to historic levels by the year 2030. To accomplish this goal, tougher lake trout take restrictions are needed. Restrictions have been debated by the Great Lakes Fishery Commission for several years, and by the end of 1984 the Great Lakes states were close to endorsing a lake trout rehabilitation plan.

Cutthroat Trout

The cutthroat trout (*Salmo clarki*) is a native of western North America. Eleven subspecies of cutthroat have been identified in the United States. Most inhabit streams and rivers, but the Lahontan and Yellowstone cutthroat inhabit lakes, and the coastal cutthroat is anadromous.

In general, the cutthroat has experienced a dramatic decline in numbers and distribution. Three subspecies — Lahontan, greenback, and Paiute — are listed as threatened species under the Endangered Species Act and are found only in a very small portion of their original range. Four other subspecies — Colorado River, Rio Grande, Bonneville, and Humboldt — also have been extirpated from much of their original range, but are not yet listed as threatened with extinction. For example, the

---

*Canada has its own control program

Colorado River cutthroat is found in only one percent of its historic range, and only two areas are known to have pure populations. Other cutthroat subspecies have been widely propagated and distributed. No specific population data on the species as a whole or on the individual subspecies are readily available from FWS.

The decline of the cutthroat is attributed to several factors. Small streams have been dewatered or modified by reservoir construction; riparian habitats have been destroyed by livestock; brook trout and brown trout introduced by federal and state agencies have displaced the cutthroat, and rainbow trout — also introduced — have hybridized with it to the extent that pure cutthroats have almost disappeared.* Today, new threats to habitat include mineral and oil development and water pollution.

FWS responsibilities and objectives for the cutthroat vary from subspecies to subspecies and even within a subspecies. Lacking direct management authority for the cutthroat, except for populations listed as threatened or endangered or resident on national wildlife refuges, FWS functions as a technical adviser to federal land-managing agencies, Indian tribes, and the states and propagates cutthroats in federal hatcheries to meet the management objectives of those entities. FWS lists these goals for some cutthroat subspecies in its NSSE objectives:

1. Greenback. Establish 20 pure, stable populations within the South Platte and Arkansas River drainages of Colorado to remove the species from the threatened list by 1995.
2. Colorado River. Re-establish five naturally reproducing populations in Rocky Mountain National Park and the Uintah and Ouray Indian Reservation by 1998, with the goal of establishing a controlled sport fishery.
3. Snake River. Starting by 1986, annually stock 50,000 pounds of cutthroat fish yearly in Palisades Reservoir, Wyoming, to meet federal mitigation requirements. Stock another 75,000 pounds annually in state, military-reservation, and Indian-reservation waters to support sport fishing. Evaluate by 1986 the annual stocking of six-inch, hatchery-propagated trout in lakes and reservoirs of Indian reservations in New Mexico and Arizona for sport-fishing use and ensure that these stocks do not become self-sustaining and disrupt or displace existing resident trout populations.
4. Yellowstone. Provide information, technical assistance and broodstock in support of National Park Service's management of the cutthroat in Yellowstone National Park.
5. Bonneville. Develop by 1984 with the state of Wyoming a memorandum of understanding that defines roles and responsibilities for preserving and restoring this extremely rare subspecies.**
6. Westslope. Establish at the Northwest Montana Fishery Center by 1984 an additional brood stock of pure-strain westslope cutthroat capable of producing 500,000 fry annually, and reintroduce this stock into Glacier National Park in accordance with park service management plans.***

---

*The stocking of nonindigenous trout species in cutthroat habitat commenced before the turn of the century and continued until about 10 years ago, according to FWS. FWS no longer stocks nonindigenous trout in cutthroat areas.

**The memorandum had not been completed as of May 1, 1985.

***An additional brood stock has been established but currently it produces only 25,000 to 30,000 fry yearly. These go to the Flathead Indian Reservation. Reintroduction to Glacier has yet to begin.

7. Coastal. By 1995, restore and maintain naturally reproducing populations in the Klamath River Basin.

In FY 1983, FWS propagated some three million cutthroats in federal hatcheries for stocking in federal, state, and Indian waters.

References

1. Act of February 9, 1871, 16 Stat. 593 (repealed).
2. Roy J. Wahle and Robert Z. Smith, "A Historical and Descriptive Account of Pacific Coast Anadromous Salmonid Rearing Facilities and A Summary of Their Releases by Region, 1960-76," NOAA Technical Report NMFS SSRF-736 (Washington, D.C.: U.S. Department of Commerce, 1979), p. 2.
3. James B. Trefethen, *An American Crusade for Wildlife* (New York: Winchester Press and the Boone and Crockett Club, 1975), pp. 107-108.
4. Act of February 14, 1903, Ch. 552, 32 Stat. 825.
5. Op. cit., James B. Trefethen, *An American Crusade for Wildlife*, p. 260.
6. Reorganization Plan No. 4 of 1970, 84 Stat. 2090 (currently codified in Appendix to Title 5, U.S.C.A.).
7. Pub. L. 93-271, 88 Stat. 92 (currently codified at 16 U.S.C.A. 7426).
8. Act of June 17, 1902, Ch. 1093, 32 Stat. 388 (current version at 43 U.S.C.A. 372 et seq.).
9. Act of June 10, 1920, Ch. 285, 41 Stat. 1063 (currently codified at 16 U.S.C.A. 791a et seq.).
10. 16 U.S.C.A. 811.
11. Act of March 10, 1934, Ch. 55, 48 Stat. 401 (currently codified at 16 U.S.C.A. 661 et seq.).
12. Pub. L. 90-454, 82 Stat. 625 (currently codified at 16 U.S.C.A. 1221 et seq.).
13. 16 U.S.C.A. 823; 2705 et seq.
14. Act of May 11, 1938, Ch. 193, 52 Stat. 345 (currently codified at 16 U.S.C.A. 755 et seq.).
15. Pub. L. 94-587, 90 Stat. 2917 (current version codified in scattered sections of Titles 16, 33, and 42 U.S.C.A.).
16. 16 U.S.C.A. 3301 et seq.
17. 16 U.S.C.A. 839 et seq.
18. Northwest Power Planning Council, Columbia River Basin Fish and Wildlife Program (Portland, OR: N.W.P.P.C., 1984).
19. Convention on Great Lakes Fisheries, September 10, 1954, 6 U.S.T. 2826; T.I.A.S. 3326.
20. Act of June 4, 1956, Ch. 358, 70 Stat. 242 (currently codified at 16 U.S.C.A. 931 et seq.).
21. 43 U.S.C.A. 620.
22. Pub. L. 89-304, 79 Stat. 1125 (currently codified at 16 U.S.C.A. 757a et seq.).
23. Convention for the Conservation of Salmon in the North Atlantic Ocean, T.I.A.S. 10789.
24. 16 U.S.C.A. 3601 et seq.
25. 16 U.S.C.A. 757g.
26. Act of August 9, 1950, Ch. 658, 64 Stat 430 (currently codified at 16 U.S.C.A. 777 et seq.).

27. 16 U.S.C.A. 670a et seq.
28. 16 U.S.C.A. 742a et seq.
29. 16 U.S.C.A. 460k.
30. 16 U.S.C.A. 668dd-ee.
31. 16 U.S.C.A. 3101 et seq.
32. 16 U.S.C.A. 778.
33. 16 U.S.C.A. 2801.
34. Joint Subcommittee on Aquaculture, National Aquaculture Development Plan, Volumes I and II (Washington, D.C.: Joint Subcommittee, 1983).
35. 16 U.S.C.A. 779-779f.
36. 16 U.S.C.A. 1801 et seq.; 22 U.S.C.A. 1978.
37. U.S. Department of the Interior, Fish and Wildlife Service, Service Management Plan (Washington, D.C.: Fish and Wildlife Services, September 1982).
38. U.S. Fish and Wildlife Service, Fishery Resources Program Management Document (Washington, D.C.: U.S. Fish and Wildlife Service, March 17, 1982).
39. U.S. Fish and Wildlife Service, Fishery Resources Program Advice, FY 1985-86 (Washington, D.C.: U.S. Fish and Wildlife Service).
40. U.S. Fish and Wildlife Service, Statement of Responsibilities and Role, Fishery Resources Program (Washington, D.C.: U.S. Fish and Wildlife Service, March 20, 1985).
41. U.S. Department of the Interior, Fish and Wildlife Service, National Objectives for National Species of Special Emphasis (Washington, D.C.: U.S. Fish and Wildlife Service, 1983).
42. Environmental Protection Agency, The Chesapeake Bay Program: Findings and Recommendations, September 1983.
43. U.S. Department of the Interior, Fish & Wildlife Service and U.S. Department of Commerce, National Marine Fisheries Service, Emergency Striped Bass Research Study, 1983-84.
44. Robert Boyle, "Rain of Death on the Striper?" *Sports Illustrated* (April 23, 1984, pp. 40-54).
45. Letters of Howard Larsen, FWS, to Colonel Griffith Flecher, Army Corps of Engineers, July 13, 1984; in U.S. Army Corps of Engineers and U.S. Department of Transportation, Final Supplemental Environmental Impact Statement, Vol. III, Part I, November 1984, pp. III-34.
46. New York Times, Nov. 29, 1984.
47. Letter from Bruce Higgins, NMFS, to Colonel F. H. Griffis, Corps of Engineers, Aug. 6, 1984 in Corps of Engineers and U.S. Department of Transportation, Final Supplemental Environmental Impact Statement - Westway Highway Project, Vol. III, Part 1, Nov. 1984.
48. 16 U.S.C.A. 803.
49. 16 U.S.C.A. 2705 et seq.
50. Congressman Jim Weaver, Testimony before the Subcommittee on Energy, Conservation, and Power (Sept. 11, 1984).
51. Terrence L. Thatcher, The National Wildlife Federation, Testimony before the Subcommittee on Energy, Conservation and Power (Sept. 11, 1984).
52. Krister, Colquhorun, and Pfeiffer, "Acid Rain and the Adirondack Sportfishery," *The Conservationist* (March - April, 1983), p. 24.
53. Pub. L. 98-360, 98 Stat. 403; Pub. L. 98-381, 98 Stat. 1341; Pub. L. 98-396, 98 Stat. 1369.
54. Pub. L. 98-541, 98 Stat. 2721.
55. Pub. L. 98-138, 97 Stat. 866.

56. Pub. L. 98-613, 98 Stat. 3187 (to be codified at 16 U.S.C.A. 1851).
57. Atlantic States Marine Fisheries Commission, Interstate Fisheries Management Plan for the Striped Bass, October 1981.
58. Op, cit., Joint Subcommittee on Aquaculture, National Aquaculture Development Plan, Volumes I and II.
59. Pub. L. 98-623, 98 Stat. 3407 (to be codified at 16 U.S.C.A. 2809).
60. Michael J. Bean, *The Evolution of National Wildlife Law* (New York: Praeger Publishers, 1983).
61. 103 S. Ct. 2817 (1983).
62. 536 F. Supp. 1225 (S.D. N.Y. 1982); aff'd sub. nom. *Sierra Club v. United States Army Corps of Engineers*, 701 F.2d 1011 (2d Cir. 1983).
63. *Escondido Mutual Water Co. v. LaJolla Band of Mission Indians*, 104 S. Ct. 2105 (1984).
64. 16 U.S.C.A. 811.
65. *Confederated Tribes and Bands of the Yakima Indian Nation v. the Federal Energy Regulatory Commission*, F.2d (9th Cir. 1984).
66. David S. Lee, et al., *Atlas of North American Freshwater Fishes* (Raleigh: North Carolina State Museum of Natural History, 1980).
67. Pacific Fishery Management Council, "1984 Ocean Salmon Fisheries Review" (Portland: PFMC, March 1985).
68. Congressional Research Service, The Library of Congress, General Economic Considerations for Policy Decisions Concerning Federal Fish Hatcheries, p. 17 (cited in U.S., Congress, House, Committee on Merchant Marine and Fisheries, Serial No. 98-55, p. 405).

The coyote, blamed by many for livestock losses, is the primary target of the federal Animal Damage Control Program.

The Federal Animal Damage Control Program

by *Roger L. Di Silvestro*
National Audubon Society Staff

INTRODUCTION

PROGRAMS DESIGNED TO reduce wildlife damage to agriculture and other economic interests were among the first federal wildlife management endeavors. Current wildlife control programs trace their roots to the late 19th century, when an agency was established within the Department of Agriculture to gather information on crop damage caused by birds and insects. The first direct federal control program was initiated in 1915 to kill wolves.

The U.S. Fish and Wildlife Service (FWS) of the Department of the Interior presently supervises control efforts on private, state, and local government lands and on federal lands that are not under FWS jurisdiction. The bulk of federal control efforts takes place west of the Mississippi, where coyotes are a primary target. Other targets include mountain lions, pocket gophers, prairie dogs, and other rodents. In the East, control work focuses mainly on teaching local officials and private citizens how to limit conflicts with birds.

To accomplish the agency goal — reduction of wildlife-caused damage without significant long-term adverse effects on targeted wildlife populations — FWS field personnel perform or supervise control operations or teach affected parties how to limit wildlife damages. Except for certain migratory bird problems, FWS initiates control programs only when requested to do so by states, counties, individuals, or organizations such as the National Woolgrowers Association. FWS enters into formal cooperative agreements with interests such as these in order to attempt control of three categories of wildlife — predators, migratory birds, and rodents. Control efforts range from the use of devices to frighten away damaging species to lethal means such as poisoning and shooting.

HISTORY AND LEGISLATIVE AUTHORITY

Federal animal damage control began in 1885, when the Department of Agriculture's Branch of Economic Ornithology sent out questionnaires asking farmers about damage caused by birds.[1] In 1886, the branch was elevated to division status, a sign of its expanding role. The following year the division began recommending animal damage control methods to farmers, ranchers, and other affected parties.

From 1888 to 1914 the division conducted studies and demonstrations of animal damage control techniques in the western United States. It also tested poisons for controlling the English sparrows that were spreading unchecked across the continent following their introduction in New York in 1851.[2] During this period the division also compiled natural history and other information on a variety of wild animals to determine which were beneficial and which harmful to agriculture.[3] This research grew in importance until finally, in 1896, the agency was renamed the Division of Biological Survey. The division expanded into full bureau status in 1905. Published materials based on the bureau's life-history studies included material on control methods.

In 1915, Congress gave the Bureau of Biological Survey $125,000 to be used in Texas to kill wolves, a term that in the jargon of the period included both true wolves and coyotes. This was the first appropriation for direct federal control efforts. Passage of the 1916 Convention with Great Britain for the Protection of Migratory Birds,[4] and the 1918 Migratory Bird Treaty Act,[5] which implemented the treaty, authorized issuance of permits for the taking of migratory birds "injurious to agriculture and other interests in any particular community."

By 1929, the federal control program had become extensive enough to warrant a distinct subdivision within the bureau. Thus was born the Division of Predatory Animal and Rodent Control. That same year, Westerners initiated a drive to reduce wildlife damage to crops and livestock. Because federal lands harbored many of the predators that livestockmen feared and because ranchers paid fees to graze cattle on those lands, the federal government inevitably became further involved in wildlife control.

The major outgrowth of the Westerners' push was congressional enactment in 1931 of the Animal Damage Control Act.[6] It provided the first clear statutory authority for federal control efforts and remains the legal foundation for FWS predator and rodent control programs. The act authorized the secretary of Agriculture to conduct research on the best means for eradicating, suppressing, or bringing under control mountain lions, wolves, coyotes, bobcats, prairie dogs, gophers, ground squirrels, jackrabbits, and other animals thought to be harmful not only to agricultural crops and livestock, but also to "wild game animals, fur-bearing animals, and birds. . . ." Additionally, it authorized and directed the secretary to conduct campaigns for the destruction or control of injurious animals.

The act also considerably broadened federal control horizons. Earlier federal control activities, authorized by various appropriations statutes, had been restricted to federal lands. The 1931 act authorized federal control activities on state, territorial, and private lands as well.

Animal damage control remained within the Agriculture Department until 1939, when President Franklin Roosevelt undertook a far-reaching plan to reorganize the government. One of Roosevelt's goals was to consolidate within the Department of the Interior all federal activities dealing primarily with wildlife. Reorganization Plan Number II 4(f) put animal damage control under Interior's new Branch of Predator and Rodent Control.

In 1946, the Fish and Wildlife Coordination Act of 1934[7] was amended to authorize the Interior Secretary to cooperate with other federal, state, and private agencies in minimizing damage caused by "overabundant" species. In 1948 the Lea Act[8] was passed, authorizing the rental or purchase of up to 20,000 acres of California land to provide migrating geese and ducks with a feeding site in an effort to keep them from raiding unharvested crop lands. The Waterfowl Depredations Control Act of

1956[9] authorized the Interior secretary to requisition Commodity Credit Corporation surplus grain for use in luring waterfowl away from agricultural crops.

Throughout the 1930s, 1940s, and 1950s the federal government operated its animal damage control program with little major opposition. For instance, as late as 1962 the Bald Eagle Protection Act[10] of 1940 was amended to permit the secretary of the Interior, on request from the governor of any state, to authorize the killing of golden eagles to protect livestock.

However, as citizens became more environmentally aware in the 1960s, animal damage control came under closer scrutiny. Concurrently, the teaching of wildlife management in major universities changed to reflect a realization among biologists that predators fulfilled an important role in natural communities. Moreover, the widespread use of poisons to kill predators increasingly was subject to sharp criticism even from traditionally conservative interests, including the editors of national hunting

POISONS USED IN FEDERAL ANIMAL DAMAGE CONTROL PROGRAMS

Reg. No.	Toxicant	Concentration	Species	Restrictions
6704-6	Zinc Phosphide	1.82%	Field Mice	
6704-15	Strychnine	5.79%	Porcupine	Not to be used in area occupied by Gray Wolf or Grizzly Bear
6704-20	Zinc Phosphide	2.0%	Field Mice	
6704-28	Zinc Phosphide	63.0%	Orchard Mice	
6704-36	Zinc Phosphide	63.0%	Rats	
6704-42	Strychnine	.6%	Pigeons	Feral & Domestic
6704-43	Zinc Phosphide	.92%	Field Mice	
6704-52	Zinc Phosphide	63.0%	Muskrats Nutria	
6704-56	DRC-1339	98.0%	Starlings Blackbirds	Concentrate for mixing baits
6704-57	Strychnine	.35%	Ground Squirrels Jackrabbits Kangaroo Rats Cotton Rats Pocket Gohpers	Burrow Builder Only for Pocket Gophers
6704-58	Strychnine	.50%	Ground Squirrels Kangaroo Rats Cotton Rats Pocket Gophers	Burrow Builder Only for Pocket Gophers
6704-73	PA-14	99.5%	Red-winged Blackbirds Rusty Blackbirds Common Grackles Brown-headed Cowbirds Starlings	
6704-74	Zinc Phosphide	2.0%	Prairie Dogs	

and fishing magazines. Many believed that the methods for distributing broad-spectrum lethal poisons such as Compound 1080 (sodium fluoroacetate) caused the deaths of too many nontarget animals. During this time, FWS relied heavily on the use of carcass baits — whole livestock carcasses laced with Compound 1080 — to kill coyotes. However, these baits killed many eagles, bears, badgers, and other animals that fed on them. Moreover, evidence suggested that the poison was so lethal that anything feeding on the carcass of a predator killed with Compound 1080 also would die.

It also was believed that overzealous control agents were ignoring the rules governing the use of poisons, putting out more baits in a given area than was legally allowed and giving to ranchers upon request poisons that were supposed to be restricted to use by trained control agents. One reason given for the presumed overzealousness of the agents was their close relationship with the livestock producers whose contributions to the federal animal damage control program funded part, and sometimes all, of an agent's salary.

One response to the new dubiousness about animal damage control was the 1964 Leopold Report. This was the product of the Advisory Board on Wildlife Management, a special committee appointed the previous year by Interior Secretary Stewart Udall to investigate federal control efforts. Officially the report was entitled "Predator and Rodent Control in the United States,"[11] but the controversial document was nicknamed after the chairman of the committee that produced it, noted zoologist A. Starker Leopold.

"It is the unanimous opinion of this Board that control as actually practiced today is considerably in excess of the amount that can be justified in terms of total public interest," the board declared in its report. The committee explained that control efforts often were undertaken at the behest of livestockmen with little investigation by control agents to determine the legitimacy of the livestockmen's complaints. "In short, the federal predator and rodent control program is to a considerable degree shaped and designed by those who feel they are suffering damage from wildlife," the report said. "There is no mechanism to assure that the positive social values of wildlife are given any weight in decision making nor that control, when it is undertaken, will be limited to minimal needs." The committee also pointed out that distribution of highly lethal poisons to control predators and rodents often was done in violation of control program rules and regulations.

To remedy the problems it perceived in the federal control program, the Leopold Committee made six recommendations:

1. Appoint a special control advisory board with a balanced membership that would include representatives of the livestock and agricultural industries, conservation organizations, and scientific societies.
2. Redefine control-program goals to encompass broad public interests, not just the interests of agriculture.
3. Develop a better control operation system, including better criteria for justifying control programs, more state funding of control efforts, and replacement of the permanent rabies control program in the eastern United States with squads of agents who would work only in areas where rabies becomes a problem.
4. Amplify research to find more species-specific control methods and to develop nonlethal controls such as repellents and fences.
5. Rename the Branch of Predator and Rodent Control to reflect a concern not only for the control but also for the conservation of wildlife.
6. Tighten legal controls over poisons.

Subsequent to the report, the Branch of Predator and Rodent Control in 1965 was renamed the Division of Wildlife Services and given responsibility not only for control but also for wildlife management and for monitoring pesticide use. A wildlife biologist was appointed as its chief. Also, increased efforts were made to develop nonlethal control techniques, such as use of chemical sterilization. However, most of the other recommendations met with resistance. For this reason and also because predator control continued as a special focus of public concern, a seven-man Advisory Committee on Predator Control, headed by Leopold Committee-member Stanley Cain, was appointed in 1971 by the Department of the Interior and the Council on Environmental Quality. The committee released its findings, dubbed the Cain Report,[12] the following January.

The Cain Report reaffirmed the recommendations of the earlier study and concluded that:

> the claimed ecological benefits of predator control have been exaggerated. Even granting that some reduction in sheep losses may have been achieved, the evidence leads us to suspect that these losses are a fairly minor part of the total, and that the stockman should be directing his concern toward more important mortality sources. There are claims that uncontrolled coyote populations are sources for rabies outbreaks; but the evidence here is scanty. And despite the claimed benefit of coyote control for deer management, this benefit would, in general, appear at best to be a minor one.

Moreover, the report said that since wildlife resources belong to all citizens, the "right of any limited segment of society to reduce or eliminate predators is increasingly open to question."

The Cain Report outlined 15 recommendations, among them:

1. End the financial and operational partnership that exists between the control program and private livestock interests by funding the program entirely with federal and state money. This recommendation, an effort to end a system that Cain in 1978 said "justifies favoritism to local interests and neglect of national interests,"[13] has never been adopted.

2. Suspend the registration of all toxic chemicals used in predator control. Adoption of this recommendation was initiated in February 1972 when President Richard Nixon banned the use of poisons against predators on federal lands and in federal programs.[14] The following month the Environmental Protection Agency cancelled the predacidal uses of Compound 1080, strychnine, and sodium cyanide, the poisons used most widely against predators.[15] This order basically prohibited use of the chemicals against predators by anyone anywhere. However, use of some poisons later was revived.

3. Require professional training of all control agents. Only trained wildlife biologists now are hired as control supervisory personnel and researchers. However, control agents and trappers still generally lack professional training.

4. Shift from federal poison-based control programs to state trapping programs. This recommendation has never been adopted because the 1931 Animal Damage Control Act, which directs the Department of the Interior to share control responsibilities with the states, has never been amended.

5. Create an insurance program to protect against the economic burden of exceptional losses to predators. This recommendation has never been adopted because losses are too difficult and expensive to validate.

6. Prohibit predator control on designated wilderness areas. No predator control currently is conducted in wilderness areas.

The committee also recommended tighter restrictions on the shooting of coyotes from aircraft, initiation of studies on the cost-benefit ratio of predator control relative to livestock losses, establishment of state trapper training programs for livestock owners, suspension or revocation of grazing permits belonging to those who violate predator control laws, study of the ecological role of predators and of the epidemiology of rabies, stronger protections from control efforts for species listed under the federal Endangered Species Act, and a banning on the broadcast distribution of toxicants for the control of rodents, rabbits, and other pests on federal and possibly private lands.

Since publication of the report, research into control economics, predator roles, and rabies has been initiated and endangered species protection strengthened, according to the 1978 Interior report, "Predator Damage in the West: A Study of Coyote Management Alternatives."[16] The other recommendations still await formal legislative or administrative adoption.

In 1974, the Division of Wildlife Services was replaced with the Office of Animal Damage Control, providing better conformance with a budgeting process that separates control functions from other FWS responsibilities. Responsible only for animal damage control, the office was expanded in 1976 into the Division of Animal Damage Control. In 1980 it was reduced to a branch of the Division of Wildlife Management. It is the largest branch of that division, which also is responsible for implementation of the Marine Mammal Protection Act, eagle management, and all FWS aircraft operations.

Sharp criticism of the federal animal damage control program surfaced in 1978 in an inspector general's report to the assistant secretary for Fish and Wildlife and Parks. The report concluded that FWS did not provide meaningful financial reports on the total control program, conducted insufficient year-end performance evaluations of individual FWS-state control programs, did not thoroughly document the need for regional office funding allocations, was slipshod in reaching agreements for control on private property, did not conduct adequate annual operational inspections of district field assistants, and did a poor job of monitoring and enforcing the administration of a control contract with the state of Washington.[17] Moreover, the report said that FWS did not have data to justify the existence of its control program since it could not show the total amount of livestock protected by control programs, total livestock losses to coyote predation, numbers of coyotes causing damage, or the relation of control methods to predator damage reduction. Finally, the report declared that the Animal Damage Control Policy Handbook governing the control program was outdated and obsolete.

As a direct result of these criticisms, Interior Secretary Cecil Andrus in 1979 initiated sweeping reforms in the government's predator control policies.[18] The new policy represented an effort to move away from killing predators and toward activities aimed at preventing damage caused by them. Andrus ended research on the use of Compound 1080 against predators and emphasized development of such nonlethal methods as predator-proof fencing and the use of guarding dogs. Andrus also recommended tight new controls on aircraft use in shooting predators, demanded that traps be used in such a way as to increase the chance of taking only target species, and outlawed denning, the killing of coyote pups in their dens.

Andrus soon partially reversed his new policy, permitting completion of Compound 1080 toxic-collar research already under way.* Then, shortly after taking office, President Reagan repealed Nixon's executive order banning the use of poisons

---

*Toxic collars are rubber bladders filled with the poison and put around the necks of sheep to kill attacking predators.

against predators on federal lands.[19] The Reagan Administration subsequently revived the use of denning and encouraged an attempt by FWS to have the Environmental Protection Agency lift its ban on Compound 1080.

The federal animal damage control program is governed today by the 1931 act and by four migratory bird treaty acts — the 1916 treaty with Great Britain, the 1936 treaty with Mexico,[20] the 1972 act with Japan,[21] and the 1976 treaty with the Soviet Union.[22] However, conduct of the program also must comply with other laws that provide strong protection for wildlife and the environment. Among these are the Endangered Species Act,[23] the National Environmental Policy Act,[24] the Federal Insecticide, Fungicide and Rodenticide Act,[25] and the Federal Environmental Pesticide Control Act.[26] These help safeguard against abusive use of toxins and against the 1931 act's call for the eradication of certain species. In fact, the Endangered Species Act expressly forbids federal agencies to engage in activities that could cause the extinction of any species, with the exception of certain injurious insects. All control activities also are subject to the laws of the states in which they take place.

ORGANIZATION AND OPERATIONS

Responsibilities and Roles[27]

The goal of the animal damage control (ADC) program is reduction of losses caused by nonendangered wildlife on private, state, and non-FWS federal lands. Control activities on FWS refuges are not part of the ADC program but rather are conducted by personnel of the Division of Refuge Management. Similarly, control actions to benefit endangered or threatened species or to reduce problems caused by endangered or threatened species are administered by the Office of Endangered Species.

Federal ADC activities include reducing livestock and crop losses to wildlife, reducing bird/aircraft conflicts, checking the spread of wildlife-borne diseases to humans, advising and cooperating with private individuals and other agencies to assure that control activities have minimal adverse biological and social impacts, and conducting research.

ADC operations are initiated by request only. Requests come from other government agencies and from private citizens and organizations. Before starting an ADC campaign, FWS is supposed to review evidence showing when and where a need for control exists. All control agreements are subject to a master agreement with the state in which the control will be conducted. This agreement outlines the cost and funding of the control efforts and the responsibilities of the federal and state personnel, including who will conduct control programs and how reports will be filed. Cooperative agreements are made with other federal agencies, state agencies, private organizations, and individual citizens. These are more detailed than the master agreements and specify who will conduct the control measures used, which techniques will be applied, and what resources will be protected.

In many cases, the agents who carry out ADC programs in the field — setting traps, distributing poisons, or initiating other controls — are not FWS personnel. They may be paid by livestock associations, county governments, or other private or government agencies. However, all agents are supervised by FWS which, in accordance with cooperative agreements, administers the funds for their salaries.

FWS has ADC agreements with 45 states. FWS also has ADC-related memoranda of understanding with other federal agencies, including various military bases, the U.S. Forest Service, the National Park Service, the Federal Aviation Administration, the Department of Agriculture's extension service, and the U.S. Agency for International Development. In all, FWS has more than 700 cooperative agreements with federal and state agencies, local municipalities, Indian tribes, universities, and private organizations, including agreements with state fish and wildlife agencies, health and agriculture departments, livestock boards, county commissioners, timber companies, and livestock associations.[28] Control efforts in 1984 required a total work force equivalent to 648 full-time employees.[29]

In the West, where most control work is conducted, the coyote is a primary target. Some 52,000 were taken by animal damage control agents in the West in 1983.[30] In the East, FWS control agents act mainly as disseminators of information. They provide instructions on how to solve problems with birds such as gulls that gather near airports and create hazards to aircraft. They also assist in the control of blackbirds that gather in large roosts. Blackbirds are controlled because in large concentrations they can become vectors for human diseases and damage crops and property. Other control-program targets include rodents, such as pocket gophers, prairie dogs, and rats, and wild geese introduced as permanent residents by state and local agencies to town parks and other areas where the birds' increasing numbers have created conflicts with private citizens.

Congressional Committees

The Senate Subcommittee on Environmental Pollution, of the Committee on Environment and Public Works, and the House Subcommittee on Fisheries, Wildlife Conservation, and the Environment have jurisdiction over federal animal damage control. The House and Senate appropriations committees determine how much money the control program will receive yearly. The annual animal damage control budget is reviewed by the subcommittee on the Interior Department and related agencies, which also allocates funds to the program.

Agency Structure and Function[31]

ADC is the responsibility of the associate director for wildlife resources, who reports directly to the FWS director. Under the associate director for wildlife resources is the deputy associate director for wildlife management, direct superior of the chief of the Division of Wildlife Management. ADC is administered by this division.

Line authority, the capacity to issue orders to a lower organizational level, is held by the director, regional directors, assistant regional directors, animal damage control regional supervisors, and state supervisors.

ADC programs are administered by individual FWS state offices in accordance with master project agreements between FWS and appropriate state agencies or non-government bodies.

The regions receive overall ADC program and operational directions from the associate director for Wildlife Resources. The program manager, through his support staff in the Division of Wildlife Management, monitors progress in attaining ADC program objectives and evaluates program performance. The division recommends ADC budget and manpower allocations and ADC program objectives to the associate director for Wildlife Resources. The division chief measures the quality and efficiency of operations and recommends ADC operational policies, regulations, and procedures to the associate director. The associate director allocates money and manpower and issues the annual Program Advice, a document that outlines specific program objectives for each region and for the FWS research facility headquartered in Denver.

U.S. Fish and Wildlife Service
Animal Damage Control Program

Planning[32]

ADC programs receive direction from FWS management plans, documents issued every 10 years to outline FWS goals, policies, and strategies; from the wildlife resources program management document, a major planning document that gives broad management guidance to ADC for one to five years by delineating goals, strategies, and policies; from annual work-plan advices issued each fiscal year by regional offices to provide more detailed guidance than is contained in the associate director's program advice; and from annual work plans, documents prepared by state supervisors to describe work to be accomplished by each ADC office during a fiscal year. ADC personnel receive specific instructions on their goals and conduct from the Animal Damage Control Manual,[33] issued by the associate director of Wildlife Resources in conjunction with the chief of the Division of Wildlife Management.

Budgeting

ADC budgeting begins when the directors of the seven FWS geographical regions submit their budget requests to the FWS Program Development Branch.[34] Branch staff works with the FWS director to determine the ADC funding request. The FWS proposal is then sent to the Department of the Interior, which subsequently sends it to the Office of Management and Budget (OMB). Interior or OMB may make changes in the proposal, which is sent back to FWS before being forwarded to Congress as part of the president's annual budget. Authorizing committees in both houses hold hearings on the budget requests and then make recommendations to their respective budget committees. The appropriations committees decide how much money is actually appropriated to animal damage control work as part of the annual Interior and Related Agencies Appropriations bill, usually approved between June and November for the following federal fiscal year, which begins October 1.

FWS allocates the appropriated funds to its various programs. Annual work plans are finalized at this time. Periodic evaluations conducted by FWS are supposed to insure that annual work objectives are being met.

State, county, and private sources that have joined with FWS in cooperative control agreements also provide funds for control activities. Although in some areas livestock associations pay up to half of control-program expenses, FWS at the state level retains administrative control of all funds.

Since 1979, ADC appropriations have remained largely stable. Declining dollar

Animal Damage Control Funding Summary for Fiscal Years 1980-85

Operations

Fiscal Year	Amount Requested	Amount Appropriated
1979		$11,461,000
1980	$7,360,000	11,488,000
1981	10,477,000	11,612,000
1982	11,814,000	11,429,000
1983	9,873,000	11,605,000
1984	10,485,000	12,018,000
1985	12,111,000	15,299,000

Research

Fiscal Year	Amount Requested	Amount Appropriated
1979		$5,240,000
1980	$4,024,000	4,028,000
1981	5,127,000	4,307,000
1982	4,073,000	3,978,000
1983	3,541,000	3,850,000
1984	3,495,000*	3,837,000
1985	3,602,000	4,235,000

*New budget format with maintenance deleted ($237,000).
(Source: USFWS)

value therefore has limited some programs. Congress sought to remedy this by adding $3.5 million to the agency's budget request for fiscal 1985, bringing the total appropriation for ADC operations and research to $19,534,000.

Research

ADC research, headquartered at the Denver Wildlife Research Center, has investigated such control techniques as the use of lethal poisons, guarding dogs, and food aversion, also called taste aversion, to control coyote depredations. Food aversion presently is being tested for use against crop-damaging birds and rodents. Food aversion involves lacing a bait with a chemical that sickens rather than kills whatever eats it. Coyotes and all tested species of rodents and birds learn to avoid the food, such as mutton or grain crops, that was used as bait. Dimethylanthranilate, a chemical harmless to humans and used in grape-flavored carbonated beverages, is being tested for use against blackbirds. When exposed to grains treated with the chemical, the birds react as humans do when exposed to ammonia. Genetic research is being conducted in an attempt to develop breeds of crop species that are more resistant to depredation.

CURRENT PROGRAM TRENDS

Many of the reforms recommended by various investigative committees in 1964, 1971, and 1978 have yet to be implemented. When data were sought for this report, FWS was unable to provide adequate figures for documenting the effectiveness of its programs in reducing animal-caused damage. Nor can FWS readily quantify the livestock and crop damage that its control program attempts to reduce. However, the Division of Wildlife Management now is developing a computer-based information system that should help to better fulfill the program's data needs. The system should be in operation in two to three years.

Reforms proposed by Interior Secretary Cecil Andrus to shift control programs from an emphasis on lethal techniques to one using nonlethal, preventative methods have been reversed by the Reagan Administration. Compound 1080, banned for use against predators in the early 1970s, in 1983 was approved by the Environmental Protection Agency for certain types of predacidal use.[35] EPA now is drawing up rules for such use.

Every year the seven FWS geographical regions turn in reports covering such topics as expenses, numbers of animals killed, and value of property lost to wildlife. The regional reports have been summarized only once into a complete national report.[36] That was in 1980. That year FWS reported a national take of 82,240 animals, including wolves, javelinas, rats, bats, mountain lions, grizzly bears, foxes, bobcats, coyotes, black bears, pigs, house cats, calves, and other target and nontarget animals. An additional 121,771 starlings were reported killed but not included in the overall figure. Confirmed and unconfirmed losses to wildlife for that year totaled a reported $8,612,303. The animal damage control program for 1980 cost a bit more than twice that, $17,621,206, in federal and nonfederal funds.

CURRENT ISSUES

Ban The Leghold Trap

Many conservation and humane groups are seeking a federal leghold-trap ban, arguing that the trap causes unnecessary suffering, results in the killing of too many nontarget animals, and could be replaced with more humane and precise techniques. A federal ban theoretically could be established by barring interstate commerce of traps and of furs caught in traps, according to one FWS official, but difficulties in identifying trapped furs would make the law unenforceable. Moreover, FWS "isn't prepared" to ban the trap because, with the exception of poisons, traps are the best tools for controlling animal damage, the official said.

Alaska Aerial Wolf Hunting

FWS received more mail in 1984 on this issue than any other, according to one official. The letters asked FWS to stop the Alaska Department of Fish and Game from killing hundreds of wolves in selected parts of the state over a three-year period. State personnel shoot the wolves from aircraft in a program that is supposed to protect reduced moose and caribou populations from wolf predation. Conservationists argued that the ungulate populations are down in some areas not because of wolves but because of a combination of other factors, including unusually harsh winters and overhunting.

Overhunting could in fact be a component of the problem, one federal source said. But, he added, in some areas wolves can reduce or suppress already reduced ungulate populations if the herds have been fragmented by roads or pipelines. Thus ungulate reductions may more properly be blamed on the roads or the pipelines than on wolf predation.

In January, the Alaska Department of Fish and Game suspended the hunt after receiving notice from the Federal Communications Commission (FCC) that the state was violating an FCC permit by using research radio collars to track down and shoot packs of wolves. The FCC, which administers the use of radio frequencies, said the department was permitted use of the collars for research only and that using the collars to locate wolves to kill them is not research. The department agreed to review its wolf-control program before continuing it.

So far FWS, which lacks direct jurisdiction over the state wolf hunt and therefore cannot stop it, has no wolf hunt of its own. FWS, under the Alaska National Interest Lands Conservation Act,[37] has the authority to control wolves for the benefit of subsistence hunters, but subsistence hunters do not want federal wolf control because the hunters themselves make money killing wolves for furs.

Compound 1080

The Environmental Protection Agency late in 1983, at the behest of various livestock associations and Western senators and representatives, and following public hearings, dropped its ban on the use of Compound 1080 in toxic collars, reviving predacidal use of the poison. Now EPA is examining current evidence to draw up the rules under which toxic collars will be used. Once the rules are made, Compound 1080 in toxic collars will be reregistered for use. EPA also determined that Compound 1080 single-lethal-dose baits should be reregistered for use. FWS currently is doing research on the baits to justify the reregistration. Until that work is done, rules for use of the baits cannot be drawn up and the baits cannot be used.

Meanwhile, 12 conservation groups have gone to court to stop Compound 1080 use against predators. These groups are Defenders of Wildlife, the National Audubon Society, Environmental Defense Fund, Natural Resources Defense Council, Sierra Club National Wildlife Committee, Friends of the Earth, National Parks and Conservation Association, Humane Society of the United States, American Humane Association, Animal Protection Institute of America, Society for Animal Protective Legislation, and Fund for Animals. They argue that the Federal Insecticide, Fungicide and Rodenticide Act permits the reregistration of poisins only if substantial new evidence exists to warrant the change. In the case of Compound 1080, no such evidence exists, the groups say. A 10-year study by FWS of coyote population trends in the West indicates that although coyote populations made small increases in the two years following the Compound 1080 ban, the populations decreased in 1975, 1976, and 1977 and did not change significantly again through 1981, the last year of the study.[38] Moreover, the groups fear that Compound 1080 reregistration will lead to widespread misuse of the poison.

These groups oppose Compound 1080 use because, they say, the poison kills too many nontarget species that eat either the baits or parts of predators killed by the poison. Moreover, killing predators such as coyotes and mountain lions can lead to increases in predation, some conservationists say. This can happen for two reasons. One is that litter size often increases after predator populations have been reduced by some factor such as control, helping to boost local numbers. The second reason is that predators usually are territorial. Killing resident animals, including those that do not prey on livestock, invites new predators into the vacated territory. New animals often are younger animals seeking a home. Young animals and older individuals new to an area are more likely to prey on easily killed livestock.

Nonlethal controls such as guarding dogs — special breeds whose natural inclination to socialize with livestock makes them easily trained to protect sheep, goats, and cattle — and food aversion would make better control substitutes, according to conservationists opposed to killing predators. For example, use of guarding dogs has reduced predation to zero on some Oregon ranches that had suffered heavy lamb losses.[39] Conservationists also point out that Saskatchewan, Canada, successfully used food aversion as the province's first line of defense against predators for several years, until a change in administrators brought revival of lethal controls. However, FWS is reluctant to fund further studies of these methods. FWS currently is researching the use of guarding dogs only because Congress in 1984 appropriated $45,000, over FWS objections, for the first year of a three-year study. Some FWS officials say that research already shows that the dogs work well under certain conditions and so more studies are not needed, while others say the dogs do not work at all. FWS has dropped its coyote food-aversion studies because, officials say, the technique has practical limits on its use in predator control. However, some experts say that FWS food-aversion reseach was improperly conducted and therefore gave inconclusive or inaccurate results.[40]

Most federal ADC personnel remain staunchly skeptical about the usefulness of nonlethal controls. Some conservationists believe this is because ADC staffers traditionally prefer lethal controls. FWS officials who admit they have no data to support their own claims that guarding dogs do not work seem to support the conservationist claim. Moreover, although these officials want to revive use of Compound 1080 single-lethal-dose baits, they agree that FWS research is still three to four years away from conclusions that might justify any need for reregistration of the baits.

The suit to stop Compound 1080 reregistration is accompanied by a second suit brought by Western livestockmen who say that reregistration of toxic collars and single-lethal-dose baits only is too restrictive. They seek the use of carcass baits — whole sheep or horses injected with the poison and left in the field. EPA so far has not approved their use. The agency banned the baits in 1972 because evidence indicated that carcass baits kill many nontarget animals, including dogs.

The Compound 1080 issue may surface in another form in 1985. FWS in February 1984 asked the EPA to issue a two-year experimental-use permit so FWS can drop 100,000 Compound 1080 single-lethal-dose baits from airplanes and helicopters on Kiska Island in Alaska's Aleutian Island chain.[41] The purpose will be to extirpate the island's introduced arctic foxes in order to protect endangered Aleutian Canada geese that nest there. Although the Aleutian Canada Goose Recovery Plan calls for extirpation of the foxes, the plan does not specify use of Compound 1080.[42] A few conservation groups can be expected to oppose this attempt to use the poison.

Minnesota Wolves

Minnesota's gray wolves were listed as endangered in 1973, but in 1978 Minnesota farmers and hunters persuaded FWS to change the listing to threatened. This permitted federal control agents to kill wolves suspected of livestock depredations. Under this approach the wolf population has remained stable at about 1,200 animals, the only major wolf population in the lower 48 states. Scarcely 50 gray wolves survive in the lower 48 outside of Minnesota.

Since 1978, the federal government has conducted a highly selective trapping program designed to kill individual wolves suspected of depredations. But in 1983 the Department of the Interior under Secretary James Watt proposed to transfer wolf management to the state, which intended to reopen sport trapping of the animals. Trappers would be permitted to take up to 160 wolves yearly and sell the hides. This toll would be added to the estimated 450 wolves already killed illegally each year.

The state also proposed to loosen regulations governing the taking of depredating wolves by control agents. Under federal guidelines, trapping of depredating wolves is restricted to within a quarter mile of farms with losses. Trapping is limited to 10 days unless further losses occur, in which case trapping is extended up to 21 days. Young wolves are released since they cannot kill large livestock.

Under the proposed state plan, control agents could kill any and all wolves, including pups, within half a mile of farms with losses to wolves. The proposal sets no criteria for selecting trappers or for verifying wolf kills and sets no limit on the length of time trapping is to be conducted following a kill.

The move to transfer wolf management to the state was opposed in court by 14 conservation groups. Federal District Judge Miles Lord in January 1984 ruled against the transfer of wolf management to the state. He said that the sport trapping season was illegal and the control changes unjustified and argued that the wolves needed increased protection to stop the illegal kill.

FWS appealed. In February 1985 the Eighth Circuit Court of Appeals upheld the ban against sport hunting of the threatened wolves, but reversed and sent back for trial Judge Lord's ruling against expansion of the wolf-control program. The appellate court said the trial court should give additional consideration to the reasons for the changes.

Conservationists will continue opposition to state wolf management, a sport season on wolves, and expansion of a wolf-control program that already has a reputation for success in a state where only one-tenth of one percent of the livestock is lost to wolves.[43]

Killing of Nontarget Wildlife

The FWS control program has been criticized by conservationists because of its failure to ensure that only livestock-depredating and crop-damaging animals are killed. A 1961 study showed that control operations in New Mexico, Colorado, and Wyoming that used leghold traps to capture bobcats and coyotes killed 1,199 animals, only 259 of them from the target species, a 78 percent failure rate.[44]

FWS tends to ignore threats to nontarget animals, and agents are not encouraged to search for nontarget animals killed by poisons. Although the FWS application for use of Compound 1080 on Kiska Island lists no threats to nontarget animals, one FWS official said he is certain some Kiska bald eagles will be lost to the poison.

Conservationists continue to urge FWS to use more selective control methods and to be more accountable in recording nontarget losses.

LEGISLATION

FY 1985 Appropriations Increase

At the request of Representative Tom Loeffler (R-Texas), the House Appropriations Committee recommended an additional $3.5 million for the FY 1985 animal damage control budget. Loeffler's district suffers heavy predator losses, his staff says. That sum, approved by the 98th Congress, included $300,000 for bird control near Eastern airports, $300,000 for blackbird control in Louisiana and South Dakota, and $2.9 million for coyote control. The increase was designed to bring the control budget up to the equivalent of 1979 spending levels.

A New Home for Animal Damage Control

A potential legislative storm began brewing in 1984 when Senator Steven D. Symms (R-Idaho) led several other senators in an effort to wrest the animal damage control program from the Interior Department and place it in the Department of Agriculture. Symms was supported in this effort primarily by the National Association of State Departments of Agriculture and also by livestock associations and the American Farm Bureau.

A Symms aide explained that animal damage control was moved from Agriculture to Interior by an error in the interpretation of the 1939 governmental reorganization under Franklin Roosevelt. Symms is basing this conclusion on a president's message that accompanied the legislation. In the message Roosevelt said, ". . .I intend to direct that facilities of the Department of Agriculture shall continue to be used for research studies which have to do with the protection of domestic animals from diseases of wildlife, and also where most economical for the protection to farmers and stockmen against predatory animals."

If the control program were moved it probably would go into the Agriculture Department's Animal, Plant and Health Inspection Services (APHIS), Symms' aide said. One executive for the National Audubon Society indicated that this could prove an alarming development, since APHIS has a reputation for favoring the widespread use of poisons. The Symms aide, however, argued that the Agriculture Department might be less likely to kill predators than would FWS, which sees predator damage as a wildlife-management problem, not a livestock-protection problem.

One FWS official said, however, that livestock interests are behind the desire to move control to Agriculture because they believe FWS is not trying hard enough to poison predators. The livestock interests believe that the Department of Agriculture would be more likely to seek eradication of coyotes and other predators, the official speculated.

Interior Secretary William Clark said he supported the transfer. However, he differed with Symms on how it should be accomplished. Symms believes the move should be made administratively by an agreement between the Agriculture and Interior secretaries. Clark recommended that the transfer be accomplished by congressional action.

Leghold Trap Ban

The House Health and Environment Subcommittee of the Committee on Energy and Commerce in August held a hearing on a bill introduced by Representative Clarence D. Long (D-Maryland) to ban interstate commerce in leghold traps and in products derived from animals caught in leghold traps. Hearings on a national trap ban have not been held since 1975. However, the bill died in subcommittee, and Representative Long was defeated for re-election. Representative Tom Lantos (D-California) is expected to introduce a trap-ban bill this year.

LEGAL DEVELOPMENTS

With the exception of the Compound 1080 suit discussed in the issues section, no legal developments occurred last year regarding federal animal damage control.

RESOURCE STATUS

No reliable data exists to show whether target and nontarget species killed in control programs are declining, stable, or increasing. Neither state nor federal wildlife managers can provide specific data on the numbers of coyotes, badgers, bobcats, foxes, and other predators in any given population. Instead, wildlife managers dealing with predators usually look for trends to determine if populations are stable. As long as the same numbers of each predator species are killed each year, it is presumed the population is stable. However, with one exception, FWS has never graphed its annual predator-kill records over several years, to reveal these telltale trends.

The exception was a 1981 report on a 10-year survey of coyote population trends.[45] The survey was conducted in nine Western states and Illinois, starting the year after compound 1080 was banned for predator control. The report indicates that coyote populations had small but significant increases in 1973 and 1974, decreases in 1975, 1976, and 1977, and no significant changes from 1978 through 1981.

Federal control officials also are unable to provide figures showing whether livestock and crop losses to predators and birds are increasing or decreasing. Although figures are available on the amount of livestock thought to be lost to predators each year, FWS has not sought to use these figures to reveal livestock loss trends over several years or decades.

REFERENCES

1. U.S. Department of the Interior, Fish and Wildlife Service, Animal Damage Control Manual (Washington, D.C.: USDOI, 1983), p. 1.8.
2. Nathaniel P. Reed and Dennis Drabelle, *The United States Fish and Wildlife Service* (Boulder and London: Westview Press, 1984), p. 75.
3. Op. cit., U.S. Department of the Interior, Animal Damage Control Manual, p. 1.8.
4. Convention for the Protection of Migratory Birds, August 16, 1916, United States-Great Britain (on behalf of Canada), 39 Stat. 1702, T.S. No. 628.
5. Act of July 3, 1918, Ch. 128, 40 Stat. 755 (Current version at 16 U.S.C.A. 703 et seq.).
6. Act of March 2, 1931, 46 Stat. 1468 (Currently codified at 7 U.S.C.A. 426-426b).
7. Act of March 10, 1934, Ch. 55, 48 Stat. 401 (Current version at 16 U.S.C.A. 661 et seq.).
8. Act of May 18, 1948, Ch. 303, 62 Stat. 238 (Currently codified at 16 U.S.C.A. 695 et seq.).
9. Act of July 3, 1956, Ch. 512, 70 Stat. 492 (Current version at 7 U.S.C.A. 442 et seq.).
10. Act of June 8, 1940, Ch. 278 54 Stat. 250 (Current version at 16 U.S.C. 668 et seq.).
11. U. S. Department of the Interior, Fish and Wildlife Service, "Predator and Rodent Control in the United States" (Washington, D.C.: USDOI, 1964).
12. Stanley A. Cain, chairman, Predator Control — 1971 (Ann Arbor: University of Michigan, 1972).
13. Stanley A. Cain, "Predator and Pest Control," in *Wildlife and America*, Howard Brokaw, ed., Committee on Environmental Quality, U.S. Fish and Wildlife Service, U.S. Forest Service, and the National Oceanic and Atmospheric Administration, 1978, p. 393.
14. Exec. Order 11643, 3 C.F.R. 664 (1971-75 Comp.).
15. 77 Fed. Reg. 5718 (March 18, 1972).
16. U.S. Department of the Interior, Fish and Wildlife Service, "Predator Damage in the West: A Study of Coyote Management Alternatives" (Washington, D.C.: USDOI, 1978). p. 4.
17. U.S. Department of the Interior, Office of Audit and Investigation, "Review of the Animal Damage Control Program U.S. Fish and Wildlife Service" (Washington, D.C. USDOI, 1978), pp. 5-7.
18. Michael J. Bean, *The Evolution of National Wildlife Law* (New York: Praeger, 1983), p. 238. Also see Sara Polenick, "Controlling Animal Damage" (Washington: Defenders of Wildlife, 1980), p. 9.

19. Exec. Order 12342, 47 Fed. Reg. 4223 (Jan. 29, 1982).
20. Convention for the Protection of Migratory Birds and Game Mammals, February 7, 1936, United States-Mexico, 50 Stat. 1311, T.S. No. 912.
21. Convention for the Protection of Migratory Birds and Birds in Danger of Extinction, and Their Environment, March 4, 1972, United States-Japan, 25 U.S.T. 3329.
22. Convention Concerning the Conservation of Migratory Birds and Their Environments, November 19, 1976, United States-USSR, 29 U.S.T. 4647.
23. Pub. L. 93-205, 87 Stat. 884 (Current version at 16 U.S.C.A. 1531 et seq.).
24. Pub. L. 91-190, 83 Stat. 852 (Current version at 42 U.S.C 4321 et seq.).
25. Act of June 25, 1947, Chap. 125, 61 Stat. 163 (Current version at 7 U.S.C.A. 135 et seq.).
26. Pub. L. 92-516, 86 Stat. 975 (Current version at 136 et seq.).
27. This section is based on U.S. Department of the Interior, Fish and Wildlife Service, Animal Damage Control Manual (Washington, D.C. : USDOI, 1983); U.S. Department of the Interior, Fish and Wildlife Service Division of Wildlife Resources, Animal Damage Control Program Management Document (Washington, D.C.: Government Printing Office, 1982); U.S. Department of the Interior, Fish and Wildlife Service, Animal Damage Control Program Final Environmental Impact Statement (Washington, D.C.: USDOI, 1979); and U.S. Department of the Interior, Fish and Wildlife Service, Predator Damage in the West: A Study of Coyote Management Alternatives (Washington, D.C.: USDOI, 1978).
28. U.S. Department of the Interior, Fish and Wildlife Service Division of Wildlife Resources, Animal Damage Control Program Management Document (Washington, D.C.: USDOI, 1982), pp. 3-4.
29. U.S. Department of the Interior, Fish and Wildlife Service, "A-76 Review for Animal Damage Control," 1984, Attachment 1.
30. U.S. Department of the Interior, Fish and Wildlife Service, Animal Damage Control Regional Reports 1983 (Washington, D.C.: USDOI, 1984).
31. Op. Cit. U.S. Department of the Interior, Animal Damage Control Manual, p. 1.7.
32. Ibid. p. 2.1.
33. Op. Cit. U.S. Department of the Interior, Fish and Wildlife Service, Animal Damage Control Manual.
34. Op. Cit. Nathaniel P. Reed and Dennis Drabelle, *The United States Fish and Wildlife Service*, pp. 143-145.
35. 37 Fed. Reg. 5718 (March 18, 1972).
36. U.S. Department of the Interior, Fish and Wildlife Service, Animal Damage Control Program National Summary, 1980 (Washington, D.C.: USDOI 1981).
37. Pub. L. 96-487; 94 Stat. 2371 (Currently codified in scattered sections of titles 16 and 43 U.S.C.A.).
38. U.S. Department of the Interior, Fish and Wildlife Service, Indices of Predator Abundance in the Western United States 1981 (Washington, D.C.: USDOI 1982), p. 4.
39. Dick Yost, "Oregon Goes For Guarding Dogs," *Defenders*, vol. 60, no. 2 (March/April 1985).
40. Carl Gustavson, "A Review of Taste Aversion Control of Coyote (Canis latrans) Predation." Paper presented to the Portland Wolf Symposium, Portland, Oregon, August 1979. Also, Debra Forthman, "The Science and Politics of Taste Aversion As A Method of Predator Control, or Guess Who's Coming To Dinner?" (Unpublished manuscript, 1980.)

41. U.S. Department of the Interior, Fish and Wildlife Service, "Application for EPA Experimental Use Permit for Use of Sodium Monofluoracetate for Control of Artic (sic) Foxes on Kiska Island, Aleutian Islands, Alaska" (Washington, D.C.: USDOI, 1984), p. G-4.
42. U.S. Department of the Interior, Fish and Wildlife Service, Aleutian Canada Goose Recovery Plan (Washington, D.C. USDOI, 1984).
43. Steven H. Fritts, "Wolf Depredation on Livestock in Minnesota," U.S. Fish and Wildlife Service Res. Publ. 145 (Washington, D.C.: U.S. Department of the Interior, 1982).
44. Weldon B. Robinson, "Population Changes of Carnivores in Some Coyote Control Areas," *J. Mammal.* 42, No. 4 (1961), pp. 510-515.
45. U.S. Department of the Interior, Indices of Predator Abundance in the Western United States 1981, p. 4.

The nation's 425 national wildlife refuges were created primarily for the protection of wildlife, such as this elk.

The National Wildlife Refuge System

by *Dennis Drabelle*
Special to National Audubon Society

INTRODUCTION

THE NATIONAL WILDLIFE Refuge System is a 90-million-acre network of lands and waters managed by the U.S. Fish and Wildlife Service (FWS) of the Department of the Interior primarily for the benefit of wildlife. The system includes:

National Wildlife Refuges (NWRs). These 425 units encompass approximately 88 million acres, 77 million of them in Alaska. The goal of the refuge system is "to provide, preserve, restore, and manage a national network of lands and waters sufficient in size, diversity, and location to meet society's need for areas where the widest possible spectrum of benefits associated with wildlife and wildlands is enhanced and made available."[1] Included in refuge system acreage are two kinds of wildlife management areas. FWS-managed areas are acquired in fee or by easement for the protection of migratory birds and other species. State-managed areas, also known as "coordination areas," are federally owned lands managed under FWS cooperative agreements by the states in which they are located. About 423,000 acres are encompassed in 58 coordination areas.

Waterfowl Production Areas (WPAs). Located in 149 counties, WPAs encompass 1,685,146 acres primarily in the prairie wetlands of Iowa, Michigan, Minnesota, Montana, Nebraska, North Dakota, South Dakota, Wisconsin, and Wyoming. WPAs are small wetlands managed to preserve wetland habitat, increase waterfowl production, sustain indigenous wildlife, and benefit the public using them. WPAs consist of either fee or easement areas. A fee area is owned outright by the United States and usually is open to hunting, trapping, bird-watching, and other wildlife-oriented activities. An easement area is under control of the private landowner, except that drainage, burning, or filling of wetlands is prohibited under the terms of a perpetual conservation easement. WPAs acquired in Iowa, Michigan, and Wisconsin are managed by the states under cooperative agreement with FWS. All other WPAs are managed directly by FWS.

In addition, several refuges are managed with another federal agency in cooperation with FWS. An example is Merritt Island NWR in Florida, managed by cooperative agreement between FWS and the National Aeronautics and Space Administration, which also controls the adjacent Kennedy Space Center. In these cases, wildlife purposes may be secondary to the other agency's goals.

The refuge system is widespread and varied. Every state but West Virginia has at least one refuge. The system is sufficiently comprehensive and ecologically diverse that some 600 of the 813 bird species recorded in the United States have been observed on refuges.[2] Refuge ecosystems range from maritime islands that harbor pelagic birds and mammals, to prairie potholes that breed waterfowl by the millions, to desert oases that serve as the sole habitat of pupfish and other highly specialized creatures. Although some refuges were established primarily to enhance the well-being of a single species (Key Deer NWR in Florida, for example), insofar as possible FWS theoretically manages its lands and waters as ecosystems for the benefit of all wildlife. About three-fourths of all refuges have been established primarily to conserve wetlands and waters for the benefit of migratory waterfowl.

HISTORY AND LEGISLATIVE AUTHORITY

The National Wildlife Refuge System has grown piecemeal, largely in response to perceived wildlife crises. The devastating effects of the millinery trade on bird populations around the turn of the century and the destruction of populations of big-game species, such as bears, deer, and elk, prompted conservationists and hunting organizations to promote the establishment of federal refuges for the protection of wildlife. The effects of drought conditions and disappearing wetlands on duck populations in the 1920s and 1930s led to enactment of legislation authorizing the establishment of migratory bird refuges. Finally, recognition of the worldwide decline in wildlife populations after World War II led to enactment of the Endangered Species Act, which authorized the purchase of refuge lands to protect a wide variety of wildlife and plants.

The concept that government should take responsibility for protecting wildlife habitat first took root in California where, in 1870, the state set aside as a bird sanctuary what is now Lake Merritt in downtown Oakland. At about the same time, the federal government was creating the predecessor agencies of the U.S. Fish and Wildlife Service. An independent Commission of Fish and Fisheries was established in 1871. In 1886, the Department of Agriculture established a Division of Economic Ornithology and Mammalogy, later renamed the Division of Biological Survey. In 1892, the United States established its first wildlife preserve when President Benjamin Harrison set aside federally owned Afognak Island in Alaska to protect island wildlife, salmon, and sea animals.

For the most part, however, American wildlife preservation during the late 19th and early 20th centuries depended on the efforts of private parties. Federal interest in wildlife accelerated, however, when Theodore Roosevelt became president. A lifelong conservationist as well as big-game hunter, Roosevelt issued an executive order in 1903 that reserved federally owned Pelican Island off the east coast of Florida as "a preserve and breeding ground for native birds." Before leaving office in 1909, Roosevelt created 52 more wildlife refuges on federal land.

In 1905, Congress became directly involved in refuge creation when it authorized the president to establish a refuge for the benefit of the bison on part of the Wichita Forest Reserve in Oklahoma Territory. In 1908, Congress itself established a refuge and authorized the use of federal funds for purchasing refuge lands when 12,800 acres were bought from the Flathead Indians in Montana and set aside for what is now called the National Bison Range.*

---

*Several other federal wildlife areas established primarily for big-game species have been called ranges. All of them are now units of the National Wildlife Refuge System.

Between 1913 and 1925, new refuges were established in 24 states. In 1924, Congress appropriated funds for the purchase of waterfowl habitat along the upper Mississippi River in several states. This marked the first time federal money was spent to acquire land for general wildlife habitat rather than as a benefit for a particular species. In 1929, Congress responded to a decade-long decline in waterfowl populations, caused primarily by market hunting, drought, and draining of wetlands for agriculture, by passing the Migratory Bird Conservation Act.[3] This authorized the establishment of migratory-bird refuges. In 1934, Congress passed the Migratory Bird Hunting Stamp Act,[4] providing a method for financing acquisition and management of migratory bird refuges by requiring all persons 16 years of age or older who hunt migratory waterfowl to buy a federal "duck stamp." Receipts from duck-stamp sales still are used to acquire refuge lands.*

The refuge system has grown in fits and starts. Many additions were made in the 1930s and modified with the help of the Civilian Conservation Corps and Works Progress Administration to contain more wetlands. By 1943, the system contained 272 units. From then until 1956 the system experienced little growth. In that year, Congress passed the Fish and Wildlife Act,[5] establishing a national fish and wildlife policy and authorizing the secretary of the Interior to acquire refuge lands for all forms of wildlife. The funding source for these acquisitions is the Land and Water Conservation Fund, established in 1964. In the two decades after 1956, refuge acreage was doubled by withdrawal of federal lands and acquisition.

In 1966, Congress, in the National Wildlife Refuge System Administration Act, provided general guidelines for management of the refuge system.[6] Among other provisions, this act authorized the secretary of the Interior to permit a variety of uses of wildlife refuges — such as recreation, grazing, and oil and gas leasing — so long as they were "compatible" with the basic purposes for which the refuges were each established. The Endangered Species Act of 1973[7] reaffirmed a long-standing FWS objective of conserving endangered and threatened species and authorized the use of Land and Water Conservation Fund moneys to acquire refuge lands for endangered species conservation.

GROWTH OF THE NATIONAL WILDLIFE REFUGE SYSTEM

Period	Number of Currently Existing Refuges Established
1900-20	36
1921-40	138
1941-60	71
1961-76	164
1977-Present	15
Total:	424

Source: FWS, Division of Refuge Management.

---

*However, the vast majority of refuge land — almost 95 percent — has been obtained by withdrawal from the federal estate. Withdrawal of federal land for refuges in Alaska accounts for about 85 percent of the system's acreage.

In 1980, Congress enacted the Alaska National Interest Lands Conservation Act (ANILCA),[8] which reorganized and expanded several existing Alaskan refuges and established several new ones. The new acreage more than doubled the size of the refuge system.*

ORGANIZATION AND OPERATIONS

Responsibilities and Roles

FWS manages the National Wildlife Refuge System. Several states have their own refuge systems, as do some private organizations, notably the National Audubon Society and the Nature Conservancy. Another private organization, the National Wildlife Refuge Association, composed largely of current and retired FWS employees, seeks to promote the refuge system and to obtain increased funding for it.

Congressional Committees

Like other programs and functions within FWS, the refuge system is dependent on Congress for the legislation that authorizes and guides its operations and for its annual appropriations. Authorizing committees are the House Committee on Merchant Marine and Fisheries and the Senate Committee on Environment and Public Works. Appropriations are made by the Appropriations Committees of the House and Senate with recommendations from each committee's Subcommittee on Interior and Related Agencies.

The authorizing committees periodically conduct oversight hearings, providing background for possible legislation. The most recent oversight hearings on the National Wildlife Refuge System were held in October 1979 by the Subcommittee on Fisheries and Wildlife Conservation and the Environment, a subdivision of the House Committee on Merchant Marine and Fisheries. Congress also is involved with the refuge system through its representation on the Migratory Bird Conservation Commission, which reviews all land acquisition proposed under the Migratory Bird Conservation Act. Two members of the commission are senators chosen by the president of the Senate. Two others are members of the House of Representatives and are chosen by the speaker.**

Agency Structure and Function

FWS organizes its activities into eight programs, each supervised by a national program manager. The National Wildlife Refuge System is a component of the Wildlife Resources Program, which carries out the agency's responsibilities for non-endangered and non-threatened mammals, birds, reptiles, amphibians, crustaceans, and terrestrial mollusks. Yet the refuge system itself supports other programs as well — such as the protection and restoration of endangered species — by serving as a land base for the accomplishment of a variety of FWS program objectives.

The refuges themselves are run by managers who report to refuge supervisors in the regional offices. From the latter, the chain of command runs to the assistant

---

*All NWRs in Alaska are treated as if they were created by ANILCA in 1980, even though some existed before that year.

**The congressional members of the Commission as of January 1, 1985, are Senator Thad Cochran, Senator David Pryor, Representative Silvio O. Conte, and Representative John D. Dingell.

regional directors of wildlife resources, to regional directors, and to the director of FWS in Washington. Within the office of the associate director for Wildlife Resources is the Division of Refuge Management. Its function, is to develop programs, plans, standards, and procedures which facilitate the accomplishment of FWS program objectives in the refuge system.

Over the same period, the number of full-time personnel engaged in refuge operations declined from 1,587 in FY 1983 to 1,550 in FY 1985, while the number engaged in maintenance has risen from 300 in FY 1983 to 458 in FY 1985. These figures reflect the Reagan administration's emphasis on maintenance and, especially, on the initiatives contained in the Accelerated Refuge Maintenance Management program (see next section).

Planning

FWS prepares plans at the national, regional, and field-station levels. Together, these plans provide an integrated form of guidance for all activities conducted on refuges.

The Service management plan provides guidance for FWS as a whole over a 10-year period. The first such plan appeared in 1980 and set goals for various FWS management categories. For example, the migratory bird goal was "To conserve and manage migratory birds in a way that provides optimum opportunity for their use and enjoyment by people."[9]

Program management documents identify and define five-year objectives for each program and set policy guidance and strategies for achieving these objectives. For planning, evaluation, and budgeting purposes, refuge operations and maintenance are part of the Wildlife Resources Program.

Regional resource plans provide more detailed guidance for national objectives for species of special emphasis. These are species and groups of fish, wildlife, and plants of notable biological, legal, or public interest that call for special attention from FWS. The species include some, but by no means all, species listed as endangered or threatened under the Endangered Species Act.

Regional resource plans, reviewed at least every five years, function as links between national priorities and the activities of field stations such as research centers, fish hatcheries, and national wildlife refuges. Regional plans also serve to promote coordination between FWS activities and those of state wildlife agencies.

Leaving aside the comprehensive management plans mandated for Alaskan refuges by ANILCA (see below), individual refuges are involved in three field station planning processes: master plans, refuge management plans, and annual work plans.

There generally have a 10- or 20-year horizon and set long-term objectives for land-use management of certain refuges. They are developed as needed. Currently about 100 master plans are in effect, with 15 more in various stages of preparation. The decision as to whether a refuge should have a master plan or revise an existing one is up to the regional director, who weighs such factors as the role of the refuge in meeting regional and national objectives, the adequacy of existing data and documentation supporting the current refuge program, and the extent of public interest and controversy associated with the current program.

Management Plans. Whether or not it has a master plan, each unit of the refuge system operates in accordance with one or more management plans covering such operations as public use, habitat management, fire management, oil and gas leasing, etc. These plans provide the broad framework for planning and budgeting. They also serve to identify long-term refuge needs and objectives for refuges that lack master plans.

NATIONAL WILDLIFE REFUGE FUNDING SINCE 1983			
	FY 1983	*FY 1984*	*FY 1985*
operations	$62.2 million	$63.5 million	$67.8 million
maintenance	$11.6 million	$26.8 million	$32.9 million
construction & dam safety	$8.6 million	$14.5 million	$4.6 million

Source: FWS. These figures do not include Fishery Resources and Endangered Species program funds. Nor do they include the appropriations for construction and dam safety for the three years covered: $8.618 million in FY 1983, $14.5 million in FY 1984, and $4.627 million in FY 1985.

Annual Work Plans. These are the basic documents that outline the jobs to be done at each refuge in a given year and budget the necessary money and personnel. These plans are essential components of the FWS budget process.

Budgeting

The refuge system is funded primarily as part of the Wildlife Resources Program budget, although various FWS program budgets also provide funds. For example, the Fishery Resources and Endangered Species programs together provided $2.8 million for refuge operations in 1985. No single item for refuges appeared in the FWS budget until FY 1983, when FWS began keeping separate accounts for refuge operations and maintenance expenditures. In FY 1984, FWS changed its budget to show all funds spent on refuges as a separate item.

Refuge Establishment

Refuges may be created by the president, the secretary of the Interior, or Congress. All refuges have been created by one of four methods:

Executive or Secretarial Order. Theodore Roosevelt pioneered the use of the executive order to "withdraw" land from the public domain for refuge purposes. Withdrawals were made by unnumbered executive order until 1907 and by numbered executive order from then until 1942. In 1942, authority to establish refuges by withdrawal was delegated to the secretary of the Interior, who does so by issuing numbered public-land orders. The secretary may use this authority to establish refuges in conjunction with the Fish and Wildlife Act and the Endangered Species Act and by cooperative agreement with other federal agencies.

General Authority Provided by Acts of Congress. Eleven separate statutes provide general authority for establishing national wildlife refuges — that is, a refuge may be established pursuant to any one of these acts without an additional congressional act. The most important of these general authorities are:

● The Endangered Species Act, which authorizes the secretary of the Interior to establish refuges as part of a program to conserve fish, wildlife, and plants determined to be endangered or threatened. Examples of such refuges include Mississippi Sandhill Crane NWR in Mississippi and Watercress Darter NWR in Alabama.

● The Fish and Wildlife Act, which authorizes the secretary of the Interior to take steps necessary for the conservation of fish and wildlife resources, including acquisition by purchase or by exchange of land and water or interests therein. Among refuges established pursuant to this authority is Harbor Island NWR in Michigan.

● The Migratory Bird Conservation Act, which authorizes the secretary of the Interior to establish refuges for migratory birds. To be established in this manner, proposed refuges must first receive the legislative consent of each state in which land would be acquired. Then the proposal must be approved by the Migratory Bird Conservation Commission, which consists of the secretary of the Interior as chairman, the secretaries of Transportation and Agriculture, two members of the Senate, two members of the House of Representatives, and an ex-officio state-government member from each involved state. Among the hundreds of refuges established in this manner are Ruby Lake NWR in Nevada and Lake Woodruff NWR in Florida.

Special Act of Congress. Dating back to 1905, this method typically is used to establish a refuge having some special purpose or needing special provisions. An example is the act establishing San Francisco Bay NWR,[10] a refuge where recreation, including environmental education, is a mission coequal with wildlife conservation and management. ANILCA established several new refuges and expanded several existing ones in Alaska.

Donation or Transfer. Other refuges have been established by donation of land to the federal government, cooperative agreement with other federal agencies, and transfer of land to FWS from other agencies. Authority for incorporating these lands into the refuge system derives from the Endangered Species Act, the National Wildlife Refuge System Administration Act of 1966, the Fish and Wildlife Coordination Act of 1934,[11] the Fish and Wildlife Improvement Act of 1978,[12] and others. A notable example of a donated refuge is Sevilleta in New Mexico, a 220,000-acre expanse given to FWS by the Campbell Family Foundation in 1973.

Funding for Refuge Acquisition

Two primary funding sources exist for acquiring land and waters for refuges. One is the Migratory Bird Conservation Fund, supported by money from the sale of duck stamps and from direct appropriations made under the authority of the Wetlands Loan Act.[13] The Migratory Bird Conservation Fund is used exclusively to acquire lands or interests therein for use as migratory bird refuges and waterfowl production areas.

The second funding source is the Land and Water Conservation Fund, which draws revenues from a tax on motorboat fuels, from the sale of surplus federal real property, and from outer continental shelf oil and gas leases. This fund is used to acquire lands and interests therein for endangered species, interpretation and recreation, and specially authorized refuges — essentially for any kind of refuge except a migratory bird refuge established by the Migratory Bird Conservation Commission. This fund also is used by the National Park Service, Bureau of Land Management, and U.S. Forest Service to acquire land for their systems.

Under the Reagan administration, expenditures from the migratory bird fund have remained steady at an average of about $15 million a year. Budget requests and congressional appropriations from the Land and Water Conservation Fund have fluctuated widely as the Reagan administration has sought to stifle land acquisition.

LAND AND WATER CONSERVATION FUND		
FY	*Budget Request*	*Appropriation*
1981	$11,420,000	$9,303,000
1982	1,139,000	16,491,000
1983	1,567,000	35,200,000
1984	-0-	46,297,000
1985	45,540,000	63,218,000

Removal of Refuge Land

Since enactment of the Game Range Act in 1975,[14] removal of land from the refuge system, other than by exchange, has been tightly restricted. The secretary of the Interior must obtain the approval of the Migratory Bird Conservation Commission before disposing of land acquired to benefit migratory birds. For land acquired for other purposes the secretary must obtain the approval of Congress. In either case the disposal must be predicated on the secretary's finding that the land is no longer needed for refuge purposes. Proceeds from disposal of land acquired for migratory birds go into the Migratory Bird Conservation Account to finance new land acquisitions.

Only one disposal of refuge lands has been made since 1975. In 1982, Congress approved a transaction whereby FWS relinquished its management of Jones Island in the San Juan Islands NWR and transferred the island to the state of Washington, which for several years had managed a public park there by cooperative agreement with FWS. In return, the state released 78 other islands to the sole jurisdiction of FWS for refuge purposes.

Prior to 1975, the following disposals were made:[15]

- 14 refuges were consolidated into others;
- 40 refuges comprising 1,604,234 acres were transferred to other federal or state agencies;
- four refuges comprising 1,795 acres were discontinued when it was determined that the lands were not in fact owned by the United States;
- three refuges comprising 59,939 acres were discontinued when it was determined that they were not useful for the purpose for which they had been acquired, namely, the preservation of waterfowl;
- 23 refuges consisting of easements only and comprising 14,244 acres were discontinued; and
- three leased refuges comprising 8,849 acres were discontinued.

Refuge Management

Methods used by FWS managers to carry out their wildlife mission can be grouped into several broad categories:

Water Management. Water and marshland are extremely important to refuges, especially for the production and conservation of waterfowl. On many refuges FWS uses dikes, pumps, and impoundments to make up for inadequacies in natural habitat.

Grassland Management. Grasses can be important as cover for ground-nesting birds such as Attwater's prairie chicken, as forage for mammals, and as components in the diversity of habitat necessary to sustain a variety of wildlife species. FWS manipulation of grasslands includes cultivation of grasses as well as grazing and haying. In FY 1982, 2.1 million acres of refuge lands were grazed, and 22,200 acres were hayed.

Forest Management. Like grasses, trees on refuges may be seeded or cut, protected from fire, or purposely burned, depending on whether resident wildlife would benefit from climax forests or earlier stages of plant succession. Totaling about 5.2 million acres, refuge forest lands are managed pursuant to forest management plans drawn up for each refuge.

Cropland Management. FWS farms or permits farming on refuges in order to supplement natural food sources. An example is crop farming on Bosque del Apache NWR to provide feed for whooping and sandhill cranes. Farming also provides cover for wildlife and alleviates wildlife depredations on adjacent private lands. In FY 1983, refuge personnel farmed about 25,000 refuge acres and private permittees about 115,000 additional acres.

Fire Management. In addition to preventing and fighting fires on refuges, FWS personnel engage in controlled burning to enhance habitat for wildlife, for example by thinning out underbrush to allow growth of small, edible plants. In FY 1983, controlled burning was practiced on about 100,000 refuge acres, and wildfires affected about 20,000 acres outside of Alaska.

Wildlife Management. Wildlife itself is managed by means of a variety of techniques, including banding or tagging to keep track of individuals, captive breeding to restore declining species, and hunting and trapping to reduce overpopulation.

Alaska's Unique Refuge Lands

The 77 million acres of refuge land in Alaska are administered under the same rules and regulations that govern other refuges. However, owing to long-standing tradition, the state's entirely different physical scale and climate, and legislative compromises that preceded the law's enactment, many provisions governing management of Alaska refuges are unique. Section 1002 of the act, for example, directs the secretary of the Interior to analyze the impacts of oil and gas production on the coastal plain of the Arctic National Wildlife Refuge and to authorize related mineral exploration on that plain. This approach to development contrasts with the typical situation — establishment of refuges for wildlife protection only.*

ANILCA also preserves the subsistence rights of rural Alaskans. These Alaskans will be able to continue their cultural traditions of gathering food from refuge lands insofar as this is consistent with "the conservation of healthy populations of fish and wildlife." Again, this contrasts with the situation outside Alaska, where subsistence is not a lifestyle, and hunting and fishing are recreational activities permitted only if compatible with the purposes for which a refuge was established.

Finally, ANILCA directs FWS to submit to Congress by 1987 comprehensive management plans for all Alaska refuges. Again, this directive is tailor-made for Alaska. The pace and degree of planning for the remainder of the system are largely within the discretion of FWS.

Wilderness

The 1964 Wilderness Act[16] applies to the refuge system. Where consistent with other responsibilities, the secretary of the Interior, on advice from FWS, recommends to Congress which areas within refuges should receive wilderness designation. The secretary must manage both designated and proposed areas so as to preserve them in a pristine state. FWS frequently manipulates habitat in an attempt to benefit wildlife, however, and such activities are usually inconsistent with the hands-off philosophy of wilderness management. Consequently, FWS does not recommend for wilderness designation those areas where manipulation is contemplated.

The Wilderness Act required FWS to review all roadless refuge areas of at least 5,000 acres and all roadless islands of any size. FWS took the position that the Wilderness Act requires it to conduct wilderness reviews only of refuges in the system in 1964, the year the bill was enacted. This review, completed in 1974, has led to enactment of 67 refuge wilderness areas totaling 19,332,901 acres by the end of FY 1984. Pending in Congress are 26 proposed refuge wilderness areas totaling 3,437,199 acres. As part of the ANILCA implementation process, FWS is conducting wilderness reviews of 16 study areas, comprising almost 58 million acres, on Alaskan refuges.

---

*FWS has acquired some refuges in which subsurface minerals are in private ownership. FWS allows private access to these minerals.

Research on Refuges

Research on national wildlife refuges is funded through several FWS program budgets, including endangered species, wildlife resources, and fisheries, so a total figure for research dollars spent on refuges in a given fiscal year is not available. Refuge-related research projects are initiated in two ways. The formal channel involves submitting proposals originating at the refuge level through the regional director's office, where they are assigned priorities, to the FWS Wildlife Resources Research Committee. To be approved and funded, such proposals must have national importance. An informal process is used for proposals of less than national significance. The regional director may approve such refuge research projects and fund them with moneys in the regional budget. In addition, refuge managers are encouraged to permit outside scientists to conduct research on refuges insofar as compatible with the purposes for which the refuge was established. Examples of major, federally funded refuge research projects in FY 1984 include:

- Havasu NWR, Arizona: study of desert bighorn sheep ecology, $10,000.
- Barnegat NWR, New Jersey: study of the effects of mosquito-control techniques on waterfowl, $10,000.
- DeSoto NWR, Iowa: study, involving computer modeling, of the effects of such land uses as hunting and farming on snow goose populations, $10,000.
- Great Dismal Swamp NWR, Virginia: pre-hunt study of black bear management, $35,000.
- Laguna Atascosa NWR, Texas: study of the effects of various water levels on food supply for waterfowl, $35,000.

CURRENT PROGRAM TRENDS

Current program trends in the management of the refuge system include FWS initiatives to improve maintenance of facilities and equipment and to allow increased use of refuges for purposes other than wildlife preservation. Both initiatives have been promoted strongly by the Reagan administration.

The Accelerated Refuge Maintenance and Management Program

The preservation and protection of wildlife on the national wildlife refuges is accomplished in large part through the manipulation of habitat. Manipulation, in turn, depends heavily on equipment and structures — for example, tractors used in farming to provide forage for geese and impoundments used to control water levels for breeding ducks. By the late 1970s, it was widely recognized that FWS was not doing an adequate job of maintaining its facilities and equipment, as refuge expenditures show.

Until FY 1984, each refuge manager was given one sum of money annually to run the refuge under the broad rubric of "operations and maintenance." The allocation of that sum between the two activities was largely up to the refuge manager, and the percentage spent on maintenance fluctuated markedly, from five percent on some refuges to 40 percent on others. Overall, however, the maintenance expenditure was about $12 million yearly, half of it for salaries. This left $6 million annually for upkeep of a capital investment with an estimated value of over $2 billion — far short of the roughly $66 million a year considered necessary to protect such an investment.

The Reagan administration in 1984 responded to this shortfall by instituting the Accelerated Refuge Maintenance and Management Program (ARMM), the counterpart of a similar new program in the national park system. In addition to rehabilitation and replacement of equipment and facilities, the program encompasses wildlife-population maintenance (for example, studies of declining species and rehabilitation of nesting sites) and habitat maintenance (for example, controlling noxious plants and erosion).

ARMM money is allocated to refuges under priorities determined by the FWS director. Half of the annual appropriation is set aside for small miscellaneous projects costing less than $15,000 each and the other half for specified major projects, which are grouped under seven categories: Managed Waters, Natural Wetlands, Managed Uplands, Wildlands, Wildlife Populations, Facilities, and Vehicles and Equipment. ARMM funding will alleviate many of the threats and conflicts reported in the Resource Problems survey (see the Resource Status section of this report). Among the projects scheduled for FY 1985 are:

- DeSoto NWR, Iowa: repair visitor-center entrance walk and dumpster pad, $15,000.

- Blackwater NWR, Maryland: continue marsh restoration, $35,000.

- Alaska Peninsula NWR: acquire a new forklift, $60,000.

- Koyukuk NWR, Alaska: survey trumpeter-swan habitat, $15,000.

- Desecheo NWR, Puerto Rico: remove exotic rhesus monkeys, $40,000.

Funding for ARMM is scheduled to grow by $8 million increments to a peak figure of $56 million a year after FY 1989. That figure, when added to the $6 million base amount that FWS traditionally spent on refuge maintenance each year, is estimated as adequate to maintain the $2 billion-plus capital investment in refuges. This schedule, however, is not being met. In FY 1984, the first year of ARMM, Congress appropriated $14.6 million in ARMM funding. In FY 1985, the administration requested $15.9 million, an increase of only $1.3 million, for ARMM. Congress appropriated this amount plus $8 million in a separate category for solving resource problems. Some of the money in this separate category was spent on projects that would otherwise have been funded through ARMM.

Other Uses of Refuges

The National Wildlife Refuge Administration Act of 1966 authorizes the secretary of the Interior to permit by regulation "such uses as are compatible with the major purposes for which such areas were established." Those purposes emphasize protection, management, and restoration of wildlife and wildlife habitat. However, the standard is applied flexibly. Consequently, farming, cattle grazing, timber harvesting, oil and gas production, and a variety of recreational activities, including hunting, fishing, boating, hiking, wildlife observation, and environmental education occur on refuges. Some of these uses have spawned controversies.

Commercial Uses. By agreement with private parties, generally by contract, lease, or permit, a number of commercial activities are allowed on refuges and waterfowl production areas where compatible: cattle grazing, timber harvesting, oil and gas production (most of which takes place in accordance with rights that predate establishment of the refuge in question), haying, trapping, concessions (for example, boat rentals), and others. In addition, a few refuges sell surplus animals — primarily bison and longhorn cattle — to the public.

In fiscal year 1983, receipts from all of these activities on refuges and WPAs amounted to approximately $11 million, $7 million of it from oil and gas production. This money does not directly benefit the refuges. Much of it is used to make payments

REVENUES RECEIVED FROM ECONOMIC AND PUBLIC USES OF NWRs*

| | Fiscal Year | | |
| Use | 1981 | 1982 | 1983 |
		(000)	
Grazing	$1,108	$1,215	$1,285
Haying	219	173	194
Forest products	653	813	564
Oil and gas	2,387	2,827	2,391
Sand and gravel	14	19	2
Surplus animal disposal	368	501	460
Furbearers (trapping)	236	212	89
Sale of salmonoid carcasses and eggs	20	46	14
Other (bee hives, rentals, etc.)	837	1,195	1,163
Concessions	48	44	89
Total	$5,890	$7,045	$6,251

*These revenues do not represent all revenues generated from wildlife refuges. Oil and gas receipts shown are only for acquired refuge lands. The Government Accounting Office identified an additional $4.7 million from oil and gas operations on public lands (in FY 1983). Source: FWS, *Analysis of Receipts by Commodity*. National Wildlife Refuge Fund.

to counties in which refuges are located, as compensation for the counties' inability to tax refuge land in federal ownership.

The appropriate extent of commercial activities on refuges became a controversial issue during the early Reagan years. The FWS director twice sent memoranda to the regional directors calling for an evaluation of opportunities to expand commercial uses of refuges. A third memo, dated April 1, 1983, specified means by which FY 1981 receipts of nearly $6 million from such activities (exclusive of oil and gas production on public domain lands) could be increased by some $2 million yearly. Most of the projected increase was to come from "sales of the backlog of merchantable refuge timber that has resulted from several years of depressed timber markets." In the meantime, Interior was preparing draft regulations to ease the way for federal oil and gas leasing on certain acquired refuge lands in the contiguous 48 states. This action would have reversed a long-standing policy against opening up refuges outside of Alaska to new federal oil and gas leasing; production normally is allowed only for necessary drainage and under valid rights in effect at the time a refuge was established.

These initiatives drew sharp responses from environmentalists, who charged that the increased commercial activities would come at the expense of habitat and wildlife. Representative John Dingell (D-Michigan), the chairman of the Subcommittee on Oversight and Investigations, House Committee on Energy and Commerce, subsequently asked the General Accounting Office (GAO) to report on the initiatives and their likely impacts. In its report,[17] GAO concluded that economic uses of refuges were "unlikely to increase significantly." Because of limited demand for timber, hay, and crops as well as "the low quality and small volume of products and the remote location of refuges," GAO saw little opportunity for increasing revenues from the sales of these commodities. GAO also noted that FWS had few data by which to determine whether more oil and gas should be extracted from refuge lands. In any event, that aspect of the initiative died. Although the policy change had resulted in 174 lease applications covering 806,000 acres in 19 states, Congress prohibited the processing of these applications until new regulations and an environmental impact statement were prepared. The dispute was resolved when Interior Secretary William P. Clark in January 1984 reversed the department's position by issuing a statement that no new federal oil and gas activity would be permitted on refuge lands.

The GAO report recommended that the secretary of the Interior issue regulations clarifying the manner in which oil and gas activities, especially seismic surveys for purposes of exploration, are to be conducted on refuge lands and explaining how access to commercial operations would be controlled. The report also recommended that "any expansion of existing [economic] uses . . . be weighed carefully against any uncorrected resource problems and an individual refuge's capability to manage new or expanded uses."[18] In light of the public controversy, the congressional prohibition, and the GAO report, it does not appear likely that the economic-use initiatives will be resurrected soon.

Hunting on Refuges. The most controversial non-commercial use of refuges is hunting. Some people are philosophically opposed to all hunting. Others are puzzled by a policy that allows the sport killing of refuge wildlife.

On many refuges the absence of natural predators permits certain species to become so numerous that they destroy habitat and reduce forage to the point that the population as a whole suffers. FWS permits hunters to kill these animals because it considers hunting, in the words of the Refuge Manual, "an acceptable, traditional, and legitimate form of wildlife-oriented recreation."[19]

The decision to allow hunting on a refuge (except those in Alaska) is made by the appropriate regional director, who receives advice from the refuge manager and then applies the compatibility test — would the proposed hunting be consistent with the purposes for which the refuge was established? The regional director's decision is reviewable by the FWS director and the assistant secretary for Fish and Wildlife and Parks. At the end of 1984, 231 refuges — 54 percent of the total — were open to hunting. During fiscal year 1983, the latest for which figures are available, hunters made 1,120,000 visits to national wildlife refuges and killed about 620,000 animals.

Hunting on refuges has increased in fits and starts. Before 1949, hunting was allowed primarily on refuges where it had been a traditional activity before the refuge was incorporated into the system, but was prohibited on migratory bird refuges, which were considered to be "inviolate sanctuaries" under the Migratory Bird Conservation Act. In 1949, an act of Congress[20] that raised the price of the duck stamp also authorized the secretary of the Interior to set aside "wildlife management areas" on up to 25 percent of any land acquired with duck-stamp revenues and, for the first time, to allow the hunting of resident and migratory game birds in these areas.

In 1958, further amendments to the Duck Stamp Act expanded the secretary's authority to allow hunting on migratory bird refuges. The secretary was authorized to administer as a wildlife management area up to 40 percent of any refuge set aside for migratory birds under any law and to permit the hunting of migratory game birds and other resident wildlife species on the area. The hunting of resident species was further expanded in 1966 with enactment of the National Wildlife Refuge System Administration Act. This act authorized the secretary to permit the hunting of any resident wildlife species on any lands within the system if the secretary determined that such hunting was compatible with the primary purposes for which the refuge was established. It should be kept in mind that a refuge may be open to one form of hunting but not others. Several refuges, for example, are open to the hunting of migratory waterfowl but not big game.

NUMBER OF REFUGES NEWLY OPENED TO HUNTING AND FISHING BY YEAR CURRENT AS OF: November 1, 1984

Year	Type of Hunting			Sport Fishing
	Migratory Bird	Upland Game	Big Game	
pre-1960	41	31	50	85
1960	0	0	0	0
1961	5	3	0	7
1962	0	0	0	0
1963	4	6	4	6
1964	9	5	5	2
1965	9	15	6	6
1966	9	9	5	8
1967	10	12	9	7
1968	3	4	1	1
1969	5	7	7	1
1970	5	4	5	4
1971	3	4	4	2
1972	1	0	3	0
1973	1	1	1	0
1974	4	0	0	1
1975	0	0	0	0
1976	5	3	2	2
1977	6	2	5	7
1978	3	1	1	0
1979	8	4	5	4
1980	20	21	26	19
1981	6	5	7	9
1982	12	13	11	4
1983	0	0	2	0
1984	10	13	12	10

Source: FWS, Division of Refuge Management, November 1, 1984.

A prolonged lull during the late 1960s and 1970s was followed by a marked increase in refuges opened to hunting in four of the last five years. This trend has alarmed some groups, such as the Humane Society of the United States, which questions whether the compatibility test is being applied strictly.

A recent FWS decision has added to the controversy. Traditionally, refuge managers have adopted state hunting regulations, with appropriate modifications, for refuge hunts. This policy seems to foster good federal-state relations, which is important because state wildlife officers often assist short-handed refuge personnel in patrolling refuge lands during hunting season. Moreover, basic responsibility for resident wildlife species legally and traditionally lies with the states.

Since 1960, FWS has issued annual hunting regulations for each open refuge. Since then, however, the number of refuges open to hunting has almost doubled, and the annual issuance has become burdensome. In 1984, FWS replaced this approach with a single, codified set of refuge hunting regulations, with variations for individual refuges as needed. This code is to be reviewed yearly for necessary changes, but remains in effect on each refuge until amended by subsequent notices in the *Federal Register*. As in the past, this consolidated approach relies heavily on state regulations, with modifications as necessary.

Codification of refuge hunting regulations prompted the Humane Society of the United States to sue FWS, alleging that the agency had illegally delegated to the states its responsibility to control hunting on refuges and had abandoned the annual FWS evaluations of hunting impacts on individual refuges. FWS says that the new regulation does not diminish its ability to set refuge hunting rules independent of state rules and of those contained in the published regulation. The suit, filed in November, 1984, has not yet come to trial.

Subsistence Uses. Title VIII of ANILCA, "Subsistence Management and Use," recognized the traditional subsistence uses of public-land resources in Alaska by native and non-native rural residents. Section 802 of the act declares that "consistent with sound management principles, and the conservation of healthy populations of fish and wildlife, the utilization of the public lands in Alaska is to cause the least adverse impact possible on rural residents who depend upon subsistence uses of the resources of such lands."

Section 803 defines subsistence as the "customary and traditional uses by rural Alaska residents of wild, renewable resources for direct personal or family consumption as food, shelter, fuel, clothing, tools, or transportation; for the making and selling of handicraft articles out of nonedible byproducts of fish and wildlife resources taken for personal or family consumption; for barter or sharing for personal or family consumption; and for customary trade." Section 813 calls for periodic reports by the secretary of the Interior on the nature and extent of subsistence uses on Alaska's public lands and on the status of fish and wildlife populations subject to subsistence use. FWS has been designated the lead agency in preparing these reports.

In November 1984, FWS published a draft[21] of the first periodic subsistence report. The draft report presents its information based on the six resource-management regions established by the Alaska Department of Fish and Game in conjunction with ANILCA.

Although the report points out that subsistence patterns transcend jurisdictional boundaries, for purposes of this chapter the most important information contained in the report is the discussion of "Specific Problem Populations on Federal Lands." The report identifies the following wildlife populations "as currently exhibiting population declines or low levels which may adversely affect or be affected by subsistence use:"[22]

Region 1 (Southeast):	Sitka black-tailed deer and moose in Tongass National Forest.
Region 2 (Southcentral):	Chisana caribou herd in Wrangell-St. Elias National Park and Preserve.
Region 3 (Southwest):	Sea birds, especially tufted puffins and shearwaters in Aleutian Islands NWR; moose in Becharof and Alaska Peninsula NWRs.
Region 4 (Western):	Geese (cackling Canada geese, Pacific white-fronted, black brant, and Emperor geese) in Yukon Delta NWR; moose and caribou in the Yukon-Kuskokwim Delta; musk ox immigrating to the mainland from Nunivak Island.
Region 5 (Arctic):	Wolverines in Selawik NWR; Dall sheep in Cape Krusenstern National Monument.
Region 6 (Interior):	Moose in Yukon Flats and Tetlin NWRs; caribou and wolves in Denali National Park; caribou and wolves in Yukon Charley Rivers National Preserve.

A pending lawsuit illustrates the complexity of the task FWS faces in enforcing the laws and treaties that apply to consumptive uses of wildlife in Alaska. The case pits sport hunters against Alaska natives, with FWS in the middle. The problem arose when FWS tried, by negotiating an agreement with local natives, to improve the management of several declining waterfowl populations that nest in the Yukon-Kuskokwim Delta. Under this agreement, the natives would cut back on their spring subsistence kill of the declining species, and FWS would reduce the fall bag limit for sport hunters in the Pacific Flyway. In *Alaska Fish and Wildlife Federation and Outdoor Council v. Jantzen*, brought in 1984 in the Federal District Court in Alaska, some Alaska hunting clubs sued FWS on the basis that any hunting or egg-collecting of migratory bird species during the spring nesting season is in violation of the migratory bird treaty with Canada, making the agreement with the natives illegal. The Alaska Federation of Natives filed a counterclaim, asserting that the treaty does not restrict subsistence uses.

FWS agrees that treaty restrictions on subsistence take prohibit spring taking of nesting birds. Thus, FWS concedes that the agreement it negotiated with the natives does not in fact live up to the letter of the treaty. FWS argues, however, that given the immense difficulties of law enforcement in remote rural Alaska, the agreement would be the best practical method of reversing the species' declines and represents an appropriate use of FWS administrative discretion to manage migratory birds.

The hunting club's request for an injunction against allowing natives to take any birds during the spring has been denied, but the natives' claim has yet to be heard.

Fishing on Refuges. The decision as to whether a refuge should be open to fishing is made, for all practical purposes, by the regional director, who weighs the recommendation of the refuge manager in determining whether — in accordance with the National Wildlife Refuge System Administration Act — the use would be compatible with the purpose for which the refuge was established. In 1984, 188 refuges were open to fishing. In 1983, the last year for which figures are available, about 8.1 million fish and amphibians were caught on refuges. Fishing on refuges generally is conducted in accordance with state law, and usually all that is required to fish is a state license. In late 1984, however, FWS was preparing a draft rule that would consolidate refuge-by-refuge fish regulations in somewhat the same way as it has hunting regulations.

Recreation and Education. Approximately 30 million people visited refuges during 1983, about one-tenth the number who visited national parks, which comprise about nine million fewer acres. The visitation included 1,120,000 visits made by hunters and about five million by fishermen. An April 1, 1983, memorandum from the FWS director to the regional directors called for, among other things, increased use of refuges by the general public for interpretation, wildlife observation, hunting and fishing, boating and hiking, and other activities. This memorandum reflects a widespread feeling among supporters of the refuge system that it is not living up to its potential to provide these activities. For example, a number of refuges close their visitor centers on Saturday and Sunday, when more visitors generally show up than on weekdays. At the opposite end of the spectrum is San Francisco Bay NWR, whose excellent facilities and interpretive programs, staffed largely by volunteers, are models for the system.

In October 1984, FWS prepared a Public Use Requirements document[23] for all refuge managers to follow insofar as funding and the compatibility test permit. These requirements include such broad directions as "welcome and orient visitors" and such specific recommendations as "install . . . 'You Are Here' map-posters." Congressional interest in improving the system in this way was shown by the $500,000 add-on appropriation for increasing public use in FY 1985.

CURRENT ISSUES

A number of problems currently affect refuge management. These include off-site threats to the resources of various refuges, FWS management actions seen by critics as detrimental to refuge wildlife, and lack of funding for management activities authorized by statute. Many of the controversies stem from the broad discretion given to the secretary by the Refuge Administration Act to allow various refuge uses that may conflict with wildlife conservation. Thus the act inherently pits refuge users against conservation groups and others who believe that the primary purpose of a refuge is to protect and conserve wildlife resources. A sample of recent conflicts is discussed here.

Boating Conflicts with Wildlife at Ruby Lake National Wildlife Refuge

Ruby Lake National Wildlife Refuge, a wetland area in the desert region of northeast Nevada, is of tremendous importance to Pacific Flyway waterfowl. No other place in the lower 48 states supports a greater population of nesting canvasbacks. Annual production of canvasbacks exceeds that of any other refuge, and redhead production is nearly as great. While FWS management of Ruby Lake focuses on producing waterfowl, public recreational use of the area is extensive. Virtually the entire marsh is used by fishermen.

Wildlife conservationists and recreational boaters and fishermen have been at odds for years over recreational use of Ruby Lake National Wildlife Refuge. The most recent conflict developed in 1984, when FWS issued on March 29 a proposed rule to extend the boating season. Environmentalists opposed the proposal, claiming that it would be incompatible with the primary purpose of Ruby Lake as a refuge and breeding ground for migratory birds and other wildlife.

The use of the refuge for recreational purposes had provoked controversy before. In July 1978, FWS issued boating regulations that permitted unlimited-horsepower boating and waterskiing within the refuge. Environmentalists filed suit in opposition, and in *Defenders of Wildlife v. Andrus*, Judge John H. Pratt held that the regulations violated the compatibility standard, since the degree and type of boating use permitted were not incidental to other activities, and were inconsistent with and disruptive of the refuge's primary purpose of protecting migratory birds.

In its 1984 proposal, FWS wanted to open the boating season two weeks early in alternate years for a five-year period in order to permit a research project on the effects of motorized boating on duck-brood survival. Opponents to this plan claimed that nesting ducks would be imperiled, that productivity would decrease significantly, and that FWS was responding to pressure from recreationists rather than to a real need for the research project. They pointed to a statement made by the refuge manager in the FWS 1981 Threats and Conflicts study: "The most important threat to Ruby Lake National Wildlife Refuge is public pressure for water-based recreation. The most important conflict at Ruby Lake National Wildlife Refuge is the Fish and Wildlife Service granting concesssions to recreational interests detrimental to wildlife."

Despite intense opposition, on June 12, 1984, FWS issued a final rule implementing the boating regulations as proposed. Defenders of Wildlife, the National Audubon Society, and the Humane Society of the United States filed suit on July 5. The suit was settled when FWS agreed to withdraw the new rule and replace it with a rule that would reinstate the former restriction on power boating. This rule was proposed on March 7, 1985.

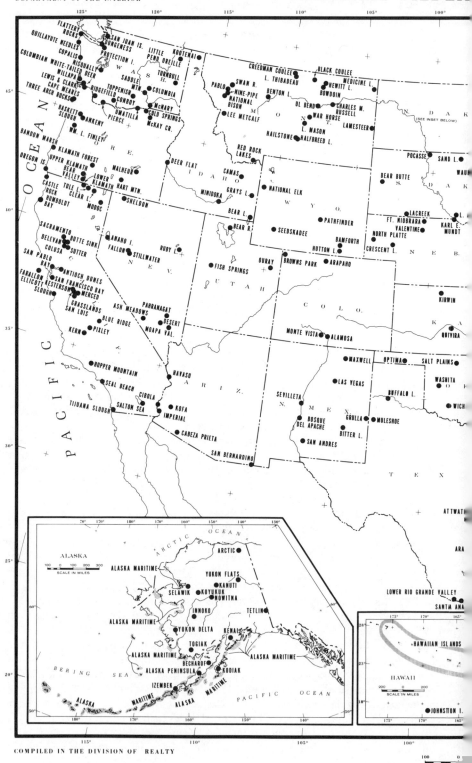

COMPILED IN THE DIVISION OF REALTY

WASHINGTON, D.C. SEPTEMBER 30, 1984

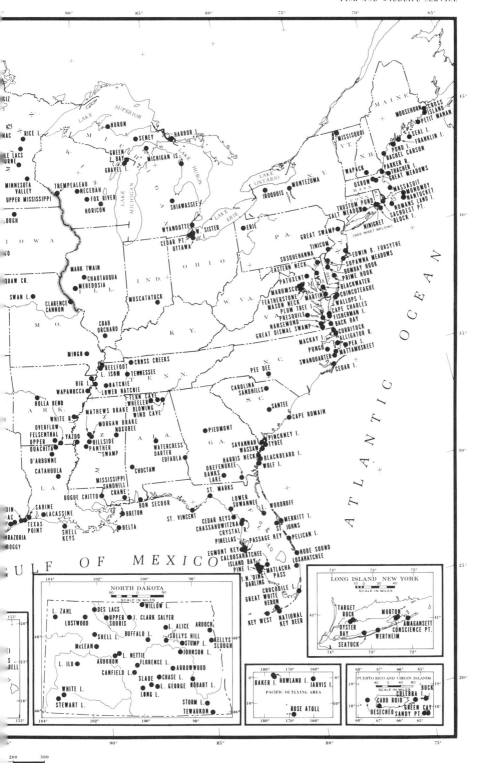

Deer Hunting on Loxahatchee National Wildlife Refuge

In an effort to expand the public use of refuges, the Department of the Interior announced a plan in 1982 to initiate a deer hunt on Loxahatchee National Wildlife Refuge in Florida. Ensuing controversy forced cancellation of the hunt as well as subsequently proposed hunts for 1983 and 1984. At issue is the compatability of hunting with the purposes for which northern Loxahatchee lands traditionally have been managed.

Since 1963, 48,000 acres in the northern part of the 143,000-acre refuge have been closed to entry by anyone, unless for research or law-enforcement purposes. A major reason for the closure of this area was protection of the fragile ecosystem, which provides habitat for such federally protected wildlife species as the wood stork, Everglades kite, peregrine falcon, bald eagle, American alligator, indigo snake, and perhaps the Florida panther. In addition to these protected species, the refuge is home for between 300 and 1,000 white-tailed deer. However, Loxahatchee generally is considered marginal deer habitat since it normally is flooded ten or more months each year. The deer herd is stable, but it is believed by some that a few animals could be killed without adversely affecting the population.

Opponents of the hunt have cited the following as reasons for their position: the hunt is not necessary to control the deer herd because the population is stable; the costs to the taxpayers of the hunt — including planning, biological surveys, environmental reviews, public hearings, and law enforcement — which totaled $93,000 in 1983, greatly outweigh the limited benefit to hunters, since hunt regulations that year permitted no more than 600 hunters to participate in killing not more than 30 deer; and the hunt threatens to disrupt a virtually pristine environment, at the northern extent of the Everglades.

In November 1984, FWS announced that for the third straight year the hunt had been cancelled. According to FWS officials, no future hunting proposals for the area are contemplated.

Toxic Chemicals on Crab Orchard National Wildlife Refuge

At least 42 refuges are known to have toxic waste dumps or hazardous materials within their borders. One of the most difficult cleanup problems faced by FWS is the PCB dump recently discovered on Crab Orchard National Wildlife Refuge in Illinois.

Crab Orchard — a 43,000-acre refuge — was established in 1946 to protect a series of lakes, marshes, and other lands used as migratory and wintering habitat by Canada geese and to provide public recreational, agricultural, and industrial uses. Prior to the transfer of lands to FWS, the area was used by the War Department for an ordnance plant site. In addition, the refuge contains buildings that are leased out to private tenants, one of whom manufactured electrical capacitors and transformers between 1946 and 1962. Highly toxic chemicals, PCBs, used as coolants in these electrical devices, wound up in the on-site dump used by the plant for its chemical and electrical-parts waste.

FWS stumbled upon the PCB dump in early 1984 when it took soil samples on the refuge in an attempt to verify a university research study that showed high concentrations of lead in deer tissue. FWS now is working with various federal and state agencies to clean up the three-acre dump site. The owner of the firm that originally dumped the PCBs has agreed to fund a cleanup feasibility study. In addition, the Corps of Engineers is examining the problem on behalf of the Department of Defense.

FWS is conducting other studies to see if the PCB contamination has affected refuge wildlife, especially its fish. So far, PCB levels in fish test samples do not exceed the Pure Food and Drug Administration standard of three parts per million.

Alaska Refuge Planning

Section 304(g) of ANILCA requires that comprehensve conservation plans be prepared for each of Alaska's 16 refuges. Plans for five refuges were to be finalized by 1983, and plans for all refuges were to be completed by 1987, but appropriations have not been sufficient to permit FWS to meet this schedule. Only four plans have been developed so far — for Kenai, Izembek, Becharof, and Alaska Peninsula refuges. Not only has the planning process been slow, but the plans have been roundly criticized by environmentalists who claim that the proposed management strategies support high levels of economic and recreational use detrimental to wildlife and the ecosystem.

The first completed draft plan was for Kenai National Wildlife Refuge. Many conservation groups opposed the management alternative preferred by FWS. Under this alternative, oil and gas leasing would have been allowed on 74 percent of the refuge's non-wilderness lands, commercial timber harvesting would have been permitted on 44 percent of the non-wilderness area, trapping and big-game hunting would have continued on 97 percent of the refuge, 43 percent of the refuge would have remained open to aircraft, and 64 percent of the refuge would have been open to snowmobile use.

Criticism by the public resulted in a final plan somewhat more favorable to conservationists. It calls for reductions in oil and gas leasing to 66 percent of the refuge's non-wilderness part and reduces the areas open to aircraft to 37 percent of the refuge. But the final plan also opens the entire refuge to trapping and big-game hunting. Environmentalists say that the final plan is still far from the congressional intent in establishing the Alaskan refuges. Conservationists will continue to participate in the planning process for Kenai and other refuges in Alaska to ensure that wildlife is protected properly.

Oil and Gas Development at D'Arbonne National Wildlife Refuge

A major controversy erupted in 1984 over FWS supervision of a private firm that drills gas wells on the D'Arbonne National Wildlife Refuge in Louisiana, habitat for the endangered red-cockaded woodpecker. The mineral estate underlying the refuge is privately owned, and FWS in the past has granted the mineral owners access to drill on the refuge. About 145 gas wells exist on the refuge now, most of them drilled before creation of the refuge.

The current controversy began when a private company entered the refuge and began drilling operations without an FWS permit. The company plans to drill 58 new wells on the 17,000-acre refuge.

The local chapter of the Sierra Club sought a court order to stop the drilling on the grounds that FWS had failed to issue a permit and had not done an environmental analysis of the drilling activity. This helped prompt FWS to obtain a biological opinion from its endangered species staff on how the drilling operation might affect the woodpeckers. After the opinion found that the woodpeckers would be driven from the refuge, the federal government sought a restraining order to require the drilling operator to obtain a permit. As a result, a permit was negotiated between FWS and the drilling company. It included various conditions to protect woodpecker habitat.

Meanwhile, the Sierra Club pressed its own lawsuit. Intervenors on the side of the local Sierra Club chapter included the Sierra Club Legal Defense Fund and Defenders of Wildlife. The plaintiffs seek to block the drilling on the grounds that FWS did not comply with the National Environmental Policy Act; that the drilling would destroy habitat of the red-cockaded woodpecker and that such destruction represented a taking of wildlife prohibited by the Endangered Species Act; and that FWS was not properly following mandates under existing authorities to protect the refuge.

Resource Problems Reported by Units of the National Wildlife Refuge System

Resource Affected	TYPE*	RF**	FH**	RES**	Total	% Stations Reporting
1. Water Quality	BIO	288	71	6	365	77
2. General Scene (public, etc.)	AES	306	37	6	349	74
3. Waterfowl	BIO	318	0	3	321	68
4. Health/Safety (public-employee)	OPS	241	69	7	317	67
5. Other Migratory Birds	BIO	313	0	2	315	67
6. Wetland Communities/Habitats	BIO	294	1	3	298	63
7. Building & Utility Systems	OPS	184	63	6	253	54
8. Large Mammals	BIO	242	4	3	249	53
9. Habitat Protection Facilities	OPS	222	19	1	242	51
10. Fish	BIO	165	65	4	234	50
11. Outdoor Experience	AES	220	12	0	232	49
12. Air Quality & Visibility	PHY	225	4	2	231	49
13. Water Supply	PHY	154	68	5	227	48
14. Plants (land & water)	BIO	221	0	2	223	47
15. Vehicles & Heavy Equipment	OPS	161	51	3	215	46
16. Invertebrates (land & water)	BIO	197	6	4	207	44
17. Small Mammals	BIO	202	2	2	206	44
18. Public Use Facilities	OPS	196	7	1	204	43
19. Water Management Facilities	OPS	166	35	1	202	43
20. Non-Migratory Birds	BIO	183	1	1	185	39
21. Grassland Communities/Habitats	BIO	173	1	1	175	37
22. Forest Communities/Habitats	BIO	160	2	4	166	35
23. Roads & Trails	OPS	160	3	1	164	35
24. Endangered/Threatened Species	BIO	154	0	2	156	33
25. Wildlife Observation	AES	122	10	1	133	28
26. Soils	PHY	129	1	0	130	28
27. Other-Operational	OPS	122	2	5	129	27
28. Wilderness (natural scene)	AES	111	7	0	118	25
29. Odor	AES	94	9	2	105	22
30. Other-Biological	BIO	74	1	1	76	16
31. Sites (historic, archeological)	CUL	69	0	2	71	15
32. Amphibians & Reptiles	BIO	59	1	1	61	13
33. Beach/Dunes	PHY	60	0	1	61	13
34. Scientific Equipment	OPS	23	29	4	56	12
35. Plankton/Microbiota	BIO	53	1	0	54	11
36. Landscapes (historic)	AES	29	0	1	30	6
37. Structures (historic, archeological)	AES	25	1	0	26	6
38. Other-Physical	PHY	23	0	1	24	5
39. Other-Aesthetic	AES	21	0	0	21	4
40. Desert Communities/Habitats	BIO	19	0	0	19	4
41. Geological Features (unique)	PHY	13	0	0	13	3
42. Tropical Communities/Habitats	BIO	12	0	0	12	3
43. Tundra Communities/Habitats	BIO	12	0	0	12	3
44. Minerals	PHY	8	0	0	8	2
45. Other-Cultural	CUL	5	0	0	5	1

*TYPE: BIO — Biological
      OPS — Operational
      PHY — Physical
      AES — Aesthetic
      CUL — Cultural

**Field Stations: RF — National Wildlife Refuge
      FH — National Fish Hatchery
      RES — National Fish or Wildlife Research Center

In response to the complaint of the intervenors, FWS agreed to conduct an environmental analysis of the drilling project. Meanwhile, a district court denied the plaintiff's request for an injunction. Some wells already have been drilled.

In 1985, FWS issued a draft environmental assessment that included new recommendations for additional requirements for the drilling permit, such as a spacing requirement of one well per 40 acres in certain parts of the refuge. The issue now is whether or not FWS actually implements recommendations for stronger woodpecker protection.

The D'Arbonne controversy exposed a weakness in the FWS policy covering access to subsurface minerals and management of drilling operations on refuges. FWS now is considering a revision of its subsurface mineral development policy.

The D'Arbonne controversy also is significant because it tests how far the Interior Department will go to protect refuge surface lands from activities designed to extract subsurface minerals. According to a Sierra Club Legal Defense Fund attorney, the federal government has all the legal power it needs, under the property clause of the Constitution, to protect the lands it manages from activities that would adversely affect them or the wildlife on them.

Pollution of Refuge Waters

On March 15, 1985, the Department of the Interior announced that it would immediately shut off the flow of contaminated irrigation water to Kesterson National Wildlife Refuge in California. This action was taken after department lawyers had determined that continued operation of the refuge would violate the 1916 migratory bird protection treaty and thus might subject the agency to criminal penalties.

Kesterson's wetlands have provided sanctuary for many species of migratory waterfowl, cranes, herons, eagles, falcons, and hawks. In the last few years, however, the refuge has turned into a death trap where thousands of birds have been poisoned by high levels of selenium in the water. The refuge staff has been forced to resort to using guns to scare the birds from the area.

The 5,900-acre refuge, near Los Banos, lies at the end of one of the Bureau of Reclamation's most elaborate drainage systems, the San Luis Drain. The drain collects waste water from 8,000 acres of irrigated farmland on the west side of the San Joaquin Valley and discharges it into the refuge's 1,200-acre complex of ponds. The original plans for the drainage project called for the waste water to be discharged into a watershed above San Francisco Bay, but the project was halted in 1975 when federal construction funds ran out.

Farmers whose irrigation system drains into the refuge grow cotton, fruit, and vegetables in one of the most productive and diversified farming regions in the world. They protested the department's move to cut off federal irrigation water, saying it would force them to take 42,000 acres of land out of production and would eliminate at least 1,650 jobs, costing them tens of millions of dollars a year.

The first reports of widespread deaths and deformities in refuge birds came in late 1983 and subsequently were linked to the concentration of selenium in refuge waters — up to 4,200 parts per billion, more than 400 times the level considered safe for drinking. When biologists later discovered toxic levels of selenium in other areas around Kesterson, public concern intensified. In February 1985, the California Resources Board declared that the selenium-contaminated water eventually could prove harmful to humans, including millions of people in Los Angeles whose water supply is channeled through the Westlands farming area. The board ordered the Bureau of Reclamation to either develop a method to end the pollution or to close Kesterson in three years. The Department of the Interior then moved on March 15 to shut off the flow of irrigation water to the refuge.

On March 28, 1985, Secretary of the Interior Donald Hodel announced that an agreement had been reached between the department and the Westlands Water District that would provide for a phased reduction of drain water into Kesterson, leading to a complete termination after June 30, 1986. Other methods for disposing of the tainted irrigation water will be considered. The settlement faces legal challenges, as the Merced County government and environmental groups have filed seperate lawsuits asking for an immediate and complete closure of the refuge.

Opposition to Creation of an Arizona Refuge

For fiscal year 1985, Congress appropriated $63,218,000 from the Land and Water Conservation Fund for acquiring national wildlife refuges. Twenty-seven projects were funded. One item proved controversial — a $4,000,000 appropriation to purchase a ranch in southern Arizona for recovery of the critically endangered masked bobwhite quail. The Buenos Aires Ranch is considered by FWS as the best remaining habitat for the species, which once ranged throughout the grasslands of southern Arizona but is now found only in Mexico. The species recovery plan calls for release of captive-bred birds in prime habitat on just a portion of the ranch, but the owner was willing to sell only the entire property, valued at $9,000,000.

The project was strongly supported by Governor Bruce Babbitt, the Arizona Department of Game and Fish, Senator Dennis DeConcini (D-Arizona), Senator Barry Goldwater (R-Arizona), and Congressman Morris Udall (D-Arizona). However, local citizens protested that the change in land ownership would have dire consequences for the local economy and school. FWS held several public hearings to present its finding, as stated in the environmental assessment, that turning the working ranch into a wildlife refuge would have a positive socioeconomic impact on the local community.

As the controversy intensified, the issue came to the attention of Congressman Eldon Rudd (R-Arizona), who appealed to then-secretary of the Interior Clark to rescind the FY 1985 appropriation. The decision was delayed for months while Clark was briefed by the FWS realty and endangered species offices. Finally, Clark's replacement Secretary Donald Hodel, gave the go-ahead, and FWS closed the deal on February 28, 1985. Quail are scheduled for release in the fall of 1985.

Purposes of the Refuge System

In 1968, two years after enactment of the National Wildlife Refuge System Administration Act, a distinguished panel of wildlife experts appointed by Interior Secretary Steward Udall and headed by A. Starker Leopold in effect declared that the law was an inadequate expression of refuge management policy. "What is still lacking," their report concluded, "is a clear statement of policy or philosophy as to what the National Wildlife Refuge System should be and what are the logical tenets of its future development."[24]

In the years since 1968, attempts to redefine the purposes of the refuge system have been confined largely to articles in conservation journals.[25] One notable exception was an effort in the mid-1970s to frame a refuge organic act.* That effort did not succeed, partly because — again in the words of the Leopold report — "Nearly everyone has a slightly different view of what the refuge system is, or should be."[26]

Need for clear management guidelines is felt most keenly during disputes, par-

---

*An organic act is a comprehensive statute that provides the purposes, authorities, and managerial guidelines that govern an agency, program, or system.

ticularly those involving commercial and recreational activities that may conflict with wildlife needs. Some conservationists believe that the current compatibility test provided by the Refuge Administration Act is vague and has not worked to protect refuges adequately. They argue that the proper criterion for allowing any use of a wildlife refuge is whether it contributes directly to the benefit of wildlife.

Another issue is whether the compatibility test is applied uniformly, based upon adequate data. The Government Accounting Office report noted an apparent inconsistency in the fact that FWS was promoting multiple use of refuges while at the same time, pursuant to a congressional directive, it was identifying threats to refuge integrity. The accounting office recommended that "the Secretary of the Interior resolve the conflicting goals of (1) promoting the multiple use of refuge lands and (2) resolving resource problems on refuges."[27] The resolution of those conflicting goals might require a re-examination of the basic rationale for the refuge system itself.

LEGISLATION

Military Uses of Refuges

Hearings in 1984 were held by the House Interior and Senate Energy committees on a bill (H.R. 4932) that would give the Department of Defense greater authority to use Desert National Wildlife Refuge in Nevada for Air Force training and gunnery purposes. Although the legislation was not reported out of committee, it is expected to be reintroduced during the 99th Congress.

Desert NWR was withdrawn from the public domain to help save the desert bighorn sheep from extinction. During World War II, the refuge and surrounding lands were set aside by executive order for military use. The withdrawal was to remain in effect until the war ended. However, the Defense Department sought and obtained continued use of the area. Later, a memorandum of understanding was signed between FWS and the Air Force regarding management of the refuge and the protection of its wildlife from the adverse effects of training and gunnery exercises.

Under the terms of the new bill, the Department of the Air Force would be given exclusive jurisdiction over the management of refuge lands for military purposes. While the refuge still would be administered by FWS according to the terms of the National Wildlife Refuge System Act, the Air Force would override this law for national defense purposes.

Conservation groups, including National Audubon, Wilderness Society and Defenders of Wildlife, are not happy with the bill because they say it would give the Air Force primary authority over the refuge. Moreover, the bill would relieve the Air Force of a requirement for cleaning up live shells left in the area after gunnery practice. Conservationists believe the legislation is a Defense Department attempt to secure permanent use of refuge lands. If the attempt succeeds, detrimental effects on the desert bighorn and other species could follow. Conservation groups already note that Air Force use of the area has hampered resource management. FWS access to withdrawn lands is restricted, and the Air Force largely ignores clean-up and minimum altitude overflight requirements. Moreover, the Air Force is opposing a proposal to designate the area as wilderness.

The 99th Congress is likely to take up one major piece of legislation affecting the refuge system: an Emergency Wetlands Resources bill that passed the House in the 98th Congress but stalled in the Senate. The bill would provide increased funding for the purchase of wetlands by FWS and state governments. (This bill is discussed in the legislation section of the Migratory Birds chapter.)

LEGAL DEVELOPMENTS

Two recent cases affect management of the refuge system.

The St. Matthew Island (Alaska) Land Exchange

In a case brought by the National Audubon Society and other conservation organizations, a federal district court in 1985 established important limits on the secretary's power to convey lands out of the refuge system.[28] The case concerned St. Matthew Island, a national wildlife refuge and wilderness area in the Bering Sea. Invoking the land-exchange authority granted by ANILCA, the secretary had conveyed part of the island to private developers, who planned to build an air base and tanker port to support offshore oil development. In return, the developers conveyed to the secretary a variety of land interests, principally unadjudicated native claims to various federal lands and a conservation easement over other private lands. FWS assessment of the exchange found that the proposed development would have caused serious harm to the island's important wildlife resources, adversely affecting some half a million nesting sea birds and several endangered whale species.

Although ANILCA's land exchange provisions were intended to facilitate acquisition of refuge inholdings, Secretary James Watt asserted that those provisions gave him *carte blanche* authority to convey into private hands refuge, park, and wilderness lands that were desired for development and that his exercise of that authority was immune from judicial review.

On November 30, 1984, the court overruled the secretary and declared the St. Matthew Island land exchange invalid. Two holdings in the court's opinion are of particular importance. First, the court held that the secretary's land-exchange decisions are subject to judicial review under the arbitrary and capricious standard. Second, the court held that any lands that were part of a national wildlife refuge in 1971 and that are conveyed to Alaskan natives under ANILCA or the Alaska Native Claims Settlement Act remain subject to the laws and regulations governing the refuge system. Thus the court's decision makes clear that any activities on such lands must be compatible with the purposes for which they were included in the refuge. Preliminary Interior Department calculations indicate that approximately two million acres of inholdings are affected by this ruling.

Grazing

Montana ranchers in the vicinity of Charles M. Russell NWR for years have been resisting FWS efforts to reduce the amount of grazing on this refuge in order to curtail the damage livestock is causing to wildlife habitat. Their congressional delegation has introduced legislation to declare Russell a dual-purpose refuge — grazing and wildlife management — and the ranchers also sued FWS on the theory that this particular refuge already had dual purposes. A federal district court judge in Montana agreed with the ranchers, holding that certain language in the executive order establishing the refuge meant that livestock and wildlife were to be given coequal consideration. This decision was overturned in *Secretary of the Interior v. Schwenke*[29] by the Ninth Circuit Court of Appeals. Based on the court ruling, FWS can now move to protect the refuge from overgrazing. The ranchers are likely to take their case to Congress, as they have previously, asking that language protecting their grazing rights be enacted into law.

RESOURCE STATUS

FWS does not yet have the capability to compile and analyze comprehensive information on the condition of the lands, wildlife, and facilities that the National

Wildlife Refuge System contains. For this reason it is virtually impossible to assess the status of the resources in the system as a whole. Such an assessment is being developed, however, and FWS probably will enter into a preliminary contract for its design in 1985. A wealth of information is available in the narrative reports prepared yearly by each refuge manager for the units under his or her control. But although all refuge managers follow somewhat the same format in making these reports, the writers vary in their emphases, inclusiveness, and writing styles. Moreover, no convenient means exists for compiling information from the hundreds of reports to show trends for the entire system.

FWS does compile certain kinds of information, such as the number of animals killed on refuges each year and the extent to which each refuge is used annually by waterfowl, but these data are collected primarily to meet program-manager needs rather than for the management of the refuge system itself. Without a mechanism for inventorying national or regional refuge resources and for updating that information, FWS cannot manage the refuge system in a way that would fulfill its potential.

FWS has a better information base concerning the condition of refuge facilities than it does concerning the lands and wildlife that use them. In 1982 FWS initiated a study to identify resource problems on all field stations, including national wildlife refuges, national fish hatcheries, and research facilities. Answering a detailed questionnaire, field-station managers and other personnel specified threats to the lands and species which they managed. The terms threat, conflict, problem, and resource problem were — and are — used more or less interchangeably to refer to what the questionnaire defines as "those pollutants, land uses, public uses, exotic species, individual development projects, etc. that are currently causing or have the potential to cause significant damage to Service-managed natural resources or physical facilities, or to those phenomena which seriously degrade important Service-managed values or visitor experiences."[30] A total of 473 field stations was surveyed: 373 of the then 410 refuges, 89 hatcheries, and 11 research facilities. The survey was completed in March 1982 and the results published the following July.[31]

The 1983 report identifies 65 problems grouped in seven categories: Water Quality and Quantity, Land Use, Air Pollution, Exotic and Feral Species, Public Use, Aesthetic Degradation, and Field Station Operations. All 65 problems were found to affect some refuges, 55 of them to affect some hatcheries, and 47 to affect some research stations.

FWS regional offices were instructed to prepare strategies for addressing the problems occurring in their regions by January, 1984. The ARMM program was made available to alleviate those problems stemming from inadequate maintenance of refuge facilities and equipment, the third most frequently reported problem. In FY 1983, FWS received a special $20-million congressional appropriation, to be obligated over a two-year period, under the so-called Jobs Bill Program. This money was spent on rehabilitation and maintenance of refuge facilities in areas of high unemployment. In FY 1985, FWS received an appropriation of $5 million to be used in solving resource problems. FWS has initiated an annually updated, five-year capital development plan for new construction and large rehabilitation projects. It also has established a new servicewide Maintenance Management Branch within the Office of Facility Services* to coordinate these maintenance activities.

Planning for FWS as a whole, for the regions, and for individual field stations has

---

*The Office of Facility Services reports to the associate director for Fishery Resources, an organizational anomaly that has arisen from an FWS desire to even out the workload of its associate directors.

been adapted to resolving the resource problems identified. In response to a request by the chairman of the House Appropriations Committee, FWS has prepared comprehensive plans for correcting the problems reported in 1982. For example, the 1984 plan for Sabine NWR in Louisiana identified chemical and thermal pollutants from industrial sources and alligator poaching among the 19 resource problems occurring on the refuge. Corrective actions called for by the plan include conducting frequent water-quality tests to monitor pollution and intensifying law-enforcement training to prevent illegal hunting of alligators.

Even the resource problems initiative, however, does not meet the need for a comprehensive maintenance management system that compiles information on the condition of refuge facilities, sets standards and priorities, and makes sure that they are carried out. Efforts to develop such a system are under way, and may be in place within two or three years.

REFERENCES

1. U.S. Fish and Wildlife Service, Refuge Manual, 1.3.
2. Nathaniel P. Reed and Dennis Drabelle, *The U.S. Fish and Wildlife Service* (Boulder: Westview Press, 1984), p. 19.
3. 45 Stat. 1222.
4. 48 Stat. 452.
5. 70 Stat. 1119.
6. 80 Stat. 927.
7. 87 Stat. 884.
8. 94 Stat. 2371.
9. Department of the Interior, U.S. Fish and Wildlife Service, Service Management Plan (revised version), (Washington, DC: September, 1982) p. 4.
10. 86 Stat. 399.
11. 48 Stat. 401.
12. 92 Stat. 3110.
13. 75 Stat. 813.
14. 90 Stat. 199.
15. These figures are derived from U.S. Fish and Wildlife Service, Modification of National Wildlife Refuges, an internal document prepared by Philip A. Dumont and Henry W. Thomas and printed in December 1975.
16. 78 Stat. 890.
17. Government Accounting Office, Economic Uses of the National Wildlife Refuge System Unlikely to Increase Significantly, (Washington, DC: June 15, 1984).
18. Ibid., p. 22.
19. Op. cit. Refuge Manual, 5.1.
20. 50 C.F.R. Part 32: Refuge Specific Hunting Regulations.
21. Department of the Interior, U.S. Fish and Wildlife Service, Subsistence Management and Use: Implementation of Title VIII of ANILCA (Washington, DC: November, 1984).
22. Ibid., p. IV-65.
23. Department of the Interior, U.S. Fish and Wildlife Service, Public Use Requirements (Washington, DC: October, 1984).
24. Department of the Interior, U.S. Fish and Wildlife Source, The National Wildlife Refuge System, Report of the Advisory Committee on Wildlife Management, in Final Environmental Statement: Operation of the National Wildlife Refuge Sys-

tem (Washington, DC: 1976), Appendix W, p. W-3.

25. See, e.g., Jim Doherty, "Refuges on the Rocks," *Audubon*, vol. 85, no. 4 (July, 1983), and Dennis Drabelle, "Going It Alone," *Wilderness*, vol. 47, no. 162 (Fall 1983).

26. Op. cit., The National Wildlife Refuge System, Report of the Advisory Committee on Wildlife Management, in U.S. Fish and Wildlife Service, Final Environmental Statement: Operation of the National Wildlife Refuge System (1976), p. W-3.

27. Op. cit., Government Accounting Office, "Economic Uses of the National Wildlife Refuge System Unlikely to Increase Significantly," p. 22.

28. *National Audubon Society v. Clark*. No. A83-425 CIV (D. Alaska).

29. *Secretary of the Interior v. Schwenke*. 720 F. 2d 571 (9th Cir. 1983).

30. Department of the Interior, U.S. Fish and Wildlife Service, Resource Problems (Washington, DC: July 1983), p. 1.

31. Ibid.

The walrus, once threatened by overhunting but now thriving, is among the marine mammal species protected by the federal government.

Marine Mammal Protection

by Michael Weber
W.J. Chandler Associates

INTRODUCTION

FEDERAL AUTHORITY TO conserve marine mammals is based upon several treaties and federal laws, the most comprehensive of which is the Marine Mammal Protection Act (MMPA) of 1972.[1] The MMPA placed a moratorium on taking or importing marine mammals or their products into the United States. Exceptions to this moratorium are limited.

MMPA restrictions apply to United States citizens wherever they may be, unless they are engaged in authorized activities in waters under foreign jurisdiction, and to foreign nationals within the fishery conservation zone of the United States, which extends 200 miles offshore. The MMPA divides the responsibility for the protection of marine mammals between the Department of the Interior and the Department of Commerce, which respectively have delegated responsibility to the Fish and Wildlife Service (FWS) and the National Marine Fisheries Service (NMFS). FWS is responsible for dugongs, manatees, polar bears, sea otters, and walruses. NMFS is responsible for whales and dolphins and all seals and sea lions, with the exception of the walruses.

A unique feature of federal marine mammal management under the MMPA is the creation of the Marine Mammal Commission. This independent commission reviews permits for the taking of marine mammals and serves as a watchdog over NMFS and FWS in their implementation of the MMPA. It also supports research and studies to identify and determine how best to resolve problems affecting the conservation and protection of marine mammals and their habitat.

With the passage of the MMPA, the federal government preempted state authority for the management of marine mammals within territorial waters. Although the MMPA provides a means whereby states may regain management authority, no states now exercise management responsibility for marine mammals. However, several states have entered into cooperative agreements with FWS and NMFS to enforce MMPA regulations.

While the MMPA is the principal basis for the nation's marine mammal programs, other federal laws and international treaties also provide guidance, authority, and responsibilities in this area. For example, the Endangered Species Act of 1973 provides various types of protection for endangered and threatened species of marine mammals. Other laws, such as the Marine Protection, Research, and Sanctuaries Act of 1972,[2] offer tools useful for the protection of habitat important to the conservation of marine mammals.

Finally, because of their highly migratory nature, some marine mammals are subject to international treaties to which the United States is a party. Most of these predate the MMPA. In the MMPA, Congress directed the executive branch to undertake an effort to conform these international agreements to the principles found in the MMPA, but progress has been slow.

NMFS focuses its research and management efforts upon exploited species, species whose management may be returned to the states, and species captured incidentally in fishing operations. FWS efforts focus on species that are hunted for subsistence purposes in Alaska and on southern sea otters and manatees, both listed under the Endangered Species Act.

HISTORY AND LEGISLATIVE AUTHORITY

The management of marine mammals, like the management of many other commercially exploited species, has evolved rather fitfully, generally in response to the overexploitation and collapse of one species after another. By the 1970s, management of marine mammals began to change in response to concerns about the humaneness of marine mammal exploitation. Until passage of the MMPA, which gave official recognition to their aesthetic and ecological importance, marine mammals had been valued primarily for commercial purposes. The management of northern fur seal populations, the first to attract federal attention, provides a good example of how this attitude affected marine mammal conservation.

The Fur Seal Treaties

In 1786, Captain Pribylova, a Russian explorer, discovered the major breeding ground of the northern fur seal on two islands in the Bering Sea. By 1805, the intense commercial hunt of these animals had so reduced the population that the hunt was suspended for a few seasons. In 1867, ownership of the Pribilof Islands was transferred from Russia to the United States, which leased the islands to a sealskin merchant for 20 years. The merchant was allowed an annual harvest of 100,000 male fur seals.

So lucrative was the hunt for fur seals that soon after discovery, other nations in the region began hunting the animals on the open sea. Pelagic sealing was quite inefficient, leading to the killing of five to nine seals for every one recovered. More significantly perhaps, pelagic sealing created considerable competition for the United States. In 1881, the United States declared the eastern Bering Sea closed,[3] and by 1886 a U.S. Navy ship had seized Canadian sealing vessels. Repeated attempts to fashion a management regime acceptable to the interested nations of Japan, Russia, Great Britain, and the United States failed. Pelagic sealing continued.

Finally, President Theodore Roosevelt made the conclusion of a treaty a priority of his administration and convened a successful meeting of the Russians, Japanese, British, and Americans. In 1911, the four nations agreed to the Treaty for the Preservation and Protection of Fur Seals.[4]

The preamble to the convention states that the party nations were "desirous of adopting effective means for the preservation and protection of the fur seals which frequent the waters of the North Pacific Ocean." The main features of the convention, many of which are still in effect, included a ban on pelagic sealing throughout the range of the northern fur seal, authority for one signatory nation to arrest nationals of another party nation engaging in pelagic sealing, and a prohibition on the import of fur seal skins that had not been taken in a supervised hunt. Aboriginal natives were allowed to hunt fur seals if traditional means were used. In return for halting pelagic sealing, Japan and Canada were to receive a share of the sealskins taken in hunts on American and Russian rookeries. The treaty itself provided no guidance or standards for setting quotas.

In response to perceived impacts of fur seals on its fisheries, Japan withdrew from the treaty just before World War II. Not until 1957 did the United States, the Soviet Union, Great Britain, and Japan enter into a new agreement, the Interim Convention on the Conservation of North Pacific Fur Seals.[5] The preamble of the Interim Convention states clearly the management objective of the party nations:

> . . . to take effective measures towards achieving the maximum sustainable productivity of the fur seal resources of the North Pacific Ocean so that the fur seal population can be brought to and maintained at the levels which provide the greatest harvest year after year, with due regard to their relation to the productivity of other living marine resources of the area.

This convention, renewed and amended slightly in 1963, 1969, 1976, and 1980, left the final determination of harvest levels up to the nation within which a particular rookery was located. However, it did establish a North Pacific Fur Seal Commission responsible for providing signatory nations with quota recommendations and for coordinating research regarding northern fur seal populations.

The Interim Convention is implemented in the United States under the Fur Seal Act of 1966.[6] The act prohibits the hunting of fur seals by United States citizens other than "Indians, Aleuts, and Eskimos who dwell on the coasts of the North Pacific Ocean." Trade in sealskins taken in an unauthorized manner also is prohibited.

The hunt of northern fur seals on the Pribilof Islands was one of the most controversial issues confronted by Congress in fashioning the MMPA. On the one hand, government officials cited the hunt as an outstanding example of wildlife management. However, other witnesses presented evidence that the fur seal herds had declined dramatically since the 1940s.[7] Congress dodged the controversy by leaving ambiguous the relationship between the MMPA and the international treaties regulating marine mammals.

Congress did direct the executive branch to undertake a full-scale review of the Interim Convention and its compliance with the principles of the MMPA. The departments of State and Commerce prepared a superficial three-page review that declared the two laws compatible.

Since passage of the MMPA, however, the United States has had to press for changes in the implementation of the convention. Some changes have been effected, although the Interim Convention's purposes still depart widely from those of the MMPA.[8] Furthermore, the fur seal hunt has become so controversial within the United States that there are considerable pressures to withdraw from the convention. The most recent protocol extending the convention expired in 1984. The Senate will consider ratification of a new protocol in 1985.

Whaling Treaties and Laws

Mismanagement of the world's whale populations also contributed significantly to the momentum of concern that resulted in the passage of the MMPA. Although concern about the decimation of whale populations blossomed most fully in the late 1960s and early 1970s, earlier attempts had been made to bring commercial whaling under control. Dramatic technological improvements in the early 20th century stream-lined the processing of whales at sea. More powerful engines allowed whalers to pursue successfully the swifter rorqual whales and to exploit the hitherto untouched populations of great whales in Antartica.

Concern for the future of the whales and the whaling industry led the League of Nations to adopt the Convention for the Regulation of Whaling in 1931.[9] This convention, which came into effect in 1935, prohibited only the hunting of endangered right whales and of calves, immature whales, and females accompanied by calves.

Increasing competition among Great Britain, Norway, Japan, and the Soviet Union led to the signing of the International Agreement for the Regulation of Whaling[10] in 1937. This convention included provisions for open and closed seasons, sanctuaries, minimum-length requirements for hunted whales, and restrictions on the use of factory ships and catcher boats.

The United States convened a conference in Washington, DC, in the fall of 1946 that resulted in the International Convention for the Regulation of Whaling.[11] This convention is implemented in the United States by the Whaling Convention Act of 1949.[12]

The principal purpose of the 1946 convention is "to provide for the proper conservation of whale stocks and thus make possible the orderly development of the whaling industry. . . ." To this end, the convention establishes a decision-making body, the International Whaling Commission (IWC), composed of a representative from each of the member nations. It is the role of the commission to amend the Schedule, a separate section of the convention that contains IWC regulations, including quotas for particular stocks or populations and open and closed seasons. The commissioners, who receive advice from a scientific committee, in some cases may amend the IWC regulations by a two-thirds vote. To amend the Schedule, a three-quarters majority is required. Any country may exempt itself from a decision by formally objecting to it within 90 days.

The IWC reached a turning point in 1972, when the United Nations Conference on the Human Environment overwhelmingly approved a resolution proposed by the United States delegation calling upon the IWC to pass a 10-year moratorium upon commercial whaling. Although proponents of the moratorium initially did not obtain the necessary three-fourths majority, the IWC did amend the way in which it set quotas in 1975. As whale populations continued to decline, pressure mounted in favor of the moratorium, which finally passed in 1982 to become effective in late 1985.

In pursuing the elimination of commercial whaling, the executive branch of the United States government has been given two very powerful tools by Congress. The first is the 1971 Pelly Amendment to the Fisherman's Protective Act of 1967,[13] which requires the secretary of Commerce to notify the president that the nationals of a foreign country "are conducting fishing operations in a manner or under circumstances which diminish the effectiveness of an international fishery conservation program." The president may then direct the secretary to prohibit the importation of fish products from the offending country. Originally passed to pressure compliance of other nations with international fishing treaties, the Pelly Amendment has never been fully invoked with regard to the IWC. Although in 1974 the Commerce Department certified both Japan and the Soviet Union for violating IWC quotas, the president declined to invoke economic sanctions against these two nations, which subsequently complied with IWC regulations.

In 1979, Congress passed the Packwood-Magnuson Amendment to the Fishery Conservation and Management Act of 1976.[14] Under this amendment, the secretary of Commerce is required to reduce by at least 50 percent the allocation of fish made to a foreign nation fishing in United States waters if that nation jeopardizes the effectiveness of the IWC. The Packwood-Magnuson Amendment was invoked in 1985 when the Soviets exceeded their take of Minke whales from the Southern Hemisphere.

The primary purpose of the IWC and the Fur Seal Treaty is to ensure sustainable exploitation at the highest possible levels. However, the gruesome details of the killing of marine mammals, combined with the obvious failures of management, created in the 1960s a powerful demand for change, which in turn led to a comprehensive marine mammal conservation law.

The MMPA

By 1971, Congress had before it a number of bills intended to revolutionize the conservation of marine mammals in the United States. The MMPA,[15] passed by Congress and signed by President Nixon in 1972, is an uneasy balance between preservation and management.

In its declaration of findings and policy, Congress stated in the act that

> . . . marine mammals have proven themselves to be resources of great international significance, esthetic and recreational as well as economic, and it is the sense of the Congress that they should be protected and encouraged to develop to the greatest extent feasible commensurate with sound policies of resource management and that the primary objective of their management should be to maintain the health and stability of the marine ecosystem. Whenever consistent with this primary objective, it should be the goal to obtain an optimum sustainable population keeping in mind the optimum carrying capacity of the habitat.[16]

Thus, management for maximum sustainable yield gave way to management for optimum sustainable populations that continue to play their role in the functioning of marine ecosystems. Also gone was the marketplace as the only measure of value for marine mammals — the MMPA recognized that marine mammals have esthetic and recreational values as well.

The primary feature of the act is the establishment of a moratorium on the taking of all marine mammals by persons subject to United States juridiction. "Taking" includes not only hunting, capturing, or killing but also harassment, which is defined by regulation as negligent or intentional acts resulting in the disturbing or molesting of a marine mammal. The act also prohibits most importations and sale of marine mammals or their products.

Under certain circumstances, the taking of marine mammals is permitted. Marine mammals may be taken for scientific research and public display and incidental to commercial fishing. In this latter category, the original MMPA called for the tuna purse-seine fishing industry to reduce its incidental capture of porpoises to "insignificant levels approaching a zero mortality and serious injury rate." In 1981, Congress amended the MMPA to allow tuna fishermen to achieve this goal by applying the "best marine mammal safety techniques and equipment that are economically and technologically feasible." The 1981 amendments also added two categories of allowable "small take,"* one for other commercial fishing operations and one for operations such as oil and gas exploration. The final exception to the moratorium on taking allows certain Alaskan natives to take any marine mammal species for subsistence use and handicrafts.

---

*"Small take" means the taking of a marine mammal in such small numbers that its population is not significantly affected.

Central to the MMPA is its requirement that marine mammals be restored to their optimum sustainable population levels. Unlike earlier management regimes that aimed at maximum exploitable productivity, optimum sustainable population is much more expansive and ambiguous. Congress defined "optimum sustainable population" as

. . . with respect to any population stock, the number of animals which will result in the maximum productivity of the population or the species, keeping in mind the carrying capacity of the habitat and the health of the ecosystem of which they form a constituent part.[17]

Making this definition work in practice has proved difficult. The Department of Commerce appears to have hit upon an operating definition acceptable to Congress:

". . . Optimum sustainable population" is a population size which falls within a range from the population level of a given species or stock which is the largest supportable within the ecosystem to the population level that results in maximum net productivity. Maximum net productivity is the greatest net annual increment in population numbers or biomass resulting from additions to the population due to reproduction and/or growth less losses due to natural mortality.[18]

Before the MMPA, various states managed marine mammal populations within their territorial waters. Concern that marine mammal populations, often shared among several states, were not being managed effectively led Congress to pre-empt state management authority with the MMPA. From the beginning, the MMPA has included procedures for returning management of individual species or populations of species to a state if the state can demonstrate compliance with a variety of criteria. Soon after passage of the act, Alaska requested management authority over 10 species found in its waters. The secretary of the Interior granted Alaska authority over the Pacific walrus in 1975.

The departments of Commerce and Interior also were preparing to return management of the other nine species when Alaska natives filed a lawsuit challenging the state's restrictions on walrus hunting.[19] When the court decided that the federal government could not approve any state laws that restricted native taking allowed under the MMPA, the state of Alaska returned walrus management authority to the federal government and dropped its request for authority to manage the other nine species.

During debate over 1981 amendments to the MMPA, both Alaska and Oregon stressed that marine mammals were important natural resources for the states and should be used wisely and managed to prevent conflicts with fisheries. Moreover, states that wanted control over marine mammals had some legitimate complaints about the existing procedure for returning management authority.

In response, the 1981 amendments facilitated return of management of marine mammals to the states and specified requirements for state programs. The amendments also authorized the secretary to make grants to the states for the development and implementation of management programs.

Before returning management authority to a state, the secretary must find that the state's management program is consistent with the purposes of the act. A state with management authority can initiate the taking of marine mammals, but only after it first determines that the species for which it intends to allow taking is at its optimum sustainable population and will not be reduced below that by the proposed level of taking. Public hearings also must be held. If marine mammal management were to be returned to a state, the federal government would retain overview authority to regulate incidental take in commercial fishing operations outside the state's jurisdiction and all taking for research and display purposes except when undertaken by or on behalf of the state.

Other Legislation

In addition to the MMPA, Congress has passed other legislation and approved various treaties that provide some degree of protection for marine mammals. In 1971, Congress prohibited all sport hunting of wildlife from aircraft.[20] Between 1961 and 1972, an average of 260 polar bears had been shot yearly, 87 percent of them from the air. Since the MMPA a year later banned all non-native hunting of polar bears, the effect of the airborne hunting prohibition on polar bear conservation may have been negligible.

The United States was not alone in recognizing that sport hunting of polar bears was having a devastating impact upon the species. Each of the circumpolar nations — Canada, the Soviet Union, Norway, Denmark, and the United States — had adopted restrictions on polar bear hunting. There appeared to be mutual interest in replenishing the species. In 1972, Congress passed a joint resolution calling upon the executive branch to negotiate an international agreement for the protection of polar bears.[21]

Negotiations in Oslo, Norway, in November 1973 led to the Agreement on the Conservation of Polar Bears,[22] the first international marine mammal treaty entered into by the United States after the passage of the MMPA. The agreement has been roundly criticized for falling far short of the standards of the MMPA.[23] It prohibits the taking of polar bears, with certain exceptions. Subsistence hunting of polar bears is allowed under the agreement if "polar bears have or might have been subject to taking by traditional means." "Traditional means" are not defined, but the parties have agreed that these means include snowmobiles and modern rifles. Polar bears also may be taken for scientific or conservation purposes or when polar bears interfere with the management of other species.

The agreement does require the parties to take appropriate action to protect the ecosystem of which polar bears are a part. But, as is true of the other provisions of the agreement, crucial terms are not defined, and there is no mechanism for concerted management actions by the party nations.

The Endangered Species Act [24] provides some tools for marine mammal protection that are not available under the MMPA. Currently, marine mammals listed as threatened or endangered under the act include the northern sea otter, the southern sea otter, the dugong, all species of manatees and monk seals, the Gulf of California harbor porpoise, and blue, bowhead, finback, gray, humpback, right, Sei, and sperm whales. Any species listed under the act is automatically considered "depleted" under the MMPA, and taking of such species is allowed only for scientific or subsistence purposes.

Like the MMPA, the Endangered Species Act sets conditions under which listed species may be taken or traded. It requires federal agencies to ensure that their activities do not jeopardize listed species and provides for the designation of critical habitat for listed species to protect areas essential for their survival. There is no such mechanism in the MMPA. Nor does the MMPA provide for the acquisition of habitat, as does the Endangered Species Act.

The Endangered Species Act also mandates recovery programs for listed species. Recovery plans for several listed marine mammals, including West Indian manatees, southern sea otters, and Hawaiian monk seals, have been completed and adopted.

The Convention on International Trade in Endangered Species of Flora and Fauna

(CITES),[25] to which 88 nations are now party, is implemented under the Endangered Species Act in the United States. International trade is prohibited in all species listed under Appendix I of the Convention, including four species of pinnipeds, the marine and southern sea otters, four species of dolphin, the finless porpoise, the Amazonian and Caribbean manatees, and all whales consistent with the regulations of the IWC. All other species of whales, dolphins, porpoises, and the West African manatee are listed on Appendix II of CITES. Trade in them is allowed only if the exporting country determines that the export will not be detrimental to the species.

The Convention on Nature Protection and Wildlife Preservation in the Western Hemisphere[26] was ratified by the United States Senate in 1941. Mentioned by the Endangered Species Act but not the MMPA, this convention has as its principal purposes "to protect and preserve in their natural habitat representatives of all species and genera . . ." in the Western Hemisphere. Among other things, the treaty restricts trade in listed species. The United States has had listed among such species a number of whales, seals, manatees, and sea otters. The Western Hemisphere Convention, which has been largely dormant, remains a potential means of conserving marine mammals within the waters of the hemisphere.

Marine mammal populations in Antarctica reach sizes unknown elsewhere in the world. The inaccessibility of the continent has protected its seal populations, numbering perhaps more than 60 million animals, from exploitation on the scale of commercial whaling operations in the area. Nonetheless, with an exploratory sealing expedition in 1964, Norway urged other nations party to the Antarctic Treaty[27] to conclude an agreement on the regulation of any future sealing in the area.

The exploratory sealing was unsuccessful and, although no commercial sealing has taken place, the Convention on the Conservation of Antarctic Seals[28] was concluded in February 1972. The United States is party to this convention as well as the Antarctic Treaty. The convention prohibits pelagic sealing and restricts any future hunting to levels that would maintain optimum sustainable yield. The convention provides that a regulatory body will be established when and if commercial sealing begins.

In 1980, the 13 nations party to the Antarctic Treaty concluded the Convention on the Conservation of Antarctic Marine Living Resources.[29] Concerns that expanding krill fisheries would disrupt the food supply of other species, including marine mammals, led to this very ambitious effort at ecosystem protection. Implementation of the convention is left to a Commission for the Conservation of Antarctic Marine Living Resources. The commission is empowered to acquire data, acting on advice from a scientific committee also established by the convention, and to adopt conservation measures, including restrictions on the harvest of living marine resources in the Southern Ocean and the creation of protected areas. All parties to the convention, including the United States, are represented on the commission.

The United States is signatory to several fisheries agreements that affect the conservation of marine mammals. The MMPA directed the secretaries of Commerce and State to pursue the reduction of incidental taking of marine mammals in the tuna purse-seine fishery through the Inter-American Tropical Tuna Commission, established in 1949.[30] While the MMPA provided authority for compelling United States fishermen to reduce incidental capture, tens of thousands of porpoises continue to be drowned in the nets of foreign tuna boats. Progress in attacking this problem has been hampered by a variety of factors, including withdrawal of some nations from the international commission and the difficulty in gathering data from foreign ships. This latter problem hampers the application of Section 101(a)(2) of the MMPA, under which the secretary of Commerce is to embargo fish products from nations that do not undertake conservation programs comparable to those instituted by the United States.

In recent years, the incidental capture of Dall's porpoise in the Japanese salmon drift-net fishery in the North Pacific has come under the increasing scrutiny of the International North Pacific Fisheries Commission, established under the International Convention for the High Seas Fisheries of the North Pacific Ocean.[31] Each year, the Japanese drift-net fishery has incidentally drowned several thousand Dall's porpoises under an MMPA incidental take permit. In December 1982, Congress amended the implementing legislation, the North Pacific Fisheries Act, and extended this permit through June 1987 while requiring Japan's continued commitment to research and installation of gear modifications to reduce the take.

Although the MMPA emphasizes the importance of ecosystem protection to marine mammals, the act provides no means itself for directly protecting important marine mammal habitat. Other federal laws do provide authority for programs that may protect habitat important to marine mammals either directly or indirectly.

Title III of the Marine Protection, Research and Sanctuaries Act of 1972 provides the secretary of Commerce with the authority to designate areas of the marine environment as national marine sanctuaries and to regulate activities in such areas in order to protect the area's resources. The Channel Islands and Point Reyes-Farallon Islands National Marine Sanctuaries off California protect two important breeding areas for pinnipeds in the United States.

Finally, the Fishery Conservation and Management Act of 1976[32] affects the conservation of marine mammals directly and indirectly. Fashioned in response to the declaration of 200-mile offshore fishing conservation zones by a number of nations and the depletion of fisheries near United States shores by foreign factory ships, the Fishery Conservation and Management Act declares waters within 200 miles of the United States shoreline as the United States Fishery Conservation Zone, and claims United States management authority over all marine life within the zones except for marine mammals, birds, and highly migratory species. However, the act also amended the MMPA to expand its jurisdiction to 200 miles offshore. As a result, whaling ships of the Soviet Union were forced from waters around the Hawaiian Islands, where they had pursued sperm whales in previous years.

In conclusion, there is ample statutory authority for the conservation and management of marine mammals. Indeed, marine mammal management law incorporates very progressive concepts that insist on viewing these animals as parts of their ecosystems. Whether these progressive concepts can be implemented where other values compete with ecological values remains to be seen. The relative lack of information on these species of animals compounds the difficulties confronting the responsible agencies.

ORGANIZATION AND OPERATIONS

The MMPA, as the nation's principal marine mammal conservation law, divides management responsibility between the Department of Commerce and the Department of the Interior. Commerce has responsibility for all whales, porpoises, sea lions, and seals, except for walruses. Interior is responsible for manatees, polar bears, sea otters, and walruses. This split is a result of Executive Reorganization Plan No. 4 of 1970,[33] which established the National Oceanic and Atmospheric Administration (NOAA) within the Commerce Department and transferred to it most of the functions vested in Interior's Bureau of Commercial Fisheries, including management responsibility for oceanic marine mammals. Marine mammals considered land-oriented remained with

Interior's Bureau of Sport Fisheries and Wildlife, which later was renamed the U.S. Fish and Wildlife Service (FWS).

Congress considered and rejected amendments to the MMPA that would have placed all authority for marine mammals in the Department of Interior. Instead, Congress reaffirmed the split responsibility but suggested it would review its decision if FWS and NOAA were not merged into a Department of Natural Resources. That never occurred, but Congress has not reviewed the bifurcation of responsibility.

Established under the MMPA, the Marine Mammal Commission is an independent agency responsible for developing, reviewing, and making recommendations on actions and policies of all federal agencies with respect to marine mammal protection and conservation and for carrying out a research program.

Although no states have been granted management authority for marine mammals, a number of states do carry on active research programs and cooperate with federal agencies in management. In addition, FWS provides funding under Section 6 of the Endangered Species Act to the state of California for southern sea otter work and to the state of Florida for West Indian manatee work.

Many nonprofit organizations conduct public awareness programs on marine mammals. Some organizations also operate centers that rehabilitate stranded marine mammals. Other private organizations conduct field research on marine mammals.

Congressional Committees

Several congressional committees have primary jurisdiction over marine mammal issues. The Senate Committee on Commerce, Science, and Transportation and the House Committee on Merchant Marine and Fisheries are responsible for all authorizing legislation regarding marine mammal matters.

Appropriations for marine programs of the National Marine Fishery Service and of the Marine Mammal Commission are set by the Senate Subcommittee on Appropriations for Commerce, Justice, State and the Judiciary and Related Agencies and the House Subcommittee on Appropriations for Commerce, Justice, State and the Judiciary and Related Agencies. Appropriations for FWS marine mammal programs under both MMPA and the Endangered Species Act are set by the Senate and the House Subcommittees on Appropriations for Interior and Related Agencies. Appropriations for the Marine Mammal Commission under the MMPA are set by the Senate and House Subcommittees on Housing and Urban Development — Independent Agencies.

Agency Structure and Function

The secretary of Commerce has delegated his authority for marine mammal management to the administrator of the National Oceanic and Atmospheric Administration (NOAA). Besides providing overall supervision, the NOAA administrator often serves as the United States commissioner to the IWC. The NOAA assistant administrator for Fisheries, who heads the National Marine Fisheries Service (NMFS), oversees the day-to-day implementation of the MMPA.

Within NMFS, the Office of Protected Species and Habitat Conservation under the direction of the deputy assistant administrator for Fisheries Resource Management handles marine mammal management. Marine mammal research is directed by the Office of Resource Investigations under the deputy assistant administrator for Science and Technology.

This division between management and research also is found at the field level. The five NMFS regional offices are responsible for management of marine mammals and other marine resources. Four fisheries centers and the National Marine Mammal Laboratory conduct research on marine mammals.

Key Offices Involved in Marine Mammal Management, National Marine Fisheries Service, NOAA, Department of Commerce

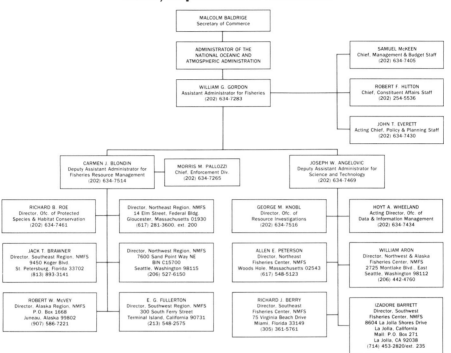

Implementation of the MMPA is a minor, if very visible, part of the NMFS mission, which is directed primarily at managing and, where possible, expanding the United States commercial fishing industry. NMFS grants or denies requests for exemptions from the moratorium on taking marine mammals; issues taking permits; carries out management, research, and enforcement programs; issues rules and regulations; and participates in international programs.

The secretary of the Interior has delegated authority for marine mammal management to FWS. Within FWS, responsibility is further divided between the Wildlife Resources Program, Division of Wildlife Management, and the Federal Assistance Program, Office of Endangered Species. The Wildlife Resources Program exercises management, research, and enforcement responsibility for marine mammals not listed as endangered or threatened under the Endangered Species Act. In essence, this restricts the Division of Wildlife Management's marine mammal responsibilities to the management of walruses, polar bears, and northern sea otters. The Endangered Species Office, on the other hand, exercises responsibility for manatees and southern sea otters. This restricts its activities to Florida for West Indian manatees and California for southern sea otters.

The Marine Mammal Section of the Denver Wildlife Research Center is responsible for coordinating FWS marine mammal research under both the MMPA and the ESA. FWS staff and programs at several national wildlife refuges assist in management and research programs for marine mammals under the aegis of NMFS. For instance, marine mammal funds appropriated under the Endangered Species Act have been provided to the Northwestern Hawaiian Islands National Wildlife Refuge for research and recovery work on endangered Hawaiian monk seals, which haul out on beaches within the refuge. Finally, the FWS Division of Law Enforcement investigates violations of the MMPA involving illegal take or importation of marine mammals for which FWS is responsible.

The Marine Mammal Commission serves as watchdog over the implementation of the MMPA. Three commissioners, appointed by the president, are assisted by a professional staff and a Committee of Scientific Advisors, composed of nine scientists knowledgeable in marine ecology and marine mammal affairs. In carrying out their MMPA responsibilities, the secretaries of Commerce and Interior are required to consult with the commission. If an agency does not accept formal committee recommendations, it must explain its reasons for rejecting them. The committee's role is crucial to implementation of the MMPA in several ways, not the least of which is its ability to fund research on emerging issues.

Planning

No long-term planning or policy documents describe the objectives of the NMFS marine mammal program. NMFS has developed 31 statements of its agency objectives, some of which touch directly or indirectly upon marine mammal management. For example, while there is a specific statement of objectives for northern fur seals, the management of porpoise populations incidentally captured in the tuna purse-seine fishery is only indirectly the subject of an objectives statement on the tuna fishery in the Eastern Tropical Pacific.

NMFS is required to develop recovery plans for marine species listed as endangered or threatened under the Endangered Species Act. Recovery plans are meant to guide agency efforts in promoting the recovery of listed species. NMFS has prepared a recovery plan only for the highly endangered Hawaiian monk seal. The agency has not convened recovery teams to develop recovery plans for other listed marine mammal species over which it has jurisdiction.* In FWS, the key planning documents guiding marine-management efforts are recovery plans for the West Indian manatee and southern sea otter and regional resource plans. Each FWS regional office prepares regional resource plans for the management of National Species of Special Emphasis (NSSEs) within their geographic area. The plans establish population and distribution goals for all NSSEs. All five marine mammals under FWS jurisdiction have been designated as NSSEs.

Budgeting

In its annual budget request, the region asks for the funds it needs to help conserve all NSSEs. Regional requests are reviewed and consolidated into the FWS budget. FWS and NMFS also receive pass-through funds from agencies such as the Minerals Management Service and the National Parks Service for research on marine mammals affected by the actions of these agencies. Funds authorized under the Endangered Species Act also are available to NMFS and FWS for management and research on listed species of marine mammals.

---

*Endangered and threatened marine mammals under NMFS jurisdiction include the gray whale, humpback whale, fin whale, blue whale, right whale, bowhead whale, sperm whale, Gulf of California harbor porpoise, sei whale, and the Hawaiian, Mediteranean, and Caribbean monk seals.

National Marine Fisheries Service Funding (000s)

	Requested	Appropriated
1981	$7,875	$7,080
1982	7,416	7,416
1983	7,416	7,475
1984	5,571	7,700
1985	5,615	9,270

Source: National Marine Fisheries Service.

The allocation of funds directed to marine mammal research and management in the NMFS budget has changed in recent years. Before 1984, marine mammal research and management funds were requested under two line items, marine mammal conservation and Pribilof Islands operations. Both line items included funds for research and management.

In fiscal year 1984, this format changed. Since then, marine mammal research has appeared as part of the sub-line item called protected species biology, which includes funding for research on marine mammals and other marine species listed under the Endangered Species Act. This sub-line item is part of the resource-information line item. Marine mammal management funds are part of the protected-species-management line item, which now includes funding for management of the northern fur seal hunt under the Fur Seal Act of 1966.

Funding for NMFS marine mammal management, research, and enforcement has increased from $7 million in FY 1981 to $9.3 million in FY 1985. By comparison, the president's request for FY 1985 was $5.6 million. Most of the growth in the NMFS marine mammal budget is for specific problems. For example, in FY 1985 Congress allocated $1 million beyond the base level for research and action on the entanglement of marine mammals in discarded fish nets. Congress also appropriated $500,000 for research on marine mammal/fishery food chains in Alaskan waters and $175,000 in additional funding for Hawaiian monk seal recovery efforts.

Prior to 1984, funding for marine mammal work conducted by the Office of Endangered Species in FWS came from two different line items, endangered species, and mammals and nongame birds. After 1984, most funds for Office of Endangered Species marine mammal work appeared in two line items, endangered species research and endangered species management. Additional funds are allocated under a line item for marine mammal protection.

Office of Endangered Species funding for marine mammal work has increased from $932,200 in fiscal year 1982 to $1.5 million in 1985. Fiscal year 1985 saw considerable increases in recovery efforts for marine mammals. Additional funds were devoted to the opening of a field station in Sacramento, California, for the purposes of

Fish and Wildlife Service Funding (000s)

	MMPA		ESA	
	Requested	Appropriated	Requested	Appropriated
1981	$2,000	$2,000	$ 561	$ 561
1982	1,600	1,600	502	502
1983	1,600	1,600	604	604
1984	N/A	N/A	1,100	1,100
1985	N/A	N/A	1,394	1,394

Source: FWS, Office of Endangered Species and Division of Wildlife Management.

preparing an environmental impact statement on the translocation of southern sea otters called for by the Recovery Plan. It is expected that this office will close when the translocation has been completed and determined successful.

Before fiscal year 1984, the Division of Wildlife Management's Wildlife Resources Program received all FWS appropriations for marine mammals. A portion of this was passed through to the Office of Endangered Species for work on endangered marine mammals. Since 1984, however, when the resources program budget was restricted to species not listed under the Endangered Species Act, funds have been appropriated under the line items "wildlife management" and "wildlife research" in the wildlife resources budget. FWS funding for research and management work on nonendangered marine mammal species has decreased from $2 million in FY 1981 to $1.6 million in FY 1983 and afterwards.

Funding for the Marine Mammal Commission is separate from all other marine mammal funding. The Commission's budget has increased from $734,000 in FY 1981 to $929,000 in FY 1985. By comparison, the administration's budget request for FY 1982 was $591,000 and for FY 1985, $781,000.

The development of annual budget requests drives NMFS planning of its marine mammal research and management programs. As is true of NMFS administration in general, the budget process is highly decentralized. Generally, the directors of NMFS management and research efforts in a given region determine new initiatives and other changes in existing regional programs. These determinations are reviewed and accepted or rejected by a group known as the board of directors, which includes the directors of the regional offices and fisheries centers and NMFS officials in Washington, DC. The set of priorities and budgets is then sent up through NMFS, NOAA, and the Department of Comerce to the Office of Management and Budget, and, from there, to Congress as part of the president's annual budget request.

Once funding has been approved by Congress, it is allocated to the regions. Each regional office and fishery center then prepares a current-year operating plan that sets out objectives, tasks, and milestones for the year.

Research

Spending much of their lives hidden from human sight, marine mammals pose considerable obstacles to scientists wishing to study their biology, life histories, and population dynamics. The passage of the MMPA and increasing human use of the oceans, particulary for offshore oil and gas exploration and production, have spurred a tremendous increase in marine mammal research.

The MMPA requires the Marine Mammal Commission to review, undertake, or instigate marine mammal research. The commission annually conducts a comprehensive survey of marine mammal research, the results of which indicate that at least 14 agencies are conducting or supporting such research. These include: The Department of State, the Minerals Management Service, the National Institutes of Health, NMFS,

Marine Mammal Commission Funding (000s)		
	Requested	Appropriated
1981	$641	$734
1982	591	672
1983	594	822
1984	638	929
1985	648	929

Source: Marine Mammal Commission.

the National Park Service, the National Ocean Service, the National Science Foundation, the North Pacific Fishery Management Council, the Office of Naval Research, the National Sea Grant Program, the Smithsonian Institution, FWS, and the U.S. Geological Survey. The Minerals Management Service, NMFS, and FWS conduct the largest programs.

Primary responsibility for gathering biological and ecological data on marine mammals rests with NMFS and FWS. The Marine Mammal Commission plays an important role in the federal research effort by supporting research that is critically needed but for which no funds are available in the budgets of other agencies.

NMFS conducts research mainly in direct response to management issues, such as the review of permits, conflicts between marine mammals and commercial fisheries, the status of species exploited under international treaty, and the anticipated return of management authority for marine mammals to states. In some cases NMFS conducts population surveys, in others it investigates technologies for reducing marine mammal/fishery conflicts.

FWS research is conducted under authority of both the MMPA and the Endangered Species Act. Research on polar bears, walruses, and northern sea otters is conducted in response to management issues. In anticipation of a request from the state of Alaska for return of management authority for these species, FWS has been gathering data that would help the state make the prerequisite findings required under the MMPA before the state assumes managment responsibility. Research emphases recently have shifted slightly, since Alaska may decide not to seek management authority for marine mammals. Current emphases of FWS research conducted under the MMPA include:

- determination of the movement, distribution, size, and trends of the polar bear populations in Alaska;
- determination of the annual and seasonal abundance, distribution, and composition of northern sea otter populations;
- investigation of hauling-out patterns and behavior of walruses on hauling-out grounds.

FWS also conducts research in response to information needs identified in recovery plans for species listed under the Endangered Species Act. Thus, FWS conducts research on such matters as manatee mortality in Florida, behavior of manatees and southern sea otters, and interactions between southern sea otters and other marine life. A major focus of research recently has been the gathering of base-line data for the San Nicolas Island ecosystem in anticipation of the translocation of southern sea otters to this area in 1985 or 1986.

The Marine Mammal Commission convenes workshops and provides funding for research or studies regarding threats to marine mammal populations and other relevant matters. Since 1974, the commission has authorized contracts for more than 400 projects. Recently, the commission has sponsored research regarding oil-spill risks in and near the range of the southern sea otter, observations of gill- and trammel-net fisheries in California, plans for the detection and monitoring of the effect of Antarctic krill harvest on whales and seals, and studies of the entanglement of marine mammals, particularly northern fur seals, in discarded fish nets.

State agencies, nonprofit organizations, and industry groups also sponsor marine-mammal research. Research on marine mammal populations that enter United States waters also is conducted with other nations. For example, under the auspices of the bilateral US-USSR Environmental Agreement, FWS, NMFS, the Soviet Ministry of Fisheries, and the Soviet Academy of Sciences have conducted joint research on Pacific walruses, including population surveys and studies of feeding habits.

CURRENT TRENDS

While program emphases have shifted among species, the marine mammal management programs of both FWS and NMFS have focused upon a few recurring areas. NMFS, for instance, has focused its efforts upon issuance of permits for taking marine mammals, law enforcement, fishery conflicts, species exploited under international treaties, and return of management authority to the states. Recently, NMFS, FWS, the Coast Guard, and other agencies were directed by Congress to undertake an effort to reduce the entanglement of marine mammals and other animals in discarded fish nets and other debris.

The program emphases of FWS focus on species listed under the Endangered Species Act, especially manatees and southern sea otters, and on those being exploited, including polar bears and Pacific walruses. These and the northern sea otter have been designated national species of special emphasis and given special management attention. In addition, FWS ensures the enforcement of laws relating to species under its authority.

Permits and Enforcement. Both NMFS and FWS, with the advice of the Marine Mammal Commission, may grant permits for incidental take of marine mammals and for taking or importing species for scientific research or display. In addition, NMFS and FWS are responsible for enforcing the prohibitions of the MMPA. These responsibilities are central to the conservation of marine mammals and form an important part of the missions of NMFS and FWS.

NMFS has processed 613 permit requests since the MMPA was enacted. Of these, 445 involving some 650,000 animals were approved. Only 10 were disapproved. Many of the others were withdrawn by the applicants.

FWS grants permits for the taking or import of marine mammals, for the purchase or sale of raw marine mammal parts or products by non-Alaskan natives, and for the tanning of marine mammal hides to facilitate trade among Alaskan natives. During 1983, FWS issued four new scientific research permits, three new public-display permits, and eight new tanning permits.

Law enforcement efforts by NMFS focus upon illegal importation and sale of marine mammals and their products and the incidental capture of marine mammals in fisheries. From June 1983 to June 1984, NMFS investigated 172 alleged violations of the MMPA.

Although NMFS and FWS coordinate some enforcement efforts, FWS retains authority for all enforcement actions involving marine mammals listed under the Endangered Species Act. During the calendar year 1983, FWS closed 89 new investigations, 18 of which ended with civil penalties being assessed and collected, and 89 new investigations were opened.

The Marine Mammal Commission and its Committee of Scientific Advisors review requests for permits under the MMPA. During 1983, the commission made recommendations on 40 applications submitted to NMFS and five submitted to FWS. The commission also made recommendations on 18 requests to amend existing permits.

Fisheries Conflicts

While the issue of incidental capture of porpoises by United States tuna fishermen largely has been resolved, other marine mammal conflicts with fisheries have become more apparent. Two types of interaction can be identified. First, marine mammals can be killed, intentionally or unintentionally, during fishing operations or by becoming entangled in discarded nets. Second, marine mammals, sometimes competing with fishermen for the same food resources, may damage a fisherman's catch or gear. The principal areas where these interactions are known to occur are California, the Pacific Northwest, the southeastern Bering Sea, and the southeastern and Gulf states.

Federal and state agencies have been studying marine mammal/fishery interactions off California since 1979. In recent years, the increasing use of gill and trammel nets in nearshore waters has been responsible for the drowning of harbor porpoises, harbor seals, and sea otters in significant numbers. Restrictions on the placement of gill nets were enacted by the California legislature in 1984, and further restrictions are being considered.

The southeastern Bering Sea is one of the world's richest marine ecosystems. The expansion of foreign and domestic fishing in areas where there are large numbers of marine mammals already has led to conflicts. A pollock fishery in Shelikof Strait expanded from a catch of 900 metric tons in 1980 to more than 130,000 metric tons in 1983. With this expansion has come the incidental capture of Steller sea lions in fish nets. The sea lion population in the area has declined more than 50 percent in the last several years. The size of the pupping colonies in the Shelikof area also has declined. The Marine Mammal Commission and the North Pacific Fishery Management Council have initiated efforts to develop and implement an ecosystem approach to the management of marine mammals and fisheries in the area.

Since 1980, NMFS has funded research on marine mammal/fishery interactions in the Columbia River and adjacent waters, an area known for its salmon fishery. Recent research confirms that harbor seals are responsible for damage to gear and catch in a significant number of cases. The harbor seal population in the area has increased about 11 percent annually between 1976 and 1982. NMFS is funding research on methods of mitigating these marine mammal/fishery conflicts.

As marine mammal populations expand and recover in these and other areas, conflicts with commercial and recreational fishermen also will increase. Resolution of these conflicts probably will require increasing research and special management attention. The MMPA's balance between protection and management also may be tested.

Entanglement

Since the mid-1970s, the entanglement of marine mammals and other marine species in discarded net fragments and other materials has been recognized as a serious problem. Since 1976, the parties to the Interim Convention on the Conservation of Northern Fur Seals have undertaken various efforts to reduce the entanglement of northern fur seals. In 1982, entanglement was implicated as the principal cause of the four to eight percent annual decline in northern fur seal populations. Entanglement also appears to be a significant mortality factor for endangered Hawaiian monk seals and other marine mammals.

The issue gained congressional attention in 1984, when Congress appropriated $1,000,000 for FY 1985 to research means of reducing this problem. With considerable prodding by the Marine Mammal Commission, NMFS conducted a workshop on entanglement in the North Pacific in November 1984 in Honolulu, Hawaii. Cosponsors included FWS, the Marine Mammal Commission, the Pacific, Western Pacific, and North Pacific Fishery Management councils, and the Pacific Sea Grant College programs. The workshop developed an extensive set of recommendations, now under study by NMFS. Since this issue involved so many individuals and nations, it will require a complex response and continued commitment of the various actors, most particularly NMFS.

Return of Management to the States

Although Congress provided means for return of marine mammal management authority to the states in the original MMPA and streamlined these means through amendments to the act in 1981, no states currently exercise management authority over resident marine mammal populations. Nor has any state requested return of management authority since the short-lived request of Alaska in 1975.

Both Alaska and California periodically have made tentative moves toward requesting marine mammal management authority. NMFS and FWS have, in turn, initiated research programs to help gather the information that would be necessary for making the required determinations under the MMPA for return of management. The lack of information on marine mammal populations, the difficulty in making a determination of the optimal sustainable population for many marine mammal populations, and the competing demands of animal protection groups, fishermen, aboriginal natives, commercial and recreational hunters, and others have all conspired to convince the states to leave marine mammal management to the federal government, however reluctant the federal agencies might be to have it. As a result, federal agencies are likely to retain management authority over marine mammals for the foreseeable future.

Southern Sea Otters

The southern sea otter subspecies inhabits a 200-mile stretch of the California coast. Decimated by 18th- and 19th-century hunters, the southern sea otter population was driven nearly to extinction. Now numbering about 1,200 animals, the southern sea otter is listed as threatened under the Endangered Species Act. Like polar bears and fur seals, sea otters lack blubber and must rely on their thick fur coat to protect them from the cold. If their fur becomes matted, it loses its insulating ability and the animals can die of exposure. As a result, sea otters are one of the most vulnerable of marine mammals in an oil spill.

The threat of an oil spill was a major factor in the 1977 listing of the species. Since a major spill could affect much of the remaining southern sea otter population and threaten its recovery, FWS, which exercises responsibility for this animal under the Endangered Species Act and the MMPA, has prepared a recovery plan. Among its recommendations, the recovery plan urged FWS to establish a second colony of sea otters so that a large oil spill would be less likely to affect the entire population.

FWS is still considering potential sites for the new colony and is trying to determine which area is favorable otter habitat, has the fewest conflicts with other ocean users, and poses the fewest risks to the new colony. The most likely site is San Nicolas Island, outermost of the California Channel Islands. The target date for translocation is autumn 1985, but it probably will be delayed until completion of an environmental impact statement.

CURRENT ISSUES

Passage and implementation of the MMPA has led to the resolution of some controversies regarding marine mammals. However, several issues remain unresolved, while new ones continue to emerge. The hunting of the great whales and of northern fur seals, both conducted under international treaties, remains very controversial, as does the hunt of bowheads by Alaska natives. In addition, a growing controversy surrounds the keeping of marine mammals in captivity at aquaria.

Moratorium on Commercial Whaling

The decision of the United States not to apply available economic sanctions against Japan to force compliance with IWC regulations restricting whaling has been hotly disputed. With IWC passage of a temporary moratorium in 1982 by a vote of 25 to one and the subsequent filing of objections by several whaling nations including Japan, the stage was set for a showdown on the commitment of the United States to its long-standing policy of pursuing an end to commercial whaling. The moratorium will apply first to the 1985-86 pelagic whaling seasons and to the 1986 coastal whaling season.

Late in 1984, the Japanese caught sperm whales in spite of a decision by the IWC to prohibit hunting of North Pacific sperm whales. This set off renewed calls for applying economic sanctions against the Japanese under the Pelly Amendment to the Fisherman's Protective Act and the Packwood-Magnuson Amendment to the Fishery Conservation and Management Act. When the Commerce Department did not apply sanctions but instead negotiated an agreement with the Japanese that basically ignores the IWC decisions on sperm-whale quotas and the moratorium, 10 United States environmental organizations filed suit in federal court to force application of sanctions. The court held that sanctions are required under both the Pelly and the Packwood-Magnuson Amendments. The Commerce Department is appealing the case.

The clash of federal marine mammal policy with balance-of-trade concerns and the increasingly close relationship between some American and Japanese fishing industries have brought the issue of commercial whaling to a point of explosiveness only dimly foreseen even five years ago.

Bowhead Whales

The bowhead whale, federally listed as an endangered species, is one of several whale species still legally hunted in United States waters. Although the MMPA forbids the commercial hunting of marine mammals and the Endangered Species Act forbids the hunting of endangered species, both statutes contain provisions that allow Alaskan Eskimos to hunt bowheads for traditional subsistence purposes.

Prior to 1977, the bowhead hunt, which the Aleuts of Alaska's northern shores have conducted for centuries, had been regulated solely by the federal government. However, the IWC claimed management authority over this species in 1977 when they learned that exceptionally high numbers of bowheads were being killed or harpooned but not retrieved. The IWC first set a zero quota, then established separate quotas for animals harpooned and animals retrieved.

In the United States, some conservationists called for an end to the hunt while others argued for continuation of a limited harvest for subsistence and traditional purposes. The Aleuts demanded a continuation of the hunt and rejected IWC jurisdiction on principle.

Initially, scientists estimated the population at 800 animals. After several years and several millions of dollars of study, scientists have revised their population estimates upward to about 3,800 animals. Nonetheless, the IWC Scientific Committee is unlikely to recommend a higher quota than has been allowed in recent years. The United States, pressed by Alaskan interests, is likely to continue seeking higher bowhead harvest quotas.

Northern Fur Seals

The hunt of northern fur seals in the Pribilof Islands has continued to be very controversial for two reasons. First, the northern fur seal population has declined steadily since the mid-60s. In 1984, the Humane Society of the United States petitioned NMFS to list the northern fur seal as threatened. Although NMFS rejected the petition, disagreement continues among government scientists as to whether the population is threatened. Some conservationists are seeking to prevent extension of the Interim Convention, which expired in October 1984. Among other things, they argue that fur seals would be better protected under the MMPA. Proponents of the convention, including NMFS and the Aleuts, suggest that without the treaty other nations, such as Japan, will renew pelagic sealing and that research on these animals will cease.

Second, there is disagreement about whether the federal government should be subsidizing the hunt. Until recently, the federal government annually spent nearly $6 million administering the northern fur seal hunt. In reauthorizing the Fur Seal Act in 1983, Congress established a $20 million trust fund for the residents of the Pribilofs to develop "a stable, diversified, and enduring economy not dependent on sealing." The state of Alaska also has spent more than $10 million for development of a fishing harbor for the Aleuts. Even conservationists who are critical of the hunt support additional funding for economic alternatives to the hunt, but are becoming impatient with continued pleas from the Aleuts for more money and more time.

In addition, controversy over the humaneness of the hunt animates much of the public concern about the Pribilof fur seal harvest. Although clubbing of the seals is relatively humane, groups that oppose the killing of wildlife argue that the hunt is needless since no market exists for the animals' furs, which are being stockpiled in government warehouses.

The treaty parties have negotiated a protocol to extend the treaty. The Senate will be taking up the ratification of the protocol in 1985. The government and Aleut groups will seek ratification, while some animal protection groups will oppose renewal of the treaty.

Cetaceans in Captivity

Controversy over the keeping of cetaceans in captivity is breaking into the open and testing the balance between management and protection in the MMPA. In 1984, Sea World, Inc., applied to NMFS for a permit to capture 100 killer whales over a period of five years. Of these, Sea World intended to release 90 after conducting various physiological tests and to retain 10 for attempts at captive breeding.

NMFS planned to grant the permit upon a number of conditions in response to recommendations from the Marine Mammal Commission and environmental groups. However, NMFS refused to conduct a full-scale environmental impact statement, and environmental groups sued in federal court. The court held that an environmental impact statement had to be prepared. The Department of Commerce is considering an appeal of the decision.

LEGISLATION

The 98th Congress passed two measures affecting marine mammal conservation. Both the MMPA and the Marine Sanctuaries Program were reauthorized, and in the process amendments were made to both.

Marine Mammal Protection Act

On June 27, 1984, the House of Representatives and the Senate unanimously approved H.R. 4997, which amends and reauthorizes the MMPA for four years.[34] Among other things, H.R. 4997 amends the MMPA to require that the secretary of Commerce obtain documentary evidence of a regulatory program for tuna-fishing practices of foreign countries before tuna from those countries may be imported into the United States. Previously, foreign vessels were not subject to the controls that have reduced by more than 90 percent the incidental kill of porpoises by the United States tuna-fishing industry.

Another provision extends the United States tuna industry's incidental catch permit for an indefinite period, subject to certain conditions. The maximum number of porpoises that may be killed annually by the fleet is set at 20,500. For the first time, this figure includes a maximum of 250 coastal spotted dolphins and 2,750 eastern spinner dolphins. These species were taken in previous years but were considered accidental and were not counted against the ceiling. Taking of these species in excess of the limits will be a violation of the MMPA. A research program to determine population trends of the affected dolphin species in the eastern tropical Pacific is mandated with an authorization of $4 million over the next five years.

The reauthorization bill also clarifies the method by which members of the Marine Mammal Commission are selected, by requiring that the list of candidates from which the president names commissioners be approved unanimously by the Smithsonian Institution, the Council on Environmental Quality, the National Science Foundation, and the National Academy of Sciences. The Marine Mammal Commission staff was increased from eight to 11.

Marine Sanctuary Program Reauthorized

The 98th Congress also passed S. 1102,[35] which reauthorizes for four years the National Marine Sanctuary Program conducted by the Office of Ocean and Coastal Resource Management in the Commerce Department. The bill substantially amended Title III of the Marine Protection, Research, and Sanctuaries Act of 1972 by codifying many of the program standards and procedures developed by NOAA in the preceeding three years. Among other things, S. 1102 requires that the secretary of Commerce provide a report on proposed sanctuaries to the Senate Commerce Committee and the House Committee on Merchant Marine and Fisheries, including a management plan for the area and an environmental impact statement. The bill also requires the secretary to consult closely with affected Fishery Management Councils and federal and state agencies before designating a sanctuary. The legislation increased the authorization levels for this program significantly from $2.2 million in FY 1984 to $3.9 million by FY 1988.

Upcoming Legislation

The Fishery Conservation and Management Act is up for reauthorization in 1985, and attempts may be made to eliminate the act's economic sanctions against nations that jeopardize IWC effectiveness. Conservation organizations brought suit against NOAA late in 1984 to force the Department of Commerce to invoke economic sanctions against Japan, which had caught sperm whales despite an IWC ban. Both the departments of State and Commerce have opposed invoking the sanctions because of ramifications for United States-Japanese trade relations.

The protocol extending the Interim Convention on the Conservation of North Pacific Fur Seals, which expired in 1984, will be considered by the Senate for ratification during 1985. Some humane organizations are seeking to block ratification of the treaty and to end the Pribilof seal hunt.

LEGAL DEVELOPMENTS

Recent litigation under the MMPA has revolved around NOAA's continuing efforts to regulate the incidental take of porpoises by yellowfin-tuna fishermen. In

1984, the Ninth Circuit overturned NOAA regulations setting quotas for porpoise taking by the fishermen, finding NOAA's methodology arbitrary.[36] More importantly, however, the Ninth Circuit upheld NOAA's authority to place observers on the tuna boats to enforce porpoise quotas. The tuna fishermen argued that the observer program exceeded NOAA authority under the MMPA and violated their right to protection against illegal search as granted by the Fourth Amendment of the Constitution. Rejecting these arguments, the court found that NOAA's general rule-making powers under the MMPA were adequate authority for the observer program and that the program had been implicitly approved by Congress. The court further held that even if the observer program were assumed to be a "search" under the Fourth Amendment, no warrant was required for such a closely regulated industry and, in any case, the regulations establishing the program were an acceptable substitute for the warrant requirement.[37]

RESOURCE STATUS

Neither FWS nor NMFS has a systematic procedure for routinely monitoring and assessing the biological status of all marine mammals and habitats under their jurisdiction. Different types of data are collected on species of management interest, but such data are scattered throughout the regional and field offices of both agencies rather than aggregated and assessed by a central office. Furthermore, the reliability of population trend and population estimates varies. Some species, like the polar bear and bowhead whale, have been relatively well studied, and the reliability of data on their status is relatively high. The status of less intensively studied species, such as the bottlenose dolphin and right whale, is more difficult to determine. The conservation status of some species that are of active management concern to NMFS and FWS are discussed here.

Pinnipeds (Seals and Sea Lions)

Pinnipeds are divided into two families: Otariidae (sea lions and fur seals) and Phocidae (earless seals). NMFS has responsibility under the MMPA for all species of seals and sea lions except walruses.

California Sea Lion. Three subspecies of California sea lions inhabit the Pacific Ocean from the Galapagos Islands to British Columbia. The largest population breeds along the Channel Islands off southern California and along the oceanic islands off Mexico. The California population numbers about 74,000, the Mexican population about 83,000, and the Galapagos Island population about 20,000.

California sea lions feed day or night on squid, Pacific whiting, sardines, and opaleye fish. The weather disruption known as El Niño appears to have so reduced prey abundance in 1982-83 that pup production of California sea lions in California and the Galapagos was reduced substantially.

This is the most exhibited species of marine mammal in the world. The species has bred in captivity, and captive individuals have lived 20 to 25 years. Both commercial and recreational fishermen complain that California sea lions destroy their catch and gear. Animals have been and are being killed as a result.

Northern (Steller) Sea Lion. This species is found in the Sea of Japan, the Bering Sea, Aleutian Islands, Gulf of Alaska, and the Channel Islands. The Alaska population is approximately 200,000 animals, the Soviet population 20,000 to 30,000, the British Columbia population about 5,000, the Oregon population about 2,000, and the California population about 3,000. The Alaskan population has been declining by six and a half percent yearly since the 1970s.

Steller sea lions feed on cephalopods and on fish such as walleye, pollock, cod, herring, shad, and lamprey. Killer whales prey upon both California and Steller sea lions.

Northern Fur Seal. Female and juvenile northern fur seals are highly migratory, ranging in an arc from the Sea of Japan through the Bering Sea and down to the Channel Islands of California. The largest breeding colonies are found on the Pribilof Islands in the Bering Sea and on the Commander Islands in the Sea of Okhotsk. The population numbers about 865,000 animals in Alaskan waters, 463,000 in Soviet waters, and 4,000 off Southern California.

All major breeding populations, except that on the Commander Islands, continue to exhibit marked long-term declines. On the Pribilof Islands alone, the total number of pups born each year has declined 50 percent from 1940 to 1980. The population established within the last 20 years found in the Channel Islands has increased, although the number of pups born in 1983 was below that for previous years.

An average of 26,000 sub-adult males has been harvested annually on the Pribilof Islands pursuant to the Interim Convention on the Conservation of Fur Seals. Recently, entanglement of fur seals in discarded fishing gear and garbage has been implicated in the four to eight percent decline in the Pribilof population.

Fur seals prey on herring, walleye, anchovy, Pacific whiting, capelin, salmon, and squid. Killer whales and sharks prey upon northern fur seals, and sea lions prey upon fur seal pups. This predation probably has no significant effect on population size or productivity.

Guadalupe Fur Seal. As recently as 1923, biologists believed this species had become extinct as a result of commercial hunting. However, a male was sighted in the Channel Islands in 1949, and a breeding colony was found on Guadalupe Island off Mexico in 1954. At least 20,000 fur seals are estimated to have lived on Guadalupe Island, before commercial sealing. About 1,600 animals now live on Guadalupe Island, and others have been seen at the Channel Islands. The population is steadily increasing. In 1984, the Center for Environmental Education petitioned NMFS to list the species as endangered.

Harbor Seal. There are three subspecies of harbor seals — Atlantic, Arctic, and Pacific. These animals generally are solitary and monogamous.

Considered abundant in most of their range, harbor seals have increased in numbers substantially over the past 10 years. There are about 48,000 to 51,500 harbor seals in European waters, 20,000 to 30,000 off eastern Canada, and 10,000 to 15,000 off the Atlantic coast of the United States. At least 312,000 harbor seals inhabit the Pacific Ocean.

Harbor seals feed on squid and a variety of fish, including salmon, cod, herring, and smelt. Eagles, foxes, and coyotes prey upon newborn and young. Adult harbor seals are prey for sharks, killer whales, northern sea lions, bears, and walruses.

Ringed Seal. The most abundant seals in the northern hemisphere, ringed seals confine themselves to advancing and retreating ice in the Arctic. The ringed seal also is the only pinniped to hide its young in a lair. Current estimates for this species range between six and seven million animals. Subsistence hunting of ringed seals occurs throughout the species' Arctic range.

The diet of ringed seals varies according to season. In the autumn and winter they prey principally upon polar cod. At other times of the year they feed primarily upon plankton and crustaceans. Arctic foxes feed on ringed seal pups, and polar bears feed on pups and adults.

Harp Seal. The harp seal also is found with Arctic ice, its preferred habitat. Like several other species of haired seals, newborn harp seals have a white coat called a lanugo. There are three distinct populations. The Norwegian population numbers between 500,000 and one million. The population in the White Sea north of the Soviet Union numbers 100,000 to 150,000, and the population that breeds in the Gulf of St. Lawrence and off Newfoundland is estimated at one to two million adults and juveniles.

The hunt for baby harp seals of the western Atlantic population galvanized public concern about seals in the 1970s, contributing to the passage of the MMPA. During the 1983 season, 55,914 harp seals were taken, all adults. The importation of harp seal pelts was prohibited by the European Economic Community during 1984 and 1985, sharply reducing demand for hides. Recent reports indicate that 9,000 to 10,000 harp seals are caught incidentally each year in the cod fishery off Norway.

Harp seals feed on capelin, cod, herring, squid, and crustaceans. Sharks, killer whales, and polar bears prey upon harp seals.

Gray Seal. There are three stocks of gray seals, all of which seem to be increasing. The western Atlantic, or Canadian, stock numbers about 24,000 to 55,000, including a few breeding animals near Nantucket Island, Massachusetts. The eastern Atlantic stock around Ireland, Britain, and Norway numbers about 75,000. The Baltic population, which breeds on ice, numbers about 1,000. During 1980, about 3,000 gray seals were killed in Canadian and British waters.

Gray seals feed on halibut, cod, haddock, lamprey, salmon, herring, cephalopods, and crustaceans. Commercial fishermen complain that gray seals prey on marketable fish, damage gear, and transmit codworm to the Atlantic cod.

Bearded Seal. Appearing somewhat like a walrus, the bearded seal feeds on bottom-dwelling invertebrates in a habitat dominated by ice. Distributed throughout the Arctic Ocean, these animals may range with advancing ice as far south as the Gulf of St. Lawrence, Scotland, and Japan. About 10,000 to 13,000 animals are taken annually in Norwegian, Soviet, and United States waters by subsistence hunters. The total world population is estimated at more than 500,000 animals. Polar bears and killer whales prey upon bearded seals.

Hawaiian Monk Seal. The genus *Monachus* includes three species. The Caribbean monk seal is considered extinct. The Mediterranean monk seal survives in small numbers along the Atlantic coast of Africa and the Mediterranean coast of Europe and Africa. The Hawaiian monk seal population, numbering about 1,500 animals, inhabits the waters and beaches of the northwestern Hawaiian Islands.

Listed as endangered under the Endangered Species Act, the Hawaiian monk seal is the object of considerable recovery efforts by NMFS and FWS. The monk seal is intolerant of human activities and has abandoned breeding areas in the past as a result of human disturbance.

Recovery efforts for this species are plagued by a number of factors. Monk seals depend upon reef organisms for food. Foraging exposes them to attack by sharks. Monk seals also are susceptible to the toxic disease cigutera. Finally, in some areas sex ratios have been altered and adult females are killed or injured by bands of competing males.

Northern Elephant Seal. This species provides a dramatic case of recovery of a severely depleted species. Numbering about 100 animals in 1892 and confined to Guadalupe Island off Mexico, the species now numbers about 100,000 and ranges from Baja California to Point Reyes, north of San Francisco. Unlike other phocid species, male northern elephant seals establish territories and harems of females. These animals feed primarily upon fish.

Cetacea (Whales, Dolphins, and Porpoises)

NMFS has responsibility under the MMPA for all species in the order Cetacea. Within this order are two suborders: the Mysticeti or baleen whales, and the Odontoceti or toothed whales, which include all dolphins and porpoises. All baleen whales are greater than 25 feet in length as adults. The baleen whales and sperm whales have been the object of the most intense commercial exploitation of any cetaceans. Some species, such as blue and right whales, may never recover from past exploitation, while the Pacific gray whale provides an example of a cetacean recovering to what is thought to be its original population size.

Gray Whale. The Pacific or California gray whale summers in the Bering and Chukchi Seas and calves in the lagoons of Baja California. Juveniles sometimes do not complete this 11,000-mile migration but linger about the shores of California. Unlike many other cetaceans, gray whales prefer to remain on the continental shelf. Gray whales rake the bottom with their stiff baleen and feed upon bottom-dwelling invertebrates.

Once severely reduced by Russian and American coastal whaling, the species has increased to about 17,000 animals. Each year, the IWC allows the Soviet Union a quota of about 180 gray whales under a subsistence exemption.

The Mexican government declared the breeding lagoons of California gray whales as sanctuaries, although here, as elsewhere in the species range, industrial development is increasing. Harassment by private and charter whale-watching boats is a source of concern for this and other species of great whales.

Minke Whale. The smallest of baleen whales, minkes are found in all the world's oceans. An estimated 80,000 to 120,000 inhabit the North Atlantic, where they feed primarily upon capelin. No population estimate has been made for the North Pacific. Minkes migrate between temperate tropical waters and the high latitudes. Approximately 300,000 live in the Southern Hemisphere; their principal prey is krill.

Minkes are hunted commercially in the Southern Ocean and off Norway. The IWC moratorium on all commercial whaling will end this hunt in 1986 if the Japanese, Soviets, and Norwegians comply. Minke whale population dynamics are still very much a matter of debate.

Sei Whale. Sei whales migrate between high and tropical latitudes in both the Northern and Southern Hemispheres, feeding on small crustaceans, herring, sardines, anchovies, and sauries. The total world population is about 42,000. Commercial whaling of sei whales in the North Pacific and the southern seas is prohibited by IWC regulations. Small numbers of sei whales are hunted off Iceland. An estimated 280 sei whales live in United States waters from Cape Hatteras to the Gulf of Maine.

Bryde's Whale. Often confused with the sei whale, Bryde's whales do not migrate to high latitudes but remain in warm temperate waters.

Because of the confusion between Bryde's and sei whales, population estimates for the Bryde's whale are only now being developed. The North Pacific population numbers about 20,000 animals, and the population off Peru about 15,000 to 20,000.

Fin Whale. This is the second largest of the whales, measuring up to 82 feet in length. This species does not regularly migrate to the high latitudes, although it is found in all oceans.

Heavily exploited in this century, fin whales are nonetheless not as seriously depleted as some other large whales. The world population of fin whales is estimated at 114,000. Some 5,400 fin whales are found in United States waters from Cape Hatteras to the Gulf of Maine. Icelandic whalers take small numbers of these animals. Some biologists fear that the population is so reduced that it will never recover.

Blue Whale. The blue whale is the largest animal that ever lived. The largest recorded individual measured 102 feet in length. Ruthlessly exploited during the first half of this century, blue whale populations were reduced from about 200,000 to less than 10,000. The current estimate is 11,000 blue whales throughout the world's oceans. The species has been protected since 1966 by the IWC, but it is not known whether the species has responded.

Humpback Whale. Humpbacks, whose songs and acrobatics have been a source of popular and scientific fascination, migrate between tropical and polar latitudes. Humpbacks feed on sand lances, anchovies, sardines, and krill. Humpbacks prefer shallow coastal waters for feeding and calving, where whale-watching boats, cargo ships, fishing boats, and nets may disrupt their behavior.

Humpback whales also were exploited heavily in this century and now are depleted severely, numbering about 10,275 animals worldwide. IWC regulations prohibit commercial whaling of this species, but allow a small take by Greenland natives for subsistence purposes.

Right Whale. Right whales were the target of choice of the 16th-century Basques, the earliest organized whalers, because these whales prefer coastal waters, are slow swimmers, and float when killed. Right whales are now found in small numbers in the North Pacific, the western North Atlantic, and the southern seas. Right whales migrate to tropical waters for breeding and calving. Like other baleen whales, right whales feed on small crustaceans and schooling fish.

This species of great whale has been protected since 1938, but remains perhaps the most severely depleted of the great whales. Up to 3,000 animals may live in the southern seas, 100 to 200 animals in the North Pacific, and fewer than 500 in the North Atlantic. About 380 right whales inhabit the waters of the Gulf of Maine and Georges Banks during the spring.

Bowhead Whale. Bowhead whales are in the same family as right whales, but bowheads are found only in the Northern Hemisphere and do not migrate to tropical waters to breed and calve. Instead, these animals follow the movement of the arctic ice.

Bowheads were exploited heavily by Yankee whalers in the 19th century, and the species now is severely depleted. The western arctic population numbers about 3,800 animals in the Bering, Beaufort, and Chukchi Seas. Since 1977, the IWC has set quotas for a hunt of the species by Alaskan Eskimos. Previous to this, the IWC did not regulate this hunt.

Toothed Whales

This suborder includes 65 species of whales, dolphins, and porpoises. Toothed whales are marked by a large brain, a sophisticated ability to echolocate, and the best diving abilities of all whales.

Sperm Whale. Sperm whales are found throughout the world's oceans, preferring deep, oceanic waters. Large solitary bulls migrate as far north as the polar pack ice, returning to breed. Other age groups form schools of up to 100 animals. Sperm whales frequently strand in large groups throughout the world.

The Southern Hemisphere population numbers about 410,000 animals. About 22,000 occur in the North Atlantic and in the North Pacific about 472,000. The age and sex distribution of the North Pacific population has been altered by commercial whaling, resulting in a decline in the population. The IWC enacted a moratorium on sperm whaling effective 1984.

Pygmy Sperm Whale. This species is one of the most frequently stranded marine mammals. Known only from research on stranded individuals, this species apparently prefers the edge of the continental shelf and the open sea. No population estimates have been made.

Bottlenose Dolphin. Known to the millions familiar with the "Flipper" television show, the bottlenose dolphin was the first dolphin species to be bred successfully in captivity. Two forms occur, one darker and found principally offshore, the other lighter and found inshore. Bottlenose dolphins range worldwide. In United States waters they are found in the Gulf of Mexico and off the southeastern coast, the Hawaiian archipelago, and central and southern California. Total population estimates are uncertain, but NMFS estimates 14,000 to 23,000 bottlenose dolphins off the Atlantic and Gulf coasts.

Spinner Dolphin. Found in the tropical waters of all oceans, spinner dolphins travel in the company of other species of dolphins and accompany yellowfin tuna in the eastern tropical Pacific, where they were drowned in significant numbers until the late 1970s. These animals number about 900,000 in the eastern tropical Pacific and are considered abundant elsewhere.

Spotted Dolphin. Also found in all tropical waters, spotted dolphins associate with other species of dolphins. They have been caught and drowned incidentally by the tuna fishery of the eastern tropical Pacific. Some populations in the eastern tropical Pacific may be increasing, and the total population in the eastern tropical Pacific is about 2.2 million.

Common Dolphin. This species is found in tropical and temperate deep waters. Like several other species of dolphin, common dolphins may travel in groups of several thousand. About 900,000 inhabit the eastern tropical Pacific, where they are taken in the tuna fishery. In winter, some 31,000 common dolphins may be found offshore from Cape Hatteras to the Gulf of Maine.

Striped Dolphin. Like several other dolphin species, striped dolphins feed on midwater fishes and crustaceans. Striped dolphins are found in the warmer waters of the Atlantic, Pacific, and Indian oceans. They too are taken in the Pacific tuna fishery, where they number about 2.3 million animals. In spring, some 4,000 striped dolphins frequent the Gulf of Maine. Elsewhere their numbers are unknown.

Atlantic White-sided Dolphin. Preferring deep waters on the continental shelf and beyond, Atlantic white-sided dolphins are found in the western Atlantic from Georges Bank and Cape Cod to the Gulf of Maine. This species is often found with pilot and humpback whales, feeding on mackerel, herring, halse, sand lance, capelin, and cod. Large numbers may strand at one time. The western Atlantic population varies from a low of 3,200 in winter to more than 36,000 in spring, when dolphins arrive from other areas.

Pacific White-sided Dolphin. This species is found in the North Pacific Ocean between Japan and California, but not in the Bering Sea. It seems to prefer deeper water but is sometimes found in large bays. Like many other species of dolphin, Pacific white-sided dolphins are gregarious, occurring in groups of 15 to thousands. They feed upon squid, as well as herring, sardines, anchovies, and sauries. Current estimates, considered unreliable, are 30,000 to 50,000 animals in the North Pacific.

Long-finned Pilot Whale. Preferring deeper waters, these animals are found around banks and other shallow areas. They live in the North Atlantic and the Southern Hemisphere, primarily in schools of hundreds or thousands. They feed mostly on squid.

Since the 1500s, these animals have been hunted on both sides of the Atlantic. Although no reliable estimates have been made for populations worldwide, it is believed that some populations, once depleted, have recovered.

Killer Whales. Instantly recognizable to millions from captive specimens on display at aquaria, killer whales are the largest of the dolphin species. They are found worldwide, but seem to prefer cool coastal waters and polar ice. Killer whales feed on squid, sea turtles, fish, whales, dolphins, seals, and sea birds. Often hunting in packs, killer whales are the pre-eminent marine predator and play an important role in the ecology of some marine ecosystems.

Only very preliminary population estimates are available for the Antarctic. No estimates are available for other areas, although the species is thought to be abundant in Puget Sound.

Harbor Porpoise. Harbor porpoises are found from far northern ice-free waters to warm temperate waters. They frequently are found inshore in the mouths of large rivers, harbors, and bays. Generally, their occurrence depends heavily upon prey availability. No reliable worldwide population estimates exist for this species. An estimated 18,000 are found in the North Atlantic. Harbor porpoises are taken incidentally in large numbers in some fisheries.

Dall's Porpoise. This species is distributed in an arc from Japan to the Aleutian Islands through the Gulf of Alaska to Baja California. Often found in small groups, this species may migrate. Its principal prey is squid and fish.

Each year, several thousand Dall's porpoises are drowned accidentally in the Japanese high-seas salmon gill-net fishery in the central North Pacific and Bering Sea. This species is caught incidentally in gill-net fisheries and is hunted off the coast of Japan. The population currently is estimated to number about 920,000.

Beluga Whale. Like its cousin the narwhal, the beluga associates primarily with the moving pack ice, but some populations are found as far south as Cook Inlet, Alaska. This species is found in shallow waters and estuaries of large rivers. Belugas feed on a wide variety of fish, including salmon, cod, and pike, as well as on squid and various crustaceans.

Subsistence hunting of this species occurs in polar waters. Local populations fluctuate widely in size. The circumpolar population is estimated to number between 62,000 to 88,000 animals.

Narwhal. Found throughout the Arctic Ocean, narwhals prefer deep water and travel in small groups. Males are recognizable by tusks protruding from their jaws. Narwhals feed on cod, halibut, squid, and several crustaceans.

This species is hunted by natives. The total population is estimated at 30,000 animals.

Species Managed by the U.S. Fish and Wildlife Service

FWS has responsibility for several species under the MMPA. The following summaries are based on an FWS report to Congress.[38]

Polar Bear. Polar bears are found only in the Northern Hemisphere and in association with ice of the Arctic Ocean. Of six possible populations, two are suspected to exist off the coast of Alaska. Polar bears are known to move with the receding and advancing of ice.

Although aerial hunting and its abuses have been halted, concern still exists that the native take of polar bears, totaling about 85 animals during the 1982-83 season, is reducing the size of the reproductive female population. FWS has estimated that the population within 100 nautical miles of the Alaska coast is between 3,000 and 5,000 animals.

Walrus. The only pinniped under FWS jurisdiction, the Pacific walrus is distinguished by its ivory tusks, which have been used as a material for crafts. This species is found only in the Bering Sea and is associated with the pack ice.

After a period of overexploitation, the Bering Sea populations of walrus in-

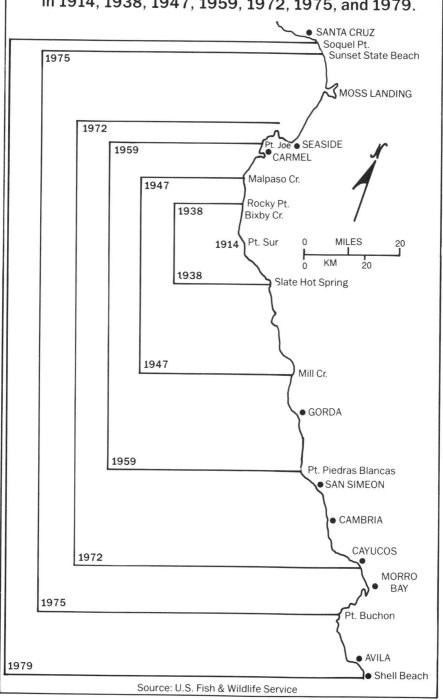

Chronological Expansion of Sea Otter Range
Established Sea Otter Range
Along California Coast
in 1914, 1938, 1947, 1959, 1972, 1975, and 1979.

1975

1972

1959

1947

1938

1938

1914

1947

1959

1972

1975

1979

SANTA CRUZ
Soquel Pt.
Sunset State Beach

MOSS LANDING

Pt. Joe ● SEASIDE
● CARMEL

Malpaso Cr.

Rocky Pt.
Bixby Cr.

Pt. Sur

Slate Hot Spring

Mill Cr.

● GORDA

Pt. Piedras Blancas
● SAN SIMEON

● CAMBRIA

CAYUCOS

MORRO
BAY

Pt. Buchon

● AVILA
● Shell Beach

MILES
0   20
0   KM   20

Source: U.S. Fish & Wildlife Service

creased from about 100,000 to about 300,000 in 1980. FWS estimates the optimum sustainable population to be between 140,000 and 300,000. Annual take by Alaskan natives has averaged between 6,500 and 8,000. However, FWS is concerned that walruses killed but unretrieved would add another 50 percent to the annual take and possibly damage the population. Some indications suggest that the population is declining.

Northern Sea Otter. Both northern and southern sea otters depend upon their fur, rather than blubber, for insulation. Feeding upon shellfish of various sorts, sea otters most often are associated with kelp beds and are considered a key species of these habitats.

Between 1742 and 1911, commercial fur hunters reduced northern sea otter populations to extremely low levels. Now numbering as many as 150,000 to 200,000 animals, northern sea otters may be above their optimum sustainable population levels in some locations. They occupy a range reduced from their historical distribution. Small populations are found in portions of southeast Alaska, along the Alaska Peninsula, and through the Aleutian Islands. Small populations have been transplanted to the Pribilof Islands and elsewhere.

Southern Sea Otter. Listed as threatened under the Endangered Species Act, this sea otter subspecies has been the focus of considerable effort by state and federal agencies. The original size of this population along the California coast is estimated to have been 16,000 and 18,000 animals. Nearly extirpated by commercial fur hunters, the animal was rediscovered in 1938. Since that time, the population has expanded to 1,200 to 1,500 animals. The population size and range have not expanded in recent years.

West Indian Manatee. Listed as endangered under the Endangered Species Act, this species has been the object of considerable efforts by state and federal agencies and nonprofit organizations. This large, docile vegetarian is found in shallow coastal waters throughout much of the tropical and subtropical regions of the New World Atlantic coast. Within the United States it is found principally in Florida.

FWS scientists currently estimate a minimum of 800 to 1,000 manatees in the Florida population. The principal causes of mortality for the species are boat and barge collision, capture in floodgates, and long periods of cold weather. In 1984, 128 manatees are known to have died in Florida waters. The principle long-range conservation problem is habitat degradation and destruction.

REFERENCES

1. 16 U.S.C.A. 1361-1407.
2. 16 U.S.C.A. 1431-1434.
3. 36 Stat. 326,4 Whiteman's Digest of International Law 37.
4. July 7, 1911, 37 Stat. 1542, T.S. 564.
5. Feb. 9, 1957 [1957], 8 U.S.T. 2283, T.I.A.S. 3948, 314 U.N.T.S. 105.
6. 16 U.S.C.A. 1511-1187.
7. Sanford E. Gainer & Dale Schmidt, *Laws and Treaties of the United States Related to Marine Mammal Protection Policy* (Springfield, Virginia: National Technical Information Service, 1978), p. 205.
8. Ibid., p. 210.
9. Sept. 24, 1931, 49 Stat. 3079, T.S. 880.
10. 52 Stat. 1460, T.S. 933.
11. Dec. 2, 1946, 62 Stat 1716, T.I.A.S. 1849.

12. 16 U.S.C.A. 916-91 (1976).
13. 22 U.S.C.A. 1978.
14. 16 U.S.C.A. 1821(e)(2).
15. 16 U.S.C.A. 1361-1407.
16. 16 U.S.C.A. 1361(a)(6).
17. 16 U.S.C.A. 1362(a)(9).
18. 50 C.F.R. 216.3 (1981).
19. *People of Togiak v. United States* (470(f) Supp. 423 [D.D.C. 1979]).
20. 116 U.S.C.A. 742(j)-7421 (1976).
21. H. J. Res. 1268, 92nd Congress, 2d Sess. (1972).
22. Nov. 15, 1973, T.I.A.S. No. 8409.
23. Michael J. Bean, *The Evolution of National Wildlife Law* (New York: Praeger, Publishers, 1983), pp. 267-268.
24. 16 U.S.C.A. 1531-1543.
25. March 3, 1973, 27 U.S.T. 1087, T.I.A.S. 8249.
26. Oct. 12, 1940, 56 Stat. 1354, T.S. 981, U.N.T.S. 193.
27. Dec. 1, 1959, 12 U.S.T. 794, T.I.A.S. 4780.
28. June 1, 1972, 29 U.S.T. 441, T.I.A.S. 826.
29. Executive X, 96th Cong., 2nd session.
30. May 13, 1949, 1 U.S.T. 230, T.I.A.S. No. 2044.
31. May 9, 1952, United States-Canada-Japan, 4 U.S.T. 380, T.I.A.S. 2786.
32. 16 U.S.C.A. 1801-1882.
33. 84 Stat. 2090, 35 *Fed. Reg.* 15677 (Oct. 3, 1970).
34. Pub.L. 98-364.
35. Pub.L. 98-498.
36. *American Tuna Boat Association v. Baldrige*, 738 F. 2d 1013 (9th Cir. 1984).
37. *Balelo v. Baldrige*, 724 F. 2d 753 (9th Cir. 1984).
38. Department of the Interior, U.S. Fish and Wildlife Service, Administration of the Marine Mammal Protection Act of 1972 for Calendar Year 1983, (Washington, DC: U.S.D.O.I., 1984).

Wetlands preservation is critical to many species, from birds, such as this great blue heron, to the fish, frogs, and insects upon which wading birds prey.

Wetlands Preservation

W.J. Chandler Associates

INTRODUCTION

THE NATION'S WETLANDS — totaling roughly 95 million acres* —
provide important and often vital habitat for much of the nation's wildlife. Although
wetlands make up only five percent of the land surface in the lower 48 states, they
comprise nearly 40 percent of the National Wildlife Refuge System.[1] Wetlands generally have high plant productivity, which gives them a high carrying capacity for
wildlife populations.

The various wetlands across the nation provide habitat for a diversity of fish and
wildlife. Wetlands include red maple swamps and black spruce bogs in the northern
states, salt marshes along the coasts, bottomland hardwood forests in the Southeast,
prairie potholes in the Midwest, playa lakes and cottonwood-willow riparian wetlands
in the western states, and the wet tundra of Alaska. Some 5,000 species of plants, 190
species of amphibians, and a third of all bird species in the United States occur in
wetlands. Species that are heavily dependent on wetlands include migratory waterfowl, mammals, alligators, freshwater game fish, and crayfish. More than 12 million
ducks breed annually in United States wetlands, and millions more overwinter here.
Thirty-five endangered and threatened species are dependent on wetlands. More than
half the marine sport fish caught in the United States are dependent on wetland
estuaries, particularly in the early part of their life cycles.

In addition to supporting wildlife, wetlands serve a variety of ecological functions, depending on their type and location. Wetlands store and convey floodwaters,
reducing flooding frequency and peak flood levels downstream. They improve water
quality by trapping pollutants in their sediments, by converting toxic pollutants
through biochemical processes to less harmful substances, and by the uptake of
pollutants by wetland vegetation. They can facilitate groundwater recharge and stabilize shorelines. And they are vital to the nation's commercial fisheries: approximately
two-thirds of the major United States commercial fish depend on estuaries and salt
marshes for nursery or spawning grounds.

---

*The most recent data on the amount of wetlands in the U.S. is from 1974, when the U.S. Fish
and Wildlife Service estimated 99 million acres existed. Estimates of the rate of wetlands loss
indicate that three to five million acres have probably been lost since that time.

Wetlands are a seriously threatened resource. According to the U.S. Fish and Wildlife Service (FWS), less than 46 percent of the nation's original 215 million acres of wetlands exist today, and in some areas the loss has been far more severe — such as in the important bottomland hardwood wetlands of the lower Mississippi, where 80 percent of the original wetlands have been lost. Wetlands continue to be destroyed at an estimated rate of from 300,000 to 458,000 acres per year, in spite of several federal programs intended to stem this loss.*

Federal wetland policy has evolved significantly over the past century. The federal interest in wetlands began in the mid-1800s, when the federal government gave 65 million acres of wetlands to 15 states for reclamation, an action responsible for a large portion of wetland losses. By the 1930s, the federal government began purchasing wetlands to protect habitat for migratory waterfowl, and in the 1970s the federal government undertook the regulation of certain activities in wetlands to protect water quality and other values. Today, the major federal wetlands protection programs are land acquisition and the permit program under Section 404 of the Clean Water Act, which requires a permit for the disposal of dredged or fill material in wetlands.

A variety of other federal laws and policies also provide some protection for wetlands, including the Fish and Wildlife Coordination Act,[2] which requires the equal consideration of fish and wildlife values in federal water resources development; the National Environmental Policy Act (NEPA),[3] which requires environmental review of federal activities in general; and the Coastal Zone Management Act,[4] which encourages and funds states to develop coastal plans that include wetland protection measures. In spite of the number of federal programs that afford wetlands some protection, federal wetland policies have developed piecemeal over time and do not form a comprehensive protection program.

The states also operate a variety of programs to protect wetlands, primarily through land acquisition and regulation of development. All coastal states except Texas have regulatory programs for coastal wetlands, although they vary considerably in their degree of protection. The states have taken far less initiative to regulate inland wetlands: as of 1983 only seven states had adopted such programs. Some local wetlands protection efforts have been initiated as well, primarily through zoning and local building ordinances. Several private organizations, most notably the Nature Conservancy, the Trust for Public Lands, Ducks Unlimited, and the National Audubon Society, also protect wetlands through acquisition or leasing programs.

This chapter discusses three major aspects of federal wetlands policy: federal water project policy and fish and wildlife mitigation as it applies to projects constructed by the Corps of Engineers; the Section 404 permit program of the Clean Water Act; and federal acquisition and leasing of wetlands. In spite of growing concern about and interest in wetland protection, federal funding for acquisition has declined and regulatory relief efforts have reduced the effectiveness of the federal 404 permit program in stemming wetland loss. On the other hand, approval for new Corps water projects has been placed on hold for the past eight years and mitigation plans are being prepared for previously approved projects that contained inadequate measures to compensate for fish and wildlife losses. But federal water policy reforms established by the Carter administration have been dismantled by the Reagan administration, and the push continues in Congress for massive new water-project bills that do not address basic conservationist concerns about the program.

---

*Loss rates are from FWS and from an Office of Technology Assessment report, discussed in the Resource Status section.

HISTORY AND LEGISLATIVE AUTHORITY

A number of federal laws directly or indirectly provide some protection for the nation's wetlands, but this body of law has developed largely in a haphazard manner and does not form a comprehensive federal wetlands protection program. In addition, the perception of how wetlands should be used has changed. In the latter part of the 19th century, wetlands were considered essentially worthless. The Swamp Lands Acts of 1849, 1850, and 1860 gave approximately 65 million acres of wetlands to 15 states for development.

Federal efforts to protect wetlands began around 1930 as part of a program to conserve migratory waterfowl. Only since the 1970s have wetlands conservation efforts addressed the need to protect the broad array of ecological values provided by the nation's wetlands.

This section discusses the development of four basic approaches to wetlands protection policy. These include: ensuring the protection of wetlands from development through fee acquisition, the purchase of easements, or leases; ensuring that the effects on wetlands of projects undertaken or authorized by the federal government are mitigated where necessary; removing federal subsidies and incentives for wetlands destruction or degradation; and regulating certain activities in the nation's waters that could degrade or destroy wetlands.

Acquisition and Leasing

Federal wetlands protection began with the acquisition of waterfowl habitat, and for many years this remained the sole purpose of federal wetlands protection. Today, acquisition or other federal payments to prevent wetland development remain the primary method of federal wetlands protection, although the purpose of acquisition has been expanded to include protection of endangered and threatened species as well as other wildlife. Although the cost of acquiring wetlands has risen dramatically since the federal government began purchasing them, and although there is a growing realization that acquisition alone cannot meet all wetlands conservation needs, acquiring wetlands is still the surest method of protecting them.

Federal wetlands acquisition was first authorized by the Migratory Bird Conservation Act of 1929,[5] which provided for federal acquisition of land by purchase, donation, or rental agreements.* The purpose of the act was to establish a national system of publicly financed bird refuges. But few appropriations were made for purchases, prompting the passage in 1934 of the Migratory Bird Hunting Stamp Act,[6] which established a special fund to finance land acquisition under the Migratory Bird Conservation Act. The fund was financed by requiring all migratory waterfowl hunters aged 16 or over to purchase a federal migratory bird hunting stamp.

Funds from the Migratory Bird Conservation Fund could be withdrawn for expenditure on bird refuges at any time, without congressional appropriation. But for nearly 25 years, the funds were used principally for refuge operation, development, and administration, with little expended for land acquisition.[7] In response, Congress amended the Stamp Act in 1958[8] to require exclusive use of fund revenues, less the cost of administration, for land acquisition. The 1958 act also authorized the acquisition in fee or by easement of small prairie wetlands known as prairie potholes, which are called "waterfowl production areas."

Congress quickly realized, however, that even with the use of nearly all of the

---

*Laws governing migratory bird habitat protection are discussed in more detail in the chapter on migratory birds.

History of the Migratory Bird Conservation Fund
Waterfowl Land Acquisition Program by Habitat Type,
FY 1962–1984 (in acres)

Fiscal Year	Refuges	Fee	Easement	Total	Migra-tion	Wintering	Total
1962	2,273	11,682	4,968	18,923	2;703	13,939	35,565
1963	10,643	12,554	12,774	35,971	12,134	40,476	88,581
1964	13,758	16,668	71,575	102,001	11,116	24,277	137,394
1965	17,896	27,089	177,796	222,781	5,888	25,483	254,152
1966	17,631	36,739	146,031	200,401	9,713	15,473	225,587
1967	10,069	30,676	106,954	147,699	2,481	11,741	161,921
1968	17,653	22,531	87,770	127,954	4,673	20,788	153,415
1969	6,756	24,617	61,354	92,727	1,736	18,468	112,931
1970	8,686	42,427	100,411	151,524	1,213	6,860	159,597
1971	15,765	50,422	60,258	126,445	1,790	4,046	132,281
1972	6,197	32,761	51,349	90,307	2,547	9,422	102,276
1973	4,269	26,243	58,289	88,801	82	4,563	93,446
1974	9,823	13,508	57,149	80,480	3,292	8,495	92,267
1975	1,766	15,951	34,072	51,789	327	1,842	53,958
1976	2,035	29,094	28,472	59,601	1,877	13,905	75,383
1977	870	23,018	36,796	60,684	1,008	13,260	74,952
1978	4,342	15,974	23,216	43,532	1,487	10,777	55,796
1979	304	7,999	17,015	25,318	—	30,222	55,540
1980	761	13,914	16,168	30,843	1	51,587	82,431
1981	—	3,215	14,320	17,535	6	6,808	24,349
1982	—	1,768	16,535	18,303	140	14,095	32,538
1983	—	3,621	9,413	13,034	—	13,231	26,265
1984	—	5,596	8,312	13,908	188	15,693	29,789
Total, 1962–1984	151,497	468,067	1,200,997	1,820,561	64,402	375,451	2,260,414

Source: Fish and Wildlife Service, Division of Realty

duck stamp receipts, acquisition of waterfowl habitat could not keep pace with its drainage. So in 1961, Congress enacted the Wetlands Loan Act,[9] authorizing an advance appropriation to the fund of $105 million for the purchase of refuges and waterfowl production areas. This authorization level later was increased to $200 million. At the end of FY 1984, about $177 million had been appropriated for land and easement purchases. The Loan Act is currently set to expire in 1986, when FWS must begin repaying the loan out of duck stamp receipts.

Although federal acquisition of migratory waterfowl habitat did accelerate after passage of the Wetlands Loan Act, drainage of wetlands for agricultural use continued at a rapid pace, particularly in the prairie pothole region. To address this problem and provide an additional mechanism to protect these areas, Congress in 1970 passed the Water Bank Act.[10] The prime motivation for the passage of the Water Bank Act — like its predecessor statutes — was the protection of habitat for migratory waterfowl. But the act gave recognition to the broader benefits of wetlands protection, evidence of the growing awareness of the multiple values of wetlands. It includes among its purposes conserving surface waters; reducing runoff, soil, and wind erosion; enhancing the natural beauty of the landscape; and contributing to flood control, improved water quality, reduced stream sedimentation, and improved subsurface moisture.

To accomplish these goals, the Water Bank Act authorizes the secretary of Agriculture to enter into 10-year renewable agreements with landowners or operators for the conservation of wetlands and adjacent uplands in important waterfowl nesting and breeding areas. The secretary is authorized to make annual payments to the landowners in exchange for their agreement not to destroy the wetlands. The secretary also may share the cost of establishing and maintaining conservation practices on set-aside areas. The act authorizes appropriations necessary to fulfill the agreements but directs the secretary not to enter into agreements that will cost the government more than a total of $10 million yearly.

One other important source of funds for wetlands acquisition is the Land and Water Conservation Fund. It was established by the Land and Water Conservation Fund Act of 1965,[11] which has the broad purpose of "preserving, developing, and assuring accessibility to all citizens . . . of outdoor recreation resources." The fund is comprised of proceeds from the disposal of federal surplus property, certain user fees, and receipts from outer continental shelf leasing. The fund is authorized at $900 million a year but, unlike the Migratory Bird Conservation Account, funds from the Land and Water Conservation Fund are available for expenditure only to the extent that they are appropriated by Congress.

Although the primary purpose of the land water fund is to acquire and develop outdoor recreation areas, it can be used in several different ways to purchase wetlands. Up to 60 percent of the annual appropriation may be used to cost-share, on a 50-50 matching basis, certain activities carried out by the states, including "planning, acquisition, and development of needed land and water areas and facilities," which includes acquisition of wetlands. The remaining funds are to be used by the federal government for the "acquisition and development of certain lands," including the acquisition of lands for national parks, national forests, and national wildlife refuges, all of which

Summary of Status of Agreements Carried Out Under the Water Bank Program, 1975 Through September 30, 1984

| State | Number of Agreements (Number) | Designated Acres | | | Annual Payment Dollars |
		Total (Acres)	Wetlands (Acres)	Adjacent (Acres)	
Arkansas	215	44,363	22,069	22,294	307,439
California	103	23,879	5,711	18,168	379,368
Louisiana	214	28,109	8,310	19,799	361,917
Maine	134	8,206	2,546	5,660	61,390
Michigan	127	5,311	1,496	3,815	96,559
Minnesota	1,405	79,710	20,609	59,101	1,896,145
Mississippi	202	38,099	14,606	23,493	318,201
Montana	115	18,185	3,147	15,038	291,355
Nebraska	89	7,768	2,956	4,812	171,305
North Dakota	1,551	227,508	62,861	164,647	3,711,875
South Dakota	898	122,015	25,584	96,431	1,846,592
Vermont	89	4,520	1,873	2,647	38,497
Wisconsin	500	21,955	8,439	13,516	473,052
Total	5,642	629,628	180,207	449,421	9,953,695

may include wetlands. The Land and Water Conservation Fund cannot be used, however, to acquire migratory waterfowl areas authorized for acquisition by the Migratory Bird Conservation Act. The fund provides an additional mechanism for wetlands acquisition, but wetlands must compete with other uses of the fund.

Reducing Impacts of Federal Projects

At about the same time that Congress authorized the federal government to acquire migratory bird habitat, it also began an effort to require federal development agencies to attempt to reduce or offset the fish and wildlife impacts of their projects. The primary statute providing for this is the Fish and Wildlife Coordination Act of 1958.[12] Although the Coordination Act is not specifically a wetlands protection statute, it does have particular importance for wetlands because it focuses on the impacts of federal or federally authorized water resource development, which has caused major wetlands losses in this century.

The first version of the Coordination Act was enacted in 1934.[13] The act was broad in scope, calling for federal and state cooperation in developing a nationwide wildlife conservation program and authorizing a variety of federal efforts to improve wildlife conservation. The 1934 act included provisions aimed at water resource development, but they were rather limited. The act required consultation with the Bureau of Fisheries for the construction or permitting of any dam by the federal government, but did not require any measures to reduce project impacts on wetland or terrestrial habitat. It did, however, permit the use of waters impounded by federal water projects for migratory-bird resting and nesting areas and authorized the Bureau of Biological Survey to consult with federal water resource agencies about obtaining wildlife uses of existing impoundments.

Although the 1934 act had a broad vision, it contained few mandatory requirements and thus had little effect. In 1946, Congress amended the law to narrow its overall scope and to strengthen its consultation requirements with respect to water resource development.[14] The act was expanded to cover all federally undertaken or permitted projects that "impounded, diverted, or otherwise controlled for any purpose whatever" the waters of any stream or body of water. For both federally undertaken and permitted projects, the sponsoring agency was required to consult with FWS as well as with state fish and wildlife agencies "with a view to preventing loss of and damage to wildlife resources" and was required to include their recommendations on measures that should be adopted to achieve this goal as part of the project report. In addition, for federal construction projects, the 1946 amendments required that "adequate provision" be made for use of project land and waters for wildlife conservation and management, as long as such measures were consistent with the primary purposes of the project. The costs of such measures were required to be included as part of the project costs. The act broadly defined wildlife resources to include "birds, fishes, mammals and all other classes of wild animals and all types of aquatic and land vegetation upon which wildlife is dependent."

In spite of these additional provisions, the act produced poorer results than anticipated, and Congress again revised the law in 1958.[15] The 1958 law, still in effect, retained the basic provisions of the 1946 act, but again expanded and strengthened them. Most notably, it requires that wildlife conservation "shall receive equal consideration . . . with other features of water resource development." The types of development covered are expanded to include channel deepening and modifications "for any purpose whatever, including navigation and drainage." Project reports submitted by federal agencies are to give "full consideration" to the recommendations of federal and state wildlife agencies, and the project plan is required to include "such justifiable means and measures for wildlife purposes as the reporting agency finds should be adopted to obtain maximum overall project benefits." The 1958 act also expanded the law's goal to include "the development and improvement" of wildlife resources; authorized federal water resource agencies to alter incomplete projects to incorporate wildlife protection measures; and provided for the acquisition of land to achieve fish and wildlife conservation measures if specifically authorized by Congress or if included in the plans of a project authorized by Congress.

Today, the Coordination Act, along with NEPA, provides the basic authority for the involvement of FWS, the National Marine Fisheries Service, and the state fish and wildlife agencies throughout the planning process for federally sponsored water resource projects and for the participation of these agencies in the review of permits for the disposal of dredged or fill material into water bodies and wetlands under Section 404 of the Clean Water Act. Nevertheless, the act has had limited success in protecting fish and wildlife, in part because its requirements are vague regarding standards and procedures. Efforts have been made in Congress to strengthen the act, and the Carter administration proposed regulations to improve its implementation, but neither of these efforts has been concluded successfully.

Removing Federal Incentives for Wetlands Destruction

A relatively recent approach to stemming wetlands destruction has been the removal of federal incentives, particularly financial assistance, for activities that degrade or destroy wetlands. This has been one way in which the federal government has tried to discourage the drainage and conversion of wetlands for agricultural use, an activity that for the most part has not been addressed by federal wetlands protection programs.*

Beginning in 1940, the Department of Agriculture was authorized to assist landowners in wetlands drainage by providing both technical assistance and cost-sharing under the Agricultural Conservation Program. As of 1980, this program had assisted in the drainage of approximately 57 million acres of wet farmland, including some wetlands.[16] In 1962, Congress passed an amendment to the Soil Conservation and Domestic Allotment Act,[17] prohibiting federal assistance for the drainage of wetlands in North Dakota, South Dakota, and Minnesota if the secretary of the Interior determined that such drainage would materially harm wildlife preservation. Within a year, the secretary of the Interior was required to offer to lease or purchase the wetland, or the prohibition expired. If the secretary made such an offer but the landowner refused it, the prohibition remained in effect for five years.

No figures exist to show the amount of conversion prevented by or lands acquired under this law, but it signaled the beginning of a move away from federal funding of wetlands drainage. In 1975, the Soil Conservation Service adopted a wetlands protection policy that prohibited technical assistance to farmers for draining certain types of wetlands. In 1977, after issuance of President Carter's executive order on wetlands protection (see below), the policy was strengthened. In 1978, the Agricultural Stabilization and Conservation Service eliminated cost-sharing for draining wetlands.

Although no good data exist on the effects these policy changes have had on wetlands drainage, it is widely agreed that many federal incentives for wetlands conversion remain, including tax incentives, commodity programs, disaster payments, crop insurance, Farmers Home Administration loans, and other cost-sharing and technical-assistance programs. One analyst, for example, has calculated that the

---

*Federal courts have recently ruled that the 404 permit program does apply in many cases to the clearing of land for conversion to agriculture use, but other agricultural activities, particularly drainage, are still uncontrolled under the 404 program.

application of tax provisions could lower the cost of bottomland clearing in east Arkansas by about 30 percent.[18] A study of drainage costs in the prairie pothole region of Minnesota found that inclusion of the effects of property tax and state and federal income taxes were enough to offset a before-tax loss on drainage investments.[19]

In May 1977, President Carter issued two executive orders that required all federal agencies to limit support for activities that destroy wetlands. Executive Order 11990, "Protection of Wetlands,"[20] requires each agency in carrying out its responsibilities to take action to minimize wetlands destruction, loss, or degradation and to preserve and enhance the natural and beneficial values of wetlands. Each agency is directed to avoid undertaking or providing assistance for new construction in wetlands unless no practical alternative exists and unless the action includes all practical measures to minimize harm to wetlands. The order does not apply, however, to the issuance of licenses and permits for activities involving wetlands on non-federal property.

Executive Order 11988, "Floodplain Management,"[21] requires each agency to take action to reduce the risk of flood loss, to minimize the impact of floods on human safety, health, and welfare, and to restore and preserve the natural and beneficial values served by floodplains. Each agency is required to consider alternatives to proposed actions to avoid adverse impacts in floodplains and to modify the action to minimize potential harm if the agency finds the only practical alternative is to locate it in a flood plain. Because many wetlands are located in floodplains, the order has the potential for providing them with some protection.

Both orders required the agencies to issue new procedures or amend existing ones to comply with their requirements. In a 1983 review of compliance with the floodplain management executive order, the Federal Emergency Management Agency reported that application of the order "has resulted in a reduction in the amount of floodplain development as well as a noticeable improvement in the development that has occurred," but noted that considerable opportunities for improvement remained.[22] No similar survey has been done on compliance with the executive order on wetlands protection. Although the orders generally are credited with raising the awareness of the public and federal agencies as to the value of wetlands, most observers believe they have had little impact on wetlands losses.

Another program that removes some federal subsidies and incentives for wetlands destruction is the Coastal Barrier Resources Act of 1982,[23] which eliminated most new federal expenditures and financial assistance for development purposes on approximately 700 miles of undeveloped coastal barriers on the Atlantic and Gulf coasts. Prohibited expenditures include new federal funding for construction or purchase of buildings, roads, and bridges, as well as federal loans, grants, subsidies, and flood insurance assistance for private development projects. "Undeveloped coastal barriers" are defined to include associated aquatic habitats, including wetlands marshes, estuaries, inlets, and nearshore waters as long as they meet the "undeveloped" criteria set forth in the law and are not already protected by a governmental or private agency for conservation or recreational purposes.

Funding prohibitions currently apply to areas designated on official maps as part of the Coastal Barriers Resources System and should have their greatest impact on reducing coastal wetlands loss in Alabama, Florida, North and South Carolina, and Texas.[24] The secretary of the Interior is required to report to Congress by October 1985, recommending possible additions to or deletions from the system. It is too early to judge the effectiveness of this law on reducing wetlands conversion, but its general approach is being investigated for possible application to wetlands throughout the nation.

Regulating the Disposal of Dredged and Fill Material

The major federal regulatory program controlling the destruction of wetlands is Section 404 of the Clean Water Act,[25] which requires the issuance of a permit from the U.S. Army Corps of Engineers for the discharge of dredged or fill material into the waters of the United States. The 404 permit program has prevented the destruction of hundreds of thousands of acres of wetlands, but in part because the program does not cover all activities that destroy wetlands, and in part because of the limited way in which the Corps has administered the program, many more wetlands are destroyed each year than are saved.

The federal government's involvement in regulating activities in navigable waters dates from the passage of the Rivers and Harbors Act of 1899.[26] Various sections of the act establish permit requirements to prevent unauthorized obstruction or alteration of any navigable waters of the United States. In particular, Section 10 of the act requires that permits be obtained from the Corps for construction of structures such as piers, wharfs, breakwaters, bulkheads, jetties, weirs, transmission lines, or any other obstacles or obstructions, and for work such as dredging or disposal of dredged material or excavation, filling, or other modification of navigable waters. Navigable waters covered by Section 10 permits are those that are subject to the ebb and flow of the tide and/or are presently used, have been used in the past, or may be susceptible to use in the transport of interstate or foreign commerce. Today this definition extends to the mean high-tide line in coastal waters and the normal high-water line in rivers.

The Rivers and Harbors Act was enacted primarily to facilitate navigation, and at first the Corps confined its permit reviews to the impact of proposed activities on navigation and anchorage. The 1958 amendments to the Fish and Wildlife Coordination Act, however, required the Corps of Engineers to consult with FWS on the issuance of Section 10 permits and to give full consideration to the agency's recommendations for preventing damage to fish and wildlife. At first this requirement had little effect on Corps permit procedures. But in 1967 the secretaries of the Army and Interior signed a formal memorandum of understanding regarding permit review, and in 1968, the Department of the Army revised its permit review policy to include the additional factors of fish and wildlife, conservation, pollution, aesthetics, and the general public interest. The Corps' authority to deny a permit based on environmental factors was supported by a 1970 court decision, *Zabel v. Tabb*,[27] in which the court upheld denial of a permit by the Corps for fish and wildlife reasons.

In 1972, Congress passed the Federal Water Pollution Control Act Amendments "to restore and maintain the chemical, physical, and biological integrity of the Nation's waters."[28] The act prohibits the discharge of any pollutant, except in accordance with various standards and permit programs. The most important provision for wetlands is the prohibition on the discharge of dredged spoil or fill material into the nation's waters except in accordance with Section 404, which authorizes the issuance of a permit for such activities at specified disposal sites.

Primary authority for implementing the Clean Water Act generally is placed with the Environmental Protection Agency (EPA), but the issuance of Section 404 permits was placed with the Corps, since the Corps had already established a permit program for certain activities in navigable waters under Section 10 of the Rivers and Harbors Act. Section 404(b)(1) of the act directs that the selection of disposal sites be made in accordance with guidelines developed by EPA in conjunction with the secretary of the Army. Section 404(c) authorizes EPA to prohibit or restrict the use of an area as a disposal site if the administrator determines that the discharge will have an unacceptable adverse effect on municipal water supplies, shellfish beds and fishery areas (including spawning and breeding areas), wildlife, or recreational areas. This provision essentially gives EPA a veto over Corps 404 permit decisions.

Although the 404 permit program applies to navigable waters, the act broadly defines this term to include "the waters of the United States, including the territorial seas." However, when the Corps of Engineers issued regulations to implement the 404 program in 1974, it limited the program's jurisdiction to the same waters covered under the Rivers and Harbors Act. This left much of the nation's waters, and particularly wetlands, unregulated, including a major portion of coastal wetlands, most freshwater wetlands and tributary streams, and many lakes and isolated wetlands such as prairie potholes, playa lakes, and wet tundra. A 1975 district court decision, *Natural Resources Defense Council v. Calloway*,[29] ruled that the "waters of the United States" were intended to include all waters that Congress may constitutionally regulate under its commerce-clause authority and directed the Corps to revise and expand its regulations.

In July 1975, the Corps published interim final regulations that included an expanded definition of navigable waters and established a schedule to phase in jurisdiction over these areas by July 1977, at which time the Corps would issue final regulations governing the program. Public reaction to the program's increased scope, fueled largely by inflammatory press releases issued by the departments of the Army and Agriculture, led to a congressional battle over the extent and scope of the program when Congress took up reauthorization of the Federal Water Pollution Control Act in 1977.

The 1977 amendments, known as the Clean Water Act,[30] however, made no changes in the definition of navigable waters, and Congress confirmed the broad jurisdiction of the 404 program by rejecting specific amendments to limit it. But the amendments did make a number of other changes to clarify the program's scope and to streamline parts of the program. Section 404(f) of the act exempts certain activities from the permit requirement, as long as their primary purpose is not to convert wetlands to a new use. In another effort to reduce the number of individual permits required, Section 404(e) of the act authorizes the Corps to issue general permits on a state, regional, or nationwide basis for any category of activities that are similar in nature and that will have only minimal adverse effects, including cumulative effects, on the environment. Sections 404(g) through (l) provide for state assumption of the 404 program in most non-tidal waters if EPA, with advice from FWS, approves the state's program. To streamline the program's implementation, Section 404(q) directs the secretary of the Army to enter into agreements with the various federal agencies responsible for consulting with the Army on 404 permit applications to minimize needless paperwork and delays, with the goal of issuing permits within 90 days of public notice.

No amendments have been made to Section 404 since the 1977 Clean Water Act, but the scope of the program, both in terms of its geographical coverage and types of activities to be regulated, continues to be debated and modified in the judicial and regulatory arenas, where many of the key decisions regarding the implementation of the 404 program have been made. These and other issues surrounding the 404 program are discussed later in this chapter.

FEDERAL WATER PROJECTS — CORPS OF ENGINEERS

Program Description

Most federal water resource development projects are carried out by one of four agencies: the Army Corps of Engineers, the Bureau of Reclamation, the Soil Conservation Service, and the Tennessee Valley Authority. This section discusses only the Corps of Engineers, which has the largest construction program and is responsible for the projects that generally have had the most impact on wetlands. The Corps of Engineers is responsible for the construction and maintenance of navigation projects, including ports, harbors, and inland waterways, as well as flood control, shore and beach restoration, erosion control, and multipurpose projects for hydropower, water supply, and recreation. No exact figures exist on the amount of wetland losses caused by Corps projects, but the projects have destroyed hundreds of thousands of acres of wetlands and, more significantly, through levees, flood control, and other projects, have made possible the conversion of many millions of acres more.

Agency Structure

The Corps of Engineers is within the Department of the Army and is a mixture of military personnel and civilians. The chief of engineers, headquartered in Washington, DC, reports to the secretary of the Army. Under the chief of engineers is the directorate of Civil Works, which oversees Corps water resource programs. The directorate's work is overseen by the assistant secretary of the Army for Civil Works. Most of the civil works program is accomplished through the 11 Corps divisions, each of which is responsible for a major watershed or group of contiguous lesser watersheds. Division engineers supervise 36 district offices, each headed by a district engineer, which are responsible principally for the planning and implementation of water projects.

The Corps and Congress

Most Corps projects must be authorized by Congress through a multistep process. Requests for federal water projects generally come from local interests. To initiate a study for a project, the Corps must receive authorization from Congress. Depending on the status of the project, this may simply require a resolution by the House or Senate Public Works Committee, or it may require the passage of legislation. When funding for the study is appropriated, the Corps prepares a feasibility report, which is generally accompanied by an environmental impact statement or environmental assessment. After undergoing internal and public review and approval, the feasibility report, final environmental impact statement, and the secretary of the Army's recommendation on the project are transmitted to Congress. Congress then must pass legislation authorizing the project's construction, generally an omnibus rivers and harbors bill authorizing multiple projects. Construction funds for approved projects are appropriated by Congress yearly.

The Fish and Wildlife Coordination Act[31] requires the Corps in planning water resource projects to consult with state and federal fish and wildlife agencies for recommendations on ways not only to prevent harm to wildlife resources but also to develop and improve such resources. The Corps is required to give full consideration to these recommendations and to incorporate wildlife needs in its plans in order to maximize project benefits. The reports and recommendations made by the fish and wildlife agencies must be included in the final Corps project report to Congress.

Consultation is carried out by the Corps at the district level and generally begins during the preparation of the project's feasibility study and continues throughout the planning process. At FWS, the consultation process and studies are overseen by the Federal Projects Branch of the Ecological Services Division and are carried out by the FWS Ecological Services field offices.

The Corps also must consult with the National Marine Fisheries Service (NMFS), an agency under the National Oceanic and Atmospheric Administration in the Department of Commerce, if the project may affect living marine resources or anadromous fish under NMFS jurisdiction. National consultation oversight responsibilities within NMFS reside in the Habitat Conservation Division within the Office of Protected Species and Habitat Conservation. Responsibility for project recommendations lies with the five NMFS regional offices. Most on-site work is conducted by staff located in 13 field offices. Both NMFS and FWS generally coordinate their activities closely with the fish and wildlife agency of the state in which the project is located.

The degree to which the Corps consults with state and federal fish and wildlife agencies varies from district to district. No regulations exist to implement the requirements of the Fish and Wildlife Coordination Act and to outline when and how the fish and wildlife agencies are to be brought into the process. Under the Carter administration, the Department of the Interior and the Department of Commerce twice proposed such rules. But following review by the President's Task Force on Regulatory Relief, the proposed rulemaking was withdrawn by the Reagan administration in 1982 "in favor of administrative actions preparing memoranda of agreement and other Executive instructions."[32] No such memoranda or other formal coordinating instructions have been issued.

The Corps does issue planning guidance to its district offices, but it is general and non-binding regarding consultation requirements. Basically it directs the district engineer to invite the agencies to participate in study scoping and to provide them with the opportunity to comment on project alternatives. Thus, the degree of involvement of fish and wildlife agencies in the planning process can range from a fully integrated role starting at the initial stages of project planning to as little as being given the opportunity to review a draft of the project plan and its alternatives, depending on the interpretation of the consultation requirements by the Corps project study manager.

The one sure mechanism that exists for coordination between the Corps and FWS is their memorandum of agreement regarding the transfer of funds. Section 662(e) of the Coordination Act authorizes federal construction agencies, including the Corps, to transfer to FWS, out of project-investigation funds, the monies necessary for FWS to conduct studies or projects needed to meet the act's consultation requirements. The level of funding is negotiated between the district office and the FWS field office on an annual basis, after reviewing the status of projects and identifying fish and wildlife information needs. The Corps requests the funds from Congress as part of its annual budget request, and when project appropriations are made, the Corps and FWS field officials renegotiate as necessary for each project the scope of work to be completed that year. FWS expenditures are reimbursed at the end of the fiscal year. Fund transfers are not made to NMFS or to state agencies, but these agencies may be involved in the planning meetings held pursuant to the FWS/Corps agreement, and certain activities may be contracted to them by FWS.

How to predict and evaluate fish and wildlife losses from water projects and determine what compensation or improvement measures should be taken always has been a matter of dispute. Until recently, the Corps generally based compensation on the loss of a "man-day of use." The Corps arrived at the compensation figure by estimating the number of hunting and fishing days that would be lost to project construction. After assigning this number a dollar value, the Corps calculated how much mitigation could be bought. The man-day use method addressed the amount of recreational use rather than the condition and type of resource. Mitigation under this approach often did not involve similar resources; for example, lake-fishing days on the project's reservoir might be considered as compensation for stream-fishing days lost to impoundment.*

Since 1976, FWS has measured habitat loss by using a methodology known as Habitat Evaluation Procedure or simply HEP. This procedure is based on identifying habitat types within a proposed project site and assigning a numerical value to each habitat type based on the habitat's relative value for selected wildlife species. This procedure focuses on wildlife habitat rather than human use.

HEP, however, provides only the technical procedure for evaluating habitat loss, not the policy guidance for how this loss should be mitigated. In 1981, FWS issued a Mitigation Policy[33] to guide its field offices in making such recommendations. Depending on the value and scarcity of the resource, the policy indicates what type of measures should be recommended. In general, the policy favors in-kind replacement of habitat rather than substituting one type of resource for another.**

In recent years, as HEP has been refined, the Corps has largely switched from its man-day use process to using this and other habitat-based methodologies. A report issued by the Corps and FWS in 1983, after a Corps-funded demonstration program involving four projects, called HEP a "viable" methodology that allows "complete and accurate documentation of results" and said that it should "improve both agencies' ability to comply with the Fish and Wildlife Coordination Act."[34]

Nevertheless, it is not uncommon to find that the Corps and the fish and wildlife agencies disagree on what mitigation measures should be included in a project. A 1984 Army report to the Office of Management and Budget[35] found that on 38 Corps projects awaiting congressional authorization, Corps and FWS recommendations for mitigation were the same in 57 percent of the cases, with FWS recommending more mitigation in 37 percent. In seven special mitigation projects awaiting authorization to correct lack of mitigation at previously authorized Corps projects, the Corps recommended less mitigation in five of the cases (71 percent).

These differences arise for several reasons. First, the accuracy or effectiveness of HEP depends on the expertise of the person applying it. Thus several agencies can use HEP on the same project and come up with significantly different results.*** Second, the agencies have different views on how much and what type of mitigation is needed to offset identified losses. The Corps does not use the FWS mitigation policy and does not itself have a mitigation policy per se, although it provides some general guidance to the field. Some officials on the construction side have criticized FWS policy as requiring "in-kind" replacement of habitat in a majority of cases and have charged FWS field staff with making unreasonably costly or difficult recommendations. FWS officials say excessively expensive recommendations occasionally have been made, and field staff have been directed to be sure their recommendations can be justified, although not necessarily on a strict economic basis. Finally, the Corps places a heavier

---

*There were exceptions to the man-day use method for especially rare, critical, or valuable resources, such as rare plant communities, heron rookeries, and critical elk wintering grounds, but this was not the norm.

**The National Marine Fisheries Service has not established a national habitat evaluation procedure, since HEP is only partially applicable in marine and estuarine habitats. Nor does NMFS have a national mitigation policy. The NMFS Habitat Conservation Policy, however, encourages mitigation as a planning tool, and some NMFS regions have developed policies appropriate to their circumstances and ecosystems.

***For this reason, conservationists have sometimes criticized the reliance on HEP in making mitigation decisions, which they say can mask important resource questions by reducing them to a numerical interpretation.

emphasis on mitigation costs, citing the requirement of the Coordination Act that construction agencies are to include "justifiable" measures that maximize project benefits. The Corps uses a process called "incremental justification" to determine which mitigation measures should be included in the project report. Essentially, the Corps looks at the value of the resource versus the cost of the proposed mitigation measure and the cost of alternative measures to determine if the proposed federal expenditure is reasonable and prudent.

No nationwide records exist on which to base an assessment of wildlife or wetland losses to Corps water projects. Similarly, no figures are available for measuring success in mitigating these losses. Data from sample studies, however, show that mitigation historically has been largely a failure. For example, in 1978 FWS conducted a study of 58 Corps of Engineer projects in the Lower Mississippi River Valley for which FWS had made significant mitigation recommendations. Fifty of these projects were active, authorized projects or were under construction. FWS estimated these 50 projects would cause the direct and indirect loss of 2.1 million acres of bottomland hardwood habitat and the channelization or modification of 6,657 miles of stream habitat. FWS requested a total of 610,740 acres of mitigation land under the Coordination Act. At the time of the study, only 182,765 acres, 30 percent of the lands recommended by FWS, had been authorized for acquisition by Congress, and only 36,683 acres, six percent of the recommended lands (and only 20 percent of authorized lands), actually had been acquired and placed under management for fish and wildlife.[36]

In 1983, the Army Corps of Engineers issued a report prepared for the Corps by the Sport Fishing Institute reviewing the success of mitigation at 20 Corps projects.[37] The 20 projects were constructed after implementation of the consultation requirements of the 1946 amendments to the Coordination Act and were selected because they were the only projects subject to both pre-construction recommendations by fish and wildlife agencies and post-impoundment investigations of fish and wildlife benefits. The report found that the 20 projects inundated 354,958 acres. The fish and wildlife agencies had recommended acquisition of 45,957 acres. At the time of the study, only 5,870 acres, 13 percent of recommended mitigation acreage, had been acquired.* The study reported that the projects caused an average tenfold increase in aquatic habitat over pre-project conditions (from 40,000 acres to 401,000), thus creating some new wetlands. However, no evaluation of the type of aquatic habitat or amount of wetlands was made. The study did note that conversion of bottomland wildlife habitat to agriculture accelerated after construction of two projects that provided substantial downstream flood protection and that the loss of riparian and associated bottomland timber habitat within the reservoir basin was particularly adverse to indigenous wildlife communities. However, use of the areas for fishing and hunting generally increased substantially after project construction, even in excess of Corps and FWS expectations.

Failure to provide sufficient mitigation generally is attributed to several factors. Many of the most environmentally destructive projects were planned and authorized before the strengthened fish and wildlife requirements of the 1958 Fish and Wildlife Coordination Act. Other subsequent projects were authorized without mitigation measures, which were to be considered later. Frequently, even when mitigation measures were authorized, Congress would put off funding their implementation until the end of a project's construction. This particularly hurt land-acquisition efforts. By the time a

*The study did not report how much of the recommended acquisition acreage had been authorized by Congress.

Pattern of Wetland loss by Physiographic Region

Region	Wetland portion of region (mid-1950s) (%)	New loss of wetlands (mid-1950s– mid-1970s) (%)	Actual loss (acres)	Actual gain (acres)	Standard error for net change (%)
1. Atlantic coastal zone[a]	16	3	84,000	48,000	52.3[c]
2. Gulf coastal zone[b]	28	9	371,000	70,000	11.3[d]
3. Atlantic coastal flats[a]	36	11	1,274,000	74,000	15.0[e]
4. Gulf coastal flats[b]	27	13	1,872,000	341,000	14.5[f]
5. Gulf-Atlantic rolling plain	8	13	2,310,000	291,000	31.2[g]
6. Lower Mississippi Alluvial Plain	36	32	3,749,000	331,000	8.6[h]
7. Eastern highlands	2	2	322,000	211,000	68.8[g]
8. Dakota-Minnesota drift and lake bed flats	10	9	816,000	424,000	33.6[g]
9. Upper Midwest	8	7	2,286,000	754,000	16.8[g]
10. Central	1	3	763,000	637,000	[i]
11. Rocky Mountains	4	1	125,000	112,000	[i]
12. Intermontane	1	12	685,000	320,000	[i]
13. Pacific mountains	1	31	473,000	94,000	77.1

[a]Atlantic regions do not include Florida.
[b]Gulf regions include Florida.
[c]Standard error given is for saltwater wetlands. The freshwater wetlands had a net gain of 10,626 acres with a standard error of 86.9 percent.
[d]Standard error given is for saltwater wetlands. The freshwater wetlands had a net gain of 2,137 acres with a standard deviation greater than this value.
[e]Standard error given is for saltwater wetlands. Saltwater wetlands had a net loss of 866 acres with a standard deviation greater than this value.
[f]Standard error given is for saltwater wetlands. Saltwater wetlands had a net loss of 933 acres with a standard error of 81.6 percent.
[g]Standard error is for all vegetated wetlands measured in region which included exclusively freshwater types.
[h]Standard error is for freshwater wetlands. Saltwater wetlands had a net loss of 22,282 acres with a standard error of 67.8 percent.
[i]Standard deviation is greater than estimated net change.
Source: Wetlands; Their Use and Regulation, OTA, 1984. Original data from FWS National Wetland Trends Study, 1983.

project was completed, Congress might be reluctant to appropriate necessary funds, or mitigation lands surrounding the project might have been rendered unsuitable by development or clearing. Sometimes public opposition would solidify against the condemnation of any more land for the project, and Congress and the Corps lacked the will to acquire it. Even if land was available and possible to acquire, wildlife and habitat losses might by this time be permanent and irreplaceable. In addition, the man-day use method of determining mitigation needs failed to address habitat needs.

The days of constructing projects without consideration of wildlife values other than the use of wildlife by humans largely are gone. But many problems remain. They include failure of some Corps districts to fully integrate fish and wildlife into project planning, disagreement between the Corps and Fish and Wildlife agencies on the amount and type of mitigation that should be required, and a variety of other issues, some of which are discussed below.

Program Trends and Issues

With the advent of the environmental movement of the late 1960s and passage of NEPA in 1969,[38] the Corps water project program began to change. NEPA require-ments for environmental impact statements necessitated a more thorough review of project impacts than had occurred under the Coordination Act, and pre-authorization consultation — although of varying degrees of quality — became the norm. Also, the Corps began to look at using the habitat-oriented methodology for assessing wildlife impacts, beginning the move away from man-day use.

Most significant, however, the public began taking a hard look at federal water resources development policy overall. By the mid-1970s, opposition to the large-scale, destructive projects of the past was strong. President Carter developed a "hit list" of projects to be deauthorized, vetoed the 1978 omnibus water projects bill, and undertook a major effort to reform federal water project planning to make it more subject to public involvement, oversight, and enforcement and to reduce its environ-mental damage. The Reagan administration, out of its concern for economic efficiency and reduced federal spending, also has tackled the federal water project pork barrel by trying to get the beneficiaries to pay more of the costs. At the same time, however, the Reagan administration has dismantled some of the reforms instituted by the Carter administration, because the Reagan administration considered them too burdensome and inflexible.

As a result, the traditional biennial congressional authorization of multiple new Corps projects has ground to a halt. The last omnibus water projects bill was enacted in 1976, and the last bill with a large number of new project authorizations passed in 1970. Thus in recent years, while concern continues for improving the Coordination Act process, public debate has focused more on what to do about the hundreds of projects that have been authorized without sufficient mitigation in the past and on how federal water resources policy should be changed to address modern environmental concerns.

Post-Authorization Mitigation. With the passage of NEPA, the Corps was re-quired to review its ongoing water projects, in part to determine if fish and wildlife impacts had been addressed adequately. This review, combined with pressure from environmental groups and lawsuits filed on specific projects, caused the Corps to undertake mitigation plans for a number of unmitigated projects with significant wildlife impacts. During the last several years, the Corps, working with fish and wildlife agencies, developed a number of special mitigation reports that one long-time water projects observer called "probably the greatest wildlife effort ever made by the Corps." Ten reports have been completed so far, recommending some 250,000 acres of acquisition at a cost of $300 million — most of it in the rapidly vanishing bottom-land hardwood wetlands. Several additional studies still are being developed.

Two of the mitigation projects covered by the special reports have been undertak-en so far: the Lower Snake River Compensation Plan in Washington, a salmon and wildlife restoration project, and mitigation at the Richard B. Russell Dam and Lake in South Carolina and Georgia. At the Russell Dam, however, all the wildlife mitigation, including acquisition of 32,000 acres (much of it bottomland hardwood wetlands), was deleted from the project, leaving only some fish mitigation and increased management on existing lands at nearby Corps projects. The remainder of the projects, still awaiting approval by the secretary of the Army, nevertheless were included for authorization in the omnibus water projects bills considered but not passed by the 98th Congress (discussed under legislation).

These projects appear to have run into trouble from the Office of Management and Budget (OMB), which has discouraged the acquisition of land for mitigation. In May 1984, OMB wrote the Army expressing concern that mitigation actions planned by the Corps of Engineers increasingly consist of land acquisition. In response, the Corps conducted a study[39] of the mitigation recommendations included in 150 projects awaiting authorization or initiation of construction funding in legislation before the 98th Congress (S. 1739, H.R. 3678, H.R. 3958). The report found that 44 of the projects (29 percent) contained mitigation recommendations, and 22 (15 percent of the total 150) recommended the acquisition of mitigation land, for a total of 140,479 acres. However, 120,280 acres, 86 percent of the total recommended mitigation lands, are associated with seven special mitigation projects. The Army wrote OMB in November 1984, saying that while the Corps report did not reveal any alarming trend toward excessive mitigation by land acquisition in reports recommending new project authorizations, "the special mitigation reports noted previously do concern us and we will be giving each a critical review."[40]

Principles and Standards. One important controversy in the planning and evaluation of water projects has been the Reagan administration revision of the Principles, Standards and Procedures[41] for the development and evaluation of federal water resource projects required by the Water Resources Planning Act.[42] The Carter administration promulgated them as regulations, thus making them binding on federal agencies, and elevated the consideration of environmental impacts. Among other things, the principles and standards required agencies to recommend a best plan from among three different alternative project plans that focused on different overall goals: one plan for national economic development, another for environmental quality, and one for non-structural alternatives. The principles and standards required that the environmental quality plan be considered coequal with national economic development.

In mid-1983, the Reagan administration revised the principles and standards and repealed their status as regulations, making the requirements non-binding.[43] The revised planning procedures, renamed the Principles and Guidelines,[44] eliminate the requirement that environmental quality be considered coequal with economic development in project planning. Instead, the guidelines establish "national economic development consistent with protecting the nation's environment" as the single federal objective in water resource planning. The guidelines eliminate the requirement for fully developed non-structural alternatives or environmental quality plans and require that the national economic development plan — designed to "reasonably maximize net national economic development" — be the recommended plan unless the secretary of the department grants an exception based on "overriding reasons." The environmental quality procedures for placing a value on and demonstrating environmental effects may be used, but again are not required. The administration said the changes were intended to reduce the burden on agencies in complying with detailed and legally binding technical rules, which it said forced project planners to concentrate on mechanical compliance with the regulations at the expense of planning itself.

Environmental groups and state water resource officials opposed the changes made by the Reagan administration, including the decision to make them non-regulatory, on the grounds that these changes would reduce consideration of environmental values, skew water resource decisions in favor of larger, potentially more destructive projects, substantially limit public participation in water resources planning, and make it impossible to enforce the guidelines through third-party lawsuits. Some sources within the Corps and others on the construction side of the water-project business say that the principles-and-standards requirement for preparation of environmental quality plans was never achieved in reality, but there is some feeling that the requirement was important as a statement of a new philosophy in water-project planning.

Efforts to overturn the administration's decision and restore the regulatory principles and standards are proceeding on two tracks. Both the House and Senate versions of the omnibus water projects legislation in the 98th Congress (H.R. 3678 and S. 1739) would establish a new National Water Policy Board to issue regulatory principles and standards and would reinstate the previous principles and standards in the interim. Both bills also would restore environmental quality as a coequal objective of water-project planning, although the House bill establishes several other goals as well.

In addition, the National Wildlife Federation filed suit against the government in July 1984 for repealing the principles and standards. The suit charges that the action was arbitrary and capricious, that the issuance of non-regulatory guidelines violated the Water Resources Planning Act, and that the decision should have been accompanied by an environmental impact statement. The federation has asked the court to direct the government to reinstate the previous principles and standards, to prepare an environmental impact statement on any subsequent modification or repeal, and to cease project planning based on the new guidelines unless such planning is augmented to comply with the principles and standards.

Discontinuation of Transfer Funds. The Corps of Engineers traditionally has transferred funds to FWS to conduct studies necessary to meet the requirements of the Fish and Wildlife Coordination Act. In October 1982, however, Assistant Secretary of the Army for Civil Works William Gianelli wrote Interior Assistant Secretary for Fish and Wildlife and Parks G. Ray Arnett that the Army planned "to review the past performance of the Transfer Funding Agreement and the Corps/FWS relationship thereunder to determine if the present means of funding the Fish and Wildlife Coordination Act activities of the Corps should be continued."[45] The areas identified for review were: FWS efficiency in performing Coordination Act studies, the adequacy of data supplied by FWS, and the feasibility of using alternative means of acquiring Coordination Act studies. However, a survey conducted by the Corps of its districts earlier that year indicated that most Corps divisions were satisfied with the transfer-funding arrangement. A majority of divisions said that FWS costs were not substantially higher than the cost of providing the services in-house or from other sources, that FWS overhead was much lower than that of other institutions, that FWS provided quality reports in a timely manner, and that the transfer-funding agreement should not be revised. In response to the threat of the recision of the transfer agreement, Representative John Breaux (D-Louisiana) included language in his proposed amendments to the Fish and Wildlife Coordination Act (H.R. 5755) that would make the transfer mandatory, although this legislation did not clear Congress in 1984 (see section on legislation). In May 1984, Gianelli resigned from his position with the Army, and the Army has taken no further steps to terminate the agreement.

Legislation

Omnibus Water Projects Authorization Legislation. The 98th Congress tried but failed to pass legislation authorizing a host of new water resources development projects and making a number of changes in national water resources policy. The legislation generally was opposed by conservation groups, including the National Audubon Society, because it would have approved construction of a number of projects with serious environmental impacts, including impacts on wetlands and wildlife, and failed to make what they considered adequate changes in the nation's water resource development policy. The legislation did, however, contain some favorable conservation measures, including authorizing the acquisition of habitat to compensate for losses caused by previously authorized water projects and making reforms in current mitigation policy.

At the center of the debate is the question of how much of the cost of water projects should be paid by users and beneficiaries. Traditionally, the federal government has shouldered most of the costs, particularly for ports, harbors, and inland waterways. Conservation groups long have advocated requiring beneficiaries to pay a larger portion of the cost. This would encourage the project's proponents to evaluate more carefully their needs and would lead to smaller, more efficiently planned projects with less damaging environmental impacts. The Reagan administration also has pushed heavily for increased cost sharing, although the administration's goal is economic efficiency and reduced federal spending.

The 98th Congress came close to passing a final omnibus water projects bill at the end of the congressional session by attaching it to a massive federal agency funding bill that had to be approved that year. However, President Reagan said he would veto the bill because it failed to contain adequate cost-sharing reforms, and the Senate voted not to include the measure. In 1985, it will be nine years since a new authorization package has been approved, and the push to pass a bill in the 99th Congress probably will be stronger than ever.

Two major versions of the water projects legislation appeared before the 98th Congress: one passed by the House in July 1984 (H.R. 3678) and one that was approved by three Senate committees but did not clear the full Senate (S. 1739). On the downside, in conservationists' eyes neither the House nor Senate bill went far enough in increasing the non-federal share of project costs. In addition, conservation groups opposed the inclusion of such large numbers of new projects, since many would have significant environmental impacts. The House bill included some 300 new projects at a cost of $18 billion. The more modest Senate bill still included some 130 projects at a cost of $8 billion. The House bill in particular contained a number of negative policy changes or exceptions, including numerous waivers of standard cost-sharing requirements, new authority for river channelization without specific approval by Congress, and congressional declaration for a number of projects that their benefits exceed their costs.

However, both bills did include a number of positive measures for conservation. They moved to reduce the $43.3 billion backlog of inactive or incomplete projects and to prevent such backlogs from accruing in the future. The House bill immediately deauthorized 330 projects at an estimated cost of $11.1 billion and automatically terminated authorization for those projects in the bill if construction had not begun in five years. Under the Senate bill, projects automatically would have been deauthorized after 10 years if construction had not begun, unless the Corps determined a project remained justified. A total of 593 projects with a cost of $18.3 billion would have been eligible for automatic deauthorization in one year.

Both House and Senate bills would have established a National Board of Water Policy similar to the old Water Resources Council to oversee water-project planning. The board would have been required to establish regulatory principles and standards (see discussion above) and to reinstate the principles-and-standards regulations issued under the Carter administration, until new ones were promulgated. The bills also would have restored environmental quality as an objective of water resource planning. Currently the only official objective is national economic development.

Both bills contained improvements upon mitigation policy. They addressed the mitigation failure by requiring that lands needed for fish and wildlife mitigation be acquired prior to or concurrent with a project's construction. The Senate bill additionally required that all mitigation work occur during construction. Both bills authorized the Corps to undertake small mitigation efforts on any project if the cost were less than $7.5 million, thus allowing the Corps to conduct mitigation for existing projects without obtaining funds from Congress. In addition, the House bill would have established a $35 million Environmental Protection and Mitigation Fund that the Corps could use to begin mitigation efforts in advance of construction. The Corps would have been required to reimburse the fund out of the first appropriations for the project. The Senate bill did not include a mitigation fund, but attempted to insure that mitigation work was fully coordinated with the project design by requiring future project proposals to include a specific mitigation plan outlining project features, land acquisition and preparation, and operation and maintenance procedures.

In addition, both bills authorized a number of fish and wildlife mitigation measures for previously authorized projects. Most notably, the House bill authorized the acquisition of 67,000 acres of fish and wildlife mitigation for the Tennessee-Tombigbee Waterway and almost 400,000 acres (mostly in easements) in Louisiana's Atchafalaya Basin for flood control, which also would have provided important wildlife habitat. The House bill included a number of other post-authorization mitigation projects that authorized acquisition of an additional 140,000 acres of habitat. The Senate bill had fewer such projects, for a total of some 60,000 acres. Finally, both bills authorized modifications to central and southern Florida projects to help restore the natural water balance in the Everglades National Park, and authorized the mitigation features of the Upper Mississippi River Basin Master Plan in conjunction with the construction of a second lock at Alton, Illinois.

Fish and Wildlife Coordination Act Amendments. On September 10, 1984, the House of Representatives passed the Fish and Wildlife Coordination Act Amendments of 1984, H.R. 5755. This bill would have made four significant changes in the act:

- It would have made the transfer funding provisions of the Coordination Act mandatory rather than discretionary and authorized the transfer of funds to NMFS as well as to FWS. Currently this fund transfer is authorized but is not mandatory, and the Army has indicated an interest in terminating the arrangement. Also, because the transfer-funding provisions are voluntary, FWS has not always had the consistent and reliable funding needed to adequately meet the consultation requirements of the Coordination Act.
- The bill would have authorized FWS and NMFS to enter into long-term contractual agreements with project sponsors and license applicants regarding the value and extent of habitat to be conserved or enhanced, the mitigation to be provided for affected wildlife resources, and the nature and extent of habitat modifications to be permitted. This provision was intended to add a measure of certainty to the fish and wildlife mitigation requirements of large-scale, long-term projects. Currently, applicants often have to negotiate individual actions rather than plan mitigation for a project as a whole.
- H.R. 5755 would have recognized the authority of fish and wildlife agencies to recommend on-site as well as off-site mitigation measures. This provision was intended to boost the concept of mitigation banking, in which an area of valuable habitat is set aside in advance so that it can be used to provide

"credits" against losses caused by future projects. Mitigation banking already is in use, primarily in permit and licensing programs, and is discussed in the section on the permit program.

- Finally, the bill would have required FWS and NMFS to compile an inventory of water projects for which recommendations were made under the Coordination Act, including recommendations on 404 permit decisions. Following the inventory, the agencies would have been required to evaluate a representative sample of projects to determine the extent to which their recommendations were incorporated as conditions of the project, the extent to which those recommendations were applied, and the result and effectiveness of their application.

Currently no comprehensive figures on compliance with mitigation requirements are available, but a 1982 study by the NMFS Southeast Region found that one in five projects investigated was in violation of permit conditions and that the percentage of violations in Corps districts ranged from zero to 64 percent. The Reagan administration has objected to the last provision of the bill, maintaining that fish and wildlife agencies should not be reviewing compliance with programs that are under the jurisdiction of other agencies. In the meantime, however, both FWS and NMFS have begun to conduct follow-up studies to determine the effectiveness of their recommendations in compensating for wildlife damages.

The Senate took no action on the House bill, and no similar bill was introduced in the Senate.

THE 404 PERMIT PROGRAM

Program Description

The 404 permit program was established in Section 404 of the Clean Water Act.[46] Section 404 requires anyone discharging dredged or fill materials into United States waters to have a special permit. The 404 program is the federal government's principal regulatory program for controlling wetlands destruction. It is administered by both the Corps of Engineers and EPA. The Corps is responsible for processing and issuing permits and for setting regulations regarding permit issuance procedures. EPA, however, is responsible for issuing the environmental guidelines required by Section 404(b)(1) of the Clean Water Act, which specify some of the environmental standards that a discharge project must meet to receive a permit. The project must comply with other federal environmental laws as well.

EPA also has authority under Section 404(c) of the act to specify areas in which discharges are prohibited or restricted, essentially giving it veto power over Corps permit decisions, but this authority has seldom been exercised. EPA is responsible for issuing regulations regarding state assumption of 404 responsibilities in certain waters and wetlands and for the approval and oversight of such programs. EPA also defines activities exempted from the permit requirement under Section 404(f).

Certain other program responsibilities are shared by EPA and the Corps. EPA determines what lands will be considered wetlands for purposes of 404 administration. But for delineating wetlands in the field, the agencies have signed a memorandum of understanding allowing the Corps to make the determination except in areas called "special cases," where EPA specifically has said that it wants to make the determination. EPA has identified two special cases — the bottomland hardwoods and a bay in California — but has taken little action to enforce the provision in recent years. The memorandum of understanding on jurisdiction currently is being renegotiated between EPA and the Corps. EPA and the Corps also share authority for enforcing Section 404, with the Corps responsible for permit violations and EPA responsible for unauthorized activities, but in fact almost all enforcement has been carried out by the Corps.

Permit issuance by the Corps is carried out primarily by the district engineers. When the district engineer receives a permit application, he issues a public notice soliciting comments on the proposed action from the public and from local, state, and federal agencies. These include state fish and wildlife agencies, FWS, and, as appropriate, NMFS, all of which the Corps is required to consult under the Fish and Wildlife Coordination Act.[47] These agencies make recommendations on whether permits should be approved as is or modified, conditioned, or denied in order to protect fish and wildlife resources, including the habitat on which they depend. EPA also reviews permits and makes recommendations based on their environmental impacts. Permit review is carried out within FWS by the 59 Ecological Services Field Offices, within NMFS by the 13 Habitat Conservation field offices, and within EPA by the 10 regional offices.

The district engineer uses two basic standards when evaluating a project proposed in a permit application. First, the project must comply with the Environmental Protection Agency's 404(b)(1) guidelines.[48] An important provision of these guidelines is the so-called water dependency test, which imposes a strong presumption against allowing discharges in wetlands. The guidelines require that no discharge be approved if a practicable alternative would have less adverse impact on the aquatic environment, provided that the alternative does not have other significant adverse environmental consequences. For activities that do not have to be located in or next to water, such as a housing development or a restaurant, the guidelines presume that such a practicable alternative exists, unless it is clearly demonstrated otherwise. The guidelines also require that practicable steps be taken to minimize impacts of discharges and prohibit discharges that will cause or contribute to significant degradation of waters of the United States, including wetlands.

The second standard that the Corps uses is the public interest review, a process in which the Corps balances the benefits that may accrue from the activity against its reasonably foreseeable detriments.[49] The Corps applies three general criteria in making this review: the relative extent of the public and private need for the proposed structure or work, the desirability of using appropriate alternative locations and methods to accomplish the objective of the proposed structure or work, and the extent and permanence of the beneficial or detrimental effects on public and private uses to which the area is suited. Factors to be considered go far beyond the impact on wetlands and include conservation, fish and wildlife values, general environmental concerns, aesthetics, cultural values, flood hazards and floodplain values, land use, navigation, shore erosion and accretion, recreation, water supply and conservation, water quality, safety, energy and mineral needs, food and fiber production, considerations of property ownership, and in general the needs and welfare of the people. Cumulative impacts — that is, the cumulative effect of numerous potential piecemeal changes — as well as the project's individual impacts are to be considered.

If a project meets the requirements of the 404(b)(1) guidelines, a permit will be issued unless it is determined that it would be contrary to the public interest. However, for activities that modify wetlands defined as "important" in Corps regulations, the permit must be denied unless the benefit of the proposed activity outweighs the damage to the wetlands resource. If the project does not comply with the 404(b)(1) guidelines, the permit must be denied.

Several other constraints govern a district engineer's permit decisions. He is required to give full consideration to recommendations from the state and federal fish and wildlife agencies. These recommendations need not be followed, however. Little guidance has been developed for determining the extent to which fish and wildlife agency recommendations are to be included in issued permits. Thus, great variability occurs from district to district on these questions. Some variability also occurs within resource agencies as to how environmental guidelines are to be applied and their requirements met.

If FWS, NMFS, or EPA disagrees with the district engineer's permit decision, the agency can request elevation of the proposed permit for review at upper levels within the Corps' hierarchy. The procedures and timing for elevation requests are outlined in memoranda of agreement, required by Section 404(q), between the Department of the Army and the departments of the Interior and Commerce and EPA. These memoranda were revised in 1982 as a result of recommendations by the President's Task Force on Regulatory Relief and currently are a matter of significant controversy (see discussion below).

In addition, EPA can veto a Corps permit decision under Section 404(c) by prohibiting discharges into an area if the discharge will have unacceptable adverse effects on municipal water supplies, shellfish beds and fishery areas, wildlife, or recreational resources. Section 404(c) also authorizes EPA to designate areas as off-limits to such discharges even if no permit application has been made, but EPA has never used this authority.

The states also have several opportunities to challenge or influence Corps permit decisions. Section 401 of the Clean Water Act[50] requires state certification or waiver of certification prior to issuance of a Section 404 permit. In addition, if a required state or local permit is denied before the Corps has made its decision on a 404 permit, the Corps will deny the 404 permit. Even if the Corps has issued a 404 permit, this does not absolve the permit applicant from the need to obtain other approvals required under state or local authority. In addition, no Corps permit may be issued in states that have federally approved coastal zone management plans under the Coastal Zone Management Act,[51] unless the state certifies that the activity is consistent with the state plan or waives its right to do so.

Not all dredge and fill activities require the issuance of an individual 404 permit. A number of activities that cause the discharge of dredged and fill material are exempted from the permit requirement under Section 404(f)(1), as long as they are not intended to bring the wetlands into a new use, as provided in Section 404(f)(2). These exemptions include normal farming, silviculture, and ranching activities; maintenance and emergency reconstruction of structures such as dikes, dams, levees, groins, etc.; construction or maintenance of farm or stock ponds or irrigation ditches; maintenance of drainage ditches; construction of temporary sedimentation basins on construction sites; and construction or maintenance of farm, forest, or temporary mining roads if they are constructed in accordance with best management practices. Also, under Section 404(r), federal projects specifically authorized by Congress are exempt if the information on their effects required by Section 404 is included in an environmental impact statement.

The Corps also can forego review of individual activities by issuing general permits on a state, regional, or nationwide basis as provided for in Section 404(e) of the Clean Water Act. General permits can be issued for categories of activities that are similar in nature and that will cause only minimal individual and cumulative adverse effects on the environment. For example, the Corps has issued nationwide permits for activities such as the placement of navigation markers and of devices for the taking of fish and wildlife such as crab pots and lobster traps, and survey activities such as core sampling. General permits are issued in a process similar to individual permits, but once they are approved the activities specified in them can be carried out without the issuance of an individual permit. However, in many cases the activities are expected to be conducted in accordance with specified practices to minimize their impacts.

As of 1981, the Corps had issued 374 general permits, eliminating the need to review an estimated 60,000 to 90,000 individual permits yearly.[52] In the meantime, a number of additional general permits have been issued, which the Corps says has resulted in a 20-percent reduction in annual permit applications.[53]

Not all wetlands are regulated by 404. As a result of a 1975 court decision, *Natural Resources Defense Council v. Calloway*,[54] the Corps has extended its jurisdiction to include most of the nation's waters as follows: waters used for interstate navigation; non-navigable streams and tributaries that lead to navigable waters; wetlands that border rivers, lakes, and streams or are the headwaters of interstate waters; and isolated lakes and wetlands that contribute to interstate commerce. Nevertheless, because of differences in agency definitions, the extent of wetlands determined by the Corps and EPA to be covered by 404 is considerably less than total wetland acreage in the United States as determined by FWS. While FWS estimated in the mid-1970s that there were 99 million acres of wetlands in the lower 48 states, the Corps estimates that its jurisdiction under 404 extends over approximately 64 million acres of wetlands. In general, the definition under 404 requires wetlands to be "wetter" than wetlands defined by FWS.

Even within these limitations, arguments over the geographic scope of the 404 program and the type of activities it is meant to regulate have been at the center of the debate over the program since its inception. Some of these issues are discussed later under Program Issues and Trends.

Little solid information exists for measuring the success of 404 in protecting wetlands. Very few 404 permits are denied. In 1984, for example, the Corps issued 5,850 Section 404 permits and denied 351, about 5.6 percent of the total. This denial rate is roughly equal to that of 1983 and is up somewhat from 1981 and 1982, when about 3.5 percent of permits were denied.[55] However, a number of projects are modified in the permit-review process to reduce their wetland impact. Corps officials estimate that more than half are modified to some extent, and a 1984 report by the congressional Office of Technology Assessment said that about a third of permit applications are modified significantly to reduce wetland impacts.[56]

The report by the Office of Technology Assessment attempted to estimate the amount of wetlands saved by 404. According to Corps of Engineers estimates for 1980-81,* Corps districts excluding Alaska processed permits for projects that, if completed as planned, would have resulted in the direct and indirect conversion of approximately 100,000 acres of wetlands per year. If the projects subsequently authorized by the Corps were completed in accordance with the conditions of the Corps permits, the amount of wetlands lost to conversion would have been halved. The overall rate of compliance is unknown, but probably less than 50,000 acres of conversion actually was prevented. This contrasts with an estimated rate of wetlands loss of 300,000 to 458,000 acres per year.** On the other hand, increased public awareness of wetland values and pre-application consultations probably cause fewer projects to be undertaken and cause applicants to modify projects to reduce wetland impacts before actually submitting a permit application, masking the overall effect of the 404 program. In addition, the Office of Technology Assessment reported that about 5,000 acres of vegetated wetlands a year either are created or restored for mitigation purposes as a direct result of the conditioning of 404 permits.

---

*This is prior to the many regulatory and administrative changes made in the program in the name of regulatory relief.
**See Resource Status section for the derivation of these numbers.

Program Trends and Issues

The 404 program has been in flux since its inception. Through court decisions, regulatory changes, and legislative amendments, the scope, standards, and procedures of the program have been redefined repeatedly. From 1972 to 1974, the Corps was developing rules to implement the program. From 1975 to 1977, the Corps phased in its jurisdiction over the nation's wetlands, as required by *Natural Resource Defense Council v. Calloway*. From 1977 to 1980, the Corps and EPA worked to develop rules to implement the 1977 legislative changes and to make other changes to cope with increased jurisdictional responsibilities.

Throughout the history of the 404 program, the Army consistently has interpreted and applied the program in a narrow and limited way — especially by trying to limit the area the program covers and the activities to which it applies. Environmental groups have responded by pressing for and often winning expansion of the program. Environmental groups also have criticized both the Corps and EPA on their implementation and enforcement of the program. Some of the specific issues at debate in this ongoing battle are discussed below.

In addition, however, in the past three years, the 404 program has been the subject of a massive regulatory reform effort. When the Reagan administration came into office with its anti-regulatory philosophy, its Presidential Task Force on Regulatory Relief targeted 404 program reform as a top priority. During the past three years, the regulatory relief effort has moved to reduce the federal presence in the 404 program by issuing more general and nationwide permits and shifting responsibility to the states. It also has tried to limit the ability of the environmental agencies to influence permit conditions and decisions and to relax the program's environmental requirements while giving more deference to private property rights. Some of these proposals have been blunted by lawsuits brought by environmental groups, and others have been at least temporarily stalled by objections from EPA. Nevertheless, the effectiveness of 404 as a wetland-protection program has been reduced, and the reform effort continues.

The other major trend related to 404 has been a growing realization that, although 404 has helped reduce wetlands loss, wetlands continue to disappear at a rapid rate, and other protective measures are needed as well. This has led to efforts to focus attention on areas where wetlands loss is most serious, such as the lower Mississippi Valley bottomland hardwoods, and the consideration of the need for new legislation or other approaches to provide more comprehensive or effective protection for the nation's wetland resources.

Ongoing Issues: Jurisdictional Scope and General Implementation and Enforcement

Environmental groups and the Corps of Engineers have struggled since the inception of the 404 program over two key issues: its geographic scope and the type of activities it covers. The question of scope first arose in 1974, when the Corps issued regulations applying Section 404 only to navigable waters covered by Section 10, which excluded a large portion of the nation's wetlands. A 1975 court decision, however, required the Corps to extend its jurisdiction to include most wetlands, and Congress affirmed this broad interpretation of the law during consideration of the 1977 amendments to the Federal Water Pollution Control Act. Even with this expanded jurisdiction, however, disputes occur over some of the Corps' delineations of wetland boundaries as well as other Corps determinations of its jurisdiction.

Another important limitation on the 404 program is that the majority of activities responsible for wetlands loss have not been regulated by the program. A 404 permit is required for the discharge of dredged or fill material. But a variety of other activities responsible for wetland conversion, many of which result in incidental deposits of fill, have not been regulated by the Corps, including projects involving excavation, drainage, clearing, and flooding of wetlands. According to a report by the congressional Office of Technology Assessment, 80 percent of wetland losses from the mid-1950s to the mid-1970s involved draining and clearing wetlands for agricultural purposes, which generally have not been regulated under 404.[57]

Bottomland Hardwoods. The area where these disputes have provoked the greatest controversy is the bottomland hardwood wetlands of the lower Mississippi alluvial plain. These forested wetlands have suffered the greatest rate of loss in the nation in the recent past, more than three times the national average. Only 20 percent of their original acreage remains today. The majority of the loss comes from land clearing for agricultural conversion to grow soybeans, an activity the Corps traditionally has not regulated under 404. In addition, the bottomland hardwoods have been the subject of major disputes between the Corps and EPA over wetland boundaries. In one case, the Corps determined that 35 percent of a tract was wetlands under 404, while EPA determined that 80 percent of the tract was wetland.

The issues of how to determine which bottomland hardwoods are covered by 404 and whether a 404 permit is required for land clearing for agricultural conversion were resolved legally in a 1983 decision by the Fifth Circuit Court of Appeals, *Avoyelles Sportsmen's League v. Marsh.*[58] That decision upheld EPA's more expansive determination of how much of the tract of land in question fell under 404. On the land-clearing question, the court ruled that the clearing of vegetation in the case did result in the discharge of fill, which the Corps defines in part as replacing aquatic areas with dry land. In addition, the court said the land clearing was not a normal farming activity exempt under 404(f)(1) because it was intended to change the use of the wetlands. Such activities are required to obtain a permit under 404(f)(2).

Although both these issues were decided legally in favor of more protection for the bottomland hardwoods, it remains to be seen how they are carried out in practice. So far, the Corps has been slow in applying the ruling. After the first decision on the case was issued in 1979 by the U.S. District Court for the Western District of Louisiana, which found that the land clearing itself was regulated by 404, the Corps issued guidance to its district engineers stating that land clearing would be regulated only in that particular judicial district. The February 1984 settlement agreement in *National Wildlife Federation v. Marsh* (discussed later) directed the Corps to apply the Fifth Circuit's 1983 ruling on land clearing nationwide, and in March 1985 the Corps issued a regulatory guidance letter to the field detailing how to interpret the court's decision. Many environmental attorneys, however, are skeptical that this guidance will have much practical effect, since the Corp program in this region has been weak. According to the Environmental Defense Fund, since the Fifth Circuit Court issued its decision in September 1983 few, if any, public notices requesting comment on agricultural-conversion permit applications have been issued by the southern Corps districts.[59] In addition, the Corps still has made restrictive determinations as to what qualifies as wetlands under 404, and environmental groups are suing on the issue.

In October 1984, EPA began a more ambitious if belated effort to implement the court decisions and place high priority on the bottomland hardwoods. EPA issued detailed interim policy guidance on administering the 404 program in the bottomland hardwoods, focusing on how to define areas and land-clearing activities subject to a 404 permit. The guidance states that it is EPA policy to ensure that determinations of jurisdiction in bottomland hardwoods reflect EPA interpretations. In addition, in December 1984 EPA began a series of three technical workshops in order to better characterize the ecosystem and to evaluate the impacts on the ecosystem of different activities and management approaches. The agency intends to issue final policy guidance by January 1, 1986. In the meantime, additional staff and resources have been allocated to the 404 program in the bottomland hardwoods.

Isolated Wetlands. Another emerging jurisdictional controversy concerns the circumstances under which isolated lakes and wetlands contribute to interstate commerce and thus can be regulated by the federal government under the Commerce Clause of the Constitution. Again, conservation groups and fish and wildlife officials charge the Corps is taking too restrictive an approach. The Corps generally identifies such wetlands on a case-by-case basis and narrowly defines what it considers to be interstate commerce. For example, migratory bird nesting areas are considered by the Corps to contribute to interstate commerce because the birds are protected by federal law pursuant to international treaty.

Conservation groups maintain that the commerce clause gives the Corps authority to regulate isolated waters as a class, without a case-by-case determination, and that the definition of interstate commerce being used by some Corps districts is too narrow. For example, the Charleston, South Carolina, district issued a wetlands policy statement in 1984 that called for regulating wetlands used for nesting and feeding by migratory birds, but omitted mention of certain other important migratory bird habitat areas, such as wetlands used for resting during migration and pair bonding. One major problem cited with the case-by-case approach to determining 404 jurisdiction, as well as the Corps' lack of clarity on its jurisdictional authority in other areas, is that dischargers may fail to understand when they must obtain a permit for their activities, resulting in unauthorized fills.

Implementation and Enforcement. In addition to these limitations, conservationists charge that the program's effectiveness is reduced further by inadequate implementation and enforcement by the Corps and EPA. EPA is criticized for its lack of priority on enforcing 404 in the field. In fact, EPA has left almost all enforcement to the Corps, and, more significantly, has failed to use its 404(c) authority to veto Corps permits or to designate areas as off-limits or restricted to discharges. Prior to 1984, EPA had initiated a 404(c) veto action on only two permits. However, recently EPA appears to be taking a more active role in 404. When William Ruckelshaus took over as EPA administrator in 1983, 404 was identified as a high priority. During 1984, EPA dramatically stepped up its use of 404(c), beginning six additional actions. EPA officials note, however, that 404(c) actions require substantial documentation and estimate that each action requires about one man-year of work.

A major criticism of the Corps, in addition to its narrow implementation of 404 discussed above, is its failure to follow natural resource agency recommendations for permit denials or modifications. Some local studies show clearly that problems do exist. For example, a 1982 study of the NMFS Southeast Region found that even when the Corps had accepted NMFS permit recommendations, one in five applicants failed to comply.[60] An FWS study of 40 of the most significant northern New Jersey wetlands fillings since 1980 found that 23 projects destroying 115 acres were unauthorized, four projects destroying 84 acres were conducted under a nationwide permit intended for activities with minimal environmental impacts, and 12 fills affecting more than 260 acres were granted permits over FWS recommendations for denial or modification. The remaining fill of 300 acres originally was authorized under a nationwide permit but was determined a year later to require an individual permit. FWS said the inability to protect wetlands was due to Corps unwillingness or inability to protect wetlands under 404, lack of enforcement by EPA, and an FWS inability to elevate permits for review (discussed below).[61]

Regulatory Relief Efforts

In 1981, in response to the Reagan administration's Task Force on Regulatory Relief and to Executive Order 12291, which requires agencies to conduct a regulatory impact analysis of their major regulations, the Corps, under Assistant Secretary of the Army William Gianelli, led an interagency review of ways to reform the 404 program. In early 1982, the Corps submitted its recommendations to the task force, and in May 1982 the task force announced the initiation of major administrative reforms of 404 to "dramatically reduce the delays in processing permit applications" and to eliminate the "seemingly endless layers of bureaucratic review associated with the permit system." According to rough estimates by the Corps, the reforms "could save $1 billion annually."[62] The task force made five major recommendations:

1. Reduce uncertainty and delay, primarily by revising the memoranda of agreement with other federal agencies responsible for commenting on 404 permits in order to limit their ability to challenge permit decisions made by district engineers. Internal Corps review procedures were to be streamlined as well.

2. Give states more authority and responsibility by issuing general permits for state programs that are substantially similar to the Army's program, reducing Corps review of state land-use decisions and making it easier for the states to assume program administration.

3. Reduce conflicting and overlapping policies by reducing the time for state action on certification requests, shortening and simplifying EPA environmental guidelines, and proposing changes to other regulations that impede implementation of the reform measures, such as NEPA.

4. Expand the use of general permits on a regional and nationwide basis.

5. Clarify the scope of the program by developing new and more specific criteria to redefine wetlands subject to the 404 program.

These initiatives over the past three years have formed the basis for a concerted push by the Department of the Army and the Office of Management and Budget for changes in the 404 program. At least initial steps have been taken to implement each of the recommendations, as discussed in the items below. To date, many have been finalized, while others remain on the regulatory relief agenda.

At the time the task force review was initiated, the Corps' research arm, the Institute for Water Resources, began an internal Regulatory Impact Analysis of the 404 program. A draft of the study[63] suggested that the benefits of the program outweighed its administrative burdens and costs. In addition, the study estimated that project modifications developed during review of permit applications resulted in less costly projects 30 to 50 percent of the time, for total annual savings to permit applicants of from $135.5 million to $271 million. The study was never released.

Revised Memoranda of Agreement. In June and July 1982, the Department of the Army promoted revisions of the interagency memoranda of agreement with FWS, NMFS, and EPA regarding procedures for reviewing and elevating 404 permit decisions. These agreements were required by the 1977 amendments to the Clean Water Act "to minimize duplication, needless paperwork and delays in permit issuance. . . ."[64] The initial agreements, signed in 1980, allowed resource agencies to request that permit decisions made by Corps district engineers be referred for further review to higher authorities in the Corps and the Department of the Army. Depending on the type of controversy involved, a permit could be elevated through as many as four levels. In fact, permit elevation was not used frequently. NMFS reported that between March 1980 and November 1981, it reviewed approximately 18,000 permit applications, including other programs as well as 404, and elevated 17 to the Division Engineer level, three of which were elevated further to Washington. FWS reported that in a six-month period in 1980, it reviewed 6,442 permit applications and elevated 11 to the division engineer, of which two went to Washington. EPA elevated 11 permit applications over the two-year lifespan of the 1980 memorandum of agreement.

The 1982 revised memoranda of agreement made several significant changes. They require the resource agencies to request a permit elevation within 20 days after a district engineer's decision to issue a permit over the agency's objections. The request must be made of the assistant secretary of the Army for Civil Works by comparable agency heads within EPA and the departments of Interior and Commerce. An elevation may be sought only if there has been insufficient agency coordination at the district level, if there is significant new information, or if policy issues of national importance are involved. The significance of the environmental impact of the permit is not in itself a permissible criteria on which to request elevation under the revised memoranda of agreement. The revised agreements also allow the assistant secretary of the Army for Civil Works to decide whether or not elevation to a higher level will be permitted. If it is permitted, the agreements provide for only one review, at whatever level the assistant secretary chooses.

All three resource agencies have experienced problems with the revised agreements, and EPA and FWS have sought to renegotiate their terms. The three agencies have the same major criticisms:

1. The agencies should be able to request elevation based on a permit's environmental impacts, not just on procedural and national policy criteria.

2. There should be an interim level of appeal at the division engineer/regional director or administrator level. The single-review policy has resulted in too many decisions on permits being made at the Washington level. In 16 months of operating under the revised agreement, FWS elevated 20 permits to the Washington level,* compared to three permits in the 26 months under the old agreement.

3. The assistant secretary of the Army should not have the unilateral right to refuse elevation requests. FWS reported that in roughly the first year under the revised agreement, the assistant secretary rejected nearly 40 percent of the FWS elevation requests.

One of the major effects of the revised agreements is that permit applicants and district engineers feel far less compelled to incorporate the mitigation recommendations of the natural resource agencies. Under the previous procedures, concern about potential delays if the permit were elevated was the only leverage that encouraged applicants to take steps to lessen or mitigate damages. With the new procedures that incentive has been removed.** The Corps agrees that the reduced threat of elevation has led to fewer mitigation requirements. In the Corps' view, however, under the previous agreement applicants were forced to agree to conditions that the Corps considered unreasonable or unnecessary simply in order to avoid further delays.

According to FWS, failure to resolve disagreements through negotiations has caused a sharp increase in the number of permit decisions that FWS believes warrant elevation, because adequate mitigation measures are not included. However, because FWS cannot elevate a permit on the grounds of its environmental impacts, the number of actual elevation requests has been reduced dramatically. Even those permits that have been elevated have not fared well in the resource agencies' opinions. In the first

---

*The total number of elevation requests, however, has gone down because of limitations imposed by the new memorandum of agreement, discussed below.

**FWS personnel report that the Army has in some cases advised permit applicants not to negotiate with the fish and wildlife agencies about such measures.

year under the new memorandum of agreement, the Corps issued all 15 permit applications that had been elevated successfully by FWS, resulting in the loss of 6,700 acres of wetlands.[65]

In addition, the resource agencies charge that the new procedures for elevation do not meet the regulatory reform goals of a more streamlined or predictable program. In the first year under the memorandum of agreement, FWS reported a 13-fold increase in the number of permit reviews that had to be conducted at the assistant secretarial level. Furthermore, FWS said that of 23 permits for which elevation was requested and rejected, four resulted in lawsuits and four resulted in EPA implementing its 404(c) authority to declare the site off-limits to discharges, an action rarely taken by EPA under the old memorandum of agreement. EPA officials say, however, that the increased use of its 404(c) authority also may be due to the high priority EPA began to place on the 404 program when William Ruckelshaus took over as EPA administrator in 1983.

Both FWS and EPA have requested renegotiation of their memoranda of agreement, but have made little progress. After more than two years of correspondence with the Corps failed in reaching an agreement, Interior Assistant Secretary G. Ray Arnett wrote the Corps in November 1984 saying, "It is now abundantly clear that further correspondence on this issue is pointless and that Army's regulatory program is so flawed, it is no longer a useable tool to adequately protect wetlands."[66] In June 1984, EPA proposed modifications to its memorandum of agreement and gave notice of intent to revoke the existing agreement in six months. The agreement had not been renegotiated at the end of 1984, but EPA and the Corps had agreed informally to continue operating under the existing agreement procedures on an interim basis. Although NMFS sees the value of a revised memorandum of agreement, agency officials have not requested renegotiation in light of the failure of FWS and EPA to make any headway on the issue.

Revisions to the Corps' Regulatory Program. Over the past several years, significant revisions have been made in Corps regulations for issuing 404 permits, and additional revisions are still pending. The process began in September 1980 when the Corps proposed revisions to incorporate changes made to Section 404 by the 1977 Clean Water Act, as well as by certain other laws, policy changes, and executive orders, and to expand the nationwide permit program. While the rules were pending, the Reagan administration came into office and the Task Force on Regulatory Relief began reviewing the 404 program. The rules were revised and issued as interim final regulations on July 22, 1982.[67] Major changes included the issuance of 27 nationwide permits, including permits for activities in all isolated wetlands and wetlands above the headwaters, and a number of changes to shorten the permit-issuance process.

In December 1982, 16 environmental groups, including the National Wildlife Federation, the National Audubon Society, and the Environmental Defense Fund, filed suit (*National Wildlife Federation v. Marsh*) seeking to revoke certain portions of the regulations that they said would substantially weaken federal protection of the nation's wetlands. While this suit was pending, the Corps on May 12, 1983, proposed another set of regulatory changes[68] that contained numerous provisions to implement the recommendations of the Task Force on Regulatory Relief.

The Corps and environmental groups reached an out-of-court settlement agreement in February 1984, and regulations implementing some of its provisions were issued in final form on October 5, 1984.[69] The agreement also addressed some of the issues in the May 1983 regulations even though these rules were only in proposed form and were not part of the initial suit. A number of the proposals made in the May 1983 rules, however, are still pending. The Corps plans to issue final rules on the remaining proposals in 1985. The major issues addressed in this regulatory battle are described below.

Nationwide Permits for Headwaters and Isolated Waters. The most prominent issue has been the Corps' issuance, in the July 1982 rules, of a nationwide permit for all discharges into two classes of waters: nontidal rivers, streams, and their lakes and impoundments, including adjacent wetlands, that are located above the headwaters (defined as having five cubic feet per second mean annual flow); and other nontidal waters and adjacent wetlands that are not part of a surface tributary system. Prior to this change, the Corps had required an individual permit for activities in isolated natural lakes and adjacent wetlands 10 acres or larger. According to FWS, dropping the 10-acre limitation removed the individual permit requirement from 700,000 to 900,000 acres of prairie potholes; one to two million acres of lakes and associated wetlands in Minnesota, Michigan, and Wisconsin; 150,000 to 200,000 acres of interior waters in Florida; 335,000 acres of wetlands adjacent to the Great Salt Lake in Utah; and 70 percent of the lakes in Alaska that are subject to 404, which provide breeding habitat for the vast majority of Pacific Flyway waterfowl. In addition, EPA estimated that 90,000 acres, 60 percent of the wetlands in the Pocono Mountains, and thousands of acres of inland freshwater wetlands in New Jersey and New York would fall under the new nationwide permit.

The environmental groups charged that Section 404(e) authorizes general permits only for categories of activities, not for classes of waters and wetlands, and then only if the activities will cause only minimal individual and cumulative adverse environmental effects, a determination that they said the Corps could not have reasonably made for all activities, regardless of size, in these varied waters.

The final rules issued as a result of the out-of-court settlement change the nationwide permit for isolated waters and headwaters to require an individual permit for activities that would cause the loss or substantial modification of 10 or more acres of water of the United States, including wetlands. In addition, the rules set up a special review process for discharges that will cause the loss or substantial adverse modification of one to 10 acres. Before conducting such an activity, the discharger must notify the Corps of Engineers. For activities proposed in areas of particular interest to EPA, FWS, NMFS, or the appropriate state natural resource agencies, the Corps must seek their views on whether to require an individual permit. If the Corps disagrees with the agency views, the division engineer must respond to the agency's comments in writing, but the permittee may be immediately notified that he can proceed under the nationwide permit. If the Corps decides the discharge would have more than minimal adverse environmental effects when viewed either separately or cumulatively, it must require an individual permit.*

The requirements for a pre-discharge notice for activities causing the loss or substantial adverse modification of one to 10 acres has the potential to strengthen protection for headwaters and isolated waters and wetlands, since such areas less than 10 acres in size were completely covered by a nationwide permit in previous rules, even prior to the 1982 revised regulations. The effectiveness of these requirements, however, will depend on their implementation by the Corps. So far, FWS officials charge, the program is not being implemented effectively. For example, two FWS regions have requested review of all pre-discharge notices in their area of jurisdiction, but the Corps has refused, saying the rules require that such notices be forwarded only

---

*The Corps rules grandfathered certain activities from these more stringent requirements for a period of up to 18 months. The environmental groups charged that this was a breach of the settlement agreement, which had not provided for grandfathering, but the court disagreed and the rules stand as is.

for specific classes of waters designated by the regional director, and that the director cannot specify all waters. In addition, FWS and EPA officials say the Corps has not made a concerted effort to publicize the pre-discharge notice requirement, nor has any guidance been issued to the field on implementing the new requirements. Corps officials say no real problems have arisen under the new provision so far and that guidance probably will be issued after it becomes apparent what types of situations need to be addressed.

Environmental Guidelines and the Water Dependency Test. Another major issue dealt with in the rules is the extent to which the Corps must follow the 404(b)(1) guidelines developed by EPA. A key issue of concern is the presumption against discharges in wetlands if practical alternatives are available, particularly for activities that are not water-dependent.

The 404(b)(1) guidelines were one of the issues targeted for review by the Task Force on Regulatory Relief. Related to this review, Assistant Secretary of the Army for Civil Works William Gianelli argued that the guidelines were advisory in nature rather than regulatory and requested the task force to reinterpret them as such. In addition, changes in both the 1982 and 1983 regulations raised questions as to how the Corps intended the guidelines to be applied. Although it was not part of the original lawsuit, this issue was addressed in the settlement agreement, and the resulting October 1984 rules require the Corps to deny a permit if it does not comply with the EPA guidelines, clearly making their application by the Corps mandatory.

However, the content of the EPA guidelines is still at issue. In May 1982, the Task Force on Regulatory Relief directed EPA and the Corps to work together to revise the guidelines in order to shorten and simplify their requirements. EPA was working on revisions to the guidelines when William Ruckelshaus took over as administrator at EPA in 1983, and 404 was identified as a high priority within the agency. Ruckelshaus said there was no indication that the guidelines were causing problems and that they should not be changed. The Army said that it would demonstrate that the guidelines cause unnecessary regulatory burdens, although no data have been produced to support this view. Thus, the guidelines remain unchanged.

Consultation and Mitigation. The July 1982 regulations forbade the Corps to require mitigation in 404 permits unless no local, state, or other programs or policies existed to achieve the objective. The October 1984 rules make it clear that the Corps must add conditions when necessary to satisfy legal requirements or to otherwise satisfy the public interest. In addition, the May 1983 regulations proposed dropping the requirement that the Corps give "great weight" to the views of federal and state fish and wildlife agencies in making permit decisions. The final rules use the Coordination Act language that these views be given "full consideration."

Redefining Wetlands. Another key change proposed by the May 1983 regulations was clarification of which wetlands are covered by the 404 permit program. The rules proposed to redefine three terms used to define wetlands: what constitutes a "prevalence of vegetation," when soils are considered "saturated," and what type of hydrologic connection constitutes wetlands that are "adjacent" to waters of the United States. According to the National Wildlife Federation, the proposed clarification could leave two-thirds of the nation's wetlands unregulated by 404, including bottomland hardwoods, wet tundra, freshwater marshes dominated by submerged plants, and shrub bogs such as North Carolina's pocosins.

This issue was not addressed in the settlement agreement or in the October 1984 rules and is not expected to be included in the remaining rules scheduled for issuance in 1985. The Corps cannot redefine wetlands without EPA concurrence. However, EPA does not agree with the Corps proposal, and no negotiations on the matter were under way at the end of 1984. The issue, however, is still considered a priority by the Corps and Office of Management and Budget, although Corps officials acknowledge that the 1983 proposal was problematic. In addition, the definition of wetlands will be at issue in an important case to be heard by the U.S. Supreme Court in 1985, *United States v. Riverside Bayview Homes, Inc.*, discussed in the legal developments section of this chapter.

Increased Responsibility to States. The administration has pursued two approaches to turn over more responsibility to the states in accordance with the recommendations of the Task Force on Regulatory Relief. Since 1982, the Corps has made a concerted effort to issue so-called state program general permits. These permits, sometimes referred to within the Corps as anti-duplication permits, are issued for activities and/or waters that are subject to some degree of regulation under existing state programs. To the extent that an activity is covered by a state-program general permit, it is exempted from obtaining a federal individual permit. If the state regulatory program does not include all the requirements of the federal 404 program, conditions are to be included in the general permit to address the discrepancies. The Army first directed its field offices to issue state-program general permits in late 1981, but few were issued before the task force issues its recommendations. Today, Corps officials estimate that perhaps 50 such permits have been issued in 35 states.

The state-program general permits were challenged in December 1982 by the 16 environmental groups in *National Wildlife Federation v. Marsh*. The suit said that at least 22 district engineers had proposed to issue state program general permits that would have removed all 404 permitting requirements for all activities within certain waters subject to state regulation. For example, the Corps proposed to issue a general authorization for dredge and fill activities in the coastal zone of Louisiana, since the Louisiana Department of Natural Resources administers a permit program in the coastal zone. The suit charged that these permits did not meet the requirements of 404(e) and that general permits authorize only activities that are similar in nature and have only minimal adverse impacts on the environment. The groups also charged that the issuance of the permits was not based on the 404(b)(1) environmental guidelines. The Corps made little headway on issuing such broad state-program general permits, and this count in the lawsuit was dismissed in the settlement agreement in February 1984. Corps officials say most state-program general permits that have been issued apply only to certain actions and only in certain waters.

The second aspect of handing more responsibility over to the states has to do with state adoption of the 404 program under Sections 404(g) through (l). These sections allow the states to assume 404 permit responsibility, subject to EPA approval, for all waters except tidal waters and adjacent wetlands and waters that presently are or potentially could be used for navigation and their adjacent wetlands. At the end of 1984, only one state, Michigan, had assumed 404 permit responsibility. The states have given several reasons for lack of interest in the program, including primarily lack of federal funds for conducting the program and lack of jurisdiction over tidal waters and adjacent wetlands. States also have criticized the requirements of the state-delegation regulations as being too burdensome.

In October 1984, EPA began to carry out the directive of the Task Force on Regulatory Relief to make it easier for states to assume the 404 program by proposing revisions to the state-delegation regulations. The rules require less detail when a state submits its program for approval, require less specificity in state general permits, reduce required information on state permit applications, and simplify federal oversight procedures. Environmental groups, including the National Wildlife Federation and the Environmental Defense Fund, have criticized the proposed changes. The federation said in comments to EPA that the revisions would limit the grounds on which EPA may veto a state permit and restrict the opportunity of other federal agencies to review permit applications, eliminate the requirement that state 404 agencies consult with the state wildlife agency on all wetland permit applications, remove the requirement that conditions mandating mitigation and restoration be included in permits where necessary, and more. The Corps, on the other hand, says the proposed rules do not go far enough in streamlining the delegation requirements and is seeking further revisions. Final state-delegation rules are expected to be issued by EPA in mid-1985.

Revisions to Corps NEPA Regulations. On January 11, 1984, the Corps proposed a set of regulatory changes[70] to its procedures for meeting the environmental assessment and environmental impact statement requirements of NEPA.[71] The environmental review requirements of NEPA apply to the issuance of 404 permits, and often the most controversial 404 permits require the preparation of an environmental impact statement that entails a more exhaustive investigation of project environmental impacts and alternatives than would otherwise be conducted in the 404 permit review. Thus the NEPA regulations make an important contribution to the effectiveness of the 404 program.

According to the notice of the proposed revisions, the purpose of the changes with regard to Corps regulatory activities was to make the rules consistent with the recommendation of the Presidential Task Force on Regulatory Relief, to reduce paperwork and delay, and to reduce unnecessary burdens on permit applications. The proposal was criticized sharply by environmental groups and EPA on a number of points. In response, the Corps made some revisions but planned to issue final regulations that still contained a number of controversial provisions. Prior to the issuance of the rules in final form, EPA referred the matter to the Council on Environmental Quality for resolution of the outstanding issues of concern between the Corps and EPA. EPA said the proposed revisions "would have an adverse effect on EPA's program . . . to prevent unacceptable adverse effects of dredge and fill discharges under Section 404 of the Clean Water Act."[72] EPA said the changes would increase the likelihood of coordination problems between EPA and the Corps and would necessitate increased EPA requests to elevate 404 permit decisions to the Washington level, as well as increased use of the 404(c) veto. EPA's position was supported by a number of conservation groups.

EPA's strongest objections are to two major proposed revisions. The Corps proposes to restrict the scope of its NEPA review to include an assessment of the environmental impacts of the specific activity for which the permit is being considered, not the entire project. This would mean, for example, that if the Corps received an application for constructing a pipeline as part of an oil-refinery construction project, it would consider the impacts of only the pipeline and not of the refinery.

Second, EPA objected to changes in guidance as to what constitute reasonable alternatives that must be analyzed in the NEPA process. Currently, Corps regulations interpret alternatives broadly, requiring, for example, that "the need for a water intake structure requiring a Corps permit as part of a fossil fuel power plant shall be stated as the need for energy and not be limited to the need for cooling water."[73] In contrast, EPA said the new guidance appears to "limit alternatives to the narrowest possible scope." EPA also objected to the elimination of specific requirements for analysis of alternatives to projects that are not water dependent.

Other Issues

Wetlands Assessments. One offshoot of the growing awareness that the 404 program and other federal conservation programs cannot adequately protect wetlands is the suggestion that wetland functions and values should be identified and wetland programs tailored to fit them accordingly. Several federal agencies have conducted some initial study in this area, and the Office of Technology Assessment focused heavily on the "tailoring" approach to wetland protection in its 1984 report, Wetlands: Their Use and Regulation.[74]

The Office of Technology Assessment report suggested a four-step program for tailoring and integrating federal wetlands policies:

1. Continue or accelerate FWS mapping of wetlands.

2. Categorize wetlands based on the combined importance of their ecological services and their intrinsic values, such as wilderness and aesthetics.

3. Tailor existing policies and programs according to the relative values of the wetlands and the values and impacts of the development. For example, under 404, individual permits could be required for high-value wetlands and general permits for those with lesser values. Some wetlands perhaps would be left unregulated.

4. Integrate wetlands policies and programs to address the full range of wetlands values. For example, acquisition and leasing programs, which currently focus on acquiring waterfowl habitat, could be given flexibility to acquire wetlands identified as having high value for other types of purposes.

The National Wetlands Technical Council, a private organization of scientists that was involved in the development and writing of the Office of Technology Assessment report, plans in 1985 to begin a series of regional workshops to assess wetlands functions and values and to identify important wetlands in each region. The goal of the assessment is to provide public agencies with the information they need to tailor wetland regulation on the basis of the value and importance of the wetland.

The concept of ranking wetlands by their significance is highly controversial. The idea has received some support from developers, who say it would help them know which wetlands are important and should be avoided. But many conservation groups and some wetland scientists and FWS personnel have expressed serious reservations about the approach — particularly about how the ranking would be done and if it would be accurate. Wetlands functions are varied and complex, and the process of ranking some types of values against others could prove extremely difficult. Another key concern is that ranking and tailoring decisions would be subject to political pressures and influence and would not be scientific. This could mean the undertaking of a complicated, controversial, and costly process that in the end could afford little or no more protection for wetlands, and possibly could result in less.

Because of these types of concerns, the Office of Technology Assessment suggested experimenting with targeting in small-scale pilot projects. The implementation of such an effort, if it gains support, first would require an assessment of wetlands values and would be several years away.

Removing Federal Incentives for Wetlands Destruction. Concern has been growing over the inconsistency of federal policies governing wetlands use. While the federal government moves to protect wetlands through acquisition and the 404 permit program, other federal programs and policies encourage their destruction. Both the administration and Congress have shown interest recently in attempting to address this issue.

The Emergency Wetlands Resources Act (H.R. 3282), which passed the House in 1984, would have required FWS to conduct a study and report to Congress on the impacts of federal wetlands policies and the potential impacts and benefits of revising them. This legislation failed to clear Congress, but in the meantime the administration had requested and Congress had appropriated some funds to carry out a more limited version of the study.

FWS has chosen the bottomland hardwood forests of the lower Mississippi alluvial plain as the focus of the study, primarily because of their high environmental value and rapid rate of loss. However, FWS expects the study's findings to be applicable to other areas. The programs to be analyzed include flood control and small watershed projects, agricultural assistance, and tax incentives, among others. The study will be used to develop a report to Congress, to be transmitted by the secretary with recommendations on establishing a consistent federal role with regard to wetlands. A draft of the study is expected to be completed in 1985.

Mitigation Banking. FWS and NMFS have begun to experiment with a new approach to mitigation called mitigation banking. In essence, the technique allows a developer to establish mitigation "credits" by such actions as managing a certain portion of his lands for wildlife, developing wildlife habitats, or contributing funds for the management of land owned by a wildlife conservation organization. These credits then can be used by the developer to compensate for unavoidable habitat losses from future development actions. For example, the first and most widely publicized mitigation banking project was undertaken by Tenneco in Louisiana. Tenneco established a system of weirs, dikes, and dams to maintain and enhance 5,000 acres of wetlands on land it currently owns. The credits from managing this area for wildlife are used to offset impacts from Tenneco's oil and gas activities in the area. At the end of 1984, FWS was involved in 13 such banks, and NMFS in two.

Mitigation banking can be attractive to developers, especially those that require repeated permit authorizations, because it speeds the approval of permit applications by allowing mitigation requirements to be met in advance in some cases. It also can provide benefits to wildlife in that a larger habitat area may be provided under the banking concept than might be established through piecemeal mitigation conditions attached to individual permits.

While almost everyone agrees that mitigation banking is beneficial in theory, some conservation groups and FWS officials are worried about how it may be applied in practice. They fear that the determination of how many wildlife credits the bank would provide relies too heavily on FWS Habitat Evaluation Procedures. Habitat evaluation has not been proved in the field to produce accurate predictions, and the quality of the evaluation varies depending on the skill of the person applying it. Problems also arise in crafting the specific agreements. For example, under the Tenneco agreements the company is guaranteed a certain number of credits from its bank whether or not the area actually produces anticipated wildlife benefits. In addition, Tenneco is required to manage the area intensively for only 25 years, at which time the area potentially could be reopened to development. Finally, it is possible that the existence of a bank and the offering of compensation lands could improperly influence permit-issuance decisions, perhaps resulting in decisions to allow destruction of wetlands in cases where it would be avoidable, allowing use of the bank credits when on-site mitigation would otherwise be called for, and so forth.

In recognition of these problems, FWS has issued interim guidance on mitigation banking specifying that determinations as to whether the bank can be used to offset specific habitat losses are to be made in accordance with the FWS Mitigation Policy[75] and specifying that the banks should be maintained for an appropriate length of time based in part on the life of the development project. In mid-1984, FWS directed its field offices to enter additional agreements only on a limited basis while FWS evaluates the success of the test cases. FWS has not adopted a formal position on the use of mitigation banks.

Legal Developments

Section 404 of the Clean Water Act has been the source of numerous lawsuits from all sides — citizens challenging permits issued, developers challenging permit denials, and the government enforcing permit requirements. The following discussion will focus on the most important recent decisions.

Courts reviewing cases under Section 404 have, by and large, affirmed broad authority, as well as broad discretion, in the secretary of the Army to implement that provision. With one notable exception, the courts have rejected attempts to limit Corps authority both under the statute and under the Constitution.

In perhaps the most important decision, *Avoyelles Sportsmen's League v. Marsh*,[76] 713 F.2d 897 (5th Cir. 1983), the Fifth Circuit enunciated a broad interpretation of Corps jurisdiction under the statute. At issue was the application of Section 404 to the clearing of 20,000 acres of bottomland hardwood forest for conversion to soybean production. Affirming the Corps demand that the landowner apply for a permit, the court upheld the broad definition of wetlands promulgated by the Corps and EPA, held that the proposed land-clearing operations were a "discharge of pollutants" for which a permit can be required, and further held that the conversion of forest to soybean fields was not exempt from the permit requirement as a normal farming activity under Section 404(f).*

The Fifth Circuit's broad application of Section 404 recently was extended by a District Court in New Jersey. In an enforcement action brought by the Corps, the court held that Section 404 protects all lands within Corps jurisdiction, even if the lands became wetlands because of man-made alterations.[77] Section 404 does not apply to wetlands created solely by Corps river-maintenance projects.

In perhaps the most startling decision under Section 404, the Sixth Circuit recently broke ranks with the *Avoyelles* decision, imposing new limitations on Corps jurisdiction. In *United States v. Riverside Bayview Homes*,[78] the Corps and the district court had found that the lands in question fell within the Corps definition of wetlands, which includes "those areas that are inundated or saturated by surface or ground water at a frequency and duration sufficient to support . . . a prevalence of vegetation typically adapted for life in saturated soil conditions," and thus was subject to Section 404. The court of appeals reversed. Although the regulation includes areas that are "inundated or saturated by surface or ground water," the Sixth Circuit held that Section 404 applies only if the government can demonstrate that the land is "frequently flooded [by adjacent streams or seas] and that the flooding causes aquatic vegetation to grow there." The Supreme Court has agreed to review the Sixth Circuit's decision.[79]

Where a permit is required, the courts have given similarly broad scope to Corps review of the proposed project. Most notably, in *Riverside Irrigation District v. Andrews*,[80]** the court held that, in its review of a dam under Section 404, the Corps may consider harm to whooping cranes 250 miles downstream in another state caused

---

*For similarly strict interpretations of the agricultural exemptions of Section 404(f), see *United States v. Huebner*, 752 F.2d 1235 (7th Cir. 1985); *United States v. Akers* (Civ. No. S-84-1276 RAR) (E.D. Cal. Jan. 15, 1985) (Findings of Fact and Conclusions of Law; Order Granting Preliminary Injunction).

**This case is discussed in more detail in the chapter on endangered species and under Legislation, below.

by reduction in stream flows due to operation of the dam. Thus the court affirmed that in making 404 permit decisions the Corps may consider not only water quality, but also water quantity, and effects not only on the site, but also off the site.

Legislation

Amendments to Section 404. Representative James J. Howard (D-New Jersey), chairman of the Committee on Public Works and Transportation, included two amendments to Section 404 in his package of amendments to the Clean Water Act (H.R. 3282) introduced in June 1983. One amendment arose out of concerns that the Corps was trying to reverse the presumption against granting a 404 permit. The amendment would have incorporated into the Clean Water Act the requirement currently contained in EPA environmental guidelines that a permit be denied unless the discharge will not have an an unacceptable adverse impact on the aquatic environment and that there is no practicable alternative with fewer adverse effects.

The second amendment was prompted by the changes in the memoranda of agreement (discussed earlier) between the Corps and EPA, FWS, and NMFS regarding permit review and elevation. The amendment specified how the review and elevation were to be conducted. It provided the resource agencies with a longer review period, required the Corps to review the district engineer's permit decision if the resource agencies so requested, and returned permit review to the division engineer rather than to the assistant-secretarial level.

Both amendments were dropped from the bill before it was reported by the committee in June 1984, in part because the Corps by that time had agreed under its settlement of *National Wildlife Federation v. Marsh* to deny a permit if it did not meet the 404(b)(1) guidelines. No further amendments to 404 were considered as part of the Clean Water Act amendments in the 98th Congress. Congress failed to complete action on the Clean Water Act, and it will be under consideration again in the 99th Congress.

State Water Rights and 404. In August 1983, Senator Malcolm Wallop (R-Wyoming) announced that he intended to offer an amendment to Section 404 of the Clean Water Act to keep the Corps and EPA from considering the effects of water diversions allowed under state water rights when determining whether to issue a 404 permit. The impetus for this amendment was a District Court ruling, *Riverside Irrigation District v. Andrews,** that upheld a Corps of Engineers decision to deny a 404 general permit for the construction of a dam on a tributary of the South Platte River in Colorado.

The Corps had determined that the withdrawal of water from the South Platte to fill the dam's reservoir would reduce the flow of water in the river, adversely affecting whooping crane habitat some 250 to 300 miles downstream. FWS determined the issuance of the permit would violate Section 7 of the Endangered Species Act, which prohibits federal actions that could jeopardize the continued existence of an endangered species.

The Corps said the project could proceed under the general permit only if the project sponsors agreed to meet certain conditions intended to protect crane habitat. Otherwise it would require the sponsors to file for an individual permit. Wallop maintained that the Corps permit denial violated the state's right to allocate water as it sees fit for "beneficial use."

---

*Decision upheld by Fifth Circuit Court of Appeals on March 26, 1985. See section on legal developments.

Wallop, however, never did introduce such an amendment. Instead, Wallop attached an amendment to the FY 1985 Interior appropriations bill directing the secretary of the Interior to work with other federal and state agencies to study the cumulative effects of water resource development activities on endangered species in the Upper Colorado and Platte River basins and to develop plans to protect both endangered species and state water rights. The amendment was dropped from the bill on the ground that the secretary already had sufficient authority to undertake such a study, although language was retained in the conference report urging the secretary to do so. The issue may arise again in 1985, but the Western water interests are more likely to try to solve their problem by amending the Endangered Species Act than by amending 404, since it was the former law that forced the Corps to deny the permit.

WETLANDS ACQUISITION

The federal government began purchasing wetlands in the 1930s and today holds several million acres of wetlands in fee and in easement for conservation purposes. The two major sources of acquisition are discussed in this section: the Migratory Bird Conservation Fund, which has been the primary funding source; and the Land and Water Conservation Fund, which has funded a variety of federal acquisitions for conservation purposes, including some wetlands. This section also covers the Water Bank program, through which the federal government protects wetlands from development or conversion by leasing them from private landowners.

Migratory Bird Conservation Fund

The Migratory Bird Conservation Fund is the primary vehicle for federal wetlands acquisition. Since 1934, 3.6 million acres of wetlands have been acquired by FWS under the fund, either in fee or easement. Nearly two-thirds of the total, about 2.3 million acres, have been acquired since the wetlands acquisition program was accelerated in 1961 with passage of the Wetlands Loan Act.[81] All lands acquired with the fund become part of the National Wildlife Refuge System.

Monies for the migratory bird fund are derived primarily from two sources: proceeds from the sale of migratory bird hunting stamps (duck stamps) and appropriations made under the Wetlands Loan Act.* Duck stamp revenues come primarily from waterfowl hunters, who are required to purchase a federal duck stamp in addition to their state hunting license. Since 1934, sale of more than 88 million duck stamps has yielded receipts of $284.4 million, although these funds generally were not used for acquisition until 1958. The Wetlands Loan Act, which authorizes appropriations of up to $200 million, has provided $175.1 million for land acquisition since 1961, leaving $24.9 million of the loan still available. These advances are to be paid back using 75 percent of the annual duck stamp receipts starting in 1987. This would reduce the duck stamp funds available for land acquisition, but it is likely that legislation will be introduced in the 99th Congress to forgive repayment of the loan.

The decision of what lands will be purchased with Migratory Bird Conservation Fund dollars is made by the FWS director in consultation with the associate directors, the Division of Realty, and the FWS Office of Migratory Bird Management. However, refuges purchased with the Migratory Bird Conservation Fund must be approved by the Migratory Bird Conservation Commission upon recommendation by the secretary

---

*Additional information on these funds can be found in chapter on migratory birds.

of the Interior. The commission also must approve prices paid for individual tracts.

It is FWS policy to acquire lands only when they are insufficiently protected by other means, such as regulation or local zoning. FWS uses an informal evaluation system in choosing lands to be acquired. In general, to be considered for acquisition an area must be valuable nesting, breeding, or feeding habitat, must face an imminent threat, and must be available from a willing seller. However, lands can be acquired through condemnation in order to prevent irreparable damage to an existing FWS unit or to important resources. A new acquisition policy currently is being drafted by FWS in order to give the process greater quantification and will be used on a trial basis to identify areas for acquisition in the 1987 budget.

The fund is used to acquire three types of waterfowl habitat: breeding, migration, and wintering habitat. Most of the acreage acquired since acquisition was accelerated in 1962* — 1.8 million of the 2.3 million acres, 80 percent, is breeding habitat. Wintering habitat totals 375,000 acres (17 percent) and migration habitat 64,000 acres (three percent). Wintering and migration areas become wildlife refuges. Breeding habitat is classified either as a refuge or a waterfowl production area.

Although the Migratory Bird Conservation Fund has been responsible for protecting more than two million acres of wetlands, it has fallen far short of its goals in recent years. In 1959, FWS, working with the states and the International Association of Fish and Wildlife Agencies, determined that a minimum of 12.5 million acres of waterfowl habitat needed to be protected under public ownership in order to maintain waterfowl populations at existing levels. The federal responsibility for habitat acquisition was placed at eight million acres, including 3.5 million already owned or managed by FWS, and the state share at 4.5 million acres, including two million already owned by the states. In 1976, FWS determined that 1.9 million acres of the federal government's share remained to be acquired, and it set a goal of completing this acquisition by 1986. Through 1984, only about 382,000 acres had been acquired, less than 20 percent of the target.

Land and Water Conservation Fund

The Land and Water Conservation Fund provides funding for the majority of federal land acquisition for conservation purposes, but is of only secondary significance for wetlands acquisition. While the Migratory Bird Conservation Fund can be used only by FWS, the Land and Water Conservation Fund also allows acquisitions by the other major land managing agencies — the National Park Service, the Forest Service, and the Bureau of Land Management — for which wetlands acquisition is often a lower priority. Furthermore, FWS uses Land and Water Conservation Fund monies to acquire a variety of land types, not just wetlands.

Land and Water Conservation Fund monies are made up of revenues from several sources, including proceeds from federal surplus property sales, certain user fees, and $1 million from the motorboat fuels tax. To the extent that these revenues do not add up to the $900 million annual ceiling authorized for the fund, miscellaneous receipts from offshore oil and gas activities are added to the fund. Unlike the Migratory Bird Conservation Fund, monies in the Land and Water Conservation Fund can be expended only when appropriated by Congress.

Acquisitions under the Land and Water Conservation Fund are not broken down specifically for wetlands, so precise wetlands acquisition figures under Land and

---

*Separate figures on breeding, wintering, and migratory habitat were not kept prior to 1962.

Water Conservation Fund are not available. FWS does most of the wetlands acquisition accomplished under the fund. The fund provides FWS with monies for the acquisition of threatened and endangered species habitat, other important fish and wildlife habitat, and congressionally authorized refuges. Within FWS, the decision of what lands to recommend for purchase with Land and Water Conservation Fund monies follows the same informal criteria used for Migratory Bird Conservation Fund monies. Value, threat, and availability must be considered, and fee acquisition is to be used only as a last resort. Land and Water Conservation Fund monies cannot be used to purchase migratory waterfowl habitat authorized for acquisition under the Migratory Bird Conservation Act.

Not all Land and Water Conservation Fund monies appropriated in a given year are spent that same year, often due to owner unwillingness to sell or the time required to start up a project. Such monies are carried forward to following years. Should FWS desire to spend funds in other than the manner appropriated, it may internally re-program amounts less than $100,000. Expenditure of amounts greater than this must be approved by the congressional appropriations committees before they can be spent on some other project.

As of 1984, more than $318 million in Land and Water Conservation Fund monies had been appropriated to FWS. These funds were used as follows: approximately $136 million were spent to acquire endangered species habitat; $107 million were appropriated specifically for acquiring land for new refuges; and $36 million went to purchase additions to existing areas. FWS used an additional $30 million to purchase new refuges through standing authority under the Fish and Wildlife Act of 1956. The remaining $9 million went for the acquisition of deficiencies and contingencies and for acquisition management.[82]

In 1984, FWS acquired more than 164,000 acres under the Land and Water Conservation Fund, compared to an average of nearly 14,000 acres per year between 1967 and 1983. The large number in 1984 represents increased funding from congressional add-ons and the donation of 120,000 acres at Alligator River, North Carolina. For 1985, Congress appropriated $63.2 million, the largest single-year total FWS has ever had. When combined with the $39 million in carry-over funds from 1984, this gives FWS $102 million in Land and Water Conservation Fund monies in 1985.

The Water Bank Program

The Water Bank Program, administered by the Agricultural Stabilization and Conservation Service of the Department of Agriculture, is the only major federal wetlands preservation program outside FWS. Like the Migratory Bird Conservation Fund, the primary purpose of the Water Bank is to preserve and improve wetlands as habitat for migratory waterfowl, but unlike both the Migratory Bird Fund and the Land and Water Conservation Fund, the Water Bank makes no outright acquisitions. Instead, the secretary of Agriculture enters into agreements with farmers to preserve wetlands and adjacent uplands on their lands.

When a person enters into an agreement under the Water Bank Program, he agrees not to burn, drain, fill or otherwise destroy the area's wetland characteristics. In return, the Agricultural Stabilization and Conservation Service makes annual payments to the owner or operator at a rate determined at the time of agreement. Agreements are for 10 years and can be renewed. At the beginning of an agreement, cost-sharing payments are available, if needed, to install conservation measures for the following purposes: to establish or maintain shallow-water areas and improve habitat; to conserve surface water, contribute to flood control, and improve subsurface moisture; and to provide bottomland hardwood management.

The Water Bank program operates only in states and counties designated by the Agricultural Stabilization and Conservation Service deputy administrator for State and County Operations in consultation with FWS. These generally are regions with the most important waterfowl breeding and wintering habitat. The program operates primarily in the northern part of the Central Flyway and the northern and southern portions of the Mississippi Flyway. In total, 169 counties in Arkansas, California, Louisiana, Minnesota, Mississippi, Montana, Nebraska, North Dakota, South Dakota, and Wisconsin participate in the program.

The Water Bank is administered through farmers elected to Agricultural Stabilization and Conservation Service county committees, which are authorized to approve Water Bank agreements on behalf of the secretary of Agriculture. The county committees monitor program activities and issue annual and cost-sharing payments to participants. The administrator of the Agricultural Stabilization and Conservation Service is in charge of general administration, with the Soil Conservation Service providing planning and technical assistance.

To enter into an agreement under the Water Bank program, an individual must file a request with the local Agricultural Stabilization and Conservation Service county committee and must agree to designate a specified amount of his acreage under the agreement. Generally, the minimum amount is 10 acres, including at least two acres of year-round wetlands. In addition to wetlands, adjacent uplands deemed "essential for nesting, breeding, or feeding of migratory waterfowl" within a quarter mile of a designated wetland also are eligible for the program. The adjacent acreage may not exceed four times the designated wetlands for a given unit. The Soil Conservation Service must certify that the acreage designated by the farmer constitutes a viable wetland unit, contains sufficient adjacent land to protect the wetland, and provides essential nesting, breeding, or feeding habitat for migratory waterfowl. Less than 10 acres can be entered into the program upon recommendation by the Soil Conservation Service.

In 1984, annual payments to farmers in the program ranged from $8 to $66 per acre, for an average payment of $16 per acre. Payment rates are subject to review and can be revised after four years and again upon renewal. An agreement can be renewed an unlimited number of times. Since the program's inception in 1972, the 1972, 1973, and 1974 agreements have expired. The renewal rate for 1972 agreements was 46 percent; for 1973, 58 percent; and for 1974, 50 percent. As of September 30, 1984, 5,642 agreements were in force, covering 629,628 acres. Roughly a third of the acreage under agreement is wetlands. The remainder is adjacent uplands.

Funding for the Water Bank comes from direct congressional appropriations. From 1972 through 1985, Congress appropriated almost $130 million for the program. From 1972 to 1981, the program was funded at an annual rate of $10 million, but in 1982 this dropped to $8.8 million, where it has remained through 1985. At this level of funding, the Agricultural Stabilization and Conservation Service cannot even renew all expiring agreements. The agency estimates that in 1985 the cost of renewing all 1976 expiring contracts alone would run $9 million. With the limited amounts of funding available in the last few years, it also has been impossible to honor all requests for new agreements. Thus under current appropriation levels the Water Bank has reached its capacity at 630,000 acres.

Overall Acquisition Trends

Federal wetlands acquisition has slowed significantly during the past four years, with a dramatic drop since the 1960s, when acquisition with funds advanced under the Wetlands Loan Act was most active. From 1981 to 1984, acquisition under the

Migratory Bird Conservation Fund averaged about 28,000 acres per year, a 58-percent drop from the previous four-year annual average of 67,000 acres, and an 81-percent drop from the 10-year average between 1961 and 1972 of 146,000 acres per year. Even when FWS acquisition under the Land and Water Conservation Fund, which only partly funds wetlands acquisition, is taken into account, total FWS acquisition has dropped substantially: from 95,525 acres per year from 1977 to 1980 to 52,903 acres per year from 1981 to 1984, a 44-percent drop.

This reduction stems from a significant decline in appropriations under the Wetlands Loan Act and from a rapid rise in land prices that have further decreased the buying power of these limited funds. Money appropriated by Congress under the Wetlands Loan Act went from $15 million in 1980 to only $1.25 million in 1981. Appropriations remained below $2 million until 1984, when Congress appropriated $7 million. In 1985, however, Congress appropriated $21.3 million under the Wetlands Loan Act, the highest single appropriation ever. The average cost of acquiring refuge lands in fee was $668 per acre from 1981 to 1984, up 83 percent from the average cost of $365 per acre for the previous four-year period. Looking at the same time frames, the cost of acquiring refuge easements rose 34 percent, from $247 to $329. The cost of acquiring waterfowl production areas in fee rose 13 percent, from $395 to $448. The cost of acquiring easements rose 65 percent, from $127 per acre to $210. Since 1962, easement costs have increased 34-fold, fee acquisition costs have increased 1,400 percent, and refuge fee acquisition costs have increased 500 percent. During this same period, the cost of a duck stamp has increased a comparatively low 250 percent, from $3 in 1959 to $5 in 1972 to $7.50 today.

For 1985, Congress has broken the pattern of lowered wetland-acquisition funds. It appropriated $21.3 million to the Migratory Bird Conservation Fund under the Wetlands Loan Act and $63.2 million under the Land and Water Conservation Fund. Both were record high appropriations from these funding sources. This one-time increase, however, can have only limited effect. Without legislation to provide new sources of funds for wetlands acquisition and/or a strong federal commitment to appropriating increased funds over an extended time period, little hope exists for making timely, significant progress on the wetlands acquisition program. Only $24.9 million remain available for appropriation under the Loan Act. Duck stamp receipts continue to lose their buying power as land prices rise, and even these limited funds may have to be used instead to pay back advances made under the Loan Act if Congress does not forgive the loan. Furthermore, although the Land and Water Conservation Fund could provide an important source of funds for additional wetlands acquisition, the administration has proposed a moratorium on its use from 1986 to 1988 as a deficit-reduction measure, and any significant expansion of Land and Water Conservation Fund appropriations for wetlands seems unlikely.

The 98th Congress considered but did not pass two measures that could increase wetlands acquisition or protection: the Emergency Wetlands Resources Act (H.R. 3082 and S. 1329), which would have authorized up to $100 million for federal and state wetlands acquisition and conservation projects, and H.R. 5900, which would have provided tax credits for private landowners who protect or enhance wetlands and other tax benefits for the donation of wetlands conservation easements. These bills are discussed further in the chapter on migratory birds.

RESOURCE STATUS

In spite of the various federal efforts to protect wetlands, a substantial portion of the nation's wetlands have been destroyed. FWS estimates that in the mid-1970s less than half of the nation's original wetland acreage remained and that losses were occurring at a rate of about 458,000 acres per year. And although no good data exists on wetlands losses during the decade since implementation of the 404 permit program, FWS wetlands experts say they have no cause to believe that the rate of loss has been reduced substantially.

The best available data on the status of wetlands is the status and trends analysis of the FWS National Wetlands Inventory completed in 1982.[83] According to FWS estimates,* in 1974 the lower 48 states contained approximately 99 million acres of wetlands, an area about the size of California and representing five percent of the land surface in the contiguous United States. About 94 percent of these are inland fresh-water wetlands, over half of which are forested. The remaining six percent, 5.2 million acres, are saltwater coastal wetlands. Estimates of Alaska's wetlands resources vary, but probably 200 million acres exist.

In certain areas, the losses have been even more extreme.** For example, California has lost 90 percent of its wetlands, and Iowa is reported to have less than five percent of its natural wetlands remaining. In the bottomland hardwood forests of the lower Mississippi alluvial plain, approximately 80 percent of the wetlands have been lost. Michigan, Minnesota, Louisiana, North Dakota, and Connecticut have lost more than half of all or certain types of their wetlands. Data for Ohio, Indiana, and Illinois are inadequate to be sure of the amount of loss, but these states probably have lost more than half their wetland resource.

In some areas, much of this loss occurred from the mid-1800s to the early 1900s due to the passage of the Swamp Land Acts of 1849, 1850, and 1860, which granted 65 million acres of wetlands to 15 states for reclamation. But wetlands continue to be destroyed at a significant rate today, particularly in certain areas.

According to the FWS trends analysis, from the mid-1950s to the mid-1970s 11 million acres of wetlands were lost, an average annual loss rate of approximately 550,000 acres. The highest proportional loss was from inland wetlands, which accounted for 97 percent of the reduction. This included losses of 400,000 acres in coastal marshes and mangroves, six million acres of forested wetlands — both bottomland hardwoods and pocosins — 4.7 million acres of inland marshes, and 400,000 acres of shrub wetlands. Wetlands conversion in coastal areas occurred at a rate of about 25 percent less than inland conversion rates.

During the same period, some wetlands gains were made. Some 200,000 acres were gained in unvegetated inland wetland flats and 2.1 million acres in inland ponds, primarily because of farm-pond construction, with about a quarter of this occurring at the expense of forested and emergent wetlands. Taking these increases into account, FWS reports a net wetlands loss of nine million acres from the mid-1950s to the mid-1970s, or an average wetlands loss of 458,000 acres yearly — 440,000 acres of inland wetlands and 18,000 of coastal wetlands.

The proportion of wetlands and the percentage of loss vary considerably in different regions. Much of the data on regional loss, especially in the West, is weak,

---

*These findings are based on a statistical survey of United States wetlands in the mid-1950s and mid-1970s, conducted using conventional air photointerpretation techniques. Although estimates of the original amount of wetland acreage vary, the best data suggest that approximately 50 percent of the wetlands in the lower 48 had been lost by 1974.[84] FWS estimates 215 million acres of wetlands originally existed, which would mean that 56 percent had been lost by the mid-1970s.

**Data on historical losses is from the FWS status and trends report previously cited, which compiled findings from a variety of scientific papers and is of varying accuracy.

Percentage of Vegetated Wetland Loss to Different Uses by Physiographic Region[a] (mid-1950s to mid-1970s

Region	Agriculture	Urban	Other	Water/ nonvegetated
1. Atlantic coastal zone[b]	5	36	5	54
2. Gulf coastal zone[c]	1	19	2	78
3. Atlantic coastal flats[b]	89	6	2(+)	3
4. Gulf coastal flats[c]	66	19	4(+)	11
5. Gulf-Atlantic rolling plain	84	3	4(+)	9
6. Lower Mississippi Alluvial Plain	90	3	3(+)	4
7. Eastern highlands	38	22	5(+)	35
8. Dakota-Minnesota drift and lake bed flats	83	1	4(+)	12(+)
9. Upper Midwest	71	8	3(+)	18
10. Central	63	5	15(+)	17(+)
11. Rocky Mountains	71	0	19(+)	10(+)
12. Intermontane	88	1	7(+)	4(+)
13. Pacific mountains	87	1	7(+)	5

[a](+)indicates there was a net gain in wetland from the use category in the region. If (+) is not indicated, then there was a net loss from that use category.
[b]Atlantic regions do not include Florida.
[c]Gulf regions include Florida.
Source: Wetlands: Their Use and Regulation, OTA, 1984. Original data from FWS National Wetland Trends Study, 1983.

but may indicate potential trouble spots. According to an Office of Technology Assessment analysis of FWS data by physiographic region, wetlands loss in five regions exceeds the national average proportional to the amount of wetlands the regions contain:* the lower Mississippi alluvial plain (which had the highest loss rate of any region), the Gulf coastal states of Texas and Louisiana, the Gulf Atlantic rolling plain, the Pacific mountains, and the Intermontane region (primarily Nevada and Arizona). Looking at state-by-state figures, the heaviest acreage losses in this 20-year period were in Louisiana, Arkansas, Mississippi, Minnesota, Michigan, Wisconsin, Illinois, Alabama, North Carolina, Florida, Georgia, South Carolina, Maryland, New Jersey, Delaware, South Dakota, North Dakota, Nebraska, and Texas.

According to FWS, agricultural conversion was responsible for 87 percent of this loss. Urban development was responsible for eight percent, and other development for the remaining five percent. Agricultural conversion is particularly a threat to inland wetlands, accounting for 80 percent of the loss of freshwater wetlands from the mid-1950s to the mid-1970s, according to the Office of Technology Assessment.[85] The remainder of inland wetland loss came from urbanization, the construction of impoundments and large reservoirs, and other causes such as mining, forestry, and road

*Standard error on much of this data is high.

construction. For coastal wetlands, most of the loss came from activities that converted these wetlands to deeper water — such as dredging for marinas, canals, and port development — and to a lesser extent from shoreline erosion. The remaining coastal wetlands losses were caused by urbanization, the disposal of dredged material or beach creation, natural or man-induced conversion to freshwater wetlands, and agriculture. Agriculture was responsible for the majority of wetlands losses in all but three regions: the Atlantic and Gulf coastal zones and the Eastern highlands.

No comprehensive survey of wetlands losses has been made since the mid-1970s. FWS believes its 458,000-acre net annual loss figure (550,000-acre gross loss) is the best estimate of current wetlands losses. The 1984 Office of Technology Assessment's report estimated that the current rate of wetland loss is about 300,000 acres yearly in gross losses — about half the 550,000 acre-per-year gross loss rate — but the Office of Technology Assessment's analysis has been criticized strongly by FWS personnel. The analysis was based on Department of Agriculture records of technical and financial assistance for farmland drainage. FWS scientists charge that this data does not include drainage done without technical assistance; off-farm activities such as channelization, diking, and water projects which drain wetlands or prevent their flooding; and non-agricultural drainage activities.

In the popular version of the status and trends report,[86] FWS identified nine problem areas where wetlands are in greatest jeopardy from the standpoint of the national interest. Data used in identifying these areas came from the trends survey as well as a review of current scientific literature. These are areas of high resource value that need special attention to stem further serious losses. These areas are discussed below.*

Forested Wetlands of the Lower Mississippi Alluvial Plain. Only 20 percent of these most important bottomland hardwood wetlands remain today. These forested wetlands provide wintering habitat for millions of migratory birds, especially mallards and wood ducks; serve as spawning and nursery grounds for numerous fin fishes; support a variety of mammals; play a vital role in flood reduction; and trap pesticides, herbicides, and sediment from adjacent agricultural lands. Since the 1950s, the primary cause of wetland loss in this area has been agricultural conversion to grow soybeans. Short-term economic returns on farming in this area are so much higher than returns for forestry that conversion is expected to continue. The federal government, through construction of Corps of Engineers flood-control projects, has fostered much of this drainage. In addition, in the past the Corps of Engineers considered only a limited amount of this area to be wetlands under the 404 permit program and failed to require permits for clearing for agricultural conversion. Court decisions favoring the broader EPA delineation of wetlands and requiring the Corps to regulate certain land-clearing activities could help slow this loss.

Estuarine Wetlands of the Coastal Zone. The rate of loss of coastal wetlands — highly valuable for commercial and recreational fisheries — increased from an historical rate of two-tenths of a percent yearly to half a percent yearly from the mid-1950s to the mid-1970s. More than half the coastal wetlands in the lower 48 states have been destroyed, with the most serious losses occurring in five states: California, Florida, Louisiana, New Jersey, and Texas. Outside of Louisiana, coastal wetlands losses are related directly to population density: more than 90 percent of the losses are caused by urbanization. The 404 permit program and the state regulatory programs provide some protection for these areas, although the degree of protection varies from Corps district to Corps district.

---

*All data in these examples are from the status and trends report.

Louisiana's Coastal Marshes. Louisiana coastal marshes comprise roughly a third of the coastal marshes in the lower 48 states and support Louisiana's multi-million-dollar commercial inshore shrimp fishery. These marshes are being lost to a combination of natural and man-induced factors at a rate of 25,000 acres — 40 square miles — per year. Coastal subsidence, a rise in sea level, and the cyclical processes of Mississippi River delta growth and deterioration represent the major natural forces, but these problems are aggravated by human interference. For example, the Corps of Engineers is controlling Mississippi and Red River flows into the Atchafalaya River, reducing the potential for natural marsh building. Other human impacts include channelization and levee construction on the Mississippi, canal dredging, and subsidence from extraction of groundwater, minerals, and oil and gas.

Chesapeake Bay's Submerged Aquatic Beds. The largest estuary in the United States, the Chesapeake Bay provides important wintering grounds for several species of waterfowl and vital spawning areas for estuarine-dependent fish. The sea-grass beds that support these uses have been declining since the 1960s and declined in the Maryland portion of the bay by almost 65 percent from 1971 to 1978. Declining populations of canvasback and redhead ducks as well as striped bass have been attributed in part to the loss of sea-grass beds. Natural stresses, such as hurricanes and disease, in addition to industrial and municipal sewage, agricultural and urban runoff, and channelization in nearby bottomland-hardwood wetlands, have contributed to the problem. EPA has established a Chesapeake Bay program to address the problem and the governors of Maryland, Virginia, and Pennsylvania have joined together to address water-quality problems in the Chesapeake Bay watershed. In 1984, Maryland established a Critical Areas Commission that will establish regulatory criteria for land development, setting aside inadequately regulated areas within the bay, its tributaries, and adjacent lands, including wetlands.

South Florida's Palustrine Wetlands. South Florida encompasses a 9,000-square-mile area of lakes, rivers, and wetlands extending from Orlando to the Keys. These wetlands provide breeding and wintering grounds for numerous bird species and support a number of endangered and threatened species. In addition, freshwater runoff from the area helps maintain the salinity balance of estuaries that support 85 percent of South Florida's offshore fishery. Channelization has destroyed 40,000 acres of wetlands and facilitated drainage of more than 100,000 acres of adjacent wetlands.

A massive Corps flood control project has encouraged wetlands destruction for agricultural and urban use, disrupted the sheet flow of water through Everglades National Park, and brought the threat of saltwater intrusion into freshwater wetlands areas. As a result, fish nurseries in estuaries have been disrupted, colonial wading-bird populations have declined from about 1.5 million in 1935 to 250,000 today, and alligators have been eliminated in many areas. Some scientists have suggested that wetlands losses have altered local rainfall patterns, causing recent severe droughts. Recently the state has embarked on a multi-million-dollar program to save the Everglades, including the acquisition of 250,000 acres of wetlands, and the Nature Conservancy and National Audubon Society have been acquiring wetlands as well.

Prairie Pothole Region Emergent Wetlands. The prairie potholes, extending from south-central Canada to the north-central United States, are the continent's most valuable inland marshes for waterfowl production. About a third of the potholes are in the United States, but they have been depleted seriously. In North and South Dakota they are down from seven million acres to three million acres. Ninety-nine percent of Iowa's prairie potholes have been lost, and nine million acres have been drained in Minnesota. Prairie potholes continue to be destroyed at a rate of 33,000 acres per year, primarily due to agricultural drainage and other agricultural activities. This is a high-priority area for FWS wetlands acquisition, but acquisition has slowed in recent years — in the early 1980s because a North Dakota state law, eventually overturned by the Supreme Court, prohibited FWS acquisition, and more recently because of reduced wetlands acquisition funds. Prairie potholes also have received limited and irregular protection under the 404 permit program because the Corps policy on regulation of isolated wetlands has been in dispute.

Wetlands of Nebraska's Sandhills and Rainwater Basin. Wetlands in these areas are important for 2.5 million migratory ducks and geese. They provide staging areas for 90 percent of the mid-continent's white-fronted geese and for 80 percent of the continent's sandhill cranes. This area also provides roosting habitat for the endangered whooping crane. Fifteen percent of the Sandhills wetlands have been lost to drainage, filling, and reduced groundwater levels. Reduced water flows in the Platte River, caused by upstream diversions, have reduced the river's channel width by 80 to 90 percent in many areas, destroying sandhill crane roosting areas. This has caused crowding at remaining roost sites, increasing crane susceptibility to catastrophic losses from storms or disease. In the Rainwater Basin, only 10 percent of the original 94,000 acres of wetlands remain. The rest have been lost primarily to agriculture. The resulting crowding of ducks and geese in this area actually has caused massive outbreaks of disease. Eighty-thousand waterfowl died in 1980, and breeding populations have been so reduced that the Nebraska Game and Parks Commission has discontinued its aerial breeding-bird survey. Water-rights disputes, lower funding for the Water Bank, and reduced effectiveness of 404 have all contributed to the problem.

North Carolina's Pocosins. These evergreen forested and scrub-shrub wetlands provide important habitat for many animals, including black bears. In addition, because they are linked with riverine and estuarine systems, they help stabilize water quality and balance salinity in coastal waters, thus playing a key role in maintaining productive estuaries for commercial and recreational fisheries. Most of the loss of these wetlands has occurred in recent years, caused primarily by agriculture, forestry, and peat mining. The pocosins in North Carolina have been reduced from an historical level of 2.5 million acres to one million acres. If the trend continues, resulting changes in estuarine salinity patterns may adversely affect North Carolina's multi-million-dollar commercial fishery. Corps regulation of these wetlands under the 404 permit program has been inconsistent, and the National Wildlife Federation currently is suing the Corps for failing to assert jurisdiction over a large pocosin.

Western Riparian Wetlands. Throughout the arid and semi-arid West, lands along the margins of ponds and lakes and in the floodplains of streams provide essential habitat for a large variety of wildlife. A disproportionate number of birds, mammals, and fish depend on these limited, moist zones for food, cover, water, and migration routes. Riparian ecosystems have been so mistreated that FWS calls them "the most modified land type in the West." They have been lost largely to agricultural conversion, overgrazing, dam construction, and groundwater withdrawal. The magnitude of loss is alarming. For example, more than 90 percent of riparian habitats along the Colorado River in Colorado have been destroyed, and only two percent of riparian forests along the Sacramento River in California remain. Much of the area is public land and subject to federal control, but losses continue.

National Wetlands Inventory

In 1975, growing interest in wetlands conservation and the increasing need for reliable scientific information on wetlands stimulated FWS to establish the National Wetlands Inventory project to generate and disseminate scientific information on the characteristics and extent of wetlands. Full-scale wetlands mapping began in 1979, and in 1980 FWS adopted a new wetlands classification system. FWS emphasizes, however, that its identification of wetlands areas does not define jurisdiction of any federal, state, or local government or the scope of any regulatory programs.

The major activity of the inventory project is to produce maps of the nation's wetlands. Mapping priorities are based primarily on the needs of FWS and of cooperating state and federal agencies. The top-priority areas include the coastal zone, including that of the Great Lakes; prairie wetlands; and the floodplains of major rivers. These areas total 55 percent of the continental United States and 32 percent of Alaska. By September 30, 1985, the inventory is scheduled to complete maps for 40 percent of the lower 48 states and 10 percent of Alaska. Maps have been completed for Massachusetts, Rhode Island, Vermont, Arizona, Connecticut, New Jersey, Delaware, Hawaii, and Guam. In addition, Wisconsin has completed its own state wetlands inventory using the FWS classification system. Maps for the remainder of the high-priority areas in the lower 48 states and half of the priority areas in Alaska are scheduled to be completed by 1988. The status of the mapping effort in various regions is available by contacting the FWS Regional Wetland Coordinators.

The other major inventory-project activity is producing reports on wetlands status and trends. The first report, which examined trends from 1954 to 1974, was issued in 1982. The study was designed and conducted by a team of Colorado State University researchers, with essential survey data produced by the inventory project. The next status and trends report will cover wetlands trends from 1954 through 1984 and is scheduled for completion in 1989.

REFERENCES

1. U.S. Congress, Office of Technology Assessment, *Wetlands: Their Use and Regulation* (Washington, DC: Government Printing Office, 1984), p. 52.
2. 16 U.S.C.A. 661 et seq.
3. 42 U.S.C.A. 4321 et seq.
4. 16 U.S.C.A. 1451 et seq.
5. Act of February 18, 1929, Chap. 257, 45 Stat. 1222 (current version at 16 U.S.C.A. 715-715d, 715e, 175f, 715-k, 715n-715r).
6. Act of March 16, 1934, Ch. 71, 48 Stat. 451 (current version at 16 U.S.C.A. 718 et seq.).
7. Michael J. Bean, *The Evolution of National Wildlife Law* (New York: Praeger Publishers, 1983), p. 216.
8. Pub. L. 85-585, 72 Stat. 486 (current version at 16 U.S.C.A. 718 et seq.).
9. Pub. L. 87-383, 75 Stat. 813 (current version at 16 U.S.C.A. 715k-3 to 715k-5).
10. Pub. L. 91-559, 84 Stat. 1468 (current version at 16 U.S.C.A, 1301 et seq.).
11. Pub. L. 88-578, 78 Stat 897 (current version at 16 U.S.C.A. 460-4 to 460-ll).
12. 16 U.S.C.A. 661 et seq.
13. Act of March 10, 1934, Ch. 55, 48 Stat. 401.
14. Act of August 14, 1946, Ch. 965, 60 Stat. 1080.
15. Pub. L. 85-624, 72 Stat. 563 (currently codified at 16 U.S.C.A. 661 et seq.).
16. Op. cit., Office of Technology Assessment, *Wetlands: Their Use and Regulation*, p. 77.
17. Pub. L. 87-732, 76 Stat. 696 (current version at 16 U.S.C.A. 590p-1).

18. Op. cit., Office of Technology Assessment, *Wetlands. Their Use and Regulation*, p. 78.
19. *Id.*, p. 79.
20. Exec. Order No. 11990, 3 CFR (1978 Comp.), 42 U.S.C.A. 4321 note.
21. Exec. Order No. 11988, 3 CFR (1978 Comp.), 42 U.S.C.A. 4321 note.
22. Federal Emergency Management Agency, "The 100-Year Base Flood Standard and the Floodplain Management Executive Order: A Review Prepared for the Office of Management and Budget by the Federal Energy Management Agency" (Washington, DC, 1983) p. III-51.
23. Pub. L. 97-348, 96 Stat. 1653 (codified at 16 U.S.C.A. 3501 et seq.).
24. U.S. Department of the Interior, Fish and Wildlife Service, *Wetlands of the United States: Current Status and Recent Trends* (Washington, DC: Government Printing Office, 1984), p. 37.
25. 33 U.S.C.A. 1344.
26. Act of March 3, 1899, Ch. 425, 30 Stat. 1151 (current version at 33 U.S.C.A. 401, 403).
27. *Zabel v. Tabb*, 430 F.2d 199 (5th Cir. 1970) cert. denied, 401 U.S. 910 (1971).
28. Pub. L. 92-500, 86 Stat. 816 (current version at 33 U.S.C.A. 1251 et seq.).
29. 392 F. Supp. 685 (D.D.C. 1975).
30. Pub. L. 95-217, 91 Stat. 1600 (current version at 33 U.S.C.A. 1251 et seq.).
31. 16 U.S.C.A. 661 et seq.
32. 47 Fed. Reg. 31299 (1982).
33. 46 Fed. Reg. 7644-7663 (1981).
34. Department of the Army, U.S. Army Corps of Engineers, and U.S. Department of the Interior, Fish and Wildlife Service, "Washington-Level Synthesis Report on the Evaluation of the Habitat Evaluation Procedures (HEP) Demonstration Program" (Washington, DC, 1983), p. 8.
35. U.S. Army Corps of Engineers, Corps of Engineers Fish and Wildlife Mitigation Practices, Main Report, (Washington, DC: October 5, 1984) p. 5.
36. Steven W. Gard, "Unmet Mitigation in the Lower Mississippi River and Tributaries" in U.S. Department of Agriculture, Forest Service, The Mitigation Symposium: A National Workshop on Mitigating Losses of Fish and Wildlife Habitats (Fort Collins, Colo., 1979), pp. 419-423.
37. Department of the Army, U.S. Army Corps of Engineers, Evaluation of Planning for Fish and Wildlife: Adequacy and Predictive Value of Recommendations at Corps Projects (Washington, DC: Government Printing Office, 1984).
38. 42 U.S.C.A. 1452 et seq.
39. Op. cit., Corps of Engineers, Fish and Wildlife Mitigation Practices, pp. 3-4.
40. Letter from Robert K. Dawson, Acting Assistant Secretary of the Army (Civil Works) to Don B. Cluff, Chief, Water Resources Branch, Office of Management and Budget, Nov. 20, 1984.
41. Previously codified at 18 CFR Parts 711, 713, 714, and 176.
42. 42 U.S.C.A. 1962a-2.
43. Repeal notice at 48 *Federal Register* 10250-10258 (1983).
44. 47 Fed. Reg. 12297 (1983).
45. Letter from William R. Gianelli to G. Ray Arnett, Oct. 1, 1982.
46. 33 U.S.C.A. 1344.
47. 16 U.S.C.A. 661 et seq.
48. 40 CFR Part 230, 45 *Federal Register* 85336 (1980).
49. 33 CFR Part 320.4, 49 *Federal Register* 39478 (1984).
50. 33 U.S.C.A. 1341.

51. 16 U.S.C.A. 1451 et seq.
52. Op. cit., Office of Technology Assessment, *Wetlands: Their Use and Regulation*, 1984, p. 71.
53. Lt. General E.R. Heiberg III, Chief of Engineers, U.S. Army Corps of Engineers, in testimony before the Subcommittee on Energy and Water Development, Committee on Appropriations, U.S. House of Representatives, Feb. 20, 1985.
54. 392 F. Supp. 685 (D.C. 1975).
55. Data from Corps of Engineers, extracted from district quarterly reports on permit processing.
56. Op. cit., Office of Technology Assessment, *Wetlands: Their Use and Regulation*, 1984, p. 144.
57. Id., p. 3.
58. 715 F.2d 897, 13 ELR 20942 (5th Cir. 1983).
59. James T.B. Tripp and David W. Hoskins, "Implementation of a Section 404 Bottomland Hardwood Wetlands Regulatory Program: Rethinking Lower Mississippi Valley Resource Objectives and Priorities," *National Wetlands Newsletter* (March-April, 1985).
60. W.N. Lindall, Jr., and G.W. Thayer, "Quantification of National Marine Fisheries Service Habitat Conservation Efforts in the Southeast Region of the United States," Marine Fisheries Review 44(12):18-22 (1982).
61. State College Field Office, Ecological Services (U.S. Fish and Wildlife Service), "An Assessment of the Corps of Engineers' Section 404 Permit Program in Northern New Jersey, 1980-1984," August, 1984.
62. Vice President, Office of the Press Secretary, "Announcement of Administrative Reforms to the Regulatory Program Under Section 404 of the Clean Water Act and Section 10 of the Rivers and Harbor Act," Washington DC, May 7, 1982.
63. U.S. Army Corps of Engineers, Institute for Water Resources report, draft, 1981, cited in National Wildlife Federation, "Section 404 — A Response to the Army — OMB Regulatory Reform Proposals" (unpublished document, March 2, 1982).
64. 33 U.S.C.A. 1344(q).
65. Letter from G. Ray Arnett, Assistant Secretary of the Interior for Fish and Wildlife and Parks to William R. Gianelli, Assistant Secretary of the Army for Civil Works, June 27, 1983.
66. Letter from G. Ray Arnett to Robert K. Dawson, Acting Assistant Secretary of the Army for Civil Works, Nov. 7, 1984.
67. 47 Fed. Reg. 31800-31834 (1982).
68. 48 Fed. Reg. 21466-21476 (1983).
69. 49 Fed. Reg. 39478-39485 (1984). (Correction at 49 Fed. Reg. 39843 (1984)).
70. 49 Fed. Red. 1387-99 (1984).
71. 42 U.S.C.A. 4321 et seq.
72. Letter from Lee M. Thomas, EPA Administrator, to A. Alan Hill, Chairman, Council in Environmental Quality, Feb. 25, 1985.
73. 40 CFR 1500.1-1517.7 (1983) Appendix B par. 8.a.
74. Op. cit., Office of Technology Assessment, *Wetlands: Their Use and Regulation*, 1984, pp. 19-21.
75. 46 Fed. Reg. 7644-7663 (1981).
76. 713 F. 2d 897 (5th Cir. 1983).
77. *United States v. Ciampitti*, 583 F. Supp. 483 (D. N.J. 1984); see also *Swanson v. United States*, 608 F. Supp. 802 (D. Idaho 1985); cf. *United States v. City of Fort Pierre*, 747 F. 2d 464 (8th Cir. 1984).
78. 729 F. 2d 391 (6th Cir. 1984).

79. 105 S. Ct. 1166 (1985).
80. 568 F. Supp. 583 (D. Colo. 1983), aff'd 758 F. 2d 508 (No. 83-2114) (10th Cir. 1985).
81. 16 U.S.C.A. 715k-3 to 715k-5.
82. 16 U.S.C.A. 742(a)-754.
83. W.E. Frayer et al., *Status and Trends of Wetlands and Deepwater Habitats in the Conterminous United States, 1950's to 1970's* (Fort Collins: Colorado State University, 1983).
84. Op. cit., Office of Technology Assessment, *Wetlands: Their Use and Regulation*, 1984, pp. 90-91.
85. Id., p. 3.
86. Op. cit., U.S. Department of the Interior Fish and Wildlife Service, *Wetlands of the United States*, 1984.

LEONARD LEE RUE III

Wild turkeys were wiped out in some areas by overhunting. Using federal funds, some states have re-introduced the bird to parts of its former range.

Federal Funding for Wildlife Conservation

by Dennis Drabelle
Special to National Audubon Society

INTRODUCTION

ONE OF THE legacies of the 1930s — years of depression, drought, and the decline of wildlife populations — is the Federal Aid in Wildlife Restoration Program, more commonly known as the Pittman-Robertson (P-R) Program after its congressional sponsors. The program's purpose is to restore wildlife populations by generating projects at the state level. Its method is grants-in-aid. It apportions among the states and territories the annual receipts from federal excise taxes on hunting and recreational shooting equipment and ammunition. At least one state dollar is required to match every three federal dollars. Each state or territory is free to spend the money on qualifying projects within the categories of land acquisition, management, planning, surveys and inventories, research, development, and hunter education. Since its inception in 1938, the P-R program has apportioned well over a billion dollars. Most of it has been spent on restoration of game species.

In 1950, Congress established a similar grant-in-aid program for fish-restoration projects by enacting the Federal Aid in Sport Fish Restoration Act, commonly known as the Dingell-Johnson (D-J) Act after its congressional sponsors. Monies for D-J grants are derived from federal excise taxes on fishing tackle and equipment. By law, grant monies must be spent on land acquisition, research, development, and management for the benefit of sport fishes. Since its inception, the D-J program has apportioned almost $400 million.

In 1980, Congress enacted the Fish and Wildlife Conservation Act, commonly known as the Forsythe-Chafee (F-C) Act after its sponsors. The F-C program was intended to generate state projects for nongame species, but Congress has yet to establish a source of revenue.*

Together these three grant-in-aid programs — Pittman-Robertson, Dingell-Johnson, and Forsythe-Chafee — constitute the Federal Aid Program of the U.S. Fish and Wildlife Service (FWS), Department of the Interior. In FY 1985, the $124 million collected for these programs constituted 21 percent of the FWS budget.

---

*D-J grants are limited by law to sport-fish projects. P-R grants are limited by regulation to wild birds and mammals; in practice, the great majority of P-R funding has gone to projects for game species.

267

HISTORY AND LEGISLATIVE AUTHORITY

The Pittman-Robertson Act

As did many federal efforts on behalf of wildlife — the establishment of water-fowl refuges, the funding of refuge acquisitions through the sale of duck stamps, and others — the Federal Aid Program originated in the midst of the Depression. In 1932, Congress enacted an excise tax on arms and ammunition. The revenues were put into the General Fund of the Treasury. In 1936, at the first North American Wildlife Conference, J. N. "Ding" Darling, the editorial cartoonist and conservationist who also directed the Bureau of Biological Survey (a predecessor of FWS), issued a call for a national wildlife policy to stem the decline of wild species, particularly waterfowl.

Three other conservationists — Senator Key Pittman of Nevada, Representative Willis Robertson of Virginia, and Carl Shoemaker, secretary of the Senate Special Committee on Wildlife — followed up on the conference by approaching the wildlife problem from the standpoint that federal activity alone would be insufficient to solve it. Then, as now, the majority of the nation's wild creatures were found on non-federal land, and the states had primary responsibility for their well-being.

The proposed solution was to transfer revenues from an excise tax on guns and ammunition into a special fund that would aid the states in undertaking projects to restore wildlife populations. In particular, the program was designed to place funding of state wildlife agencies on a solid footing. This, in turn, would allow the agencies to hire biologists to staff wildlife-restoration efforts and to make the long-term commitments necessary to survey populations, acquire habitat, and undertake wildlife-oriented improvements such as the construction of water impoundments for ducks and geese.

Hunting groups supported the measure as a means of saving the resources on which they relied for recreation. Sporting and ammunition manufacturers supported it as a means of perpetuating their industry. The states supported it as a way of overcoming the perennial unwillingness of their fiscally strapped governments to spend money on wildlife. On September 2, 1937, the Pittman-Robertson bill was signed into law.[1] The program went into effect the following year.

Under the act, a special "federal aid to wildlife restoration fund" was established in the U.S. Treasury. Originally the fund consisted of revenue derived from a federal excise tax on firearms, shells, and ammunition. Currently it consists of revenues from an 11-percent federal excise tax on firearms, shells, and ammunition, a 10-percent tax on handguns, and an 11-percent tax on archery equipment. The secretary of the Interior is authorized to use up to eight percent of annual revenues for administration of both the P-R Act and the Migratory Bird Conservation Act.[2]

The remainder of the revenues supplied to the fund is available for apportionment among the states according to a dual formula. Half is apportioned according to state area as compared with the total area of all states. The other half is apportioned by number of paid-hunting-license holders in a state, as compared with the total holders for all states. This formula, however, has lower and upper limits. No state is to receive less than one half of one percent nor more than five percent of the amount apportioned in any year.*

To qualify for receiving any money from the fund at all, each state is required to meet a fundamental condition. Its legislature must pass a law prohibiting "the diver-

---

*The upper limits for "non-states" are specifically set by the act: Puerto Rico is to receive no more than one half of one percent per year; Guam, the Northern Mariana Islands, the Virgin Islands, and American Samoa are each to receive no more than one sixth of one percent per year.

sion of license fees paid by hunters for any other purpose than the administration of [the] State fish and game department." The point of this requirement is to ensure that the states do their part to implement the federal purpose of providing sustained funding and management of wildlife programs. All 50 states plus Guam, American Samoa, the Northern Mariana Islands, Puerto Rico, and the Virgin Islands have enacted such a prohibition.

Within the limits of their annual apportionment, states* are free to submit wildlife projects for funding on a 75-percent federal, 25-percent state basis.** To be funded, an individual project must be "substantial in character and design," a provision that in the early years of the program enabled FWS biologists to exercise a good deal of control over state projects. In recent years, however, FWS has loosened its control as the states have developed their own biological expertise.

Currently, under regulations that apply to both the P-R and D-J acts, a project is considered to be substantial in character and design if it:

- Identifies and describes a need within the purposes of the relevant act to be utilized;
- Identifies the objectives to be accomplished based on the stated need;
- Utilizes accepted fish and wildlife conservation and management principles, sound design, and appropriate procedures; and
- Will yield benefits which are pertinent to the identified need at a level commensurate with project costs.

Other regulations forbid the use of Federal Aid funds for income-producing purposes unless these are "incidental to the accomplishment of approved purposes" and require that real property acquired or constructed with federal funds must continue in use for the purpose for which acquired or constructed. The regulations impose a freeze on the eligibility of a state to participate in the program until diverted assets are restored.

In 1970, amendments to the P-R Act[3] gave the states an option. Instead of submitting individual projects, they could submit a "comprehensive fish and wildlife resource management plan" covering a period of at least five years. Once the secretary of the Interior had approved such a plan, projects encompassed by it would be routinely funded. (The planning option will be discussed more fully in connection with the Fish and Wildlife Conservation Act of 1980, below.) Amounts apportioned to the states but not obligated by them in the fiscal year of apportionment or the succeeding fiscal year revert to the secretary of the Interior, who may spend them to implement the Migratory Bird Conservation Act, including the purchase of land.

Other amendments to the act have further loosened FWS control over the purposes for which apportioned monies could be spent. In 1946,[4] the term "wildlife restoration project" was redefined to include the maintenance of completed projects. In 1955, management of wildlife areas and resources, except for law enforcement and public relations, was made a purpose for which funds apportioned under the act could be spent.[5]

In 1970, the act was amended to increase revenues and add to the program's purposes.[6] Half of the federal excise tax on pistols, revolvers, and — since 1975 — bows and arrows was established as a fund within the fund, to be apportioned among the states "in proportion to the ratio that the population of each State bears to the population of all the States," with the proviso that in any fiscal year, no state shall

---

*For convenience, the term "states," as used in this chapter, generally should be construed to mean the 50 states and the qualifying territories.
**The five territorial areas are not required to provide a matching share.

receive more than three percent of the total amount nor less than one percent. Although the act suggests that amounts apportioned in this way be spent "to pay up to 75 per centum of the costs of a hunter safety program and the construction, operation, and maintenance of public target ranges, as a part of such program," the states may opt to spend this money on traditional wildlife-restoration projects.

The Dingell-Johnson Act

During World War II, Congress enacted excise taxes on several items, including fishing equipment. After the war, these taxes were marked for repeal, and the tax on fishing equipment was likely to be eliminated until Representative John Dingell of Michigan* and Senator Edwin Johnson of Colorado decided to use it for fisheries restoration. In 1950, their bill was enacted as the Federal Aid in Sport Fish Restoration Act,[7] more commonly known as the Dingell-Johnson Act.

The D-J program is modeled closely after the P-R program, but some differences are apparent. Whereas P-R projects theoretically can embrace all forms of wildlife, game and nongame alike, D-J projects are limited to those involving "fish which have material value in connection with sport or recreation in the marine and/or fresh waters of the United States." In practice, the program has been especially beneficial to species favored by anglers, such as trout, bass, catfish, and other pan fish. The revenues apportioned under D-J originally derived from the 10-percent federal excise tax on fishing rods, creels, reels, and artificial lures, baits, and flies — made available for apportionment according to a slightly different dual formula from that for P-R: 40 percent is allocated on the basis of each state's geographical area and 60 percent on the basis of the number of the state's paid fishing-license holders. In addition to the states and territories eligible for the P-R program, the District of Columbia recently has qualified for the D-J program. As with P-R, the fundamental D-J requirement is for the state to enact a prohibition against diverting fishing-license revenues from any purpose other than administering its fish and game department. Reverted D-J funds may be spent by the secretary of the Interior on research concerning "fish of material value for sport and recreation."

In 1984, amendments to the Deficit Reduction Act[8] transformed the D-J program by establishing a new Aquatic Resources Trust Fund consisting of a Boat Safety Account and a Sport Fish Restoration Account. The latter replaces the old D-J Account. The new fund, which should more than triple the amount of money available for D-J grants, derives its revenues from the following sources:

- an expansion of the excise tax on fishing equipment to include tackle boxes, trolling motors, and flasher-type fish finders;
- an extension of the D-J excise taxes to certain importers who had previously escaped paying the taxes;
- transfer from the Federal Highway Trust Fund of certain revenues derived from federal taxes on motorboat fuels; and
- transfer of certain revenues from import duties on yachts, pleasure craft, and imported fishing equipment.

The amendments require each state to use at least 10 percent of its annual apportionment under the D-J program for development of facilities for recreational boating. The amendments also permit each state to use up to 10 percent of its apportionment to provide "an aquatic resource education program for the purpose of increasing public understanding of the nation's water resources and associated aquatic life forms." In addition, the new law directs each coastal state to allocate, to the extent

*Father of the incumbent representative of the same name.

practical, its annual Sport Fish Account apportionment between marine-fish projects and freshwater-fish projects according to the number of resident anglers who participate in each activity. The purpose of this directive is to ensure that in coastal states, one group of fisherman or the other is not unduly favored in project expenditures. Finally, the amendments reduce the amount of annual revenues available for federal administration of the D-J program from eight percent to six percent.

The Fish and Wildlife Conservation Act of 1980

As previously mentioned, D-J monies are available only for projects involving sport-fish species. Moreover, although P-R monies are available for all wild birds and mammals, the amount spent for nongame species over the years has been small — according to one estimate, perhaps 12 or 13 percent in recent years, a smaller percentage in earlier years.[9] In 1980, Congress sought to redress this imbalance by enacting the Fish and Wildlife Conservation Act of 1980,[10] also known as the Nongame Act.

The act is predicated on a finding that "Historically, fish and wildlife conservation programs have been focused on the more recreationally and commercially important species within any particular ecosystem." In response to that fact, the act encourages the states to address the conservation of their nongame wildlife species through the preparation of conservation plans and the submission of projects in accordance with those plans. Under Section 4 of the act, conservation plans must meet various criteria, which include the following:
- provide for an inventory of "plan species," namely nongame fish and wildlife that are determined by the state wildlife agency to be "valued for ecological, educational, esthetic, cultural, recreational, economic, or scientific benefits by the public;"
- provide for determination of plan species' ranges and habitats; and
- determine actions that should be taken to conserve the plan species and their significant habitats.

Once a state's conservation plan has been approved, it becomes eligible for, in most cases, 75-percent reimbursement of costs of nongame projects related to the plan.

Under Section 5(b) of the Nongame Act, an approved conservation plan may double as a comprehensive plan under the P-R and D-J Acts. That is, if approved, the wildlife portion of the conservation plan "shall be deemed to be an approved plan for purposes of" the P-R Act, and the fish portion "shall be deemed to be an approved plan for purposes of" the D-J Act. States that lack an approved comprehensive plan can obtain federal funding for their nongame projects only through fiscal year 1986 — a marked difference from the P-R and D-J programs. Also unlike those programs, the Nongame Act program was authorized for funding by means of general appropriations from the Treasury. So far, the executive branch has not requested appropriations, and the program has never been funded.

ORGANIZATION AND OPERATIONS

Responsibilities and Roles

FWS is responsible for administering the Pittman-Robertson, Dingell-Johnson, and Nongame Acts. The states are responsible for developing and carrying out the wildlife-restoration projects authorized and funded by the three statutes. FWS encourages state agencies to consult with the National Marine Fisheries Service in the Department of Commerce concerning any project relating to marine species.

FWS relies upon state audits of P-R and D-J expenditures for assurance that Federal Aid monies are being spent for the intended purposes. FWS personnel do, however, review audits and conduct periodic field inspections of project sites. The most serious enforcement problems arising under the program usually have to do with a state fish and wildlife agency losing control over the expenditure of hunting and fishing-license revenues, with the result that they are spent for purposes unrelated to administering the agency, or with the use of apportioned monies for purposes unrelated to fish and wildlife restoration. For example, one state legislature recently considered a bill to use license fees for purchase of a lake that would have served primarily as water supply for a pump-storage project. After the regional office warned legislators that enactment of the bill would result in ineligibility for future D-J apportionments, the bill was killed.

Congressional Committees

The House Committee on Merchant Marine and Fisheries and the Senate Committee on Environment and Public Works have substantive jurisdiction over the Federal Aid Program. These committees exercise oversight over the program and periodically hold hearings concerning its operation, usually in connection with proposed changes in the laws. In the House, oversight or action on federal aid legislation begins with the Subcommittee on Fisheries and Wildlife Conservation and the Environment. In the Senate it begins with the Subcommittee on Environmental Pollution.

The P-R and D-J funds, including the new Sport Fish Account, are available on a "permanent-indefinite basis." That is, by virtue of parallel amendments to the Interior Appropriation Act[11] contained in the P-R and D-J laws, the House and Senate appropriation committees routinely approve administration disbursements of P-R and D-J receipts. The Nongame Act is structured in the traditional fiscal way: it calls for annual appropriations from the Treasury, which must be approved annually by Congress.

Agency Structure and Function

The three components of the Federal Aid Program — P-R, D-J, and Nongame — are managed by the FWS Division of Federal Aid, which reports to the associate director for federal assistance. In the early years of the program, FWS played a quasi-paternal role in project approval, largely because state wildlife agencies lacked the biological expertise that the P-R and D-J statutes were designed to develop. This FWS role was reflected in the centralization of project approval at Washington, D.C., headquarters.

In 1958, FWS decentralized the approval process for both P-R and D-J projects, vesting approval authority for projects and plans with the various regional directors. Since then, the program's Washington staff has merely distributed apportioned funds, provided policy guidance to the regional directors and their federal aid staffs, coordinated information concerning the program, and evaluated program compliance and accomplishments.

Thus, FWS regional offices have the basic responsibility for administering the Federal Aid Program. This includes the review and approval of state project documents, monitoring project implementation, maintaining adequate records, reviewing progress on projects, providing technical assistance to states, ensuring that policy and regulations are carried out, and ensuring that properties acquired are used for their intended purpose and adequately maintained. To carry out this responsibility, each region has an assistant regional director for federal assistance who is responsible for administering both federal aid and endangered species programs and a regional federal aid office supervised by a regional federal aid chief.

The regional offices seek to become involved with state projects in their early stages. This means that by the time the project is submitted for approval, FWS concerns about compliance with the various statues and the substantiality test often have been addressed. It is common for project proposals to be unveiled in tentative form at meetings of fish and game agency associations, at private fish and game society meetings, or at university colloquia, where they are subject to peer review.

Planning

Like other FWS programs, the Federal Aid Program is guided by the "Service Management Plan,"[12] which provides broad guidance and long-term policy direction for agency programs. Federal aid also is the subject of its own program-management document, which encompasses goals, objectives, strategies, and policies for the program over a five-to-ten-year period. The first such document was issued for the Federal Aid Program on December 18, 1979. A new program-management document now is circulating in draft form and is expected to be made final in 1985. FWS publishes an annual Federal Aid Report summarizing the previous fiscal year's activities on a project-by-project basis.

Budgeting

The funding process for the Federal Aid Program bypasses the normal Executive Branch and congressional process. Rather than submitting an appropriations request for the program, FWS draws up an annual estimate of monies to be apportioned, which is included in the Interior Department's budget as a matter of information. Excise-tax collections made in a given fiscal year are apportioned in the next fiscal year. Annual apportionments are made in two installments: a preliminary one, which FWS attempts to make no later than October 1 (the beginning of the federal fiscal year) and which may amount to a half or more of the final figure apportioned that year; and a final apportionment, which FWS attempts to make no later than January 31. Before making the apportionments, FWS will have made the deductions for administration of the programs. Some states have reported problems with FWS accuracy in predicting the funding level for a given year. If the total allocation for a state falls drastically short of the projected amount, havoc can result and one of the program's primary purposes — to put funding of state wildlife programs on a solid sustained basis — can be stymied.

Although D-J apportionments have increased over the past few years from about $31 million in FY 1981 to $35 million in FY 1985, P-R apportionments have been up and down.

Apportionments FY 1981–1985

	FY 1981	FY 1982	FY 1983	FY 1984	FY 1985
D-J	$30,950,000	$29,970,000	$32,780,000	$31,380,000	$35,059,730
P-R Wildlife Restoration	69,194,000	99,980,000	88,240,000	73,000,000	64,909,600
P-R Hunter Education	14,200,000	16,980,000	18,820,000	15,450,000	14,190,000
Total P-R	$83,394,000	$116,960,000	$107,060,000	$88,450,000	$79,099,600
Total Fed. Aid	$114,344,000	$146,930,000	$139,840,000	$119,830,000	$114,159,330

Source: U.S. Fish and Wildlife Service.

Percentages of Collected Federal Aid Spent on Program Administration — FY 1981–1984

FY	P-R	D-J
1981	7.9	8.0
1982	4.0	6.2
1983	3.9	6.3
1984	5.6	5.9

Source: U.S. Fish and Wildlife Service.

Research

Since 1964, when careful records began to be kept, the cost of administering the program have averaged 5.3 percent of annual revenues collected for P-R and 6.4 percent for DJ. Each year the Federal Aid Program uses a part of its administrative monies for special projects, including research that benefits all the states but is too demanding and costly to be undertaken by any one of them. These projects may be as general as national surveys of hunting and wildlife-oriented recreation, or as specific as research on the suitability of diaminopimelic acid as an indicator of the energy derived by deer and elk during normal feeding — a technique that could lend itself to assessments of these ungulates' health. The common feature of these projects is that they are designed to aid the states in restoring and managing species that are primarily under state jurisdiction.

CURRENT PROGRAM TRENDS

Streamlining of the Process

Perhaps the most significant recent trend in the administration of the Federal Aid Program has been the streamlining of the project approval process. This trend — already under way as over the years Congress loosened the statutory requirements and FWS deferred more and more to the developing biological expertise possessed by state wildlife agencies — accelerated following an audit report on the program issued in July 1981 by the inspector general of the Interior Department. That report criticized FWS administration of the P-R and D-J grant programs as being characterized by excessive, nonproductive paperwork. In conclusion, the report recommended that "FWS take action necessary to adopt a block grant approach for funding Federal Aid in fish and wildlife restoration, and hunter safety. Under this concept, a separate block grant for each of the Federal Aid programs will be awarded to the cognizant state agency responsible for these programs, normally a state game and fish department."[13]

In response, the assistant secretary of the Interior for Fish and Wildlife and Parks, who supervises FWS, instructed FWS to conduct a study, in consultation with the states, of alternative means for administering the P-R and D-J grants. The resulting survey of the states elicited broad agreement that the essentials of the federal-state relationship in the two programs should remain in place but that greater flexibility should be allowed the states in program execution, along with "relief from certain peripheral laws, regulations and orders."[14] Thus, the states rejected the suggestion that a block-grant system — by which they would enjoy almost total discretion in the spending of their P-R and D-J apportionments — should replace project-by-project or plan approval.

It may seem odd for the states to affirm the desirability of federal control over P-R

Federal-Aid Administration Expenditures ($000s)

FY		D-J	P-R	
1981	Program Administration	1,971	4,823	
	Special Projects	2,083	3,686	
	(FTP)	(20)	(43)	
1982	Program Administration	1,920	4,446	
	Special Projects	816	1,362	
	(FTE)	(?)	(?)*	
1983	Program Administration	2,030	4,580	
	Special Projects	415	785	
	(FTE)	(27)	(65)	(92)
1984	Program Administration	2,230	4,928	
	Special Projects	567	808	
	(FTE)	(27)	(64)	(91)
1985	Program Administration	2,287	4,592	
	Special Projects	1,204	2,468	
	(FTE)	(26)	(64)	(90)

*The question marks in these columns reflect confusion caused by a mid-year change in the way employees were counted: the FTP system counted only "full-time permanent" employees as of the last day of the fiscal year; the FTE (full-time equivalent) system counts person-years worked by all employees on hand at any time during a fiscal year.
Source: U. S Fish and Wildlife Service.

and D-J expenditures. This stance, however, apparently is based upon a fear among wildlife-management professionals that too much state discretion could result in a politicization of spending decisions at the state level. In most states, the fish and wildlife agency is small and lacking in the kind of political clout that would enable it to resist the pressures brought to bear by various interest groups regarding how agency funds should be spent.

In a memorandum to the assistant inspector general for auditing dated June 16, 1982, the assistant secretary of the Interior for Fish and Wildlife and Parks presented his conclusions concerning administration of federal aid. In essence, he determined that the best method of administering the programs was to retain federal monitoring and supervision but allow states greater flexibility in the manner of seeking federal approval. Under the new system, which the assistant secretary's memo directed FWS to begin implementing, a state may adopt a "pattern of administration consistent with its resources and its desire for Federal involvement," with three basic options to choose from:

- Execute all or part of the program on a project-by-project basis, providing traditional documentation for each project, and/or
- Prepare and maintain a strategic plan for the entire fish and wildlife program or for separable components of it, and provide minimum annual documentation describing the proposed undertakings and estimated costs for approval and fund obligation, or
- Prepare and maintain a comprehensive plan for the entire fish and wildlife agency, and maintain adequate fiscal and performance control systems to protect plan integrity. After the plan and management systems are approved, the state needs no prior federal approval to select undertakings, implement the plan, or to make reprogramming changes. The state will keep FWS advised of the most recent programming of federal funds.[15]

Federal Aid Reversions*

	D-J	*P-R*
1981	$115,278.19	$981,220.42
1982	160,608.84	968,424.00
1983	76,051.68	682,749.63
1984	96,583.00	51,046.00

Source: U.S. Fish and Wildlife Service.
*One of the most common reasons for reversions is failure of states to complete projected land acquisitions.

State Planning

In a related development, the states have begun to administer their side of the P-R and D-J programs through either comprehensive or modular planning. Four states have obtained formal FWS approval of their comprehensive plans, which cover all aspects of the state's fish and wildlife mission: Kansas, Colorado, Wyoming, and Tennessee. Modular plans are those that cover only a part of the state mission. One state, Maryland, has obtained FWS approval of its modular plan, which covers wildlife but not fish.

The primary reason that so few states have obtained approval of plans since amendment of the P-R and D-J acts in 1970 is that it has taken a number of years for both FWS and the states to assimilate the notion of planning and to develop standards for the activity. Currently 27 states are developing either comprehensive or modular plans, and many of them are already in effect, though not approved by FWS. The number of states with approved plans is expected to rise sharply in the next few years. Although some states have developed superb planning capabilities, others resist the use of planning because, again, their wildlife agency directors are reluctant to expose projects and strategies to the conflicting pressures exerted by various interest groups.

CURRENT ISSUES

Efforts to Change D-J Funding

The predominant federal aid issue is the Reagan administration's initiative to eliminate automatic appropriation for the D-J program and subject it to the routine budget process. Although automatic transferrals of federal money generally are objectionable to any administration because they elude the planning and budgeting process, the D-J program has drawn special scrutiny because the revenues contributed to it have just increased substantially during a time of rapidly increasing federal deficits. It has been estimated that revenues from the motorboat fuel and other taxes recently made available for the D-J program will triple the annual state apportionments more than $100 million yearly. The administration presumably would prefer to be able to recommend reduced or zero funding for the program during certain years and to use the freed-up tax revenues to fund higher-priority programs.

Opponents of the administration's attempt, such as hunting, fishing, motor boating, and conservation groups, point to inconsistencies in its politics. In October, 1984, the Reagan-Bush '84 Committee took out full-page ads in such publications as *Field & Stream*, urging "sportsmen and outdoor enthusiasts" to vote to re-elect the president in part because "he signed the Federal Aid to Fish Restoration law which increases funding for fishery management and boat access facilities."[16] Shortly after the election, however, that law was the target of budget-cutters at the president's Office of Management and Budget (OMB).

The first cutback attempt by OMB involved interpreting the 1984 D-J amendments as having repealed the permanent-indefinite appropriation provision for that program. But the solicitor's office of the Interior Department issued a contrary opinion, and in a letter to Senator Malcolm Wallop, a proponent of full D-J funding, OMB Director David Stockman stated his conclusion that "no change in the funding mechanism of the program was intended by the amendments."[17]

Subsequently, the administration has requested legislative repeal of the new transfers of motorboat-fuel tax and other revenues into the D-J program and of the D-J permanent-indefinite provision as part of the FY 1986 budget request for the Interior Department. The justification is deficit reduction. Whether or not Congress will enact the proposed changes is questionable. It is expected that the changes will face strong opposition by the sports equipment industry, hunting and fishing groups, environmentalists, and the states, all of which are concerned not only about D-J but also P-R, which they feel would be subjected to the same approach if the D-J initiative were to succeed.

Funding for the Nongame Act

The other major issue facing the Federal Aid Program is funding of the Nongame Act. Section 12 of the act directed FWS to "conduct a comprehensive study to determine the most equitable and effective mechanism for funding state conservation plans and actions under this chapter, including, but not limited to, funding by means of an excise tax on appropriate items." The study was delivered to the Senate Committee on Environment and Public Works and the House Committee on Merchant Marine and Fisheries in February 1985.[18] In the meantime, the Nongame Act has not yet been funded.

Although the report listed several possible new excise taxes as funding mechanisms, e.g. a tax on backpacking equipment and a tax on recreational diving equipment, the administration rejected any new taxes or the use of appropriations from the general fund of the Treasury. In his letter transmitting the FWS report to Congress, the director made no recommendation for funding the Nongame Act, but cited the issuance of semipostal stamps as a method of funding that "would encourage voluntary contributions." Semipostal stamps are special stamps on which the buyer pays a surtax that is dedicated for a specified purpose. Although this practice is a common revenue-generating mechanism in Europe and Canada, it has never been used in the United States, and the U.S. Postal Service objects to it because it discerns no sound way of limiting the fund-raising purposes to which the stamps would be put. FWS has estimated that, depending on the amount of the surcharge, such a mechanism could have raised between $11.3 and $203.4 million for nongame funding in 1980.

LEGISLATION

The most important legislative development to affect the Federal Aid Program — the expansion of the D-J program in the 1984 amendments to the Deficit Reduction Act — has been discussed in the History and Legislative Authority section of this chapter. In addition, the administration's proposal to transform the D-J funding process from one involving automatic transfers of money to one shaped by the customary budget and appropriations channels has been discussed in the Current Issues section.

The other major federal-aid item on the legislative agenda for the near term is the need to reauthorize the Nongame Act, which expires at the end of fiscal year 1985.

LEGAL DEVELOPMENTS

There has not been any significant litigation under the federal aid statutes in recent years.

RESOURCE STATUS

By its nature the Federal Aid Program is designed to accommodate the states' priorities for the use of available revenues, with a minimum of federal second-guessing about project purposes. For that reason, short of conducting detailed evaluations of each state's use of P-R and D-J grants over the years, it is difficult to draw concrete conclusions about the program's effectiveness. Nor is there any valid way to compare the benefits obtained by Federal Aid expenditures with those that might have been obtained by other uses of the same money.

FWS does not maintain a comprehensive data base on the many uses of P-R and D-J monies by the states or on the results obtained. FWS does, however, keep statistics on some uses of the funds by project type on an annual and cumulative basis. For example,

- from the beginning of the P-R program through the end of FY 1982, nearly 38 million acres of land had been acquired, developed, or managed as wildlife management areas and wildlife refuges; and through the end of FY 1983 some 1,350,000 birds and mammals had been stocked;
- from the beginning of the D-J program through FY 1983, more than 192,000 acres of land and water were acquired and 350 fishing lakes comprising about 43,000 acres were created or restored;
- a grand total of approximately $1.7 billion has been turned over to the states since the programs began.

The only certain way to assess the status of the fish and wildlife resources conserved by the Federal Aid Program would be for FWS to request the states to adopt a tracking system that correlated the progress of benefited species and resources within a state with the expenditure of federal aid monies from one year to the next. The Interior Department assistant inspector general recently recommended that the burden of paperwork on the states be lightened, and all the recent history of the program militates against imposition of such a requirement.

REFERENCES

1. 50 Stat. 917 (codified at 16 U.S.C.A. 669-669i).
2. 45 Stat. 1222 (codified at 16 U.S.C.A. 715-715d, 715e, 715f-715r).
3. 84 Stat. 1097.
4. 60 Stat. 656.
5. 60 Stat 698.
6. See reference 3.
7. 64 Stat. 430 (codified at 16 U.S.C.A. 777-777k).
8. P. L. 98-369.
9. The source for this estimate is an FWS staff employee.
10. P.L. 96-366.
11. For P-R, the amendment is contained in 64 Stat. 693, for D-J in 65 Stat. 262.

12. U.S. Fish and Wildlife Service, "Service Management Plan" (revised), September 1982.
13. Quoted in U.S. Department of the Interior memorandum, "Administration of the Federal Aid Program", from the Assistant Secretary for Fish and Wildlife and Parks to the Assistant Inspector General for Auditing, June 16, 1982.
14. Quoted in U.S. Fish and Wildlife Service, "The Federal Aid Program and Alternative Methods for Administering It", April 7, 1982, p. 1.
15. Ibid., Appendix E.
16. See *Field & Stream*, October 1984.
17. October 18, 1984.
18. U.S. Fish and Wildlife Service, "Report and Recommendations on Funding Sources to Implement the Fish and Wildlife Conservation Act of 1980," December 19, 1984.

The national parks are the last sanctuary for many wildlife species, including the bison, symbol of the unmastered plains.

Wildlife and the National Park Service

by Chris Elfring
W.J. Chandler Associates

INTRODUCTION

THE NATIONAL PARKS play a clear and critical role in preserving the nation's wildlife heritage. When Congress established the National Park Service in 1916, it declared that one of the goals of the park system was "to conserve the wildlife therein." While the 334 units now in the system vary tremendously in character and include historic, recreational, and cultural sites, the parks, set aside for their spectacular natural environments, provide irreplaceable habitat for wildlife. The survival of certain wildlife species — the gray wolf and the grizzly bear in the lower 48 states for example — can be directly attributed to the existence of national parks.

In the years that have elapsed since the nation's first national park, Yellowstone, was established in 1872, the park service has evolved in its understanding of both nature and its own mission. Originally, the service protected "things" — grand scenery, unique land forms. Little or no awareness was shown of the need to preserve complete ecosystems when parks were established. Today, the park service more often takes an ecosystem approach to resource management — planning and carrying out activities designed to keep ecosystems and their natural processes functioning in perpetuity. Wildlife is considered a key element of park ecosystems, but the service rarely manages exclusively for wildlife. Instead, it attempts to integrate wildlife considerations into its other activities.

Although natural resource management is an essential part of the park service's mandate, its enabling legislation also identifies the enjoyment of people as a primary concern. Thus, the modern park service has a strong visitor-use orientation. At the same time, it is now clear that park natural resources are subject increasingly to a complex array of influences, both internal and external to the parks, that threaten their long-term preservation. Wildlife, perhaps more than other park resources, suffers because of threats emanating from activities on land adjacent to the parks. The reason is simple: Wildlife does not recognize boundaries contrived by people, and habitat outside the parks often is critical to its survival.

HISTORY AND LEGISLATIVE AUTHORITY

The evolution of wildlife policy in the national parks can be traced from 1872, when Yellowstone National Park was established. The first national park, Yellowstone, was dedicated as a "pleasuring ground for the benefit and enjoyment of people" in order to protect for all time this outstanding natural area. Yellowstone's first superintendent lacked both staff and salary for park management, and park wildlife often were killed by hunters. In 1883, Congress authorized the use of U.S. Army troops to protect Yellowstone wildlife and scenery — a policy that predated the actual establishment of the National Park Service by 33 years.

Between the creation of Yellowstone and the establishment of the National Park Service in 1916, Congress increased the size of the park system. Sequoia, General Grant (later to become part of Kings Canyon), and Yosemite national parks were added in 1890. Mt. Rainier was set aside in 1899. Crater Lake joined the system in 1902, followed by Mesa Verde, Glacier, Rocky Mountain, and Lassen Volcanic national parks between 1906 and 1916. The Army provided haphazard protection for the new system, but people still killed wildlife, cut trees, grazed livestock, and used the land as if it were any other part of the public domain.

Recognizing the need to protect and manage the parks it was creating, in 1916 Congress passed the National Park System Organic Act.[1] This act created the National Park Service and set the basic purpose of the parks that still guides their management today. "The fundamental purpose of said parks," reads the act, is "to conserve the scenery and the natural and historic objects and *the wildlife therein* and to provide for the enjoyment of the same in such manner and by such means as will leave them unimpaired for the enjoyment of future generations" (emphasis added).

With the passage of the Organic Act, Congress was no longer just setting aside areas of spectacular scenery and scientific curiosities, it also was requiring the protection of park resources, including wildlife. But that protection was colored by the attitudes of the era. "Good" animals such as deer, elk, and bison were to be protected, but "bad" animals — basically predators such as wolves, grizzly bears, and mountain lions — were to be eliminated. This attitude prevailed for several decades.

In 1929, George M. Wright, the service's first scientist, suggested that systematic study of the parks' wildlife was necessary. Under Wright's direction, the park service for the first time delineated the status of wildlife in the parks, analyzed unsatisfactory conditions, and proposed a plan for the orderly development of wildlife management. In 1932, the park service created its first Wildlife Division, with Wright as its chief. This division was directed to plan, review, and assist in ecological research and the management of biological resources. With the establishment of this division, the National Park Service began to adopt a more ecologically based approach to wildlife management. The importance of predators, for instance, was recognized and the service stopped its lethal control programs. By 1936, the park service had 27 staff biologists. Their efforts produced a series of faunal monographs that quickly attained status as classic wildlife field studies. But despite auspicious beginnings, Wright's untimely death in 1936 left the service without an advocate for a strong ecological perspective.

In the late 1930s and 1940s, National Park Service wildlife management attitudes regressed. In Yellowstone, for example, the service resumed the killing of coyotes to "protect" antelope, deer, and bighorn sheep. Some scientists within the service called for sounder management, and wildlife policy might have shifted yet again, but World War II interfered.

During the war, staff and funds for the parks were scarce and wildlife management was minimal. World War II put new demands on the parks, which were considered for use as sites for mountain-warfare training and cattle grazing and, in the case of some Pacific Northwest parks, as sources of Sitka spruce, a light wood needed to make airplanes. After the war, the management emphasis shifted strongly in favor of construction of facilities and visitor services, while research and resource management suffered. In the 1950s the park service began its "Mission 66" program, considered the height of user-oriented park policy. Mission 66 was an ambitious, decade-long program of facilities improvement named for its planned termination date in 1966, the 50th anniversary of the National Park Service. Appropriations for the program totaled more than $1 billion over the 10-year period. In all, 2,000 miles of roads were built or upgraded and 144 visitors' centers were built.[2] The program was an attempt to build stronger public support for the parks, but its focus on increased use was not always compatible with resource-protection goals.

During this period there was a growing awareness of problems in wildlife management and the need for better technical advice and information. In the late 1950s, the shooting of Yellowstone elk to reduce a perceived overpopulation problem rallied members of the conservation community to criticize park service wildlife management. As a result of these pressures, an advisory board was appointed to review park service wildlife management activities and policies.

In 1963, the board issued a landmark study known as the "Leopold Report,"[3] that has influenced policy to this day. In strong language, the Leopold Report, named for the board's chairman, A. Starker Leopold, asserted: "Maintenance of suitable habitat is the key to sustaining animal populations, and . . . protection, though it is important, is not of itself a substitute for habitat. . . . Moreover, habitat is not a fixed or stable entity that can be set aside and preserved behind a fence, like a cliff dwelling or a petrified tree. Biotic communities change through natural stages of succession." The report also established the still-current doctrine that the national parks should provide "a reasonable illusion of primitive America." And it raised three questions that remain relevant today:

1. What should be the goals of wildlife management in the national parks?
2. What general policies of management are best adapted to achieve the predetermined goals?
3. What are some of the methods suitable for on-the-ground implementation of policies?

While these changes in natural-resource management were occurring, the park service gained a variety of new management responsibilities. The crown-jewel natural areas were joined by new categories of parks: national recreation areas, national preserves, national seashores and lakeshores, national wild and scenic rivers, national memorials, national parkways, national historic sites, national scenic trails, even the national capital parks of Washington, D.C. Not only did the variety of park units increase, but visitation grew as well. Between 1960 and 1979, 84 new areas encompassing 49 million acres were added to the park system, while total visits grew from 135 million to 282 million.*

Three important occurrences mark 1964. First, within the park service, a three-part classification system was adopted to help deal with the problem of managing the now-varied units of the system. Each unit was classified either recreational, historic, or natural so that resources could be appropriately identifed and managed in terms of

---

*Most of the park service's new units entered the system through individual acts of Congress, but there were some exceptions. The 1906 Antiquities Act[4] allows the president to declare objects of historic or scientific interest to be national monuments, provided the land is federally owned or controlled. This act has been used fairly frequently to preserve unique areas, including areas important for their wildlife values. Some of the areas set aside under the act include Petrified Forest in 1906, Grand Canyon in 1908, Dinosaur in 1915, Acadia in 1916, and Katmai in 1918. Once established, many of the early national monuments later were changed to national parks by acts of Congress.

their inherent values and appropriate uses. This three-part classification has since been changed. The service now recognizes that any one park may have different components of use. Thus, the parks themselves are not classified, but areas within each park are zoned to designate where various management strategies will be used. The four management zones used are natural, historic, park development, and special use.

Another important event was passage of the 1964 Wilderness Act,[5] which established on federal lands a system of protected wilderness areas where management emphasis is on preserving the natural ecological character of the area. The act directed the park service to study park lands for wilderness potential and to recommend areas to Congress for inclusion in the system. To date, approximately 36.8 million acres of park land have been designated wilderness (32.3 million in Alaska), and the National Park Service has recommended wilderness designation for another 31.6 million acres, 25.5 million of it in Alaska. Wilderness designation can benefit wildlife populations by providing an extra measure of protection for some habitat.

Also passed in 1964 was the Land and Water Conservation Act,[6] which created an important funding mechanism — the Land and Water Conservation Fund — to help buy park lands. This fund, authorized to provide up to $900 million a year, is made up of certain user fees, a portion of motorboat fuel taxes, and receipts from outer continental shelf oil and gas leasing. The fund has been used to acquire lands for new parks as well as to acquire inholdings or additions to existing units. By the end of 1984, the conservation fund had provided nearly $2 billion for the acquisition of almost 1.5 million acres of national park lands.

The climate of the late 1960s and 1970s was a positive one for natural resources and wildlife in the parks. During the 1970s, the park service refined its management policies to reflect a more ecological perspective. Park policy today strives, though with some debate and inconsistency, to perpetuate a park's natural processes and total systems rather than merely preserve individual species or unique landforms.

Accompanying this shift in perspective, during the first half of the 1970s the number of field scientists and amount of funding for research and natural resource management in the parks increased significantly. But wildlife populations suffered anyway, in large part because the pressures of modern society were fast encroaching upon the parks.

In 1980 the park service, by issuing its State of the Parks report, made an important step toward identifying the many resource management problems faced by the parks.[7] This report surveyed park managers to learn what problems they perceived to be threatening the parks. The resulting study provides the first broad overview of activities that are degrading park resources. In a 1981 follow-up document, "State of the Parks: A Report to the Congress on a Servicewide Strategy for Prevention and Mitigation of Natural and Cultural Resources Management Problems,"[8]* the National Park Service outlined ways to respond to the threats. Both reports will be discussed in more detail later in this chapter.

ORGANIZATION AND RESPONSIBILITIES

Since its beginning in 1872, the National Park System has grown to include 334 areas in 49 states, the District of Columbia, Puerto Rico, Guam, the Trust Territories, and the Virgin Islands. Parks range in size and character from the immense roadless wilderness of Gates of the Arctic National Park in Alaska to Federal Hall National

---

*This report surveyed park personnel about what threats they perceived at that time. The perceptions were not documented, so the findings should be interpreted judiciously.

Memorial in lower Manhattan. Overall, the service is responsible for 74.8 million acres (including 52.1 million acres in Alaska), an area larger than the state of Arizona. An additional 4.6 million acres within the National Park System boundaries are owned by private individuals or other public entities. Visitation is projected to reach 360.5 million in 1985.

Roles and Responsibilities

The National Park Service is mandated to manage its lands to keep them in an unimpaired state in perpetuity. Under park service policy, areas in the parks designated as natural zones must be managed to ensure that natural ecological processes operate unimpaired unless otherwise specifically provided for in the law, and the historic zones must be managed to provide full protection for cultural resources.[9] Simultaneously, the service is mandated to provide for the highest quality of use and enjoyment of the National Park System by visitors today and in the future.

Regarding wildlife in the parks, the park service's Management Policies states:

> . . . The Service will perpetuate the native animal life of the parks for their essential role in the natural ecosystems. Such management, conformable with the general and specific provisions of law and consistent with the following provisions, will strive to maintain the natural abundance, behavior, diversity, and ecological integrity of native animals in natural portions of parks as part of the park ecosystem.[10]

Under park service law, policy, and regulations, native animal life in the National Park System is protected from harvest, removal, destruction, harassment, or other harm through human actions, with the following exceptions:

1. Hunting and trapping may be allowed where specifically permitted by law. To date, Congress has authorized hunting in 55 units managed by the park service, primarily national recreation areas, national seashores, and national preserves. Trapping also is allowed in 24 of these units.
2. Sport fishing is allowed unless specifically prohibited.
3. Park service officials may use necessary control measures for specific populations of wildlife where required for the maintenance of a healthy park ecosystem.
4. Animals may be removed or controlled where necessary for human health and safety.

It is National Park Service policy to rely to the greatest extent possible on natural processes to regulate populations of native species. Unnatural concentrations of native species, caused by human activities, may be regulated if the activities causing the concentrations cannot be controlled. Non-native species are not to be allowed to displace native species if the displacement can be prevented by management. The need for and results of any manipulation of animal populations is documented and evaluated by research studies.

Wildlife management within the national parks is the responsibility of the National Park Service unless otherwise specifically stated in law. Some park enabling legislation that allows hunting, fishing, or trapping specifies that such activities shall be regulated by the states. Even in cases where the federal government has legal jurisdiction over these activities, the park service generally manages them according to state regulations, unless it determines more restrictive management is needed. The park service stresses the importance of cooperation between state and federal authorities.

Congressional Committees

In Congress, four committees share primary responsibility for national park issues. In the House of Representatives, the Subcommittee on National Parks and Recreation (separated from the Subcommittee on Public Lands and National Parks in January 1985) of the Committee on Interior and Insular Affairs has jurisdiction over park service lands and management. In the Senate, jurisdiction over park issues comes under the Committee on Energy and Natural Resources, in particular the Subcommittee on Public Lands and Reserved Water. Interior appropriations subcommittees under the appropriations committees in both the House and the Senate also affect National Park Service policy because they determine the funding the agency receives to carry out its planning and management activities and how that funding generally is to be allocated.

Agency Structure and Function

The National Park Service is a bureau within the Department of the Interior and is headed by a director and a deputy director. The National Park Service consists of the headquarters staff in Washington, D.C., and the following field units:

- 10 regional offices responsible for designated geographic areas;
- 334 parks, monuments, historic sites, recreation sites, etc., located within the regions;
- a Denver Service Center responsible for providing technical assistance in park planning and development;
- a Harpers Ferry Center that helps prepare interpretive plans and media; and
- training centers at Grand Canyon National Park, Arizona, and Harpers Ferry, West Virginia.

The headquarters staff reports to the director and is responsible for developing policies, programs, and regulations and for coordination with Congress, the Office of Management and Budget, other agencies, and the public. The director is assisted by four associate directors and two assistant directors, each responsible for certain program areas.

The associate director for Natural Resources has the most important responsibilities relating to wildlife. He oversees the natural, social, and physical sciences in the parks, including the inventorying, monitoring, and preservation of natural resources. This directorate also provides scientific and resource management assistance to the National Park System. The associate director supervises five divisions: Air Quality; Water Resources; Special Science Projects; Energy, Mining, and Minerals; and Biological Resources.

The Biological Resources Division oversees natural history, natural science, and natural resources activities in the National Park System, including wildlife. It is responsible for policy and program review for exotic species, endangered species, aquatic and terrestrial resources, research proposals and contracts, research permits, resource monitoring, and publications.

The next level of management in the National Park Service is the region. A region consists of all the parks in one geographic section of the country. The regional director supervises all the park superintendents within the region and is the principal representative of the service in the designated region. The regional director approves all programs, plans, and activities in accordance with park service policy. Each region also has a chief scientist who oversees research throughout the region and a resource management specialist knowledgeable about resource concerns, including wildlife.

The basic management unit of the National Park System is the park. Wildlife activities are planned and carried out at the park level. Each park is headed by a

National Park Service

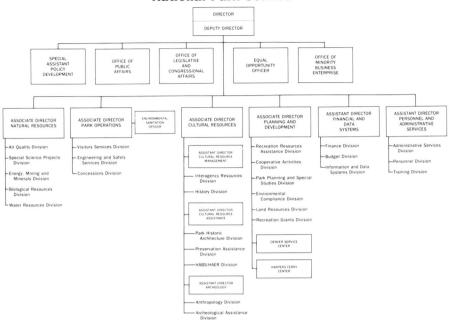

superintendent responsible for day-to-day management. Depending on the size and complexity of the park, there may be an assistant superintendent and various staffers trained in administration, interpretation, resource management, and maintenance. Some parks also are staffed with biologists, ecologists, landscape architects, or other specialized personnel, some of whom may have special responsibilities for wildlife.

Planning

Park planning has a long history in the national parks. In 1915, even before the establishment of the National Park Service, landscape architects were calling for each park to have a plan to guide its use. In 1918, two years after the park service was created, each park was directed to prepare a master plan. Since these early plans were inspired by landscape architects, they tended to concentrate on site design — such as where headquarters should be located and where roads should be built—with little attention to planning for natural resources management. But despite the limitations of the early plans, the long history of planning has had a strong influence, and today the idea of planning is deeply ingrained in the National Park Service. As one service staffer explained: "That planning is so ingrained in the National Park Service is a real strength — it has kept park managers [in the past and today] from making their decisions in a vaccuum . . . . The most important thing planning tells you is what you're not going to do."

Planning is done to assure that the purpose for which each park was created is achieved through specific guidance on park preservation, use, and development. The general purpose of each national park unit, and sometimes specific instructions for its management, usually is included in its enabling legislation, presidential proclamation, or executive order.

Planning is initiated at the park level and begins with the identification of issues, problems, and objectives to be addressed in the plan. This process is begun by the park superintendent, who, with help from regional and Denver Service Center personnel,

287

prepares what is called a statement for management. The statement attempts to provide an up-to-date inventory of the park's condition and an analysis of its problems. In theory, statements are to be reviewed and updated every two years to reflect the current condition of each park. The statement does not prescribe solutions. It is a base-line assessment from which the park can determine its next steps.

The park then uses the information in the statement for management to prepare its most important planning document, the general management plan. The general management plan, a more sophisticated version of the park service's early master plans, sets forth the basic management philosophy for a park and provides strategies for resolving problems and achieving management objectives. Resource management, visitor use, and all aspects of park operations are addressed. Any assessments of environmental impacts and other required compliance documents are included in the general management plan. These plans must be prepared with public involvement, providing an important opportunity for public participation in basic park management decisions.

General management planning is conducted by an interdisciplinary team that normally includes specialists from the park, the region, and the Denver Service Center. Through extensive research, review, and discussion with both agency personnel and the public, the general management planning team identifies the major areas of concern and develops alternative strategies to address them. A general management plan may be fairly general or very specific with regard to wildlife, depending upon the nature of the park, the planning issues, available information, and time and funding. At a minimum, each draft plan must provide information on the park's purpose, objectives, and legal constraints and a brief description of the park. It also includes the issues addressed by the plan; describes proposed actions and alternatives; presents the environmental impacts of the proposal and alternatives; and contains other necessary back-up documentation. The draft document is then circulated to the public and other agencies for review and comment and is revised as necessary. The regional director reviews the plan, and, if all requirements have been met, approves it.

General management plans are required by law for all units of the National Park System. Of the 334 units, 276 have approved plans and 58 are without plans. The park service, however, many never prepare plans for some very small units, such as Federal Hall National Monument in New York, may go without plans purposefully. The National Park Service expects each plan to have a useful life of 10 to 20 years, depending on circumstances. The general management plan is intended to be dynamic, to receiving periodic revaluation and revision to reflect changes in management objectives or ecological, social, or economic conditions. Plans are updated as needed, provided that funds are available for doing so. Need for updating is identified in the statements for management prepared by each park every two years.

The park service also prepares more specific plans which delineate management activities needed to deal with particular resource problems in a park. These are called resource-management plans. Resource management plans were initiated in the late 1960s but did not receive high priority. In 1981, however, in response to the extensive resource problems identified in the 1980 State of the Parks report, Congress directed the park service to give resource management planning greater emphasis. Resource management plans lay out the principal projects needed to protect, preserve, and perpetuate an individual park's natural and cultural resources for the next five to ten years. Priority for implementing the projects listed in the plan normally is based on the significance of the resource.

Resource management plans may identify needed research, discuss the impacts of development, plan measures to mitigate such impacts, or describe site-specific management actions to deal with a resource problem. No research can be funded unless it is first identified in a plan, but being listed in a management plan in no way assures funding. Wildlife-related activities are one of many types of projects included in the plans. For instance, Yellowstone's resource management plan calls for more detailed study of the impact on the grizzly bear of the Fishing Bridge Village development. Other wildlife activities in resource-management plans might include projects to address overpopulation of native species such as elk or bison, wildlife disease problems such as rabies and encephalitis, restoration of extirpated species, removal of exotic species, and wildlife monitoring.

A park's resource management plan may present a number of issues, the most important of which may become designated natural resource preservation problems. These are determined in each park and then are submitted to the appropriate regional director, where they are ranked, compiled with preservation problems from other regions, and funded according to importance. The identification and funding of natural resource preservation problems grew out of the park service's identification of significant resource problems as a result of the 1980 State of the Parks report. From 1983 through 1985, approximately $7.5 million was provided yearly to fund corrective efforts for about 60 natural resource preservation problems.

Until 1983, all resource management plans were reviewed by the Biological Resources Division in Washington, D.C. At that time, 246 park units had plans. The plans are now reviewed at the regional offices, and more recent plans are not logged at National Park Service headquarters. Service officials estimate, however, that about 280 units now have resource management plans.

In spite of this extensive planning, some critics argue that the park service continues to be shortsighted in its management of park resources. In addition, the service has been criticized for its lack of national planning. Although some early efforts were made at planning on the regional level, almost all planning to date has been park oriented. As one critic explained:

. . . The National Park Service has no systemwide, long-range planning process to assess resource needs, develop programs, and implement programs over time. As a result, the Service often finds itself reacting to crises, rather than anticipating needs.[11]

Budgeting

Funding is key to carrying out park management plans. Like planning, the formulation of the budget is a complex process, involving interactions between park superintendents, regional directors, the director of the National Park Service, the secretary of the Interior, the Office of Management and Budget, and Congress. In general, budget planning begins in the parks but is guided and ultimately controlled at the national level.

It is not possible to track specific wildlife-related expenditures in the National Park Service budget because activities focused exclusively on wildlife are a relatively small part of management programs and because of the great variety of park management activities that can directly and indirectly affect wildlife. For instance, monitoring elk populations or restoring peregrine falcons are activities directly focused on wildlife. Conducting a controlled burn is an ecosystem-management activity with both direct and indirect impacts on wildlife. Building a visitor center is an activity that may appear unrelated to wildlife, but in fact may have profound effects — for example, if the siting interferes with migration routes. The National Park Service considers that its ecosystem-management approach integrates wildlife concerns into all its management activities. Also, it is difficult to determine how much time and resources are devoted to

National Park Service Budget
FY 1981–1985

FY	Natural Resources Mgmt. Appropriated	Requested	NPS Budget* Operating Bgt.	Total Funds	Natural Resources Percent of Total
1981	$34,337,000	—**	$479,562,000	$844,217,000	4.1
1982	39,239,000	—**	538,347,000	803,036,000	4.8
1983	48,468,000	48,750,000	619,670,000	1,123,769,000	4.3
1984	48,906,000	48,156,000	629,309,000	954,919,000	5.1
1985	50,916,000	51,955,000	628,498,000	964,098,000	5.3

*The NPS operating budget is the amount appropriated for normal operating expenses. The total NPS budget also includes funds authorized for specific land acquisiton or construction, which can vary greatly from year to year. For instance, the increase in 1983 reflects funds for the Park Restoration and Improvement Program.
**Amounts requested natural resources management funds are not available for years prior to 1983 because this category was combined with cultural resources management funds.
Source: National Park Service Budget Office, 1985.

wildlife because park personnel typically have many and varied duties and cannot account precisely for all wildlife-related activities.

Although wildlife funds cannot be tracked specifically, most funds allocated for direct wildlife-related activities are contained within the park-operations account under the subheading "natural resources management."

Natural resources management appropriations have increased $16.6 million, 48 percent, since 1981, but as a percentage of the total National Park Service budget, natural resources management funds have remained relatively constant — constituting about four to five percent of the budget. The most significant increase came in 1983, when Congress appropriated an additional $10 million specifically for natural resources management under the Park Restoration and Improvement Program, a stepped-up park-construction and maintenance program that had focused almost exclusively on facilities improvements prior to 1983. The additional funding was used primarily to fund the Natural Resource Preservation Program described earlier, which provides funding for top-priority resource projects identified by the parks. The National Park Service has since kept the restoration and improvement increase in its base funding for natural resources management at a level of about $7 million. Under the Park Restoration and Improvement Program, the National Park Service spent through FY 1985 $21.8 million on natural resources preservation, $431 million on capital improvements (mainly water and sewer systems), $275 million on park roads, $115.2 million on other health and safety improvements, and $97 million for historic rehabilitation. Less than $1 million went to the new Natural Resource Management Specialist Training Program, another response to the State of the Parks report, which is intended to provide more natural resources managers for the parks.

Although these budget figures indicate some increased attention to natural resources, they should be interpreted cautiously because of changing definitions of what constitutes resource management, changes in accounting procedures, and difficulties in separating resource-management activities from other park management. What is clear is that natural resources management funding remains a small portion of total National Park Service expenditures.

Research

National Park Service headquarters does not maintain a separate research division. Research policy and program oversight relating to wildlife is part of the responsibilities of the Biological Resources Division or the Special Science Projects Division. Also, each region has a chief scientist responsible for overseeing research in that region. In general, however, most research occurs at the park level, and the degree of attention it receives depends on the superintendent. Research priorities are identified in the resource management planning process and research will not be funded by the park service unless it is identified in the resource management plan. Because the work is often site specific, and because budgets are tight, research results generally are not disseminated widely.

About 150 research scientists are assigned to the national parks themselves.* The types of research and monitoring projects conducted by the park service vary considerably. Research projects include air- and water-quality monitoring; ecological base-line data surveys; impacts of and methods for controlling exotic species; animal and plant surveys and censuses; studies on the ecology, management, or restoration of threatened or rare species; the role of fire in maintaining natural ecosystems; human impacts on back country and other fragile resources; hydrologic studies; inventories of significant park features; and more.

The park service also gets research information on important concerns, including wildlife, from its cooperative park study units. The service has cooperative agreements with about 20 universities and other institutions of higher learning to facilitate research and provide technical assistance to the parks. Under the agreements, a park service scientist may be stationed at the unit, where he or she has improved access to current information and expertise. The scientist also is a liaison to enlist faculty and graduate students for research needed by the parks. The cooperative units serve two important functions: they help keep National Park Service scientists up to date, and they provide expertise unavailable among park service staff. At present, the cooperative unit program is small.

A significant part of the research conducted in the parks is contracted directly with universities by regional chief scientists and park staff and not through cooperative units. In addition, a substantial amount of research in the parks is funded and carried out by other government agencies and private researchers such as the National Science Foundation, the Environmental Protection Agency, the National Oceanic and Atmospheric Administration, university scientists, and others. These projects must be approved by the National Park Service, but generally are independent of service research.

The need for research in the national parks was highlighted in the 1980 State of the Parks report. The National Park Service found that all park units suffered from a wide range of perceived threats affecting their resources. Of a total of 4,345 threats reported, 33 percent were designated as "suspect, and need documentation" and 42 percent were designated as "known, but need further documentation." Only 25 percent were designated as "known, adequately documented by available research." Thus, 75 percent of all the perceived threats reported are in need of verification and documentation.

Research serves a critical function in park management, providing information on which to base management decisions. Research is not a funding priority in the National

---

*People who devote at least 51 percent of their time to research or research administration at the park level.

Park Service. In 1985, for example, research and development funding was $15 million, or only 1.5 percent of the total service budget. While park personnel acknowledge the need for adequate research and monitoring on resource issues, including wildlife, in the face of budget declines more tangible concerns such as health, safety, and maintenance have been top priority.

CURRENT TRENDS AND ISSUES

If we are going to succeed in preserving the greatness of the national parks, they must be held inviolate. They represent the last stands of primitive America. If we are going to whittle away at them, we should recognize, at the very beginning, that such whittlings are cumulative and the end result will be mediocrity. —Newton Drury, Director of the National Park Service, 1940-1951.

Despite the protective mandate given the National Park Service, wildlife in the nation's parks is increasingly threatened by human development and other factors. These threats emanate from both internal and external sources and affect natural resources in all parks, regardless of size, use, or location. The resulting degradation affects wildlife and threatens the ability of the parks to serve their fundamental purpose of protecting the scenic, natural, and historic resources of the parks "and the wildlife therein." Despite these threats, parks resource management today receives low priority in comparison with visitor use, law enforcement, and maintenance needs. The low commitment of staff and funding for resource management, including wildlife, in the face of visitation pressures within the parks and development pressures outside is likely to lead to continued and increasingly visible problems in the future.

Threats* in the Parks

In 1980, in response to a request by Congress, the park service issued its State of the Parks report, which showed that the natural and cultural resources of the national parks are endangered both from within and from without by a broad range of problems, causing significant and demonstrable damage. Parks set aside primarily to protect natural areas, which include the parks most valuable for wildlife, are especially hard hit. The 63 national parks greater than 30,000 acres reported twice as many threats as the servicewide norm.** The Biosphere Reserve Parks, internationally recognized for their scientific importance through the United Nations' Man and the Biosphere program,*** reported an average number of threats three times the servicewide norm. This is particularly disturbing because the biosphere reserve parks are considered to be global bench marks of ecological health and outstanding examples of the world's ecosystems and biological diversity.

More than 50 percent of the reported threats emanated from sources outside the parks. Industrial and commercial development, air pollution, urban encroachment,

---

*The term "threats" as used here and in the State of the Parks-1980 refers to pollutants, visitor activities, exotic species, industrial development projects, etc., that have the potential to cause significant damage to park resources or to seriously degrade important park values or visitor experiences. All the data presented in this section are from the 1980 report.
**This may be partly due to the fact that the larger areas have more professionally trained staff who are more capable of recognizing threats.
***As of March 1985, 21 National Park Service areas were included in the international network of biosphere reserves, a network containing 243 units in 65 countries (41 in the United States).

National Park Service Research and Development Funding*
FY 1981–1985

| | Funds |
FY	Appropriated
1981	10,351,000
1982	11,203,000
1983	13,746,000
1984	14,000,000
1985	15,000,000

*These funds are devoted specifically to national park research projects, including money for college and university research, technical assistance, and other hands-on aspects of research. It does not include salaries for the regional chief scientists or Washington office staff.
Source: NPS Budget Office, 1985.

and roads were the most frequently identified external threats (discussed later). The most frequently perceived internal threats that can cause significant degradation of park resources, park values, and visitor experiences were associated with heavy visitor use, utility access corridors, vehicle noise, soil erosion, and exotic plants and animals. The report found that scenic resources were threatened in more than 60 percent of the parks; air quality in more than 45 percent; and mammal, plant, and freshwater resources in more than 40 percent. A disturbing 75 percent of the threats were cited as inadequately documented and in need of research.

Threats specifically affecting wildlife included direct threats such as hunting and poaching, competition from exotic species, harrassment, and habitat destruction. Other threats indirectly harming wildlife included air pollution, adjacent land development, and some visitor use.

The report divided threatened resources into five categories: operations and biological, physical, aesthetic, and cultural resources. Many of the problems related to wildlife habitat and populations were included in the biological category, which covered a wide variety of living organisms and biological systems in the parks. Collectively, biological resources in the national parks constituted 32 percent of all the reported threatened resources. The biotic group most frequently identified as threatened was mammals, followed by plants and wetland communities. Vertebrate animals accounted for some 35 percent of the threatened biological resources. When considered together, the various ecological communities represented in the parks comprised the single largest threatened resource — 39 percent. Endangered species problems were reported in few parks.

In 1981, the National Park Service prepared a follow-up report, "State of the Parks: A Report to Congress on a Servicewide Strategy for Prevention and Mitigation of Natural and Cultural Resources Management Problems."[12] This prevention and mitigation strategy consisted of a short-term program that included the determination and ranking of significant resource problems throughout the system and a mid-term program that called for each park to formulate and use comprehensive resource-management plans.

Today the significant resource problem idea has been incorporated into National Park Service planning and budgeting as the Natural Resource Preservation Problems Program. For several years, natural resource preservation problems have received annual funding of approximately $7.5 million. Resource management plans have been prepared for a majority of the parks, and a new program to train additional natural resource managers for the park system has been established. In spite of these new efforts, however, budget, staff, and research for natural resources management still are inadequate to address the need.

Pressures from Adjacent Lands

The national parks are affected by a variety of pressures emanating from adjacent lands. These range from observable habitat destruction caused by various types of land-use development to more insidious problems such as air pollution, ground water depletion, and acid rain. Problems caused by outside sources often are complex and frequently more difficult to deal with than internal problems because the park service has no authority to control them.

The 1980 State of the Parks report explored the extent to which events occurring outside park boundaries caused damage to park resources. More than 50 percent of the perceived threats were attributed to outside sources or activities. These included residential, commercial, industrial, and road development; grazing; logging; agriculture; energy extraction and production; mining; recreation; and many others. The extent and rapid expansion of these external threats has introduced new economic, legal, and technical issues into park management.

When the large natural national parks such as Yellowstone, Glacier, and Yosemite were established, they were surrounded by huge expanses of undisturbed, often federally owned lands. These adjacent lands served as convenient buffers between the parks and civilization and often filled gaps in the park ecosystems. But as the nation's population has grown, the public lands adjacent to the parks have become increasingly subject to a variety of uses. When management activities on land surrounding a national park differ greatly from the management inside, the park may become an

Rank of Threatened Biological Resources

Threatened Resource	Number of Parks Reporting
1. Mammals (land and water)	136
2. Plant Species (land and water)	132
3. Wetland Communities/Habitats	87
4. Birds (land and water)	71
5. Woodland Communities/Habitats	67
6. Fishes	67
7. Forest Communities/Habitats	60
8. Endangered Species/Threatened Species	43
9. Invertebrates (land and water)	41
10. Grassland Communities/Habitats	34
11. Amphibians and Reptiles	33
12. Desert Communities/Habitats	20
13. Meadow Communities/Habitats	18
14. Tropical Communities/Habitats	15
15. Scrub Communities/Habitats	10
16. Cave Species (animals and plants)	8
17. Plankton	4
18. Tundra Communities/Species	4
19. Coral Communities/Species	3

Source: State of the Parks - 1980, National Park Service.

ecological island. The natural ebb and flow of wildlife into and out of the park can be disturbed. Habitat vital to park species— for example, winter range for a species — can be lost.

Conflicts between people and wildlife can only increase as human activities occur closer to the parks. For example, Shenandoah National Park in Virginia is losing black bears to poaching, road kills, and loss of habitat as the land around the park is developed. Predator control on adjacent lands also is a continuing issue. Near Carlsbad Caverns in New Mexico, ranchers claim that mountain lions kill their livestock and then retreat into the park. The ranchers argue that the lions should be followed into the park and killed to prevent future depredations. When Interior in 1983 announced plans to do this, Defenders of Wildlife and the Sierra Club sought an injunction. Interior subsequently dropped the plan.

Other examples of adjacent-lands problems include:

• Glacier National Park in Montana, where minerals extraction, timber harvesting, road construction, and oil and gas leasing on United States Forest Service lands adjacent to the park are degrading grizzly bear migration corridors, elk calving grounds, and spring feeding grounds for moose populations.

• Yellowstone National Park in Montana and Wyoming, where geothermal development, oil and gas leasing, and ski-resort development on adjacent lands are threatening or destroying vital habitat for threatened grizzly populations, concentrating the bears in reduced territories and increasing conflicts with people.

• Dinosaur National Monument in Colorado and Utah, where cricket-control programs conducted by the Bureau of Land Management on adjacent lands may interfere with the breeding success of the park's peregrine falcon.

• Canyonlands National Park in Utah, where the Department of Energy is considering a site less than one mile from the eastern boundary of the park for a proposed high-level nuclear-waste dump.

• Everglades National Park in Florida, where diversion of natural fresh water flows by Army Corps of Engineers projects and overfishing by commercial operators regulated by the National Marine Fisheries Service have affected the environment so seriously that wading-bird populations have declined 90 percent since the park was established.

• Bryce Canyon National Park in Utah, where the forest service has identified a contiguous tract of the Dixie National Forest for possible sale, a tract that lies in the immediate foreground of many park vistas.

Activities on adjacent lands can have less obvious effects on wildlife. For example, ground-water depletion in Everglades National Park is destroying habitat and changing the ecosystem's character. Threats to air and water quality, which constituted 24 percent of all the reported threats in the State of the Parks report, also can have effects on wildlife. Even small changes in lake or stream acidity caused by acid rain, for example, can inhibit reproduction in fish, and higher levels can impair body organs, alter growth rates, and decrease resistance to environmental stresses. Frogs and salamanders may be affected similarly. The loss of such species can affect other wildlife through the food chain. The elimination of fish from a lake, for example, would reduce the use of that lake by loons, mergansers, or other species dependent upon the fish for food. A recent study by the World Resources Institute identified acid precipitation as a problem in Yosemite, Sequoia, Mount Rainier, North Cascades, and Rocky Mountains national parks. Other parks, including Yellowstone, King's Canyon, Devil's Postpile, Olympic, Crater Lake, and Glacier, were found to be sensitive to acid rain damage.[13]

All the national parks will become more stressed as incompatible adjacent land uses continue. Because the viability of an important park resource — wildlife — often is dependent upon habitat outside the park, the future is likely to bring this issue increasingly into the limelight. Yet the National Park Service has limited authority and methods to deal with the problem of incompatible adjacent land uses. It has little voice even when the adjacent landowners are other federal agencies. No clear legislative statements declare which land-use practice is to take precedence where conflicts occur.

Two bills have been considered in Congress to deal at least partially with the adjacent-lands problem: the Park Protection Act, passed by the House of Representatives in the last two Congresses, which would require the park service to review other agency activities on adjacent lands to determine if the activities would harm park resources; and the Wildlife and the Parks Act, which would prohibit the expenditure of federal funds for activities that would have an adverse impact on important habitat areas within the parks and on adjacent federal lands. Both bills (discussed further under Legislation) have been highly controversial and are heavily opposed by development interests. Another partial solution, would be the adoption or issuance of administrative procedures for consultation between the National Park Service and other federal agencies, or other agencies within Interior, on activities that might affect the parks. Such a measure was considered by Interior in 1984, but no action was taken to implement such a directive.

Exotic Species

A major source of problems for park wildlife, and one of the most difficult issues for park managers, is the introduction of non-indigenous or "exotic"* species into the parks. In the 1980 State of the Parks report, more than 300 park units reported a total of 602 threats related to exotic species. Because of the seriousness of these problems, in recent years this natural-resource-management issue has received more time and funds than any other.

The most common problems caused by exotic animals concern habitat destruction. Some exotic species have become established so firmly and are so destructive of the local ecosystem that populations of native species have been reduced or even extirpated. Exotics can change normal ecological processes, such as nutrient and energy cycling; modify predator-prey and herbivore-plant relationships; and affect soil building and erosion. Because exotic species have few, if any, predators and parasites in their new environments, their population growth can overwhelm native species and destroy resources critical to the survival of the native inhabitants.

Exotic-species problems are varied and widespread. They include wild boars at Great Smoky Mountain, Haleakala, and Hawaiian Volcanoes national parks; mountain goats at Olympic National Park; Barbary sheep at Carlsbad Caverns and Guadalupe Mountains national parks; and feral burros in a number of western parks. Exotic fish introduced in earlier years to improve sport fishing also are an issue. European brown trout and western rainbow trout out-compete native Appalachian brook trout in the Great Smokies. Ironically, introduced eastern brook trout are causing similar problems in western parks. A more detailed description of a few exotic species problems follows:

Wild Boars at Great Smoky Mountains. European wild boars were introduced to a private hunting preserve in Tennessee in 1912. In an ecosystem lacking natural checks and balances, the boars multiplied and extended their range. They now inhabit three-quarters of the park and have been causing serious problems, primarily destruction of forest-floor plants and related animal communities. In the most damaged sites, the voracious boars have reduced herbaceous ground cover by as much as 98 percent. Their rooting disturbs spring wildflowers, they eat native small animals, and they radically change the upper soil structure, affecting small mammals such as voles and shrews. They also compete with native black bears for fruits and nuts, especially in the fall. Two endemic species — a salamander and a snail — are threatened because of the wild boars. Management is extremely difficult, in part because the animals are elusive and in part because local people view the boar as a desired game species and want it maintained for sport hunting.

Mountain Goats at Olympic. Mountain goats, while native to Washington's Cascade Range, were introduced into the Olympic Mountains around 1925. Now numbering more than 1,100 animals, the goats reduce plant cover, shift the dominant species of plants, and cause severe soil erosion in fragile alpine areas. Goats eat at least three rare plant species endemic to the Olympic Range and eventually could cause their extinction. The National Park Service is studying the response of the native vegetation and soil systems to the goats and is testing several goat removal and sterilization techniques.

Feral Burros in Grand Canyon, Death Valley, and Bandelier. Burros were left in these areas by miners and prospectors in the late 1800s. As their numbers grew, these animals became a major threat to park resources. Large populations destroyed vegetation, caused severe erosion, damaged prehistoric sites, and may have competed with native species such as bighorn sheep and mule deer. Historically, populations were kept in check by routine shooting. However, public pressure stopped that procedure. In Grand Canyon, live capture and removal proved costly, but most or all of the burros have been eliminated from the park. Similarly, most or all of the burros have been removed from Bandelier and two-thirds of the burros have been removed from Death Valley.

Exotic Plant Species. Another related issue with indirect effects on wildlife is the problem of exotic plant species. Like exotic animals, exotic plants can replace native flora and alter park ecosystems. Exotic plants tend to lower the level of diversity in an ecosystem, which can interrupt the food chain, harm birds and insects, and change animal population dynamics.

For example, African ice plants have taken over eroded areas in Channel Islands National Park in California, where they effectively out-compete rare native species. Tamarisk, native to the Mediterranean, has invaded springs and waterways in several desert parks. The plant's deep roots lower the water table and eliminate surface water essential to native wildlife. Hawaii Volcanoes National Park has serious problems with exotic plant species, especially with those that disrupt plant communities in the rain forests.

In Everglades National Park in Florida, Australian pines *(Casuarina)*, introduced as a windbreak and now common in Florida, change the deposition of sand on beaches, thus reducing nesting sites for the American crocodile and for sea turtles. Another troublesome exotic, *Melaleuca*, was aerially seeded in 1936 to help "dry up" the Everglades. A third exotic, Brazilian pepper, also is widespread and prevents native species from occupying certain areas. Management consists of pulling small plants out or using herbicides on larger specimens, but efforts are small compared to the size of the problem. Further, because the park is surrounded by other land where exotics are common, exotic control will always be at least a maintenance problem for the park.

The most visible success with exotic animals has been the removal of feral burros. On the whole, however, removal of exotics is tedious, expensive, and sometimes impossible. Species such as the wild boars of the Smokies, require different management approaches. Shooting, perhaps the most effective and economic technique, generally arouses tremendous controversy. Eradication of exotic plant species, while it does not arouse the controversy often associated with exotic-animal control, can be just as difficult. In general, much remains to be learned about the effects of exotic species and about ways to control their populations to prevent irreversible damage to park ecosystems and native wildlife.

Low Priority for Natural Resource Management

The National Park Service has a dual mandate: to protect park resources and to provide for the public's enjoyment of them. Historically, emphasis within the agency has shifted between the two priorities, more often focusing on visitor enjoyment. But a strong and consistent commitment to resource protection is essential to maintain the values for which the parks were set aside. The diversity and complexity of the many problems currently facing the parks emphasizes the need for an expanded program to protect and preserve park resources.

Since the issuance of the 1980 State of the Parks report, some steps have been taken to improve the management of park natural resources. These include the preparation of Resource Management Plans for a majority of park units, the identification and funding of natural resource-preservation problems, and the establishment of the Natural Resource Management Specialist Trainee Program. In addition, week-long courses in natural resource management and related specialized courses — in air and water quality for example — have been developed for park superintendents, mid-level managers, and resource specialists.

But these increases pale in comparison to the size of the task and leave natural resource management still low in park service priorities. While the effort is providing roughly $7.5 million per year for approximately 60 projects, a preliminary list of 63 priority projects developed in 1981 projected a three-year funding need of $57 million for their completion — and these 63 projects were just the most important out of a list of 266 priority projects identified at the park level. Even with this and other lesser increases, the natural resources management budget remains about five percent of the total National Park Service budget. Only about four percent of the total permanent staff — 300 people — specialize in natural resource management, although the trainee program's eventual goal is to place at least one trained natural resource specialist in each park having sufficient natural resources to warrant a full-time specialist.

Another factor limiting wildlife and other natural resource protection in the parks is lack of funding and staff to support scientific research. About 150 research scientists serve the entire National Park System. Only 20 percent of the parks have basic inventories, and the State of the Parks report said 75 percent of the threats to the parks are inadequately documented. Accurate base-line data are essential to monitoring changes in the resources and to knowing if they are caused by some outside influence or if the variability is normal. Further, such data are needed to justify management priorities, support the will to take difficult or controversial management actions, and to allocate scarce management funds effectively.

One reason for the relatively low level of natural resource funding is that visitor needs — particularly construction and repair of roads, facilities, and support systems such as water supply — are more visible, immediate, and seemingly imperative. In addition, long-time park supporters say that one of the major underlying problems for natural resource management in the park system is the generally low priority it has been given in recent years by some high-level National Park Service administrators as well as by Interior Department officials. In addition, decisions about park management priorities are influenced today by political pressure from a variety of sources. Michael Frome, one of the most published authors on the national park system, describes this phenomenon:

> Disruptions of park values come in diverse forms, but among the most devastating are those political in nature. Years ago the National Park Service built for itself a reputation as a bureau powered by professional ethics and uniquely free of political pressures. This is no longer the case. Democratic and Republican administrations alike and congressional power brokers have politicized the agency, influencing personnel selection and treating the parks like political pork on a par with roads, dams, and military bases.[14]

While it may be debatable whether wildlife and natural resources management should be given more consideration in National Park Service priorities, there can be little debate as to whether the current level of effort on natural resources management is sufficient. The fundamental purpose of the National Park System is to conserve the parks' scenic, natural, historic, and wildlife resources and to leave them unimpaired for future generations. Today, the parks are not meeting that goal.

Visitation

Many of the problems faced by the national parks are caused by people — it has been said that Americans are "loving their parks to death." In 1916, 356,000 people visited national parks. By 1930, 10 million visited. By 1950, the number jumped to 30 million. In 1984, the National Park System's 334 units hosted some 280 million visits. Throughout its history, much of the park service budget and management efforts have

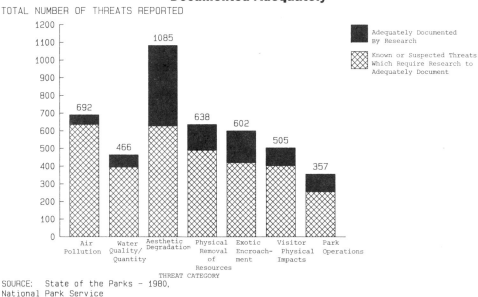

Known and Suspected Threats Requiring Adequate Documentation Compared with Threats that Are Documented Adequately

TOTAL NUMBER OF THREATS REPORTED

Adequately Documented By Research

Known or Suspected Threats Which Require Research to Adequately Document

THREAT CATEGORY

SOURCE: State of the Parks - 1980, National Park Service

been allocated to addressing the increasing demands of this growing visitation. These programs sometimes have harmed park resources, such as through construction of roads and facilities, or have diverted funding from important natural resource needs. In addition, increasing numbers of people in the parks have caused increased resource damage, including conflicts with wildlife.

In recent years, however, this growth pattern has changed. Attendance at rural parks, which generally are most important for wildlife, stopped increasing in 1978 and has since declined two percent, from 80 million visitors in 1978 to 78 million visitors in 1983. Visitation at urban parks, meanwhile, has increased from 65 million in 1978 to 90 million in 1983. Part of this increase is due to the addition of more urban parks to the National Park System, but the cause of the decrease in visits to rural parks appears to be more complex.

According to the park service's chief statistician, changing social and economic factors may be working to alter permanently the nature of park use.[15] The cost of gas and accommodations is one obvious economic factor. In the past decade, average size of cars in America has shrunk from intermediate to compact and the average driver now drives 1,500 fewer miles each year. A less obvious possible cause is the trend toward dual-income families. While these families have more money available, they have less leisure time and are less likely to drive cross-country to a rural park. Further, many who delayed marriage and children now are changing lifestyles, and people with small children travel less.

LEGISLATION

Congress considered four bills relating to wildlife in the national parks during the 98th session (1983-1984), but none of these bills was enacted:

National Park Protection and Resources Management Act.
This bill (H.R. 2379), sponsored by Representative John Seiberling (D-Ohio) and generally referred to as the Park Protection Act, required increased National Park Service efforts to address natural and cultural resource problems and required cooperative planning between the service and other government agencies that conduct development activities on lands adjacent to national parks. The legislation was a response to the 1980 State of the Parks report, which listed some 4,000 threats to the parks, more than half of them emanating from outside park boundaries.

The version of the bill passed by the House in 1983 required the Department of the Interior to conduct a variety of activities to improve resource management, including preparation of a state of the parks report every two years; the annual submission to the appropriations committees of a list of the 50 most critical natural resource and 50 most critical cultural resource problems and an estimate of the funds necessary to address them; the preparation of resource management plans for all parks, with updates every two years; and the development of a plan for the National Park Service to conduct resource inventories and to research threats to park resources, to be prepared by the National Academy of Sciences.

The most significant and controversial portion of the bill concerned the Interior secretary's review of federal activities that might harm park resources. The bill required the secretary to determine if the actions authorized by Interior — such as the issuance of grazing permits or oil and gas leases — would be likely to have a significant adverse effect on the values for which the park was established. The secretary would be required to refuse authorization for harmful activities within the parks. He also would be required to consider refusing authorization for harmful activities on adjacent lands if the adverse effects on the parks significantly outweighed the benefits of the proposed projects.

The bill required a less stringent review procedure for activities undertaken or authorized by federal agencies not in the Interior Department. If these agencies determined that a proposed action within or adjacent to a park unit might have a significant adverse effect on park resources, the bill required them to notify the secretary of the Interior. The secretary would then make recommendations regarding the protection of park resources and would submit a copy of his recommendations and the agency's decision to Congress. However, no requirement was made for congressional action on the measure, nor was the federal agency directed to delay undertaking its action to give time for congressional review. Moreover, the federal agency was not required to accommodate any of the secretary's recommendations. The bill also directed the Interior Department to initiate cooperative planning efforts with all government agencies and other entities regarding lands within or adjacent to parks and provided for small grants to local governments for the development of land-use plans.

The Park Protection Act passed the House in both the 97th and 98th Congresses. No action was taken in the Senate during either session, and the bill probably will not be reintroduced. The administration and the National Park Service opposed the bill, claiming that it created buffer zones around the parks and that the bill's major provisions were provided for elsewhere in law.

Wildlife and the Parks Act of 1984.

This bill (Amendment No. 2807 to S. 978) shared some similar goals with the Park Protection Act, but focused specifically on wildlife. Sponsored by Senator John Chafee (R-Rhode Island), the legislation was intended to protect fish and wildlife in the national park system from detrimental federally supported activities occurring both within and outside of park boundaries. The bill affected only parks larger than 5,000 acres, thus including most of the national parks with significant wildlife populations but exempting many smaller areas such as historic sites and urban recreation areas.

The bill called for the secretary of the Interior to designate wildlife-resource habitat areas on lands both within park units and on federally managed lands contiguous to the parks. It did not provide any new authority over activities on private lands outside the parks, but did cover activities on private inholdings within the parks. Federal expenditures and financial assistance detrimental to wildlife would be prohibited in these wildlife-resource habitat areas. The bill established procedures for interagency review of any proposed activities and called for periodic reports to Congress.

This amendment was attached to a bill under the jurisdiction of the Environmental Pollution Subcommittee of the Committee on Environment and Public Works, which has jurisdiction over wildlife matters, rather than the Public Lands Subcommmittee of the Energy and Natural Resources Committee, which normally has jurisdiction over park matters. The Environmental Pollution Subcommittee held a hearing on the bill, but no further action was taken, and it is not expected to be reintroduced in the 99th Congress.

Trapping in the Parks.

Two bills dealing with trapping in the national parks were introduced in the last Congress. One bill (H. R. 4962) proposed to allow the secretary of the Interior to permit trapping in 11 national park units where it is not now specifically authorized. The other, H. R. 2122, authorized trapping only in the Ozarks National Scenic Riverways. The sponsors of that bill contend that the unit's enabling legislation intended trapping to be included when it specified that hunting and fishing would be allowed as applicable with state laws.

The bills were introduced in response to rules issued by the National Park Service that confirmed a long-standing policy of prohibiting trapping in park areas unless it was specifically authorized by Congress. Trapping is specifically permitted in 20 national park units, but while reviewing its regulations, the National Park Service discovered 11 other park areas in which trapping was occurring in violation of that policy. In these areas, park managers had interpreted broadly their authority to allow hunting to encompass trapping as well. A compromise on the Ozarks bill, authorizing a two-year study of trapping in the area, passed the House in the waning moments of the 98th Congress, but was not acted upon in the Senate. The broader trapping bill was not voted upon. Concurrently, the National Rifle Association filed suit to overturn the National Park Service rules. The rules have been amended to allow trapping to continue in the 11 parks until 1987 or until the lawsuit is concluded, whichever comes first.

Alaska Sport Hunting Bill.

This bill, S. 49 by Senator Ted Stevens (R-Alaska), would have redesignated 12 million acres, later amended to 4.9 million acres, of national parks in Alaska to the category of national park preserves, thus opening the lands to sport hunting. In an unusual move, the bill was reported from the Senate Energy and Natural Resources Committee "without recommendation," and no further action was taken. This amendment seems unlikely to gain much additional support in the future. The issue of how much acreage and what areas should be open to hunting was debated hotly during the consideration of the Alaska Lands Act[16] passed in 1980, and many members of Congress are reluctant or unwilling to reopen the issue. In addition, supporters of the Alaska Lands Act believe any effort to amend the law could reopen debates on other provisions, such as energy and mineral development.

RESOURCE STATUS

The National Park Service does not have a comprehensive, coordinated system to inventory or monitor the types, amounts, or status of wildlife populations in national park units. Some data are available at the park level, either in resource management plans or among staff, but this information is not aggregated at the national level nor readily available without extensive efforts to contact numerous regional and park personnel.

Despite recent efforts to prepare resource management plans for all parks, few parks actually have a complete inventory of their wildlife. Good knowledge of the identity and status of such natural resources and how they function within ecosystems is a prerequisite to their wise stewardship. At the park level, adequate knowledge about wildlife and other natural resources is key to producing good general-management plans, documenting threats to the resources, and implementing appropriate management actions. Similarly, such basic information is critical for national planning. Although the resource management plan process has helped to provide better information on a park-by-park basis, no effort has been made to pull this information together at the national level and assess overall status and trends.

Approximately half of the 249 species of animals listed as threatened or endangered in this country occur in units of the National Park System. The National Park Service does not have an inventory of all endangered or threatened species that live in the parks. This limits the agency's ability to comprehensively protect these species, especially some of the lesser-known species.

The National Park Service's Geographic Information Systems field unit, located at the Denver Service Center, conducts some useful monitoring activities. The Remote Sensing Program, for instance, uses satellites and aerial photography to collect data on land use and to document changes around park borders. These techniques are not directly useful in monitoring wildlife because they cannot register small-scale differences. However, they are useful in monitoring vegetative changes. In the late 1970s, for example, satellite data on the perimeter of Olympic National Park discovered some trespass clearcuts.

Another program, Digital Cartography, works to compile and synthesize a range of map data, such as geologic and vegetation maps, for national park units. Computer technology allows the staff to produce various composite maps and do many more analyses than previously possible. At present, computerized data bases have been compiled for 10 to 20 parks. The content of the data bases varies from park to park, depending on the type of park and the amount of funding available.

The National Park Service has developed another data base: NPFLORA. This growing compilation of information on vascular park plants is a review of existing literature and an update of plant nomenclature, not a field inventory of park flora. About 85 parks now are represented, with about 30 parks to be added each year. Some interest has been expressed in creating a similar data base for animals, NPFAUNA, but it will not be considered until the plant system is complete.

One problem that arises from the lack of national data on wildlife status and trends is that it becomes difficult to determine the priority of various wildlife-related activities during planning at the regional or national levels. Without base-line data, no means exists for making comparisons from year to year or to chart long-term progress. Thus, changing attitudes, more than actual need, can sometimes play too large a role in determining wildlife-management priorities and funding.

REFERENCES

1. Act of August 26, 1916, Ch. 408, 39 Stat. 535 (current version at 16 U.S.C.A. 1, 2-3).
2. Ronald A. Foresta, *America's National Parks and Their Keepers* (Washington, D.C.: Resources for the Future, 1984).
3. A. Starker Leopold, "Study of Wildlife Problems in National Parks," reprinted in *Reports of the Special Advisory Board on Wildlife Management for the Secretary of the Interior, 1963-1968* (Washington, D.C.: Wildlife Management Institute, 1969).
4. Act of June 8, 1906, Ch. 3060, 34 Stat. 225 (current version at 16 U.S.C.A. 431, 432, 433).
5. 16 U.S.C.A. 1131-1136.
6. 16 U.S.C.A. 460l-4 through 460l-11.
7. U.S. Department of the Interior, National Park Service, Office of Science and Technology, "State of the Parks - 1980," May 1980.
8. U.S. Department of the Interior, National Park Service, "State of the Parks: A Report to Congress on a Servicewide Strategy for Prevention and Mitigation of Natural and Cultural Resources Management Problems," January 1981.
9. Gary Gregory, "State of the Parks 1980: Problems and Plans," *National Parks in Crisis* (Washington, D.C.: National Parks and Conservation Association, 1982).

10. U.S. Department of the Interior, National Park Service, Management Policies 1978.
11. William E. Shands, The Conservation Foundation, Testimony before the Subcommittee on Public Lands and National Parks of the Committee on Interior and Insular Affairs, U.S. House of Representatives, April 7, 1983.
12. Op. cit., U.S. Department of the Interior, National Park Service, "State of the Parks: A Report to Congress on a Servicewide Strategy for Prevention and Mitigation of Natural and Cultural Resources Management Problems," 1981.
13. World Resources Institute, *The American West's Acid Rain Test*, 1985.
14. Michael Frome, "The Ungreening of Our National Parks," *National Parks in Crisis* (Washington D.C.: National Parks and Conservation Association, 1982).
15. Kenneth E. Hornback, "Social Trends and Leisure Behavior," paper delivered at the 1985 National Outdoor Recreation Trends Symposium II, Myrtle Beach, S.C., February 24-27, 1985.
16. 16 U.S.C.A. 3101-3233.

The Forest Service faces the challenge of protecting forest-dependent species, such as this spotted owl, while planning the harvest of timber.

Wildlife and the U.S. Forest Service

by Whit Fosburgh
National Audubon Society Staff

INTRODUCTION

THE 191 MILLION acres managed by the Department of Agriculture's U.S. Forest Service include half the big game and cold-water fish habitat in the nation and habitat for 64 federally listed threatened or endangered species. But conservation and propagation of the 3,000 wildlife species found on Forest Service lands is only one of several objectives pursued concurrently by the service in its land management program.

The first national forests were created at the turn of the century to protect watersheds and to provide reserves for timber supply. Over the years other uses were added, such as grazing, recreation, energy development, and mining. Wildlife conservation was not added to the service's statutory objectives until 1960.

Today, wildlife objectives are set through the Forest Service's land management planning process as required by the 1974 Forest and Rangeland Renewable Resources Planning Act and the 1976 National Forest Management Act. Planning is done at the national, regional, and individual forest levels and is implemented by district rangers in each forest. With certain exceptions — threatened and endangered species, migratory birds, marine mammals, animal damage control, and wild horses and burros — the states have the lead responsibility for wildlife management on national forests within their borders. The Forest Service, however, manages wildlife habitat on its lands.

The traditional focus of the Forest Service's wildlife habitat management program has been big game. But with the enactment by Congress of such laws as the Endangered Species Act of 1973, which requires federal agencies to protect federally listed species, and the National Forest Management Act, which directs the Forest Service to preserve biological diversity and manage for game and nongame species, the scope of management has broadened significantly. Today the Forest Service is at the forefront of fish and wildlife research and the implementation of new habitat management techniques. Recently, however, the emphasis in the National Forest System has been directed strongly toward such areas as timber production and oil, gas, and mineral leasing, and away from wildlife. As a result, much wildlife habitat work has been diverted from habitat improvement to mitigation of the impacts of other resource management activities.

Forest Service activities are organized into three major programs: the National Forest System, Forest Research, and State and Private Forestry. Although each has significant impacts on wildlife, only the National Forest System and Forest Research will be dealt with here.*

HISTORY AND LEGISLATIVE AUTHORITY

In the second half of the 19th century, the federal government embarked on a program of massive land disposals in order to encourage and facilitate the settlement and development of the West. Eventually the government disposed of 62 percent of its 1.8 billion acres of public domain, primarily by means of land sales, land grants, and homesteading. Most of the valuable lands were given away or sold, including lands adjacent to water or transportation routes, mineral-rich lands, and highly arable lands. Much of what was left was either desert or forest.

The idea that public land should be preserved as a national resource gained support toward the end of the century as it became apparent that much of the land given away had been exploited and then abandoned. The Forest Reserve Act of 1891[1] was the first act to authorize the creation of forest reserves from the public domain. It empowered the president to create public reservations from any wholly or partially forested public lands "whether of commercial value or not."

Between 1891 and 1898, Presidents Harrison and Cleveland set aside 33 million acres as forest reserves managed by the Government Land Office in the Department of the Interior. Although no mention was made of wildlife in the Forest Reserve Act, the reserves served as inviolate sanctuaries for wildlife because timber harvest, mining, trespassing, and hunting were banned within them. These restrictions angered many Westerners, who pressured Congress to revise the law. This pressure resulted in passage of the Forest Service Organic Administration Act of 1897.[2]

The 1897 Organic Act established three purposes for the forest reserves: forest protection, watershed protection, and establishment of a perpetual source of timber. Again, no mention was made of wildlife. In 1905, the Forest Reserve Transfer Act moved the reserves from the General Land Office to the Division of Forestry in the Department of Agriculture. The Division of Forestry became the Forest Service in 1905. In 1907, forest reserves were designated "national forests."

Although wildlife was neglected in the 1897 act, strong public support existed for having federal forest reserves serve as refuges where game populations could live free from hunting pressures, reproduce, and naturally restock surrounding lands. After much debate concerning the number, size, and legality of such refuges, it finally was agreed that sections of certain forests would be designated as refuges. After President Theodore Roosevelt designated a four-acre island in Florida as a federal wildlife refuge (the beginning of the National Wildlife Refuge System), the way was paved for the establishment of game refuges. In 1905, Roosevelt signed a proclamation establishing under Forest Service jurisdiction what is now the Wichita Mountains National

---

*State and Private Forestry (often called Cooperative Forestry) works with state forestry departments, forest products industries, and smaller private landowners in order to improve forest quality. Areas of concern include better land management techniques, pest and disease control, fire control, and reforestation. Some cooperative work is done to develop wildlife habitat. In 1983, 539,917 acres were developed for this purpose, primarily in the South and Northeast.

Wildlife Refuge.[3]* The Forest Service now administers 21 national game refuges totaling 1,229,657 acres.**

Much of the success of federal conservation initiatives during the early part of the 20th century is attributable directly to the efforts of President Theodore Roosevelt and Gifford Pinchot, director of the Forest Service. After Roosevelt left Washington in 1908 and Pinchot in 1910, much of the momentum for conservation slackened. During Roosevelt's administration, 132 million acres of public domain were added to the National Forest System. Between 1910 and 1940, another 20 million acres were added, for the most part acquired from private landowners under authority granted in the 1911 Weeks Act[4] and the 1924 Clark-McNary Act.[5] The acquisitions were primarily in the East and gave the Forest Service lands in 41 states.

Aside from the periodic designation of game refuges, very little attention was paid to wildlife between the end of Roosevelt's term as president and World War II. The post-war economic boom caused an increased demand for timber, which coincided with a recreational boom in forest use. By the late 1950s it was clear that the national forests no longer could meet increased demands and that some sort of planning was needed in order to establish priorities for resource use. This situation was addressed in the Multiple Use-Sustained Yield Act of 1960,[6] the first act to recognize fish and wildlife conservation objectives specifically on national forests.

The Multiple Use-Sustained Yield Act states, "It is the policy of Congress that the national forests be administered for outdoor recreation, range, timber, watershed, and wildlife and fish purposes." The act also states that in determining national forest use, "Due consideration shall be given to the relative values of the various resources," but that the selection of uses need not be the combination "that will give the greatest dollar return or the greatest unit output."

The act frequently has been criticized as too vague, achieving little more than codifying the Forest Service's longstanding motto of "the greatest good for the greatest number in the long run." But the law did raise other resources, such as wildlife, at least theoretically to a level equal to that of timber.

In 1964, wilderness was added to the list of multiple-use considerations. As early as 1919 the Forest Service voluntarily had created the first "primitive areas"*** by administrative fiat, but increased timber harvest in the 1950s led many to fear that these unofficial wilderness areas would be declassified and harvested. Although a wilderness bill was first proposed in 1956, the same year the Multiple Use-Sustained Yield bill was introduced, wilderness legislation proved far more controversial. The Forest Service was opposed to the bill because congressionally designated wilderness areas were viewed as a detriment to the service's management flexibility and as a threat to the multiple-use approach, which was strongly supported by the Forest Service. Proponents of the wilderness bill, led by the Sierra Club and the Wilderness Society, pointed to the greatly increased recreational pressures on the forests and to the need for wilderness to meet these demands. Passage of the Wilderness Act[7] in 1964 highlighted the escalating power of environmental organizations. But despite the benefits wilderness can have for some wildlife, statutory recognition of wildlife still was limited to the Multiple Use Act. This remained true until 1974.

The Sikes Act Extension of 1974,[8] an amendment to the 1960 Sikes Act, directed the secretaries of Interior and Agriculture to develop comprehensive plans with the

---

*Now administered by the U.S. Fish and Wildlife Service.
**Hunting is now allowed on all game refuges as a population control mechanism.
***Called "wilderness" areas after 1937.

appropriate state fish and game departments in order "to develop, maintain, and coordinate programs for the conservation and rehabilitation of wildlife, fish, and game." Although the act did lead to the development of cooperative wildlife management agreements, it did little to change the virtually unlimited discretion of the Forest Service in exercising its multiple-use mandate.

The debate that preceeded and followed the Multiple Use-Sustained Yield Act regarding forest resource allocation was addressed in the 1974 Forest and Rangeland Renewable Resources Planning Act.[9] The act was concerned with long-term resource planning, going beyond the year-to-year approach often employed. As a first step, the act required the secretary of Agriculture to prepare "a comprehensive assessment of present and anticipated uses, demand for, and supply of renewable resources from the Nation's public and private forests and rangelands." The first assessment was due in 1975, the next in 1980. Subsequent assessments are to be made every ten years. Based on the first Resources Planning Act assessment, a Renewable Resources Program was to be developed, setting specific multiple-use goals for the national forests. These goals were subject to review by the president and Congress. System-wide goals were to be accomplished through "land and resources management plans" prepared by the individual units of the National Forest System. The first Renewable Resources Program was issued in 1975, with five-year updates required. The 1985 program currently is being formulated.

In 1973, the Forest Service practice of clear-cutting was challenged in a lawsuit by the Izaac Walton League. The league alleged that a clear cut in the Monongahela National Forest, West Virginia, was illegal due to a provision of the 1897 Organic Act that authorized the sale of only "dead, matured, or large growth" trees. The courts upheld the suit, and the Forest Service turned to Congress for help.[10] Help came in the form of the National Forest Management Act,[11] which repealed the language of the Organic Act upon which the suit was based. In addition, Congress took the opportunity to repair flaws in the Resources Planning Act and, in doing so, further defined the multiple-use mandate of the Forest Service.

A major flaw of the planning act was its failure to establish how land and resources management plans, also referred to as forest plans, were to be developed. The law also failed to state what these plans should contain.[12] The National Forest Management Act attempted to correct this by directing the secretary of Agriculture to develop regulations describing the development and revision of the land-management plans. To assist in this, the secretary was required to establish advisory boards "to secure full information and advice on the execution of his responsibilities. The membership of such boards shall be representative of a cross section of groups interested in the planning for and management of the National Forest System." In addition, the act called for public hearings to allow for comment on the plans.

The management act established detailed requirements for the content of the plans. Those with the greatest significance for fish and wildlife included: limitations on clear-cutting and the size and extent of even-age timber stands; provision for plant and animal diversity; restrictions against timber harvesting that seriously affects watershed and fish habitat integrity; consideration of wildlife habitat in planning; and the designation and monitoring of indicator species* whose populations and habitat needs, to the extent practicable, must be studied in cooperation with the states.

Another important aspect of the management act was its amendment to the 1930 Knutson-Vandenberg Act.[13] The Knutson-Vandenberg Act, primarily concerned with

---

*An indicator species is a species whose status is considered representative of other species with similar niche requirements.

reforestation and timber stand improvements following timber harvest, requires the purchaser of National Forest System timber to make a deposit to help pay for rehabilitation of logged areas. The National Forest Management Act amended the Knutson-Vandenberg Act to allow use of the deposited funds for the protection and improvement of fish and wildlife habitat as well. Although these funds have greatly benefited wildlife habitat management, the amendment applies only to the actual sale area and not to outside areas that also may be affected by logging activities. This has proved especially limiting in fish habitat management because timber companies are not required to rehabilitate rivers and streams that become heavily silted after timber harvest and road building in adjacent areas. In addition, since Knutson-Vandenberg funds are calculated as a percentage of the proceeds of the sale, only profitable timber sales generate improvement dollars.

In 1978 Congress passed an organic act for research, the Forest and Rangeland Renewable Resources Research Act.[14] Intended to be an accompaniment to the Forest and Rangeland Renewable Resources Planning Act, the research act updated, clarified, and consolidated forest and range research authorities to provide scientific data useful to the planning act process.

ORGANIZATION AND OPERATIONS

Responsibilities and Roles

The National Forest System covers 191 million acres, including 155 national forests, 19 national grasslands, and 18 land utilization projects.* These lands are located in 48 states. The greatest acreage in any single state is the 23,043,437 acres in Alaska. The national forests make up the bulk of the system, accounting for 186.53 million acres National grasslands account for 3.81 million acres, and land utilization projects for 59,000 acres. The great majority of the system is located in the western states. Only 24.28 million acres are located in the southern and eastern regions.

Congressional Committees

The congressional committees that handle the Forest Service are:

- Forests created from public domain (mostly western and Alaskan forests): House Interior and Insular Affairs Committee (Subcommittee on General Oversight, Northwest Power and Forest Management and Subcommittee on Public Lands and National Parks) and the Senate Energy and Natural Resources Committee (Subcommittee on Public Lands and Reserved Waters).
- Acquired forests (mostly eastern) and general forestry: House Agriculture Committee (Subcommittee on Forests, Family Farms, and Energy) and the Senate Agriculture and Forestry Committee (Subcommittee on Soil and Water Conservation).
- Budget: House Appropriations Committee (Subcommittee on Interior and Related Agencies) and the Senate Appropriations Committee (Subcommittee on Interior).

Agency Structure and Function

The Forest Service is an agency within the Department of Agriculture, supervised by the assistant secretary for Natural Resources and Environment. It is headed by a

---

*Land utilization projects are small tracts of land transferred to the Forest Service from the Soil Conservation Service (SCS) in 1973 under Title III of the Bankhead-Jones Farm Tenant Act.[15]

The Audubon Wildlife Report 1985

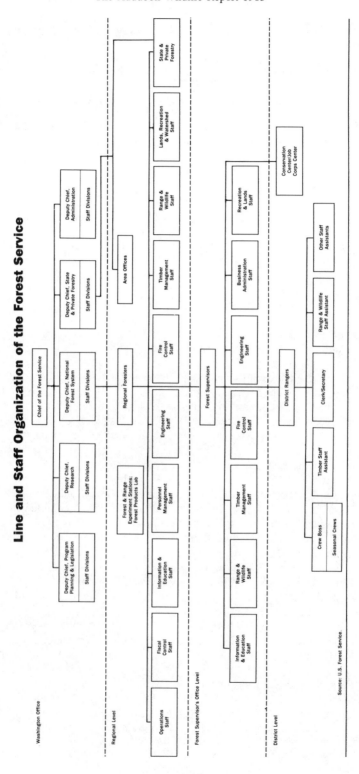

Line and Staff Organization of the Forest Service

Source: U.S. Forest Service.

312

chief who is assisted by five deputy chiefs, one each for State and Private Forestry, the National Forest System, Forest Research, Planning and Legislation, and Administration.

In Washington, the deputy chief for the National Forest System supervises 10 staff divisions: Air and Watershed Management, Wildlife and Fisheries Management, Minerals and Geology Management, Range Management, Recreation Management, Timber Management, Aviation and Fire Management, Lands, Land Management Planning, and Engineering. The function of the Wildlife and Fisheries Management Division is development of a national program for fish and wildlife resources on National Forest System lands and coordination of that program in the planning stage so that it can be carried out by field personnel.

The National Forest System is divided into nine regions, numbered 1 through 10 (Region 7 was combined with Regions 8 and 9.) Each is headed by a regional forester responsible for supervising the national forests, grasslands, and land utilization projects within his region. Regional foresters report directly to the chief of the Forest Service.

Overseeing the forest as a whole is the forest supervisor, who may oversee a neighboring national grassland or land utilization project as well. Sometimes two or more forests are combined under the supervision of a single forest supervisor, examples being the Grand Mesa, Uncompaghre, and Gunnison national forests in Colorado.

Each forest is broken down into ranger districts numbering three to eight per forest depending upon the size and needs of the forest. Each district within a forest is headed by a district ranger who, along with his staff, is in charge of the daily management of the forest.

Just under 50 percent of the districts have a fisheries or wildlife biologist on staff, but all the forests have at least one. Four hundred and fourteen wildlife and 123 fisheries biologists work for the National Forest System, a small part of a total work force of some 38,300, which includes nearly 5,800 foresters and 3,700 engineering personnel.

Forest Research's Washington office is divided into seven functional areas: Forest Environment Research, Fire and Atmospheric Sciences Research, Insects and Disease Research, Timber Management, Resource Economics Research, Forest Products and Harvesting Research, and International Forestry. Research for fish, wildlife, and range falls under Forest Environment Research. The staff director for each of the functional areas supports the deputy chief for Research and provides overall leadership, direction, and coordination in each given area.

Research is carried out at the Forest Products Laboratory in Madison and at 66 field locations that are part of eight geographically situated Forest and Range Experiment Stations. Each station is headed by a station director who oversees research activities, generally known as research "work units," in that region. Currently 201 research work units are in progress. Generally each is given a five-year authorization at the end of which it is reviewed and either revised, updated, or terminated. Changes in administration policies or funding cutbacks, however, can cause the abrupt ending of many "low priority" units.

Planning

Planning for the National Forest System is done at the national, regional, and forest level under authority granted in the 1974 planning act and 1976 National Forest Management Act, closely following steps set forth in the 1970 National Environmental Policy Act (NEPA),[16] which requires public involvement and development of environmental impact statements in the formulation and adoption of all plans. The process is designed to provide a dynamic program for determining how forest and range resources can best be managed to meet present and estimated future demands. Wildlife is among the resources that must be considered.

Forest Planning. At the base of the system's planning pyramid are the individual forest plans required by the Resources Planning Act. In the formulation of a forest plan, consideration must be given to the resources available, local demand, and national objectives. A forest plan is developed in 10 stages:

- Identification of issues and concerns
- Development of criteria for evaluation
- Inventory of the resources
- Analysis of the management situation defining maximum physical and biological production potential
- Formulation of management alternatives
- Estimated effect of alternatives
- Evaluation of alternatives
- Selection of an alternative
- Plan approval
- Monitoring

In the formulation of the plan, the forest supervisor is required to include as alternatives the maximum and minimum resource potentials; a no-action plan that continues the current level of goods and services being produced by the forest; and a program to meet national resource objectives. Forest plans have a two-way relationship with the national program: Not only do the plans reflect national objectives allocated to the forests by regional guidelines, but they also are intended to serve as a data base, complete with inventory, estimated local demand, and resource potential, that guides the formulation of the national program. Since the first round of forest plans is not due until 1985, national programs for 1975, 1980, and 1985 were not able to use the plans in program formulation.

Forest plans are to be reviewed every five to 10 years and revised at least every 15 years, except when a forest is unable to meet its objectives either because of miscalculation of supply or demand, lack of funding, or shifting national priorities. In those cases the National Forest Management Act process must begin again and a new plan must be produced. Should an adopted plan be seen as unsatisfactory by an individual or group who participated in the plan's formulation, recourse can be found in the form of an administrative appeal to the chief of the Forest Service. The secretary of Agriculture has the option of reviewing the decision of the chief. Should the appeals be denied, legal action can be taken.

Regional Guidelines. The regional guidelines serve as the link between the Resources Planning Act and the forest plans. The act establishes output requirements for each region, and the regional forester distributes them among the forests under his supervision. Although each forest can vary from the planning act objectives, the region as a whole must meet compliance. A forest supervisor can request adjustment of the unit goals if they appear unattainable. A three-month period for public review and comment follows the adoption of a regional guideline, after which the chief must approve the guideline. As with the forest plans, interested parties can appeal an approved regional guide.

National Planning. National planning consists of two main steps: the assessment and the program. The assessment describes the forest and range situation and projects future supply and demand for these resources. The most recent assessment was done in 1979. The next is due in 1989 and will be updated every 10 years thereafter. Much of the data for the 1989 assessment will come from information gathered in the forest plans.

Based on the findings of the assessment, a program is developed for the management of the National Forest System as well as for Forest Research and State and Private Forestry. The process by which the national program is developed is nearly identical to that used in the development of the forest plans, except that Congress has the final say in what the program will look like.

After the program is formulated by the Forest Service, it is given by the secretary to the president. The president reviews the program and presents it to Congress with a statement of policy that gives a justification for the chosen program, including what the national priorities are as seen by the president. Then Congress reviews the program and the president's statement of policy. The 1980 program was presented to President Carter with a "high-bound" and "low-bound" alternative from which to choose. The high-bound alternative is the costlier but more productive of the two. President Carter opted for the low-bound alternative but Congress overrode him and directed him to implement the high-bound level. Congress has since requested the Forest Service not to include a choice, but instead to recommend the program it sees as best.

Some problems with the planning act have arisen since the 1980 program was approved. Although Congress directed the president to follow the high-bound program, there is no legal requirement for the president to comply. In the five years since the program was approved, the Forest Service has been funded far below the congressionally recommended program. Some forest uses have suffered more than others. Fish and wildlife habitat management, for example, has received less than half of the recommended level of funding. Timber, on the other hand, has been funded at nearly full levels.

Congress has the power to keep all resource funding levels up but has failed to do so. Each year's annual budget reflects administration priorities or areas that are being recommended for high-level funding. For the National Forest System in 1985 the stated priorities are:

- increased timber-sales offerings and harvest administration,
- advance timber sale preparation work,
- oil, gas, and mineral leases and claims, and
- fuels management.

Research

Research is a separate program within the Forest Service, but works closely with the National Forest System in providing information for a successfully balanced management. In the context of research and development, research provides the information that is then developed on the ground by the system personnel. Fish and wildlife research presently is done at 22 locations in 24 research work units, employing 50 Forest Service biologists plus supporting university cooperators. From FY 1979 through 1983 research has resulted in publication of 633 wildlife or fish papers in scientific journals, Forest Service and other agency technical papers, symposium proceedings, and other outlets. Among these were five books on wildlife subjects.

Research Branch funding has gone from $127,812,000, including general administration, in 1981 to $120,964,000 for 1985. In 1981 there were 242 research work units, down to 207 in 1984. Following Reagan administration budget cuts the number of scientists dropped from 965 to 794. Wildlife, range, and fish habitat research has suffered a 10.5 percent decline during this same period, going from $9,905,000 to $8,876,000. Funding within this division is roughly broken down as follows: wildlife—65 percent; range—25 percent; and fish—10 percent.

Forest Research
Research Work Units

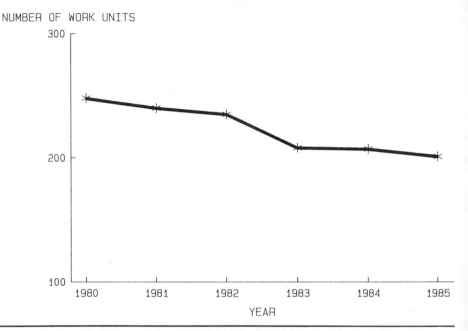

Research priorities traditionally follow priorities set in the National Forest System. Increasingly, fish and wildlife research has focused on the study of whole species complexes in the biotic community and the integration of wildlife and fisheries resources with other uses and products of the forests and rangelands. Due to limited funding in recent years, research has had to focus on high priority needs such as old-growth, anadromous fish, certain endangered species, and management indicator species.

Presently there are four major areas of wildlife and fish habitat research: anadromous fish, threatened, endangered, and sensitive species and their habitats; grazing/ wildlife relationships; and forest management and wildlife.

Anadromous Fish. Anadromous fish research focuses on chinook, coho, sockeye, pink, and chum, salmon, steelhead and cutthroat trout, and one species of char, the Dolly Varden. All depend heavily on the forested watersheds of the Pacific Northwest and Alaska to complete their life cycles. The role of research is to clarify the often confusing relationships between land management activities and the anadromous fish and its habitat. A predictive relationship between habitat quality and fish numbers can be established only if the fish's habitat requirements are thoroughly known.

Although results of several major studies on this subject have been published, more information is needed. Present research focuses on understanding habitat needs for fish rearing, the influence of timber harvesting activities on habitat, hydrologic processes of habitat formation, and cost-effective methods to improve habitat. The units working on anadromous fish research are centered in Juneau, Alaska; Corvallis, Oregon; Arcata, California; and Boise, Idaho.

Recent accomplishments of the anadromous fish research program include:
- development of a compendium of the effects of forest and rangeland management on anadromous fish habitat;

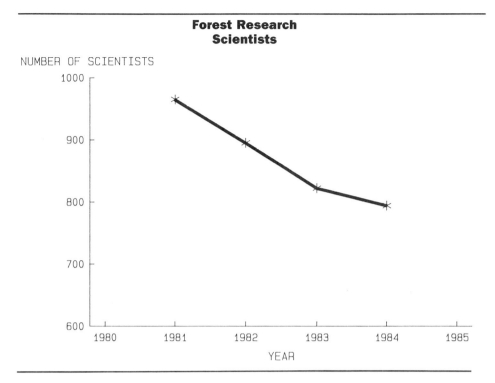

**Forest Research
Scientists**

- development of a preliminary stream classification system and sediment model;
- studies of how fish use submerged branches and other debris for habitat, and development of a risk-rating system to assess the potential effects of debris torrents on salmonoid habitat;
- major breakthroughs in development of instrumentation to measure the quality of subsurface stream gravel, so that managers can determine the quality of spawning riffles and provide a means to study the subsurface gravel environment of salmonoid eggs;
- determination of spawning habitat requirements of several anadromous salmonoids;
- definition of the importance of large organic debris for salmonoid habitat and development of guides for debris management; and
- definition and quantification of hydrologic events in controlling the formation of salmonoid habitat.

Threatened, Endangered, and Sensitive Species. Presently highlighted in this research area are species that have come into direct conflict with Forest Service resource uses. The two primary examples are research on the endangered red-cockaded woodpecker and on the spotted owl, a sensitive species. In both cases, emphasis is on the linkage between old growth and species habitat requirements. Researchers also are looking for other old-growth dependent species.

In addition to this, several research locations are investigating habitat requirements and developing management methods for cavity-nesting species, a group whose habitat is very sensitive to intensive forest management.

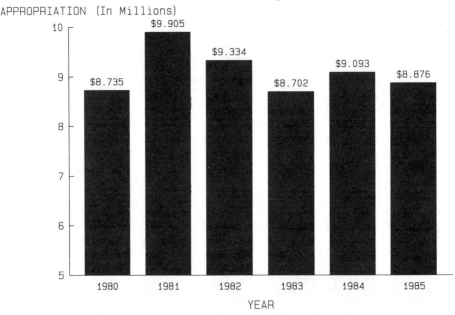

Wildlife, Range and Fish Habitat
Research Funding

Recent accomplishments in the threatened, endangered, and sensitive research area include:

- Research on the habitat requirements of and development of management guidelines for several species, including the Kirtland's warbler, bald eagle, peregrine falcon, eastern timber wolf, Indiana bat, gray bat, Gila trout, Gila topminnow, masked bobwhite, Puerto Rican parrot, several Hawaiian birds, and the California condor.
- Other research on the requirements of species that, although not threatened or endangered, are sensitive to management activities. Habitat requirements for several species of raptors have been defined for the Pacific northwest, south, and north-central United States. Management guides have been defined for nesting accipiter hawks in the western United States. Bioenergetics of hawks in the central United States have been studied in connection with interactions with timber harvesting. In Alaska, a major effort has highlighted the management of black-tailed deer in old-growth forests.
- Snags, or standing dead trees, provide an essential part of the life support system for some 85 species of birds and 49 species of mammals and are among habitats most sensitive to intensive forest management. Research has defined the specific habitat requirements for cavity-using species such as the pileated woodpecker and the northern flying squirrel. Other research has examined life expectancy of snags and developed ways to produce snag habitat.

Wildlife and Fish and Livestock Grazing. Two main phases of this research area presently are under way. The first is examining the interactions between cattle and wildlife and fish in critical riparian zones, with activities headquartered in Tempe, Arizona; Boise, Idaho; and LaGrande, Oregon. The second area of concentration is dietary competition and other kinds of direct interaction between livestock and wild ungulates, such as antelope, elk, and deer, in non-riparian areas. Current efforts here center in Fresno, California; LaGrande, Oregon; Alexandria, Louisiana; and Missoula, Montana. The Forest Service's Forest Environment Research staff points out that additional research is needed for the development of grazing schemes for protection of riparian zones.

Recent accomplishments:

- Some grazing interactions with anadromous fish have been defined in riparian zones in the Pacific northwest and intermountain west. In the northern plains, a method of regenerating woody draws under a grazing regime has been developed.
- The relationship between livestock and wild herbivores has been examined in several locations. Dietary competition has been quantified, for example, among cattle, sheep, and pronghorns in the southern Great Plains, knowledge useful in the allocation of forage. Elsewhere, the relationship between lifestock watering areas and distribution and productivity of pronghorns has been studied. In the northern plains, a grazing-vegetation-prairie dog interaction has been demonstrated.
- Research has resulted in quantification of rangeland habitat used by various wildlife species and has shown how range management can affect these species. In California, wildlife communities on annual grasslands have been surveyed. Similar studies have been completed in woody draws of the northern plains and riparian zones of the Pacific Northwest. In the southern Great Plains, information on the habitat requirements of scaled quail, lesser prairie chicken, mule deer, and white-tailed deer has been developed.
- Research by the intermountain station has developed means for reclaiming unproductive rangeland and wildlife habitat, and the Rocky Mountain station has produced methods for reclamation of surface-mined lands for wildlife habitat.

Forest Management and Wildlife. Because of the National Forest System's priority on increased timber production, research has emphasized understanding how the multiple species complexes that make up forest wildlife communities change following the cutting of timber. In connection with this, studies are being carried out on management indicator species to determine the effects of timber harvesting on their populations. In addition, research is developing methods to monitor the effects of timber harvesting on wildlife. Still needed is further study of different species habitat needs so that predictive models can be developed to assess proposed resource activities.

Recent accomplishments:

- Research on the habitat requirements of several forest species has produced information that has been used to develop management guides and/or predictive habitat models. Species include the black bear, fisher, red squirrel, Abert's squirrel, northern flying squirrel, beaver, elk, whitetailed deer, wild turkey, cow bird, yellowthroat, and other forest birds.
- Research has shown how habitat and/or whole species complexes change with timber harvesting, stand development, and forest succession. Such work, for example, has been done in the Great Lakes states' aspen forests, central states' oak-hickory, the ponderosa pine forests of the Southwest, and southern pine forests.
- Breakthroughs in management and planning include the Southern Station's discovery that bird songs change depending on the habitat quality which could

The Forest Service
United States Department of Agriculture

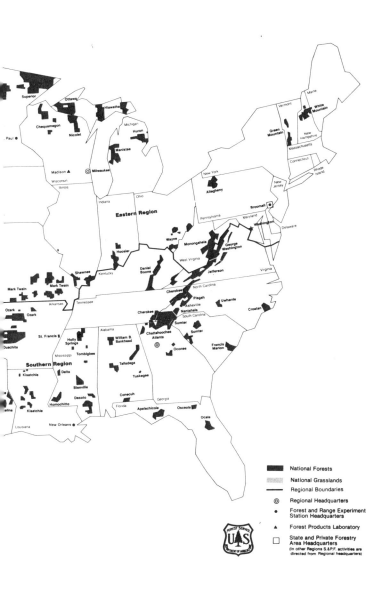

National Forests	
National Grasslands	
Regional Boundaries	
◎ Regional Headquarters	
• Forest and Range Experiment Station Headquarters	
▲ Forest Products Laboratory	
▢ State and Private Forestry Area Headquarters (In other Regions S.&P.F. activities are directed from Regional headquarters)	

prove important in monitoring habitat condition, and a new framework and system for cost-effective monitoring of avian populations and their habitat, developed by the Pacific-southwest station.

Budget

In the Forest Service budget, fish and wildlife habitat management is classified as "habitat improvement" or "wildlife support." Habitat improvement, also called direct habitat management, is defined by the Forest Service as ". . . an activity applied to the land or stream or lake that is not dependent on some other resource function for its support." Activities include prescribed burning to stimulate forage for big game animals, water developments, installing nesting structures for waterfowl, and stream or lake spawning bed or fish-cover development. Direct habitat management includes work done through Knutson-Vandenberg funding.

Wildlife support, or indirect habitat management, is intended to "minimize adverse impacts from other resource programs to fish and wildlife habitats and, whenever possible, to design those projects to produce concurrent fish and wildlife outputs." Specific activities may include streamside protection measures for fish habitats affected by timber harvesting, roading, or grazing; timber sales designed to meet wildlife habitat objectives; and livestock grazing plans modified to protect wildlife needs in riparian zones.

In the past six years the National Forest System has received a funding increase of approximately 12.5 percent, rising from $927,774,000 in the 1980 Forest Service budget to $1,045,680,000 in 1985. Individual programs within the National Forest System are difficult to track over this period because general administration costs were included in each program prior to the 1982 budget, when general administration became a separate line item.

Since the first Reagan adminstration budget in 1982, the wildlife and fish habitat management program has increased from $33,136,000 to $36,626,000 in the 1985 budget, approximately a 10 percent increase without adjusting for inflation. However, the current funding level is less than half the 1984 level of $83 million recommended by the 1980 Resource Planning Act program. Moreover, although overall wildlife and fish dollars have remained fairly constant, emphasis within the program has shifted from habitat improvement to wildlife and fisheries support. Whereas habitat improvement received more funding in 1980 and 1981 than did wildlife fisheries support, by the 1985 budget, support funding was nearly double that for improvement. The primary reason is additional mitigation needs resulting from accelerated resource development programs such as timber (funded at $159,836,000 in 1982 and $194,226,000 in 1985, a 21.5 percent increase over four years) and minerals ($18,691,000 in 1982 to $26,479,000 in 1985, a 41.6 percent increase). The increase in the mineral program is furthur shown by the fact that in the 1980 Carter budget, which includes general administration, the program was only funded at $15,892,000. Within the Habitat Improvement section of the budget are four subdivisions: wildlife (45 percent of the habitat improvement budget in 1985); resident fish (12.5 percent); threatened, endangered, and sensitive species (17 percent); and anadromous fish (26.5 percent).

The Forest Service is charged with responsibility for maintaining wildlife populations and a diversity of species within the National Forest System. The great majority of the habitat management work concentrates on species that the Forest Service is either legally required to manage, such as threatened and endangered species, or on species that are in especially high public demand and sensitive to other resource uses,

National Forest Service
Wildlife and Fish Habitat Management Funding

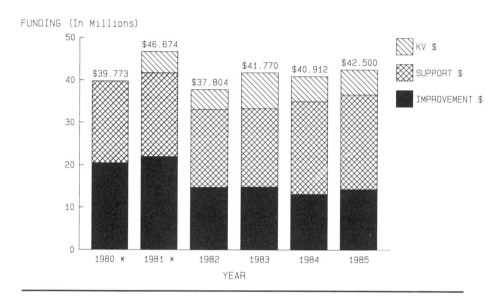

FUNDING (In Millions)

including elk, deer, waterfowl, and anadromous fish. Although 64 threatened and endangered species occur within the National Forest System, management is essentially limited to 13 species: grizzly bear, California condor, Kirtland's warbler, red-cockaded woodpecker, Lahonton cutthroat trout, Paiute trout, woodland caribou, bald eagle, peregrine falcon, Puerto Rican parrot, and, to a lesser degree, the gray, Indiana, and Virginia big-eared bats. In 1984, a push to do more with threatened and endangered plants has meant that of the 20 listed plant species, eight have FWS approved recovery plans and seven others have plans currently in agency draft.

CURRENT TRENDS

The primary trend in wildlife and fish habitat management on the National Forest System in the past five years has been the shift in emphasis from habitat improvement to wildlife support. While funding and acres mitigated have increased from 1980 to the present under wildlife support, both have declined dramatically for habitat improvement. In addition, much of the habitat improvement money allocated is being used to mitigate other resource uses, primarily timber sales, instead of being used to improve existing habitat. As a result, Forest Service fisheries and wildlife personnel are trying merely to maintain current population levels in the face of increased resource development priorities.

Other trends during the past five years have been increased recreational demand on the National Forest System, development of a new habitat management program, and a new initiative to conserve anadromous fish.

Estimated Consumptive and Non-consumptive Recreation Visitor Days on National Forests and Grasslands — Fiscal Year 1984

Region	Cold Water Fishing	Warm Water Fishing	Salt Water Fishing	Ice Fishing
1 RVDs	894,500	11,900	0	16,500
Percent	96.9	1.3	0	1.8
2 RVDs	1,628,000	38,500	0	11,200
Percent	97.0	2.3	0	.7
3 RVDs	659,000	296,500	0	1,500
Percent	68.9	31.0	0	.2
4 RVDs	2,184,300	4,200	0	2,100
Percent	99.7	.2	0	.1
5 RVDs	2,339,900	390,700	43,900	12,500
Percent	84.0	14.0	1.6	.4
6 RVDs	1,743,500	10,400	27,200	2,200
Percent	97.8	.6	1.5	.1
8 RVDs	787,400	1,966,900	11,500	700
Percent	28.5	71.1	.4	0
9 RVDs	639,500	1,327,600	300	161,200
Percent	30.4	62.4	0	7.6
10 RVDs	249,500	0	137,300	3,200
Percent	64.0	0	35.2	.8
TOTAL	11,125,600	4,046,700	220,200	211,100
	71.3	25.9	1.4	1.4

Use expressed in recreation visitor days (RVDs) as provided by the recreation information management data base (RIM).

Recreational Use

The decrease in habitat improvement funding has coincided with an increase in recreational use of the National Forest System. Overall there were 228 million recreational visitor days * on the national forest system in 1983, which made up 42 percent of the recreational visitor days of all federal lands. In 1984 wildlife and fisheries resources accounted for 32.1 million user days, or approximately 15 percent of the total recreational use. Fishing made up 48.5 percent of this, hunting 47.5 percent, and nature study the final four percent. Sale of hunting and fishing licenses have increased 45 percent and 49 percent respectively in the last 20 years. These upward trends are expected to continue, with the Forest Service predicting a 90 percent increase in angling demand by the year 2030.

Wildlife and Fish Habitat Relationships

The Wildlife and Fish Habitat Relationships Program, pioneered by Jack Thomas in the 1979 Forest Service publication "Wildlife Habitats in Managed Forests: The Blue Mountains of Oregon and Washington," guides the system employed by the Forest Service to predict the effects of development activities on fish or wildlife

*A visitor day, or user day, is described as one person using an area (in this case a national forest or grassland) for 12 hours, or 12 persons for 1 hour, or any equivalent.

Estimated Consumptive and Non-consumptive Recreation Visitor Days on National Forests and Grasslands — Fiscal Year 1984 (Continued)

Big Game Hunting	Small Game Hunting	Upland Game Bird Hunting	Water-fowl Hunting
1,089,300	73,000	188,000	55,200
77.5	5.2	13.4	3.9
1,324,600	101,700	54,200	29,900
87.7	6.7	3.6	2.0
820,300	154,200	110,800	61,800
71.5	13.4	9.7	5.4
1,327,600	76,800	123,800	49,400
84.3	4.9	7.9	2.9
850,300	134,000	103,500	28,200
76.2	12.0	9.3	2.5
1,866,100	99,300	136,300	46,500
86.9	4.6	6.3	2.2
2,006,600	1,278,700	411,600	100,200
52.8	33.7	10.8	2.6
1,222,500	584,500	399,700	188,300
51.0	24.4	16.7	7.9
104,700	12,300	13,300	19,300
70.0	8.2	8.9	12.9
10,612,000	2,515,300	1,541,200	575,800
69.6	16.5	10.1	3.8

habitat. Using information about an individual species' relationship with its habitat, a model is developed that predicts the overall suitability of a particular habitat for the species and the habitat's potential production capability. The system can be used during development planning to predict a fish or wildlife habitat response to a potential alteration of this habitat.

The effect of this system has been to allow the Forest Service greater latitude in habitat management. Whereas elk and deer dominated in the past, the system can be used on whole species complexes. In addition, it allows for the prediction of resource development conflicts and trade-offs as opposed to purely reactive management. This predictive function, along with a cumulative effects analysis that relates past resource development activities to present habitat conditions, was upheld legally in 1984 in National Wildlife Federation v. the Forest Service (Mapleton),[17] which found a proposed clear cut of the Siuslaw National Forest threatening to anadromous fish habitiat.

Anadromous Fish Initiative

In 1982 the Forest Service embarked on a major initiative to restore instream habitats for anadromous fish in the Northwest, where steelhead and salmon populations are at an all-time low. Some 50 percent of the salmon and steelhead spawning and rearing habitat in California, Oregon, Washington, and Idaho is on national forests. In Alaska, the figure is 27 percent. In 1983, fishermen took from these habitats approximately 118 million pounds of fish with a dockside commercial value of $123 million. In addition, sport fishing accounted for some 721,000 user days which, combined with the indirect commercial value, makes the total economic value of these fisheries $349

Estimated Consumptive and Non-consumptive Recreation Visitor Days on National Forests and Grasslands — Fiscal Year 1984 (Continued)

Total Nature Study	Total Fishing	Total Hunting	Total Recreation Visitor Days
99,800	922,900	1,406,300	2,429,000
4.1	38.0	57.9	100
140,600	1,677,700	1,510,400	3,328,700
4.2	50.4	45.4	100
189,900	957,000	1,147,100	2,294,000
8.3	41.7	50.0	100
106,200	2,190,600	1,574,600	3,871,400
2.7	56.6	40.7	100
262,800	2,787,000	1,116,000	4,165,800
6.3	66.9	26.8	100
147,300	1,783,300	2,148,200	4,078,800
3.6	43.7	52.7	100
191,900	2,766,500	3,797,100	6,755,500
2.8	41.0	56.2	100
106,400	2,128,600	2,395,000	4,630,000
2.3	46.0	51.7	100
24,700	390,000	149,600	564,300
4.4	69.1	26.5	100
1,269,600	15,603,600	15,224,300	32,117,500
4.0	48.6	47.5	100

Source: U.S. Forest Service

Wildlife and Fish Acres of Habitat Improvement

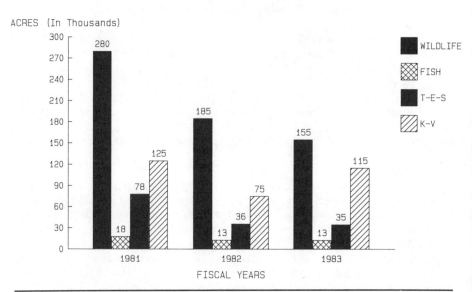

million. The Forest Service estimates that fish production could be increased more than 60 percent, angling use tripled, and fisheries-related employment doubled to nearly 20,000 by improving of the spawning and rearing habitat on national forests.

The current population decline for salmon and steelhead is attributable to over-fishing, dams, and deterioration of spawning and rearing habitat. The Forest Service, in cooperation with the states and to a lesser degree with other federal agencies, the Northwest Power Planning Council, individual Indian tribes, and private aquaculture and sportsmen's organizations, has begun to correct this problem. The service is encouraging habitat improvement, barrier removal, instream pool and cover develop-ment, streambank stabilization, streambank fencing, and lake fertilization. The initia-tive is to be supported primarily by increased funding from Congress. The Forest Service estimates that an initial $7.7 million, rising to $14.2 million in five years, is needed to successfully implement the program, which by the year 2000 will have required a $200 million investment. In 1985, Congress appropriated the Forest Service only $3.8 million for anadromous fish habitat improvement. At the present level of funding, the Forest Service predicts an additional 10 percent reduction in habitat quality by the year 2000.

CURRENT ISSUES

All 191 million acres of the National Forest System serve as wildlife or fish habitat to some extent, so any action affecting these lands has potential consequences for these resources. Current fish and wildlife issues include the effects of harvesting old-growth forests, management of the grizzly bear, the impacts of below-cost timber sales and roading, and the adverse effects of livestock grazing in riparian zones.

Old-Growth Timber Harvest and Wildlife

Over the past century, old-growth timber stands have been almost totally depleted on private lands by widespread initial harvest and subsequent cutting on short rotations in order to maximize profits. Because the Forest Service traditionally has employed a far less intensive management scheme, often following a policy of non-declining yield, the National Forest System has become the principal area of remaining old-growth stands of timber in the United States today. But accelerated harvest schedules over the past decade have rapidly reduced existing old-growth stands, and this has raised a storm of controversy. Much of the controversy surrounds the impacts of such harvest on various old-growth-dependent wildlife species. The question has arisen of how to maintain sufficient quantities of old growth for wildlife, recreational, scienti-fic, and water-quality needs while still allowing timber harvest.

Old growth is defined in two ways. The first, traditional definition is age. Any trees over a specified age (250 years for Douglas fir in the Pacific Northwest, 80 years for loblolly pine in the Southeast) are considered old growth. The second is an ecological, or functional, definition. This definition is based on the forest having certain characteristics that make it perform the functions of old growth.

The Forest Service's legal imperative to preserve old-growth is unclear. Nowhere is old growth specifically mentioned in the principal laws governing forest manage-ment, but certain statutes imply that old-growth stands should be conserved. Some conservationists and biologists have advocated the preservation of old-growth timber as a multiple-use objective of forest management. In addition, the National Forest Management Act required the Forest Service to maintain biological diversity, a provi-sion that has direct application to old growth. Yet the Forest Service still has no set

Population Estimates of Big-game Animals on National Forests and Grasslands in 1983

	Northern Region	Rocky Mountain Region	South-western Region	Inter-mountain Region	Pacific Southwest Region	Pacific Northwest Region	Southern Region	Eastern Region	Alaska Region	Total
Alligator	0	0	0	0	0	0	8,105	0	0	8,105
Barbary Sheep	0	0	332	0	0	0	0	0	0	332
Bighorn Sheep (Desert)	0	524	107	845	601	0	0	0	0	2,077
Bighorn Sheep (Other)	4,665	7,819	667	2,959	739	582	0	0	0	17,431
Bison	0	0	100	66	0	0	0	0	0	166
Black Bear	19,809	7,364	5,630	8,872	9,218	18,332	8,027	12,097	13,250	97,599
Black-tailed Deer	0	0	0	0	183,644	222,133	0	0	158,500	564,277
Caribou	20	0	0	0	0	6	0	0	0	26
Dall Sheep	0	0	0	0	0	0	0	0	1,840	1,840
Elk Rocky Mtn	119,704	138,939	24,580	79,146	316	66,395	0	0	0	429,079
Elk Roosevelt	0	0	0	225	200	32,694	0	0	0	33,119
Grizzly Bear	387	95	0	0	0	4	0	0	0	486
Javelina	0	0	24,701	0	0	0	0	0	0	24,701
Moose	6,806	1,144	0	7,772	0	45	0	6,978	4,880	27,625
Mountain Goat	4,234	1,017	0	2,399	0	4,471	0	0	11,180	23,301
Mountain Lion	1,574	887	2,549	2,310	1,382	1,867	0	0	0	10,569
Mule Deer	147,356	270,735	145,239	508,691	184,450	217,600	0	0	0	1,474,071
Pronghorn Antelope	5,395	30,674	5,673	12,722	3,137	2,080	0	0	0	59,681
Turkey	5,415	19,480	35,749	719	5,537	1,849	124,133	39,438	0	232,320
White-tailed Deer	73,071	57,906	34,136	1,250	5	15,665	275,526	318,042	0	775,601
Wild Boar	0	0	0	50	1,015	0	1,954	5,954	0	8,984
Wolf	15	0	0	15	0	2	0	348	765	1,145

From 1983 FS Wildlife & Fisheries Annual Report.

policy on old growth conservation. Three species currently demonstrate the old-growth controversy: the spotted owl, red-cockaded woodpecker, and Sitka black-tailed deer.

Spotted Owl. The northern spotted owl (*Strix occidentalis*) is a medium-sized owl native to the coniferous old-growth forests of the Pacific Northwest. The U.S. Fish and Wildlife Service (FWS), in its 1982 status review of the spotted owl, named timber harvest as the greatest existing threat to the survival of the species:

> . . . Timber harvesting continues to decrease spotted owl habitat. Demand for all types of forest products has depleted old-growth stocks to the point where there is only limited acreage remaining. The existing habitat is confined mostly to federal lands. There are no threats to the habitat of the owl on National Park Service land, but almost all good habitat on Forest Service and Bureau of Land Management lands is or will be in the near future subject to timber sale consideration. Sale and subsequent logging of the habitat is occurring at a rapid rate today and will result in serious damage or destruction of spotted owl habitat.[18]

FWS estimates that almost all the old-growth timber stands within the spotted owl's range will be harvested within the next five to 20 years if present management objectives are not changed.

A great deal of scientific uncertainty surrounds the spotted owl. There is little agreement as to the present population size of the birds, although FWS estimated the number of pairs at 2,500 in 1982. It generally is agreed that these numbers are decreasing, but at an estimated rate that varies depending on whom one asks. The habitat requirements of the owl also are subject to dispute.

Harvest Estimates of Big-game Animals on National Forests and Grasslands in 1983

	Northern Region	Rocky Mountain Region	South-western Region	Inter-mountain Region	Pacific Southwest Region	Pacific Northwest Region	Southern Region	Eastern Region	Alaska Region	Total
Alligator	0	0	0	0	0	0	0	0	0	0
Barbary Sheep	0	0	28	0	0	0	0	0	0	28
Bighorn Sheep (Desert)	0	16	1	16	0	0	0	0	0	33
Bighorn Sheep (Other)	258	200	11	94	0	9	0	0	0	572
Bison	0	0	19	0	0	0	0	0	0	19
Black Bear	1,873	761	456	886	651	1,572	364	1,255	572	8,390
Black-tailed Deer	0	0	0	0	8,934	18,036	0	0	8,133	35,103
Caribou	0	0	0	0	0	0	0	0	0	0
Dall Sheep	0	0	0	0	0	0	0	0	23	23
Elk Rocky Mtn	18,621	31,083	2,969	13,151	0	14,019	0	0	0	29,813
Elk Roosevelt	0	0	0	0	3	4,166	0	0	0	4,169
Grizzly Bear	19	0	0	0	0	0	0	0	0	19
Javelina	0	0	3,865	0	0	0	0	0	0	3,865
Moose	519	87	0	1,003	0	0	0	0	375	1,984
Mountain Goat	179	44	0	40	0	198	0	0	440	901
Mountain Lion	192	82	435	227	7	120	0	0	0	1,063
Mule Deer	21,061	46,649	18,738	81,630	6,300	25,123	0	0	0	199,501
Pronghorn Antelope	640	7,443	263	961	180	125	0	0	0	9,612
Turkey	679	2,623	2,080	24	151	38	11,569	7,377	0	26,541
White-tailed Deer	14,317	5,404	3,486	24	0	2,095	49,120	56,564	0	131,010
Wild Boar	0	0	0	1	61	0	171	2,360	0	2,593
Wolf	0	0	0	0	0	0	0	0	87	87

From 1983 FS Wildlife & Fisheries Annual Report.

Realizing that there was a decline in the spotted owl's population, the Forest Service classified the species as "sensitive" in 1975. Sensitive species designation is applied when a potentially unfavorable management situation exists for a fish, wildlife, or plant species. The aim is to avoid actions that would make the species threatened or endangered under the Endangered Species Act.[19] Since the range of the spotted owl, which is restricted to the Far West from just north of the Canadian border south to central California, overlaps the most economically valuable timber stands in the nation, a federal listing could have very severe economic consequences. Such a listing would prohibit the Forest Service from taking any action that would jeopardize the continued existence of the owl, and this could curtail a significant amount of old-growth harvest.

In 1979, the Forest Service adopted a spotted owl management plan based on the findings of a federal-state interagency task force. The plan called for providing each pair of owls with a home range of 300 acres of old-growth, surrounded by 1,200 acres of other forest, 50 percent of which had to be more than 30 years old. After the Forest Service adopted this plan, the National Wildlife Federation appealed the decision on the grounds that no environmental impact statement had been done before its adoption. In 1980, the chief of the Forest Service denied the appeal.

In 1981, after more extensive research, the area to be preserved for each owl pair's home range was increased from 300 to 1,000 acres of old growth. This was incorporated into the regional guide, which did not finally come out until 1984. Again, the National Wildlife Federation and several other local conservation groups appealed adoption of the spotted owl management plan without the formulation of an environmental impact study. Should the appeal be denied again, the federation and other groups are likely to sue the Forest Service. The legal basis for their suit would be the allegation that the Forest Service is in violation of the National Forest Management Act, which requires the Forest Service to maintain viable populations of all species. Again the problem of scientific uncertainty enters in. Some, including the Forest Service, believe that a minimum viable population is as low as 500 pairs, whereas others feel that the present number already is below the minimum. The National Wildlife Federation and the other groups want the Forest Service to halt the destruction of the old-growth spotted owl territory until an environmental impact statement can be done.

The specter of federal listing as threatened or endangered still remains, but many conservation groups are reluctant to pursue this course for fear that the spotted owl could cause harmful revision of the Endangered Species Act, which is up for congressional reauthorization in 1985. A proposed solution is the listing of the spotted owl as threatened or endangered over parts of its range. The biggest obstacle to this is that any decision as to where to list the owl is bound to be very controversial, because few jurisdictions would want the harvest restrictions that would be imposed. Since the appeal by the federation, the spotted owl has been given more time because decreased timber demand in the region has slowed harvest. It is hoped that this will allow more research to be done on the important questions of the owl's home range and minimum viable population.

The Red-cockaded Woodpecker. The red-cockaded woodpecker (*Picoides borealis*) is at the center of a dispute in the old-growth softwood forests of the Southeast. This controversy has simmered since the species was federally listed as endangered in 1970. The controversy may come to a head in 1985. The principal actors in this drama are the Forest Service, FWS, and conservation organizations led by the National Wildlife Federation.

The red-cockaded woodpecker is a native of old-growth (80 to 150 years old) conifer forests from Texas to Virginia, primarily continuous stands of mature loblolly and longleaf pines. Although many woodpecker species are quite social, the red-cockaded's behavior is unique. It lives in family groups called clans. A clan's nesting territory, called a colony, is defended from other red-cockadeds. Each clan has one nesting pair and several "helpers." These helpers usually are young male offspring of one or both of the nesting pair, and they help the pair in incubating the eggs, feeding the young, excavating cavities for nest sites, and defending the territory. Each colony may contain anywhere from two to nine birds.

The red-cockaded makes its nests in cavities in living pine trees. These trees are usually between 80 and 100 years of age, old enough for the trees to become susceptible to red-heart fungus, which weakens the tree's heartwood and allows it to be excavated by the woodpecker. The red-cockaded will stay in its territory unless undergrowth becomes high enough to reach the nests, allowing predators easy access, or until the trees are taken over by competitors or destroyed by other habitat alterations.

It is estimated that the acreage of mature pines in the Southeast has declined by 60 percent in the last 40 years. The decrease has been mostly a result of harvests on private lands, followed by reforestation and then harvesting on short rotational cycles, usually about 30 years. In the Southeast, the Forest Service traditionally has employed a policy of much less intensive harvest, so although the Forest Service owns only about five percent of the southeastern pine forests, its lands contain approximately 70 percent of the remaining red-cockadeds, or about 2,000 nesting colony sites. Over the past two decades, an estimated 13 percent decline has occurred in usable habitat on the national forests of the Southeast.

In 1980, FWS, which legally has the lead in the management of endangered species, issued a biological opinion declaring that the timber harvest plans in the Southeast, outlined in the regional guide, would jeopardize the continued existence of the red-cockaded. The biological opinion gave the Forest Service two alternatives for timber harvesting that would protect the red-cockaded. The first alternative was to manage the forest within one mile of existing red-cockaded colonies on a rotation of 100 + years old for longleaf pine and 80 + years old for loblolly and other pines. The second alternative allowed for shorter rotation, 80 + years for longleaf and 70 + years for loblolly, to be offset by the use of "recruitment stands," 25-acre areas of old growth that theoretically could be used by red-cockadeds as colony sites if they abandoned or were forced out of their existing colony sites, or as sites to attract new colonies. This alternative called for one recruitment stand within a quarter to three-quarters of a mile of each existing colony.

The Forest Service required individual forests to achieve compliance with one of the two alternatives by the time the new forest plans, in which the management changes were to be incorporated, were released. The National Forest Management Act requires these plans to be made before September 30, 1985. The Forest Service began to release these draft plans in 1984. According to the National Wildlife Federation and other conservation organizations, the first draft plans released, those of the Francis Marion and Kisatchie national forests, fell short of the requirements of the 1980 FWS biological opinions. At the same time, a scientific consensus had developed that Alternative 2 was inadequate to preserve the species. This was pointed out by the fact that no new colonies had been proved to use the recruitment areas and that red-cockaded numbers were still declining. Among those proclaiming the inadequacy of the alternatives were the FWS Environmental Project Review Office in Atlanta in comments on the Francis Marion draft forest plan, FWS in its draft revised recovery plan currently being circulated, and biologists of the National Wildlife Federation.

On November 7, 1984, the National Wildlife Federation filed a "notice of violation" with FWS and the Forest Service. A notice of violation informs an agency that it is thought to be in violation of the Endangered Species Act and gives the agency a 60-day period for consultation. At the end of 60 days, the plaintiff can issue a notice of suit.

The notice by the federation centered on two points. First, according to the Endangered Species Act, FWS and the Forest Service must ensure that a biological opinion is based on the best scientific information available. Since the 1980 opinion is deficient, consultation must be reinitiated and a new biological opinion developed. Second, the federation cited a lesser known and tested part of Section 7 of the Endangered Species Act that requires an "affirmative conservation obligation" on the part of the agencies dealing with endangered species. Affirmative obligation means that not jeopardizing a listed species is not enough, that the agency also must strive for recovery. Until a new and adequate biological opinion is issued, the federation called for a halt to all "irretrievable and irreversible commitments of resources."[20]

Under this pressure, the Forest Service and FWS have reinitiated formal consultation. New red-cockaded management guidelines will be issued by the Forest Service in 1985, after which FWS will issue a new biological opinion.

The Sitka Black-tailed Deer. The Sitka black-tailed deer (*Odocoieus hemionus sitkensis*) occupies a very narrow area between the ice-capped Coast Range in southeast Alaska and the sea, at the northwest extent of the black-tailed deer's natural distribution. It is dependent in winter on old growth stands at low elevation. Winter may be the most important factor limiting Sitka deer populations. In winter, deer food plants that retain living parts above ground throughout the winter are far scarcer in cutover areas than in the old-growth. Moreover, old-growth, because of its uneven canopy, provides deer with open forage areas even during times of heavy snowfall.

The commercial clear cutting of old-growth stands that began in the 1950s has generated a continuing controversy on the impact of timber harvests on habitat capacity for the deer. Much of the controversy has focused on the Tongass National Forest in southeast Alaska. This 17-million acre area includes between five and six million acres of good commercial forest. Beyond the densely forested coastal strip the land rises into the glaciers and ice fields that make up the bulk of the Tongass. The Forest Service plans to subsidize the cut of about two million acres of the best Tongass forest, trees nearly 10 centuries old that tower 200 feet. About 86 percent of the area slated for cutting is classified as important to deer.

Principals in the Tongass controversy include the timber industry, the Forest Service, the Alaska Department of Fish and Game, native Alaskans (who depend in part upon venison for subsistence), conservationists, and sportsmen groups. Opponents are concerned that harvest of the old growth will greatly reduce habitat carrying capacity, and thus greatly reduce the herd. They desire to maintain herds at approximately existing size, even though present demands for sport and subsistence hunting are beneath the level the population could sustain. Further, opponents question whether second-growth stands can be managed so as to provide habitat comparable to that provided by old growth.

Research on the black-tailed deer in Alaska has been limited, particularly in regard to the effects of timber harvest and other silvicultural practices on the deer. Moreover, management of second-growth stands via thinning, slash treatments, etc. has only begun in the last few years. The Forest Service and the Alaska Department of Fish and Game are studying the key relationships between the Sitka deer and its habitat in order to assess the importance of both old-growth and second-growth habitat and to develop a management system for second growth that will enhance habitat capability for the deer. The Second Growth Management Project, as it is called, is being hurt by underfunding, especially in the research phase of the project, which is necessary before actual management can be done.

Grizzly Bear

The Forest Service mandate to conserve federally listed threatened and endangered species again clashed with resource uses in 1984 in the management of the grizzly bear. The grizzly bear issue became prominent nationally via major articles in such publications as *Sports Illustrated* and *Life*. In addition, the grizzly was the subject of heated debate in Congress between those who felt protection of the bear infringed upon resource uses in the region and those who believe the bear should be preserved as a national treasure. The Forest Service finds itself heavily involved both in the management of the bear and in the controversy.

The grizzly bear in 1975 was listed federally as threatened in the lower 48 states. Today its range is limited to parts of Wyoming, Idaho, Montana, and Washington, where numbers are estimated to be around eight hundred. Well over half of the bears are found on national forests, though precise numbers are not known.

The service has a three-part role in the management of the grizzly bear habitat:

- To protect grizzly habitat and insure that no Forest Service activities, nor activities by others on the national forests, jeopardize the recovery of the species. Of particular concern is the prevention of human-caused mortality. To reduce the risk of human-bear conflict, the Forest Service has bear-proofed all its garbage facilities in occupied grizzly bear habitat and has posted signs and distributed pamphlets to promote public awareness of the bear.
- To participate in the Interagency Grizzly Bear Committee for the coordination of research and recovery. A major aspect of the work now being done involves

habitat component mapping in an effort to determine the forests' proper carrying capacity for the bear. When that has been determined, population numbers can be assigned and managed. In addition, the mapping allows for a cumulative effects analysis on any proposed resource activities.

● To participate in interagency law enforcement efforts, including the monitoring of outfitters, sheep and livestock, timber, and camping activities.

In order to help protect the grizzly, national forests with major known grizzly bear populations were directed to "stratify their land according to a system of 'management situations,'" which are to be incorporated into their forest plans. Grizzly bears in Management Situation 1 receive priority over all other resource uses, this being deemed as essential grizzly bear habitat. Management Situation 2 also is occupied grizzly bear habitat, and other resource activities must use mitigation to avoid grizzly bear harm. In Situation 2, however, conflicts between the bear and other users are usually resolved in favor of the user. In Management Situation 3, grizzly bear presence is possible, though infrequent, and is discouraged because of high human use in the area. The bear will be removed if conflict appears to be imminent or occurs. Management Situations 4 and 5 are areas outside of grizzly bear habitat but have the characteristics of potentially good and fair grizzly bear habitat, respectively. Designation of management situations, especially Management Situation 1, can be very controversial, because of the potential restrictions these management guidelines impose.

The controversy surrounding the bear was surfaced in Congress during the hearings for the 1985 budget. The Senate included wording in its appropriations bill that allowed for no funds to be expended for "the designation, management, or enhancement of the grizzly bear habitat until the public has had an opportunity to review and comment on the alternative management proscriptions and until the funds have been budgeted and approved by Congress." The language was inserted by Senator James McClure (R-Idaho) in response to constituent sentiments that the bear too heavily dominates land management policies and is responsible for many limiting restrictions, especially in sheep grazing and in access to Management Situation 1 areas. The Forest Service, FWS, and the National Audubon Society worked with Senator McClure, and the final language was modified to prohibit funding for the augmentation of grizzly bear populations in either the National Forest System or the National Park System unless such augmentation is included in the appropriate park system general management plans or forest plans, both of which require public participation in their development. Any activities concerning the grizzly bear must be included in that agency's budget justification and be approved by the appropriations committees in Congress. In addition, the Park Service and the Forest Service were directed to develop management guidelines for the grizzly in the Yellowstone ecosystem, again using public input. Expressly allowed in the new language was the relocation of bears that have a history of conflicts with humans.

Congress also appropriated money for four grizzly bear projects. A $50,000 appropriation was made for each of the following: the development of a state of the art compendium on grizzly bear research (being done by the National Wildlife Federation's Institute for Wildlife Research and due out in December 1985); a determination of the best grizzly bear habitat; an analysis of road-access needs and closure criteria; and an analysis of the impact of backcountry recreation on the grizzly. The aim of the studies is to aid in the recovery of the grizzly within its 1975 habitat range and to keep that recovery from threatening people or resource uses.

Below-Cost Timber Sales

The most controversial issue for the Forest Service in 1984 was its practice of selling timber on the National Forest System below cost. At issue are the Forest

Service's timber sale accounting system, the relative economic value of the forest resources, and the basic question of how much timber harvest is enough. The outcome of the controversy will have direct implications for wildlife and fish.

The Forest Service has no legal responsibility to turn a profit. The Multiple Use-Sustained Yield Act of 1960 calls for the Forest Service to manage its resources for "not necessarily the combination of uses that will give the greatest dollar return or greatest unit output." But in 1983 the Natural Resources Defense Council and nine other national and local conservation organizations filed appeals under the National Forest Management Act against the forest plans of the San Juan and Grand Mesa/Uncompaghre/Gunnison (GMUG) national forests on the grounds that these forests are economically unsuitable for timber production. The appeals cited Section 6 of the management act, which states, "In developing land management plans pursuant to this Act, the Secretary shall identify lands within the management area which are not suited for timber production, considering physical, economic, and other pertinent factors to the extent feasible. . . ." In 1983, the San Juan and GMUG forests returned to the Forest Service three and four cents, respectively, for each dollar spent. Planned future timber production is almost double the 1983 level. The National Resource Defense Council estimates that the harvest schedule for the San Juan National Forest alone will cost taxpayers $68 million dollars over the next 100 years.[21]

In 1984 the issue ballooned. The Wilderness Society, the House Interior Appropriations Committee, the Congressional Research Service, and the General Accounting Office (GAO) all issued reports attacking the Forest Service's timber sale accounting system and, in some cases, the practice of selling timber in areas where sale revenues do not repay the costs of implementing the sale. Some figures used in demonstrating the problem are:

- Thirty-seven percent of all timber sold on national forests in 1983 was sold below cost. (Forest Service, 1984.)
- In its nine regions the Forest Service lost $114 million on its below-cost sales in 1983. (House of Representatives, 1984.)
- One hundred and seven of 788 timber sales in California in 1982 and 1983 involved only a single bidder. It is estimated that the Forest Service would have collected an additional $58 million in California, Oregon, and Washington if the sales had been competitive. (GAO, 1984.)
- Sales programs in 23 states over the 1972-82 period lost $140 million to $155 million annually. In 21 of these states, losses were so great that they did not cover a third of the sales cost to the agency. The 21 states contained almost half of the nation's timber base. (Congressional Research Service, 1984.)
- In two Rocky Mountain regions, which had at least 60 percent of their timberland classified as low productivity land and which accounted for only about seven percent of the Forest Service's timber volume sold, more than 88 percent of the sales were below cost in 1981 and more than 96 percent were below cost in 1982. (GAO, 1984.)
- In Alaska, each dollar expended on federal timber sales in 1983 returned only two cents in timber sale receipts. (Wilderness Society, 1984.)

Opponents of the sales go on to say that these figures show the fallacy of the current administration's emphasis on timber production. Because high national objectives are being set for timber production, the regional foresters, in trying to fulfill their set goals, are assigning high-harvest goals to many forests that have low timber producing capability. Since lagging demand has not kept pace with the supply being offered for sale, the Forest Service has had to bear the brunt of the costs in many of these regions. Five of the nine regions are chronic money losers. Critics also suggest that by offering timber at artificially low prices, the Forest Service is hurting private timber landowners.

In response to these arguments, the Forest Service points out that, although some specific sales lost money, overall sales returned $650 million to the treasury in 1983. In addition, says the service, some costs now attributed to a sale, such as road building, should be spread out over subsequent sales, since the same road can be used again. The below-cost sales may themselves be beneficial as well, as when harvesting is done for insect and disease control, to prevent forest fires, to increase yields on future stands, for wildlife habitat improvement, or to satisfy the needs of local mills and communities dependent on national forest timber. High national production levels are needed because of expected increased demand due to the good economy, and the need for the National Forest System to meet this expected increase because of the poor condition of so many private forests, and the even poorer condition of the Canadian forests, from which comes much of America's pulp and timber.

The affects of these below-cost sales on wildlife and fish vary. There are no benefits for fish habitat. Timber harvesting often causes erosion, which results in sediment deposit in streams. At best there are no impacts. But some wildlife can benefit from timber harvesting. Such popular game species, such as white-tailed deer and grouse, thrive in recently cut areas, using the low growth for cover and browse. Moreover, some below-cost sales are designed expressly for habitat improvement, a figure that does not show up on balance sheets.

Opponents of the sales question these alleged wildlife benefits. The first point raised is that bulldozers making roads and 30-ton trucks running back and forth are not wildlife benefits. Roads themselves are detrimental (see discussion below), and although timber harvest can benefit many species, many more are adversely impacted, including elk, cavity-nesting birds, fish, and turkeys. The opponents also stress that certain below-cost sales are justifiable, such as those designed specifically for wildlife improvement, but add that closer scrutiny must be paid to all sales and that below-cost sales must be justified rigorously.

The National Resources Defense Council appeal currently is being reviewed by the secretary. Should it be denied, litigation likely will begin. In the 1984 appropriations hearings, Congress directed the Forest Service to devise a new, more comprehensive, timber sales accounting system that is to take into account many of the intangibles that the Forest Service claims make their sales profitable even when a cost-receipt analysis shows a deficit. The 99th Congress is sure to scrutinize this issue very closely.

Road Building

An issue closely related to, though distinct from, timber sales, road building is a major issue for the Forest Service and wildlife. The building of roads is done in preparation for timber sales. Often no timber sale is scheduled for an area which is roaded, but the timber will at some future date be put up for sale. The current roading controversy centers in the Rocky Mountains, but the issue is spread system-wide.

In 1984, the National Wildlife Federation filed suit against the Forest Service on the ground that road plans in the northern region (Idaho-Montana) did not meet National Environmental Policy Act requirements, namely the development of an environmental impact statement and the chance at public review that goes along with this. In the Idaho-Montana area, 30 new road projects are scheduled, 15 into currently roadless areas. A preliminary injunction was sought against further road construction and denied by a U.S. district court. The ruling has been appealed to the Ninth Circuit Court of Appeals in San Francisco.

Excessive roading not only has the obvious results of disturbing wildlife, but also more serious potential consequences for many species, one example being elk. Research has shown that elk require a 60/40 cover-to-forage ratio and that the security of the cover decreases as open-road mileage increases past 1.5 miles per 640 acres. In many forests in the Rocky Mountain and northern regions, present road density already exceeds optimum levels, yet the Forest Service has called for more roading and timber harvesting increases. Traditionally, the National Forest System has been a haven for elk, with approximately three-fourths of all elk harvested in the United States, about 80,000, coming from the system. Road building, because it increases human access to remote areas, also can jeopardize grizzly bears, Northern Rocky Mountain wolves, and woodland caribou, all listed species that tend to decline as contact with man is increased. Forest Service biologists have intensified their efforts to work with foresters in designing road systems and providing for road closures during critical wildlife-use periods, alleviating some problems.

Another aspect of the roading controversy involves wilderness designations. Many pro-wilderness groups see the Forest Service plans to escalate road building in currently roadless (RARE II) areas as a deliberate attempt to remove these areas from future consideration for wilderness designation. In response, the Forest Service denies any increases in roading and points out that only areas classified as non-wilderness are being considered in plans to build new roads. Resource development is allowed on the 27,721,600 acres released by Congress in 1984 from wilderness consideration. This land will be eligible for reconsideration for wilderness designation in 15 years, but only if it still meets wilderness qualifications, one of which is no roads.

Wildlife and Grazing in Riparian Zones

An issue of continuing controversy is the relationship between livestock grazing and the ecologically critical riparian zones. Because of the wide extent of grazing on the National Forest System, the service finds itself heavily embroiled in the issue, a controversy that has pitted ranchers against environmentalists.

A riparian zone is the transitional zone between water and upland habitat and, generally, is the most critical wildlife habitat area. In the Blue Mountains of Oregon and Washington, for example, 285 of the 378 terrestrial species known to occur are either directly dependent on riparian zones or utilize them more than other habitats.[22] Fish and amphibians are completely dependent on riparian and adjacent aquatic zones. Big game species use riparian zones for forage, water, cover, and migration routes. Elk calving areas generally are located adjacent to riparian zones, and elk will spend a disproportionate amount of its time in the riparian zones when on summer range. Riparian zones also act as brooding areas for many species, including the sage grouse.

Because riparian zones are fertile lands with good grass growth and plenty of water, they are subject to extremely high forage utilization, soil compaction, and streambank damage by livestock. This has been a problem for many years, but as more research is done on the ecological importance of riparian zones, the urgency of the issue has increased.

Livestock grazing in the National Forest System occurs on about 105 million acres of grassland, open forests, and other forage-producing areas. This area is divided into approximately 10,000 range allotments in 36 states, with the allotments administered through a grazing permit system that currently allows for 9.9 million animal unit months (AUMs) to occur.

Grazing that affects riparian zones is usually done by either sheep or cattle. Sheep grazing generally is less of a problem because it is declining and because flocks are accompanied by a herder who can keep them from doing too much damage to the riparian zone. Cattle, on the other hand, are often unsupervised and will remain on riparian zones for indefinite periods, causing extensive damage to the forage and streambanks. Loss of streambank stability, shade, and instream fish and wildlife cover results. Flood peaks increase as runoff time over compacted, devegetated soils decreases. The result has been a significant decline in resident trout, salmon, and steelhead production in the 16 western states in recent years. Research shows that some streams have lost more than 50 percent of their trout populations.

The issue is how to protect riparian ecosystems, either by allowing no grazing, reduced grazing, or better supervised grazing. Among the solutions proposed are: fencing riparian areas, either completely or "gap" fencing (where sections of the riparian zones are fenced and given time to recover); grazing systems based on a rotation of grazing areas to allow for recovery periods; herding and salting to keep cattle away from riparian zones; or increased mitigation to counter grazing's adverse effects. It is not known if any of these systems, alone or in combination with another, will provide the necessary relief for the riparian zones or if these solutions will be politically feasible.

The issue is heavily politicized. The Forest Service issues grazing permits at prices ($1.37/AUM in 1984) that average five times lower than going market rates for comparable private lands. Critics say that this encourages overgrazing and allows little money to be spent for range management and wildlife and fisheries habitat improvement or support. Grazers reply that low fees are essential to continue their traditional way of life and say that raising fees would hurt the already depressed livestock industry. In addition, grazers resist efforts to keep livestock out of riparian areas because these areas are by far the most productive of the forage lands.

Since the grazing-fee system is scheduled to come up for review in the 99th Congress's first session, this issue will be very important in 1985. For a more detailed account of the grazing/wildlife issue, see the chapter on the Bureau of Land Management.

Wilderness

In 1964, Congress passed the Wilderness Act to "secure for the American people of present and future generations the benefits of an enduring resource of wilderness." The National Wilderness Preservation System classified about nine million acres of the National Forest System as wilderness. All additions to the system must be passed by Congress. Today, the wilderness system totals 88.8 million acres on lands administered by four agencies; 32.3 million acres are in the lower 48 states. The remaining 56.5 million acres are in Alaska.

In order to identify land eligible for wilderness designation within the National Forest System, the Forest Service embarked on a system-wide Roadless Area Review and Evaluation (RARE) between 1971 and 1973. This evaluation was challenged in court, and a second Roadless Area Review and Evaluation (RARE II) was done between 1977 and 1979 under the Carter administration. The purpose of RARE II was to inventory all roadless areas within the National Forest System and to designate them in one of three ways:

- Wilderness. These areas were to be recommended to Congress for inclusion in the wilderness system. Fifteen million acres were recommended as such.
- Further planning. The 10.8 million acres placed in this category would be protected pending completion of forest management plans that would consider whether to recommend the area for inclusion in the wilderness system.
- Non-wilderness. Some 36 million acres.

The first two designations were relatively uncontroversial, but the non-wilderness designation resulted in a lawsuit filed by the state of California and others against the Forest Service. The basis of the suit, upheld by the Ninth Circuit Court in California (California v. Block),[23] was that an insufficient environmental impact study had been done on the non-wilderness designation.

The decision meant that RARE II was invalidated in California, a precedent that could have been followed, probably with similar results, around the nation. But environmentalists, fearing that a RARE III conducted by the Reagan administration, with its pro-development policies, would cut back seriously the wilderness and further planning designations made in RARE II, have resisted following California's example. California, in fact, faced this very problem after the circuit court decision, but Congress intervened and passed the California wilderness bill, for the most part implementing the RARE II designations. The recommendations of RARE II have been implemented primarily through a series of state wilderness bills.

The wilderness system is made up of lands under the jurisdiction of the four major land agencies: the Forest Service, Bureau of Land Management, National Park Service, and FWS. More than three-fourths of the system is administered by the National Park Service (35.3 million acres, 91 percent of it in Alaska) and the Forest Service. The Forest Service controls 32,086,580 acres of wilderness, 16.8 percent of all service lands. Of this, 5,453,366 acres are in Alaska. Some 6,800,000 acres of the National Forest System were added to the wilderness system in 1984.

Currently, 4,054,913 acres are designated as "Congressional Wilderness Study Areas" and 2,458,670 acres as "pending recommended wilderness" within the National Forest System. Some 5,300,000 acres of RARE II lands remain in the further planning designation, and the 98th Congress released 27,721,600 acres of RARE II lands from wilderness consideration. Resource development is allowed on released lands, but they are eligible to be reconsidered by the service for wilderness in 15 years if they still meet wilderness criteria.

Wilderness is defined as an area protected in order to preserve its natural conditions, in which there are to be no permanent structures and "man is a visitor, who does not remain." No roads, no motorized vehicle transportation, and no manipulation of the habitat are allowed. These constraints do not allow for much active wildlife habitat management, but certain activities are permitted on National Forest System wilderness.

Wildlife research is considered a legitimate activity in wilderness, and methods that temporarily infringe on the wilderness character may be used. This includes helicopters and fixed wing aircraft when approved, and the continuation to their normal end of any research activities occurring before designation.

Threatened and endangered species occurring on wilderness are to be provided maximum protection, and the transplanting of an endangered species to wilderness can be permitted. Wilderness designation, however, should not be made if some other designation would serve species interests better. For example, the Forest Service's condor sanctuary in southern California once was considered for designation as wilderness, but it was decided that a wilderness designation would attract too many visitors and that prescribed burning may be needed to maintain suitable habitat. The sanctuary allows access to no one except the guards and researchers on duty because of the condor's critical situation. (For more information on the condor, see the species account by John Ogden.)

Fishing is considered acceptable in National Forest System wilderness. As is true on other federal lands, the states regulate and enforce fishing regulations. Other acceptable activities include the removal of debris from critical spawning streams, spawn-taking when practiced prior to designation, sampling fish populations by such means as gill netting and battery operated electrofishing, and even chemically treating waters where certain undesirable non-native fish are present because of human actions. The purpose of the removal of undesirable fish would be to reintroduce desirable native species to the waters. In addition, dams, water developments, and diversion ditches in existence prior to designation and deemed necessary for wildlife management are permitted to remain.

Wilderness management in the National Forest System allows hunting and trapping, again under state laws and regulations. Animal damage control is allowed on a case by case basis and only with Forest Service approval. The management plan for a wilderness should specify the wildlife population and habitat conditions that are to be maintained.

A problem in the management of wilderness areas is too much recreational demand. It has been shown that recreational use increases greatly when an area is designated as wilderness. Although this is a testament to the popularity of the wilderness system, the situation makes management much harder, especially when mitigation means are so limited. Wildlife is among the resources adversely affected. As a result, many wildlife conservation organizations traditionally have opposed wilderness designations. This has changed in recent years because these groups perceive that Reagan administration development policies have created a polarized choice: either wilderness or massive roading projects and timber sales. Many claim that the Forest Service's plans for increased roading are a thinly veiled effort to remove huge tracts of land from future wilderness consideration. The service responds that only congressionally released RARE II lands are being considered for roading and timber harvest.

LEGAL DEVELOPMENTS

Four recent cases have helped delineate the responsibilities of the Forest Service to protect wildlife interests as required by the National Environmental Policy Act and the Endangered Species Act.

In *Foundation for North American Wild Sheep v. U.S. Department of Agriculture*,[24] the Ninth Circuit reviewed a special-use permit that allowed a mining company to reopen and use an existing road through the Angeles National Forest in California. The road passed through an area occupied by a herd of 400 to 700 bighorn sheep. The court found that the Forest Service environmental assessment was inadequate because it failed to estimate the amount of traffic likely on the road and failed to consider the effects of the traffic on the sheep and, in particular, on their use of a nearby mineral lick. The court held that the Forest Service determination that an environmental assessment was not required was unreasonable and therefore unlawful.

In *National Wildlife Federation v. Forest Service*,[25] the district court reviewed the Seven Year Action Plan for the Mapleton District of the Siuslaw National Forest. The plan proposed sale of 100 million board feet of timber, to be harvested principally by clearcutting. NWF challenged the plan under NEPA. The Forest Service had prepared an Environmental Impact Statement on its 10-year Timber Resource plan for the entire forest and planned to prepare environmental assessments for each individual sale. The court found that these documents did not, or would not, adequately consider the effects of the Mapleton District plan on anadromous fish. Most important, the court held that NEPA required the Forest Service to consider the cumulative effects on the fish of the proposed timber harvest and the harvesting planned on adjacent Bureau of Land Management and private lands in the same watershed.

In *Cabinet Mountains Wilderness/Scotchman's Peak Grizzly Bears v. Peterson*,[26]

Habitat Capability for Selected Management Indicator Species or Species Groups on the National Forest System (1980 = 100)

Species Species Groups	Recommended Program High	Recommended Program Low	Current (1985) Level	Difference from Recommended High
Mule Deer	120	95	95	−25
White-tailed Deer	120	95	95	−25
Black-tailed Deer	125	95	100	−25
Elk	118	90	95	−23
Wild Turkey	133	95	100	−33
Cavity-nesting Birds	100	95	95	−5
Resident Trout	120	95	95	−25
Anadromous Fish	130	105	95	−35

Source: U.S. Forest Service.

the District of Columbia Circuit upheld a Forest Service decision to allow exploratory drilling for minerals in the Cabinet Mountains Wilderness Area. Citing harm to grizzly bears, the Sierra Club and others challenged the decision under NEPA and the Endangered Species Act. The court ruled that measures adopted to mitigate the project's effects on the grizzly and to compensate for any harm done were sufficient to support the Forest Service's conclusion that an Environmental Impact Statement was not required and that the grizzly would not be jeopardized.

In *Thomas v. Peterson*,[27] the Ninth Circuit strengthened the cumulative effects analysis requirement under NEPA and the consultation requirements of the Endangered Species Act. Under NEPA the court held that, before building a road through a roadless area, the Forest Service must prepare an Environmental Impact Statement assessing the cumulative impacts of the road and the timber sales it would facilitate. Under the Endangered Species Act the court held that once the Forest Service is aware that an endangered species may be present in the area of a proposed action, the service must prepare a biological assessment to determine whether the action is "likely to affect the species" and therefore requires consultation with FWS. Failure to prepare such an assessment, the court held, compelled issuance of an injunction.

RESOURCE STATUS

The Forest Service does not have a comprehensive system for regularly monitoring the biological status of wildlife and plant species occurring on its lands, either at the national level or the forest level. Even if such a system were in place, it would provide only a partial picture of wildlife status since few species, other than endemic plants, occur exclusively on Forest Service lands.

The Forest Service does monitor 22 big game species, in an attempt to estimate populations within the system and annual hunter harvest. But wildlife professionals in the Forest Service point out that these numbers are estimates, not a good measurement of species health.

The best measure of species status on a limited area such as a national forest is to determine the habitat's carrying capability for a given species. Habitat capability is defined as the estimated ability of an area, given existing or predicted habitat conditions, to support a wildlife, fish, or plant population. The capability is measured in terms of potential population numbers. The 1980 Resources Planning Act Program listed species that are indicative of certain habitat types. These species' populations are monitored to serve as a barometer of the quality of the fish and wildlife habitat on the National Forest System.

Although Congress approved a high bound program level for the 1980 planning act, habitat quality has declined for six of the eight indicator species/species groups between 1980–85. In the case of anadromous fish, the current situation does not even meet the low recommended level.

REFERENCES

1. Forest Reserve Act of 1891, (Ch. 561, 24, 26 Stat. 1103 (repealed 1976)).
2. Act of June 4, 1897 (Ch. 2, 30 Stat. 11, as amended; 16 U.S.C.A. 475).
3. James B. Trefethen, *An American Crusade for Wildlife* (New York: Winchester Press and the Boone and Crockett Club, 1975), Chapters 4 and 5.
4. Act of March 1, 1911, (Ch. 186, 36 Stat. 961, as amended (codified in scattered sections of 16 U.S.C.A.)).
5. 16 U.S.C.A. §499, 505, 568, 568a, 569, 570.
6. Act of June 12, 1960 (P.L. 86-517, 74 Stat. 215; 16 U.S.C.A. §528(note), 528-531).
7. Act of September 3, 1964 (P.L. 88-577, 78 Stat. 890; 16 U.S.C.A. 1121 (note), 1131-1136).
8. Act of October 18, 1974 (P.L. 93-452, 88 Stat. 1369, as amended; 16 U.S.C.A. 670g, 670h, 670o).
9. Act of August 17, 1974 (P.L. 93-378, 88 Stat. 476, as amended; 16 U.S.C.A. 1601 (note), 1600-1614).
10. Paul J. Culhane, *Public Land Politics: Interest Group Influence on the Forest Service and the Bureau of Land Management*, Resources for the Future, Inc. (Baltimore: Johns Hopkins University Press, 1981), Chapter 2.
11. Act of October 22, 1976 (P.L. 94-588, 90 Stat. 2949 as amended (codified in scattered sections of 16 U.S.C.A.).
12. Michael Bean, *The Evolution of National Wildlife Law* (New York: Praeger, 1983), p. 148.
13. 16 U.S.C.A. 576-5766.
14. Act of June 30, 1978 (P.L. 95-307, 92 Stat. 353, as amended; 16 U.S.C.A. §1600(note), 1641(note), 1641-1647).
15. 7 U.S.C.A. §1010-1012; 16 U.S.C.A. 551.
16. 42 U.S.C.A. §4321(note), 4321, 4331-4335, 4341-4347.
17. 592 Supp. 931, 1984.
18. U.S. Department of Interior, Fish & Wildlife Service, The Northern Spotted Owl: A Status Review, 1982, p. 22.
19. 16 U.S.C.A. §1531-1536, 1538-1540.
20. Letter from Lynn A. Greenwalt to William Clark, November 7, 1984.
21. *Land Letter*, February 1, 1985.
22. Department of Agriculture, U.S. Forest Service, Wildlife in Managed Forests: The Blue Mountains of Oregon and Washington, 1979.
23. 690 F. 2d 753 (9th Cir. 1982).
24. 681 F.2d 1172 (9th Cir. 1982).
25. 592 F.Supp. 931 (D.Ore. 1984).
26. 685 F.2d 678 (D.C.Cir. 1982).
27. 753 F.2d 754 (9th Cir. 1985).

Use of Bureau of Land Management holdings for livestock grazing is one of the biggest threats to wildlife on federal lands.

Wildlife on Bureau of Land Management Lands

by Katherine Barton
W.J. Chandler Associates

INTRODUCTION

THE BUREAU OF Land Management (BLM) oversees approximately 300 million acres — more land than any other federal or state agency. This land, located primarily in the West and Alaska, provides habitat for substantial and important populations of fish and other wildlife. One BLM publication claims that one of every five big game animals resides on BLM land, although this figure has probably declined since wildlife-rich BLM lands in Alaska have been transferred into state and native ownership.[1] Nevertheless, BLM lands support significant populations of pronghorns, elk, deer, and bighorn sheep. These lands also are increasingly in demand for wildlife-related recreational use. In 1983, the public lands supported approximately 113 million visitor hours of hunting and fishing activities and some 220 million visitor hours of nonconsumptive recreation not necessarily related to wildlife. These lands also provide habitat for a variety of small game and nongame wildlife and for 86 federally listed endangered and threatened species.

Technically, BLM manages wildlife habitat as opposed to wildlife species. Management of resident species, including regulation of hunting and fishing and propagation of wildlife, is carried out by the states. In practice, BLM habitat management generally is coordinated closely with the states through a variety of cooperative arrangements and agreements. BLM has increased responsibility for threatened or endangered species under the requirements of the Endangered Species Act. The bureau is also responsible for the direct management of wild horses and burros, animals that are not native to the United States but that have well-established populations on BLM lands.

BLM is mandated by the Federal Land Policy and Management Act[2] to manage its lands for multiple use, with wildlife identified as one of six principle or major uses of the land. In addition to managing its lands for fish and wildlife enhancement, BLM also manages them for the development of energy fuels such as coal and oil and gas; hard-rock mining; timber production; livestock grazing; rights-of-way; recreation, scenic, and archeological resources; and range for wild horses and burros. In contrast to the Fish and Wildlife Service (FWS) and state wildlife agencies, where wildlife needs are the primary concern, in BLM wildlife habitat management is one of many responsibilities, and trade-offs are common.

Wildlife has never achieved the coequal role in BLM's management scheme that wildlife conservationists believe would represent truly balanced, multiple-use management. Instead, the agency traditionally has focused heavily on livestock grazing and timber production and more recently on energy and mineral development. And in spite of the clear multiple-use mandate of the Federal Land Policy and Management Act, wildlife continues to take a back seat to commodity uses of the land. The result is that most habitat-management efforts have focused on two extremes. The main emphasis has been on the popular, relatively healthy big-game species that are in demand for hunting. A secondary emphasis is on species listed as endangered or threatened under the Endangered Species Act, which BLM is mandated to protect by law. Wildlife values did begin to gain a more dominant role in BLM land management in the latter part of the 1970s. But in the past several years, budget cuts and changes in management philosophy at the top agency and department levels have relegated wildlife management to a minor consideration in comparison with development uses. Thus, BLM's wildlife program today is primarily reactive, focusing the vast majority

Public Lands Under Exclusive Jurisdiction of the Bureau of Land Management, FY 1983

State	Acres
Alabama	3,100
Alaska	166,674,087*
Arizona	12,280,027
Arkansas	1,820
California	17,149,997
Colorado	8,347,464
Florida	2,332
Idaho	11,919,172
Illinois	28
Kansas	728
Louisiana	3,962
Michigan	766
Minnesota	61,275
Mississippi	627
Missouri	400
Montana	8,094,892
Nebraska	8,581
Nevada	48,065,097
New Mexico	12,707,432
North Dakota	68,198
Ohio	120
Oklahoma	6,988
Oregon	15,716,608
South Dakota	275,248
Utah	22,191,979
Washington	315,110
Wisconsin	589
Wyoming	18,417,149
Total	342,313,776

Source: *Public Land Statistics, 1983*, published by the Bureau of Land Management.
*Figures for Alaska are high. Several million acres have subsequently been transferred to the State or to Alaska Native Corporations.

of its efforts on trying to identify and mitigate the impacts of other activities affecting wildlife on BLM lands.

In addition to the wildlife program per se, this chapter covers several other BLM programs that have significant importance for, or impacts on, wildlife. These include the livestock grazing program, the Oregon and California grant lands, special management areas such as wilderness and areas of critical environmental concern, and wild horses and burros. Each of these is dealt with in a separate section of this chapter.

HISTORY AND LEGISLATIVE AUTHORITY

BLM derives its main authority for managing its lands from three laws: The Taylor Grazing Act of 1934,[3] which authorized federal regulation of grazing on public lands; the Federal Land Policy and Management Act (FLPMA),[4]* which gave BLM its permanent multiple-use management authority, and the Public Rangeland Improvement Act of 1978,[5] which directed BLM to improve the condition of the range and authorized funding for such an effort. This section addresses the history and evolution of these laws, drawing primarily on information contained in *Politics and Grass*, by Phillip Foss[6] and *Public Land Politics*, by Paul Culhane.[7]

Two additional laws contain important but narrower management authority: the Oregon and California Lands Grant Act of 1937,[8] which provides for the management of BLM's productive timberlands in western Oregon; and the Wild Free-Roaming Horses and Burros Act of 1971,[9] which provides for the protection and management of wild horses and burros by BLM on the public lands and by the Forest Service within the national forests. These two laws are discussed later in the chapter.

The public domain at one time consisted of almost all the land in the lower 48 states except the 13 original colonies and Texas. The federal government over time acquired ownership of some 1.4 billion acres. Since the Revolutionary War and throughout the 1800s, however, the primary goal with respect to the public lands was to dispose of them. Today, the federal government retains only about 30 percent of its original holdings and has sold or given away approximately one billion acres.

The disposal of the public lands was overseen by the General Land Office, which was established in 1812 as part of the Treasury Department and transferred to the newly created Department of the Interior in 1849. The disposal policies were developed piecemeal over time and proceeded without any unified plan or objective. Initially, Congress moved to dispose of the lands by selling them, primarily to raise revenue for the federal government. However, when this policy failed either to encourage much settlement or to raise much money, Congress began simply to grant lands to the states for a variety of uses, including the construction of railroads, canals, and wagon roads, and to support local schools and colleges. In 1850, Congress began granting land directly to railroad companies to encourage railroad construction.

These land grants caused the checkerboard pattern of state, private, and federal land ownership that characterizes the West today. The school grants generally consisted of one to four non-adjacent sections each a square mile in size per each 36-section township. Revenues from these lands were to be used to support the state's schools. The railroad grants generally consisted of a certain number of sections of land on alternating sides of the track.

The first homesteading law was approved in 1862. It provided for the transfer of 160 acres of land to anyone who would make improvements and maintain a residence on the land for five years. The goal was to encourage farming, but the policy was

---

*This law is commonly referred to by its acronym, FLPMA, pronounced "flip-ma."

inappropriate for the arid lands in the West, where farming was impractical and where 160 acres was too small to support a ranch. As this problem became apparent in the late 1800s, Congress tried to find other ways to encourage the productive use of these lands, including the passage of laws to encourage the planting of trees and to provide incentives for irrigating the land, but these policies also proved impractical. In 1916, Congress finally authorized homesteading specifically for stock raising and increased the acreage to 640 acres, but this acreage still was too small for survival in the West.

These homesteading policies further contributed to the checkerboard pattern of land settlement in the West. Under the original homesteading law, which allowed ownership of only 160 acres, ranchers located their homesteads on lands that contained water supplies. A rancher could then control the water supply and graze his livestock on the surrounding public lands for free. Without access to water, other settlers had little interest in laying claim to these lands. Thus, throughout the West, the most productive lands and the best water supplies were transferred into private ownership, leaving vast amounts of arid, often less productive lands in the public domain.

This land-ownership pattern encouraged overgrazing and led to the infamous range wars over use of the range. Belonging to no one, the public lands belonged to everyone, and each rancher tried to get as much production out of them as possible. After the Civil War and the expansion of the railroads into the West, livestock use of the western lands suddenly burgeoned, and by the 1870s reports of extensive overgrazing began to emerge. Overgrazing and bad weather combined in the late 1880s to cause disastrous livestock losses and the beginning of concern about the condition of the range. By the early 1900s even many stockmen, who generally objected to government interference, began to call for some kind of federal intervention in range management in order to reduce conflicts over the use of the range.

Throughout the early 1900s a number of bills were introduced in Congress to provide a federal role in range management, but these proposals were stalled by supporters of homesteading and by those who saw such federal management as an unwarranted intervention of the states' rights to manage the land within their borders. In addition, the Forest Service, which began to charge fees for grazing on its forest reserves in 1906, moved to increase grazing fees and reduce grazing levels, adding to the livestock industry's fear of federal control.

The push for a grazing law came to a climax in the early 1930s with two key events. First, a congressionally authorized grazing demonstration project in Montana, known as the Mizpah River-Pumpkin Creek experiment, proved a success. This project gave a local stockman's association authority to control the use of the range under the direction of the Department of the Interior. Within three years, the area was producing twice as much grass, and its livestock carrying capacity had nearly doubled. Then, in the spring of 1934, the nation suffered one of the worst droughts and accompanying dust storms in its history. Congress was prompted to action by the devastation caused to the range by the storms, which Senator Gore of Oklahoma called "the most tragic, the most impressive lobbyists that have ever come to this Capital."[10]

In the summer of 1934, Congress passed the Taylor Grazing Act, which declared the following purposes: "to stop the injury to the public grazing lands by preventing overgrazing and soil deterioration; to provide for their orderly use, improvement, and development; to stabilize the livestock industry on the public range."[11] To achieve these goals, the act authorized the secretary of the Interior to establish grazing districts in order to regulate their use and occupancy, preserve the land and its resources from destruction or unnecessary injury, and provide for the orderly use, improvement, and development of the range. Within the grazing districts the secretary was to issue permits in order to control livestock grazing, giving preference to nearby landowners engaged in the livestock business, bona fide occupants or settlers, or owners of water or water rights; charge "reasonable" annual fees for the use of the range, with a portion of the receipts allocated for range improvements; and specify from time to time the allowable number of livestock and seasons of use.

The Taylor Grazing Act authorized the first federal management of the range and, by requiring the establishment of grazing districts, essentially ended homesteading on the western public lands. But Congress apparently did not yet envision the permanent retention of these lands in federal ownership. The Taylor Grazing Act stated that the purpose of the grazing districts was "to promote the highest use of public lands pending it's [sic] final disposal."[12]

Wildlife was mentioned only briefly in two sections of the act. The law specified that nothing in the act was intended to restrict the right to hunt or fish within a grazing district or to give any grazing permittee the right to interfere with hunting or fishing in the district. It also directed the secretary of the Interior to cooperate with local associations of stockmen, state land officials, and state agencies "engaged in conservation or propagation of wildlife."[13]

The clear purpose of the act was to rescue the livestock industry, and it was implemented in a manner designed to serve the livestock operators. Responsibility for administering the law was given to a new agency called the Division of Grazing (renamed the Grazing Service in 1939). A stockman from Colorado, Farrington Carpenter, was appointed as the division's first chief. Carpenter construed the law's directive calling for the Department of the Interior to cooperate with local associations of stockmen as authorizing the creation of grazing district advisory boards. Carpenter established the boards through administrative directives and gave them a strong voice in the overall management of the public lands. The establishment of these boards was ratified in 1939 amendments to the act,[14] which required the boards to be composed of five to 12 stockmen plus one wildlife representative.

The enactment of the Taylor Grazing Act was followed by a decade of controversy and struggle over the federal management of the public range. From 1939 to 1946, the Grazing Service was headed by former Forest Service professionals who believed overgrazing should be controlled and grazing fees should be raised. These proposals were aggressively fought by the livestock interests and their congressional supporters, most notably Senator Pat McCarran of Nevada. At the same time, other members of Congress, notably the House Appropriations Committee, criticized the agency for not collecting sufficient grazing fees to cover its administrative costs. The result of this battle was a massive cut in the agency's budget and personnel to the point where it had to be supported by funds from the grazing district advisory boards and was rendered almost completely ineffective.

In 1946, in an effort to remedy the situation, President Truman consolidated the Grazing Service and the General Land Office into one new agency, the Bureau of Land Management. Under BLM's first director, Marion Clawson, the newly organized agency began in the 1950s a 10-year effort to bring grazing use into balance with the capacity of the range and initiated a study of grazing fees. During this period, BLM also began to attract significant numbers of range professionals and the agency internally developed an interest in moving toward more conservation-oriented, multiple-use management. But progress was relatively slow, and although BLM did address some wildlife concerns during this period, it was not until 1961 that the agency began to hire trained wildlife personnel.

The push for multiple-use management authority for BLM really got under way in the 1960s. In 1964, Congress established the Public Land Law Review Commission to examine federal land laws and policies and to make recommendations on the disposal or retention of the public lands. At the same time, Congress enacted the Classification and Multiple Use Act,[15] a temporary law proposed by the Department of the Interior to guide BLM's land management while the review commission study was under way. This act made two key changes in the management of the public lands. It gave BLM the authority to classify public domain lands either for retention in federal ownership or for disposal, the first official recognition that much of the public domain should remain in public ownership. Second, it directed that the public lands be managed according to multiple-use and sustained-yield principles and included fish and wildlife as one of the basic purposes for such management.

With the strength of the Classification Act behind it, BLM continued to move in the direction of multiple-use management. In 1967 the agency completed its allocation of range use, which generally was criticized as giving in to demands by ranchers for higher grazing levels, and began for the first time to develop allotment management plans for the individual grazing allotments. In 1969, the agency began comprehensive, long-range planning to guide the overall management of all of its lands. With the growth in concern for multiple-use management came an increased attention to the needs of wildlife. By the end of the 1960s, every western state had at least one BLM wildlife biologist.[16]

Two key events were responsible for turning BLM into a multiple-use agency and for the growth of the wildlife program in the late 1970s. The first was a lawsuit brought by the Natural Resources Defense Council (NRDC) against BLM under the National Environmental Policy Act of 1969. BLM had attempted to comply with the law's requirement for assessing the environmental impacts of its grazing program by preparing a single environmental impact statement covering the entire program on its 170 million acres of rangeland. The court agreed with NRDC that the single statement was inadequate and directed the bureau to prepare individual impact statements for 212 specific areas, later reduced to 141. The preparation of the impact statements has caused BLM to consider environmental effects, including effects on wildlife, when making major decisions about livestock use on specific tracts of public land.*

Finally, in 1976 Congress enacted a comprehensive law for multiple-use management of BLM lands, FLPMA.[17] FLPMA finally resolved the two long-standing questions about public land management. It declared that it was federal policy to retain the public domain in federal ownership, reversing the 200-year-old policy of federal lands disposal and limiting transfer, exchange, or selling of lands to certain circumstances that would serve the national interest. In addition, FLPMA gave BLM a permanent mandate to manage the public domain according to multiple-use and sustained-yield principles. The law declared that it is federal policy to manage the public lands in a manner "that will protect the quality of scientific, scenic, historical, ecological, environmental, air and atmospheric, water resource and archeological values; that, where appropriate, will preserve and protect certain public lands in their natural condition; that will provide food and habitat for fish and wildlife and domestic animals; and that will provide for outdoor recreation and human occupancy and use."[18]

FLPMA is referred to as the BLM organic act because it guides all agency activities. Among its major provisions, it:

- directs BLM to manage its lands according to land-use plans developed with public participation and involvement;
- directs the agency to prepare and maintain an inventory of the public lands and their resource values;

---

*BLM had completed 104 of the court-ordered environmental impact statements as of February 1985 and was scheduled to complete the remainder by September 1988.

- establishes a policy of requiring fair market value for the use of the public lands and their resources;
- directs BLM to conduct a wilderness review of its roadless areas, with recommendations due by 1991;
- authorizes the establishment of citizen's advisory councils to "represent the various major citizen's interests concerning problems relating to land use planning or the management of public lands." The grazing advisory boards established under the Taylor Grazing Act are continued until December 1, 1985. Current grazing advisory boards are composed solely of livestock permitees and lessees and their purview is restricted to the development of grazing allotment management plans and the use of range improvement funds.

FLPMA also contains several other provisions specifically related to wildlife. It directs BLM to give priority to designating and protecting "areas of critical environmental concern" in order to protect fish and wildlife resources as well as other natural values. It mandates that 50 percent of grazing fees and certain other revenues from the public lands be used for rehabilitation, protection, and improvement of the range, including fish and wildlife habitat enhancement. It also directs the secretary to consider the needs of fish and wildlife in determining whether it is in the public interest to make a land exchange. And while FLPMA specifies that the act is not intended to enlarge or diminish state authority for the management of fish and wildlife, it does authorize the secretary, after consultation with the states, to designate areas of public land where hunting or fishing is not allowed for reasons of public safety, administration, or compliance with other laws.

In addition, fish and wildlife development and utilization is included as one of the six principal or major uses of the public lands, along with livestock grazing, mineral exploration and production, rights-of-way, outdoor recreation, and timber production. These principal or major uses receive special consideration in FLPMA as follows: any management decision or action that would eliminate totally one of these uses for two years or more on a tract of 100,000 acres or more must be reported to Congress. Congress has 90 days to adopt a concurrent resolution of non-approval of the management decision, in which case the decision must be terminated promptly by the secretary.

Since the enactment of FLPMA, one last law of particular significance for BLM has been passed: the Public Rangelands Improvement Act of 1978.[19] The act contains three main provisions. First, it establishes a grazing-fee formula tied to meat prices and livestock operating costs that has kept the fee low and actually has caused the fee to decrease in recent years. The fee was set for a trial period of seven years. The Department of Agriculture and the Department of the Interior are directed to evaluate the new fee formula and make recommendations to Congress for future grazing fees by December 31, 1985.

The Rangelands Act also addressed continuing concerns about the poor condition of the public range. It declared that "vast segments of the public rangelands are producing less than their potential for livestock, wildlife habitat, recreation, forage, and water and soil conservation benefits, and for that reason are in an unsatisfactory condition." To remedy the situation, the act directs both BLM and the Forest Service to maintain up-to-date inventories of range conditions and a record of condition trends on public rangelands. In addition, it directs BLM to manage the public rangelands to improve their condition in order to make them as productive as is feasible and authorizes $365 million over a 20-year period for rangeland improvements, although none of this funding has been appropriated.

The rangelands act also authorized a temporary experimental stewardship program to provide incentives to livestock operators to make range improvements of their own. The Department of Agriculture and the Department of the Interior were directed to report on the success of this program by December 31, 1985.

ORGANIZATION AND OPERATIONS

Roles and Responsibilities

As of the end of 1984, BLM was responsible for managing approximately 300 million acres of public land: 176 million acres in the lower 48 states and 124 million acres in Alaska. In the lower 48, most of the land, approximately 175.5 million acres, is located in what generally are referred to as the 11 Western states: Arizona, California, Colorado, Idaho, Montana, Nevada, New Mexico, Oregon, Utah, Washington, and Wyoming. BLM lands account for about half the total acreage in these states. The remainder of BLM land — some 430,000 acres — is scattered throughout 17 other states. Most of the land in the lower 48 — about 170 million acres — is rangeland, and it is on these lands that most of this chapter will focus. In the Pacific Northwest, BLM has jurisdiction over 2.4 million acres of highly productive forest land, which is dealt with later in this chapter.

Congressional Committees

In the Senate, BLM falls under the jurisdiction of the Committee on Energy and Natural Resources, with wildlife and other resource issues under the jurisdiction of the Subcommittee on Public Lands and Reserved Water. On the House side, the responsible committee is the Committee on Interior and Insular Affairs, with wildlife matters falling under the jurisdiction of the Subcommittee on Public Lands. Appropriations for BLM are made by the Interior subcommittees of the appropriations committees in both the House and Senate.

Agency Structure and Function

The Bureau of Land Management is an agency within the Department of the Interior and is under the assistant secretary for Land and Minerals Management, who also oversees the Minerals Management Service, Bureau of Mines, and Office of Surface Mining. BLM is headed by a director and an associate director who are supported by three deputy directors: for Energy and Mineral Resources, for Lands and Renewable Resources, and for Management Services.

Bureau of Land Management

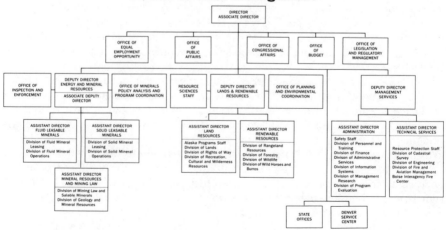

The deputy director for Energy and Mineral Resources oversees all the energy and mineral leasing and production-oversight activities. These responsibilities include the identification of lands subject to competitive leasing; issuance of oil and gas leases on 520 million acres of public lands, national forests, and private lands on which the federal government owns the mineral rights; and leasing for the recovery of geothermal resources, oil shale, tar sands, and coal. This deputy director also oversees leasing of non-energy minerals such as phosphate, potassium, and sodium, and oversees the mining of hardrock minerals under the 1872 Mining Law.

The deputy director for Lands and Renewable Resources oversees all land, recreation, and renewable-resource programs, including wildlife habitat management. He is supported by two assistant directors and the chief of the Office of Planning. The assistant director for Land Resources oversees four separate divisions: the Division of Lands, which includes land sales, exchanges, and other transactions; the Division of Recreation, Cultural, and Wilderness Resources, which oversees wilderness studies and provides policy guidance and technical assistance regarding a variety of natural and scientific areas, including areas of critical environmental concern, the Division of Rights-of-Way, and Alaska Programs. The assistant director for Renewable Resources supervises four other divisions: the Division of Wildlife; the Division of Rangeland Resources; the Division of Forestry; and the Division of Wild Horses and Burros.

BLM has 12 state offices: one in Alaska, one in Virginia to oversee BLM land in 31 states east of Kansas City, and one in each of the 11 Western states except Washington. These offices, each headed by a state director, are responsible for managing and operating all BLM programs within their geographic area of responsibility and for supervising the district offices. Each state office includes a wildlife staff of one or two biologists.

At the local level are 55 district offices, responsible for program implementation, operations, land-use planning, and user supervision in their area.* Districts vary greatly in size, but average about three million acres, an area about the size of Connecticut. The 55 districts are divided into 154 Resource Areas, with an average of two to four areas per district. Each area has an area manager who is responsible for day-to-day resource-management activities and implementation of on-the-ground actions for use of the public lands.

Planning

Most of the major decisions regarding public-land management, including decisions affecting wildlife, are made within BLM's extensive and rather complex planning system. BLM's planning system is organized into three "tiers": the policy tier, which consists of national policy established in public laws, federal regulations, executive orders, and other policy documents, as well as policy guidance established by state directors; the land-use plans, which are developed for each resource area and address multiple-use conflicts and generally allocate resources and select appropriate uses for the public lands; and the activity plans, which are more detailed, site-specific plans for carrying out particular uses provided for in the land-use plans, such as habitat management plans for wildlife.

The land-use plans are where most basic and significant decisions about on-the-ground management of BLM lands are supposed to be made. BLM currently uses two types of plans: management framework plans and resource management plans. Management framework plans were being used at the time FLMPA was enacted, and the agency continued to prepare the plans until regulations implementing FLPMA's new

---

*The number of district offices has varied over time. The figure here is for the end of 1984.

planning requirements were issued in September 1979. Resource management plans are the new plans issued in accordance with the FLPMA planning requirements. From 1980 to 1983, BLM had a transition period in which it allowed both resource management plans and management framework plans to be prepared, but today only resource management plans are prepared.

Resource management plans generally are prepared for individual resource areas, although a state director may approve a more appropriate area for plan coverage. The plans are prepared by the area manager under the guidance of the district manager and receive final approval from the state director. The approval of a resource management plan is considered a "major federal action significantly affecting the human environment," and resource management plans must be accompanied by an environmental impact statement. Both the resource management plan and the environmental impact statement are developed under one integrated process and published as a single document.

In general, resource management plans set forth decisions that identify what land areas are to be restricted to limited uses, designate what kinds of uses of different resources will be allowed and at what level of use, and establish goals for resource conditions. The plans also specify support actions needed to reach the objectives specified in the plan and outline the order or implementation of those actions. BLM headquarters is currently preparing supplemental program guidance for resource management planning that will clarify further the decisions for each resource program, including wildlife-habitat management, that should be included in the plans. This guidance will become part of the BLM planning-manual series, which is available to the public.

More specifically, resource management plans set forth decisions and related terms and conditions on a number of issues of particular importance to wildlife:

- Activity Plans. Resource management plans identify, where appropriate, site-specific actions to be carried out under the more detailed activity plans. Examples include habitat management plans, allotment management plans for managing livestock grazing, herd management plans for wild horses and burros, coal activity plans, transportation plans, and recreation area management plans. Clearly, decisions identifying areas for wildlife habitat management, intensive livestock grazing, or coal development are critical decisions for wildlife.
- Forage Allocation. Resource management plans establish general goals for allocating forage among livestock, wildlife, and wild horses and burros. Under current BLM policies, however, forage-allocation decisions generally have been deferred, since BLM has decided not to implement decisions on livestock grazing reductions until additional data is collected through monitoring.
- Areas of Critical Environmental Concern. FLPMA directs BLM to give priority to designating and protecting areas of critical environmental concern in developing its land use plans. Areas of critical environmental concern are defined in the law as areas where special management attention is required to protect and prevent irreparable damage to important "historic, cultural, or scenic values, fish and wildlife resources, or other natural systems or processes, or to protect life and safety from natural hazards."
- Areas of Surface Mining Unsuitability. The resource management plan process is the chief means by which BLM lands are assessed to determine whether there are areas that should be designated as unsuitable for all or certain types of surface mining under the Surface Mining Control and Reclamation Act of 1977.[20]

FLPMA requires public participation in the land use planning process, and BLM provides both formal and informal opportunities for involvement by the public, federal and state agencies, and other interested parties throughout the process.* There are several key points for formal participation:

Identifying Issues. Under the 1983 regulations, BLM focuses its planning on specific issues, such as concerns or controversies about existing and potential land and resource allocations; levels of resource use, production, and protection; and related management practices. An issue could be, for example, whether to manage a particular area primarily for wildlife. This is a critical point in the process that sets the tone and scope for the rest of the planning effort.

Development of Planning Criteria. The planning criteria establish standards, rules, and measures to guide subsequent actions in the planning process. They also may help set the scope of inventory and data collection and identify the range of reasonable alternatives. This is another key determinant of the entire planning process. Draft planning criteria are made available for public review before they are approved.

Review of the Draft Resource Management Plan and Environmental Impact Statement. The draft resource management plan and environmental impact statement identify the preferred alternative selected by the state director and provide an analysis of other possible alternatives. A 90-day public comment period occurs at this stage, during which public workshops, hearings, or other sessions may be held.

Protesting a Proposed Resource Management Plan. Once the district manager makes his final recommendation on the resource management plan to the state director, the state director files the proposed resource management plan and final environmental impact statement with the Environmental Protection Agency. Any member of the public or any agency or group that has participated in the planning process has 30 days to submit comments on the plan or to file a protest with the director of BLM objecting to approval of the plan or to any part of it that may affect their interests adversely. The governor of the affected state also reviews the resource management plan during this period. If the director determines that significant changes should be made to the proposed plan, a public notice is issued providing an additional public comment period. If no protest is filed, or if the protest is rejected, the state director may approve the plan.

No timetable has been set for the preparation of resource management plans. By the time BLM began preparing resource management plans, approximately 80 percent of the public lands outside of Alaska were covered by management framework plans. Current planning regulations allow continued use of these framework plans as long as they meet FLPMA standards. BLM's planning staff say that some management framework plans could remain in place for as long as 10 to 15 years if conflicts do not arise and if the plans are useful in managing the land. Nor is there a requirement to revise resource management plans after a certain time. The initial resource management plan regulations, issued in 1979, required the revision of the plans every 10 years, but this requirement was dropped in the 1983 rules.

However, whenever a proposed action is not in conformance with the land-use plan — either a resource management plan or a management framework plan — the proposal must be rejected or the plan must be changed. A plan can be changed either by amending the plan or by completely revising it. The process of amending a plan is similar to that for preparing new resource management plans except that an amend-

---

*For more information on public participation in the land use planning process, refer to "BLM Planning: A Guide Resource Management Planning on the Public Lands," a 22-page pamphlet available from BLM.

ment may require only an environmental assessment rather than a full environmental impact statement. Under the Reagan administration, BLM has emphasized the use of plan amendments over the total revision of existing plans.

The first resource management plan prepared in accordance with FLPMA received final approval on January 3, 1984. As of January 1, 1985, BLM's planning office reported that a total of six resource management plans had been approved since the passage of FLPMA, 10 had been completed but were under protest, and 40 resource management plans were under preparation. Based on information from the BLM state offices, the bureau estimates the need to start about a dozen new resource management plans in both 1985 and 1986, but budget and other constraints compel the agency to initiate only about half that number. These figures do not represent the total land use planning effort. Numerous amendments to existing plans have been prepared since the passage of FLPMA. With the heavier reliance on the amendment process under the Reagan administration, this process has taken on increased importance for decision making within the agency. But the figures do show how slowly the envisioned comprehensive FLPMA planning has proceeded.

Budgeting

Funds for the BLM wildlife program are allocated through the Interior Department budget process. Overall BLM spending levels, as well as target spending levels for the various BLM programs, are set by the assistant secretary for Land and Minerals Management. The director of BLM then sets overall spending goals for each of the BLM state offices. Following directives from BLM headquarters identifying spending priorities and projections, each of the state directors prepares a budget allocating funding among the various programs as he or she sees fit. Based on these state budgets, the bureau prepares its budget justification, although the BLM director or the assistant secretary may reallocate the funds differently from the state budgets. The budget is then reviewed by the White House Office of Management and Budget, which also may make revisions.

Next the budget is submitted to Congress as part of the president's annual budget. Hearings are held by both the authorizing committees, which make recommendations on the proposal to the House and Senate appropriations committees, and by the appropriations subcommittees on Interior and related agencies. Additions and deletions to the budget are made by the appropriations subcommittees, and a final budget is approved sometime between June and November for the federal fiscal year, which begins October 1. Funds appropriated for wildlife-habitat management are allocated by the Division of Wildlife to the state directors based on the previously submitted state budgets, on specific congressional directives from the appropriations committees, and on program priorities for that year.

Major problems of the wildlife program over the past several years have been consistently low levels of funding and a continually declining number of biologists and botanists at a time when program workload has been increasing. Some historical perspective is useful to understanding the current situation. In the early 1970s, the program was funded at less than $5 million a year. But with the push for balanced multiple-use management of BLM lands, court-ordered grazing environmental impact statements, and passage of FLPMA, the wildlife program budget steadily grew throughout the late 1970s. From 1978 to 1981, funding for the wildlife program more than doubled, from $7.8 million to $16 million in the last Carter administration budget.

In 1982, this trend was reversed when the Reagan administration requested a 20-percent cut in the wildlife program's budget, from $16 million to $12.6 million.

Wildlife Program Budget Request and Appropriations, FY 1981–1985

Year	Request (millions)	Appropriations (millions)
1981*	—	$16.017
1982*	$12.594	14.918
1983	13.642	15.160
1984	10.515	13.515
1985	11.705	15.783

*Note: Prior to 1983, BLM included general administration costs in the program accounts. The 1981 and 1982 appropriations and the 1982 request shown here have been recalculated to remove general administration costs for accurate comparison. No similar figure is available for the 1981 request. The actual request was $20.070; estimates without general administration range from $15.894 to $17.104.

Congress appropriated $14.9 million, a seven-percent cut. Congress continued through 1984 to provide funds below the 1981 level but above the yearly request from the Reagan administration. The lowest level of funding was in FY 1984, when Congress approved only $13.5 million for wildlife, a 15-percent cut from FY 1981 levels, not accounting for inflation. Funding for the renewable resources program overall followed a similar pattern. In 1984 the renewable resources program received appropriations of $100.4 million, a nine-percent cut from 1981, not adjusted for inflation.

At the same time, funding for the BLM energy and minerals program increased 45 percent, from $5 million in 1981 to $82 million in 1984.* It is important to note that BLM has a unique accounting system in which wildlife activities related to other programs — for example, assessment of impacts on wildlife from a proposed energy lease — are charged to and paid for out of the other program's account. Therefore, some of the increase in the energy and mineral budget has been used to assess the wildlife impacts of the stepped-up program. However, the BLM accounting system does not track the level of such expenditures.

A major concern has been the continuing reduction in BLM wildlife staff. Full-time-equivalents (FTEs) listed in the bureau's annual budget justifications show that the wildlife program staff was cut 13 percent, from 360 to 312 FTEs, between 1982 and 1984.** With such low levels of personnel, BLM lacks wildlife biologist expertise in many of its resource areas, although a few areas do have more than one biologist.

The personnel reductions have been most severe with respect to aquatic biologists and botanists. From 1981 to 1984, the number of aquatic biologists was cut from 53 to 31 and the number of botanists from 15 to nine. Cuts in these types of scientists are especially significant in light of the importance of the resources for which they are responsible. Streams and associated riparian zones in the arid West are essential to maintaining wildlife diversity. As for plants, 24 endangered or threatened species are

*The increases between 1982 and 1984 were partly but not entirely due to BLM assumption of certain mineral-leasing activities from the Minerals Management Service in December 1983. The BLM accounting system does not show what portion of the increases were due to this change.
**Staff cuts since 1981 are even greater, but because BLM did not use FTEs prior to 1982, no accurate estimate of the size of the cut can be made.

located on BLM lands, and as many as 900 additional plant species in the West that may be on BLM lands have been identified as possibly qualifying for listing.

For fiscal year 1985, Congress has boosted the wildlife budget to $15.8 million, almost back up to 1981 levels, not including inflation. This increase will allow BLM to step up its wildlife activities, including preparation of habitat management plans and implementation of endangered species recovery plans. Personnel, however, continued to be cut, down to 295 FTEs, an 18-percent drop since 1982.

WILDLIFE HABITAT MANAGEMENT

The FLPMA multiple-use mandate requires BLM to manage its lands for wildlife. The provisions of FLPMA most significant for wildlife have been described in the legislative authority section of this chapter. Additional authority for wildlife or wildlife-habitat management on BLM lands derives from the following sources: the Migratory Bird Conservation Act of 1929,[21] which provides for habitat protection and enhancement for migratory birds; the Endangered Species Act of 1973,[22] which provides for the protection of endangered species and their habitats; the Public Rangelands Improvement Act of 1978, which directs that rangelands be improved to provide productive wildlife habitat; and the Executive Orders on Floodplain Management (E.O. 11988) and Wetlands Protection (E.O. 11990), which provide for the protection of beneficial floodplain values as well as wetland and riparian values on the public lands. In addition, the Sikes Act Extension of 1974[23] directs BLM to cooperate with the states in developing comprehensive plans and programs for the conservation of fish and wildlife and their habitat, including endangered species. The Sikes Act also authorizes the states, under agreement with BLM, to charge a fee for hunting, trapping, or fishing on public lands, with the receipts to be used to carry out cooperative wildlife programs established under the act.

All BLM programs — livestock grazing, forestry, energy, and minerals — have impacts on wildlife and are in part responsible for meeting the wildlife requirements of FLPMA's multiple-use mandate and for complying with other wildlife laws. This section, however, focuses specifically on the wildlife program carried out by the Division of Wildlife.

Program Management

The wildlife program in BLM is highly decentralized. Overall priorities, policies, and annual budget levels for each state are set by the Washington office, but the allocation of funds within each state are set by the state director. As of FY 1984, reports on wildlife-program accomplishments in each state were limited to the number of acres inventoried. monitored, improved, and maintained. With this type of general information, it is difficult to provide a comprehensive assessment of the program's achievements. Beginning in FY 1985, the state reporting requirements changed. Instead of reporting accomplishments in terms of acreage, the state offices must report to headquarters the number of plans monitored, the number of habitat management plans written, and the number of habitat-development projects completed and maintenance projects maintained. It appears that this data will provide even less real information about wildlife-program accomplishments.

The major activities of the BLM wildlife program are conducting the inventorying and monitoring necessary for planning decisions, undertaking specific projects to maintain or improve wildlife habitat, and carrying out BLM responsibilities for the protection of federally listed threatened and endangered species. Wildlife field staff also work to assess and mitigate the impacts of other BLM actions, such as livestock grazing and energy and mineral leasing, but these activities are paid for from the budgets of other programs and technically are not part of the program carried out under the Division of Wildlife.

Under FLPMA, BLM is directed to prepare and maintain on a continuing basis an inventory of all public lands and their resource values, including fish and wildlife values. Under current policy, however, inventories generally are conducted as a one-time activity and are limited to providing data for resource management plans and for environmental impact statements relevant to other proposed BLM actions, and to providing the basis for monitoring. Wildlife monitoring helps to determine whether BLM land-use decisions are meeting wildlife-management objectives, such as whether a particular livestock grazing program is having the intended effect on wildlife habitat. Monitoring also is used to determine if wildlife improvement projects are meeting their goals.

Habitat maintenance and improvement generally are carried out in the context of habitat management plans. These are site-specific plans for the management of wildlife habitat and are intended to address the needs of either a particular species or group of species. The need for a habitat management plan and its objectives are identified in the land use planning process. A habitat management plan may involve simply identifying and protecting important habitat areas through changes in management emphasis, or it may involve improvements, such as the development of water facilities, installation of protective fencing or removal of fence barriers, and brush control. The implementation of most habitat management plans includes both management changes and project work. Since the states are responsible for management of resident wildlife, the plans usually are developed in cooperation with the states. States also may assist in funding and carrying out the plans.

With regard to endangered species, BLM — like all federal agencies — is charged with two major responsibilities under the Endangered Species Act. BLM is required to insure that any action it authorizes, funds, or carries out does not jeopardize the continued existence of any threatened or endangered species or result in the adverse modification of its critical habitat. The act also directs federal agencies to implement positive management programs to bring about the recovery of these species.

The wildlife program's top priority for endangered species is to provide the information and recommendations necessary to insure that land use decisions do not jeopardize a species or adversely affect its habitat. As with the rest of the BLM wildlife program, this is done primarily by conducting inventories and by monitoring, with the emphasis on collecting information in areas where there are significant conflicts or critical issues. Second in importance to this effort is BLM participation in the development and implementation of recovery plans for the threatened and endangered species on its lands. The FWS is the lead agency in the development of these plans, but the plans generally are prepared with input and review by affected agencies. After the recovery plan is complete, BLM prepares an action plan for implementing its portion of the effort.

BLM also identifies three other groups of species as special status species that are to be managed in order to avoid having to add them to the endangered species list in the future. These include proposed, candidate, and sensitive species. Proposed species are species that the U.S. Fish and Wildlife Service (FWS) has proposed for listing as endangered or threatened. Candidate species are those that FWS is considering for addition to the list but has not yet actually proposed for listing.[24] Sensitive species are those designated by BLM state directors because the species are declining in numbers, their habitat is restricted or in poor condition, or their population levels are so low that any further adverse impacts could lead to the need to add them to the endangered species list.

Program Trends and Issues

The trends in the wildlife program over the past several years under the Reagan administration reflect the pressures of a tight budget for the federal government in general and an increasing emphasis on development uses of BLM lands. With reduced funds, the BLM wildlife program has been forced to address only the most serious problems or areas of most intense conflict, making the program primarily reactive and largely unable to initiate positive actions either to head off future problems or to capitalize on opportunities. With reduced personnel, the program has had to conduct inventory and monitoring for increasing numbers of development activities, creating growing concern among wildlife professionals that these essential and basic surveys are not being done adequately. In addition, habitat-improvement funds have been reduced deliberately as the agency tries to encourage the states and private groups to undertake and contribute to this type of work.

Finally, wildlife professionals and conservationists repeatedly report that in recent years BLM top-level management philosophy has placed increased emphasis on economic uses of the land and often has both explicitly and implicitly discouraged non-commercial renewable-resource efforts in the field.

Reduced Inventory. Under the Reagan administration, BLM general policy has been to cut back on inventories and to increase monitoring. BLM budget justifications state that inventories for one point in time are expensive to conduct and that it is more cost-effective to conduct base-line inventories followed by monitoring. At the same time, the agency is decreasing the inventory effort by focusing only on areas where a specific controversy or planned action has been identified in a resource management plan. BLM also claims the need for inventories is decreasing as the grazing environmental impact statements ordered by the court in the NRDC lawsuit are nearing completion.

The wildlife-inventory data eventually is to be kept in an automated data-processing system so that it will be easily retrievable. That system, however, currently is operational only on a limited basis. The lack of comprehensive and periodically updated inventories forces decisions to be made case by case, without information on the cumulative impacts of various actions.

Reduction in Habitat Improvement. BLM habitat-improvement efforts generally are carried out under habitat management plans. The most recent data available on the status of habitat management plans show that by 1983, 268 habitat management plans had been prepared in 10 western states and Alaska, covering more than 38 million acres of terrestrial habitat and almost 2,000 miles of streams. Twenty-three of these plans, or nine percent of the total, had been fully implemented and 137 of them, or more than 50 percent, were less than half complete. BLM estimates it would cost $27.13 million to complete these plans. At the present rate of funding (FY 1984) these existing plans would not be fully implemented until about 1997. Meanwhile, habitat management plans in need of updating are being identified in the new resource management plans. Many of the existing habitat management plans were developed years ago and may be obsolete. The bureau plans to review existing habitat management plans in 1985 to identify those that should be dropped and those that warrant continued implementation, and to establish priorities to guide their completion.

Current BLM policy is to defer the development of new habitat management plans, but it is unclear whether this has had much effect in the field. BLM estimates

Status of Habitat Management Plans by State as of December 31, 1983

State	Number of Plans	Acres	Miles of Stream	Funds Spent (Millions)	Total Estimated Cost (Millions)
Alaska	4	1,380,711	173	$.207	$.508
Arizona	15	4,707,988	125	1.542	3.524
California	50	2,417,922	53	1.601	3.512
Colorado	15	2,528,866	652	2.110	4.842
Idaho	32	2,085,554	143	1.739	4.808
Montana	15	7,527,114	64	.983	6.034
Nevada	43	6,574,952	122	1.084	4.528
New Mexico	22	3,343,050	32	1.504	5.836
Oregon	31	1,338,574	161	1.784	2.961
Utah	27	5,012,474	184	1.991	4.464
Wyoming	14	1,428,239	256	.775	1.362
Total	268	38,345,444	1,965	$15.32	$42.459

Compiled from state reports, Wildlife Habitat Management Statistics, BLM.

that approximately 50 new plans were written in 1984 compared to 60 in 1981. However, it does appear that the implementation and maintenance of existing habitat management plans for non-critical areas is being reduced. In particular, habitat improvement has decreased significantly. According to figures from BLM annual budget justifications, terrestrial habitat improved dropped from 7.75 million acres in 1981 to 1.8 million in 1984, and aquatic habitat improved dropped from 2,996 miles in 1982 to 212 miles in 1984.

Endangered Species. While the overall wildlife program budget in BLM generally has declined over the past several years, funding for endangered species has increased somewhat. These increases should help BLM catch up with some neglected activities, such as the implementation of recovery plans. But funding at the current level will be inadequate if, as expected, the number of listed species on the public lands increases significantly over the next several years.

The endangered species program in BLM always has been relatively small. The program is estimated to have operated on less than $1 million in FY 1978. In FY 1983, the first year that funding for the program appeared separately in the budget, it received $1.65 million. In the past two years, the program has been increased, for a total of $2.65 million in FY 1984 and $3.9 million in FY 1985.

As of the end of 1984, public lands provided part or all of the habitat used by 86 species listed as endangered or threatened: 62 animals and 24 plants. Forty-four recovery plans had been prepared for 41 species on BLM lands, and BLM was implementing recovery for 26 of these. For the remaining 18 plans, implementation is limited to avoiding activities that would cause further habitat deterioration. With the FY 1985 increase, BLM expects to more fully implement the 26 plans, for which recovery actions are under way, and to assist FWS in the preparation of 15 additional plans.

While funding for the endangered species program is increasing, so are its needs. Increased development activities that could affect endangered species have accelerated wildlife inventory and consultation needs. At the same time, FWS has stepped up its listing of endangered species, and BLM's endangered species responsibilities could double over the next three years. In addition, BLM has hundreds of special status species for which it has essentially taken no action. These include:

- Proposed Species — 30 animal and 24 plant species proposed by FWS for addition to the endangered or threatened list during 1983 and 1984.
- Candidate Species — 34 vertebrate and 30 invertebrate species for which FWS has substantial information to support listing and for which listing is anticipated, and 108 vertebrate species for which FWS has some information indicating that listing may be appropriate but for which additional data is still being collected. In addition, perhaps as many as 900 candidate plant species may be located on BLM lands.
- Sensitive Species — approximately 116 species identified by BLM state directors as future candidates for the endangered list if they are not properly managed. These may include candidate or proposed species.

In its report on the FY 1985 Interior Department appropriations, the House Committee on Appropriations directed BLM to use part of the funding increase for endangered species "to develop recovery plans to prevent additional species from becoming federally listed." This is the first explicit congressional recognition of the BLM special status species effort. As a result, BLM allocated $250,000 for the development of this program in FY 1985.

Encouraging Non-federal Contributions. A major new thrust of the BLM wildlife program has been to encourage non-federal participation in wildlife-habitat management activities on the public lands. Four of 11 major points in the most recent BLM fish and wildlife resources management policy, issued October 20, 1983, address this issue. The bureau began implementing this policy in FY 1984 by issuing an instruction memorandum to the field identifying the encouragement of state and private investment and cooperation as a major objective of the wildlife program and identifying four specific incentives to encourage this activity:

- Field officers are to encourage state or private organizations to file for water rights in areas where they have participated in a wildlife project.
- BLM will give priority to retaining lands in federal ownership where a state or private investment has been made in a wildlife project. If the land is disposed of, BLM will try to provide for state management of the improvement through a lease, permit, or easement, or will compensate the parties for their investment.
- For wildlife projects that BLM considers to be of equal priority, BLM will give higher priority to undertaking those with state or private investments.
- Field officers are encouraged through various recognition programs to reward the efforts of those who contribute to wildlife projects.

In addition, in December 1983 BLM expanded use of cooperative management agreements, originally devised to give ranchers more independence in their use of BLM grazing lands, to a number of other programs, including wildlife, recreation, and wild horses and burros. The agreements are signed with state and private organizations willing to assume part of the responsibility for wildlife projects on BLM lands. BLM has no clear guidelines for determining which wildlife projects should be carried out under cooperative management agreements or what the advantages of developing agreements are. Although the wildlife cooperative-management-agreements effort gives BLM one more tool to encourage state and private contributions, it does not provide the program with any new authority. Many conservationists believe the extension of the cooperative management-agreements concept from the range program to the wildlife and recreation programs was done simply to defuse criticism that the agreements are a special concession to ranchers. Others say extending the agreements to the wildlife program opens it up to a broader constituency and tends to counterbalance domination by a single-interest group. As of the end of 1984, BLM had some 15 wildlife cooperative management agreements in effect and was working on 15 more, most of them developed with state fish and wildlife agencies.

In FY 1984, BLM cstimated that the wildlife habitat management program received some $1.5 million in contributions. Nearly two-thirds of this was labor at an estimated value of $940,000. About 20 percent was in materials, such as fencing, gates, seeds, plants, and watering facilities. The remainder, or about $240,000, was in monetary contributions, primarily from companies that jointly sponsored research where their interests were affected directly.

Since 1984 was the first year that BLM tracked the level of non-federal contributions, it has no data by which to determine if the contributions were increased in 1984 over previous years. Officials estimate, however, that contributions were slightly higher. For 1985, BLM has allocated $500,000 among the states to be used as matching funds for non federal contributions and again expects about $1.5 million worth of donated time, money, and materials.

Sikes Act User Fee. Another effort designed to increase non-federal investment in wildlife habitat management on public lands is a BLM/Forest Service initiative to encourage a Sikes Act user-fee program administered voluntarily by each state. The authority for such an initiative is in Section 203 of the Sikes Act, which authorizes state wildlife agencies, in agreement with the secretary of Interior or Agriculture, to collect a fee for hunting, fishing, or trapping on public lands and to use these monies for habitat conservation and rehabilitation programs.[25] Such a public-land fee would be in addition to currently required hunting and fishing licenses. User fees already are collected on some national forests in the eastern United States.

As of the end of 1984, no Sikes Act user fees had been established, but New Mexico was in the process of holding public hearings on a proposed fee of $5.25 per year. BLM officials say that other states are beginning to consider the fee as an option and that resistance among user groups appears to be declining somewhat. One hurdle that may prevent or slow the adoption of such fees is that many states require the approval of state legislatures to set such fee structures.

A major concern expressed by conservationists about the user fees and the effort to encourage more state and private investment is that the administration will try to reduce the wildlife program's budget by equivalent amounts. The administration record thus far sustains this concern. On the other hand, some suggest that a constituency that actually has made an investment in wildlife habitat on the public lands might become a stronger and more persistent advocate for public-land wildlife resources.

Riparian Habitat and Livestock Grazing. Because the vast majority of public lands are arid, with relatively sparse vegetation, the riparian zones — particularly in the desert area of the Southwest — are critical to the survival of a vast array of wildlife. The dense trees and shrubs in these zones provide shade, keep aquatic habitat cool for fish, and provide vital habitat for many terrestrial species. Riparian habitat also is important to many big-game species for cover and food. These wet and well-vegetated areas provide an important source of water, food, and cover and receive proportionately heavier use than any other habitat type. Without sufficient riparian habitat, wildlife diversity and abundance would be reduced substantially.

Riparian zones also may be the most threatened habitat on BLM lands. Riparian and wetland habitats have been reduced vastly from their original extent across the United States, and the loss has been proportionately greater in the arid western states.

A variety of problems have contributed to the loss of riparian habitat, including floods, dams, drought, roads, logging, gravel pits, and recreation. The most extensive impacts, however, have been from livestock grazing. The same qualities that make these lands attractive to wildlife — water, lush vegetation, and shade — also make them attractive to livestock. A number of individual studies have documented the impact of livestock upon riparian habitat. For example, a study in Nevada reported that livestock grazing had caused extensive destruction of or damage to 883 miles of streams.[26] Another study in Montana found that an ungrazed segment of stream produced 268 percent more trout than did a grazed segment of the same stream.[27]

In recognition of the importance of riparian zones to wildlife and the extent of the threat to them, BLM has directed its state offices to address habitats in the following priority: (1) wetland/riparian habitats, (2) aquatic/fisheries habitats, and (3) terrestrial habitats. But wildlife conservationists maintain that the only real solution to the riparian habitat problem may be fencing or the termination of livestock grazing. Fencing and planning livestock distribution to protect critical riparian habitat areas may provide a feasible compromise in some circumstances.

The question of livestock impacts on riparian habitats is only one of many conflicts — although perhaps the most critical one — between livestock use and wildlife habitat on the public lands. Thus it may be addressed as part of the larger range and wildlife issue if the 99th Congress considers some type of omnibus range legislation (see discussions on grazing fees and legislation later in this chapter).

WILDLIFE AND THE LIVESTOCK PROGRAM

Livestock grazing is the broadest economic use of public lands. BLM authorizes livestock grazing on 170 million acres, 98 percent of its 174 million acres in the lower 48 states. The agency currently issues about 26,200 grazing permits, leases, or adjustments yearly to authorize grazing for 4.3 million animals, including two million cattle and 2.3 million sheep and goats. About four percent of the nation's beef cattle and 28 percent of the sheep depend on the public lands for all or part of their yearly forage requirement.[28]

Many major and basic decisions affecting the public lands and the wildlife that depends on them are related to livestock grazing: How many animals will be allowed to graze? At what times and in what locations? Which lands will receive improvements? What type of improvements will they be? These decisions are critical in determining whether wildlife has adequate forage, the right type of forage, sufficient wintering grounds, access to and adequate amounts of water, and more.

BLM reports that at least 60 percent of the public rangelands are in unsatisfactory condition because of overgrazing.[29] Livestock grazing also serious impacts on riparian zones and contributes to high rates of soil erosion. Wildlife professionals also charge that range improvements for livestock use are hurting wildlife. The range program is of continuing and increasing concern to wildlife conservationists.

Program Management

Livestock grazing is managed by the Division of Rangeland Resources. Grazing is authorized through permits and leases, which generally are issued for a period of 10 years and which are required by FLPMA to specify allowable numbers of livestock and seasons of use.

The basic goals and objectives of the livestock management program are supposed to be determined in the land-use plan, including setting overall targets for levels of grazing and establishing priorities for managing the various grazing allotments. For some of the allotments in an area, BLM will prepare an allotment management plan, an activity plan that describes how livestock grazing is to be conducted and managed. Allotment management plans may vary from a simple documentation of existing management to a complex plan for grazing-management and range improvement. Key decisions affecting wildlife are made in the plans. In fact, according to a 1981 report by the Wildlife Management Institute, "In practice, the most important of all BLM plans to wildlife is the allotment management plan."[30]

The other major facet of the range management program is range improvements. FLPMA directs that 50 percent of grazing fees from the public lands be credited to an account called the range-betterment fund and be available for appropriation for "on-the-ground range rehabilitation, protection, and improvements" on the public lands.[31] FLPMA specifies that these improvements are to include "seeding and reseeding, fence construction, weed control, water development, and *fish and wildlife habitat enhancement*" (emphasis added).[32] Half of the funds are to be made available for use in the district, region, or national forest from which they were derived. The remainder are to be allocated by the secretary. This provision was modified slightly in the Public Rangelands Improvement Act of 1978. Because it appeared that grazing fees would decrease under the new formula established in the act, causing a decrease in funds available for range improvement, Congress directed that 50 percent of these receipts or $10 million, whichever is greater, be authorized for annual range improvements.[33]

Program Trends and Issues

In the past several years, BLM has made a number of significant changes in the range program, most of which have drawn criticism from wildlife conservationists, environmental groups, and others interested in non-commercial uses of the public lands. The agency's decentralized management makes the effects of these changes difficult to track. Moreover, some of the effects may not show up for a number of years.

Delaying Grazing Reductions. After the passage of the Taylor Grazing Act in 1934, the Grazing Service spent its early years allocating grazing privileges among potential users. In 1942 it issued its first 10-year permits. This reduced the number of users of the public range, but still allowed grazing to continue at a high level. When the 10-year permits expired in the early 1950s, BLM embarked on an effort to adjudicate the range, that is, to bring livestock use into balance with forage capacity and with forage consumption by wildlife. This effort was completed in the late 1960s, but generally was regarded as not reducing livestock numbers to the appropriate carrying capacity. Thus in the 1970s, as BLM began to prepare management framework plans and to develop environmental impact statements on its grazing programs as a result of the NRDC lawsuit, the agency conducted intensive inventories on the lands to determine their available forage. In many cases, BLM decided that grazing reductions were needed and called for grazing cutbacks in its land-use plans.

This process initially was continued by the Reagan administration. On March 5, 1982, BLM issued a grazing management policy that required allotments to be identified as belonging to one of three categories — maintain, improve, or custodial management — to better help the bureau set priorities. In the instruction memorandum issuing the policy (No. 82-292), the director noted that BLM still intended to issue grazing-use decisions within 17 months following publication of a final environmental impact statement.

But on September 1, 1982, BLM issued another instruction memorandum (No. 82-644) that changed this policy. The memorandum ordered that all 1982 grazing environmental impact statements contain a cautionary statement saying that although the vegetation-production data in the statements was used to help determine areas suitable for continued livestock grazing and to provide the basis for developing a rangeland management program, the data also "must be supported by the results of monitoring studies before making forage allocation decisions." BLM range officials say the change was necessary to head off an American Farm Bureau Federation lawsuit that challenged the adequacy of BLM's one-point-in-time inventories as a basis for making grazing adjustment decisions. The instruction memorandum thus reversed the BLM policy of adjusting livestock use based on data in the grazing environmental impact statement and allowed grazing to continue at existing levels for an indefinite period.

This policy subsequently was added to the new BLM grazing regulations that went into effect March 22, 1984.[34] In response to criticisms that the regulations placed no limit on the amount of monitoring to be completed before implementing grazing adjustments, BLM issued another instruction memorandum (No. 84-495) on May 15, 1984. It said that in the absence of acceptable data, grazing-allotment decisions would be delayed up to five years while monitoring data was collected. However, the memorandum also instructed BLM personnel to issue decisions "as soon as data are available to support the change." In addition, the new grazing regulations allow grazing adjustments to be phased in over a five-year period unless an agreement can be developed with the livestock operator to phase in the use more quickly. These two changes together mean that grazing reductions may not be implemented for 10 years — five years of monitoring and five of implementation.

Some conservationists are concerned that the monitoring necessary to support decisions to reduce grazing in the future is not being done, or at least is not being done adequately. Whether this is the case is difficult to discern at the national level. One indicator in support of this charge is the fact that while BLM has a total of 26,686 grazing allotments, it currently is monitoring only about 4,000 to 4,500 a year. BLM officials counter that many allotments do not need to be monitored every year. But at this level of monitoring, BLM cannot conduct annual monitoring even on those allotments that it has designated for most intensive management — the improve allotments.* As of November 1984, BLM had placed 4,740 allotments in the improve category. Additional allotments will be added as BLM classifies the 9,000 allotments that have not yet been categorized. The failure to conduct adequate monitoring could cause future grazing reduction decisions to be challenged again in court or by Congress.

Grazing Regulations and Cooperative Management Agreements. On February 21, 1984, BLM published new grazing regulations that the agency said eliminated redundant items, clarified existing language and terms, and reorganized the regulations for easier understanding.[35] On May 9, 1984, NRDC and four other environmental groups filed suit in the U.S. District Court for the Eastern District of California, charging that the rules made numerous substantive changes in BLM policy that are contrary to the mandatory requirements of FLPMA and the Public Rangelands Improvement Act.

The major issue at debate is the new BLM Cooperative Management Agreement Program. BLM first adopted the use of the agreements in instruction memorandum No. 83-485, issued April 22, 1983. BLM said the purpose of the cooperative management agreements was to provide livestock operators who have demonstrated good rangeland-management practices with recognition of good stewardship, a larger role in managing grazing on the public lands, and the assurance of tenure needed to encourage

---

*Improve allotments are those that have moderate to high resource-production potential but that are producing at only low to moderate levels.

private investment in rangeland improvements. According to the agency, through the use of agreements, BLM will be "encouraging operators to maintain or initiate good grazing management practices, while also reducing federal expenditures for improving and managing the public lands."

The memorandum defined cooperative management agreements as a formal written agreement between the BLM and a livestock operator. Through the agreement, the livestock operator agrees to graze livestock in a manner that will achieve the allotment objectives, which may include fish and wildlife habitat improvement objectives. The objectives, as well as the operator's management flexibility, are to be defined by the agreement. Initially, cooperative management agreements are to be limited to operators who graze livestock in allotments that have satisfactory resource conditions and in which land-use objectives are being met. In addition, a grazing environmental impact statement must have been completed for the area, the district advisory board and multiple-use advisory council must recommend approval of the agreement, and the operator must agree to contribute to the construction of range improvements.

Initially, the cooperative management agreements concept received quiet support from some conservation organizations. But implementation of the program and the regulations issued for it have been criticized severely. Prior to the issuance of the regulations, at least seven cooperative management agreements were signed and agreed to by BLM and individual livestock operators. According to NRDC, two of the cooperative management agreements simply allowed the rancher to manage livestock grazing on the public lands "as he determines appropriate," and three others allowed the rancher to increase numbers of livestock by 10 percent or more over levels allowed by existing permits.

In addition, the regulations governing cooperative management agreements are very general and give BLM and the livestock operator wide latitude. They authorize BLM to enter into a cooperative agreement with any permittee or lessee "who has demonstrated exemplary rangeland practices."[36] The rules say the agreement simply is to establish the "responsibilities and performance standards" of the cooperating parties and must be consistent with the land-use plan for the area.[37] They authorize the issuance of a cooperative management agreement for a period of 10 years and require BLM to periodically review the agreement and the operator's performance under it. A cooperative management agreement does not allow the livestock operator to exclude or limit other authorized uses on the allotment.

NRDC charges that the agreement regulations violate the requirement in FLPMA that BLM specify in grazing permits and leases the numbers of animals to be grazed and the seasons of use. NRDC also charges that cooperative management agreements allow ranchers to make grazing decisions for a period of 10 years, contrary to FLPMA's requirements that grazing permits must specify that BLM may "reexamine the condition of the range at any time" and may require "adjustment in the amount or other aspect of grazing use."[38] Also, the rules do not require cooperative management agreements to be altered to meet changes in the land-use plan. In addition, conservation groups say that the agreement program does not provide for any formal public notice or comment on the proposed provisions of individual agreements nor on the actual range-management decisions made by the livestock operator, thus violating the FLPMA requirement that the public be given "adequate notice and opportunity to comment upon . . . and participate in" the management of the public lands.[39]

While the main focus of the lawsuit is the Cooperative Management Agreement Program, it addresses other aspects of the new grazing rules as well. Among other things, the plaintiffs charge that the rules could lead to the exclusion of wildlife and conservation groups from the administrative appeals process by allowing only affected interests, as defined by BLM field staff, to participate; that they eliminate the requirement for issuing rangeland program summaries and updates — a requirement established by BLM in 1981 to provide a clear public record for which BLM and users can be held accountable; and that they remove the requirement that grazing permits be modified or cancelled in order to be consistent with the area's land-use plan.

In sum, NRDC and other conservation groups charge that the 1984 grazing regulations will seriously impair BLM's ability to curb the improper and excessive livestock use that has destroyed wildlife habitat, accelerated soil erosion and desertification, and caused the deterioration of the recreational and scenic values of the public lands.

The court heard arguments on the case November 19, 1984. While the case is pending, BLM has continued to prepare additional cooperative management agreements, although it has agreed not to put any into effect until the case is decided. BLM estimates that it could have a total of 60 to 80 agreements ready for implementation when the court issues a decision.

Range Improvements. On October 15, 1982, BLM issued a new range-improvement policy that also has been criticized as posing problems for wildlife conservation. The policy addresses four major areas:

Distribution and Use of the Funds. Prior to the new policy, half the range-betterment funds were distributed to the districts in proportion to the amount of grazing fees collected by each district and half by the secretary of the Interior. The revised policy distributes all the range betterment funds to the district, where the district grazing advisory boards — composed entirely of livestock operators — make recommendations on their use. This reduces the agency's ability to target the funds to areas of most need and increases the grazing advisory board's influence in determining how the funds are spent. These changes could reduce spending on improvements that benefit wildlife.

Private Contributions. The revised policy contains a number of provisions to encourage grazing permittees to contribute labor, materials, equipment, or funding for range improvements. One of the changes is to give top priority to range improvements funded entirely by contributions and to assign higher ranking to improvements funded in part by contributions. This could mean that improvements with the most benefits for livestock would be given highest priority.

Assigning Maintenance. The policy calls for assigning the maintenance of structural improvements to the primary beneficiaries of the improvements. Thus, if an improvement, such as a watering facility, produced 40 percent of its benefits for wildlife and 60 percent for livestock, maintenance responsibilities would be given to the livestock operator. Wildlife conservationists are concerned that livestock operators will not properly maintain the improvements for use by wildlife. Although BLM says the operator would be required to maintain the improvement in a way that protects its benefits for wildlife, it is doubtful that such requirements could be enforced adequately. BLM had planned to complete its assignments of maintenance responsibilities by the end of FY 1984, but this effort was slowed by Congress. However, as of FY 1985 no maintenance costs will be paid out of range betterment funds. These funds will be used solely for on-the-ground improvements. Remaining maintenance costs will be paid out of other portions of BLM funding.

Rangeland Investments. The policy establishes how BLM will set priorities among rangeland improvements. The policy requires an investment analysis to ensure that range improvements are cost-effective. This analysis attempts to place economic values on the wildlife and recreational benefits yielded by the investment, although generally it is agreed that the agency does not have a good basis for valuing these benefits. On the one hand, the values used in this process generally are perceived as underestimating wildlife values. On the other hand, wildlife benefits in these analyses sometimes tip the scales and make cost-effective a proposed range investment intended primarily for livestock use. Sometimes this analysis also is suspect.

Whether it is the fault of this new policy or not, wildlife conservationists charge that although FLPMA and the Public Rangelands Improvement Act include fish and wildlife enhancement as one of the goals of range improvements, in fact few improvements are made for the benefit of wildlife. In FY 1984, for example, $10.3 million was spent on range improvements. Ninety-eight percent of this was for improvements for grazing, while one percent was spent on improvements for wildlife. BLM generally maintains that almost all range improvements produce some benefits for wildlife. Wildlife conservationists, however, say that many of these improvements not only fail to benefit wildlife, but actually are harmful to wildlife. For example, livestock watering facilities have been placed in areas where livestock previously did not graze, encouraging livestock to move into areas that previously provided habitat for wildlife. Another example is livestock fencing that interrupts wildlife migratory patterns.

Grazing Fees. The current grazing-fee formula, established in the Public Rangelands Improvement Act in 1978, expires December 31, 1985. This will provide an opportunity for wildlife conservationists, who consistently have criticized the fees as being too low and therefore encouraging overgrazing, to suggest changes.

Grazing fees have been the focus of controversy throughout the history of federal range management. Fees for grazing on the public domain lands were first charged by the Grazing Service in 1936, which set its fees at five cents per animal unit month (AUM). The Grazing Service's fee originally was intended to cover the administrative costs of the federal range-management program, but by the mid-1940s the cost of the grazing program was more than $5 million, while grazing fees were bringing in less than $1 million. The House Interior Appropriations Subcommittee pressured the Grazing Service to raise fees, while Senator Pat McCarran of Nevada campaigned to refuse to allow an increase. This led to a massive cut in appropriations for the Grazing Service, which resulted in its demise and the establishment of the Bureau of Land Management.

Grazing fee fights continued at BLM, with the agency proposing some increases and then compromising to lower levels. By 1969 both BLM and the Forest Service were brought under a fair market value formula. Based on this formula, it was determined that the 1966 rate should be $1.23. Forest Service fees, averaging 56 cents, and BLM fees, at 33 cents, were to be raised to this level — adjusted annually to account for changes in private lease rates — in 10 equal installments. This new fee, however, was the subject of several court suits and of moratoriums in 1970 and 1972. Nevertheless, by 1974 the fee had reached $1.00 for BLM lands and $1.11 for Forest Service lands.

In 1976, Congress declared in FLPMA that it was the policy of the United States to receive fair market value for the use of the public lands. But rather than requiring fair market value for grazing fees, Congress froze fees at their current levels and ordered another study, due in 1977. In 1978, Congress adopted a new fee formula in the rangelands improvement act that was based not on fair market value but on the livestock operator's ability to pay. Grazing fees under the new formula at first began to rise, from $1.89 per AUM in 1979 to $2.36 per AUM in 1980, but fees then began to drop and were down to $1.37 per AUM in 1984.

Almost everyone except the livestock permittees and lessees on BLM lands and their supporters thinks the fees should be increased. In 1983, the grazing fee under the rangelands improvement act was $1.40 compared to an average fee of $8.85 on private lands.[40] Livestock operators argue that fees for public lands should not be as high as for private lands because the forage is not as good, and the rancher must shoulder more costs when using public lands. However, ranchers clearly are receiving a significant public subsidy in the form of artificially low fees.

Virtually all wildlife interests also support an increase in grazing fees, although for several different reasons. One of the main arguments is that the artificially low fees encourage livestock operators to pressure BLM for the highest level of livestock use possible and make it difficult for the agency to reduce overgrazing. This is because permit value, generally is estimated to run about $1,000 to $1,500 per head. An additional allotment of 500 cattle can be worth $500,000 to $750,000 to the rancher. The permit value is commonly considered the permittee's private property and is included in the market price and loan value of the property to which the public land permit is attached. At least in part because the fee for grazing on public lands is below that on private lands, the demand of livestock operations for public lands exceeds the number of permits. Thus purchasers of private grazing lands and livestock have been willing to pay large premiums to sellers where the sellers have permits to graze on public range lands.

Wildlife interests argue that keeping permit value high is top priority for livestockmen, whose operations often are only marginally profitable, and that the value is kept high by keeping permit AUMs high. Raising grazing fees to market rates would eliminate permit value, they say, and eliminate this incentive for overgrazing.

Another reason that wildlife conservationists are interested in raising grazing fees is that 50 percent of the fees are used for range improvements. Conservationists would also like some kind of assurance that the funds would be used for multiple-use purposes or that a certain portion of the funds would be used in the interests of wildlife.

Legislation

In addition to the grazing-fee formula, two other aspects of the range program expire at the end of 1985. These are the grazing advisory boards and the Experimental Stewardship Program. Wildlife interests would like to see the elimination of the rancher-controlled boards, which they see as giving the livestock industry undue influence over BLM. They argue that the multiple-use advisory councils established by FLPMA are more appropriate forums for advising BLM on all types of land-use decisions, although they say that even these councils need to be improved to establish balanced representation of the many different users of BLM lands.

The Experimental Stewardship Program was authorized by the Rangelands Improvement Act as an experiment in providing incentives or rewards for permittees who manage grazing in a manner that improves range condition on the public lands. The secretaries of Interior and Agriculture are directed to report on the results of the experimental program at the same time that they report on their evaluation of the grazing fee formula.

With these programs up for reauthorization, and a likely fight brewing over grazing fees, the Congressional Research Service, in November and December 1984, convened a series of workshops for the key parties likely to be involved in such a legislative battle. The goal of the workshops was to air the issues of top concern to both conservationists and the livestock industry and to establish a process for negotiating legislation that addresses these concerns.

After the December workshop, both conservationists and committee staff involved in the workshops reported that the negotiation process showed some promise. The result is likely to be consideration by the 99th Congress of an omnibus range bill that would address a number of different issues, including the fee formula, wild horses and burros, wildlife habitat and range condition, riparian-zone protection, monitoring, grazing advisory boards, experimental stewardship, and cooperative management agreements.

LANDS UNDER SPECIAL MANAGEMENT

BLM has several land-management categories that can provide a measure of protection for wildlife as well as for other resources. These include a variety of natural-area designations, areas of critical environmental concern, and wilderness. At BLM headquarters, these programs are coordinated by the Division of Recreation, Cultural, and Wilderness Resources. Planning for and coordinating the management of natural areas and areas of critical environmental concern in the field is undertaken by whatever division or divisions have jurisdiction over the resources designated for protection. For example, the wildlife division would oversee an area that was designated for the protection of an endangered species. More than one division may share responsibility for an area.

Program Management

Natural Areas. The least protective of these three land management categories is the natural-area designation. BLM for years has identified areas that are important for a variety of natural or recreational values and has given them a designated title to indicate their significance. These include research natural areas, outstanding natural areas, primitive areas, recreation lands, and national natural landmarks, as well as some other miscellaneous designations. For the most part, these designations are not specifically authorized by law and protection of the areas is not required legally. The designations simply provide notice that an area has an important resource value.

ACECs. Areas of critical environmental concern (ACECs) are potentially the most important tools for protecting fish and wildlife habitat on the public lands. This designation was established in FLPMA, which defined areas of critical environmental concern to include "areas within the public lands where special management attention is required (when such areas are developed or used or where no development is required) to protect and prevent irreparable damage to important historic, cultural, or scenic values, fish, and wildlife resources or other natural systems or processes, or to protect life and safety from natural hazards."[41] FLPMA directed BLM to give priority to the identification of potential ACECs in its inventory of all public lands. FLPMA also directs BLM to give priority to the designation and protection of these areas in the development and revision of its land-use plans.

ACECs are designated through the land-use planning process. It is an administrative designation and does not require congressional approval. A potential ACEC may be nominated by the public; by representatives of other federal, state, or local agencies; or by BLM personnel. A nomination may be made at any time and may be considered within the context of the preparation or revision of a resource management plan, as an amendment to an existing plans, or through a planning analysis if there is no existing plan.

After receiving an ACEC nomination, the district manager is to determine in writing whether the area should be considered as a potential ACEC in the planning process. If the district manager determines that it should be considered for ACEC status, he must determine whether the area requires some interim protection to prevent undue degradation until a final decision is made. An ACEC is considered officially designated when the state director approves the plan in which it is proposed.

Areas of Critical Environmental Concern Designated as of October 1, 1984

State	Wildlife-related ACECs Number	Acres	Plant or Ecosystem-related ACECs Number	Acres	Total Number	Acres
Alaska	—	—	—	—	—	—
Arizona	—	—	—	—	—	—
California	29	388,214	7	20,081	80	708,990
Colorado	1	750	—	—	5	21,327
Idaho	4	196,345	—	—	5	228,345
Montana	1	12,048	—	—	1	12,048
Nevada	1	307	2	100	4	1,479
New Mexico	3	5,419	3	5,026	7	29,392
Oregon	16	95,033	38	50,828	64	240,061
Utah	1	7,592	3	11,200	7	89,231
Wyoming	9	126,506	4	2,526	13	208,385
Total	65	832,214	57	89,761	186	1,529,258

Compiled from ACEC Data Summary, Division of Recreation, Cultural, and Wilderness Resources, BLM.

No specific protective actions are automatically required to accompany an ACEC designation. Neither FLPMA nor BLM regulations set specific standards for ACEC protection, and the areas are open to mineral entry and some homesteading, since only a secretarial withdrawal of an ACEC can protect it from such activities. The decision on what actions and limitations are necessary to protect an ACEC are made by the district manager with the approval of the state director on a case-by-case basis. Key planning and management information, such as activities and uses considered compatible or incompatible with the ACEC and other special management terms and conditions, are to be described in the land-use plan. More specific information on management actions are to be included in an ACEC activity plan. Once an ACEC is designated, any actions that would be incompatible with the purposes for which it was established can proceed only if the land-use plan is revised or amended accordingly.

Wilderness. In the latter part of the 1980s, BLM will be completing wilderness studies on its lands and making recommendations to Congress for wilderness designations. This could result in the designation of millions of acres of wilderness on the public lands in the West, although it undoubtedly will be a relatively small percentage of total BLM acreage. The designation of wilderness can provide some additional protection for fish and wildlife on public lands, since these areas are to be managed for naturalness and non-degradation even though a number of existing uses will be allowed to continue.

BLM is directed to conduct wilderness studies under FLMPA Section 603, which requires BLM to review "roadless areas of five thousand acres or more and roadless islands of the public lands" identified as having wilderness characteristics and to make recommendations on their suitability for wilderness preservation.[42] These recommendations are to be submitted to the president by no later than October 21, 1991, and the president is to submit his recommendations for wilderness designations to Congress within two years of the date on which he receives a recommendation from the secretary. While the lands are being studied they are to be managed so as not to impair their suitability for wilderness designation, although existing mining and grazing uses and mineral leasing may continue. Once an area is designated for wilderness it is to be managed according to the provisions of the 1964 Wilderness Act. Section 603 also directed BLM to undertake an accelerated review of areas that were designated as primitive or natural areas prior to November 1, 1975, known as "instant study areas."

In addition to the review under Section 603, which focuses primarily on areas 5,000 acres or larger, BLM also conducts wilderness reviews of smaller areas as part of its land-use planning process. This is sometimes referred to as Section 202 wilderness study, after the section in FLPMA that applies to land-use plans.

BLM completed its wilderness inventory in the western states in 1980 and identified approximately 24 million acres in 930 separate tracts for further wilderness study. Although recommendations on the suitability of these areas is not due until 1991, BLM has accelerated the study process and is scheduled to complete all studies in 1987. Before the secretary recommends an area to the president for wilderness designation, however, the area must undergo a mineral survey by the U.S. Geological Survey. Thus, wilderness recommendations may not be made to Congress for several years after the initial completion of a study.

BLM has completed studies on 38 instant study areas. Five of these had been designated wilderness by Congress as of 1984. The other 33 still are under administrative review. In addition, studies of the remaining 16 natural and primitive areas have been integrated with studies of contiguous wilderness study areas scheduled between 1984 and 1987.

As of December 31, 1984, 368,739 acres of wilderness had been designated on BLM lands, most of it by Congress in 1984. Management of these lands currently is guided by the BLM Wilderness Management Policy, issued in September 1981. BLM proposed regulations on the management of designated wilderness on June 12, 1983, but final rules had not been issued by the end of 1984.

Program Trends and Issues

Lack of Priority for ACECs. Although FLPMA requires BLM to give priority to the designation and protection of areas of critical environmental concern, nearly eight years after the passage of FLPMA little use has been made of this designation. As of October 1, 1984, 186 areas of critical environmental concern had been designated, totaling slightly more than 1.5 million acres. This is less than .005 percent of the total BLM acreage. Sixty-five of these, totaling 832,000 acres, were designated at least in part for wildlife purposes. Another 57, totaling 90,000 acres, were established to protect unique plants, vegetation, or ecosystem types. However, looking at only the aggregate numbers gives an appearance of greater overall progress on ACEC designations than is the case. Seventy-three of the total were designated as part of the California Desert Conservation Area Plan, which was ordered in FLPMA to be completed by September 30, 1980. Another 64 are in Oregon, which designated many of its natural areas as areas of critical environmental concern in recent land-use plans. Oregon and California aside, the ACEC designation has been used very little. Only 43 areas of critical environmental concern in seven other states have been designated to date.

In addition, it appears that little progress has been made on developing plans for the management of ACECs. BLM headquarters does not monitor the status of these plans, but as of October 1, 1984, the Division of Recreation was aware of only 18 plans that had been completed for the 186 areas.

The program has suffered from a lack of direction from BLM headquarters, which has failed to indicate that the designation of ACECs should be a priority in the field. Environmental groups charge, in fact, that under the current emphasis on development uses, protective designations such as areas of critical environmental concern are discouraged.

In addition, the BLM policy on natural areas and their relationships to areas of critical environmental concern is in disarray. Some districts or states, such as Oregon, have designated their natural areas as ACECs during the development of their land-use plans, others have not. Some natural areas still are being designated in land-use plans without being granted ACEC status. No deadlines or criteria have been established for directing the type of designation an area should receive.

At the end of 1984 the Recreation Division was developing guidance on the designation of these various areas and considering use of the ACEC category as an umbrella designation for all the various natural areas. This would help assure that these areas get the recognition and protection they need.

Deletion of Wilderness Study Areas. The wilderness study has been surrounded with controversy. The action that raised the most furor among conservation groups was the decision by former Secretary of the Interior James Watt to delete more than 1.6 million acres from wilderness study. Citing several decisions by Interior's Board of Land Appeals, Watt concluded that three types of areas were improperly included for wilderness study by the Carter administration: areas under 5,000 acres; areas where the federal government owns the surface rights, but a non-federal entity owns the subsurface mineral rights (known as split-estate lands); and areas that do not by themselves have wilderness characteristics but are contiguous to wilderness areas or wilderness study areas.

In January 1983, six conservation organizations and the late Representative Phillip Burton (D-California) filed suit against Interior charging that the decision to drop wilderness study areas from further examination violated FLPMA and the 1969 National Environmental Policy Act. On September 9, 1983, the U.S. Eastern District Court in California issued a preliminary injunction requiring the Department of the Interior to protect the wilderness values of the 1.5 million acres until the court makes a final ruling on the case. All the briefs on the lawsuit have been filed. The court's decision was still pending at the end of 1984.

Inadequacies of the Wilderness Study. The wilderness study has been plagued with a host of other criticisms as well, a situation that could mean that BLM will run into trouble when it gets to the actual wilderness recommendation and designation stage, if not before. These complaints were voiced at hearings held June 19 and 21, 1984, by the House Subcommittee on Public Lands and National Parks of the Committee on Interior and Insular Affairs. The criticisms, made by representatives of environmental groups throughout the West, fell into three general categories. They charged that too many areas were deleted from wilderness review at the wilderness inventory stage (aside from the areas dropped by Watt); that wilderness study areas are not being adequately protected and are being subjected to activities such as expanded and intensified grazing, damaging off-road vehicle use, road construction, and mineral development even where there were no valid existing rights; and that the studies have been so accelerated that they are inadequate and biased against wilderness. In response to threats of oil and gas leasing in BLM wilderness study areas, Congress added provisions to the Interior Department's appropriations bills for fiscal years 1984 and 1985 that banned such activity, but this is the only substantive action taken by Congress so far to deal with environmental-group complaints.

These issues are important because they are likely to be raised again and again throughout the BLM wilderness-designation process. Subcommittee Chairman John Seiberling (D-Ohio) said that the testimony showed "literally flagrant violations of the spirit and the letter of the law" by BLM and warned that BLM might be backing itself into the same situation as the Forest Service did with its Roadless Area Review and Evaluation process, which went through two entire cycles and was legally challenged at both stages. The subcommittee plans further oversight hearings in the 99th Congress.

OREGON AND CALIFORNIA GRANT LANDS

The vast majority of land managed by BLM in the lower 48 states is rangeland. But in western Oregon, BLM manages 2.4 million acres of land that the agency describes as containing "some of the most productive forests in the world."[43] Most of this acreage is known as the Oregon and California Grant Lands, generally referred to as the O and C Grant Lands. The O and C lands are administered largely under a law different from those governing other BLM lands and pose different management and wildlife problems.

Most BLM land in western Oregon is comprised of two land parcels: the revested Oregon and California Railroad Grant Lands (comprising two million acres) and the reconveyed Coos Bay Wagon Road Lands (74,500 acres). These lands originally were granted to private companies for transportation purposes but were reclaimed by the federal government in 1916 when it became apparent that they were not going to be put to their intended uses.

In 1937, Congress passed the Oregon and California Sustained Yield Act,[44] placing these lands under the Department of the Interior and providing for their management. The O and C Lands Act primarily addresses the use of these lands for timber production. It directs that they be managed "for permanent forest production, and the timber thereon shall be sold, cut, and removed in conformity with the principle of sustained yield. . . ."[45] The law does address other values of these lands, stating that the purpose of their management shall be "for a permanent source of timber supply, protecting watersheds, regulating stream flow and contributing to the economic stability of local communities and industries, and providing recreational facilities."[46] It does not, however, include any specific mention of wildlife. FLPMA, passed in 1976, also applies to the O and C lands, but says that "in the event of conflict or inconsistency" between FLPMA and the O and C Lands Act "insofar as they relate to management of timber resources," the O and C Lands Act shall prevail.[47]

BLM also manages 239,000 acres of public domain land that is intermingled with the O and C and Coos Bay Wagon Road lands. In theory, these public domain lands are to be managed in accordance with FLPMA, not the Sustained Yield Act. In practice, however, all the BLM western Oregon lands are managed as a unit under a single management philosophy.

Program Management

BLM manages its western Oregon lands primarily for timber production. Of the 2.4 million acres, BLM designates 2.1 million acres as commercial forest land (land capable of producing at least 20 cubic feet per acre per year of commercial forest species). These highly productive timber lands account for about half of BLM's commercial forest land in the lower 48 but are far more significant in terms of timber sales and production. In 1983, the O and C lands accounted for 92 percent of BLM timber sales (1.1 billion board feet) and for 97 percent of BLM timber sale revenues ($130.4 million).

BLM's lands in western Oregon are divided into five districts: Coos Bay, Eugene, Medford, Roseburg, and Salem. Each district operates under a land-use plan.

373

Currently, all districts are covered by the older management framework plans. However, the most significant management decisions are made in the timber management plans, which are revised every 10 years. In 1981 through 1983, BLM completed a new round of timber management plans that will guide the agency's activities in western Oregon over the next decade. The next planning cycle will begin in 1991, with preparatory work beginning in 1987.

Program Trends and Issues

Old-growth Habitat and the Spotted Owl. Although the final timber management plans for all five districts have been completed, their preparation was riddled with controversy over the effects of proposed timber management on wildlife, particularly on old-growth-dependent species, and the debate promises to continue. The fight has focused primarily on the spotted owl, a species listed as threatened by the state of Oregon, but the overall outcome is important for a wide variety of other species that depend on old-growth forest.

The focal point for the controversy was the Coos Bay District plan, the first plan to reach the completion stage under the Reagan administration. The first final environmental impact statement for the plan was issued for public comment in March 1981. The plan proposed to place 15 percent of the mid-aged and old-growth stands in the commercial forest under constrained management for wildlife. BLM biologists had said that preservation of 25 percent of these age classes in the commercial forest overall would provide optimum conditions for wildlife, but that 15 percent would maintain most species at minimum populations. The plan generally was considered to conform to the requirements of the Interagency Spotted Owl Management Plan, under which BLM agreed to protect 1,000 acres of habitat for each of 90 pairs of spotted owls on BLM western Oregon land, including 16 pairs in the Coos Bay district.

The timber industry and other economic interests objected to the plan, however, prompting BLM to ask the Interior solicitor's office to rule on whether the proposed multiple-use management policy met the requirements of the O and C Lands Act. In September 1981, the solicitor found that the policy required only "minor modifications." But on July 15, 1982, BLM Director Robert Burford issued new management criteria for making final decisions on timber management plans.

The major effect of the new criteria was to increase the emphasis on timber production and to prohibit the preservation of habitat within the commercial forest for state-listed endangered or threatened species. It said the previous BLM agreement to adhere to the Spotted Owl Management Plan was "an interim measure to be used until timber-management decisions were reached through the planning process." In September 1982, BLM issued a new Coos Bay proposal that increased timber harvest and provided no old-growth set-asides for wildlife, deleting protection for the 36,500 acres included for wildlife in the original plan. However, the revised plan included a new withdrawal of about 25,000 acres of mid-aged and old-growth timber to preserve plant-animal relationships thought to play a part in forest regeneration and therefore potentially important to maintaining long-term timber production capacity.* BLM is conducting additional research to determine if in fact such old-growth is necessary. In the meantime, the set-aside provides some old-growth habitat for wildlife.

The release of the new policy and plan caused a torrent of criticism from conservation and wildlife groups. The Oregon Natural Resources Council and the National

---

*Actually, the revised plan protected as much existing mid-aged and old-growth forest as the original plan, but did not include 11,000 acres of younger growth that the original plan set aside for future old-growth.

Audubon Society began to consider petitioning FWS to place the spotted owl on the federal endangered species list. Some discussion centered on trying to get Congress to amend the O and C Lands Act to eliminate the timber bias, a possibility that worried the counties in which the O and C lands are located. They feared that Congress also might see fit to eliminate the unusually generous share of timber receipts that the O and C Lands Act grants to these counties.*

In addition, the Oregon Department of Fish and Wildlife charged that the plan was not consistent with Oregon's coastal management program and thus did not meet the requirement in the Coastal Zone Management Act that federal activities affecting the coastal zone be consistent, to the maximum extent practicable, with the state's coastal plan. The department said that the allocations for retention of mid-aged and old-growth timber did not provide sufficient protection for the spotted owls, were inconsistent with the statewide planning goal "to conserve open space and protect natural and scenic resources," and could ultimately affect wildlife in the coastal zone. In response, the Oregon Land Conservation and Development Commission, which was responsible for making the consistency determination, held up its consistency finding and asked BLM and the Department of Fish and Wildlife to negotiate a settlement.

The upshot of all this controversy was that BLM both revised its O and C Forest Resources Policy and entered into a temporary agreement with the Department of Fish and Wildlife on the spotted owl. The new policy, revised in March 1983, still emphasizes timber management on the O and C lands, but does allow for the management of some commercial forest lands to meet other resource needs.[48] With respect to wildlife, this includes protection of wetlands and riparian zones, conservation of specifically identified habitats for federally listed threatened and endangered species, consideration of habitat needs of native species, and consideration of state goals and objectives concerning state-listed threatened and endangered species in land-use planning and management. In each case, however, timber harvesting is to be restricted or excluded only in areas where mitigating measures will not be effective.

The agreement on the spotted owls was signed September 26, 1983. Under the agreement, BLM is to maintain 90 pairs of spotted owls on the O and C grant lands for five years. Although it is not specified in the agreement, BLM has said it will maintain 1,000 acres per pair. This is a temporary agreement, to be reviewed in light of any new scientific information and the condition of the spotted owl as of October 1, 1988, in order to determine what continued actions are necessary for the protection of the owls. The high timber-harvest levels and limited old-growth set-asides specified in the timber management plans have not been changed.

As of the end of September 1983, all the timber management plans for the O and C lands had received final approval. Taken together, the plans provide for an allowable timber-cut increase of 1.1 percent over 1971 levels on a commercial forest acreage that is 11 percent smaller than it was in 1971. Seventy-seven percent of the commercial forest is in unconstrained management, three percent is set aside or in constrained management for old-growth, and another 20 percent is protected for other reasons, most of this (14 percent) because it is too fragile to log.

With the completion of the plans and the temporary agreement to maintain spotted owl populations for five years, the controversy has somewhat abated, but it is

---

*Currently these counties receive 50 percent of receipts from the O and C and Coos Bay Wagon Road lands, versus 25 percent of receipts from national forest lands. The law actually grants them 75 percent of receipts, but in recent years the countries voluntarily have returned 25 percent to the federal government.

likely to erupt again soon. The Pacific Northwest Legal Clinic, representing Lane County Audubon, the Oregon Natural Resources Council and the Oregon Chapter of the Sierra Club, has filed an appeal with the Interior Board of Land Appeals against the spotted owl agreement, arguing that BLM should have prepared an environmental assessment. In addition, a number of groups, including the National Wildlife Federation, Seattle Audubon, Lane County Audubon, and the Oregon Natural Resources Council, have appealed the Forest Service's regional guide and have requested a joint BLM-Forest Service regional environmental impact statement on the spotted owl.*

Finally, it appears there will be problems with implementing the BLM spotted owl agreement. The Department of Fish and Wildlife has begun its review of the Spotted Owl Management Areas set aside by BLM and, according to a preliminary summary, only 54 of the 90 sites definitely are occupied by spotted owls. In addition, early findings of the review indicate that the old-growth in some of these areas is too fragmented or is insufficient to meet the owl's habitat requirements and that the protection of only 90 pairs of owls on BLM lands might not be adequate for meeting the goal of keeping owls no more than six miles apart. The department intends to have at least the problems of location and composition of owl management areas decided by October 1985.

WILD HORSES AND BURROS

Wild horses and burros were introduced to the western range from Spain. Some of these animals escaped from captivity and established wild populations and, as the range became settled, were captured for saddle animals, rounded up and sold, or shot as nuisances. Population levels dropped from an estimated two to seven million in the early 1800s to 150,000 by the 1930s. With the establishment of grazing districts and the new use of wild horses and burros for pet food, populations continued to decline. By the early 1970s, BLM estimates that only some 25,000 wild horses and burros remained.

Concern for protection of these animals was first expressed by Congress in 1959 with passage of a law that made it a crime to use aircraft or motor vehicles to hunt wild horses or burros on the public lands.[49] In 1967, BLM adopted a wild horse policy requiring, among other things, that consideration be given to reserving forage for wild horses and burros where it is needed and is definitely in the public interest. But population declines continued and the inhumane methods used by the "mustangers" to capture these animals for commercial purposes continued to gain notoriety. In 1971, Congress passed the first law designed specifically to protect these animals, the Wild Free-Roaming Horses and Burros Act.[50]

This act declared wild horses and burros to be "living symbols of the historic and pioneer spirit of the West" and found their populations to be "fast disappearing from the American scene."[51] It protected them from capture, branding, harassment, or death and directed that they be considered "an integral part of the natural system of the public lands"[52] in areas where they were found at the time of passage. The act applies to both BLM and the Forest Service, but 95 percent of the populations are on BLM lands.

Although the act was designed to protect and stabilize populations of these animals, Congress placed certain limits on their protection. The act directs the secretaries to manage wild horses and burros in a manner designed to maintain a "thriving natural ecological balance" on the public lands,[53] and all management activities are to

*See the Forest Service chapter for further details.

be conducted in consultation with state wildlife agencies "to protect the natural eco-logical balance of wildlife species."[54] Any adjustments in allocation of forage for wild horses and burros are to take into consideration the needs of native wildlife.

To assure this balance, the act gives the secretaries authority to remove or destroy "excess" animals. Amendments to the act in 1978, included in the Public Rangelands Improvement Act, established priorities for disposal of excess animals. Old, sick, or lame animals are to be destroyed as humanely as possible. Other excess animals are to be put up for adoption by qualified individuals. Those for which no adoption demand exists are to be destroyed in "the most humane and cost-efficient manner possible."[55]

Program Management

The protection and management of wild horses and burros are considered part of the BLM land-use planning process, in which the two primary issues — where herds will be maintained and what population levels will be allowed — are addressed. The Wild Horse and Burro Act restricts the location of herds to areas in which they were located in 1971. BLM has identified 303 such sites, called herd areas. Through 1983, BLM had designated 142 of these areas for the maintenance of permanent populations and had developed herd-area management plans for 58 of the designated sites. These plans specify the size of the herd, specific objectives for the herd and its habitat, and management methods to be used to attain the objectives. BLM still must review the remaining 161 original herd areas in the planning process, but expects that many of these will be identified for continued wild horse and burro populations.

Soon after passage of the act, BLM found that wild horse and burro populations were rising sharply. BLM estimates that there were about 25,400 wild horses and burros on the public lands in 1971 when the act was passed. By 1974, population levels had increased to an estimated 57,000, causing alarm about the rate of increase in these populations and their potential for causing serious resource damage. BLM responded to the population increases with the start of a removal effort and adoption program in 1973. The national "Adopt-a-Horse" program was launched three years later. After certifying that a potential adopter is qualified to give the horse or burro proper care, BLM arranges to transfer the animal into the individual's private care for one year. Adopters may be awarded title to the animals after a year if they have provided proper care and treatment. Through 1983, some 46,000 horses and burros had been adopted through this program.

Program Trends and Issues

Slowdown in Removal. In spite of years of efforts to reduce populations of wild horses and burros on the public lands, in 1984 populations were at near record highs. Although BLM began removing animals in 1973, population levels continued to increase throughout the 1970s. In 1973, however, Congress included a provision in FLPMA that authorized the use of helicopters in capturing wild horses and burros and also substantially increased the agency's budget for removals. By 1981, BLM was making clear progress in reducing wild horse populations, capturing 11,000 animals that year.

In January 1982 BLM and the Forest Service, in response to directives from the Office of Management and Budget and the House Subcommittee on Public Lands and National Parks, decided to establish a uniform adoption fee to help cover the costs of the adoption program. Although the government had charged for some costs prior to the uniform fee, the revenues were far below the cost of running the adoption program. The fees were raised from an average of $65 per animal in 1980 to $200 for a horse and

$75 for a burro. In addition, adopters were required to pay transportation costs if the animal had to be moved from one adoption center to another.

This fee increase, perhaps combined with the economic recession, resulted in a sharp drop in the rate of adoptions. In 1982, about 6,000 animals were adopted, compared with 11,000 the year before. This in turn led to an increase in the number of animals being held in BLM corrals. The uniform fees also provoked a lawsuit by the American Horse Protection Association, which charged that BLM had failed to go through proper regulatory procedures for revising the fee. BLM subsequently agreed to use the rulemaking process for revising the fees, and the suit was dismissed. In March 1983, BLM issued final regulations establishing adoption fees of $125 for horses and $75 for burros.

Nevertheless, adoption rates continued at a slow pace. By early 1984, BLM was maintaining as many as 3,000 animals in its corrals at an estimated average daily cost as high as $2 per animal. The increased costs forced BLM to slow down its removal program, and by 1984 population levels were estimated to have increased again to some 60,000 animals.

In the FY 1985 appropriations for the Department of the Interior, Congress provided approximately $17 million, an increase of some $12 million over FY 1984, to provide for the removal of 17,000 animals from the public lands and to care for excess unadopted animals in BLM corrals. Anticipating even further increases in the excess animals, BLM in October 1984 dropped the transportation-fee requirement as a further incentive for adopters. Clearly, however, this one-time appropriation will not solve the problem, and the controversy will continue.

Debate Over Appropriate Management Levels. The underlying question in the management of horses and burros is how many of these animals should be retained on the public lands. A report completed by the National Academy of Sciences in late 1982 raised a number of questions about the traditional assumptions.[56] Although the study was limited severely because of a lack of funds, it did address two key questions related to the BLM removal program: What is the rate of population increase, and what is the level of resource damage caused by the animals?

The apparently alarming rate of increase in these populations has provided much of the impetus and sense of urgency for the removal effort. But the National Academy of Sciences said that BLM population-increase estimates, which generally range from 18 to 22 percent per year, probably are high. The academy, however, said BLM underestimated the number of horses and burros on the public lands in 1971, perhaps by as much as half. This could mean that as many as 50,000 animals were on the range when the act was passed and that the rate of increase is more likely 10 percent or less. This raises questions about BLM's target management level of 25,000 animals and about the need for quick, urgent removals.

The National Academy of Sciences also questioned the general assumption that wild horses and burros are causing widespread resource damage, such as competition with wildlife, soil erosion, and vegetative damage. The academy found no evidence that such damage was widespread or common. The chairman of the academy committee, Frederic H. Wagner of Utah State University, reported that the committee asked to be shown areas of severe horse impacts "but was told by BLM that such areas were few and inaccessible."[57] The National Academy of Sciences did note that many studies have concluded that wild burros pose a serious problem for desert bighorn sheep in some areas, but said that even most of this evidence was circumstantial.

The academy also was asked to address the question of how to define which animals were "excess." The academy noted that this was not a scientific question but an economic, political, and social question of what is the proper allocation of forage on the range. To put the current allocation in perspective, the National Academy of Sciences calculated that the ratio of forage consumption by livestock to that of wild horses and burros was 23 to one. The academy noted, however, that the situation cannot be generalized. This ratio varies considerably throughout the West. In Nevada, for example, the ratio is only 4.8 to one, and is as high as two to one in certain districts. The National Academy of Sciences made no findings on what is "excess."

Legislation

One result of the increase of wild horses and burros in the government's hands — as well as the increased interest in trying to recover the costs of the program — is a proposal to authorize the government to sell unadopted animals for commercial purposes. Two such bills first were introduced in 1982 but saw no action. In early 1983, the legislation was reintroduced as H.R. 1675 by Representative Barbara Vucanovich (R-Nevada) and S. 457 by Senator James McClure (R-Idaho). No action was taken on the House bill. The Senate bill was reported by the Committee on Energy and Natural Resources on November 17, 1983.[58]

As reported, the Senate bill also would revise and streamline the program in other ways. Its major provisions include the following:

1. It would recognize that wild horses and burros are no longer in danger of disappearing and would require that the animals be managed in accordance with multiple-use principles and the resource management objectives of the land-use plans.
2. It would authorize public auctions of unadopted animals, with revenues to be used to reimburse costs of the wild horse and burro program. Sales authority is limited to 3,500 animals per year for four years. Prior to such sale, the secretary is to offer to transfer the animals at no cost into the care of qualified animal-protection groups.
3. It would reduce other program requirements, allowing BLM to transfer title to all adopters after one year unless there is evidence of improper care — eliminating the application requirement and reducing compliance checks — and eliminating the requirement for a public hearing prior to the use of helicopters and motor vehicles in animal-removal efforts, although public notice still would be required.

Opponents of the legislation argue that BLM exaggerates the damage done to the public lands by wild horses and burros, that the land can support larger numbers than BLM has estimated, and that selling the animals for commercial purposes represents a fundamental departure from the purposes of the Wild Horse Act and essentially would authorize the government to do what the act forbade the mustangers to do: round up wild horses and sell them for pet food.

This highly controversial issue will continue in some form in the 99th Congress. Increased funding for removal of wild horses and burros in FY 1985 is likely to result in increased animals in BLM corrals and increased costs to the government, a situation that proponents of sales authority are likely to use in support of their position. The issue of wild horses and burros is expected to be addressed in a larger range-management package, discussed in the range section of this chapter.

Litigation

Two recent court decisions portend potentially dramatic changes in the BLM wild horse and burro program. Both involve actions brought under Section 4 of the Wild Horses and Burros Act, which requires the secretary to remove wild horses from private lands upon request of the landowner. In these decisions, the courts have imposed upon the secretary an affirmative duty to prevent wild horses from "trespassing" on private lands, and possible constitutional liability for damages caused by such trespass, even where those lands are interspersed with public lands.

In *Fallini v. Watt*,[59] the plaintiff owned lands scattered among public lands in an area roamed by wild horses. Reasoning that trespass of wild horses from public lands onto private lands should be governed by the same rules that apply to trespass of private livestock onto public lands, the court held that BLM must not only remove all wild horses found on the plaintiff's lands, but also must ensure that the wild horses do not enter those lands in the future. In effect, this holding requires BLM to remove all wild horses from the area, even though much of the land in the area is publicly owned. The government has appealed.

In *Mountain States Legal Foundation v. Clark*,[60] plaintiffs' lands were dispersed among public lands in a checkerboard pattern. They sued to compel BLM to reduce the wild horse herd in the area to a "reasonable" level, and sought to recover damages for the forage eaten by the horses, claiming that their property had been taken without just compensation, in violation of the Fifth Amendment. Plaintiffs asked the court to assess $500,000 in damages personally against Frank Gregg, who was director of BLM from 1978 to 1981, and $10 nominal damages from the United States. The district court ordered BLM to remove "excess" horses, but denied the request for damages.

Plaintiffs appealed the denial of damages, and the three-judge panel of the Tenth Circuit reversed. Although refusing to assess any personal liability against BLM officials, the Tenth Circuit found that the landowners could recover compensation from the United States, under the Fifth Amendment, for forage on their lands eaten by wild horses, and remanded the case for factual findings by the district court. As the dissent points out, this decision has astounding implications for federal wildlife-protection programs far beyond the Wild Horse Act. By the court's reasoning, the United States could be held liable for damage to private property caused by almost any protected animal — including eagles, other endangered species, and migratory birds. As the dissent also demonstrates, the court's decision seems flatly inconsistent with the Supreme Court's interpretation of "take" as defined by the Fifth Amendment. The Tenth Circuit court has agreed to a government request to rehear the case. All Tenth Circuit judges will participate in the hearing.

RESOURCE STATUS

No reliable information exists on the biological status of wildlife on the public lands or on the adequacy of wildlife habitat there. BLM does not maintain population estimates for wildlife species. The states prepare population estimates every five years for 11 big-game animals, which are reported each year in the Department of Interior's *Public Land Statistics*, but BLM wildlife officials say these numbers are not reliable enough to be used to show population trends. BLM's informal assessment is that the big-game populations, with the exception of the desert bighorn sheep, are in pretty good shape. Even less is known about the status of small-game and nongame animals, except for those whose populations already have reached dangerously low levels.

In spite of the lack of reliable data, it is clear that today's wildlife populations on public lands are far below the pre-settlement levels. One speculative but interesting estimate was made in 1975 by wildlife biologist Frederic Wagner.[61] These estimates are for wildlife in the 11 Western states, including state and private land as well as public land. Extrapolating largely from a 1929 report by Ernest Thompson Seton, Wagner estimated that there were 20 to 30 million big-game animals in the 11 western states in the pre-Columbian era. This included five to 10 million bison, 10 to 15 million pronghorn antelope, one to two million bighorn sheep, five million mule and blacktail deer, and two million elk. Wagner notes, however, that the estimates for deer and bighorn sheep may be high. Compared with 1975 population estimates, Wagner estimated that overall populations of these animals are only 15 to 20 percent of their original levels. The climax species — bison, pronghorn, and bighorn — are estimated to be at less than five percent of original levels. Elk also have decreased significantly, though not as seriously as these other species, and deer are generally thought to exceed their pre-settlement populations.

Reduced populations of two species — the desert bighorn sheep and the desert tortoise — have caused particular concern in recent years. Eighty percent of the desert bighorn sheep population in the United States occurs on public land in Arizona, Nevada, New Mexico, California, and Utah. Current studies show that a number of distinct bighorn sheep populations have been extirpated from their ranges in recent times. Of the remaining herds, some still are declining. The reason for the decline is not clear, but it appears to be due to a combination of factors. This includes increased use of sheep habitat by livestock, encroachment from power lines, pipelines, and other rights-of-way, and increased recreational use of the public lands. BLM has been working with wildlife agencies in the southwestern states to develop joint programs for management of the desert bighorn sheep habitat to reverse the downward population trends, with some initial success. In the FY 1985 budget, Congress specifically provided $300,000 for a challenge grant to continue efforts to facilitate the recovery of this species.

The desert tortoise is another southwestern species directly affected by BLM actions. Within the past several years, the desert tortoise population in Utah was listed as threatened under the federal Endangered Species Act, and a number of studies have indicated that desert tortoise populations in Arizona, California, and Nevada are being seriously affected by livestock grazing, off-road vehicle use, and oil and gas exploration, although the extent and severity of the threat are debated. In late 1984, the Desert Tortoise Council — an organization dedicated to tortoise protection — petitioned FWS to add all desert tortoise populations in these three states to the federal endangered species list. FWS has determined that substantial scientific evidence exists to show that the species may warrant listing and is scheduled to determine by late 1985 whether or not to propose its addition to the list.

Another approach to assessing the status of wildlife on the public lands is to look at the condition of its habitat. Since the first range condition study was conducted in 1936, assessments of the range have shown consistently that the public range is in poor condition. In 1936, about 84 percent of the public range was classified as being in unsatisfactory condition, defined as producing at less than 50 percent of its vegetative potential. Only 1.5 percent was classified as being in excellent condition. The most recent comprehensive study on range condition, conducted in 1975,[62] came up with similar figures, although that study is frequently criticized as possibly overstating the case in an effort to build support for more funding and more range improvements for the public lands.

According to the 1975 study, the outlook for the improvement of the range was not good. The report estimated that only 31 million acres, 19 percent of the range, was improving, while 65 percent was remaining static and 16 percent was declining. However, most range-management professionals agree that the condition of the range has improved somewhat under federal management, a claim backed up by figures released by BLM in 1984 which show 60 percent of the range in unsatisfactory condition and 5 percent in excellent condition. These 1984 figures were based not on a new study but on range inventories conducted on 98 million acres to provide information for grazing impact statements, with the condition of the remaining 70 million acres based on "professional knowledge and judgment."[63] Although the accuracy of these figures may be questionable as well, the irrefutable conclusion is that a large portion of the public range is in poor shape.

A number of problems prevent application of these range-condition figures directly to wildlife habitat. First, a determination that the range is in a satisfactory condition begs the question: Is it satisfactory for wildlife or for livestock? For what species or mix of wildlife? In addition, while an assessment of overall range condition may tell something about the wildlife habitat in general, it does not address the significant habitat areas that really control the survival of wildlife populations, such as riparian zones, winter habitat, and nesting grounds.

The 1975 range-condition study did include some specific figures on the condition of wildlife habitat on the range. Oddly enough, these figures were somewhat more favorable than those for range condition. The study found that 53 percent of big-game habitat was in satisfactory condition, although it found only 17 percent of the range to be in satisfactory shape. It found that 60 percent of fishable streams and 87 percent of the fishable lakes fell into the satisfactory category. It has been suggested, however, that since deer account for most of the big game on BLM lands, the figures for big-game habitat were sharply skewed in the direction of the vegetation preferred by deer — that is, brushy species that invade overgrazed grasslands — rather than giving a useful picture of habitat conditions overall.[64] At any rate, the trend for wildlife habitat generally was worse than for overall range condition, with nearly a third of big-game, small-game, and nongame acres in a declining condition. The report estimated that if the present trend continued, the amount of habitat in unsatisfactory condition would reach 50 percent by the year 2000. More specifically, it predicted a seven-percent decrease in antelope, an eight-percent decrease in bighorn sheep, and a 16-percent decrease in elk.

Still, these figures do not give information on critical zones, such as wintering and riparian habitat, and give only a very general picture of habitat condition on the public lands. In summary, very little reliable data exists on wildlife in an agency that manages more habitat than any other state or federal agency in the United States.

Comparative Percentages of the Public Rangelands in Excellent, Good, Fair, and Poor Condition, 1936–1984

| Year | Percent by Condition Class | | | |
	Excellent	Good	Fair	Poor or Bad
1936[a]	1.5	14.3	47.9	36.3
1966[b]	2.2	16.7	51.6	29.5
1975[c]	2.0	15.0	50.0	33.0
1984[d]	5.0	31.0	42.0	18.0

Sources:

[a]Data adapted from *The Western Range,* Senate Document 199, 75th Congress, 2nd Session.

[b]*The Forage Resource,* Pacific Consultants (1969).

[c]*Range Condition Report,* Department of the Interior (1975).

[d]Aggregation of all baseline resource records maintained at each of the Resource Areas within the BLM. Total acreage = 96 percent; the remaining four percent has not been rated for range condition.

Table taken from: *50 Years of Public Land Management,* U.S. Department of the Interior, Bureau of Land Management, Washington, DC.

REFERENCES

1. U.S. Department of the Interior, Bureau of Land Management, *Wildlife on the Public Lands* (Washington, D.C.: Government Printing Office, 1978), p. 1.
2. 43 U.S.C.A. 1701 et seq.
3. 43 U.S.C.A. 315 et seq.
4. 43 U.S.C.A. 1701 et seq.
5. 43 U.S.C.A. 1901 et seq.
6. Phillip Foss, *Politics and Grass* (Seattle, Wash.: University of Washington Press, 1960).
7. Paul J. Culhane, *Public Lands Politics: Interest Group Influence on the Forest Service and the Bureau of Land Management*, Resources for the Future, Inc. (Baltimore, Md.: Johns Hopkins University Press, 1981), Chap. 3.
8. 43 U.S.C.A. 1181 et seq.
9. 16 U.S.C.A. 1331 et seq.
10. Op. cit., Foss., *Politics and Grass*, p. 58.
11. Act of June 28, 1934, Ch. 865, 48 Stat. 1269 (currently codified at 43 U.S.C.A. 315).
12. *Id.*
13. *Id.*, Sec. 9.
14. Act of July 14, 1939, 53 Stat. 1002 (currently codified at 43 U.S.C.A. 315).
15. Pub. L. 88-607, 78 Stat. 986 (terminated six months after submission to Congress of report by Public Lands Law Review Commission, due June 30, 1970).
16. Frederic H. Wagner, "Progress and Problems, 1934-1984, in Improvement of Wildlife Habitat," unpublished manuscript, (presented before the National Celebration of the 50th Anniversary of the Taylor Grazing Act, Grand Junction, Colo., July 8-10, 1984).
17. Pub. L. 94-579, 90 Stat. 2743 (currently codified at 43 U.S.C.A. 1701 et seq.).
18. *Id.*, Section 1701(8).
19. Pub. L. 95-514, 92 Stat. 1803 (currently codified at 43 U.S.C.A. 1901 et seq.).
20. 30 U.S.C.A. 1281.
21. 16 U.S.C.A. 1531 et seq.
22. 16 U.S.C.A. 715.
23. Pub. L. 93-452, 88 Stat. 1371 (current version at 16 U.S.C.A. 670a-670o).
24. 47 Fed. Reg. 58454-58460 (1982).
25. 16 U.S.C.A. 670i.
26. Denzel and Nancy Ferguson, *Sacred Cows at the Public Trough* (Bend, Ore.: Maverick Publications, 1983), p. 74.
27. *Id.*, p. 76.
28. U.S. General Accounting Office, *Public Rangeland Improvement — A Slow Costly Process in Need of Alternate Funding*, (Washington, D.C.: U.S. Government Printing Office, 1982) p. 5.
29. U.S. Department of the Interior, Bureau of Land Management, *50 Years of Public Land Management*, (Washington, D.C., 1984).
30. Wildlife Management Institute, *Evaluation of Bureau of Land Management Program Interactions with Rangeland Management* (Washington, D.C.: Wildlife Management Institute, 1981), p. 13.
31. 16 U.S.C.A. 1751(b)(1).
32. *Id.*
33. *Id.*

34. 49 Fed. Reg. 6440-6455 (1984).
35. *Id.*
36. 43 CFR 4120.1.
37. *Id.*
38. 43 U.S.C.A. 1752(e).
39. *Id.*, Section 1739(e).
40. U.S. Congress, House Committee on Appropriations, Surveys and Investigations Staff, "A Report to the Committee on Appropriations, U.S. House of Representatives, on the BLM Grazing Management and Rangeland Improvement Program, "April 1984 in *Department of the Interior and Related Agencies Appropriations for 1985*: Hearings before a subcommittee of the Committee on Appropriations, Part II, 1984, p. 922.
41. 43 U.S.C.A. 1702(a).
42. *Id.*, Section 1782(a).
43. U.S. Department of the Interior, Bureau of Land Management, *Timber Management for the 1980s*, 1984.
44. Act of Aug. 28, 1937, Ch. 876, 50 Stat. 875 (currently codified at 43 U.S.C.A. 1181 et seq.).
45. 43 U.S.C.A. 1181(a).
46. *Id.*
47. Op. cit., Pub. L. 94-579, Section 702(b).
48. The current policy is printed in USDI's *Timber Management for the 1980s*, cited above.
49. Pub. L. 88-234, Sec. 1(a), 73 Stat. 470 (currently codified at 18 U.S.C.A. 47).
50. Pub. L. 92-195, 85 Stat. 649 (currently codified at 16 U.S.C.A. 1331 et seq.).
51. *Id.*
52. *Id.*
53. 16 U.S.C.A. 1333(a).
54. *Id.*
55. *Id.*, Section 1333(b).
56. National Research Council, Board on Agriculture and Renewal Resources, Committee on Wild and Free-Roaming Horses and Burros, *Wild and Free-Roaming Horses and Burros, Final Report*, (Washington, D.C.: National Academy Press, 1982).
57. Frederic H. Wagner, "Status of Wild Horse and Burro Management on Public Rangelands," unpublished manuscript (presented at the 48th North American Wildlife and Natural Resources Conference, Kansas City, Mo., March 18-23, 1983), p. 14.
58. U.S. Congress, Senate Committee on Energy and Natural Resources, *Amending the Wild Free-Roaming Horses and Burros Act of 1971 (16 U.S.C. 1331-1340), as Amended*: Report to Accompany S. 457, 98th Cong., 1st Sess., 1983, S. Rpt. 98-339.
59. Civil L.V. 81-536 RDF (D. Nev. October 4, 1984).
60. No. 82-1485 (10th Cir. 1984).
61. Frederic H. Wagner, "Livestock Grazing and the Livestock Industry," in Howard Brokaw, ed., Council on Environmental Quality, *Wildlife and America: Contributions to an Understanding of American Wildlife and Its Conservation* (Washington, D.C.: Government Printing Office, 1978), p. 121.
62. U.S. Department of the Interior, Bureau of Land Management, *Range Condition Report Prepared for the Senate Committee on Appropriations*, 1975.

63. Op. cit., Bureau of Land Management, *50 Years of Public Land Management*, p. 19.
64. Maitland Sharpe, "Rangeland Condition" in U.S. Department of Agriculture, Forest Service, *Proceedings of a Symposium, Jan. 28-31, 1979, Tucson, Arizona* (Washington, D.C.: Government Printing Office, 1979), pp. 29-33.

PART III.
Species Accounts

A California condor stretches its wings. Biologists are trying desperately to ensure the survival of the species, now reduced to fewer than 20 birds.

The California Condor

by *John Ogden*
National Audubon Society Staff

SPECIES DESCRIPTION AND NATURAL HISTORY

THE CALIFORNIA CONDOR (*Gymnogyps californicus*), with a weight of 18 to 22 pounds and a wingspan of approximately nine feet, is one of the largest land birds in the Western Hemisphere. It is one of seven species of New World vultures in the family Cathartidae, which includes the more familiar and much smaller North American species, the turkey vulture (*Cathartes aura*).[1]

Like most species in its family, the California condor is predominantly black. The unfeathered skin of the head and neck is a brightly colored mosaic of rose reds, orange, and yellow in adults, and dark gray in immature birds up to the age of three or four years. The most conspicuous field mark on a flying condor is the large and showy white triangular area on the underside of each wing near the body and at the wing's leading edge. This white patch is mottled with varying amounts of gray on immature birds. A flying condor differs from the smaller golden eagle, a common bird throughout the condor's range, in showing proportionally wider wings and a shorter tail.

Two cathartid species are called condors. Both are characterized by large size and a ruff of feathers around the neck. The Andean condor (*Vultur gryphus*) is a fairly common bird in parts of its range in the Andes Mountains between extreme southwestern Venezuela and southern Chile. The California condor presently has a very restricted range in the mountains bordering the southern San Joaquin Valley in California. It occurs regularly only as far north as San Luis Obispo County in the coastal mountains and Tulare County on the western slopes of the Sierra Nevada range, and as far south as the northern corner of Los Angeles County.[2] Included in this range are portions of Kern, Ventura, and Santa Barbara counties.

All nesting sites and many of the condor's important roosting sites are in rugged chaparral and pine-covered mountains between 2,000 and 6,000 feet above sea level. Roosting sites may be on ledges of large rocky escarpments, but frequently are on the largest horizontal branches in the upper parts of tall conifer trees, both living and dead. Many of the important roosts are located on public lands, primarily lands administered by the U.S. Forest Service and the Bureau of Land Management. Nesting sites are in small caves, potholes, or ledges located on rock escarpments and, much more rarely, in natural cavities in the upper portions of large, living sequoia trees. All known

389

nesting sites are in Sequoia, Angeles, and Los Padres national forests.

Condors are carrion feeders and do most of their searching for food in fairly open terrain. The important feeding areas are in the broad grassland and oak-savanna habitats in the foothills below the nesting sites. The foraging areas are almost entirely on private land used principally for ranching.

The California condor is a long-lived animal with delayed maturity and a low annual reproductive rate.[3] This combination results in a relatively prolonged investment by adult pairs in care of their offspring and low rates of potential recruitment and population increase. As with other species sharing the same reproductive pattern, once reduced to small numbers condors recover slowly even under the best of natural conditions. Losses of any breeders will have a major detrimental effect on condor recovery.

Adult condors form pair bonds that last more than a year, in fact in most cases for as long as both birds are alive.[4] The time required to complete a single nesting cycle may be more than 12 months, so some pairs nest only in alternate years. Courtship and mating usually occur during late winter, primarily in January and February, and the single egg is laid during February or early March. The adults take turns incubating. The adult that is not incubating may stay away from the nest for as long as two to six days, sometimes longer. Presumably it is on the foraging grounds most of this time. The incubation period is 56 to 58 days.

The adults take turns brooding the small chick and going out to search for food for about the first four weeks after hatching. After that both adults spend much of their time searching for food. The chick is fed daily when small, but the frequency of feedings declines as the chick matures so that a large, mostly feathered nestling may be fed only three to five days per week.

Generally about five to six months after hatching, the chick takes its first short flight. This flight can be extremely awkward, usually ending in a controlled crash rather than a smooth landing, and anyone watching invariably finds heart in throat before the flight is ended. The art of graceful flying requires much practice, and a young condor may not make its first trip to a distant foraging ground for three or four months after that first short adventure. During this training period, the juvenile condor remains entirely dependent upon the adults for food.

Whether the adult pair nests the following year or skips a year seems to depend upon several factors, most notably on how dependent the present chick remains on the parents for food. Initially, the chick travels with the parents, learning the location of favorable foraging areas from them and from associations with other condors at the feeding sites. Young condors may continue to be fed intermittently by their parents or occasionally by other adult condors well through the next breeding season.

Young condors retain the gray head until about three years old. Between three and four years a change in color is apparent, and the heads of birds four to five years old are colored like those of adults.[5] Birds four to five years old do not breed in the wild, and it is thought that condors must be at least six years old to nest.

Since most foraging by condors occurs on ranch lands, it is not surprising that the condor's principal food is dead calves, cattle, and sheep.[6] In addition, one common native mammal, the mule deer, is an important food source, especially during the hunting season and severe winters and droughts.

Although the total death toll among livestock and deer herds seems to be low at any given season, condors can quickly search large areas of country and go days between feedings, important adaptations for dealing with a relatively sparse food resource. In a typical week, a non-breeding condor will feed only two or three times. Condors spend the intervening days roosting and preening, soaring near roost sites, and flying 40 to 125 miles round-trip to foraging grounds. During these long flights the birds learn the locations of new carcasses, so that when they are hungry again they often know where to find one or more dead animals.

Condors apparently locate food entirely by sight. Perhaps of considerable importance to locating food is the condor's frequent habit of keying in on concentrations of other avian scavengers, most frequently ravens and golden eagles. The activities of several ravens or eagles at a carcass are conspicuous from miles away and certainly are seen by high-soaring condors.

The only regular competitor at a carcass is the golden eagle. Eagles usually discover a carcass early in the day, before condors begin soaring, and one or more eagles may be feeding by the time a condor arrives. The presence of eagles at a carcass may prevent a condor from feeding immediately. However, condors will wait to the side, often for an hour or more, or return to the same carcass the next day. They also may drive an eagle away from a carcass.

California condors may shift their foraging activities seasonally between different portions of the range.[7] Typically, mated adults operate nearly year-round from roosts near their nesting sites, but seasonally change the direction and distance when they fly for food. Non-breeding condors, especially immatures with no ties to a particular area, are much more mobile and shift both their roosts and foraging sites throughout the total condor range, often in seasonally predictable ways. One-way flights of 100 to 150 miles may be made in a single day. Changes in foraging sites by either age class apparently is related to changing food abundance.

SIGNIFICANCE OF THE SPECIES

The California condor story is an important case history for the entire endangered species recovery program. Worldwide attention has been directed to the bird and the efforts to save it.[8] Most conservationists, outdoorsmen, birdwatchers, and professional ornithologists know of at least some details of this story. The massive effort has made the condor symbolic of the effort to save endangered species.[9]

HISTORICAL PERSPECTIVE

Condors are wide-ranging birds that live in rugged country where human access can be difficult. Efforts to count or estimate accurately the number of condors in the wild have been plagued with problems. For example, should two condors spotted 40 miles and three hours apart be counted as two different birds, or can one condor move that far in that time? The sometimes almost arbitrary decisions that census takers have been forced to make, in the absence of sound data on condor movement patterns, have meant that census results are subject to valid criticisms and that their overall value has been in showing trends rather than absolute numbers.

The number of condors in the wild at any time in the 19th or early 20th centuries is almost anyone's guess. Lewis and Clark shot condors on the lower Columbia River in 1805-06, Douglas shot condors in the same region in 1826-27, and Townsend shot one there in 1834.[10] At the other end of their range, condors may have occurred regularly in the mountains of northern Baja California as recently as the early part of this century. But none were known to nest anywhere north of the San Francisco Bay region or in Baja. The number seen at any one time in these non-breeding regions usually was low, only a single bird or a few together. Since individual birds may move over large geographical areas in the course of a year, it is likely that the wild population in the early to mid-19th century was surprisingly small, perhaps fewer than 500.

Carl Koford, whose 1939 to 1946 research sponsored by the National Audubon Society was the first intensive study of the California condor, estimated the total number at 60.[11] He thought that number probably had been fairly constant for 30 years or more. Sanford Wilbur, another condor researcher, suggested that Koford's estimate was too low and that a more realistic estimate for the early 1940s was in excess of 70 condors.[12] Wilbur's reasoning was based upon his belief that two separate subpopulations of condors existed and that a total count could be produced most accurately by combining the maximum counts of condors from two different geographical portions of the species' range. Wilbur's theory of subpopulations recently has been shown to be incorrect, so his estimates may have been too high.

Whatever the actual number, no doubt exists that condor numbers declined considerably in the century preceding 1930. Wilbur suggested that much of this decline occurred between 1840 and 1890. Koford listed 11 California counties ranging the full length of the state (Humboldt and San Diego counties at the extremes) in which condors disappeared between 1850 and 1940.

Both Wilbur and Koford listed reasons for the decline. Wanton shooting headed both lists, but the lists also included collecting for museum specimens. At least 177 condors and 71 eggs were taken for this purpose, including 111 birds and 49 eggs in the short span between 1886 and 1910.[13] The mortality lists also included poisoning and various types of direct human disturbance as primary causes for declines. The poisonings probably were caused by strychnine placed in carcasses for control of carnivores and by the application of thallium and Compound 1080 treated grain for rodents. Opinions vary widely over what number of condors may have been poisoned, either directly or secondarily, largely because deaths from predator control activities on privately owned rangelands probably were not reported.

Causes of direct disturbance included a large array of human activities such as wildlife photography, bird watching, oil and gas drilling, road and trail building, and increased access to remote backcountry regions, as well as habitat loss to house construction, lumbering, and other causes.

Following Koford, the next intensive survey was by Ian and Eben McMillan in 1963 and 1964.[14] Using survey techniques similar to those used by Koford, the McMillan brothers concluded that a 30 percent decline had occurred since the mid-1940s and that the 1964 total was about 40 condors. They considered shooting and poisoning as the two most frequent causes of unnatural mortality during the intervening years, although evidence for both was primarily hearsay and circumstantial.

Wilbur, still believing the wild population was divided into two subpopulations, estimated the 1968 total at 50 to 60 condors, and the 1976 total at between 40 and 50 birds.[15] He also added to the list of factors responsible for the decline, suggesting that inadequate food supplies were causing an overall reduction in nesting success. At about the same time, it was suggested that DDE poisoning may have been responsible for some of the decline.[16]

Using data collected during a series of surveys conducted in October for all years between 1965 and 1978, Wilbur estimated populations of 25 to 35 condors for 1978.[17] Although these October surveys still reflected Wilbur's belief in two subpopulations, they were the most systematic attempt yet to accurately estimate condor numbers. In most years they involved between 50 and 140 trained observers who manned strategically selected mountaintop observation posts for two consecutive days. Yet as was readily acknowledged by Wilbur, the translation of the raw counts into an accurate estimate was fraught with pitfalls, including observer biases and the uncertainty of assumptions about the speed and distance traveled by individual condors. Neverthe-less, the fourteen-year trend was shockingly apparent. It was these data perhaps more than any others that brought greatly increased attention to the plight of the condor.

CURRENT TRENDS

An intensified research and recovery program initiated in 1980, jointly organized by the U.S. Fish and Wildlife Service (FWS) and the National Audubon Society, included an assessment of the accuracy of the census techniques as a means for determining how rapidly the birds were declining. This information was particularly important in understanding what kind of recovery program would be needed.

The new look at census techniques eventually resulted in the development of a photography study technique far more accurate than earlier censuses.[18] Beginning in 1982, biologists on the condor research team photographed every condor they saw. With so few birds in the wild, the prolonged molt characteristics of the condor and other individual plumage features, such as broken or split feathers, made possible the recognition of each condor photographed. Files were kept for each bird and yielded a growing record of the plumage characteristics and location of each wild condor. From this record the wild population was estimated to contain between 21 and 24 birds in late 1982, between 19 and 22 in late 1983, and approximately 16 in late 1984.[19]

Although some of the decline during these three years was due to removal of condors from the wild for creation of a captive-breeding program (see below), it was clear that the total number remaining in the wild was frightfully low and that unnatural mortality continued to occur. In fact, during these three years, two wild condors were found dead. Both died of unnatural causes, the first apparently due to sodium cyanide poisoning and the second from lead poisoning.[20] Although not proved, the cyanide-poisoned condor most likely had contact, directly or secondarily, with a sodium cyanide predator control device known as a "coyote getter." The lead-poisoned bird most likely ingested one or more lead bullets from carcasses it had fed upon. These dead condors were the first in years that were located soon enough for the cause of death to be determined. Interestingly, neither died from the more frequently suggested causes, shooting and strychnine or 1080 poisoning. But both may have died because of what they ate, a clue for where to direct attention in the desperate effort to reduce mortality.

MANAGEMENT

The present condor research and recovery program is the culmination of 80 years of growing concern and attention. In 1905, California passed a law banning the take of all nongame birds, the first protection for the condor and its eggs. Three years later a $50 fine was levied against an individual who shot a condor in Los Angeles County.

In 1953, the condor was given special protection under California law, and in 1967 it was put on the first federal endangered species list. Three years later the California endangered species act was passed, and the condor was state-listed as endangered.

Condor-habitat protection began in 1939, when the 1,200-acre Sisquoc Condor Sanctuary was set aside on Los Padres National Forest. In 1947, another 53,000 acres of the forest were reserved as the Sespe Condor Sanctuary. More roosting and condor habitat was protected in 1975 when FWS established Hooper Mountain National Wildlife Refuge.

Although the Forest Service hired a full-time condor biologist in 1968, the first condor recovery plan was not approved until 1975. Three years later, an independent panel of ornithologists, selected by the American Ornithologists' Union and the National Audubon Society, recommended a more aggressive research and captive breeding program. FWS, Audubon, the California Department of Fish and Game (CDFG), the Forest Service, and the Bureau of Land Management signed an agreement in 1979 to implement such a program.

By the time work was under way in 1980, the wild condor population had declined to an estimated 20 to 30 birds, and the factors responsible for the decline were unknown.[21] At that time, CDFG, the state agency responsible for permitting endangered species work in California, became embroiled in a dispute stimulated by a hands-on, radiotelemetry research and captive-breeding program proposed by FWS and the National Audubon Society. All major North American ornithological societies supported the program, holding the view that the proposed techniques were well proven and that no other program had the potential to be successful in the time remaining for the wild population.[22] However, several local environmental groups viewed such hands-on techniques as a direct threat to the birds.[23] They argued that enough already was known about the wild population and the causes of the decline and that the emphasis of the recovery program should be protection and improvement of condor habitat.

The inadequacy of the habitat-protection counterproposal was that in the absence of telemetry, no means existed for closely monitoring recovery success or for determining where and why condors were dying. Also, without more precise habitat and condor-location information than was available in 1980, land protection efforts could not be focused efficiently to the sites where protection actually was needed, and any effort to stem the decline would be by trial and error.

After two years of debate on these issues, and while the wild population apparently continued to decline, CDFG agreed to proceed with the captive-breeding and telemetry projects. The complicating factor was the death of a young condor as it was being measured by a biologist at a nest site in 1980. The death prolonged the debate, further delaying the initiation of the recovery program.[24]

Since 1980, efforts to save the California condor have involved a complex mix of state, federal, and private groups that include the San Diego Zoo, San Diego Wild Animal Park, Los Angeles Zoo, Santa Barbara Natural History Museum, California Polytechnic State University, and the Western Foundation of Vertebrate Zoology. At the heart of this effort is the Condor Research Center in Ventura, California, presently made up of a team of FWS, CDFG, and National Audubon Society biologists.[25] The center has the task of conducting original research on the condor and coordinating the recovery program. The goals of this endeavor are to maintain and eventually to increase the wild condor population and to establish a captive-breeding flock for the production of young condors for release into the wild.

The maintenance of a wild flock of condors is a high priority in the present recovery program. Studies of the wild population by the Condor Research Center and associated research personnel offer the only opportunity for discovering in a relatively brief time the causes of the condor's continued decline and the characteristics and boundaries of habitat critical to its long-term survival. In addition, a key factor in the release of captive-bred condors is integration of released birds with wild condors, so that the former will learn more quickly the locations of important foraging and roosting sites. Although the releases probably would be successful without a wild flock, in its absence survival of released condors may be lower, and the speed with which they become independent slower.[26]

The primary research tool for the field studies has been radiotelemetry.[27] Between

October 1982 and December 1984, nine wild condors were trapped and small radio transmitters were attached to the upper, leading edge of each wing. The telemetry program has, in two years, provided more new information on condor daily activity patterns and foraging behavior than was learned in the preceding 40 years. By tracking daily the locations of individual birds, substantial progress has been made toward identifying habitat types and specific areas utilized by wild condors, especially foraging sites located on large and to some extent inaccessible privately owned ranches. Daily tracking also has helped determine the daily and seasonal movements of individual birds, the frequency of feeding, and preliminary correlations between bird movements and the location of food resources.

These data show that each condor visits yearly all or large portions of the remaining range. Although movement of adult breeding pairs is limited somewhat during nesting, the overall impression is that condors are not being stressed by food shortages. These data now are being used in the preparation of precise habitat maps showing nesting, roosting, and foraging areas as well as the regularly used flight corridors that connect the roosting and feeding sites. These maps will be critical in the development of a long-range habitat protection scheme designed to assist land-management and conservation agencies and organizations.

The captive-breeding program is viewed as an essential part of the recovery effort for two important reasons.[28] First, it provides insurance against extinction in the event that the field studies do not uncover the factors responsible for the species' decline before the wild population disappears or that these limiting factors cannot be controlled quickly enough. Second, releases of young captive condors might help maintain the wild flock until the adverse factors are controlled and eventually may speed recovery by producing many more young condors than would be possible by natural reproduction.

A major breakthrough in the effort to develop a captive flock was the discovery that condors will lay a second egg if the first is lost during early incubation. This led to a highly successful test in 1983 to determine if multiple-clutching could become the primary means for obtaining condors for captivity. Multiple-clutching has several features that make it especially attractive. It allows a high level of selectiveness in choosing which egg will be brought into captivity, an important consideration in balancing the genetic representation in the captive flock. It also has the potential of having the least impact on the size of the wild population. If a wild pair almost invariably lays a second egg, and that egg has as much chance of hatching as the first, then natural reproduction will not be curtailed while the captive flock is being formed.

Also tested in 1983 and 1984 was whether a third egg would be laid if the second were taken early enough, and whether the pair would lay again the following year if its final egg or nestling of the present year were removed. The answer to both questions is still unresolved, but some pairs did lay third eggs when the second was taken, and pairs that had their entire reproduction taken in 1983 did produce eggs in 1984. An important unanswered question, however, is how long this level of pressure on the wild pairs can be maintained, and whether any negative consequences will occur.

Since maintaining a wild population is the highest long-term priority, a decision was made early in 1984 to begin small, periodic releases of birds from the captive flock so long as the integrity of the captive-breeding program is not jeopardized.[29] The initial proposal was for three yearling condors to be released in 1985. That decision was supported so long as most of the five pairs known in the wild in 1984 continued to survive. But only one of these five pairs had attempted to breed as of March 1985, so the present recommendation is to postpone any releases pending further monitoring of the wild population.

Habitat

Relatively little is known about how condors use the vast tracts of privately owned rangelands where most foraging occurs. If condors are having habitat-related problems, they most likely occur on these private lands. Certainly a great potential exists for severe habitat degradation, depending upon how well ranching survives into the distant future. Potential habitat problems on the rangelands could include inadequate food resources for condors, food quality problems, and disturbance to condors caused by increasing levels of human interference and changing land-use practices.[30]

The telemetry studies begun in 1982 already have provided considerable new information on where condors feed and roost on private lands and where potential conflicts between human activities and condors are greatest. As part of this process, it was learned that a 13,000-acre ranch identified as a primary foraging area for condors was scheduled to be converted to a multi-use housing area. This site, known as the Hudson Ranch, is so important to the remaining condor population that its loss would constitute an enormous disaster to the recovery program. This information was used by the National Audubon Society's Washington staff to help set spending priorities for Land and Water Conservation Funds for FY 1985 and to provide a $9 million appropriation for acquisition of the Hudson Ranch. Through early 1985, negotiations were still in progress between the willing sellers of the Hudson Ranch and FWS. Once acquired, the ranch will be managed as a national wildlife refuge, primarily as a foraging area for condors. The management plan for the refuge probably will allow leasing of cattle-grazing rights to a private rancher and call for supplemental carcasses during the seasons of highest condor activity.

PROGNOSIS

By 1984, biologists at the Condor Research Center were expressing cautious optimism regarding the overall condor recovery program. Although no assurances of success were in hand, the feeling was that significant progress has been made toward developing a captive-breeding population and answering important habitat questions. As yet no large amount of information on causes of death among the wild population had been collected, but progress has been made in this direction. In addition to the known causes of death for two condors, a much greater understanding of the dynamics of the entire wild flock has been obtained.

Close observations at a series of active nests strongly indicated that in 1984 condors were not having important problems with reproduction. The fact that as many as five mated pairs were still producing eggs in a total population of fewer than 20 birds seemed remarkable.

On the foraging grounds, condors were having no apparent problems finding enough food. Even adult condors with dependent chicks seemed to be collecting enough food for both themselves and the nestlings. The problem, then, seemed to be one of excessive mortality rather than reproductive problems or a shortage of suitable habitats.

Then, early in 1985, only two known breeding pairs returned to nest sites. Only one pair has attempted to breed. Until this occurred, no evidence suggested that the remaining four pairs had any problems or that any of these birds were missing. Biologists are still trying to determine whether losses of adults from these four pairs caused the nesting decline. The sharp downward turn in reproductive effort in 1985 is most disturbing, and places additional pressure on the entire recovery program.

RECOMMENDATIONS

A major concern resulting from the poor nesting effort in 1985 is that the recovery program may not be able to stay on track in its highly important studies of habitat needs and limiting factors and in attempting to maintain a wild population. Since it now seems that excessive mortality is the cause of the condor's decline, highest priority should be given to attaching radio transmitters to additional wild condors in an effort to document causes of death or injury. Field studies of radio-tagged condors should take a strong precedence over other field studies, both as a means for dealing with the mortality questions and for continuing to measure habitat needs and food habits.

Although the proposed release of three yearling condors from the captive flock in 1985 apparently has been abandoned, the idea should be kept alive. Every effort should be made to maintain a wild population, since it is the best means of ensuring the long-term survival of the condor and its habitat.

Releasing captive condors assumes that a geographically limited and free-ranging wild population such as that of the condors almost certainly is genetically homogeneous, and that the present captive flock should have no inbreeding problems. Additionally, wild condors should be added to the captive flock, though more slowly than was done in 1983 and 1984. These birds should include one adult or older immature female to be used in an attempt to breed Topatopa, the mature captive male, at the earliest possible time. Offspring from this pairing potentially could be produced several years sooner than from any other captives and could be used for further releases or for building the captive flock.

Although the preliminary indications are that habitat per se is not one of the factors causing the condor's decline, it seems quite clear that the long-term survival of a wild condor flock will require a vigilant habitat protection program. Specific sites and habitat types being identified now as important to condors, plus those known to have had regular use in the past, should become the basis for developing an inviolate habitat reserve. Working with local and regional government and conservation organizations to develop creative ways of ensuring that these lands hold their attractions for condors should become a permanent feature of the recovery effort. The habitat specialist position on the Condor Research Center staff should be made permanent. The specialist should be given lead responsibility for developing and coordinating long-term habitat preservation plans and for integrating the ecological data collected by the research team with the land-use and planning activities being conducted within the condor's range.

REFERENCES

1. Sir A. Landsborough Thomson, ed., *A New Dictionary of Birds* (New York: McGraw-Hill Book Co., 1964), p. 867.
2. California Condor Recovery Team, Revised California Condor Recovery Plan (Portland, Oregon: U.S. Fish and Wildlife Service, 1984).
3. E.R. Pianka, "On r and k Selection," *American Naturalist*, vol. 104 (1970), p. 592.
   N.G. Hairston, D.W. Tinkle and H.M. Wilbur, "Natural Selection and the Parameters of Population Growth," *Journal of Wildlife Management*, vol. 34 (1970), p.681.
4. Op. cit., California Condor Recovery Team, Condor Recovery Plan.
   Jennifer Meyer, "Field work seeks cause of decline," *Outdoor California*, vol. 44, No. 5 (Sept.-Oct. 1983), p. 19.

5. Carl B. Koford, *The California Condor* (New York: Dover Publications, 1966).
F.S. Todd and N.B. Gale, "Further Notes on the California Condor at Los Angeles Zoo," *International Zoo Yearbook*, vol. 10 (1970), p.15.
Sanford R. Wilbur, "California Condor Plumage and Molt as Field Study Aids," *California Fish and Game*, vol. 64, no. 3 (1975), p. 144.
6. Sanford R. Wilbur, "Food Resources of the California Condor" (Administrative Report, U.S. Department of the Interior, Washington, D.C., 1972).
7. Op. cit., Koford, *The California Condor*.
Alden H. Miller, Ian I. McMillan, and Eben McMillan, "The Current Status and Welfare of the California Condor," National Audubon Society Research Report, no. 6 (1965).
Sanford R. Wilbur, "The California Condor, 1966-76: A Look at its Past and Future," *North American Fauna*, no. 72, U.S. Fish and Wildlife Service (1978).
8. Warren B. King, ed., *Endangered Birds of the World* (Washington, D.C.: Smithsonian Institution Press, 1981).
9. S. Dillon Ripley, "Take the Ultimate Risk," Point Reyes Bird Observatory newsletter 53 (Spring 1981), p. 1.
New York Times, July 3, 1984
10. Op. cit., Koford, *The California Condor*.
11. Ibid.
12. Op. cit., Wilbur, "The California Condor," *North American Fauna*.
13. Ibid.
14. Op. cit., Miller et al., "Current Status of the Condor."
15. Op. cit., Wilbur, "The California Condor," *North American Fauna*.
16. Lloyd F. Kiff, David B. Peakall, and Sanford R. Wilbur, "Recent Changes in California Condor Eggshells," *The Condor*, vol. 81 (1979), p. 166.
17. Sanford R. Wilbur, "Estimating the Size and Trend of the California Condor Population (1965-1978)," *California Fish and Game*, vol. 66, no. 1 (1980), p. 40.
18. Noel F.R. Snyder and Eric V. Johnson, "Photographic Censusing of the 1982-1983 California Condor Population," *The Condor*, vol. 87, no. 1 (1985), p. 1.
19. Ibid.
20. Marilyn Anderson, "Necropsy Reports" (Unpublished manuscripts, Zoological Society of San Diego, November 1983 through March 1984).
Stanley N. Wiemeyer, "California Condor" (Unpublished memorandum, Patuxent Wildlife Research Center, U.S. Fish and Wildlife Service, Laurel, MD, April 30, 1984).
21. John C. Ogden, "The California Condor Recovery Program: An Overview," *Bird Conservation*, vol. 1 (1983), p. 87.
22. Robert E. Ricklets, ed. "Report of the Advisory Panel on the California Condor," Audubon Conservation Report, no. 6 (1978).
Cooper Ornithological Society, "51st Annual Meeting of the Cooper Ornithological Society," *The Condor*, vol. 83, no. 4 (1981), p. 398.
23. David Phillips, "Shedding Light on the Controversy," *Outdoor California*, vol. 44, no. 5 (Sept.-Oct. 1983), p.20.
24. Op. cit., Ogden, "Condor Recovery Program," *Bird Conservation*.
25. Ibid.
26. Stanley A. Temple and Michael P. Wallace, "Final Report: A Study of Techniques for Releasing Hand-reared Andean Condors to the Wild" (Unpublished manuscript, Department of Wildlife Ecology, University of Wisconsin, Madison, WI, 1983).

Stanley A. Temple, "To Save the Condor," *The Living Bird Quarterly*, vol. 2, no. 1 (Winter 1983), p. 21.

27. John C. Ogden, "Radio-tracking the California Condor," *Outdoor California*, vol. 44, no. 5 (Sept.-Oct. 1983), p. 11.

28. John C. Ogden and Noel F.R. Snyder, "The View from Ventura," Point Reyes Bird Observatory newsletter 53 (Spring 1981), p. 11.

29. California Condor Recovery Team, "Summary of Reasons for Captive Rearing and Release of California Condors" (Unpublished manuscript, Condor Research Center, Ventura, CA, November 1984).

30. Cynthia Dawn Studer, "Effects of Kern County Cattle Ranching on California Condor Habitat" (Masters Thesis, Michigan State University, Department of Geography, 1983).

Cynthia Dawn Studer, "An Analysis of Range Land in Kern County" (Unpublished manuscript, Condor Research Center, Ventura, CA, September 1982).

JOHN OGDEN has been with National Audubon Society since 1974. Formerly co-director of the California Condor Program, he now is director of the newly-organized Ornithological Research Unit. There he oversees research on the whooping crane, wood stork, heron, and puffin.

LEONARD LEE RUE III

Once overlord of the Great Plains, the grizzly in the lower 48 states now depends on human tolerance to survive.

The Grizzly Bear

by *Chris Servheen*
U.S. Fish and Wildlife Service

SPECIES DESCRIPTION AND NATURAL HISTORY

THE GRIZZLY BEAR (*Ursus arctos horribilis*) is one of two brown bear subspecies native to North America. It once ranged throughout the continent, except for the islands of Kodiak, Shuvak, and Afognak off the coast of Alaska. There the Kodiak subspecies (*Ursus arctos middendorffi*) is found. Brown bears also occur in Western Europe, North Africa, and Asia, including Japan.

The grizzly is characterized by a humped shoulder, a somewhat concave face, and long, curved front claws. Color is variable but the long guard hairs usually are lighter at the tips, giving the animal a silvery color and the name "grizzly." In the lower 48 states, adult males range from 300 to 850 pounds, females from 150 to 550 pounds. Generally, inland bears are smaller than those along the coast. Weight varies with physical condition and food supply. Weight is greater in autumn prior to den entry and lowest in early to mid-June. Body weight can fluctuate by as much as 25 percent over the course of a year.

The grizzly bear is an opportunistic omnivore. Up to 90 percent of its food is green vegetation, roots and tubers, and fruits and pine cone nuts. In most areas the majority of the meat in its diet is carrion, although some bears, especially in the Yellowstone area, prey efficiently on ungulates. Salmon is the major food of bears along the Alaska coast.

Grizzly bear home ranges may be among the largest of any land mammal. In exceptional cases, adult males may range over some 1,100 square miles. Home ranges typically include spring, summer, autumn, and denning habitat. Movements between these are determined by food and habitat availability. In many areas the grizzly is an altitudinal migrant, using low elevations in spring and late autumn and high elevations in summer and when denning.

The grizzly hibernates in winter.[1] Lower-48 bears do not eat, drink, urinate, or defecate for the entire four and a half to five months they spend on average in winter dens. During hibernation bears undergo reductions in heart and metabolic rates and slight reductions in body temperature. Bears are aroused easily during hibernation and are sensitive to noises and changes in their environment throughout the denning period.

The grizzly typically excavates its own den, although some bears occasionally use natural caves. The den site usually is above 6,500 feet, where there is sufficient snow throughout the winter to provide an insulating cover over the entrance.

Females first breed between four and seven years and generally have cubs every three years. Cubs are born in the den in January and emerge with the mother in spring. Typical litter size is two, although singles and triplets are not uncommon. The young usually stay with their mother for two full summers and den with her twice. During the time the young are with the mother they learn many of the food habits and behaviors they will use throughout adulthood. There is much speculation about the importance of this "cultural inheritance" and how dependent young grizzlies are on maternal training for such critical information as habitat use and response to humans.

SIGNIFICANCE OF THE SPECIES

Because the grizzly ranges widely and generally does not prosper in areas where it has frequent contact with man, its presence in viable populations is an indication of intact natural habitat. As science continues to reveal the importance of preserving the plant and animal diversity that can be found only in pristine habitats, species such as the grizzly will become increasingly important as evidence of the integrity of our wild areas.

HISTORICAL PERSPECTIVE

The grizzly bear once was present throughout most of the western United States and south into central Mexico.[2] It was regularly encountered by the Lewis and Clark expedition along the Missouri River in Montana in 1805. In fact, Lewis and Clark encountered so many grizzlies at the site of present-day Great Falls, Montana, that they did "not think it prudent to send a man alone on an errand of any kind."[3]

Grizzly bear populations declined with the country's westward expansion. In Wyoming[4] and possibly in Montana, the grizzly was thought to exist in greater numbers than the black bear (*Ursus americanus*) prior to the coming of the white man. But by 1929 Ernest Thompson Seton was expressing concern for the grizzly's survival: "Each year the number of hunters increases; each year more deadly traps, subtler poisons and more irresistible guns are out to get the Grizzly. He has no chance at all of escape. . . . He is absolutely at the mercy of those who know no mercy; and before five years or more, I expect to learn that there are no Grizzlies left in the United States, except in the Yellowstone National Park."[5]

Causes of the grizzly's decline included shooting and poisoning carried out for sport, protection of human life, livestock depredation control, commercial hunting, and fear of bears. Stockmen viewed the grizzly as a real and/or potential threat to their welfare, and it generally was believed that commercial cattle and sheep production could not coexist with the grizzly.[6] Livestock associations and individual operators often hired predator control personnel specifically to kill all grizzlies and wolves within their area.

As human populations increased in the West, the grizzly was limited to remote areas. This reduction in range resulted in isolation of subpopulations. The bear's decline accelerated because these subpopulations were small and cut off from immi-

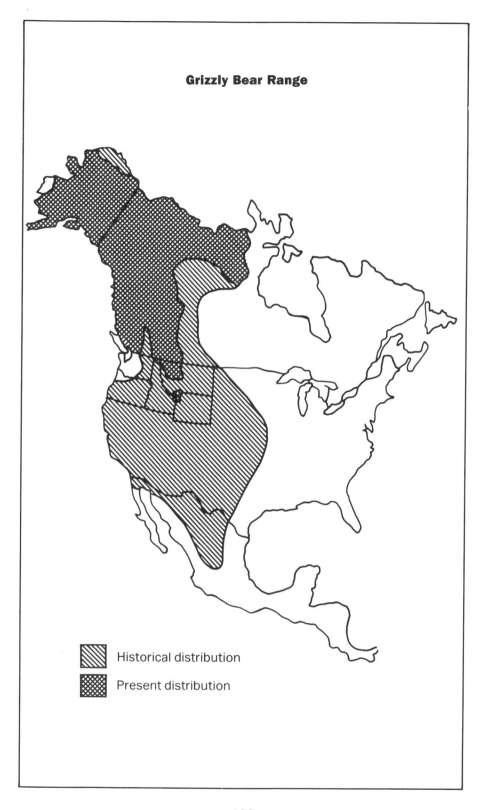

Grizzly Bear Range

Historical distribution

Present distribution

gration from adjacent areas. The grizzly disappeared from Texas in 1890, California in 1922, Utah in 1923, Oregon in 1931, New Mexico in 1933, and Arizona in 1935.[7] A grizzly killed in Colorado's San Juan Mountains in 1979 may have represented one of the last survivors in that state. Two years of intensive field work have failed to find any evidence of another grizzly in Colorado.

CURRENT TRENDS

Ownership and Management of Occupied Habitat

The present verified range of the grizzly bear is approximately 20,000 square miles in four states. This area does not include part of the North Cascades and Selway/Bitterroot ecosystems. Population estimates for the lower 48 states range between 600 and 900 bears. In 1975, grizzlies in the lower 48 states were listed as threatened under the Endangered Species Act.

About 95 percent of the habitat currently occupied by the grizzly bear is federal or state land or is owned by American Indian tribes as part of their reservations. The remaining five percent is in private ownership. The majority of the federal land is managed by the U.S. Forest Service either as multiple-use land, where resource development such as timber harvest and road building is permitted, or as designated wilderness, where only non-motorized recreational uses are allowed.

Four national parks — Glacier, Yellowstone, Grand Teton, and North Cascades — make up the majority of the federal lands in occupied range outside of national forests. Indian lands are managed by the tribal governments with the assistance of the U.S. Bureau of Indian Affairs either as multiple-use lands or as tribal wilderness. The remaining federal and state lands are managed by the U.S. Bureau of Land Management or the state land departments, usually as multiple-use lands.

Current Population Status and Distribution

Yellowstone Grizzly Bear Ecosystem. Occupied habitat in the Yellowstone Grizzly Bear Ecosystem, which surrounds and includes Yellowstone National Park, covers approximately 7,800 square miles. This population probably has been isolated by human development from other grizzly populations for approximately 60 years. Most of the Yellowstone Ecosystem is designated wilderness. Less than 85 square miles (one percent) is in private ownership.[8] This small area of private ownership has a high proportion of the bear/people management problems that occur in the ecosystem each year. Sport hunting for grizzly bears has not been permitted in the Yellowstone Ecosystem since 1974.

Yellowstone Ecosystem grizzlies have been the subject of considerable scientific study and debate for many years.[9] Despite this exhaustive effort, controversy continues,[10] and further statements on the subject usually promote more conflict. Craighead et al. (1974) reported an annual average population of 230 grizzly bears from 1959 through 1967. Based on the yearly number of unduplicated sightings of adult females with young, the most recent estimate suggests a minimum of 181 to 210 grizzly bears in 1980.[11] The most recent estimate of population trends indicates a significant decline from 1959 to 1982 in the most important part of the population, adult females with young.[12]

Northern Continental Divide Grizzly Bear Ecosystem. Occupied habitat in the Northern Continental Divide Grizzly Bear Ecosystem, which lies along the eastern edge of the Rocky Mountains in northern Montana, consists of approximately 8,900 square miles, 1,800 of it designated wilderness managed by the U.S. Forest Service and 1,600 of it in Glacier National Park. Approximately 730 square miles (eight percent) is in private ownership.[13] The rest is on national forest nonwilderness lands or in state ownership.

Recent development of private lands has increased, especially in important low-elevation range. The increasing value of private lands adjacent to pristine federal land probably will spur subdivision and second home development. Considerable commercial timber harvest occurs in federal, state, and private nonwilderness areas. The Northern Continental Divide Ecosystem sits on top of the Overthrust Belt geological formation, an area of considerable interest to oil and gas developers.

This ecosystem is open to sport hunting of grizzly bears. The Montana Department of Fish, Wildlife and Parks from 1976 to 1981 sold an average of 614 grizzly bear licenses yearly. No limit is placed on the number of licenses that can be sold or on the areas open to hunting. The season runs from September 15 to November 30. The state can close the season on a 48-hour notice if an annual quota of 25 bears dead from all causes is approached. From 1974 through 1982 the mean annual kill by sport hunters was 10.75, while the mean number of grizzly bears removed for control and by illegal and accidental kills was 10.[14]

The exact size and stability of this populations is unknown. Defenders of Wildlife, a conservation group headquartered in Washington, DC, has told the department that it will sue to stop the hunt unless the department is able to establish reliable data on the status of the population, which is contiguous with Canadian grizzly bear populations along the United States-Canada border.

The grizzly bear population trend for the Northern Continental Divide Ecosystem is unknown. Data on the number of females seen with young each year are insufficient for making a trend estimate. In Glacier National Park the population estimate is 200, based upon a sighting system,[15] and has remained relatively constant to date.[16] The population outside Glacier National Park has been estimated at between 240 and 480, based upon an extrapolated density estimate from three intensively studied areas.[17] Glacier National Park's estimate of one bear per eight square miles is probably the highest density in the ecosystem.

Human recreation in the wilderness portion of the Northern Continental Divide Ecosystem, one of the largest remaining grizzly bear habitats in the lower 48 states, is intense. In 1982, the park tallied 342,700 visitor-use days. That year more than 10,000 pack animals entered the wilderness areas outside Glacier Park.[18] The wilderness area also is the operating zone of more than 45 commercial outfitters who guide recreationists during summer and hunters, including grizzly bear hunters, during autumn. The area contains a significant amount of wilderness, yet human recreational impacts on the wilderness must be considered in the recovery of the grizzly.

Cabinet/Yaak Grizzly Bear Ecosystem. The Cabinet/Yaak Grizzly Bear Ecosystem in northwest Montana and northeast Idaho covers a total of approximately 2,000 square miles,[19] only five percent of it privately owned. Some controversy exists about whether the east and west Cabinet Mountains and the Yaak River drainage are contiguous populations, or if Cabinet Mountain bears are an insular population cut off from immigration from the north by the Kootenai River and human development. The probability of immigration of grizzly bears into this area also may be so low as to be negligible. The Yaak River area, which includes the Northwest Peaks area along the Montana-Idaho border, is contiguous with occupied habitat in British Columbia. No sport hunting is permitted on either side of the border.

The Cabinet Mountain Wilderness is the grizzly habitat core in the east Cabinet Mountains. This area is being explored for silver deposits by ASARCO Inc. and U.S. Borax Corporation. Grizzly habitat in this ecosystem is fragmented, reducing the

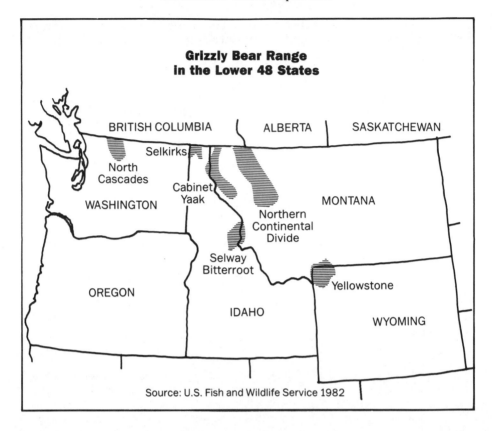

**Grizzly Bear Range
in the Lower 48 States**

Source: U.S. Fish and Wildlife Service 1982

opportunity for individual animals to have entire home ranges within areas of secure habitat.

The number of grizzly bears and the population trend in the Cabinet/Yaak Ecosystem is unknown because of the low density of bears in the area. It was estimated in 1978 that 12 bears lived in the Cabinet Mountain portion of the ecosystem.[20] No estimates have been made for other portions of the ecosystem, but sightings of grizzly bears occur each year.

Selkirk Mountains Grizzly Bear Ecosystem. Occupied habitat in the Selkirk Ecosystem in north Idaho and extreme northeast Washington is approximately 1,100 square miles, four percent of it private land. This population is contiguous with populations in British Columbia. The current range is the southernmost extension of occupied habitat in the Selkirk Mountain chain. The main resource use is commercial timber harvest. The area is sparsely populated by man. No grizzly bear hunting is allowed on the United States side. Sport hunting on the Canadian side is by permit and limited to four animals per year.[21]

North Cascades Grizzly Bear Ecosystem and Selway/Bitterroot Grizzly Bear Ecosystem. Current population levels for North Cascades Ecosystem in northwest Washington are thought to be low, but little can be said without further surveys.

The Selway/Bitterroot Ecosystem in central Idaho also has little current information available. Each year a few sightings are reported, but none have been confirmed since 1946.[22] In conjunction with the River-of-No-Return Wilderness in Idaho, the area is the largest contiguous wilderness in the lower 48 states. Parts of it have been surveyed to measure its suitability as grizzly bear habitat,[23] but little else is known.

San Juan Mountains, Colorado. In 1979, a hunter shot an old female grizzly bear in Colorado's San Juan Mountains, the first verified record of a grizzly in Colorado since 1952. This incident prompted the state Division of Wildlife and the U.S. Forest Service to begin a grizzly bear status survey. Two summers were spent searching for evidence of grizzly bears, but no bears were found. It seems likely that this population is or was the last remnant population in the United States south of the Yellowstone Ecosystem.

Population Status

Research in the Yellowstone Ecosystem[24] has determined distribution and movement patterns, population dynamics, and population trends. Home ranges are large and variable and movement across the ecosystem is common, especially for adult males. From 1975 to 1983, 111 grizzly bears were captured. Thirty-four (30.6 percent) have since died. Thirty of these deaths were human-caused, three natural, and one unknown.[25] Litter size is down. The Craigheads estimated an average litter size of 2.1 between 1959 and 1970. Litter size for 1974 to 1982 is estimated to be 1.9. Average female age at first pregnancy has been delayed for as yet unknown reasons from five years of age from 1959 to 1970 to six years of age from 1974 to 1982.[26] Mortality has varied since 1974 .

Known Man-caused Grizzly Bear Mortalities in the Yellowstone Ecosystem 1975–1983.

	1975	1976	1977	1978	1979	1980	1981	1982	1983	Nine year Total
Yellowstone National Park	0	1	3	2	1	2	0	3	3	15
Montana	0	1	2	2	1	2	4	3	3	18
Wyoming	0	2	3	0	1	1	2	8	0	17
Idaho	0	0	2	0	0	0	0	0	0	2
Total	0	4	10	4	3	5	6	14	6	52

Source: K.R. Greer.

Population status information in the Northern Continental Divide Ecosystem has been limited to selected study areas where intensive trapping and radio tracking have allowed estimates of population density and demography.[27] Limited information on adult male movement[28] indicates that distinct subpopulations do not exist within the ecosystem since individual bears range throughout the area. Home-range size is large and varies by sex, age, and reproductive status.

From 1975 to 1982, 117 grizzlies have been captured in this ecosystem, including 33 just north of the Canadian border.[29] As of 1982, 20 had died of human causes, one from natural causes, and one from unknown causes.[30] Average litter size on the Rocky Mountain Front study area, based on data from eight female bears, was 2.5 from 1980 to 1982.[31] Limited data are available for female age at first pregnancy in the Northern Continental Divide, but three females were known to have produced cubs at four years of age.[32] Such early reproduction has not been recorded in the Yellowstone area. Reported bear mortality in the ecosystem has remained relatively constant since 1975, but the total mortality including unreported deaths is unknown.[33]

Known Man-caused Grizzly Bear Mortalities in Northwest Montana
1975–1983

	1975	1976	1977	1978	1979	1980	1981	1982	1983	Nine year Total
Hunting	13	11	5	7	11	11	10	17	8	93
Other	9	12	8	7	7	12	5	7	7	74
Total	22	23	13	14	18	23	15	24	15	167

Source: K.R. Greer.

Population status information is not yet available for the Cabinet/Yaak, Selkirk, North Cascades, or Selway/Bitterroot Ecosystems. One subadult female grizzly was captured in the Selkirk Mountains, and at least six other grizzly bears were sighted in the area in 1983 and 1984.[34] Two grizzly bears were captured in the Cabinet Mountains, one in 1983 and one in 1984.[35] One of these, a 29-year-old female, may be the oldest wild grizzly bear ever captured in North America. A survey of historic and recent grizzly sightings was completed for North Cascades National Park[36] and the entire North Cascades in 1983.[37] Sullivan (1983) reviewed 233 reports over the past 130 years. The last grizzly verified in this area was a bear killed by a hunter in 1967, although reports occur every year.

MANAGEMENT

Habitat Requirements

Habitat-use information has been analyzed for the Yellowstone Ecosystem using habitat-type base maps and location data gathered since 1975 from radio-collared bears.[38]

In the Northern Continental Divide Ecosystem, habitat preference has been studied by comparing habitat use based on radio locations of bears to habitat availability within the home range of radio-collared animals.[39] This analysis has enabled biologists to predict habitat preference and, therefore, importance by season. In most Northern Continental Divide areas, grizzly bears tend to be altitudinal migrants moving to low-elevation riparian zones in spring and late autumn and up to high-elevation habitats in summer and early autumn in response to plant food and prey availability.[40]

Road building and timber harvest affect the habitat use of some grizzly bears,[41] but other grizzlies apparently adapt to certain levels of road use and human disturbance.[42] Road building and habitat development increased 88 percent around Glacier National Park from 1938 to 1968.[43] Increasing human access around Glacier National Park may be isolating the park grizzly population and increasing human-caused mortality.[44]

Grizzly bear habitat in the Cabinet/Yaak Ecosystem has been intensively mapped by Kootenai National Forest biologists as part of a habitat management program.[45] Important habitats in the Cabinet/Yaak have been determined by extrapolation from Northern Continental Divide Ecosystem habitat-use data. Grizzly habitat in this area has been divided into 13 components on the basis of structural habitat differences. Seasonal importance and availability of each component are considered in managing human resource use.[46]

The Selkirk Ecosystem in Idaho and Washington has been surveyed for grizzly habitat suitability.[47] Further mapping is planned in this area by Idaho Panhandle National Forest biologists as part of the habitat management program. Habitat in the

North Cascades Ecosystem has not been mapped or surveyed. A portion of the Selway/Bitterroot Ecosystem has been surveyed for grizzly habitat suitability.[48]

Recovery Goals

The grizzly in 1975 was listed as threatened in the lower 48 states. The U.S. Fish and Wildlife Service (FWS) in 1980 initiated development of a grizzly bear recovery plan completed and signed by the director in January 1982.

The recovery plan objective[49] is to establish viable, self-sustaining populations in areas where the grizzly bear occurred in 1975. There are no plans to re-establish grizzly bear populations where they do not now exist or to expand the ecosystem boundaries beyond currently occupied habitat.

The plan lists population goals for the Yellowstone, Northern Continental Divide, and Cabinet/Yaak Ecosystems. No recovery goals have been set yet for the other ecosystems. However, since 70 to 90 bears is considered the minimum number necessary for long-term survival, this figure may provide a guideline.[50] Recovery goals are based on information that includes estimates of minimum viable population size[51] and estimates of population sizes in historic times. The current recovery goal is 301 bears for the Yellowstone Ecosystem, 560 for the Northern Continental Divide, and 70 for the Cabinet/Yaak. Recovery goals also are defined in terms of a set of reproductive parameters that must be maintained for at least six years.

The recovery plan outlines a series of tasks and assigns responsibility for the completion of these tasks to state and federal management agencies within the remaining range of the species. The plan does not spell out specific types of agency guidelines nor does it require adherence. Implementation of the plan is contingent upon funding and other budgetary constraints. Federal agencies are required to comply with Section 7 of the Endangered Species Act,[52] which states, "Each Federal Agency shall . . . ensure that any action authorized, funded, or carried out by such agency is not likely to jeopardize the continued existence of any endangered or threatened species or result in the destruction or adverse modification of its habitat." Examples of federal activities involved under Section 7 include timber sales and road construction on national forest lands, oil and gas exploration and development of federal surface or subsurface mineral rights, and bear management plans in national parks.

Cooperation among agencies is sometimes complicated by the different legal mandates under which each agency operates. The Interagency Grizzly Bear Committee (IGBC) was established in 1983 to facilitate cooperation among the various agencies. The IGBC was created by a memorandum of agreement signed by the governors of Idaho, Montana, Washington, and Wyoming, the assistant secretary of Agriculture, and two assistant secretaries in the Department of Interior. The IGBC is composed of representatives of the Idaho, Montana, Washington, and Wyoming state game and fish departments, three regional foresters, the regional director of the National Park Service, the FWS regional director, and the state director of the Bureau of Land Management in Montana. The IGBC has as *ex officio* members representatives of the Bureau of Indian Affairs and the Salish/Kootenai and Blackfoot tribes and Canadian wildlife managers from Alberta and British Columbia. The IGBC serves as the coordinating mechanism to implement the management and research necessary for recovery of the grizzly bear.

Current management actions attempt to minimize bear mortality, especially of adult females, and habitat destruction and disturbance. Management activities under direction of the IGBC include:

1. A major public education effort to inform users of grizzly bear habitat about the needs of the species and how confrontations with bears can be avoided.

2. A coordinated law-enforcement campaign that involves cooperation among all state and federal agencies to prevent illegal killing of grizzlies.

3. Development of a computer-based cumulative effects analysis procedure that helps land managers recognize the potential cumulative effects of land-use decisions on grizzly habitat and bear survival.

4. Intensive mapping of all important habitat so that important seasonal-use areas can be identified and carefully managed.

5. Placement of food storage facilities in backcountry areas to allow recreationists to keep human foods away from bears and thus prevent bears from linking people-use areas with feeding areas.

6. Classification of all occupied habitat as one of three management situations— 1) areas necessary for survival, where bear management is the major but not exclusive management concern; 2) areas perhaps necessary for survival, where other land uses can be maintained in conjunction with bear management; and 3) areas where bear use will be discouraged because of existing high human use, e.g. town sites and large campgrounds.

These management efforts will continue to improve as research develops more information on the effects of human activity on bears and as managers improve the tools for making land-use decisions, such as the cumulative effects analysis process.

PROGNOSIS

Direct mortality and loss factors include legal and illegal kills, removals to zoos and research centers of bears that have had repeated conflicts with man, accidental kills, and self-defense kills. Indirect mortalities are much more difficult to measure but no less damaging to the population. These include animals forced to move out of suitable habitat because of human-related disturbance and which subsequently suffer increased mortality or lowered reproductive fitness because of poor food supply or inability to compete with resident bears.

Increasing resource demands of particular importance to the survival of the grizzly include oil and gas exploration and development, commercial timber harvest, recreation, housing development on private lands, and livestock grazing. The cost of maintaining the grizzly may involve delay or modification of development opportunities or forgoing development altogether.

Human influence cannot be completely eliminated from grizzly habitat because resource demands will not allow removal of people from such large areas. Public land managers must determine the tolerance limits of the grizzly for human activity and carefully manage resource use with these limits in mind. Grizzly survival is dependent upon maintenance of suitable habitat, limitation of human-induced mortality, and minimization of conflicts between bears and people.

RECOMMENDATIONS

Population Trend Monitoring Systems

The development of a population-monitoring system is identified as a high-priority item in the Grizzly Bear Recovery Plan, because a need exists to assess population change over time to validate management efforts. Several design criteria must be met by any trend-monitoring system: 1) it should be cost-effective; 2) it must measure a representative sample of an acceptable size; 3) it must not cause more than minimal disturbance to the bears and the ecosystem; and 4) it must be easy to use.

Current efforts to develop population trend monitoring techniques have involved using aircraft to locate females with young and establishing scent stations on transect lines through representative habitats. Radio-location data are being used to develop survey timing and routes. Current population size and trend estimates for the Yellowstone Ecosystem are based on the number of unduplicated yearly sightings of adult females with cubs. These estimates are somewhat flawed because the efficiency of sighting adult females is unknown. Future work in the Yellowstone Ecosystem will be directed at improving the accuracy of this estimate.

In the Northern Continental Divide Ecosystem, several methods to assess population trends were tested from 1982 to 1984. These included helicopter surveys of known denning areas when bears were emerging in spring, helicopter surveys of shrub fields in autumn when the shrub fruit crop was at its peak, and aerial and ground surveys of open alpine areas in summer. Flights were made in early morning or late evening when bears were thought to be most active.

Quantification of the Impact of Human Disturbance

Human-related disturbance can take two forms. One is habitat or ecological disruption caused by such activities as timber harvest, petroleum development, housing subdivisions, developed campgrounds, and livestock grazing. The other is behavioral disruption resulting from such activities as helicopter flights, recreation, or road use. Disturbance of the physical landscape or ecological disturbance can be a long-lasting or permanent change, while behavioral disturbance is usually transient. Ecological disturbance changes the availability of resources, while behavioral disturbance changes the bear's use of resources.

The effects of disturbance must be predictable and quantifiable if resource development and recreation are to be managed successfully. Predicting the effects of ecological disturbance in a given area depends on having disturbance information from other similar areas.

Before making assumptions about behavioral disturbance it is important to consider whether an area is pristine or previously disturbed, and what the effects of this history have been on the behavioral response of resident bears. At present, little information is available about the bear's ability to change learned habitat-use patterns in response to disturbance. Some evidence suggests that bears living in highly disturbed habitat learn to avoid activity areas, habituate to activities, or vary their own activity to avoid conflict with man.[53] The predictability of human presence appears important for successful grizzly bear adaptation to human disturbance.[54] The adaptability of bears may be related to behaviors learned from their mothers, a type of cultural inheritance from generation to generation.

Grizzly bears living in pristine areas may not be able to coexist with human disturbance.[55] The effect of habitat disturbance may be most profound in pristine areas. If so, then documentation of this fact is very important to management of much of the remaining grizzly bear habitat in the lower 48 states. Increased oil and gas exploration and development is a prime example of a disturbance that soon will be introduced into most occupied grizzly habitat outside national parks and some wilderness areas.[56] Because much occupied range is multiple-use land, exclusion of human activity is not possible. Successful minimization of negative effects of human disturbance will be dependent upon management decisions based on sound information.

REFERENCES

1. G.E. Folk Jr., *Textbook on Environmental Physiology* (Philadelphia: Lea and Febiger, 1974), pp. 280-309.
2. T.I. Storer and L.P. Tevis, *California Grizzly* (Lincoln and London: University of Nebraska Press, 1955).
3. B. Devoto, *The Journals of Lewis and Clark* (Boston: Houghton Mifflin Corp., 1953).
4. C.A. Long, "The Mammals of Wyoming," *University of Kansas Publications*, vol. 14 (1965), pp. 493-758.
5. Ernest Thompson Seton, *Lives of Game Animals* (New York: Doubleday, Doran and Co., Inc., 1929), vol. II part 1. p. 21.
6. V. Bailey, "Mammals of New Mexico," U.S.D.A. Biological Survey (1931).
7. Op. cit., Storer and Tevis, *California Grizzly.*
8. U.S. Department of the Interior, Fish and Wildlife Service, Grizzly Bear Recovery Plan (Washington, D.C.: U.S.D.I., 1982).
9. I. McT. Cowan, Report of Committee on the Yellowstone Grizzlies (Washington, D.C.: National Academy of Sciences, 1974).
J.J. Craighead, J. Varney, and F.C. Craighead Jr., "A Population Analysis of Yellowstone Grizzly Bears," MT for Conserv. Exp., Sta. Bull. No. 40 (Missoula: University of Montana, 1974).
G.F. Cole, U.S. Department of the Interior, "Management Involving Grizzly and Black Bears in Yellowstone National Park, 1970-75," National Park Service Natural Resources Report No. 9 (1976).
S.F. Stringham, "Possible Affects of Hunting on the Grizzly/Brown Bear, A Threatened Species," in C.J. Martinka and K.L. McArthur, eds., *Bears—Their Biology and Management*, Bear Biologists Association Conference Series 3 (Kalispell: Bear Biologists Association Conference, 1980), pp. 337-349.
D.R. McCullough, "Population Dynamics of the Yellowstone Grizzly," in C.W. Fowler and T.D. Smith, eds., *Dynamics of Large Mammal Populations* (New York: J. Wiley and Sons, 1981), pp. 173-196.
R.R. Knight, B.M. Blanchard, and K.M. Kendall, *Yellowstone Grizzly Bear Investigations*, 1982 (Washington, D.C.: U.S. Department of the Interior, National Park Service, 1982), 70 pp.
10. A.S. Johnson, "Yellowstone's Grizzlies: Endangered or Prospering?" *Defenders of Wildlife News* (Oct., 1973), pp. 557-568.
S. Seater, "Vanishing Point: The Grizzly Bear," *Environmental Quality*, vol. 4 (1973), pp. 28-34.
B. Gilbert, "The Great Grizzly Controversy," *Audubon*, vol. 78 (1976), pp. 63-92.
C. Cauble, "The Great Grizzly Grapple," *Natural History*, vol. 86 (1977), pp. 74-81.
F.C. Craighead Jr., *Track of the Grizzly* (San Francisco: Sierra Club Books, 1979).
P. Schullery, *The Bears of Yellowstone* (Yellowstone National Park: Yellowstone Library and Museum Assoc., 1980), 176 pp.
T. McNamee, "Breath-Holding in Grizzly Country," *Audubon*, vol. 84 (1982), pp. 68-83.
T. McNamee, *The Grizzly Bear* (New York: Alfred A. Knopf, 1984), 308 pp.
11. Interagency Grizzly Bear Committee, "Report of the ad hoc Task Force to Review the Population Status of the Yellowstone Grizzly Bear" (Unpublished Report, 1983), 7 pp.

12. Ibid.
    R.R. Knight and L.L. Eberhardt, "Projected Future Abundance of the Yellowstone Grizzly Bear," *Journal of Wildlife Management*, vol. 48 (1984), pp. 1434-1438.
13. Op. cit., U.S.D.I., Grizzly Bear Recovery Plan.
14. K.R. Greer, "Grizzly Bear Mortality Studies, 1981," State of Montana, Department Fish, Wildlife and Parks, Wildlife Investigations Lab Project W-120-R-13, Project No. V., Study No. WL-1.0 (1982), 20 pp.
15. C.J. Martinka, "Population Characteristics of Grizzly Bears in Glacier National Park," *Journal of Mammalogy*, vol. 55 (1974), pp. 21-29.
16. C. Martinka, pers. commun.
17. Op. cit., U.S.D.I., Grizzly Bear Recovery Plan.
18. Unpublished U.S. Forest Service data.
19. Op. cit., U.S.D.I., Grizzly Bear Recovery Plan.
20. H. Wright, *The Grizzly Bear* (Lincoln and London: University of Nebraska Press, 1909).
    C.H. Merriman, "Distribution of Grizzly Bears in the United States," *Outdoor Life* (Dec., 1922), pp. 405-406.
    P.E. Zager, "Grizzly Bears in Idaho's Selkirk Mountains: An update," *Northwest Science*, vol. 57 (1983), pp. 299-309.
    J. Almack, pers. commun.
21. G. Woods, pers. commun.
22. W.R. Moore, "The Last of the Bitterroot Grizzlies," *Montana Magazine*, No. 68 (1984), pp. 8-12.
23. G.B. Scaggs, "Vegetation Description of Potential Grizzly Bear Habitat in the Selway-Bitterroot Area, Montana and Idaho" (M.S. Thesis, University of Montana, Missoula, 1979).
24. R.R. Knight, B.M. Blanchard, and K.M. Kendall, *Yellowstone Grizzly Bear Investigations, 1980* (Washington, D.C.: U.S.D.I., 1980), 55 pp.
    Op. cit., R.R. Knight et al., *Yellowstone Grizzly Bear Investigations*, 1982.
    J. Basile, "Grizzly Bear Distribution in the Yellowstone Area, 1973-79," U.S. Department of Agriculture-Forest Service, Intermountain Forest and Range Experiment Station Resources Note (1981).
    Op. cit., Knight et al., "Abundance of Yellowstone Grizzly Bear," *Journal of Wildlife Management*.
    R.R. Knight and L.L. Eberhardt, "Population Dynamics of Yellowstone Grizzly Bears," *Ecology*, vol. 66 (1985), in press.
25. R.R. Knight, pers. commun.
26. Op. cit., Knight and Eberhardt, "Abundance of Yellowstone Grizzly Bear," *Journal of Wildlife Management*.
27. R. Mace and C. Jonkel, "Grizzly Bear Response to Habitat Disturbance," in C. Jonkel, ed., Border Grizzly Project, Annual Report No. 5 (Missoula: University of Montana, Missoula, 1980), pp. 70-98.
    C. Servheen, "Denning Ecology, Food Habits, Habitat Use, and Movements of Grizzly Bears in the Mission Mountains, Montana" (Ph.D. dissertation, University of Montana, Missoula, 1981).
    K. Aune and T. Stivers, Rocky Mountain Front Grizzly Bear Monitoring and Investigation (Helena: Montana Department Fish, Wildlife and Parks, 1981).
    K. Aune and T. Stivers, Rocky Mountain Front Grizzly Bear Monitoring and Investigation (Helena: Montana Department Fish, Wildlife and Parks, 1982).
    K. Aune and T. Stivers, Rocky Mountain Front Grizzly Bear Monitoring and

Investigation (Helena: Montana Department Fish, Wildlife and Parks, 1983).
B. McLellan, pers. commun.
28. Op. cit., Servheen, "Denning Ecology of Grizzly Bears in the Mission Mountains."
29. B. McLellan, pers. commun.
30. Op. cit., Greer, "Grizzly Bear Mortality Studies."
Unpublished data, B. McLellan, J. Almack and R. Klaver, pers. commun.
31. B. McLellan, pers. commun.
32. Unpublished data, B. McLellan and C. Servheen.
33. Op. cit., Knight and Eberhardt, "Abundance of Yellowstone Grizzly Bear," *Journal of Wildlife Management.*
34. J. Almack, pers. commun.
35. W. Kasworm, G. Brown and A. Olsen, Cabinet Mountains Grizzly Bear Study Annual Report, June-December, 1983, Report submitted to U.S. Fish and Wildlife Service (Helena: Department Fish, Wildlife and Parks, 1984).
36. J. Bjorklund, Habitat and Vegetative Characteristics of a Remote Backcountry Area as Related to the Reestablishment of a Grizzly Population in the North Cascades National Park Complex, Miscellaneous Research Paper NCT-10 (Sedro-Wooley, Washington: North Cascades National Park, 1980).
37. P.T. Sullivan, "A Preliminary Study of Historic and Recent Reports of Grizzly Bears, *Ursus arctos,* in the North Cascades Area of Washington" (Unpublished Report, Washington Dept. of Game, Olympia, Washington, 1983).
38. Op. cit., Knight and Eberhardt, "Abundance of Yellowstone Grizzly Bear," *Journal of Wildlife Management.*
39. Marcum and Loftsgaarden, "A Nonparametric Technique for Studying Use vs. Availability of Environmental Components," *Journal of Wildlife Management,* vol. 44 (1980), pp. 963-968.
40. C. Servheen and L.C. Lee, "Mission Mountains Grizzly Bear Studies, An Interim Report, 1976-78," Montana Forest and Range Experiment Station School of Forestry, University of Montana, Missoula (1979).
R. Mace and C. Jonkel, "Seasonal Food Habits of Grizzly Bears in Northwestern Montana," in C. Jonkel, ed., Border Grizzly Project, Annual Report No. 5 (Missoula: University of Montana, 1980).
A. Schallenberger and C. Jonkel, "Rocky Mountain East Front Grizzly Studies, 1978," Border Grizzly Project, Annual Report (Missoula: School of Forestry, University of Montana, Missoula, 1979).
P.E. Zager, "Influence of Logging and Wildfire on Grizzly Bear Habitat in Northwestern Montana" (Ph.D. dissertation, University of Montana, Missoula, Dept. Botany, 1980).
Op. cit., Aune and Stivers, Grizzly Bear Monitoring and Investigation, 1981.
Op. cit., Aune and Stivers, Grizzly Bear Monitoring and Investigation, 1982.
Op. cit., Aune and Stivers, Grizzly Bear Monitoring and Investigation, 1983.
41. R. Mace and C. Jonkel, "The Effects of a Logging Activity on Grizzly Bear Movements," in C. Jonkel, ed., Border Grizzly Project, Annual Report No. 5 (1980), pp. 133-147.
42. B. McLellan, pers. commun.
43. C.J. Martinka, "Effects of Conterminous Land Use on Grizzly Bears in Glacier National Park," *American Association for the Advancement of Science Symposium on Threats to Ecosystems of National Parks* (1981).
44. Ibid.
45. A.C. Christensen and M.J. Madel, "Cumulative Effects Analysis Process: Griz-

zly Bear Habitat Componant Mapping," Department of Agriculture, Kootenai National Forest (1982).
46. Ibid.
47. Op. cit., Zager, "Grizzly Bears in Idaho," *Northwest Science.*
48. Op. cit., Scaggs, "Vegetation Description of Potential Grizzly Bear Habitat."
49. Op. cit., U.S.D.I., Grizzly Bear Recovery Plan.
50. M.L. Shaffer, *Determining Minimum Viable Population Sizes—A Case Study of the Grizzly Bear* (Ursus arctos) (Durham: Duke University, School of Forestry and Environmental Studies, 1978).
51. Ibid.
52. Pub. L. No. 93-205, 87 Stat. 884.
53. Op. cit., Aune and Stivers, Grizzly Bear Monitoring and Investigation, 1981.
Op. cit., Aune and Stivers, Grizzly Bear Monitoring and Investigation, 1982.
Op. cit., Aune and Stivers, Grizzly Bear Monitoring and Investigation, 1983.
Op. cit., Servheen, "Denning Ecology and Movements of Grizzly Bears in the Mission Mountains."
B. McLellan, pers. commun.
54. Unpublished data, B. McLellan and C. Servheen.
55. Op. cit., Mace and Jonkel, "Effects of Logging on Grizzly Movements."
56. Op. cit., Schallenberger and Jonkel, "Rocky Mountain Grizzly Studies."

CHRISTOPHER SERVHEEN received his doctorate from the University of Montana in 1981 after completing his dissertation on the ecology, denning activities, habitat, and eating habits of the grizzly in the Mission Mountains of Montana. He has since been working as the Grizzly Bear Recovery Coordinator for the U.S. Fish and Wildlife Service.

Maryland biologist captures a female striped bass during the annual Chesapeake Bay spawning-population survey, part of an effort to reverse the decline of this commercially important species.

The Striped Bass

By *Whit Fosburgh*
National Audubon Society Staff

SPECIES DESCRIPTION AND NATURAL HISTORY[1]

THE STRIPED BASS (*Morone saxatilis*) is perchlike in shape, with an elongated and moderately compressed body and a slightly arched back. Its color is its most distinguishing characteristic. The sides are dark olive-green varying to bluish above, paling on the sides, and silvery on the belly. Each side has seven or eight dark, usually continuous, longitudinal stripes that follow the scale rows. One of these stripes always follows the lateral line, with three or four above it and three below.

Striped bass are relatively long-lived and can attain great size. The heaviest striper on record weighed 125 pounds, and the current rod and reel record is 76 pounds. When caught, bass generally range from three to 35 pounds, but fish heavier than 50 pounds are not exceptional. A fish of 50 pounds is probably a female at least 15 years old. Females live longer and grow considerably larger than males. Reported maximum lengths are 72 inches and 45.5 inches respectively for females and males. An average 10-year-old female bass weighs 28.2 pounds; a male, 22.3 pounds.

Historically, the range for the striped bass was the Atlantic coast of North America from the St. Lawrence River in Canada south to northern Florida and west along the northern Gulf of Mexico to the Atchafalaya Basin in Louisiana. In the last quarter of the 19th century, it was introduced on the Pacific coast, where its range extends from Frays Harbor, Washington, to Los Angeles County in California. In addition, the bass now has been extensively transplanted into inland lakes, reservoirs, and streams for sport fishing. Scientists identify four distinct races of the coastal striped bass — the North Atlantic, South Atlantic, Gulf coast, and Pacific coast races. The North Atlantic race, which occurs from Maine to the Albemarle Sound in North Carolina, is the most important in terms of numbers and overall commercial and recreational value, and is the focus of this account.

Striped bass are anadromous, ascending coastal rivers and streams in early spring to spawn. They may travel little farther than the brackish waters in the heads of estuaries or more than 100 miles, as is often the case on the Hudson and Roanoke rivers. Spawning areas characteristically are areas of fresh, turbulent water. Turbulence allows the eggs to drift and stay clean of sediment that would smother them. The semibuoyant eggs may drift all the way to tidewater before hatching, but need a salinity of less than five parts per thousand to survive. The eggs hatch in about 70 to 74 hours at a water temperature of 58 to 60 degrees, 48 hours at 67 degrees, and 30 hours at 71 or 72 degrees.[2]

There is a strong correlation between the size and age of the female striped bass and the number of eggs she produces. A six-year-old female, weighing approximately 10 pounds, may carry as many as one million eggs. A bass 14 years old, weighing nearly 50 pounds, may have as many as five million eggs.

Upon hatching, striped bass larvae derive nourishment from their yolk sac for seven to 14 days, depending upon water temperature. Larvae less than five days old are unable to swim continuously and require some turbulance in order to remain suspended. From four to 10 days after hatching, active feeding begins, initially on only small, mobile, pelagic planktonic forms. By 13 days, the stomach is well-developed and feeding, expands to benthic forms such as mysid shrimp larvae. Since the air bladders are not fully inflated, energy expenditure is high in these early life stages, and it is necessary to have large concentrations of food available.

Within three or four weeks of hatching, the bass have grown from an average of a tenth of an inch to more than an inch, acquiring the features of adult bass, including well-developed scales and fins. The young bass usually remain on or near the nursery areas where they were spawned until they reach sexual maturity, which generally is in their fourth year for the females and second year for the males. By their second summer, young striped bass go from a diet consisting almost entirely of invertebrates to one including small fish. By their third year they subsist predominantly on fish.

The characteristic most clearly separating the North Atlantic race of striped bass from the other races is its migratory habits. Bass of the South Atlantic and Gulf coast races are endemic to particular river systems and are fairly non-migratory. In contrast, it has been determined that the North Atlantic race and, in particular, the Chesapeake Bay stocks make seasonal movements of considerable distance.

Three spawning areas are most important to this coastal migratory stock: Chesapeake Bay and the Hudson and Roanoke rivers. A study by Texas Instruments in 1975 showed that 90 percent of the stock came from the Chesapeake, 6.5 percent from the Hudson, and 2.7 percent from the Roanoke. More recent studies have shown that a shift has occurred in this breakout. Some experts estimate that more than half the stock now comes from the Hudson, because Chesapeake stocks are so depleted.

Although the Hudson and Roanoke stocks appear to be less migratory than those in the Chesapeake, all show evidence of northward migration in the summer, southward movement in the fall, and a return to natal rivers in the winter and spring to spawn. Studies have shown that the Chesapeake Bay stocks migrate to the southern shore of Long Island, with many continuing north to the New England coast. For the most part, females from Chesapeake Bay join the migratory schools, while males remain in the bay. However, Hudson River males appear to migrate with the females. The bass migration corresponds with the northward migration of the menhaden, a favorite bass food fish. Bluefish and weakfish also follow the pattern of the striped bass and menhaden, providing direct dietary competition with the striped bass. There is no evidence that fluctuations in the abundance of any one of these predatory species has affected levels of the others.

A migrating bass is known for its voracious appetite, eating whatever is available, vertebrate or invertebrate. Menhaden, alewives, anchovies, eels, herring, squid, crabs, shrimp, worms, and small mussels all make up its diet. Fishermen have found that when the bass are gorging on any particular prey, they largely ignore all others. After the school gorges on plentiful prey, it generally stops to digest its food, then begins feeding again. Such stops and starts are done largely in unison.

The bass in migration closely follow the shoreline, rarely venturing more than two miles from shore. Their location is governed by the availability of food. In fall, the migrants move southward to winter in deeper coastal waters. Males precede females by several weeks into the spawning rivers. In the Chesapeake's tributaries and in the Roanoke River, this movement occurs from December through February. The actual spawning season runs from March through June, with most activity concentrated between mid-April and mid-May. In the Hudson, spawning generally runs from mid-May through mid-June. For the bass in general, peak spawning activity occurs when water temperatures are between 60 and 65 degrees.

About 55 to 85 percent of the fish on the spawning grounds are males. Mating activity generally is greatest at dawn or dusk and can be very dramatic and spectacular to observe. Often a single female may be accompanied by 10 to 50 males. When the female broadcasts her eggs, which is done near the water's surface, the males may roll and splash in a frantic effort to fertilize the eggs. This phenomenon is known as a "rock fight." Egg shedding usually is a single event completed in several hours.

Significance of the Species

The striped bass is a highly effective predator. Its voracious appetite, aggressive nature, and large adult size place the bass at the top of the food chain, giving it an important biological role. Because the bass eats other fish, its flesh is highly valued for human consumption. Because the bass is gregarious and aggressive, it is popular for commercial and sport fishing. In 1980, commercial and sport striped bass fisheries supported 5,600 jobs, generated $90 million in spending, and created $200 million in related economic activity in coastal areas from North Carolina to Maine.

But the value of the bass to man goes beyond dollars and cents for the millions of sport fishermen who have pursued it. The fabled run of the bass when hooked, and its unrelenting fight for liberty among the rollings of the surf, have given the bass a nearly unequaled place in the lives and lore of those who have made it a premier game fish.

Historical Perspective

Since Colonial times, the striped bass has been a source of admiration, economic livelihood, and controversy. The first minister of Salem, Massachusetts, the Reverend Francis Higginson, who died in 1630, wrote of the striped bass:

> There is a fish called bass, a most sweet and wholesome fish as ever I did eat; it is altogether as good as our fresh salmon, and the season of their coming was begun when we first came to New England in June, and so continued about three months' space. Of this fish our fishers take many hundreds together which I have seen lying on the shore, to my admiration: yea, their nets ordinarily take more than they are able to haul to land, and for want of boats and men they are constrained to let many go after they have taken them, and yet sometimes they fill two boats at a time with them[3]

The striped bass was the subject of the first conservation law in North America. In 1639, the Massachusetts Bay Colony forbade the use of the fish as fertilizer. In 1670, the first public school on the continent was financed in Plymouth Colony by profits from the sale of striped bass, herring, and mackerel. Captain John Smith wrote of seeing Chesapeake Bay so teeming with bass that a man could almost walk on their backs.[4] Local problems such as dams and water pollution eliminated striped bass populations in several rivers during the 1800s, but the overall coastal population appears to have remained fairly high until the 1970s.

Today, striped bass populations are monitored through two principal means: commercial harvest surveys and young-of-the-year indices. Harvest surveys are compiled by the individual states and published annually on a coast-wide basis by the National Marine Fisheries Service (NMFS).

Young-of-the-year indices are taken by individual states and center on particular waters, such as Chesapeake Bay or the Hudson River. The index is an indicator of the rate of spawning success in a geographically distinct area as measured by the average number of immature fish found in various seine-net samples. The samples are done in Chesapeake Bay at four nursery areas: the Potomac River, the Choptank River, the Nanticoke River, and the uppermost part of the bay. Seine hauls are done at each of these locations in July, August, and September, and the numbers are averaged for the index. In the Chesapeake Bay, the long-term average for the young-of-the-year index is 9.3. Traditionally, the index has a strong positive correlation with harvest numbers. For example, in 1970 the young-of-the-year index for the Chesapeake was 30.4, the highest index ever recorded. In 1973, the year these fish reached a catchable size, total commercial landings were 14.7 million pounds, also a record.

Fish from a plentiful spawning year are referred to as a dominant-year class. Evidence has shown that such classes are necessary to keep the overall bass population high. Through 1970, dominant-year classes had occurred on average every six years in the bay. Chesapeake Bay has not produced another since 1970. The Hudson River produced a dominant-year class in 1983.

CURRENT TRENDS

From 1929 to 1973, the overall trend in striped bass commercial harvest was upward, from around two million pounds landed in 1929 to 14.7 million in 1973. The young-of-the-year indices, which were not collected in Chesapeake Bay until 1954, show that while striped bass reproduction remained fairly constant from year to year, improved efficiency in the commercial take had led to a far greater catch.

These trends dramatically reversed beginning in 1973. The annual commercial catch dropped to 1.7 million pounds in 1983, a 90-percent decline in 10 years. No dominant-year class has emerged since 1970, and the corrected 1984 young-of-the-year index for Chesapeake Bay was a mere 3.2,* indicating that the catch decline will continue. Commercial striped bass fishing in the Hudson River has been banned since 1976 because of unsafe levels of PCBs in the bass. Although young-of-the-year indices have remained fairly high in the Hudson, these bass historically have made up only a small portion of the coastal migratory stock, and their success has done little to prevent a coastal decline in the catch. Commercial take in North Carolina also is depressed, down from 1.7 million pounds in 1973 to 360,000 in 1983. The young-of-the-year index in the Roanoke River went from 10.52 in 1976 to 0.36 in 1984.** It is estimated that in 1980 alone the coastal decline cost 7,500 jobs and $218 million in economic activity.

---

*The official young-of-the-year index for 1984 was 4.2, but an inadvertent bass stocking a week before one of the samples artificially raised the sample number at one of the sites. The removal of this sampling site resulted in an index of 3.2.
**The 1984 figure is based on a trawl sample.

Two questions continually arise: What has caused the decline? And what should be done to reverse it? Initially, the decline was blamed on two factors: commercial overkill and chemical contamination. Blaming either factor alone for the decline is too simplistic. The level of contaminant-related mortality affects the magnitude of fishing mortality that a striped bass population can withstand, and vice versa.

The majority of past and present research focuses on contaminants. In 1975, Congress authorized the Environmental Protection Agency (EPA) to do a five-year study on the biological decline of the Chesapeake Bay. The study, completed after seven years and $27 million, pointed out the extent of the decline of the bay. For instance, subaquatic vegetation had declined 84 percent since 1971. Areas suffering from anoxic conditions (no dissolved oxygen) had increased 15-fold since 1950, and in Baltimore Harbor more than 450 organic compounds, mostly toxins, were identified. The study documented corresponding declines in the native species of the bay, including dramatic declines in the pounds of oysters, shad, yellow perch, and striped bass taken.[5]

In 1979, Congress passed an amendment to the Anadromous Fish Conservation Act authorizing NMFS and the U.S. Fish and Wildlife Service (FWS) to conduct an Emergency Striped Bass Research Study. Annual reports from this study have been released since 1981. Neither the EPA study nor the Emergency Research Study has determined a precise cause for the bass decline. The Emergency Research Study noted that young striped bass are relatively more susceptible to toxins than many other estuarine species and that the degree of contaminant-induced mortality decreases as salinity increases, suggesting that larval and juvenile bass living in predominantly freshwater are the most severely affected by contaminants.[6]

The striped bass spawns and spends its early life stages in the lower reaches of coastal rivers, watersheds that are highly developed by agriculture, industry, or municipalities. Point and non-point pollution sources dump a variety of heavy metals and organic and inorganic chemicals into these areas. Research has shown a direct correlation between heavy rains and Chesapeake larval striper mortality. The research has not determined whether the mortality is a result of toxic runoff alone or in combination with a new variable in the striped bass equation: acid rain.

Although acid rain is not a new phenomenon, it has only recently been considered in reference to striped bass. Striped bass prefer alkaline water. Larvae do best in water with a pH of 7.5 to 8.5 and have difficulty tolerating pH levels below 7. Moreover, the larvae are very sensitive to sudden chages in pH, even within the optimal range. Precipitation in Maryland averages from a pH of 4.5 to 3.5. Maryland Department of Natural Resources (DNR) scientists monitored the headwaters of 23 streams that feed the bay and historically supported spawning runs of white perch, yellow perch, American shad, hickory shad, alewives, or blueback herring, all species that tend to spawn much farther upstream than the bass. Monitoring took place in April and May, months associated with the acid pulses occurring after heavy rains. All 23 streams monitored fell to pH 5.8 at least once, and six suffered slumps to between pH 4.9 and 4.5. In addition, scientists have noted extremely high levels of dissolved aluminum in many streams. The mobilization of toxic heavy metals, such as aluminum, is a characteristic effect of acid rain.

Overharvest, chemical contamination, and declining pH levels appear to be the dominant causes of the decline in the coastal migratory stock of the North Atlantic striped bass. In addition, several other, more localized factors have reduced and threaten to further reduce bass populations, including dams, hybridization, and highway development.

The Susquehanna River, once possibly the most important bass spawning river in the Chesapeake Bay, now has only a remnant population because dams have left only the first 10 miles open to the bass.

In June 1983, the Maryland Department of Natural Resources released 100,000 white bass/striped bass hybrids into the Patuxent River. Later seine samplings showed that the hybrids survival rate was approximately three times that of the striper. Seen as a possible means of augmenting the depleted striped bass stocks and increasing angling opportunity, the hybrid stocking was to be a major initiative by the state of Maryland. But questions arose as to whether this hybrid would compromise the genetic integrity of the native striped bass. Research has yet to determine if the hybrid will reproduce naturally with the striped bass, but concerns over genetic integrity persist, and Maryland has stopped its hybrid stocking program. Now concerns are being raised that hybrids stocked in surrounding states, and especially in the Susquehanna River in Pennsylvania, are intermingling with striped bass in Maryland's waters.

The coastal decline of the striped bass has fueled heated controversy over a proposed highway and real-estate development off lower Manhattan. Westway, as the project is called, proposes creating 169 new acres of land in the Hudson River on top of what is now a major nursery area for young striped bass. As the Chesapeake Bay striped bass population has declined, the Hudson's importance in the overall East-coast stock has increased greatly. Estimates are that between 20 and 50 percent of the striped bass from North Carolina to Maine may come now from the Hudson. The area proposed for the Westway dredge and fill operation contains old piers that provide shelter for wintering juvenile bass. The Army Corps of Engineers estimates that 20 to 33 percent of the Hudson's bass population could be displaced by the project.[8] FWS suggested that losses could be higher.[9] Mitigation is not seen as a viable possibility.[10]

Some bright spots exist for the striper. On September 23, 1984, two members of the Committee to Restore Resident Stripers to the Kennebec River in Maine worked with the Maine Department of Marine Resources to release some 2,300 striper fingerlings into the estuary formed by the Kennebec and Androscoggin rivers. Although tidal, the estuary's water is fresh because of the large volume of water in the rivers. Historically it supported a striped bass population. Pollution from upstream pulp and paper mills reduced dissolved oxygen levels in the estuary to near zero in the early 1970s, but the levels have risen since, prompting speculation that a return of the striped bass is possible. Committee's funds for the 1984 stocking were raised privately; the state committed manpower and transportation from a federal hatchery in South Attleboro, Massachusetts, where larval bass captured in the Hudson River were raised to fingerlings. Maine officials hope to increase the stocking to 30,000 fingerlings in 1984 and beyond.

A similar reintroduction initiative is being attempted for the Navasink River in New Jersey. In 1984, the New Jersey Division of Marine Fisheries stocked 50,000 striped bass of various sizes into the Swimming River, a tributary of the Navasink, in hopes of establishing a naturally reproducing fishery. The fish used for the stocking came from the FWS Edentown Hatchery in North Carolina and are far less migratory than those stocked in the Kennebec. Thus, the proposed fishery would be limited essentially to the Navasink and its tidal estuary. New Jersey plans to stock another 50,000 in 1985 and 1986.

With $5 million dollars already appropriated under the governor's Chesapeake Bay Initiative, Maryland currently is looking for a site to construct a striped bass hatchery. The hatchery will be an "intercept" hatchery — constructed on a spawning ground. Construction is scheduled to begin in 1987.

A major FWS striped bass stocking is planned for the bay in 1985. FWS, in cooperation with Maryland, has taken larval bass from a number of the bay's tributary streams to several federal hatcheries in the mid-Atlantic area, where the bass will be reared to around six inches, then restocked into the bay. Plans call for more than one million fish to be stocked in 1985 under this program.

MANAGEMENT

Management responsibility for the striped bass is divided among several federal and state authorities. The states have primary management authority within their waters, which include all inland waters and coastal waters within three miles of shore. This authority includes the power to regulate the harvest of striped bass. The states cooperate on fishery matters through the Atlantic States Marine Fisheries Commission. Two federal agencies, NMFS and FWS, share responsibility, but their roles are limited essentially to research, advice, and assistance and, in the case of FWS, bass culture at hatcheries. The present management program has come under increasing criticism because it failed to foresee and prevent the decline in the bass population.

As researchers have been unable to determine that any single chemical is dominant in the decline of the bass, management has focused on the only factor positively identified as a player in the decline, and which can be immediately controlled — overharvest. In 1984, federal legislation was enacted mandating a 55-percent reduction in the striped bass take from Maine to North Carolina by July 1, 1985. The bill, introduced by Representative Gerry Studds (D-Massachusetts) and Senator John Chaffee (R-Rhode Island) was a watered-down version of a bill introduced by Representative Claudine Schneider (R-Rhode Island) that had called for a complete moratorium on the catching of the bass. The Atlantic States Marine Fisheries Commission is responsible for monitoring state compliance. If it finds that a state has not implemented the requirements necessary to meet the goals, then the secretary of Commerce may impose a moratorium on striped bass harvest in that state. The law is a step in the right direction but may not go far enough.

Realizing the gravity of the situation, Maryland in September 1984 implemented a moratorium on the harvest of striped bass in its waters. The moratorium will remain in effect for four years or until the young-of-the-year index is at least 8.0 for three consecutive years.

The ban has highlighted the problems in striped bass management. First, the Potomac River, legally a Maryland water but overseen by a Maryland-Virginia commission, was exempted from the ban. The commission elected to close only the six-week spring season on the river, allowing harvest between June and December. The Potomac is the most productive river for Chesapeake Bay striped bass. In 1984, 631,000 pounds were caught there, compared to less than 500,000 pounds for all other Maryland waters combined. In addition, Virginia fishermen fish heavily in the bay, yet Virginia has resisted implementing a moratorium. Needless to say, Maryland fishermen are unhappy with Virginia, and Maryland now is considering prematurely ending its moratorium if Virginia does not join it.

PROGNOSIS

The striped bass is in trouble, on that there is agreement. Uncertainty surrounds the causes for the decline, and consequently any prognosis is difficult. Research currently is under way on the state and federal levels, and a great deal depends upon its findings.

If overharvest of brood stock proves to be the dominant cause of the decline, then the future of the bass is bright, provided stringent harvest reductions are implemented and enforced. However, if a contaminant or combination of contaminants is found to be the primary cause, recovery will be slower, again dependent upon regulation and enforcement. If acid rain is the cause of the decline, there is little that can be done at the local level. As the buffering ability of the soils diminishes, the problem will escalate, and only comprehensive national legislation controlling sulfur dioxide and nitric oxide emissions can restore the striper.

The striped bass has proved resilient and adaptive to past environmental degradations. If given half a chance, the species might rebound quickly. But it will require decisive and immediate action. The Atlantic States Marine Fisheries Commission plan being adopted to achieve the 55-percent harvest reduction likely will prove inadequate. The 24-inch-minimum size limit recommended in the committee plan is inadequate because less than 50 percent of the fish this size have ever spawned. Other states must follow Maryland's lead and implement a moratorium. It is unlikely that commercial harvest will ever return to levels of the early 1970s.

RECOMMENDATIONS

Continue and expand current research efforts.

Implement an immediate coastal harvest moratorium. When bass populations return to historical levels, manage the species first as a game fish and second, to the extent that populations allow, as a commercial fish. No harvest of any sort should be allowed on spawning or nursery grounds. No deep-water gill netting should be allowed. Initiate a 28-inch minimum because it would allow approximately 90 percent of the fish to spawn before being taken.

Agricultural and industrial pollution control should be accelerated. Attention should be paid to heavy metals, phosphates, and nitrates.

Immediate and comprehensive national emission controls should be implemented to reduce acid rain. Until national controls are implemented, Maryland and other states should implement their own control programs, as New York already has done.

REFERENCES

1. Except where noted, information in this section comes primarily from The Atlantic States Marine Fisheries Commission, *Interstate Fisheries Management Plan for the Striped Bass*, October 1981.
2. Henry B. Bigelow and William C. Schroeder, *Fishes of the Gulf of Maine* (United States Department of the Interior, Fish and Wildlife Service), First Revision, Fisheries Bulletin 74 (Washington, D.C.: U.S. Government Printing Office, 1953), pp. 389-395.
3. Raymond McFarland, A.M., *A History of the New England Fisheries* (New York: University of Pennsylvania Press, 1911), p. 53.
4. George Will, *Baltimore Sun*, October 8, 1984.
5. Environmental Protection Agency, *The Chesapeake Bay Program: Findings and Recommendations*, September 1983.
6. Department of the Interior, Fish and Wildlife Service, *Emergency Striped Bass Research Study*, Report for 1983-84.
7. Robert Boyle, "Rain of Death on the Striper?" *Sports Illustrated*, April 23, 1984, pp. 40-54.

8. Corps of Engineers and U.S. Department of Transportation, *Final Supplemental Environmental Impact Statement - Westway Highway Project*. vol. II, November 1984, p. 38.

9. Letters of Howard Larsen, FWS, to Colonel Griffith Flecher, Army Coprs of Engineers, July 13, 1984; in U.S. Army Corps of Engineers and U.S. Department of Transportation, *Final Supplemental Environmental Impact Statement*, vol. III, Part I, November 1984, p. III-34.

10. Letter of Bruce Higgins, NMFS, to Colonel F. H. Griffis, Corps of Engineers, August 6, 1984, in Corps of Engineers and U.S. Department of Transportation, *Final Supplemental Environmental Impact Statement - Westway Highway Project*, vol. III, Part 1, November 1984.

An emperor goose on its nest in Alaska. Alaska-nesting geese face several threats, including overhunting by man.

Arctic-Nesting Geese

Introduction by David Cline
National Audubon Society Staff

INTRODUCTION

THE VAST AND remote tundra wetlands of Alaska have long provided secure breeding habitat for a host of swans, geese, and ducks. The state's four species, including seven subspecies, of nesting geese are of particular interest because of their popularity with sportsmen, subsistence users, and other wildlife enthusiasts.

Despite the fact that most waterfowl habitats in Alaska are still in essentially pristine condition, the future of arctic-nesting geese appears increasingly precarious. They, like other waterfowl, are limited to specific types of breeding, molting, migration, and wintering habitats. The demands of growing numbers of people are accelerating the loss of these habitats to drainage, reclamation, and pollution. Meanwhile, the birds are becoming more vulnerable to mounting hunting pressure throughout their ranges.

Prompt adoption throughout the flyway of cooperative, coordinated conservation strategies is essential if the skeins of arctic-nesting geese that wing their way south from Alaska each fall are not to become yet another lost North American wildlife spectacle.

The Cackling Canada Goose

by *William Butler*
U.S. Fish and Wildlife Service

Species Description and Natural History

"GOOSE" CONJURES A vision in the minds of many people of the white cheek patches and black head and neck of the Canada goose. The cackling Canada goose (*Branta canadensis minima*), smallest of the 12 races of Canada goose,[1] fits that vision in miniature. Only slightly larger than a mallard, this diminutive Canada goose can be distinguished from others of its species by its small size, short neck, stubby bill, and dark brown, almost purplish breast feathers. Its repeated high-pitched call contrasts with the deeper "honking" of its larger cousins and is the reason for its name.

The cackler's range spans 3,000 miles, from its breeding grounds on the coastal fringe of the Yukon–Kuskokwim Delta (YKD) in Alaska to its wintering area in the central valleys of Oregon and California.[2] Fall migration carries the birds south from the YKD to Bristol Bay and the Alaska Peninsula and across 1,000 to 1,500 miles of the Pacific Ocean to landfall near the mouth of the Columbia River in Oregon. From this area of the rugged Pacific coast, cacklers move inland and disperse southward along the east side of the Cascade Mountains to their wintering grounds.

With the lengthening days of April, spring migration begins, and cacklers venture northward through Oregon and Washington to the coast of British Columbia and the Alaska Panhandle. Upon reaching the secluded marshes and bays of Cook Inlet near Anchorage, Alaska, cacklers rest before moving westward through the majestic passes of the Alaska range to their summer home on the YKD.[3]

Cacklers arrive on the YKD in late April or early May. Nesting occurs on small islands in shallow coastal ponds adjacent to the Bering Sea. Four to five eggs are laid in bowl-like nests lined with grass and down. Incubation is by the female while the male stands guard. Hatching occurs within 26 days,[4] and both parents protect and raise the goslings. Young of the year are on the wing by mid-August. With the freezing temperatures and north winds of September, families of cacklers begin moving south toward Bristol Bay.

Significance of the Species

In 1979 the United States and Canada signed a protocol to amend the Migratory Bird Convention of 1916[5] to legalize spring and summer harvest of waterfowl by natives in the arctic for nutritional and other essential needs. The signers recognized that subsistence harvest by aboriginal peoples is legitimate, that traditional hunting activities are continuing, and that it is not possible to manage an illegal harvest. A legal, regulated spring harvest may be a means for limiting waterfowl take and ensuring that populations are managed properly. As of this writing, however, the Migratory Bird Convention has not been amended.

A major challenge facing waterfowl management in the 1980s is implementation of subsistence harvest regulations without causing damage to waterfowl populations or significantly compromising the interests of other users.[6] Cackling Canada geese are important in the diet of Yupik Eskimos on the YKD and in the hunter's bag in the Pacific Flyway. The cackling Canada goose is highlighted here because its numbers are at the lowest levels ever recorded and intensive management actions are needed to restore its population. It is significant because its plight will focus our attention on solving one of the major waterfowl management challenges of the decade.

HISTORICAL PERSPECTIVE

Historical evidence suggests cacklers in Alaska once were considerably more numerous than they are today. Biologists studying geese in the coastal zone of the YKD during the late 1940s and early 1950s indicated cacklers were the most abundant species present.[7] They made up 60 percent of a post-breeding goose population described as "almost uncountable." In 1959, cackler populations were estimated at 250,000 to 300,000 birds.[8]

During the past 20 years, peak winter counts at Tule Lake and Lower Klamath national wildlife refuges in California have indicated an alarming decline in cackling Canada goose populations.[9] Numbers dropped from 380,000 in 1965 to 26,200 in 1983.

CURRENT TRENDS

Many factors have been identified as potential causes for declines. These include habitat loss and sport hunting on the wintering grounds, spring subsistence hunting and egging by Yupik Eskimos on the YKD, and predation and successive years of poor weather on the breeding grounds. Inadequate annual data on population numbers, spring harvest on YKD, and sport harvest in the Pacific Flyway have made it difficult to manage the population effectively. The failure of management agencies to recognize the problem and the difficulties in balancing legitimate subsistence harvest by an indigenous culture with sound wildlife management practices have further delayed implementation of appropriate management actions. Subsistence harvest on the YKD[10] and sport harvest on the wintering grounds currently are the most important factors affecting the population trends.

MANAGEMENT

Management actions to protect cackling Canada goose populations have been slow in coming. Seventy-five to 89 percent of the cackling goose kill in the Pacific Flyway occurs in California.[11] Hunting regulations implemented in 1975 in California, designed to protect the endangered Aleutian Canada goose (*Branta canadensis leucopareia*) benefited the cackling Canada goose. Further restrictions, specifically aimed at protecting cackling Canada geese, were implemented in 1979. These restrictions resulted in a 39 percent and 65 percent reduction in the kill of cacklers in California after 1975 and 1979.[12]

Studies to provide improved population estimates of cacklers on the wintering grounds and a better understanding of distribution and habitat use began in 1982.[13] Pilot Point on the Alaska Peninsula and Redoubt Bay near Anchorage were identified as critical fall and spring stopover areas in recent migration studies.[14] Efforts to document harvest levels on the YKD were begun in 1980 by staff of the Yukon Delta National Wildlife Refuge.[15]

Representatives from federal agencies, state wildlife management agencies, and sport hunting groups met with native leaders from the YKD during the winter of 1983-84 to cooperatively address the problem of declining cackling Canada geese. These meetings resulted in a revolutionary agreement by the YKD natives to voluntarily stop all hunting and egging of cackling geese. California enacted an emergency closure of cackling Canada goose hunting for the last 12 days of its 1983-84 season. Since the initial agreement, now titled "The Yukon Delta Goose Management Plan," negotiations have continued with the objective of extending the voluntary restrictions on harvest of cackling geese on the YKD through 1985. A total closure of cackling Canada goose hunting in California was enacted for the 1984-85 season. These cooperative efforts represent the first step in restoring cackler populations.

PROGNOSIS

The difficulty of the recovery problems faced by the cackler is suggested by the length of time for population growth.[16] Assuming a starting population of 30,000 birds and an average reproduction of 20 percent in the autumn population, with 85 percent survival, it would take 10 years for the cackler population to reach 150,000 to 200,000 birds. All hunting would have to be eliminated to reach this population goal.

The cooperative efforts begun in 1984 to address declining goose numbers are a start toward meaningful solutions. Currently, restrictions on harvest by the Yukon Delta natives are voluntary, and means to measure and ensure compliance are being developed. However, it will take several years of intensive management efforts before cackler harvest on the YKD can be eliminated. Limited accidental take also will continue in the Pacific Flyway because of difficulties in differentiating cacklers from other "small" subspecies—the dusky Canada goose (*B.c. occidentalis*) and the Taverner's Canada goose (*B.c. taverneri*).

The cackler population probably will continue to decline, but at progressively slower rates. As management actions become effective over the next several years, the population should stabilize. Restoration of cacklers to harvestable levels after the decline is stopped is clearly a long-term process. If the historic Yukon Delta Goose Management Plan is the beginning of cooperative development and implementation of a long-term management plan, hope exists for increasing cackler populations in the future.

RECOMMENDATIONS

Through the cooperative process already begun, a long-term management plan should be developed that outlines time frames, population goals, and management actions to be taken. No sport or subsistence kill should be allowed until a population of at least 110,000 cacklers is reached. Methods for obtaining adequate population information must be implemented on the wintering and breeding grounds. Because subsistence harvest agreements are voluntary, it is especially important to develop a public information program to educate and inform the people of the YKD on all aspects of the Cackling Canada Goose Management Plan. Amending the Migratory Bird Convention of 1916 should be a high priority because it would allow legalization and regulation of subsistence harvest for successful management.

REFERENCES

1. J. Delacour, *The Waterfowl of the World*, vol. 1 (London: Country Life, Limited), 1954.
2. U.C. Nelson and H.A. Hansen, "The Cackling Canada Goose: Its Migration and Management," *North American Wildlife Conference Transactions*, vol. 24 (1959), pp. 174-186.
3. D.E. Timm, "Some Observations of Spring Migratory Waterfowl 1982" (Unpublished Report, Alaska Department of Fish and Game, Anchorage, Alaska, 1982).
4. P.G. Mickelson, "Breeding Biology of Cackling Canada Geese and Associated Species on the Yukon-Kuskokwim Delta, Alaska," *Wildlife Monographs*, No. 45 (1975), pp. 1-35.
5. Convention for the Protection of Migratory Birds, August 16, 1916, United States-Great Britain (on behalf of Canada), 39 Stat. 1702, T.S. No. 628.
6. L.R. Jahn and C. Kabat, "Current Challenges," in A.S. Hawkins, R.C. Hansen, H.K. Nelson and H.M. Reeves, eds., *Flyways Pioneering Waterfowl Management in North America* (Washington, D.C.: Government Printing Office, 1984), pp. 385-386.
7. D.L. Spencer, U.C. Nelson and W.A. Elkins, "America's Greatest Goose-brant Nesting Area," *North American Wildlife Conference Transactions*, vol. 16 (1951), pp. 290-295.
   J.A. Gabrielson and F.C. Lincoln, *The Birds of Alaska* (Washington, D.C.: The Wildlife Management Institute, 1959).
8. Op. cit., Nelson and Hansen, "Cackling Canada Goose," *North American*.
9. E.J. O'Neill, "Fourteen Years of Goose Populations and Trends at Klamath Basin Refuges," in R.J. Jarvis and J.C. Bartonek, eds., *Management and Biology of Pacific Flyway Geese* (Corvallis: Oregon State University Book Stores, Inc., 1979), pp. 316-321.
   D.G. Raveling, "Geese and Hunters of Alaska's Yukon Delta: Management Problems and Political Dilemmas," *North American Wildlife Conference Transactions* (in press).
10. Ibid.
11. Ibid.
12. Ibid.
13. J.C. Johnson and D.G. Raveling, Distribution and Abundance of Cackling Canada Goose During Winter 1982-83, Progress Report to California Department of Fish and Game and U.S. Fish and Wildlife Service (Anchorage: Fish and Wildlife Service, 1983).
14. K.S. Bollinger, Sightings of collared Canada geese. Unpublished report. U.S. Fish and Wildlife Service. Anchorage, Alaska. (1983).

15. J.D. Copp and M. Smith, "A Preliminary Analysis of the Spring Take of Migrating Waterfowl by Yupik Eskimos on the Yukon-Kuskokwim Delta," U.S. Fish and Wildlife Service Report, Bethel, Alaska (1981).
16. P.G. Raveling, "Recovery Potential of Cackling Geese" (Unpublished Report, University of California, Davis, Division of Wildlife and Fisheries Resources, Davis, Calif., 1983).

WILLIAM BUTLER is an FWS migratory bird biologist and pilot in Anchorage, Alaska. He also has worked as a biologist for the Yukon Delta National Wildlife Refuge in Bethel, Alaska, and as environmental specialist for the U.S. Bureau of Reclamation in Nevada.

The Dusky Canada Goose

by David Cline and Cynthia Lenhart
National Audubon Society Staff

SPECIES DESCRIPTION AND NATURAL HISTORY

THE DUSKY CANADA goose (*Branta canadensis occidentalis*) is one of the largest and darkest of the seven subspecies of Canada geese that nest in Alaska. It is second in size only to the Vancouver Canada goose.

The dusky goose nests only on the Copper River Delta, near Cordova, Alaska, and winters primarily in the Willamette Valley of western Oregon, along the lower Columbia River below Portland, and in southwestern Washington, where extensive agricultural lands and a mild, wet climate make the area especially attractive to geese.

SIGNIFICANCE OF THE SPECIES

The dusky is somewhat unusual because it nests in only one specific area. While its numbers are relatively few, it is one of the most heavily hunted of Canada goose subspecies. Management of the dusky, because of the bird's importance to hunters and its relatively small population size, has a major impact on management of other Canada goose subspecies in the same breeding and winter range.

HISTORICAL PERSPECTIVE

The dusky goose was first described by Baird from a specimen collected at Port Townsend, Washington Territory, in 1857.[1] Although specimens were collected in western Oregon in 1914 and in the 1920s,[2] for many years dusky geese were considered nonmigratory.[3] Duskies were uncommon in the Willamette Valley until the late 1940s. Historically, duskies comprised most of the Canada goose population in the valley.[4] However, in the early 1970s the number of Taverner's Canada geese (*B. c. taverneri*) wintering in the valley began to increase. Taverner's now comprise about 80 percent of the valley's wintering Canada goose population.[5]

Two events in the mid-1960s significantly influenced the dusky goose population. In 1964 and 1965 three national wildlife refuges were established in the Willamette Valley. The distribution of geese on the wintering grounds changed accordingly, and in the first six years after the refuges were established, the post-breeding season dusky goose population increased by 40 percent.[6]

In 1964, a severe earthquake uplifted the Copper River Delta by six feet, reducing the quality and quantity of nesting habitat. The nesting grounds were changed from a predominantly brackish-water marsh — maintained by periodic tidal flooding — to a freshwater marsh with tall shrub. Prior to the earthquake, nest density and nesting success were high compared to those of other Canada goose subspecies.[7] For a few years after the earthquake, production may have been influenced favorably by the abundance of flood-free habitat. However, long-term changes apparently have not favored the dusky goose. While the geese continue to nest in the same locations, they are now in a different habitat type as plant succession proceeds. In the last 10 years, changes in vegetation have led to a dramatic increase in predation on both eggs and geese.

The dusky goose midwinter population has ranged from a low of 8,000 in 1952 to a high of 28,000 in 1959. In recent years the population has declined drastically: In 1975 the population was estimated at 26,500, and until 1981 population estimates exceeded 20,000. By 1984, however, the population had plummeted to 10,100.

CURRENT TRENDS

In eight of the past 14 years estimated mortality exceeded estimated production by an average of more than 1,000 birds per year. Hunting is the most significant cause of mortality for the dusky and appears to be the primary factor now controlling population size.

Biologists had hoped that the increase in Taverner's geese would take some of the hunting pressure off the dusky geese, but Taverner's geese have proved to be less vulnerable to hunting.[8] In 1984 duskies accounted for 46 percent of the bagged geese, but only 11.5 percent of the Canada geese on the wintering grounds. Taverner's geese comprised 86.5 percent of the wintering geese, but only 51 percent of the kill. Such disproportionate mortality rates may be explained by differences in behavior and activity patterns between the two races and by possible hunter preference for shooting larger Canada geese to avoid hitting the protected — and relatively small — cackling Canada goose.

In a healthy goose population, the number of young harvested usually outnumbers the number of adults harvested. Between 1964 and 1966, 22.3 to 38.5 percent of the duskies harvested were adults.[9] Between 1975 and 1983, the number of adults in the bag jumped to between 46.7 and 64.1 percent (an average of 55.8 percent),[10] further evidence of the dusky's poor reproductive success and overall population decline.

MANAGEMENT

In 1973 the Pacific Flyway Council adopted a management plan with the principal objective of maintaining an annual population of between 20,000 and 25,000 dusky geese. In 1983, however, the population started to show signs of a severe decline, and the hunting season in western Oregon and southwestern Washington was shortened. The take still was heavy that year, however, and the population declined to the new low of 10,100 in 1984. The season length and bag limit were reduced, but even so the dusky kill was too high, finally prompting an emergency closure of the season.

A primary objective of the management plan is balancing mortality with production. In order to estimate the number of duskies killed, five management areas in the Willamette Valley and along the Columbia River are being closely monitored. These areas are estimated to make up 16 percent of the total dusky take. In 1984, an estimated 2,184 duskies were produced on those five management areas. Any hunter kill exceeding 350 birds would indicate overharvest. As of December 2, 1985, — only 16 days into the 30-day season — 561 duskies had been harvested on the five areas. This indicated a total kill of approximately 3,500 geese, well above the acceptable level. Through emergency procedures, the dusky hunting season was closed.

PROGNOSIS

If the downward slide in the dusky population is not reversed, federal designation as a threatened species under the Endangered Species Act is a distinct possibility. No magic number has been established for such a designation, but a population level of 7,000 has been discussed as a possible trigger for a formal status review. Biologists see no reason to believe that production on the breeding grounds will improve and calculate that — even with no hunting — it would take the dusky a minimum of five to seven years to recover to the population objective of 20,000.

RECOMMENDATIONS

Recommendations for recovery of the dusky include a closure of the season in portions of western Oregon, southwestern Washington, and the Copper River Delta, and a ban on the collection of eggs or goslings on the breeding grounds.

REFERENCES

1. S. F. Baird, *Birds, Reports of Explorations and Surveys for a Railroad Route from the Mississippi River to the Pacific Ocean.* vol. 9 (1858), p. 766.
2. S. G. Jewett, "The white-cheeked goose in Oregon," *Condor*, vol. 34, (1932), p. 136.
3. P. A. Taverner, "A study of *Branta canadensis* (*Linnaeus*) The Canada Goose," *Ann. Rept. Natl. Mus. Canada*, (1931), pp. 28-40.
   I. N. Gabrielson and S. G. Jewett, *Birds of Oregon* (Corvallis, Oregon: Oregon St. College, 1940), 650 pp.
   J. Delacour, *The Waterfowl of the World*, Vol. 1, (London: Country Life Lmtd., 1954), 284 pp.
4. H. A. Hansen, "Canada geese of coastal Alaska," *Transactions of the North American Wildlife Conference,* vol. 27, (1962), pp. 301-329.
   J. A. Chapman, C. J. Henny, and H. M. Wight, "The status, population dynamics and harvest of the dusky Canada goose." *Wildlife Monograph*, vol. 18 (1969), p. 1-48.
   S. G. Simpson and R. L. Jarvis, "Comparative ecology of several subspecies of Canada geese during winter in western Oregon," in *Management and biology of*

Pacific Flyway Geese, R. L. Jarvis and J. C. Bartonek, eds., (Corvallis, Oregon: OSU Book Stores, Inc., 1979), pp. 223-241.

5. R. L. Jarvis and J. E. Cornely, "Recent changes in wintering populations of Canada geese in western Oregon/southwestern Washington," in *Waterfowl in Winter*, M. W. Weller, ed., in press.

6. D. E. Timm, R. G. Bromley, D. E. McKnight, and R. S. Rodgers, "Management evolution of dusky Canada geese," in *Management and Biology of Pacific Flyway Geese*, R. L. Jarvis and J. C. Bartonek, eds., (Corvallis, Oregon: OSU Book Stores, Inc., 1979), pp. 322-330.

7. S. T. Olsen, Copper River Delta banding operations, USFWS Federal Aid for Wildlife Restoration Quarterly Progress Report, Project W-3-R-9, Work Plan C., (Juneau, Alaska: USFWS, 1953), pp. 34-40.
C. E. Trainer, "The 1959 western Canada goose (*Branta canadensis occidentalis*) study on the Copper River Delta, Alaska," in Annual Waterfowl Report (Juneau, Alaska: USFWS, 1959), 9 pp.
H. A. Hansen, "Loss of waterfowl production to tide floods," *Journal of Wildlife Management*, vol. 25 (1961), pp. 242-248.

8. Op. cit., Simpson and Jarvis, "Comparative ecology of several subspecies of Canada geese during winter in western Oregon," 223-241.
Op. cit., Jarvis and Cornely, "Recent changes in wintering populations of Canada geese in western Oregon/southwestern Washington."

9. Op. cit., Chapman, et al., "The status, population dynamics and harvest of the dusky Canada goose."

10. Op. cit., Jarvis and Cornely. "Recent changes in wintering populations of Canada geese in western Oregon/southwestern Washington."

The Aleutian Canada Goose

by Michael J. Amaral
U.S. Fish and Wildlife Service

SPECIES DESCRIPTION AND NATURAL HISTORY

ALEUTIAN CANADA GEESE (*Branta canadensis leucopareia*) are small, white-cheeked geese that resemble other Canada geese such as cackling Canada geese (*B. c. minima*), Taverner's Canada geese (*B. c. taverneri*), and lesser Canada geese (*B. c. parvipes*). Cackling Canada geese are the smallest of these races, while lessers are the largest. Measurements of Aleutians overlap at the upper end of the range of cacklers and at the lower end of Taverner's and lessers.[1] Aleutians also have a more tapered bill than Taverner's when viewed from above.

Although no known single characteristic absolutely distinguishes Aleutian Canada geese from other subspecies, a combination of morphological characteristics can reliably separate most of the birds.[2] Nearly all Aleutians have a ring of white feathers at the base of their black necks. The ring averages about an inch in width in adults and half that in immatures. Some but not all cacklers, Taverner's, and lessers also have white neck rings. Other characteristics that are more pronounced in Aleutians than in other small subspecies are an abrupt forehead, separation of the cheek patches by black feathering along the throat, and a narrow border of dark feathering along the bottom of the white neck ring.[3]

Aleutian Canada geese currently nest on Buldir and Chagulak islands in the Aleutian Archipelago, Alaska. A small breeding population recently was reestablished on Agattu Island, which lies approximately 80 miles west of Buldir in the western Aleutians. During migration, Aleutian geese sometimes stop along the Oregon coast (Tillamook, Coos, and Curry counties) and occasionally are reported from Washington state. Aleutian geese winter primarily in the San Joaquin Valley of California. Northwest California, particularly Castle Rock and nearby pastures around Crescent City, is a major spring staging area.[4] Byrd and Woolington (1983)[5] have summarized the breeding biology of the Aleutian Canada goose from their work on Buldir Island. The geese arrive in their Aleutian Island breeding grounds in early May, and egg laying peaks during the last week in June. Average clutch size is 5.6 eggs. Hatching occurs in late June or early July, and goslings usually can fly by August 21.

Unlike most other Canada geese, Aleutian geese do not nest near water but instead seek out steep, densely vegetated slopes. Most geese migrate from the breeding grounds in September, sometimes stopping along the Oregon coast en route to the wintering grounds in California, where they begin arriving in October.

SIGNIFICANCE OF THE SPECIES

The Aleutian Canada goose is the only subspecies of the large and successful *Branta canadensis* group whose range once included both the North American and Asian continents. When the Aleutian goose was abundant, it was an important item in the diet of Aleuts in the Aleutian Islands. Numbers of geese were even domesticated by these native peoples for winter food. Until 1975, it also was among waterfowl hunted recreationally and for food by hunters in the Pacific Flyway, particularly California. The Aleutian Canada goose is now protected by both the Endangered Species Act and the Migratory Bird Treaty Act. It is one of only two geese in the world currently recognized as endangered with extinction. The other, the Hawaiian Island Nene (*Nesochen* [= *Branta*] *scandvicensis*), is thought to be a close descendant of the Aleutian goose. Perhaps the greatest significance of the Aleutian Canada goose is that its steady recovery over the past decade symbolizes what can be accomplished when state and federal agencies and waterfowl interest groups work together toward a common goal.

HISTORICAL PERSPECTIVE

The Aleutian Canada goose is listed as an endangered species pursuant to the Endangered Species Act of 1973,[6] as amended. The precipitous decline of this subspecies occurred as a result of arctic fox introductions to most of its Aleutian Islands breeding habitat. Hunting along migration and wintering areas probably prevented remnant populations from recovering.

Aleutian geese once numbered in the thousands in just the Near Island portion of their range.[7] By the mid-1970s the Aleutian goose was reduced to fewer than 800 birds. Delineating the historic range of this subspecies is difficult, but the range appears to have included most of the larger Aleutian Islands from the Islands of Four Mountains to Attu Island,[8] Bering Island in the Commander Islands,[9] and some of the Kuril Islands.[10] Aleutian Canada geese are said to have wintered historically in Japan and from British Columbia to California.[11] Almost nothing is known of the former abundance of the birds. In 1910 they were reported to be the most abundant bird on Agattu where they bred in the thousands.[12] Thousands also were reported on Attu Island during fall migration in the 1880s.[13]

The Russian–American Company, a fur-trading firm, introduced arctic foxes in the Aleutians about 1836,[14] a practice continued by United States citizens until about 1930. By 1962, the only known breeding population of Aleutian Canada geese was on Buldir Island,[15] one of the few Aleutian Islands to escape fox introduction. The breeding population discovered on Chagulak Island in 1982[16] is also probably a remnant population.

Other factors that may have contributed to the decline of Aleutian Canada geese include hunting by natives on the nesting area and during migration in Alaska[17] and hunting on the wintering grounds,[18] as well as loss of habitat there. Historic accounts[19] indicate that considerable numbers of the birds were domesticated by natives in the western Aleutians.

CURRENT TRENDS

The wild population now numbers about 4,000 birds,[20] a fivefold increase since the active recovery effort was initiated in the early 1970s. The Aleutian Canada goose has been increasing steadily since hunting was halted in the migration and wintering grounds in 1975. These closures continue today. Approximately 100 birds are being held in captivity at private and university waterfowl facilities in the United States, Canada, and Japan. However, release of captive-raised birds is not presently an integral part of the recovery effort.

Foremost among the many factors responsible for the positive population trend is complete protection from hunting in the migration and wintering grounds. The recognition and protection provided by the Endangered Species Act has facilitated the acquisition or easement of important Aleutian Canada goose migration and wintering habitat in California. In the Aleutians, arctic fox eradication efforts have eliminated these introduced predators from several former breeding islands, including Alaid/ Nizki, Agattu, Amchitka, and Rat. By capturing wild geese and transplanting them to Agattu Island, a small breeding population recently was reestablished there. Public support for the recovery program continues to be an important contributing factor to the remarkable progress this subspecies has made.

MANAGEMENT

The Aleutian goose is the focus of a comprehensive recovery program both in the Aleutian Islands and in the California wintering grounds. Fox eradication efforts presently are under way on selected smaller Aleutian Islands. Efforts to secure Environmental Protection Agency authorization for use of toxicants on larger target islands were initiated in 1984. Former nesting islands such as Kiska and Kanaga appear too large and fox populations too great for removal by mechanical means.

Unless these introduced predators can be removed, these larger islands will remain unavailable as breeding habitat for Aleutian geese and other ground nesting birds in the Aleutians. Concurrent with the fox removal program is the effort to reintroduce Aleutian geese to these nesting islands where foxes have been eliminated. Agattu and Amchitka currently are targets for Aleutian goose reintroductions. A small number of nesting pairs found on Agattu Island in 1984 marked the first nesting of this species on the island since the 1930s.

In the wintering grounds, efforts to maintain and protect habitat needed by migrating and wintering flocks continue. State and federal biologists monitor the number, movements, and distribution of the population in the wintering grounds. The success of these efforts is demonstrated clearly in the population increases observed over the past decade. It also is noteworthy that annual mortality to illegal hunting usually amounts to far less than one percent of the total population. As an endangered species, the Aleutian Canada goose is protected by law. Activities that are federally funded or authorized must be evaluated for their impact on the Aleutian goose or its essential habitat.

The captive flock is important for education, research, and display and to maintain a gene pool separate from the wild population. Aleutian geese formerly wintered in Japan, and the geese loaned to Japan in 1983 are part of an effort to re-establish this wintering tradition. The captive propagation of Aleutian geese for release in the wild is not part of the current recovery program in the United States.

All of the Aleutian Island breeding habitat is part of the Aleutian Island Unit of the Alaska Maritime National Wildlife Refuge and thus is quite secure. The continued presence of arctic foxes remains the only impediment to the eventual repopulation of former breeding habitat.

Key migration and wintering habitats have been identified by closely monitoring the movements of the birds over the past decade. Many areas have been acquired and added to the National Wildlife Refuge System, for example Castle Rock in Del Norte County and the Butte Sink Wildlife Area in Butte County, California. Other areas, such as the Lake Earl Wildlife Area and State Park in Del Norte County and the San Joaquin Grasslands in Merced County, California, are protected through easements or state management practices. Aleutian geese are protected from hunting on all key migration and wintering habitat.

After early efforts to reintroduce captive-raised Aleutian geese to the wild proved unsuccessful, a program in which wild family groups were transplanted to fox-free islands was initiated. Thus far, geese have been reintroduced successfully to Agattu Island. Geese also are observed frequently on Alaid/Nizki islands. However, nesting here has not yet been confirmed. Aleutian geese have been released on Attu and Amchitka Islands but have not become reestablished there. Amchitka remains an important target island for reintroduction.

Currently, two research efforts involve Aleutian geese. One is an effort to identify and monitor the incidence of coccidial parasitism in the breeding populations on Buldir and Chagulak Island. The other is studying a small population of *Branta canadensis* discovered on Kaliktagik Island (south of the Alaska Peninsula) in the Semidi Island group to determine its taxonomic relationship to the endangered Aleutian Canada goose.*

PROGNOSIS

The future of the Aleutian Canada goose appears very bright. If the population trend continues at the present rate, it is likely that this subspecies will be delisted within five years. Numbers of geese have increased fivefold in the past decade, and the fall 1984 population estimate, 4,000 birds, is a new high. With the exception of remnant populations of foxes, the Aleutian Island breeding habitat appears secure. Most of the key migration and wintering areas also have been protected through acquisition, easements, land-use agreements, and hunting closures. The remaining potential threats to the full recovery of this subspecies are mortality factors such as disease or weather-related catastrophes and the continued presence of arctic foxes on former breeding islands.

RECOMMENDATIONS

Current recovery activities, including protection and closure to hunting of key migration and wintering areas, removal of introduced arctic foxes from as many Aleutian Islands as possible, and reintroduction of wild family groups to fox-free islands, should continue until the subspecies is restored to a secure status within its range. The Aleutian Canada Goose Recovery Team[21] has recommended specific criteria for reclassification from endangered to threatened status and, eventually, for removal from the list of threatened and endangered species.

---

*By mid-1985, this project had provided genetic evidence indicating that the 80 to 85 Kaliktagik birds are Aleutian geese.

REFERENCES

1. P. H. Johnson, D. E. Timm and P. F. Springer, "Morphological Characteristics of Canada Geese in the Pacific Flyway," in R. L. Jarvis and J. C. Bartonek, eds., *Management and Biology of Pacific Flyway Geese* (Corvallis: Oregon State University Bookstore, Inc., 1979), pp. 56-80.
2. Ibid.
3. Ibid.
4. J. L. Martin, Aleutian Canada Goose Recovery Plan (Anchorage: U. S. Fish and Wildlfie Service, 1982).
5. G. V. Byrd and D. W. Woolington, "Breeding Biology, Habitat Utilization and Populations Structure of Aleutian Canada Geese on Buldir Island" (Unpublished manuscript, Aleutian Islands NWR, 1983).
6. Pub. L. 93-205, 87 stat. 884.
7. O. J. Murie and V. B. Scheffer, *Fauna of the Aleutian Islands* (Washington, D.C.: Government Printing Office, 1959).
8. A. C. Bent, Notes on Birds Observed During a Brief Visit to the Aleutian Islands and Bering Sea in 1911, *Smithsonian Miscellaneous Collections*, 56(32) (1919), pp. 1-29.
   A. H. Clark, "Birds Collected and Observed During the Cruise of the United States Fisheries Steamer 'Albatross' in the North Pacific Ocean, and in the Bering, Okhotsk, Japan, and Eastern Seas, from April to December 1906." *Proceeding U. S. National Museum*, vol. 38 (1910), pp. 25-74.
   W. Jochelson, "History, Ethnology, and Anthropology of the Aleut." *Carnegie Institute Washington Publications*, 432 (1932).
   Op. cit., Murie and Scheffer, *Fauna of the Aleutian Islands*.
   E. W. Nelson, Birds of the Bering Sea and the Arctic Ocean. *Cruise of the Revenue-Steamer Corwin in Alaska and N.W. Arctic Ocean in 1881* (Washington, D.C.: Government Printing Office, 1883).
   L. M. Turner, U. S. Army, *Contributions to the Natural History of Alaska*, Results of investigations made chiefly in the Yukon District, and the Aleutian Islands; conducted under the auspices of the Signal Service U.S. Army, extending from May 1874, to August 1881. No. II. (Washington, D.C.: Government Printing Office, 1886).
9. L. Stejneger, "Results of Ornithological Expeditions in the Commander Islands and Kamtschatak." *Bulletin U.S. National Museum*, vol. 29 (1885), pp. 1-382.
10. H. J. Snow, *Notes in the Kuril Islands*, (London: Royal Geographical Society, 1897).
11. J. Delacour, *The Waterfowl of the World*, vol. 1 (London: Country Life, Limited, 1954).
12. Op. cit., Clark, "Birds Collected and Observed," *Proceedings U.S. National Museum*.
13. Op. cit., Turner, *Contributions to the Natural History of Alaska*.
14. P. A. Tikhmenev, *Historical Review of the Formation of the Russian-American Company and Its Activities Up to the Present Time* (Berkeley: Library of Congress and Bancroft Library, 1863).
15. R. D. Jones, "Buldir Island, Site of a Remnant Breeding Population of Aleutian Canada Geese," *Wildlife Trust Annual*, vol. 14 (1963), pp. 80-84.
16. E. P. Bailey and J. L. Trapp, "A Second Wild Breeding Population of Aleutian Canada Goose," *American Birds* (1984) pp. 284-286.

17. Op. cit., Turner Contributions to the Natural History of Alaska.
18. J. Grinnel, H. C. Bryant, and T. I. Storer, The Game Birds of California (Berkeley: University of California Press, 1918).
19. Op. cit., Nelson, Birds of the Bering Sea and the Arctic Ocean.
20. Paul Springer, personal communication.
21. Op. cit., Martin, Aleutian Canada goose Recovery Plan.

MICHAEL AMARAL for the past five years has worked with the Endangered Species Division in Anchorage, Alaska, particularly on the recovery programs for both the Aleutian Canada goose and peregrine falcon. He received his masters in wildlife science from the University of Washington researching tufted and horned puffins in the Barren Islands of Alaska.

The Black Brant

by Christian P. Dau and Mary E. Hogan
U.S. Fish and Wildlife Service

SPECIES DESCRIPTION AND NATURAL HISTORY

THE PACIFIC BLACK brant (*Branta bernicla migricans*) is a small, stocky, short-necked goose. The head is dark with a short bill and sloping forehead. The white collar at the top of the neck is incomplete behind. The breast and belly of the black brant are a uniform dusky brown, making it one of the darkest waterfowl.[1] Pacific brant are truly marine waterfowl, spending all but summer in salt and brackish waters. Eelgrass determines brant distribution from fall through early spring. During nesting season grasses and sedges of coastal salt meadows are the brant's principal food.

The black brant nests in coastal areas from the central Canadian arctic west to Wrangel Island in the Soviet Union. Up to 50 percent of this population is thought to breed on the coastal fringe of the Yukon-Kuskokwim Delta (YKD) in Alaska. Molt occurs on or near production areas. A key molting area is in the vicinity of Teshekpuk Lake on Alaska's North Slope, where nearly 32,000 brant summer. The most critical fall-use areas are Izembek Lagoon and associated bays and lagoons at the tip of the Alaska Peninsula. Probably the entire black brant population spends six to nine weeks there each fall accumulating the energy reserves needed to complete the fall migration to wintering areas as far south as the west coast of Mexico.

Black brant migrating in spring arrive at Izembek Lagoon in late April and early May. They reach maximum numbers on the Yukon Delta breeding grounds by the last week in May[2] and in arctic and western Canada by the middle of June.[3] The birds tend to nest in colonies. Eggs are laid at the rate of one per day, and the average clutch is four eggs.[4] The incubation period averages 24 days, and another 50 days are required to bring the young to fledging. Young birds are led to tidal flats, and the adults undergo a month-long flightless period at this time. Non-breeding brant molt earlier than breeding birds and undergo a molt migration.[5]

Brant leave the breeding areas in late August and early September. They appear at Izembek Lagoon during the third week of August and stay until late October or early November. Brant usually arrive in the Puget Sound area, on the California coast, and in Mexico sometime between November 5 and November 20, depending on when they left Izembek Lagoon.[6] During mild winters, several thousand brant may remain at Izembek.

In winter, brant are found from Alaska into Mexico, with largest numbers on the outer coast of Baja California. In February and March the birds shift northward, with concentrations in Humboldt Bay, California. They continue northward and follow the Alaskan coast. A few stop in the Kodiak area. Arrivals at Izembek continue from April to very early June.[7]

SIGNIFICANCE OF THE SPECIES

Because the brant breeds in the Soviet Union, Alaska, and Canada and winters from Alaska to Mexico, it is of international importance. Natural climatic phenomenon such as delayed spring breakup and flooding due to storm surges, in combination with human and animal predation, have caused dramatic fluctuations in annual production and population size.

The three-year moving mean population, determined by midwinter aerial counts, has declined from 156,000 in 1979-81 to 121,000 in 1981-83. The 1981 Black Brant Management Plan, as recommended by the Pacific Flyway Council, calls for closing all sport hunting of brant if the three-year running average drops below 120,000.

HISTORICAL PERSPECTIVE

Early explorers of arctic regions reported little statistical data on brant but frequently mentioned "large numbers." Immense numbers of migrating "Eskimo geese," as brant were known locally, were reported along the Yukon River, Alaska, in 1884.[8] The YKD was identified as an important breeding ground for brant.[9] Since the mid-1960s, staff of the Yukon Delta National Wildlife Refuge (formerly Clarence Rhode National Wildlife Refuge) have monitored brant reproduction on the refuge and prepared an annual density index to document trends in numbers of breeding birds. While these inventories were limited in scope, biologists were able to make some qualitative assessments of waterfowl productivity, and in 1979 field biologists began to voice concerns about declining numbers of breeding brant.[10]

Changes also have occurred on the wintering grounds. The distribution of wintering black brant has changed significantly in recent years. From 1954 through 1958, the average number of brant along the coasts of Washington, Oregon, and California was 54,491. Since 1969, wintering brant along the Pacific coast states have averaged about 9,850, with the majority wintering in Washington. A corresponding increase in numbers of brant wintering in Mexico began in 1960. The wintering population in Baja continued to increase until 1972, and since then a slight decrease has occurred.[11] The reasons for this shift are not documented but may be related to food, disturbance, and/or hunting. Human disturbance in the coastal waters of California increased considerably during the period when the southward shift of wintering brant occurred and is believed to be the most important factor in the decrease of brant there.

CURRENT TRENDS

Brant numbers have been determined yearly since 1954 by midwinter aerial counts conducted by the U. S. Fish and Wildlife Service (FWS) in cooperation with the three Pacific coast states and Mexico. The population remained relatively stable at approximately 140,000 birds along the Pacific coast, at least until 1970,[12] but began to decline in 1972, reaching a low estimate of 109,314 black brant in 1983. In 1984,

133,430 birds were counted with a three-year moving average of 121,262.[13] Fall counts at Izembek National Wildlife Refuge in 1984 suggested the population had declined 16 percent to 123,607 brant after a summer of poor production on the YKD.[14] However, the 1985 midwinter count on the Pacific coast totaled 144,800 brant. The total population count does not reflect the decline that is occurring on the Yukon Delta. Years of poor reproduction obviously contributed to reduced fall flights, but a less measurable contributing factor is subsistence harvest of adults, young, and eggs by natives throughout the Alaskan breeding areas.

MANAGEMENT

In January 1984, FWS, the Alaska Department of Fish and Game (ADFG), California Department of Fish and Game (CDFG), and Association of Village Council Presidents agreed to restrict subsistence take of black brant to the pre-nesting and post-fledging periods. This agreement was known as the "Hooper Bay Agreement," but was updated in 1985 and titled "The Yukon Delta Goose Management Plan." Talks are under way between the United States and Canada to amend the Migratory Bird Treaty Act[15] in order to enable legal regulation of spring harvest, with options to set bag limits, seasons, zone closures, and harvest checks.

A goal of 50 percent reduction in sport harvest of black brant was adopted by the Pacific Flyway Council in 1984. For the 1984-85 season, bag limits in Alaska were halved. The California bag limit was cut by a third.

In 1980, FWS initiated a program to obtain spring subsistence harvest information in 11 villages on the YKD. Each year two volunteers interview members of goose-hunting households throughout the season. A cooperative information/education program implemented by FWS, ADFG, and the association provides information to villages about the need to conserve geese on the YKD.

Other management actions include a cooperative effort between FWS and the Direccion General De Fauna Silvester of Mexico to obtain sport harvest information for brant wintering there. A management plan for Pacific coast brant that serves as a guide to regional agencies and states has been prepared by the Technical Committee of the Pacific Flyway Council.

Loss or alteration of habitats has been significant on the Pacific coast. In spite of protection, eelgrass beds are threatened by enterprises ranging from mariculture to the construction of canal towns.[16] Even where eelgrass beds are protected, human use of some bays may simply crowd out the brant.

Some 50 percent of the most important waterfowl nesting habitat within 15 miles of the coast on the YKD soon will be conveyed to native corporate ownership under the Alaska National Interest Lands Conservation Act. Commercial and recreational development, oil and gas exploration, and commercial reindeer grazing are potential threats.

Virtually all major staging, migration, and nesting areas in Alaska are threatened with the impacts of oil and gas development. Principal nesting areas of brant on the Yukon Delta, on the Alaskan arctic coast, and in the Canadian western arctic are adjacent to areas either already leased or scheduled for lease sales for petroleum development. Up to 25 percent of the Pacific brant population molt in the Teshekpuk Lake area within the National Petroleum Reserve-Alaska, 37,000 square miles of federal lands lying between the Brooks Range and the Arctic Ocean on the North Slope. Congress gave the secretary of the Interior the authority to conduct a competitive oil and gas leasing program in the reserve.[17] Oil spills and increased human activity and disturbance threaten this area. The principal staging area of brant at Izembek Lagoon will be threatened by development of the petroleum resources of the St. George Basin and the North Aleutian Shelf. Increased air traffic associated with oil exploration already has disturbed staging brant at Izembek.

The potential for reintroduction of brant in Alaska appears good. In the past, large colonies of nesting geese occurred on the Seward Peninsula, but it is suspected that exploitation of the birds by local residents eliminated most nesting geese. However, since good habitat remains, the expansion of nesting areas in Alaska may be feasible provided protection is given during spring and summer.

Management of a species is dependent upon a data base. Numbers, distribution, survival, and recruitment of brant are important data needs. Studies to determine brant colony dynamics and annual production of the Yukon Delta National Wildlife Refuge will continue, as will annual counts of brant at key Pacific Flyway staging and wintering areas.

PROGNOSIS

Cooperative efforts among federal and state agencies, subsistence users, and sportsmen's groups are cause for optimism about the future of black brant. Management actions initiated in the past four years have been designed specifically to halt the black brant decline.

Hunting during fall and winter was reduced significantly by 1984 restrictions. If the three-year average kill falls below 120,000, all hunting will be stopped. Agreements calling for restrictions on take during spring and summer on the YKD are promising.

Perhaps one of the most important needs is a comprehensive, nationwide education and information program. FWS has established an education program to promote understanding of wildlife conservation, research, and management concepts as they relate to goose populations on the Yukon Delta. The intent of the program is to teach that geese are a shared resource and management responsibility. Through understanding and subsequent management actions, the decline of brant can be halted and populations restored to optimum levels.

RECOMMENDATIONS

The population objective for Pacific coast black brant is a midwinter count of 185,000 birds.[18] The sport kill should be maintained at reduced levels until the population rises above 140,000. Reduced subsistence take should be encouraged through voluntary agreements that ban egg gathering and hunting during nesting, rearing, and molting.

Habitat must be available in sufficient quality and quantity to support the desired population levels. Threats to all production, molting, staging, and wintering areas should be determined, and any steps needed to protect threatened habitat should be taken. Strategies for habitat protection include land exchanges, state or federal refuge acquisitions, easements, or cooperative management agreements.

REFERENCES

1. F.C. Bellrose, *Ducks, Geese, and Swans of North America* (Harrisburg: Stackpole Books, 1976), 544 pp.
   R.S. Palmer, "Waterfowl," *Handbook of North American Birds*, vol. 2, part 1 (New Haven and London: Yale University Press, 1976).

2. P.G. Mickelson, "Breeding Biology of Cackling Goose and Related Species on the Yukon-Kuskokwim Delta, Alaska," *Wildlife Monograph*, vol. 45 (1975), pp. 1-35.
3. T.W. Barry, "The Geese of the Anderson River Delta, Northwest Territories" (Ph.D. dissertation, Univ. of Alberta, Edmonton, 1966).
4. Op. cit., Mickelson, "Breeding Biology," *Wildlife Monograph*
5. J.G. King, "The Swans and Geese of Alaska's Arctic Slope," *Wildfowl*, vol. 21 (1970), pp. 11-17.
   D.V. Derksen, M.W. Weller and W.D. Eldridge, "Distributional Ecology of Geese Molting Near Teshekpuk Lake National Petroleum Reserve-Alaska," in R.L. Jarvis and J.C. Bartonek, eds., *Management and Biology of Pacific Flyway Geese* (Corvallis: OSU Book Stores, Inc., 1979), pp. 189-207.
6. Op. cit., Palmer, *Handbook of North American Birds.*
7. Ibid.
8. S.F. Baird, T.M. Brewer, and R. Ridgway. 1884. Waterbirds of North America 1:473. *Memoirs of the Museum of Comparative Zoology*, Harvard University, vol. 7.
9. J.A. Gabrielson and F.C. Lincoln. *The Birds of Alaska* (Washington, D.C. : The Wildlife Management Institute, 1959).
10. R.L. Garrett, W.I. Butler, and M.L. Wege, An Evaluation of Productivity and Mortality Factors Influencing Goose Populations, U.S. Fish and Wildlife Service Report, Bethel, Alaska (1983).
11. Pacific Flyway Technical Committee, "Management Plan Pacific Coast Brant," Pacific Flyway Council Report (1981).
12. R.H. Smith and G.H. Jensen, "Black Brant on the Mainland Coast of Mexico," *Transaction of the 35th North American Wildlife and Natural Resources Conference* (1970), pp. 227-241.
13. J.C. Bartonek, Pacific Flyaway Waterfowl Report. No. 91. May 1984. 170pp.
14. B. Conant and J.I. Hodges, "Ocular Estimates of Fall Staging Black Brant Near Cold Bay, Alaska," (Abstract) Alaska Bird Conference and Workshop, Anchorage, Alaska (1985).
15. Convention for the Protection of Migratory Birds, August 16, 1916, United States-Great Britain (on behalf of Canada), 39 Stat. 1702, T.S. No. 628.
16. Op. cit., Pacific Flyway Technical Committee, "Management Plan," Pacific Flyway Council Report.
17. J.G. King and J.I. Hodges, "A Preliminary Analysis of Goose Banding on Alaska's Arctic Slope," in R.J. Jarvis and J.C. Bartonek, eds., *Management and Biology of Pacific Flyway Geese* (Corvallis: OSU Book Stores, Inc., 1979), pp. 176-188.
18. Op. cit., Pacific Flyway Technical Committee, "Management Plan," Pacific Flyway Council Report.

CHRISTIAN P. DAU is wildlife biologist for the Izembek National Wildlife Refuge, Alaska. Primarily interested in waterfowl biology and management, he helps draft flyway management plans for the tundra swan, cackling Canada goose, black brant, and others for the Pacific Flyway Technical Committees.

MARY HOGAN, before joining the FWS as assistant migratory bird specialist in the Alaska region, worked as a biologist in the FWS Special Studies Division. She has studied breeding seabirds, wintering waterbirds, and avian use of wetlands.

The Pacific White-fronted Goose

by Calvin J. Lensink
U.S. Fish and Wildlife Service

SPECIES DESCRIPTION AND NATURAL HISTORY

THE PACIFIC WHITE-fronted goose (*Anser albifrons frontalis*) — usually known more simply as the white-fronted goose or white-front, and often as specklebelly or yellow-legs — is aptly described by both its technical and common names. It is a medium sized (five to seven pounds), grayish-brown goose characterized by white face, orange legs, black barring or splotches on the breast, and pinkish bill. Immature birds in their first year lack the white face and black barring on the breast, but are distinguished from other geese by yellowish bills and legs. The taxonomy of white-fronted geese is much confused and the subject of continuing debate, but the Pacific white-front usually is considered one of only two subspecies of white-fronted goose in North America. The other is the rare Tule white-fronted goose (*A. a. gambelli*), a slightly larger bird with a darker, chocolate brown head and neck.

Chances are that almost any white-fronted goose you see in North America will be the Pacific white-front. Tule geese are known to nest only in the Cook Inlet region of Alaska and winter primarily in a few localities in the central valley of California, although a few individuals may migrate through the Central Flyway into Texas and Mexico.[1] On the other hand, Pacific white-fronts are a hundred or so times more abundant and nest in areas that are widespread throughout northern Alaska and northern Canada. Moreover, they migrate through both the Pacific and Central flyways to wintering areas in California's central valley and in the coastal regions of Louisiana and Texas and to widespread localities in Mexico.[2]

Although white-fronted geese nest as many discrete breeding populations, perhaps with distinctive migration patterns and wintering areas, they are managed collectively as Pacific Flyway and midcontinent populations. The midcontinent population is arbitrarily divided into eastern and western subpopulations. The Pacific population nests almost exclusively on the Yukon Delta in western Alaska, with only a few birds, probably less than 10 percent, originating in the adjacent Innoko and Bristol Bay regions. Survey and banding records indicate that in late September and early October most geese from the delta migrate nonstop more than 3,000 miles to major fall staging areas at Tule Lake and the Klamath Basin in northern California. From there they gradually disperse to suitable habitat throughout the central valley of California and into Mexico. Fall counts of white-fronted geese at Tule Lake and the Klamath Basin indicate that the population has declined precipitously from nearly 500,000 geese in the late 1960s to fewer than 100,000 in recent years.[3]

Most geese from the Innoko and all those from other nesting areas in interior and northern Alaska and northwestern Canada are part of the midcontinent population. Nesting areas of most importance include the Innoko and Koyukuk river drainages in interior Alaska, the region of Kotzebue in northwestern Alaska, the Colville Delta on Alaska's arctic slope, the Mackenzie and Anderson river deltas in the Northwest Territories, and the region of Queen Maud Gulf in the central Canadian arctic. Smaller populations and scattered pairs are found throughout this range.[4]

It might be expected that migration routes of geese from these widespread nesting areas would differ appreciably, but while these differences occur, similarities in migration patterns are more obvious and of more importance to current management programs. The main migration pattern of all midcontinent geese from Alaska and Canada to as far east as the Anderson River appears to be a direct flight from nesting areas to staging areas in the Kinderly region on the border between Alberta and Saskatchewan. From this staging area geese move to wintering areas in the coastal regions of Louisiana and Texas.[5] Spring migration in March and early April tends to be the reverse pattern, but movement is more gradual, more dependent on weather conditions, and includes the buildup of major concentrations at staging areas in Nebraska.

During migration the distribution of white-fronted geese nesting in the central Canadian arctic overlaps that of geese from Alaska and western Canada. Most move directly south to staging areas further east, to Saskatchewan, to southwestern Manitoba, or to the Souris National Wildlife Refuge in North Dakota, then proceed to wintering areas in Louisiana. These birds, with part of those from Alaska and western Canada, comprise the eastern midcontinent subpopulation.

SIGNIFICANCE OF THE SPECIES

Hunters seek out white-fronts throughout their range as the most delectable of all wild geese. Eskimos take them in nesting areas in Alaska and the Canadian arctic and recreational hunters take them in staging areas in Alberta, Saskatchewan, the Dakotas, and Nebraska and on wintering areas in Louisiana, Texas, California, and Mexico. The enthusiasm with which hunters pursued this species, combined with inadequate information on size of populations and kills, contributed most importantly to the precipitous decline of white-fronts in the Pacific Flyway. Hunters now are in the forefront of efforts to restore populations to former levels.

HISTORICAL PERSPECTIVE

Early naturalists were not concerned with populations statistics such as those now required for waterfowl management and kept no reliable records of white-fronted goose numbers. Clearly, however, the nearly unrestricted hunting that prevailed until early in this century must have reduced the population greatly.

Changes in hunting regulations give some indications of how waterfowl populations fared at the turn of the century. In 1913, spring hunting was prohibited throughout the United States, but bag limits still were set by the states. It would have been possible to shoot 10 white-fronted geese in Nebraska, 15 in Louisiana, North Dakota and Texas, and 25 in California. Spring hunting was prohibited in Canada in 1917, the year the United States imposed a bag limit of eight geese aggregated from all species. Diminished numbers of geese caused Texas unilaterally to reduce the federal limit to four in 1925. Nebraska took similar action, cutting the limit to five in 1927. The federal limit was reduced to four in 1931.

White-fronted geese in the Pacific Flyway responded to the more restrictive regulations by increasing during the following decade. Although bag limits were raised to three dark geese in 1953, the population continued to expand, reaching a peak in the late 1960s. The Central Flyway population, however, remained depressed, and the bag limit was reduced in 1958 to only one white-front. The population responded, increased steadily, and now is near peak numbers.

CURRENT TRENDS

Coordinated mid winter and spring goose surveys by the U.S. Fish and Wildlife Service (FWS) and states of the Mississippi and Central flyways indicate that the midcontinent population has more than tripled since surveys were begun in 1958. Spring counts in recent years average nearly 300,000. The fall population is much larger and usually includes about 38 percent young hatched the preceding summer. The relatively stable annual production supports a yearly kill averaging 100,000 geese in recent years.

Although a few geese from the Pacific and midcontinent populations may intermingle in Mexico, most are well separated. Ninety percent of those from the Pacific population winter in Sonora, Chihuahua, and Nayarit in northwestern Mexico, while 85 percent of the geese in the midcontinent population winter in Tamaulipas on the east coast and inland in San Luis Potosi, Zacatecas, and Durango. A few midcontinent birds cross also to the west coast and winter south of geese from the Pacific population.

PROGNOSIS

Clearly, causes for the precipitous decline of the Pacific population and the potential actions that may be taken to restore this population are of immediate concern. Although preserving habitat quality and quantity is a long-term priority, nesting areas are pristine, and the nature of the decline in goose populations from the Yukon Delta indicates that habitat change in wintering areas was not a significant cause of losses. Unusual losses from pollution, disease, predators, or other natural causes were not observed, nor could they have accounted for the precipitous decline in populations. Annual production as indicated by studies of nesting in the delta and of age composition and sizes of family groups in wintering areas indicated that production was normal throughout the period of decline.

On the other hand, the yearly kill clearly seems to have been excessive. From 1966 to 1969, the kill in the Pacific Flyway averaged about 68,000 white-fronts. Significant but unknown numbers of geese also were killed in Mexico and on nesting areas of the Yukon Delta. Total hunting mortality, including crippling losses, was certainly more than 100,000 geese annually, exceeding production. The precipitous decline in populations became inevitable, a situation exacerbated by lack of adequate information on both size of populations and yearly kills.

Severe restrictions on Pacific Flyway hunting appear to have halted the decline of white-fronts, though other goose species nesting along the Yukon Delta coast (black brant, cackling Canada geese, and emperor geese) have continued to decline. Obviously, restoration of the white-front population will require continued or further restriction of hunting in the Pacific Flyway and termination of unrestricted subsistence harvests on the Yukon Delta. Efforts to restrict hunting on the delta have focused on the voluntary cooperation of native organizations and hunters and were at least partially successful in 1984. Cooperative agreements with native organizations are being continued with the hope and expectation of better compliance with restrictions in 1985. If these efforts are successful, the prognosis for the population is good, but in any case successful goose management will require continuing effort over many years.

RECOMMENDATIONS

Considering the precipitous decline of the Pacific population, could the situation be repeated for the midcontinent population? Probably not. The diverse origin of midcontinent white-fronts and the minimal kill in nesting areas largely precludes such disaster. However, it is not possible to be entirely complacent given the large kills and inadequate information on the size, status, and productivity of discrete nesting populations. Major nesting populations have different migration patterns, reproductive success, and mortality rates, and may be affected quite differently by current harvest regulations, which are based on average counts from surveys in staging and wintering areas. Because the status of geese in specific nesting areas is largely ignored, the nesting population of a given area could well be jeopardized even though the overall population is stable or increasing. Management programs should increasingly focus attention on populations in major nesting areas.

Overall, both Pacific Flyway and midcontinent populations of white-fronted geese seem reasonably secure at existing levels. It is reasonable to presume that the Pacific population can be restored to more acceptable numbers.

REFERENCES

1. R.D. Bauer, "Historical and Status Report of the Tule White-Fronted Goose," in R.L. Jarvis and J.C. Bartonek, eds., *Management and Biology of Pacific Flyway Geese: A Symposium* (Corvallis: OSU Book Stores, Inc., 1979), pp. 44-55.
   D.E. Timm, M.L. Wege and D.S. Gilmer, "Current Status and Management Challenges for Tule White-Fronted Geese," *Transactions 47th North American Wildlife and Natural Resources Conference* (1982), pp. 453-463.
2. F.C. Bellrose, *Ducks, Geese and Swans of North America* (Harrisburg: Stackpole Books, 1979).
   G.B. Saunders and D.C. Saunders, "Waterfowl and Their Wintering Grounds in Mexico," U.S.D.I., U.S. Fish and Wildlife Service, Research Publication, vol. 138 (1981).
3. E.J. O'Neil, "Fourteen Years of Goose Populations and Trends at Klamath Basin Refuges," in R.L. Jarvis and J.C. Bartonek, eds., *Management and Biology of Pacific Flyway Geese: A Symposium* (Corvallis: OSU Book Stores, Inc., 1979), pp. 316-326.
   D.G. Raveling, "Geese and Hunters of Alaska's Yukon Delta: Management Prob-

lems and Political Dilemmas," *Transactions 49th North American Wildlife and Natural Resources Conference* (in press).
4. Op. cit., Bellrose, *Ducks, Geese and Swans of North America.*
   J.G. King and J.I. Hodges, "A Preliminary Analysis of Goose Banding on Alaska's Arctic Slope," in R.L. Jarvis and J.C. Bartonek, eds., *Management and Biology of Pacific Flyway Geese: A Symposium* (Corvallis: OSU Book Stores, Inc., 1979), pp. 176-188.
   J.G. King and C.J. Lensink, "An Evaluation of Alaska Habitat for Migratory Birds" (Unpublished report, U.S. Department of the Interior, Bureau of Sport, Fish, Wildlife, Washington, D.C., 1971).
5. Op. cit., Bellrose, *Ducks, Geese and Swans of North America.*
   C.J. Lensink, "The Distribution of Recoveries from White-Fronted Geese (*Anser albifrons frontalis*) Banded in North America" (Unpublished report, U.S. Fish and Wildlife Service, Bethel, Alaska, 1969).

CALVIN J. LENSINK has been studying the ecology and management of Alaskan mammals and migratory birds since 1951. The National Wildlife Federation has named him Alaska Conservationist of the Year, and he has earned the FWS award for superior performance five times.

The Emperor Goose

by *Margaret R. Petersen*
U.S. Fish and Wildlife Service

SPECIES DESCRIPTION AND NATURAL HISTORY

MANY ORNITHOLOGISTS BELIEVE the emperor goose (*Chen canagicus*) is the most beautiful goose in North America. Detailed descriptions of its plumage can be found in Palmer[1] and a general description in Bellrose.[2] Emperor geese are rather short and squatty, with yellow-orange feet and pink bills. Their bluish-gray body feathers are banded in black and fringed on the outside edge with white. The heads and necks of adult emperors are white except for a wide, dark-gray band that begins at the throat and extends down the neck to the breast. The plumage of immatures more than four months old is similar to that of adults. Before four months their heads are gray.

The emperor goose is a truly northern species. It nests along the west coast of Alaska and east coast of the Soviet Union in arctic tundra habitats. About 90 percent of the world population nests on the Yukon Kuskokwim Delta (YKD), Alaska. The birds winter primarily in the Aleutian and Commander islands and along the Kamchatka Peninsula. A few winter along the Kodiak-Afognak Island area and on the south side of the Alaska Peninsula.[3] As with other geese, emperors migrate to several key staging areas in spring and fall. These include several lagoons and estuaries in coastal Alaska between Izembek Lagoon, Alaska Peninsula, and Chagvan-Nanvak Bays in Bristol Bay.

Emperor geese begin migrating in March from their Aleutian Islands wintering areas to stage at lagoons along the north side of the Alaska Peninsula. There they remain until May, when they move north[4] to arrive on the breeding grounds of the YKD in mid-May.[5] Once they reach the tundra breeding grounds, the pairs establish territories and hold them until the spring thaw makes nest sites available. Commencement of nesting can vary substantially from year to year, depending on the amount of ice and snow and how quickly it melts from the nesting areas. Emperors choose a wide variety of nest locations, including high spots in open areas between ponds; the shores, peninsulas, and islands of ponds of all sizes; and the sides of grass-covered mounds of frozen soil called pingos.[6]

Females generally lay between four and seven eggs, with nests containing eight to 12 eggs not uncommon. The female incubates almost continuously from the day she lays the last egg until the eggs hatch 25 days later. During this time the male remains at an inconspicuous location away from the nest, returning only if a predator approaches the nest.

Little is known about the biology of the emperor goose from the time of hatching until fledging. Observations of dyed broods suggest that adults may move their young several miles to brood-rearing areas.[7] However, observations of collared adults suggest that some families may be found within a mile of their nest areas, while others may be found six or more miles away from their nest sites. Most concentrations of broods are associated with tidal sloughs and shallow estuaries that contain extensive mud flats, although the molting and brood-rearing habitat of this goose is virtually undescribed.

Once the young are flying, emperors tend to congregate along the coast. Then they follow the coastline, staging at each major lagoon or estuarial system below the Seward Peninsula. Emperor geese can be found along the north side of the Alaska Peninsula after mid to late August, and some individuals may remain through winter unless the estuaries freeze.[8] Incidental observations of staging geese suggest that these estuaries may provide food resources essential for accumulating body reserves needed for migration in fall and reproduction in spring. Except for the general timing of migration, the importance of estuaries along the north side of the Alaska Peninsula,[9] and observations of feeding behavior of geese at Nelson Lagoon,[10] little is known about the ecology of emperor geese in these areas. Even less is known about the ecology of emperor geese in winter. This is not surprising, considering the inaccessibility of the Aleutian Islands in winter.

SIGNIFICANCE OF THE SPECIES

Emperor geese are unique in that no major man-induced changes have occurred in their wintering, staging, or breeding environments, and no abrupt environmental changes have occurred in any portion of their range. However, the number of emperor geese has been declining consistently over the past 20 years.[11] It is apparent that the degree of success we can achieve by managing arctic nesting geese on the YKD will be most apparent with the emperor goose, since there are no confounding man-induced factors influencing their winter survival. Thus, the emperor goose serves as an indicator of successful management of geese on their summer breeding range on the YKD.

HISTORICAL PERSPECTIVE

Observers on the breeding grounds of the emperor goose in the YKD found emperors plentiful at numerous locations around the mouth of the Kuskokwim River, on Nelson Island, and in Hazen Bay.[12] In the late 1870s, they reportedly were so plentiful that Yupiks discarded goslings they captured and killed during land drives to get them out of the way of the next drive.[13] Presently, emperors are plentiful at only two locations on the YKD — Kokechik Bay (Igigak Bay) and along the Manokanak River in Hazen Bay.

Since the 1970s, nesting densities of emperor geese at Kokechik Bay have dropped dramatically. Studies conducted on the bay found nesting there had been reduced 49 percent between 1971 and 1984.[14]

CURRENT TRENDS

Population levels of this goose have never been high. King and Lensink[15] estimated about 150,000 emperors in the early and mid-1960s. More recent estimates have suggested that the population declined by 34 percent between the 1960s and 1981.[16] Recent surveys have shown a continuous decline of about 10 percent per year to a spring population of 71,200.[17] Factors affecting the present decline generally are believed to be the take of birds and their eggs in excess of what the population can sustain and a poor reproductive season in 1982. Data on marked adults suggests that adult female survival currently is about 70 percent.[18] This adult mortality ratio, when combined with a reproductive rate of 12 to 21 percent per year,[19] will result in a continuous decline.

MANAGEMENT

Emperor goose management focuses primarily on the taking of birds and eggs and on protection of key estuaries used by staging geese. Threats to these estuaries are associated with offshore and nearshore oil and gas development and consist primarily of increased disturbance by aircraft flights, increased human use of estuaries for recreational purposes, disturbance of birds in estuaries by exploratory testing (shock waves and underground blasting), and direct effects on geese of oil and gas leaks and spills. Current efforts by state and federal agencies and local citizens groups along the Alaska Peninsula have minimized human impacts successfully. However, as economic pressures and mineral development increase, threats to these estuaries also will increase.

Excessive taking of emperors and their eggs seems the likely explanation for the bird's decline. Data collected between 1969 and 1984 show no change in productivity in terms of the average clutch size, percent of hatching success, or average brood size.[20] Rates of predation by foxes, gulls, and jaegers on eggs and small young have remained relatively constant. Mortality rates on the wintering areas are unknown, but U.S. Fish and Wildlife Service (FWS) personnel have reported no substantial losses to disease or weather in the Aleutian Islands nor any losses of wintering habitat that might result in increased mortality.

A kill of about 2,500 emperors has occurred each fall in the Alaska Peninsula since 1976.[21] The total kill of adult geese in spring on the YKD is unknown. In 1964, Klein[22] estimated that 6,500 emperors were taken by YKD residents in spring and an additional 1,700 in fall. Recent surveys of spring waterfowl mortality are inadequate to estimate accurately the current take of geese and eggs,[23] but those data and others suggest that emperors currently are the most important goose taken in spring on the YKD.[24] It seems reasonable to assume that the current take of emperors there is substantial.

PROGNOSIS

Emperor geese are protected under the Migratory Bird Treaty Act,[25] and bags and seasons are established annually by FWS and the Alaska Department of Fish and Game (ADFG). In response to the decline of the emperors, ADFG has proposed a reduction in the Unit 9 (Alaska Peninsula) bag limit beginning in fall 1985. Similarly, a coalition that includes the representatives of the Association of Village Council Presidents, FWS, ADFG, and other states in the Pacific Flyway has placed limitations on the taking of emperor geese during the 1985 spring and summer hunts. If a reduction in the hunter kill reduces total mortality below total productivity, the population should begin to increase.

RECOMMENDATIONS

Prognosis for the recovery of emperor geese to former levels of abundance is good if the harvest can be managed adequately and if there is continued protection of environmentally sensitive habitats.

Several gaps in our knowledge about this goose are becoming increasingly deleterious as our need to manage emperor geese increases. Closing these gaps requires:

1. An accurate evaluation and determination of sport and subsistence take of adults, immatures, and eggs. This information is necessary to most effectively set bag limits and seasons.
2. An evaluation and understanding of the seasonal importance and vulnerability of Bristol Bay and the Alaska Peninsula estuaries and lagoon systems used by emperor geese during spring and fall migration. Such an understanding will enhance our ability to manage areas for minimal impacts on the species and perhaps more accurately delineate areas that may be particularly vulnerable.
3. Studies of geese on molting and brood-rearing areas to characterize habitat needs and factors influencing growth and survival of goslings and to delineate important molting areas on the YKD, Seward Peninsula, and Saint Lawrence Island. As private lands in these areas become available for development we will need to have a detailed understanding of which areas are important to this goose.

REFERENCES

1. R.S. Palmer, ed., *Handbook of North American Birds*, vol. 2 (New Haven: Yale University Press, 1976).
2. F.C. Bellrose, *Ducks, Geese and Swans of North America* (Harrisburg: Wildlife Management Institute, Stackpole Books, 1976).
3. Op. cit., Palmer, *Handbook of North American Birds*.
   J.A. Gabrielson and F.C. Lincoln, *The Birds of Alaska* (Washington, D.C.: The Wildlife Management Institute, 1959).
4. M.R. Petersen and R.E. Gill, "Population and Status of Emperor Geese Along the North Side of the Alaska Peninsula," *Wildfowl*, vol. 33 (1982), pp. 31-38.
5. D.I. Eisenhauer and C.M. Kirkpatrick, "Ecology of the Emperor Goose in Alaska," *Wildlife Monographs*, vol. 57 (1977).
6. Ibid.
   M.R. Petersen, "Nesting Ecology and Habitat Requirements of Geese at Kokechik Bay, Yukon-Kuskokwim Delta, Alaska," (Unpublished report, U.S. Fish and Wildlife Service, Anchorage, Alaska, 1984).
7. Op. cit., Eisenhauer and Kirkpatrick, "Emperor Goose in Alaska," *Wildlife Monographs*.
8. Op. cit., Petersen and Gill, "Population and Status of Emperor Geese," *Wildfowl*.
9. Op. cit., Petersen and Gill, "Population and States of Emperor Geese," *Wildfowl*.
10. M.R. Petersen, "Observations of Emperor Geese Feeding at Nelson Lagoon, Alaska," *Condor*, vol. 85 (1983), pp. 367-368.

11. Op. cit., Petersen and Gill, "Population and Status of Emperor Geese," *Wildfowl*.
12. Op. cit., Gabrielson and F. C. Lincoln, *The Birds of Alaska*.
13. E. W. Nelson, "The Emperor Goose," in E. Ingersoll, *Alaskan Bird-life*. (National Association of Audubon Societies, New York, 1914).
14. Op. cit, Petersen, "Nesting Ecology and Habitat Requirements of Geese at Kokechik Bay, Yukon-Kuskokwim Delta, Alaska," Eisenhauer and Kirkpatrick, *Ecology of the Emperor Goose in Alaska*.
15. J.G. King and C.J. Lensink, "An Evaluation of Alaskan Habitat for Migratory Birds," (Unpublished report, Bureau of Sport Fisheries and Wildlife, Juneau, Alaska, 1971).
16. Op. cit., Petersen and Gill, "Population and Status of Emperor Geese," *Wildfowl*.
17. C.P. Dau, "Spring Survey of Emperor Geese in Southwestern Alaska, 28-30 April, 4 May," (Unpublished report, U.S. Fish and Wildlife Service, Cold Bay, Alaska, 1984).
18. Unpublished data, M.R. Petersen.
19. Op. cit., Petersen and Gill, "Population and Status of Emperor Geese," *Wildfowl*.
20. Anonymous, Draft Emperor Goose Management Plan (Unpublished report, Emperor Goose sub-committee, Pacific Flyway Technical Committee, U.S. Fish and Wildlife Service, Anchorage, Alaska, 1981).
    Op. cit., Petersen, "Nesting Ecology and Habitat Requirements."
21. Op. cit., Anonymous, Draft Emperor Goose Management Plan.
    Unpublished data, Fish and Wildlife Service.
22. D.R. Klein, "Waterfowl in the Economy of the Eskimos on the Yukon-Kuskokwim Delta, Alaska," *Arctic*, vol. 19 (1966), pp. 319-326.
23. J.Copp and R. Garrett, "Results of the 1982 Survey of Spring Waterfowl Hunting by Eskimos on the Yukon-Kuskokwim Delta, Alaska" (Unpublished report, U.S. Fish and Wildlife Service, Bethel, Alaska, 1983).
24. Unpublished data, U.S. Fish and Wildlife Service.
25. Convention for the Protection of Migratory Birds, August 16, 1916, United States-Great Britain (on behalf of Canada), 39 Stat. 1702, T.S. No. 628.

MARGARET R. PETERSEN, as an FWS wildlife biologist, has conducted extensive studies on the breeding, migration, behavior, and feeding ecology of waterfowl along coastal Alaska. Her current research project focuses on the nesting ecology and behavior of emperor geese at Kokechik Bay, Yukon-Kuskokwim Delta.

Lacking marketable feathers, the woodstork survived the plume hunters that ravaged many Florida bird populations, but now is jeopardized by land development.

The Wood Stork

by John C. Ogden
National Audubon Society Staff

SPECIES DESCRIPTION AND NATURAL HISTORY

THE WOOD STORK (*Mycteria americana*) is one of three species of New World storks. It is the only one that nests or regularly occurs in the United States. The largest of the long-legged wading birds native to the United States, it stands between five and five and a half feet tall. The stork's plumage is entirely white except for glossy black flight feathers on the wings and a short black tail. The feathered heads and necks of immature wood storks are drably colored. Adult birds have blackish, unfeathered heads and necks that are the basis for colloquial names such as flinthead, ironhead, and gourdhead. The stork's bill is long, tapers to a blunt point, and is massive compared with the bills of herons and egrets. The heavier bill is an adaptation for capturing fish larger than those caught by most other wading birds.

The wood stork is related to the European white stork (*Ciconia ciconia*) famous for its habit of nesting on rooftops and chimneys. The wood stork differs from the white stork, however, in being much more social.

The American wood stork's principal range is in wetlands across the southern United States, from South Carolina to southern California south through the tropical and subtropical regions of Mexico, Central America, and South America to central Argentina. Storks have nested historically in all coastal states from eastern Texas to South Carolina,[1] although the largest and most consistently used nesting sites are in Florida. In recent decades, storks in the United States have nested in peninsular Florida, in a few small colonies in southeastern Georgia, and, rarely, in southeastern South Carolina.

During nonbreeding months large numbers of storks leave the nesting regions, generally moving northward. In the past, when the number of storks was greater, dispersing birds occurred regularly as far north in the United States as southern California, Arizona, northern Texas, southern Illinois, and North Carolina.[2] Presently, storks from Florida nesting colonies are known to disperse in summer as far as coastal South Carolina and central Mississippi. Storks that appear each summer in coastal Louisiana and Texas, as well as the smaller numbers found in the southern Salton Sea area of California and along the lower Colorado River, come from nesting colonies along both coasts of central and southern Mexico. No known interchange occurs between storks that nest in Mexico and those that nest in the southeastern United States.

Wood storks are highly social birds that nest in colonies and roost and forage for food in flocks. Nesting colonies, often called "rookeries" in Florida, traditionally have been located in cypress or mangrove swamps. Less often they occur in thickets of low, woody vegetation on islands or in marshes or in stands of other swamp hardwoods. In recent years some colonies have been located in tall trees standing in water in man-made impoundments. Colonies range in size from only a few nests to as many as several thousand. Storks may nest in "pure" colonies containing no other species or in mixed colonies containing many herons, egrets, ibis, cormorants, or pelicans.

Storks feed almost entirely on small freshwater fish that usually range in size between about two and 10 inches.[3] Because the stork's specialized grope-feeding technique works most efficiently when fish are concentrated in drying pools, ditches, or swampy depressions, nesting coincides with the seasons when rainfall and temperatures are most likely to yield the highest fish densities. In southern Florida, storks begin nesting during the winter dry season when water levels are dropping in interior marshes and swamps and fish are being concentrated in ever-diminishing volumes of water. In northern Florida and Georgia, where winter temperatures and storms are a more important factor, storks nest in spring and summer. In this region, food is found in streams, isolated ponds, and swampy depressions where high summer evaporation rates seem important to maintaining good foraging habitat.

Male and female storks participate about equally in the construction of nests, incubation of eggs, and feeding of chicks. Nests are large bulky platforms of sticks. In a crowded colony they may be located within two or three feet of each other. Clutches vary from two to four large white eggs. Incubation lasts about 30 days. Parent birds feed chicks by regurgitating whole fish into the bottoms of their nests, where the fish are quickly consumed by the nestlings. One adult remains at or near the nest to shade and protect the young while the nestlings are downy. When chicks are about four to five weeks old, growing rapidly and beginning to develop feathers, both adults spend most of each day collecting food. Young birds make their first short flights at about 55 to 60 days, although they continue to return to the nest to be fed until 75 days or older.[4]

Nestlings usually are fed three to six times daily, less often when food is scarce or adults are traveling great distances to find it. The general daily pattern is for an adult stork to leave the colony during midmorning, once warm-air thermals have developed, and return to feed the chicks sometime between early and late afternoon. An incoming adult usually will bring enough food to regurgitate several separate loads of small fish into the nest over a period of one hour or more.

Although the most common clutch size is three eggs, the number of chicks successfully raised to fledging varies depending upon food supply. When high winds, heavy rainfall, drought, or other factors interrupt routine feeding, the youngest chick is the first to suffer. It will die if the food shortage becomes acute.

Storks travel between colony and feeding grounds almost entirely by soaring, typically by circling to the top of a well-developed thermal and sailing off in the desired direction, gradually losing altitude until another thermal is encountered. Much foraging occurs within 10 to 35 miles of a colony, although flights up to 60 and 70 miles are taken when necessary.[5] Longer flights often result in the adults remaining overnight on the foraging grounds and returning to the colony on morning thermals.

Information from a small number of marked storks indicates that for the first two years after fledging the birds are in an immature plumage characterized by a pale yellowish bill and feathered necks and heads. Third-year plumage seems to be transitional. Four-year-old storks are in adult plumage, with black bill and unfeathered head and neck. A few four-year-old storks are known to have nested successfully.[6] Nothing is known of annual mortality rates or of the birds' usual life span.

Wood storks are not truly migratory, although they do participate in regular, post-breeding-season dispersals. Heavy summer rains in southern Florida and relatively cold winter temperatures and storms in the northern parts of the breeding range cause storks to shift seasonally between northern and southern regions. The early to midsummer dispersal is northward, primarily into northern Florida and coastal Georgia and South Carolina, less commonly as far west as central Mississippi. South Florida storks disperse at the same time that nesting colonies in north Florida and Georgia are active. The south Florida storks, perhaps with post-breeding adults from more northerly colonies, move back into the southern peninsula by late fall and early winter. Yearly differences in the timing and magnitude of summer rains, as well as the degree of nesting success in the southern colonies, seem to influence considerably the timing and number of birds that participate in each year's dispersal. During periods of unusual drought or excessively prolonged heavy rains, storks may disperse much further north than usual, appearing in coastal locations in the mid-Atlantic and northern Atlantic states or up the Mississippi Valley as far north as the southern Great Lakes.

SIGNIFICANCE

The wood stork formerly was an abundant and ecologically important element in many swamps and marshes in the southeastern coastal plain of the United States. Its decline forcefully attests to the considerable degradation that has occurred in many freshwater wetlands. Both the biological character and the complex moods of beauty and mystery that are a part of large swamps and marshes have suffered from the loss of storks and other large wading birds.

The wood stork is a valuable indicator species for the biological well-being of freshwater wetlands. A foraging stork locates fish by probing with its partially open bill into several inches of water. Fish are captured by split-second reflex closures of the bill. Considering the nature of this foraging technique and the stork's large size, it is readily apparent that the bird requires high fish densities. Such optimal feeding conditions are more often met in naturally functioning ecosystems than in those that have been altered. Any factor that reduces fish density — whether changes in water quality, reduced hydroperiods, or unseasonable manipulations in water levels — often will have greater adverse effects on a specialized forager such as the stork than on more generalized visual foragers such as most herons and egrets.

Reduced densities of fish over large regions of freshwater wetlands in fact have resulted in a decline in the carrying capacity of these regions for wood storks, and declines in other wading birds in freshwater regions have been documented[7].

The challenge of dealing with the deteriorating status of the wood stork will be difficult because the stork's problem is habitat loss. Successful endangered species recovery programs generally deal with species whose endangered status is due to some direct mortality problem rather than to a habitat factor. The recovery of the brown pelican and bald eagle, for example, was accomplished by the reduction of a single primary mortality-causing factor: pesticides.[8] In contrast, when a species' decline has been due to habitat loss, as was the case with the ivory-billed woodpecker and dusky seaside sparrow, the task of correctly identifying the necessary habitat and taking the steps to protect it always has been a more difficult undertaking, sometimes an impossible one.[9]

A real test of the entire concept of endangered species recovery programs is how well the combined efforts of federal, state, and private conservation organizations can deal with the more complex habitat issues. In the case of the wood stork, the nature of the problem presumably has been recognized while enough birds remain in the wild so that the lengthy process of habitat identification and protection still may be a reachable goal.

HISTORICAL PERSPECTIVE

At the turn of the century, when many species of long-legged wading birds apparently were at their lowest numbers after several decades of shooting for the plume trade,[10] wood storks apparently still occurred in large numbers. For example, Oscar Baynard and F.M. Phelps[11] visited in 1912 and 1914, respectively, a large stork nesting colony located in southwest Florida's Big Cypress Swamp and estimated that it contained 5,000 to 8,000 stork nests. The storks survived those difficult decades because they neither had attractive plumes nor were good to eat.

Estimates of the number of breeding pairs of storks in the United States for any period prior to the late 1950s are little more than educated guesses. The difficulty in making these estimates is that no systematic surveys of all nesting colonies were conducted, while estimates of the number of storks in individual colonies for several consecutive years rarely were attempted.[12]

Only by comparing a series of historical estimates from a single persistent colony with more recent information and making some assumptions about the total number of colonies active during any given period can we develop an estimate for the total number of storks in the United States prior to the late 1950s. Elsewhere,[13] an attempt was made to do this for the early 1930s, a period when a surge of activity by Audubon wardens in south Florida produced several colony visits. The estimate was 60,000 wood storks, including 10,000 adults in the southwestern Florida mangrove colonies (now Everglades National Park), 20,000 adults in the Big Cypress colonies, 10,000 adults in the smaller colonies scattered northward from central Florida, and approximately 20,000 nonbreeding storks, mainly immatures, throughout the range.

Whether the early 1930s stork population represents a pristine level or an already reduced population is debatable. Most likely the numbers in each region already were reduced, perhaps considerably, by the cumulative effects of cypress logging and a miscellany of other human-caused direct disturbance factors.

Between the early 1930s and the late 1950s, the stork population in the United States dropped by a half. A series of drought-induced nesting failures during the mid-1950s called attention to the decline and lead to the organization of several aerial and ground surveys over much of Florida. The surveys were conducted cooperatively by the National Audubon Society, the Florida Audubon Society, and the Florida Game and Fresh Water Fish Commission. They revealed a minimum adult stork population of about 20,000 birds.

Good nesting success from 1959 to 1961 served to mask the more long-term trend, which was a continuing decline. Everglades National Park colonies contained 2,500 pairs in 1960 and only about 1,300 pairs in 1975. Between 1961 and 1975 the park colonies had only five years of good stork reproduction—1961, 1963, 1967, 1974, and 1975.[14] A similar pattern occurred in the Big Cypress region, where the number of nesting pairs declined from 6,300 in three colonies in 1960 to 3,000 in two colonies in 1975.[15]

This decline prompted the National Audubon Society to initiate annual aerial surveys of all stork nesting colonies in the United States. It also stimulated an expansion of studies, begun in Everglades National Park in the early 1970s, to several colonies scattered throughout Florida. The aerial surveys showed a total breeding population in all Florida and Georgia of approximately 6,000 pairs in 1975, down to about 4,800 pairs in 1980[16] and approximately 5,000 pairs in 1984.[17]

In summary, between 1960 and 1980 the total number of nesting pairs declined by 52 percent. In the southern Florida region, where declines were sharpest and where historically the largest nesting colonies occurred, the decline was 75 percent.

The aerial surveys also revealed several geographical and habitat shifts that are of special interest for understanding the present condition of the wild population. These shifts included a northward relocation by nesting storks, a change from nesting in the historically important cypress swamps to nesting in man-made water impoundments, and a shift in colony location from inland to coastal sites.

CURRENT TRENDS

The northward shift by nesting birds needs to be documented, although no other explanation for certain observations seems plausible. The decline in numbers of storks nesting in certain traditionally large South Florida colonies has been more rapid during the past decade than can be reasonably explained by mortality alone. Concurrent with the declines in South Florida, several small colonies have formed in north Florida and Georgia, and other nothern colonies have remained stable or have increased in size. In some years, failure of large numbers of storks to nest in South Florida has correlated directly with sudden and comparable increases in the number of storks in many northern colonies, presumably due to their somewhat better northern nesting success compared to south Florida colonies and to the northern immigration of south Florida storks into the north. The relative importance of these two factors in maintaining northern colonies is presently unknown.

The other two trends — shifting to nesting in impoundments or to coastal sites — seem related to a deterioration in the quality of nesting habitat. This habitat loss has been especially noticeable in central and northern Florida, where the percentage of storks nesting in impoundments increased from 10 percent in 1959 to 40 percent in 1984. In the same region the number nesting on coastal islands increased from only two pairs in 1959 to about 680 pairs in 1984.

Without doubt, the more important factors for the decline have been various forms of habitat destruction or alteration. Direct mortality or serious chemical poisoning have not been major factors.[18] The loss of traditional cypress-swamp nesting habitat, mainly to drainage, is a factor in central and northern Florida. However, storks in that region have found other nesting sites, so the overall importance of the habitat change to the stork's decline may not be great.

In southern Florida, where the decline has been severe, the colony sites have been the best protected of any in the species' range. These colonies have included the large Corkscrew Swamp, owned by the National Audubon Society since 1954, and several traditional colony sites in Everglades National Park protected by the National Park Service since 1947 and before that by Audubon wardens.

Storks in southern Florida have declined so greatly because the freshwater wetland foraging habitat has been reduced considerably in area or adversely altered by water-management practices. Between 1900 and 1973, the total acreage of South Florida freshwater wetlands in five habitat categories used by foraging storks —

cypress domes and strands, wet prairies, scrub cypress, freshwater marshes and sloughs, and sawgrass marshes — were reduced 35 percent.[19]

Many of the remaining wetlands are either impounded or subject to shortened hydroperiods. It appears certain that these systems no longer provide fish for foraging storks in anywhere near the numbers that once occurred. Unfortunately, no quantitative data on fish numbers, sizes, or density from the pre-drainage wetlands of Florida are available, so the magnitude of the change is unknown.

A strong circumstantial case can be made that many remaining wetlands have been so altered that they no longer provide the food needed to support large numbers of nesting storks. Many examples of changing patterns of feeding and nesting in south Florida seem explicable only on the basis of such an assumption. One key example is the delay in nesting by storks in Everglades National Park since the 1960s. Approximately coinciding with the construction of new water-control structures along the north and east (upstream) park boundaries during the 1960s, storks in the park began to set back the yearly initiation of their nesting season from November or December to between January and March.[20] It appears that the new water-control structures had a profound effect on the seasonal distribution of fish. The problem with delayed nesting has been that in many years storks nest too late in the winter dry season to successfully fledge their young before the summer rainy season begins. Once the rains start, usually in May or June, the concentrations of fish in freshwater foraging sites rapidly became diluted by rising water. The adult storks can no longer obtain enough food and are forced to abandon the colonies and move north out of the region.

MANAGEMENT

The deterioration of the United States wood stork population has been well documented.[21] Florida was the first state to give official recognition to the species' serious decline. In 1972 the wood stork was listed preliminarily as endangered by the Florida Game and Fresh Water Fish Commission. The status of the stork in Florida was changed by the commission to threatened in 1974 and back to endangered in 1975. The endangered classification was reaffirmed in 1978 by the Florida Committee on Rare and Endangered Plants and Animals.[22] The wood stork was listed as endangered by South Carolina in 1985, Alabama in 1983, and Mississippi in 1984. Texas listed it in 1978 as a protected nongame species, a classification equivalent to threatened. It is not state-listed in Arizona, California, Georgia, Louisiana, or Arkansas.

The United States breeding population of the wood stork was listed by the U.S. Fish and Wildlife Service (FWS) as endangered in 1984.[23] Since wood storks breed only in Florida, Georgia, and South Carolina, it is the storks in these three states, plus Alabama, that are listed federally. The storks that occur west of Alabama are presumed to be birds from Mexican colonies, a population not considered endangered.[24]

The FWS Endangered Species Field Station in Jacksonville, Florida, currently is preparing a wood stork recovery plan, of which a first draft should be completed in 1985.

Of 27 colony sites used by wood storks in the 1983 and 1984 nesting seasons, 10 were protected by either federal, state, or private conservation organizations. Storks nesting at several other locations, primarily on large, privately owned ranches, also receive a high degree of protection because of their isolation and because most ranching activities do not directly disturb nesting storks.

The 10 protected colonies include six that have been in government or private conservation ownership for a relatively long time. One is in Everglades National Park, two are in national wildlife refuges administered by FWS, one is in Corkscrew Swamp Sanctuary, owned by the National Audubon Society, and two are at sites owned by the state of Florida (Chaires in Leon County, North Port Charlotte in Charlotte County). The remaining four colonies more recently have received state protection — the Birdsville colony in Jenkins County, Georgia, and three sites in Florida: Little Gator Creek (Pasco Co.), Tolomato (St. Johns Co.), and Hillsborough River (Hillsborough Co.).

The Birdsville stork colony is protected by the Georgia Department of Natural Resources through a cooperative agreement with the landowners, I.T.T. Raynier, Inc., which cuts timber in Georgia.

The Little Gator Creek site was acquired by the state of Florida in 1982 with money from an annually renewed Conservation and Recreation Land Program Fund. This fund was established by the state legislature in 1979 and is supported by a severance tax on the phosphate industry. The same fund is being used to purchase the Tolomato site, with acquisition to occur over a four-year period that began in 1984. The Hillsborough River colony is part of a state water-management district and is managed by the Florida Game and Fresh Water Fish Commission as the Hillsborough River Wildlife Management Area. One unprotected colony in Florida, at River Styx, Alachua County, has been proposed for acquisition by a coalition of Micanopy, Florida, landowners who are concerned about intrusion of major urban development into a region that still retains its rural character. This proposal also would draw upon Conservation and Recreation Land funds.

Presently, about 48 percent of Georgia and Florida's 5,000 pairs of storks receive full protection at nesting sites. That figure could be increased to 76 percent with acquisition of three additional colonies in Florida — Reedy Creek in Osceola County, Telegraph Swamp in Sarasota County, and El Clair Ranch colony in Hardee County. In 1983 and 1984 these sites had a combined total of about 1,450 pairs of nesting storks.

Although many nesting sites are protected, that protection does not extend to most feeding areas. Storks generally feed within 35 miles of their colonies, but may go much further when conditions require. Circles with a 35-mile radius drawn on a map, with the location of an active colony at the center of each circle, would reveal generally where the major foraging wetlands must be located. But for most colonies the precise sites within that circle that actually are used for foraging are poorly known and therefore hard to designate for protection. The few colonies where data on location and importance of foraging sites have been collected include the Birdsville colony in Georgia and the Everglades National Park, Corkscrew Swamp, El Clair, Moore Creek, and Dee Dot colonies in Florida. In 1983 and 1984, these six colonies contained between 40 and 46 percent of the total nesting pairs.

At any one time, storks may feed at a few primary sites as well as at several other sites of secondary importance.[25] The pattern is for birds to shift constantly from one foraging site to another, as old sites become dry or fished out and dropping water levels create new sites in new locations.

The present inadequate state of knowledge about the location of many foraging sites is especially unfortunate since it appears that inadequate food resources during the nesting seasons have been major factors responsible for many recent colony failures or overall poor reproduction, especially in southern Florida. The major challenges to the wood stork recovery effort will be to identify the key foraging sites associated with each colony and to work to protect or re-establish the biological viability of these wetlands. Only through such steps can the long-term stability of nesting colonies and the success of the recovery program be assured. Many of the foraging sites undoubtedly are located on private land, where future land practices will not necessarily be compatible with the needs of wood storks.

A significant effort to mitigate the loss of a foraging site for storks nesting at the Birdsville, Georgia, colony is presently under way. The U.S. Department of Energy (DOE) is reactivating a plutonium reactor at the Savannah River Plant near Aiken, South Carolina. Large volumes of cooling water will be discharged from the plant into Steel Creek, flooding downstream foraging sites. The lower Steel Creek delta apparently is an important foraging site for wood storks nesting about 30 miles away.[26]

DOE, following advice from the FWS Endangered Species Field Station in Asheville, North Carolina, is attempting to compensate for the loss by constructing manageable foraging ponds at some alternate location. An existing 30-acre pond located at Silver Bluff Plantation, adjacent to the Savannah River Plant, has been selected as the replacement foraging site. Silver Bluff Plantation, owned by the National Audubon Society, is managed as a wildlife area. Modification of the pond, called Kathwood Lake, is planned for the spring of 1985, perhaps in time for the pools to provide foraging habitat for storks from the Birdsville colony during the summer 1985 nesting season. Funding for the project will be provided by DOE through DuPont Company contractors at the Savannah River Plant. Kathwood Lake will be redesigned so that gravity flow and a series of weirs will control water depths and fish densities. Ideally, the managed ponds will provide no less than the amount of fish that will be lost to storks when the water level in Steel Creek is raised.

The concept of managed ponds to provide fish for wood storks to supplement deteriorating natural supplies was tested at Corkscrew Swamp Sanctuary in southwestern Florida between 1969 and 1978. Eight ponds with a total of 30 acres, each with independently regulated water levels, were managed to maximize fish reproduction and growth rates to sizes suitable for foraging storks. Water levels in the ponds, either separately or in combination, were lowered by pumping to concentrate fish in the proper densities and depths to make them available to storks. Although the Corkscrew ponds were not large enough to make an important contribution to the food resources of a colony as large as the nearby Corkscrew rookery (some 1,000 pairs), they did demonstrate the feasibility of the concept. For example, between March 4, 1976, and May 13, 1976, 2,297 stork-use days (number of storks x number of days when feeding occurred) were recorded at the Corkscrew ponds.[27]

Research on wood storks has been increasing since the early 1970s. Between 1974 and 1979, National Audubon Society biologists studied relationships between reproductive success of colonies in central and southern Florida and the quality and quantity of available food. Reproductive success was measured by determining clutch size, hatching success, nestling growth rates, and fledging rates. Food characteristics were determined by measuring feeding rates at nests and collecting large samples of the fish that were brought in by adult birds. These data are being analyzed and will be correlated with rainfall and temperature data to show relationships between nesting success and the environmental factors thought to have the greatest influence on food supply. The Audubon biologists also tagged about 1,000 nestlings as a means of gathering certain demographic and post-fledging movement data.

More recently, biologists with the Florida Game and Fresh Water Fish Commission and the Savannah River Ecology Laboratory have initiated long-term wood stork studies. The Florida Game Commission study, started in 1981, is looking at nesting success in north and central Florida colonies and locating foraging sites by radio-tracking adult storks. Earlier studies of foraging locations for nesting storks — conducted in Everglades National Park during the late 1960s and early 1970s,[28] at Corkscrew Swamp Sanctuary,[29] and at the Moore Creek coastal colony in central Florida[30]

— used small airplanes to follow birds flying between colonies and feeding sites.

The Savannah River Ecology Lab study, funded by DOE, began during the summer of 1983 to look at nesting success and foraging behavior of storks from the Birdsville, Georgia, colony. A key feature of this ongoing project is to determine the importance of wetlands on the Savannah River Plant as foraging habitat for these storks. This study includes use of radio-telemetry and aircraft tracking for locating foraging sites. It is this study that revealed the probable importance of the Steel Creek delta as a foraging site for the Birdsville storks and led to the Lake Kathwood mitigation plan.

PROGNOSIS

The future of the United States wood stork population is uncertain. The task of identifying and protecting habitats necessary for an endangered species often is the most difficult challenge faced by recovery programs. In the case of the wood stork, the sites that seem to be most in need of protection are the wetland foraging habitats, since they are particularly sensitive to disturbance by human activities. There is little doubt, for example, that large areas of the remaining Everglades in southern Florida, which superficially appear as they did a century ago, are much degraded today in terms of the size distribution of fish and of fish availability to wading birds. The resolution to this problem is complicated by lack of the historical quantitative information needed to measure the degree of alteration of these ecosystems and to set standards for their recovery. Equally important are biological and political disagreements over ways to restore the Everglades and where such a goal should stand in the list of overall south Florida water-management priorities.

An interesting and possibly short-term phenomenon is the slightly improved reproduction that recently has been seen in colonies located between central Florida and Georgia, while the historically large south Florida colonies continue to decline. The apparent abandonment of south Florida colonies and the corresponding increase in the size and number of colonies to the north during the past 15 years was first noticed during the aerial surveys of the mid-1970s.[31]

Although it appears that south Florida colonies, when they were in good shape, were capable of higher rates of nesting success than generally occurred in the northern colonies,[32] the recent trend has been toward a reversal of this pattern. It is possible that this northward shift will result in an overall improvement in nesting success as more of the population moves into regions where the potential for successful nesting seems better than in present southern colonies.

A close look at wading-bird populations in the southeastern United States between 1930 and 1975[33] reveals several important trends. A most interesting one is the overall decline that has occurred in freshwater regions, while species in estuarine zones generally have been stable or increasing. This suggests that freshwater habitats, relative to coastal wetlands, have suffered considerable degradation.

RECOMMENDATIONS

The following are needed:

1. Greatly enlarged effort to identify and map the key foraging habitats used by wood storks throughout the year. This would include the important wetlands surrounding each nesting colony as well as those used by nonbreeding storks during the post-breeding dispersal into Georgia, South Carolina, and other southeastern regions.

2. Expansion of studies of stork movements to examine the frequency and causes for exchanges of adult birds between colonies in different years, specifically the dynamics of the northward population shift.

3. Detailed foraging-site studies that look at the yearly ecological events contributing to the creation of good feeding habitats and that characterize these sites in terms of water quality and quantity, fish populations and densities, and vegetative characteristics.

4. Long-range studies of marked wood storks to determine the species' demography. Preliminary information from storks marked as nestlings during the 1970s suggests that the age of first breeding is four years.[34] Annual mortality rates and life spans are still unknown. Without these data, establishment of annual reproductive requirements for a stable population will not be possible.

Two basic improvements are needed:

1. Seek a means to coordinate county, state, federal, and private interests in monitoring and protecting essential wood stork habitat. The focus of this approach should be a recovery plan that identifies the agencies responsible for wetland preservation at each governmental level and develops a method of involving representatives of these agencies in the process. A wood stork council, composed of key environmental and biological personnel, may help ensure communication on these matters.

2. A wide-scale educational program supported by both government and private conservation organizations should be implemented to convey the overall picture of freshwater-habitat degradation in the southeastern coastal plain and what we are losing as a result. A key recipient of this message should be the county agencies that make the land-use decisions that often result in loss of these wetlands.

REFERENCES

1. A.C. Bent, "Life Histories of North American Marsh Birds," *U.S. National Museum Bulletin* 135 (1926).
W. Cone and J. Hall, "Wood Ibis Found Nesting on Okefenokee Refuge," *Chat*, vol. 35 (1970), p. 14.
J. Dusi and R. Dusi, "Evidence for the Breeding of the Wood Stork in Alabama, 1968," *Alabama Birds*, vol. 16 (1968), pp. 14-16.
A.H. Howell, *Florida Bird Life* (New York: Coward-McCann, 1932).
H.C. Oberholser, "The Bird Life of Louisiana," Bulletin 28 (New Orleans: Louisiana Dept. Conservation, 1938).
H.C. Oberholser and E.B. Kincaid Jr., *The Bird Life of Texas*, vol. 1 (Austin: Univ. Texas Press, 1974).
A.T. Wayne, *Birds of South Carolina*, (Charleston: Contributions of the Charleston Museum, 1910).
2. Op. cit., Bent, "Life Histories of North American Marsh Birds," *U.S. National Museum Bulletin.*
T.G. Pearson, C. Brimley and H. Brimley, *Birds of North Carolina* (Raleigh: North Carolina Department of Agriculture, 1942).
3. J.R. Ogden, J. Kushlan and J. Tilmant, "Prey Selectivity by Everglades Wood Storks," *Condor*, 78 (1976), pp. 324-330.
4. M.P. Kahl, "Food Ecology of the Wood Stork (*Mycteria americana*) in Florida," *Ecology Monograph*, vol. 34 (1964), pp. 97-117.
5. J. Ogden, J. Kushlan and J. Tilmant, "The Food Habits and Nesting Success of Wood Storks in Everglades National Park, 1974," U.S. Dept. Interior, National Park Services, Natural Resources Report, No. 16 (1978), 25 pp.

6. Unpublished J. Ogden field notes.
7. J. Ogden, "Recent Population Trends of Colonial Wading Birds on the Atlantic and Gulf Coastal Plains," in A. Sprunt IV, J. Ogden, and Suzanne Winckler, eds., *Wading Birds*, National Audubon Society, Research Rept. No. 7 (New York: National Audubon Society, 1978), pp. 137-153.
8. P. Anderson, J. Jehl, R. Risebrough, L. Woods Jr., L. Derveese, and W. Edgecomb, "Brown Pelicans: Improved Reproduction Off the Southern California Coast," *Science*, vol. 190 (1975), pp. 806-808.
9. J. Tanner, *The Ivory-billed Woodpecker*, National Audubon Society Research Report No. 1 (New York: National Audubon Society, 1942).
10. W.B. Robertson Jr. and J. Kushlan, "The Southern Florida Avifauna," In P.J. Gleason, ed., *Environments of South Florida: Present and Past*, Memoir 2, (Miami: Geological Society, 1974), pp. 414-451.
11. Op. cit., Bent, "North American Marsh Birds," *U.S. National Museum Bulletin*
12. Op cit., Ogden, "Population Trends of Colonial Wading Birds," *Wading Birds*.
13. J. Ogden and B. Patty, "The Recent Status of the Wood Stork in Florida and Georgia," in R. Odom and J. Guthrie, eds., *Proceedings of the Nongame and Endangered Wildlife Symposium*. Georgia Department Natural Resources, Technical Bulletin WL5 (1981) pp. 97-103.
14. Unpublished Everglades National Park files.
15. J. Ogden and S. Nesbitt, "Recent Wood Stork Population Trends in the United States," *Wilson Bulletin* vol. 94 (1979) pp. 512-523.
16. ibid.
    Op cit., Ogden and Patty, "The Recent Status of the Wood Stork," *Proceedings of the Nongame and Endangered Wildlife Symposium*.
17. Unpublished B. Patty, National Audubon Society.
18. H. Ohlendorf, E. Klaas and T. Kaiser, "Organochlorine Residues and Eggshell Thinning in Wood Storks and Anhingas," *Wilson Bulletin*, vol. 90 (1978), pp. 608-618.
    J. Ogden, W. Robertson Jr., G. Davis, and T. Schmidt, Pesticides, Polychlorinated Biphenols and Heavy Metals in Upper Food Chain Levels, Everglades National Park and Vicinity (Washington, D.C.: U.S. Dept. Commerce, National Technical Information Service, 1974).
19. J. Browder, C. Littlejohn, and D. Young, The South Florida Study (Gainesville: Center for Wetlands, University of Florida, and Tallahassee: Bureau Comprehensive Planning, Florida Dept. Administration, 1976).
20. J. Kushlan, J. Ogden, and H. Higer, "Relation of Variations of Water Level and Fish Availability to Wood Stork Reproduction in the Southern Everglades, Florida," Open File Report 75-434 (Tallahassee: U.S. Geol. Survey, 1975).
21. Ibid.
    Op. cit., Ogden and Nesbitt, "Recent Wood Stork Population Trends," *Wilson Bulletin*.
    Op. cit., Ogden and Patty, "The Recent Status of the Wood Stork," *Proceedings of the Nongame and Endangered Wildlife Symposium*.
    J. Ogden, "The Abundant, Endangered Flinthead," *Audubon*, vol. 85 (1983), pp. 90-101.
22. H.W. Kale II, ed., "Rare and Endangered Biota of Florida," *Birds*, vol. 2 (Gainesville: University of Presses of Florida, 1978).
23. D.J. Wesley, pers. comm. January 17, 1985.
24. Unpublished J. Ogden field notes.
25. Op. cit., Ogden et al., "Food Habits and Nesting Success."

26. Ibid.
27. J. Hansen, "Wood Stork Feeding Project: A Progress Report Covering the Period April 1, 1975 - June 30, 1976" (Unpublished report, National Audubon Society, Tavernier, Florida, 1976).
28. Op. cit., Kushlan et al., "Variations of Water Level and Fish Availability." Op. cit., Ogden et al., "Food Habits and Nesting Success of Wood Storks."
29. J. Browder, "Water, Wetlands and Wood Storks in Southwest Florida" (Ph.D. dissertation, University of Florida, Gainesville, 1976).
30. E.S. Clark in "A Continuation of Baseline Studies for Environmentally Monitoring Space Transportation Systems at John F. Kennedy Space Center" (Orlando: Department of Biological Sciences, Florida Technical Univ., 1978) pp. 598-607.
31. Op. cit., Ogden and Patty, "Recent Status of the Wood Stork," *Proceedings of the Nongame and Endangered Wildlife Symposium.*
32. Op. cit., Kahl, "Food Ecology of the Wood Stork," *Ecological Monograph*
33. Op. cit., Ogden, "Population Trends of Colonial Wading Birds," *Wading Birds.*
34. Unpublished J. Ogden field notes.

JOHN OGDEN has been with National Audubon Society since 1974. Formerly co-director of the California Condor Program, he now is director of the newly-organized Ornithological Research Unit. There he oversees research on the whooping crane, wood stork, heron, and puffin.

Equipped by nature to survive the rigors of the arid Southwest, the desert bighorn has coped poorly with the inroads of man.

The Desert Bighorn

by Allen Cooperrider
Bureau of Land Management

SPECIES DESCRIPTION AND NATURAL HISTORY

THE TERM "DESERT bighorn" is a popular or ecological description rather than a formal taxonomic subdivision. Taxonomists recognize seven subspecies of bighorn sheep (*Ovis canadensis*). Of these, the four southern subspecies—*nelsoni*, *mexicana*, *cremnobates*, and *weemsi*—typically are found in desert habitat.

Desert bighorns have, however, adapted to the desert in their behavior, physiology, and anatomy. Physically, desert bighorns tend to be smaller and lighter than the California and Rocky Mountain bighorns. They are capable of living during summer on desert shrubs and dry grass, marginal forage at best. Furthermore, they can endure temperatures over 115 degrees during the peak heat of summer and can go without drinking for up to three days under these conditions. The desert bighorn is the only native ungulate that inhabits many of the southwestern desert mountain ranges.

Physical Characteristics

Desert bighorn sheep are about the size of mule deer, but are shorter legged and blockier in appearance. Adult males average about 160 pounds but may weigh as much as 200 pounds, whereas adult ewes average about 105 pounds.[1] Desert bighorns are not particularly fast runners on flat terrain, but are very sure-footed in rugged, rocky, precipitous terrain and are adept at running and escaping from predators in such habitat.

Pelage varies among individuals and regions from dark slate gray to buff tan. The typical desert bighorn is medium gray-brown with white on the rump, backs of legs, and muzzle. The fur is shed in spring only and becomes increasingly washed out throughout the year. Pure white animals occasionally are reported.

Both sexes have horns, but the ewes' horns are smaller and seldom exceed 12 inches in length. The rams' horns continue to grow in a characteristic circle throughout their lives and may measure 30 to 40 inches along the outsides of the curls.[2] Annual growth rings on rams can be distinguished with the naked eye, providing a means of aging animals in the field.

Desert bighorns appear to have well developed senses of smell, hearing, and sight, although no studies have been done on the subject. Most observers have concluded that the bighorn's vision is particularly acute.[3] Bighorns prefer to remain in open country where their vision is unimpaired and to avoid areas of thick brush or trees where they cannot see predators.

Lambing Cycle

Lambing may begin as early as January in some populations. At this time ewes usually are separate from the older rams. Ewe bands typically consist of ewes, young of the year, and rams less than two and a half years old. A typically small band will include two or three ewes and their recent offspring for a total of five to 10 animals. However, on some more populated ranges bands may number more than 50.

As lambing time approaches, individual ewes leave the bands and move to lambing areas. These areas typically contain extremely rugged terrain with shelter from weather and are close to water and good forage supplies.[4] Limited evidence suggests ewes return each season not only to the same general vicinity but even to the same lambing-bed site. Because bighorns appear to be very intolerant of human activity and disturbance at such times, protection of lambing areas is very important.

Desert bighorns give birth to single lambs that are capable of moving around almost immediately following birth. Unlike deer fawns, which hide when the mothers leave to obtain forage or water, bighorn lambs stay with their mothers almost from birth. Because lambs are quite vulnerable to predators at this time, ewes often stay close to lambing grounds for a week to 10 days before joining up with other ewes. After this time lambs occasionally are left for several hours in nursery bands of up to eight lambs tended by one or more ewes. Lambs may be six months old before they are completely weaned. However, by three months most of their nutrition is from the plants they consume rather than from milk.

Weaning typically coincides with the beginning of dry periods in the desert. Herbaceous plants cease growing and become desiccated, and ephemeral water sources dry up. Desert bighorns must turn to alternative foods and limit their activities to areas within about two miles of water. Forage in such areas can be overused. Furthermore, since they concentrate at the limited water sources, desert sheep are more vulnerable to predators at this time. Any increase or decrease in the size of the herd will be largely a function of how many animals, particularly how many young of the year, survive this period.

With the onset of late-summer thunderstorms and colder weather, bighorns once again spread out into areas with ephemeral waters. This typically coincides with the onset of the rut. Rams rejoin ewes. Younger, smaller horned rams are chased off by larger, older rams so that most of the breeding is done by the older animals. On occasion old rams fight over ewes by butting heads. As the rutting season ends, the rams move back into male bands that may use ranges separate from those of the ewe bands.

Young are born from January to June, and the rut may occur from July to December depending on location.[5] The gestation period of 173 to 185 days is quite consistent.[6] The rut, and thus the breeding season, usually does not last more than three and a half months for a given herd.

The extended breeding season of desert bighorns has been cited as evidence that desert bighorns are not particularly well adapted to desert environment. It is suggested that the Pleistocene extinction of most North American ungulates has allowed the more northern-adapted bighorns to survive as relics in the Southwest, but that exotic species such as Barbarry sheep (*Ammotragus lervia*) and the feral burro (*Equus asinus*) are far better adapted to the deserts. This idea has stimulated some strong rebuttals and resulted in a provocative series of papers.[7] Although these papers are largely speculative, they raise many interesting issues relevant to management.

Significance

Desert bighorn sheep are the only native North American ungulate capable of surviving in our harshest deserts. They are indicators of the wilderness characteristics that still exist in our southwestern desert mountains. A desert range that has lost its bighorn herd is a poorer place, and residents and visitors in the Southwest prize these animals and the opportunity to view or hunt them in their natural habitat.

Historical Perspective

An estimated 1.5 to two million bighorn sheep were present in North America at the beginning of the 19th century. One biologist concluded that in 1960 populations were between 15,000 and 18,200, of which 6,700 to 8,100 were the desert subspecies *nelsoni* and *mexicana*.[8] If these numbers are realistic, and if desert bighorn numbers have declined in about the same proportion as those of their northern counterparts, then as many as a million desert bighorn sheep may have occupied our southwestern desert ranges. The 1960 estimate suggests a decline to less than one percent of that number.

In 1974, desert bighorn numbers were estimated at between 8,500 and 9,100.[9] This represented an increase of 10 to 20 percent from the estimates made in 1960. However, given the primitive nature of such estimates, wildlife biologists were reluctant to regard this as solid evidence that bighorn herds were recovering. Probably the higher number reflected improvements in the methods used to determine bighorn numbers and distribution.

The geographic distribution of the sheep has not changed as drastically. Desert bighorns still occupy most of the ranges they had prior to the 19th century — from Baja California to northern Nevada and Utah, then southeast to New Mexico, west Texas, and the Mexican provinces of Sonora, Chihuahua, and Coahuila.

This is arid country, a region of isolated mountain ranges surrounded by an extensive area of flat to rolling terrain. One ecologist aptly described the area as one of mountain islands and desert seas. Bighorns are found only in the mountain islands. The intervening valleys and basin floors are used by sheep only to move from one range to another.

Prior to 1800, distinct herds of sheep could be found in these isolated ranges. With the arrival of European settlers, many whole herds were extirpated and the routes between many ranges were cut off by highways, fences, towns, canals, and other obstructions. The combination was devastating to bighorns. Their movements between ranges always were quite limited, so they were slow at best in colonizing new areas. But once movement corridors were blocked, natural re-establishment of the animals became impossible.

Entire herds can be lost in many ways. Many herds live in ranges with only one or two year-round springs. If these springs dry up during a drought or are usurped by man for other purposes, sheep must move to another range or perish. But such movement may be impossible now because of human development. Moreover, small isolated herds are more vulnerable to extirpation from epidemics and more likely to suffer from the effects of inbreeding.

Although probably only a few herds were lost in any given year, the cumulative effect over the period from 1800 to 1960 was devastating. By 1960, only isolated remnant herds survived.

The Causes of Decline

Four primary problems have caused the decline of desert bighorn sheep: over-hunting; disease; competition from livestock, feral burros, and other exotics; and human disturbance and competition. Often these factors operated simultaneously, making it difficult to isolate a single factor responsible for the decline. In addition, the increased isolation of herds has prevented recovery.

Hunting. Hunting caused much of the decline from 1850 to 1900.[10] Few regulations were in effect and their enforcement was minimal or nonexistent. This was a period of rapid settlement and exploitation in the Southwest. Meat was required for the new settlements and many mining camps that sprang up throughout the desert. For many reasons, particularly their preference for open country and dependence on a limited number of waterholes, desert bighorns were relatively easy prey for hunters with long-range rifles.

By 1900, most states and territories had enacted some form of protective legislation for desert bighorn. California, one of the earliest to do so, passed legislation in 1873 providing complete protection from hunting. Although hunting groups consistently have sought in recent years to re-open the season, it has remained closed to this day. A closed season was first declared in Mexico in 1922. However, poaching probably continued to be a detrimental factor well into the 1950s and still may be a serious problem in local areas.

Legal hunting has been reinstated in the last 35 years in most states and Mexico. Annual hunts have been held in Arizona since 1953, New Mexico since 1968, Nevada since 1956, and Mexico since 1964. These hunts vary in specifics but are generally carefully controlled permit hunts for older rams only. Bighorns have been protected from hunting in Texas since 1903.[11] There is no evidence that legal hunting is either preventing or aiding recovery of bighorn sheep herds.

Disease. Desert bighorns seem to be particularly vulnerable to epidemic diseases. Some diseases, such as pneumonia, contagious ecthyma ("soremouth"), scabies, bluetongue, and chronic sinusitis, typically are associated with die-offs. Lungworm, associated with many die-offs of Rocky Mountain bighorns, does not appear to be particularly detrimental to desert bighorns.[12]

Why desert sheep are so susceptible to contagious diseases is not well understood. Two factors certainly contribute. First, bighorns concentrate in summer around a limited number of waterholes, creating ideal conditions for transmission of diseases through either water or direct contact. Second, the bighorn's fragmentation into small, isolated populations makes them particularly susceptible to introduced diseases.

Domestic livestock continue to be a prime source of new diseases. Most of the documented disease problems of desert bighorns, including die-offs, involve diseases carried by domestic livestock.[13] Domestic sheep, closely related to bighorns, seem to carry many diseases to which desert bighorn are quite vulnerable. Die-offs following introduction of domestic sheep into bighorn habitat have occurred many times.[14] And although it is not always possible to determine that disease from the domestic sheep was the cause, much evidence supports that conclusion. In any case, introduction of domestic sheep into bighorn range is not a prudent management practice if preservation of bighorn sheep is a primary objective.

The situation with cattle is less conclusive. Some bighorn die-offs have been triggered by diseases introduced by cattle. Yet many bighorn herds survive reasonably well on ranges used by domestic cattle. Some biologists believe that livestock grazing should be phased out on bighorn ranges and that desert bighorns should not be reintroduced into areas where livestock grazing continues. Others believe that some overlap in range use may be possible under carefully controlled conditions. Guidelines have been developed for managing livestock in such situations.[15]

Some cattle operations may be much safer than others for bighorns. In a cow-calf operation a rancher maintains a herd of cows and sells the young each year as either calves or yearlings. Typically, the only new animals introduced into the range are bulls that have been chosen carefully and inspected for disease. Such an operation may not pose a great risk to bighorns since the sheep will be exposed to the same diseases each year. By contrast, in a stocker operation cattle are bought each year as calves or yearlings and put out on the range. Thus, new animals and new diseases are introduced onto the range each year. Such an operation probably poses much more of a threat.

Competition from Livestock, Feral Burros, and Exotics. Competition for forage and water between livestock and desert bighorns began with livestock introductions in the Southwest by the Spanish in the late 1700s. However, livestock reached their peak on southern ranges about 1900, following rapid settlement and development of the ranching industry.[16]

Feral burros were introduced into the Southwest during the same period. Although domesticated for thousands of years, burros originally evolved in arid regions similar to the desert Southwest. When domesticated burros escaped or were released into the wild by prospectors and others, they thrived and increased in numbers. This is not surprising. The animals were not only in a familiar habitat, but as one biologist[17] has observed, they had been selected for thousands of years to survive in the presence of man and diseases of other domestic ungulates. Extensive field studies support the view that competition from burros for food and water can be detrimental to desert bighorns.[18]

Exotic ungulates also have been introduced or have spread into bighorn ranges or adjacent areas. Of particular concern are the aoudads or Barbarry sheep that have been introduced into desert mountain ranges in New Mexico and Texas. They have thrived in these areas. If they spread or are moved into desert bighorn ranges, the desert bighorns probably would decline.[19]

Competition for forage between desert bighorns and domestic and feral animals is especially intense during summer, when bighorn sheep are confined to ranges within a few miles of water. If the preferred forages have been removed previously by livestock or burros, the bighorns will be forced to turn to inferior forages and their nutritional status will deteriorate.

Competition for water also is most severe during the dry months of summer. Desert water sources are widely spaced and may be very limited. Desert bighorns in midsummer may wait more than an hour for other sheep to leave before getting a drink at a spring. If domestic livestock or feral burros also are competing for this water the effects can be detrimental.

Human Disturbance and Competition. Human disturbance and competition include so many varied activities that it is hard to generalize about their effects on desert bighorns. Furthermore, the types of activities have changed over the years. When miners in the 1800s set up camp next to a desert spring, they not only were competing for water but also, by their presence, were preventing bighorns from watering. In modern times, a myriad of activities — seismic testing, diversion of water to remote locations, powerlines, pipelines, highways, fences, and even residential development — disturb sheep and disrupt their behavior.

The Beginning of Recovery (1950 - Present)

Beginning around 1950, wildlife biologists and the public became more interested in desert bighorn and their management. Many articles were written, surveys of bighorn numbers and distribution were conducted, and habitat management programs were initiated. In 1950, studies of the distribution and life history of desert bighorns in Arizona were initiated, resulting in the publication in 1956 of the first monograph on the subject.[20] Similar statewide surveys in other states were reported in 1972 in California[21] and 1978 in Nevada.[22] Many other regional and local studies were conducted. In 1957, the Desert Bighorn council was formed to provide a forum for exchange and publication of information through annual meetings and published transactions.

In 1974, desert bighorn numbers were estimated at between 8,500 and 9,100.[23] This represented an increase of 10 percent to 20 percent from the estimates made in 1960. However, given the primitive nature of such estimates, wildlife biologists were reluctant to regard this as solid evidence that bighorn herds were recovering. Probably the higher numbers reflected improvements in survey methods.

CURRENT TRENDS

Habitat

The majority of desert bighorn sheep habitat is in public ownership. The U.S. Bureau of Land Management (BLM) manages the largest acreage of it, although the National Park Service and the U.S. Fish and Wildlife Service (FWS) also manage large areas. BLM manages some 100 million acres of public lands in Arizona, California, Nevada, New Mexico, and Utah. In 1982, BLM biologists estimated that 7,700 desert bighorns in 103 separate herds ranged on these lands.

Three features provide the essential components of desert bighorn habitat: open, rocky, mountainous terrain; adequate forage; and year-round sources of drinking water. Open country permits bighorns to detect intruders easily. Rugged, rocky terrain is used for escape. Preference for this type of habitat is very strong. The sheep will make little use of habitat that is more than a half to one mile from escape cover.

Forage supplies for desert bighorns are marginal at best and unpredictable because rainfall is intermittent in the desert. Consequently, desert bighorns are opportunistic foragers that make use of a wide variety of plants. During the wetter and cooler periods of fall, winter, and spring, desert bighorns eat many species of grass and other herbaceous plants that are relatively nutritious when they are green and succulent. Sheep need to put on weight and build up fat reserves during these seasons in order to survive the harsher dry periods. Dry periods come at different times in the various deserts that bighorns occupy, but all deserts have such times. During these periods, desert bighorns must turn to alternative forages such as leaves and twigs of shrubs as well as many cactus species.

What an animal eats in a given locality will depend primarily on what is available and how palatable and nutritious these plants are. Desert bighorns require about four pounds of dry-weight forage per day. However, plants vary considerably in their nutritional value. Some, such as creosote bush, are nearly worthless. To determine if forage supplies are adequate, wildlife biologists must estimate not only the total amount of plant biomass but also how much of that potential forage consists of palatable and nutritious plants. Such determinations are difficult and time-consuming, but crucial to sound desert bighorn management.

Of the three essential habitat components, water is the one that is most frequently limiting.[24] Desert water sources are used by feral burros and livestock, and water frequently is piped to remote sites for livestock, mining operations, and other activities. Furthermore, recreational activities such as camping and hunting tend to concen-

Important Desert Bighorn Forage Plants

Item	Common Name	Scientific Name
Grasses	galleta grass	*Hilaria* sp.
	desert needlegrass	*Stipa* sp.
	gramma grasses	*Bouteloua* sp.
	Muhly grass	*Muhlenbergia* sp.
	triodia	*Triodia* sp.
	three awn	*Aristida* sp.
	chess	*Bromus* sp.
Forbs*	buckwheats	*Eriogonum* sp.
	globe mallow	*Sphaeralcea* sp.
	spurge	*Euphorbia* sp.
	penstemon	*Penstemon* sp.
	filaree	*Erodium* sp.
	Indian wheat	*Plantago* sp.
Shrubs	Mormon tea	*Ephedra* sp.
	mountain mohogany	*Cercocarpus* sp.
	saltbush	*Atriplex* sp.
	blackbrush	*Coleogyne ramosissima*
	brittle bush	*Encelia* sp.
	agave	*Agave* sp.
	yucca	*Yucca* sp.
	whiteratang	*Krameria grayi*
Cacti	prickly pear	*Opuntia englemannii*

*Over 50 species of the composite family are utilized.
Source: Bruce Browning, 1971, unpublished manuscripted cited in *Transactions of the Desert Bighorn Council 1980.*

trate around water sources. Competition for water in the desert is fierce and often involves complicated legal, financial, and political issues. Not surprisingly, desert bighorns often do not fare well in such competition. In some areas permanent or intermittent streams provide water for bighorns. However, springs and seeps together with tanks and "tinijas" provide the only source of water on many ranges. The latter are natural rock formations that catch and store rainwater. Although bighorns may range widely and make use of many seasonal springs and other water sources, to survive they need to have sources that do not dry up during the critical hot summer months.

MANAGEMENT

Conservation and management of desert bighorns and their habitat consists primarily of habitat protection and improvement, re-introduction, and research.

Habitat Protection and Improvement

Conserving, improving, and protecting bighorn habitat are the most critical needs, since most desert bighorn populations are protected adequately by state legislation from overhunting.

Wildlife biologists are concentrating their efforts on three major areas related to habitat: water development, protection and enhancement of forage resources, and protection from human disturbance.

Water development has been one of the most successful management programs for desert bighorns. This is done by improvement of existing springs or other water sources and by building artificial catchments.

Springs can be improved in several ways. Marginal springs can be dug out so that standing water is available. Brush or other vegetation may be removed from the site so that bighorns will make use of it. In some cases, runoff from an ephemeral spring is caught and stored in large tanks. These tanks then can feed a "drinker" or small basin equipped with a float valve. Such a development converts a seasonal source of water into a year-round supply. Horizontal drilling has been quite effective in increasing flow of water from marginal springs.

The big game "guzzler" is probably the most important water-development technique for desert bighorns since it can provide water even in the absence of an existing water source. A guzzler consists of a concrete dam in a dry wash, one or more storage tanks, and a drinker. There are many different types of dams and drinkers. A typical construction will consist of a concrete dam about two feet high and eight feet wide, leading to three 1,500-gallon steel water tanks that feed a small concrete drinker about the size of a bathroom basin. A half-inch rain will fill up all three tanks, a supply that can last desert bighorns for more than a year.

The development of water in existing bighorn ranges can have quite dramatic effects on the population. In the late 1960s, a water treatment plant was developed in the River Mountains about five miles southeast of Las Vegas, Nevada. As part of this development, water was provided for desert bighorns. The population increased in a few years from approximately 80 animals to some 240. More than 100 desert bighorns from this herd have been re-introduced to other areas throughout the Southwest.

Water development can be quite expensive. In addition to the cost of materials and equipment, suitable locations for such development often are in remote areas where access is difficult. Supplies and even labor often must be flown in by helicopter at considerable expense.

Volunteer groups such as Nevada's Fraternity of the Desert Bighorn Sheep and southern California's Volunteer Desert Water and Wildlife Survey have helped considerably in these efforts. Between 1969 and 1982, members of the latter group contributed some 11,000 person-days of labor, more than 750,000 vehicle miles, and $170,000 worth of other goods and services.[25] Volunteers will continue to play an important role in such efforts in the future.

Improvement of forage conditions for desert bighorns is a more complex problem. Because rainfall typically is sparse and unpredictable in desert regions, plantings and seedings to improve forage for desert bighorns have met with limited success, although on some ranges with higher rainfall such efforts are possible. With increasing development of arid-land plants and reseeding techniques, such efforts may become more successful.

Controlled burning is another potential tool for improving forage conditions, although it has not been used extensively. Burning can improve forage conditions and also increase visibility by removing brush, which makes the habitat more usable by bighorns. In some cases brush can be removed by chaining or cutting.

If livestock or feral burros or other exotic ungulates are the primary cause of unsatisfactory forage conditions, control of these animals can improve conditions substantially. Feral-burro control usually requires removing the animals. Shooting them is the most efficient and cost effective way to do it, and state and federal legislation allows this on public lands. However, shooting is used only as a last resort because of substantial public sentiment against such methods.[26] Control by livetrapping and transplanting is feasible although very costly. In some cases, private organizations have paid for transplanting. The Fund for Animals spent in excess of $1,000 per animal to remove 600 burros from Grand Canyon.[27]

Control of domestic livestock also can bring significant improvement in forage conditions and increases in bighorns. Livestock were removed from Canyonlands National Park in 1975, and the bighorn populations have been increasing steadily since.[28] On BLM lands, changes in seasonal use, animal distribution, and number of animals are potential alternatives to removal.

Control of human disturbance is perhaps the most complex and difficult task of habitat management. On private land, few legal constraints prevent a landowner from making an area unsuitable for desert bighorns. On public land the management agency has some control, but the demands on these lands are ever increasing. BLM manages much of the public land that is actual or potential desert bighorn habitat. However, these lands also are in demand for mining and recreation, pipeline and powerline rights-of-way, and many other activities that can harm desert bighorn sheep. In some cases, the impacts can be minimized or mitigated by choosing alternative sites or routes, but when the activities are incompatible with maintenance of bighorn habitat and populations, the land manager must decide between the welfare of the desert bighorn or the competing activity.

Re-introductions

Re-introduction of sheep into historic range has been done with mixed success, but has great potential. Some herds, such as the one in the River Mountains, have increased until they are approaching the carrying capacity of the habitat. Animals can be transplanted to other mountain ranges without risk to the mother herd. Techniques for capturing, transporting, and releasing bighorn sheep with minimum mortality have been developed and tested in the past 15 years.

A review of published information on 13 re-introductions discovered that 11 were successful and two were failures.[29] Unfortunately, failures usually are not as well publicized as successes, so those numbers are undoubtedly misleading. The tendency to publicize only successes is unfortunate since we can learn much from studying failures. In many cases, however, funds are not available to follow up and monitor re-introductions. Some of the re-introductions within the past 15 years, including those in Zion National Park in Utah and the Virgin Mountains of Arizona and Nevada, have been monitored carefully.[30] Information from such efforts will be extremely valuable in the future in developing better techniques for successful re-introductions. Re-introductions probably will fail in areas where causes of the original extirpation of a herd have not been removed.

Inventory, Studies, and Research

Most successful management programs are based upon sound knowledge of the managed resources. A bibliography[31] of nearly 600 publications on desert bighorn has been compiled, yet much remains to be learned. As one Arizona biologist said, "Although desert bighorn sheep are well studied, many of their most pressing problems remain a mystery."[32] Solving some of these mysteries is necessary for proper management.

Three types of efforts will be required: basic inventories of the animals and their habitat, site-specific studies to determine what is happening with individual bighorn herds, and basic research on the biology and ecology of desert bighorns and their habitat.

The habitat and population inventory is the most basic information required for management. A basic inventory for desert bighorns consists of an estimate of population size, a map showing all areas used by sheep by season along with migration routes between such areas, a map of all actual or potential lambing areas, a map of all water sources and a listing of their status (permanent, ephemeral, etc.), and a description of any significant or potential problems for each herd.

Every mountain range has its own unique characteristics. Bighorn herds use the resources of each range in different ways and are affected differently by habitat disturbances. Site-specific studies often are needed to determine what is happening with a herd. These efforts go beyond the mere listing of resources and attempt to get at the causes of problems as well as at the reasons for management success.

Finally, basic research is needed on the biology and ecology of desert bighorns and their habitat. BLM biologists in 1982 identified five subjects that should be emphasized in future research: disease and genetics, nutritional requirements, impact of domestic livestock and feral animals, habitat evaluation techniques, and methods for mitigating human disturbance and improving habitat.

PROGNOSIS

Man has the capability to restore desert bighorn sheep herds to numbers far beyond what they are now, although probably not to the prehistoric levels of 500,000 to one million animals. Increasing desert bighorns in the United States from roughly 10,000 to 50,000 in the next 25 years is a realistic goal. This represents an annual increase of roughly seven percent per year. Obviously, this would require an organized long-term effort and commitment.

Many critical tools are available now. Wildlife biologists know how to provide stable water sources, how to trap and transplant desert bighorns, and how to protect critical ranges and habitats. Knowledge of how to rehabilitate desert forage is advancing steadily. However, application of this knowledge is limited by lack of money and manpower.

RECOMMENDATIONS

Restoration of desert bighorns will not occur naturally. It will require a substantial commitment on the part of many agencies, organizations, and individuals. The agencies involved will need to fund management programs, research, and, in some cases, acquisition of private lands in critical bighorn areas. An immediate need is a range-wide management plan that identifies priorities for management and estimates of what will be required to achieve the objectives.

Research into basic biology of desert bighorns slowly is providing new knowledge that can be used in management. Basic research techniques such as field immobilization and radiotelemetry now allow biologists to capture and study animals in the wild in ways impossible 15 years ago. However, research needs to be expanded.

Funds for such efforts must be used efficiently. The public and its elected representatives increasingly are aware of the need to spend taxpayers' money frugally and wisely. Those seeking to restore desert bighorns cannot afford to spend money on duplicative research.

The effort will require cooperation among federal and state agencies, private landowners, users of public lands, and conservation organizations. Many such efforts already are in effect. State wildlife agencies are responsible for managing the animals, whereas most habitat is on federal land. Cooperative efforts and agreements have been used for many years for activities such as water developments and re-introductions. For some 10 years, habitat management plans for desert bighorns have been implemented under cooperative management agreements between BLM and state agencies, and in some cases with private landowners and organizations. Such efforts need to be expanded and implemented at all levels of government.

Finally, such an effort will require organized and sustained support from the public. Volunteers can continue to contribute significantly to desert bighorn recovery programs. Equally important is the need for citizens to let management agencies know what they expect in terms of desert bighorn management.

For FY 1985 Congress appropriated a $300,000 challenge grant to BLM to initiate a program for the recovery of desert bighorn sheep. This money is to be matched by donations of equivalent value. This is a positive sign of the interest at the national level in such a program.

REFERENCES

1. C.G. Hansen, "Physical Characteristics," in G. Monson and L. Sumner, eds., *The Desert Bighorn—Its Life History, Ecology and Management* (Tucson: University of Arizona Press, 1980), pp. 52-56.
2. Ibid.
3. Ibid.
   R.E. Welles and F.B. Welles, "The Bighorn of Death Valley," National Park Service, Fauna Series No. 6 (1961).
4. J.C. Turner and C.G. Hansen, "Reproduction," in G. Monson and L. Sumner, eds., *The Desert Bighorn—Its Life History, Ecology and Management* (Tucson: University of Arizona Press, 1980), p. 147.
5. Ibid, p. 146
6. J.A. Bailey, "Desert bighorn forage competition and zoogeography," *Wildlife Society Bulletin*, vol. 8 (1980), pp. 208-216.
7. H.E. McCutchen, "Desert Bighorn Zoogeography and Adaptation in Relation to Historic Land Use," Biological Bulletin, No. 6 (1978).
   M.C. Hansen, "Desert Bighorn Sheep: Another View," *Wildlife Society Bulletin*, vol. 10 (1982), pp. 133-140.
   J.E. Wehausen, "Comment on Desert Bighorn as Relicts: Further Considerations," *Wildlife Society Bulletin*, vol. 12 (1984), pp. 82-85.
   J.A. Bailey, "Bighorn Zoogeography: response to McCutchen, Hansen, and Wehausen," *Wildlife Society Bulletin*, vol. 12 (1984), pp. 86-89.
8. H. Buechner, "The Bighorn Sheep in the United States, Its Past, Present, and Future," *Wildlife Monograph*, No. 4 (1960).
9. W. Wishart, "Bighorn Sheep" (Chap. 11), in *Big Game of North America* by J. L. Schmidt and D. L. Gilbert (eds.), Stackpole Books, (Harrisburg, PA, 1978), pp. 160-171
10. W.E. Kelley, "Hunting," in G. Monson, L. Sumner, eds., *The Desert Bighorn—Its Life History, Ecology and Management* (Tucson: University of Arizona Press, 1980), pp. 336-342.
11. Ibid, pg. 336.
12. R.W. Allen, "Natural Mortality and Debility," in G. Monson and L. Sumner, eds., *The Desert Bighorn — Its Life History, Ecology and Management* (Tucson: University of Arizona Press, 1980), pp. 172-285.

13. P.R. Krausman, J.R. Morgart and M. Chilelli, *An Annotated Bibliography of Desert Bighorn Sheep Literature* (Phoenix, Arizona: Southwestern Natural History Association, 1984), 204 pp.
14. N.J. Goodson, "Effects of Domestic Sheep Grazing on Bighorn Sheep Populations: a Review," *Biennial Symposium of the Northern Wild Sheep and Goat Council* No. 3 (1983), pp. 287-313.
15. Desert Bighorn Council Technical Staff, Desert Bighorn Habitat Requirements and Management Recommendations, *Transactions of the Desert Bighorn Council* (1980), pp. 1-7.
16. F.H. Wanger, "Livestock Grazing and the Livestock Industry," in H.P. Brokaw, ed., *Wildlife and America*. (Washington, D.C.: Council on Environmental Quality), pp. 121-145.
17. H.E. McCutchen, Desert Bighorn Restoration at Zion National Park, Utah, *Transactions of the Desert Bighorn Council* (1975), pp. 19-27.
18. R.F. Seegmiller and R.D. Ohmart, "Ecological Relationships of Feral Burros and Desert Bighorn Sheep," *Wildlife Monograph,* No. 78 (1981).
19. R.F. Seegmiller and C.D. Simpson, "The Barbary Sheep: Some Conceptual Implications of Competition With Desert Bighorn," *Transactions of the Desert Bighorn Council* (1979), pp. 47-49.
20. J.P. Russo, "The Desert Bighorn in Arizona," Ariz. Game and Fish Dept., Wildlife Bulletin, No. 1 (1956), 153 pp.
21. R.A. Weaver, Conclusion of the Bighorn Investigation in California, *Transactions of the Desert Bighorn Council* (1972), pp. 56-65.
22. R.P. McQuivey, "The Desert Bighorn Sheep of Nevada," Nevada Department of Fish and Game, Biological Bulletin, No. 6 (1978), 81 pp.
23. W. Wishart, "Bighorn Sheep," in J.L. Schmidt and D.L. Gilbert, eds., *Big Game of North America* (Harrisburg: Stackpole Books, 1978), pp. 160-171.
24. J.C. Turner and R.A. Weaver, "Water," in G. Monson and L. Sumner, eds., *The Desert Bighorn — Its Life History, Ecology and Management*. (Tuscon: University of Arizona Press, 1980), pp. 100-112.
25. V.C. Bleich, V.C., L.J. Coombes, and G.W. Sudmeier, "Volunteer Participation in California Wildlife Habitat Improvement Projects," *Transactions of the Desert Bighorn Council* (1982), pp. 56-58.
26. S.D. Kovach, "Report of the Feral Burro Committee," *Transactions of the Desert Bighorn Council* (1982), pp. 101-102.
27. Ibid.
28. T.C. Wylie and J.W. Bates, "Status of Desert Bighorn Sheep in Canyonlands National Park—1978," *Transactions of the Desert Bighorn Council* (1979), pp. 79-80.
   J. Connors, 1984, pers. commun.
29. M.M. Rowland and J.L. Schmidt, "Transplanting Desert Bighorn Sheep — a Review," *Transactions of the Desert Bighorn Council* (1981), pp. 25-28.
30. Op. cit., McCutchen, "Desert Bighorn Restoration at Zion National Park, Utah."
   R.P. McQuivey and D. Pulliam, "Preliminary Results of a Wild-Release Desert Bighorn Sheep Transplant in Nevada," *Transactions of the Desert Bighorn Council* (1980), pp. 57-61.
   J.R. Morgart and P.R. Krausman, "The Status of a Transplanted Bighorn Sheep Population in Arizona Using an Enclosure," *Transactions of the Desert Bighorn Council* (1981), pp. 46-49.

31. Op. cit., Krausman et al., *An Annotated Bibliography of Desert Bighorn Sheep Literature*.
32. D.E. Brown, "Publishers Preface," in P.R. Krausman, J.R. Morgart and M. Chilelli, *An Annotated Bibliography of Desert Bighorn Sheep Literature* (in press), pp. i-iv.

ALLEN COOPERRIDER has been with BLM for the past 11 years, studying the effects of grazing on bighorn sheep and establishing new water projects for them. Currently he is staff biologist at the BLM service center in Colorado and assists in wildlife projects throughout the West.

Scarcely 30 Puerto Rican parrots remain, with only five breeding pairs among them, a pressing challenge to biologists struggling to save the species.

The Puerto Rican Parrot

by Kirk M. Horn
U.S. Forest Service

SPECIES DESCRIPTION AND NATURAL HISTORY

THE PUERTO RICAN parrot (*Amazona vittata*) is a medium-sized, bright-green parrot, with blue outer-wing primaries, red lores and flesh-colored bill and legs. It measures 11 to 12 inches in length. At an average weight of 10 ounces, it is the smallest of the nine extant *Amazona* parrots in the West Indies. Wetmore describes the males as being slightly larger than the females,[1] though this cannot be distinguished in the field.

Since about 1940, the bird has been confined to about 0.2 percent of its original range. It now is restricted completely to the Luquillo Mountains of the Caribbean National Forest, managed by the U.S. Forest Service.[2]

The parrot's present habitat is characterized by extremes. Elevation ranges from about 100 feet to 3,532 feet. Air temperature averages about 80 degrees at lower elevations and about 65 degrees in higher areas. The upper forests are often cloud-laden, with rain falling nearly every day. On the higher peaks, yearly rainfall averages approximately 200 inches.

The forest habitat can be divided into three major cover types — Tabonuco-tree, Sierra-Palms, and Colorado-tree types — not including the dwarf forests on the upper peaks and ridges and the small forest openings. The fruit eating, cavity nesting parrot is rarely observed far from old-growth forests. It is critically dependent on large trees for nests and shelter. The bird eats mostly the fruit of the Sierra Palm (*Enterpe globosa*), a tree found in disturbed areas.

Sexually mature at three to five years of age, Puerto Rican parrots appear to pair for life or at least for extended periods. Each pair stays together during the entire year. The female incubates the eggs and cares for the young, and the male assumes foraging responsibilities during incubation. Mated pairs often engage in vicious combat with other pairs in defense of their territories.

Clutches average three eggs per nest and are completed by late February or early March. The average 26-day incubation period is accomplished solely by the female. Replacement clutches for eggs lost during the early part of the season have been observed[4] — an important trait that facilitates the captive-breeding program now under way to help the species recover.

Hatchlings are nearly naked with closed eyes, but will take food almost immediately after hatching. They are fed day and night for the first few weeks. The female may leave the nest for her first foraging sojourn about one week after the eggs hatch. The chicks normally fledge about nine weeks after hatching.

SIGNIFICANCE OF THE SPECIES

Conservation of the parrot has special importance to wildlife biologists and public natural resource managers throughout the Americas. Most other *Amazona* species of the West Indies are similarly threatened with extinction. What can be gleaned from efforts to recover the Puerto Rican parrot will be valuable in the conservation of other *Amazona* parrots. The Puerto Rican parrot also deserves special consideration because it is the last native species of parrot still surviving within United States territory. An additional noteworthy feature is that it lives in the only tropical rainforest in the National Forest System.

HISTORICAL PERSPECTIVE

The Puerto Rican parrot once was abundant throughout most of Puerto Rico, and the species probably ranged over three or four of the larger offshore islands around Puerto Rico.[5] When Columbus arrived in 1493, the parrot probably inhabited the entire island, especially its optimum habitat in the lower elevations.[6] At that time, the island was almost entirely forested.

The colonization of Puerto Rico marked the beginning of a long decline for the parrot. Man converted the parrot's forest home to crop lands and other uses. By 1912, less than one percent of the original Puerto Rican forest remained.[7] In addition, the parrots frequently were taken for pets, shot for food, killed to reduce depredations on crops, and used for trade. By the late 1930s, the population of Puerto Rican parrots was approximately 2,000 birds,[8] down from conservative estimates of 100,000 birds in the 1800s.[9] From about 1963, and with certainty from 1966, population numbers dropped to a frightening low. Actual counts of known individuals were 24 in 1968, 18 in 1969, 16 in 1970, and 12 in 1971. Since 1975, the population has increased to about 30 individuals in the wild, though only five pairs are known to be actively attempting to breed.

Causes for Decline

Many natural and human-caused events have interacted to reduce the parrot almost to extinction. These factors include habitat destruction, nest robbing, shooting, and natural factors such as predation and parasitism.

Habitat Destruction. By 1912, more than 80 percent of the island had been deforested,[10] primarily to obtain logs for charcoal production. The Luquillo Mountains escaped man's ravage mainly because of the difficult terrain and poor access. The area became a public forest reserve in 1903, a national forest in 1918, and a commonwealth wildlife refuge in 1946.

Nest Robbing by Man. Until the 1960s, man probably was raiding nearly every nest site in the Luquillo Mountains. Not only did nest robbing cause a significant loss of wild birds but it probably also played a significant role in decreasing nest-site availability. To avoid risk of injury, nest robbers sometimes felled nest trees in order to avoid climbing them. Although habitat loss to timber harvest for charcoal production was a major factor in the parrot's decline, nest robbing probably was sufficient by itself to cause a sharp reduction in the population.[11]

Recreational Use. A rapidly growing dispersed recreational use on the Caribbean National Forest poses a threat to the parrots. While difficult to quantify, human recreational activities near feeding areas and especially, nesting sites apparently is incompatible with recovery success.

Shooting and Hunting. During this century, the ever-increasing human population of Puerto Rico placed increasing demands on the parrot population for food, pets, and feathers. Additionally, both recreational shooting and the killing of parrots by farmers occurred. Early in the century, the parrot was considered a threat to agricultural crops.

Shooting of the bird for food apparently was spotty on the island, and little evidence exists of shooting in the Luquillo Mountain area. However, the hunting and killing of *Amazona* parrots was a common activity in the past. Parrot hunting was a boy's occupation. One observer described it as follows: "A boy would put on a large straw hat to hide his face, then climb a tree with a live parrot in his hand. When he made the parrot scream, other parrots would come nearby and he would catch them with a lasso. The Indians liked parrot meat, and parrots were abundant in those times."[12] Other references discuss similar accounts of Indians hunting and eating parrots in Santo Domingo. Apparently, the Puerto Rican parrot was hunted for food in the northwest portion of the island.[13]

Other Human Effects. Several additional activities played an uncertain role in causing the parrot decline during the 1960s. These included: guerilla-warfare training maneuvers between 1966 and 1971 in connection with the Vietnam War, microwave radiation from at least two of the peaks in the area, and a radiation experiment involving a 10,000-curie cesium source at ground level near a parrot use site.

CURRENT TRENDS

Several natural factors threaten the remaining population. These include interspecies competition for nest sites, predation, and parasitism.

Pearly-eyed thrasher (Margarops fuscatus). The pearly-eyed thrasher, a recent invader in the national forest, represents a serious threat to parrot nesting success. The thrasher, like the parrot, nests in tree cavities. In its search for a nest site, the thrasher will explore parrot nesting cavities and attack unattended eggs and nestlings for food. Since parrots do not constantly attend their nests, the thrasher poses a serious threat to increased reproduction. To check the depredations of the thrasher, man-made nest boxes that are preferred by thrashers have been installed in the vicinity of each parrot nest. Once the thrasher occupies a box, it will drive other nest-prospecting thrashers from the vicinity. This technique appears to have eliminated depredations by thrashers.[14]

Red-tailed hawk (Buteo jamaicensis). Second to the thrasher, the red-tailed hawk represents an important predator of nesting parrots. Red-tailed hawks are abundant on the island and have been observed raiding parrot nests and taking parrots on the wing.[15]

Rat (Rattus rattus). This introduced pest probably is not a significant problem to nesting success, although rats were blamed circumstantially for the loss of four nests from 1953 to 1955. However, it now is believed that rats are not a threat to nests that are properly attended by parrot pairs.[16]

Warble flies (Philornis pici). Warble flies are a significant parasitic threat to nestling parrots, as they are to other avian species on the island. The parrot has a moderate infestation rate. Of the 44 nestlings raised in the wild since 1973, 11 became infested with warble-fly larvae. It is estimated that four of these would have died without human intervention.[17]

Honeybees (Apis mellifera). Honeybees are a constant competitor for nest cavities. While no records of honeybees driving nesting parrots from a nest have been documented, bees are known to take over nest cavities after parrot nesting season. As a consequence, the bees must be removed before parrot nesting begins the next year.

Other Biological Enemies. Several additional species should be mentioned as possible threats. They are now being monitored by specialists during the nesting season. The Puerto Rican boa (*Epicrates inornatus*), also an endangered species, is an excellent tree climber and may prey on parrot nestlings. This may have been true especially in earlier times when the parrots nested in the lower elevations. Domestic cats (*Felis catus*) frequent parrot nesting areas. At least one nest is known to have been destroyed by a cat.[18] Potential competition from other *Amazona* parrot species that have become established on the island also is a concern.[19]

Weather puts additional limitations on recovery. Compared to the original range of the Puerto Rican parrot, the Luquillo Mountains are extremely wet. The high rainfall must be regarded as a limiting factor in nesting success. Besides the rain, the constant threat of hurricanes in the area also must be considered.

MANAGEMENT

In 1968, the Puerto Rico Department of Natural Resources, (DNR), the U. S. Fish and Wildlife Service (FWS), and the U.S. Forest Service initiated a cooperative recovery and research program. The effort is directed at improving the nesting success and productivity of wild parrots.

The very small population of 12 wild birds in 1971 is more than doubled today, but the population remains extremely vulnerable to rapid extinction from disease or hurricane.[20] Because of this, a captive-propagation program was established in 1969 to augment wild populations with young birds.

Recovery of the Puerto Rican parrot will require at least two separate, stable wild populations. Currently, 23 parrots are in the captive population.[21] The first experimental releases of free-flying, captive-reared parrots into the wild is planned for the 1985 breeding season.

Progress toward recovery for the Puerto Rican parrot has been slow, but promising. Because no more than 60 adult birds have remained at any one time for at least 17 years, genetic viability has become a major concern.

The densities needed to secure a viable, self-sustaining wild population still are unknown. Tentatively, a goal of 250 breeding pairs in at least two separate populations is proposed in the draft recovery plan. [22]

Current management activities include: guarding of nests, renovation of natural cavities or their replacement with artificial nesting structures or cavities, provision for alternative nest sites for pearly-eyed thrashers, protection of nests from honeybee takeover, inventories of wild populations, and rat control near nest sites.

The Puerto Rican parrot research program, like the recovery effort, is an interagency effort of DNR, FWS and the Forest Service. The recovery program focuses on the ecology and behavior of the wild population, development of techniques to increase bird densities, and the maintenance of the captive population to augment wild birds and serve as insurance against a catastrophic loss.

PROGNOSIS

With adequate funding, the chances for parrot recovery are good. The occupied remaining habitat of the parrot is predominantly in public ownership, as are the primary sites where additional populations could be established. In addition, strong political commitment to save the parrot has been made by all involved government agencies.

RECOMMENDATIONS

The improved status of the parrot population is attributable largely to the coordinated interagency recovery effort. At the same time, this effort is not problem free. A constant struggle is waged for funding and recruitment of qualified personnel, including volunteers, to manage the recovery effort. Though the professional and political commitment among agencies is high, continued public support is the key to parrot recovery. Most recovery problems have been identified and are being dealt with. Now what is needed is long-term financial support to keep the parrot population increasing and to establish a second population elsewhere on the island.

REFERENCES

1. A. Wetmore, *The Birds of Puerto Rico and the Virgin Islands*. Scientific Survey of Puerto Rico and the Virgin Islands. (NY Academy of Science, 1927) pp. 412-413.
2. James Wiley, *The Puerto Rican Parrot:* (Amazona vittata): *Its Decline and the Program for Its Conservation*; Puerto Rico Field Station, Patuxent Wildlife Research Center U.S. Fish and Wildlife Service, P.O. Box 21, Palmer, Puerto Rico 00721, U.S.A.:133-159—in Pasquier R. (ed). Conservation of New World Parrots. International Council for Bird Preservation Technical Publication No. 1; Smithsonian Inst. Press, Washington D.C.
3. F. Wadsworth, in *Puerto Rican Parrot* (Amazona vittata vittata) *Study*; Monographs of the Department of Agriculture and Commerce, Jose A. Rodgiguez Vidal, ed. (San Juan, Puerto Rico: Division of Information, 1959) No. 1 15pp.
4. F. Wadsworth, Team Leader, et al., Puerto Rican Parrot Recovery Plan-Draft; The Puerto Rican Parrot Recovery Team (Denver, Colorado: U.S. Fish and Wildlife Service, 1982).
5. op. cit., Wiley, *The Puerto Rican Parrot* (Amazona vittata): *Its Decline and The Program For Its Conservation*.
6. ibid.
7. ibid.
8. Wadsworth, 1949.
9. op. cit., Wiley, *The Puerto Rican Parrot* (Amazona vittata): *Its Decline and The Program For Its Conservation*.
10. op. cit., Wadsworth, Puerto Rican Parrot Recovery Plan-Draft.
11. ibid.
12. op. cit., Jose A. Rodgiguez Vidal, ed., *Puerto Rican Parrot* (Amazona vittata vittata) *Study*
13. op. cit., Wadsworth, Puerto Rican Parrot Recovery Plan-Draft.
14. ibid.

15. op. cit., Wiley, *The Puerto Rican Parrot:* (Amazona vittata): *Its Decline and The Program For Its Conservation.*
16. ibid.
17. ibid.
18. op. cit., Wadsworth, Puerto Rican Parrot Recovery Plan-Draft.
19. op. cit., Wiley, *The Puerto Rican Parrot:* (Amazona vittata): *Its Decline and The Program For Its Conservation.*
20. F. Stormer, Briefing Paper—Puerto Rican Parrot, (Washington DC: U.S. Department of Agriculture-Forest Service, Research, 1985), 6pp.
21. ibid.
22. op. cit., Wadsworth, Puerto Rican Parrot Recovery Plan-Draft.

KIRK HORN co-authored the revised 1979 Spotted Owl Management Plan. For the past six years Horn has specialized in threatened and endangered species as national program manager for the U.S. Forest Service.

LEN RUE, JR.

The Selkirk caribou may be the rarest mammal in the lower 48 states; a tiny remnant herd of about two dozen teeters toward extinction.

The Woodland Caribou

by Michael Scott
Idaho Department of Fish and Game

SPECIES DESCRIPTION AND NATURAL HISTORY

CARIBOU ARE MEDIUM-sized members of the deer family, intermediate between deer and elk. The largest males, from western Canada and Alaska, weigh approximately 600 pounds; the smallest, from the Canadian arctic archipelago, weigh about 240 pounds. Caribou are distinguished from other deer by their large hooves, broad muzzles, and distinctive antlers. Both sexes have antlers that are somewhat flattened in cross section. The antlers of females tend to be small and inconspicuous, and some individuals may be missing one or both antlers. The antlers of adult males seem ostentatious with their sweeping arcs, numerous points, and palmate "shovels."

Color varies geographically. Northern animals tend to be palest, while animals inhabiting the forests of central and western Canada are darkest, varying annually from a deep chocolate brown in midsummer to a grayish-tan the next spring. Adult males develop a conspicuous white mane during the rut. Newborn calves are dark brown and unspotted.

Range

Currently, the most widely accepted classification of caribou places all of the North American animals into one species, *Rangifer tarandus*.[1] Four living subspecies are recognized: three barren-ground races that inhabit northern Canada and Alaska and the woodland subspecies (*R.t. caribou*) that ranges across central Canada virtually from coast to coast. Most caribou populations, particularly the barren-ground animals, still exist in large numbers. The woodland caribou formerly occupied parts of New England, Michigan, and Minnesota, but was extirpated by a combination of habitat destruction and overharvest following European settlement, plus the spread of a severely detrimental brain parasite associated with white-tailed deer.[2] Historical records indicate that caribou occurred in western Montana, northeastern Washington, and northern Idaho.[3]

Woodland, or mountain, caribou calves, dark brown, unspotted, and precocious, are born in mid-June. Their first view of the world is forbidding — high, isolated ridges still frozen under the winter snowpack. Snow, rain, and wind are the rule rather than the exception. The warmth and lush green forage of summer are weeks away. The calves are born in some of the most severe and isolated habitats the cow can find. This rather remarkable aspect of mountain caribou biology, as with many other aspects of the animal's life, until recently was unknown.

Spring finally reaches the high elevation world of the Selkirk caribou by late May. After a long, severe winter on a steady diet of lichens, caribou body condition is at its lowest ebb. Prominent ribs and hip bones offer evidence of winter stress. When snowmelt on the lower southerly slopes exposes the first green forage of the year, caribou respond. They eagerly seek out those sites and concentrate their activities there for the next few weeks, slowly regaining body fat reserves. This is a period of intense, concentrated feeding activity. Caribou, typically unwary animals, are even less cautious during this period. They often can be approached within a few yards before showing any apparent concern.

Soon, however, an even stronger biological imperative strikes the pregnant cows. Forsaking the highly nutritious green buds at a time when their bodies most need them, they climb 2,000 feet to the snowy ridgetops. There, alone, they give birth to their calves. Three to four feet of hard-packed snow still cover the ground. Green forage is largely unavailable. Spring weather in the Selkirks, typically bad, is even worse on the high ridges. Yet there the cow remains for the better part of a month as her calf grows stronger. Should the calf die, she will abandon the ridges immediately to rejoin the rest of the band at lower elevations. In addition to this mysterious choice of calving habitats, the cow's basic demeanor changes. Formerly unwary, she suddenly becomes vigilant. Skittish and shy, she bolts at the hint of an intruder.

Similar calving behavior has been described for other caribou herds in British Columbia.[4] Apparently, it is an adaption to predation. A dense population of black bears plus a handful of grizzly bears inhabit the Selkirk Moutains. Aside from occasional bits of carrion, spring bear diets largely revolve around growing green vegetation. Consequently, in spring, bears move to the same sites caribou choose. For adult caribou, bears are not a particular threat. A newborn calf, however, would be easy prey for any opportunistic bear who happened upon it. Apparently, caribou move to areas least likely to be used by predators and become much less tolerant of the presence of other large animals in order to help ensure the survival of their young. Over the long run, the benefits of predator avoidance have outweighed the physiologic costs of a harsher environment.

Although female caribou in the wild can conceive at 18 months of age, most cows in the wild do not breed until they are three and a half years old.[5] Thereafter, adult pregnancy rates are high, more than 80 percent. Virtually all births are single calves. Age-specific reproductive performance of the Selkirk caribou is not known. However, overall pregnancy rates apparently are comparable to those of other caribou populations.[6] Currently three to five calves are produced annually from an adult cow segment of 10 to 12 animals. Asumming an 80 percent pregnancy rate, annual calf mortality must be in the range of 40 percent to 70 percent. Observations of cow behavior, physical condition, and herd composition suggest that most calf mortality is occurring within a very few days after birth. To date, specific causes of that mortality have not been identified. Disease, predation, and weather may all play a role. A more likely possibility, given that calves are disappearing so quickly after birth, is that malnourished females are producing small, weak offspring that have a poor chance of survival.

By mid-July, the surviving calves are strong and agile enough to travel at an adult pace. At this point, the cow-calf pairs rejoin the groups of barren cows and juvenile bulls. They now enter upon a period of relative ease and forage abundance. The days are warmer, snowmelt has proceeded from the open south slopes to the more sheltered sites, and succulent green forage is available beneath the forest canopy. Where caribou had been using low elevation openings during spring and high ridges during calving, they now turn to the mature spruce and subalpine fir forests in the high glacial basins.

The Selkirk Mountains are in a high precipitation zone. Forage growth in the open-canopied subalpine forests is lush and abundant, far in excess of the caribou's needs. Caribou are adaptable feeders in the summer, shifting from one grass, sedge, or flowering plant species to the next as each plant reaches its most nutritious and palatable growth stage. One consistent mainstay of the summer diet is huckleberry leaves delicately plucked from their twigs. Summer is a period for caribou to restore body condition and stockpile the reserves necessary for the coming winter.

The adult bull caribou is perhaps at his least attractive in early summer. Swollen knobs of velvet cover the rapidly growing antlers. Last year's faded grayish-tan coat is being replaced in great blotches by this year's rich chocolate brown. Each time he shakes, a nimbus of discarded hair surrounds him. By early September, however, nature has transformed the clown into a prince. The velvet is gone from the sweeping, impressive antlers, replaced by a hardened sheen of deep reddish-brown. The once-gaunt body is now sleek and well muscled. A cape of white hair over his neck and shoulders provides contrast to his dark, chocolate-colored body. The rut will soon begin.

Adult bulls tend to be loners much of the year. In recent years, they have been the only population segment known to use the United States portion of the herd's range regularly.[7] However, by early September the mature bulls begin to seek out the cow/calf and immature bull bands on their summer range. The rut begins in mid-September and lasts until late October, peaking in early October. Typical rutting groups consist of one mature bull at least four or five years old, six to 10 cows and calves, and, on the periphery of the group, one to three immature bulls. While the other animals feed or rest, the adult bull is almost continuously active. He is challenged constantly with the task of keeping the cows together and at the same time preventing young bulls from entering the group. To this end he is ever vigilant, rushing back and forth between the cows and the young bulls while regularly emitting a series of hoarse, coughing grunts. He apparently is rewarded for his efforts by doing most of the breeding, but he will pay for this profligate expenditure of energy the following winter. Through the late summer and into the rut, caribou increasingly seek more dense timber stands and moist areas in search of the dwindling supply of succulent green forage. Now they can be found near the seeps and wet meadows along the streams, lakes, and ponds in the glacial basins.

In caribou habitats high in the Selkirks, the change from fall to winter is abrupt. Typically the first part of November brings permanent snow. Deep, soft snow piles up rapidly, often reaching 60 inches or more by the first of January. The snowpack works two changes in the caribou's life. Suddenly the grasses and forbs of summer are buried and unavailable. Furthermore, the uncompacted snow will not support caribou high enough to reach many of the lichens hanging in the trees. To compound the problem, moving through the wet, heavy snow requires tremendous exertion. It is a time of limited forage availability and greatly increased energy expenditure. Early winter marks a transition in survival strategy from energy collection to energy conservation. From now until spring the caribou will use more energy than they take in and must rely on stored energy reserves to carry them through.

Caribou respond to these new conditions by shifting their habitat-use patterns. They come down out of the spruce-fir forests into the upper reaches of the cedar and hemlock. They choose dense cedar-hemlock stands hundreds of years old. The closed overstory canopy of such old-growth stands, often totally blocking out the sky, significantly alters snow conditions underneath. Snow depths are dramatically reduced, particularly next to the boles of larger trees. Here, scraps of evergreen forage may still be found. More importantly, the energy costs of locomotion are reduced greatly.

These early winter habitats, along with early spring range, probably are the critical habitats in the annual caribou cycle. As a complement to early winter habitats, early spring range, with its highly nutritious forage, probably allows the pregnant female to recover some of the winter's losses prior to calving, thus giving her calf a better chance for survival. In contrast to spring range, which easily can be created by judicious logging, early winter range can be created only by the patient accumulation of at least 150 years of forest growth, assuming growth starts with the proper mix of tree species.

Gradually, through the agents of sun, wind, and gravity, the snowpack begins to metamorphose and solidify. Instead of sinking 20 to 30 inches into the snow, caribou sink only six to 10 inches. When this occurs, usually in mid-January, caribou abandon the old-growth cedar-hemlock forests and move to the upper slopes and ridges above 6,000 feet. Here they prefer the more exposed southerly slopes covered by scattered, stunted subalpine fir and whitebark pine trees. They will spend the next four months in a leisurely cycle of feeding and resting, usually covering only a small area each day. The typical winter pattern for a band of six to 12 animals is to forage slowly one long ridgeline for several weeks, then move to the next ridge. Caribou have inhabited their winter world virtually alone in the past, since most other animals either hibernate or move elsewhere in winter. Today, snowmobiles and backcountry skiers increasingly disturb their isolation.

Snow continues to accumulate through the winter, peaking at eight to 12 feet in early April. This much snow buries all ground forage, including shrubs. Caribou must subsist on the only palatable forage remaining — arboreal lichens growing on conifer limbs. The moss-appearing lichens, or "old man's beard," actually are the result of a poorly understood symbiotic relationship between an algae and a fungus. Lichens derive no nourishment from the trees they grow upon. All of their sustenance comes from the air. Furthermore, the optimum combination of growing conditions occurs only briefly each year. This makes lichens slow-growing. Once a forest is destroyed by fire or logging, usable caribou winter range may be 100 to 150 years away.

Lichen growth rates are regulated chiefly by humidity and light. For instance, the dense cedar-hemlock forests produce few lichens in their gloomy interiors.[8] On the other hand, the very open, exposed ridges tend to be deficient in humidity, and hence have lower lichen densities. However, these are the very sites preferred by caribou during winter.[9] Optimum lichen production occurs in the moist glacial basins, areas rarely frequented by caribou during the period they are subsisting on lichens.

Why, when their sole forage is arboreal lichens, do caribou not choose areas with the greatest abundance of lichens, particularly when doing so often would involve moving only a few yards across the ridgeline? The answer probably is a combination of two factors. First, lichens are poor forage.[10] Although high in digestible energy, the protein content is very low. Caribou partially compensate for the low-protein diet by being more efficient at recovering nitrogen from their urea.[11] Nevertheless, their physical condition apparently is on a steady decline throughout the winter. Second, on the high, exposed ridges, wind and sun have more opportunity to operate on the snow, creating a consistently firmer snowpack. Apparently caribou are choosing ease of movement over forage abundance. It probably is more efficient for the caribou to choose habitats that allow them to meet minimum forage needs and, at the same time, conserve energy than it is for them to expend more energy to maximize the intake of low-quality forage.

During the latter part of April and May, snow depth declines rapidly as the snowpack melts and condenses. This produces a very firm snow pavement on which caribou sink very little. At this time caribou often become very mobile, moving from one drainage to the next and then back again. When they encounter the first green forage in late May they again become sedentary, and the annual cycle is complete.

A year in the life of a caribou is a long-term balancing act. Energy and nutrients must be accumulated and stored during the abundant periods of spring and summer, and then carefully doled out during the deficit periods. Survival strategies must therefore switch annually from active acquisition to passive conservation of resources. Any breakdown in this system, particularly at key points such as early winter, can lead to reproductive failure that particular year or, in more drastic instances, to death.

SIGNIFICANCE OF THE SPECIES

Caribou in the United States are of a type found in the cordilleran region of southeastern British Columbia and are commonly known as mountain caribou to distinguish them from the typical woodland caribou of northern British Columbia and eastern Canada. In the past, taxonomists have classified the mountain caribou as a separate species or subspecies. Currently they are classified as a local ecotype of the woodland subspecies.[12] Approximately 2,000 mountain caribou exist, virtually all of them in British Columbia.[13] In contrast, about 250,000 woodland caribou persist across North America.[14] Although sporadic sightings have been reported recently from northwestern Montana and northeastern Minnesota,[15] the only place in the lower 48 states where caribou now regularly occur is in the Selkirk Mountains of northeastern Washington and northwestern Idaho. In the last decade, most of the Selkirk population, currently 25 to 30 animals, apparently has remained in British Columbia just north of the international border. Thus, the Selkirk caribou is one of the rarest large mammals in the contiguous 48 states.

HISTORICAL PERSPECTIVE

Caribou were found in Idaho, Montana, and Wyoming hundreds of miles south of their present location during the 1800s,[16] but these apparently were small, isolated relict bands that soon disappeared.

More recent reports have come from the Cabinet and Purcell mountains of northern Idaho and adjacent Montana,[17] plus the Whitefish Range of northwestern Montana. However, the great bulk of historical records comes from the Selkirk Mountains,[18] where caribou numbers apparently were greatest. Reliable estimates of the population size are not available prior to the early 1970s. In the late 1800s, Selkirk caribou were common enough to be hunted regularly by the local Kootenai Indians.[19] Early homesteaders in the area described the caribou as "numerous." Trappers and miners often dined on caribou. Caribou briefly supported a limited amount of commercial activity in the form of outfitting, guiding, and market hunting.

In the period from 1900 to 1950, caribou were seen regularly throughout the Selkirks in groups of one to 20 animals. Based on this information and the assumption that the population was highly mobile and would gather into one post-rut congregation, one biologist[20] argued that the population never exceeded 50 animals after 1900.

More recent information indicates the Selkirk animals are relatively sedentary and unlikely to gather into one group.

During the mid-1950s, winter logging began at high elevations in the Selkirks, exposing caribou to frequent human contact. An Idaho Department of Fish and Game conservation officer, Paul Flinn,[21] spent considerable time in the northern Idaho Selkirks documenting caribou presence and numbers from 1955 to 1960. In the small area he was able to cover on his snowshoes, less than five percent of the total known range for this population, he estimated there were at least 100 caribou, although he could account for no more than 28 at any one time. Thus, the earlier estimate of no more than 50 animals prior to 1950 almost certainly is too low. A reasonable estimate of the population size between 1900 and 1950 is between 100 and 200.

After a relatively quiescent first half of the 20th century, two major changes came rapidly to caribou habitat: the construction of road access and loss of mature forest habitat. Severe winds in 1949 created large blocks of blowdown spruce, precipitating a spruce-bark beetle epidemic that infested the remaining standing spruce trees.[22] Previously pristine high-elevation habitat rapidly was roaded in an effort to salvage the spruce. In 1963, British Columbia completed a major highway through the heart of caribou habitat just north of the border. Several utility corridors soon followed. New logging systems arose as the early selective cutting techniques, more or less compatible with caribou habitat, gave way to the massive clearcuts of the 1960s. Much prime habitat was destroyed. A series of major fires roared across the Idaho Selkirks in 1967, compounding the habitat loss. In two short decades, the 20th century had come to the Selkirks.

Perhaps more devastating than habitat loss was the sudden influx of people associated with all the new access into the Selkirks. Normally a very docile, unwary creature, caribou had avoided overharvest by virture of their inaccessibility. Now exposed, they were slain easily by ignorant or unethical hunters. A new menace, high-speed vehicle traffic, appeared with the construction of Highway 3 in British Columbia. Dave Gray, a conservation officer in Creston, British Columbia, reported that he personally knew of five caribou killed by vehicles and five illegally shot along the highway in the first seven years of operation.[23]

Prior to 1970, what little was known about the Selkirk caribou was gleaned primarily from compendiums of anecdotal accounts. In February 1972, Dave Freddy, from the University of Idaho, began his graduate research into the status of the Selkirk population.[24] Based upon ground surveys and a series of 17 aerial flights over the next 14 months, he estimated the population to number 16 to 23 animals. Groups of 17 to 20 caribou seen by others during the same period suggest a minimum population of 20. Freddy's estimate was based upon the apparently invalid assumption that these animals were highly nomadic. This implied that if groups were seen in a particular area on one flight but not the next, they were shifting to a new area. However, a more likely alternative was that the caribou still were present, but unseen. Freddy observed caribou that were distributed more widely than the current population of 25 to 30 animals. For instance, some 10 to 20 animals apparently were residing in Idaho and Washington at that time, in addition to the group that still remains in British Columbia. A reevaluation of Freddy's data suggests the population probably was in the range of 30 to 50 animals. In any case, the Selkirk caribou experienced a significant decline between 1950 and 1970.

CURRENT TRENDS

Intensive helicopter surveys during April and early May (the optimum time to census mountain caribou) in 1983, 1984, and 1985 revealed a total population of 26 to

28 animals.[25] It is unlikely that many caribou went uncounted in these surveys. In 1984, the population included four mature bulls, three immature bulls, 13 cows, and three unidentified animals, probably immature bulls. Three calves born in 1982, five in 1983, and three in 1984 survived the first year of life. The only known mortality in recent years has come from animals shot by hunters — one each year from 1980 to 1983. An animal reportedly was hit on the highway in British Columbia during the summer of 1984, but this was not verified. One calf born to a radio-collared female in 1984 developed a severe limp in the fall, presumably because of some accident, and subsequently disappeared. At present, the population appears to be stagnant or slowly declining. Reproduction is relatively low, barely keeping pace with mortality.

Current population trends exist because habitat alteration, either through logging, wildfire, or insect attacks, has reduced the availability of apparently critical habitat components such as old-growth cedar-hemlock forests. The proliferation of access associated with mining and logging activities surely has led to increases in caribou poaching. Disease, predation, and accidents all take their toll, but are not considered significant factors in the decline. Although not a problem at this stage, the small remnant band is genetically isolated and vulnerable in the long term to the deleterious effects of inbreeding.

MANAGEMENT

The first modern management effort directed at the Selkirk caribou came in 1957 when British Columbia closed the legal season on this herd north of the international border.[26] In 1971, a cooperative agreement among state, provincial, and federal agencies formed the International Mountain Caribou Technical Committee to coordinate caribou research and management efforts.[27] Membership in the committee later was broadened to include representatives from the timber industry and sportsmen's and environmental groups. As a result of research in the early 1970s, guidelines for managing human activities within caribou range were adopted by both the British Columbia and the United States forest services.[28]

In 1977, the Idaho Fish and Game Commission listed caribou as a threatened or endangered species in the state of Idaho. A similar listing in the state of Washington followed. Idaho petitioned the U.S. Fish and Wildlife Service (FWS) for a caribou status review in 1980 and protection under the Endangered Species Act in 1982. Federal emergency listing was granted in 1983 and permanent listing in 1984. As a result of new sources of funding for nongame management, the Idaho Department of Fish and Game in 1982 initiated an intensive three-year study of caribou status, distribution, and habitat requirements.[29] Federal classification as an endangered species also generated new sources of research and management funding via the U.S. Forest Service and FWS. In 1982, members of the Caribou Committee developed a comprehensive cooperative caribou management plan[30] that recently was adopted as the official Selkirk caribou recovery plan to guide the recovery effort. The plan, which details research and management objectives, priorities, and strategies, set a short-term population recovery goal of approximately 100 animals.

Current caribou management efforts fall into three broad categories: animal protection, habitat protection, and population enhancement. Although caribou have not been hunted legally in Idaho and Washington since the turn of the century, and in British Columbia since 1957, poaching has been a continual problem.[31] If one assumes a natural adult mortality rate of five percent to 10 percent annually in this population of 25 to 30 animals, then two to three animals will die of natural causes each year. This is very near the recruitment rate of three to five calves per year. Any additional adult mortality, such as from poaching or highway accidents, probably causes a net population decrease for that particular year. The proliferation of road access into the Selkirks since 1950 and the increased human presence that access created probably played a major role in the caribou decline.

Most of the poaching that occurs apparently is not intentional. It happens during legal seasons when hunters are searching for deer or elk. Even today, many hunters are unaware that caribou are in the area. When they see an antlered animal they presume it is a legal deer or elk and shoot, often to find out much later that they have killed a caribou. Although state, provincial, and federal penalties for poaching a caribou can be substantial, they cannot act as a deterrent for someone who does not know that he is violating the law. The appropriate antidote for ignorance is education. That has been the primary focus of anti-poaching efforts in recent years. Prior to legal hunting seasons, caribou articles are placed in local newspapers and warning posters are placed along all access routes into caribou habitat. Numerous caribou presentations have been given in the local area. Recently pamphlets, videotapes, and slide-tape presentations have been developed. Larger permanent caribou signs are planned for major access roads. Finally, the Audubon Society and local sportmen's groups offer rewards for information about illegal shootings. Such reward systems are a highly effective public education tool.

A second anti-poaching strategy is to separate the hunters from the caribou. British Columbia has accomplished this since 1983 by closing the herd's range to hunting of any type. Intended as a stopgap measure until an effective information and education program is in place, this is not viewed as a desirable long-term management program. The risks of eroding local support for caribou recovery and generating an anti-caribou backlash are too great, particularly where other management options are available. One of those options is to restrict vehicular access into caribou habitat during hunting seasons. Although this does not eliminate hunters, it does reduce hunting pressure and favors more careful target selection, since the hunter knows he will have to pack out whatever he kills. Some roads on both sides of the international border have been closed to protect caribou. Perhaps one of the least socially painful alternatives for separating hunters and caribou is simply to set hunting seasons to coincide with snowfall at higher elevations. When this occurs, game populations and hunters move to lower elevations while caribou remain higher. Idaho's current seasons generally accomplish this.

The second potential source for human-related caribou mortality is accidents along British Columbia Highway 3 just north of the border. Caribou are attracted to the salt used to erode ice on the highways. Although highway accidents apparently have not been as much of a problem in recent years, the danger always exists that one disastrous accident could eliminate a major portion of the herd. Deicing agents have been suggested as alternatives to salt. Another solution might be establishment of salt licks away from the highway, but little has been accomplished. Small warning signs have been placed where the highway enters caribou habitat, but these probably have a negligible effect on vehicle speeds. The British Columbia Ministry of Transportation and Highways has been reluctant to consider different signs or a reduction in the speed limit, even though the presence of animals on the highway represents a significant human safety hazard.

The second phase of caribou management, habitat protection, primarily involves integrating caribou habitat needs into timber harvest programs. Northern Idaho is one of the major lumber-producing areas in the Northwest, and the timber industry is a mainstay of the local economy. Fortunately, recent research indicates that potential caribou-timber harvest conflicts are not severe and unmanageable.[32] Logging is being used to enhance caribou habitat. Timber harvest on the correct site can open up the dense forest canopy and create more of the critical early spring range where it is deficient. Similar improvements are possible in some areas of potential winter range but are unlikely to occur since those sites typically have low timber values. Summer and fall habitats do not benefit from logging, but, on the other hand, they apparently are not harmed by a judicious selective harvesting system, as opposed to a clearcut system. In any case, summer and fall probably are the least critical habitats. Finally, where present timber stands and forest succession patterns are not producing usable caribou habitat, timber harvest can be used to alter stand characteristics so that caribou habitat will be created in the future.

The primary conflict in timber-caribou management occurs on early winter range. The critical old-growth cedar-hemlock forests are not desirable from a purely silvicultural standpoint. Foresters would prefer to eliminate these stagnant stands and replace them with faster growing, more highly valued tree species. Enough information has not been collected to predict whether different kinds of timber stands could function as early winter caribou range. How large or small a stand can be and still be usable, or if an interspersion of openings or solid forest canopy is optimal, has not been determined. Data do not even show how much of the early winter habitat is necessary to support the population. In this ecosystem, the effect of a mistake is drastic. Once destroyed, these old-growth forests cannot be recreated even in our grandchildren's lifetime. Lacking information, management must be conservative in order to retain all options for the future. If it is proved that these old-growth stands are not as critical as we thought, they still will be here and available for harvest 20, 50, or 100 years from now. For now, it is vital to retain what is left.

Several entities are responsible for managing caribou habitat. In the United States, the most important is the Forest Service, with 175,000 acres of identified caribou habitat on the Idaho Panhandle National Forest and 36,000 acres on the Colville National Forest in Washington. An additional 50,000 acres are primarily state-owned lands. In British Columbia, the Ministry of Forests administers 79,000 acres; the Park Service, 3,000 acres; and private timber companies, 30,000 acres.

The U.S. Forest Service must abide by the Endangered Species Act and the National Forest Management Act of 1979, both of which require the service to manage habitat for a viable caribou population. In accordance, the service is making a concerted effort to protect and enhance potential caribou habitat. Although not under similar constraints, the British Columbia Forest Service is cooperating in an effort to maintain caribou habitat north of the border. In contrast, state and private landowners have no legal obligation to manage for caribou. The most worrisome problems this creates are the potential wholesale liquidation of old-growth cedar-hemlock stands and the proliferation of uncontrolled road access. Therefore it is imperative that federal lands be managed appropriately.

The third major recovery effort after animal and habitat protection is population enhancement. Beginning in 1983, after it became obvious that much of the current habitat could support caribou but was unoccupied, representatives from the cooperating agencies began developing a herd-augmentation plan.[33] The draft of this plan will be undergoing public and agency review during the spring of 1985 and could be finalized by fall, 1985. If the final decision to tranplant caribou is made, 18 to 36 caribou during a three-year period will be captured and removed from a healthy mountain caribou population near Revelstoke, British Columbia. Since dispersal of transplanted animals into inappropriate habitats is a major concern, the plan direction is aimed at minimizing initial animal movements. Under the preferred option, caribou will be captured and moved during early winter when the animal's behavior and snow conditions make dispersal unlikely. At the release site, caribou will be held about a week in a large temporary pen to allow social bonds to form within the transplant group and to allow the initial flight response to subside. One evening the gate will be opened and the animals allowed to move out at their leisure.

The British Columbia Wildlife Branch attempted a similar transplant within British Columbia (not in the Selkirks) during the winter of 1984-85. To date, that transplant appears successful. However, should the preferred alternative appear likely to fail, other options include a holding period that lasts through calving or maintaining a permanent captive nursery herd and releasing the offspring. A major part of any transplant effort will be radio collared and tracked by a full-time biologist for at least two years after release. Other plan details call for intensive law enforcement and public information efforts, plus temporary restrictions on public access to minimize disturbance during critical periods. Funding is available for the first year of a transplant effort, but continued funding is questionable in times of budget restraint. If all goes well, the first transplant could occur in the late fall of 1985.

PROGNOSIS

Caribou in a sense are more fortunate than other threatened or endangered species in the West. As a large mammal, they capture the public's imagination yet are not viewed as potentially dangerous as are the wolf and grizzly bear. Therefore more support exists for recovering their population. Most of the opposition comes from those who see caribou as a threat to their economic well-being. Furthermore, the infrastructure necessary to coordinate caribou management already is in place and functioning well. Mangement of the Selkirk caribou herd is often cited as a model of international cooperation.

Caribou habitat, though diminished, is still apparently more than adequate to support a recovered population. The outlook is bleak for habitat management on state lands, which must by law be managed for maximum economic return to the state, and on private lands. However, some excellent habitat is economically inoperable from a timber-management standpoint and is, therefore, unlikely to be seriously disturbed by man. Federal timber lands, which comprise the bulk of caribou habitat, are now and will continue to be managed under guidelines designed to protect that habitat. Now that it has been identified as a problem, the direct impact of people on caribou is being addressed through an aggressive program of law enforcement, public education, recreation management, and access control. However, human population growth in north Idaho, particularly that associated with massive development proposals in the Priest Lake area, could swamp the regulatory system.

Two of the keys to caribou recovery — animal and habitat protection — already are in place and, given time, could lead to recovery by themselves. However, given the low reproductive rates of this population, recovery could require decades of very conservative management. In the intervening years, a chance disaster easily could tip the scales against this small isolated band. Furthermore, as time goes on, inbreeding could become more and more a problem. The obvious solution is to re-establish other bands within the Selkirks to speed up the recovery process, provide new genetic material, and provide insurance against catastrophe. If this third recovery key, transplanting, is turned, the recovery of the Selkirk caribou could occur in a matter of years, not decades. That is an opportunity that exists with few other endangered species.

RECOMMENDATIONS

Current management direction[34] should continue. Few options exist on state or private lands except where caribou habitat protection is incidental to other activities. On federal lands, maintenance of the key early winter habitats and access control are top priorities. Areas in which caribou habitat could be enhanced by logging should be identified, particularly on potential spring ranges. Alternatives to clear-cut logging systems need to be evaluated for the spruce-fir forest zone. Detailed contingency plans for dealing with natural catastrophes such as wildfire or forest insect epidemics are lacking and should be developed. The currrent caribou habitat management guidelines should be revised in light of the most recent research information. The current efforts of the U.S. Forest Service and Idaho Department of Fish and Game personnel to develop a computer model of the cumulative effects of all human activities on caribou habitat should continue.

The potential impact of greatly increased recreational activity in the Selkirks needs to be addressed. Efforts to maintain broad public exposure to caribou research and management efforts should continue via slide and video presentations, pamphlets and posters, and media contacts. Law enforcement, particularly of access closures, should be stressed. Big game hunting seasons should be arranged to minimize the possibility of a caribou shooting. Some potentially deleterious recreation activies such as snowmobiling or heli-skiing should be monitored closely to preclude problems. During very sensitive periods, particularly during winter and calving, disturbance of caribou should be minimized.

Research should focus first on more closely identifying early winter habitat preferences and requirements. Physiologic research aimed at developing an annual energy and nutrient budget, particularly for reproductive females, could prove invaluable in identifying the most critical time periods and the factors that limit population growth. Causes of early calf mortality have not yet been identified. Similarly, possible genetic, pathological, or mineral deficiencies have yet to be investigated. Behavioral responses to human disturbances have been studied only casually.

Finally, but most important, the transplant program should be approved and carried out. No other activity has as great a chance of leading to the recovery of the Selkirk caribou herd.

REFERENCES

1. A.W.F. Banfield, "Revision of the Reindeer and Caribou, Genus *Rangifer*," National Museum of Canada Bulletin, No. 177, 1961.
2. R.C. Anderson, "Neurologic Disease in Reindeer, (*Rangifer tarandus*) Introduced into Ontario," *Canadian Journal of Zoology*, vol. 49, 1971, pp. 159-166. D.O. Trainer, "Caribou Mortality Due to the Meningeal Worm *Parelaphostrongylus tenuis*," *Journal of Wildlife Diseases*, vol. 9, 1973, pp. 376-378.
3. E.F. Layser, "A Review of the Mountain Caribou of Northeastern Washington and Adjacent Northern Idaho," *Journal of the Idaho Academy of Science*, Special Research Issue No. 3, 1974.
4. K. Simpson, K.B. Hebert, and G.P. Woods, "Mountain Caribou (*Rangifer tarandus caribou*) Ecology in the Columbia Mountain of British Columbia," (unpublished manuscript, British Columbia Fish and Wildlife Branch, Nelson, B.C., May 1984). British Columbia Ministry of Recreation and Conservation, Fish and Wildlife Branch, "The Status and Management of Caribou in British Columbia," (Victoria, B.C., 1978).

5. F.L. Miller, "Caribou: *Rangifer tarandus*," in J.A. Chapman and G.A. Feldhamer, eds., *Wild Mammals of North America* (Baltimore: Johns Hopkins University Press, 1982), pp. 923-959.
6. Idaho Department of Fish and Game, "Caribou Ecology," Job Progress Report, Project No. W-160-R-10 (Boise, ID, 1983).
7. Idaho Department of Fish and Game, "Caribou Ecology," Job Progress Report, Project No. W-160-R-10 (Boise, ID, 1984).
8. R. Detrick, "Arboreal Lichens Available to Caribou: Selkirk Mountains, Northern Idaho," (unpublished manuscript, University of Idaho, Department of Biological Sciences, Moscow, ID, 1983).
9. Op. cit. Idaho Department of Fish and Game, "Caribou Ecology," Job Progress Report, Project No. W-160-R-10 (Boise, ID, 1984).
10. T. Ahti, "Ecological Investigations on Lichens in Wells Gray Provincial Park, with Special Reference to Their Importance to Mountain Caribou," (unpublished manuscript, British Columbia Parks Branch, Victoria, B.C., 1962).
11. R. Wales, L. Milligan, and E.H. McEwan, "Urea Recycling in Caribou, Cattle and Sheep," in J.R. Luick, P.C. Lent, D.R. Klein, and R.G. White, eds., *Proceedings of the First International Reindeer and Caribou Symposium*, Biological Papers of the University of Alaska, Special Report No. 1, 1975, pp. 297-307.
12. Op. cit., Layser, "A Review of the Mountain Caribou of Northeastern Washington and Adjacent Northern Idaho."
13. British Columbia Ministry of Environment, "Woodland Caribou in the Thompson-Nicola Resource Region," (June 1981).
14. A.T. Bergerud, "Status of *Rangifer* in Canada. I. Woodland Caribou (*Rangifer tarandus caribou*)," in E. Reimers, E. Gaare, and S. Skjenneberg, eds., *Proceedings of the Second International Reindeer/Caribou Symposium*, Direktoratet for Vilt OG Ferskvannsfisk, (Trondheim, Norway, 1980, pp. 748-753).
15. L.D. Mech and M.E. Nelson, "Reoccurence of Caribou in Minnesota," *The American Midland Naturalist*, vol. 108, No. 1, 1982, pp. 206-208.
16. D.R. Johnson, "Historic Record of Caribou in Central Idaho," *The Murrelet*, vol. 48, No. 3 (September-December 1967), p. 57.
    H.F. Evans, "An Investigation of Woodland Caribou in Northwestern United States," *Transactions of the North American Wildlife and Natural Resources Conference*, vo. 29, 1964, pp. 445-453.
17. Op. cit., Layser, "A Review of the Mountain Caribou of Northeastern Washington and Adjacent Northern Idaho."
18. Ibid.
19. Ibid.
20. D.J. Freddy, "Status and Management of the Selkirk Caribou Herd," (M.S. Thesis, University of Idaho, Zoology Department, 1973).
21. P. Flinn, "Caribou of Idaho," (unpublished manuscript, Idaho Department of Fish and Game, Boise, ID, 1956).
    P. Flinn, "The Caribou of Northern Idaho," *Idaho Wildlife Review*, vol. 11, No. 5 (March-April 1959), pp. 10-11.
22. U.S. Department of Agriculture, Forest Service, "Selkirk Mountain Caribou Management Plan," (Idaho Panhandle National Forests, Coeur d'Alene, ID, 1983).
23. Op. cit., Layser, "A Review of the Mountain Caribou of Northeastern Washington and Adjacent Northern Idaho."
24. Op. cit., D.J. Freddy, "Status and Management of the Selkirk Caribou Herd."

25. Op. cit., Idaho Department of Fish and Game, "Caribou Ecology," Job Progress Report, Project No. W-160-R-10 (Boise, ID, 1983).
Op. cit., Idaho Department of Fish and Game, "Caribou Ecology," Job Progress Report, Project No. W-160-R-10 (Boise, ID, 1984).
26. Op. cit., P. Flinn, "Caribou of Idaho."
27. Op. cit., U.S. Department of Agriculture, Forest Service, "Selkirk Mountain Caribou Management Plan."
28. D.R. Johnson, D.R. Miller and J.M. Peek, "Guidelines for Human Activity Within the Range of Mountain Caribou, Southern Selkirk Mountains," University of Idaho, College of Forestry, Wildlife and Range Sciences, Misc. Publication No. 3, 1977.
29. Op. cit., Idaho Department of Fish and Game, "Caribou Ecology," Job Progress Report, Project No. W-160-R-10 (Boise, ID, 1983).
Op. cit., Idaho Department of Fish and Game, "Caribou Ecology," Job Progress Report, Project No. W-160-R-10 (Boise, ID, 1984).
30. Op. cit., U.S. Department of Agriculture, Forest Service, "Selkirk Mountain Caribou Management Plan."
31. Op. cit., Layser, "A Review of the Mountain Caribou of Northeastern Washington and Adjacent Northern Idaho."
Op. cit., P. Flinn, "Caribou of Idaho."
Op. cit., Idaho Department of Fish and Game, "Caribou Ecology," Job Progress Report, Project No. W-160-R-10 (Boise, ID, 1984).
32. Op. cit., Idaho Department of Fish and Game, "Caribou Ecology," Job Progress Report, Project No. W-160-R-10 (Boise, ID, 1984).
33. U.S. Department of Agriculture, Forest Service, "Environmental Assessment: Selkirk Mountains Caribou Herd Augmentation" (Idaho Panhandle National Forests, Coeur d'Alene, ID, 1985).
U.S. Department of Agriculture, Forest Service, "Selkirk Mountains Caribou Herd Augmentation, A Cooperative Interagency Plan" (Idaho Panhandle National Forests, Coeur d'Alene, ID, 1985).
34. Op. cit., U.S. Department of Agriculture, Forest Service, "Selkirk Mountain Caribou Management Plan."

MICHAEL D. SCOTT began ungulate research during graduate work at the University of Montana. After completing an elk research project for the University of Idaho, he began a three-year stint with the Idaho Fish and Game Department studying caribou. Now principal wildlife research biologist with the Idaho department, he has recently been assigned to study California bighorn sheep.

Its numbers increasing in the lower 48 states, the bald eagle may prove to be one of wildlife management's surest successes.

The Bald Eagle

by Nancy Green
Bureau of Land Management

SPECIES DESCRIPTION AND NATURAL HISTORY

THE DARK BODY and pure white head and tail of an adult bald eagle (*Haliaeetus leucocephalus*) are unmistakable. Prior to attaining this coloration, however, immatures go through a sequence of five other plumage types and sometimes are mistaken for golden eagles (*Aquila chrysaetos*). These plumages include a uniformly dark phase in the first year, followed by phases with varying amounts of white on the belly, back, wings, tail, and head. The coloration of some four-year-olds is similar to that of the distinctive adult plumage, which usually occurs at about age five. Eye and beak color also change with age, from dark brown at hatching to yellow in adults.[1]

Bald eagles show a gradual decrease in size and weight from the northern to the southern portions of their range. Females are larger than males, as is the case with many birds of prey. Measurements range from three to three and a half feet for body length, six to eight feet for wingspan, and eight to 14 pounds for weight.[2] Of the North American birds of prey, only the California condor (*Gymnogyps californianus*) is larger.[3]

Range

Bald eagles occur only in North America. Their range encompasses most of the continent, from south of the arctic tundra in Alaska and Canada to the southern United States and Baja California in Mexico. Breeding areas are primarily along the coasts and inland lakes and rivers.[4] During the fall, thousands of bald eagles from Alaska and Canada migrate to the lower 48 states and winter there from October through March. The birds occur in nearly every state during part or all of this time. Winter range includes arid terrestrial habitats as well as areas associated with water.[5]

Taxonomy

The bald eagle is one of eight species in the genus *Haliaeetus*, the "fish" or "sea" eagles, and is the only member of the genus that regularly occurs in North America. Early taxonomists described two subspecies, the southern bald eagle (*H. l. leucocephalus*) and the northern bald eagle (*H. l. alascanus*), but the validity of such a distinction now is questioned.[6] Other than a gradual decrease in the birds' weight and size from northern to southern nesting areas, no distinct morphological characteristics separate the so-called subspecies, nor are their breeding ranges clearly separable.[7]

Longevity

Bald eagles in captivity have lived 36 years, but it is unlikely that many individuals reach that age in the wild.[8] Of the young birds that fledge, probably at least 50 to 70 percent die within a year, and it has been estimated further that more than 90 percent may die prior to attaining adult plumage. Mortality is believed to be low for adults and is estimated to range from five to 10 percent per year.[9]

Reproduction

Bald eagles are monogamous and are believed to mate with the same individual for several years, possibly for life. However, if a pair bond is broken for some reason, for example by the death of a mate, a new pair bond usually is formed.

The age at first breeding is variable for most birds of prey. For bald eagles, records of breeding age are for captive-reared and hacked birds (see below for a description of hacking). The youngest confirmed age of bald eagles breeding and successfully rearing young is four years for both the male and female.[11] One record exists of a three-year-old at a successful nest, although it is not certain that this eagle was the parent of the chick.[12] The percentage of wild-reared eagles that actually breed as three- or four-year-olds probably is quite low, particularly in areas with relatively large nesting populations where young, inexperienced adults face stiff competition for nest sites from older eagles with established breeding areas.

The breeding period begins with courtship and nesting activity and ends five to seven months later, when the young become independent of their parents. Breeding activity is not necessarily synchronized within a particular area, and dates of egg laying sometimes vary by four to eight weeks among nests in the same vicinity.[13]

Breeding periods also vary along a latitudinal gradient. Most courtship and nest building occurs from late September through November in Florida and Texas,[14] from November to January in central Arizona,[15] Janaury to early March in Colorado, late February through March in Washington,[17] and late March through April in Alaska.[18] The breeding season also can vary with elevation. Nesting activity begins approximately one month later in Yellowstone National Park, at 7,000 to 8,000 feet, than in surrounding areas 1,000 feet or so lower. This difference is related to the longer period of ice cover, which affects prey availability at higher elevations.[19]

Mated pairs do not necessarily produce eggs each year. Factors that could account for nonbreeding include both human related and naturally occurring problems such as chemical contamination, disturbance, poor physical condition due to severe weather, shortages in prey during the nonbreeding period, or low prey availability at the beginning of the nesting season.

A breeding female lays a single clutch of one to three eggs. Although bald eagles have been known to lay a second clutch if the first is destroyed,[20] this apparently is rare. Incubation begins when the first egg is laid and usually lasts 34 to 36 days. The young fledge from 70 to 98 days after hatching. They usually remain dependent on the adults for another 60 to 80 days while they learn to hunt.[21]

Characteristics of Nesting Habitat

Water is the feature common to bald eagle nesting habitat throughout the continent. Nearly 100 percent of all bald eagle nests are within two miles, and the vast majority are within a half mile, of a coastal area, bay, river, lake, or other body of water.[22] Proximity to water reflects the dependence of bald eagles on fish, waterfowl, and seabirds as primary food resources. The minimum abundance of available prey required for successful bald eagle reproduction is not known, and the prey base, if described at all, generally is characterized as "abundant" or "regularly available."

Most bald eagles nest in trees. The particular types of trees used for nesting vary across the country, but one or two species usually contain most of the nests within a particular geographic locale. Consequently, the physical characteristics of nest trees are similar within a given area, but vary widely when considered over the entire nesting range. Two characteristics — a clear flight path to at least one side of the nest and excellent visibility, often with an unobstructed view of water — are common to nearly all bald eagle nests. These characteristics usually are provided by dominant or co-dominant trees within wooded areas, trees at the edge of wooded areas, and trees in open areas. Most nest trees also have a stout limb structure or a branching pattern that is suitable for supporting a large nest near the treetop. Although a few nests are in the tops of dead trees, most are in the top third of a living tree, with live foliage above the nest providing shade or protection during inclement weather.[23]

Nests typically are used for a number of years and become immense in size because the birds add to them each year. However, pairs sometimes build a new nest near an old one. The maximum number of nests reported for a single breeding area is seven.[24] Only one nest is used for rearing young in a particular year. The others, so-called alternate or "supernumerary" nests, often are used as feeding platforms or perch sites.

Nests on cliffs and rock pinnacles were reported in historic habitat in southern California, Kansas, Nevada, New Mexico, and Utah.[25] Currently, occupied nests on these substrates are known to occur only in Alaska and Arizona.[26]

Bald eagles rarely nest on the ground, probably because such sites are highly susceptible to predators. Ground nesting has been reported in Canada's Northwest Territories and in Ohio, Michigan, Alaska, and Texas.[27]

Nests on man-made structures are rare. The top of an airport approach light was used as a nest platform by a pair on Amchitka Island, a nest was reported in an abandoned barn near the Niagara River, and wooden observation towers have been used twice in the Chesapeake Bay area.[28] Recently, bald eagles used a man-made nest platform in Arizona.[29]

Food Habits

Fish are the primary diet of most bald eagles. Both live and dead fish are taken. When capturing prey, an eagle extends its talons only a few inches below the water's surface. Consequently, live fish are vulnerable only when near the surface or in shallows. Species taken vary throughout the continent as a result of local differences in availability. Species most commonly reported in the literature include catfish (*Icatalurus spp.*), carp (*Cyprinus carpio*), and gizzard shad (*Dorosoma cepedianum*). At several well-known bald eagle wintering areas, including Glacier National Park in Montana, the Chilkat River near Haines, Alaska, and the Skagit River in Washington, the birds take advantage of the large numbers of salmon carcasses (*Oncorhynchus spp.*) available after spawning.[30]

Bald eagles are opportunistic. The amount of fish they eat depends in part on the ease with which they can obtain other food items. In the Chesapeake Bay region, for example, prey items collected beneath bald eagle nests during the 1984 breeding season included 29 species of birds, six species of mammals, and five species of turtles.[31] Waterfowl and seabirds have been reported in a few locations as being of equal or greater importance than fish in the eagles' diet.[32] Bald eagles can capture healthy birds, and some are relatively efficient at doing so,[33] but most of the birds they take are injured, sick, or dead. Eagles undoubtedly are more successful and expend less energy capturing injured or sick birds or scavenging on dead ones.

Remains of numerous species of mammals have been found at bald eagle nests, but the regular use of mammalian prey probably occurs only when such prey is readily available. For example, when carrion of the European hare is abundant, it rivals fish as the major food item for some nesting pairs on San Juan Island, Washington.[34]

Winter Habitat Characteristics

Abundant, readily available food resources are a primary characteristic of bald eagle wintering habitat. Most wintering areas are associated with open water where eagles feed on fish or waterfowl, often taking dead or injured animals that are obtained easily. Wintering bald eagles also use habitats with little or no open water if other food resources, such as rabbit or deer carrion, are regularly present.[35]

Night roost sites are the other major characteristic of winter habitat. Roosts also may be occupied for significant portions of the daytime, particularly during inclement weather. Communal roosting by two or more eagles is quite common, and a few sites regularly have more than 100 bald eagles present during periods of high use. The same roosts are used from year to year, probably by many of the same birds. Levels of use vary during the winter, but as a general rule certain roosts are used by many more eagles than others.

As is the case with nesting, the structural and site characteristics of a roost are more important than the particular tree species. Roost trees usually are the oldest and largest trees within a stand and most have stout horizontal limbs and an open branching pattern that allows plenty of room for takeoff and landing. Visibility to the surrounding areas is unobstructed, and little or no human activity occurs in the immediate vicinity. Finally, the microclimate is more favorable than it is in areas which are not used for roosting.[36]

The distance between roost sites and feeding areas is highly variable. Some are immediately adjacent, others are several miles apart. The greatest reported distance is approximately 18 miles for a site in Utah.[37] This suggests that proximity to food is far less critical than other roost-site characteristics. The warmer microclimate at roosts is a particularly important factor because it means that the eagles do not have to spend as much energy to maintain body temperature. They therefore require less food and can better withstand periods of food shortage.[38] This not only enhances survival but also helps ensure that adults enter the breeding season in good condition, which is important for reproductive success.

SIGNIFICANCE OF THE SPECIES

The bald eagle has unique cultural significance because it is the national symbol and is of special interest to Native Americans who use eagle feathers and talons for rituals. Consequently, public concern for and interest in bald eagles is unusually great. Bald eagles have special biological significance as they occur at the top of the food chain and are susceptible to certain types of environmental contaminants. Thus, their status is one indicator of the health of the environment.

HISTORICAL PERSPECTIVE

Historic Distribution and Abundance

Information about the historic distribution and abundance of bald eagles during the winter is incomplete, and several states have no records of wintering eagles prior to this century, although the birds probably were present. Many of the historic accounts describe major threats to wintering eagles. For example, a report from 1668 in Maine states that many of an "infinite number" of wintering eagles at Casco Bay were shot and fed to hogs.[39] In New York, 60 to 70 were shot on Long Island during one winter in the mid-1800s.[40]

Historic records of nesting eagles are more numerous and indicate clearly that their number and range has declined significantly over the past two centuries. Documented records or good indications of historic nesting habitat in the lower 48 states exist for all but Rhode Island and West Virginia.[41]

Several historic accounts mention that noticeable population declines occurred prior to 1900, and in 1921 an article in the journal *Ecology* included a plea for the protection of bald eagles to prevent their extinction.[42] By 1940, declines had been mentioned in articles describing nesting populations in at least 12 states — California, Illinois, Indiana, Iowa, Kansas, Minnesota, Missouri, Montana, New Jersey, New York, Pennsylvania, and Washington.[43] Concern for the species was widespread, and Congress, believing the national symbol was threatened with extinction, passed the Bald Eagle Protection Act of 1940. At that time, the major problems affecting the species were habitat loss and shooting.[44]

Beginning in 1947, reproductive success in several nesting areas plummeted and remained at extremely low levels through the early 1970s. Some of the best documentation is for a 100-mile segment of Florida's west coast, where the number of breeding pairs dropped from 73 with 103 young in 1946 to 43 with just eight young in 1957.[45] Similar catastrophic declines were recorded elsewhere in Florida and in parts of Maine, New Jersey, Michigan, and the Chesapeake Bay area.[46]

Data on the percentage of immature bald eagles observed during the winter also reflected the decline in reproductive success. For example, from 1931 to 1945 about 36 percent of the bald eagles migrating past Hawk Mountain, Pennsylvania, were immatures. Between 1954 and 1960, just 23 percent were immatures. Midwinter surveys sponsored by the National Audubon Society in the early 1960s also yielded 22 to 26 percent immatures.[47]

After several years of study, the low level of reproductive success exhibited by bald eagles and many other birds was linked conclusively to organochlorine insecticides, particularly DDE, a persistent metabolite of the insecticide commonly known as DDT. The history of DDT and its effects is well known.[48] Used extensively on agricultural lands and forested areas beginning in 1947, DDT entered watersheds and became part of aquatic-based food chains. Eventually, it was stored as DDE in the fatty tissue of fish and waterfowl. As bald eagles fed on these animals, they accumulated DDE in their systems.

Although occasionally implicated as a cause of death,[49] DDE mainly affected bird reproduction. Laboratory studies on selected species revealed that some affected birds failed to lay eggs and that many produced thin eggshells that broke during incubation. Intact eggs often were addled or contained dead embryos, and the mortality rate was unusually high among the young that hatched.[50]

By the late 1960s, the detrimental effects associated with DDT were becoming widely known, and its use was curtailed sharply. On December 31, 1972, the Environmental Protection Agency banned the use of DDT in the United States. Recent analyses show that DDE residues in bald eagle eggshells have dropped significantly since the ban, with a concomitant increase in reproduction.[51]

Other chemicals and toxicants may have played a role in the decline of bald eagles, but their impact is less clear. Lethal levels of the pesticides dieldrin, banned in 1974, and endrin, withdrawn from the United States market in 1984, have been documented in bald eagles, as have lethal levels of mercury. The high levels of dieldrin found in some bald eagle eggs may have contributed to reproductive failure. High residues of polychlorinated biphenyls, known as PCBs and widely used by the electric power industry as an insulating fluid and by other industries as a plasticizer, have been documented in bald eagles and their eggs and might have contributed to mortality or reproductive failures.[52]

Of the human-related mortality factors that have contributed to the decline or extirpation of historic nesting populations, shooting is the most significant. Quantitative data concerning bald eagles found dead in the wild have been available since the early 1960s, when shooting was diagnosed as the cause of death about 60 percent of the time. This percentage has declined fairly steadily since then to roughly 18 percent in the late 1970s.[53]

Other mortality factors directly attributable to humans include electrocution on powerlines, poisoning from substances such as thallium and strychnine, collisions, and accidental trapping (usually in open-bait traps set for predators or furbearers). An additional, recently documented mortality factor is lead poisoning, which can occur when bald eagles feeding on waterfowl or other prey that have been shot ingest lead shotgun pellets . Procedures for identifying bald eagle mortality due to lead poisoning have been developed only recently,[54] and consequently the magnitude of this problem in the past cannot be assessed.

Human disturbance is cited frequently as a major cause of population declines, but little quantitative data exists on this topic. Activities associated with logging, mining, construction of various types, recreational activity, and many other land uses certainly disturbs bald eagles in some instances. However, the impact depends on factors such as the type of action, its frequency and duration; the distance between the activity and the areas regularly used by eagles; the extent to which it modifies nest trees, hunting and loafing perches, roosts, and prey habitat; the timing of the activity in relation to the birds' reproductive cycle; and the level of disturbance already existing in the area. The issue is further complicated by the fact that some birds are far more tolerant of disturbance than others. Previous experience could account for some of the individual differences. Age is a factor, too, with adults generally less tolerant than immatures.[55]

Despite this variability, disturbance near nests unquestionably has caused nesting failures. Short-term disturbance might affect reproduction for only one year, but long-term presence of people in the immediate vicinity of a nest can cause permanent abandonment. Even in these cases, the effects depend on whether the pair can locate suitable unoccupied nesting habitat and successfully raise young. The loss of suitable habitat due to disturbance decreases available habitat and limits the potential for population maintenance and growth.

How disturbance in nonbreeding habitat affects population levels is even less clear. Studies of wintering eagles show that some sites have been abandoned as a result of human intrusion of various types. If the birds are forced into less suitable habitat, the results could be poor physiological condition and subsequent reproductive failures or even starvation.

The factor most consistently associated with population declines over the past 200 years is habitat loss. Increasing human populations have resulted in significant alterations of land near water — the type of habitat in which all bald eagle nesting areas and most wintering areas are located. Some of this habitat loss has been offset, however, by land uses that have created favorable habitat conditions for bald eagles. For example, the construction of dams along the Mississippi and other rivers in the Midwest resulted in open water and provided eagles with winter-killed fish or fish stunned, injured, or killed by dam turbines. Use of these unfrozen areas by wintering eagles is quite high. The extent to which this positive change in winter habitat suitability has led to increased survival and reproductive success is unknown. New nesting habitat also has been created at some reservoirs and other water impoundments, such as Shasta Lake in northern California, which is used by several nesting pairs.

CURRENT TRENDS

The bald eagle is listed as an endangered species throughout the lower 48 states except in Washington, Oregon, Minnesota, Wisconsin, and Michigan, where it is listed as threatened.

The most current informaton on the nationwide distribution and abundance of nesting bald eagles is for the 1982 breeding period, when 31 of the lower 48 states reported at least one occupied nesting area.[56] Overall, 1,482 occupied nests were reported. Pairs that successfully raised young totaled 954, roughly 65 percent of the number of nesting pairs. The number of young that were raised and presumably fledged from nests was 1,487.

Broad geographic assessment shows that almost 90 percent of the remaining nesting pairs occur in 11 states covering five areas: the Great Lakes region (Wisconsin, Minnesota, Michigan); Florida; the Pacific Northwest (Washington, Oregon, northern California); the Chesapeake Bay area (Maryland, Virginia, Delaware), and Maine.

Productivity, as measured by the number of young raised per occupied nest, provides an important index of population status. Nationwide, productivity was one young per occupied nest in 1982, but natural factors cause productivity to vary widely across the country. For example, biologists in Wyoming attributed the low level of productivity in 1982 to severe weather conditions during a critical time in the nesting cycle. The next year, productivity was up to 1.19 young per occupied nest.

In a few states, productivity is chronically low and merits concern. Productivity in Washington was approximately 0.8 for 1982, up slightly from 1981, when it was 0.7. Data going back several years indicate that productivity in Washington has been relatively low since at least 1975.[57] Whether this is caused by natural or human factors is unknown.

Maine's productivity of 0.8 was higher than in the past, but still not particularly good. Bald eagle populations in Maine were seriously affected when DDT was in widespread use, and it is possible that some breeding females are still affected by contaminants.

The Chesapeake Bay population had productivity of about 0.9 in 1982. This is slightly below the national average, but considerably higher than the levels found 10 to 20 years ago when pesticide contamination was a more severe problem and productivity was only 0.2 to 0.4 young per pair.[58]

The status of bald eagle populations during the winter months has received vastly increased attention since 1979, when the National Wildlife Federation initiated the annual midwinter bald eagle survey. This popular event, with approximately 4,000 participants each year, involves counting bald eagles during a two-week period each January. The counts show a minimum winter population of about 14,000 bald eagles in the conterminous states.[59] The majority of these, probably at least 75 percent, are migrants from Alaska and Canada.

Hundreds of wintering sites exist. The length of time wintering bald eagles remain at any one of them varies. Food availability and weather conditions influence the duration of winter use. Some locations receive their highest use early in winter, others during the middle, still others toward the end. The number of eagles present also varies tremendously, from sites used by only one or two eagles to those with hundreds.

Survey coverage for wintering eagles is highly variable both in timing and areas covered. The most complete data on winter distribution is for January, when the midwinter survey is held. Major areas of use at that time include portions of the Mississippi, Illinois, and Missouri rivers in the Midwest, the Skagit River in Washington, and the Klamath Basin area along the border of California and Oregon. These locations account for about half the eagles observed during the January count. The majority of the other eagles are found west of the Mississippi River. The relatively low number of wintering eagles observed in the eastern United States probably reflects a smaller amount of suitable wintering habitat plus the size of nesting populations in eastern Canada, which are considerably smaller and therefore contain fewer migrants than those in central and western Canada and Alaska.

Bald Eagle Reproduction in the Conterminous 48 States, 1982*

State	Occupied Nests	Successful Nests	Young Raised	Productivity (Young Per Occupied Nest)
Alabama	0	—	—	—
Arkansas	1	1	1	1.00
Arizona	10	8	14	1.40
California	52	31	48	0.92
Colorado	6	4	9	1.50
Connecticut	0	—	—	—
Delaware	4	2	3	0.75
Florida	340	240	356	1.05
Georgia	3	3	5	1.67
Idaho	15	8	15	1.00
Indiana	0	—	—	—
Illinois	2	1	2	1.00
Iowa	1	0	—	0.00
Kansas	0	—	—	—
Kentucky	0	—	—	—
Louisiana	18	16	18	1.12
Maine	72	36	56	0.78
Maryland	58	35	55	0.96
Massachusetts	0	—	—	—
Michigan	96	57	87	0.91
Minnesota	207	145	245	1.18
Mississippi	0	—	—	—
Missouri	2	0	—	0.00
Montana	37	25	44	1.19
Nebraska	0	—	—	—
Nevada	0	—	—	—
New Hampshire	0	—	—	—
New Jersey	1	0	—	0.00
New Mexico	1	0	—	0.00
New York	2	1	2	1.00

State	Occupied Nests	Successful Nests	Young Raised	Productivity (Young Per Occupied Nest)
North Carolina	0	—	—	—
North Dakota	0	—	—	—
Ohio	7	5	7	1.00
Oklahoma	2	1	2	1.00
Oregon	93	51	72	0.77
Pennsylvania	4	3	4	1.00
Rhode Island	0	—	—	—
South Carolina	21	15	20	0.95
South Dakota	0	—	—	—
Tennessee	0	—	—	—
Texas	14	10	16	1.14
Utah	0	—	—	—
Vermont	0	—	—	—
Virginia	48	27	40	0.83
West Virginia	1	1	2	2.00
Washington	135	75	101	0.78
Wisconsin	207	145	251	1.21
Wyoming	22	8	12	0.55
TOTALS	1,482	954	1,487	

*For a few states the number of occupied nests includes sites where only one adult was present. Productivity is based on young per occupied nest with known outcome.

Trend

Variability in the use of wintering areas, combined with differences in survey efforts and coverage from year to year and place to place, makes it difficult to assess the nationwide trend of bald eagles based on the numbers reported for the winter period. Information on the number and success of nesting pairs gives a better indication of trend. The first attempts to assess the nationwide status of nesting bald eagles occurred in 1962 and 1963 as part of the National Audubon Society Continental Bald Eagle Project.[60] Nationwide data also were compiled in 1973 and 1974 by the U.S. Fish and Wildlife Service (FWS),[61] in 1978 by the National Wildlife Federation,[62] and in 1981 and 1982 by the Bureau of Land Management.[63] A comparison of these reports shows declines since the early 1960s in Georgia, New Jersey, North Carolina, Ohio, and Tennessee. Nesting surveys in these states have remained the same or increased over the years, indicating that the declines are real, not just an artifact of changes in survey effort.

Despite these decreases in specific states, on a nationwide basis the data suggest a tremendous increase in nesting pairs, from about 500 in the early 1960s to approximately 1,500 in the early 1980s. However, most biologists agree that much of this increase is the result of greater survey efforts and expanded coverage. The extent of actual population increases is unknown, but generally is believed to have been small until very recently. The present situation looks more encouraging than it has in years. Biologists in the Great Lakes states, Maine, Texas, and the Chesapeake Bay area believe small increases in the number of nesting pairs have occurred over the past few years. Also, pairs are becoming established in previously unoccupied and historic habitat in the Great Lakes region, Georgia, Missouri, and Colorado. Further, produc-

Distribution of Occupied Bald Eagle Nests by Regions, 1982

Region/State	Occupied Nests	Percent of Total
Lake states	510	34
Florida	340	23
Pacific Northwest	280	19
Chesapeake Bay	110	7
Maine	72	5
All other states	170	12
Total	1,482	100

tivity has improved in populations that once were severely affected by DDE. For example, a survey of the Chesapeake Bay region in 1936, 11 years prior to the use of DDT, indicated productivity of about 1.6 young per active nest. In 1962, the next time the area was surveyed, productivity had declined to about 0.2 young per active nest. By 1977, five years after the DDT ban, productivity was 0.8.[64] In 1984, the number of young per active nest was 1.1,[65] still below the level observed in the 1936 survey but well above the level observed when DDT was widely used.

MANAGEMENT

Laws, Regulations, Policies

In 1940, Congress passed the Bald Eagle Protection Act, giving special protection to the nation's symbol. This law prohibits the possession, sale, or transport of bald eagles or any parts thereof (e.g., feathers, talons), nests, or eggs. Pursuing, shooting, poisoning, wounding, killing, capturing, trapping, collecting, molesting, or disturbing bald eagles also is prohibited under this act.

Bald eagles in Alaska were exempted from the act until 1959, when the law was amended to include them. Another amendment in 1962 extended protection to the golden eagle, a species subject to considerable illegal shooting. This amendment was designed primarily to discourage the shooting of immature bald eagles, which in some plumages are similar in appearance to golden eagles.

Maximum civil and criminal penalties for violation of the Bald Eagle Protection Act are a fine of $5,000 and imprisonment for one year for the first offense, and a fine of $10,000 and two years imprisonment for subsequent violations. Also, the head of any federal agency that authorizes livestock grazing on public land may revoke the grazing permit of a permittee convicted of violating the act.

A recent court ruling on a violation of the Bald Eagle Act in South Dakota casts doubt on its application to lands owned by Native Americans. The case involved the killing of bald and golden eagles and sale of feathers and other parts. Basically, the court ruling was that the defendants were not liable for killing the eagles because the taking occurred on tribal lands where centuries-old treaties give tribal members the right to hunt. The ruling was upheld by the Eighth U.S. Circuit Court of Appeals. The Department of the Interior currently is considering whether the case should be taken to the Supreme Court. In the same case, the sale of feathers and other parts was determined to be illegal under the Bald Eagle Act, the Migratory Bird Treaty Act, and the Endangered Species Act.

The Migratory Bird Conservation Act was passed in 1918 to provide for the preservation, introduction, and restoration of migratory birds. This law contains most

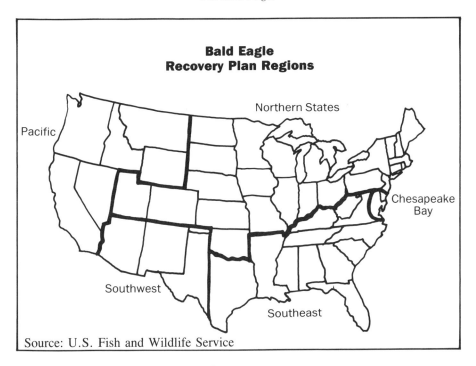

**Bald Eagle
Recovery Plan Regions**

Northern States

Pacific

Chesapeake
Bay

Southwest

Southeast

Source: U.S. Fish and Wildlife Service

of the same prohibitions as the Bald Eagle Act. Bald eagles and other raptors were not covered under this act until 1972, when the Migratory Bird Treaty between the United States and Mexico was amended to include them.

The Endangered Species Act probably is the single most important piece of legislation affecting bald eagles. The act directs federal agencies to ensure that any action they fund, authorize, or carry out is not likely to jeopardize the continued existence of listed species or result in the destruction or adverse modification of habitat designated as critical for the species. What constitutes jeopardy for bald eagles never has been defined firmly, so proposed actions in nesting and wintering habitat are reviewed case by case. With appropriate planning, many actions can be designed and carried out in a manner compatible with the continued presence of bald eagles in an area. Provisions of the act that involve critical habitat do not apply to the bald eagle because no critical habitat has been designated for them.

Four recovery plans for bald eagles have been approved by the U.S. Fish and Wildlife Service. They cover the Chesapeake Bay area, the Southwest, the Southeast, and the northern states. A fifth plan, covering the Pacific region, is under preparation.

The five plans differ in details, but collectively they recommend an approximate doubling of the current nesting population, re-establishment of pairs in states where nesting populations occurred historically, minimum average productivity of 0.9 to 1.1 young per occupied nest, and adequate habitat protection to assure population maintenance. All of the plans contain specific recommendations for research and management activities by federal and state agencies.

Captive Breeding

The major captive breeding program for bald eagles is at the FWS Patuxent Wildlife Research Center in Laurel, Maryland. The 14 pairs at the facility are all wild birds that have permanent injuries and cannot be released. Since the program's inception in 1976, 71 Patuxent eaglets have been placed in the wild. Successful production of young also has occurred at the Columbus Zoo, the Cincinnati Zoo, and the Cleveland Museum of Natural History.

Re-introduction

Techniques for establishing new populations or bolstering existing ones have involved translocation of eggs, fostering, and hacking. Translocation of eggs involves moving eggs produced by wild or captive adults to nests where wild pairs consistently have failed to produce young of their own, usually because of reproductive failures related to environmental contaminants. This technique has not generally succeeded. Between 1974 and 1978, only five young were fledged from 18 translocated eggs. An additional problem is that removal of all or most of the eggs from wild parents often results in abandonment of the donor nests. Consequently, egg translocation is not recommended for bald eagle population restoration.[66]

Fostering is a technique in which young are placed in nests and raised by adults that are not their parents. The young usually are two to four weeks old when placed with foster parents, which typically are wild pairs with a poor history of reproductive success. Most of the young are from captive breeding facilities. Young from the wild usually are from a destroyed nest, such as one blown down in a storm. At least 53 young have been fostered since 1978, with about 85 percent successfully fledged.[67]

Hacking involves raising young bald eagles in a large cage on a tower. Hack sites are suitable but unoccupied nesting habitat. The eagles, taken mostly from nests in the wild, usually are six to eight weeks old when placed in the hack tower. Food is provided through a tube or in some other manner that does not allow the young birds to associate humans with being fed. The hack cage is large enough to allow the young to exercise their wings, just as they would at a natural nest site. When the birds are ready to fledge, the front of the cage is opened and the eagles are free to fly.

Hacking has been tremendously successful. Some 266 eaglets have been hacked and fledged in 11 states since 1976.[68] In 1976, New York — where the nesting population has been reduced to just one pair — was the first state to try hacking bald eagles. The two eaglets hacked that year paired four years later, built a nest approximately 85 miles from their hack site, and successfully raised young.[69] Hacked eagles subsequently have been observed at another nest in New York and at one in Tennessee.[70] Eagles hacked in historic habitat on Santa Catalina Island, California, now are beginning to show nesting activity there, too.[71]

Research

Research activities are occurring in several areas and cover numerous topics, including energetics, daily activity patterns and habitat utilization, migratory movements, characteristics of nesting and wintering habitat, and responses to disturbance. One of the most interesting research techniques involves satellite tracking of a bald eagle fitted with a solar-powered transmitter. This has the potential to provide excellent data on long-distance movements.[72] At Patuxent, research on bald eagles includes work on lead poisoning, hematology, and artificial insemination techniques.

Habitat Management

To the extent possible, biologists manage bald eagle habitat through site-specific management plans based on data for individual nesting or wintering areas. However, it is not always possible to conduct the detailed studies needed to deal with adverse impacts from proposed habitat alterations such as highway construction, timber management, or other activities in bald eagle habitat.

A wildlife biologist on the Chippewa National Forest in northern Minnesota has developed guidelines for protecting bald eagle nesting areas when detailed, site-specific information is not available. These guidelines[73] are based on concentric buffer zones around a nest site, with fewer restrictions on human activity as the distance from the nest increases. In the "primary zone," extending a minimum of 330 feet from the nest, all land-use actions except those that involve habitat improvement are prohibited. In the "secondary zone," extending at least 660 feet from the nest, no significant changes in the landscape from activities such as clear cutting or major construction are allowed. The "tertiary zone" extends a quarter mile from the nest or up to a half mile if there is direct visibility from the nest to activities at that distance. This is the least restrictive zone, with several activities permissible if they cannot be seen from the nest or if they take place during the nonbreeding period.

Additional management practices include restricting the presence of humans during the nesting season, particularly before the young are six weeks old; retaining abandoned nest trees if the surrounding habitat is still suitable; preserving dominant or co-dominant trees near the nest for perching, roosting, or construction of new nests; planting trees, if necessary, to provide potential nest sites; and maintaining an adequate prey base.

The buffer zone approach can be modified to fit local conditions. For example, a primary zone radius of 1,500 feet is recommended for nesting areas covered by the Southeast Bald Eagle Recovery Plan, except for Florida, where the recommended radius is 750 feet. The larger zone for states other than Florida reflects more intensive management because of the relative scarcity of nesting bald eagles in those states. The loss of even one suitable nest site in those states would have a very serious and potentially devastating impact on an individual state's total nesting population.[74]

Site-specific management plans have been written for bald eagle nesting areas in several states, mostly on federal land. Some involve application of the concentric zone approach around individual nests. Others involve zones with irregular boundaries that are determined on the basis of detailed studies. Some of the zones include feeding habitat as well as the nest tree.

A new and very promising approach is being used in the Greater Yellowstone Ecosystem, which includes portions of Idaho, Wyoming, and Montana. Researchers and biologists from the three states have formed a working group to incorporate site-specific management recommendations into a regional management strategy encompassing approximately 50 nesting areas in the vicinity of Yellowstone and Grand Teton national parks.[75] This coordinated ecosystem approach is designed to maintain habitat for the existing population and protect habitat for future population growth. The procedure should serve as a model for other locations with concentrations of nesting pairs and habitat.

Encouraging private landowners to recognize the unique and special significance of nest sites on their property, a conservation measure pioneered by the Florida Audubon Society, has been an excellent means of assuring habitat protection in Maine. Similar attempts to inform and involve landowners are now under way in the Great Lakes and Chesapeake Bay states, Washington, and perhaps a few other states.

Management of wintering habitat has developed more slowly than for nesting areas. As is the case for nesting areas, site-specific and regional plans are preferred. General guidelines for maintaining habitat suitability include prohibiting or minimizing human activity within a quarter-mile zone of night roosts and major feeding areas during the time of year when bald eagles are present (this can be reduced to 330 feet if vegetation screens the view of human activity); maintaining night roost trees and preferred hunting and loafing perches in feeding areas; prohibiting habitat alterations such as road construction, land clearing, and clear cutting in roosting and feeding areas, and controlling livestock use in riparian zones where such use has a significant negative impact on tree regeneration in roosting or feeding areas. Recommended habitat enhancement practices include improvements for prey species, planting trees in areas where regeneration appears to be a problem that will limit the future availability of roosts and hunting perches, and planting vegetation to help visually screen bald eagle habitat from human activity. These guidelines for habitat protection and enhancement also could be applied to roosts and feeding areas used by immatures and by nonbreeding adult bald eagles during the nesting season.[76]

PROGNOSIS

The precipitous decline of bald eagle nesting populations that began in the late 1940s has ended. Improved productivity, higher numbers of nesting pairs, and reoccupancy of some historic nesting habitats are encouraging signs. Also, increasing attention is being given to habitat protection and maintenance. Nevertheless, current populations are only about half of the target levels recommended in the five bald eagle recovery plans, and the prognosis is uncertain.

For any species, population growth depends on rates of reproduction and survival for different age classes. A computer model of bald eagle population dynamics, based on a range of hypothetical but realistic values for reproduction and survival rates, has demonstrated that the survival rate is by far the more critical factor affecting bald eagle populations.[77] One major implication of this model is that management of nesting habitat with the goal of maximizing reproduction will not guarantee population growth or even population stability unless accompanied by an adequate rate of survival. Human-related mortality factors such as shooting and lead poisoning could limit populations in some areas. Because much of the mortality occurs during the winter period, the identification and management of important winter habitat, in addition to management of nesting areas, is essential.

Another implication of the model is that recovery of the species will be a slow process. Like most large, long-lived animals, bald eagles have a relatively low reproductive rate and are slow to reach sexual maturity. Under these conditions, particularly if the local breeding population is small, population growth will be slow, even if survival is relatively high.

Small populations are a major concern because they are particularly vulnerable to extinction. Fifteen states reported 10 or fewer nesting pairs in 1982. The long-term viability of populations containing so few pairs is questionable. For example, the entire nesting population in Arizona—10 pairs in 1982—is concentrated along segments of two adjacent rivers, the Salt and the Verde. Any significant changes in habitat

Comparison of Status Reports for Nesting Pairs of Bald Eagles

Year	Pairs Reported
1962	515
1963	487
1973	632
1974	708
1978	1,116
1981	1,424
1982	1,482

suitability in this river system could jeopardize the whole Arizona nesting population. Even some of the large populations cannot be considered secure. In places like Florida and the Chesapeake Bay area, the expansion of human populations continues to affect bald eagle habitat. Construction of waterfront homes and subdivisions, increased boating and other recreational activity, alteration and drainage of wetlands, and land development for highways, airports, and other public or commercial purposes are continuing problems. Acid rain, through its impact on lake ecosystems and the bald eagle prey base, has the potential to affect habitat suitability seriously over large portions of the species' range. Hazardous waste that contaminates groundwater supplies also could lead to widespread problems for the prey species that bald eagles depend upon.

In summary, the incremental, cumulative loss of habitat; human-related mortality; and nesting failure are the crucial factors influencing the survival and recovery of bald eagle populations today. The future status of bald eagles in the conterminous states depends largely on the extent to which suitable habitat can be retained and survival and reproductive success maximized.

RECOMMENDATIONS

Implementation of the Endangered Species Act and the recommendations in the five bald eagle recovery plans is crucial to the long-term survival of the species in the conterminous United States. For managers of federal land, this means doing more than simply avoiding activities that could jeopardize the continued existence of the species. Positive management actions to facilitate recovery are needed. The recovery plans contain specific recommendations for actions by federal and state agencies and cooperating private organizations. Although the details of the plans vary, the basic recommendations are similar in all of them:

1. Protect all of the remaining occupied nesting habitat, including feeding areas and prey populations. Federal and state agencies can accomplish this through site-specific or regional management plans for nesting habitat under their jurisdiction, or by ensuring that the land-use plans and actions they authorize contain appropriate stipulations for habitat protection. Significantly increased effort is needed to enlist the cooperation and support of private landowners to maintain habitat suitability.

2. Identify and maintain suitable historic and unoccupied nesting habitat to allow for population expansion. This is important everywhere, but particularly in states with relatively limited suitable habitat.

3. Monitor the status of nesting populations yearly by determining nest occupancy and reproductive success. Also, adopt standard procedures and terminology to improve the comparability of data over time and from different areas.

4. Continue population restoration through hacking and fostering. Focus on areas with very small populations that need to be bolstered to ensure long-term viability and on areas where historic populations have been extirpated. Continue support for captive breeding programs to provide young for these efforts.

5. Reduce human-related mortality from shooting, lead poisoning, and other factors through changes in laws and regulations and through increased public education programs.

6. Continue support for facilities and personnel to analyze causes of mortality and reproductive failure.

7. Give continuing attention to acid rain, hazardous wastes, and other environ-

mental contamination problems that affect or could affect habitat suitability, survival, and reproductive success.

8. Identify and protect important roosts and feeding areas used by wintering and nonbreeding bald eagles. Give greater emphasis to identifying habitat used during the early and late winter by conducting surveys during those times. Initiate surveys to identify important roosts and feeding areas used by immatures and by nonbreeding adults during the nesting season. These habitats have received little attention. Federal and state agencies should maintain and enhance key wintering and nonbreeding habitats by addressing them in land-use plans, preparing site-specific or regional management plans, and placing stipulations on other land uses in order to maintain habitat suitability. Public relations programs are needed to ensure the cooperation of private landowners in maintaining habitat suitability.

9. Promote increased communication and coordination among the many biologists, researchers, and land managers who deal with bald eagles throughout the country. Better coordination would ensure the most efficient use of available funds by focusing attention on the highest priority problems and management activities. Successful management strategies would be more widely known and adopted. Public relations materials would be more likely to be shared, rather than developed independently at greater cost. Duplication of research efforts would be minimized, as would the potential for unnecessary disturbance of the birds. Increased coordination also would facilitate the use of standard procedures and terminology, so that the information needed to monitor the species' status will be comparable for different locations. This could be accomplished by forming working groups on local, regional, and national levels.

REFERENCES

1. W.S. Clark, "Plumage Sequences of the Bald Eagle" (Unpublished manuscript presented at the Raptor Research Foundation Annual Meeting, Blacksburg, Virginia, 1984).
2. Ralph H. Imler and E. R. Kalmbach, "The Bald Eagle and Its Economic Status," U.S. Department of Interior, Fish and Wildlife Service Circular no. 30 (1955). Arthur C. Bent, *Life Histories of North American Birds of Prey*, Order Falconiformes, Part I. U.S. National Museum Bulletin no. 167 (Washington, D.C., 1937), pp. 321-349.
3. Leslie Brown and Dean Amadon, *Eagles, Hawks, and Falcons of the World* (New York: McGraw-Hill Book Company, 1968).
4. Ibid.
5. Donald A. Spencer, *Wintering of the Migrant Bald Eagle in the Lower-Forty Eight States* (Washington, D.C.: National Agricultural Chemicals Association, 1976).
6. Dean Amadon, "The Bald Eagle and Its Relatives", in *Biology and Management of Bald Eagles and Ospreys*, David M. Bird, Chief Ed. (Ste. Anne de Bellevue, Quebec: Harpell Press, 1983), p. 1-4.
7. American Ornithologists' Union, *Checklist of North American Birds*, 5th ed. (Ithaca, NY: American Ornithologists Union, 1957).
8. Ian Newton, *Population Ecology of Raptors* (Vermillion, SD: Buteo Books, 1979).
9. Steve K. Sherrod, Clayton M. White, and Francis S.L. Williamson, "Biology of the Bald Eagle on Amchitka Island, Alaska," *Living Bird*, vol. 15 (1977), pp. 143-182.

J.W. Grier, "Modeling Approaches to Bald Eagle Population Dynamics." *Wildlife Society Bulletin*, vol. 8, no. 4 (1980), pp. 316-322

10. Op. cit., Newton, *Population Ecology of Raptors.*

11. P.E. Nye, "A Biological and Economic Review of the Hacking Process for the Restoration of Bald Eagles," in *Biology and Management of Bald Eagles and Ospreys*, David M. Bird, Chief Ed. (Ste. Anne de Bellevue, Quebec: Harpell Press, 1983), pp. 127-135.

12. Donald A. Hammer, John L. Mechler, Marcus E. Cope, and Richard L. Lowe, "Successful Wild Nesting of a Three-Year-Old Captive-Reared Bald Eagle" (Unpublished manuscript, Raptor Research Foundation, Blacksburg, Va., 1984).

13. C.L. Broley, "Migration and Nesting of Florida Bald Eagles," *Wilson Bulletin*, vol. 59 (1947), pp. 3-20.

14. Ibid.
    Doris Mager, "The Life and the Future of the Southern Bald Eagle," in *Proceedings of the Bald Eagle Conference on Eagle Movements* (Apple River, IL: Eagle Valley Environmentalists, 1977), pp. 115-117.
    J. Smith, Pers. comm., Texas Div. Parks and Wildlife (1982).

15. T.G. Grubb, "A Survey and Analysis of Nesting Bald Eagles in Western Washington" (Thesis, University of Washington, Seattle, 1976).

16. Pers. observation (Green).

17. Op. cit., Grubb, "A Survey and Analysis of Nesting Bald Eagles in Western Washington."

18. Op. cit., Sherrod et al., "Biology of the Bald Eagle on Amchitka Island, Alaska."
    R. J. Hensel and W. A. Troyer, "Nesting Studies of the Bald Eagle in Alaska," *Condor* vol. 66, no. 4 (1964), pp. 282-286.

19. J. E. Swenson, "Ecology of the Bald Eagle and Osprey in Yellowstone National Park" (Thesis, Montana State University, Bozeman, 1975).

20. W. J. Hoxie, "Notes on the Bald Eagle in Georgia," *Auk*, vol. 127, no. 4 (1910), p. 454.
    Herrick, F. H., *The American Eagle: A Study in Natural and Civil Liberty* (New York: Appleton-Century Co., 1934).
    Craig Koppe, Pers. comm., U.S. Fish and Wildlife Service, Washington, D.C. (1985).

21. Op. cit., Bent, *Life Histories of North American Birds of Prey.*
    J. R. Maestrellin and S. N. Wiemeyer, "Breeding Bald Eagles in Captivity," *Wilson Bulletin*, vol. 87, no. 1 (1975), pp. 45-53.
    J. D. Fraser, "The Breeding Biology and Status of the Bald Eagle in the Chippewa National Forest" (Ph.D. dissertation, University of Minnesota, St. Paul, 1981).

22. Op. cit., Grubb, "A Survey and Analysis of Nesting Bald Eagles in Western Washington."
    R. N. Lehman, "A Survey of Selected Habitat Features of 95 Bald Eagle Nest Sites in California," State of California Department of Fish and Game, Wildlife Management Branch Administration Report No. 79-1 (1979).
    J. E. Mathisen, "Nest Site Selection by Bald Eagles on the Chippewa National Forest," in Biology and Management of Bald Eagles and Ospreys, David M. Bird, ed. (Ste. Anne de Bellevue, Quebec: Harpell Press, 1983), pp. 95-100.
    J. M. Andrew and J. A. Mosher, "Bald Eagle Nest Site Selection and Nesting Habitat in Maryland," *Journal Wildlife Management*, vol. 46, no. 2 (1982), pp. 385-390.
    Linda C. McEwan and David H. Hirth, "Southern Bald Eagle Productivity and

Nest Site Selection," *Journal Wildlife Management*, vol. 43, no. 3 (1979), pp. 585-594.

J. R. Murphy, "Nest Site Selection by the Bald Eagle in Yellowstone National Park," *Utah Academy of Sciences Proceedings*, vol. 42, no. 2, pp. 261-264.

23. Op. cit., Grubb, "A Survey and Analysis of Nesting Bald Eagles in Western Washington."

Op. cit., Mathisen, "Nest Site Selection by Bald Eagles on the Chippewa National Forest."

24. C. M. Pruett-Jones Nash and G. T. Allen, "The San Juan Island Bald Eagle Nesting Survey, in *Proceedings of the Washington Bald Eagle Symposium*, R. L. Knight, G. T. Allen, M. V. Stalmaster, and C. W. Servheeen, eds. (Seattle, Wa.: The Nature Conservancy, 1981), pp. 105-115.

25. Op. cit., Bent, *Life Histories of North American Birds of Prey*.

N.S. Goss, 1886. In Ohmart and Sell, op. cit. (ref. 55).

Ridgway, R. 1877. In Ohmart and Sell, op. cit.

Ligon, J. S. 1961. In Ohmart and Sell, op. cit.

26. Op. cit., Sherrod, et al., "Biology of the Bald Eagle on Amchitka Island, Alaska."

D. M. Rubink and K. Podborny, "The southern bald eagle in Arizona (a status report)" (Albuquerque, NM: Fish and Wildlife Service, 1976), Endangered Species Report No. 1., 33 pp.

27. Op. cit., Bent, *Life Histories of North American Birds of Prey*.

Op. cit., Sherrod, et al., "Biology of the Bald Eagle on Amchitka Islands, Alaska."

R. G. Bromley and D. L. Trauger, "Ground Nesting of Bald Eagles Near Yellowknife, Northwest Territories," *Canadian Field-Naturalist*, vol. 88, no. 1 (1974), pp. 73-75.

Anonymous. "Bald Eagles in Ohio," *The Surveyor*, vol. 3, no. 1, (1976), p. 1.

E. M. Brigham, Jr., "Larry Eagles," *Jack-Pine Warblers*, vol. 17, no. 3 (1939), pp. 59-63.

O. J. Murie, "Fauna of the Aleutian Island and Alaska Pennsula," Fish and Wildlife Service, North American Fauna No. 61 (1959).

28. Op. cit., Sherrod, et al., "Biology of the bald eagle on Amchitka Islands, Alaska."

J. H. Lagille, (1884), quoted in S. Postupalsky, "Artificial Nesting Platforms for Ospreys and Bald Eagles," in *Endangered Birds: Management Techniques for Preserving Threatened Species*, S. A. Temple, ed. (Madison, WI: Univ. Wisc. Press, 1977), pp. 35-45.

J. M. Abbott, Chesapeake Bay Bald Eagles, *Delaware Conservationist*, vol. 22, no. 2 (1978), pp. 3-9.

29. T. G. Grubb, D. M. Rubink, S. W. Hoffman and L. A. Forbis, "Management of Breeding Bald Eagles in Arizona: Problems and Perspectives," in *Proceedings of the Bald Eagle Conference on Bald Eagle Restoration*, Terrence N. Ingram ed., (1982), pp. 73-88.

30. Op. cit., Bent, *Life Histories of North American Birds of Prey*.

F. H. Herrick, "The Daily Life of the American Bald Eagle: Late Phase," *Auk* vol. 41, no. 3 (1924), pp. 389-422.

B. S. Wright, "The Relation of Bald Eagles to Breeding Ducks in New Brunswick," *Journal of Wildlife Management*, vol. 17, no. 1 (1953), pp. 55-62.

K. Steenhof, "The Ecology of Wintering Bald Eagles in Southeastern South Dakota" (Thesis, University of Missouri, Columbia, 1976).

B. R. McClelland, "Autumn Concentrations of Bald Eagles in Glacier National Park," *Condor* vol. 75, no. 1 (1973), pp. 121-123.

Stephen M. Waste, "Winter Ecology of the Bald Eagles of the Chilkat Valley, Alaska," in *Proceedings of a Symposium and Workshop on Raptor Management and Biology in Alaska and Western Canada*, W. N. Ladd and P. F. Schempf, eds. (Anchorage, AK: U.S. Fish and Wildlife Service, 1982), pp. 68-81.

S. W. Servheen, "Ecology of the Winter Bald Eagles on the Skagit River, Washington" (Thesis, University of Washington, Seattle, 1975).

T. C. Dunstan and J. F. Harper, "Food Habits of Bald Eagles in North-Central Minnesota," *Journal of Wildlife Management*, vol. 39, no.1, pp. 140-143.

31. K. W. Cline, *Chesapeake Bay Bald Eagle Banding Project Report*, (Washington, D.C.: National Wildlife Federation, 1984).

32. Op. cit., Bent, *Life Histories of North American Birds of Prey*.
Ecological Land Use Planning in Northern Saskatchewan," in *Proceedings of Bald Eagle Days*, T. N. Ingram, ed. (Apple River, IL: Eagle Valley Environmentalists, 1976), pp. 84-93.

C. G. Thelander, "Bald Eagle Reproduction in California, 1972-1973," State of California Dept. of Fish and Game, Wildlife Management Branch Admin. Report No. 73-5 (1973), 17 pp.

33. Op. cit., Bent, *Life Histories of North American Birds of Prey*.
Op. cit., Sherrod, et al., "Biology of the Bald Eagle on Amchitka Island, Alaska."

34. L. I. Retfalvi, "Food Nesting Bald Eagles on San Juan Island, Washington," *Condor*, vol. 72, no. 3 (1970), pp. 358-361.

35. Op. cit., Spencer, *Wintering of the Migrant Bald Eagle in the Lower 48 States*.

36. Ibid.
A. J. Hansen, M. V. Stalmaster, and J. R. Newman, "Habitat Characteristics, Function, and Destruction of Bald Eagle Communal Roosts in Western Washington," in *Proceedings of the Washington Bald Eagle Symposium*, R. L. Knight, G. T. Allen, M. V. Stalmaster, and C. W. Servheen, eds. (Seattle, WN: The Nature Conservancy, 1981), pp. 221-229.

R. Bowes, "Pere Marquette Eagle Roost," in Bald Eagle Land: Preservation and Acquisition, *Proceedings of Bald Eagle Days 1975* (Apple River, IL: Eagle Valley Environmentalists, 1975), pp. 12-24.

M. V. Stalmaster, "Ecological Energetics and Foraging Behavior of Winter Bald Eagles" (Ph. D. dissertation, Utah State University, Logan, 1981).

K. Steenhof, S. S. Berlinger, L. H. Frederickson, "Habitat Use by Wintering Bald Eagles in South Dakota," *Journal of Wildlife Management*, vol. 44 (1980), pp. 798-805.

L. A. Forbis, B. Johnston, A.M. Camarena, and D. McKinney, Bald Eagle Habitat Management Guidelines, USDA Forest Service (1977).

G. P. Keister, Jr., "Characteristics of Winter Roosts and Populations of Bald Eagles in the Klamath Basin" (Thesis, Oregon State University, Corvallis, 1981).

R. G., Anthony, R. L. Knight, G. T. Allen, B. R. McClelland, and J. I. Hodges, "Habitat Use by Nesting and Roosting Bald Eagles in the Pacific Northwest," in *Transactions of the Forty-Seventh North American Wildlife and Natural Resources Conference*, K. Sabol, ed. (Washington, D.C.: Wildlife Management Institute, 1982), pp. 332-342.

37. J. F. Swisher, "A Roosting Area of the Bald Eagle in Northern Utah," *Wilson Bulletin*, vol. 76, no. 2 (1964), pp. 186-187.

38. M. V. Stalmaster, "Ecological Energetics and Foraging Behavior of Winter Bald

Eagles in South Dakota," *Journal of Wildlife Management*, vol. 44 (1981), pp. 798-805.

39. R.S. Palmer, (1949), in *Annotated Bibliography of Historical Bald Eagle Records: An Appendix to the Northern States Bald Eagle Recovery Plan*, James P. Mattsson, Joel V. Kussman, and Francis J. Gramlich (Twin Cities, MN: U.S. Fish and Wildlife Service, 1982).

40. J. P. Giraud, Jr. (1844.), in *Annotated Bibliography of Historical Bald Eagle Records: An Appendix to the Northern States Bald Eagle Recovery Plan*, James P. Mattson, Joel V. Kussman, and Francis J. Gramlich (Twin Cities, MN: U.S. Fish and Wildlife Service, 1982).

41. Jeffrey L. Lincer, William S. Clark, and Maurice N. LeFranc, Jr., *Working Bibliography of the Bald Eagle*, National Wildlife Federation Scientific/Technical Series, no. 2 (Washington, D.C.: National Wildlife Federation, 1979), 219 pp.
James P. Mattsson, Joel V. Kussman, and Francis J. Gramlich, *Annotated Bibliography of Historical Bald Eagle Records: An Appendix to the Northern States Bald Eagle Recovery Plan* (Twin Cities, MN: U.S. Fish and Wildlife Service, 1982), 96 pp.
Thomas M. Murphy, Fred M. Bagley, Wayne Dubuc, Doris Mager, Stephen A. Nesbitt, William B. Robertson, Jr. and Ben Sanders, Southeastern States Bald Eagle Recovery Plan (Atlanta, GA: U.S. Fish and Wildlife Service, 1984).

42. W. G. V. Name, "Threatened Extinction of the Bald Eagle," *Ecology*, vol. 2 (1921), pp. 76-78.

43. Op. cit., Lincer, et al., *Working Bibliography of the Bald Eagle*.
Op. cit., Mattsson, et al., *Annotated Bibliography of Historical Bald Eagle Records*.

44. J. C. Howell, "Comparison of 1935 and 1940 Populations of Nesting Bald Eagles in East-Central Florida," *Auk*, vol. 58, no. 3 (1941), pp. 402-403.

45. C. L. Broley, "Plight of the American Bald Eagle," *Audubon*, vol. 60 (1958), pp. 162-163, 171.

46. Alexander Sprunt, IV, "Population Trends of the Bald Eagle in North America," in *Peregrine Falcon Populations: Their Biology and Decline*, Joseph J. Hickey, ed., (Madison, WI: University of Wisconsin Press, 1969), pp. 347-351.

47. J. M. Abbott, "Status Report on the Bald Eagle," *Virginia Wildlife*, vol. 23, no. 7 (1962), pp. 4-6.
Alexander Sprunt, IV and Richard L. Cunningham, "Wisconsin Has a Stake in the Continental Bald Eagle Project: A Progress Report," *Passenger Pigeon*, vol. 24, no. 3 (1962), pp. 63-68.
Alexander Sprunt, IV and Frank J. Ligas, "The 1963 Bald Eagle Count," *Audubon*, vol. 66, no. 1 (1964), pp. 45-47.

48. J. J. Hickey and D. W. Anderson, "Chlorinated Hydrocarbons and Eggshell Changes in Raptorial and Fish-Eating Birds," *Science*, vol. 162 (1968), pp. 271-273.
David B. Peakall, "Physiological Effects of Chlorinated Hydrocarbons on Avian Species," in *Symposium on Environmental Dynamics of Pesticides* (New York: Plenum Press, 1975), pp. 343-360.
Robert W. Risebrough, "Pesticides and Other Toxicants," in *Wildlife and America*, H. P. Brokaw, ed. (Washington, D.C.: Council on Environmental Quality, 1978), pp. 218-236.

49. B. M. Mulhern, W. L. Reichel, L. J. Locke, T. G. Lamont, A. A. Belisle, E. Cromartie, G. E. Bagley, and R. M. Prouty, "Organochlorine Residues and

Autopsy Data from Bald Eagles 1966-68," *Pesticide Monitoring Journal*, vol. 4, no. 3 (1970), pp. 141-144.

50. D. B. Peakall, "Pesticides and the Reproduction of Birds," *Scientific American*, vol. 222, no. 4 (1970), pp. 72-78.

51. James W. Grier, "Ban of DDT and Subsequent Recovery of Reproduction in Bald Eagles," *Science*, vol. 218 (1982), pp. 1232-1235.

52. Op. cit., B. M. Mulhern, et al., "Organochlorine Residues and Autopsy Data from Bald Eagles 1966-68."
Op. cit., Grier, "Ban of DDT and Subsequent Recovery of Reproduction in Bald Eagles."
A. A. Belisle, W. L. Reichel, L. H. Locke, T. G. Lamont, B. M. Mulhern, R. M. Prouty, R. B. DeWolf and E. Cromartie, "Residues of Organochlorine Pesticides, Polychlorinated Biphenyls, and Mercury and Autopsy Data for Bald Eagles, 1969 and 1970," *Pesticide Monitoring Journal*, vol. 6, no. 3, pp. 133-138.
E. Cromartie, W. L. Reichel, L. N. Locke, A. A. Belisle, T. E. Kaiser, T. G. Lamont, B. M. Mulhern, R. M. Prouty and D. M. Swineford, "Residues of Organochlorine Pesticides and Polychlorinated Biphenyls and Autopsy Data for Bald Eagles, 1971-72," *Pesticide Monitoring Journal*, vol. 9, no. 1 (1975), pp. 11-14.
R. M. Prouty, W. L. Reichel, L. N. Locke, A. A. Belisle, E. Cromartie, T. E. Kaiser, T. G. Lamont, B. M. Mulhern, and D. M. Swineford, "Residues of Organochlorine Pesticides and Polychlorinated Biphenyls and Autopsy Data for Bald Eagles, 1973-74," *Pesticide Monitoring Journal*, vol. 11, no. 3 (1977), pp. 134-137.

53. Op. cit., Mulhern, et al., "Organochlorine Residues and Autopsy Data from Bald Eagles, 1966-1968."
Op. cit., Belisle, et al., "Residues of Organochlorine Pesticides, Polychlorinated Biphenyls, and Mercury and Autopsy Data for Bald Eagles, 1969 and 1970."
Op. cit., Cromartie, et al., "Residues of Organochlorine Pesticides and Polychlorinated Biphenyls and Autopsy Data for Bald Eagles, 1971-72."
Op. cit., Prouty, et al., "Residues of Organochlorine Pesticides and Polychlorinated Biphenyls and Autopsy Data for Bald Eagles, 1973-74."
N. C. Coon, L. N. Locke, E. Cromartie and W. L. Reichel, "Causes of Bald Eagle Mortality, 1969-1965," *Journal of Wildlife Disease*, vol. 6, no. 1 (1970), pp. 72-76.
T. E. Kaiser, W. L. Reichel, L. N. Locke, E Cromartie, A. J. Krynitsky, T. G. Lamont, B. M. Mulhern, R. M. Prouty, C. J. Stafford, and D. M. Swineford, "Organochlorine Pesticed, PRC, and PBB Residues and Necropsy Data for Bald Eagles from 29 States—1975-77," *Pesticide Monitoring Journal*, vol. 13, no. 4 (1980), pp. 145-149.
Louis Locke, "A Brief Review of Bald and Golden Eagle Mortality 1975-1981 With Some Comments on Possible Management Procedure," in *Proceedings of the Bald Eagle Conference on Bald Eagle Restoration*, Terrence N. Ingram, ed. (Apple River, IL: Eagle Valley Environmentalists, 1982), pp 113-114.

54. O. H. Pattee, S. N. Wiemeyer, B. M. Mulhern, L. Sileo, and J. W. Carpenter, "Experimental Lead-Shot Poisoning in Bald Eagles," *Journal of Wildlife Management*, vol. 45 (1981), pp. 806-810.

55. J. W. Grier, J. B. Elder, F. J. Gramlich, N. F. Green, J. V. Kussman, J. E. Mathisen, and J. P. Mattson, Northern States Bald Eagle Recovery Plan (Twin Cities, MN: U.S. Fish and Wildlife Service, 1983).
Mark V. Stalmaster and James R. Newman, "Behavorial Responses of Wintering

Bald Eagles to Human Activity," *Journal of Wildlife Management*, vol. 42, no. 3 (1978), pp. 506–513.

56. N.F. Green, "Bald Eagle Distribution, Abundance, and Status in the Conterminous United States" (Unpublished manuscript, Bald Eagle Habitat Management Workshop, Corvallis, OR, 1982).

57. Teryl G. Grubb, Richard L. Knight, Duane M. Rubink, and Charles M. Nash, "A five-year comparison of Bald Eagle Productivity in Washington and Arizona," in *Biology and Management of Bald Eagles and Ospreys*, David M. Bird, Chief Ed. (Ste. Anne de Bellevue, Quebec: Harpell Press, 1983).

58. G. J. Taylor, J. M. Abbott, M.A. Byrd, D. R. Perkuchin, and S. N. Weimeyer, The Chesapeake Bay Region Bald Eagle Recovery Plan (Boston, MA: U.S. Fish and Wildlife Service, 1982).

59. B. A. Millsap, *Results of the National Wildlife Federation Midwinter Bald Eagle Survey, 1979-1982* (Washington, D.C.: National Wildlife Federation, in prep.).

60. A. Sprunt, IV. and R. L. Cunningham, "Continental Bald Eagle Project, Progress Report No. 2," (Paper presented at the National Audubon Society's 58th Annual Convention, Corpus Christi, TX, November 1962).
A. Sprunt, IV and F. J. Ligas, "Continental Bald Eagle Project, Progress Report No. 3," in *A Florida Notebook, Proceedings of the National Audubon Society Annual Convention*, (November 1963), pp. 2-7.

61. P. Nickerson, "The National Bald Eagle Nesting Surveys — 1973 and 1974" (Unpublished manuscript, U.S. Fish and Wildlife Service, 1974).

62. M. Pramstaller and W. Clark, "Symposium on the Status of the Bald Eagle and Bald Eagle Research" (Washington, D.C.: National Wildlife Federation, 1979), 12 pp.

63. Op. cit, Green, "Bald Eagle Distribution, Abundance, and Status in the Conterminous United States."
N. F. Green, "Status of Nesting Bald Eagles in the Conterminous United States During 1981," in *Proceedings of the Bald Eagle Conference on Bald Eagle Restoration*, Terrence N. Ingram, ed. (Apple River, IL: Eagle Valley Environmentalists, 1982), pp. 89-97.

64. Op. cit., Taylor, The Chesapeake Bay Region Bald Eagle Recovery Plan.

65. Op. cit., Cline, Chesapeake Bay Bald Eagle Banding Project Report.

66. J. M. Engel and F. B. Isaacs. Bald Eagle Translocation Techniques: North Central Region Report (Twin Cities, MN: Fish and Wildlife Service, 1982).

67. Ibid.
U.S. Fish and Wildlife Service, Bald Eagle Translocations Fact Sheet (Washington, D.C.: Fish and Wildlife Service, 1984).

68. D. Garcelon, pers. comm., 1985.
Op. cit., U.S. Fish and Wildlife Service, Bald Eagle Translocations Fact Sheet.

69. Op. cit., Nye, "A Biological and Economic Review of the Hacking Process for the Restoration of Bald Eagles."

70. Op. cit., Hammer, et al., "Successful Wild Nesting of a Three-Year-Old Captive-Reared Bald Eagle."
M. Allen, "The Second Record of a Hacked Bald Eagle Nesting in the Wild," in *Proceedings of the Bald Eagle Conference on Bald Eagle Restoration*, Terrence N. Ingram, ed., (Apple River, IL: Eagle Valley Environmentalists, 1982), pp. 5-7.

71. D. Garcelon, pers. comm., 1985.

72. M. R. Fuller, W. S. Seegar, F. P. Ward, P. W. Howey, T. Strikewerda, J. Wall, N. Levanson, H. D. Black, and J. Daniels, "A Bird-Borne Transmitter for

Tracking Via Satellite" (Unpublished manuscript, presented as a paper at the Raptor Research Foundation Annual, Blacksburg, VA, October 1984).

73. J. W. Grier, J. B. Elder, F. J. Gramlich, N. F. Green, J. V. Kussman, J. E. Mathiase, and J. P. Mattson, Northern States Bald Eagle Recovery Plan (Twin Cities, MN: U.S. Fish and Wildlife Service, 1983).

74. Op. cit., Murphy, et al., Southeastern States Bald Eagle Recovery Plan.

75. GYE Working Team, A Bald Eagle Management Plan for the Greater Yellowstone Ecosystem (Wyoming Game and Fish Dept., 1983).

NANCY GREEN has been wildlife management biologist with BLM in Washington, DC, since 1978. Her primary interest and ongoing research efforts as a doctoral candidate center around conflicts involving management of bald eagles and other raptors. She is a member of the Northern States Bald Eagle Recovery Team.

Because the Endangered Species Act protects plants only on federal land, the rare carnivorous green pitcher plant may still succumb to collectors and developers.

The Green Pitcher Plant

by E. LaVerne Smith
U.S. Fish and Wildlife Service

SPECIES DESCRIPTION AND LIFE HISTORY

THE GREEN PITCHER plant (*Sarracenia oreophila*) is a carnivorous species restricted to limited areas in the southern United States. It is a perennial herbaceous plant that arises from a branched rhizome, or underground stem. The leaves are of two types. The unique pitcher-like leaves, for which the genus is best known, appear in spring and summer and measure seven to 30 inches high and two to four inches in diameter at the orifice, gradually narrowing toward the base. These leaves, with their hooded orifices, are green to yellow-green and variously mottled with maroon or purple. The second type of leaf measures only two to six inches long and one-half to one inch broad and persists throughout the year. Pitcher plant flowers are as unique and attractive as the leaves. Borne singularly on erect stalks measuring 17 to 27 inches tall, the flowers measure two to four inches in diameter. Their petals are yellow and hang from a broad umbrella-shaped disk that also is yellow. The plants flower from mid-April to early June. The fruits, which appear shortly after flowering, are capsules about an inch wide.[1]

The green pitcher plant and all other carnivorous (also referred to as insectivorous) plants have for hundreds of years attracted the interest of botanists, horticulturists, and the general public. Carnivorous plants trap and then digest insects, small birds, small amphibians, and aquatic invertebrates. They usually occur in acidic, mineral-poor bogs, swamps, marshes, and savannas. By extracting needed minerals from small trapped animals, these plants are able to survive in their mineral-poor habitats.[2]

Flytraps, sundews, butterworts, bladderworts, and pitcher plants all possess different trap mechanisms. The tubular leaves of the pitcher plants have several features that enable them to trap prey.[3] Pitchers are brightly colored and secrete a nectar that lures prey to their slippery edges. Downward-pointing stiff hairs that line the pitcher lids encourage descent into the pitchers and discourage ascent. Once inside, the prey is digested and absorbed. These carnivorous adaptations have been the subject of much evolutionary and ecological research, are a wonderful educational tool illustrating plant-animal interactions, and have sparked horticultural interest in the plants.

Green pitcher plants occur in three habitat types: mixed-oak woodlands, seepage bogs, and streambanks. The plants occur widely scattered in the mixed-oak woodlands that usually are situated in flat areas with poor drainage. Springhead bogs, usually dominated by shrub thickets, host locally concentrated populations of the green pitcher plant. The plants occupy the edges of the bog and do not commonly occur in standing water. Sandy or rocky deposits and banks atop sandstone streambeds support small populations of the pitcher plant. Streambank sites often are fairly open, with alders or mountain laurels present. Green pitcher plants occur in full sun in some bog and streambank habitats and in moderate to heavy shade conditions in oak woodlands and in some bogs. The soils of these habitats are consistently sandy, varying from pure sand along streambanks to sandy clays at woodland sites.[4]

SIGNIFICANCE OF THE SPECIES

The green pitcher plant is especially interesting because it is one of only three pitcher plant species occurring outside the coastal plain and because it occupies disjunct coastal plain communities.[5] Ecologically the species is interesting because it sometimes occupies habitats unusual for the genus: oak woodlands and nonwetland sites.[6] The aesthetic value of the plant's attractively colored pitchers and flowers is high. Moreover, the species may have medicinal value, since extracts from a closely related pitcher plant, *Sarracenia flava*, have shown anticancer properties.[7]

HISTORICAL PERSPECTIVE

Sarracenia oreophila, known since 1900, has been found only in limited areas in northeastern Alabama, northern Georgia, and eastern Tennessee. The number of known green pitcher plant populations always has been limited, and reductions have occurred. Historically, the plant was restricted to 60 populations in 14 counties in the three states. Today it remains in only six counties in two states, Alabama and Georgia.[8] The number of plants in each of the remaining 26 populations ranges from three to more than 1,000.

Most historical and extant populations were recorded in Alabama, where populations still occur in five counties: Cherokee, DeKalb, Etowah, Jackson, and Marshall. Of the 26 known populations, 23 occur on Lookout and Sand mountains on the Cumberland Plateau in Alabama. Two other populations occur in Alabama's Coosa River Valley in the Ridge and Valley Province.[9]

The only known extant Georgia population occurs in Towns County and was discovered in 1979[10] in a seepage bog on the margins of Lake Chatuge in the Blue Ridge Province. Historical records of populations of the green pitcher plant exist for five additional Georgia counties—Bibb, Chattooga, Gilmer, Taylor, and Troup—but no populations are known from these counties today.[11] A population was reported from Fentress County, Tennessee, but recent searches have failed to locate it.[12]

The green pitcher plant's habitat is not as wet as that of other pitcher plant species. Fire probably historically reduced competition from other plants and maintained the proper successional state for the green pitcher plant in many areas.[13]

The geographical range of the green pitcher plant always has been limited, and reductions have occurred. The optimum ecological conditions under which it exists are found only occasionally and at widely scattered sites. Elimination of these conditions has led to reductions as well.

CURRENT TRENDS

The U.S. Fish and Wildlife Service (FWS) in September 1979 published a final rule listing the green pitcher plant as an endangered species under the Endangered Species Act of 1973.[14] The final rule, and the prohibitions and restrictions applicable to endangered species, were to take effect on October 21, 1979. However, FWS subsequently postponed the effective date in order to accommodate requests from business and agricultural interests for a public meeting on the listing. Requests for the public meeting arose from concerns that the listing would have adverse economic impacts. Following the public meeting in February 1980, no economic impacts were identified and the listing became effective in April 1980. Litigation surrounding the listing was brought later in 1980 by various business and agricultural interests, including the Alabama Power Company. The plaintiffs argued that FWS had violated the proper listing process and had failed to consider economic impacts. The case was settled out of court early in 1982. Requirements of the settlement include expedited development and implementation of a recovery plan for the green pitcher plant, investigation of the biological and economic feasibility of transplantation, and development of conservation agreements with landowners to secure colonies of the green pitcher plant. The settlement also stipulated the situations where Alabama Power Company development activities could proceed.

The green pitcher plant is recognized as endangered by the three states in which it occurred historically. It is an endangered species on the Alabama state list.[15] Tennessee lists the plant as endangered and possibly extirpated.[16] Georgia's Protected Plants Program has been working actively toward proper state management of the green pitcher plant. However, the species does not appear on the official Georgia list,[17] since it was not known to occur in the state until 1979.

Residential, recreational, business, and agricultural development have resulted in the loss of green pitcher plant populations.[18] The same land uses could eliminate extant populations if proper protection is not assured. The Weiss Reservoir near Centre, Alabama, and a recreational dam in Alabama's DeSoto State Park reportedly destroyed populations of the green pitcher plant. The Alabama Power Company's tentative plans for impoundments along the Little River could eliminate additional populations. This potential threat received much attention during the litigation surrounding the listing and is being addressed through the recovery planning process. The possibility of strip mining still threatens much of the area containing green pitcher plant populations. Direct disturbance and associated runoff, erosion, and siltation could jeopardize the continued existence of some populations.

Carnivorous plants, including the green pitcher plant, have been threatened by collecting for many years. Removal of these unique plants from their natural habitats by curious individuals, carnivorous plant enthusiasts, botanists, and commercial dealers has resulted in the depletion and destruction of whole populations.[19] The exact locations of green pitcher plant populations have been withheld by many authors in order to deter collection and vandalism. Federal listing of the green pitcher plant did not include critical habitat because publication of maps might encourage or facilitate collection. If interest in carnivorous plants continues to increase, as it has in past years, pressure from collectors on natural populations also will increase. Unfortunately, federal listing does not protect plants on private land.

In addition to actual changes in land use and depletion by collection, two other important factors threaten the green pitcher plant. Elimination or control of fire and fluctuating water levels in wetlands have long been considered major threats to carnivorous plants.[20] Although the green pitcher plant tolerates more shade than most pitcher plants, periodic fire seems to reduce competition and promote green pitcher plant success. Unfortunately, wildfire has been all but removed from America's rural lands. Although the green pitcher plant does not seem to require as much moisture as most pitcher plants,[21] it does require summer water tables near the surface. Modifications of water tables through nearby drainage or other alterations could affect it adversely.

MANAGEMENT

The Endangered Species Act requires that recovery plans be developed and implemented for endangered and threatened species. In 1982 a green pitcher plant recovery team was formed with representation from the Alabama Forestry Commission, the Georgia Department of Natural Resources, FWS, universities, and the private sector. A green pitcher plant recovery plan was approved by FWS in May 1983. That plan now is under revision. The 1985 revised draft will be the basis for discussions to follow.[22]

The major conservation needs addressed by the recovery plan include:
- protection and management of existing populations;
- re-establishment, protection, and management of selected extirpated populations;
- transplantation and propagation experimentation;
- perpetuation of the optimum hydrological and successional state of the sites;
- alleviation or reduction of over-collection and vandalism;
- development and implementation of public information programs.

Protection and management of the extant populations are of primary importance in securing the continued existence of the species. The 26 extant populations occur on private, corporate, and state owned and/or administered lands.[23] Alabama's DeSoto State Park historically has attempted to protect populations that occur within the park. The remainder of the Alabama populations are located on private and corporate-owned lands. Conservation agreements are being negotiated between all landowners and FWS. These agreements will be for 10 years or longer and will contain provisions for either the owner or FWS to carry out management activities, conduct periodic monitoring, and allow transplantation/salvage of the plants if the site is to be destroyed. Conservation agreements already have been negotiated to protect 10 populations.

The Georgia population is privately owned, but the Tennessee Valley Authority (TVA) is involved since the population occurs on the margins of a TVA reservoir. Because the Endangered Species Act protects plants only on federal land, this is the only known site where the act can be used to stop harmful activities. The owners of this site are cooperating with TVA and the Georgia Department of Natural Resources in attempting to manage the population properly.

Transplantation experiments were called for as a stipulation in the stay and eventual settlement of the litigation surrounding federal listing.[24] Re-establishment of green pitcher plant populations will be attempted by FWS or the states at a minimum of three extirpated sites. Information gained from propagation and transplantation research will be important to the success of re-establishment efforts. Populations will be re-established primarily at sites where the green pitcher plant previously existed or at protected suitable sites within the historical range of the species. These sites will be chosen after careful consideration of their protection status and ecological suitability. Protection and management agreements will be negotiated for all re-established populations as well as for extant populations.

Transplantation can be employed to salvage plants from imminent destruction. However, transplantation is not the optimum solution to land-use conflicts, and efforts will be made to protect natural populations. Since a majority of the populations occur on private and corporate-owned lands with no federal involvement, the Endangered Species Act cannot save the plant's habitat. FWS will work, however, to encourage voluntary protection. If destruction cannot be prevented, the plants will be relocated or used to develop educational displays and botanical garden plots.

Management activities for all protected sites will include reduction of competition, protection of optimum hydrological conditions, pest control, and creation of seedling-establishment areas. Removal of competing vegetation may be done by hand, through prescribed burning, or by chemical injection. Prescribed burning may be the most effective method since it destroys competing vegetation, creates bare soils for seedling establishment, and eliminates litter that may harbor pest infestations. The Alabama Forestry Commission, working cooperatively with FWS, has been setting up a prescribed burning program for the green pitcher plant. Initial efforts began with the burning of seven sites during the early part of 1984. Prescribed burning and mowing of vegetation for several areas at the Georgia site has improved habitat conditions, and higher rates of seedling germination and establishment have occurred. Careful monitoring and negotiations with landowners are under way to maintain the hydrological integrity of the sites.

Monitoring of all sites is important not only to detect new threats and monitor the health of the populations but also to gather data concerning the success of various management and re-establishment techniques. Little data currently exist on which to base rare-plant management. The optimum time and frequency of burns, the optimum hydrological conditions, the best source of material (wild vs. garden) for reestablishments, and the success of relocated plants will be understood only after years of monitoring and analysis of the resulting data.

PROGNOSIS

Identification of the green pitcher plant as endangered and completion of its recovery plan have been major advances in checking its decline. It is to be hoped that implementation of the recovery plan will reduce sufficiently the threats to the species so that its continued existence will be ensured. Progress toward this goal has begun. Several conservation agreements have been completed, and management actions and research have been initiated. A primary challenge will be careful monitoring of sites following management activities and gathering of data on which to base future management recommendations. Management experience gained here can be of use in formulating protection strategies for other endangered plants as well. Data concerning survivability of transplanted and reestablished populations will enable managers to better determine the desirability of this approach.

RECOMMENDATIONS

The effects of collection must be evaluated and alleviated. Interstate commerce, import, export, and removal from federal lands of endangered and threatened plants for personal possession are prohibited by the Endangered Species Act. Permits are available for scientific study and propagation if the activities will enhance species survival. An education program to discourage taking from the wild is recommended in the recovery plan. Propagated sources will be identified by FWS or the states, and anyone who wants specimens of the plants will be encouraged to use such sources. Educational efforts also are under way to reduce the local apprehension that surrounded listing of the plant.

Cooperation of private landowners, state and federal agencies, and carnivorous-plant collectors will be crucial to the success of the green pitcher plant recovery program. Early indications are that most of the private landowners will enter into conservation agreements. DeSoto State Park personnel historically have been stalwart allies. Elimination of taking from the wild is a message that has begun to show up in carnivorous plant newsletters, journals, and catalogs. This message will need further dissemination.

REFERENCES

1. S. McDaniel, "The genus *Sarracenia* (Sarraceniaceae)," *Bull. Tall Timbers Res. Stat.*, vol. 9 (1971), p. 1-36.
   R. L. Troup and S. McDaniel, *Current Status Report on* Sarracenia Oreophila (Atlanta, Georgia: U. S. Fish and Wildlife Service, 1980).
2. D. E. Schnell, *Carnivorous Plants of the United States and Canada* (Winston-Salem, North Carolina: John F. Blair Publisher, 1976).
3. Op. cit., Schnell, *Carnivorous Plants of the United States and Canada*
4. Op. cit., Troup and McDaniel, *Current Status Report on* Sarracenia Oreophila.
5. Ibid.
6. Ibid.
7. D. H. Miles and U. Kokpol, "Tumor Inhibitors II: Constituents and Antitumor Activity of *Sarracenia Flava*," *Journal of Pharmacological Science,* vol. 65 (1976), p. 284-285.
8. U.S. Department of the Interior, Fish and Wildlife Service, Green Pitcher Plant Recovery Plan. Revised Version of 1983 Plan (Atlanta, Georgia: U.S. Department of the Interior, 1985).
9. Ibid.
10. W. M. Dennis, "*Sarracenia oreophila* (Kearney) Wherry in the Blue Ridge Province of Northeastern Georgia," *Castanea*, vol. 45 (1980), p. 101-103.
11. Op. cit., U.S. Department of the Interior, Green Pitcher Plant Recovery Plan.
12. Op. cit., Troup and McDaniel, *Current Status Report on* Sarracenia oreophila.
13. Ibid.
14. Pub. L. 93-205, 87 Stat. 884 (1973).
15. J. D. Freeman, A. S. Causey, J. W. Short, and R. R. Haynes, *Endangered, Threatened, and Special Concern Plants of Alabama* (Auburn, Alabama: Auburn University, 1979).
16. Tennessee Department of Conservation, Ecological Services Division, *Official Rare Plant List of Tennessee*, issued pursuant to E. O. No. 11 (March 7, 1980) (Nashville, Tennessee, 1984).
17. J. L. McCollum and D. R. Ettman, *Georgia's Protected Plants* (Atlanta: Georgia Department of Natural Resources, 1977).
18. Op. cit., Troup and McDaniel, *Current Status Report on* Sarracenia oreophila.
19. Ibid.
20. Op. cit., Schnell, *Carnivorous Plants of the United States and Canada*.
21. Op. cit., Troup and McDaniel, *Current Status Report on* Sarracenia oreophila.

22. Op. cit., U.S. Department of the Interior, Green Pitcher Plant Recovery Plan.
23. Op. cit., Troup and McDaniel, *Current Status Report on* Sarracenia oreophila.
   Op. cit., U.S. Department of the Interior, Green Pitcher Plant Recovery Plan.
24. U. W. Clemon, Civil Action Number 80-C-1242-M (U. S. District Court, Northern District of Alabama, 1981).

E. LaVERNE SMITH earned her bachelor's and master's degrees in botany from North Carolina State University. As assistant branch chief for the FWS Office of Endangered Species, she is involved in listing threatened and endangered species and establishing guidelines for their recovery.

Stronger protections seem to be slowing the decline of the West Indian manatee, now numbering about 1,000 in Florida waters.

The West Indian Manatee

by Patrick M. Rose
Florida Department of Natural Resources

SPECIES DESCRIPTION AND NATURAL HISTORY

THE WEST INDIAN manatee (*Trichechus manatus*) is a large aquatic mammal that belongs to the order Sirenia. This group is represented by only two living genera, the manatee (*Trichechus*) and the dugong (*Dugong*). Until as recently as 1768, the order had a third member, the Steller's sea cow (*Hydrodamalis*), but it was hunted to extinction just 21 years after it was discovered.[1]

The manatee, or sea cow, has a large spatulate tail and two flipperlike forelimbs. Its prehensile upper lip is split in two and can be used like fingers to draw food into the mouth. Weighing as much as 3,500 pounds and reaching lengths in excess of 12 feet, these herbivores eat as much as 100 pounds of food daily during five to eight hours of feeding. Manatees eat a wide variety of emergent, floating, and submergent aquatic and marine plants. Their plant food preferences often vary with geographical areas.[2]

Although the manatee life span is unknown, evidence suggests the animals may live as long as 50 years.[3] Female manatees have an estrus period of about two weeks, during which they are pursued constantly by entourages of up to 20 males. Females apparently mate with several males during estrus. The manatee calving interval is between two and three years. Although twinning has been documented, usually only one calf is born following a gestation of 12 to 14 months.

Births occur during all months of the year. Calf dependence on the mother usually lasts one to two years. Females can be sexually mature as early as four years of age, while males may take up to seven.

The only long-term social relationship is between a cow and her precocial calf. Although manatees do not form stable herds, they often are seen in groups of two or more and frequently engage in social interactions for days and even weeks.[4]

Manatees are nonterritorial and may cover up to 150 linear miles of river or coastline during summer. Many manatees undertake north-south migrations in response to seasonal changes in water temperature. During winter, aggregations of up to 335 manatees form at artificial and natural warm water refuges. As many as 90 percent of the individuals using a particular wintering site may return to the same place each year. Individual manatees in Florida are known to travel more than 350 miles during trips between summer and winter areas, and some evidence suggests journeys of greater distance.[5]

A few manatees range in summer as far north as Chesapeake Bay, Virginia. In winter the range is from Jacksonville, Florida, south through the southern Gulf of Mexico, the Caribbean Islands, and the east coast of South America to Recife, Brazil.[6]

This docile animal has no natural enemies. It is, perhaps, the only mammal incapable of aggression, even in defense of its young. When threatened, it merely retreats.

Manatees in Florida occupy a wide range of habitat, including shallow coastal waters, bays, estuaries, lagoons, river mouths, rivers, springs, and lakes connected to the coast. Manatees tend to avoid large expanses of water shallower than four and a half feet. They are thought to require freshwater as they often are found drinking from various freshwater sources.

Significance of the Species

The manatee is a sign of the health and integrity of the Florida ecosystems on which it depends. Many other flora and fauna depend upon the same essential elements to survive. If the manatee fails, so will these many other species. Since Florida's human population also depends on manatee habitat for fisheries, recreation, in some cases drinking water, and for crops, a decline in manatee numbers would be a warning to humans that their own environment is in serious jeopardy.

Historical Perspective

Early reports suggest that thousands of manatees once lived in Florida waters. By the early 18th century, some concern about the need to protect manatees from hunting was raised. However, significant hunting pressures continued until the late 1930s and early 1940s. Although no accurate estimates of manatee abundance are available, manatee numbers probably reached a low around the early 1940s and then began to increase to somewhat more than 1,000 by the 1970s.[7] The species was listed as endangered in 1967.

Current Trends

The single greatest cause of manatee mortality today is collisions with boats and barges. Virtually all except the youngest manatees bear scars from boat propellers. Some have 10 sets of scars. In fact, scars are used by biologists to identify individual manatees, and the scar pattern data has to be updated yearly as the animals become freshly scarred. Often manatees are killed by impact alone without being struck by the propellers. Boat/barge mortalities, together with other human-related mortality, such as entrapment in locks and dams, shooting, and entanglement in fishing gear, are likely to increase as Florida's human population expands.[8]

During unusually harsh winters, cold-related deaths may exceed those caused by humans. Warm-water discharges from power plants and other industries have augmented manatee winter range, but elimination or failure of these artificial refuges cause great harm during critically cold periods.[9]

Human introduction of exotic plants to Florida waterways has enhanced manatee

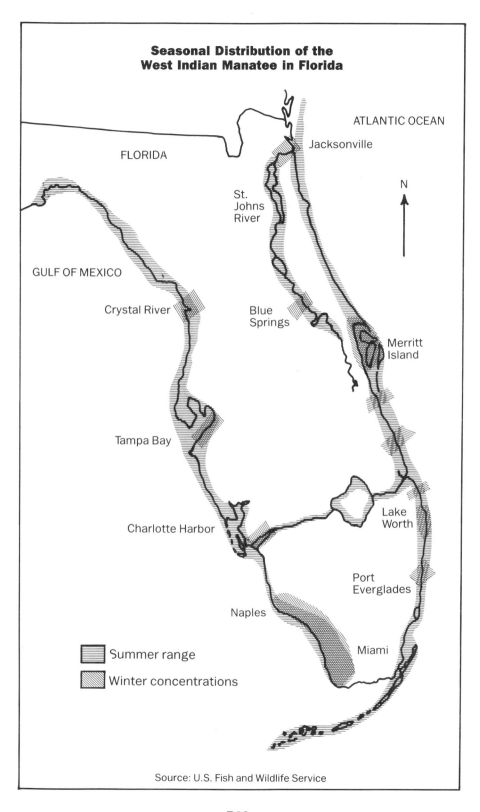

Seasonal Distribution of the West Indian Manatee in Florida

ATLANTIC OCEAN

FLORIDA

Jacksonville

St. Johns River

N

GULF OF MEXICO

Crystal River

Blue Springs

Merritt Island

Tampa Bay

Charlotte Harbor

Lake Worth

Port Everglades

Naples

Miami

Summer range

Winter concentrations

Source: U.S. Fish and Wildlife Service

freshwater habitat by increasing the food supply in some areas. On the other hand, use of poisons to control introduced plants, such as hydrilla and the water hyacinth, has exposed manatees to contamination.

MANAGEMENT

Present recovery efforts are directed toward both immediate mortality reduction and future habitat protection. In an effort to understand and then reduce manatee mortality, biologists from the U.S. Fish and Wildlife Service (FWS) have undertaken a salvage and necropsy program that will be continued after June 1, 1985, by the Florida Department of Natural Resources. About 100 manatees are necropsied each year, but many are too badly decomposed to determine the cause of death. Nevertheless, the data collected on the causes, rates, and locations of manatee mortality have helped in the planning of recovery efforts.

Although the manatee is protected by the Marine Mammal Protection Act of 1972, the Endangered Species Act of 1973, and the Florida Manatee Sanctuary Act of 1978, man still is responsible for about half the manatee's annual mortality for which a cause could be established. Attempts are being made to control this through establishment of regulatory zones in which speed limits are placed on water craft or in which all water activities are prohibited. These measures are effective locally, but cover only a small fraction of the manatee's preferred habitat. Even though additional regulatory zones will be established, it is impractical to try to regulate large areas this way. Other management strategies are required.

Comparison Between Human Related & Natural Manatee Mortality for Known Causes of Death 1978 Through 1984
Death Category

YEAR	HUMAN RELATED		NATURAL	
	DEATHS	PERCENT	DEATHS	PERCENT
1978	31.00	70.45	13.00	29.55
1979	41.00	75.93	13.00	24.07
1980	26.00	56.52	20.00	43.48
1981	30.00	57.69	22.00	42.31
1982	26.00	32.10	55.00	67.90
1983	26.00	52.00	24.00	48.00
1984	39.00	43.33	51.00	56.67
TOTAL	219.00	52.52	198.00	47.48

As Florida continues to grow, so will the number of boats and developments such as marinas, boat ramps, and boat slips. Current growth-management practices, while helpful, are inadequate and will not control future increases in manatee mortality from boat collisions. Even though individual development projects may not increase significantly the probability of manatee injury, mortality, and harassment, the cumulative effects of development may render certain essential habitat areas unavailable. Efforts are being made to identify areas where increased boating activity poses the greatest threat, to determine specific areas where new permit applications should receive more detailed permit review, to develop manatee-related criteria to be used in the permit process, and to consider alternative actions and/or permit conditions that will address recreational boating facilities and manatee protection needs.[10]

Manatee research efforts are carried out by state, federal, and private agencies and organizations. Information is being obtained relative to manatee abundance and distribution, dietary requirements, reproductive biology, causes of mortality, individual movements, and habitat requirements.

The most significant advancement in manatee research has come through the adaptation of a radio harness for use in salt and brackish waters. The new design developed by the FWS allows the transmitter to float to the surface on a six-foot tether attached to a belt placed just in front of the flattened tail, the manatee's narrowest part. For several years the belt has been used successfully without a tether in freshwater. In saltwater, however, the antenna must protrude above the water in order to transmit its signal. The tether allows the floating transmitter's antenna to break the surface whenever the manatee rises to breathe or when it is resting near the surface.[11]

By following the movements of individual manatees in brackish and saltwater habitats, valuable information can be obtained about manatee behavior and preferred habitat. Although radio tracking of manatees is expected to increase, the relatively high cost of the technique will limit its use. For this reason, less costly aerial surveys will continue as the primary tool of manatee research and management.

Information acquired in various studies is being applied to management practices as quickly as possible. For example, the number of manatees killed in flood gates decreased from seven or eight yearly to no more than three following modifications of gate opening sequences. The modifications allowed the gates to be opened wide enough to sweep a manatee through, rather than allowing it to become pinned by the rush of water against an opening too narrow to allow passage.

Habitat protection has taken several forms, ranging from acquisition to regulatory control. High costs have limited acquisition to areas that cannot be protected otherwise or that will be used directly for manatee research or for facilities that teach about manatees. Other manatee protection efforts revolve around preventing or minimizing habitat alteration or destruction. This may be achieved through a case-by-case review of development projects or through establishment of well-defined preserves or of areas in which development is limited. The rudiments of these controls now exist but must be refined in order to provide adequate protection.

The potential benefits and detriments of a large-scale captive breeding program have been debated recently. Successful reproduction in the wild, coupled with the possibility that captive-bred manatees suffer reductions in fitness, makes large-scale captive breeding unnecessary for now. In the meantime, propagation of the 18 manatees already in captivity is continuing. The fitness of captive-bred manatees should be better understood after some of the captive-bred manatees are radio collared and released next year. Biologists will monitor the manatees as the animals attempt to adapt to the wild.

PROGNOSIS

Although no large increase in manatee abundance is likely, proper remedial action in some areas should keep mortality at tolerable limits. By coupling development controls with habitat protection programs, subpopulations in some areas may even increase. Under the best of circumstances, however, the recovery of manatees from their endangered status will take many years.

RECOMMENDATIONS

Recovery of the manatee is within our grasp, but a consolidated state, local, and federal effort must be made in order to protect the animal and its habitat. Efforts to assess manatee population trends must be intensified so that changes in manatee abundance can be monitored and effective remedial actions taken.

Effective growth-management controls will have to be developed and instituted for waterfront developments. Some condominiums occupy 400 to 500 feet of waterfront and plan to build boat slips for all residents. This increases the number of boats and the number of collisions with manatees. Slips should be limited to one for every 100 feet of waterfront. Areas of special importance to manatees should be protected from all development.

Florida residents must be taught that failure of the manatees to survive would be a sign that Florida's ecosystems are seriously degraded, and that by protecting manatee habitat, residents are in fact preserving the environment upon which their own health and livelihood depends.

REFERENCES

1. J.F. Brandt, *Contributions to Sirenology, Being Principally an Illustrated Natural History of* Rhytina, *a Translation TT-72-56004* (Washington, D.C.: Smithsonian Institution, 1974), p. 122.
2. Unpublished data, Sirenian Project, United States Fish and Wildlife Service.
3. J.J. Betz, "Sea Cow Deception," *Sea Frontiers*, vol. 14 (1968).
4. Op. cit., Sirenian Project.
5. Ibid.
6. D.S. Hartman, "Ecology and Behavior of the Manatee (*Trichechus manatus*) in Florida," American Society of Mammalogists, Special Publication Number 5 (1979).
7. T.S. O'Shea, C. Beck, R. Bonde, H. Kochman, and D. O'Dell, "An Analysis of Manatee Mortality Patterns in Florida 1976-81," *Journal of Wildlife Management*, vol. 49 (in press), p. 11.
8. Ibid.
9. P.M. Rose and S.P. McCutcheon, "Manatees (*Trichechus manatus*): Abundance and Distribution In and Around Several Florida Power Plant Effluents," P.O. Number 31534-86626 (Unpublished report prepared for Florida Power and Light Company, 1980), p. 128.
10. P.M. Rose, J. Baker, and D. Peterson, "Comprehensive Work Plan for the West Indian Manatee (*Trichechus manatus*)" (Unpublished manuscript, United States Department of the Interior, Fish and Wildlife Service, 1981), p. 45.
11. Op. cit., Sirenian Project.

PATRICK M. ROSE has been the Manatee Coordinator for the Florida Department of Natural Resources since 1983. In conjunction with the Florida Audubon Manatee Program, later called the Save the Manatee Committee, he coordinated workshops in Florida and South Carolina promoting public awareness of manatees. He is vice chairman of Save the Manatee Committee.

The problems besetting the nene goose and other native Hawaiian bird species are typical of those jeopardizing island wildlife throughout the world.

Hawaiian Birds

by *J. Michael Scott*
U.S. Fish and Wildlife Service
and
John L. Sincock
U.S. Fish and Wildlife Service, retired

HISTORICAL PERSPECTIVE

HAWAII'S 132 ISLANDS, reefs, and shoals extend 1,523 miles from the southernmost island of Hawaii to the northernmost islands at Kure Atoll. The northernmost islands, now eroded almost to sea level, are about 27 million years old, whereas the still-forming island of Hawaii is only about 750,000 years old. The Hawaiian Islands are the most isolated in the world and, as such, have developed many species and subspecies of plants and animals found nowhere else. The arrival of few ancestral species and the isolation of the islands, with their varying ages, elevations, climates, and microhabitats, were ideal for creating this great endemic biota through adaptive radiation.

The eight main islands — Hawaii, Maui, Oahu, Kauai, Molokai, Lanai, Niihau, and Kahoolawe, in their order of size — make up 99 percent of the total land area of 6,425 square miles. The remaining one percent, less than six square miles, is made up of islands off the shores of the main islands and the northwestern (or Leeward) Hawaiian islands, from Kure Atoll in the north to Nihoa Island in the south (Armstrong 1973).[1] Until about 1,500 years ago, when the Polynesians arrived, this was a land of Eden — the only terrestrial mammal was the Hawaiian hoary bat, there were no mosquitoes to carry avian disease, and no influx of man-introduced competitors: Only nature was at work.

Undoubtedly during the past 27 million years, natural extinctions of Hawaiian birds occurred of which no evidence remains. In historic times dating from the arrival of Captain Cook in 1778, at least 90 species and subspecies of endemic and indigenous birds occurred on the Hawaiian Islands. This assemblage included 57 passerines, 22 oceanic species, one heron, one goose, two ducks, one hawk, two rails, one gallinule, one coot, one stilt, and one owl. Additionally, there have been more than 100 migrant or accidental species.

At least 23 (40 percent) of the passerines and both rails have become extinct in the past century. Of the 34 remaining passerines, 23 are classified as endangered (U.S. Fish and Wildlife Service 1983). Thus, 80 percent of the passerine birds discovered in Hawaii in the past 200 years are either extinct or endangered. Of the 22 oceanic birds, two are classified as endangered or threatened. Of the remaining nine bird species, seven are classified as endangered. Only 37 percent of the endemic and indigenous Hawaiian birds known in historic times are neither extinct nor endangered, and in truth there are some very real threats to them.

For many years biologists thought that in the 1,400 years prior to the arrival of western man, the Polynesians and their pigs, dogs, rats, and fowl had caused some destruction of the native ecosystems and that the direct killing of birds for food and feathers had acted adversely on their populations. However, recent research[2] has revealed the widespread destruction the Polynesians wrought on the land by clearing and burning forests below 3,300 feet. Studies of fossils conducted since 1971[3] have caused a reevaluation of what has happened to Hawaiian birdlife since man first put his foot on Hawaiian lava. One study[4] of fossils from five of the main islands doubled the known number of land birds. Researchers found 40 extinct species known only from bones, including one petrel, two ibises, seven geese, one small hawk, one eagle, seven rails, three species of a new genus of owl, two large crows, one honeyeater, and at least 15 species of Hawaiian finches. Evidence shows that these extinct birds survived into the period of Polynesian colonization. At least five other species known only from fossils have been added to the list, and it is estimated that only 25 percent of the original taxa of Hawaiian birds still survive.[5]

Human-caused extinction of Hawaii's unique birds began with the Polynesians, but it was accelerated vastly after the arrival of western man. The introduction of livestock in the late 18th century had dire consequences for all the main islands.[6] Mosquitoes were introduced about 1826 and became a vector for the spread of avian diseases. Avian diseases now are considered among the major factors jeopardizing the survival of some bird species.[7] Many undesirable animals have been introduced deliberately or accidentally and include, among others, European boars, axis deer, mule deer, mouflon sheep, mongooses, three more species of rats, prairie dogs, cats, rabbits, wallabies, snakes, and iguanas. Thoughtless introductions continue to the present day.

To fill the void in birdlife in the lowlands and outer forests, settlers began the importation of foreign birds, beginning with the common pigeon (*Columba livia*) in 1796. Since then more than 160 species of exotic birds have been released in Hawaii, including at least 78 kinds of game birds.[8] About 50 of these species have become established, and a few have invaded the native koa (*Acacia koa*) and ohia (*Metrosideros polymorpha*) forests that are the last retreat for most of the native forest birds. These forest invaders include the Japanese white-eye (*Zosterops japonicus*), red-billed leiothrix (*Leiothrix lutea*), nutmeg mannikin (*Lonchura punctulata*), melodious laughing-thrush (*Garrulax canorus*), Northern cardinal (*Cardinalis cardinalis*), white-rumped shama (*Copsychus malabaricus*), and spotted dove (*Streptopelia chinensis*). The common myna (*Acridotheres tristis*) was imported in 1865. Reportedly it had invaded the deepest rainforests by 1900, but it since has retreated to more disturbed areas. These birds and a few others are potential competitors for food and living space and could serve as hosts for avian diseases such as avian pox and malaria as well as parasites.[9]

The high specialization of some of the Hawaiian forest birds and native insects probably makes them vulnerable to extinction, for they are ill-adapted to change.[10] Inbreeding also may contribute to extinction of birds with localized habitat or of those restricted in their normal range by decreased habitat.[11] Habitat and range reduction have been estimated for all of the native forest birds. Many of the rarer species occupy less than five percent of their original range, and even the commoner, non-endangered species now seldom occupy more than 40 percent of their original range.[12]

Interest in the Hawaiian avifauna intensified during the 1960s when U. S. Fish and Wildlife Service (FWS) biologists undertook a major literature review[13] of the birds of the northwestern Hawaiian Islands[14] and of Kauai.[15] The Smithsonian Institution launched a major investigation of Pacific seabirds that added tremendously to knowledge of the Northwestern Hawaiian Islands.[16] From 1976 to 1982, the U.S. Forest Service funded a major research program to study the behavior of native birds. This study focused on a limited number of sites and obtained a perspective on seasonal and year to year variation. During the 1970s, the International Biological Program focused research efforts on the mid-elevation east slope of Mauna Loa; these results were reviewed in Mueller-Dombois and others.[17]

SPECIES MANAGEMENT AND RECOMMENDATIONS

Obviously, all of the birds of Hawaii cannot be discussed here. A few examples that illustrate some of the birds' varied problems and potentials for management have been selected.

Newell's Shearwater

One research and management success story is that of the Newell's race of the Townsend's shearwater (*Puffinus auricularis newelli*), accomplished by joint efforts of FWS and the Hawaii Department of Land and Natural Resources. The Newell's shearwater is a small, black and white seabird that was discovered in 1894,[18] extirpated from most Hawaiian islands by mongooses, cats, dogs, rats, and pigs by 1908,[19] considered extinct by 1931,[20] but confirmed to still exist in 1954.[21] It was believed to have nested on all of the major islands. The first nesting colony known to science was discovered in the fern-covered mountains of Kauai in 1967.[22]

Autumn crash landings by fledgling shearwaters disoriented by bright lights became common on Kauai in the early 1960s[23] and remain commom at present[24]. In the late 1960s the public was asked to pick up the fallen fledglings each October and November and release them in the ocean. In 1978, biologists asked the public through this Save Our Shearwater (SOS) program to turn in the birds to Shearwater Aid Stations located at fire stations and other collection points. From 1978 through 1984 almost 10,000 fledgling Newell's shearwaters and more than two dozen endangered dark-rumped petrels (*Pterodroma phaeopygia sandwichensis*) were accounted for. Many of the shearwaters died, but 8,853 of them, with the other birds, were released alive and given further chances for survival. Even with this program, about 1,000 died on the highways. Probably more than 50 percent of the annual production came down around streetlights and the lights of hotels, tennis courts, football fields, etc. Unshaded lighting is increasing rapidly on Kauai and the other Hawaiian Islands and if unabated will threaten the survival of the Newell's shearwater and possibly that of the dark-rumped petrel.

While the SOS program is highly successful in saving these birds and undoubtedly has contributed to a growing population, it did not get at the real source of the problem. Research by scientists at the University of Wisconsin, conducted under contract to FWS since 1979, has indicated that this fallout could be reduced significantly by shading upward radiation of lights.[25] FWS and the Nature Conservancy of Hawaii have started a joint effort with the excellent cooperation of the Citizens Utility Company of Kauai to shade all streetlights on the island. Reduction of unshaded lights is recommended in the recovery plan for the Newell's shearwater and the dark-rumped petrel.[26] Presently, the Citizen's Utility Company is testing a flat-lens light that makes

551

the point source invisible except from almost directly below the lamp. Use of this light may replace the shading effort.

Predation by pigs, cats, dogs, and probably rats is sometimes very destructive to Newell's shearwater nesting colonies on Kauai. Adults at least three years old return in April to their mountain nesting colonies. A single white egg is laid in a burrow in late May to early June, and hatching peaks in late July and early August. The birds fledge in October and November and are believed to go south of Kauai some 1,500 to 2,000 miles, returning to the fern-covered nesting colonies when they are ready to breed.

The potential for even more serious predation on Newell's shearwaters was increased when a lactating mongoose was found dead on a Kauai highway in 1976. Since then, several dozen mongoose sightings have been reported by the public, but it still has not been determined that the mongoose has become established on Kauai. However, in response to this threat, the known predation, and the high mortality of fledglings around lights, FWS and the Hawaii Department of Land and Natural Resources began an experimental program to establish a new colony of Newell's shearwaters away from lights and predators. From 1978 through 1980, 90 Newell's shearwater eggs were placed under foster wedge-tailed shearwaters (*Puffinus pacificus*). Sixty-seven of the Newell's shearwaters were fledged. During the past two years several of these banded birds have returned to their natal area, where they may establish a new colony.

It appears that the expanding population of Newell's shearwaters now exceeds 10,000. The birds have tried to recolonize other islands, but these efforts are not likely to succeed without effective control of mongooses and other predators. FWS started new research in 1984 to obtain a label for a pesticide that could be used to control mongooses around ground nesting birds such as the Newell's shearwater, dark-rumped petrel, and nene (*Nesochen sandvicensis*).

Recommendations. The proposal to shade streetlights and hotel lights on Kauai should be carried out and fully evaluated, and all possible efforts should be made to prevent establishment of a mongoose population on Kauai. Evaluation of the efficacy of the Newell's shearwater transplant program should continue for several more years.

Nene

The nene, or Hawaiian goose, is the state bird. It is a medium-sized, heavily barred, grayish-brown goose with a black face, head, and nape of neck. Its feet are adapted to rough lava flows and have lost much of their webbing. The nene weighs about five pounds. It is known from fossils on the islands of Kauai and Molokai[27] and still survives on the island of Hawaii. It was reported to have occurred on Maui. Originally all of the main islands probably were home to the Hawaiian goose or closely related taxa. During the latter part of the 18th century the population may have numbered 25,000.[28]

Hunting, habitat changes, and predation caused a rapid decline between 1850 and 1900, and by the early 1940s the population on the island of Hawaii numbered only 50 birds.[29] By 1952 the wild population was estimated at less than 30 birds. For the past 36 years FWS, with the Hawaii Department of Land and Natural Resources, has conducted an intensive propagation program to restore the nene on Hawaii and Maui. The National Park Service also has started a captive propagation program and has conducted extensive research. The present population on Hawaii is estimated at 300 and occupies only 10 percent of its original range. The population on Maui is about 100 birds and possibly occupies 27 percent of its original range.

The propagation program continues, but recent surveys[30] indicate that the population cannot be sustained without a release program. The nesting season is from about

October through March, and the clutch size is two to five eggs. Goslings suffer about a 95 percent mortality, and the wild population already would have vanished were it not for augmentation with captive-reared birds. The reasons for the nene's failure to establish a self-sustaining population in the wild is not fully known, but predation and loss of primary habitat in the lowlands have certainly played a role.[31]

Recommendations. Research initiated by FWS in 1984 to obtain a label for a pesticide to use on mongooses eventually may lead to better control of predators and increase nene survival, but for the present a propagation program must be continued. Semen from producing ganders should be placed in a sperm bank at Patuxent Wildlife Research Center, an effort that also could prove valuable for several other endangered species of Hawaiian birds.

Hawaiian Stilt

The Hawaiian stilt (*Himantopus mexicanus knudseni*) is a race of the black-necked stilt. This 16-inch-tall wading bird has a black back, white underparts and forehead, and long pink legs. It is found on all major islands except Lanai. Reduction in taro and rice production and the draining and filling of many of the lowland marsh areas such as the Mana marsh on Kauai, which was the largest in the state until the late 1920s, has caused serious loss of habitat for the Hawaiian stilt, as well as for the Hawaiian coot (*Fulica americana alai*) and Hawaiian gallinule (*Gallinula chloropus sandvicensis*).

The Hawaiian stilt was hunted until 1939, but now has full protection under state and federal laws. Only 200 stilts were thought to survive in 1940.[32]

Stilts feed on fish, crabs, worms, and aquatic insects. Nests are built close to the water in a shallow depression. The normal clutch is four eggs. Both adults and young are subject to predation by mongooses, cats, and dogs.[33]

Because of the rapid drainage and filling of wetland habitats in Hawaii, FWS gave first priority in the mid-1960s to the identification of these vanishing areas. In 1968, cooperative semiannual surveys of Hawaiian wetland birds were begun by FWS and the Hawaii Department of Land and Natural Resources. The surveys are reasonably good for the Hawaiian stilt and the Hawaiian coot but inadequate for the Hawaiian gallinule. The estimates of the annual numbers of Hawaiian stilts from 1968 through 1985 generally have varied from 1,200 to 1,500 birds. Based on information from habitat and population surveys, FWS began a habitat-acquisition program in the early 1970s resulting in two refuges on Kauai, two refuges on Oahu, and one refuge on Molokai, totalling about 1,431 acres. The U.S. Department of Defense also manages a 507-acre wetland refuge on Oahu. The Hawaii Department of Wildlife Resources and the Honolulu Zoo have initiated a small propagation program using salvaged birds.

Recommendations. A monitoring program should be maintained to determine if insecticides or other chemicals may be adversely affecting Hawaii's wetland birds or their habitats. Implementation of full management activities on all of the national wildlife refuges on the main islands should do much to benefit the Hawaiian stilt. The acquisition of one important marsh on Maui would do a great deal to insure the survival of the Hawaiian stilt. The labeling of a pesticide to control mongooses and its appropriate use should enhance productivity of wetland birds on existing refuges.

Laysan Finch

Even birds on the remote Hawaiian Leeward Islands have not escaped damage from herbivores and predators. In 1909 these northwestern Hawaiian islands were declared the Hawaiian Bird Reservation. This provided some legal protection for millions of nesting seabirds, the Hawaiian monk seal (*Monachus schauinslandi*), green sea turtle (*Chelonia mydas*), Laysan duck (*Anas laysanensis*), Laysan finch (*Telespyza cantans*), Nihoa finch (*Telespyza ultima*), Laysan honeycreeper (*Himatione sanquinea freethii*), Laysan millerbird (*Acrocephalus familiaris familiaris*), Nihoa millerbird (*Acrocephalus f. kingi*), and the Laysan rail (*Porzana palmeri*). All these birds were endemic to either Laysan or Nihoa Islands. The Laysan finch will be discussed here because its problems and their potential solutions once were common to all seven of the Leeward Island birds.

The overall length of the Laysan finch is six inches. Females are brownish and streaked with black. The males have a yellow head. The heavy bill is pale bluish gray. The natural range of the Laysan finch is the two-square-mile island of Laysan. The bird is believed to be one of the closest relatives of the ancestors of the Hawaiian honeycreepers or finches. Fossils found on Oahu and Molokai are apparently of this species.[34]

Both the Laysan finch and the Laysan rail were translocated to Midway Island and became well established at about the turn of the century. Introduced rabbits devegetated Laysan Island between 1904 and 1923, causing the near extinction of the Laysan finch and Laysan duck, the extinction of the Laysan millerbird and the Laysan honeycreeper, and the extirpation of the Laysan rail in its natural habitat. Some 4,000 finches were estimated on Laysan in 1915.[35] These were reduced to an estimated 100 by 1923.[36]

An expedition for the Biological Survey, an FWS forerunner, in cooperation with the Bishop Museum of Honolulu in 1923 succeeded in destroying the last of the rabbits on Laysan.[37] FWS surveys since 1966 indicate an average of 10,000 Laysan finches. The population varies from 7,000 to 21,000. The only other surviving endangered bird on Laysan, the Laysan duck, also has come back and numbers about 300 to 500 birds, although population estimates were far fewer than 100 birds in the early 1970s.

The Laysan rail and the Laysan finch continued to flourish on the island of Midway until 1943, when the roof rat (*Rattus rattus*) arrived, and both bird species were eliminated quickly. The Laysan rail was last seen in June 1944. One biologist lamented the fact that the rails at Midway were not returned to Laysan Island after the vegetation was reestablished, stating simply, "Hence a species needlessly became extinct."[38]

In March 1967, Eugene Kridler, first refuge manager assigned to the Northwestern Hawaiian Islands National Wildlife Refuge, transplanted some 100 Laysan finches to Pearl and Hermes reefs, an atoll in the refuge system. These birds have become well established and average about 500 to 700 individuals, which appears near carrying capacity for the small islands. This second population provides some protection to the Laysan finch in the event that rats or other predators are introduced to Laysan Island and cause quick loss, such as what occurred at Midway. The threat to the survival of the Laysan finch and the Laysan duck grows greater because of the increased interest in commercial fishing in those waters, which enhances the opportunity for arrival of predators.[39]

Recommendations. Many ship wrecks have occurred in the northwestern Hawaiian islands, and it is likely that someday rats or cats will be introduced to Laysan or Nihoa, severely jeopardizing the Laysan finch, Laysan duck, Nihoa finch, Nihoa millerbird, and millions of seabirds of several species. Rat populations could build so swiftly that the annual FWS visits would not be adequate to prevent extinction of some of these endangered species. A detection and control system should be developed for rats and implemented on each of the major islands within the refuge. Surveys of the endangered birds should be conducted not less than once a year. The Nihoa millerbird should be translocated to Laysan Island to enhance its chances for survival. The

Laysan Duck Recovery Plan[40] recommends the maintenance of a captive flock of good genetic quality for reintroduction to Laysan Island in the event of catastrophe.

Kauai 'o'o

The Kauai 'o'o (*Moho braccatus*) is a medium-sized bird about eight inches in length with a black head, wings, and tail, and a cinnamon-brown rump and upper tail coverts. The bend of the wing and the undertail coverts are white. The black throat has white feathers that give a barred appearance, which is more prominent in the female. The feathers of the legs are golden yellow. The eye is yellowish white.

The Kauai 'o'o was common to locally abundant in the 1890s,[41] but it was rapidly dying out by 1915.[42] Munro[43] considered it in danger of extinction in 1943. It is the last of at least five representatives of the family Meliphagidae (Australian honeyeaters) that resided in Hawaii. The Hawaiians killed many 'o'os for their yellow feathers, but the Kauai 'o'o or 'o'o' a'a (meaning dwarf 'o'o) probably was not taken as extensively as the 'o'os of the other islands. An unidentified bird putatively regarded as a Bishop's 'o'o (*Moho bishopi*) was reported recently from Maui.[44] The Kauai 'o'o illustrates the demise of an aggressive bird in relatively pristine habitat. It formerly occurred in most of the forests of Kauai, but for several decades has been found only in the Alakai Swamp, a ohia rain forest at 4,000 feet in the middle of the island.[45] One Kauai 'o'o was collected in 1960 by biologists who estimated they heard at least 12. That may have been an overestimate, for the birds move rapidly through the forest and under favorable conditions their calls can be heard for a third of a mile.

Extensive forest-bird surveys were conducted in all the forests of Kauai from 1968 through 1973, and although the Kauai 'o'o was heard twice it was not seen until 1971. The first nest of any of the Hawaiian 'o'os was discovered in a tree cavity on May 31, 1971, deep in the Alakai Swamp. This was also the first tree-cavity nest found for any of the Hawaiian birds. When the nest was checked on June 11 it contained two downy young. A tree cavity nest also was found in 1972 and 1973. An 'o'o was observed fledging on May 24, 1973. It frequently was fed spiders and moths by both parents. The adult 'o'os defend their nesting territory aggressively, chasing away all intruders in an area almost 100 yards across. They feed mostly on the nectar of ohia flowers and on moths, spiders, and insect larvae dug from tree moss.

In 1971 six Kauai 'o'o were observed at one time, but despite extensive searching and listening for the bird's loud melodious call only one pair was found through 1982. For the past two years only one bird, presumably a male, has been found calling and periodically checking an old tree cavity nest site. Some 50 nest boxes were placed in the area from 1972 through 1976, but none were used by the Kauai 'o'o or other birds.

It is possible that a few more Kauai 'o'o reside in some remote valley in the Alakai Swamp, but the extensive, multi-person Hawaiian Forest Bird Survey conducted on Kauai in 1981 failed to reveal more than the one known 'o'o. It resides in less than one percent of its former range, and that is in the Alakai Swamp State Sanctuary set aside many years ago for the preservation of native biota. The Kauai 'o'o is not alone in its route to extinction in a relatively pristine forest, for the Kauai akialoa (*Hemignathus procerus*) and the Kauai nuku-pu'u (*Hemignathus lucidus hanapepe*) have been seen only a few times this century. The formerly abundant large Kauai thrush (*Phaeornis obscurus myadestina*) and the small Kauai thrush (*Phaeornis palmeri*) now number in the low hundreds. The ou (*Psittirostra psittacea*) numbers fewer than 100 birds on Kauai and only about 400 on Hawaii.

Recommendations. It is probable that avian disease has contributed to the demise of these species. The Kauai Forest Bird Recovery Plan[46] recommends captive propagation and inclusion in a sperm bank as the only possible hope for long-term survival. If this is to be accomplished it should be done soon, while there is at least a chance of capturing the ou, as well as the large and small Kauai thrushes. The recovery plan also recommends against the building of a proposed hydroelectric dam in the Alakai Swamp.

Palila

The palila (*Loxioides bailleui*) is a grayish, plump Hawaiian finch about six inches in length, with a large yellow head, a big, dark bill, and a dark eyestripe. Intensive studies have been done on the palila and its habitat,[47] making it perhaps the best studied of the endangered Hawaiian passerines. It was formerly thought to have occurred only on the island of Hawaii, but fossils of the palila have been found in the lowlands of Oahu.[48]

In the 1890s, the palila was extremely numerous above 4,000 feet both in North Kona and in Mauna Kea on the island of Hawaii. It has disappeared in North Kona and now exists only in the narrow band of mamane (*Sophora chrysophylla*)/naio (*Myoporum sandwicense*) forest between 7,000 to 9,000 feet on the southern and western slopes of Mauna Kea. The destruction of this forest by clearing for pasture and the introduction of feral and mouflon sheep has resulted in a 95 percent reduction in the palila's range.

The palila provides a good example of what concerned conservationists can do to maintain some of Hawaii's native biota.[49] In 1940, there were an estimated 40,000 feral sheep in the mamane forest. Despite a reduction in the sheep population in the 1940s, the habitat continued to deteriorate.[50] Conservationists protested against the state's maintenance of the feral sheep and took the case to court in behalf of the palila in 1979. The judge ruled that feral sheep should be removed from the mountain, and this was done in 1982. Mouflon sheep still continue to threaten the upper levels of mamane forest and the survival of the palila.[51]

Palila breed in late spring and early summer. They feed on flowers and seed pods of the mamane and associated caterpillars. Since the first intensive surveys of their populations in the 1970s, estimates have run from 1,600 to 6,400. The birds now number about 2,200. Introduced plants, particularly fountain grass (*Pennisetum setaseum*) and German ivy (*Senacio mikanoides*), are modifying the habitat and increasing the threat of fire.[52]

Recommendations. If a fire management plan is developed and mouflon sheep are removed from the mountain, the chance of long-term survival for the palila is good.

Crested Honeycreeper

The crested honeycreeper (*Palmeria dolei*) is about seven inches in length. It has a black back and wings, an orange collar, and a tuft of white, gray, or golden feathers forming a crest that bends forward from the forehead. It was collected on Maui in 1888 and was considered locally abundant on both Molokai and Maui.[53] Perkins noted that it deserted the forests opened by cattle and was believed extirpated from Molokai about 1907.[54] It also is gone from its former habitat on west Maui. It still occupies about 6 percent of its former range. About 3,800 birds remain near the 6,000-foot level of the ohia rain forests on east Maui.

No known record exists of the nests, eggs, or nestlings of the crested honeycreeper.[55] One biologist believed they generally were paired and ready to nest in February and March.[56] The species feeds primarily on nectar gleaned from ohia flowers.

Recommendations. Honeycreepers continue to undergo destruction by pigs and goats. Significant portions of the crested honeycreeper's critical habitat on Maui are controlled by the Haleakala National Park and the Nature Conservancy's Waikamoi Preserve. Management plans for removing pigs and fencing out goats should help in preserving this habitat for the crested honeycreeper, the Maui parrotbill (*Pseudnestor xanthophrys*), the Maui akepa (*Loxops coccineus ochraceus*), and the recently discovered poo-uli (*Melamprosops phaeosoma*).[57] Significant increases in the Maui parrotbill and poo-uli should occur after fencing and then eliminating feral pigs and goats from the high montane rain forest in the Hanawi and Kuhiwa watersheds. These areas are national park and state forest reserve lands. Recently, Haleakala National Park signaled its intention to help fence essential forest-bird habitat. The area with the highest priority for fencing is the watershed between the two forks of the Hanawi, where the greatest numbers of poo-uli are known to occur.

All other endangered Maui forest birds also occur in this area. The adjacent Waikamoi Reserve supports a fairly intact koa-ohia forest west of Koolau Gap, with key populations of Maui parrotbill, Maui akepa, and crested honeycreeper. Management rights to this area recently have been acquired by the Nature Conservancy, which will be fencing it and eliminating feral ungulates. Management rights to the Haiku Uka lands, owned by East Maui Irrigation Co. and lying between Waikamoi Reserve and the Koolau Forest Reserve, also need to be acquired so that this essential connecting forest can be managed similarly. If the restoration of the Nature Conservancy's Kamakou Preserve on Moloki is successful, consideration should be given to translocation of some crested honeycreepers back to Molokai.

Akiapolaau

The akiapolaau (*Hemignathus munroi*) is a resident of a few widely scattered koa-mamane-naio-ohia forests at elevations above 4,900 feet only on the island of Hawaii. It is about five and a half inches long, olive green above with bright yellow underparts, sometimes yellow on the head, and black lores. It has an unusual bill with a strongly decurved upper mandible and a short, straight lower mandible.

It was distributed widely over the island at the turn of the century and was numerous from 3,500 feet upwards.[58] The habitat of the akiapolaau, the less endangered Hawaiian akepa (*Loxops c. coccineus*), and the Hawaii creeper (*Oreomystis mana*) is being destroyed by domestic cattle. It is estimated that the akiapolaau now occupies less than five percent of its former range and that the population is only 1,500 birds.

Nests and nestlings were discovered in 1972, but the eggs have not been described.[59] Immature birds have been seen in June, October, and December.[60] It feeds on insects and insect larvae.

Recommendations. Acquisition and management of some of the high-elevation koa-ohia forests, which would include removal of cattle and control of pigs, is recommended to preserve habitat for the akiapolaau, Hawaii creeper, and Hawaii akepa.[61] All efforts should be made to prevent the introduction of a mosquito capable of breeding at high elevations and spreading avian disease.

Alala

The alala, or Hawaiian crow (*Corvus tropicus*), differs from North American crows in being duller black and having the wings tinged with brown. The feathers of the throat are stiff, with hairlike webs and grayish shafts. Total length is 18 to 20 inches.[62] The alala is known historically only from the island of Hawaii, but two other crow species have been found in fossil deposits on Molokai and Oahu.[63]

The endangered alala's population estimated at 76 birds in 1978 has reached the point where intensive management is required immediately if it is to survive. At the turn of the century the alala was numerous in all of its originally known range from 1,000 to 8,000 feet elevation, but it now occupies less than five percent of it former range. By the 1930s and 1940s it was reduced greatly in numbers. It has had legal protection since 1931.

The reasons for the drastic reduction in the alala population are not fully known, but shooting, predation, disease, habitat destruction, and inadequate food all may have played a part.

The Alala Recovery Plan[64] has synthesized most of what is known of the alala. Sexual maturity occurs in the second or third year. The breeding season extends from March into July. Only 0.5 to 0.9 birds are fledged per nest; post-fledgling survival is even lower. The alala is omnivorous and includes fruits of trees and shrubs, nectar, arthropods, mice, lizards, and nestling birds in its diet.

Recommendations. The recovery plan recommends improving habitat at elevations above high-elevation mosquito populations, direct treatment of diseased birds, and captive propagation to develop immunizations. Without immediate implementation of these management actions, the prognosis for the survival of the alala, along with numerous other Hawaiian birds, is poor. Someday biologists may be able to control mosquito vectors of avian diseases more effectively than at present, but for the moment, captive propagation and sperm banks may be the only means to ensure alala survival.

SUMMARY

Federal legislative actions that have benefited Hawaiian birds include the Lacey Act of 1900, the Weeks-McLean Law of 1913, the Migratory Bird Treaty Act of 1918, indirectly the Pittman-Robertson Federal Aid in Wildlife Restoration Act of 1937, and the Endangered Species Act and its revisions of the past 20 years. Land protection began with the establishment of the Hawaiian Bird Reservation in 1909 and the Hawaii National Park in 1916, which included 17,755 acres at Haleakala on Maui and 211,668 acres at Kilauea-Mauna Loa on Hawaii.

We know as much now about the status and distribution of Hawaii's birds as we are apt to know for many decades. Through numerous recovery plans, recommendations have been made for actions required to ensure the survival of the fragile biota of Hawaii.

The federal actions taken on behalf of Hawaiian wildlife have been made possible only by the excellent cooperation of the Hawaii Department of Land and Natural Resources, the Bishop Museum, the National Audubon Society and its Hawaii chapter, most landowners and residents of Hawaii, and the Nature Conservancy.

Heroic efforts will be required to restore habitats, and they will be costly. New techniques will be required to control predators and feral ungulates and even to begin to abate avian disease, and they will be costly. Research and management should address realistically the feasibility and future potential for control of vectors of avian disease. The lesson has been well demonstrated in Hawaii and elsewhere that the mere acquisition of land and designation as a wildlife sanctuary does little to preserve the biota.[65] The preservation of genetic material through propagation programs and sperm banks means little unless the causes of the demise of these animals in the wild can be identified and corrected.

REFERENCES

1. R. W. Armstrong, ed., *Atlas of Hawaii* (Honolulu: University Press of Hawaii, 1973), pp. 8-9.
2. P. Kirch, "The impact of the prehistoric Polynesians on the Hawaiian ecosystem," *Pacific Science*, vol. 36 (1982), pp. 1-14.
3. S. L. Olson and H. F. James, *Prodromus of the Fossil Avifauna of the Hawaiian Islands* (Washington: Smithsonian Contributions to Zoology, no. 365, 1982).
4. Op. cit., Olson and James, *Prodromus of the Fossil Avifauna of the Hawaiian Islands*.
5. S. L. Olson, personal communication.
6. Op. cit., Olson and James, *Prodromus of the Fossil Avifauna of the Hawaiian Islands*.
7. R. E. Warner, "The Role of Introduced Diseases in the Extinction of the Endemic Hawaiian Avifauna," *Condor*, vol. 70, 101-120.
   D. van Riper, III, S. G. van Riper, M. L. Gof, and M. Laird, "The Impact of Malaria on Birds in Hawaii Volcanoes National Park," *Ecology* (in press).
8. A. J. Berger, *Hawaiian Birdlife* (Honolulu: University Press of Hawaii, 1972).
   A. J. Berger, *The Exotic Birds of Hawaii* (Norfolk Island, Australia: Island Heritage Limited, 1977).
9. Op. cit., Warner, "The Role of Introduced Diseases in the Extinction of the Endemic Hawaiian Avifauna."
   S. Mountainspring and J. M. Scott, "Interspecific Competition Among Hawaiian Forest Birds," *Ecological Monograph* (in press).
   J. L. Sincock, R. E. Daehler, T. Telfer and D. H. Woodside, Kauai Forest Bird Recovery Plan (Portland, Oregon: U. S. Fish and Wildlife Service, 1984).
   Op. cit., Berger, *Hawaiian Birdlife*.
   V. Lewin and J. C. Holmes, "Helminths from the Exotic Game Birds of the Puu Waawaa Ranch, Hawaii," *Pacific Science*, vol. 25 (1971), pp. 372-381.
   Op. cit., van Riper et al., "The Impact of Malaria on Birds in Hawaii Volcanoes National Park."
10. R. C. L. Perkins, "Vertebrata," in *Fauna Hawaiensis*, D. Sharp (ed.), vol. 1, part IV (Cambridge, England: The University Press, 1903), pp. 365-466.
    E. C. Zimmerman, *Insects of Hawaii*, vol. 1 (Honolulu: University of Hawaii Press, 1948).
11. H. W. Henshaw, "Introduction of Foreign Birds into the Hawaiian Islands with Notes on Some of the Introduced Species," *The Hawaiian Annual*, vol. 27 (1901), pp. 132-142.
    H. W. Henshaw, "Letter in Report of the Board of Commissioners of Agriculture and Forestry of the Territory of Hawaii," in Report of the Committee on the Introduction of birds into the Hawaiian Islands, Hawaiian Gazette Co. Ltc. (1910), pp. 61-64.
12. J. M. Scott, S. Mountainspring, F. L. Ramsey and C. B. Kepler, "Forest Bird Communities of the Hawaiian Islands: Their Dynamics, Ecology and Conservation," *Studies in Avian Biology* (in press).
13. W. E. Banko, "History of Endemic Hawaiian Birds, Part I. Population histories - species accounts," *Avian History Reports*, Cooperative National Park Research Studies Unit (Honolulu: University of Hawaii, 1980-1984) p. 4-8.
    W. E. Banko and P. C. Banko, "Role of Food Depletion by Foreign Organisms in Historical Decline of Hawaiian Forest Birds," in C. W. Smith (ed.), *Proceedings of the First Conference in Natural Sciences in Hawaii Cooperative National Park*

Research Studies Unit (Honolulu: University of Hawaii, 1976), pp. 29-34.

14. J. L. Sincock and E. Kridler, "The Extinct and Endemic Endangered Birds of the Northwestern Hawaiian Islands" (Unpublished manuscript, U.S. Fish and Wildlife Service).

15. J. L. Sincock, R. E. Daehler, T. Telfer and D. H. Woodside, Kauai Forest Recovery Plan (Portland, Oregon: U. S. Fish and Wildlife Service, 1984).

16. C. B. Kepler, "Polynesian Rat Prediation on Nesting Laysan Albatrosses and other Pacific Seabirds," *Auk*, vol. 84 (1967), pp. 426-430.

    C. B. Kepler, "Breeding Biology of the Blue-faced Booby, sula dactylatra personata on Green Island Kure Atoll" *Nuttall Ornithology Club*, vol. 8 (1969).

    R. B. Clapp and P. W. Woodward, "New Records of Birds From the Hawaiin Island," *Proceedings of the U.S. National Museum*, vol. 124i (1968) pp. 1-39.

    A. B. Amerson, "The Natural History of French Frigate Shoals, Northwestern Hawaiin Islands," *Atoll Research Bulletin*, no. 150 (1971).

    R. B. Clapp, "The Natural History of Gardner Pinnacles, Northwestern Hawaiin Islands," *Atoll Research Bulletin*, no. 163 (1972).

    P. W. Woodward, "The Natural History of Kure Atoll, Northwestern Hawaiin Islands," *Atoll Research Bulletin*, no. 164 (1972).

    C. A. Ely and R. Clapp, "The Natural History of Laysan Island, Northwestern Hawaiian Islands," *Atoll Research Bulletin*, no. 171 (1973), 361 pp.

    A. B. Amerson, et al., "The Natural History of Pearl and Hermes Reef, Northwestern Hawaiian Island," *Atoll Research Bulletin*, no. 174 (1974).

    R. R. Fleet, "The Red-tailed Tropicbird on Kure Atoll," Ornithological Monograph, no. 16 (1974).

    R. B. Clapp and W. O. Wirtz, "The Natural History of Lisianski Island, Northwestern Hawaiian Islands," *Atoll Research Bulletin*, no. 186 (1975).

    R. B. Clapp and E. Kridler, "The Natural History of Necker Island, Northwestern Hawaiian Islands," *Atoll Research Bulletin*, no. 206 (1977).

    R. B. Clapp, et al., "The Natural History of Nihoa Island," *Atoll Research Bulletin*, no. 207 (1977).

17. D. Mueller-Dombois, K. W. Bridges, and H. L. Carson (eds.), *Island Ecosystems: Biological Organization in Selected Communities* (Stroudsburg, PA: Hutchinson Ross, 1981).

18. H. W. Henshaw, "Description of a New Shearwater From the Hawaiian Islands," *Auk*, vol. 17 (1900), pp. 246-247.

19. G. C. Munro, *Birds of Hawaii* (Honolulu: Tongg Publ. Co., 1944).

    J. L. Sincock, "Saving the Newell's shearwater," in *Hawaii Forestry Wildlife Conference Proceedings*, 1981.

20. J. L. Peters, *Check-list of Birds of the World* (Cambridge: Harvard University Press, 1931).

21. F. Richardson, "Reappearance of Newell's Shearwater in Hawaii," *Auk*, vol. 72 (1955), p. 412.

22. J. L. Sincock and G. Swedberg, "Rediscovery of the nesting grounds of Newell's Manx Shearwater with Initial Observations," *Condor*, vol. 71 (1969), pp. 69-71.

23. T. Hadley, "Shearwater Calamity on Kauai," *Elepaio*, vol. 21, no. 8 (1961), pp. 60-61.

24. T. C. Telfer, "Successful Newell's Shearwater Salvage on Kauai," *Elepaio*, vol. 39, no. 7 (1979), p. 71.

    D. V. Byrd, J. L. Sincock and T. Telfer, "The Status of the Newewell's Manx Shearwater, a Threatened Species," *Pacific Seabird Group Bulletin* (1978).

    T. C. Telfer, J. L. Sincock, J. R. Reed and G.V. Byrd, "Salvage of Downed

Seabirds in Relation to Photo-pollution and Lunar Events" (Unpublished manuscript).

25. J. R. Reed, J. L. Sincock, and J. P. Hailman. "Light Attraction in Endangered Procellariform birds: Reduction by Shielding Upward Radiation," *Auk*, vol, 102, no. 2 (1985), pp. 377-383.

26. T. C. Telfer, Recovery Plan for the Newell's shearwater and dark-rumped petrel (Portland, Oregon: U. S. Fish and Wildlife Service, 1983).

27. Op. cit., Olson and James, *Prodromus of the Fossil Avifauna of the Hawaiian Islands*.

28. P. H. Baldwin, "The Hawaiian goose, Its Distribution and Reduction in Numbers," *Condor*, vol. 47 (1945), pp. 27-37.

29. Op. cit., Baldwin, "The Hawaiian Goose, Its Distribution and Reduction in Numbers".

30. W. S. Devick, *Status of the Nene Population on the Island of Hawaii Between 1975 and 1980* (Honolulu: Hawaii Dept. Land and Nat. Resources, 1981).
W. S. Devick, *Status of the Nene Population on the Island of Maui Between 1975 and 1980* (Honolulu: Hawaii Dept. Land and Nat. Resources, 1981).

31. P. C. Banko, "Productivity of Wild and Captive Nene Populations," in *Hawaii Volcanoes National Park*, Coop. National Park Res. Studies Unit, Proceedings: Fourth Conference in Natural Science, Universisty of Hawaii, Honolulu.
C. P. Stone, R. L. Walker, J. M. Scott and P. C. Banko, "Hawaiian Goose Management and Research — Where Do We Go from Here?" *Elepaio*, vol. 44 (1983), pp. 11-15.

32. Op. cit., Munro, Birds of Hawaii.

33. R. J. Shallenberger, "A Seal Slips Away," *Natural History*, vol. 91, no. 1248-63 (1982).

34. Op. cit., Olson and James, *Prodromus of the Fossil Avifauna of the Hawaiian Islands*.

35. W. H. Munter, "Reporting Destruction of Bird Life on Laysan Island," Annual Report, Coast Guard (1915).

36. Op. cit., Ely and Clapp, "The Natural History of Laysan Island, Northwestern Hawaiian Islands."

37. A. Wetmore, "Bird Life Among Lava Rock and Coral sand," *National Geographic Magazine*, vol. 48 (July 1925), pp. 76-108.

38. Op. cit., Berger, *Hawaiian Birdlife*.

39. Op. cit., Shallenberger, "A Seal Slips Away."
Op. cit., Sincock and Kridler, "The Extinct and Endemic Endangered Birds of the Northwestern Hawaiian Islands."

40. B. Giezentanner, D. Woodside, J. Sincock and E. Kridler, Laysan Duck Recovery Plan (Portland, Oregon: U. S. Fish and Wildlife Service, 1982).

41. Op. cit., Perkins, "Vertebrata."

42. W. A. Bryan, *Natural History of Hawaii* (Honolulu: Hawaiian Gazette Co., 1915).

43. Op. cit., Munro, *Birds of Hawaii*.

44. S. R. Sabo, "The Rediscovery of Bishop's O'o on Mauai," *Elepaio*, vol. 42 (1982), p. 69-70.

45. F. Richardson and J. Bowles, A Survey of the Birds of Kauai, Hawaii, B. P. *Bishop Museum Bulletin*, no. 227, 1964.

46. J. L. Sincock, R. E. Daehler, T. Telfer and D. H. Woodside, Kauai Forest Bird Recovery Plan (Portland, Oregon: U. S. Fish and Wildlife Service, 1984).

47. C. van Riper, III, "The Breeding Biology of the Amakihi (*Loxops virens*) and

Palila (*Psittirostra bailleui*) on Mauna Kea, Hawaii" (Ph.D. dissertation, University of Hawaii, Honolulu, 1978).

C. van Riper, III, "Observations on the breeding of the palila (*Psittirostra bailleui*) of Hawaii," *Ibis*, vol. 122 (1980), pp. 462-475.

C. van Riper, III, et al., "Distribution and Abundance Patterns of the Palila on Mauna Kea, Hawaii," *Auk* vol. 95 (1978), pp. 518-527.

Scott, et al., "Annual Variation in the Distribution, Abundance, and Habitat of the Palila (*Loxioides bailleui*)," *Auk* vol. 101 (1984) pp. 647-667.

48. Op. cit., Olson and James, *Prodromus of the Fossil Avifauna of the Hawaiian Islands*.
49. S. Yates, "On the Cutting Edge of Extinction," *Audubon* (July 1984), pp. 62-85.
50. R. E. Warner, "A Forest Dies on Mauna Kea," *Pacific Discovery*, vol. 13, no. 1 (1960), pp. 6-14.
51. J. Giffin, "Ecology of the Mouflon Sheep on Mauna Kea," Pittman-Robertson Prog. W-17-R, Study R-III (Honolulu: Hawaii Dept. Land and Nat. Resources, 1982).
52. A. J. Berger, E. Kosaka, J. M. Scott, P. Scowcraft, C. Wakida, D. Woodside and C. van Riper, III, Palila Recovery Plan (Portland, Oregon: U. S. Fish and Wildlife Service, 1977).

Op. cit., Scott, et al., 1984.
53. Op. cit., Perkins, "Vertebrata."
54. Op. cit., Munro, *Birds of Hawaii*.
55. J. M. Scott, J. Baker, A. Berger, E. Kosaka, L. Landgraf, C. Ralph, D. Woodside, R. Bachman and T. Burr, Hawaii Forest Bird Recovery Plan, (Portland, Oregon: U. S. Fish and Wildlife Service, 1982).
56. Op. cit., Perkins, "Vertebrata."
57. C. B. Kepler, T. A. Burr, C. B. Cooper, D. Dunatchik, J. Medeiras, J. M. Scott, M. Ueoka and W. Wong, Maui-Molokai Forest Bird Recovery Plan (Portland, Oregon: U. S. Fish and Wildlife Service, 1984).
58. Op. cit., Perkins, "Vertebrata."
59. J. M. Scott, J. L. Sincock and A. J. Berger, "Records of Nests, Eggs, Nestlings, and Cavity Nesting of Endemic Passerine Birds in Hawaii," *Elepaio*, vol. 40, no. 12 (June 1980), pp. 163-168.
60. R. J. Shallenberger, ed., *Hawaii's Birds* (Honolulu, Hawaii Audubon Society, 1978).
61. Op. cit., Scott et al., Hawaii Forest Bird Recovery Plan.
62. Op. cit., Berger, *Hawaiian Birdlife*.
63. Op. cit., Olson and James, *Prodromus of the Fossil Avifauna of the Hawaiian Islands*.
64. Burr et al., Alala Recovery Plan (Portland, Oregon: U.S. Fish and Wildlife Service, 1981).
65. Op. cit., Mueller-Dombois et al., *Island Ecosystems*.
66. C. B. Kepler and J. M. Scott, "Conservation of Island Ecosystems," *International Council for Bird Preservation World Conference Proc. XVIII* (in press).

J. MICHAEL SCOTT for 10 years was the biologist in charge of the FWS Mauna Loa field station, where he helped initiate the Hawaii Forest Bird Survey. He currently is project leader of the Condor Research Center in California.

JOHN L. SINCOCK retired in 1984 after 28 years with FWS. His research and management efforts in Hawaii led to the discovery of the nesting sites of the Newell's shearwater and the threatened Kauai'o'o.

PART IV.
Appendices

Appendix I.
Directory of Key Personnel

U.S. Fish and Wildlife Service

WILDLIFE RESOURCES PROGRAM

CENTRAL OFFICE

Ronald E. Lambertson
Associate Director - Wildlife Resources
Main Interior Building, Rm 3252
18th & C Streets, NW
Washington, DC 20240
(202) 343-5333

Walter O. Stieglitz
Deputy Associate Director - National Wildlife Refuge System
Main Interior Building, Rm 3252
18th & C Streets, NW
Washington, DC 20240
(202) 343-5333

James F. Gillett
Chief, Division of Refuge Management
Main Interior Building, Rm 2341
18th & C Streets, NW
Washington, DC 20240
(202) 343-4311

Walter R. McAllester
Chief, Division of Realty
Matomic Building, Rm 520
1717 H Street, NW
Washington, DC 20006
(202) 653-7650

Conley L. Moffett
Chief, Office of Public Use Management
Main Interior Building, Rm 3438
18th & C Streets, NW
Washington, DC 20240
(202) 343-4128

Donald H. Boyd
Chief, Office of Youth Activities
Main Interior Building, Rm 2414
18th & C Streets, NW
Washington, DC 20240
(202) 343-4404

Russell D. Earnest
Chief, Program Development Staff - Wildlife
Main Interior Building, Rm 2542
18th & C Streets, NW
Washington, DC 20240
(202) 343-6351

Don W. Minnich
Deputy Associate Director - Wildlife Management
Main Interior Building, Rm 3252
18th & C Streets, NW
Washington, DC 20240
(202) 343-5333

Rollin D. Sparrowe
Chief, Office of Migratory Bird Management
Matomic Building, Rm 536
1717 H Street, NW
Washington, DC 20006
(202) 254-3207

LeRoy W. Sowl
Chief, Division of Wildlife Management
Matomic Building, Rm 514
1717 H Street, NW
Washington, DC 20006
(202) 632-7463

Clark R. Bavin
Chief, Division of Law Enforcement
Hamilton Building, Suite 300
1375 K Street, NW
Washington, DC 20005
(202) 343-9242

REGIONAL OFFICES

Assistant Regional Directors - Wildlife Resources

Lawrence W. De Bates (Region 1)
Lloyd 500 Building, Rm 1552
500 NE Multnomah Street
Portland, OR 97232
(503) 231-6214

W. Ellis Klett (Region 2)
P.O. Box 1306
Albuquerque, NM 87103
(505) 766-1829

Harold W. Benson (Region 3)
Bishop Henry Whipple Building
Fort Snelling
Twin Cities, MN 55111
(612) 725-3507

Crayton J. Lankford (Region 4)
R. B. Russell Federal Bldg, Rm 1240
75 Spring Street, SW
Atlanta, GA 30303
(404) 221-3538

Suzanne Mayer (Region 5)
One Gateway Center
Newton Corner, MA 02158
(617) 965-5100 (ext. 222)

Nelson B. Kverno (Region 6)
P.O. Box 25486
Denver Federal Center
Denver, CO 80225
(303) 234-4608

John P. Rogers (Region 7)
1011 E Tudor Road
Anchorage, AK 99503
(907) 786-3538

Special Agents-in-Charge

David McMullen (District 1)
Lloyd 500 Building, Suite 1490
500 NE Multnomah Street
Portland, OR 97232
(503) 231-6125

John E. Cross (District 2)
P.O. Box 329
Albuquerque, NM 87103
(505) 766-2091

Robert A. Hodgins (District 3)
Bishop Henry Whipple Building
Fort Snelling
Twin Cities, MN 55111
(612) 725-3530

Dan M. Searcy (District 4)
P.O. Box 4839
Atlanta, GA 30302
(404) 221-5872

James V. Sheridan (District 5)
P.O. Box 129
New Town Branch
Boston, MA 02258
(617) 965-2298

Terry L. Grosz (District 6)
P.O. Box 25486
Denver Federal Center
Denver, CO 80225
(303) 234-4612

James H. Hogue (District 7)
P.O. Box 4-2597
Anchorage, AK 99509-2597
(907) 276-3800

FISHERY RESOURCES PROGRAM

WASHINGTON OFFICE

Dr. Joseph H. Kutkuhn
Associate Director - Fishery Resources
(202) 343-6394

Gary Edwards
Deputy Associate Director - Fishery Resources
(202) 343-4266

William P. Atchison
Chief, Office of Program Development - Fisheries
(202) 343-6307

John T. Brown
Chief, Division of Program Operations - Fisheries
(202) 653-8746

G. Donald Weathers
Chief, Office of Facility Services
(202) 653-8232

Mailing Address:
U. S. Fish and Wildlife Service
U. S. Department of the Interior
Washington, DC 20240

REGIONAL OFFICES

Assistant Regional Directors - Fisheries Resources

Wally Steucke (Region 1)
Lloyd 500 Building, Suite 1692
500 NE Multnomah Street
Portland, OR 97232
(503) 230-5967

Conrad Fjetland (Region 2)
P.O. Box 1306
Albuquerque, NM 87103
(505) 766-2323

John Popowski (Region 3)
Bishop Henry Whipple Building
Fort Snelling
Twin Cities, MN 55111
(612) 725-3505

Frank Richardson (Region 4)
R. B. Russell Federal Bldg, Rm 1200
75 Spring Street, SW
Atlanta, GA 30303
(404) 221-3576

Dr. James Weaver (Region 5)
One Gateway Center, Suite 700
Newton Corner, MA 02158
(617) 965-5100

Danny Regan (Region 6)
P.O. Box 25486
Denver Federal Center
Denver, CO 80225
(303) 236-8154

Jon Nelson (Region 7)
1011 E Tudor Road
Anchorage, AK 99503
(907) 786-3539

Law Enforcement: Special Agents-in-Charge

Loren K. Parcher (District 1)
Lloyd 500 Building, Suite 1490
500 NE Multnomah Street
Portland, OR 97232
(503) 231-6125

John E. Cross (District 2)
P.O. Box 329
Albuquerque, NM 87103
(505) 766-2091

Robert A. Hodgins (District 3)
Bishop Henry Whipple Building
Fort Snelling
Twin Cities, MN 55111
(612) 725-3530

Dan M. Searcy (District 4)
P.O. Box 4839
Atlanta, GA 30302
(404) 221-5872

James V. Sheridan (District 5)
P.O. Box 129
New Town Branch
Boston, MA 02258
(617) 965-2298

Terry L. Grosz (District 6)
P.O. Box 25486
Denver Federal Center
Denver, CO 80225
(303) 234-4612

James H. Hogue (District 7)
P.O. Box 4-2597
Anchorage, AK 99509-2597
(907) 276-3800

ANIMAL DAMAGE CONTROL PROGRAM

WASHINGTON OFFICE

LeRoy Sowl
Chief, Division of Wildlife Management

Gary Simmons
Acting Chief, Branch of Animal Damage Control

Mailing Address:
Department of the Interior
18th and C Streets, NW
Washington, DC 20240
(202) 632-7463

REGIONAL SUPERVISORS

Vern Cunningham (Region 1)
U. S. Fish and Wildlife Service
500 NE Multnomah Street
The Lloyd 500 Building, Suite 1692
Portland, OR 97232
(503) 231-6167

Norm Johnson (Region 2)
U. S. Fish and Wildlife Service
500 Gold Ave, SW
P.O. Box 1306
Albuquerque, NM 87103
(505) 766-2839

Ralph Town (Region 3)
U. S. Fish and Wildlife Service
Federal Building
Fort Snelling
Twin Cities, MN 55111
(612) 725-3313

Royston (Rudy) Rudolph (Region 4)
U. S. Fish and Wildlife Service
R. B. Russell Federal Bldg
75 Spring Street SW, Suite 1200
Atlanta, GA 30303
(404) 221-3538

Gerry Atwell (Region 5)
U. S. Fish and Wildlife Service
1 Gateway Center, Suite 700
Newton Corner, MA 02158
(617) 965-5100 (ext. 222)

Darrell Gretz (Region 6)
U. S. Fish and Wildlife Service
P.O. Box 25486
Denver Federal Center
Denver, CO 80225
(303) 234-4291

Jim Baker (Region 7)
U. S. Fish and Wildlife Service
1011 E Tudor Road
Anchorage, AK 99503
(907) 263-3534

REGIONAL WETLAND COORDINATORS

(National Wetlands Inventory Maps are
available from the Fish and Wildlife
Service's regional wetland coordinators)

Dennis Peters (Region 1)
U. S. Fish and Wildlife Service
Lloyd 500 Bldg, Suite 1692
500 NE Multnomah Street
Portland, OR 97232
(503) 231-6154

Warren Hagenbuck (Region 2)
U. S. Fish and Wildlife Service
P.O. Box 1306
Albuquerque, NM 87103
(505) 766-2914

Ron Erickson (Region 3)
U. S. Fish and Wildlife Service
Bishop Henry Whipple Federal Bldg
Twin Cities, MN 55111
(612) 725-3536

John Hefner (Region 4)
U. S. Fish and Wildlife Service
R. B. Russell Federal Bldg
75 Spring Street, SW
Atlanta, Georgia 30303
(404) 221-6343

Ralph Tiner (Region 5)
U. S. Fish and Wildlife Service
One Gateway Center, Suite 700
Newton Corner, MA 02158
(617) 965-5100 (ext. 379)

Charles Elliott (Region 6)
U. S. Fish and Wildlife Service
P.O. Box 2548
Denver Federal Center
Denver, CO 80225
(303) 234-5586

Jon Hall (Region 7)
U. S. Fish and Wildlife Service
1011 E Tudor Road
Anchorage, AK 99503
(907) 786-3403

BUREAU OF LAND MANAGEMENT

ALASKA
*Laun Buoy, State Office Biologist
Bureau of Land Management
701 C Street
Anchorage, AK 99513
(907) 271-3349

ARIZONA
*John Costellano, State Office Biologist
Bureau of Land Management
3707 North 7th Street
Phoenix, AZ 85011
(602) 261-5512

CALIFORNIA
*Mike Ferguson, State Office Biologist
Bureau of Land Management
Federal Office Bldg
2800 Cottage Way
Sacramento, CA 95825
(916) 484-4701

COLORADO
*Lee Upham, State Office Biologist
Bureau of Land Management
2020 Arapahoe Street
Denver, CO 80205
(303) 837-4325

DENVER SERVICE CENTER
*Allen Cooperrider, Service Center Biologist
Bureau of Land Management
Denver Service Center
Denver Federal Center, Bldg 50
Denver, CO 80225
(303) 236-0161

EASTERN STATES OFFICE
*Gene Ludlow, State Office Biologist
Bureau of Land Management
Eastern States Office
350 South Pickett Street
Alexandria, VA 22304
(703) 274-0069

IDAHO
*Allen Thomas, State Office Biologist
Bureau of Land Management
3380 Americana Terrace
Boise, ID 83706
(208) 334-1835

MONTANA
Ray Hoem, State Office Biologist
*Dan Hinckley
Bureau of Land Management
222 North 32nd Street
Billings, MT 59107
(406) 657-6655

NEVADA
David Goicoechea, State Office Biologist
*Osborne Casey
Bureau of Land Management
300 Booth Street, Rm 3038
Reno, NV 89520
(702) 784-5455

NEW MEXICO
*Brian Mills, State Office Biologist
Bureau of Land Management
Montoya Federal Bldg
South Federal Place
Santa Fe, NM 87501
(505) 988-6231

OREGON
Art Oakley, State Office Biologist
*Bill Nietro
Bureau of Land Management
825 NE Multnomah Street
Portland, OR 97208
(503) 231-6866

UTAH
*Jerry Farringer, State Office Biologist
Bureau of Land Management
324 South State Street
Salt Lake City, UT 84111-2303
(801) 524-3123

WYOMING
*Dick Felthousen, State Office Biologist
Bureau of Land Management
2515 Warren Avenue
Cheyenne, WY 82003
(307) 778-2086

(* = Biologist for Endangered Species)

MARINE MAMMAL MANAGEMENT

MARINE MAMMAL COMMISSION

James C. Nofziger, Ph.D., Commissioner (Chairman)

Donald K. McCallum, Ph.D., Commissioner

Robert B. Weeden, Ph.D., Commissioner

John R. Twiss, Jr., Executive Director

Douglas G. Chapman, Ph.D., Chairman,
Committee of Scientific Advisors

Mailing Address:
Marine Mammal Commission
1625 Eye Street, NW
Washington, DC 20006
(202) 653-6237

FISH AND WILDLIFE SERVICE

WASHINGTON OFFICE

John L. Spinks, Jr., Chief
Office of Endangered Species
18th & C Streets, NW
Washington, DC 20240
(703) 235-2771

LeRoy W. Sowl, Chief
Division of Wildlife Management
18th & C Streets, NW
Washington, DC 20240
(202) 632-7463

REGIONAL AND FIELD PERSONNEL

Skip Ladd
Sea Otter Coordinator
2800 Cottage Way, Rm E-2727
Sacramento, CA 95825
(916) 484-4731

Earl Possardt
Manatee Coordinator
Endangered Species Field Station
2747 Art Museum Drive
Jacksonville, FL 32207
(904) 791-2580

Dr. Robert E. Putz (Region 7)
Regional Director
Alaska Regional Office
1011 E Tudor Road
Anchorage, AK 99503
(907) 786-3542

Appendix II.
U.S. Fish and Wildlife Service

REGIONAL OFFICES

Region 1: California, Hawaii, Idaho, Nevada, Oregon, Washington, Pacific Trust Territories.
Lloyd 500 Building, Suite 1692
500 NE Multnomah Street
Portland, OR 97232
(503) 231-6118

Region 2: Arizona, New Mexico, Oklahoma, Texas.
P.O. Box 1306
Albuquerque, NM 87103
(505) 766-2321

Region 3: Iowa, Illinois, Indiana, Michigan, Minnesota, Missouri, Ohio, Wisconsin.
Bishop Henry Whipple Building
Fort Snelling
Twin Cities, MN 55111
(612) 725-3563

Region 4: Alabama, Arkansas, Florida, Georgia, Kentucky, Louisiana, Mississippi, North Carolina, South Carolina, Tennessee, Puerto Rico, Virgin Islands.
R. B. Russell Federal Building
75 Spring Street, SW
Atlanta, GA 30303
(404) 221-3588

Region 5: Connecticut, Delaware, Maine, Maryland, Massachusetts, New Hampshire, New Jersey, New York, Pennsylvania, Rhode Island, Vermont, Virginia, West Virginia.
One Gateway Center, Suite 700
Newton Corner, MA 02158
(617) 965-5100

Region 6: Colorado, Kansas, Montana, Nebraska, North Dakota, South Dakota, Utah, Wyoming.
P.O. Box 25486
Denver Federal Center
Denver, CO 80225
(303) 236-7926

Region 7: Alaska
1011 E Tudor Road
Anchorage, AK 99503
(907) 786-3542

ECOLOGICAL SERVICES FIELD OFFICES

REGION 1
Boise Field Office
U.S. Fish and Wildlife Service
4696 Overland Road, Rm 209
Boise, ID 83705
(208) 334-1931

Great Basin Complex
U.S. Fish and Wildlife Service
4600 Kietzke Lane, Suite C
Reno, NV 89502
(702) 784-5227

Pacific Area Office
U.S. Fish and Wildlife Service
300 Ala Moana Blvd, Rm 5302
P.O. Box 50167
Honolulu, HI 96850
(808) 546-5608

Honolulu Field Office
U.S. Fish and Wildlife Service
300 Ala Moana Blvd, Rm 6307
P.O. Box 50167
Honolulu, HI 96850
(808) 546-7530

Olympia Field Office
U.S. Fish and Wildlife Service
2625 Parkmont Lane SW, Bldg B3
Olympia, WA 98502
(206) 753-9440

Moses Lake Suboffice
U.S. Fish and Wildlife Service
P.O. Box 1157
517 Buchanan Street
Moses Lake, WA 98837
(509) 765-6125

Marrowstone Suboffice
U.S. Fish and Wildlife Service
Marrowstone, Nordland, WA 98358
(206) 385-1007

Portland Field Office
U.S. Fish and Wildlife Service
727 NE 24th Avenue
Portland, OR 97232
(503) 231-6179

Laguna Niguel Field Office
U.S. Fish and Wildlife Service
Federal Building, 24000 Avila Road
Laguna Niguel, CA 92677
(714) 643-4270

Sacramento Field Office
U.S. Fish and Wildlife Service
2800 Cottage Way, Rm E1803
Sacramento, CA 95825
(916) 484-4731

REGION 2
Albuquerque Field Office
U.S. Fish and Wildlife Service
P.O. Box 4487
Onate Hall, Room 137
University of New Mexico
Albuquerque, NM 87196
(505) 766-3966

Corpus Christi Field Office
U.S. Fish and Wildlife Service
Corpus Christi State University
6300 Ocean Drive, Campus Box 338
Old Science Hall, Rm 118
Corpus Christi, TX 78412
(512) 888-3346

Fort Worth Field Office
U.S. Fish and Wildlife Service
9A33 Fritz Lanham Building
819 Taylor Street
Fort Worth, TX 76102
(817) 334-2961

Clear Lake Field Office
U.S. Fish and Wildlife Service
17629 El Camino Real, Suite 211
Houston, TX 77058
(713) 229-3681,2,3,4

Phoenix Field Office
U.S. Fish and Wildlife Service
2934 West Fairmount Avenue
Phoenix, AZ 85017
(602) 241-2493

Tulsa Field Office
U.S. Fish and Wildlife Service
222 South Houston, Suite A
Tulsa, OK 74127
(918) 581-7458

REGION 3
Bloomington Field Office
U.S. Fish and Wildlife Service
718 North Walnut Street
Bloomington, IN 47401
(812) 334-4261

Columbia Field Office
U.S. Fish and Wildlife Service
705 Hitt Street
Columbia, MO 65201
(314) 875-5374

Columbus Field Office
U.S. Fish and Wildlife Service
P.O. Box 3990
Columbus, OH 43216-5000
(614) 231-3416

East Lansing Field Office
U.S. Fish and Wildlife Service
301 Manly Miles Building
1405 South Harrison Road
East Lansing, MI 48823
(517) 337-6650

Green Bay Field Office
U.S. Fish and Wildlife Service
University of Wisconsin
Green Bay, Rm SE 480
Green Bay, WI 54302
(414) 465-2682

Rock Island Field Office
U.S. Fish and Wildlife Service
1830 Second Avenue
Rock Island, IL 61201
(309) 793-5800

Marion, Illinois Suboffice
(Under Rock Island Field Office)
U.S. Fish and Wildlife Service
Route 3, Box 198A
Crab Orchard National Wildlife Refuge Head
Marion, IL 62959
(618) 997-5491

St. Paul Field Office
U.S. Fish and Wildlife Service
570 NalPak Building
333 Sibley Street
St. Paul, MN 55101
(612) 725-7131

REGION 4
Brunswick Field Office
U.S. Fish and Wildlife Service
801 Gloucester Street
Brunswick, GA 31520
(912) 265-9336

Charleston Field Office
U.S. Fish and Wildlife Service
P.O. Box 12559
217 Fort Johnson Road
Charleston, SC 29412
(803) 724-4707

Cookeville Field Office
U.S. Fish and Wildlife Service
P.O. Box 845
9 E Broad Street
Cookeville, TN 38503
(615) 528-6481

Daphne Field Office
U.S. Fish and Wildlife Service
P.O. Drawer 1197
2001 Daphne East Office Plaza, Suite A
Highway 98
Daphne, AL 36526
(205) 626-1880

Lafayette Field Office
U.S. Fish and Wildlife Service
P.O. Box 4305
Postal Square Bldg, Rm 102
103 E Cypress Street
Lafayette, LA 70502
(318) 234-7478,9

Mayaguez Field Office
U.S. Fish and Wildlife Service
P.O. Box 3005, Marina Station
Mayaguez, PR 00708
(809) 833-5760

Panama City Field Office
U.S. Fish and Wildlife Service
1612 June Avenue
Panama City, FL 32405
(904) 769-0552

Raleigh Field Office
U.S. Fish and Wildlife Service
P.O. Box 25039
Raleigh, NC 27611-5039
Actual location:
Federal Building, Rm 468
310 New Bern Avenue
Raleigh, NC 27601
(919) 755-4520

Vero Beach Field Office
U.S. Fish and Wildlife Service
P.O. Box 2676
1323 21st Street
Vero Beach, FL 32960
(305) 562-3909

Vicksburg Field Office
U.S. Fish and Wildlife Service
900 Clay Street, Rm 235
Vicksburg, MS 39180
(601) 638-1891,2

REGION 5
Annapolis Field Office
U.S. Fish and Wildlife Service
1825-B Virginia Street
Annapolis, MD 21401
(301) 269-5448,9

Elkins Suboffice
U.S. Fish and Wildlife Service
P.O. Box 1278
Elkins, WV 26214
Actual location:
USDA Forestry Building, Rm 311
Sycamore Street
Elkins, WV 26241
(304) 636-6586

Gloucester Point Suboffice
U.S. Fish and Wildlife Service
P.O. Box 729
Route 1208, Box 729
Gloucester Point, VA 23062
(804) 642-7180

Cortland Field Office
U.S. Fish and Wildlife Service
100 Grange Place, Rm 202
Cortland, NY 13045
(607) 753-9334,5

Long Island Suboffice
U.S. Fish and Wildlife Service
c/o Brookhaven National Laboratory
Building 134
Upton, NY 11973
(516) 345-3300

State College Field Office
U.S. Fish and Wildlife Service
315 S Allen Street, Suite 322
State College, PA 16801
(814) 234-4090,2

Absecon Suboffice
U.S. Fish and Wildlife Service
705 White Horse Pike
P.O. Box 534
Absecon, NJ 08201
(609) 646-9310,1

Concord Field Office
U.S. Fish and Wildlife Service
P.O. Box 1518
55 Pleasant Street
Condord, NH 03301
(603) 224-2585,6

REGION 6
Billings Field Office
U.S. Fish and Wildlife Service
Federal Building, Rm 3035
316 North 26th Street
Billings, MT 59101
(406) 657-6750

Cheyenne Suboffice
(Under Billings Field Office)
U.S. Fish and Wildlife Service
2120 Capital Avenue, Room 7010
Cheyenne, WY 82001
(307) 778-2220 (ext. 2374)

Bismarck Field Office
U.S. Fish and Wildlife Service
1500 Capitol Avenue
Bismarck, ND 58501
(701) 255-4011

South Dakota Field Office
U.S. Fish and Wildlife Service
227 Federal Building
P.O. Box 986
Pierre, SD 57501
(605) 224-8693

Kansas-Nebraska Ecological Services Office
U.S. Fish and Wildlife Service
1811 W 2nd Street, Rm 430
Grand Island, NE 68801
(308) 381-5571,2,3

Kansas Suboffice
U.S. Fish and Wildlife Service
Division of Biology, Ackert Hall
Kansas State University
Manhattan, KS 66506
(913) 539-3152

Salt Lake Field Office
U.S. Fish and Wildlife Service
2060 Administration Building
1745 West 1700 South
Salt Lake City, UT 84104-5110
(801) 524-5637

Grand Junction Suboffice
U.S. Fish and Wildlife Service
551 25 ½ Road, Suite B-113
Independence Plaza
Grand Junction, CO 81501
(303) 243-2778

Lakewood Suboffice
U.S. Fish and Wildlife Service
730 Simms Street
MSHA Building, Suite 292
Golden, CO 80401
(303) 236-2675

REGION 7
Project Investigations (Special Studies)
(907) 786-3492

Western Alaska Field Office
U.S. Fish and Wildlife Service
Western Alaska Ecological Services (WAES)
Sunshine Mall, 605 West 4th Ave, Suite 2-B
Anchorage, AK 99501
(907) 271-4575

Northern Alaska Field Office
U.S. Fish and Wildlife Service
Northern Alaska Ecological Services (NAES)
101 12th Ave, Federal Bldg, Box 20
Fairbanks, AK 99701
(907) 456-0203

Southeast Alaska Field Office
U.S. Fish and Wildlife Service
P.O. Box 1287
Southeast Ecological Services (SEES)
Federal Building, Room 417
Juneau, AK 99802
(907) 586-7240

Ketchikan Suboffice
U.S. Fish and Wildlife Service
P.O. Box 3193
Ketchikan, AK 99901
(907) 225-9691

Petersburg Suboffice
U.S. Fish and Wildlife Service
P.O. Box 1108
Petersburg, AK 99833
(907) 772-3866

Sitka Suboffice
U.S. Fish and Wildlife Service
P.O. Box 810
Sitka, AK 99835
(907) 747-8882

Appendix III.
National Park Service Regional Offices and Contacts

North Atlantic Regional Office
National Park Service
15 State Street
Boston, MA 02109
(617) 223-3793

Regional Chief Scientist:
Dr. Michael Soukup
Regional Natural
Resource Specialist:
Dr. Michael Soukup

The region includes Connecticut, Maine, Massachusetts, New Hampshire, New Jersey, New York, Rhode Island, and Vermont.

Mid-Atlantic Region
Regional Chief Scientist:
National Park Service
John Karish
143 South Third Street
Regional Natural
Philadelphia, PA 19106
Resource Specialist:
(215) 597-3679
Mike Maule

The region includes Delaware, Maryland, Pennsylvania, Virginia, and West Virginia.

National Capital Region
National Park Service
1100 Ohio Drive, SW
Washington, DC 20242
(202) 426-6700

Regional Chief Scientist:
Dr. William Anderson
Regional Natural
Resource Specialist:
Stan Locke

The National Capital Region covers parks in the metropolitan area of Washington, D.C. and certain field areas in Maryland, Virginia, and West Virginia.

Southeast Regional Office
National Park Service
75 Spring Street, SW
Atlanta, GA 30303
(404) 221-3448

Regional Chief Scientist:
Dr. G. Jay Gogue
Regional Natural
Resource Specialist:
Dr. G. Jay Gogue

The region includes Alabama, Georgia, Kentucky, Mississippi, North Carolina, South Carolina, Tennessee, and Puerto Rico, and the Virgin Islands.

Midwest Regional Office
National Park Service
1709 Jackson Street
Omaha, NE 68102
(402) 221-3448

Regional Chief Scientist:
Dr. Michael Ruggiero
Regional Natural
Resource Specialist:
Ben Holmes

The region includes Illinois, Indiana, Iowa, Kansas, Minnesota, Michigan, Missouri, Nebraska, Ohio, and Wisconsin.

Rocky Mountain Regional Office
National Park Service
655 Parfet Street
Denver, CO 80225
(303) 236-4648

Regional Chief Scientist:
Neil J. Reid
Regional Natural
Resource Specialist:
Jim Olson

The region includes Colorado, Montana, North Dakota, South Dakota, Utah, and Wyoming.

Southwest Regional Office
The National Park Service
Old Santa Fe Trail
P.O. Box 728
Santa Fe, NM 87501
(505) 988-6375

Regional Chief Scientist:
Dr. Milford Fletcher

Regional Natural
Resource Specialist:
Dr. Milford Fletcher

The region includes part of Arizona, Arkansas, Louisiana, New Mexico, Oklahoma, and Texas.

Western Regional Office
National Park Service
450 Golden Gate Avenue
P.O. Box 36063
San Francisco, CA 94102
(415) 556-5186

Regional Chief Scientist
(Acting):
Gene Wehunt
Regional Natural
Resource Specialist:
Francis Jacot

The region includes part of Arizona, California, Hawaii, and Nevada.

Pacific Northwest Regional Office
National Park Service
Westin Building
2001 Sixth Avenue, Room 1920
Seattle, WA 98121
(206) 442-4830

Regional Chief Scientist:
James Larson

Regional Natural
Resource Specialist:
Dick Praisl

The region includes Idaho, Oregon, and Washington.

Alaska Regional Office
National Park Service
2525 Gambell Street, Room 107
Anchorage, AK 99503
(907) 271-4196

Regional Chief Scientist:
Al Lovass
Regional Natural
Resource Specialist:
Al Lovass

The region includes the State of Alaska.

Appendix IV.
U.S. Forest Service

ALABAMA
William B. Bankhead, Conecuh, Talladega
and Tuskegee National Forests
Joe J. Brown, Supervisor
National Forests in Alabama
1765 Highland Ave
Montgomery, AL 36107
(205) 832-7630

ALASKA
Chugach National Forest
Dalton DuLac, Supervisor
2221 E Northern Lights Blvd, Suite 238
Anchorage, AK 99504
(907) 279-5541

Tongass-Chatham Area National Forest
William P. Gee, Supervisor
Box 1980
Sitka, AK 99835
(907) 747-6671

Tongass-Ketchikan Area National Forest
Win Green, Supervisor
Federal Bldg
Ketchikan, AK 99901
(907) 225-3101

Tongass-Stikine Area National Forest
John Hughes, Supervisor
Box 309
Petersburg, AK 99833
(907) 772-3841

ARIZONA
Apache-Sitgreaves National Forest
Nick W. McDonough, Supervisor
Federal Bldg, Box 640
Springerville, AZ 85938
(602) 333-4301

Coconino National Forest
Neil R. Paulson, Supervisor
2323 E Greenlaw Lane
Flagstaff, AZ 86001
(602) 527-7400

Coronado National Forest
Robert B. Tippeconnic, Supervisor
301 W Congress
Tucson, AZ 85702
(602) 629-6789

Kaibab National Forest
Leonard A. Lindquist, Supervisor
800 South 6th Street
Williams, AZ 86046
(602) 635-2681

Prescott National Forest
Donald H. Bolander, Supervisor
344 S Cortez
Prescott, AZ 86301
(602) 445-1762

Tonto National Forest
James L. Kimball, Supervisor
102 S 28th Street
P.O. Box 29070
Phoenix, AZ 85038
(602) 261-3205

ARKANSAS
Ouachita National Forest
John V. Orr, Supervisor
Box 1270, Federal Bldg
Hot Springs National Park, AR 71902
(501) 321-5202

Ozark and St. Francis National Forests
James R. Crouch, Supervisor
Box 1008
Russellville, AR 72801
(501) 968-2354

CALIFORNIA
Angeles National Forest
Paul C. Sweetland, Supervisor
150 South Los Robles, Suite 300
Pasadena, CA 91101
(213) 577-0050

Cleveland National Forest
Ralph C. Cisco, Supervisor
880 Front Street
San Diego, CA 92188
(619) 293-5050

Eldorado National Forest
Robert R. Lusk, Supervisor
100 Forni Rd
Placerville, CA 95667
(916) 622-5061

Ínyo National Forest
Eugene E. Murphy
873 North Main Street
Bishop, CA 93514
(619) 873-5841

Klamath National Forest
Robert L. Rice, Supervisor
1312 Fairland Rd
Yreka, CA 96097
(916) 842-6131

Lassen National Forest
David M. Jay, Supervisor
707 Nevada
Susanville, CA 96130
(916) 257-2151

Los Padres National Forest
Frederik G. deHoll, Supervisor
42 Aero Camino
Goleta, CA 93117
(805) 968-1578

Mendocino National Forest
R. Lyle Laverty
420 E Laurel Street
Willows, CA 95988
(916) 934-3316

Modoc National Forest
Glenn S. Bradley, Supervisor
441 N Main Street
Alturas, CA 96101
(916) 233-5811

Plumas National Forest
Lloyd R. Britton, Supervisor
159 Lawrence Street
Box 1500
Quincy, CA 95971
(916) 283-2050

San Bernardino National Forest
Robert Tyrrel, Supervisor
144 N Mountain View
San Bernardino, CA 92408
(714) 383-5588

Sequoia National Forest
James A. Crates, Supervisor
900 W Grand Ave
Porterville, CA 93257
(209) 784-1500

Shasta-Trinity National Forest
Bernard A. Coster, Supervisor
2400 Washington Ave
Redding, CA 96001
(916) 246-5222

Sierra National Forest
Richard Stauber, Supervisor
Federal Bldg
1130 O Street, Rm 3017
Fresno, CA 93721
(209) 487-5155

Six Rivers National Forest
James L. Davis, Jr., Supervisor
507 F Street
Eureka, CA 95501
(707) 442-1721

Stanislaus National Forest
Blain L. Cornell, Supervisor
19777 Greenley Road
Sonora, CA 95370
(209) 532-3671

Tahoe National Forest
Robert G. Lancaster, Supervisor
Highway 49
Nevada City, CA 95959
(916) 265-4531

COLORADO

Arapaho and Roosevelt National Forests
Ray Benton, Supervisor
240 W Prospect Street
Fort Collins, CO 80526
(303) 221-4390

Grand Mesa, Uncompahgre and Gunnison
National Forests
Raymond J. Evans, Supervisor
2250 Highway 50
Delta, CO 81416
(303) 874-7691

Pike and San Isabel National Forests
Bruce H. Morgan, Supervisor
1920 Valley Dr
Pueblo, CO 81008
(303) 545-8737

Rio Grande National Forest
George W. Whitlock, Jr., Supervisor
1803 West Highway 160
Monte Vista, CO 81144
(303) 852-5941

Routt National Forest
Jack A. Weissling, Supervisor
Hunt Bldg
Steamboat Springs, CO 80477
(303) 879-1722

San Juan National Forest
Paul C. Sweetland, Jr., Supervisor
Federal Bldg
701 Camino Del Rio
Durango, CO 81301
(303) 247-4874

White River National Forest
Richard E. Woodrow, Supervisor
Old Federal Bldg, Box 948
Glenwood Springs, CO 81602
(303) 945-2512

FLORIDA
Apalachicola, Ocala and Osceola
National Forests
Donald E. Percival, Supervisor
National Forests in Florida
Hobbs Federal Bldg
227 No. Bronough Street, Suite 4061
Tallahassee, FL 32301
(904) 681-7265

GEORGIA
Chattahoochee and Oconee National Forests
W. Pat Thomas, Supervisor
601 Broad Street, SE
Gainesville, GA 30501
(404) 536-0541

IDAHO
Boise National Forest
John J. Lavin, Supervisor
1750 Front Street
Boise, ID 83702
(208) 334-1516

Caribou National Forest
Charles J. Hendricks, Supervisor
250 S 4th Ave, Suite 282
Federal Bldg
Pocatello, ID 83201
(208) 236-6700

Challis National Forest
Jack E. Bills, Supervisor
Forest Service Bldg
P.O. Box 404
Challis, ID 83226
(208) 879-2285

Clearwater National Forest
James C. Bates, Supervisor
12730 Highway 30
Orofino, ID 83544
(208) 476-4541

Idaho Panhandle National Forest
William E. Morden, Supervisor
1201 Ironwood Drive
Coeur d'Alene, ID 83814
(208) 765-7223

Nezperce National Forest
Tom Kovalicky, Supervisor
Rt. 2, Box 475
Grangeville, ID 83530
(208) 983-1950

Payette National Forest
Kenneth D. Weyers, Supervisor
Forest Service Bldg, Box 1026
McCall, ID 83638
(208) 634-8151

Salmon National Forest
Richard T. Hauff, Supervisor
Forest Service Bldg
Salmon, ID 83467
(208) 756-2215

Sawtooth National Forest
Roland M. Stoleson, Supervisor
1525 Addison Ave, East
Twin Falls, ID 83301
(208) 733-3698

Targhee National Forest
John E. Burns
420 N Bridge Street
P.O. Box 208
St. Anthony, ID 83445
(208) 624-3151

ILLINOIS
Shawnee National Forest
Kenneth D. Henderson, Supervisor
U.S. Rt. 45S, South
Harrisburg, IL 62946
(618) 253-7114

INDIANA
Wayne-Hoosier National Forest
Harold L. Godlevske, Supervisor
3527 10th Street
Bedford, IN 47421
(812) 332-4340

KENTUCKY
Daniel Boone National Forest
Richard H. Wengert, Supervisor
100 Vaught Road
Winchester, KY 40391
(606) 745-3100

LOUISIANA
Kisatchie National Forest
Robert C. Joslin, Supervisor
2500 Shreveport Hwy
Pineville, LA 71360
(318) 473-7160

MAINE
White Mountain National Forest
See New Hampshire

MICHIGAN
Hiawatha National Forest
Roy E. Droege, Supervisor
2727 N Lincoln Road
Escanaba, MI 49829
(906) 786-4062

Huron-Manistee National Forest
Wayne R. Mann, Supervisor
421 S Mitchell Street
Cadillac, MI 49601
(616) 775-2421

Ottawa National Forest
Joseph Zylinski, Supervisor
East U.S. 2
Ironwood, MI 49938
(906) 932-1330

MINNESOTA
Chippewa National Forest
James E. Brewer, Supervisor
Cass Lake, MN 56633
(218) 335-2226

Superior National Forest
Clay C. Beal, Supervisor
Box 338
Duluth, MN 55801
(218) 727-6692

MISSISSIPPI
Bienville, Delta, Desoto, Holly Springs,
Homochitto and Tombigbee National Forests
B. F. Finison, Supervisor
National Forests in Mississippi
100 W Capital Street, Suite 1141
Jackson, MS 39269
(601) 960-4391

MISSOURI
Mark Twain National Forest
Leon Cambre, Supervisor
401 Fairgrounds Road
Rolla, MO 65401
(314) 364-4621

MONTANA
Beaverhead National Forest
Joseph J. Wagenfehr
Box 1258
610 N Montana Street
Dillon, MT 59725
(406) 683-2312

Bitterroot National Forest
Robert S. Morgan, Supervisor
316 N 3rd Street
Hamilton, MT 59840
(406) 363-3131

Custer National Forest
James F. Mann, Supervisor
Box 2556
Billings, MT 59103
(406) 657-6361

Deerlodge National Forest
Frank E. Salomonsen, Supervisor
Federal Bldg, Box 400
Butte, MT 59703
(406) 496-3400

Flathead National Forest
John L. Emerson, Supervisor
Box 147
1935 3rd Ave, East
Kalispell, MT 59901
(406) 755-5401

Gallatin National Forest
John T. Drake, Supervisor
Federal Bldg, Box 130
Bozeman, MT 59771
(406) 585-5011

Helena National Forest
Robert S. Gibson, Supervisor
Federal Bldg, Drawer 10014
Helena, MT 59626
(406) 449-5201

Kootenai National Forest
James F. Rathbun, Supervisor
W Highway 2
Libby, MT 59923
(406) 293-6211

Lewis and Clark National Forest
J. Dale Gorman, Supervisor
Box 871
1602 2nd Ave, North
Great Falls, MT 59403
(406) 727-0901

Lolo National Forest
Orville L. Daniels, Supervisor
Bldg 24, Fort Missoula
Missoula, MT 59801
(406) 329-3557

NEBRASKA
Nebraska National Forest
Deen E. Boe, Supervisor
270 Pine Street
Chadron, NE 69337
(308) 432-3367

NEVADA
Humboldt National Forest
Bobby Joe Graves, Supervisor
976 Mountain City Hwy
Elko, NV 89801
(702) 738-5171

Toiyabe National Forest
R. M. (Jim) Nelson, Supervisor
1200 Franklin Way
Sparks Way, NV 89431
(702) 784-5331

NEW HAMPSHIRE
White Mountain National Forest
James R. Jordan, Supervisor
Federal Bldg
719 Main Street, Box 638
Laconia, NH 03246
(603) 524-6450

NEW MEXICO
Carson National Forest
Jack S. Crellin, Supervisor
Forest Service Bldg, Box 558
Taos, NM 87571
(505) 758-2238

Cibola National Forest
Chester P. Smith, Supervisor
10308 Candelaria, NE
Albuquerque, NM 87112
(505) 766-2185

Gila National Forest
Kenneth C. Scoggin, Supervisor
2610 N Silver Street
Silver City, NM 88061
(505) 388-1986

Lincoln National Forest
James R. Abbott, Supervisor
Federal Building
11th and New York
Alamogordo, NM 88310
(505) 437-6030

Santa Fe National Forest
James L. Perry, Supervisor
Pinon Building
1220 St. Francis Drive, Box 1689
Santa Fe, NM 87501
(505) 988-6940

NORTH CAROLINA
Croatan, Nantahala, Pisgah, and
Uwharrie National Forests
George A. Olson, Supervisor
National Forests in North Carolina
Plateau Building
50 S French Broad Ave, Box 2750
Asheville, NC 28802
(704) 253-2352

OHIO
Wayne National Forest
Harold L. Godlevske, Supervisor
3527 10th Street
Bedford, IN 47421
(812) 332-4340

OREGON
Deschutes National Forest
David G. Mohla, Supervisor
211 NE Revere Ave
Bend, OR 97701
(503) 382-6922

Fremont National Forest
Orville D. Grossarth, Supervisor
Box 551
Lakeview, OR 97630
(503) 947-2151

Malheur National Forest
Kenneth Evans, Supervisor
139 NE Dayton Street
John Day, OR 97845
(503) 575-1731

Mt. Hood National Forest
Richard J. Pfilf, Supervisor
2955 NW Division Street
Greshaw, OR 97030
(503) 667-0511

Ochoco National Forest
William McCleese, Supervisor
Box 490, Federal Bldg
Prineville, OR 97754
(503) 447-6247

Rogue River National Forest
Robert J. Devlin, Supervisor
Federal Building
333 W 8th St, Box 520
Medford, OR 97501
(503)776-3600

Siskiyou National Forest
Vacant, Supervisor
Box 440
Grants Pass, OR 97526
(503) 479-5301

Siuslaw National Forest
Larry A. Fellows, Supervisor
Box 1148
Corvallis, OR 97339
(503) 757-4480

Umatilla National Forest
John E. Lowe, Supervisor
2517 SW Hailey Ave
Pendleton, OR 97801
(503) 276-3811

Umpqua National Forest
Richard D. Swartzlender, Supervisor
Box 1088
Roseburg, OR 97470
(503) 672-6601

Wallowa-Whitman National Forests
Jerry G. Allen, Supervisor
Box 907
Baker, OR 97814
(503) 523-6391

Willamette National Forest
Michael A. Kerrick, Supervisor
Box 10607
Eugene, OR 97440
(503) 687-6521

Winema National Forest
Art Dufault, Supervisor
Box 1390
Klamath Falls, OR 97601
(503) 883-6714

PENNSYLVANIA
Allegheny National Forest
John P. Butt, Supervisor
Spiridon Bldg, Box 847
Warren, PA 16365
(814) 723-5150

PUERTO RICO
Caribbean National Forest
Juan E. Munoz, Supervisor
Box AA
Rio Piedras, PR 00928
(8-809) 753-4335

SOUTH CAROLINA
Francis Marion and Sumter National Forests
Donald W. Eng, Supervisor
1835 Assembly St, Box 2227
Columbia, SC 29202
(803) 765-5222

SOUTH DAKOTA
Black Hills National Forest
James R. Mathers, Supervisor
Box 792
Custer, SD 57730
(605) 673-2251

TENNESSEE
Cherokee National Forest
Donald L. Rollens, Supervisor
2800 N Ocoee St, NW, Box 2010
Cleveland, TN 37311
(615) 476-9700

TEXAS
Angelina, Davy Crockett, Sabine
and Sam Houston National Forests
William M. Lannan, Supervisor
National Forests in Texas
Homer Garrison Federal Bldg
701 N 1st Street
Lufkin, TX 75901
(409) 629-8501

UTAH
Ashley National Forest
James R. Craig, Supervisor
Ashton Energy Center
1680 W Highway 40, Suite 1150
Vernal, UT 84078
(801) 789-1181

Dixie National Forest
Ed Fournier, Supervisor
82 N 100 E St
Cedar City, UT 84720
(801) 586-2421

Fishlake National Forest
J. Kent Taylor, Supervisor
115 East 900 North
Richfield, UT 84701
(801) 896-4491

Manti-LaSal National Forest
Reed C. Christensen, Supervisor
499 West Price River Drive
Price, UT 84501
(801) 637-2817

Uinta National Forest
Don T. Nebeker, Supervisor
88 West 100 North
Provo, UT 84603
(801) 377-5780

Wasatch-Cache National Forest
Arthur J. Carroll, Supervisor
8226 Federal Building
125 S State Street
Salt Lake City, UT 84138
(801) 524-5030

VERMONT
Green Mountain National Forest
Stephen C. Harper, Supervisor
Federal Building
151 West Street, P.O. Box 519
Rutland, VT 05701
(802) 775-2579

VIRGINIA
George Washington National Forest
George M. Smith, Supervisor
210 Federal Building
Harrisonburg, VA 22801
(703) 433-2491

Jefferson National Forest
Thomas A. Hoots, Supervisor
210 Franklin Rd, SW, Rm 954
Roanoke, VA 24001
(703) 982-6274

WASHINGTON
Colville National Forest
William D. Shenk, Supervisor
695 S Main
Colville, WA 99114
(509) 684-3711

Gifford Pinchot National Forest
Robert Williams
500 W 12th Street
Vancouver, WA 98660
(206) 696-7500

Mt. Baker-Snoqualmie National Forest
J. D. MacWilliams, Supervisor
1022 First Ave
Seattle, WA 98104
(206) 442-5400

Okanogan National Forest
William D. McLaughlin, Supervisor
1240 S Second
Okanogan, OR 98840
(509) 422-2704

Olympic National Forest
Richard D. Beaubien, Supervisor
Box 2288
Olympia, WA 98507
(206) 753-9534

Wenatchee National Forest
Donald H. Smith, Supervisor
Box 811
Wenatchee, WA 98801
(509) 662-4335

WEST VIRGINIA
Monongahela National Forest
Ralph F. Mumme, Supervisor
USDA Building
Sycamore St, Box 1548
Elkins, WV 26241
(304) 636-1800

WISCONSIN
Chequamegon National Forest
John C. Wolter, Supervisor
157 N 5th Ave
Park Falls, WI 54552
(715) 762-2461

Nicolet National Forest
James S. Berlin, Supervisor
Federal Building
68 S Stevens
Rhinelander, WI 54501
(715) 362-3415

WYOMING
Bridger-Teton National Forest
H. Reid Jackson, Supervisor
Forest Service Bldg
340 N Cache
Jackson, WY 83001
(307) 733-2752

Bighorn National Forest
Edward L. Schultz, Supervisor
1969 S Sheridan Ave
Sheridan, WY 82801
(307) 672-0751

Medicine Bow National Forest
Sonny O'Neal
605 Skyline Drive
Laramie, WY 82070
(307) 328-0471

Shoshone National Forest
Stephen P. Mealey, Supervisor
225 West Yellowstone Ave, Box 2140
Cody, WY 82414
(307) 587-6241

FIELD OFFICES

Forest Service, USDA
Northern Region (R-1)
Federal Building
P.O. Box 7669
Missoula, MT 59807
(406) 329-3011

Forest Service, USDA
Rocky Mountain Region (R-2)
11177 West 8th Ave
P.O. Box 25127
Lakewood, CO 80225
(303) 234-3711

Forest Service, USDA
Southwestern Region (R-3)
Federal Building
517 Gold Ave, SW
Albuquerque, NM 87102
(505) 766-2401

Forest Service, USDA
Intermountain Region (R-4)
Federal Building
324 25th Street
Ogden, UT 84401
(801) 625-5412

Forest Service, USDA
Pacific Southwest Region (R-5)
630 Sansome Street
San Francisco, CA 94111
(415) 556-4310

Forest Service, USDA
Pacific Northwest Region (R-6)
319 SW Pine Street
P.O. Box 3623
Portland, OR 97208
(503) 211-3625

Forest Service, USDA
Southern Region (R-8)
1720 Peachtree Road, NW
Atlanta, GA 30367
(404) 881-4177

Forest Service, USDA
Eastern Region (R-9)
310 West Wisconsin Ave, Rm 500
Milwaukee, WI 53203
(414) 291-3693

Forest Service, USDA
Alaska Region (R-10)
Federal Office Building
P.O. Box 1628
Juneau, AK 99802
(907) 586-7263 (through Seattle, WA)

Forest Service, USDA
Northeastern Area—S&PF
370 Reed Road
Broomall, PA 19008
(215) 461-1660

Intermountain Forest and Range
Experiment Station
Forest Service Building
507 25th Street
Ogden, UT 84401
(801) 625-5412

North Central Forest Experiment Station
1992 Folwell Avenue
St. Paul, MN 55108
(612) 642-5207

Northeastern Forest Experiment Station
370 Reed Road
Broomall, PA 19008
(215) 461-3006

Pacific Northwest Forest and Range
Experiment Station
P.O. Box 3890
Portland, OR 97208
(503) 231-2052

Pacific Southwest Forest and Range
Experiment Station
1960 Addison Street
P.O. Box 245
Berkeley, CA 94701
(415) 486-3291

Rocky Mountain Forest and Range
Experiment Station
240 West Prospect Street
Fort Collins, CO 80526
(303) 221-4390

Southeastern Forest Experiment Station
200 Weaver Blvd
Asheville, NC 28804
(704) 257-6758

Southern Forest Experiment Station
Room T-10210
U.S. Postal Service Building
701 Loyola Avenue
New Orleans, LA 70113
(504) 589-6787

Forest Products Laboratory
Gifford Pinchot Drive
P.O. Box 5130
Madison, WI 53705
(608) 264-5600

Appendix V.
Fishery Assistance Offices

ALASKA (R-7)
King Salmon FAO
Chris Dlugokenski
P.O. Box 277
King Salmon, AK 99613
(907) 246-3339

Kenai FAO
Jack Dean
P.O. Box 2800
Kenai, AK 99611
(907) 262-9863
(907) 262-9329

Fairbanks FAO
Michael Smith
P.O. Box 20
101 12th—Court House
Fairbanks, AK 99701
(907) 456-0454

Kodiak NWR
Tony Chatto, Fishery Biologist
P.O. Box 825
Kodiak, AK 99615
(907) 487-2600

ARIZONA (R-2)
Parker
Vacant
P.O. Box 830
Parker, AZ 85344
(602) 669-2928

Pinetop
James Hanson
P.O. Box 39
Pinetop, AZ 85935
(602) 336-2651

ARKANSAS (R-4)
Greers Ferry
Richard B. Eager
Rt. 3, Box 71
Heber Springs, AR 72593
(501) 362-3615

CALIFORNIA (R-1)
Red Bluff
David A. Vogel
P.O. Box 667
Red Bluff, CA 96080
(916) 527-3043

Arcata
Robert A. Adair
791 8th Street, Suite S
Arcata, CA 95521
(707) 822-7201

Stockton
Martin A. Kjelson
4001 North Wilson Way
Stockton, CA 95205
(209) 466-4421

COLORADO (R-6)
Lakewood
Bruce D. Rosenlund
330 S. Garrison Street
Lakewood, CO 80226
(303) 234-5899

FLORIDA (R-4)
Panama City
Edouard J. Crateau
1612 June Avenue
Panama City, FL 32405
(904) 763-1059

IDAHO (R-1)
Dworshak
William H. Miller
P.O. Box 18
Ahsahka, ID 83520
(208) 476-7242

ILLINOIS (R-3)
Carterville
Charles Surprenant
P.O. Box J
Carterville, IL 62918
(618) 997-6869

LOUISIANA (R-4)
Natchitoches
John S. Forester
615 Highway 1, South
Natchitoches, LA 71357
(318) 352-5324

MASSACHUSETTS (R-5)
Hadley
Steven G. Rideout
Connecticut River
Anadromous Fish Program
4 Whalley Street
Hadley, MA 01035
(413) 586-4416

MICHIGAN (R-3)
Elmira
Charles L. Maas
Route 1, Box 64-A
Elmira, MI 49730
(616) 584-2461

MINNESOTA (R-3)
Winona
Hannibal Bolton
51 E 4th Street, Rm 101
Winona, MN 55987
(507) 452-4390

MONTANA (R-6)
Creston Fishery Center
Bruce Haines, Complex Manager
Ron Skates, Fishery Biologist
780 Creston Hatchery Road
Kalispell, MT 59901
(406) 755-7870

NEBRASKA (R-6)
Valentine
Alan J. Sandvol
Hidden Timber Star Route
Valentine, NE 69201
(402) 376-3558

NEVADA (R-1)
Reno
(Great Basin Complex)
Donald King
4600 Kietzke Lane, Bldg C
Reno, NV 89502
(702) 784-5227

NEW HAMPSHIRE (R-5)
Laconia
Alexis A. Knight
Federal Bldg, Rm 124
Laconia, NH 03246
(603) 524-6809

Concord
Lawrence W. Stolte
Merrimack River Coordination
Box 1518
Concord, NH 03301
(603) 224-2585

NEW JERSEY (R-5)
Rosemont
Joe Miller
P.O. Box 95
Rosemont, NJ 08556
(609) 397-0115

NORTH DAKOTA (R-6)
Valley City
J. Monte Millard, Complex Manager
Frank Pfeifer, Fishery Biologist
Valley City Fishery Center
Route 1
Valley City, ND 58072
(701) 845-3464

PENNSYLVANIA (R-5)
Harrisburg
Richard St. Pierre
Susquehanna River Coordination
P.O. Box 1673
Harrisburg, PA 17105-1673
(717) 657-4547

Warren
John D. Anderson
RD 1, Box 1050
Warren, PA 16365
(814) 726-1241

UTAH (R-6)
Vernal
Don Toney, Complex Manager
Ken Harper, Fishery Biologist
447 E Main Street, Suite 4
Vernal, UT 84078
(801) 789-0351

Colorado River Fishery Investigation Team
Donald Archer
Administration Building
1745 S 1700 West, Rm 2010
Salt Lake City, UT 84104

VERMONT (R-5)
Montpelier
Carl F. Baren
Federal Bldg, Rm 326
Montpelier, VT 25602
(802) 223-5900

VIRGINIA (R-5)
Gloucester Point
Gary Swihart
Box 729
Gloucester Point, VA 23062
(804) 642-7181

WASHINGTON (R-1)
Leavenworth
James Mullan
Route 1, Box 123-A
Leavenworth, WA 98826
(509) 548-7573

Olympia
Ralph Boomer
2625 Parkmont Lane, Bldg A
Olympia, WA 98502
(206) 753-9460

Vancouver
Curtis Burley
9317 Highway 99, Suite 1
Vancouver, WA 98665
(206) 696-7605

WISCONSIN (R-3)
Iron River
William B. Ziegler
P.O. Box 37
Iron River, WI 54847
(715) 372-8570

WYOMING (R-6)
Lander
Richard Baldes
170 North First Street
Lander, WY 82520
(307) 332-2159

Yellowstone
Ronald Jones
P.O. Box 184
Yellowstone National Park, WY 82190
(307) 242-7248 (summer)
(307) 344-7381 (winter)

Appendix VI.
Cooperative Fish and Wildlife Research Units

FISHERY RESEARCH UNITS

Alaska Cooperative Fishery Research Unit
James B. Reynolds, Unit Ldr
Jacqueline LaPerriere, Asst Ldr
U.A.F. 138 Arctic Health Research Bldg
University of Alaska
901 Koyukuk Avenue South
Fairbanks, AK 99701
(907) 474-7661

Arizona Cooperative Fishery Research Unit
Jerry C. Tash, Unit Ldr
Charles D. Ziebell, Asst Ldr
210 Biological Sciences East
University of Arizona
Tucson, AZ 85721
(602) 621-1959

California Cooperative Fishery Research Unit
Roger A. Barnhart, Unit Ldr
Thomas J. Hassler, Asst Ldr
Humboldt State University
Arcata, CA 95521
(707) 826-3268

Hawaii Cooperative Fishery Research Unit
James D. Parrish, Unit Ldr
Vacant, Asst Ldr
2538 The Mall
University of Hawaii
Honolulu, HI 96822
(808) 948-8350

Iowa Cooperative Fishery Research Unit
John G. Nickum, Unit Ldr
Vacant, Asst Ldr
Science Hall II
Iowa State University
Ames, IA 50011
(515) 294-3057

Louisiana Cooperative Fishery Research Unit
Charles F. Bryan, Unit Ldr
William H. Herke, Asst Ldr
Parker Coliseum, Room 245
Louisiana State University
Baton Rouge, LA 70803
(504) 388-6051

Massachusetts Cooperative Fishery Research Unit
Henry E. Booke, Unit Ldr
Boyd E. Kynard, Asst Ldr
204 Holdsworth Hall
University of Massachusetts
Amherst, MA 01003
(413) 545-0398

Montana Cooperative Fishery Research Unit
Robert G. White, Unit Ldr
William R. Gould, Jr., Asst Ldr
Biology Department
Montana State University
Bozeman, MT 59717
(406) 994-3491

North Carolina Cooperative Fishery Research Unit
Melvin T. Huish, Unit Ldr
J. Howard Kerby, Asst Ldr
Department of Zoology
Gardner Hall, Box 7617, Rm 4105
Raleigh, NC 27695-7617
(919) 737-2631

Ohio Cooperative Fishery Research Unit
Joseph Margarf, Acting Unit Ldr
Vacant, Asst Ldr
Department of Zoology
1735 Neil Avenue
Ohio State University
Columbus, OH 43210
(614) 422-8961

Oregon Cooperative Fishery Research Unit
Carl B. Schreck, Unit Ldr
Hiram W. Li, Asst Ldr
Department of Fisheries and Wildlife
Oregon State University
Corvallis, OR 97331
(503) 754-4531

Tennessee Cooperative Fishery Research Unit
R. Don Estes, Unit Ldr
James B. Layzer, Asst Ldr
Biology Department, Box 5063
Tennessee Technical University
Cookeville, TN 38505
(615) 528-4194

Washington Cooperative Fishery Research Unit
Gilbert B. Pauley, Unit Ldr
Vacant, Asst Ldr
College of Fisheries WH-10
Unversity of Washington
Seattle, WA 98195
(206) 543-6475

Wisconsin Cooperative Fishery Research Unit
Daniel W. Coble, Unit Ldr
Vacant, Asst Ldr
College of Natural Resources
University of Wisconsin
Stevens Point, WI 54481
(715) 346-2178

WILDLIFE RESEARCH UNITS

Alaska Cooperative Wildlife Research Unit
David R. Klein, Unit Ldr
209 Irving Building
University of Alaska
902 Koyukuk Avenue North
Fairbanks, AK 99701
(907) 474-7673

Arizona Cooperative Wildlife Research Unit
Lyle K. Sowls, Unit Ldr
Norman S. Smith, Asst Ldr
214 Biological Sciences East
University of Arizona
Tucson, AZ 85721
(602) 621-1193

Iowa Cooperative Wildlife Research Unit
Robert B. Dahlgren, Unit Ldr
Erwin E. Klaas, Asst Ldr
Science Hall II
Iowa State University
Ames, IA 50011
(515) 294-3056

Louisiana Cooperative Wildlife Research Unit
Philip J. Zwank, Acting Unit Ldr
Vacant, Asst Ldr
School of Forestry & Wildlife Management
Louisiana State University
Baton Rouge, LA 70803
(504) 388-4131

Massachusetts Cooperative Wildlife Research Unit
Wendell E. Dodge, Unit Ldr
Vacant, Asst Ldr
Holdsworth Hall
University of Massachusetts
Amherst, MA 01003
(413) 545-2757

Montana Cooperative Wildlife Research Unit
Bart W. O'Gara, Unit Ldr
Joseph Ball, Asst Ldr
107 Health Sciences
University of Montana
Missoula, MT 59812
(406) 243-5372

Ohio Cooperative Wildlife Research Unit
Theodore A. Bookhout, Unit Ldr
Jonathan Bart, Asst Ldr
1735 Neil Avenue
Ohio State University
Columbus, OH 43210
(614) 422-6112

Oregon Cooperative Wildlife Research Unit
E. Charles Meslow, Unit Ldr
Robert G. Anthony, Asst Ldr
104 Nash Hall
Oregon State University
Corvallis, OR 97331
(503) 754-4531

Wisconsin Cooperative Wildlife Research Unit
Donald H. Rusch, Unit Ldr
Vacant, Asst Ldr
226 Russell Laboratories
University of Wisconsin
Madison, WI 53706
(608) 263-6882

FISH AND WILDLIFE RESEARCH UNITS

Alabama Cooperative Fish and Wildlife Research Unit
Vacant, Unit Ldr
Daniel W. Speake, Asst Ldr
John S. Ramsey, Asst Ldr
Wildlife Building
Auburn University
Auburn, AL 36830
(205) 826-4796

Colorado Cooperative Fish and Wildlife Research Unit
David Anderson, Unit Ldr
Eric Bergersen, Asst Ldr
J.V.K. Wagar Building, Rm 201
Colorado State University
Fort Collins, CO 80523
(303) 491-1416

Florida Cooperative Fish and Wildlife Research Unit
Vacant, Unit Ldr
Franklin Percival, Asst Ldr
117 Newins-Ziegler Hall
University of Florida
Gainesville, FL 32611
(904) 392-1861

Georgia Cooperative Fish and Wildlife Research Unit
Michael Van Den Avyle, Unit Ldr
Vicki S. Blazer, Asst Ldr
School of Forest Products
University of Georgia
Athens, GA 30602
(404) 546-2234

Idaho Cooperative Fish and Wildlife Research Unit
Theodore C. Bjornn, Acting Unit Ldr
James Congleton, Asst Ldr
College of Forestry, Wildlife and Range Sciences
University of Idaho
Moscow, ID 83843
(208) 885-6336

Maine Cooperative Fish and Wildlife Research Unit
John R. Moring, Acting Unit Ldr
Vacant, Asst Ldr
313 Murray Hall
University of Maine
Orono, ME 04469
(207) 581-2581

Mississippi Cooperative Fish and Wildlife Research Unit
Robert J. Muncy, Unit Ldr
Edward P. Hill, Asst Ldr
Dorman Hall, Box BX
Mississippi State University
Mississippi State, MS 39762
(601) 325-2643

Missouri Cooperative Fish and Wildlife Research Unit
Vacant, Unit Ldr
Richard O. Anderson, Asst Ldr
Charles Rabeni, Asst Ldr
112 Stephens Hall
University of Missouri
Columbia, MO 65201
(314) 882-3234

New York Cooperative Fish and Wildlife Research Unit
Milo E. Richmond, Unit Ldr
Richard A. Malecki, Asst Ldr
Steven P. Gloss, Asst Ldr
Fernow Hall
Cornell University
Ithaca, NY 14853
(607) 256-2014

Oklahoma Cooperative Fish and Wildlife Research Unit
O. Eugene Maughan, Unit Ldr
Vacant, Asst Ldr
Life Sciences West Bldg, Rm 433
Oklahoma State University
Stillwater, OK 74078
(405) 624-6342

Pennsylvania Cooperative Fish and Wildlife Research Unit
Robert F. Carline, Unit Ldr
Gerald L. Storm, Asst Ldr
Dean E. Arnold, Asst Ldr
113 Ferguson Building
Pennsylvania State University
Unversity Park, PA 16802
(814) 865-4511

South Dakota Cooperative Fish and Wildlife Research Unit
Charles R. Berry, Jr., Unit Ldr
Vacant, Asst Ldr
Department of Wildlife and Fishery Science
South Dakota State University
Brookings, SD 57006
(605) 688-6121

Wyoming Cooperative Fish and Wildlife Research Unit
Stanley H. Anderson, Unit Ldr
Wayne A. Hubert, Asst Ldr
Fred G. Lindzey, Asst Ldr
University Station, Box 3166
University of Wyoming
Laramie, WY 82071
(307) 766-5415

Utah Cooperative Fish and Wildlife Research Unit
Vacant, Unit Ldr
Vacant, Asst Ldr
UMC 52
Utah State University
Logan, UT 84322
(801) 750-2466

Virginia Cooperative Fish and Wildlife Research Unit
Vacant, Unit Ldr
Richard J. Neves, Asst Ldr
Michael R. Vaughan, Asst Ldr
106 Cheatham Hall
VPI and SU
Blacksburg, VA 24061
(703) 961-5927

Appendix VII.
FWS Research Laboratories and Centers

FISH LABORATORIES AND CENTERS

Columbia National Fisheries Research Laboratory
U.S. Fish and Wildlife Service
Route 1
Columbia, Missouri 65200
Director: Dr. Richard A. Schoettger
Telephone: 314-875-5399
Congressional District: Missouri — Eight
Land Holdings: 33 acres, donated by the University of Missouri. Office space for field laboratories and research stations is provided through arrangements with agencies or universities.
Number of Laboratory Buildings on Property: Seven
Special Equipment: Flow-through toxicity testing systems, computers, chemical ionization and ion-impact GC-mass spectrometers, inductively coupled plasma emission spectrophoto osometer, polygraph, and liquid scintillation counters.
Estimated Value for Replacement: $8,500,000
Historical Background: Original facility completed in 1966 as Fish-Pesticide Research Laboratory. In 1975, the laboratory was given responsibility to monitor fish from across the nation for contaminant residues as part of the National Pesticide Monitoring Program. In 1977, the laboratory was given additional responsibility to conduct field ecological research on contaminants in strategic watersheds across the nation.
Budget:

Major Programs	FY 1984 Budget Allocation
Environmental Contaminant Evaluation	$3,571,000
Special Appropriation — Striped Bass	344,000
Other (including FY 1983 carry over)	61,800
TOTAL	$3,976,800

Personnel: Full-Time Equivalent: 87
Purpose: Attempts are being made to anticipate potential aquatic contaminants and thus prepare for their consequences. The program strongly links laboratory research with field ecological stations located in strategic watersheds around the country.
Current Research: Laboratory Research is oriented toward toxicology and analysis of chemical contaminants in fish and fish food organisms. Field research centers around a multitude of known and suspected contaminants and is closely integrated with the laboratory activities. Major research emphasis is directed toward contaminant from energy developments, irrigation drainage waters, acid rain, carcinogenic contaminants including fish tumors of the Great Lakes, sediment/contaminant interaction in northern prairie wetlands, development of biological indicators of contaminant stress on fish, and contaminant impacts on striped bass.

Great Lakes Fishery Laboratory
U.S. Fish and Wildlife Service
1451 Green Road
Ann Arbor, Michigan 48105
Director: Dr. Bernard L. Griswold
Telephone: 313-994-3331
Congressional District: Michigan — Two
Land Holdings: 2.7 acres at Ann Arbor. Cheboygan Vessel Base is on U.S. Coast Guard leased space; all other field stations are on GSA-leased space (less than one acre total).
Number of Buildings on Property: Two
Special Equipment: Large continuous-flow water system supplied from wells (Ann Arbor);

wet laboratories with fish respirometer (stamina tunnel); well-equipped chemistry laboratories with a mass spectrometer, etc.; John Van Oosten Memorial (Fisheries) Library: Biometrics and Computer Services Unit; and various water craft (12′ to 75′) for work on the Great Lakes and connecting waters.

Estimated Value for Replacement: $4,224,500

Historical Background: The laboratory was established in 1927 and the present facility built in 1964. Land for the laboratory was donated by the University of Michigan.

Budget:

Major Programs	FY 1984 Budget Allocation
Fishery Resources	$2,119,700
Environmental Contaminant Evaluation	568,000
Other	747,800
TOTAL	$3,465,500

Personnel: Full-Time Equivalent: 84

Purpose: Research on Great Lakes fishery resources and fish habitat.

Current Research: Research centers on fishery resource assessment, ecology-limnology, fish physiology, and contaminant chemistry. Results facilitate measuring and projecting the impact of fishing, habitat alteration, and contamination on Great Lakes fishery resources.

National Fisheries Center-Leetown
U.S. Fish and Wildlife Service
Box 700
Kearneysville, West Virginia 25430
Director: James A. McCann
Assistant Director-Technical Services: David. W. McDaniel
Assistant Director-Research: James E. Weaver
Telephone: 304-725-8461
Congressional District: West Virginia — Two
Land Holdings: 232 acres
Number of Buildings on Property: 23
Special Equipment: PDP 11/23 Digital computer and VT 180 microcomputers for data base management, word processing, data analysis, and communication with other center laboratories. Tektronix 4052 with plotter printer, digitizer, disc drives, communication interface, and dot matrix printer.
Estimated Value for Replacement: $25,000,000
Historical Background: The concept of a national fisheries center was realized in 1977–78 when realignment of the administrative and program activities of six husbandry laboratories and certain developmental and training activities allowed formation of the Leetown Center. The center assumed the administration of these various functions into a comprehensive program.

Budget: (Center administration and support services)

Major Programs	FY 1984 Budget Allocation
Fishery Resources	$533,000
Biological Services	6,200
TOTAL	$539,200

Personnel: Full-Time Equivalent: 12.0

Budget: (All Functions-NFC)

Major Programs	FY 1984 Budget Allocation
Fishery Resources	$4,851,400
Other (ESBS, NMFS, NPS)	724,000
TOTAL	$5,575,400

Personnel: Full-Time Equivalent: 119

Purpose: The Leetown Center administers and interrelates the various geographically scattered fish husbandry research development and fishery training activities of the Service to provide timely research and development through the most efficacious and least costly means.

603

Current Research: The Center provides management and support services to the research development and training components.

National Fishery Research Laboratory
P.O. Box 818
LaCrosse, Wisconsin 54601
Director: Fred P. Meyer
Telephone: 608-783-6451
Congressional District: Wisconsin — Three (3)
Land Holdings:
    LaCrosse, Wisconsin — 63 acres
    Millersburg, Michigan — 54 acres
Number of Buildings on Property:
    LaCrosse — Nine
    Hammond Bay — Three
Special Equipment: The facility possesses one of the most sophisticated toxicology laboratories in the world for testing the toxicity of chemicals to fish and aquatic organisms in both acute and long-term exposure systems. Chemistry and physiology capability encompasses ultra-sophistication in analytical detection of residues in water, soil, and tissues. Numerous concrete and earthen ponds provide capability to culture test fish and to test chemicals in natural environments before conducting large-scale field trials. The laboratory also maintains the most extensive reference library in the world on fish culture, management, and research.
Estimated Value for Replacement:
    LaCrosse — $14,586,600
    Millersburg — $1,990,000
Historical Background: In 1960, the Fish and Wildlife Service began operation of a fishery research laboratory at Riverside Park, LaCrosse, Wisconsin, known as the Fish Control Laboratory. After 18 years of highly productive research, laboratory needs far exceeded the available water supply, electrical service, and floor space. A new laboratory, known as the National Fishery Laboratory-LaCrosse, was constructed during 1973–1980 on French Island. The laboratory complex includes three large buildings, numerous smaller buildings, a waste treatment facility, and many ponds and tanks for fish holding and testing. The Hammond Bay Biological Station is located on the northwest shore of Lake Huron. Built in 1895, the facility initially was operated as a lifeboat rescue station by the U.S. Coast Guard. In 1950, the Bureau of Commercial Fisheries established a biological station at the site. Since that time, the station has figured prominently in research on the life history and control of the parastic sea lamprey. The Bureau of Sport Fisheries and Wildlife accepted supervision of the facility in 1970. Direction of the program was assigned to the Fish Control Laboratory, LaCrosse, Wisconsin, 14 June 1981, in keeping with its emphasis on the control of the sea lamprey. Research at the Hammond Bay Biological Station presently is directed toward biological controls of sea lamprey, sea lamprey attractants and repellents, evaluation of various new formulations of registered lampricides and fish toxicants against sea lamprey ammocetes, and the development of a better understanding of sea lamprey biology.
Budget:

Major Programs	FY 1984 Budget Allocation
Fishery Resources — 1390	$ 806,100
Federal Aid — 4100	325,000
Great Lakes Fishery Commission — Sea Lamprey Research — LaCrosse — 7320	163,325
Great Lakes Fishery Commission — Sea Lamprey Research — Hammond Bay — 7320	421,100
SUBTOTAL	$1,715,525
St. Paul Field Office — Ecological Services (outside contract)	54,000
TOTAL	$1,769,525

Personnel: Full-Time Equivalent: 35

Purpose: The laboratory has four missions: (1) conduct and coordinate studies to fulfill registration requirements for chemicals used in fisheries; (2) research and development of chemical tools needed to resolve existing problems in fishery management and fish culture, especially for the control of nuisance aquatic organisms; (3) ecological studies on issues identified by operational units of the Fish and Wildlife Service relating to major river systems; and (4) research on control of the sea lamprey.

Current Research: Directed toward (1) toxic effects, modes of action, residue dynamics, and ecological impacts of chemicals used to manage fishery resources or to culture fishes; (2) interrelationships between water chemistry variations, pollutants and contaminants, and biological strains and their effects on the activity of fishery chemicals; (3) techniques for counteracting, neutralizing, or synergizing the activity of fishery chemicals; (4) alternate control techniques; (5) screening candidate compounds to meet needs identified by resource managers, and (6) the effects of navigation and development on fishery and related resources in large river systems.

Seattle National Fishery Research Center*

U.S. Fish and Wildlife Service
Building 204, Naval Station
Seattle, Washington 98115
Director: Dr. Alfred C. Fox
Telephone: 206-526-6282
Congressional District: Washington — One
Land Holdings: 4.4 acres at Seattle (U.S. Navy property); 5.4 acres at Marrowstone Field Station (USFWS property). The Alaska Field Station is located within the Regional Office complex on GSA-leased space.
Number of Laboratory Buildings on Property: 3 at SNFRC; 6 at MFS; 2 at Willard; and 1 at AFS.
Special Equipment: Seattle — physiology, pathology, chemistry, and water quality laboratories; fish culture capabilities; temperature gradient incubator; ELISA automatic processor; atomic absorption spectrophotometer with graphite furnace; Marrowstone — fresh and seawater culture capabilities; Willard — full complement of equipment required for population dynamics studies in streams and reservoirs; Alaska — Arctic research capability including wet labs.
Estimated Value for Replacement: SNFRC — $6,000,000; MFS — $2,700,000; Willard Substation — $1,500,000; Alaska — $1,000,000.
Historical Background: In 1950, the center was founded as the Western Fish Disease Laboratory. In 1959, the center moved from the University of Washington College of Fisheries, where it had been located since its inception, to the present location in a converted warehouse at Sand Point Naval Station. In 1975, the center became known as the Seattle National Fishery Research Center with research responsibilities in fish health, environmental factors impacting fish populations, and established field stations to respond to specific study areas.

Budget:

Major Programs	FY 1984 Budget Allocation
In House Funding	$1,105,700
Other	260,674
TOTAL	$1,366,374

Personnel: Full-Time Equivalent: 24

*Currently a laboratory; upon completion of new facility, long-range plans call for a functional center.

Purpose: The function of the Seattle center is to conduct research to identify and quantitate environmental factors limiting the distribution and abundance of fish populations of the western U.S., including Alaska, and to develop new and improved methods for increasing efficiency in the use of artificially propagated juveniles for anadromous fisheries enhancement programs.

Current Research: The center's research program is aimed at (1) fish health research including development of new and improved fish disease control methods; (2) fishery ecology research including development of new and improved methods, concepts and standards for predicting the environmental impact of proposed development projects. To accomplish this, studies involving physiological ecology, life histories, population dynamics, smoltification physiology, diagnostic and control methods for infectious diseases, and fish cultural methods are carried out with the emphasis on anadromous fishes. A major goal is to provide relevant biological information in a form resource managers can use to enhance consideration of fish and wildlife values in resolving land-use and water-use conflicts.

Wildlife Laboratories and Centers

Denver Wildlife Research Center
U.S. Fish and Wildlife Service
Building 16, Federal Center
Denver, Colorado 80225
Director: Paul A. Vohs, Jr.
Telephone: 303-236-2283
Congressional District: Colorado — Six
Land Holdings: The Denver Wildlife Research Center headquarters is located on the Denver Federal Center, where some 19 buildings and about five acres are leased from GSA. Overseas field stations are leased through the Department of State. Twenty-five acres at Gainesville, Florida, are owned by the Fish and Wildlife Service as is a small station at Laredo, Texas. Other field stations are leased or provided by cooperative agreements through GSA, BLM, U.S. Coast Guard, Forest Service, Smithsonian Institution, universities, and, for the Philadelphia station, the Monell Chemical Senses Center.
Number of Laboratory Buildings on Property: Six at headquarters in Denver.
Special Equipment: (1) computerized system for continuous measurement of food intake of rodents or other small animals; (2) infrared total darkness television camera for studying the behavior of animals under captive total darkness conditions; (3) timelapse video recorder capable of recording up to three days of behavioral data; (4) olfactometer, taste preference devices for measuring sensory responses to potential attractants, repellents, and food additives; (5) wide variety of chromatographs; (6) spectrometry instrumentation; (7) enzyme research instrumentation; (8) anechoic chamber and sonograph; (9) radio transmitters; (10) markers — microtaggants to topically mark birds and mammals; (11) behavioral instrumentation and electrophysiological instrumentation to measure responses to various stimuli; and (12) extensive scientific collections of birds, mammals, fish, reptiles, and amphibians.
Estimated Value for Replacement: $8,500,000
Historical Background: The center's origins can be traced to Dr. A. K. Fisher who, in 1887, began work on animal damage problems. In 1920, S. E. Piper formed the Control Methods Laboratory to pursue this same purpose. In 1940, the Control Methods Laboratory merged with the Food Habits Laboratory of the newly formed Fish and Wildlife Service to form the Denver Wildlife Research Laboratory. Because of its wide diversity of research and interests, the laboratory was merged with the Denver Wildlife Research Center in 1959. The Research Center has been located in Denver since its creation in 1940. In 1980 the Service's National Fish and Wildlife Laboratory merged with the Denver Center, thus adding museum, marine mammal, and expanded ecology research functions. In 1983 all wildlife research programs in Alaska, exclusive of the Cooperative Wildlife Research Unit, were placed under the supervision of the Denver Wildlife Research Center. This added three marine bird projects to the center's migratory bird research program.
Budget:

Major Programs	FY 1984 Budget Allocation
Wildlife Resources	$7,428,129*
Endangered Species	714,700
TOTAL	$8,142,829

*Includes $1,551,129 anticipated AR/CF funds.

Personnel: Full-Time: 190 authorized in FY 1984.

Purpose: Research is concerned with two primary areas: (1) status and distribution of wildlife populations and ecological relationships between wildlife and man's continual use and modification of the land and water and associated resources; and (2) reducing the damage wildlife causes to agriculture, forests, industry, or other areas of human endeavor.

Current Research: Field research is conducted from the center and at field stations throughout the United States. Research in animal damage control includes damage assessment; laboratory and field studies of behavior and ecology of the damaging species; and the development and testing of chemical, physical, or cultural methods for minimizing or eliminating the problem situation. Emphasis is given to ensuring that the methods developed are biologically sound, effective, safe, and economically acceptable within the broad context of environmental concerns.

Center scientists at Denver and overseas field stations, in cooperation with the U.S. Agency for International Development, are developing methods for reducing severe agricultural damage by a variety of rodents, birds, and by vampire bats in Latin America, Africa, and Asia. The international programs are designed to develop and test appropriate technology for reducing animal damage in developing countries and to train scientists of host countries in these specialized types of research and management.

A laboratory facility located in Denver performs much of the basic scientific support for animal damage control. This includes pharmacology, application of biochemical techniques and methods to wildlife management, electronic development for wildlife research and management, applications of physiological and behavioral biology to wildlife management, chemical research and analytical services, and chemosensory applications in animal damage control.

The Museum Section is responsible for the acquisition, care, permanent preservation, and systematic study of wildlife species; carries out biological surveys and related studies of geographic and ecological distribution of wildlife; conducts life history studies and provides identification of wildlife.

The Marine Mammal Section is responsible for carrying out the Service's mandates under the Marine Mammal Protection Act and the Endangered Species Act, especially with regard to determining the ecological effects on marine wildlife and ecosystems of man's activities related to development and exploitation of the marine environment.

Field studies in the Ecology Section relate primarily to wildlife population biology and the relationships between land uses and natural resource management and wildlife in the lower 48 states and Alaska. Such studies relate to assessments of timber management practices, grazing, habitat, and wildlife management practices, effect of surface mining and other development projects on selected wildlife species, and population dynamics.

National Wildlife Health Laboratory

6006 Schroeder Road
Madison, Wisconsin 53711
Director: Dr. Milton Friend
Telephone: 608-271-4640
Congressional District: Wisconsin — Two
Land Holdings: 23.7 acres at Madison.
Number of Laboratory Buildings on Property: One garage/shop maintenance building (1950 sq. ft.) and one laboratory facility (31,700 sq. ft.).
Special Equipment: Zeiss photo microscope, laminar flow biological cabinets, ultralow freezers, refrigerated centrifuges, sterilizers, autoclaves, pathological incinerator, fluoroscope, autopsy tables, CO_2 incubators, and a variety of other equipment used for infectious disease studies.
Estimated Value for Replacement: 8 million.
Historical Background: The laboratory was organized in 1975 and, until recently, was housed in temporary facilities provided by the University of Wisconsin and other facilities leased from the Wisconsin Department of Agriculture. In 1979 these facilities were replaced by a modular temporary building (trailers) erected on univesity property at 5707 Mineral Point Road. Dedication of permanent facilities at 6006 Schroeder Road occurred during June 1983 following

completion of construction of the main laboratory building. Construction funds for a second building have been received and construction is anticipated to begin by October 1984.

Budget:

Major Programs	FY 1984 Budget Allocation
Wildlife Resources	$1,304,000
Endangered Species	51,100
TOTAL	$1,355,000

Personnel: Full-Time Equivalent: 33

Purpose: The laboratory represents service capabilities in wildlife disease investigations. Emphasis is on prevention and control of disease in wildlife to benefit populations under service stewardship. Field and laboratory studies are carried out and activities can be categorized as Research, Diagnostic Services, and Training. Training efforts are oriented for refuge biologists and other field personnel and involve identification and control of disease problems as well as collection and preservation of diagnostic specimens.

Current Research: Wildlife Resources research is directed at avian cholera with special emphasis on problems in the Rainwater Basin of Nebraska, a cooperative effort with NPS, and evaluation of control techniques for management of nuisance Canada goose problems. Endangered species research is limited to determining causes of mortality in bald eagles and development of an associated data base.

Support is also provided law enforcement regarding causes of mortality for court cases; advice and assistance in animal health care and disease prevention is provided service installations, and considerable cooperative efforts are undertaken with state fish and wildlife agencies in combatting wildlife disease problems.

Northern Prairie Wildlife Research Center
U.S. Fish and Wildlife Service
P.O. Box 1747
Jamestown, North Dakota 58401
Director: Dr. Rey C. Stendell
Telephone: 701-252-5363
Congressional District: North Dakota — 38 01
Land Holdings: 3,200 acres at Jamestown and the Woodworth Field Station
Number of Buildings on Property: Nine
Special Equipment: Waterfowl propagation facility, water chemistry laboratory, lipid analysis laboratory, second largest herbarium in North Dakota, aerial and ground telemetry tracking equipment, and a large vehicle fleet specially equipped for field work on migratory birds.
Estimated Value for Replacement: $12,700,000
Historical Background: The center was dedicated officially on September 18, 1965. Seven years earlier, the idea of a new facility for wildlife research in the north-central states was first brought to the public's attention.

Budget:

Major Programs	FY 1984 Budget Allocation
Migratory Birds	$1,816,700
Endangered Species	56,000
Other	435,000
TOTAL	$2,307,700

Personnel: Full-Time Equivalent: 41

Purpose: The Northern Prairie Wildlife Research Center (NPWRC) was established to conduct research to provide guidelines for effective management of wildlife populations and their habitats in the north-central United States. Increased demands for renewable resources and a diminished habitat base have indicated a need for more intensive management of wildlife on remaining habitats. Research at NPWRC has helped to identify important problems and issues facing these resources and provided information needed to understand and manage them. Studies conducted here have emphasized the breeding biology, habitat requirements, and population dynamics of waterfowl and other migratory birds in the northern prairie region of the United States and the prairie and parkland regions of Canada. One of our goals is to provide information for management activities on National Wildlife Refuges and other federal, state, and private lands.

During the past 15 years, NPWRC has made important contributions to the understanding of habitat rquirements of prairie nesting ducks. Emphasis has been on the mallard and canvasback, but much information has been collected for other species. In addition, research has documented the role of the aquatic food chain in maintaining waterfowl breeding populations and evaluated the ecological factors that limit production. Understanding the adverse impact that mammalian predators have on prairie nesting ducks has been a valuable contribution that called attention to the development of management techniques to limit predator impacts on nesting areas. In addition to research in the prairie region, NPWRC conducts studies in major migration and wintering areas including California and the Upper Mississippi River.

In the years since NPWRC was established, changes have occurred in the migratory bird and habitat resource picture and in the priorities of the FWS. A Service Management Plan, Program Management Documents, Important Resource Problems, Species of Management Concern, Regional Resource Plans, and a National Waterfowl Management Plan reflect these changes and provide guidance on issues of highest concern to FWS. Research conducted at NPWRC and elsewhere has prepared FWS to better deal with these changes and meet the challenges of the future.

Current Research: Current research is directed toward: 1) factors influencing productivity of upland nesting ducks, 2) breeding biology and migrational ecology of diving ducks, 3) management of wetlands, 4) land management practices for upland nesting waterfowl, 5) relationships of Pacific Flyway wetlands to migratory birds, 6) predator management practices, and 7) nongame birds.

Patuxent Wildlife Research Center
U.S. Fish and Wildlife Service
Laurel, Maryland 20708
Director: Dr. David L. Trauger
Telephone: 301-498-0300
Congressional District: Maryland — Five
Land Holdings: 4,700 acres in Prince Georges and Anne Arundel Counties; includes three Research Natural Acres constituting 2,950 acres, representing the three major habitat types of the Upper Coastal Plain: bottomland forest, terrace woodland, and upland forest. Parallel areas of each type are maintained in successional ecological stages.
Number of Laboratory Buildings on Property: 19
Special Equipment: Atomic absorption spectrophotometers, computerized gas chromatographs and mass spectrometers, gel permeation chromatographs, liquid scintillation and gamma counters, serum enzyme analyzer, spectrophotofluorometer, environmental chambers, computer terminals, various types of field equipment, radio-tracking receivers for following bird movements.
Estimated Value for Replacement: $22,000,000
Historical Background: Land was acquired in 1936 through the Federal Resettlement Administration. The Patuxent Wildlife Research Center was the first major wildlife research station in the United States. Acreage was increased in 1970 by purchase acquisition and in 1975 by transfer from USDA through presidential directive; increases were made in order to increase capability for ecological and experimental research and to maintain natural areas.
Budget:

Major Programs	*FY 1984 Budget Allocation*
Endangered Species	$1,777,000
Habitat Resources	3,450,000
Wildlife Resources	1,176,000
Construction and Maintenance	1,000,000
TOTAL	$7,400,000

Personnel: Full-Time Equivalent: 167

Purpose: The center conducts research in three program areas.

(1) *Environmental Contaminant Evaluation.* The ecological impacts of contaminants on wildlife and wildlife habitat are measured, predicted, and monitored in an integrated program that combines field and laboratory studies conducted by scientists in several disciplines: ecologist, behaviorists, physiologists, chemists, and biometricians.

(2) *Endangered Species Research.* Ecological research on endangered and threatened wildlife identifies and evaluates limiting factors and provides recommendations to improve the status of the populations. Behavioral, physiological, and nutritional needs of the species are studied with captive animals to extend and interpret the field observations. Methods of propagation are developed for critical species and certain of these are propagated for release to the wild.

(3) *Wildlife Resources Research.* Provides information for more management of migratory birds and in so doing (1) evaluates existing methods and develops new procedures for measuring the population status of migratory birds; (2) determines factors which affect the population status of migratory birds; and (3) determines habitat requirements and the ecology of waterfowl and nongame birds, especially in the eastern part of the United States. Methods are developed to evaluate and improve conditions for wildlife in urban environments.

Current Research:

(1) *Environmental Contaminant Evaluation Program.* Research focuses on contaminant problems in the principal wildlife habitats: marine, estuarine, freshwater, woodlands, grasslands, and croplands. Primary emphasis is on nongame species: birds of prey, seabirds, wading birds, and songbirds; although a significant effort is directed toward problems of waterfowl. More limited studies are made of mammals (marine mammals, mink, and bats) and other species (quail, prairie chicken). Agricultural pesticides as well as industrial and energy-related chemicals such as heavy metals and oil are included.

(2) *Endangered Species Program.* Ecological studies are conducted on Hawaiian forest birds, eastern timber wolf, California condor, bald eagle (southeast), Everglade kite, yellow-shouldered blackbird, Puerto Rican parrot, Puerto Rican plain pigeon, whooping crane, masked bobwhite quail, Kirtland's warbler, and several endangered bats. Behavioral, physiological, and nutritional studies are conducted on whooping cranes, sandhill cranes, and Andean condors. Propagation for release is underway with whooping cranes, masked bobwhite quail, Mississippi sandhill cranes, bald eagles, and Puerto Rican plain pigeons and parrots.

(3) *Wildlife Resources Program.* Research is conducted on migratory birds in three primary areas. Nongame bird communities, especially songbirds, are studied to aid federal agencies and other groups in the management of both large and small tracts of land. Game bird populations, mainly waterfowl, are studied to obtain reliable data with which to manage hunted species and populations, while also providing maximum benefit for nonconsumptive users. Research also is conducted on migratory shore and upland game birds. Urban wildlife research includes developing and testing of census methods that can be used in cities, developing management practices to enhance wildlife populations, recommending building and design improvements to deter nuisance species; and measuring the relationships between highways and wildlife populations.

Appendix VIII.
Regional Species of Special Emphasis

Region 1
Lahontan Cutthroat Trout
Region 2
Mottled Duck
Rainbow Trout
Humpback Chub
Woundfin
Gila Topminnow
Knowlton Cactus
Peebles Navajo Cactus
Region 3
Common Tern
Great Blue Heron
Higgin's Eye Pearly Mussel
Indiana Bat
Gray Bat
Ozark Big-eared Bat
Iowa Pleistocene Snail
Northern Monkshod
Region 4
Brook Trout
Rainbow Trout
Brown Trout

Snail (Everglade) Kite
Tennessee Coneflower
Wood Stork
Yellow-shouldered Blackbird
Eastern Bluebird
Florida Duck
Mottled Duck
Caribbean Waterfowl Group:
  —West Indian Whistling Duck
  —Masked Duck
  —West Indian Ruddy Duck
  —White-cheeked Pintail
Red-headed Woodpecker
Seaside Sparrow
White-crowned Pigeon
Region 5
Colonial Nesting Waterbirds
American Shad
Region 6
Paddlefish
Rainbow Trout
Region 7
Emperor Goose

Appendix IX.
National Species and Species Groups of Special Emphasis

Mammals

Grizzly bear (*Ursus arctos horribilis*)
 (Lower 48 states population)
Polar bear (*Ursus maritimus*)
Black-footed ferret (*Mustela nigripes*)
Sea otter (*Enhydra lutris*)
Coyote (*Canis latrans*)
Gray wolf (*Canis lupus*)
 (Eastern and Rocky Mt. populations)
Walrus (*Odobenus rosmarus*)
West Indian manatee (*Trichechus manatus*)

Birds

Brown pelican (*Pelecanus occidentalis*) }Seabird group
Tundra swan (*Cygnus columbianus*)
Trumpeter swan (*Cygnus buccinator*)
White-fronted goose (*Anser albifrons*)
Snow goose (*Chen caerulescens*)
Brant (*Branta bernicla*)
Canada goose (*Branta canadensis*)
Wood duck (*Aix sponsa*)
Black duck (*Anas rubripes*) } Surface feeding duck group
Mallard (*Anas platyrhynchos*)
*Pintail (*Anas acuta*)
Canvasback (*Aythya valisineria*)
Redhead (*Aythya americana*) } Bay duck group
*Ring-necked duck (*Aythya collaris*)
California condor (*Gymnogyps californianus*)
Osprey (*Pandion haliaetus*)
Bald eagle (*Haliaeetus leucocephalus*)
Golden eagle (*Aquila chrysaetos*)
Peregrine falcon (*Falco peregrinus*)
Attwater's greater prairie-chicken (*Tympanuchus cupido attwateri*)
Masked bobwhite (*Colinus virginianus ridgwayi*)
Yuma clapper rail (*Rallus longirostris yumanensis*)
Light-footed clapper rail (*Rallus longirostris levipes*)
Sandhill crane (*Grus canadensis*)
Whooping crane (*Grus americana*)
*Piping plover (*Charadrius melodus*) } Shorebird group
American woodcock (*Scolopax minor*)
*Roseate tern (*Sterna dougallii*)
Eastern least tern (*Sterna antillarum antillarum*) } Gull and tern group
Interior least tern (*Sterna antillarum athalassos*)
California least tern (*Sterna antillarum brownii*)
White-winged dove (*Zenaida asciatica*)
Mourning dove (*Zenaida macroura*)
Spotted owl (*Strix occidentalis*)
Red-cockaded woodpecker (*Picoides borealis*)

Kirtland's warbler (*Dendroica kirtlandii*)
Reptiles
American alligator (*Alligator mississippiensis*)
Fish
Sea lamprey (*Petromyzon marinus*) (Great Lakes)
Coho salmon (*Oncorhynchus kisutch*)
  (Anadromous populations — Pacific coast/Alaska)
*Sockeye salmon (*Oncorhynchus nerka*)
  (Alaska populations) ⎱ Pacific salmon group
Chinook salmon (*Oncorhynchus tshawytscha*)
  (Anadromous populations — Pacific coast/Alaska)
Cutthroat trout (*Salmo clarki*)
  (Western U.S.) ⎱ Stream trout group
Steelhead (Anadromous populations — Pacific coast/Alaska)/
  Rainbow trout (*Salmo gairdneri*)
Atlantic salmon (*Salmo salar*)
  (Anadromous populations)
Lake trout (*Salvelinus namaycush*)
  (Great Lakes)
Cui-ui (*Chasmistes cujus*)
  (Historical range)
Striped bass (*Morone saxatilis*)
  (Anadromous populations — Atlantic/Gulf coasts)
Great Lakes Percidae
Molluscs
(No specific species identified.)
Plants
(No specific species identified.)

Appendix X.
Permit Office Under Various Laws
Types of Permits Issued by the FWS

Endangered Species Act[1]

Endangered Species:[2]   Scientific research, enhancement of propagation or survival, incidental taking.

Threatened Species:[2]   All of the above, as well as for zoological, horticultural, or botanical exhibition; educational purposes; special purposes consistent with the purposes of the Act.

Captive-Bred Wildlife: Endangered or threatened species not native to the U.S. that have been born in the U.S. can be bought, sold, transported for interstate commerce, and exported or reimported if a permit is obtained.

Exemptions: Exemptions from obtaining a required permit may be granted under special circumstances. Contact WPO for more details.

[1]Permits must also comply with other federal, state, and foreign laws as required by the Lacey Act.

[2]Sea turtles are within the jurisdiction of NMFS when they are at sea.

Marine Mammal Protection Act (MMPA)

The WPO has jurisdiction only over polar bears, sea and marine otters, walrus, dugong, and West Indian and Amazonian manatees. Of these, only the polar bear and walrus are not also protected by the ESA. Permits are issued for scientific purposes, public display, incidental taking in commercial fisheries, and for special purposes consistent with the Act. The National Marine Fisheries Service, Office of Protected Species, handles permits for 11 other marine mammals listed under the MMPA. For more information about permits or exemptions contact the appropriate office.

Convention on International Trade in Endangered Species of Wild Flora and Fauna (CITES)[3]

Appendix I: Species threatened with extinction   Two permits: one from the importing country (obtained first), and another from the exporting country. A permit is issued only if import is not primarily commercial and will not be detrimental to the survival of the species.

Appendix II: Species which could be threatened with extinction in the future   Only a foreign export or reexport permit is required. Permits may be issued for any purpose as long as export will not be detrimental to the survival of the species.

Appendix III: Species not endangered or threatened but that are regulated for conservation by a party nation.   Only an export permit from the country that listed the species, or a reexport certificate or certificate of origin from any other country.

[3]Species listed under CITES may also be covered under ESA or MMPA which impose more restrictive export/import conditions.

For Permit Information Contact:

Federal Wildlife Permit Office
Fish and Wildlife Service
U.S. Department of the Interior
Washington, D.C. 20240
(703) 235-1903

Office of Protected Species
National Marine Fisheries Service
Department of Commerce
Washington, D.C. 20235
(202) 634-5729

Appendix XI.

Origin, Size, and Cost of National Wildlife Refuges

State and Unit	Reserved from Public Domain — Sole or Primary	Reserved — Secondary	Acquired by Other Federal Agency — Sole or Primary	Acquired — Secondary	Devise or Gift	Purchased — Acres	Purchased — Cost	Agreement Easement or Lease	Total Acres
Alabama									
Blowing Wind Cave						264	575,000		264
Bon Secour						3,350	13,379,760	415	3,765
Choctaw				E 4.218					4.218
Eufaula (1)				E 7.929					7,929
Fern Cave						199	110,000		199
Watercress Darter						7	36,150		7
Wheeler			8,323	T 25,674		122	149,700		34,119
7 TOTAL			8,323	37,821		3,942	14,250,610	415	50,501
Alaska									
Alaska Maritime	3,364,784	N 62,220				3,000	1,920,000	121,779	3,551,783
Alaska Peninsula	3,500,000								3,500,000
Arctic	17,988,855				971,800	19,958		65,769	19,046,382
Becharof	1,200,000								1,200,000
Innoko	3,850,000								3,850,000
Izembek	302,201	FA 893						17,799	320,893
Kanuti	1,430,000								1,430,000
Kenai	1,904,752							65,248	1,970,000
Kodiak	1,656,180							208,820	1,865,000
Koyukuk	3,550,000								3,550,000
Nowitna	1,560,000								1,560,000
Selawik	2,150,000								2,150,000
Tetlin	700,000								700,000
Togiak	4,097,430							7,570	4,105,000
Yukon Delta	19,131,581	IA 63						492,814	19,624,458
Yukon Flats	8,630,000								8,630,000
16 TOTAL	75,015,783	63,176			971,800	22,985	1,920,000	979,799	77,053,516
Arizona									
Cabeza Prieta	860,000								860,000
Cibola (2)	45	R 3,573		R 4.173					7,791
Havasu (2)	13,075	R 12,383		R 11.071		1,575	1,600,000		38,104
Imperial (2)		R 16.501		R 1.305					17,806
Kofa	660,000								660,000
San Bernardino						2,309	816,000		2,309
6 TOTAL	1,533,120	32,457		16,549		3,884	2,416,000		1,586,010
Arkansas									
Big Lake	8,876		1,597			563	30,918		11,036
Felsenthal				E 64.510		89	100,000		64,599
Holla Bend			4,068			15	2,500		4,083
Overflow						6,790	4,716,131		6,790
Wapanocca						5,484	1,351,416		5,484
White River	6		83,478	E 46	1,050	27,819	163,961		112,399
6 TOTAL	8,882		89,143	64,556	1,050	40,760	6,364,926		204,391
California									
Antioch Dunes						55	2,135,000		55
Blue Ridge						897	642,500		897
Butte Sink						440	1,100,700	1,050	1,490
Castle Rock						14	41,250		14
Cibola (3)*		R 1.255		R 2.095				297	3,647
Clear Lake		R 33.440							33,440
Colusa						4,040	291,281		4,040
Delevan						5,634	2,019,739		5,634
Ellicott Slough						126	556,000		126
Farallon		91	CG 120						211
Grasslands								24,484	24,484
Havasu (3)*		R 4,672	10	R 3,065					7,747
Hopper Mountain						1,871	510,000		1,871
Humboldt Bay			C 1			558	1,335,410		559
Imperial (3)*		R 6,309		R 1,649					7,958
Kern						10,618	579,912		10,618
Kesterson				R 5,900					5,900
Lower Klamath (4)	39,316				448	531	2,130		40,295
Merced						2,562	510,000		2,562
Modoc	40					6,243	1,119,618		6,283
Pixley			4,121			1,056	1,121,000		5,187
Sacramento						10,783	162,998		10,783
Salton Sea		R 23,425	160			9,342	294,462	4,451	37,378
San Francisco Bay			37		198	15,922	8,698,890	1,061	17,218
San Luis		8				7,422	2,171,055		7,430

NATIONAL WILDLIFE REFUGES (CONTINUED)

State and Unit		Reserved from Public Domain — Sole or Primary	Reserved — Secondary	Acquired by Other Federal Agency — Sole or Primary	Acquired — Secondary	Devise or Gift	Purchased — Acres	Purchased — Cost	Agreement Easement or Lease	Total Acres
San Pablo Bay						249	185	167,500	11,200	11,634
Seal Beach					N 852				59	911
Sutter							2,591	292,282		2,591
Tijuana Slough							407	7,655,000	65	472
Tule Lake		39,396								39,396
27	TOTAL	78,851	69,222	4,328	13,561	895	81,297	31,406,727	42,667	290,821
Colorado										
Alamosa		86					9,655	1,399,464	611	10,352
Arapaho		3,073					13,941	3,242,086	640	17,654
Browns Park		6,794					5,276	594,976	1,305	13,375
Monte Vista		800					13,389	1,374,909		14,189
4	TOTAL	10,753					42,261	6,611,435	2,556	55,570
Connecticut										
Salt Meadow						177	6	2,000		183
Delaware										
Bombay Hook			542				14,580	437,739		15,122
Prime Hook							8,817	3,471,337	884	9,701
2	TOTAL		542				23,397	3,909,076	884	24,823
Florida										
Caloosahatchee		40								40
Cedar Keys		379					342	681,190		721
Chassahowitzka		321					30,115	456,746		30,436
Crocodile Lake						11	1,455	1,880,642		1,466
Crystal River							33	383,600		33
J.N. Ding Darling		407			CG 54	180	4,373	2,071,907		5,014
Egmont Key		328								328
Great White Heron		770			265	80	5,087	2,758,327	1,202	7,404
Hobe Sound						957	4	18,000	8	969
Island Bay		20								20
Key West		1,865	N, CG 154							2,019
Lake Woodruff						3	18,503	1,405,710		18,506
Lower Suwannee							13,265	2,628,200	9,556	22,821
Loxahatchee							2,550	118,512	143,085	145,635
Matlacha Pass		10				221				231
Merritt Island				NA 139,228						139,228
National Key Deer		53				603	5,160	5,735,825		5,816
Okefenokee	(1)						3,678	52,636		3,678
Passage Key		36								36
Pelican Island		43							4,353	4,396
Pine Island		31					373	1,034,000		404
Pinellas							15	18,000	377	392
St. Johns							6,254	2,683,917		6,254
St. Marks		93		32,516		39	31,952	284,014		64,600
St. Vincent		45					12,445	2,035,000		12,490
25	TOTAL	4,441	154	32,781	139,282	2,094	135,604	24,246,226	158,581	472,937
Georgia										
Banks Lake									3,550	3,550
Blackbeard Island				4,659			959			5,618
Eufaula	(5)*				E 3,231					3,231
Harris Neck				2,687						2,687
Okefenokee	(6)*			1,860		15,404	374,138	1,780,185		391,402
Piedmont				24,821			10,042	44,000		34,863
Savannah	(7)			4,015			7,484	702,852		11,499
Tybee					E 100					100
Wassaw						10,050			20	10,070
Wolf Island				538			4,588	120,814		5,126
8	TOTAL			38,580	3,331	25,454	397,211	2,647,851	3,570	468,146
Hawaii										
Hanalei							917	1,289,081		917
Hawaiian Islands		254,418								254,418
Huleia							238	309,573		238
James C. Campbell									145	145
Kakahaia							45	684,550		45
Pearl Harbor					N 61					61
6	TOTAL	254,418			61		1,200	2,283,204	145	255,824
Idaho										
Bear Lake		16,978					627	212,279		17,605
Camas							10,578	202,530		10,578
Deer Flat	(4)	1,008	R 9,993			21	226	19,616		11,248
Grays Lake		43					3,110	1,149,135	13,000	16,153
Kootenai							2,764	633,100		2,764
Minidoka		2,864	R 16,787		R 1,070					20,721
6	TOTAL	20,893	26,780		1,070	21	17,305	2,216,660	13,000	79,069

NATIONAL WILDLIFE REFUGES (CONTINUED)

State and Unit	Reserved from Public Domain — Sole or Primary	Secondary	Acquired by Other Federal Agency — Sole or Primary	Secondary	Devise or Gift	Purchased — Acres	Cost	Agreement Easement or Lease	Total Acres
Illinois									
Chautauqua					1,709	4,488	30,447		6,197
Crab Orchard			42,511			1,039	1,824		43,550
Mark Twain (8)				E 12,459	60	2,417	823,646	128	15,064
Meredosia					1,850				1,850
Mississippi River Caue (9)				E 20,120					20,120
Upper Mississippi (9)	65		288			2,788	22,120		3,141
6 TOTAL	65		42,799	32,579	3,619	10,732	878,037	128	89,922
Indiana									
Muscatatuck						7,724	3,612,778		7,724
Iowa									
De Soto (10)						3,499	735,409		3,499
Mark Twain (11)*				E 10,424		48	16,000		10,472
Mississippi River Caue (13)*				E 30,315					30,315
Union Slough						2,200	210,407		2,200
Upper Mississippi (13)*	333			E 2	1	19,988	140,295		20,324
2 TOTAL	333			40,741	1	25,735	1,102,111		66,810
Kansas									
Flint Hills				E 18,463					18,463
Kirwin				R 10,778					10,778
Quivira						21,820	2,059,237		21,820
3 TOTAL				29,241		21,820	2,059,237		51,061
Kentucky									
Reelfoot (14)						2,040	418,450		2,040
Louisiana									
Bogue Chitto (27)						17,803	6,668,220	620	18,423
Breton	9,047								9,047
Catahoula						5,309	53,085		5,309
D'Arbonne			17,420						17,420
Delta	1,408	E 2,892	10,036			34,463	233,324		48,799
Lacassine			22,992			8,132	38,156	652	31,776
Sabine			138,870			567	14,001		139,437
Shell Keys	8								8
Upper Ouachita						20,905	6,271,500		20,905
9 TOTAL	10,463	2,892	189,318			87,179	13,278,286	1,272	291,124
Maine									
Cross Island					1,355				1,355
Franklin Island			12						12
Moosehorn			6,490		333	15,842	97,261	80	22,745
Petit Manan			14		1,464	1,657	516,613	175	3,310
Pond Island			10						10
Rachel Carson					78	2,599	915,673	59	2,736
Seal Island			65						65
7 TOTAL			6,591		3,230	20,098	1,529,547	314	30,233
Maryland									
Blackwater						14,263	1,490,318		14,263
Chincoteague (16)						418	13,780		418
Eastern Neck						2,286	1,606,145		2,286
Martin					2,570	1,854	61,027		4,424
Patuxent			3,754			928	927,744		4,682
Susquehanna			4						4
6 TOTAL	—		3,758		2,570	19,749	4,099,014		26,077
Massachusetts									
Great Meadows					236	2,642	1,295,994		2,878
Massasoit						184	252,000		184
Monomoy			2			2,700	149,465		2,702
Nantucket			40						40
Nomans Land Island				N 620					620
Oxbow			662						662
Parker River			2			4,648	107,563		4,650
Thacher Island			22						22
8 TOTAL			728	620	236	10,174	1,805,022		11,758
Michigan									
Harbor Island						695	197,000		695
Huron	22		113	CG-E 12					147
Kirtland Warbler						1,896	815,566		1,896
Michigan Island	12	CG 121	230						363
Seney	2,736		7,070			85,649	177,340		95,455
Shiawassee						8,984	1,448,376		8,984
Wyandotte	304								304
7 TOTAL	3,074	121	7,413	12		97,224	2,638,282		107,844

617

NATIONAL WILDLIFE REFUGES (CONTINUED)

State and Unit	Reserved from Public Domain Sole or Primary	Secondary	Acquired by Other Federal Agency Sole or Primary	Secondary	Devise or Gift	Purchased Acres	Cost	Agreement Easement or Lease	Total Acres
Minnesota									
Agassiz	6		60,172			874	38,626		61,052
Big Stone			10,540	E 254					10,794
Mille Lacs	1								1
Minnesota Valley			275			3,321	5,580,701	1,283	4,879
Mississippi River Caue (18)*				E 15,421					15,421
Rice Lake			10,027			6,489	165,330		16,516
Sherburne						29,583	3,275,500		29,583
Tamarac	40					35,151	590,655		35,191
Upper Mississippi (18)*	241				1	17,512	209,055	3	17,757
7 TOTAL	288		81,014	15,675	1	92,930	9,859,867	1,286	191,194
Mississippi									
Bogue Chitto (28)						214	85,484		214
Hillside			15,383		23				15,406
Mathews Brake						807	484,446		807
Mississippi Sandhill Crane						15,846	19,467,637	120	15,966
Morgan Brake						1,465	715,365		1,465
Noxubee	40		35,344			10,940	145,413		46,324
Panther Swamp						22,476	12,600,089	321	22,797
Yazoo						12,471	2,142,504		12,471
7 TOTAL	40		50,727		23	64,219	35,640,938	441	115,450
Missouri									
Clarence Cannon						3,737	1,163,272		3,737
Mark Twain (13)*				E 232					232
Mingo						21,676	317,382		21,676
Squaw Creek			3,081			3,838	137,853		6,919
Swan Lake			5,245			5,424	195,568		10,669
4 TOTAL			8,326	232		34,675	1,814,075		43,233
Montana									
Benton Lake	12,235					148	5,315		12,383
Black Coulee	640							669	1,309
Bowdoin	11,937								12,577
Charles M. Russell	358,196	E 380,901	3,745	E 152,692	55	900	125,380	640	897,129
Creedman Coulee	80							2,648	2,728
Hailstone		MMS 160						760	920
Halfbreed Lake								3,097	3,097
Hewitt Lake		MMS 400	320					960	1,680
Lake Mason	18		11,392					5,558	16,968
Lake Thibadeau	19							3,849	3,868
Lamesteer								800	800
Lee Metcalf						2,696	799,180		2,696
Medicine Lake	1,089		19,311		4	2,420	25,100		22,824
National Bison Range			18,521		1	19	700		18,541
Nine-Pipe								2,022	2,022
Pablo								2,542	2,542
Red Rock Lakes	8,239	F 594	22,631			1,004	15,859		32,468
Swan River						1,569	901,645		1,569
Ul Bend	29,678	E 6,897		E 9,226		9,688	577,280		55,489
War Horse			3,192						3,192
20 TOTAL	422,131	388,952	79,752	161,918	60	18,444	2,450,459	23,545	1,094,802
Nebraska									
Crescent Lake	120		240			45,458	326,304		45,818
De Soto (19)*						4,324	761,275		4,324
Fort Niobrara	14,390		2,384			1,893	31,084		18,667
Karl E. Mundt (20)					19				19
North Platte		R 5,047							5,047
Valentine			61,782			5,315	63,573		67,097
5 TOTAL	14,510	5,047	64,406		19	56,990	1,182,236		140,972
Nevada									
Ash Meadows						11,173	5,000,000		11,173
Anaho Island	248								248
Desert	1,588,055				4	720	352,800		1,588,779
Fallon		R 17,902							17,902
Moapa Valley						31	880,000	2	33
Pahranagat	1,466					3,915	500,000		5,381
Ruby Lake	7,566	LM 120				29,946	208,437		37,632
Sheldon (4)	544,277	LM 80			2,496	23,568	151,797		570,421
Stillwater								24,203	24,203
9 TOTAL	2,141,612	18,102			2,500	69,353	7,093,034	24,205	2,255,772
New Hampshire									
Wapack					1,672				1,672

NATIONAL WILDLIFE REFUGES (CONTINUED)

State and Unit	Reserved from Public Domain		Acquired by Other Federal Agency		Devise or Gift	Purchased		Agreement Easement or Lease	Total Acres
	Sole or Primary	Secondary	Sole or Primary	Secondary		Acres	Cost		
New Jersey									
Edwin B. Forsythe					378	27,815	5,549,022	2,413	30,606
Great Swamp					2,857	3,935	6,024,167	1	6,793
Supawna Meadows			7	E 2	884	825	469,744		1,718
3 TOTAL			7	2	4,119	32,575	12,042,933	2,414	39,117
New Mexico									
Bitter Lake	12,396					10,954	52,304		23,350
Bosque Del Apache	140					56,850	125,311	201	57,191
Grulla (12)	3,231								3,231
Las Vegas						8,672	2,121,151		8,672
Maxwell				R 439		2,792	423,371	468	3,699
San Andres		LM 57,215							57,215
Sevilleta					220,200	7,871	1,270,766	63	228,134
7 TOTAL	15,767	57,215		439	220,200	87,139	3,992,903	732	381,492
New York									
Amagansett			36						36
Conscience Point					60				60
Elizabeth A. Morton					187				187
Iroquois						10,818	1,240,905		10,818
Montezuma					12	6,029	161,192	391	6,432
Oyster Bay					3,204				3,204
Seatuck					183				183
Target Rock					80				80
Wertheim					1,860	535	2,437,791		2,395
9 TOTAL			36		5,586	17,382	3,839,888	391	23,395
North Carolina									
Alligator River					120,000				120,000
Cedar Island			31		10	12,485	347,171		12,526
Currituck						512	500,000		512
Great Dismal Swamp (16)					10,957	13,552	4,324,579		24,509
Mackay Island (16)						6,182	388,957		6,182
Mattamuskeet			49,925			252	1,285	3	50,180
Pea Island			35	CG 21		5,859	40,402		5,915
Pee Dee						8,438	2,553,852		8,438
Pungo						12,350	1,682,158		12,350
Swanquarter					142	15,501	61,001		15,643
10 TOTAL			49,991	21	131,109	75,131	9,899,405	3	256,255
North Dakota									
Appert Lake								908	908
Ardoch					14	293	4,739	2,389	2,696
Arrowwood		4	11,240		3	2,098	46,906	2,589	15,934
Audubon				E 14,736					14,736
Bone Hill								640	640
Brumba								1,977	1,977
Buffalo Lake		24			3			2,070	2,097
Camp Lake								585	585
Canfield						3	100	310	313
Chase Lake						4,385	25,610		4,385
Cottonwood								1,013	1,013
Dakota Lake								2,756	2,756
Des Lacs		100	13,258		30	681	6,891	5,475	19,544
Florence Lake						1,468	31,486	420	1,888
Half-Way Lake								160	160
Hiddenwood								568	568
Hobart Lake		9				236	5,165	1,831	2,076
Hutchinson Lake								479	479
J. Clark Salyer		321	36,800		3	21,569	306,344		58,693
Johnson Lake					4			2,003	2,007
Kellys Slough		680						590	1,270
Lake Alice					2	7,369	1,685,184	3,583	10,954
Lake Elsie								635	635
Lake George		29						3,090	3,119
Lake Ilo					11	3,186	116,422	836	4,033
Lake Nettie						2,261	105,525	634	2,895
Lake Otis								320	320
Lake Zahl		40				3,179	53,275	604	3,823
Lambs Lake								1,207	1,207
Little Goose								288	288
Long Lake		1,170				12,579	77,174	8,561	22,310
Lords Lake								1,915	1,915

NATIONAL WILDLIFE REFUGES (CONTINUED)

State and Unit	Reserved from Public Domain — Sole or Primary	Reserved from Public Domain — Secondary	Acquired by Other Federal Agency — Sole or Primary	Acquired by Other Federal Agency — Secondary	Devise or Gift	Purchased — Acres	Purchased — Cost	Agreement Easement or Lease	Total Acres
Lost Lake								960	960
Lostwood	204		21,458			3,148	24,551		24,810
Maple River								712	712
McLean						344	12,516	416	760
Pleasant Lake								898	898
Pretty Rock								800	800
Rabb Lake								261	261
Rock Lake								5,507	5,507
Rose Lake								836	836
School Section Lake								680	680
Shell Lake						710	17,901	1,125	1,835
Sheyenne Lake								797	797
Sibley Lake								1,077	1,077
Silver Lake								3,348	3,348
Slade					3,000				3,000
Snyder Lake								1,550	1,550
Springwater								640	640
Stewart Lake					4			2,226	2,230
Stoney Slough								880	880
Storm Lake						2	161	684	686
Stump Lake	27								27
Sullys Hill	1,674								1,674
Sunburst Lake								328	328
Tewaukon	1					6,857	460,121	2,415	9,273
Tomahawk								440	440
Upper Souris	160		28,792		7	3,129	41,221	4	32,092
White Lake						1,040	28,800		1,040
Wild Rice Lake								779	779
Willow Lake					1			2,620	2,621
Wintering River								239	239
Wood Lake								280	280
63 TOTAL	4,443		111,548	14,736	3,082	74,537	3,050,092	78,938	287,284
Ohio									
Cedar Point					2,445				2,445
Ottawa						5,203	2,625,394	591	5,794
West Sister Island	77								77
3 TOTAL	77				2,445	5,203	2,625,394	591	8,316
Oklahoma									
Optima				E 4,333					4,333
Salt Plains	19,314			E 11,565		1,117	50,837		31,996
Sequoyah				E 20,800					20,800
Tishomingo				E 16,464					16,464
Washita				R 8,062				22	8,084
Wichita Mountains	58,492					527			59,019
6 TOTAL	77,806			61,224		1,644	50,837	22	140,696
Oregon									
Ankeny						2,796	893,600		2,796
Bandon Marsh						289	235,000		289
Baskett Slough						2,492	941,985		2,492
Bear Valley						1,733	1,762,200		1,733
Cape Mears	139								139
Cold Springs	50	R 1,748		R 932		387	2,760		3,117
Columbian White-Tailed Deer (26)					136	1,594	1,616,750	250	1,980
Deer Flat (21)*	162								162
Hart Mountain	183,856	LM 1,951				63,432	680,719		249,239
Klamath Forest						16,377	912,694		16,377
Lewis and Clark			875		247	2,851	469,250	34,027	38,000
Lower Klamath (2)*	6,500								6,500
Malheur	57,979		58,969			66,227	1,769,320	789	183,964
McKay Creek	24			R 1,813					1,837
Oregon Islands	575								575
Sheldon (15)*						627	4,078		627
Three Arch Rocks	15								15
Umatilla (26)		E 348	1,449	E 7,082					8,879
Upper Klamath	6	R 8,140				4,311	123,476		12,457
William L. Finley						5,325	1,421,800		5,325
17 TOTAL	249,356	12,187	61,293	9,827	383	16,441	10,833,632	35,066	536,553
Pennsylvania									
Erie						7,994	901,438		7,994
Tinicum			168		232	498	7,985,517		898
2 TOTAL			168		232	8,492	8,886,955		8,892

NATIONAL WILDLIFE REFUGES (CONTINUED)

State and Unit	Reserved from Public Domain — Sole or Primary	Secondary	Acquired by Other Federal Agency — Sole or Primary	Secondary	Devise or Gift	Purchased Acres	Purchased Cost	Agreement Easement or Lease	Total Acres
Rhode Island									
Block Island			29						29
Ninigret			408						408
Sachuest Point			157		71				228
Trustom Pond					516	63	440,000		579
4 TOTAL			594		587	63	440,000		1,244
South Carolina									
Cape Romain			5,247		6,496	22,306	52,418	180	34,229
Carolina Sandhills			44,555			631	38,353	405	45,591
Pinckney Island					1,325			2,728	4,053
Santee						4,413	521,614	39,223	43,636
Savannah (1)*			5,071		37	9,953	933,891	24	15,085
4 TOTAL			54,873		7,858	37,303	1,546,276	42,560	142,594
South Dakota									
Bear Butte								374	374
Karl E. Mundt (10)*					758			305	1,063
Lacreek			6,807		223	9,220	736,491	10	16,260
Lake Andes			320			618	92,321	2	940
Pocasse				E 2,540					2,540
Sand Lake		80	15,802			3,922	90,622		19,804
Waubay			1,901			684	74,217		2,585
6 TOTAL		80	24,830	2,540	981	14,444	993,651	691	43,566
Tennessee									
Cross Creeks			6,328	E 2,442		92	26,200		8,862
Hatchie						11,556	1,862,029		11,556
Lake Isom			1,485			361	27,291		1,846
Lower Hatchie					8	1,982	2,964,820	638	2,628
Reelfoot (22)*						541	209,532	7,847	8,388
Tennessee				T 50,830		528	247,147		51,358
5 TOTAL			7,813	53,272	8	15,060	5,337,019	8,485	84,638
Texas									
Anahuac					185	21,510	8,672,809	63	21,758
Aransas			18,999		7,568	47,261	463,532	24,893	98,721
Attwater Prairie Chicken					2,663	5,321	4,050,949		7,984
Big Boggy						3,564	1,962,905		3,564
Brazoria					46	10,361	2,013,682		10,407
Buffalo Lake			7,664						7,664
Grulla (17)*						5	5,000		5
Hagerman				E 11,320					11,320
Laguna Atascosa			8,486			36,588	1,109,166	113	45,187
Lower Rio Grande Valley			17		1,440	1,863	2,714,830	5,025	8,345
McFaddin						41,682	8,250,000	1,274	42,956
Moody								3,517	3,517
Muleshoe			3,654			2,155	25,740		5,809
San Bernard						24,454	6,624,789		24,454
Santa Ana					37	2,050	203,520	1	2,088
Texas Point						8,952	1,719,000		8,952
15 TOTAL			38,820	11,320	11,939	205,766	37,815,922	34,886	302,731
Utah									
Bear River	44,083				4,272	16,674	43,061	1	65,030
Fish Springs	14,217					3,775	93,325		17,992
Ouray	3,111					4,872	461,984	3,500	11,483
3 TOTAL	61,411				4,272	25,321	598,370	3,501	94,505
Vermont									
Missisquoi					70	5,769	188,884		5,839
Virginia									
Back Bay						4,589	120,000		4,589
Cape Charles			174					9	183
Chincoteague (23)*						9,513	635,404		9,513
Featherstone						164	486,800		164
Fishermans Island			1,000	N 25					1,025
Great Dismal Swamp (24)*			27		49,097	28,236	9,784,022	4	77,364
Mackay Island (24)*						874	26,856		874
Marumsco			63						63
Mason Neck						1,146	3,202,859	789	1,935
Nansemond			208						208
Plum Tree Island			3,276						3,276
Presquile					1,329				1,329
Wallops Island			373	NA 3,000					3,373
10 TOTAL			5,121	3,025	50,426	44,522	14,255,941	802	103,896

NATIONAL WILDLIFE REFUGES (CONTINUED)

State and Unit	Reserved from Public Domain — Sole or Primary	Secondary	Acquired by Other Federal Agency — Sole or Primary	Secondary	Devise or Gift	Purchased Acres	Purchased Cost	Agreement Easement or Lease	Total Acres
Washington									
Columbia	10,978	R 1,387	1	R 1,275		15,062	458,277	249	28,952
Columbian White-Tailed Deer (4)*						2,621	1,787,821	156	2,777
Conboy Lake						5,509	795,600		5,509
Copalis	61								61
Dungeness	45	CG 190			125	75	348,500	321	756
Flattery Rocks	125								125
Little Pend Oreille	8,791		25,841			5,543	37,718		40,175
McNary			234	E 3,029	5	331	122,955	30	3,629
Nisqually			486			2,311	2,780,216	27	2,824
Pierce					319				319
Protection Land						4	16,900		4
Quillayute Needles	300								300
Ridgefield					25	2,992	1,389,600		3,017
Saddle Mountain		NR 440		NR 30,370					30,810
San Juan Islands	451								451
Toppenish						1,763	599,138		1,763
Turnbull						14,489	252,533	1,076	15,565
Umatilla (4)*		E 103	1,466	E 11,567				870	14,006
Willapa	2,059					9,117	5,150,011	3,121	14,297
17 TOTAL	22,810	2,120	28,028	46,241	474	59,817	13,739,269	5,850	165,340
Wisconsin									
Fox River						641	371,558		641
Gravel Island	27								27
Green Bay	2								2
Horicon						20,976	553,988		20,976
Mississippi River Caue (25)*				E 40,341					40,341
Necedah	30		39,176			343	3,194		39,549
Trempealeau						5,617	897,242		5,617
Upper Mississippi (25)*	662		20		4	46,972	300,687	20	47,678
6 TOTAL	721		39,196	40,341	4	74,549	2,126,669	20	154,831
Wyoming									
Bamforth	201					965	6,368		1,166
Hutton Lake	153					1,275	7,943		1,428
National Elk	4,322				4,470	15,415	5,556,475	40	24,247
Pathfinder	2,295	R 11,502		R 3,010					16,807
Seedskadee	7,500		6,316					1,026	14,842
5 TOTAL	14,471	11,502	6,316	3,010	4,470	17,655	5,570,786	1,066	58,490
413 GRAND TOTAL	79,966,599	689,927	1,137,163	803,247	1,463,667	2,379,724	325,570,914	1,468,826	87,909,153
Territories									
American Samoa									
Rose Atoll			1,613	C 37,453					39,066
Johnston Atoll									
Johnston Island				N 100					100
Puerto Rico									
Cabo Rojo			587						587
Culebra			1,478						1,478
Desecheo			360						360
Pacific Islands									
Baker Island			31,737						31,737
Howland Island			32,550						32,550
Jarvis Island			37,519						37,519
Virgin Islands									
Buck Island			45						45
Green Cay						14	250,000		14
Sandy Point						327	2,500,000	4	331
11 TOTAL			105,889	37,553		341	2,750,000	4	143,787
424 GRAND TOTAL	79,966,599	689,927	1,243,052	840,800	1,463,667	2,380,065	328,320,914	1,468,830	88,052,940

(1) Also in Georgia	AF	— Department of the Air Force
(2) Also in California	BIA	— Bureau of Indian Affairs, Department of the Interior
(3) Also in Arizona	C	— Department of Commerce
(4) Also in Oregon	CG	— Coast Guard, Department of Transportation
(5) Also in Alabama	E	— Corps of Engineers, Department of the Army
(6) Also in Florida	F	— Forest Service, Department of Agriculture
(7) Also in South Carolina	FA	— Federal Aviation Administration, Department of Transportation
(8) Also in Iowa and Missouri	FP	— Federal Power Administration
(9) Also in Iowa, Minnesota, and Wisconsin	LM	— Bureau of Land Management, Department of the Interior
(10) Also in Nebraska	MMS	— Minerals Management Survey, Department of the Interior

NATIONAL WILDLIFE REFUGES (CONTINUED)

(11) Also in Illinois and Missouri	N	— Department of the Navy
(12) Also in Texas	NA	— National Aeronautics and Space Administration
(13) Also in Illinois, Minnesota, and Wisconsin	NR	— Nuclear Regulatory Commission
(14) Also in Tennessee	T	— Tennessee Valley Authority
(15) Also in Nevada	(CAUE)	— Corps of Engineers, Department of the Army, within reach of Upper Mississippi River Wild Life and Fish
(16) Also in Virgina		Refuge
(17) Also in New Mexico	R	— Bureau of Reclamation, Department of the Interior
(18) Also in Illinois, Iowa, and Wisconsin	*	Counted in another State
(19) Also in Iowa		
(20) Also in South Dakota		
(21) Also in Idaho		
(22) Also in Kentucky		
(23) Also in Maryland		
(24) Also in North Carolina		
(25) Also in Illinois, Iowa, and Minnesota		
(26) Also in Washington		
(27) Also in Mississippi		
(28) Also in Louisiana		

Source: FWS

Appendix XII. Endangered and Threatened Wildlife and Plants

Title 50—Wildlife and Fisheries
PART 17—ENDANGERED AND
THREATENED WILDLIFE AND PLANTS

*　　*　　*　　*　　*

Subpart B—Lists

Source: 48 FR 34182, July 27, 1983, unless otherwise noted.

§ 17.11　Endangered and threatened wildlife.

(a) The list in this section contains the names of all species of wildlife which have been determined by the Services to be Endangered or Threatened. It also contains the names of species of wildlife treated as Endangered or Threatened because they are sufficiently similar in appearance to Endangered or Threatened species (see § 17.50 *et seq.*).

(b) The columns entitled "Common Name," "Scientific Name," and "Vertebrate Population Where Endangered or Threatened" define the species of wildlife within the meaning of the Act. Thus, differently classified geographic populations of the same vertebrate subspecies or species shall be identified by their differing geographic boundaries, even though the other two columns are identical. The term "Entire" means that all populations throughout the present range of a vertebrate species are listed. Although common names are included, they cannot be relied upon for identification of any specimen, since they may vary greatly in local usage. The Services shall use the most recently accepted scientific name. In cases in which confusion might arise, a synonym(s) will be provided in parentheses. The Services shall rely to the extent practicable on the *International Code of Zoological Nomenclature.*

(c) In the "Status" column the following symbols are used: "E" for

Endangered, "T" for Threatened, and "E [or T] (S/A)" for similarity of appearance species.

(d) The other data in the list are nonregulatory in nature and are provided for the information of the reader. In the annual revision and compilation of this Title, the following information may be amended without public notice: the spelling of species' names, historical range, footnotes, references to certain other applicable portions of this Title, synonyms, and more current names. In any of these revised entries, neither the species, as defined in paragraph (b) of this section, nor its status may be changed without following the procedures of Part 424 of this Title.

(e) The "Historic Range" indicates the known general distribution of the species or subspecies as reported in the current scientific literature. The present distribution may be greatly reduced from this historic range. This column does not imply any limitation on the application of the prohibitions in the Act or implementing rules. Such prohibitions apply to all individuals of the species, wherever found.

(f)(1) A footnote to the **Federal Register** publication(s) listing or reclassifying a species is indicated under the column "When Listed." Footnote numbers to §§ 17.11 and 17.12 are in the same numerical sequence, since plants and animals may be listed in the same **Federal Register** document. That document, at least since 1973, includes a statement indicating the basis for the listing, as well as the effective date(s) of said listing.

(2) The "Special Rules" and "Critical Habitat" columns provide a cross reference to other sections in Parts 17, 222, 226, or 227. The term "NA" (not applicable) appearing in either of these two columns indicates that there are no

special rules and/or Critical Habitat for that particular species. However, all other appropriate rules in Parts 17, 217–227, and 402 still apply to that species. In addition, there may be other rules in this Title that relate to such wildlife, e.g., port-of-entry requirements. It is not intended that the references in the "Special Rules" column list all the regulations of the two Services which might apply to the species or to the regulations of other Federal agencies or State or local governments.

(g) The listing of a particular taxon includes all lower taxonomic units. For example, the genus *Hylobates* (gibbons) is listed as Endangered throughout its entire range (China, India, and SE Asia); consequently, all species, subspecies, and populations of that genus are considered listed as Endangered for the purposes of the Act. In 1978 (43 FR 6230–6233) the species *Haliaeetus leucocephalus* (bald eagle) was listed as Threatened in "USA (WA, OR, MN, WI, WI, MI)" rather than its entire population; thus, all individuals of the bald eagle found in those five States are considered listed as Threatened for the purposes of the Act.

(h) The "List of Endangered and Threatened Wildlife" is provided below:

Editorial Note: This is a compilation and special reprint of 50 CFR 17.11 and 17.12 and is current as of the date shown on the cover. Minor changes and corrections to the October 1, 1983, compilation of 50 CFR have been incorporated in this printing, as well as all published final rules that have subsequently appeared in the **Federal Register.** Otherwise, no entry in these lists has been significantly affected. This list has been prepared by the staff of the Office of Endangered Species, U.S. Fish and Wildlife Service, Washington, D.C. 20240. Readers are requested to advise the Service of any errors or omissions to this list. Copies are available from the Publications Unit, U.S. Fish and Wildlife Service, Washington, D.C. 20240.

Common name	Scientific name	Historic range	Vertebrate population where endangered or threatened	Status	When listed	Critical habitat	Special rules
MAMMALS							
Anoa, lowland	*Bubalus depressicornis (=B. anoa depressicornis)*	Indonesia	Entire	E	3	NA	NA
Anoa, mountain	*Bubalus quarlesi (=B. anoa quarlesi)*	do	do	E	15	NA	NA
Antelope, giant sable	*Hippotragus niger variani*	Angola	do	E	15	NA	NA
Argali	*Ovis ammon hodgsoni*	China (Tibet, Himalayas)	do	E	15	NA	NA
Armadillo, giant	*Priodontes maximus (=giganteus)*	Venezuela and Guyana to Argentina	do	E	3	NA	NA
Armadillo, pink fairy	*Chlamyphorus truncatus*	Argentina	do	E	3	NA	NA
Ass, African wild	*Equus asinus (=africanus)*	Somalia, Sudan, Ethiopia	do	E	3	NA	NA
Ass, Asian wild (=kulan, onager)	*Equus hemionus*	Southwestern and Central Asia	do	E	3	NA	NA
Avahi	*Avahi (=Lichanotus) laniger (=entire genus)*	Malagasy Republic (=Madagascar)	do	E	3	NA	NA
Aye-Aye	*Daubentonia madagascariensis*	Malagasy Republic (=Madagascar)	do	E	3	NA	NA
Babirusa	*Babyrousa babyrussa*	Indonesia	do	E	15	NA	NA
Baboon, gelada	*Theropithecus gelada*	Ethiopia	do	T	16	NA	17.40(c)
Bandicoot, barred	*Perameles bougainville*	Australia	do	E	4	NA	NA
Bandicoot, desert	*Perameles eremiana*	do	do	E	6	NA	NA
Bandicoot, lesser rabbit	*Macrotis leucura*	do	do	E	4	NA	NA
Bandicoot, pig-footed	*Chaeropus ecaudatus*	do	do	E	4	NA	NA
Bandicoot, rabbit	*Macrotis lagotis*	do	do	E	4	NA	NA
Banteng	*Bos javanicus (=banteng)*	Southeast Asia	do	E	3	NA	NA
Bat, Bulmer's fruit (flying fox)	*Aproteles bulmerae*	Papua New Guinea	do	E	139	NA	NA
Bat, bumblebee	*Craseonycteris thonglongyai*	Thailand	do	E	139	NA	NA
Bat, gray	*Myotis grisescens*	Central and Southeastern U.S.A.	do	E	13	NA	NA
Bat, Hawaiian hoary	*Lasiurus cinereus semotus*	U.S.A. (Hawaii)	do	E	2	NA	NA
Bat, Indiana	*Myotis sodalis*	Eastern and Midwestern U.S.A.	do	E	1	17.95(a)	NA
Bat, Ozark big-eared	*Plecotus townsendii ingens*	U.S.A. (MO, OK, AR)	do	E	85	NA	NA
Bat, Rodrigues fruit (flying fox)	*Pteropus rodricensis*	Indian Ocean: Rodrigues Island	do	E	139	NA	NA
Bat, Singapore roundleaf horseshoe	*Hipposideros ridleyi*	Malaysia	do	E	139	NA	NA
Bat, Virginia big-eared	*Plecotus townsendii virginianus*	U.S.A. (KY, WV, VA)	do	E	85	17.95(a)	NA
Bear, brown	*Ursus arctos pruinosus*	China (Tibet)	do	E	15	NA	NA
Bear, brown	*Ursus arctos arctos*	Palearctic	do	E	15	NA	NA
Bear, brown or grizzly	*Ursus arctos horribilis*	Canada, Western U.S.A.	Italy, U.S.A.—48 conterminous States.	T	1, 2, 9	NA	17.40(b)
Bear, Mexican grizzly	*Ursus arctos nelsoni*	Mexico	Entire	E	3	NA	NA
Beaver	*Castor fiber birulai*	Mongolia	do	E	15	NA	NA
Bison, wood	*Bison bison athabascae*	Canada, Northwestern U.S.A.	Canada	E	3	NA	NA
Bobcat	*Felis rufus escuinapae*	Central Mexico	Entire	E	15	NA	NA
Bontebok (antelope)	*Damaliscus dorcas dorcas*	South Africa	do	E	15	NA	NA
Camel, Bactrian	*Camelus bactrianus (=ferus)*	Mongolia, China	do	E	15	NA	NA
Caribou, woodland	*Rangifer tarandus caribou*	Canada, U.S.A. (AK, ID, ME, MI, MN, MT, NH, VT, WA, WI).	Canada (that part of S.E. Brit. Col. bounded by the Can.-USA border, Columbia R., Kootenay R., Kootenay L., and Kootenai R.), U.S.A. (ID, WA).	E	128E, 136E, 143	NA	NA
Cat, Andean	*Felis jacobita*	Chile, Peru, Bolivia, Argentina	Entire	E	15	NA	NA
Cat, black-footed	*Felis nigripes*	Southern Africa	do	E	15	NA	NA

Species — Common name	Species — Scientific name	Historic range	Vertebrate population where endangered or threatened	Status	When listed	Critical habitat	Special rules
Cat, flat-headed	Felis planiceps	Malaysia, Indonesia	do.	E	15	NA	NA
Cat, Iriomote	Felis (Mayailurus) iriomotensis	Japan (Iriomote Island, Ryukyu Islands)	do.	E	50	NA	NA
Cat, leopard	Felis bengalensis bengalensis	India, Southeast Asia	do.	E	15	NA	NA
Cat, marbled	Felis marmorata	Nepal, Southeast Asia, Indonesia	do.	E	139	NA	NA
Cat, Pakistan sand	Felis margarita scheffeli	Pakistan	do.	E	15	NA	NA
Cat, Temminck's (=golden cat)	Felis temmincki	Nepal, China, Southeast Asia, Indonesia (Sumatra)	do.	E	15	NA	NA
Cat, tiger	Felis tigrinus	Costa Rica to northern Argentina	do.	E	5	NA	NA
Chamois, Apennine	Rupicapra rupicapra ornata	Italy	do.	E	15	NA	NA
Cheetah	Acinonyx jubatus	Africa to India	do.	E	3, 5	NA	NA
Chimpanzee	Pan troglodytes	West and Central Africa	do.	T	16	NA	17.40(c)
Chimpanzee, pygmy	Pan paniscus	Zaire	do.	T	16	NA	17.40(c)
Chinchilla	Chinchilla brevicaudata boliviana	Bolivia	do.	E	15	NA	NA
Civet, Malabar large-spotted	Viverra megaspila civettina	India	do.	E	50	NA	NA
Cougar, eastern	Felis concolor couguar	Eastern North America	do.	E	6	NA	NA
Deer, Bactrian	Cervus elaphus bactrianus	U.S.S.R., Afghanistan	do.	E	50	NA	NA
Deer, Bawean	Axis (=Cervus) porcinus kuhli	Indonesia	do.	E	15	NA	NA
Deer, Barbary	Cervus elaphus barbarus	Morocco, Tunisia, Algeria	do.	E	50	NA	NA
Deer, Cedros Island mule	Odocoileus hemionus cedrosensis	Mexico (Cedros Island)	do.	E	10	NA	NA
Deer, Columbian white-tailed	Odocoileus virginianus leucurus	U.S.A. (WA, OR)	do.	E	1	NA	NA
Deer, Corsican red	Cervus elaphus corsicanus	Corsica, Sardinia	do.	E	50	NA	NA
Deer, Eld's brow-antlered	Cervus eldi	India to Southeast Asia	do.	E	3	NA	NA
Deer, Formosan sika	Cervus nippon taiouanus	Taiwan	do.	E	50	NA	NA
Deer, hog	Axis (=Cervus) porcinus annamiticus	Thailand, Indochina	do.	E	15	NA	NA
Deer, key	Odocoileus virginianus clavium	U.S.A. (southern Florida)	do.	E	1	NA	NA
Deer, marsh	Blastocerus dichotomus	Argentina, Uruguay, Paraguay, Bolivia, Brazil	do.	E	3	NA	NA
Deer, McNeill's	Cervus elaphus macneilli	China (Sinkiang, Tibet)	do.	E	3	NA	NA
Deer, musk	Moschus spp. (all species)	Central and East Asia	Afghanistan, Bhutan, Burma, China (Tibet, Yunnan), India, Nepal, Pakistan, Sikkim	E	15	NA	NA
Deer, North China sika	Cervus nippon mandarinus	China (Shantung and Chihli Provinces)	Entire	E	50	NA	NA
Deer, pampas	Ozotoceros bezoarticus	Brazil, Argentina, Uruguay, Bolivia, Paraguay	do.	E	15	NA	NA
Deer, Persian fallow	Dama dama mesopotamica	Iraq, Iran	do.	E	3	NA	NA
Deer, Philippine	Axis (=Cervus) porcinus calamianensis	Philippines (Calamian Islands)	do.	E	15	NA	NA
Deer, Ryukyu sika	Cervus nippon keramae	Japan (Ryukyu Islands)	do.	E	50	NA	NA
Deer, Shansi sika	Cervus nippon grassianus	China (Shansi Province)	do.	E	50	NA	NA
Deer, South China sika	Cervus nippon kopschi	Southern China	do.	E	50	NA	NA
Deer, swamp (= barasingha)	Cervus duvauceli	India, Nepal	do.	E	3	NA	NA
Deer, Yarkand	Cervus elaphus yarkandensis	China (Sinkiang)	do.	E	50	NA	NA
Dhole (= Asiatic wild dog)	Cuon alpinus	U.S.S.R., Korea, China, India, Southeast Asia	do.	E	3	NA	NA
Dibbler	Antechinus apicalis	Australia	do.	E	4	NA	NA
Dog, African wild	Lycaon pictus	Sub-Saharan Africa	do.	E	139	NA	NA
Drill	Papio leucophaeus	Equatorial West Africa	do.	E	16	NA	NA
Dugong	Dugong dugon	East Africa to southern Japan, including U.S.A. (Trust Territories)	do.	E	4	NA	NA
Duiker, Jentink's	Cephalophus jentinki	Sierra Leone, Liberia, Ivory Coast	do.	E	50	NA	NA
Eland, Western giant	Taurotragus derbianus derbianus	Senegal to Ivory Coast	do.	E	50	NA	NA

Species Common name	Species Scientific name	Historic range	Vertebrate population where endangered or threatened	Status	When listed	Critical habitat	Special rules
Elephant, African	*Loxodonta africana*	Africa	do	T	40	NA	17.40(e)
Elephant, Asian	*Elephas maximus*	South-central and Southeast Asia	do	E	15	NA	NA
Ferret, black-footed	*Mustela nigripes*	Western U.S.A., Western Canada	do	E	1, 3	NA	NA
Fox, Northern swift	*Vulpes velox hebes*	U.S.A. (northern plains), Canada	Canada	E	3	NA	NA
Fox, San Joaquin kit	*Vulpes macrotis mutica*	U.S.A. (California)	Entire	E	1	NA	NA
Fox, Simien	*Canis (Simenia) simensis*	Ethiopia	do	E	50	NA	NA
Gazelle, Clark's (= Dibatag)	*Ammodorcas clarkei*	Somalia, Ethiopia	do	E	3	NA	NA
Gazelle, Cuvier's	*Gazella cuvieri*	Morocco, Algeria, Tunisia	do	E	3	NA	NA
Gazelle, Mhorr	*Gazella dama mhorr*	Morocco	do	E	3	NA	NA
Gazelle, Moroccan (= Dorcas)	*Gazella dorcas massaesyla*	Morocco, Algeria, Tunisia	do	E	3	NA	NA
Gazelle, Rio de Oro Dama	*Gazella dama lozanoi*	Western Sahara	do	E	3	NA	NA
Gazelle, Arabian	*Gazella gazella*	Arabian Peninsula, Palestine, Sinai	do	E	50	NA	NA
Gazelle, sand	*Gazella subgutturosa marica*	Jordan, Arabian Peninsula	do	E	50	NA	NA
Gazelle, Saudi Arabian	*Gazella dorcas saudiya*	Israel, Iraq, Jordan, Syria, Arabian Peninsula.	do	E	50	NA	NA
Gazelle, Pelzeln's	*Gazella dorcas pelzelni*	Somalia	do	E	50	NA	NA
Gazelle, slender-horned (= Rhim)	*Gazella leptoceros*	Sudan, Egypt, Algeria, Libya	do	E	3	NA	NA
Gibbons	*Hylobates spp. (including Nomascus)*	China, India, Southeast Asia	do	E	3, 15	NA	NA
Goat, wild (= Chiltan markhor)	*Capra aegagrus (=falconeri chiltanensis)*	Southwestern Asia	Chiltan Range of west-central Pakistan.	E	15	NA	NA
Goral	*Nemorhaedus goral*	East Asia	Entire	E	15	NA	NA
Gorilla	*Gorilla gorilla*	Central and Western Africa	do	E	3	NA	NA
Hare, hispid	*Caprolagus hispidus*	India, Nepal, Bhutan	do	E	15	NA	NA
Hartebeest, Swayne's	*Alcelaphus buselaphus swaynei*	Ethiopia, Somalia	do	E	50	NA	NA
Hartebeest, Tora	*Alcelaphus buselaphus tora*	Ethiopia, Sudan, Egypt	do	E	50	NA	NA
Hog, pygmy	*Sus salvanius*	India, Nepal, Bhutan, Sikkim	do	E	3	NA	NA
Horse, Przewalski's	*Equus przewalskii*	Mongolia, China	do	E	15	NA	NA
Huemul, North Andean	*Hippocamelus antisensis*	Ecuador, Peru, Chile, Bolivia, Argentina	do	E	15	NA	NA
Huemul, South Andean	*Hippocamelus bisulcus*	Chile, Argentina	do	E	15	NA	NA
Hyena, Barbary	*Hyaena hyaena barbara*	Morocco, Algeria, Tunisia	do	E	3	NA	NA
Hyena, brown	*Hyaena brunnea*	Southern Africa	do	E	3	NA	NA
Ibex, Pyrenean	*Capra pyrenaica pyrenaica*	Spain	do	E	3	NA	NA
Ibex, Walia	*Capra walie*	Ethiopia	do	E	3	NA	NA
Impala, black-faced	*Aepyceros melampus petersi*	Namibia, Angola	do	E	3	NA	NA
Indri	*Indri indri (=entire genus)*	Malagasy Republic (=Madagascar)	do	E	3	NA	NA
Jaguar	*Panthera onca*	U.S.A. (TX, NM, AZ), C. and S. America.	Mexico southward.	E	5	NA	NA
Jaguarundi	*Felis yagouaroundi cacomitli*	U.S.A. (Texas), Mexico	Entire	E	15	NA	NA
Jaguarundi	*Felis yagouaroundi fossata*	Mexico, Nicaragua	do	E	15	NA	NA
Jaguarundi	*Felis yagouaroundi panamensis*	Nicaragua, Costa Rica, Panama	do	E	15	NA	NA
Jaguarundi	*Felis yagouaroundi tolteca*	U.S.A. (Arizona), Mexico	do	E	15	NA	NA
Kangaroo, eastern gray	*Macropus giganteus (all subspecies except tasmaniensis).*	Australia	do	T	7	NA	17.40(a)
Kangaroo, red	*Macropus (Megaleia) rufus*	do	do	T	7	NA	17.40(a)
Kangaroo, Tasmanian forester	*Macropus giganteus tasmaniensis*	Australia (Tasmania)	do	T	6	NA	NA
Kangaroo, western gray	*Macropus fuliginosus*	Australia	do	T	7	NA	17.40(a)
Kouprey	*Bos sauveli*	Vietnam, Laos, Cambodia, Thailand	do	E	3	NA	NA
Langur, capped	*Presbytis pileata*	India, Burma, Bangladesh	do	E	15	NA	NA
Langur, entellus	*Presbytis entellus*	China (Tibet), India, Pakistan, Kashmir, Sri Lanka, Sikkim, Bangladesh.	do	E	15	NA	NA
Langur, Douc	*Pygathrix nemaeus*	Cambodia, Laos, Vietnam	do	E	3	NA	NA
Langur, Francois'	*Presbytis francoisi*	China (Kwangsi), Indochina	do	E	16	NA	NA
Langur, golden	*Presbytis geei*	India (Assam), Bhutan	do	E	15	NA	NA

Species – Common name	Species – Scientific name	Historic range	Vertebrate population where endangered or threatened	Status	When listed	Critical habitat	Special rules
Langur, long-tailed	*Presbytis potenzlani*	Indonesia	do	T	16	NA	17.40(c)
Langur, Pagi Island	*Nasalis (Simias) concolor*	do	do	E	3	NA	NA
Langur, purple-faced	*Presbytis senex*	Sri Lanka (=Ceylon)	do	T	16	NA	17.40(c)
Langur, Tonkin snub-nosed	*Pygathrix (Rhinopithecus) avunculus*	Vietnam	do	T	16	NA	17.40(c)
Lechwe, red	*Kobus leche*	Southern Africa	do	T	3, 15, 106	NA	NA
Lemurs	Lemuridae (incl. Cheirogaleidae, Lepiemuridae); all members of genera *Lemur, Phaner, Hapalemur, Lepiemur, Microcebus, Allocebus, Cheirogaleus, Varecia.*	Malagasy Republic (=Madagascar)	do	E	3, 15	NA	NA
Leopard	*Panthera pardus*	Africa, Asia	Wherever found, except where it is listed as Threatened as set forth below.	E	3, 5, 114	NA	NA
Leopard	*Panthera pardus*	Africa, Asia	In Africa, in the wild, south of, and including, the following countries: Gabon, Congo, Zaire, Uganda, Kenya.	T	3, 5, 114	NA	17.40(f)
Leopard, clouded	*Neofelis nebulosa*	Southeast and south-central Asia, Taiwan.	Entire	E	3, 15	NA	NA
Leopard, snow	*Panthera uncia*	Central Asia	do	E	5	NA	NA
Linsang, spotted	*Prionodon pardicolor*	Nepal, Assam, Vietnam, Cambodia, Laos, Burma.	do	E	15	NA	NA
Lion, Asiatic	*Panthera leo persica*	Turkey to India.	do	E	3	NA	17.40(c)
Loris, lesser slow	*Nycticebus pygmaeus*	Indochina	do	T	16	NA	NA
Lynx, Spanish	*Felis (= Lynx) pardina*	Spain, Portugal	do	E	3	NA	17.40(c)
Macaque, Formosan rock	*Macaca cyclopis*	Taiwan	do	T	16	NA	17.40(c)
Macaque, Japanese	*Macaca fuscata*	Japan (Shikoku, Kyushu and Honshu Islands).	do	T	16	NA	17.40(c)
Macaque, lion-tailed	*Macaca silenus*	India	do	E	3	NA	NA
Macaque, stump-tailed	*Macaca arctoides*	India (Assam) to southern China.	do	T	16	NA	17.40(c)
Macaque, Toque	*Macaca sinica*	Sri Lanka (=Ceylon)	do	T	16	NA	17.40(c)
Manatee, Amazonian	*Trichechus inunguis*	South America (Amazon River Basin).	do	E	3	NA	NA
Manatee, West African	*Trichechus senegalensis*	West Coast of Africa from Senegal River to Cuanza River.	do	T	52	NA	NA
Manatee, West Indian (Florida)	*Trichechus manatus*	U.S.A. (southeastern), Caribbean Sea, South America.	do	E	1, 3	17.95(a)	NA
Mandrill	*Papio sphinx*	Equatorial West Africa.	do	E	16	NA	NA
Mangabey, Tana River	*Cercocebus galeritus*	Kenya.	do	E	3	NA	NA
Mangabey, white-collared	*Cercocebus torquatus*	Senegal to Ghana; Nigeria to Gabon.	do	E	16	NA	NA
Margay	*Felis wiedii*	U.S.A. (Texas), C. and S. America.	Mexico southward.	E	5	NA	NA
Markhor, Kabal	*Capra falconeri megaceros*	Afghanistan, Pakistan.	Entire	E	15	NA	NA
Markhor, straight-horned	*Capra falconeri jerdoni*	do	do	E	15	NA	NA
Marmoset, buff-headed	*Callithrix flaviceps*	Brazil	do	E	139	NA	NA
Marmoset, cotton-top	*Saguinus oedipus*	Costa Rica to Colombia.	do	E	16	NA	NA
Marmoset, Goeldi's	*Callimico goeldii*	Brazil, Colombia, Ecuador, Peru, Bolivia.	do	E	3	NA	NA
Marmot, Vancouver Island	*Marmota vancouverensis*	Canada (Vancouver Island)	do	E	139	NA	NA

Species		Historic range	Vertebrate population where endangered or threatened	Status	When listed	Critical habitat	Special rules
Common name	Scientific name						
Marsupial, eastern jerboa	Antechinomys laniger	Australia	do	E	4	NA	NA
Marsupial-mouse, large desert	Sminthopsis psammophila	do	do	E	4	NA	NA
Marsupial-mouse, long-tailed	Sminthopsis longicaudata	do	do	E	4	NA	NA
Marten, Formosan yellow-throated	Martes flavigula chrysospila	Taiwan	do	E	3	NA	NA
Monkey, black colobus	Colobus satanas	Equatorial Guinea, People's Republic of Congo, Cameroon, Gabon.	do	E	16	NA	NA
Monkey, black howler	Alouatta pigra	Mexico, Guatemala, Belize	do	T	16	NA	17.40(c)
Monkey, Diana	Cercopithecus diana	Coastal West Africa	do	E	16	NA	NA
Monkey, howler	Alouatta palliata (= villosa)	Mexico to South America	do	E	15	NA	NA
Monkey, L'hoest's	Cercopithecus lhoesti	Upper Eastern Congo Basin, Cameroon.	do	E	16	NA	NA
Monkey, Preuss' red colobus	Colobus badius preussi	Cameroon	do	E	139	NA	NA
Monkey, proboscis	Nasalis larvatus	Borneo	do	E	15	NA	NA
Monkey, red-backed squirrel	Saimiri oerstedii	Costa Rica, Panama	do	E	3	NA	NA
Monkey, red-bellied	Cercopithecus erythrogaster	Western Nigeria	do	E	16	NA	NA
Monkey, red-eared nose-spotted	Cercopithecus erythrotis	Nigeria, Cameroon, Fernando Po	do	E	16	NA	NA
Monkey, spider	Ateles geoffroyi frontatus	Costa Rica, Nicaragua	do	E	3	NA	NA
Monkey, spider	Ateles geoffroyi panamensis	Costa Rica, Panama	do	E	3	NA	NA
Monkey, Tana River red colobus	Colobus rufomitratus (= badius) rufomitratus.	Kenya	do	E	3, 16	NA	NA
Monkey, woolly spider	Brachyteles arachnoides	Brazil	do	E	3	NA	NA
Monkey, yellow-tailed woolly	Lagothrix flavicauda	Andes of northern Peru	do	E	16	NA	NA
Monkey, Zanzibar red colobus	Colobus kirki	Tanzania	do	E	3	NA	NA
Mouse, Australian native	Zyzomys (= Notomys) pedunculatus	Australia	do	E	15	NA	NA
Mouse, Australian native	Notomys aquilo	do	do	E	15	NA	NA
Mouse, Field's	Pseudomys fieldi	do	do	E	4	NA	NA
Mouse, Gould's	Pseudomys gouldii	do	do	E	6	NA	NA
Mouse, Key Largo cotton	Peromyscus gossypinus allapaticola	U.S.A. (Florida)	do	E	131E	NA	NA
Mouse, New Holland	Pseudomys novaehollandiae	Australia	do	E	4	NA	NA
Mouse, salt marsh harvest	Reithrodontomys raviventris	U.S.A. (California)	do	E	2	NA	NA
Mouse, Shark Bay	Pseudomys praeconis	Australia	do	E	4	NA	NA
Mouse, Shortridge's	Pseudomys shortridgei	do	do	E	4	NA	NA
Mouse, Smoky	Pseudomys fumeus	do	do	E	4	NA	NA
Mouse, western	Pseudomys occidentalis	do	do	E	4	NA	NA
Muntjac, Fea's	Muntiacus feae	Northern Thailand, Burma.	do	E	50	NA	NA
Native-cat, eastern	Dasyurus viverrinus	Australia	do	E	6	NA	NA
Numbat	Myrmecobius fasciatus	do	do	E	4, 6	NA	NA
Ocelot	Felis pardalis	U.S.A. (TX, AZ) to C. and S. America	do	E	5, 119	NA	NA
Orangutan	Pongo pygmaeus	Borneo, Sumatra	do	E	3	NA	NA
Oryx, Arabian	Oryx leucoryx	Arabian Peninsula	do	E	3	NA	NA
Otter, Cameroon clawless	Aonyx (Paraonyx) congica microdon	Cameroon, Nigeria	do	E	3	NA	NA
Otter, giant	Pteronura brasiliensis	South America	do	E	3	NA	NA
Otter, long-tailed	Lutra longicaudis (incl. platensis)	do	do	E	3, 15	NA	NA
Otter, marine	Lutra felina	Peru south to Straits of Magellan	do	E	15	NA	NA
Otter, southern river	Lutra provocax	Chile, Argentina	do	E	15	NA	NA
Otter, southern sea	Enhydra lutris nereis	West coast U.S.A. (WA, OR, CA) south to Mexico (Baja California).	do	T	21	NA	NA
Panda, giant	Ailuropoda melanoleuca	People's Republic of China	do	E	139	NA	NA
Pangolin (= scaly anteater)	Manis temminckii	Africa	do	E	15	NA	NA
Panther, Florida	Felis concolor coryi	U.S.A. (LA and AR east to SC and FL)	do	E	1	NA	NA
Planigale, little	Planigale ingrami subtilissima (formerly P. subtilissima).	Australia	do	E	4	NA	NA
Planigale, southern	Planigale tenuirostris	do	do	E	4	NA	NA
Porcupine, thin-spined	Chaetomys subspinosus	Brazil	do	E	3	NA	NA

Species Common name	Species Scientific name	Historic range	Vertebrate population where endangered or threatened	Status	When listed	Critical habitat	Special rules
Possum, mountain pygmy	*Burramys parvus*	Australia	do	E	4	NA	NA
Possum, scaly-tailed	*Wyulda squamicaudata*	do	do	E	4	NA	NA
Prairie dog, Mexican	*Cynomys mexicanus*	Mexico	do	E	3	NA	NA
Prairie dog, Utah	*Cynomys parvidens*	U.S.A. (Utah)	do	T	6, 149	NA	NA
Pronghorn, peninsular	*Antilocapra americana peninsularis*	Mexico (Baja California)	do	E	10	NA	NA
Pronghorn, Sonoran	*Antilocapra americana sonoriensis*	U.S.A. (AZ), Mexico	do	E	1, 3	NA	NA
Pudu	*Pudu pudu*	Southern South America	do	E	15	NA	NA
Puma, Costa Rican	*Felis concolor costaricensis*	Nicaragua, Panama, Costa Rica	do	E	15	NA	NA
Quokka	*Setonix brachyurus*	Australia	do	E	6	NA	NA
Rabbit, Ryukyu	*Pentalagus furnessi*	Japan (Ryukyu Islands)	do	E	50	NA	NA
Rabbit, volcano	*Romerolagus diazi*	Mexico	do	E	3	NA	NA
Rat, false water	*Xeromys myoides*	Australia	do	E	4	NA	NA
Rat, stick-nest	*Leporillus conditor*	U.S.A. (California)	do	E	6	NA	NA
Rat, Morro Bay kangaroo	*Dipodomys heermanni morroensis*	U.S.A. (California)	do	E	2	17.95(a)	NA
Rat-kangaroo, brush-tailed	*Bettongia penicillata*	Australia	do	E	4	NA	NA
Rat-kangaroo, Gaimard's	*Bettongia gaimardi*	do	do	E	6	NA	NA
Rat-kangaroo, Lesuer's	*Bettongia lesueur*	do	do	E	4	NA	NA
Rat-kangaroo, plain	*Caloprymnus campestris*	do	do	E	4	NA	NA
Rat-kangaroo, Queensland	*Bettongia tropica*	do	do	E	4	NA	NA
Rhinoceros, black	*Diceros bicornis*	Sub-Saharan Africa	do	E	97	NA	NA
Rhinoceros, great Indian	*Rhinoceros unicornis*	India, Nepal	do	E	4	NA	NA
Rhinoceros, Javan	*Rhinoceros sondaicus*	Indonesia, Indochina, Burma, Thailand, Sikkim, Bangladesh, Malaysia	do	E	3	NA	NA
Rhinoceros, northern white	*Ceratotherium simum cottoni*	Zaire, Sudan, Uganda, Central African Republic	do	E	3	NA	NA
Rhinoceros, Sumatran	*Dicerorhinus (=Didermoceros) sumatrensis*	Bangladesh to Vietnam to Indonesia (Borneo)	do	E	3	NA	NA
Saiga, Mongolian (antelope)	*Saiga tatarica mongolica*	Mongolia	do	E	15	NA	NA
Saki, white-nosed	*Chiropotes albinasus*	Brazil	do	E	3	NA	NA
Seal, Caribbean monk	*Monachus tropicalis*	Caribbean Sea, Gulf of Mexico	do	E	1, 2, 45	NA	NA
Seal, Hawaiian monk	*Monachus schauinslandi*	Hawaiian Archipelago	do	E	18	NA	NA
Seal, Mediterranean monk	*Monachus monachus*	Mediterranean, Northwest African Coast and Black Sea	do	E	3	NA	NA
Seledang (=Gaur)	*Bos gaurus*	Bangladesh, Southeast Asia, India	do	E	3	NA	NA
Serow, Sumatran	*Capricornis sumatraensis*	Sumatra	do	E	15	NA	NA
Serval, Barbary	*Felis serval constantina*	Algeria	do	E	3	NA	NA
Shapo	*Ovis vignei vignei*	Kashmir	do	E	15	NA	NA
Shou	*Cervus elaphus wallichi*	Tibet, Bhutan	do	E	3	NA	NA
Siamang	*Symphalangus syndactylus*	Malaysia, Indonesia	do	E	15	NA	NA
Sifakas	*Propithecus spp. (all species)*	Malagasy Republic (= Madagascar)	do	E	4	NA	NA
Sloth, Brazilian three-toed	*Bradypus torquatus*	Brazil	do	E	3, 4	NA	NA
Solenodon, Cuban	*Solenodon (Atopogale) cubanus*	Cuba	do	E	3	NA	NA
Solenodon, Haitian	*Solenodon paradoxus*	Dominican Republic, Haiti	do	E	3	NA	NA
Squirrel, Delmarva Peninsula fox	*Sciurus niger cinereus*	U.S.A. (DelMarVa Peninsula to South-east PA)	do	E	1	NA	NA
Stag, Barbary	*Cervus elaphus barbarus*	Tunisia, Algeria	do	E	3	NA	NA
Stag, Kashmir	*Cervus elaphus hanglu*	Kashmir	do	E	3	NA	NA
Suni, Zanzibar	*Neotragus (Nesotragus) moschatus moschatus*	Zanzibar (and nearby islands)	do	E	50	NA	NA
Tahr, Arabian	*Hemitragus jayakari*	Oman	do	E	50	NA	NA
Tamaraw	*Bubalus mindorensis*	Philippines	do	E	4	NA	NA

Species — Common name	Species — Scientific name	Historic range	Vertebrate population where endangered or threatened	Status	When listed	Critical habitat	Special rules
Tamarin, golden-rumped (=golden-headed Tamarin; =golden-lion Marmoset).	Leontopithecus (=Leontideus) spp. (all species).	Brazil	do	E	3	NA	NA
Tamarin, pied	Saguinus bicolor	Northern Brazil	do	E	16	NA	NA
Tamarin, white-footed	Saguinus leucopus	Northern Colombia	do	T	16	NA	17.40(c)
Tapir, Asian	Tapirus indicus	Burma, Laos, Cambodia, Vietnam, Malaysia, Indonesia, Thailand.	do	E	15	NA	NA
Tapir, Brazilian	Tapirus terrestris	Colombia and Venezuela south to Paraguay and Argentina.	do	E	3	NA	NA
Tapir, Central American	Tapirus bairdii	Southern Mexico to Colombia and Ecuador.	do	E	3	NA	NA
Tapir, mountain	Tapirus pinchaque	Colombia, Ecuador and possibly Peru and Venezuela.	do	E	3	NA	NA
Tarsier, Philippine	Tarsius syrichta	Philippines	do	T	16	NA	17.40(c)
Tiger	Panthera tigris	Temperate and Tropical Asia	do	E	3, 5	NA	NA
Tiger, Tasmanian (=Thylacine)	Thylacinus cynocephalus	Australia	do	E	3	NA	NA
Uakari (all species)	Cacajao spp. (all species)	Peru, Brazil, Ecuador, Columbia, Venezuela.	do	E	3	NA	NA
Urial	Ovis musimon (=orientalis) ophion	Cyprus	do	E	15	NA	NA
Vicuna	Vicugna vicugna	South America (Andes)	do	E	3	NA	NA
Wallaby, banded hare	Lagostrophus fasciatus	Australia	do	E	4	NA	NA
Wallaby, brindled nail-tailed	Onychogalea fraenata	do	do	E	4	NA	NA
Wallaby, crescent nail-tailed	Onychogalea lunata	do	do	E	4	NA	NA
Wallaby, parma	Macropus parma	do	do	E	4	NA	NA
Wallaby, Western hare	Lagorchestes hirsutus	do	do	E	4	NA	NA
Wallaby, yellow-footed rock	Petrogale xanthopus	do	do	E	6	NA	NA
Whale, blue	Balaenoptera musculus	Oceanic	do	E	3	NA	NA
Whale, bowhead	Balaena mysticetus	Oceanic (north latitudes only)	do	E	3	NA	NA
Whale, finback	Balaenoptera physalus	Oceanic	do	E	3	NA	NA
Whale, gray	Eschrichtius robustus	North Pacific Ocean: coastal and Bering Sea.	do	E	3	NA	NA
Whale, humpback	Megaptera novaeangliae	Oceanic	do	E	3	NA	NA
Whale, right	Balaena glacialis	do	do	E	3	NA	NA
Whale, Sei	Balaenoptera borealis	do	do	E	3	NA	NA
Whale, sperm	Physeter catodon	do	do	E	3	NA	NA
Wolf, gray	Canis lupus	Holarctic	U.S.A. (48 conterminous States, except MN), Mexico	E	1, 6, 13, 15, 35	17.95(a)	NA
Wolf, gray	Canis lupus	do	U.S.A. (MN)	T	35	17.95(a)	17.40(d)
Wolf, maned	Chrysocyon brachyurus	Argentina, Bolivia, Brazil, Paraguay, Uruguay.	Entire	E	4	NA	NA
Wolf, red	Canis rufus	U.S.A. (southeastern U.S.A. west to central TX).	do	E	1	NA	NA
Wombat, hairy-nosed (=Barnard's and Queensland hairy-nosed).	Lasiorhinus krefftii (formerly L. barnardi and L. gillespiei).	Australia	do	E	4, 6	NA	NA
Woodrat, Key Largo	Neotoma floridana smalli	U.S.A. (FL)	do	E	131E	NA	NA
Yak, wild	Bos grunniens	China (Tibet), India	do	E	3	NA	NA
Zebra, Grevy's	Equus grevyi	Kenya, Ethiopia, Somalia	do	T	54	NA	NA
Zebra, Hartmann's mountain	Equus zebra hartmannae	Namibia, Angola	do	T	54, 111	NA	NA
Zebra, mountain	Equus zebra zebra	South Africa	do	E	15, 111	NA	NA

BIRDS

Common name	Scientific name	Historic range	Vertebrate population where endangered or threatened	Status	When listed	Critical habitat	Special rules
Akepa, Hawaii (honeycreeper)	Loxops coccineus coccineus	U.S.A. (Hawaii)	do.	E	2	NA	NA
Akepa, Maui (honeycreeper)	Loxops coccineus ochraceus	do.	do.	E	2	NA	NA
Akialoa, Kauai (honeycreeper)	Hemignathus procerus	do.	do.	E	1	NA	NA
Akiapolaau (honeycreeper)	Hemignathus munroi (= wilsoni)	do.	do.	E	1	NA	NA
Albatross, short-tailed	Diomedea albatrus	North Pacific Ocean: Japan, U.S.S.R., U.S.A. (AK, CA, HI, OR, WA).	Entire, except U.S.A.	E	3	NA	NA
Blackbird, yellow-shouldered	Agelaius xanthomus	U.S.A. (Puerto Rico)	Entire	E	17	17.95(b)	NA
Bobwhite, masked (quail)	Colinus virginianus ridgwayi	U.S.A. (Arizona), Mexico (Sonora)	do.	E	1,3	NA	NA
Booby, Abbott's	Sula abbotti	Indian Ocean: Christmas Island	do.	E	15	NA	NA
Bristlebird, western	Dasyornis brachypterus longirostris	Australia	do.	E	15	NA	NA
Bristlebird, western rufous	Dasyornis broadbenti littoralis	do.	do.	E	15	NA	NA
Bulbul, Mauritius olivaceous	Hypsipetes borbonicus olivaceus	Indian Ocean: Mauritius.	do.	E	3	NA	NA
Bullfinch, Sao Miguel (finch)	Pyrrhula pyrrhula murina	Eastern Atlantic Ocean: Azores	do.	E	3	NA	NA
Bushwren, New Zealand	Xenicus longipes	New Zealand	do.	E	3	NA	NA
Bustard, great Indian	Choriotis nigriceps	India, Pakistan	do.	E	3	NA	NA
Cahow (=Bermuda Petrel)	Pterodroma cahow	North Atlantic Ocean: Bermuda	do.	E	3	NA	NA
Condor, Andean	Vultur gryphus	Colombia to Chile and Argentina	do.	E	4	NA	NA
Condor, California	Gymnogyps californianus	U.S.A. (OR, CA), Mexico (Baja California).	do.	E	1	17.95(b)	NA
Coot, Hawaiian (= Alae keokeo)	Fulica americana alai	U.S.A. (Hawaii)	do.	E	2	NA	NA
Cotinga, banded	Cotinga maculata	Brazil	do.	E	15	NA	NA
Cotinga, white-winged	Xipholena atropurpurea	do.	do.	E	15	NA	NA
Crane, black-necked	Grus nigricollis	China (Tibet)	do.	E	15	NA	NA
Crane, Cuba sandhill	Grus canadensis nesiotes	West Indies: Cuba	do.	E	15	NA	NA
Crane, hooded	Grus monacha	Japan, U.S.S.R.	do.	E	4	NA	NA
Crane, Japanese	Grus japonensis	China, Japan, Korea, U.S.S.R	do.	E	4	NA	NA
Crane, Mississippi sandhill	Grus canadensis pulla	U.S.A. (Mississippi)	do.	E	6	17.95(b)	NA
Crane, Siberian white	Grus leucogeranus	U.S.S.R. (Siberia) to India, including Iran and China.	do.	E	4	NA	NA
Crane, white-naped	Grus vipio	Mongolia.	do.	E	15	NA	NA
Crane, whooping	Grus americana	Canada, U.S.A. (Rocky Mountains east to Carolinas), Mexico.	do.	E	1,3	17.95(b)	NA
Creeper, Hawaii	Oreomystis (= Loxops) mana	U.S.A. (Hawaii).	do.	E	10	NA	NA
Creeper, Molokai (= Kakawahie)	Oreomystis (= Loxops) flammea	do.	do.	E	2	NA	NA
Creeper, Oahu (= alauwahio)	Oreomystis (= Loxops) maculata	do.	do.	E	2	NA	NA
Crow, Hawaiian (= alala)	Corvus hawaiiensis (= Tropicus)	do.	do.	E	1	NA	NA
Cuckoo-shrike, Mauritius	Coquus (= Coracina) typicus	Indian Ocean: Mauritius	do.	E	3	NA	NA
Cuckoo-shrike, Reunion	Coquus (= Coracina) newtoni	Indian Ocean: Reunion.	do.	E	3	NA	NA
Curassow, razor-billed	Mitu (= Crax) mitu mitu.	Brazil (Eastern)	do.	E	15	NA	NA
Curassow, red-billed	Crax blumenbachi	Brazil	do.	E	4	17.95(b)	NA
Curassow, Trinidad white-headed	Pipile pipile pipile	West Indies: Trinidad	do.	E	3	NA	NA
Curlew, Eskimo	Numenius borealis	Alaska and northern Canada to Argentina.	do.	E	1,3	17.95(b)	NA
Dove, cloven-feathered	Drepanoptila holosericea	Southwest Pacific Ocean: New Caledonia.	do.	E	3	NA	NA
Dove, Grenada	Leptotila wellsi	West Indies: Grenada	do.	E	3	NA	NA
Dove, Palau ground	Gallicolumba canifrons	West Pacific Ocean: U.S.A. (Palau Islands).	do.	E	3	NA	NA
Duck, Hawaiian (= koloa)	Anas wyvilliana	U.S.A. (Hawaii)	do.	E	1	NA	NA
Duck, Laysan	Anas laysanensis	do.	do.	E	1	NA	NA
Duck, pink-headed	Rhodonessa caryophyllacea	India, Malaysia, Indonesia, Thailand.	do.	E	15	NA	NA
Duck, white-winged wood	Cairina scutulata	do.	do.	E	3	NA	NA

Species		Historic range	Vertebrate population where endangered or threatened	Status	When listed	Critical habitat	Special rules
Common name	Scientific name						
Eagle, Greenland white-tailed	Haliaeetus albicilla groenlandicus	Greenland and adjacent Atlantic islands	do	E	15	NA	NA
Eagle, harpy	Harpia harpyja	Mexico south to Argentina	do	E	15	NA	NA
Eagle, Philippine (=monkey-eating)	Pithecophaga jefferyi	Philippines	do	E	3	NA	NA
Eagle, bald	Haliaeetus leucocephalus	North America south to northern Mexico	U.S.A. (conterminous States, except WA, OR, MN, WI, MI)	E	1, 34	NA	NA
Eagle, bald	Haliaeetus leucocephalus	do	U.S.A. (WA, OR, MN, WI, MI)	T	34	NA	17.41(a)
Eagle, Spanish imperial	Aquila heliaca adalberti	Spain, Morocco, Algeria	Entire	E	3	NA	NA
Egret, Chinese	Egretta eulophotes	China, Korea	do	E	3	NA	NA
Falcon, American peregrine	Falco peregrinus anatum	Nests from central Alaska across north-central Canada to central Mexico, winters south to South America	do	E	2, 3, 145	17.95(b)	NA
Falcon, Arctic peregrine	Falco peregrinus tundrius	Nests from northern Alaska to Greenland; winters south to Central and South America	do	T	2, 3, 145	NA	NA
Falcon, Eurasian peregrine	Falco peregrinus peregrinus	Europe, Eurasia south to Africa and Mideast	do	E	15	NA	NA
Falcon, peregrine	Falco peregrinus	Worldwide, except Antarctica and most Pacific Islands	Wherever found in wild in the conterminous 48 States	E(S/A)	145	NA	NA
Finch, Laysan (honeycreeper)	Telespyza (=Psittirostra) cantans	U.S.A. (Hawaii)	Entire	E	1	NA	NA
Finch, Nihoa (honeycreeper)	Telespyza (=Psittirostra) ultima	do	do	E	1	NA	NA
Flycatcher, Euler's	Empidonax euleri johnstonei	West Indies: Grenada	do	E	3	NA	NA
Flycatcher, Palau fantail	Rhipidura lepida	West Pacific Ocean: U.S.A. (Palau Islands)	do	E	3	NA	NA
Flycatcher, Seychelles paradise	Terpsiphone corvina	Indian Ocean: Seychelles	do	E	3	NA	NA
Flycatcher, Tahiti	Pomarea nigra	South Pacific Ocean: Tahiti	do	E	3	NA	NA
Flycatcher, Tinian monarch	Monarcha takatsukasae	Western Pacific Ocean: U.S.A. (Mariana Islands)	do	E	3	NA	NA
Fody, Seychelles (weaver-finch)	Foudia sechellarum	Indian Ocean: Seychelles	do	E	3	NA	NA
Frigatebird, Andrew's	Fregata andrewsi	East Indian Ocean	do	E	15	NA	NA
Gallinule, Hawaiian (moorhen)	Gallinula chloropus sandvicensis	U.S.A. (Hawaii)	do	E	1	NA	NA
Goose, Aleutian Canada	Branta canadensis leucopareia	U.S.A. (AK, CA, OR, WA), Japan	do	T	1, 3	NA	NA
Goose, Hawaiian (=nene)	Nesochen (=Branta) sandvicensis	U.S.A. (Hawaii)	do	E	1	NA	NA
Goshawk, Christmas Island	Accipiter fasciatus natalis	Indian Ocean: Christmas Island	do	E	3	NA	NA
Grackle, slender-billed	Quiscalus (=Cassidix) palustris	Mexico	do	E	3	NA	NA
Grasswren, Eyrean (flycatcher)	Amytornis goyderi	Australia	do	E	3	NA	NA
Grebe, Atitlan	Podilymbus gigas	Guatemala	do	E	3	NA	NA
Greenshank, Nordmann's	Tringa guttifer	U.S.S.R., Japan, south to Malaya, Borneo	do	E	15	NA	NA
Guan, horned	Oreophasis derbianus	Guatemala, Mexico	do	E	3	NA	NA
Gull, Audouin's	Larus audouinii	Mediterranean Sea	do	E	3	NA	NA
Gull, relict	Larus relictus	India, China	do	E	15	NA	NA
Hawk, Anjouan Island sparrow	Accipiter francesii pusillus	Indian Ocean: Comoro Islands	do	E	3	NA	NA
Hawk, Galapagos	Buteo galapagoensis	Ecuador (Galapagos Island)	do	E	3	NA	NA
Hawk, Hawaiian (=Io)	Buteo solitarius	U.S.A. (Hawaii)	do	E	1	NA	NA
Hermit, hook-billed (hummingbird)	Glaucis (=Ramphodon) dohrnii	Brazil	do	E	15	NA	NA
Honeycreeper, crested (=akohekohe)	Palmeria dolei	U.S.A. (Hawaii)	do	E	1	NA	NA
Hornbill, helmeted	Rhinoplax vigil	Thailand, Malaysia	do	E	15	NA	NA

633

Species — Common name	Scientific name	Historic range	Vertebrate population where endangered or threatened	Status	When listed	Critical habitat	Special rules
Honeyeater, helmeted	Meliphaga cassidix	Australia	do	E	4	NA	NA
Ibis, Japanese crested	Nipponia nippon	China, Japan, U.S.S.R., Korea	do	E	3	NA	NA
Kagu	Rhynochetos jubatus	South Pacific Ocean: New Caledonia	do	E	3	NA	NA
Kakapo (=owl-parrot)	Strigops habroptilus	New Zealand	do	E	3	NA	NA
Kestrel, Mauritius	Falco punctatus	Indian Ocean: Mauritius	do	E	3	NA	NA
Kestrel, Seychelles	Falco araea	Indian Ocean: Seychelles Islands	do	E	3	NA	NA
Kite, Cuba hook-billed	Chondrohierax uncinatus wilsonii	West Indies: Cuba	do	E	3	NA	NA
Kite, Grenada hook-billed	Chondrohierax uncinatus mirus	West Indies: Grenada	do	E	3	NA	NA
Kite, Everglade (snail kite)	Rostrhamus sociabilis plumbeus	U.S.A. (Florida)	do	E	1	17.95(b)	NA
Kokako (wattlebird)	Callaeas cinerea	New Zealand	do	E	3	NA	NA
Macaw, glaucous	Anodorhynchus glaucus	Paraguay, Uruguay, Brazil	do	E	15	NA	NA
Macaw, indigo	Anodorhynchus leari	Brazil	do	E	15	NA	NA
Macaw, little blue	Cyanopsitta spixii	...do...	do	E	15	NA	NA
Magpie-robin, Seychelles (thrush)	Copsychus sechellarum	Indian Ocean: Seychelles Islands	do	E	3	NA	NA
Malkoha, red-faced (cuckoo)	Phaenicophaeus pyrrhocephalus	Sri Lanka (=Ceylon)	do	E	3	NA	NA
Mallard, Mariana	Anas oustaleti	West Pacific Ocean: U.S.A. (Guam, Mariana Islands)	do	E	23	NA	NA
Megapode, La Perouse's	Megapodius laperouse	West Pacific Ocean: U.S.A. (Palau Island, Mariana Islands)	do	E	3	NA	NA
Megapode, Maleo	Macrocephalon maleo	Indonesia (Celebes)	do	E	3	NA	NA
Millerbird, Nihoa (old world warbler)	Acrocephalus familiaris kingi	U.S.A. (Hawaii)	do	E	3	NA	NA
Nukupu'u (honeycreeper)	Hemignathus lucidus	...do...	do	E	1, 2	NA	NA
'O'o, Kauai (='O'o 'A'a) (honeyeater)	Moho braccatus	...do...	do	E	1	NA	NA
Ostrich, Arabian	Struthio camelus syriacus	Jordan, Saudi Arabia	do	E	3	NA	NA
Ostrich, West African	Struthio camelus spatzi	Spanish Sahara	do	E	3	NA	NA
'O'u (honeycreeper)	Psittirostra psittacea	U.S.A. (Hawaii)	do	E	1	NA	NA
Owl, Anjouan scops	Otus rutilus capnodes	Indian Ocean: Comoro Island	do	E	3	NA	NA
Owl, giant scops	Otus gurneyi	Phillipines: Marinduque and Mindanao Island	do	E	15	NA	NA
Owl, Palau	Pyrroglaux (=Otus) podargina	West Pacific Ocean: U.S.A. (Palau Islands)	do	E	3	NA	NA
Owl, Seychelles	Otus insularis	Indian Ocean: Seychelles Islands	do	E	3	NA	NA
Owlet, Morden's (=Sokoke)	Otus ireneae	Kenya	do	E	3	NA	NA
Palila (honeycreeper)	Loxioides (=Psittirostra) bailleui	U.S.A. (Hawaii)	do	E	1	17.95(b)	NA
Parakeet, Forbes'	Cyanoramphus auriceps forbesi	New Zealand	do	E	3, 15	NA	NA
Parakeet, golden	Aratinga guarouba	Brazil	do	E	4	NA	NA
Parakeet, golden-shouldered (=hooded)	Psephotus chrysopterygius	Australia	do	E	3	NA	NA
Parakeet, Mauritius	Psittacula echo	Indian Ocean: Mauritius	do	E	3	NA	NA
Parakeet, ochre-marked	Pyrrhura cruentata	Brazil	do	E	3	NA	NA
Parakeet, orange-bellied	Neophema chrysogaster	Australia	do	E	4	NA	NA
Parakeet, paradise (=beautiful)	Psephotus pulcherrimus	...do...	do	E	4	NA	NA
Parakeet, scarlet-chested (=splendid)	Neophema splendida	...do...	do	E	4	NA	NA
Parakeet, turquoise	Neophema pulchella	...do...	do	E	3	NA	NA
Parrot, Australian	Geopsittacus occidentalis	...do...	do	E	3, 15	NA	NA
Parrot, Bahaman or Cuban	Amazona leucocephala	West Indies: Cuba, Bahamas, Caymans	do	E	4	NA	NA
Parrot, ground	Pezoporus wallicus	Australia	do	E	6	NA	NA
Parrot, imperial	Amazona imperialis	West Indies: Dominica	do	E	3	NA	NA
Parrot, Puerto Rican	Amazona vittata	U.S.A. (Puerto Rico)	do	E	1	NA	NA
Parrot, red-browed	Amazona rhodocorytha	Brazil	do	E	3	NA	NA
Parrot, red-capped	Pionopsitta pileata	...do...	do	E	15	NA	NA
Parrot, red-necked	Amazona arausiaca	West Indies: Dominica	do	E	50	NA	NA
Parrot, red-spectacled	Amazona pretrei pretrei	Brazil, Argentina	do	E	15	NA	NA

Species — Common name	Species — Scientific name	Historic range	Vertebrate population where endangered or threatened	Status	When listed	Critical habitat	Special rules
Parrot, St. Lucia	Amazona versicolor	West Indies: St. Lucia	do	E	3	NA	NA
Parrot, St. Vincent	Amazona guildingii	West Indies: St. Vincent	do	E	3	NA	NA
Parrot, thick-billed	Rhynchopsitta pachyrhyncha	Mexico, U.S.A. (AZ, NM)	Mexico	E	3	NA	NA
Parrot, vinaceous-breasted	Amazona vinacea	Brazil	Entire	E	15	NA	NA
Parrotbill, Maui (honeycreeper)	Pseudonestor xanthophrys	U.S.A. (Hawaii)	do	E	1	NA	NA
Pelican, brown	Pelecanus occidentalis	U.S.A. (Carolinas to TX, CA), West Indies, C. and S. America: Coastal.	do	E	2, 3	NA	NA
Penguin, Galapagos	Spheniscus mendiculus	Ecuador (Galapagos Island)	do	E	3	NA	NA
Petrel, Hawaiian dark-rumped	Pterodroma phaeopygia sandwichensis	U.S.A. (Hawaii)	do	E	2, 4, 1	NA	NA
Pheasant, bar-tailed	Syrmaticus humiae	Burma, China	do	E	3	NA	NA
Pheasant, Blyth's tragopan	Tragopan blythi	Burma, China, India	do	E	3	NA	NA
Pheasant, brown eared	Crossoptilon mantchuricum	China	do	E	3	NA	NA
Pheasant, Cabot's tragopan	Tragopan caboti	do	do	E	3	NA	NA
Pheasant, Chinese monal	Lophophorus lhuysii	China	do	E	3	NA	NA
Pheasant, Edward's	Lophura edwardsi	Vietnam	do	E	3	NA	NA
Pheasant, Elliot's	Syrmaticus ellioti	China	do	E	3	NA	NA
Pheasant, imperial	Lophura imperialis	Vietnam	do	E	15	NA	NA
Pheasant, Mikado	Syrmaticus mikado	Taiwan	do	E	3	NA	NA
Pheasant, Palawan peacock	Polyplectron emphanum	Philippines	do	E	3	NA	NA
Pheasant, Sclater's monal	Lophophorus sclateri	Burma, China, India	do	E	3	NA	NA
Pheasant, Swinhoe's	Lophura swinhoii	Taiwan	do	E	3	NA	NA
Pheasant, western tragopan	Tragopan melanocephalus	India, Pakistan	do	E	3	NA	NA
Pheasant, white eared	Crossoptilon crossoptilon	China (Tibet), India	do	E	4	NA	NA
Pigeon, Azores wood	Columba palumbus azorica	East Atlantic Ocean: Azores	do	E	3	NA	NA
Pigeon, Chatham Island	Hemiphaga novaeseelandiae chathamensis.	New Zealand	do	E	3	NA	NA
Pigeon, Mindoro zone-tailed	Ducula mindorensis	Philippines	do	E	15	NA	NA
Pigeon, Puerto Rican plain	Columba inornata wetmorei	U.S.A. (Puerto Rico)	do	E	2	NA	NA
Piping-guan, black-fronted	Pipile jacutinga	Argentina	do	E	15	NA	NA
Pitta, Koch's	Pitta kochi	Philippines	do	E	15	NA	NA
Plover, New Zealand shore	Thinornis novaeseelandiae	New Zealand	do	E	3	NA	NA
Po'ouli (honeycreeper)	Melamprosops phaeosoma	U.S.A. (Hawaii)	do	E	10	NA	NA
Prairie-chicken, Attwater's greater	Tympanuchus cupido attwateri	U.S.A. (Texas)	do	E	1	NA	NA
Quail, Merriam's Montezuma	Cyrtonyx montezumae merriami	Mexico (Vera Cruz)	do	E	15	NA	NA
Quetzal, resplendent	Pharomachrus mocinno	Mexico to Panama	do	E	15	NA	NA
Rail, Aukland Island	Rallus pectoralis muelleri	New Zealand	do	E	3	NA	NA
Rail, California clapper	Rallus longirostris obsoletus	U.S.A. (California)	do	E	2	NA	NA
Rail, Guam	Rallus owstoni	Western Pacific Ocean: U.S.A. (Guam)	do	E	146E	NA	NA
Rail, light-footed clapper	Rallus longirostris levipes	U.S.A. (CA), Mexico (Baja California)	do	E	2	NA	NA
Rail, Lord Howe wood	Tricholimnas sylvestris	Australia (Lord Howe Island)	do	E	15	NA	NA
Rail, Yuma clapper	Rallus longirostris sumanensis	Mexico, U.S.A. (AZ, CA)	do	E	1	NA	NA
Rhea, Darwin's	Pterocnemia pennata	Argentina, Bolivia, Peru, Uruguay	do	E	3	NA	NA
Robin, Chatham Island	Petroica traversi	New Zealand	do	E	3	NA	NA
Robin, scarlet-breasted (flycatcher)	Petroica multicolor multicolor	Australia (Norfolk Island)	do	E	3	NA	NA
Rockfowl, grey-necked	Picathartes oreas	Cameroon, Gabon	do	E	3	NA	NA
Rockfowl, white-necked	Picathartes gymnocephalus	Africa: Togo to Sierra Leone	do	E	3	NA	NA
Roller, long-tailed ground	Uratelornis chimaera	Malagasy Republic (= Madagascar)	do	E	3	NA	NA
Scrub-bird, noisy	Atrichornis clamosus	Australia	do	E	3	NA	NA
Shama, Cebu black (thrush)	Copsychus niger cebuensis	Philippines	do	E	3	NA	NA
Shearwater, Newell's (Townsend's, formerly Manx) (= 'A'o)	Puffinus auricularis (formerly puffinus) newelli.	U.S.A. (Hawaii)	do	T	10	NA	NA
Shrike, San Clemente loggerhead	Lamus ludovicianus mearnsi	U.S.A. (California)	do	E	26	NA	NA
Siskin, red	Carduelis (= Spinus) cucullatus	South America	do	E	15	NA	NA

635

Species — Common name	Species — Scientific name	Historic range	Vertebrate population where endangered or threatened	Status	When listed	Critical habitat	Special rules
Sparrow, Cape Sable seaside	Ammospiza maritima mirabilis	U.S.A. (Florida)	do	E	1	17.95(b)	NA
Sparrow, dusky seaside	Ammospiza maritima nigrescens	...do...	do	E	1	17.95(b)	NA
Sparrow, San Clemente sage	Amphispiza belli clementeae	U.S.A. (California)	do	T	26	NA	NA
Starling, Ponape mountain	Aplonis pelzelni	West Pacific Ocean: U.S.A. (Caroline Island).	do	E	3	NA	NA
Starling, Rothschild's (myna)	Leucopsar rothschildi	Indonesia (Bali)	do	E	3	NA	NA
Stilt, Hawaiian (=Ae'o)	Himantopus himantopus knudseni	U.S.A. (Hawaii)	do	E	2	NA	NA
Stork, oriental white	Ciconia ciconia boyciana	China, Japan, Korea, U.S.S.R.	do	E	3	NA	NA
Stork, wood	Mycteria americana	U.S.A., (CA, AZ, TX, to Carolinas), Mexico, Central and South America.	U.S.A. (AL, FL, GA, SC).	E	142	NA	NA
Teal, Campbell Island flightless	Anas aucklandica nesiotis	New Zealand (Campbell Island)	do	E	15	NA	NA
Tern, California least	Sterna antillarum (=albifrons) browni	Mexico, U.S.A. (CA)	do	E	2, 3	NA	NA
Thrasher, white-breasted	Ramphocinclus brachyurus	West Indies: St. Lucia, Martinique.	do	E	3	NA	NA
Thrush, large Kauai	Phaeornis obscurus myadestina	U.S.A. (Hawaii)	do	E	2	NA	NA
Thrush, Molokai (=oloma'o)	Phaeornis obscurus rutha	...do...	do	E	2	NA	NA
Thrush, New Zealand (wattlebird)	Turnagra capensis	New Zealand	do	E	3	NA	NA
Thrush, small Kauai (=puaiohi)	Phaeornis palmeri	U.S.A. (Hawaii)	do	E	1	NA	NA
Tinamou, solitary	Tinamus solitarius	Brazil, Paraguay, Argentina	do	E	15	NA	NA
Trembler, Martinique brown (thrasher)	Cinclocerthia ruficauda gutturalis	West Indies: Martinique.	do	E	3	NA	NA
Wanderer, plain (collared-hemipode)	Pedionomus torquatus	Australia	do	E	6	NA	NA
Warbler (wood), Bachman's	Vermivora bachmanii	U.S.A.(Southeastern), Cuba.	do	E	1, 3	NA	NA
Warbler (wood), Barbados yellow	Dendroica petechia petechia	West Indies: Barbados	do	E	3	NA	NA
Warbler (wood), Kirtland's	Dendroica kirtlandii	U.S.A. (principally MI), Canada, West Indies: Bahama Islands.	do	E	1, 3	NA	NA
Warbler (willow), reed	Acrocephalus luscinia	Western Pacific Ocean: U.S.A. (Mariana Islands).	do	E	3	NA	NA
Warbler (willow), Rodriguez	Bebrornis rodericanus	Mauritius (Rodrigues Islands)	do	E	3	NA	NA
Warbler (wood), Semper's	Leucopeza semperi	West Indies: St. Lucia	do	E	3	NA	NA
Warbler (willow), Seychelles	Bebrornis sechellensis	Indian Ocean: Seychelles Island.	do	E	3	NA	NA
Whipbird, Western	Psophodes nigrogularis	Australia	do	E	6	NA	NA
Whip-poor-will, Puerto Rican	Caprimulgus noctitherus	U.S.A. (Puerto Rico).	do	E	15	NA	NA
White-eye, Norfolk Island	Zosterops albogularis	Indian Ocean: Norfolk Islands.	do	E	3	NA	NA
White-eye, Ponape great	Rukia longirostra (=sanfordi)	West Pacific Ocean: U.S.A. (Caroline Islands).	do	E	3	NA	NA
White-eye, Seychelles	Zosterops modesta	Indian Ocean: Seychelles	do	E	3	NA	NA
Woodpecker, imperial	Campephilus imperialis	Mexico	do	E	3	NA	NA
Woodpecker, ivory-billed	Campephilus principalis	U.S.A. (southcentral and southeastern), Cuba.	do	E	1, 3	NA	NA
Woodpecker, red-cockaded	Picoides (=Dendrocopos) borealis	U.S.A. (southcentral and southeastern)	do	E	2	NA	NA
Woodpecker, Tristan's	Dryocopus javensis richardsi	Korea.	do	E	3	NA	NA
Wren, Guadeloupe house	Troglodytes aedon guadeloupensis	West Indies: Guadeloupe.	do	E	3	NA	NA
Wren, St. Lucia house	Troglodytes aedon mesoleucus	West Indies: St. Lucia	do	E	3	NA	NA
REPTILES							
Alligator, American	Alligator mississippiensis	Southeastern U.S.A	Wherever found in wild except those areas where listed as threatened as set forth below.	E	1, 11, 51, 60, 113, 134	NA	NA

Species — Common name	Scientific name	Historic range	Vertebrate population where endangered or threatened	Status	When listed	Critical habitat	Special rules
Do	do	do	U.S.A. (FL and certain areas of GA and SC, as set forth in 17.42(a)(1)).	T	20, 47, 51, 60, 134	NA	17.42(a)
Do	do	do	U.S.A. (LA and TX).	T(S/A)	11, 47, 51, 60, 113, 134	NA	17.42(a)
Do	do	do	In captivity wherever found.	T(S/A)	11, 47, 51	NA	17.42(a)
Alligator, Chinese	Alligator sinensis	China	Entire	E	15	NA	NA
Anole, Culebra Island giant	Anolis roosevelti	U.S.A. (Puerto Rico: Culebra Island)	do	E	25	17.95(c)	NA
Boa, Jamaican	Epicrates subflavus	Jamaica	do	E	3	NA	NA
Boa, Mona	Epicrates monensis monensis	U.S.A. (Puerto Rico)	do	T	33	17.95(c)	NA
Boa, Puerto Rico	Epicrates inornatus	do	do	E	2	NA	NA
Boa, Round Island [no common name]	Casarea dussumieri	Indian Ocean: Mauritius	do	E	88	NA	NA
Boa, Round Island [no common name]	Bolyeria multocarinata	Indian Ocean: Mauritius	do	E	88	NA	NA
Boa, Virgin Islands tree	Epicrates monensis granti	U.S. and British Virgin Islands	do	E	2, 86	NA	NA
Caiman, Apaporis River	Caiman crocodilus apaporiensis	Colombia	do	E	15	NA	NA
Caiman, black	Melanosuchus niger	Amazon basin	do	E	15	NA	NA
Caiman, broad-snouted	Caiman latirostris	Brazil, Argentina, Paraguay, Uruguay	do	E	15	NA	NA
Caiman, Yacare	Caiman crocodilus yacare	Bolivia, Argentina, Peru, Brazil	do	E	3	NA	NA
Chuckwalla, San Esteban Island	Sauromalus varius	Mexico	do	E	88	NA	NA
Crocodile, African dwarf	Osteolaemus tetraspis tetraspis	West Africa	do	E	15	NA	NA
Crocodile, African slender-snouted	Crocodylus cataphractus	Western and central Africa	do	E	5	NA	NA
Crocodile, American	Crocodylus acutus	U.S.A. (FL), Mexico, South America, Central America, Caribbean.	do	E	10, 87	17.95(c)	NA
Crocodile, Ceylon mugger	Crocodylus palustris kimbula	Sri Lanka	do	E	15	NA	NA
Crocodile, Congo dwarf	Osteolaemus tetraspis osborni	Congo River drainage	do	E	15	NA	NA
Crocodile, Cuban	Crocodylus rhombifer	Cuba	do	E	3	NA	NA
Crocodile, Morelet's	Crocodylus moreletii	Mexico, Belize, Guatemala	do	E	15	NA	NA
Crocodile, mugger	Crocodylus palustris palustris	India, Pakistan, Iran, Bangladesh	do	E	3	NA	NA
Crocodile, Nile	Crocodylus niloticus	Africa	do	E	3	NA	NA
Crocodile, Orinoco	Crocodylus intermedius	South America: Orinoco River Basin	do	E	15	NA	NA
Crocodile, Philippine	Crocodylus novaeguineae mindorensis	Philippine Islands	do	E	87	NA	NA
Crocodile, saltwater (=estuarine)	Crocodylus porosus	Southeast Asia, Australia, Papua-New Guinea, Pacific Islands.	Entire, except Papua-New Guinea.	E	15	NA	NA
Crocodile, Siamese	Crocodylus siamensis	Southeast Asia, Malay Peninsula	Entire	E	15	NA	NA
Gavial (=gharial)	Gavialis gangeticus	Pakistan, Burma, Bangladesh, India	do	E	3, 15	NA	NA
Gecko, day	Phelsuma edwardnewtoni	Indian Ocean: Mauritius	do	E	125	NA	NA
Gecko, Monito	Sphaerodactylus micropithecus	U.S.A. (Puerto Rico)	do	E	3	17.95(c)	NA
Gecko, Round Island day	Phelsuma guentheri	Indian Ocean: Mauritius	do	T	129	NA	NA
Gecko, Serpent Island	Cyrtodactylus serpensinsula	Indian Ocean: Mauritius	do	T	129	NA	NA
Iguana, Acklins ground	Cyclura rileyi nuchalis	West Indies: Bahamas	do	T	129	NA	NA
Iguana, Allen's Cay	Cyclura cychlura inornata	do	do	T	129	NA	NA
Iguana, Andros Island ground	Cyclura cychlura cychlura	do	do	E	3	NA	NA
Iguana, Anegada ground	Cyclura pinguis	West Indies: British Virgin Islands (Anegada Island).	do	E	3	NA	NA
Iguana, Barrington land	Conolophus pallidus	Ecuador (Galapagos Island)	do	E	3	NA	NA
Iguna, Cayman Brac ground	Cyclura nubila caymanensis	West Indies: Cayman Islands	do	T	129	NA	NA

637

Species — Common name	Species — Scientific name	Historic range	Vertebrate population where endangered or threatened	Status	When listed	Critical habitat	Special rules
Iguana, Cuban ground	Cyclura nubila nubila	Cuba	Entire (excluding population introduced in Puerto Rico).	T	129	NA	NA
Iguana, Exuma Island	Cyclura cychlura figginsi	West Indies: Bahamas	Entire	T	129	NA	NA
Iguana, Fiji banded	Brachylophus fasciatus	Pacific: Fiji, Tonga	do.	E	88	NA	NA
Iguana, Fiji crested	Brachylophus vitiensis	Pacific: Fiji	do.	E	88	NA	NA
Iguana, Grand Cayman ground	Cyclura nubila lewisi	West Indies: Cayman Islands	do.	E	129	NA	NA
Iguana, Jamaican	Cyclura collei	West Indies: Jamaica	do.	E	129	NA	NA
Iguana, Mayaguana	Cyclura carinata bartschi	West Indies: Bahamas	do.	E	129	NA	NA
Iguana, Mona ground	Cyclura stejnegeri	U.S.A. (Puerto Rico: Mona Island)	do.	T	33	17.95(c)	NA
Iguana, Turks and Caicos	Cyclura carinata carinata	West Indies: Turks and Caicos Islands	do.	T	129	NA	NA
Iguana, Watling Island ground	Cyclura rileyi rileyi	West Indies: Bahamas	do.	T	129	NA	NA
Iguana, White Cay ground	Cyclura rileyi cristata	do	do.	E	129	NA	NA
Lizard, blunt-nosed leopard	Gambelia (=Crotaphytus) silus	do	do.	E	1	NA	NA
Lizard, Coachella Valley fringe-toed	Uma inornata	U.S.A. (CA)	do.	T	105	17.95(c)	NA
Lizard, Hierro giant	Gallotia simonyi simonyi	Spain (Canary Islands)	do.	E	144	NA	NA
Lizard, Ibiza wall	Podarcis pityuensis	Spain (Balearic Islands)	do.	T	144	NA	NA
Lizard, Ibiza night	Xantusia (=Klauberina) riversiana	U.S.A. (CA)	do.	T	26	NA	NA
Lizard, St. Croix ground	Ameiva polops	U.S.A. (Virgin Islands: Green Cay, Protestant Cay).	do.	E	24	17.95(c)	NA
Monitor, Bengal	Varanus bengalensis	Iran, Iraq, India, Sri Lanka, Malaysia, Afghanistan, Burma, Vietnam, Thailand.	do.	E	15	NA	NA
Monitor, desert	Varanus griseus	North Africa to Neareast, Caspian Sea through U.S.S.R. to Pakistan, Northwest India.	do.	E	15	NA	NA
Monitor, Komodo Island	Varanus komodoensis	Indonesia (Komodo, Rintja, Padar, and western Flores Island.	do.	E	15	NA	NA
Monitor, yellow	Varanus flavescens	West Pakistan through India to Bangladesh.	do.	E	15	NA	NA
Python, Indian	Python molurus molurus	Sri Lanka and India	do.	E	15	NA	NA
Rattlesnake, Aruba Island	Crotalus unicolor	Aruba Island (Netherland Antilles)	do.	T	129	NA	NA
Rattlesnake, New Mexican ridge-nosed	Crotalus willardi obscurus	U.S.A. (NM), Mexico	do.	T	43	17.95(c)	NA
Skink, Round Island	Leiolopisma telfairi	Indian Ocean: Mauritius	do.	T	129	NA	NA
Snake, Atlantic salt marsh	Nerodia fasciata taeniata	U.S.A. (Florida)	do.	T	30	NA	NA
Snake, eastern indigo	Drymarchon corais couperi	U.S.A. (AL, FL, GA, MS, SC)	do.	T	32	NA	NA
Snake, San Francisco garter	Thamnophis sirtalis tetrataenia	U.S.A. (California)	do.	E	1	NA	NA
Tartaruga	Podocnemis expansa	South America: Orinoco and Amazon River basins.	do.	E	3	NA	NA
Terrapin, river (=Tuntong)	Batagur baska	Malaysia, Bangladesh, Burma, India, Indonesia.	do.	E	3	NA	NA
Tomistoma	Tomistoma schlegelii	Malaysia, Indonesia	do.	E	15	NA	NA
Tortoise, angulated	Geochelone yniphora	Malagasy Republic (=Madagascar)	do.	E	15	NA	NA
Tortoise, Bolson	Gopherus flavomarginatus	Mexico	do.	E	46	NA	NA
Tortoise, desert	Scaptochelys (=Gopherus) agassizii	U.S.A. (UT, AZ, CA, NV); Mexico	Beaver Dam Slope, Utah.	T	103	17.95(c)	NA
Tortoise, Galapagos	Geochelone elephantopus	Ecuador (Galapagos Islands)	Entire.	E	3	NA	NA
Tortoise, radiated	Geochelone (=Testudo) radiata	Malagasy Republic (=Madagascar)	do.	E	3	NA	NA
Tracaja	Podocnemis unifilis	South America: Orinoco and Amazon River basins.	do.	E	3	NA	NA
Tuatara	Sphenodon punctatus	New Zealand	do.	E	3	NA	NA
Turtle, aquatic box	Terrapene coahuila	Mexico	do.	E	6	NA	NA

Species Common name	Species Scientific name	Historic range	Vertebrate population where endangered or threatened	Status	When listed	Critical habitat	Special rules
Turtle, black softshell	Trionyx nigricans	Bangladesh	do.	E	15	NA	NA
Turtle, Burmese peacock	Morenia ocellata	Burma	do.	E	15	NA	NA
Turtle, Central American river	Dermatemys mawii	Mexico, Belize, Guatemala	do.	E	129	NA	NA
Turtle, Cuatro Cienegas softshell	Trionyx ater	Mexico	do.	E	15	NA	NA
Turtle, geometric	Psammobates geometricus (=Geochelone geometrica).	South Africa	do.	E	15	NA	NA
Turtle, green sea	Chelonia mydas	Circumglobal in tropical and temperate seas and oceans.	Wherever found except where listed as endangered below.	T	2, 42	NA	17.42(b) and Parts 220 and 227.
Turtle, green sea	Chelonia mydas	do.	Breeding colony populations in FL and on Pacific coast of Mexico.	E	2, 42	NA	NA
Turtle, hawksbill sea (=carey)	Eretmochelys imbricata	Tropical seas	Entire.	E	3	17.95(c)	NA
Turtle, Indian sawback	Kachuga tecta tecta	India	do.	E	15	NA	NA
Turtle, Indian softshell	Trionyx gangeticus	Pakistan, India	do.	E	15	NA	NA
Turtle, Kemp's (=Atlantic) Ridley sea	Lepidochelys kempii	Tropical and temperate seas in Atlantic Basin.	do.	E	4	NA	NA
Turtle, leatherback sea	Dermochelys coriacea	Tropical, temperate, and subpolar seas.	do.	E	3	17.95(c), 226.71	17.42(b) and Parts 220 and 227.
Turtle, loggerhead sea	Caretta caretta	Circumglobal in tropical and temperate seas and oceans.	do.	T	42	NA	17.42(b) and Parts 220 and 227.
Turtle, Olive (Pacific) Ridley sea	Lepidochelys olivacea	Tropical and temperate seas in Pacific Basin.	Wherever found except where listed as endangered below.	T	42	NA	NA
Turtle, Olive (Pacific) Ridley sea	Lepidochelys olivacea	do	Breeding colony populations on Pacific coast of Mexico.	E	42	NA	NA
Turtle, peacock softshell	Trionyx hurum	India, Bangladesh	Entire.	E	15	NA	NA
Turtle, Plymouth red-bellied	Pseudemys (=Chrysemys) rubriventris bangsi.	U.S.A. (Massachusetts)	do.	E	90	17.95(c)	NA
Turtle, short-necked or western swamp	Pseudemydura umbrina.	Australia	do.	E	3	NA	NA
Turtle, spotted pond	Geoclemys (=Damonia) hamiltonii.	North India, Pakistan	do.	E	15	NA	NA
Turtle, three-keeled Asian	Melanochelys (=Geoemyda, Nicoria) tricarinata.	Central India to Bangladesh and Burma.	do.	E	15	NA	NA
Viper, Lar Valley	Vipera latifii	Iran	do.	E	129	NA	NA
AMPHIBIANS							
Coqui, golden	Eleutherodactylus jasperi	U.S.A. (Puerto Rico)	do.	T	29	17.95(d)	NA
Frog, Israel painted	Discoglossus nigriventer	Israel	do.	E	3	NA	NA
Frog, Panamanian golden	Atelopus varius zeteki.	Panama	do.	E	15	NA	NA
Frog, Stephen Island	Leiopelma hamiltoni.	New Zealand	do.	E	3	NA	NA
Salamander, Chinese giant	Andrias davidianus davidianus	Western China	do.	E	15	NA	NA
Salamander, desert slender	Batrachoseps aridus	U.S.A. (California).	do.	E	6	NA	NA
Salamander, Japanese giant	Andrias davidianus japonicus	Japan	do.	E	15	NA	NA

Species Common name	Species Scientific name	Historic range	Vertebrate population where endangered or threatened	Status	When listed	Critical habitat	Special rules
Salamander, Red Hills	Phaeognathus hubrichti	U.S.A. (Alabama)	do	T	19	NA	NA
Salamander, San Marcos	Eurycea nana	U.S.A. (Texas)	do	T	98	17.95(d)	17.43(a)
Salamander, Santa Cruz long-toed	Ambystoma macrodactylum croceum	U.S.A. (California)	do	E	1	NA	NA
Salamander, Texas blind	Typhlomolge rathbuni	U.S.A. (Texas)	do	E	1	NA	NA
Toad, African viviparous	Nectophrynoides spp.	Tanzania, Guinea, Ivory Coast, Cameroon, Liberia, Ethiopia	do	E	15	NA	NA
Toad, Cameroon	Bufo superciliaris	Equatorial Africa	do	E	15	NA	NA
Toad, Houston	Bufo houstonensis	U.S.A. (Texas)	do	E	2	17.95(d)	NA
Toad, Monte Verde	Bufo periglenes	Costa Rica	do	E	15	NA	NA
Toad, Wyoming	Bufo hemiophrys baxteri	U.S.A. (WY)	do	E	138	NA	NA
FISHES							
Ala Balik (trout)	Salmo platycephalus	Turkey	Entire	E	3	NA	NA
Ayumodoki (loach)	Hymenophysa (=Botia) curta	Japan	do	E	3	NA	NA
Blindcat, Mexican (catfish)	Prietella phreatophila	Mexico	do	E	3	NA	NA
Bonytail, Pahranagat	Gila robusta jordani	U.S.A. (Nevada)	do	E	2	NA	NA
Bonytoungue, Asian	Scleropages formosus	Thailand, Indonesia, Malaysia	do	E	15	NA	NA
Catfish [no common name]	Pangasius sanitwongsei	Thailand	do	E	3	NA	NA
Catfish, giant	Pangasianodon gigas	do	do	E	3	NA	NA
Cavefish, Alabama	Speoplatyrhinus poulsoni	U.S.A. (Alabama)	do	E	28	17.95(e)	NA
Chub, bonytail	Gila elegans	U.S.A. (AZ, CA, CO, NV, UT, WY)	do	E	92	NA	NA
Chub, Borax Lake	Gila boraxobius	U.S.A. (Oregon)	do	E	124	17.95(e)	NA
Chub, Chihuahua	Gila nigrescens	U.S.A. (NM) Mexico (Chihuahua)	do	T	132	17.95(e)	17.44(g)
Chub, humpback	Gila cypha	U.S.A. (AZ, CO, UT, WY)	do	E	1	NA	NA
Chub, Mohave tui	Gila bicolor mohavensis (= G. mohavensis)	U.S.A. (California)	do	E	2	NA	NA
Chub, slender	Hyboposis cahni	U.S.A. (TN, VA)	do	T	28	17.95(e)	17.44(c)
Chub, spotfin	Hyboposis monacha	U.S.A. (AL, GA, NC, TN, VA)	do	T	28	17.95(e)	17.44(c)
Cicek (minnow)	Acanthorutilus handlirschi	Turkey	do	E	3	NA	NA
Cui-ui	Chasmistes cujus	U.S.A. (Nevada)	do	E	1	NA	NA
Dace, Ash Meadows speckled	Rhinichthys osculus nevadensis	U.S.A. (NV)	do	E	117E, 127E, 130	17.95(e)	NA
Dace, Kendall Warm Springs	Rhinichthys osculus thermalis	U.S.A. (Wyoming)	do	E	2	NA	NA
Dace, Moapa	Moapa coriacea	U.S.A. (Nevada)	do	E	1	NA	NA
Darter, bayou	Etheostoma rubrum	U.S.A. (Mississippi)	do	T	10	NA	17.44(b)
Darter, fountain	Etheostoma fonticola	U.S.A. (Texas)	do	E	2	17.95(e)	NA
Darter, leopard	Percina pantherina	U.S.A. (AR, OK)	do	T	31	17.95(e)	17.44(d)
Darter, Maryland	Etheostoma sellare	U.S.A. (Maryland)	do	E	1	17.95(e)	NA
Darter, Okaloosa	Etheostoma okaloosae	U.S.A. (Florida)	do	E	6	NA	NA
Darter, slackwater	Etheostoma boschungi	U.S.A. (AL, TN)	do	T	28	17.95(e)	17.44(c)
Darter, snail	Percina tanasi	U.S.A. (AL, GA, TN)	do	T	12,150	NA	NA
Darter, watercress	Etheostoma nuchale	U.S.A. (Alabama)	do	E	2	NA	NA
Gambusia, Big Bend	Gambusia gaigei	U.S.A. (Texas)	do	E	1	NA	NA
Gambusia, Clear Creek	Gambusia heterochir	do	do	E	1	NA	NA
Gambusia, Amistad (= Goodenough)	Gambusia amistadensis	do	do	E	93	NA	NA
Gambusia, Pecos	Gambusia nobilis	U.S.A. (NM, TX)	do	E	2	17.95(e)	NA
Gambusia, San Marcos	Gambusia georgei	U.S.A. (Texas)	do	E	98	17.95(e)	NA
Killifish, Pahrump	Empetrichthys latos	U.S.A. (Nevada)	do	E	1	NA	NA
Madtom, Scioto	Noturus trautmani	U.S.A. (Ohio)	do	E	10	17.95(e)	NA
Madtom, yellowfin	Noturus flavipinnis	U.S.A. (GA, TN, VA)	do	T	28	17.95(e)	17.44(c)
Nekogigi (catfish)	Coreobagrus ichikawai	Japan	do	E	3	NA	NA

Species — Common name	Species — Scientific name	Historic range	Vertebrate population where endangered or threatened	Status	When listed	Critical habitat	Special rules
Pupfish, Ash Meadows Amargosa	*Cyprinodon nevadensis mionectes*	U.S.A. (NV)	do	E	117E, 127E, 130	17.95(e)	NA
Pupfish, Comanche Springs	*Cyprinodon elegans*	U.S.A. (Texas)	do	E	1	NA	NA
Pupfish, Devils Hole	*Cyprinodon diabolis*	U.S.A. (Nevada)	do	E	1	NA	NA
Pupfish, Leon Springs	*Cyprinodon bovinus*	U.S.A. (Texas)	do	E	102	17.95(e)	NA
Pupfish, Owens River	*Cyprinodon radiosus*	U.S.A. (California)	do	E	1	NA	NA
Pupfish, Warm Springs	*Cyprinodon nevadensis pectoralis*	U.S.A. (Nevada)	do	E	2	NA	NA
Squawfish, Colorado	*Ptychocheilus lucius*	U.S.A. (AZ, CA, CO, NM, NV, UT, WY), Mexico.	do	E	1	NA	NA
Stickleback, unarmored threespine	*Gasterosteus aculeatus williamsoni*	U.S.A. (California)	do	E	2	NA	NA
Sturgeon, shortnose	*Acipenser brevirostrum*	U.S.A. and Canada (Atlantic Coast)	do	E	1	NA	NA
Tango, Miyako (Tokyo bitterling)	*Tanakia tanago*	Japan	do	E	3	NA	NA
Temolek, Ikan (minnow)	*Probarbus jullieni*	Thailand, Cambodia, Vietnam, Malaysia, Laos.	do	E	15	NA	NA
Topminnow, Gila	*Poeciliopsis occidentalis*	U.S.A. (AZ, NM), Mexico	do	E	1	NA	NA
Totoaba (seatrout or weakfish)	*Cynoscion macdonaldi*	Mexico (Gulf of California)	do	E	45	NA	NA
Trout, Apache (= Arizona)	*Salmo apache*	U.S.A. (Arizona)	do	T	1, 8	NA	17.44(a)
Trout, Gila	*Salmo gilae*	U.S.A. (New Mexico)	do	E	1	NA	NA
Trout, greenback cutthroat	*Salmo clarki stomias*	U.S.A. (Colorado)	do	T	1, 38	NA	17.44(f)
Trout, Lahontan cutthroat	*Salmo clarki henshawi*	U.S.A. (CA, NV)	do	T	2, 8	NA	17.44(e)
Trout, Little Kern golden	*Salmo aguabonita whitei*	U.S.A. (California)	do	T	37	NA	17.44(e)
Trout, Paiute cutthroat	*Salmo clarki seleniris*	...do	do	T	1, 8	17.95(e)	17.44(e)
Woundfin	*Plagopterus argentissimus*	U.S.A. (AZ, NV, UT)	do	E	2	NA	NA
SNAILS							
Snail, Chittenango ovate amber	*Succinea chittenangoensis*	U.S.A. (New York)	NA	T	41	NA	NA
Snail, flat-spired three-toothed	*Triodopsis platysayoides*	U.S.A. (West Virginia)	NA	T	41	NA	NA
Snail, Iowa Pleistocene	*Discus macclintocki*	U.S.A. (Iowa)	NA	E	41	NA	NA
Snail, Manus Island tree	*Papustyla pulcherrima*	Pacific Ocean: Admiralty Is. (Manus Is.).	NA	T	3	NA	NA
Snail, noonday	*Mesodon clarki nantahala*	U.S.A. (North Carolina)	NA	T	41	NA	NA
Snail, Oahu tree (all species)	*Achatinella* spp. (all species)	U.S.A. (Hawaii)	NA	E	108, 112	NA	NA
Snail, painted snake coiled forest	*Anguispira picta*	U.S.A. (Tennessee)	NA	T	41	NA	NA
Snail, Stock Island	*Orthalicus reses*	U.S.A. (Florida)	NA	T	41	NA	NA
Snail, Virginia fringed mountain	*Polygyriscus virginianus*	U.S.A. (Virginia)	NA	E	41	NA	NA
CLAMS							
Pearly mussel, Alabama lamp	*Lampsilis virescens*	U.S.A. (AL, TN)	NA	E	15	NA	NA
Pearly mussel, Appalachian monkeyface	*Quadrula sparsa*	U.S.A. (TN, VA)	NA	E	15	NA	NA
Pearly mussel, birdwing	*Conradilla caelata*	...do	NA	E	15	NA	NA
Pearly mussel, Cumberland bean	*Villosa* (= *Micromya*) *trabalis*	U.S.A. (KY, TN)	NA	E	15	NA	NA
Pearly mussel, Cumberland monkeyface	*Quadrula intermedia*	U.S.A. (AL, TN, VA)	NA	E	15	NA	NA
Pearly mussel, Curtis'	*Epioblasma* (=*Dysnomia*) *florentina curtisi*.	U.S.A. (Missouri)	NA	E	15	NA	NA
Pearly mussel, dromedary	*Dromus dromas*	U.S.A. (TN, VA)	NA	E	15	NA	NA
Pearly mussel, green-blossom	*Epioblasma* (= *Dysnomia*) *torulosa gubernaculum*.	...do	NA	E	15	NA	NA
Pearly mussel, Higgins' eye	*Lampsilis higginsi*	U.S.A. (IL, IA, MN, MO, NE, WI).	NA	E	15	NA	NA
Pearly mussel, Nicklin's	*Megalonaias nicklineana*	Mexico	NA	E	15	NA	NA
Pearly mussel, orange-footed	*Plethobasus cooperianus*	U.S.A. (AL, IN, IA, KY, OH, PA, TN)	NA	E	15	NA	NA
Pearly mussel, pale lilliput	*Toxolasma* (=*Carunculina*) *cylindrella*	U.S.A. (AL, TN)	NA	E	15	NA	NA
Pearly mussel, pink mucket	*Lampsilis orbiculata*	U.S.A. (AL, IL, IN, KY, MO, OH, PA, TN, WV).	NA	E	15	NA	NA
Pearly mussel, Tampico	*Cyrtonaias tampicoensis tecomatensis*	Mexico	NA	E	15	NA	NA

| Species | | Historic range | Vertebrate population where endangered or threatened | Status | When listed | Critical habitat | Special rules |
Common name	Scientific name						
Pearly mussel, tubercled-blossom	Epioblasma (=Dysnomia) torulosa torulosa.	U.S.A. (IL, IN, KY, TN, WV)	NA	E	15	NA	NA
Pearly mussel, turgid-blossom	Epioblasma (=Dysnomia) turgidula	U.S.A. (AL, TN)	NA	E	15	NA	NA
Pearly mussel, white cat's paw	Epioblasma (=Dysnomia) sulcata delicata.	U.S.A. (IN, MI, OH)	NA	E	15	NA	NA
Pearly mussel, white wartyback	Plethobasus cicatricosus	U.S.A. (AL, IN, TN)	NA	E	15	NA	NA
Pearly mussel, yellow-blossom	Epioblasma (=Dysnomia) florentina florentina.	U.S.A. (AL, TN)	NA	E	15	NA	NA
Pigtoe, fine-rayed	Fusconaia cuneolus	U.S.A. (AL, TN, VA)	NA	E	15	NA	NA
Pigtoe, rough	Pleurobema plenum	U.S.A. (KY, TN, VA)	NA	E	15	NA	NA
Pigtoe, shiny	Fusconaia edgariana	U.S.A. (AL, TN, VA)	NA	E	15	NA	NA
Pocketbook, fat	Potamilus (=Proptera) capax.	U.S.A. (AR, IN, MO, OH)	NA	E	15	NA	NA
Riffle shell, tan	Epioblasma walkeri	U.S.A. (KY, TN, VA)	NA	E	27	NA	NA
CRUSTACEANS							
Amphipod, Hay's spring	Stygobromus hayi	U.S.A. (District of Columbia)	NA	E	115	NA	NA
Isopod, Madison Cave	Antrolana lira	U.S.A. (VA)	NA	T	123	NA	17.46(a)
Isopod, Socorro	Thermosphaeroma (=Exosphaeroma) thermophilus.	U.S.A. (New Mexico)	NA	E	36	NA	NA
Shrimp, Kentucky cave	Palaemonias ganteri	U.S.A. (KY)	NA	E	135	17.95(h)	NA
INSECTS							
Beetle, Delta green ground	Elaphrus viridis	U.S.A. (California)	NA	T	100	17.95(i)	NA
Beetle, valley elderberry longhorn	Desmocerus californicus dimorphus	do	NA	T	99	17.95(i)	NA
Butterfly, Bahama swallowtail	Papilio andraemon bonhotei	U.S.A. (FL), Bahamas.	NA	T	13	NA	17.47(a)
Butterfly, El Segundo blue	Euphilotes (=Shijimiaeoides) battoides allyni.	U.S.A. (California)	NA	E	14	NA	NA
Butterfly, Lange's metalmark	Apodemia mormo langei	do	NA	E	14	NA	NA
Butterfly, Lotis blue	Lycaeides argyrognomon lotis	do	NA	E	14	NA	NA
Butterfly, mission blue	Icaricia icarioides missionensis	do	NA	E	14	NA	NA
Butterfly, Oregon silverspot	Speyeria zerene hippolyta	U.S.A. (OR, WA)	NA	T	95	17.95(i)	NA
Butterfly, Palos Verdes blue	Glaucopsyche lygdamus palosverdesensis.	U.S.A. (California)	NA	E	96	17.95(i)	NA
Butterfly, San Bruno elfin	Callophrys mossii bayensis	do	NA	E	14	NA	NA
Butterfly, Schaus swallowtail	Papilio aristodemus ponceanus	U.S.A. (Florida)	NA	T	13	NA	17.47(a)
Butterfly, Smith's blue	Euphilotes (=Shijimiaeoides) enoptes smithi.	U.S.A. (California)	NA	E	14	NA	NA
Moth, Kern primrose sphinx	Euproserpinus euterpe	do	NA	T	91	NA	NA

#—Indicates FR where species was delisted; relisting of the species is indicated by subsequent number(s).
E—Indicates Emergency rule publication (see FR document for effective dates); subsequent number(s) indicate FR final rule, if applicable.
EDITORIAL NOTE: For "When listed" citations, see list following.

1—32 FR 4001; March 11, 1967.
2—35 FR 16047; October 13, 1970.
3—35 FR 8495; June 2, 1970.
4—35 FR 18320; December 2, 1970.
5—37 FR 6476; March 30, 1972.
6—38 FR 14678; June 4, 1973.
7—39 FR 44991; December 30, 1974.
8—40 FR 29864; July 16, 1975.
9—40 FR 31736; July 28, 1975.
10—40 FR 44151; September 25, 1975.
11—40 FR 44418; September 26, 1975.
12—40 FR 47506; October 9, 1975.
13—41 FR 17740; April 28, 1976.
14—41 FR 22044; June 1, 1976.
15—41 FR 24064; June 14, 1976.
16—41 FR 45993; October 19, 1976.
17—41 FR 51021; November 19, 1976.
18—41 FR 51612; November 23, 1976.
19—41 FR 53034; December 3, 1976.
20—42 FR 2076; January 10, 1977.
21—42 FR 2968; January 14, 1977.
23—42 FR 28137; June 2, 1977.
24—42 FR 28545; June 3, 1977.
25—42 FR 37373; July 21, 1977.
26—42 FR 40685; August 11, 1977.
27—42 FR 42353; August 23, 1977.
28—42 FR 45528; September 9, 1977.
29—42 FR 58755; November 11, 1977.
30—42 FR 60745; November 29, 1977.
31—43 FR 3715; January 27, 1978.
32—43 FR 4028; January 31, 1978.
33—43 FR 4621; February 3, 1978.
34—43 FR 6233; February 14, 1978.
35—43 FR 9612; March 9, 1978.
36—43 FR 12691; March 27, 1978.

37—43 FR 15429; April 13, 1978.
38—43 FR 16345; April 18, 1978.
40—43 FR 20504; May 12, 1978.
41—43 FR 28932; July 3, 1978.
42—43 FR 32808; July 28, 1978.
43—43 FR 34479; August 4, 1978.
44—43 FR 44812; September 28, 1978.
45—44 FR 21289; April 10, 1979.
46—44 FR 23064; April 17, 1979.
48—44 FR 29480; May 21, 1979.
50—44 FR 37126; June 25, 1979.
51—44 FR 37132; June 25, 1979.
52—44 FR 42911; July 20, 1979.
54—44 FR 49220; August 21, 1979.
55—44 FR 54007; September 17, 1979.
60—44 FR 59084; October 12, 1979.
85—44 FR 69208; November 30, 1979.
86—44 FR 70677; December 7, 1979.
87—44 FR 75076; December 18, 1979.
88—45 FR 18010; March 20, 1980.
90—45 FR 21833; April 2, 1980.
91—45 FR 24090; April 8, 1980.
92—45 FR 27713; April 23, 1980.
93—45 FR 28722; April 30, 1980.
94—45 FR 35821; May 28, 1980.
95—45 FR 44935; July 2, 1980.
96—45 FR 44939; July 2, 1980.
97—45 FR 47352; July 14, 1980.
98—45 FR 47355; July 14, 1980.
99—45 FR 52803; August 8, 1980.
100—45 FR 52807; August 8, 1980.
102—45 FR 54678; August 15, 1980.
103—45 FR 55654; August 20, 1980.
105—45 FR 63812; September 25, 1980.
106—45 FR 65132; October 1, 1980.

108—46 FR 3178; January 13, 1981.
111—46 FR 11665; February 10, 1981.
112—46 FR 40025; August 6, 1981.
113—46 FR 40664; August 10, 1981.
114—47 FR 4204; January 28, 1982.
115—47 FR 5425; February 5, 1982.
117—47 FR 19995; May 10, 1982.
119—47 FR 31670; July 21, 1982.
123—47 FR 43701; October 4, 1982.
124—47 FR 43962; October 5, 1982.
125—47 FR 46093; October 15, 1982.
127—48 FR 612; January 5, 1983.
128—48 FR 1726; January 14, 1983.
129—48 FR 28464; June 22, 1983.
130—48 FR 40186; September 2, 1983.
131—48 FR 43043; September 21, 1983.
132—48 FR 46057; October 11, 1983.
134—48 FR 46336; October 12, 1983.
135—48 FR 46342; October 12, 1983.
136—48 FR 49249; October 25, 1983.
138—49 FR 1994; January 17, 1984.
139—49 FR 2783; January 23, 1984.
142—49 FR 7335; February 28, 1984.
143—49 FR 7394; February 29, 1984.
144—49 FR 7398; February 29, 1984.
145—49 FR 10526; March 20, 1984.
146—49 FR 14356; April 11, 1984.
149—49 FR 22334; May 29, 1984.
150—49 FR 27514; July 5, 1984.

Effective Date Note: At 48 FR 43043, Sept. 21, 1983, the Key Largo cotton mouse and Key Largo woodrat were added by an emergency rule to the List of Endangered and Threatened Wildlife. This emergency determination was effective September 21, 1983, and expired May 18, 1984.

§ 17.12 Endangered and threatened plants.

(a) The list in this section contains the names of all species of plants which have been determined by the Services to be Endangered or Threatened. It also contains the names of species of plants treated as Endangered or Threatened because they are sufficiently similar in appearance to Endangered or Threatened species (see § 17.50 *et seq.*).

(b) The columns entitled "Scientific Name" and "Common Name" define the species of plant within the meaning of the Act. Although common names are included, they cannot be relied upon for identification of any specimen, since they may vary greatly in local usage. The Services shall use the most recently accepted scientific name. In cases in which confusion might arise, a synonym(s) will be provided in parentheses. The Services shall rely to the extent practicable on the *International Code of Botanical Nomenclature.*

(c) In the "Status" column the following symbols are used: "E" for Endangered, "T" for Threatened, and "E [or T] (S/A)" for similarity of appearance species.

(d) The other data in the list are nonregulatory in nature and are provided for the information of the reader. In the annual revision and compilation of this Title, the following information may be amended without public notice: the spelling of species' names, historical range, footnotes, references to certain other applicable portions of this Title, synonyms, and more current names. In any of these revised entries, neither the species, as defined in paragraph (b) of this section, nor its status may be changed without following the procedures of Part 424 of this Title.

(e) The "Historic Range" indicates the known general distribution of the species or subspecies as reported in the current scientific literature. The present distribution may be greatly reduced from this historic range. This column does not imply any limitation on the application of the prohibitions in the Act or implementing rules. Such prohibitions apply to all individuals of the plant species, wherever found.

(f)(1) A footnote to the **Federal Register** publication(s) listing or reclassifying a species is indicated under the column "When Listed." Footnote numbers to §§ 17.11 and 17.12

are in the same numerical sequence, since plants and animals may be listed in the same **Federal Register** document. That document, at least since 1973, includes a statement indicating the basis for the listing, as well as the effective date(s) of said listing.

(2) The "Special Rules" and "Critical Habitat" columns provide a cross reference to other sections in Parts 17, 222, 226, or 227. The term "NA" (not applicable) appearing in either of these two columns indicates that there are no special rules and/or Critical Habitat for that particular species. However, all other appropriate rules in Parts 17, 217–227, and 402 still apply to that species. In addition, there may be other rules in this Title that relate to such plants, e.g., port-of-entry requirements. It is not intended that the references in the "Special Rules" column list all the regulations of the two Services which might apply to the species or to the regulations of other Federal agencies or State or local governments.

(g) The listing of a particular taxon includes all lower taxonomic units [see § 17.11(g) for examples).

(h) The "List of Endangered and Threatened Plants" is provided below:

Species		Historic range	Status	When listed	Critical habitat	Special rules
Scientific name	Common name					
Agavaceae—Agave family:						
Agave arizonica	Arizona agave	U.S.A. (AZ)	E	147	NA	NA
Alismataceae—Water-plantain family:						
Sagittaria fasciculata	Bunched arrowhead	U.S.A. (NC, SC)	E	53	NA	NA
Asteraceae—Aster family:						
Bidens cuneata	Cuneate bidens	U.S.A. (HI)	E	141	NA	NA
Dyssodia tephroleuca	Ashy dogweed	U.S.A. (TX)	E	152	NA	NA
Echinacea tennesseensis	Tennessee purple coneflower	U.S.A. (TN)	E	49	NA	NA
Lipochaeta venosa	None	U.S.A. (HI)	E	73	NA	NA
Senecio franciscanus	San Francisco Peaks groundsel	U.S.A. (AZ)	T	137	17.96(a)	NA
Stephanomeria malheurensis	Malheur wire-lettuce	U.S.A. (OR)	E	126	17.96(a)	NA
Berberidaceae—Barberry family:						
Mahonia sonnei (= Berberis s.)	Truckee barberry	U.S.A. (CA)	E	76	NA	NA
Betulaceae—Birch family:						
Betula uber	Virginia round-leaf birch	U.S.A. (VA)	E	39	NA	NA
Brassicaceae—Mustard family:						
Arabis mcdonaldiana	McDonald's rock-cress	U.S.A. (CA)	E	44	NA	NA
Erysimum capitatum var. angustatum	Contra Costa wallflower	do	E	39	17.96(a)	NA
Cactaceae—Cactus family:						
Ancistrocactus tobuschii (=Echinocactus t., Mammillaria t.)	Tobusch fishhook cactus	U.S.A. (TX)	E	80	NA	NA
Cereus robinii	Key tree-cactus	U.S.A. (FL), Cuba	E	153	NA	NA
Coryphantha minima (=C. nelleae, Escobaria n., Mammillaria n.)	Nellie cory cactus	U.S.A. (TX)	E	81	NA	NA
Coryphantha ramillosa	Bunched cory cactus	U.S.A. (TX), Mexico (Coahuila)	T	77	NA	NA
Coryphantha sneedii var. leei (= Escobaria l., Mammillaria l.)	Lee pincushion cactus	U.S.A. (NM)	T	61	NA	NA
Coryphantha sneedii var. sneedii (=Escobaria s., Mammillaria s.)	Sneed pincushion cactus	U.S.A. (TX, NM)	E	82	NA	NA
Echinocactus horizonthalonius var. nicholii	Nichol's Turk's head cactus	U.S.A. (AZ)	E	71	NA	NA
Echinocereus engelmannii var. purpureus	Purple-spined hedgehog cactus	U.S.A. (UT)	E	58	NA	NA
Echinocereus fendleri var. kuenzleri (=E. kuenzleri, E. hempelii of authors, not Fobe)	Kuenzler hedgehog cactus	U.S.A. (NM)	E	70	NA	NA
Echinocereus lloydii (=E. roetteri var. l.)	Lloyd's hedgehog cactus	U.S.A. (TX)	E	67	NA	NA
Echinocereus reichenbachii var. albertii (=E. melanocentrus)	Black lace cactus	do	E	68	NA	NA
Echinocereus triglochidiatus var. arizonicus (=E. arizonicus)	Arizona hedgehog cactus	U.S.A. (AZ)	E	62	NA	NA
Echinocereus triglochidiatus var. inermis (=E. coccineus var. i., E. phoeniceus var. i.)	Spineless hedgehog cactus	U.S.A. (CO, UT)	E	83	NA	NA
Echinocereus viridiflorus var. davisii (=E. davisii)	Davis' green pitaya	U.S.A. (TX)	E	81	NA	NA
Neolloydia mariposensis (=Echinocactus m., Echinomastus m.)	Lloyd's Mariposa cactus	U.S.A. (TX), Mexico (Coahuila)	T	77	NA	NA
Pediocactus bradyi (= Toumeya b.)	Brady pincushion cactus	U.S.A. (AZ)	E	63	NA	NA
Pediocactus knowltonii (= P. bradyi var. k., Toumeya k.)	Knowlton cactus	U.S.A. (NM, CO)	E	72	NA	NA
Pediocactus peeblesianus var. peeblesianus (=Echinocactus p., Navajoa p., Toumeya p., Utahia p.)	Peebles Navajo cactus	U.S.A. (AZ)	E	69	NA	NA
Pediocactus sileri (=Echinocactus s., Utahia s.)	Siler pincushion cactus	U.S.A. (AZ, UT)	E	64	NA	NA
Sclerocactus glaucus (=Echinocactus g., E. subglaucus, E. whipplei var. g., Pediocactus g., S. franklinii, S. whipplei var. g.)	Uinta Basin hookless cactus	U.S.A. (CO, UT)	T	59	NA	NA

Species Scientific name	Common name	Historic range	Status	When listed	Critical habitat	Special rules
Sclerocactus mesae-verdae (= Coloradoa m., Echinocactus m., Pediocactus m.).	Mesa Verde cactus	U.S.A. (CO, NM)	T	75	NA	NA
Sclerocactus wrightiae (= Pediocactus w.).	Wright fishhook cactus	U.S.A. (UT)	E	58	NA	NA
Caryophyllaceae—Pink family:						
Schiedea adamantis	Diamond Head schiedea	U.S.A. (HI)	E	141	NA	NA
Cistaceae—Rockrose family:						
Hudsonia montana	Mountain golden heather	U.S.A. (NC)	T	107	17.96(a)	NA
Crassulaceae—Stonecrop family:						
Dudleya traskiae	Santa Barbara Island liveforever	U.S.A. (CA)	E	39	NA	NA
Cupressaceae—Cypress family:						
Fitzroya cupressoides	Chilean false larch (= alerce)	Chile, Argentina	T	79	NA	NA
Ericaceae—Heath family:						
Arctostaphylos pungens var. ravenii (=A. hookeri ssp. ravenii).	Presidio (= Raven's) manzanita	U.S.A. (CA)	E	65	NA	NA
Rhododendron chapmanii	Chapman rhododendron	U.S.A. (FL)	E	47	NA	NA
Euphorbiaceae—Spurge family:						
Euphorbia skottsbergii var. kalaeloana	Ewa Plains 'akoko	U.S.A. (HI)	E	120	NA	NA
Fabaceae—Pea family:						
Astragalus perianus	Rydberg milk-vetch	U.S.A. (UT)	T	39	NA	NA
Baptisia arachnifera	Hairy rattleweed	U.S.A. (GA)	E	39	NA	NA
Lotus dendroideus ssp. traskiae (=L. scoparius ssp. t.)	San Clemente Island broom	U.S.A. (CA)	E	26	NA	NA
Vicia menziesii	Hawaiian vetch	U.S.A. (HI)	E	39	NA	NA
Hydrophyllaceae—Waterleaf family:						
Phacelia argillacea	Clay phacelia	U.S.A. (UT)	E	44	NA	NA
Phacelia formosula	North Park phacelia	U.S.A. (CO)	E	121	NA	NA
Lamiaceae—Mint family:						
Haplostachys haplostachya var. angustifolia	None	U.S.A. (HI)	E	73	NA	NA
Hedeoma apiculatum	McKittrick pennyroyal	U.S.A. (TX, NM)	T	118	17.96(a)	NA
Hedeoma todsenii	Todsen's pennyroyal	U.S.A. (NM)	E	110, 112	17.96(a)	NA
Pogogyne abramsii	San Diego mesa mint	U.S.A. (CA)	E	44	NA	NA
Stenogyne angustifolia var. angustifolia	None	U.S.A. (HI)	E	73	NA	NA
Liliaceae—Lily family:						
Harperocallis flava	Harper's beauty	U.S.A. (FL)	E	57	NA	NA
Trillium persistens	Persistent trillium	U.S.A. (GA, SC)	E	39	NA	NA
Malvaceae—Mallow family:						
Callirhoe scabriuscula	Texas poppy-mallow	U.S.A. (TX)	E	109, 112	NA	NA
Kokia cookei	Cooke's kokio	U.S.A. (HI)	E	74	NA	NA
Malacothamnus clementinus	San Clemente Island bush-mallow	U.S.A. (CA)	E	26	NA	NA
Nyctaginaceae—Four-o'clock family:						
Mirabilis macfarlanei	MacFarlane's four-o'clock	U.S.A. (ID, OR)	E	66	NA	NA
Onagraceae—Evening-primrose family:						
Oenothera avita ssp. eurekensis.	Eureka Valley evening-primrose	U.S.A. (CA)	E	39	NA	NA
Oenothera deltoides ssp. howellii	Antioch Dunes evening-primrose	do	E	39	17.96(a)	NA

645

Species Scientific name	Common name	Historic range	Status	When listed	Critical habitat	Special rules
Orchidaceae—Orchid family:						
Isotria medeoloides	Small whorled pogonia	Canada (Ont.), U.S.A. (CT, IL, MA, MD, ME, MI, MO, NC, NH, NJ, NY, PA, RI, SC, VA, VT).	E	122	NA	NA
Spiranthes parksii	Navasota ladies'-tresses	U.S.A. (TX)	E	116	NA	NA
Papaveraceae—Poppy family:						
Arctomecon humilis	Dwarf bear-poppy	U.S.A. (UT).	E	78	NA	NA
Pinaceae—Pine family:						
Abies guatemalensis	Guatemalan fir (=pinabete)	Mexico, Guatemala, Honduras, El Salvador.	T	84	NA	NA
Poaceae—Grass family:						
Tuctoria mucronata (=*Orcuttia m.*)	Solano grass	U.S.A. (CA).	E	44	NA	NA
Panicum carteri	Carter's panicgrass	U.S.A. (HI)	E	133	17.96(a)	NA
Swallenia alexandrae	Eureka Dune grass	do	E	39	NA	NA
Zizania texana	Texas wild-rice	U.S.A. (TX).	E	39	17.96(a)	NA
Polygonaceae—Buckwheat family:						
Eriogonum gypsophilum	Gypsum wild-buckwheat	U.S.A. (NM)	T	110, 112	17.96(a)	NA
Eriogonum pelinophilum	Clay-loving wild-buckwheat	U.S.A. (CO)	E	151	17.96(a)	NA
Ranunculaceae—Buttercup family:						
Aconitum noveboracense	Northern wild monkshood	U.S.A. (IA, NY, OH, WI).	T	39	NA	NA
Delphinium kinkiense	San Clemente Island larkspur	U.S.A. (CA).	E	26	NA	NA
Rosaceae—Rose family:						
Cowania subintegra	Arizona cliffrose	U.S.A. (AZ)	E	148	NA	NA
Potentilla robbinsiana	Robbins' cinquefoil	U.S.A. (NH, VT).	E	104	17.96(a)	NA
Sarraceniaceae—Pitcher plant family:						
Sarracenia oreophila	Green pitcher plant	U.S.A. (AL, GA, TN)	E	56, 89	NA	NA
Scrophulariaceae—Snapdragon family:						
Castilleja grisea	San Clemente Island Indian paintbrush	U.S.A. (CA).	E	26	NA	NA
Cordylanthus maritimus ssp. *maritimus*	Salt marsh bird's-beak	U.S.A. (CA), Mexico (Baja California).	E	44	NA	NA
Pedicularis furbishiae	Furbish lousewort	U.S.A. (ME), Canada (New Brunswick).	E	39	NA	NA
Taxaceae—Yew family:						
Torreya taxifolia	Florida torreya.	U.S.A. (FL, GA).	E	140	NA	NA

E—Indicates Emergency rule publication (see FR document for effective dates); subsequent number(s) indicate FR final rule, if applicable.

EDITORIAL NOTE: For "When listed" citations, see list following.

26—42 FR 40685; August 11, 1977.
39—43 FR 17916; April 26, 1978.
44—43 FR 44812; September 28, 1978.
47—44 FR 24250; April 24, 1979.
49—44 FR 32605; June 6, 1979.
53—44 FR 43701; July 25, 1979.
56—44 FR 54923; September 21, 1979.
57—44 FR 58863; October 2, 1979.
58—44 FR 58868; October 11, 1979.
59—44 FR 58870; October 11, 1979.
61—44 FR 61556; October 25, 1979.
62—44 FR 61558; October 25, 1979.
63—44 FR 61786; October 26, 1979.
64—44 FR 61788; October 26, 1979
65—44 FR 61911; October 26, 1979.
66—44 FR 61913; October 26, 1979.
67—44 FR 61916; October 26, 1979.
68—44 FR 61920; October 26, 1979.
69—44 FR 61924; October 26, 1979.
70—44 FR 61927; October 26, 1979.
71—44 FR 61929; October 26, 1979.
72—44 FR 62246; October 26, 1979.
73—44 FR 62469; October 30, 1979.
74—44 FR 62471; October 30, 1979.
75—44 FR 62474; October 30, 1979.
76—44 FR 64247; November 6, 1979.
77—44 FR 64250; November 6, 1979.
78—44 FR 64252; November 6, 1979.
79—44 FR 64733; November 7, 1979.
80—44 FR 64738; November 7, 1979.
81—44 FR 64740; November 7, 1979.
82—44 FR 64743; November 7, 1979.
83—44 FR 64746; November 7, 1979.

84—44 FR 65005; November 8, 1979.
89—45 FR 18929; March 24, 1980.
104—45 FR 61944; September 17, 1980.
107—45 FR 69360; October 20, 1980.
109—46 FR 3184; January 13, 1981.
110—46 FR 5730; January 19, 1981.
112—46 FR 40025; August 6, 1981.
116—47 FR 19539; May 6, 1982.
118—47 FR 30440; July 13, 1982.
120—47 FR 36846; August 24, 1982.
121—47 FR 38540; September 1, 1982.
122—47 FR 38927; September 10, 1982.
126—47 FR 50885; November 10, 1982.
133—48 FR 46332; October 12, 1983.
137—48 FR 52747; November 22, 1983.
140—49 FR 2786; January 23, 1984.
141—49 FR 6102; February 17, 1984.
147—49 FR 21058; May 18, 1984.
148—49 FR 22329; May 29, 1984.
151—49 FR 28565; July 13, 1984.
152—49 FR 29234; July 19, 1984.
153—49 FR 29237; July 19, 1984.

WILDLIFE REMOVED FROM THE ENDANGERED AND THREATENED SPECIES LIST

The following list of wildlife removed from the List of Endangered and Threatened Wildlife (50 CFR 17.11) is provided for informational purposes only and is not codified in the Code of Federal Regulations.

The Service's listing regulations at 50 CFR 424.11(d), state that: The data to support the removal of a species from the list must be the best scientific and commercial data available to the Director to substantiate that the species is neither endangered nor threatened for one or more of the following reasons:

1. *Extinction*—Unless each individual of the listed species was previously identified and located, a sufficient period of time must be allowed before delisting to clearly ensure that the species is in fact extinct.

2. *Recovery of the species*—The principal goal of the Service is to return listed species to a point at which protection under the Act is no longer required. A species may be delisted if evidence shows that it is no longer endangered or threatened.

3. *Original data for classification in error*—Subsequent investigations may produce data that show that the best scientific or commercial data available at the time the species was listed were in error.

| Species | | Historic range | Former vertebrate population where endangered or threatened | Former status | Delisted | |
Common name	Scientific name				Citation	Reason
Duck, Mexican	Anas "diazi"	U.S.A. (AZ, NM, TX) to central Mexico.	U.S. only	E	43 FR 32258–61; January 25, 1978.	Original data in error.
Pupfish, Tecopa	Cyprinodon nevadensis calidae.	U.S.A. (CA)	Entire	E	47 FR 2317–19; January 15, 1982.	Extinct.
Cisco, longjaw	Coregonus alpenae	U.S.A. and Canada (Lakes Michigan, Huron, Erie).	......do	E	48 FR 39941–43; September 2, 1983.	Extinct.
Pike, blue	Stizostedion vitreum glaucum.	U.S.A. and Canada (Lakes Ene, Ontario).	......do	E	48 FR 39941–43; September 2, 1983.	Extinct.
Sparrow, Santa Barbara song.	Melospiza melodia graminea	U.S.A. (CA)	......do	E	48 FR 46336–37; October 12, 1983.	Extinct.
Treefrog, Pine Barrens	Hyla andersonii	U.S.A. (FL, AL, NC, SC, NJ)	Florida	E	48 FR 52740–43; November 22, 1983.	Original data in error.
Pearly mussel, Sampson's	Epioblasma (=Dysnomia) sampsoni.	U.S.A. (IL, IN)	NA	E	49 FR 1057–58; January 9, 1984.	Extinct.
Turtle, Indian flap-shelled	Lissemys punctata punctata	India, Pakistan, Blangladesh	Entire	E	49 FR 7394–98; February 29, 1984.	Original data in error.

U.S. GOVERNMENT PRINTING OFFICE : 1984 O - 447-430

647

Index

Federal Aid in Wildlife Restoration Program, 267
Federal Aid Program, 16–17, 105, 267–278
administration expenditures, 275
apportionments, 273
budgeting, 273
congressional committees, 272
legislation, 277
percentages spent on program administration, 273
Pittman-Robertson Program, 267
planning, 273
research, 274
resource status, 278
reversions, 276
state administration options, 275
state planning, 276
streamlining the process, 274–275
see also Dingell-Johnson Act; Forsythe-Chafee Act
Federal Emergency Management Agency, floodplain management, 220
Federal Energy Regulatory Commission, 96
disregarding of environmental considerations, 114-115
licensing of, 114
small-hydro projects, 113–114
Federal Land Policy and Management Act, 343–345
development of planning criteria, 353
environmental impact statement, review, 353
identifying issues, 353
major provisions, 348–349
resource management plan
draft, review, 353
protesting a proposed plan, 353
public participation, 353
wilderness studies, 370–371
Federal Power Act of 1920, 5
Federal Power Commission, 96
Federal Water Pollution Control Act
amendments, 221, 237
reauthorization, 222
see also Clean Water Act
Federal Water Power Act of 1920, 96
Federal Wildlife Permit Office, 20
Finch, Laysan, 553–555
Fire
controlled, green pitcher plant habitat, 537
forage condition improvement, 480
management, 158–159
Fish

anadromous, see Anadromous fish
bald eagle diet, 511–512
breeding, effects of acid rain, 116
Great Lakes, 123–125
husbandry, 107
regional species of special emphasis, 111
research, 102–103
species of special emphasis, 613
see also specific types of fish
Fish and Wildlife Act of 1956, 102, 153, 156
fish research, 102
Fish and Wildlife Conservation Act of 1980, 8, 45, 267, 271
funding, 277
Fish and Wildlife Coordination Act of 1934, 5, 31, 104, 114
amendments, 31–33, 218–219, 221, 230, 232–233
fish mitigation, 96
preconstruction consultation activities, 8
proposed, 50
animal damage control, 132
Corps of Engineers, 223
fish research, 102
impacts of dams on fish, 96
wetlands, 214
protection, 218
Fish and Wildlife Research Units, 599–601
Fish and Wildlife Service, 1–23
activity accounts, 23
Administration and Related Support Services Program, 18
agency structure and function, 35–36
anadromous species, jurisdiction over, 103–104
assessment of condition of refuge facilities, 177
budget, 12–13, 106, 192–194
fishery resources, 110–111
migratory bird activities, 38–39
1985, 16
request and appropriation for migratory bird, 39–40
Bureau of Commercial Fisheries, 6, 95
Bureau of Sport Fish & Wildlife, 6, 95
Cooperative Research Units Program, 18–19
Cooperative Whooping Crane Project, 74
Corps of Engineers coordination, 223–224, 230
current program trends, 22–23
Directorate, 10
ecological services and field offices,

Please send _____ *copies of the Audubon Wildlife Report 1985, at $16.50 per copy postpaid, to:*

Name _____

Organization/Agency _____

Address _____

City _____ State _____ Zip _____

A check or money order is enclosed.

(   ) Please reserve _____ copies of the 1986 report and let me know as soon as it is available.

Allow four weeks for delivery.

Please send _____ *copies of the Audubon Wildlife Report 1985, at $16.50 per copy postpaid, to:*

Name _____

Organization/Agency _____

Address _____

City _____ State _____ Zip _____

A check or money order is enclosed.

(   ) Please reserve _____ copies of the 1986 report and let me know as soon as it is available.

Allow four weeks for delivery.

Audubon Wildlife Report
National Audubon Society
950 3rd Avenue
New York, New York 10022

Audubon Wildlife Report
National Audubon Society
950 3rd Avenue
New York, New York 10022

goose
 subsistence harvests, 47–48
 yellow-legs, *see* Pacific white-fronted
goose
Georgia
 national wildlife refuges, 616
 Protected Plants Program, 535
Gill nets, 197
Glacier National Park
 adjacent land problems, 295
 cutthroat, 126
 grizzly bear
 habitat, 408
 population, 405
Golden eagle, 391
Grand Canyon, burrors, 297
Grand Mesa/Uncompaghre/Gunnison National Forest, timber harvest, 333
Grasslands
 big-game animals on, 328
 harvest, 329
 management, 158
Grazing
 cattle, national forests, 336–337
 districts, 347
 permits, 346–347
 riparian zones, 361–362
 user fee, 366–367
 wildlife and fish, 318–319
 see also Wildlife and Livestock Program
Grazing Service, 347
Great Lakes, fish, 123–125
Great Lakes and Upper Colorado River
Fisheries, 99–100
Great Lakes Fisheries Act of 1956, 6, 99,
102
Great Lakes Fishery Commission, 99, 123
Great Lakes Fishery Laboratory, 107, 602–
603
Great Smoky Mountains, wild boars, 296–
297
Greater Yellowstone Ecosystem, bald eagle, 521
Green pitcher plant, 533–538
 current trends, 535
 historical perspective, 534
 management, 536
 prognosis, 537
 recommendations, 537
 recovery plans, 536
 significance, 534
 species description and life history, 533–
534
 transplantation experiments, 536–537
Green-winged teal, breeding populations,
55

Greenback, cutthroat, 125
Grizzly bear, 401–411
 breeding, 402
 Cabinet/Yaak Ecosystem, 405–406
 Forest Service management role, 332–
333
 habitat
 ownership and management of occupied habitat, 404
 requirements, 408–409
 hibernation, 401–402
 historical perspective, 402, 404
 home ranges, 401, 403
 known man-caused mortalities, 407–408
 management activities, 409–410
 North Cascades Ecosystem, 406
 Northern Continental Divide Ecosystem,
404–405
 old-growth timber, 332–333
 population
 status, 407–408
 trend monitoring systems, 410–411
 prognosis, 410
 project funding, 333
 quantification of the impact of human
disturbance, 411
 recommendations, 410–411
 recovery goals, 409–410
 San Juan Mountains, Colorado, 407
 Selkirk Mountains Ecosystem, 406
 Selway/Bitterroot Ecosystem, 406–407
 significance of the species, 402
 species description and natural history,
401–402
 Yellowstone Ecosystem, 404
Guns and ammunition, excise tax, Pittman-
Robertson Act, 268
Guzzler, 480

H. J. Justin & Sons v. Deukmejian, 88–89
H. R. 1675, 379
H. R. 2122, 301
H. R. 4962, 301
H. R. 5900, 255
Habitat, 283
 California condor, 396
 capability
 defined, 340
 National Forest System, 340
 critical
 endangered species, 76–77
 desert bighorn, 478–479
 protection and improvement, 479–481
 destruction, Puerto Rican parrots, 488
 fishery research, 106
 grizzly bear, 408–409

665

347–348
Public Law 98-138, 118
Public Law 98-541, 117
Public Rangelands Improvement Act of 1978, 345, 356
  Free-Roaming Horses and Burros Act, amendments
  funding for, 363
  grazing fee, 367
  provisions, 349–350
Public Utility Act of 1935, 96
Public Utility Regulatory Policies Act, 97
Puerto Rican parrot, 487–491
  causes for decline, 488–489
  current trends, 489
  historical perspective, 488
  management, 490
  nest robbing by man, 488
  prognosis, 491
  recommendations, 491
  shooting and hunting, 489
  significance, 488
  species description and natural history, 487
Puerto Rico, national wildlife refuges, 622
Puyallup Tribe v. Department of Game, 120

Rail, Laysan, 554
Rainwater Basin, 260
Range
  improvement, 363, 366–367
    outlook, 381–382
  investments, 366–367
  poor condition, 381–382
  woodland caribou, 495–499
Rangeland Act, *see* Public Rangelands Improvement Act of 1978
Rat, 489
Recreational use
  refuges, 166
  wilderness, 339
Red-cockaded woodpecker, old-growth timber, 330–331
Red-tailed hawk, 489 .
Redhead, breeding populations, 57–58
Refuge Recreation Act of 1962, 102
Refuge, *see also* National Wildlife Refuge System
Refuges, 151
  acquisition funding, 157
  establishment, 156–157
  fish conservation, primary purpose, 102
  fishery management, 101–102
  history, 7–8
  increased fishing, 109

land removal, 158
management, 158–159
migratory bird, 29–31
origin, size and cost, 615–623
for particular species, 74
waterfowl, 32
Remote Sensing Program, 303
Renewable Resources Program, 310
Reptiles, species of special emphasis, 613
Resource Planning Act, 310
Resources, threatened, 294
Resources Planning Act, 310
Reuss amendment, 32
Rhode Island, national wildlife refuges, 621
Richard B. Russell Dam and Lake, 229
Ring-necked duck, breeding populations, 59–60
Riparian wetlands, 260
Riparian zones, 318–319
  defined, 336
  livestock grazing, 361–362
  wildlife and grazing, 336–337
Rivers, zoning for hydroelectric development and protection, 115
Rivers and Harbors Act of 1899, 221
Riverside Irrigation District v. Andrews, 88, 249–250
Road building, effects on woodland caribou habitat, 500
Roadless Area Review and Evaluation, 337
Rocky Mountains
  Northern Continental Divide Grizzly Bear Ecosystem, 404–405
  road building, 335–336
Rookeries, 460
Roosevelt Campobello International Park Commission v. the Environmental Protection Agency, 88
Ruby Lake National Wildlife Refuge, boating conflicts with wildlife, 167

S. 457, 379
Sabine National Wildlife Refuge, 178
Salmon
  Atlantic
    high take in ocean fisheries, 113
    interstate compact to conserve, 118
    restoration, 100–101, 112–113
  chinook, 122
  coho, 122
  Columbia River Basin, 97, 121–123
  Pacific
    Columbia River Basin, 97
    conservation measures, 98–99
    Lower Snake River compensation